EC LAW

TEXT, CASES, AND MATERIALS

Paul Craig and Gráinne de Búrca

CLARENDON PRESS · OXFORD

Oxford University Press, Great Clarendon Street, OX2 6DP
Oxford New York
Athens Auckland Bangkok Bogota Bombay Buenos Aires
Calcutta Cape Town Dar es Salaam Delhi Florence Hong Kong
Istanbul Karachi Kuala Lumpur Madras Madrid Melbourne
Mexico City Nairobi Paris Singapore Taipei Tokyo Toronto
and associated companies in
Berlin Ibadan

Oxford is a trade mark of Oxford University Press

Published in the United States
by Oxford University Press Inc., New York

First published 1995
Paperback reprinted 1995, 1996 (twice), 1997

British Library Cataloguing in Publication Data
Data available

Library of Congress Cataloging in Publication Data
Craig, P. P. (Paul P.)
EC law: text, cases, and materials / P. P. Craig and G. de Búrca.
p. cm.
Includes bibliographical references and index.
1. Law—European Economic Community countries.
2. European Economic Community.
I. De Búrca, G. (Gráinne) II. Title.
KJE947.C73 1995 349.4—dc20 [344] 95–13322
ISBN 0–19–876272–0
ISBN 0–19–876273–9 (Pbk)

Printed in Great Britain
on acid-free paper by
Biddles Ltd,
Guildford and King's Lynn

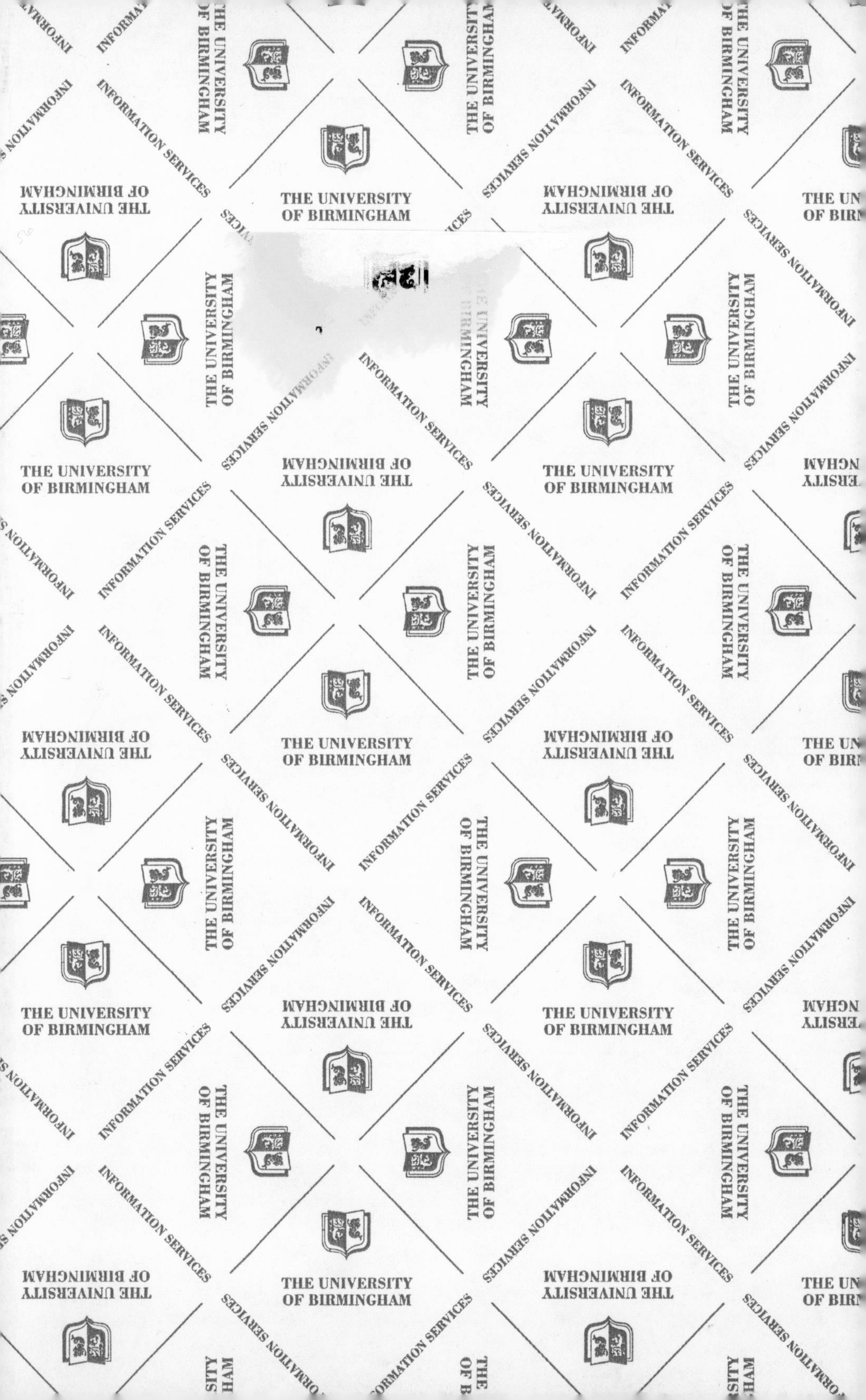

For Anita and Ciaran
P.P.C

Do mo mháthair agus i gcuimhne m'athar
G. de B.

PREFACE

European Community law has become increasingly important for students and practitioners of law alike. Consequently, there is a growing need for a good understanding of this dynamic and complex subject. This book has been written with a view to providing a comprehensive and integrated text, built around a variety of important European Community cases and materials. In addition to a full textual analysis of the areas of law which are covered, the book includes a substantial selection of case law, primary and secondary legislation, academic commentary and other relevant materials. It is designed to be used as a primary textbook, but it can also be used alongside another text.

One of the themes of the book is that EC law is a dynamic and evolving subject, which should be assessed not only in the light of contemporary political, institutional and economic development and change, but also by paying particular attention to its historical context. Accordingly, the book throughout does not aim simply to present EC law as it now is, but to explain and to evaluate it in the light of its gradual development and evolution. This is equally true of the major constitutional and administrative principles and of the substantive law of the Community. The book also highlights the importance of the interaction between the legislative and judicial branches in the attainment of Community aims. A connected theme which we have sought to emphasize is the dynamic interaction between institutional and substantive developments in Community law. Too often these are studied as separate branches of Community law. An appreciation of the necessary interrelationship between the two considerably enriches our understanding of the subject.

The book aims to cover most of the institutional, constitutional and administrative law of the Community as well as a selected range of important areas of substantive law, with an introduction to the institutional structure of the Union. The enormous range and breadth of the subject has meant that selection has been inevitable. As a result, we have not been able to include various areas, such as Environmental law or External Relations. Detailed coverage of the law of the 'intergovernmental pillars' of the Union, in Justice and Home Affairs and the Common Foreign and Security Policy, is also not included.

Several people have provided assistance during the course of preparation of the book, either in reading and commenting on various chapters, or in proof reading, or providing materials and other support. Thanks are due to Sandy Fredman, Christine Gray, Murray Hunt, Chris McCrudden, Gillian More, Aidan Robertson and Emma Wright. Additionally, many thanks are due to those at Oxford University Press for their courtesy and efficiency, in particular to Kate Elliot, Richard Hart, Jo Kuszmar and Margaret Shade.

We have aimed to state the law as it stood on 31 December 1994.

Paul Craig
Gráinne de Búrca

OUTLINE TABLE OF CONTENTS

CONTENTS

7. GENERAL PRINCIPLES I: FUNDAMENTAL RIGHTS

8. GENERAL PRINCIPLES OF COMMUNITY LAW II: PROPORTIONALITY, LEGITIMATE EXPECTATIONS, AND NON-DISCRIMINATION

TABLE OF ABBREVIATIONS

AC	Appeal Cases
All ER	All England Law Reports
Am. J. Comp. Law	American Journal of Comparative Law
Bull EC	Bulletin of the European Communities
BYIL	British Yearbook of International Law
CA	English Court of Appeal
CAP	Common Agricultural Policy
CDE	Cahiers de Droit Européen
CEE	Charges of equivalent effect
CEN	European Standardization Committee
CENELEC	European Standardization Committee for Electrical Products
CFI	Court of First Instance
CFSP	Common Foreign and Security Policy
CLJ	Cambridge Law Journal
CLP	Current Legal Problems
CMLR	Common Market Law Reports
CMLRev.	Common Market Law Review
COREPER	Committee of the Permanent Representatives (of the Member States)
Corn.L.R.	Cornell Law Review
D.&R.	Decisions and Reports of the European Commission of Human Rights
Dec.	Decision
Dir.	Directive
EAGGF	European Agricultural Guidance and Guarantee Fund
ECB	European Central Bank
ECJ	European Court of Justice
ECHR	European Convention on Human Rights
ECtHR	European Court of Human Rights
ECLR	European Competition Law Review
ECOSOC	Economic and Social Committee
ECR	European Court Reports
ECSC	European Coal and Steel Community
EC Treaty	European Community Treaty
ECU	European Currency Unit(s)
EDC	European Defence Community
EEA	European Economic Area
EEC	European Economic Community
EFTA	European Free Trade Association

EIPR	European Intellectual Property Review
EJIL	European Journal of International Law
ELRev.	European Law Review
EMU	Economic and Monetary Union
EPC	European Political Co-operation
Euratom	European Atomic Energy Community
EU	European Union
Fordham Int.LJ	Fordham International Law Journal
GATT	General Agreement on Tariffs and Trade
GNP	Gross national product
Harv.Int.LJ	Harvard International Law Journal
Harv.LR	Harvard Law Review
HRLJ	Human Rights Law Journal
ICLQ	International and Comparative Law Quarterly
ICR	Industrial Cases Reports
IGC	Inter-Governmental Conference
ILJ	Industrial Law Journal
ILO	International Labour Organisation
ILRM	Irish Law Reports Monthly
IR	Irish Reports
IRLR	Industrial Relations Law Reports
JCMS	Journal of Common Market Studies
JO	Journal Officiel de la Communauté Européenne (the French version of the OJ)
J.Pol.Econ.	Journal of Political Economy
JSWFL	Journal of Social Welfare and Family Law
JWTL	Journal of World Trade Law
LIEI	Legal Issues of European Integration
LQR	Law Quarterly Review
MCA, MCAS	Monetary Compensatory Amount(s)
MEQRs	Measures of equivalent effect to a quantitative restriction
MLR	Modern Law Review
NATO	North Atlantic Treaty Organization
NW.J.Int.Law & Bus.	Northwestern Journal of International Law and Business
NYULR	New York University Law Reports
OJ	Official Journal of the European Communities
OJLS	Oxford Journal of Legal Studies
PDB	Preliminary Draft Budget (of the Community)
PL	Public Law
QB	Queen's Bench Reports
RDI	Rivista di Diritto Internazionale
Reg.	Regulation
RMC	Revue du Marché Commun

SEA	Single European Act
Summit	European Council Meeting
TEU	Treaty on European Union ('Maastricht Treaty')
VAT	Value Added Tax
WLR	Weekly Law Reports
Yale LJ	Yale Law Journal
YBEL	Yearbook of European Law

ACKNOWLEDGEMENTS

Grateful acknowledgement is made to all the authors and publishers of extract material which appears in this book, and in particular to the following for permission to reprint material from the sources indicated:

Basic Books Inc. and HarperCollins Publishers Ltd.: Bork, R., *The Antitrust Paradox: A Policy at War with Itself*, pp. 297–8, 310–11.

Blackwell Publishers and the Modern Law Review Ltd.: Bishop, W., 'Price Discrimination under Article 86: Political Economy in the European Court' (1981) 44 *MLR* 282; McGee, A. and Weatherill, S., 'The Evolution of the Single Market—Harmonisation or Liberalisation' (1990) 53 *MLR* 578; Snyder, F., 'The Effectiveness of European Community Law' (1993) 56 *MLR* 19.

Butterworth & Co. (Publishers) Ltd.: Extracts from the *All England Reports*; Whish, R., *Competition Law* 3/ed (1993), pp. 235–6, 268, 285–6, 307, 326, 469–70, 490, 564–5, 618; Westlake, M., *The Commission and the Parliament: Partners and Rivals in the European Policy-Making Process*, pp. 19–21, 37–8, 79, 96.

Butterworths (Ireland) Ltd.: Jacobs, F., 'Is the Court of Justice of The European Community a Constitutional Court?' from Curtin and O'Keeffe (eds.) *Constitutional Adjudication in European Community and National Law*.

The Incorporated Council of Law Reporting for England & Wales for permission to reproduce extracts from the *Weekly Law Reports* and *Official Law Reports*.

John Wiley & Sons Ltd.: Toth, A. G., 'A Legal Analysis of Subsidiarity' 39–40, and 41; Steiner, J., 'Subsidiarity under the Maastricht Treaty' 57–8; and D'Oliveira, H., 'Expanding External And Shrinking Internal Borders: Europe's Defence Mechanisms in the Areas of Free Movement, Immigration and Asylum' in O'Keeffe and Twomey (eds.) *Legal Issues of the Maastricht Treaty* © John Wiley, 1994 reprinted by permission of John Wiley & Sons Ltd.

Johns Hopkins University Press: Sandholz, W. and Zysman, J., '1993: Recasting the European Bargain' 42 *World Politics* 95.

Kluwer Academic Publishers: extracts from the *Common Market Law Reports*; Bebr, B., 'The Existence of a Genuine Dispute: An Indispensable Precondition for the Jurisdiction of the Court under Article 177 EEC Treaty?' (1980) 17 *CMLRev* 525, 530–2; Forrester, I. and Norall C., 'The Laicization of Community Law: Self-Help and the Rule of Reason: How Competition is and Could be Applied' (1984) 21 *CMLRev* 11, 16, 17–18, 32, 37, 38; Gaja, G., 'New Developments in a Continuing Story: The Relationship between EEC Law and Italian Law' (1990) 27 *CMLRev* 83, 93–4.

Professor Valentine Korah: 'The Rise and Fall of Provisional Validity—The Need for a Rule of Reason in EEC Antitrust' (1981) 3 *Northwestern Journal of International Law and Business*, 320, 354–55. First published by Northwestern University School of Law.

Macmillan Press Ltd and Duke University Press: Nugent, N., *The Government and Politics of the European Union*, 3/edn., pp. 87, 118–19, 325.

MIT Press Journals: Moravcsik, A., 'Negotiating the Single Act: National Interests and Conventional Statecraft in the European Community' 1991, 45 *International Organization* 19 © MIT Press, 1991.

Oxford University Press: Jacobs, F., *The European Convention on Human Rights*; Cappelletti, M., *The Judicial Process in Comparative Perspective*; Mancini and Keeling 'From *CILFIT* to *ERT*: the Constitutional Challenge Facing the European Court', [1991] *YEL* 1; Craig 'United Kingdom Sovereignty after *Factortame*' [1991] *YEL* 221; de Búrca 'The Principle of Proportionality and its Application in EC Law', [1993] *YEL* 105.

Pinter Publishers Ltd.: Lodge, J., 'EC Policymaking: Institutional Dynamics', 11; Mazey, S. P. and Richardson, J. J., 'Pressure Groups and Lobbying in the EC', 44; Lodge, J., 'Towards a Political Union', 382 in Lodge (ed.) *The European Community and the Challenge for the Future*, 1993, 2/edn.

Sweet and Maxwell: Craig, P. P., '*Francovich*, Remedies and the Scope of Damages Liability' 109 *Law Quarterly Review*, 595, 600–1, 605, 614, 620–1; Rasmussen, H., 'Why is Article 173 Interpreted against Private Plaintiffs?' (1980) 5 *ELRev* 112, 122–7; Chard, J. S., 'The Economics of the Application of Article 86 to Selective Distribution Systems' (1982) 7 *ELRev* 83, 97, 100–1; Wyatt, D. A., 'Foglia (No. 2): The Court Denies it has Jurisdiction to Give Advisory Opinions' (1982) 7 *ELRev* 186, 187–8, 190; Petriccione, R., 'Italy: Supremacy of Community Law over National Law' (1986) 11 *ELRev* 320; Martin, J. F. M. and Stehmann, O., 'Product Market Integration versus Regional Cohesion in the Community' (1991) 16 *ELRev* 216, 228–30; Bradley, K., 'Sense and Sensibility: Parliament v. Council Continued' (1991) 16 *ELRev* 245, 251–4; von Heydebrand u.d. Lasa, H.-C., 'Free Movement of Goodstuffs, Consumer Protection and Food Standards in the European Community: Has the Court of Justice Got it Wrong?' (1991) 16 *ELRev* 391, 409–13; Wils, W. P. J., 'The Search for the Rule in Article 30 EEC: Much Ado About Nothing?' (1993) 18 *ELRev* 475, 476–8, 483; Schodermeier, M., 'Collective Dominance Revisted: An Analysis of the EC Commission's New Concepts of Oligopoly Control' (1990) 1 *ECLR* 28.

The Yale Law Journal Company and Fred B. Rothman & Company: Weiler, J., 'The Transformation of Europe', *Yale Law Journal*, vol. 100, pp. 2403–83.

TABLE OF CASES

European Court of Justice and Court of First Instance

A. ALPHABETICAL

B. NUMERICAL

Cases from Other Jurisdictions

Belgium

European Court and Commission of Human Rights

France

Germany

Ireland

Italy

United Kingdom

United States

Commission and Council Decisions

European Merger Cases

TABLE OF TREATIES, EUROPEAN LEGISLATIVE INSTRUMENTS AND NATIONAL LEGISLATION

TREATIES and CONVENTIONS

EC DIRECTIVES

EC REGULATIONS

EC DECISIONS

NATIONAL LEGISLATION

France

Germany

1

The Development of European Integration

1. INTRODUCTION

The gradual move away from a strictly analytical approach to the study of law, and the increasing emphasis on the interdisciplinary nature of its subject matter is a development which is particularly fortunate in the context of European Community law. To study and to evaluate Community law without considering something of the historical, political, and economic forces shaping its evolution would be to gain a very limited understanding of the subject. It is a fascinating area of law for many reasons. In order to approach the study of the Community legal system, one must begin by asking why the European Community exists at all. What prompted the establishment of this elaborate and often fraught political organization with its complex legal system? What are its aims and what role does law play in furthering those aims? The legal process consists of a tangled network of relationships and interaction between the substantive aims and policies of the Community, its institutional structure, and its constituent Member States. It is hoped that this will become evident during the course of this book, and that the interconnectedness of political forces, institutional structures, processes, and substantive policy in the formation of Community law will become clear.

There are no straightforward answers, of course, to the questions posed above. There are, and always have been, many different views about the aims of the Community among those who make up its population and among its political actors, and many different historical and political forces and contingencies contributed to creating the Community which exists today. Unravelling these would be a difficult task indeed, but consideration of the history of the Community helps to explain why its process of development appears such an uneven, often erratic, and sometimes even tortuous one. This history is reflected in the gradual legal shaping of the Community: in the progressive enlargement of its membership; and in the various Treaty amendments over the years, dealing with matters ranging from the mechanics of the budgetary process to the expansion of areas of policy and competence, from market integration to political integration through legislative and institutional reform.

In subsequent chapters, when examining the emergence of various legal principles and legal doctrine together with the development of areas of substantive law and policy, it is useful to consider these against the background of the Community's history, and of the various periods of change which affected law-making within both the political institutions and the Court, as well as the reception of Community law into the Member States. This chapter will examine the history of the Community, describing briefly the main events and decisions which have contributed to shaping its legal and constitutional structure, as well as providing a brief account of the theories of integration which underlay many of the attempts at progress and reform. Reference will be made to the 'European Community' to describe all three Communities even though, until the amendments made by the Treaty on European Union (TEU) in 1992, the European Coal and Steel Community (ECSC), the Economic Community (EEC) and the Atomic Energy Community (Euratom) were, properly speaking, the 'Communities'. After the TEU, the EEC is renamed the European Community, whereas the ECSC and the Euratom retain their original titles, but it is likely that the title European Community will continue to be used to refer to all three.

2. THE HISTORY AND IDEAS BEHIND EUROPEAN INTEGRATION

Most accounts of European integration begin with the aftermath of the Second World War, and with the desire to secure a lasting peace between European nations. After the destruction and ruin of the war years, and the climate of nationalism which preceded them, many people hoped for a new model of political co-operation in Europe. This important point in the story of modern European integration, however, should also be considered in a wider timeframe, and placed in the context of ideas of European unity stretching back considerably further.

D. Urwin, The Community of Europe [1]

Yet while this ferment of the months surrounding the final cessation of hostilities may have provided the seed bed for the developments in European integration in the years since 1945, the idea of and the desire for unity had had a much more prolonged prologue. Across the centuries, intellectuals and political leaders alike had dreamed of overcoming the unique historical characteristic of Europe: its extreme political fragmentation. . . .

As the Enlightenment and ideas on liberalism and democracy began to take firmer root, the focus of integrative schemes shifted away from the religious unity of Europe towards its intellectual unity, and away from the rights of princes and

[1] D. Urwin, *The Community of Europe: A History of European Integration* (Longman, 1991), 1–2. Urwin traces many of the calls for various forms of European co-operation and unity before the onset of the Second World War.

kings towards a broader institutional framework that explicitly or implicitly meant the end of independent territorial unity. The prominent English Quaker, William Penn, was one of the first to argue, in 1693, for a European Parliament and the end of the state mosaic in Europe.

During the war, the Resistance movement strongly supported the idea of a united Europe, as a way of consolidating the spirit of co-operation and fellowship of the war years and replacing the destructive forces of national pride and chauvinism.[2] However, despite the efforts and urgings of federalists such as Altiero Spinelli, the movement for integration faltered after the war, especially after the electoral defeat in the United Kingdom of Churchill, who had been a strong proponent of European unity. Promptings towards greater European co-operation, however, came from other sources. Faced with the onset of the Cold War and with Europe's severe post-war economic problems, the United States in 1947, the same year in which the General Agreement on Tariffs and Trade (GATT) was signed in an effort to liberalize world trade,[3] announced its so-called Marshall Plan. The Marshall Plan was a scheme to provide financial aid for Europe, and the United States required some form of organization to be set up which would administer the programme.[4] This became, in 1948, the Organization for European Economic Co-operation (OEEC) and eventually, in 1960, the broader Organization for Economic Co-operation and Development (OECD). Although it was essentially intergovernmental, the OEEC required a degree of institutional co-ordination and co-operation between the European states which received aid, and provided certain experience which would be useful for the more developed forms of co-operation and integration which were to come.[5]

Further examples of early co-operation in defence and other matters were agreements such as the 1948 Brussels Treaty between France, the United Kingdom and the three Benelux countries, the North Atlantic Treaty Organization (NATO), signed in 1949, and the Western European Union, created in 1954, which was itself based on the earlier Brussels Treaty. On the economic side, Belgium, The Netherlands, and Luxembourg had signed the Benelux Treaty in 1944, with the aim of establishing a customs union between them. Developments in the direction of political union were stalled by the United Kingdom, when, after the 'Congress of Europe' was convened at The Hague in 1948, with a view to drawing up proposals for European unity, the

[2] See the collection of *Documents of the History of European Integration*, ed. W. Lipgens (European University Institute, 1985).

[3] The GATT has now been replaced, after the lengthy Uruguay Round negotiations, by the GATT 1994, with an agreement setting up a new World Trade Organization to come into force by 1995.

[4] On the American enthusiasm for European integration, not simply as a means of averting the threat of Communist dominance in Europe, see F. Duchêne 'Less or More than Europe? European Integration in Retrospect' in *The Politics of 1992*, ed. C. Crouch and D. Marquand (1990), 9, 11–12.

[5] M. Holland, *European Integration From Community to Union* (Pinter, 1993) 23.

United Kingdom insisted on an organization which would be intergovernmental in nature and which did not compromise state sovereignty.[6] What emerged was the Statute on the Council of Europe, which was signed in 1949, providing for a Committee of Ministers and a Parliamentary Assembly. The latter had few powers beyond making recommendations to the Committee of Ministers, which, was in effect a twice-yearly meeting of the foreign ministers of the signatory states. However, despite its limitations—it has been likened to 'a standing diplomatic conference with a permanent secretariat'[7]—the Council of Europe became involved in many cultural, economic, and scientific acitivies, and collaborates with various other international organizations including the Community. One of the Council's best-known achievements was the adoption of the European Convention on Human Rights, which was signed in 1950 and came into force in 1953. The Convention established a Commission on Human Rights which began to operate soon thereafter, and a Court of Human Rights which came into operation in 1959. Further, the European Social Charter which was signed in 1961 and came into force in 1965, although without the same enforcement mechanisms as the Human Rights Convention, has been important in the field of social and economic rights.[8]

Given the failure to convince Britain to participate in more concrete moves towards European integration, the French foreign minister, Robert Schuman, who was a strong supporter of integration, proposed the pooling of Franco-German coal and steel resources under a single High Authority, with the option for other European states to participate, too. The plan had been drafted by Jean Monnet, a committed federalist who believed that economic co-operation between states was crucial. However, the plan was clearly not only economically inspired, but it also represented an attempt to restabilize relations between France and Germany after the war, to allay French fears about any military threat which the defeated German state might represent, and to bind them within a limited framework of peaceful co-operation in order to avert emerging rivalry over the coal-producing regions of the Ruhr and the Saar.[9] The Schuman proposal led to the setting-up of the European Coal and Steel Community (ECSC), and it was the first significant step towards European integration going beyond intergovernmentalism and establishing a supranational authority.[10]

The ECSC Treaty was signed in 1951 by six states: France, Germany, Italy, and the three Benelux countries. The Treaty aimed to establish a common market in coal and steel, beginning by abolishing import and export duties

[6] P. Kapteyn and P. VerLoren van Themaat, *Introduction to the Law of the European Communities*, ed. L. Gormley (2nd edn. Kluwer, 1989), 3.

[7] M. Westlake, *A Modern Guide to the European Parliament* (1994), 6.

[8] See Ch. 7 for discussion of the way the Court of Justice draws on the provisions of both the Convention and the Charter in its case law.

[9] M. Holland, *European Integration*, n. 5 above, 25.

[10] T. Hartley, *The Foundations of European Community Law* (3rd edn., Clarendon Press, 1994), 10, suggests that the term 'supranational' is *passé* and that the features distinguishing the Community from an intergovernmental organization are now described as 'federal'.

and trade restrictions, anti-competitive practices and state subsidies, and developing common policies for the coal and steel industries. To this end, four institutions were set up: a High Authority, made up of nine independent appointees of the six Member State governments (in practice, two from each large state), and which was to be the main executive institution with decision-making and responsibility for implementing the aims of the Treaty; an Assembly made up of delegates chosen by their respective national Parliaments, which was to exercise mainly supervisory powers; a Council made up of one representative of each of the Member State governments, which had both a consultative role and some decision-making powers—its assent was also required for various High Authority decisions—and which was to harmonize the activities of the states and the High Authority; and finally a Court of Justice of nine judges, which was to interpret and apply the Treaty provisions and to ensure that they were observed. Since the High Authority could adopt binding decisions by a majority of its members, albeit in many cases after consulting various bodies, it was effectively a supranational authority. However, its influence was countered to some extent in those areas in which its decision was not final by the Council, which, being made up of national ministers, represented the interests of the Member States. The balance of power between the High Authority (later named the Commission after the Merger Treaty in 1965) and the Council was rather different under the ECSC Treaty from under the later EEC Treaty, with a stronger supranational element and a weaker intergovernmental element on account of the dominant position of the High Authority. The other reason generally given for the enhanced role of the executive High Authority under the ECSC Treaty is the greater level of detailed policy set out in the provisions of the ECSC than in the EEC Treaty. The Assembly had fewer powers, mainly to deliver opinions and to supervise the High Authority through questions by considering its general reports. In extreme circumstances it could require the resignation of the High Authority by a vote of censure. It has been said that the inclusion of Article 21 in the ECSC Treaty, which provided for the possibility of direct elections 'although described by some as inconsequential window, was a significant conceptual step'.[11] The establishment of a Court of Justice, as we will subsequently see, was an important move in terms of its potential to contribute towards legal and political integration in Europe. On its establishment, however, it was intended primarily to rule on the validity of the acts of the High Authority, either in direct actions before the Court of Justice under Article 33 or on a reference from a national court under Article 41.[12] Article 49 enables the Coal and Steel Community to be self-financing through direct levies on coal and steel production. Article 97 provides that the lifespan of the Treaty is to be fifty years, so that it will expire in 2002.

[11] M. Westlake, *A Modern Guide*, n. 7 above, 10.

[12] It was not until Case C–221/88 *Busseni* [1990] ECR I–495 that the ECJ ruled that it had jurisdiction under Art. 41 ECSC to rule, in references from a national court, not just on the validity of ECSC law but also on its interpretation.

Although progress with the aims of the ECSC was slow and complicated, it was a very significant development, as much because of what it symbolized as because of its actual achievements in the organization of the coal and steel market. It was clear from the outset that, for its architects and proponents, this Community was not merely about coal and steel, but represented a first step in the direction of the integration of Europe. Many supporters of European unity were 'federalists', in the sense of believing in the creation of a single supranational political entity, with constitutionally defined powers, which would take over many of the functions of the individual nation-state. By contrast, Monnet, who drew up the plans on which the ECSC was based and who subsequently served as the first President of the ECSC High Authority, is generally described as a 'functionalist'. While the aims of those who supported a functional approach to integration were essentially the same as the aims of those who advocated a more federal approach, there was certainly disagreement over the proper steps or method of pursuing these aims.[13] The functionalist theory, which was subsequently rejected in this context by political scientists and other theorists of Community integration, is described below.

M. Holland, European Integration From Community to Union[14]

The earliest conceptual approach that was used to provide a framework for Community integration was the theory of functionalism as first constructed by David Mitrany in the inter-war years. The underlying assumption was very close to the idea of subsidiarity introduced into the Community's intergovernmental discussions of 1991. For Mitrany, 'the functional approach emphasises the common index of need. There are many such needs that cut across national boundaries, and an effective beginning could be made by providing joint government of them' . . . Thus, for example, coal and steel production or agriculture could be removed from national control and decision-making authority given to a functional agency separate from any nation state.

Holland describes the two main assumptions of the functionalist theory of integration: first that the establishment of institutional co-operation in particular sectors or policy areas would lead to the expansion of this co-operation into other areas, and secondly that such co-operation would lead to changes in popular opinion and mood, in favour of further integration. However, in the light of the way in which the Community developed, the functional theory was subsequently abandoned in favour of other theories which were considered to have greater explanatory weight.

According to the following author, the course of integration in the European Communities has been described as a linear development, beginning with the functionalism of the 1950s, and moving to the neofunctionalism

[13] See P. Sutherland, 'Joining the Threads: The Influences Creating a European Union' in *Constitutional Adjudication in European Community and National Law*, ed. D. Curtin and D. O'Keeffe (Butterworths, 1992), 12–14.

[14] N. 5 above, 14–15.

which developed in response to the perceived inadequacies of functional theory. Neofunctionalism, in its turn, subsequently became less popular, and other theories and views of integration became dominant at different stages in the Community's history.[15] Clearly, a linear analysis is a necessarily simplified description of what is undoubtedly a more complex picture, since there will always, at any given time, be a range of views and theories of the course of European integration, but it does provide a broad overview of the development of theories of European integration.

J. Lodge, The European Community and the Challenge of the Future[16]

The role of the nation state in the international system provides the starting point for all approaches to the study and analysis of European integration. Two such approaches—functionalism and federalism—precede the inception of the European Community system. Functionalism starts from the premise that by promoting functional cooperation among states it may be possible to deter them from settling disputes over competition for scarce resouces aggressively. The logic behind the approach is to prevent war not negatively—by keeping states apart—but positively by engaging them in cooperative ventures. The approach rests on sustaining international cooperation by collective action and the creation of cross-cutting ties, consensus and attitudinal changes at the popular level. It proposes the notion that form should follow function to establish functionally specific agencies—initially in what were then seen as non-contentious areas like welfare. These were to transcend national boundaries and be managed by rational technocrats (not swung by the vagaries of political ideology and power-hungry political parties) owing allegiance to a functionally specific organization not to a given nation state. The vehicle for cooperation is economic. This has often led to the claim that functionalism separates politics from economics: politics represents the high ground (politically charged, sensitive, combative issue areas) whereas economics is concerned with low politics—functional, non-contentious issues. Such a dichotomy is untenable. However, altruistic notions are behind its guiding principles: the idea of the collective endeavour is emphasized together with the pursuit of the common good. . . . Eventually, a web of overlapping functionally specific international organizations will be created. Their tasks will cover those areas of the economy essential to running military machines. Governments, deprived of control over those areas, will be unable to pursue war and will eventually be left to manage residual areas not covered by functional bodies. . . .

Neofunctionalists have a common starting point with functionalists in their attachment to the collective pursuit of mutually beneficial goals leading to enhanced economic prosperity. But where functionalists attach importance to learning processes, allegedly apolitical, technocratic socio-economic welfare functions, consensus-building and functional specificity, neofunctionalists adopt a pluralist perspective. They argue that competitive economic and political elites mediate in the process and not only become involved in it but become key players. . . . Neofunctional integration sees integration as a process based on

[15] The 3rd and 4th stages referred to by Lodge in the essay cited are the 'intergovernmental' phase of the 1970s and the 'neo-federal' phase of the 1980s and 1990s.

[16] Introduction, xix (1993).

spill-over from one initially non-controversial, technical sector to other sectors of possibly greater political salience, involving a gradual reduction in the power of national government and a commensurate increase in the ability of the centre to deal with sensitive, politically charged issues. . . .

Neofunctionalists' emphasis on economic activity, competition, rules of the game, the role of incremental spillover and the primacy of economic elites has led to this particular approach to integration theory being seen as the most relevant to an analysis of the economic dynamics of the single market.

However, although the ECSC did have some success in bringing about a period of co-operation and a greater degree of trust between the Member States, in particular between France and Germany, the period between 1951 and 1957 was a mixed one from the point of view of European integration. The sensitive area of defence was next to be tackled, and rather than agree to German rearmament within NATO, as the United States had suggested, France had proposed instead, in its Pleven plan of 1950, the setting up of a European Defence Community (EDC) with a European army, a common budget, and joint institutions. The EDC Treaty was signed in 1952 by the six ECSC states, with Britain once again refusing to participate, but progress towards ratification was slow. It was argued that, if there was to be a European army, a common European foreign policy would also be needed and, on this basis, plans for a European Political Community were drawn up. The 1953 draft statute which emerged represented a serious effort at designing a European federation, with a detailed institutional structure and ambitious aims, including a co-ordinated foreign policy and eventual economic integration. However, these developments were soon to be stopped in their tracks, when France, which had been wary of the remilitarization of Germany and had delayed for some time, finally submitted the EDC Treaty to its national assembly where the proposal to debate its ratification was rejected.[17] This resulted in the shelving of the plans for both defence and political union, and more generally it resulted in a very serious setback to the progress of European integration.[18] It would be thirty-nine years before the Member States would ratify another Treaty—that signed at Maastricht in 1992—which purported to establish a 'European Union'.

3. THE EEC AND EURATOM TREATIES

On the other hand, moves towards integration at the time were not entirely halted. After a conference of foreign ministers of the six states in Messina in

[17] According to J. Pinder, 'The Single Market: a step towards European Union', *ibid.* 51, this defeat was due to 'a combination of nationalists and stalinists' in the French National Assembly in 1954.

[18] See Ch. 7 for its possible effect on the exclusion of fundamental rights from the subsequent EEC Treaty.

Italy in 1955, agreement on moving in the direction of economic integration was reached. This has been described as 'triumphing over both a more limited conception advocated by West Germany that fell somewhere between supranationalism and the old sectoral route, and the doubts of France over the whole concept of the common market'.[19] A Committee chaired by Paul-Henri Spaak, who was the Belgian Prime Minister and another strong advocate of integration, published its report in 1956 which contained the basic plan for what became the European Atomic Energy Community (Euratom) and the European Economic Community (EEC). This time, although political motivation and political aims may have underlain the Treaties, the focus was specifically economic. The peaceful development of atomic energy under the responsibility of a permanent institution was considered to be of great importance, and as a clearly defined sector it was an appropriate area of energy policy which could be placed under common authority. With regard to the EEC Treaty, the following extract begins with a quote from the Spaak report, and continues by summarising some of the themes and arguments of the report.

P. Kapteyn and P. VerLoren van Themaat, Introduction to the Law of the European Communities[20]

'The purpose of a common market must be the creation of a large area with a common economic policy, so that a powerful unit of production is formed and continuous expansion is made possible, as well as an increased stability, an accelerated increase of the standard of living, and the development of harmonious relations between the Member States'. For this, a fusion of the separate national markets was absolutely essential. A division of labour on a fairly large scale can put an end to waste of economic resources. A greater certainty that the requisite sources of supply are permanently accessible makes it possible to abandon productive activities which pay no attention to costs.

This grand design is worked out further in the report around three topics. The *fusion of markets* involves the establishment of a customs union, the abolition of quantitative restrictions, free movement of services and a common agricultural policy. This fusion of markets should be accompanied by a *policy for a common market*. Indeed, in the present economic situation an expansion of markets and of competition *per se* would not yet be sufficient to ensure the more rational division of economic activities and the most favourable degree of expansion. A common competitive regime would be needed and also provisions for harmonisation of laws and the development of a common transport policy. Another essential point was a co-ordination of national economic policies, so as to avoid difficulties with the balance of payments, if possible, and also common action for eliminating these difficulties, should they arise. *To ensure the development in this common market of European economic resources and their full use*, financial aid for investments and retraining of workers would be necessary in order to promote the transformation of enterprises, the development of economically backward regions, and professional mobility. Freedom of movement should also be given to the production factors—labour and capital.

[19] Urwin, *History*, n. 1 above, 74.

[20] L. Gormley ed. (2nd edn., 1989), 13–14.

The economic impetus behind the 1957 Treaties was thus clear. In accordance with the thrust of the Spaak report, the EEC Treaty avoided the explicit political aims of the earlier draft EPC Treaty, and concentrated on economic integration, setting out its aims in the preamble and in Article 2. These reflected the recommendations of the report, being to establish a common market, progressively to approximate the economic policies of the Member States, to promote harmonious development of economic activities throughout the Community, to increase stability and to raise the standard of living, and finally to promote closer relations between the Member States. Barriers to trade were to be abolished and a common customs tariff was to be set up, undistorted competition was to be ensured, national economic and monetary policies were to be progressively co-ordinated, and fiscal and social policies gradually harmonized. Unlike the ECSC there was to be no temporal limit on the existence of the Treaty. The Parliamentary Assembly and the Court of Justice were to be shared with the ECSC,[21] but there was to be a separate Council of Ministers and executive authority—this time called the Commission rather than the High Authority. It was not until the Merger Treaty of 1965 that these two institutions were also merged and shared by the three Communities.[22] Under Article 193 of the EEC Treaty, an Economic and Social Committee with advisory status was set up, and this was to be shared with the Euratom Community.

The location of the Community institutions which, according to the Treaties, was to be decided by agreement of the Member States, was a matter of some dispute. The Assembly of the ECSC had been located in Strasbourg, with the High Authority, the Council, and the Court of Justice in Luxembourg. Now the Council of Ministers, the Commission, and their respective staffs, as well as the Economic and Social Committee are based in Brussels. Certain meetings of the Council are held, and certain departments of the Commission are based, however, along with the Court of Justice and the European Investment Bank,[23] in Luxembourg. The Parliament has continued to sit in Strasbourg, with its secretariat in Luxembourg and certain sessions and committee meetings in Brussels. These various seats were finally confirmed by the European Council (i.e. the heads of government of the Member States) at its meeting in Edinburgh in 1992, leaving the seat of other institutions to be decided by a subsequent European Council.[24]

The common market was to be established over a transitional period of sev-

[21] This was decided in the Convention on certain Institutions common to the European Communities, signed on the same day as the EEC and Euratom Treaties in 1957.

[22] Treaty establishing a Single Council and a Single Commission of the European Communities, signed on 8 Apr. 1965.

[23] The European Investment Bank was established under Art. 129 of the EC Treaty to finance projects in less-developed regions of the Community, as a kind of early regional policy. After the Treaty on European Union amendments it is now mentioned in Arts. 4b and 189d–e.

[24] It was also decided that the seat of the Court of Auditors, created in 1975 by the second budgetary treaty, and the Court of First Instance, created in 1986 by the Single European Act, should be in Luxembourg.

eral stages, during which tariff barriers between the states would be removed and a common external customs tariff set up. There were to be common policies in agriculture and transport, free movement of workers, companies, the self-employed, goods and services, and strict control of anti-competitive practices in the various states. A European Social Fund was established to improve employment opportuntites, and an Investment Bank to give loans and guarantees and to help less developed regions or sectors was set up, and a European Development Fund for overseas countries and territories of some of the Member States was set up by an implementing Convention attached to the Treaty.

The balance of power between the Commission and the Council was not the same under the EEC Treaty (or under Euratom, whose institutional provisions are essentially the same as those in the EEC Treaty) as it had been under the ECSC Treaty. The Commission was not to have the same degree of legislative autonomy under the EEC Treaty as it had under the earlier Treaty, and the Council was to have the power of approval of most Commission legislative proposals. However, the Commission was given a very important position, since it was to be the initiator of all legislation and the overall 'watchdog' of the Treaties, as well as having certain decision-making powers of its own and such implementing powers as the Council conferred upon it. It was to be the negotiator of international agreements on behalf of the Community, and had powers under various Articles to ensure compliance with the Treaty by the Member States and others.

Voting in the Council was to be weighted, but its voting procedure was to vary according to the nature of the issue. In a very few instances it could vote by simple majority, in many other matters by qualified majority, and in yet others unanimity was required. It will be seen that the issue of voting in Council is crucial to the nature and development of the Community, since it determines essentially whether intergovernmentalism—i.e. the interests of the Member States—or supranationalism—i.e. the overall interest of the Community—is to dominate. It will also become evident that the legislative process and the different voting procedures for different matters under the Treaty can be quite arbitrary, and that the procedures can represent the result of political bargaining and compromise in the course of negotiating on the terms of an amending Treaty, rather than anything intrinsically important to the issue on which a vote is being taken. On the whole, the process of weighted qualified-majority voting was intended to give greater weight to the larger member states than to the smaller, to reflect in part the differences in their population size.

The Parliamentary Assembly, which, although it called itself the Parliament, was not to be officially so named until the adoption of the Single European Act in 1986, had few powers under the original provisions of the Treaty. It now had a consultative role in legislation, but was largely a supervisory body whose powers involved questioning the Commission, receiving its annual report. It also possessed, as it had under the ECSC Treaty, a strong but never-used power of censure, whereby it could require the Commission to resign *en bloc* by a motion of censure.[25]

4. 1966–86: FROM THE LUXEMBOURG ACCORDS TO THE SINGLE EUROPEAN ACT

Despite the fact that the EEC Treaty avoided issues of political integration, calls for political co-operation between the states continued throughout the early 1960s. President de Gaulle of France clearly favoured an intergovernmental rather than a supranational model of European co-operation, and he proposed a regular forum for meetings of the heads of government of the six Member States. However, this proposal was not taken up with any enthusiasm until the emergence of European Political Co-operation in 1970. De Gaulle's view of the Community during these years was at odds with that of the other Member States, and a source of tension between France and the Commission which, under Walter Hallstein as President, had adopted a dynamic and activist approach.

(a) Crisis: The Luxembourg Accords

This tension erupted into a crisis in 1965, when the time came, under the transitional provisions of the Treaty, for the Council of Ministers to move to qualified-majority voting rather than the unanimous voting which had been in force until then. De Gaulle objected to an important institutional reform proposal made by the Commission—which was combined with a proposal to resolve a conflict over agricultural policy—for the Community to raise its own resources from agricultural levies and from tariffs on goods from outside the Community, instead of being funded by national contributions. This 'federalist-inspired' proposal was significant not just because of its strengthening of the autonomy of the Community,[26] but because it would also empower the Commission and the Parliament, since the Commission would control the budget under the supervision of the Parliament. De Gaulle strenuously objected, and after a failure to reach a compromise in the Council, France refused to attend any further Council meetings and adopted what became known as the 'empty-chair' policy. This lasted for seven months, from June 1965 until January 1966, after which a settlement was reached, which became known as the Luxembourg Compromise, or the Luxembourg Accords. These Accords, which were to have considerable impact on the direction and pace of Community development over the next two decades, were essentially an agreement to disagree over voting methods in the Council, which had been

[25] Many motions of censure have, however, been tabled over the years. See K. Bradley 'Legal Developments in the European Parliament' (1992) 12 *YBEL* 505.

[26] See J. Pinder, *European Community: The Building of a Union* (Oxford University Press 1991), p.120.

one of de Gaulle's major concerns. The first part sets out the view of the other five Member States, and the second the French view:

> I. Where, in the case of decisions which may be taken by a majority vote on a proposal from the Commission, very important interests of one or more partners are at stake, the Members of the Council will endeavour, within a reasonable time, to reach solutions which can be adopted by all the Members of the Council while respecting their mutual interests and those of the Community, in accordance with Article 2 of the Treaty.
>
> II. With regard to the preceding paragraph, the French delegation considers that where very important interests are at stake the discussion must be continued until unanimous agreement is reached.
>
> III. The six delegations note that there is a divergence of views on what should be done in the event of a failure to reach complete agreement.
>
> IV. The six delegations nevertheless consider that this divergence does not prevent the Community's work being resumed in accordance with the normal procedure.[27]

An agreement to disagree would not resolve the practical question of voting procedures in Council, of course, and in practice the French view prevailed. The Member States endeavoured to reach agreement in their meetings, and the effect of pleading the 'very important interests' of a state was treated as a veto which the other Member States would respect. Qualified-majority voting became the exception rather than the norm. The 'return to intergovernmentalism', which has been described as the next stage of integration after functionalism and neofunctionalism, greatly affected the dynamics of the Community in the following years.

D. Urwin, The Community of Europe[28]

In particular, the Luxembourg Compromise permitted a State to plead special circumstances in the Council of Ministers; in other words it would be able to exercise a veto on matters which it believed and claimed might adversely affect its own vital national interests. At heart, this was probably almost as welcome to the other five as it was to France. A further important consequence was an increase in the importance of the national governments relative to the authority of the Commission. The latter was obliged in practice to pledge that it would consult and inform governments at all stages of any initiative, that it would cooperate more closely with the Council of Ministers and that it would not seek in the future to behave like a government. In short, the crisis resolved some of the ambiguity in the Treaty of Rome between supranationalism and intergovernmentalism. The effect of the crisis and its resolution through the Luxembourg compromise was that the future development of the EEC would be much more as an intergovernmental union of independent states.

[27] Bull. EC 3–1966, 9. [28] Urwin, n. 1 above, 115.

The shift of power away from the Commission towards the Council of Ministers also had a further weakening effect on the Parliament, which exercised supervisory powers over the Commission. It also emphasized the importance of COREPER, the Committee of Permanent Representatives established under Article 151 of the EEC Treaty, which prepared the agenda for Council meetings, since it carried out most of the negotiation between the Commission and the Council on the various proposals and initiatives to be put forward by the Commission.

While the Community was experiencing internal crises, on the other hand, it was increasingly finding its voice on the international stage as a single entity rather than as six Member States. This could be seen in the GATT negotiations of 1967, and in the signing of the Yaoundé Convention between the EEC and eighteen African states in 1963, which was intended to offer preferential treatment in importation to developing countries.

(b) Enlargement of the Community

The next boost to the Community came with the first enlargement in 1973. Initially in the 1950s, the United Kingdom had chosen to remain outside the EEC, and had proposed instead a looser and wider free trade area with a simple institutional structure. When this was rejected by the six states which intended to form the EEC, the United Kingdom instead in 1960 set up the European Free Trade Association (EFTA) with six other states, Norway, Sweden, Austria, Switzerland, Denmark, and Portugal. It was in 1961, after a change of policy, that the United Kingdom made its first application for membership of the Community. De Gaulle, however, was determined that the United Kingdom should not join—since he viewed Britain's place as being within the Commonwealth rather than as part of continental Europe—and he firmly vetoed the application, not only on this occasion but also after its second application in 1967. The relationship between EFTA and the EEC at this stage was not good, and it was not until after de Gaulle's resignation that Britain's application for membership was finally accepted, together with those of Ireland and Denmark in 1973. At the same time Norway, whose application had also been accepted, delivered its first blow to Community morale when it failed to ratify the Treaty of Accesssion after a national referendum had yielded a majority opposing Community membership. In 1981 the Community expanded again when Greece became a member. Greenland, however, finally left the Community in 1985 after obtaining a degree of internal legislative independence from Denmark, and Spain and Portugal became members in 1986.

(c) Political Co-operation

Moves towards co-operation in political matters had begun again in 1970, when the Davignon Report, which was commissioned after the Hague summit of 1969, recommended amongst other things the holding of quarterly meetings of the foreign ministers of the Member States, as well as the establishment of a permanent political secretariat. This became an essentially intergovernmental forum for co-operation in foreign policy, without a developed institutional structure such as that existing within the Community. A second report in 1973 recommended its continuation as a form of co-operation, and it became known as European Political Co-operation (EPC). EPC was successful and enabled the Community to be represented as one voice in other international organizations in which all of the Member States participated, but it represented a move towards intergovernmentalism. Further, in 1974 the European Council was established to regularize the practice of holding summits. This body was to be made up of the heads of governments of the Member States, and the President of the Commission would be allowed to attend bi-annual meetings. The practice of 'summitry' represented by the European Council,[29] although it provided the Community with much-needed direction which its internal structure did not provide, represented a weakening in the supranational element of the Community. In terms of its relation to the other Community institutions, the European Council was not within the framework created by the Treaties, and it was not until the Single European Act was passed that it was actually recognized in a formal instrument—although again outside the structure of the EC Treaties. According to one commentator, the European Council as it was created symbolized 'a real triumph for advocates of intergovernmental co-operation which by its very nature eludes parliamentary supervision'.[30]

This trend within the Community from supranationalism towards intergovernmentalism from the time of the Luxembourg Compromise until the adoption of the Single European Act in 1986 has been the subject of much comment. The following extract reflects on the way the Luxembourg Accords affected the whole institutional structure and pace of progress of the Community from 1966 until 1982, when the author was writing.

P. Dankert, The EC—Past, Present and Future[31]

The dialectics of co-operation or integration have also continued to dominate the process of European unification—to an increasing extent—ever since 25th March 1957. It has been a continuous 'to and fro' for years, as can be seen from the course of development of the Community institutions. The Council of Ministers, which was originally intended to be a Community body, has now become largely an intergovernmental institution thanks to the famous Luxembourg Agreement, which, under French pressure, put an end to the majority decisions which the Council was supposed to take according to the Treaty on proposals submitted by the European Commission. This rule that decisions could only be taken

[29] Urwin, n. 1 above, 162.

[30] Pieter Dankert, 'The EC—Past, Present and Future' in *The EC: Past, Present and Future*, ed. L.Tsoukalis (Basil Blackwell, 1983).

[31] *Ibid.* 7.

unanimously had the effect of gradually transforming the Commission into a kind of secretariat for the Council which carefully checked its proposals with national officials before deciding whether or not to submit them. This in turn has a negative effect on the European Parliament which can only reach for power, under the Treaty, via the Commission. The move towards intergovernmental solutions for Community problems reached its peak—after frustrated attempts such as the Fouchet plan at the beginning of the 60s—in the creation of the European Council, the EPC and the EMS.

There were, however, forces working in the other direction: the system of the Community's own resources (a strong federalist element) and the related extension of the European Parliament's budgetary powers and, in 1979, the direct election of that Parliament.

During this period—often referred to as one of political stagnation in the Community—various reports on reforming the Community's institutional structure and strengthening the process of integration were commissioned and considered. After the Paris summit of 1974, the Belgian Prime Minister, Leo Tindemans, was asked to produce a report on the future of the Community. This report proposed a variety of far-reaching institutional reforms, including strengthening the Commission and the Parliament, providing for direct elections to the Parliament, and reform and strengthening of the European Council. Economic and monetary integration, citizenship rights, and development of social and regional policy were also suggested. However, this report, like various others, was not acted upon at the time, although many of the ideas surfaced again in later proposals for reform. In 1976, however, direct elections to the Parliament were agreed by the Member States, and the first elections took place in 1979. This event ought to have represented a significant development for the Community since the Parliament would become the first Community institution with popular legitimacy and a democratic mandate of sorts. However, the elections were not an unqualified success.

M. Holland, European Integration From Community to Union[32]

According to functional theory, popular support for the idea of the Community was believed to be a necessary condition for integration to occur. Consequently the direct elections were expected to demonstrate an awareness and support for the Community among the peoples of Europe. . . . In practice, these 'second order' elections provided only a modest advance towards European Union. . . . The supranational aspects of the election were partially camouflaged. Transnational party cooperation was at a rudimentary level and the decision to run each of the nine European elections independently and according to national electoral rules did little to persuade voters that the elections were any different from their respective national elections. The election issues were not European ones, but reflected national concerns and parochialism: as a result, turnout was disappointingly low, averaging just 62 per cent . . . the United Kingdom having the lowest figure at

[32] N. 5 above, 42.

32.6 per cent. . . . Faced with this apparent popular disinterest, the first direct elections failed to provide the anticipated springboard for accelerated integration; rather, as the Community entered the 1980s, the popular legitimacy and future development of the Community came into question and a renewed trend towards more modest intergovernmental cooperation emerged.

In 1978, after the summit of the European Council in Brussels, the so-called 'Three Wise Men' Committee was established to consider again the question of progress in the direction of greater political integration. This Committee similarly proposed institutional reforms which would strengthen the Commission, and which would weaken the intergovernmental element by introducing more qualified-majority voting in the Council.[33] Unsurprisingly, given the nature of the European Council which would consider the report, these proposals, like the Tindemans Report before them, did not cause any action to be taken. The fact that proposals for reform were continually solicited and committees regularly established to consider such proposals indicates that there was a feeling that reform of the Community structure was necessary. But since institutional reform is inextricably bound up with the intergovernmental/supranational balance within the Community, and thus with the question of the appropriate pace of political integration, it is not surprising that such change was slow to come—indeed, that it remained at a virtual standstill for some time.

It is worth noting, however, the suggestion which has been made that during this period of 'political stagnation' and 'decisional malaise' from the mid-1970s into the 1980s, less noticeable but important constitutional changes were taking place in the gradual erosion of the limits to Community competences—in other words, the substantive areas in which the Community had jurisdiction to act were expanding through the use of Article 235, the 'implied powers' provision of the Treaty, with the sanction of the Court of Justice.[34] It will be noted also in later chapters of this book that the Court, often at times when the Community's political processes were dormant or in crisis, contributed to its legal expansion and integration in various ways. Thus the doctrine of direct effect which was developed in the early 1960s was utilized in the 1970s to make effective Community policies which were provided for under the Treaty but which either the Member States or the Community institutions were failing to implement.[35] It was in the 1970s, too, that the Court developed a judicial policy of 'negative integration' by interpreting Article 30 of the Treaty, dealing with the abolition of non-tariff barriers to the free movement of goods, in a very broad manner. Again, this was done at a time when the decision-making processes in the Community were in decline, and the Court's approach was a

[33] For an official summary of the report see Bull. EC 11–1979 1.5.2.

[34] J. Weiler, 'The Transformation of Europe' (1991) 100 Yale LJ 2403, 2431–53. For further discussion of Art. 235, see Ch. 3.

[35] See Ch. 4.

very important one which subsequently influenced the Commission in its strategy.[36]

The next formal political initiative for reform, however, was brought forward by the German and the Italian foreign ministers, and became known as the Genscher–Colombo plan. This time, the proposal was not just for institutional reform, in the shape of giving the Parliament a power of proposal and making the European Council report to Parliament on progress towards union, but also on budgetary reform and expansion of Community competence in further policy areas. The European Council, after considering this report, issued a 'Solemn Declaration on European Union' in 1983, but this set out no real programme for concrete institutional change or reform.[37] The European Parliament then, in 1984, on the basis of a report put together by Altiero Spinelli, an Italian MEP and a committed federalist, overwhelmingly approved a 'Draft Treaty on European Union'. This again suggested radical institutional reform with a strengthened Commission, a Council sharing joint legislative and budgetary powers with the Parliament, and increased qualified-majority voting in the Council. Yet again, however, no action was taken on the basis of this draft Treaty. However, after the Fontainebleu European Council summit of 1984, two committees were set up to look at the question of revision of the Treaties and further political integration. One was the Adonnino Committee on a people's Europe, set up to consider the issue of furthering a European identity[38] and the second was the *ad hoc* Dooge Committee which was to look at questions of political reform. Although the Dooge Report, which again included far-reaching reform proposals, was not acted upon, the 1985 European Council meeting in Milan agreed, voting for the first time by majority only, to convene an intergovernmental conference under Article 236 of the EEC Treaty to discuss treaty amendment.[39] What emerged from the meetings of the working parties within the intergovernmental conference became the Single European Act, which was ready to be signed early in 1986.

(d) Developments in the Budgetary and Monetary Spheres

Before looking at the changes made by the Single European Act, a brief account of developments in budgetary policy, and of those towards economic and monetary union (EMU) in the interim years, will be given, since these developments were a very important part of the process of Community integration. In 1969, agreement on the principle of monetary union was reached, as well as an agreement on funding from the Community's own resources

[36] See the discussion of the 'Cassis' case, Case 120/78, *Rewe-Zentrale AG* v. *Bundesmonopolverwaltung für Branntwein* [1979] ECR 649, [1979] 3 CMLR 494 in Ch. 14.

[37] See Bull. EC. 6–1983, 1.6.1.

[38] See COM(84)446 Final.

[39] W. Nicoll and T. Salmon, *Understanding the European Communities* (Philip Allan, 1990), 38. See P. Pescatore, 'Some Critical Remarks on the Single European Act' (1987) 24 CMLRev 9, 14 for criticism of the outvoting of Denmark, Greece, and the UK in the European Council meeting, given the need for mutual consent in any revision of the Treaties.

rather than from national contributions, and on the expansion of Parliament's role in the budgetary process. The last two issues, which were brought about in the first budgetary Treaty of 1970 and the Own-Resources Decision of the same date, contained an important 'federal' element, since the funding proposal would make the Community financially independent, and any increase in Parliament's powers could be seen as strengthening its desired position as a Community legislature. The Decision provided that the Community's own resources were to come from agricultural levies, from customs duties on products from outside the Community, and from a maximum of 1 per cent Value Added Tax (VAT) as applied to an assessment basis determined in a uniform manner for the Member States. Articles 203–204 of the EEC Treaty were amended to reflect the increase in the Parliament's budgetary powers, which, amongst other things, shifted from Council to Parliament the symbolically important task of actually adopting the budget. By 1975, the date by which the Community budget was required to be financed entirely from its own resources, a second budgetary treaty had been agreed, with further increases in Parliament's budgetary role, and a Joint Declaration of the three institutions on a 'conciliation procedure' agreement was made in the same year. The Joint Declaration, followed in 1982 by a second such declaration, was intended to reconcile the views of Parliament and Council as regards legislation which has considerable financial implications. A Court of Auditors was also established by the 1975 Treaty to oversee Community revenue and expenditure and to report at the end of each financial year. In 1992, after the amendments made by the Treaty on European Union, the Court of Auditors eventually acquired official status as the fifth Community institution alongside the Parliament, Council, Commission, and Court. Little progress, however, was made towards economic and monetary union until the setting-up in 1979 of the European Monetary System, with an Exchange Rate Mechanism—although not all of the Member States at first participated—and a European currency unit (ECU).

One of the continuing problems which had faced the Community during the 1970s and 1980s was its serious financial situation, when it hovered 'on the brink of insolvency'.[40] Part of the reason for the Community's increasing levels of expenditure was the cost of one of its central policies—the common agricultural policy (CAP). This was also a very controversial policy, given its protectionism and the enormous and expanding costs of guaranteeing fixed prices for farmers. It was also a source of great divisiveness between Britain and the rest of the Community, which came to a climax in 1982 when the Council of Ministers overrode the British veto, adopting an agricultural prices agreement by qualified majority over British opposition. It was apparently felt by the other Member States that Britain was objecting, not to the agricultural prices agreement itself, but to the separate issue of what Britain considered to be its excessive contributions to the Community budget. However, at the

[40] Urwin, n. 1 above, 187.

1984 Fontainebleu summit, a formula for budget contributions which was acceptable to Britain at the time was agreed. On the other hand, spending continued to rise and in 1988 a second 'own-resources' decision was adopted to increase Community resources.[41] At the same time a more thorough budgetary reform was agreed, based on an increase in Member States' contributions in proportion to each state's share of the Community's gross national product.[42] Most recently, after the Treaty on European Union was signed, the European Council at Edinburgh agreed a further own-resources decision, which was subsequently adopted by the Council.[43]

In so far as institutional reform was concerned, however, the changes made in the Single European Act in 1986 represented the first major attempt at revising the Treaties.

5. THE SINGLE EUROPEAN ACT

In 1985 the British Commissioner, Lord Cockfield, had drawn up on behalf of the Commission a precise timetable for the completion of the single or internal market—known as the 'White Paper'—setting out a long list of the various barriers which would have to be removed before a deadline of 1992.[44] The Single European Act represented a commitment to this deadline, and despite the delay occasioned by a constitutional challenge to the Act in Ireland, the support of all of the Member States, including Thatcher's Britain, can be explained by the centrality of the 'market project' to the SEA.

Undoubtedly, at the time it was signed in 1986, the Single European Act represented the most important revision of the Treaties since they were first adopted. Despite the fact that the Act was criticized for its limited and even regressive effects,[45] there is no doubt that it heralded the revival of the Community momentum towards integration which has continued apace since then, with the adoption of the Treaty on European Union in 1992 and the plans for a further intergovernmental conference in 1996.

However, even in the specific changes and reforms it brought about, although they may not have gone as far as any of the committees or reports presented during the 1970s and 1980s had proposed, the Single European Act was significant. In the first place Title I, which did not amend the existing Treaties, gave a formal legal basis to European Political Co-operation as something which, together with the European Communities, would make progress towards European unity. Secondly, it formally recognized the European Council and provided for its twice-yearly meetings.

Title II then set out the amendments to the three existing Treaties, which introduced both institutional and substantive changes. With regard to the

[41] [1988] OJ L185/24.
[42] See J. Pinder, *European Community*, n. 26 above, Ch. 8.
[43] Council Regs. 2729/94 and 2730/94, [1994] OJ L293.
[44] COM(85)310.
[45] P. Pescatore, 'Some Critical Remarks', n. 39 above.

institutional changes, a Court of First Instance was provided for to assist the Court of Justice. Further, a new legislative procedure, to be called the 'co-operation procedure', was set out in Article 149, and was introduced into various areas of decision-making under the EEC Treaty, providing an enhanced consultative role for Parliament. Parliament was also given a power of veto over the accession of new Member States and over the conclusion of association agreements under Articles 237 and 238 of the EEC Treaty. Lastly, the so-called 'management committee' procedure under which the Council delegates powers to the Commission on certain conditions, was formally included within Article 145 of the Treaty.[46]

Then followed the substantive changes. First, Article 8a—renamed 7a after the Treaty on European Union—set out the internal market aim:

> The Community shall adopt measures with the aim of progressively establishing the internal market over a period expiring on 31 December 1992, in accordance with the provisions of this Article and of Articles 8B, 8C, 28, 57(2), 59, 70(1), 84, 99, 100A and 100B and without prejudice to the other provisions of this Treaty.
>
> The internal market shall comprise an area without internal frontiers in which the free movement of goods, persons, services and capital is ensured in accordance with the provisions of this Treaty.

A second substantive change was that qualified majority voting by the Council was introduced into a range of areas which had previously provided for unanimity, and a new Article 100A was introduced into the Treaty. Article 100A is by way of derogation from the 'harmonizing' provision in Article 100, which provides that the Council will act unanimously when issuing directives for the approximation of national laws or regulations which affect the establishment or functioning of the common market. What Article 100A provides is that, for achieving the objectives set out in Article 8a (now 7a), the Council will adopt approximating measures by qualified majority, where they have 'as their object the establishment and functioning of the internal market'. These provisions for qualified-majority voting will not apply to fiscal provisions nor to measures relating to the free movement of persons and to the rights of employed persons, and a controversial derogation for Member States from the provisions of a harmonization measure was provided in Article 100A(4).[47]

In addition to these 'internal market' reforms, Title II of the SEA also added to the existing substantive areas of Community competence, some of which had already in fact been asserted by the institutions and supported by the Court, but which had not been expressly contained in the original Treaties. The additions related to the areas of co-operation in economic and monetary union, social policy, economic and social cohesion (i.e. reducing disparities

[46] For further discussion of the management committee procedure see Ch. 3.
[47] See Ch. 25.

between the various regions of the Community),[48] research and technological development, and environmental policy.[49]

Finally, Title III, which, along with earlier provisions of the Single Act on European Political Co-operation, has since been repealed and replaced by the more detailed framework of the Treaty on European Union, set out in more detail the provisions which were to govern the operation of EPC. This Title did not amend the existing Treaties and its provisions operated outside the formal Community structures. It provided that the Commission was to be fully associated with EPC and that Parliament was to be informed and its views to be considered, and it provided for the development of common objectives and co-operation in the foreign-policy and security fields.

Responses to the SEA were mixed, some seeing it as an important and a positive step forward for the Community out of the political sluggishness which had gone before, whereas others saw it as a serious setback for the progress of the Community. The additions to Parliament's powers were minor, the Commission had gained no new powers, many of the 'new' areas of competence already existed in practice, and there had been no formal abolition of the 'Luxembourg veto'. Pierre Pescatore, formerly a judge on the Court of Justice, fell into the category of critics, and was very pessimistic about the potential of the Act.

P. Pescatore, Some Critical Remarks on the Single European Act[50]

The Act is *fundamentally* deceptive, because:

(a) It ignores all the achievements arrived at up until now and implies that all will have to be started over again. This is the impression conveyed by the new Article 8a to be inserted in the EEC Treaty when it says that 'the Community shall adopt measures with the aim of progressively establishing the internal market over a period expiring on 31 December 1992.'

(b) For the well-balanced and complex notion of a 'Common Market' the Single Act substitutes the one-sided notion of an 'internal market' based on an arbitrary selection of the Treaty objectives, ignoring essential features such as the rules on competition, freedom of current payments, economic policy, commercial policy, taxation, non-discrimination etc.

(c) No less than sixteen years after the end of the first transitional period, the Single Act opens a new period of transition of indefinite duration, the target date of 31 December 1992 being said to entail no legal obligation, as appears from a declaration inserted in the Final Act.

(d) During this indefinite period the Single Act allows for enlarged possibilities of unilateral protective measures by Member States under Article 36 of the EEC

[48] Apart from the provisions in Arts. 129 and 130 EEC establishing a European Investment Bank (and the setting up of a European Regional Development Fund in 1975—see Bull. EC 3–1975, 1201), regional policy was not developed within the Treaty framework.

[49] Various Community environmental measures were passed on the basis of Art. 100 before the adoption of the Single European Act, and the Council had adopted Environmental Action Programmes since 1973.

[50] N. 39 above, 11.

Treaty to which elusive notions such as 'safety', 'protection of the environment', and 'protection of the working environment' have been added.

Further accusations he makes against the Act are that its provisions are 'submerged in a flood of verbose vagueness', that 'pretentiousness is the principal mark of the Act', that some parts 'come close to ridicule', that 'ambiguity is the hallmark of most of the amendments introduced to the EEC Treaty', and that some clauses display 'the most vicious form of legal drafting'.[51] Pescatore was writing before the Single Act had actually come into force, in the hope that it would falter at some stage during the ratification process. However, it was duly ratified and came into force, and in the following extract, a commentator with the benefit of having observed the Act in operation for three years, compared the apparent weakness of the Act's provisions with a more optimistic assessment of what the Commission White Paper and the Act itself had actually achieved by 1991.

J. Weiler, The Transformation of Europe[52]

The bulk of the 1992 program is little more than a legislative timetable for achieving in seven years what the Community should have accomplished in the preceding thirty. The SEA is even less powerful. Its forays into environmental policy and the like fail to break new jurisdictional ground, and its majority voting provisions, designed to harmonise non-tariff barriers to trade, seem to utilise such restrictive language, and open such glaring new loopholes that even some of the most authoritative commentators believed the innovations caused more harm than good in the Community. Clearly, the new European Parliament and the Commission were far from thrilled with the new act.

And yet, with the hindsight of just three years, it has become clear that 1992 and the SEA do constitute an eruption of significant proportions. Some of the evidence is very transparent. First, for the first time since the very early years of the Community, if ever, the Commission plays the political role clearly intended for it by the Treaty of Rome. In stark contrast to its nature during the foundational period in the 1970s and early 1980s, the Commission in large measure both sets the Community agenda and acts as a power broker in the legislative process.

Second, the decisionmaking process takes much less time. Dossiers that would have languished and in some cases did languish in impotence for years in the Brussels corridors now emerge as legislation often in a matter of months.

For the first time, the interdependence of the policy areas at the new-found focal point of power in Brussels creates a dynamic resembling the almost forgotten predictions of neo-functionalist spillover. The ever-widening scope of the legislative and policy agenda of the Community manifests this dynamic. The agreement to convene two new intergovernmental conferences to deal with economic and monetary union just three years after the adoption of the SEA symbolises the ever-widening scope of the agenda, as does the increased perception of the Community

[51] *Ibid.* 15–16. [52] N. 34 above, 2454

and its institutions as a necessary, legitimate, and at times effective locus for direct constituency appeal.

What was noticeable about the Single European Act was how dominant the economic arguments—as opposed to the political arguments—were. The provisions on regional policy, the environment, and research, and even on institutional reform, seemed, in a sense, subsidiary to or merely supportive of the central aim of freeing the 'internal market' from interstate barriers. This ambiguity about its basic aim may have been one of the reasons for the support it gained, but it reveals what was noted at the outset of this chapter, i.e. that the European Community signifies very different things to different people. The following extracts illustrate the free market Europe/social and political Europe debate in relation to the Single European Act, but it is a theme which runs through the entire process of European integration, and which is as relevant after the Treaty on European Union as it was after the Single European Act.

V. Curzon Price, The Threat of Fortress Europe[53]

In fact, however, Europe could go either way. One could even take an optimistic view that the 'social dimension' will remain a list of non-binding general principles, that competition within the Single Market will shake out so many old inefficiencies (including those stemming from an excess of well-intentioned but excessively costly regulation) and generate such dramatic dynamic growth that the pressure for bedrock protection might actually shrink, thus setting the European economy on a permanently higher growth path . . . There is so much to be done by Europeans at the level of the Community that it would be missing a huge opportunity to let the socialists have their way. Above all, one must insist that a market based vision of European integration is not being anti-European, but rather the only way to achieve, in the long run, the objectives laid forth in the Single European Act.

In 1988, Margaret Thatcher, who, after signing the Single European Act, became displeased with the dynamism of the Commission under Jacques Delors, gave her famous Bruges speech in which she set out her vision of the Community, claiming that the EEC Treaty was intended as a charter for economic liberty. Ernest Wistrich, in the following extract, challenges this claim and counters the market-based vision of European integration.

E. Wistrich, After 1992: The United States of Europe[54]

This claim distorts the basic aims of the Treaty. Its explicitly declared objectives are to lay the foundations of an ever closer union among the peoples of Europe and ensure the economic and social progress of their countries by common action to eliminate the barriers that divide Europe. A further essential objective is the

[53] *Europe's Constitutional Future* (1990), 53, 68. [54] (1989) 15, 65.

constant improvement of the living and working conditions of people, and the reduction of differences in wealth between the regions.

. . .

In all progress towards European unity there has to be a trade off between the benefits to industry and commerce of a common market and the likely disadvantages to the weaker regions or sectors of society in a free-for-all environment if integration is to be acceptable to the poorer countries and to the public generally. The maintenance of a balance of advantage has thus been an essential condition of all integration. Criticisms by Mrs Thatcher, in 1988, of the Community's involvement in legislating for workers' rights, for example, had failed to recognize that these are as much part of the process of integration as the removal of barriers to trade within the Community.

Weiler, too, addresses the apparent narrowness of the internal market project in the Commission's White Paper and in the Single European Act, and the differing approaches to European integration which it concealed.

J. Weiler, The Transformation of Europe[55]

Unlike all earlier attempts and proposals to revive the Community, the 1992 White Paper, although innovative in its conception of achieving a Europe without frontiers, was entirely functional. . . . Critically, it eschewed any grandiose institutional schemes. These were to come as an inevitable result, once 1992 was in place. Because of this technocratic approach, the White Paper apparently appealed to those with different, and often opposing, ideological conceptions of the future of Europe. To some, it represented the realization of the old dream of a true common marketplace, which, because of the inevitable connection between the social and the economic in modern political economies, would ultimately yield the much vaunted 'ever closer union of the peoples of Europe'. To others, it offered a vision of the European dream finally lashed down to the marketplace, and importantly, a market unencumbered by the excessive regulation that had built up in the individual Member States.

Criticism of the excessive focus on the success or otherwise of the Community as a purely economic project has also been voiced.

W. Nicoll and T. Salmon, Understanding the European Communities[56]

The belief in the construction of a new Europe involving a new pattern of political relationships, as an experiment, has been distorted as the economic instruments identified to achieve political change and objectives have gradually become regarded as more important than the objectives themselves. The means are in danger of consuming the ends. The fact that the true nature of the European Community cannot be understood simply by focusing on the provisions of the founding Treaties has been obscured. As the cohort who lived through the rav-

[55] N. 34 above, 2457–8. [56] N. 39 above, 239.

ages of war, despair and destruction died, it was replaced by a new generation of citizens and adults which was brought up to focus on the economic dimension of the Community. In the 1970s, however, the sheen went off the economic miracle as progress ran into the wall of OPEC price increases and world recession. Given this, the shortcomings of the Community appear only too apparent to the new generations of Europeans.

Indeed, when considering perspective, the shortcomings are also apparent if the current situation is compared to the aspirations of the founding fathers. Their motivation was not the price of eggs, bacon or steel, but rather a revolution in international behaviour.

Whatever criticisms there may have been about the thrust and substance of the Single European Act, however, the Community momentum had been revived, and the renewal of qualified-majority voting affected not just the practice of the Council in a move away from consensus-based intergovernmentalism towards supranationalism, but it affected also the influence of the Commission and the Parliament in decision-making. The 'spectre of the veto' was not entirely banished, since some Member States continued to assert its existence, but it did not have its previously restraining effect on Community decision-making and qualified-majority voting became commonplace in the Council.

6. THE TREATY ON EUROPEAN UNION

The momentum which gave rise to and which was generated by the Single European Act continued after its adoption. The committee chaired by Jacques Delors on Economic and Monetary Union had presented a report in 1989 setting out a three-stage plan for reaching EMU. The European Council decided to hold an intergovernmental conference on the subject, and, significantly, to hold at the same time a second intergovernmental conference (IGC) on political union. The relationship between the two IGCs has been explained as follows:

> The second IGC on Political Union did not have such a long gestation period: it was not independently planned, but developed in response to the EMU decision. Key Community states thought it imperative to balance economic integration with political integration (or perhaps more realistically to link the latter to the more dynamic performance of the former). An economically integrated Europe without a comparable political dimension seemed the antithesis of the Community ideal.[57]

[57] M. Holland, n. 5 above, 73.

On the basis of the intergovernmental conference negotiations, a draft Treaty was presented by the Luxembourg presidency of the European Council in 1991. After various revisions of this draft at the European Council meeting in December of that year, the Treaty on European Union (TEU) was eventually agreed and signed in Maastricht in February 1992.[58] After vigorous debates leading up to the ratification process in the various Member States, which revealed a considerable amount of public disquiet and dissatisfaction with the Treaty and with the process of its negotiation, it was rejected by the Danish population in a national referendum. However, after several 'concessions' were secured by the Danish Government and formalized in a decision of the Heads of State at the Edinburgh European Council in 1992, including the right not to participate in the third and final stage of EMU and not to take on the Presidency of the European Council when defence issues were involved, a second referendum yielded a narrow majority in favour of ratification. When the last obstacle—in the shape of a challenge before the German Federal Supreme Court to the constitutionality of ratification[59]—was cleared, the Treaty entered into force in November 1993.

Undoubtedly, the popular profile of the Community has been raised more by the 'Maastricht' debate than by any previous development in the Community's history, even though some would contend that the Single European Act, with its revival of qualified-majority voting, represented a more significant step for the Community in the process of integration. Perhaps, apart from the detailed commitment to full economic and monetary union, the most obvious feature of the Treaty on European Union was the institutional change it wrought, establishing a 'three-pillar' structure for what was henceforth to be called the European Union, with the Communities as the first of these pillars. As noted above, the EEC Treaty was officially renamed the European Community Treaty.

There are seven titles in the Treaty on European Union. Title I includes the 'common provisions' which do not amend the EC Treaties but which set out the basic objectives of the TEU. Titles II, III, and IV cover the amendments to the EEC, ECSC and Euratom Treaties respectively—these are generally referred to as the first pillar. Title V constitutes the second pillar of Common Foreign and Security Policy (CFSP), Title VI the third pillar of Justice and Home Affairs (JHA), and Title VII contains the final provisions. Following these seven titles are the various protocols to the Treaty and the Declarations.

(a) Title I: The Common Provisions

Articles A to F of Title I did not amend the existing Treaties but set out the basic aims and principles of the newly created 'Union'. The controversial word

[58] For a commentary on the Treaty 'From Conception to Ratification', see R. Corbett, *The Treaty of Maastricht* (Longman, 1993).

[59] See Cases 2 BvR 2134/92 and 2159/92, *Brunner* v. *The European Union Treaty* [1994] 1 CMLR 57, discussed in Ch. 6.

'federal', which appeared in the draft Treaty as first presented after the intergovernmental conference, was dropped in favour of including in Article A the 'ever-closer union' language of the original EEC Treaty preamble. These common provisions, although non-justiciable, contain some high rhetoric: decisions are to be taken 'as closely as possible to the citizen', the Union is to organize relations between Member States and their peoples 'in a manner demonstrating consistency and solidarity' (Article A), it shall 'respect the national identities of its Member States', and it shall respect fundamental human rights (Article F). Article C provides that the *acquis communautaire*—that is the body of Community law which has been developed over the years—will be respected and built upon.

With regard to the aims of the Union, Article B provides:

> The Union shall set itself the following objectives:
>
> —to promote economic and social progress which is balanced and sustainable, in particular through the creation of an area without internal frontiers, through the strengthening of economic and social cohesion and through the establishment of economic and monetary union, ultimately including a single currency in accordance with the provisions of this Treaty;
>
> —to assert its identity on the international scene, in particular through the implementation of a common foreign and security policy including the eventual framing of a common defence policy, which might in time lead to a common defence;
>
> —to strengthen and protect the rights and interests of the nationals of its Member States through the introduction of a citizenship of the Union;
>
> —to develop close cooperation on justice and home affairs;
>
> —to maintain in full the *acquis communautaire* and build on it with a view to considering, through the procedure referred to in Article N(2), to what extent the policies and forms of cooperation introduced by this Treaty may need to be revised with the aim of ensuring the effectiveness of the mechanisms and the institutions of the Community.
>
> The objectives of the Union shall be achieved as provided in this Treaty and in accordance with the conditions and the timetable set out therein while respecting the principle of subsidiarity as defined in Article 3b of the Treaty establishing the European Community.

These common provisions are, according to Article L of the final provision of the TEU, not subject to the jurisdiction of the Court of Justice, although the Court is likely to be able to refer to them as part of the context within which provisions of the EC Treaty are to be interpreted.[60]

[60] It has also been suggested that, on the basis of Art. M TEU—which established that with the exception of the amending provisions, nothing in the TEU is to affect the Treaties establishing the European Communities—the Court of Justice could review acts of the European Council under Art. D of these 'non-justiciable' common provisions. See D. Curtin, 'The Constitutional Structure of the Union: A Europe of Bits and Pieces' (1993) 30 CMLRev 17, 27.

(b) Titles II–IV: Changes to the Existing Treaties

Within the changes made to the EEC Treaty, the TEU brought about not only institutional and legislative changes, but also a concrete timetable for economic and monetary union with provision for a European Monetary Institute and subsequently a European Central Bank. New areas of Community competence were added and existing areas expanded, a concept of European citizenship was introduced, a Parliamentary Ombudsman was provided for, the principle of 'subsidiarity' was formalized, and a 'Committee of the Regions' was established. A Social Protocol with an Agreement on Social Policy was annexed to the EC Treaty, although the United Kingdom did not sign the Agreement. Many other protocols were signed, including one which preserves the right of the United Kingdom to opt out of (or rather, if it so chooses, to opt into) the third and final stage of EMU, involving a single currency.[61] Lesser changes—principally some of the institutional amendments and the citizenship amendments—were made to the ECSC and Euratom Treaties. In all, the amendments made to the European Community by the TEU were numerous and complex and an attempt to summarize them will inevitably omit much that is important. Some of these—such as the legislative process, the principle of subsidiarity, the new powers of the institutions including the court, the notion of citizenship, and the Social Policy Agreement—will be discussed throughout the book in the chapters to which they are relevant.

Broadly speaking, however, the aims of the Community as defined in Article 2 of the EC Treaty were amended to include reference to economic and monetary union, as well as environmental concerns, convergence of economic policies, social protection, economic and social cohesion, and to emphasize not just balanced expansion but also 'sustainable' growth and 'quality of life' in addition to a raised standard of living. Article 3, which sets out the range of Community activities, in addition to listing some of the new aims mentioned in Article 2, and expanding some of the existing activities, also now includes policies relating to research and technological development, trans-European networks, health protection, education, 'the flowering of cultures', development co-operation, consumer protection, energy, civil protection, and tourism.

Article 4, in addition to placing the Court of Auditors on a footing equal to that of the other four institutions, provides that the Economic and Social Committee and the new Committee of the Regions—which are to share a common organizational structure—shall assist the Council and the Commission. Article 4a provides for both a European System of Central Banks (ESCB) and a European Central Bank (ECB), and Article 4b refers to the European Investment Bank.

A new timetable for free movement of capital was established by Article 73a–h, and the new provisions on economic and monetary policy appear in

[61] For criticism of some of the protocols, including the Irish 'abortion' protocol, the Danish 'acquisition of second homes' protocol, and the 'Barber' protocol, for 'tearing holes, of varying sizes, in the acquis communautaire veil' see Curtin, *ibid.*

Articles 102a to 109m. These provide for much closer co-ordination of economic policies, set strict 'convergence criteria' relating to the size of government deficits, and set out detailed provisions relating to the operation and powers of the ESCB and the ECB.[62] The timetable for the different stages of monetary union are then set out in Articles 109e–m, with the objective of eventually adopting a single currency.[63]

The most significant change to the existing institutions was the increase in Parliament's legislative involvement, with the introduction of what is generally referred to (although not in the Treaty itself) as the co-decision procedure. Parliament was also given the right to request the Commission to initiate legislation, and the power to block the appointment of the new Commission by refusing to give its approval.

(c) The Two Inter-governmental Pillars

The second and third pillars of the Union, which did not amend the existing Treaties and so remain outside the Community (i.e. EC, ECSC, and Euratom) institutional and legal structure, relate to a 'Common Foreign and Security Policy' and to co-operation in 'Justice and Home Affairs' respectively. However, these pillars are not entirely disconnected from the Community, since, although they concern the Member States acting together on an intergovernmental basis in these areas of policy, to some extent they involve the Community institutions and, in particular, the Council.

(i) Pillar 2, Title V: Common Foreign and Security Policy (CFSP) The area of Common Foreign and Security Policy is covered by Articles J–J.11 of the TEU. The Council may 'define a common position' based on the agreement of the Member States, to which the states must then ensure their national policies conform. On the basis of guidelines from the European Council, the Council of Ministers may decide that a certain matter should be the subject of 'joint action' and, in what may be a significant departure from the consensus-based intergovernmental approach of the second and third pillars, it is to specify those matters on which decisions may be taken by qualified majority. This is significant because, with certain limited exceptions, Member States are committed to the joint actions in the conduct of their activities. Procedural matters may also be decided by qualified majority, but otherwise the Council is to act unanimously. The Council of Ministers also has a role, along with the Western European Union, in the area of a possible future common defence policy. Article J.4(4) appears, in somewhat ambiguous terms, to safeguard the position of Member States which are neutral or which are not full members of the WEU. The Council is to draw up a report by the time the next inter-

[62] See also the various protocols on the ECB, ESCB, and EMI, as well as on the 'excessive deficit' procedure and the 'convergence criteria'.

[63] See J. Pipkorn, 'Legal Arrangements in the Treaty of Maastricht for the Effectiveness of the Economic and Monetary Union' (1994) 31 CMLRev 263.

governmental conference in 1996 is to be held, evaluating the progress which has been made and possibly proposing a revision of Article J.4, presumably with a view to moving further in the direction of a common defence policy. The Commission is to be 'fully associated' with the work carried out in CFSP and may, as may any Member State, refer any question to the Council or request the convening of an extraordinary Council meeting. In particular it is to be fully associated with the Presidency of the European Council in the tasks of representing 'the Union' and implementing any common measures adopted, as well as in keeping the European Parliament informed of the developments. Parliament is to be consulted by the Presidency 'on the main aspects and the basic choices' of the CFSP and its views are to be taken into consideration. It may ask questions of the Council and make recommendations, as well as holding an annual debate on progress in these areas of policy. A Political Committee is to assist the Council by monitoring the international situation, delivering opinions, and monitoring the implementation of agreed policies.

(ii) Pillar 3, Title VI: Justice and Home Affairs The Justice and Home Affairs Pillar—Articles K to K.9 of the TEU—deals with policies on matters such as asylum, immigration, 'third country' nationals, as well as co-operation on a range of 'international crime' issues and various forms of judicial co-operation. The Council of Ministers again has a role to play in this essentially intergovernmental policy area, where it is to adopt joint positions and draw up agreements in various specified areas on the basis of initiatives from the Member States or, on occasion, from the Commission. As in the CFSP provisions, the Council is to act unanimously except on matters of procedures and, under Article K.3(b), in the case of measures which are to implement joint action or to implement conventions which have been agreed.

The Commission again is to be 'fully associated' with the work done in the sphere of justice and home affairs, and the Parliament is to be informed and its views to be 'duly taken into consideration'. Again, as in the case of the CFSP, Parliament may question the Council or make recommendations to it, and is to hold an annual debate on progress made. A Co-ordinating Committee is to be set up to help the Council, which, like the Political Committee set up under CFSP, has a role similar to that of COREPER under the EC Treaty. Under the justice and home affairs pillar, unlike the CFSP pillar, the European Council does not appear to have the same role in first defining the principles and general guidelines of the policy before the Council of Ministers adopts joint positions.

(iii) The Court of Justice and Pillars 2 and 3 Article L of Title VII—the Title which contains the final provisions of the TEU—excludes the Court of Justice from exercising its powers in matters dealt with under the common provisions or the second or the third pillar. However, it seems that matters relating to justice and home affairs could be dealt with by the Court either if a Convention adopted under Article K.3(c) chooses to give the Court jurisdiction in

respect of its provisions, or if Article 100c of the EC Treaty is used in accordance with Article K.9 to deal with certain of the areas of action listed there. In the case of foreign and security policy, Article J.6 mentions co-operation and contribution by the Member States to the implementation of provisions referred to in Article 8c (which deals with protection of 'Union citizens' by Member States' diplomatic authorities) of the EC Treaty. The Court of Justice clearly has jurisdiction over the interpretation and enforcement of Article 8c, even if it relates to areas which could be considered to be foreign and security policy.

(iv) Enlargement of the Community after the TEU On the event of German reunification, it was decided by the European Council that it was unnecessary for there to be any revision of the Treaties in order for integration of the German Democratic Republic into the Community to take place.[64] Two of the EFTA countries, Austria and Sweden, applied for membership of the Community in 1989 and 1991 respectively.[65] At the same time, in 1991 an Agreement on the European Economic Area (EEA) between the EC and EFTA was made. The Agreement provides for free-movement provisions similar to those in the EEC Treaty—of goods, persons, services, capital, and similar competition policy and rules, as well as 'close co-operation' in the fields of research and development, the environment, education, and social policy. The EFTA members who signed the amended Agreement in May 1992 with the Community were Austria, Sweden, Finland, Iceland, Liechtenstein, Norway, and Switzerland, although the latter ultimately did not ratify the Agreement when it was rejected in a subsequent national referendum. The Agreement came into force at the beginning of 1994. The EEA Agreement established an EEA Council, consisting of members of the EC Commission and Council, and one member of the government of each of the EFTA states, with a function somewhat similar in relation to the EEA as the European Council has in relation to the Community structure. A Joint Committee was also established to implement the Agreement, made up of representatives of the contracting parties and meeting once a month, and a Joint Parliamentary Committee with mainly supervisory functions, made up of members of the European Parliament and members of the parliaments of the EFTA states. An EEA Consultative Committee was also established to provide a forum for representatives of the 'social partners' in the Community and the EFTA states. The establishment of an EEA court and the jurisdiction conferred upon it led the Court of Justice to rule that the first EEA Agreement was incompatible with the EC Treaty,[66] but after amendments which set up, instead of the EEA Court under the first version of the Agreement, an EFTA Court without any connection with the Court of Justice, the Court of Justice was satisfied that its

[64] See Bull. EC Supp.4–1990.

[65] Other applications received before this time, but which are unlikely to be accepted by the Community in the near future, were Turkey in 1987 and Cyprus and Malta in 1990.

[66] Opinion 1/91 [1991] ECR 6079, [1992] 1 CMLR 245.

ultimate interpretive authority in relation to the EC Treaty was not being undermined, and upheld the compatibililty of the amended Agreement with the Treaty under Article 228.[67]

After Austria and Sweden had applied to join the EC, Finland and Norway also applied for membership in 1992, as did Switzerland—although this was before that country's rejection by referendum of the EEA.[68] The Acts of Accession of Norway, Austria, Sweden, and Finland to the European Union were signed at the European Council meeting in Corfu in 1994, but only the latter three acceded in 1995 when, for the second time in just over twenty years, a national referendum in Norway yielded a majority opposed to accession. Given the fact of accession to the Community of three of the EFTA states, the 'shelf-life' and viability of the EEA Agreement has been questioned.[69]

Article O of the final provisions of the Treaty on European Union now provides the procedure for new states to become Members of the Union, replacing Article 237 of the EEC Treaty, Article 205 of Euratom, and Article 98 of the ECSC Treaty. Like the previous provisions of Article 237 of the EEC Treaty, which dealt with the procedure for accession to the Community, this requires the Council to act unanimously after receiving the opinion of the Commission and the assent of the Parliament.[70]

7. AFTER THE TREATY ON EUROPEAN UNION, WHERE NEXT?

The Treaty on European Union, like the Single European Act before it, has been subject to considerable analysis and commentary. The obscurity and secrecy of the processes of negotiating the Treaty, the incoherence and complexity of the new 'Union' structure, the mixed bag of institutional reforms, the partial borrowing of the Community institutions for areas of intergovernmental policy-making, and the many opt-outs and exceptions—the 'variable geometry'—have attracted a good deal of criticism. Similar fears about the next proposed intergovernmental conference have also been expressed. The feeling seems to be that the course of European integration is increasingly haphazard, that there is no clear vision of the future, and that the political process of inter-state jostling and bargaining which characterizes the drawing-up of

[67] Opinion 1/92 [1992] ECR I–2821, [1992] 2 CMLR 217.

[68] On the future applications of the eastern European states see D. Kennedy and D. Webb, 'The Limits of Integration' (1993) 30 CMLRev 1095.

[69] F. Weiss 'The Oporto Agreement on The European Economic Area—A Legal Still Life?' (1992) 12 YBEL 385. See also M. Cremona, 'The "Dynamic and Homogenous" EEA: Byzantine Structures and Variable Geometry' (1994) 19 ELRev 508.

[70] Art. N of the final provisions now governs amendments to the Treaties, replacing Arts. 236 EC, 204 Euratom, and 96 ECSC.

Treaties during and after intergovernmental conferences produces very mixed results.

The concept of 'variable geometry', which has been a particular focus for criticism, and its re-emergence in the debates leading up to the Treaty on European Union are explained in the following extract.

B. Laffan, The Governance of the Union[71]

During the long period of stagnation in the Community in the 1970s and early 1980s, there was a wide-ranging debate on the appropriateness for the Community of differentiated integration, known as 'variable geometry', two-speed Europe or Europe *à la carte*. Close examination of the Community points to the use of such formulae, notably in the EMS, in varying transitional arrangements, and in some differentiation in the application of EC law. The debate reemerged in relation to two areas of critical importance in the Inter Govermental Conferences, namely EMU and foreign and security policy. The suggestion that there could be a multi-speed approach to EMU is a central theme in the Bundesbank's thinking on EMU because of its concern for convergence. This model of EMU would involve a number of countries, whose economic performances are closely in tune, moving towards EMU at a faster pace than other EC states. The precise definition of the core or first speed countries is not yet clear.

A 'variable geometry' approach is also maintained in relation to a common foreign and security policy. When the Italian government submitted its paper on the WEU in September 1990, it proposed an 'opting-out' clause for countries like Ireland which did not want to participate in arrangements that might involve 'hard security' or defence.

The following extract forms part of a biting criticism of the whole package of the Treaty on European Union, in particular of features such as the mix of intergovernmentalism and Community institutions, and the likely impact of 'variable geometry' on the *acquis communautaire*, according to which all Member States previously were bound by the same body of legal rules and principles.

D. Curtin, The Constitutional Structure of the Union: A Europe of Bits and Pieces[72]

The result of the Maastricht summit is an umbrella Union threatening to lead to constitutional chaos; the potential victims are the cohesiveness and the unity and the concomitant power of a legal system painstakingly constructed over the course of some 30 odd years . . . And, of course, it does contain some elements of real *progress* (co-decision and powers of control for the European Parliament, increased Community competences, sanctions against recalcitrant Member States, Community 'citizenship', EMU etc.) but a *process* of integration, if it has any

[71] *Political Union*, ed. P. Keatinge (Institute of European Affairs, 1991), 3, 56.
[72] N. 60 above, 67.

meaning at all, implies that you can't take one step forward and two steps backwards at the same time. Built into the principle of an 'ever closer union among the peoples of Europe' is the notion that integration should only be one way.

It must be said, at the heart of all this chaos and fragmentation, the unique *sui generis* nature of the European Community, its true world-historical significance, is being destroyed. The whole future and credibility of the Communities as a cohesive legal unit which confers rights on individuals and which enters into their national legal systems as an integral part of those systems, is at stake.

According to Article N of the Treaty on European Union, the next intergovernmental conference is scheduled for 1996, 'to examine those provisions of this Treaty for which revision is provided' in accordance with the objectives set out in Articles A and B of the Treaty. The author of the following extract suggests that, although it is very unlikely that the Member States will take the steps necessary towards a full 'federal' union, the autonomous forces which have so far driven the Member States towards 'ever-closer union' are likely to continue to do so.

J. Pinder, The New European Federalism: The Idea and its Achievements[73]

Member Governments, with the exception of the British one, were ready to call the Maastricht Treaty 'a new stage in the process leading gradually to a Union with a federal goal'. How likely is this goal to be attained? . . . It can . . . be argued that the hardest steps are yet to come, into the citadels of sovereignty represented by currency, defence and the powers of governments in the Community's Council. Even if EMU has been agreed by eleven Member States in the Maastricht Treaty, and some further steps are taken before enlargement of the Community, will a Community in the process of enlargement towards twenty members, maybe more, be able to cover the final distance to a federal union or state?

The neofunctionalists underestimated the resistance of nation-states to integration and overestimated the power of spillover of integration from one sector to another. De Gaulle scotched their optimism and political scientists have since been reluctant to consider the prospects for the Community's development. It is indeed possible that member states will balk at the final steps, even if most of them are committed to the EMU that would take them far towards federal union. But it is also necessary to weigh in the balance the exogenous forces that have been driving them towards interdependence in security, the economy and the environment: the 'nature of the problems' that provide motives for federation.

Given the number and complexity of its provisions, it is difficult to define the exact nature of the change to the constitutional structure of the Community which was brought about by the Treaty on European Union. Equally, we can see that it is difficult to predict its future direction, or the likely agenda or outcome of the 1996 intergovernmental conference.

[73] *Comparative Federalism and Federations*, eds. M. Burgess and A. Gagnon, (1993), 45, 63.

Some of the difficulties of definition are due to the inherent ambiguity in the language which has been used both in political discussions and in legal instruments. The term 'European Union', for example, is a central part of the language in which the political debate on the future of Europe is conducted, despite—or perhaps because of—its ambiguity. In the following extract the author argues that the Member States are not in fact committed to the same end, but rather to a continuing *process* of integration. And it is argued that this lack of agreement as to the 'end', or the 'common good', is something which could undermine the process of integration itself.

J. Lodge, Towards a political union[74]

European integration differs markedly from other attempts to create a common market, or, more commonly, a free trade area. Its goal is political. Its instruments may be economic. But its essence, its *raison d'être*, is cemented by the *acquis communautaire*; by the supremacy of binding supranational legislation over national legislation; and by the decision-making authority of supranational institutions and their rules. Different governments have at various times tried to move away from the full obligations that flow from EC membership; some have canvassed different models for European integration. But for all their apparent tolerance of diversity in the pace with which integration is pursued by individual member states, the underlying assumption is that they are all moving towards a common and shared goal—however ill-defined—European Union. This applies even to the exceptions made in respect of functionally specific and lengthy transition periods for new members or similar 'opt-outs' for the United Kingdom.

Integration is seen as a process rather than an end . . . It was at the heart of the Monnet method: supranational agencies were created to instil a sense of permanent endeavour in the process. It was also assumed that each generation would subscribe to a shared set of core, often implicit values such as working to preserve and further peace, to accord each Member equal status, to work cooperatively in pursuit of the common good (however that was defined) and for the good of the community. The weakness of seeing integration as a process rather than an end lies in the potential to regress from as well as progress to an assumed common interest in closer, deeper cooperation.

It is extremely unlikely that all of the Member States, and in particular not if the membership of the Community continues to grow, could ever agree on a single ultimate aim or goal, even though most of them will subscribe to many of its aims and policies. There are as many different reasons for desiring a degree of integration which transcends the traditional model of inter-state co-operation as there are states. Even if the original motivation behind the Schuman plan—the uniting of the interests of European states so as to make another war unthinkable—had faded from the memories of many, the outbreak of war in the middle of Europe, in the former Yugoslavia, reinvoked

[74] *The European Community and the Challenge for the Future*, ed. J. Lodge (2nd edn., Pinter, 1993), 382.

the continuing relevance and force of that early aim. The remarks of Klaus Hänsch, in his address as newly elected President of the European Parliament in July 1994, provide an illustration of this perspective:[75]

> The challenges facing us at the end of this millennium mean that we need more, not less, community in Europe. We are horrified by the murder, rape and forced migration in the former Yugoslavia. Our disgust that this is possible in Europe is mixed with shame at our inability to stamp out the fire in the Balkans.
>
> But however disgusted and ashamed we may feel, we should not forget that earlier this century, almost eighty years ago to the day, a single murder in Sarajevo was enough to set the whole continent on fire, because Europe was torn apart by nationalism, suspicion and hatred. When we consider the history of Europe, it is a phenomenal achievement on the part of the European Union and European integration since the war—and one which can by no means be taken for granted—that the peoples of Europe have not resumed the dangerous game of alliances and counter-alliances. This is a phenomenal achievement when we consider the history of Europe.

Clearly there are conflicting economic views about the wisdom of European integration, there is a continuing debate over the preservation by certain states of an ideal of national sovereignty, a tension between market Europe and social Europe, a disagreement over 'deepening versus widening', a distrust of variable geometry by some and a distrust of homogenizing harmonization by others, fears by some of an inward-looking 'fortress' Europe which discriminates against non-Community nationals, and fears by others of uncontrollable immigration. Yet despite all of this and despite a constant fear of disintegration, there appears to be an overall commitment to a process of integration in Europe for a variety of reasons, backed up perhaps by the 'shadow of war' factor which served as the original stimulus, so that whatever the tensions and differences which exist, the 'journey to an unknown destination' continues.[76]

9. FURTHER READING

(a) Books

Corbett, R., *The Treaty of Maastricht* (Longman, 1993)
Holland, M., *European Integration From Community to Union* (Pinter, 1993)
Lodge, J., *The European Community and the Challenge of the Future* (Pinter, 1993)

[75] EP Debs. 1994 No. 4–449/16, 20 July 1994.

[76] The phrase is borrowed from Andrew Schonfield, *Europe: Journey to an Unknown Destination* (1973), and was used by J. Weiler in 1993 in an article entitled 'Journey to an Unknown Destination: A Retrospective and Prospective of the European Court of Justice in the Arena of Political Integration' (1993) 31 JCMS 417.

NICOLL, W., and SALMON, T., *Understanding the European Communities* (Philip Allen, 1990)

PINDER, J., *European Community: The Building of a Union* (Oxford University Press, 1991)

URWIN, D., *The Community of Europe: A History of European Integration* (Longman, 1991)

(b) Articles

CURTIN, D., 'The Constitutional Structure of the Union: A Europe of Bits and Pieces' (1993) 30 CMLRev. 17

DANKERT, P., 'The EC—Past, Present and Future' in *The EC: Past, Present and Future*, ed. L. Tsoukalis (1983)

EVERLING, U., 'Reflections on the Structure of the European Union' (1992) 29 CMLRev. 1053

WEILER, J., 'The Transformation of Europe' (1991) 100 Yale LJ 2403

2

The Institutions of the Community

1. INTRODUCTION

There are five principal institutions mentioned in Article 4 of the EC Treaty, as amended by the Treaty on European Union (TEU), which are entrusted with carrying out the tasks of the Community: the Council, the Commission, the European Parliament, the Court of Auditors, and the Court of Justice. The object of this chapter is to describe the role which each of these institutions plays in the Community and the way in which they interrelate. We shall also be considering other important institutions such as the European Council, the Economic and Social Committee, and the Committee of the Regions. Detailed discussion of the Community's legislative process will be left to the following chapter. Two general introductory points may help in understanding what follows.

The first is that the materials set out below should not be approached with any preconceptions about the traditional division of governmental functions into categories of legislative, executive, administrative, and judicial. It is of course the case that these functions are performed within the Community. But do not seek to pigeon-hole each of the institutions into one category as if it *only* undertook tasks of, for example, a legislative or executive nature. As we shall see, many of these duties are shared between different institutions in a manner which renders it impossible to describe any one of them as the sole legislator, or the sole executive. In this sense the Community does not conform to any rigid separation-of-powers principle of the sort which has shaped certain domestic political systems.

The second point which should be borne in mind is that the pattern of institutional competence within the Community has not remained static. It has altered both as a consequence of subsequent Treaty revisions and as a result of changes in the political balance of power between the institutions over time.

Our discussion of the institutions will begin with the Commission because of its centrality to so many facets of the Community's operation.

2. THE COMMISSION

(a) The College of Commissioners: Composition and Appointment

There are now seventeen Commissioners[1] and under Article 157 of the EC Treaty, as amended by the TEU, they are to be persons whose 'independence is beyond doubt', and they 'shall neither seek nor take instructions from any government or from any other body'. There shall be at least one, and no more than two, Commissioners from each state, and they take decisions by majority vote.[2] Each of the five larger countries has two Commissioners (France, Germany, Italy, Spain, and the United Kingdom), while the other seven smaller countries have one Commissioner each. The accession of Sweden, Finland and Austria will increase the number of Commissioners to twenty. The Commissioners meet collectively as the College of Commissioners.

The method of choosing Commissioners has been altered by the TEU, with the consequence that the Parliament has more say in the process than hitherto. Under Article 158 the governments of the Member States, after consulting the European Parliament, nominate the person they intend to be President of the Commission. These governments, together with the nominee for President, then nominate those who are intended to serve as Commissioners. All such nominees are then subject to a vote of approval by the European Parliament,[3] after which they are appointed by common accord of the Member State governments. Their term of office is five years, and this term may be renewed.

The Presidency of the Commission is a position of real significance. The holder of this post is clearly *primus inter pares* as compared with the other Commissioners. The President will play an important role in shaping overall Commission policy, in negotiating with the Council and the Parliament, and in determining the future direction of the Community, whether this be in relation to suggestions for the timetable for monetary union, or to the possibility of closer social/political union. How much is made of the post, over and beyond this, will depend to some extent on the personality and vision of the incumbent. Jacques Delors had both a strong personality and a vision for the Community's development. Many of the broader Community initiatives which led to further integration were in no small measure the result of his leadership within the Commission. The tensions with Member States which such an assertive Presidency could produce are well known.

Portfolios within the Commission will be decided upon principally by the President. But there will be negotiations, often intense, between the Commissioners, the President, and the Member States as to 'who gets what'. Commissioners who have seniority will press strongly for the high-profile portfolios, although Sir Leon Brittan's disappointment at not being assigned the

[1] This number can be increased by the Council acting unanimously: Art. 157(1).

[2] Art. 163 EC, as amended by the TEU.

[3] See below, 62.

portfolio of his choice in 1994 attests to the fact even senior Commissioners will not always be successful in securing their number one priority. This will be especially so after the recent enlargement of the Community.

The Commissioners will have their own personal staff (or *cabinet*), which consists partly of national and partly of Community officials. There will normally be six or seven officials in these teams, although the President of the Commission will have a larger *cabinet* of about twelve. The members of the *cabinet* perform a variety of functions: they will liaise with other parts of the Commission and with the country from which the Commissioner was appointed; they will have a role in the legislative process, scrutinizing draft regulations and directives which have emerged from other parts of the Commission bureaucracy; they will keep the Commissioner informed about developments in other connected areas; and they can undertake research initiatives for the Commissioner.

While the Council represents the interests of the Member States, the Commission is independent of any such national concerns, and, as we have seen, Article 157 stipulates that the independence of the Commissioners shall be beyond doubt. Overt and excessive partisanship is therefore precluded. However, one should not necessarily expect total neutrality as the following extract demonstrates.

N. Nugent, The Government and Politics of the European Union[4]

The Treaty insistence on complete independence of Commissioners is . . . interpreted flexibly. Indeed, total neutrality is not even desirable since the work of the Commission is likely to be facilitated by Commissioners maintaining links with sources of influence throughout the EU and this they can most easily do in their own Member States. But the requirements of the system and the necessities of the EU's institutional make-up are such that real problems arise if Commissioners try and force their own states' interests too hard. It is both legitimate and helpful to bring favoured national interests onto the agenda, to help clear national obstacles from the path, to explain to other Commissioners what is likely to be acceptable in 'my' national capital. But to go further and act consistently and blatantly as a national spokesman is to risk losing credibility with other Commissioners. It also makes it difficult for the Commission to function properly since clearly it cannot fulfil its set tasks if its divisions match those of the Council.

(b) The Commission Bureaucracy

The permanent officials who work in the Commission, and who form the Brussels bureaucracy, are organized into Directorates General (DG) covering the major differing subject matter areas. Each DG has a number and is often referred to in this manner:

DGI	External Economic Relations
DGIA	External Political Relations

[4] (3rd edn., Macmillan, 1994), 87.

DGII	Economic and Financial Affairs
DGIII	Internal Market and Industrial Affairs
DGIV	Competition
DGV	Employment, Industrial Relations, and Social Affairs
DGVI	Agriculture
DGVII	Transport
DGVIII	Development
DGIX	Personnel and Administration
DGX	Audiovisual, Information, Communication, and Culture
DGXI	Environment, Nuclear Safety, and Consumer Protection
DGXII	Science, Research, and Development
DGXIII	Telecommunications, Information Technologies, and Industries
DGIV	Fisheries
DGXV	Financial Institutions and Company Law
DGXVI	Regional Policy
DGXVII	Energy
DGXVIII	Credit and Investments
DGXIX	Budgets
DGXX	Financial Control
DGXXI	Customs and Indirect Taxation
DGXXII	Co-ordination of Structural Policy (now disbanded)
DGXXIII	Enterprise Policy, Distributive Trades, Tourism, and Co-operatives

In addition to the DGs there are a number of special units which provide services across the spectrum of Commission activities. These include: the Translation Service, the Legal Service, the Statistical Office, the Security Office, the Joint Research Centre, the Secretariat General of the Commission, and the Office for Official Publications of the European Communities.

There are essentially four layers of hierarchical division within the Commission bureaucracy. First, there is the Commissioner who has the portfolio for that area. Second comes the Director General who is the head of a particular DG. Thirdly, there are the Directors. Each Directorate General will have a number of Directorates within it, commonly somewhere between four and six, and each of these Directorates will be headed by a Director who is responsible to the Director General. The fourth and final part of the administrative organization is the Head of Division. Divisions are parts of Directorates. Each Division will have a Head of Division who will be responsible to the relevant Director.

Decisions and the drafts of legislative proposals will normally emanate from a lower part of this hierarchy, upwards towards the College of Commissioners. There will be a detailed discussion of the legislative process in the next chapter. Suffice it to say for the present that within the Commission a proposal will usually have its origins within the relevant DG. Outside experts will often be used at this formative stage, and there will be consultation with national civil servants. The draft proposal will then pass up through the DGs to the *cabinets* of the relevant Commissioners, and on to the weekly meeting which is held by the *chefs de cabinet*. From there it will proceed to the College of Commissioners, which may accept it, reject it, or suggest amendments. Matters are obviously more complex when a proposed measure affects more than one area, and hence more than one DG may be involved. It is, moreover, not uncommon for the different DGs which are involved with a measure to have a 'different angle' on the problem. It is for this reason, amongst others, that the actual meeting of the College of Commissioners will be preceded by a range of formal and informal consultations within the Commission. Formal meetings will be held by the *chefs de cabinet* before the Commissioners themselves consider the measures, the object being to try to reach agreement on as many matters as possible before the College itself convenes. The meeting of the *chefs de cabinet* will receive input from discussion sessions held by the particular member of a *cabinet* who specializes in the relevant area. In addition there will be informal exchanges between opposite numbers within the bureaucracy at all levels, including the Commissioners themselves, members of differing *cabinets* and officials who work in DGs with an interest in a measure.

The basic principle within the Commission is for positions and promotions to be based upon merit, determined by competitive examination. In this way a career structure is open to those who work in the bureaucracy. This meritocratic principle is, however, qualified by the fact that Member States will take a keen interest to ensure that their own nationals are properly represented, particularly in the senior posts. For this reason it has been traditional for an informal quota regime to operate in the allocation of such jobs. Whether this can still survive is more doubtful, given that the Court has held that job allocation should not be predetermined and should be decided on merit.[5]

There has been much carping over the years about the size of the Brussels bureaucracy. This is largely based on ignorance of the facts. In 1993 the Commission employed 18,000 people, which is far fewer than many ministries within Member States.[6]

(c) The Powers of the Commission

The powers of the Commission are set out in Article 155 of the EC Treaty:

> In order to ensure the proper functioning and development of the common market, the Commission shall:
>
> —ensure that the provisions of this Treaty and measures taken by the institutions pursuant thereto are applied;

[5] Case 105/75, *Giuffrida* v. *Council* [1976] ECR 1395.

[6] EU Member States average approximately 322 civil servants per 10,000 of the population. This is as against 0.8 per 10,000 for all EU institutions: Nugent, *The Government and Politics of the European Union*, n 4 above 89.

—formulate recommendations or deliver opinions on matters dealt with in this Treaty, if it expressly so provides or if the Commission considers it necessary;

—have its own power of decision and participate in the shaping of measures taken by the Council and by the European Parliament in the manner provided for in this Treaty;

—exercise the powers conferred on it by the Council for the implementation of the rules laid down by the latter.

A 'bare' reading of Article 155 does little to convey the central role played by the Commission in all aspects of the Community's life. The Community institutional structure is not, as noted above, characterized by any rigid doctrine of separation of powers, and the Commission is at the heart of many Community initiatives. It is important to realize that the Commission has a whole array of powers which are legislative, administrative, executive, and judicial in nature. These will be considered in turn.

The Commission plays a central part in the *legislative* process of the Community. The details of the Community's complex legislative procedures will be considered in the following chapter. An outline of the Commission's powers in this respect will be given here. These legislative powers assume a number of different forms.

One of the most important is that the Commission possesses the right of legislative initiative. The common format in the Treaties is for the Council to act on a proposal from the Commission when making legislation which fills out the Treaty Articles themselves. In this sense the Commission's right of initiative places it in the forefront of the development of policy.[7] Although these legislative proposals have to be approved by the Council and, depending on the circumstances, by the European Parliament, the Commission's right of initiative has enabled it to act as a 'motor of integration' for the Community as a whole. Having said this it should also be noted, as will become apparent from the subsequent discussion, that the Council may be the *de facto* source of legislative initiatives, even if the details of these suggestions are then given more concrete form by the Commission.

The capacity of the Commission to act as the motor of integration for the Community is also evident in a second role which it plays in the legislative process. It will be the Commission which will play a large part in the development of the Community's overall legislative plan for any single year. Planning of this nature has become of increasing importance in recent years, and the agenda-setting aspect of the Commission's work is of real significance in shaping the priorities which the Community is to tackle in the forthcoming year.[8]

Closely allied to, but distinct from, the above is a third way in which the

[7] The major qualification to this right of initiative is to be found in the provisions dealing with foreign policy and co-operation in the fields of justice and home affairs to be found in the TEU, Titles V and VI.

[8] See below, 137–42.

Commission affects the development of Community policy. This is the part which the Commission plays in the evolution of more general policy strategies for the Community as a whole. One notable example of this is to be found in the Commission's White Paper on the *Completion of the Internal Market*.[9] It proved to be of seminal importance in shaping the Single European Act. Another instance where the Commission has had an important impact on the general evolution of Community policy is in relation to Economic and Monetary Union (EMU). It was Commission initiatives under the Presidency of Jacques Delors which fashioned the EMU debate and laid the groundwork for many of the provisions on this issue which are now to be found in the TEU. Yet another area in which the Commission has had a marked impact on the Community's development is in the social field. The Commission's *Community Charter of the Fundamental Social Rights of Workers*[10] (the Social Charter) proved to be an important factor in the debate about Community social policy.

The powers discussed thus far do not exhaust the Commission's legislative responsibilities. A fourth way in which the Commission exercises legislative power is that it has the ability, in certain limited areas, to enact Community norms without the formal involvement of any other Community institution.[11]

Finally, the Commission exercises delegated legislative power.[12] This is expressly contemplated by the fourth indent of Article 155. The Council will delegate to the Commission power to make further regulations within particular areas. The most common example of the use of this delegated power is in the agricultural sphere, where it is often necessary to act expeditiously in the face of changing market circumstances. But Commission regulations made in this manner are not confined to agriculture. Important regulations relating to competition policy have been enacted by the Commission as a result of power delegated to it by the Council.

In addition to its legislative powers the Commission will also have significant *administrative responsibilities*. Policies, once made, have to be administered. Legislation, once enacted, must be implemented. In this capacity the Commission will normally act as a supervisor and overseer of policy implementation, rather than being engaged in direct implementation itself. This is because Community policies, once enacted, will often be directly administered by agencies at the national level. Thus many agricultural regulations will be executed at the grass-roots level by national Agricultural Intervention Boards. While many of the rules concerning the free movement of goods will be the responsibility of bodies such as Customs and Excise Authorities, or Veterinary Inspection Teams which check the quality of foodstuffs, none the less the Commission will try and maintain a general supervisory stance in relation to the national agencies, in order to ensure uniformity of application of the relevant rules, and also to ensure that the rules are being properly applied at national level. There are difficulties with the successful execution of this

[9] COM(85)310.
[10] See below, 710, n. 150, and 857, n. 168.
[11] See below, 121.
[12] See below, 128–31.

supervisory role. This is in part because the Commission often does not have sufficient personnel for the task; in part because the rules which the national agencies have to apply may be extremely complex; and in part because in certain areas the national agencies may be less than wholly enthusiastic about their remit, particularly where the Community regime has to subsist alongside national rules which touch on the same subject-matter.

The Commission possesses responsibilities of an *executive* nature. Once again, as in the case of its legislative responsibilities, its executive powers take a number of different forms. Two are of particular importance: those relating to finance and those concerning external relations.

The Commission plays an important role in the establishment of the Community's budget. This topic will be considered separately below,[13] since it is one which intimately involves all three of the Community's major decision-making institutions and provides an excellent example of the way in which they interrelate. In addition to the part which the Commission plays in setting the revenue side of the budget, it also has significant powers in relation to expenditure policies. Around 50 per cent of the Community's annual budget is used for agricultural support, administered by the European Agricultural Guidance and Guarantee Fund (EAGGF). Management of this fund is entrusted to the Commission, although the decisions which it reaches will often be overseen by a management or regulatory committee.[14] The Commission also has important responsibilities for expenditure of the structural funds, which now consist of the European Regional Development Fund (ERDF), the European Social Fund (ESF), and the Guidance Section of the EAGGF. The objectives of these funds is to: develop the poorer regions; convert or adjust declining industries; combat long-term unemployment; integrate young people into the job market; and help in the adjustment of agricultural structures and developing rural areas.

The Commission also exercises executive powers in the sphere of external relations. Nugent explains:

N. Nugent, The Government and Politics of the European Union[15]

First, the Commission is centrally involved in determining and conducting the EU's external trade relations. On the basis of Article 113 of the EC Treaty, and with its actions always subject to Council approval, the Commission represents and acts on behalf of the EU both in formal negotiations, such as those which are conducted under the auspices of GATT, and in the more informal and explanatory exchanges such as are common between, for example, the EU and the United States over world trade, and between the EU and Japan over access to each other's markets.

Second, the Commission has important negotiating and managing responsibilities in respect of the various external agreements which the EU has with many countries and groups of countries . . .

[13] See below, 90–4.
[14] For discussion of these committees, see below, 128–31.
[15] N. 4 above, 118–19.

Third, the Commission represents the EU at, and participates in the work of, a number of important international organizations. Four of these are specifically mentioned in the EC Treaty: the United Nations and its specialised agencies (Article 229); GATT (Article 229); the Council of Europe (Article 230); and the Organization for Economic Cooperation and Development (Article 231).

Fourth, the Commission has responsibilities for acting as a key point of contact between the EU and non-Member States. Over 140 countries have diplomatic missions accredited to the EU . . . The EU, for its part, maintains an extensive network of diplomatic missions abroad, numbering 100 delegations and offices, and these are staffed by Commission employees.

Fifth, the Commission is entrusted with important responsibilities in regard to applications for EU membership. On receipt of an application the Council normally asks the Commission to carry out a detailed investigation of the implications and to submit an opinion (an opinion that the Council need not, of course, accept . . .). If and when negotiations begin, the Commission, operating within Council approved guidelines, acts as the EU's main negotiator, except on show-piece ministerial occasions or when particularly sensitive or difficult matters call for an inter-ministerial resolution of differences . . .

Sixth, and finally, under the TEU the 'Commission shall be fully associated with the work carried out in the common foreign and security policy field' (Article J.9).

What, then, of the Commission's *judicial* powers and responsibilities? These are based on the first indent to Article 155 and fall into two principal categories.

On the one hand, it will be the Commission which will bring actions against recalcitrant Member States when they act in breach of Community law.[16] The actions will be brought under Article 169 of the Treaty and will literally assume the form of *Commission* v. *Germany* etc. Recourse to formal legal action will be a last resort and will be preceded by Commission efforts to resolve the matter through negotiation. None the less Article 169 actions form a steady part of the Court's diet and they have been used by it to propound important points of principle, as well as bringing a particular Member State to book.

On the other hand, the Commission will in certain areas act as investigator and initial judge of a Treaty violation, whether by private firms or by Member States. In practical terms two of the most important of these areas are competition policy,[17] and state aids.[18] The Commission's decision will be reviewable by the Community's judiciary, and this will now normally be by the Court of First Instance (CFI). Notwithstanding the existence of judicial review, the Commission's investigative and adjudicative powers provide it with a significant tool for the development of Community policy. It allows the Commission to devise new strategies in relation to particular aspects of, for example, competition policy or state aids; it enables it to employ the power of selective prosecution to take cases which raise significant issues; and it

[16] See below, Ch. 9. [17] See below, Ch. 22. [18] See below, Ch. 24.

provides a vehicle through which the Commission can give guidance to national courts as to the more precise meaning of broadly framed Treaty Articles.

(d) The Role of the Commission: Conclusion

The preceding discussion reveals the centrality of the Commission to the Community and to the aspirations which underlie it. The Commission has always been the single most important political force for integration and federalism, ever seeking to press forward to attain the Community's initial objectives as expeditiously as possible, with the aim of moving on to a closer form of union. The institutional structure within the Community means that the Commission must work with the Council and the Parliament. The pace of Community development has not always been steady because of this very inter-institutional dimension. What the Member States have been willing to accept, on what conditions, and how quickly, has varied over the Community's brief history. We have already touched on this when considering the history of the Community,[19] and we shall have occasion to return to this issue when discussing the Community's decision-making structure.[20] That the power of the Commission relative to the other institutions, particularly the Council, has altered over time is then undeniable. But it is equally undeniable that the general thrust of the Commission's vision for the Community has remained constant and the Commission remains a powerful force for the achievement of that objective in the present day.

3. THE COUNCIL

(a) Composition of the Council

Article 146 of the EC Treaty, as amended by the TEU, states that the Council shall consist of a representative of each Member State at ministerial level who is authorized to commit the government of that state. The members of the Council are, therefore, politicians as opposed to civil servants, but the politician can be a member of a regional government where this is appropriate.

It is common for meetings of the Council to be arranged by subject-matter with different ministers attending from the Member States. Thus there is a General Affairs Council, attended by Foreign Ministers, which deals with external relations and also many matters concerning general Community policy. The Economic and Financial Affairs Council, by way of contrast, is concerned with matters such as the implementation of the programme for the completion of the Single Market. Sectoral issues will be dealt with in the various 'Technical Councils', such as those dealing with Transport, Energy,

[19] See above, Ch. 1. [20] See below, Ch. 3.

Agriculture, Labour and Social Affairs, Health, Education, Industry, Environment, and the like. Each of these will be attended by the relevant ministers responsible for those affairs within the Member States. The ministers will be supported by their own delegations of national officials who have expertise in the relevant area.

Article 147 states that the Council shall meet when convened by the President of the Council on his own initiative, or at the request of one of its members, or at the request of the Commission. There are approximately ninety Council meetings per year, most of which take place in Brussels, although some are held in Luxembourg.

(b) *The Presidency of the Council*[21]

Article 146 provides for the Presidency of the Council to be held by each Member State in turn for six months. It establishes two six-year cycles, the purpose of this being to ensure that the same states do not have the Presidency always during the same period of the Community's affairs.

The position of President of the Council has assumed greater importance in recent years for a number of reasons. This is in part because different states have 'competed' with each other in order to see which country could achieve more within the designated period; in part because of the growing complexity of the Community's decision-making structure, which necessitates more co-ordination between the institutions; and in part it is because the Council as a whole may often wish to take a more proactive role in the development of Community policy and this requires initiatives on its part which the President can help to organize.

In more concrete terms the President will perform a number of functions. The President will normally arrange Council meetings, and set the agenda for them. He or she may develop policy initiatives within areas which are of particular concern either to the Council as a whole or to the Member State which currently holds the Presidency. The President will have an important liaison role to play with the Presidents of the Commission and the Parliament, and will represent the Council in discussions with institutions outside the Community.

While the Presidency therefore gives considerable power to the incumbent, the office is not without its stresses and pitfalls. Six months is a short time within which to get things done. The eyes of the other Member States will be focused, often critically and sharply, on the incumbent to determine the use to which the office has been put during that period. If a country tries to use its Presidency to achieve goals which are felt not to accord with the majority sentiment in the Council, and which are too narrowly nationalistic, then the criticism is likely to be particularly harsh.

[21] E. Kirchner, *Decision-Making in the European Community: The Council Presidency and European Integration* (Manchester University Press, 1992).

(c) The Committee of Permanent Representatives

The work of the Council is prepared by the Committee of Permanent Representatives (COREPER), which is, after the TEU amendments, dealt with in Article 151 of the EC Treaty. COREPER is staffed by senior national officials and it operates at two levels. COREPER II is the more important and consists of permanent representatives who are of ambassadorial rank. It deals with the more contentious matters such as economic and financial affairs, external relations, and other issues which are likely to be both significant and controversial. It also performs an important liaison role with the national governments. COREPER I is composed of deputy permanent representatives and is responsible for issues such as the environment, social affairs, the internal market, and transport.

COREPER plays an important part in the decision-making within the EC, in part because it sets the agenda for Council meetings. The agenda is divided into Parts A and B: the former includes those items which COREPER has agreed can be adopted by the Council without discussion; the latter will cover topics which do require discussion.

A large number of working groups, recently about 150 to 200 at any one time, will feed into COREPER. These groups will examine legislative proposals from the Commission. They will be composed of national experts from the Member States or from the Permanent Representations. Their role in the policy-making process will be examined more fully below.[22] In addition to these working groups the Council and COREPER will receive input from specialist committees established under the Treaty, such as the Monetary Committee set up pursuant to Article 105, and from committees created by Community legislation.

(d) The Council Secretariat

In addition to COREPER the Council also has its own Secretariat which provides direct administrative support to it. The Secretariat has a staff of about 2,000, and of these roughly 200 are 'A' grade, diplomatic level. This body will furnish administrative service to the Council itself and also to COREPER and the working parties. It will prepare documentation, give legal advice, undertake translation, process decisions, and take part in the preparation of agendas. It will also work closely with the staff of the President of the Council, helping to smooth conflicts, and providing valuable information as to the way in which such conflicts might best be resolved.

(e) The Powers of the Council

The powers of the Council are described in Article 145, albeit in a rather vague manner:

[22] See below, 142–7.

> To ensure that the objectives set out in the Treaty are attained, the Council shall, in accordance with the provisions of this Treaty:
> —ensure co-ordination of the general economic policies of the Member States;
> —have power to take decisions;
> —confer on the Commission, in the acts which the Council adopts, powers for the implementation of the rules which the Council lays down. The Council may impose certain requirements in respect of the exercise of these powers. The Council may also reserve the right, in specific cases, to exercise directly implementing powers itself. The procedures referred to above must be consonant with principles and rules to be laid down in advance by the Council, acting unanimously on a proposal from the Commission and after obtaining the opinion of the European Parliament.

Some Articles of the Treaty convey a clear impression of the powers which are being accorded to a particular institution. Some do not. Article 145 comes within the latter category. A simple reading of this provision does little to convey the reality of the Council's powers, nor does it explain their provenance. Explanation is therefore required.

The Council exercises an important role in the legislative and policy-making process of the Community in four ways.

The principal manifestation of this resides in the fact that the Council will have to vote its approval of legislative initiatives which emanate from the Commission before they become law. This is not evident from the face of Article 145. This aspect of the Council's power is derived from the fact that the Articles of the Treaty which give the Commission the right to propose legislation, impose the condition of Council approval. The details of the legislative process, and the role played by the Council within it, will be explained in the next chapter. Suffice it to say for the present that Council consent is nearly always required. Whether this must be by unanimity, or qualified or simple majority will vary depending upon the requirements which are stipulated in a particular Treaty Article.[23] Moreover, as we shall see, the draft proposal which emanates from the Commission will often be subject to considerable modification as a result of scrutiny by COREPER and the working parties.[24]

Secondly, the Council's role in the legislative process is not, however, simply one of reaction. It has in certain respects become more proactive. This is in part through the Council's use of Article 152. This states that the 'Council may request the Commission to undertake any studies which the Council considers desirable for the attainment of the common objectives, and to submit to it any appropriate proposals'. While the wording of this Article might indicate that the Council's requests would be couched in terms of some generality, this is not always so. The Council has made use of this power to frame very specific proposals which it wishes the Commission to shape into concrete

[23] For a discussion of the Council's voting requirements, see below, 133–4.
[24] See below, 145–7.

legislation.[25] In addition to this use of Article 152, the Council has increasingly made use of opinions and resolutions as a way of pressuring the Commission into generating legislative proposals. The Council's ability to trigger policy initiatives of this nature is due in part to the more sophisticated back-up machinery which it now possesses, in the form of COREPER and the plethora of working parties etc. which feed into it. It is also in part the result of the greater importance of the Council Presidency and the fact that the incumbent of this Office will often have an 'agenda' which he or she wishes to see achieved.

Thirdly, the Council can delegate power to the Commission, enabling the latter to pass further regulations within a particular area. It is now common for such delegations of power to be subject to the condition that the Commission action is acceptable to committees which are staffed by national representatives. This operates as a mechanism whereby the Council can ensure that the detail of the legislation which emerges from such delegations is in conformity with its own wishes.[26]

Finally, the increasing complexity of the Community's decision-making process, as a result of the changes introduced by the SEA and the TEU, have necessitated increased inter-institutional collaboration between the Commission, the Parliament, and the Council. This assumes various guises, from informal discussions concerning the shape of the legislative agenda at one end of the scale to the increasing usage made of Inter-Institutional Agreements at the other end of the scale. Agreements of this latter kind are becoming of real importance as a way in which principles in the Treaty, such as subsidiarity, can be fleshed out; as a mechanism for developing principles of good governance, such as transparency of decision-making; and as a method of mediating difficult inter-institutional issues, such as the budget.[27]

(f) The Role of the Council: Conclusion

The Council represents national interests and always has. Whether the framers of the original Rome Treaty would have been surprised by the way in which the Commission and Council have interrelated since the inception of the Community is unclear. They hoped that the formation of the EEC would herald an era of greater collaboration in which sectional, national interests would diminish in relation to the collective interests of the Community's development as a whole. The original decision-making structure of the Community certainly bore testimony to the central role accorded to the Commission. The range of its powers is readily apparent from the preceding discussion. To be sure, the Council had to approve legislation, but the Commission was in the driving seat, both in terms of its capacity to set the legislative agenda, and in terms of the institutional resources at its disposal for the development of Community policy. Moreover, the message from the original Treaty was clear:

[25] Sir Leon Brittan, 'Institutional Development of the European Community' [1992] PL 567.

[26] See below, 128–31.

[27] For a discussion of these agreements see below,140–2.

while Council consent was required for the passage of legislation, unanimity was also the condition for Council amendment to the Commission's proposals. It was then not to be easy for the Council to tinker with Community initiatives.

It would be wrong to depict the Commission and the Council as perpetually at odds with each other throughout the Community's history. But it would be equally mistaken to view the two institutions as co-existing in perfect harmony. There have been real tensions between the federal pro-integration perspective of the Commission, and the more cautious, intergovernmental perspective of the Council. The Treaty framers might have hoped that these tensions between Commission and Council would prove minimal and short-lived.[28] If this was so it was too optimistic a forecast. The history of the Community has witnessed a series of institutional changes, often initially outside the strict letter of the Treaty, whereby the Council strengthened its own position in relation to that of the Commission. This 'temporal' perspective on decision-making will be charted more fully below.[29] Suffice it to say for the present that the development of a veto power in the Council, the growing importance of COREPER, the creation of committees to oversee the delegation of power to the Commission, and the evolution of the European Council, all played a part in this process.

The balance of power within the Community, and the perspectives of the key institutional players, is not, however, a matter determined once and for all. We indicated in the introduction to this chapter the dynamic quality of the Community's institutional relationships, both in terms of the formal powers which they possess and the actual way in which they interrelate. This should be emphasized once again here. The SEA was the catalyst for a change of attitude on the part of the Member States as represented in the Council. There was a growing recognition that insistence on the veto, together with the attitude that if a measure did not conform wholly to a state's interests then it should be opposed, was too negative. The SEA also made the European Parliament a more active force in Community decision-making than it had been hitherto. These developments do not mean that relationships between the Council and the Commission, or for that matter between the Council and the Parliament, will always be smooth. It does mean that the nature of the inter-institutional relationships which prevail within the Community has moved on.

4. THE EUROPEAN COUNCIL[30]

(a) Evolution and Composition

The European Council consists of the Heads of Government of the Member States. The institution has evolved during the last twenty-five years. Meetings

[28] See above, Ch. 1. [29] See below, 134–7.
[30] S. Bulmer and W. Wessels, *The European Council* (Macmillan, 1987).

of Heads of Government took place during the 1960s, but the decision to institutionalize these meetings came in 1974 at the Paris summit. Meetings of the European Council continued to be held during the 1970s and 1980s, even though there was no formal remit in the Treaty for an institution of this nature. The first mention of the European Council within a Treaty came in the SEA. Its position has now been formalized further in the TEU, Article D of which states:[31]

> The European Council shall provide the Union with the necessary impetus for its development and shall define the general political guidelines thereof.
>
> The European Council shall bring together the Heads of State or of Government of the Member States and the President of the Commission. They shall be assisted by the Ministers for Foreign Affairs of the Member States and by a Member of the Commission. The European Council shall meet at least twice a year, under the chairmanship of the Head of State or of Government of the Member State which holds the Presidency of the Council.
>
> The European Council shall submit to the European Parliament a report after each of its meetings and a yearly written report on the progress achieved by the Union.

Mention of the European Council is also now to be found in certain specific provisions of the EC Treaty itself. Not surprisingly this is in the context of politically sensitive matters. Thus, under Article 103(2) it is accorded a role in relation to the co-ordination of the economic policies of the Member States, while under Article 109b it is to be presented with a report by the European Central Bank.[32]

The other explicit reference to the European Council is to be found in Article J.3 of the TEU, concerning the Common Foreign and Security Policy. This provides that the Council shall decide, on the basis of general guidelines from the European Council, that a matter should be the subject of joint action.

Meetings of the European Council will normally be held in the country which holds the Presidency of the Council at that time.

(b) Rationale and Role

The paucity of the Treaty references to the European Council should not lead one to doubt its importance. It plays a central role in setting the pace and shape of Community policy, establishing the parameters within which the other institutions will then operate.

[31] In this technical sense the European Council is an institution of the Union, although as we shall see it plays a vital role in shaping the development of the Community.

[32] Mention of Heads of Government, independently of the European Council, is also to be found in connection with appointment of members of the European Central Bank: Arts. 109a and 109f, and the final stages of the transition to Economic and Monetary Union: Arts. 109j and 109k.

Why, then, did it evolve? After all the Member States are represented in the Council. Why then does there need to be yet another institution within which Member State interests can be represented? The rationale for its evolution was mixed. It was in part due to disagreements between the Member States themselves. These would normally be resolved through the ordinary Council mechanisms, but if the disagreements were particularly severe, or on particularly important issues, then resolution might only prove to be possible by intervention at the highest possible level, through the Heads of Government themselves. Thus, one common item which has featured on European Council agendas has been the budget, and the respective contributions which should be paid by each Member State. The evolution of the European Council was also due in part to the perceived need for a focus of authority at the highest political level in order that the general strategy for the Community's development could be properly evaluated and planned.

What, then, are the types of issues which are commonly considered by the European Council? These vary, but can be grouped into the following categories.

One of the most significant types of issue to be discussed at the European Council is the very *development of the Community itself*. Major changes in the Community's Treaty foundation will be preceded by an Inter-Governmental Conference (IGC). The catalyst for the establishment of such Conferences will come from a summit meeting of the European Council. Thus the IGC which laid the groundwork for the SEA was initiated by the summit held in Milan in June 1985. The European Council will not only initiate the IGC. It will also provide the final and conclusive affirmation of the consequential Treaty changes.

Important changes in the *institutional structure* of the Community will often be confirmed by the European Council. The final decision on the enlargement of the Parliament following German unification was taken by a summit of the European Council.

The European Council can provide the focus for significant *constitutional initiatives* which affect the operation of the Community. We have already had occasion to mention Inter-Institutional Agreements, and we shall return to this topic in the next chapter. Agreements of this nature between the three major institutions will often be made, or finalized, at a summit meeting. The Inter-Institutional Agreement on Subsidiarity and the Declaration on Democracy, Transparency, and Subsidiarity were made at, or on the fringes of, such European Council meetings.

Not surprisingly, another item which frequently appears on the European Council's agenda is the *state of the European economy* as a whole. This is in part because of Treaty provisions concerning closer social and economic union, which demand growing convergence between national economic policies. It is also because of the centrality of economic issues to the very health and vitality of the Community. For this reason the European Council may, for example, take initiatives which are designed to combat unemployment, promote growth, and increase competitiveness.

Conflict resolution is another of the issues which is addressed by the European Council. We have already seen that this was one of the rationales for its evolution, and it continues to occupy some of its time. For example, budgetary matters, 'who contributes how much, and who gets what financial benefits', continued to cause conflict between the Member States in the early 1980s, and then once again in the later 1980s.

While the European Council will normally focus on broad strategies for the Community, it can also play a role in the *initiation, or development, of particular policy strategies*. Examples of this include the adoption of the Social Charter in 1989, and policies aimed to combat problems concerning drugs, terrorism, and the like.

External relations form part of the European Council's focus. The European Council will, for example, consider important international negotiations which are under way, such as those concerning the Uruguay Round of GATT. It will be the European Council which will issue declarations relating to more general international affairs, whether they be in relation to South Africa, or the civil war in what was Yugoslavia. And it will be the European Council which will set the guidelines for the relationship between the EU and the former Soviet-bloc countries.

The European Council will also consider *new accessions* to the Community. Thus it was, for example, the summit held in late 1991 in Maastricht which requested the Commission to produce a report on the applications for membership by the EFTA countries, while the Edinburgh summit of late 1992 authorized the formal opening of negotiations.

(c) The Role of the European Council: Conclusion

The European Council is a classic example of a change in the original institutional structure of the Treaty to accommodate political reality. This body evolved from a series of *ad hoc* meetings outside the letter of the Treaty to a more structured pattern of summits. Treaty-recognition was originally accorded in the SEA and it now, as we have seen, has a foundation in the TEU. Yet, as we have also seen, the brief mention of the European Council in the TEU does little to convey its real importance in the decision-making process of the Community. The reality is that no developments of genuine importance for the Community's internal structure, or for its external relations, will occur without having passed through at least one summit meeting. It is, of course, true that the concluding resolutions of such meetings do not themselves have the force of law. When this is required legislation will have to be drafted in accordance with one of the procedures to be discussed in the following chapter. None the less the conclusions reached by the European Council will almost always provide the framework within which the other institutions will consider more specific policy issues.

5. THE EUROPEAN PARLIAMENT

The story of the European Parliament is one of gradual transformation from a relatively powerless Assembly under the 1952 Coal and Steel Treaty to the active and considerably strengthened institution which it represents today. The history of its development within the Community is touched upon in Chapter 1, and its precise role in the legislative processes are examined in some detail in Chapter 3. We have already seen that the Assembly, to give the Parliament its original title—which indeed remained its formal title until the Single European Act in 1986, despite having itself adopted the title Parliament in 1962—was given few powers under the ECSC Treaty and under the original EEC and Euratom Treaties. It was intended to exercise consultative and supervisory powers, but not, as the title Parliament might suggest, to play any substantial legislative role.

However, although the elite 'government of technocrats', which the High Authority represented under the ECSC Treaty, was not to be replicated in the provisions of the EEC Treaty, the Community institutions set up by the later Treaty were not a model of democratic organization. The observation that the Community would not of itself satisfy the democratic criteria for membership is well-known. We saw in Chapter 1 how the influence of the Parliament grew, first with the two budgetary treaties of 1970 and 1975, and subsequently—after the change to direct elections rather than selection of its members—with the 'co-operation' and 'assent' procedures under the Single European Act of 1986 and the 'co-decision' procedure under the TEU in 1992. The extent of the increase in Parliament's role and influence with each of these amendments is examined further in the next chapter. However, even if these legislative additions did enhance the power of the one institution which is directly elected at a European level,[33] it is not necessarily clear that these changes render the Community or the Union a considerably more democratic organization. The problems of secrecy and impenetrability,[34] of the unaccountability of the legislative authorities, and of the non-representative nature of the decision-making institutions within the Community and the Union, are not necessarily solved simply by giving added powers to the European Parliament. Indeed some commentators claim that the national parliaments will—and should—remain the democratic focus of the Community, whatever the powers of the European Parliament.[35]

[33] See P. Raworth, 'A Timid Step Forwards: Maastricht and the Democratisation of the European Community' (1994) 19 ELRev. 16.

[34] For recent developments on this issue, see below, 140–2.

[35] See Brittan, n. 25 above, 576. One of the Intergovernmental Declarations annexed to the Final Act of the TEU stressed the importance of encouraging greater involvement and contact between the national parliaments and the European Parliament. See M. Westlake, *A Modern Guide to the European Parliament* (Pinter, 1994), 53–63 on the structures and initiatives already existing to enhance co-operation between the European Parliament and national parliaments. Another of the TEU Declarations invited the European Parliament and the national Parliaments to meet as a Conference of the Parliaments or *assises*, which they had in fact done just before the 1990 Intergovernmental Conference.

(a) Composition

In order to consider its 'democratic' character, it is necessary to consider first the composition of the Parliament. There are altogether 624 members of the Parliament, after the accession of Austria, Finland, and Sweden. One of the serious criticisms of the 'representative' nature of the Parliament is that the number of MEPs for each Member State is far from being in proportion to population size.[36] By way of illustration, the numbers for each country are set out below, together with the population of that country. It can be seen that the smaller countries are disproportionately represented, as compared to those with larger populations.[37]

Composition of Parliament

Country	*Seats*	*Population (millions)*
Austria	20	7.9
Belgium	25	10.07
Denmark	16	5.18
Finland	16	5.05
France	87	57.53
Germany	99	80.61
Greece	25	10.35
Ireland	15	3.56
Italy	87	56.93
Luxembourg	6	.95
The Netherlands	31	15.24
Portugal	25	9.86
Spain	64	39.11
Sweden	21	8.69
United Kingdom	87	57.96

A further cause for complaint has been the fact that, despite the holding of direct elections to the Parliament since 1979, in accordance with a decision of the Council in 1976,[38] the uniform electoral procedure envisaged by the original Article 138(3) of the EC Treaty is still not in existence. However, in 1993 the Court struck out an action for failure to act in accordance with Article 138(3) of the Treaty, brought under Article 175 on behalf of the Liberal Democratic Party in the United Kingdom against the European Parliament.[39] This was because Parliament, since the initiation of the legal proceedings, had adopted a resolution on a uniform electoral procedure, proposing a form of

[36] T. Hartley, *The Foundations of European Community Law* (3rd edn., Clarendon, 1994), 28–9. See also D. Curtin, 'The Constitutional Structure of the Union: A Europe of Bits and Pieces' (1993) 30 CMLRev. 17, 39.

[37] Population figures from Eurostat for 1993.

[38] Dec. 76/787, [1976] OJ L278/1.

[39] Case C–41/92, *Liberal Democrats* v. *Parliament* [1993] ECR I–3153.

proportional representation, but with a formula which would allow states such as the United Kingdom to maintain two-thirds of its seats as single-member constituencies.[40] In order for such a uniform electoral procedure to come into effect, Article 138(3) provides that:

> The European Parliament shall draw up proposals for elections by direct universal suffrage in accordance with a uniform procedure in all Member States.
>
> The Council shall, acting unanimously, lay down the appropriate provision, which it shall recommend to Member States for adoption in accordance with their respective constitutional requirements.

It is clear from this provision that, although the Parliament is to draw up proposals, it is the Council which must ultimately decide—as it had finally done in 1976 with regard to the holding of direct elections—on the provisions for a uniform electoral procedure. Whether the Council will act soon on the Parliament's resolution remains to be seen.

Prior to the first elections, MEPs had been delegates of their national parliaments. After the first direct elections, the practice of 'double-jobbing' i.e. the holding of a dual mandate by MEPs became the exception, although it is still possible. Now, after the addition of Articles 8 to 8e to the EC Treaty by the TEU, citizens of the Union who are resident in a Member State will have the right to vote and to stand as a candidate in European Parliament elections.[41]

MEPs sit in the Parliament according to political grouping, rather than according to nationality, although national parties generally remain together within the larger European Parliament groupings. There are many political groups within the Parliament, the largest three being, respectively, the European Socialists, the Christian Democrats (European People's Party), and the European Liberal Democratic and Reformist Party. Others include the Greens and the newly formed 'anti-Maastricht' group, the Europe of Nations. There are some non-aligned members, although most MEPs will join one of the political groups, which enjoy 'considerable financial and practical advantages'.[42] Article 138a of the EC Treaty, which was added by the TEU, expresses ideological support for the creation of European political parties, providing as follows:

> Political parties at European level are important as a factor for integration within the Union. They contribute to forming a European awareness and to expressing the political will of the citizens of the Union.

[40] See EP Res. A3–0381/92, [1993] OJ C115/121, based on the De Gucht Report.

[41] See Council Dir. 93/109 on exercising the right to vote in European Parliament elections, [1993] OJ L329/34. See also the resolution of the European Parliament on the implementation of this Dir.: [1994] OJ C44/159.

[42] See M. Westlake, *A Modern Guide*, n. 35 above, 189.

The Parliament elects its own President, together with fourteen Vice-Presidents, which collectively are called the Bureau of Parliament. Together with the leaders of the various political groups, they were formerly called the enlarged Bureau of Parliament, but this body is now called the Conference of Presidents. Parliament has a large range of specialist committees, with some sub-committees, on matters such as Legal Affairs and Citizens' Rights, Foreign Affairs, Security and Defence Policy, Budgets and Budgetary Control, Women's Rights, Social Affairs and Employment, Institutional Affairs, and Petitions, which carry out much of its legislative work through drawing up reports on relevant issues. Parliament is also helped by a large secretariat which provides substantial legal and administrative assistance.

After years of wrangling between Member States over the seat of Parliament, in 1992 the Member States finally decided, as they had been required to do under Article 216 of the EEC Treaty,[43] that Parliament would sit in Strasbourg, with its secretariat in Luxembourg and certain sessions and committee meetings in Brussels.

(b) Parliament's Legislative Role

We have already noted that from the originally weak, purely consultative part it played in the legislative process, the European Parliament has gradually acquired a fairly substantial role, and indeed is constantly clamouring for more. Its position alongside the Council as one of the two 'arms' of the budgetary authority, with the symbolically important task of actually adopting the Budget, was, until recently, Parliament's most significant power. However, its role in the wider legislative process since the 1975 Budgetary Treaty has been greatly enhanced as a result of the widened consultation, co-operation, assent, and co-decision procedures, which were negotiated and established in successive Treaty amendments. Parliament's legislative role is examined in greater detail in Chapter 3, but the overall picture is one of a gradually strengthening institution whose relations with the other Community institutions are in constant dynamic development.

The following extract gives an example, from 1992, of how Parliament chose to use one of the modes of its legislative involvement—the assent procedure, which is an effective veto—in a tactical manner to influence the substance of international agreements.

K. Bradley, Legal Developments in the European Parliament[44]

Parliament's now well-established use of the power to refuse assent to agreements and protocols based on Article 238 EEC as an instrument of foreign policy, particularly as a means to encourage respect for human rights in contracting third States, took on a more systematic appearance with its Resolution of 15 January on the EEC–Maghreb and EEC–Mashreq protocols. In particular, Parliament

[43] See Art. 77 ECSC and Art. 189 Euratom. [44] (1992) 12 YBEL 505, 524.

called for the insertion of a 'clause concerning democracy and human rights' in all such protocols, and offered its own services as an observer at the annual meeting of the Cooperation Council with each of the Partner countries. The Commission was requested not to implement either the fourth protocols with Syria or Morocco, until these countries comply with United Nations Security Council Resolutions on respect for human rights, or on the fourth protocol with Israel, until the human rights situation in the occupied territory improves. Assent to two protocols with Syria and one with Morocco was refused on this occasion.

After the Treaty on European Union, the substitution by Article 228(3) of the EC Treaty of a simple majority of Parliament rather than an absolute majority in various contexts in which the assent procedure is to be used—including the conclusion of association agreements and other types of international agreement—has been seen by some as a reduction in Parliament's influence. This is because it is easier for the other institutions to obtain the support of a simple rather than an absolute majority of the members of Parliament. Further, despite the increase in the use of the assent procedure occasioned by the amended Article 228, there are still certain international agreements, such as those in the common commercial policy field under Article 113(3), in which Parliament continues to play no role at all. Its involvement under the two new 'pillars' of the Treaty on European Union, in the common foreign and security policy and in justice and home affairs, is also fairly limited. Parliament is to be consulted by the Presidency 'on the main aspects and the basic choices of the common foreign and security policy' as well as 'on the principal aspects of activities' in the area of Justice and Home Affairs, and its views are to be 'duly taken into consideration'. It is to be regularly informed of developments in those areas and may ask questions of the Council or make recommendations, as well as holding an annual debate. These, however, represent a weaker form of parliamentary participation than the co-operation, co-decision, or assent procedures.

Outside the formal legislative process and the conciliation procedures within this process, however, Parliament, Council, and Commission regularly meet together in inter-institutional conferences, devoted either to particular topics or to general common problems.[45] The increasing number of occasions on which Parliament and Council meet together in the course of various procedures of this kind can only improve the dialogue and relationship between these two characteristically antagonistic institutions. Since Parliament is perceived to be an instinctively federalist institution, whereas the Council represents the Member States' interests, a certain tension is to be expected. According to Westlake, 'even today, relations between the two institutions are tinged by frustration, envy and resentment on Parliament's part and condescension on the part of the Council'.[46] However, they are certainly not always at loggerheads, and it appears that the Council sometimes chooses to

[45] M. Westlake, *A Modern Guide*, n. 35 above, 37. [46] *Loc. cit.*

consult Parliament on measures even where it is not obliged by the Treaty to do so.[47]

Parliament also now has the formal right, under Article 138b, to request the Commission to submit a proposal on any matter on which the Parliament thinks a Community act is necessary. The Commission is not bound to draw up a proposal in response to a request under Article 138b, but, if the right is exercised sensibly by Parliament in accordance with its own rules of procedure,[48] the Commission is likely to consider such requests seriously.

The Commission has always been accountable to Parliament, and after the TEU this accountability is strengthened further. Having had the power to censure the Commission and require its resignation ever since the signing of the ECSC Treaty,[49] the Parliament has now acquired the right to participate in the appointment of the Commission. Article 158(2), as amended, provides that after the nomination by the Member States—having consulted the European Parliament—of the Commission Members and the President of the Commission, the Commission 'shall be subject, as a body to a vote of approval by the European Parliament', thus giving Parliament a veto over the appointment of the Commission as a whole. Both the Commission and the Parliament, after the TEU, have the same term of five years, whereas the Commission was previously appointed for four years only. The first exercise of this power was taken seriously, when the large Socialist group was considering attempting to block the appointment of Jacques Santer, who had emerged at the last minute as a compromise candidate after the United Kingdom vetoed the appointment of Jean-Luc Dehaene, who was claimed to be 'too federalist'. The following extract from the speech of a member of the Socialist group gives a flavour of the debate which took place in the European Parliament prior to the vote on the appointment of Santer.

> The European Union is a Union of Member States and people who live in some of the most sophisticated, most developed countries in the world; countries that pride themselves on their democratic traditions, countries that lecture the world on democratic rights—one country indeed reckons it has the mother of parliaments. Yet, these same countries are willing to connive at the most squalid, shabby and ill-judged practices to put in place what is essentially the most important position in Europe, the President of the European Commission. The Council makes pious statements about improving openness, democracy, about the need to make Europe more accessible, to bring Europe closer to its people. Then on our

[47] The Commission attempted to challenge such 'optional' consultation in Case 165/87, *Commission* v. *Council* (commodity coding) [1988] ECR 5545, [1990] 1 CMLR 457 but the Court ruled in para. 20 that 'consultation of Parliament, which the Council is always entitled to do, cannot be regarded as unlawful even if it is not mandatory'.

[48] The Parliament draws up its own rules of procedure in accordance with Art. 142 EC, Art. 25 ECSC, and Art. 112 Euratom. These were amended in 1993 so as to implement the Treaty on European Union changes. See [1993] OJ C268/51.

[49] See Art. 144 EC, Art. 24 ECSC, Art. 114 Euratom. An absolute majority of Parliament, with a two-thirds majority of the votes cast, is required to carry the motion of censure.

television screens it shows us prime ministers and presidents huddled in corners trying to find a candidate acceptable to the majority.

. . .

The Maastricht Treaty gives us the right to be involved, to be consulted. We do at least in this forum have a democratic legitimacy. It is a forum where we can generate an open discussion and come forward with the names of potential candidates. The Group of the Party of European Socialists wants to see this Parliament taken seriously.[50]

Compared with its right of participation in the appointment of the other institutions, the Parliament's powers are greatest in the context of the Commission, since it can actually block the appointment of the Commission as a whole and is to be consulted on the nominations of the Member States for the individual Commission members as well as on the Commission President. In the case of members of the Court of Auditors and the President of the new European Monetary Institute, Parliament is to be consulted in the same way, but has no ultimate power of veto. Further, despite its expressed wish to participate in the appointment of judges of the Court of Justice, Parliament at present has no part to play in their selection or appointment.

One of the reasons Parliament and the Commission have always been seen as natural allies, apart from their inherent federalist tendencies or supranational leanings, is the fact that neither has control over the Council, except in so far as the Parliament has a joint legislative role in some areas. Given that the Council inevitably represents the Member States' interests, it is often seen by the other institutions as a hindrance to more dynamic Community goals. However, Parliament's increasing familiarity with the Council and with its workings not only through the budgetary process, but also as a result of the new Conciliation Committee which forms part of the 'co-decision' procedure, may draw these two institutions somewhat closer. Parliament's experience of the Conciliation Committee procedure is discussed in the following extract.

M. Westlake, A Modern Guide to the European Parliament[51]

Parliament's earliest experiences of the procedure have been revealing. In the first place, in the Parliament's eyes there has been a generalised 'de-mystification' of the Council much as had previously occurred with Parliament's budgetary specialists. The Council, its procedures, its secretariat, its personalities and even its buildings are no longer 'off limits' to Parliament. The Council is becoming more familiar and is held less in awe; MEPs are now entitled to stalk its corridors and sit at its tables in search of compromise and concession. In the second place, the Parliament rapidly realised that, on the substance of issues subject to the procedure, Parliament could only hope to 'do serious business' if it sent delegations that could winningly combine expertise, experience and good tacticians. In the third place, from the Council's point of view, the procedure has been little less than a

[50] Green, EP Debs. 1994 No. 4–449/66, 21 July 1994. [51] N. 35 above, 150.

revolution and, although in a sense conciliation could be reduced to systematic bluff-calling, the stakes are very high . . . In the fourth place, and more generally, the procedure has already been subject to *ad hoc* refinements. The most important of these is the introduction of informal conciliation meetings, typically between a reduced number of parliamentarians and the Council Presidency, in the search for the basis of a compromise solution before issues are subject to the formal procedure itself. It has been said that the Commission is like a 'thirteenth Member State' at the Council table; the co-decision procedure has clearly added a fourteenth factor.

(c) Parliament's Supervisory Role

Parliament's supervisory role can be seen in its monitoring of the activities of the other institutions through the asking of oral and written questions,[52] and the establishment of committees of inquiry. The setting up of committees of inquiry, and the establishment of the right of Member State nationals to petition the European Parliament were practices of the Parliament for many years, but these were not given Treaty status until the TEU, and they are now provided for under Articles 138c and 138d of the EC Treaty respectively.[53]

Another change made to the powers of the Parliament by the TEU—this time establishing an entirely new practice—was the provision for the appointment by the Parliament of an Ombudsman.[54] The role of the Ombudsman is said in the Treaty to be to receive complaints from Union citizens or resident third-country nationals or legal persons, concerning 'instances of maladministration in the activities of the Community institutions or bodies' as well as to 'conduct inquiries for which he finds grounds, either on his own initiative or on the basis of complaints submitted to him direct or through a member of the European Parliament'.

The Parliament in 1993 adopted draft regulations and conditions governing the performance of the Ombudsman's duties,[55] which were subsequently confirmed by the Council.[56] Article 6(2) specifies that the Parliament is to elect as an Ombudsman a Union citizen, who must have 'full civil and political rights, offer every guarantee of independence, and meet the conditions required for the exercise of the highest judicial office in their country or have the acknowledged competence and experience to undertake the duties of Ombudsman'. The Ombudsman is to be appointed for the duration of the mandate of the Parliament, and in the case of serious misconduct or non-fulfilment of the conditions of office, the Court of Justice, at the request of the Parliament, may dismiss her or him. The Court of Justice and the Court of First Instance act-

[52] Art. 140 EC, Art. 23 ECSC, and Art. 110 Euratom.

[53] On the petition procedure see E. Marias, 'The Right to Petition the European Parliament after Maastricht' (1994) 19 ELRev. 169. For criticism of the apparent narrowing, in Art. 138d, of the material scope of the right of petition, see K. Bradley, 'Better Rusty than Missin': Institutional Reforms of the Maastricht Treaty and the European Parliament', in *Legal Issues of the Maastricht Treaty*, eds. D. O'Keeffe and P. Twomey (Chancery, 1994), 193, 207.

[54] See Art. 138e EC, Art. 20d ECSC, and Art. 107d Euratom.

[55] [1993] OJ C329/136.

[56] See Council Dec. 94/114, [1994] OJ L54/25.

ing in their judicial role are excluded by Article 138e from the Ombudsman's jurisdiction, and the regulations further prohibit intervention in cases before courts or questioning the soundness of a court's ruling, which presumably applies also to national courts. Only Community institutions are to be subject to the Ombudsman's jurisdiction and they must supply information requested and give access to files, except where grounds of secrecy are pleaded. At the conclusion of an investigation the Ombudsman is to send a report to the Parliament and to the institution under investigation, and the complainant is to be informed of the outcome. An annual report of activities is also to be presented by the Ombudsman to the Parliament.

(d) Parliament as a Litigant

Apart from the gradual extension of Parliament's legislative powers, a further significant development in its status and influence came about through litigation. As in the case of its legislative role, the enhancement of Parliament's institutional role as a litigant occurred progressively, through a series of decisions of the Court of Justice from 1980 to 1990, with a considerable expansion of litigation since then. It will be seen that Parliament's use of its right to bring proceedings before the Court of Justice is often a means of reinforcing and strengthening its legislative role. That such strategic use of its litigation rights may be an irritant to the other institutions can be seen in the following comments of Council, made in the course of proceedings brought by Parliament under Article 175.

> The Council explains first of all that in its opinion the present action is to be seen as part of the Parliament's efforts to increase its influence in the decision-making process within the Community . . . The political aims of Parliament must be pursued by other means.[57]

There have been various stages in the process of recognizing Parliament as a litigant with comparable, though not equal, rights to those of the other institutions. In the first place, in 1980, the Court in the *Roquette* and *Maizena* cases confirmed that Parliament had, under Article 37 of the Statute of the Court, the right to intervene in any case before it, in the same way as the other institutions, without having to show any special interest in the outcome of the case.[58] The Council had sought Parliament's opinion on a regulation governing the sweetener 'isoglucose', as it was required to do under Article 43(2) of the Treaty. Due to disagreement within the committees of Parliament which were considering the measure, an opinion had not yet been given by the end of the parliamentary session, but the Council nevertheless went ahead and

[57] Case 13/83, *European Parliament* v. *Council* (transport) [1985] ECR 1513, para. 13.

[58] Cases 138/79, *Roquette Frères* v. *Council* [1980] ECR 3333 and 139/79, *Maizena* v. *Council* [1980] ECR 3393.

adopted the regulation. The regulation was then successfully challenged by a company which produced isoglucose, on the ground of failure to obtain Parliament's opinion. In confirming both Parliament's right to intervene under Article 37 of the Statute and the importance of actually obtaining Parliament's opinion where consultation is required, the Court of Justice gave a boost to its institutional status and significance:

> 19. The first paragraph of that article provides that all the institutions of the Community have the right to intervene. It is not possible to restrict the exercise of that right by one of them without adversely affecting its institutional position as intended by the Treaty and in particular Article 4(1).
>
> ....
>
> 33. The consultation provided for in the third subparagraph of Article 43, as in other similar provisions of the Treaty, is the means which allows the Parliament to play an actual part in the legislative process of the Community. Such power represents an essential factor in the institutional balance intended by the Treaty. Although limited, it reflects at Community level that fundamental democratic principle that the peoples should take part in the exercise of power through the intermediary of a representative assembly. Due consultation of the Parliament in the cases provided for by the Treaty therefore constitutes an essential formality, disregard of which means that the measure concerned is void.

In 1985, Parliament successfully brought proceedings against the Council under Article 175 for failure to implement the common transport policy as required by Article 75 of the Treaty. Since the wording of Article 175 permitted 'the Member States and the other institutions of the Community' to bring proceedings against the Council and Commission for failure to act, Parliament was held, on the same reasoning as that used in the isoglucose cases, to be included as one of the 'institutions'.[59]

There was equally little difficulty in persuading the Court to include Parliament as an institution against which an action for annulment under Article 173 could be brought, even though only the Council and the Commission were expressly mentioned in that Article. In '*Les Verts*', the Court reached this conclusion by reasoning that the Community was 'a Community based on the rule of law, inasmuch as neither its Member States nor its institutions can avoid a review of the question whether the measures adopted by them are in conformity with the basic constitutional charter, the Treaty', and that 'an interpretation of Article 173 which excluded measures adopted by the European Parliament from those which could be contested would lead to a result contrary both to the spirit of the Treaty as expressed in

[59] Case 13/83, n. 57 above, para. 17, and see Case 377/87, *European Parliament* v. *Council* (draft budget) [1988] ECR 4017. An action under Art. 175 has also recently been initiated in Case C–445/93, *European Parliament* v. *Commission* (frontier controls) [1994] OJ C1/24.

Article 164 and to its system'.[60] The Court explained the original rationale for Parliament's exclusion from Article 173 as a 'passive participant', a rationale which was no longer applicable.

> 24. It is true that, unlike Article 177 of the Treaty, which refers to acts of the institutions without further qualification, Article 173 refers only to acts of the Council and the Commission. However the general scheme of the Treaty is to make a direct action available against 'all measures adopted by the institutions . . . which are intended to have legal effects' as the Court has already had occasion to emphasize in its judgment of 31 March 1971 (Case 22/70 *Commission* v. *Council* [1971] ECR 263). The European Parliament is not expressly mentioned among the institutions whose measures may be contested because, in its original version, the EEC Treaty merely granted it powers of consultation and political control rather than the power to adopt measures intended to have legal effect *vis-à-vis* third parties. Article 38 of the ECSC Treaty shows that where the Parliament was given *ab initio* the power to adopt binding measures, as was the case under the last sentence of the fourth paragraph of Article 95 of that Treaty, measures adopted by it were not in principle immune from actions for annulment.

Subsequently, in proceedings brought by the Council against Parliament seeking the annulment of the budget for 1986 which had been adopted in breach of the agreed maximum rate of increase of non-compulsory expenditure, the Court granted the annulment sought but refused to intervene any further in the dispute.[61] Many other actions under Article 173 have been brought against Parliament since then, and the Court has ruled that acts which have no legal effects[62] or acts which have 'internal' legal effects only, such as a reorganization of Parliament's workplace and practices,[63] cannot be the subject of annulment proceedings.

The emphasis on the importance of Parliament's democratic credentials in the *Isoglucose* cases, the ease with which its first action for failure to act was admitted by the Court, and the readiness to acknowledge Parliament as a

[60] Case 294/83, *Parti ecologiste 'Les Verts'* v. *European Parliament* [1986] ECR 1339, [1987] 2 CMLR 343, paras. 23, 25. Earlier, in annulment proceedings brought by Luxembourg under the EEC, ECSC, and Euratom Treaties against a resolution of the Parliament relating to its seat and places of work, the action was admissible on the basis that Art. 38 ECSC expressly permitted an act of the Parliament to be annulled, even though the act in question related 'simultaneously and indivisibly to the spheres of the three Treaties', Case 230/81, *Luxembourg* v. *European Parliament* [1983] ECR 255, [1983] 2 CMLR 726, para. 20. For other such proceedings brought by Luxembourg, see Cases 108/83, *Luxembourg* v. *European Parliament* [1984] ECR 1945, [1986] 2 CMLR 507 and C–213/88 and 39/89, *Luxembourg* v. *European Parliament* [1991] ECR I–5643.

[61] Case 34/86, *Council* v. *Parliament* (Budget) [1986] ECR 2155, [1986] 3 CMLR 94. See, more recently, Case C–284/90, *Council* v. *European Parliament* [1992] ECR I–2277 in which the Court annulled the amending and supplementary budget for 1990.

[62] See e.g. Cases 78/85, *Group of the European Right* v. *Parliament* [1986] ECR 1753 and C–68/90, *Blot* v. *Parliament* [1990] ECR I–2101.

[63] See Cases 358/85 and 51/85, *France* v. *Parliament* [1988] ECR 4821, [1990] 1 CMLR 309 and Case C–314/91, *Weber* v. *Parliament* [1993] ECR I–1093. In the latter case the annulment action was successful since the contested act did have legal effects.

defendant in Article 173 annulment proceedings clearly gave the Parliament confidence that its right to bring an action for annulment under Article 173 would similarly be recognized. However, in the '*Comitology*' case[64] in 1988, the Court delivered its first blow to Parliament's developing status as a litigant, ruling that only the Council and Commission were listed in Article 173 as applicants (unlike Article 175 which referred generally to the 'institutions'), and that there were adequate alternative ways of ensuring that Parliament's legislative role was respected and that illegal acts were challenged, other than by giving Parliament itself a right of action. Two years later in the '*Chernobyl*' case,[65] however, the Court changed its position and ruled that Parliament could indeed bring proceedings under Article 173, but only where it was alleging that its prerogatives had been infringed in the adoption of the contested act:

> The absence in the Treaties of any provision giving the Parliament the right to bring an action for annulment may constitute a procedural gap, but it cannot prevail over the fundamental interest in the maintenance and observance of the institutional balance laid down in the Treaties establishing the European Communities.[66]

Thus, where no other institution or person was likely to challenge an allegedly illegal act—as was the situation in the *Chernobyl* case itself—Parliament should be entitled to bring proceedings to challenge it, since otherwise its prerogatives might be ignored without there being any adequate means of redress. However, a concomitant of this rationale for giving Parliament *locus standi* has been that the Court has refused to allow Parliament to plead a ground of annulment other than the failure to respect its prerogatives.[67]

Since then, Parliament has used its right to bring annulment proceedings a number of times, and with a measure of success.[68] The legal basis used by the institutions for the adoption of legislation has become an issue of major importance and the focus of frequent litigation since the Single European Act and the TEU, given the differing degrees of participation of different institutions—and in particular of the Parliament—under various Treaty provi-

[64] Case 302/87, *European Parliament* v. *Council* (Comitology) [1988] ECR 5616.

[65] Case C–70/88, *European Parliament* v. *Council* (Chernobyl) [1990] ECR 2041, [1992] 1 CMLR 91.

[66] *Ibid.*, para. 26 of the judgment.

[67] Case C–187/93, *European Parliament* v. *Council* (Transfer of Waste) [1994] ECR I–2857.

[68] The Court annulled the Students' Residence Dir. in Case 295/90, *European Parliament* v. *Council* [1992] ECR I–4193, [1993] 3 CMLR 281, on the basis that the Council had based it partly on Art. 235, which required only simple consultation of Parliament, rather than basing it solely on Art. 7 (now Art. 6) which required the use of the co-operation procedure. For an unsuccessful action in which the Court ruled that the measure challenged was not an act of the Community, see Cases C–181 and 248/91, *European Parliament* v. *Council and Commission* (Bangladesh aid) [1993] ECR I–3685, [1994] 3 CMLR 317.

sions.[69] In addition to challenging the legal basis for legislation, Parliament has also used its standing as a litigant to strengthen its right of consultation, and to ensure that the Council adequately reconsults it if the substance of the legislation changes after the first consultation of Parliament.[70]

We have seen that the TEU has been heavily criticized, partly on account of its failure to respect the *acquis communautaire* in attempting to undermine or to restrict principles of law which had been developed by the Court of Justice. However, in the area of Parliament's standing as a litigant, the TEU provides an example of an actual incorporation of the *acquis* into the provisions of the EC Treaty. However, this, too, has been criticized, on the basis that the Court's case law represented a minimal approach to the standing of Parliament, and that a more extensive recognition of its rights as a litigant was merited.[71] The relevant parts of Article 173[72] are now amended to provide:

> The Court of Justice shall review the legality of acts adopted jointly by the European Parliament and the Council, of acts of the Council, of the Commission and of the European Central Bank, other than recommendations and opinions, and of acts of the European Parliament intended to produce legal effects *vis-à-vis* third parties.[73]

Parliament has also been added after the TEU in Article 175 of the EC Treaty as a potential defendant. This amendment follows the spirit of the Court's case law rather than any particular decision since, although several sets of proceedings were initiated against the Parliament under Article 175 prior to its amendment, none of the cases was actually brought to judgment.

[69] After the two cases brought by the Commission against the Council in Cases C–300/89, *Commission* v. *Council* (Titanium Dioxide) [1991] ECR I–2867, [1993] 3 CMLR 359 and C–155/91, *Commission* v. *Council* (Waste Directive) [1993] ECR I–939, challenging the adoption of environment-related legislation under Art. 130s rather than Art. 100a (when Parliament's prerogatives under the latter were more substantial than under Art. 130s at the time), Parliament itself was unsuccessful in a third, Case C–187/93, n. 67 above. In the first case, the Court had ruled that Art. 100a should have been used, thus enhancing Parliament's role, whereas in the later two cases, it held that the legislation had been properly based on Art. 130s. The issue of the correct legal base for legislation is discussed in more detail in Ch. 3.

[70] See recently Cases C–65/90, *European Parliament* v. *Council* [1992] ECR I–4953 and C–388/92, *European Parliament* v. *Council* [1994] ECR I–2067 concerning measures adopted in the field of transport. On Parliament's right to be properly consulted, see also Case C–316/91, *European Parliament* v. *Council* (Lomé Convention) [1994] ECR I–625, [1994] 3 CMLR 149, paras. 16–18, although it did not succeed on the substance of the case.

[71] K. Bradley, 'Better Rusty than Missin' ', n. 53 above, 201–202.

[72] For amendments to the other Treaties see Art. 33 ECSC, and Art. 146 Euratom.

[73] For criticism of this description of the acts of Parliament which are to be reviewable, see K. Bradley, 'Better Rusty than Missin' ', n. 53 above, 200. He argues that the language of Art. 173 focuses on the subjective intention of Parliament and the existence of a third party, rather than on the effects of the measure.

6. THE EUROPEAN COURT OF JUSTICE AND THE COURT OF FIRST INSTANCE

The Court of Justice, to which the Court of First Instance is attached, is the judicial branch of the Community. The Court of Auditors, although it also bears the title of 'court', does not have a judicial function, but rather one of financial and budgetary supervision and review. The powers and function of the Court of Justice are generally considered separately from the three 'political' institutions—the Council, Commission, and Parliament—but this should not conceal the fact that the Court has very much played its part alongside the other institutions in shaping the legal and political structure of the Community.

The Court of Justice is generally perceived to have pursued a vigorous policy of integration over the years, to have taken on the task of giving flesh and substance to an 'outline' Treaty, with a distinctive vision of the kind of Europe which it sought to promote. One of its primary concerns has been the enhancement of the effectiveness of Community law and its integration into the legal systems of the Member States. However, the Court is but one of five—formerly four—institutions, and has played its part in developing Community law alongside those others. Sometimes its approach has been in tension with theirs, at other times in greater harmony with one or other of them, but the process has always been one of interaction. The Court has at times been reactive, at times proactive, and at times a mixture of both. In other words, the Court has not pursued a project of integration growing more or less 'activist' all the time. At the same period of time the Court may have been cautious in one area of law and ambitious in another, reacting perhaps to events or sentiments in the Member States on the one hand, and to those in the Community institutions on the other. There are always many factors influencing the Court, and a note of warning should be sounded against any theory or explanation of its role that is too simplistic. Like any of the institutions, its role is and has been a complex one.

Consider the many different issues on which the Court may be called upon to adjudicate. These include matters of constitutional significance such as the proper division of powers between the states and the Community, and widely varying matters of substantive law from competition policy to social policy, to agriculture, or to transport. The Court decides cases between Community institutions and Member States, between individuals and their employers, and on a wide range of legal issues between parties which have been referred from a national court. It gives opinions on the compatibility with the Treaties of international agreements, and other kinds of jurisdiction may be conferred upon it by agreement. The scope of its jurisdiction will be considered further below.

It has been argued that the Court of Justice is the 'European lawyer's hobbyhorse' and this indeed is a danger which should be kept in mind.[74] There

[74] T. Koopmans, 'The Future of the Court of Justice of the European Communities' (1991) 11 YBEL 15. Elsewhere, the same author cautioned that 'not every problem of European

is a tendency in studying and in teaching Community law to focus excessively on the Court as an institution, and on case law as a source of law. While there is no denying the importance of these, excessive concentration on them results in a neglect of the importance of the other law-making processes and dynamics within the Community. While this can be said to be true of the study and teaching of law generally, it is perhaps exacerbated in the Community context by the high profile (amongst lawyers) of the Court of Justice. It is not an undeserved profile, since undoubtedly the Court has been central to much of the development of the Community's legal system. But it is important to remember that a vast amount of Community law never comes before the Court, and either takes effect without difficulty or the difficulties are addressed other than through the Community's adjudicative process.

(a) Composition and Structure of the Court of Justice

The composition of the Court of Justice and the Court of First Instance are governed by Articles 165 to 168A of the EC Treaty, Articles 32 to 32d of the ECSC Treaty and Articles 137 to 140a of Euratom. References to the Treaty below will be to the provisions of the EC Treaty. A protocol on the Statute of the Court of Justice, which was amended in 1988 when the Court of First Instance was established, is attached to each of the three Treaties, dealing with the organization and procedure of the Court.[75] The Rules of Procedure, which build on the provisions of the Statute of the Court, are adopted by the Court of Justice under Article 188 of the EC Treaty, and require the unanimous approval of the Council of Ministers.

The Treaty provisions on the number of judges are amended upon the accession of each new Member State, most recently with the accession of Finland, Austria, and Sweden. Prior to these three accessions there were thirteen judges, one selected by the government of each of the Member States and one additional judge selected by the four large Member States—France, Germany, Italy and the United Kingdom. The European Council continued this practice by deciding in 1993 that in the event of an even number of Member States acceding (which would have been the case had Norway also acceded), those same four states and Spain could take part in a system involving the rotation of an additional judge. However, if an uneven number of states acceded—thus rendering the number of judges even—the 'thirteenth acting judge' could be allowed to become an Advocate General.[76] Thus after the recent accessions, since the number of judges would become even at sixteen, there will be fifteen judges and one additional Advocate General. The

integration can be reduced to something justiciable'. See 'The Role of Law in the Next Stage of European Integration' (1986) 35 ICLQ 925, 930.

[75] For a review of the first years of the new Court, see B. Vesterdorf, 'The Court of First Instance of the European Communities after Two Full Years in Operation' (1992) 29 CMLRev. 897.

[76] Bull. EC 12–1993, 1.18.

appointment of all judges is required by Article 167 to be 'by common accord of the Governments of the Member States'.[77] The term of office is six years, and the appointment of new judges or reappointment of the existing judges is staggered so that there will be a partial replacement of judges every three years.

Prior to the latest accessions, the Treaty provided that the Court of Justice was to be assisted by six Advocates General. It was agreed that there would be an additional two Advocates General appointed on the accession of the four new Member States, and although without Norway there are only three new Members, three new Advocates General have nonetheless been appointed, making nine in total. Two of the three were newly appointed and the extra was formerly the 'thirteenth acting judge'. It was agreed by the Member States that five of the eight Advocates General should be appointed by the five large Member States, the remaining three to be appointed by the other Member States on a system of rotation. The qualifications for selection, method of appointment, and conditions of office of the Advocates General are the same as for the judges of the Court. Their duty, which is set out in Article 166 of the EC Treaty, is 'to make, in open court, reasoned submissions on cases brought before the Court of Justice' with complete impartiality and independence.

The dangers of a fixed-term appointment for the independence—or the perceived independence—of the judiciary have been noted, but no change has been proposed to this and, in practice, most judges have been reappointed.[78] The secrecy of the Court's deliberations may be a protection against perceived 'political' appointments or refusals to renew, although this would not apply to the Advocates General, whose opinions are made public.

The qualifications for selection as a judge of the Court of Justice require 'persons whose independence is beyond doubt and who possess the qualifications required for appointment to the highest judicial offices in their respective countries or who are jurisconsults of recognized competence'.[79] The Court is to appoint its own Registrar, and to elect its President from amongst its own judges.[80]

In accordance with their respective traditions, certain Member States have appointed academics to sit as judges of the Court of Justice, whereas others—such as the United Kingdom and Ireland—have nominated existing judges from their domestic courts, or prominent practising advocates from the domestic legal profession. Although states tend to select their own nationals, the Treaty clearly requires that the judges be entirely independent of the government which chose them or indeed of any other interest group which might seek to influence their decision. Judging from the nature of much of the Court of Justice's jurisprudence, the wishes of individual Member States have had

[77] Art. 168a provides similarly for the CFI.

[78] N. Brown and T. Kennedy, *The Court of Justice of the European Communities* (4th edn., Sweet & Maxwell, 1994), 48.

[79] Art. 167(1) EC.

[80] See Art. 168 of the Treaty and Art. 7 of the Rules of Procedure.

little influence on its decision-making.[81] On the other hand, this is not to say that the Court as a body is immune from political pressures, nor that it takes no account of the general wishes of the Member States in its decision-making. Indeed, its judgments are clearly sometimes influenced by relatively 'non-legal' arguments made by Member States before the Court, or by critical responses from national and from Community sources.[82]

Judges may not hold any other political or administrative office while they are members of the Court and, apart from their normal replacement, their period of office may terminate on death, resignation, or on removal from office. Article 6 of the Statute of the Court provides that a judge or Advocate General who, in the unanimous opinion of the other judges and Advocates General, no longer fulfils the requisite conditions and obligations of office may be removed from office, but this has never yet occurred.

The Court of Justice is permitted under Article 165 of the EC Treaty to sit in chambers of three or five, as well as in plenary session. The ability to sit in chambers is vital to the Court's functioning given its ever-increasing case-load, and it is a facility which has been used extensively.[83] Until the amendment made by the TEU, Article 165 provided that cases brought by a Member State or by one of the Community institutions had to be decided in plenary session—usually nine or thirteen judges, although the quorum was seven. However, after the amendments, Article 165 now does not preclude any category of case from being heard by a chamber,[84] although it specifies that the Court shall sit in plenary session when a Member State or a Community institution which is party to the proceedings so requests. The problem of overburdening the Court apparently continues to grow despite the temporary easing of the case-load which the establishment of a Court of First Instance in 1988 initially brought about. Various suggestions for reform have been made, varying from recommending radical solutions,[85] such as the transformation of the Court of Justice into a European High Court of Justice with a more restricted category of cases appropriate to a supreme court, and the establishment of four regional courts to receive preliminary references from

[81] The irrelevance of the nationality of the judges is underscored by Art. 16 of the Statute of the Court, which provides that a party may not apply for a change in the composition of the Court or of one of its chambers on the grounds either of the nationality of a judge or the absence from the Court or chamber of a judge of the nationality of that party.

[82] The Court's decision in Case C–262/88, *Barber* v. *Guardian Royal Exchange Assurance Group* [1990] ECR I–1889, [1990] 2 CMLR 513, and the relationship between the '*Barber* Protocol' and the TEU and the Court's subsequent case law is a commonly cited example of this. For further discussion see Ch. 18. H. Rasmussen, *On Law and Policy in the European Court of Justice* (Nijhoff Dordrecht, 1986), ch. 10, refers to such critical response as 'negative policy inputs'.

[83] See N. Brown and T. Kennedy, n. 78 above, 37–9.

[84] Art. 95 of the Rules of Procedure, last amended in 1991, will be amended to take account of this change.

[85] See also Lord Slynn, former judge of the Court, in *Introducing a European Legal Order* (Stevens & Sons/Sweet & Maxwell, 1992), 171, who advocates 'a radical reexamination and rethink of, and not a mere tinkering with, the structure of the Court, of its jurisdiction and its procedures'.

national courts within each region,[86] to more modest proposals of reorganization for rendering it more efficient.[87]

(b) The Court of First Instance

The Court of First Instance[88] was established in 1988 under the terms of Article 168a of the Treaty, which had been inserted by the Single European Act.[89] The reason for its establishment was to relieve some of the burden on the Court of Justice, and it had been long argued that staff cases, which were numerous but which often involved issues of individual rather than of general importance, could be transferred to a tribunal to decide. After the new accessions there are fifteen judges, with no separate Advocates General, although any member of the Court of First Instance may be called upon to perform the task of an Advocate General.[90] This, however, has happened only rarely. The qualifications required for appointment as a judge of the Court of First Instance are slightly less exalted than those required for appointment to the Court of Justice (those 'whose independence is beyond doubt and who possess the ability required for appointment to judicial office'), although in practice the status and calibre of Member States' appointees to both courts appear to have differed little.

Like the Court of Justice, the Court of First Instance elects its own President from amongst its judges, and appoints its Registrar. Again, like the Court of Justice, it sits in chambers of three and five, sitting in plenary session with one judge acting as Advocate General only in cases of legal difficulty. There is an appeal to the Court of Justice on a point of law only within two months from the date of the decision of the Court of First Instance.[91] This is set out in Article 51 of the Statute of the Court which provides that 'it shall lie on the grounds of lack of competence of the Court of First Instance, a breach of procedure before it which adversely affects the interests of the appellant as well as the infringement of Community law by the Court of First Instance'. An appeal is not to have suspensory effect, except where the Court of First Instance has declared a regulation void, in which case the decision of the Court will take effect only after the two-month period for appeal has expired or when the appeal has been dismissed. Initially staff cases, competi-

[86] J.P. Jacqué and J. Weiler, 'On the Road to European Union: A New Judicial Architecture: An Agenda for the Intergovernmental Conference' (1990) 27 CMLRev. 185. They proposed that the European High Court of Justice would have jurisdiction in enforcement actions brought against Member States, actions for judicial review brought by Member States or Institutions, and preliminary references from highest national courts only.

[87] A. Arnull, 'Refurbishing the Judicial Architecture of the European Community' (1994) 43 ICLQ 296. For a discussion on rendering the Court more accessible to non-privileged litigants, without necessarily overburdening it further, see C. Harlow 'Towards a Theory of Access for the European Court of Justice' (1992) 12 YBEL 213.

[88] Known in French as the *Tribunal de Première Instance*, which explains the T used before the case number when a case is registered with the CFI.

[89] Council Dec. 88/591, [1988] OJ L319.

[90] See Arts. 17–19 of the Rules of Procedure.

[91] See e.g. Case C–53/92P, *Hilti* v. *Commission* [1994] ECR I–667.

tion cases brought by individuals against the Community institutions (because of their heavy and often complex factual content), and cases under the ECSC Treaty were dealt with by the new Court.[92] Since then the Council agreed, as envisaged under Article 3 of the Decision establishing the Court of First Instance, to transfer other categories of case such as anti-dumping cases, which had originally been proposed by the Court of Justice but which not all of the Member States were content to transfer. The Court of First Instance now has jurisdiction over all actions brought by 'non-privileged' parties—i.e. parties other than Member States or Community institutions—including anti-dumping cases. Article 168a, however, expressly provides that it has no jurisdiction to hear preliminary rulings. There is nothing in the Treaty to prevent other classes of cases, other than preliminary references, from being transferred to the Court of First Instance, such as cases between institutions, or brought by or against Member States, although it may be politically unlikely that the states would agree, as yet, to the transfer of some of these classes of cases.

(c) The Role of the Advocate General

The decision-making task of the Court of Justice is assisted by the existence of the office of Advocate General. The Advocate General participates at the oral stage of the judicial hearing and, more importantly, produces a written opinion for the Court. This opinion will be produced by the Advocate General who has been assigned to a given case, before the Court makes its decision. The written opinion will set out his or her understanding of the law applicable to the case, and will recommend to the Court how the case ought to be decided. This opinion is not binding on the Court, but it is generally very influential, and the opinion is indeed followed by the Court in the great majority of cases. The Advocate General's opinion is intended as impartial and independent advice, and in practice it tends to be an exhaustive and thoroughly reasoned account of the law governing every aspect of the case. The style and content of the Advocate General's opinion is virtually always far more readable than those of the Court, and often make some sense of an obscure or inadequately reasoned judgment. For this reason, even if an opinion was not followed, it is generally worthwhile reading it before attempting to understand a judgment of the Court.

(d) Procedure before the Court

Procedure before the Court of Justice and Court of First Instance is governed by their respective rules of procedure.[93] The procedure before the Court of

[92] Arnull describes the CFI as exercising 'its inquisitorial functions with gusto', n. 87 above, 300.

[93] For some of the differences between procedure before the Court and the otherwise similar procedures before the CFI, see N. Brown and T. Kennedy, n. 78 above, 81–93.

Justice takes place in two stages, the written and the oral stage.[94] Unlike in Member States with a common law background and an adversarial legal process, the written part of the proceedings before the Court of Justice is the most thorough and most important. At this stage, all applications, statements of case, defences, and indeed any written submissions or relevant documents are communicated to the parties to the case and to the institutions whose decisions are being contested. The Court itself can also request any further documents or information which it considers desirable, although in the case of refusal, Article 21 of the Statute of the Court simply provides that 'formal note' shall be taken.[95] The oral stage, by contrast, is limited and short. The *juge-rapporteur*—the judge who is assigned in a given case—prepares and presents to the Court the 'report for the hearing', which summarizes the facts of the case and the arguments of the parties. Then the legal representatives of the various parties may make oral submissions to the Court, followed by submissions of the Advocate General and the hearing of any necessary witnesses or experts. The Court itself has also adopted the practice of asking questions of the legal representatives before it. This has become an important part of the oral stage of proceedings, since it focuses attention on and clarifies the issues which the Court considers of particular significance in the case.

Other than the appeal on a point of law from the decisions of the Court of First Instance to the Court of Justice, there is no further appeal from the judgments of the Court of Justice, which is the ultimate or supreme court of the European Community. However, Member States, Community institutions, and parties may under certain conditions contest a judgment rendered without their being heard, where it is prejudicial to their rights.[96] There is also a mechanism whereby any party with an interest in a particular judgment can apply to the Court to construe the meaning or scope of a judgment which is in doubt,[97] and a method for seeking revision of a judgment within ten years of its being given 'on discovery of a fact which is of such nature as to be a decisive factor' and which was unknown at the time the judgment was given.[98] It is also apparent that the Court, although it generally builds on its own case law and follows the pattern and reasoning of its previous case law, clearly does

[94] See Art. 18 of the Statute of the Court.

[95] Compare the ruling of the Court in Case 2/88, *Zwartveld* [1990] ECR 3365, [1990] 3 CMLR 457 where it held it had inherent jurisdiction to require an institution of the Community to co-operate with national courts by producing documents requested by a national court.

[96] See Art. 39 of the Statute of the Court of Justice and Art. 97 of the Rules of Procedure.

[97] Art. 40 of the Statute of the Court and Art. 102 of the Rules of Procedure. See also the judgment of the Court in Case 69/85, *Re Wünsche* [1986] ECR 947 where it held that, although a national court cannot, in a reference to the Court under Art. 177, question the validity of a previous preliminary ruling of the Court, it can ask for an interpretation or clarification of the meaning of a previous ruling which is unclear.

[98] Art. 41 of the Statute of the Court and Arts. 98–100, of the Rules of Procedure. See e.g. Case 115/73, *Serio* v. *Commission* [1974] ECR 671, in which the Court dismissed the application for revision because no new facts were alleged, and the applicant wanted the Court to reopen an earlier case and to reconsider it on its merits.

not consider itself bound by a strict system of precedent.[99] Sometimes, where it has clearly departed from the reasoning or result of a previous case, the Court has made reference to the earlier case and explained the reason for its change.[100]

(e) Proposals for Reform

One thing on which virtually all commentators are agreed, as has been reflected in some of the extracts above, is that there is a serious need to rethink the structure and organization of the Court, in the light of its ever-expanding workload. Judge Koopmans has described the problem below, and recommends, as have others in the past, that the principle of one judge for every Member State might have to yield.

T. Koopmans, The Future of the Court of Justice of the European Communities [101]

One of the worst methods for increasing productivity is to enlarge the number of Judges and Advocates-General . . . In practice, only matters of high principle are heard by a Court of thirteen; the full Court normally sits with nine Judges (the quorum is seven). It is indeed infinitely more difficult to discuss a troublesome case with thirteen Judges. The Court's work is characterised by bringing out opposing views on new issues. Until now, the Court derived much of its strength from its custom of having deliberations where Judges personally discuss matters, without the Advocate General and the Registrar, without any personal assistants and without interpreters, and where they do so in complete openness. In this way, it is the personal contribution of each which helps to construct the Court's reasoning and decision. That working method has a strongly integrating effect, especially under a President who is capable of creating an atmosphere where everybody feels progress depends on combining diverging arguments into a real synthesis. Thus, this working method may have helped to strengthen the Court's authority; it should not needlessly be jeopardized.

. . .

If it is extremely difficult to discuss judicial decisions with thirteen persons, will it not become completely impossible to deliberate with seventeen or nineteen, and to decide on procedural and administrative problems with twenty-five?

. . .

For mid-term developments, the only way to reconcile the different aspirations consists of creating new courts of first instance for direct actions, or separate

[99] See e.g. Case 302/87, *Parliament* v. *Council* (Comitology), n. 64 above, followed a year later by Case C–70/88, *European Parliament* v. *Council* (Chernobyl), n. 65 above. See in general A. Arnull, 'Owning up to Fallibility: Precedent and the Court of Justice' (1993) 30 CMLRev. 247.

[100] See e.g. the judgment in Case C–10/89, *SA CNL-SUCAL NV* v. *Hag GF AG* [1990] ECR I–3711, [1990] 3 CMLR 571 which reached quite a different result from the ruling in a very similar previous case: Case 192/73, *Van Zuylen Freres* v. *Hag AG* [1974] ECR 731, [1974] 2 CMLR 127. In Cases 267–8/91, *Keck and Mithouard* [1993] ECR I–6097, however, although the Court was evidently departing from some of its past case law, it did not specify which decisions were 'overruled', if this term can be used. See Chapter 14.

[101] N. 74 above, 24, 32

courts for some distinct themes such as customs law, and to concentrate preliminary rulings entirely in the hands of the Court of Justice itself.

It is surprising, in the light of all of the calls for reform, in particular those coming from the Community judiciary itself, which finds the system increasingly unable to support the volume of case law, that the TEU made no major changes to the structure of the Court. No doubt when the 1996 Intergovernmental Conference is under way, the existence of three new Member States will render this problem more urgent still.

(f) Style of the Court's Judgments

The style of the Court of Justice's judgments contrasts considerably with the style and content of the opinions of the Advocate Generals. Article 33 of the Statute of the Court provides that judgments are to state the reasons on which they are based. But by way of contrast with the individual and less institutionally constrained opinions of the Advocates General, the Court's judgments are collegiate, representing the single and final ruling of all of the judges hearing the case. The fact that decisions may not often be unanimous and will require a vote is indicated by Article 15 of the Statute, which provides that decisions of the Court will be valid only when an uneven number of its members is sitting in the deliberations. And since there are no dissents or separately concurring judgments, the divergent views of a number of different judges may have to be contained within the language of the judgment. This can sometimes result in obscurity or in a ruling which is curt and ambiguous on matters of importance. Various theories can be put forward to explain the occasionally rather scanty reasoning or somewhat less than thorough legal analysis of the Court's judgments. It seems sometimes that, quite apart from the need to construct a single judgment when the judges are not fully in agreement, the Court does not always like to rule in detail on matters which are not strictly necessary for the decision in the case before it.[102] Although the Advocate General's opinion will often consider exhaustively all the legal arguments which could be relevant to the case, the Court may prefer not to commit itself on a specific legal issue until another case arises where the resolution of that issue is directly necessary for it to give a decision. This approach by the Court can be seen in particular in its preliminary rulings under Article 177 of the EC Treaty.[103]

A further reason for the inelegance and not infrequent obscurity of the Court's judgments may be the fact that they are translated into all the official languages of the Community.[104] Sentences in the judgments are often long,

[102] The converse, however, is also true, in that the Court sometimes chooses to rule, in a preliminary reference procedure, on a matter which was not expressly asked of it.

[103] See further Ch. 10.

[104] See Arts. 29–31 of the Rules of Procedure. Finnish and Swedish are added after the new accessions.

clumsy, and inadequately punctuated. The working language which the Court has adopted for its own secret deliberations is French, but the 'language of the case' will depend on the kind of proceeding before the Court. In Article 177 references, for example, the language of the case is that of the national court or tribunal from which the reference was sent, while in other cases the language will be that chosen by the applicant or that of the defendant Member State.[105]

(g) Role and Methodology of the Court

The specific tasks to be performed by the Court are described in the Treaties. Its jurisdiction is set out in various Articles of the Treaties, the main provisions being Articles 169 to 186 of the EC Treaty. The Treaty on European Union enhanced the jurisdiction of the Court under Article 171, by empowering it to impose a pecuniary penalty on a Member State which has failed to comply with a previous judgment, in which that state was found to be in breach of Treaty obligations. This, and the various other causes of action will be examined further throughout this book, in the chapters on judicial review, damages, preliminary references, enforcement actions, and so on. In accordance with Article 181, the Court can be given jurisdiction under an arbitration clause in a contract concluded by the Community, and under Article 182 it is to have jurisdiction in any dispute between Member States where the subject matter is covered by the Treaty and the dispute is submitted to it by agreement of the parties. There are also a number of international agreements which have been made between the Member States which confer jurisdiction on the Court of Justice, such as the Convention on Jurisdiction and the Enforcement of Judgments in Civil and Commercial Matters made pursuant to Article 220 of the Treaty and giving the Court jurisdiction to give preliminary rulings,[106] and the (as yet unratified) Community Patent Convention under which disputes could, in certain conditions, be referred to the Court of Justice.[107] Under the European Economic Area Agreement, too, the national courts of EFTA states may, if those states permit, make references on the interpretation of provisions of the Agreement to the Court of Justice.

However, it is Article 164, the provision which sets out its task in very general terms, which has perhaps figured most prominently in the Court's shaping of its own sphere of influence. The Court has used this provision—imaginatively described as a 'pregnant formula'[108]—to define its role very broadly. Article 164 provides that 'the Court of Justice shall ensure that in the interpretation and application of this Treaty, the law is observed'. It will be seen in subsequent chapters how the Court has utilized this provision to extend its review jurisdiction to cover bodies which were not expressly subject

[105] *Ibid.*
[106] [1972] OJ L299/32 and [1983] OJ C97/23.
[107] [1976] OJ L17/1.
[108] N. Brown and T. Kennedy, n. 78 above, 4.

to it,[109] and to measures which were not listed in the Treaty.[110] In the name of preserving 'the rule of law' in the Community, the Court has extended its functions beyond those expressly outlined in the Treaty under which it was established.[111] Given the fact that the competence of the Community, and hence of its institutions, has always been accepted to be an attributed competence,[112] limited to what was given by the Treaty, the question of an inherent jurisdiction of the Court is problematic.

A. Arnull, Does the Court of Justice have Inherent Jurisdiction?[113]

Advocates of the principle of *compétence d'attribution* may find the developments in the Court's case law discussed above difficult to accept. The decision in *Les Verts* has been criticised for its failure to respect that principle and its implication that there are few, if any, limits to the Court's jurisdiction. It is submitted, however, that the Court was faced with an almost impossible task in trying to reconcile the duty imposed on it by Article 164 and its counterparts with the incomplete system of remedies laid down in the Treaties. It has rightly chosen to give precedence to the need to ensure respect for the rule of law in the Community. Moreover, in seeking to broaden the scope of its jurisdiction, the Court is following the example set by the political institutions, which have sought to intervene, notably under Articles 100 and 235 EEC, in areas which might have seemed at first sight to fall outside the scope of the Treaties.

As we shall see below, not all commentators would agree with Arnull that the Court was justified in extending its jurisdiction as it has done. Further, in addition to extending its own review jurisdiction under Article 164, the 'gap-filling' role of the Court has also extended to developing principles of a constitutional nature as part of Community law to which it then claims to hold both the institutions and the Member States bound, when they act within the Community sphere.[114] It has also played a significant role in its interaction with the other institutions, reacting to action taken by them or prompting them to act as a result of its decisions. As interpreter of the Treaties and their

[109] It subjected Parliament to judicial review under Art. 173 in Case 294/83, n. 60 above, although it was not included in the Treaty as a body subject to review. Conversely, in Case 70/88, *Parliament* v. *Council* [1990] ECR 2041, [1992] 1 CMLR 91, it allowed Parliament to bring such an action despite not being covered by the Treaty.

[110] Case 22/70, *Commission* v. *Council* (ERTA) [1971] ECR 263, [1971] CMLR 335. More dramatically, in this case, the Court extended the international treaty-making powers of the Community beyond those expressly given in the Treaty.

[111] See Case C–2/88, n. 95 above. D. Curtin suggests that under Art. 164, the Court could even review the legality of amendments to the Treaty itself, 'The Constitutional Structure', n. 36 above.

[112] In Case 26/62, *Van Gend en Loos* [1963] ECR 1, [1963] CMLR 105, the case in which the Court laid down the basic constitutional principles of the Community, the Court said that the Member States had limited their sovereign rights in favour of the Community 'albeit within limited fields'.

[113] (1990) 27 CMLRev. 684, 707.

[114] These are the general principles of law such as proportionality, non-discrimination on grounds of nationality, legitimate expectations and legal certainty, as well as 'fundamental human rights' which the Court has claimed as part of Community law. See further Chs. 7 and 8.

limits, the Court has had to adjudicate not just among the institutions in disputes over their respective powers and competences, but also, and more contentiously still, in questions concerning the proper sphere of the Community as against that of the Member States.[115] This sort of adjudication can arise in many guises—either in direct challenges to Community action by Member States,[116] or in actions between the institutions,[117] or in preliminary references which may relate to the scope of areas of substantive Community law.[118]

In the years of so-called institutional malaise or stagnation, the Court can be seen to have played a 'political' role through law, by rendering the Treaty effective even when its provisions had not been implemented as required by the Community, and in rendering secondary legislation effective even when it had not been properly implemented by the Member States.[119] It adopted an active part in the creation of the internal market through the litigation which came before it, by the negative means of requiring the removal of national barriers to trade, at a time when progress towards completing the Single Market through positive legislative harmonization was hindered by institutional inaction.[120]

The Court has achieved the 'hobbyhorse' status which it occupies amongst European lawyers as much on account of its reasoning and methodology as on account of the impact of its decisions. Its approach to interpretation is generally described as a purposive or teleological method, although not in the sense of seeking the purpose or aim of the authors of a text.[121] The fact that the *travaux préparatoires* to the Treaties were deliberately never published means that these are not a source which can be used, and this is reflected in much of the Court's case law. In a case in which Belgium invoked an argument based on the intention of the states at the time the Treaty was drafted, the Commission argued that 'as historical interpretation plays hardly any part in Community law it would be futile to refer to the intentions of the authors of the Treaty'.[122] In the case of secondary legislation, although the discussions

[115] In a lengthy analysis of the role of all the different players and institutions, including the Court, in the gradual development of the Community, see Weiler's discussion of the Court's 'hands-off' approach to the extension of Community competence by the Community institutions under Art. 235 in 'The Transformation of Europe' (1991) 100 Yale LJ 2403.

[116] Cases 281, 283–85, 287/85, *Germany et al.* v. *Commission* (non-Community workers) [1987] ECR 3203, [1988] 1 CMLR 11.

[117] Cases 22/70, n. 110 above, and C–181/91 and C–248/91, n. 68 above.

[118] Cases C–159/90, *SPUC* v. *Grogan* [1991] ECR 4685, [1991] 3 CMLR 849 and 267–8/91, n. 100 above.

[119] For further discussion see Ch. 4.

[120] Cases 8/74, *Procureur du Roi* v. *Dassonville* [1974] ECR 837, [1974] 2 CMLR 436 and 120/78, *Rewe-Zentrale AG* v. *Bundesmonopolverwaltung fur Branntwein* (Cassis) [1979] ECR 649, [1979] 3 CMLR 494.

[121] Several works on the Court's methods of interpretation appeared in the 1970s, but there has been little since then. One of the first philosophical works on the reasoning of the Court appeared in 1993: J. Bengoetxea, *The Legal Reasoning of the European Court of Justice* (Clarendon Press, 1993).

[122] Case 149/79, *Commission* v. *Belgium* [1980] ECR 3881, 3890, [1981] 2 CMLR 413. See also the discussion of the use of *travaux préparatoires* and of 'declarations' by Member States, by Mayras A.G. in Case 2/71, *Reyners* v. *Belgium* [1974] ECR 631, 666, [1974] 2 CMLR 305.

at Council and Commission meetings are not published, declarations and extracts from the minutes have occasionally been supplied and have been argued by parties before the Court as an aid to interpretation. The Court has not been consistent in its approach to such material, occasionally referring to it for assistance,[123] but in most cases denying its relevance if it does not appear in the text of the legislation itself.[124]

Rather than adopting a narrower historical-purposive approach, the Court tends to examine the whole context in which a particular provision is situated—which often involves looking at the preamble to the Treaties or to legislation—and it gives the interpretation most likely to further what the Court considers that provision in its context was aimed to achieve. Often this is very far from a literal interpretation of the Treaty or of legislation in question, even to the extent of flying in the face of the express language, and this aspect of the Court's methodology has attracted sharp criticism. Many examples of this will be seen throughout the following chapters of this book.

Perhaps the Court's most famous critic has been Hjalte Rasmussen, whose 1986 critique of the Court's policy-making role was one of the earliest sustained attacks on what the author viewed as its illegitimate practices. His thesis is that the Court has sought 'inspiration in guidelines which are essentially political of nature and hence, not judicially applicable. This is the root of judicial activism which may be an usurpation of power.'[125] He does not criticize all 'activism', but rather that which he believes to have gone too far and to have lost popular legitimacy.

H. Rasmussen, On Law and Policy in the European Court of Justice[126]

The Court of Justice assumed the role, at an early stage of development of the Community experiment, as one of its chief architects. If it had not done so, that experiment might have crumbled under the weight of growing parochialism. It is reasonable to hypothesize that the authority of the Community's judiciary will in the future likewise be needed for the defence of the *acquis communautaire*; and it may perhaps even be needed for further cementing of the federalist and centralist values. From this perspective, judicial activism may be considered a public good.

If activism is not, on the other hand, prescribed in nicely calculated doses, it may become that dangerous social evil of which Griffith spoke, not only for the concerned court itself.

. . .

Society's declining taste for a precipitated process of integration cannot have passed unnoticed by European judicial minds. It failed, nonetheless, to leave much impact on European judicial decision. One is led, with this background, to spec-

[123] See Cases 136/78, *Ministère Public* v. *Auer* [1979] ECR 437, [1979] 2 CMLR 373, paras. 25–6 and 131/86, *UK* v. *Council* [1988] ECR 905, [1988] 2 CMLR 364, paras. 26–7.

[124] e.g. Cases 38/69, *Commission* v. *Italy* [1970] ECR 47, [1970] CMLR 77, para. 12; 143/83, *Commission* v. *Denmark* [1986] ECR 427, 237/84; *Commission* v. *Belgium* [1986] ECR 1247; 306/89, *Commission* v. *Greece* [1991] ECR 5863, [1994] 1 CMLR 803, paras. 6 and 8; C–292/89, *Antonissen* [1991] ECR I–745, [1991] 2 CMLR 373.

[125] H. Rasmussen, n. 82 above, 62.

[126] *Ibid.* 8, 14.

ulate inevitably about why an impact is largely lacking. Were the judges or their majority carried away by their personal convictions when they decided to sever the world in which they operated from the real world? Is it tenable at all to assume that the Judges had a certain idea (intimately associated, as it is, with the visions of the Founding Fathers) of their own, different from the ideas of the society surrounding them.

Another author, as well placed as Pierre Pescatore to know the answer to that question, candidly observes that the Court and its Judges actually had *une certaine idée de l'Europe* of their own. In crucial situations of choice this idea was made decisive 'and not arguments based on the legal technicalities of the matter'.

Rasmussen's book is a strongly argued and lively work, trenchant in its criticism and polemical in tone. The reaction of an academic community which was largely supportive of the Court's strategy and achievements was not unmixed.[127]

M. Cappelletti, The Judicial Process in Comparative Perspective[128]

The heart of the matter is simply that Rasmussen's criticism lacks an historical dimension. It might well be, indeed I myself am of this opinion, that no court can for an unlimited time run foul of societal, political and other pressures. A court, however, and especially one dealing with constitutional, federal, or generally transnational matters, has to have the courage to stand against temporary pressures whenever the 'higher law' which it is its mission to enforce so demands . . .

The vision of a great court, of course, should itself not be arbitrary. Now I have no difficulty in admitting that Rasmussen is right in seeing the European Court's vision as one of furthering European integration. Contrary to Rasmussen, however, I am convinced that such a vision, far from being arbitrary, is fully legitimate, for it is rooted in the text, most particularly in the Preamble and the first articles of the EEC Treaty . . .

After a thorough analysis and criticism of Rasmussen's approach, his use of case law, and his conclusions, Cappelletti ultimately challenges the philosophy on which he believes Rasmussen's work to be based:[129]

There is, however, a basic ideological difference between us which has prompted what might seem a certain hardness in my reaction to the book. I think I have detected a missionary zeal in Rasmussen's work, one which might explain its many exaggerations but also one which runs counter to those very ideals mentioned earlier. The European Court, I believe, has made and can still make a fundamental contribution to the ideals of 'a united, peaceful, and federal Europe' which I have no difficulty in acknowledging as being shared by me and which I do read into the

[127] See also J. Weiler (1987) 24 CMLRev. 555 and A. Toth (1987) 7 YBEL 411.

[128] *The Judicial Process in Comparative Perspective* (Clarendon Press, 1989), 390–1. An earlier version of this ch. appeared in (1987) 12 ELRev. 3.

[129] *Ibid.* 401.

Community basic texts. A devastating criticism such as that undertaken by Rasmussen could prove most detrimental to those ideals if it were not recast in the context of its own real limits and significance. My purpose was simply to contribute to this recasting. Only if refined of its many hyperboles and misrepresentations can Rasmussen's book have a positive impact upon the future of Europe.

A somewhat more measured response to criticisms like those of Rasmussen has come from one of the Court's Advocates General—even if, like Rasmussen and Cappelletti in their respective ways, an Advocate General also has a mission of sorts to fulfil—in his defence of the Court's 'constitutional' role.[130]

F. Jacobs, Is the Court of Justice of the European Communities a Constitutional Court?[131]

In at least two respects, the epithet 'constitutional' may be appropriate to the work of the Court. In the first place, certain of the Court's functions are incontestably constitutional. The clearest examples are, on the one hand, cases in which the Court must adjudicate on the respective powers of the other, 'political' institutions—the Council, Commission and Parliament; on the other hand, cases involving the delimitation of competence between the Community and the Member States. It also seems likely that issues of the latter kind will be increasingly significant in future years as the Community assumes and exercises new powers. The Court will have a difficult but essential role in preserving the balance between the Community and the Member States.

. . .

Secondly, and also of increasing significance, there is the emergence through the case law of many principles of a constitutional character. These include not only the historic principles of direct effect and primacy, but also the more recently emerging principles governing the scope of judicial review itself: the requirement that, the Community being subject to the rule of law, all Community and national measures must be subject to judicial review, and the requirement that such review must ensure conformity with substantive standards including respect for fundamental rights and such principles as non-discrimination and proportionality.

. . .

If then, the Court sometimes performs the task of a Constitutional Court, and if it has developed constitutional principles in its case law, we can understand why, in some quarters, the Court's activities have been misunderstood. The Court has sometimes been criticised as a 'political' Court. Such criticisms are probably based on unfamiliarity with the very notion of constitutional jurisprudence, which, as we have seen, is not familiar in all the Member States, and which requires what may seem novel judicial techniques, different approaches to interpretation, even a dif-

[130] That the Court sees itself as having a constitutional role is made clear in its first opinion on the EEA Agreement, a decision in which it jealously asserts and guards its ultimate interpretive authority. See Opinion 1/91, [1991] ECR 6079, [1992] 1 CMLR 245, paras. 21, 46. See also Case 294/83, n. 60 above, para. 23.

[131] *Constitutional Adjudication in European Community and National Law*, ed. D. Curtin and D. O'Keeffe (Butterworths (Ireland), 1992) 25, 32.

ferent conception of the law. Yet, in the Community system, which is based on the notion of a division of powers, some form of constitutional adjudication is inescapable, if indeed the Community is to be based, as its founders intended, on the rule of law. By establishing a Court of Justice, the founders of the Community intended that disputes, even constitutional disputes, should thenceforth be resolved by judicial settlement, rather than by the methods which had been tried, often unsuccessfully, sometimes disastrously, in the past.

Of course it is true that all constitutional courts engage in political issues, but given the unaccountability of courts, the real question, which Jacobs does not fully address, is the nature and origin of the 'unwritten' values which they promote, and the *extent* to which their decisions seem to depart from what their express powers under the constitution or Treaty establishing them would appear to allow. However, it appears that the Court of Justice has not been too severely damaged by what Rasmussen called the 'negative policy inputs', and indeed has adopted a strategy of disarming its critics, in particular when national courts have begun to rebel against its rulings.

N. Brown and T. Kennedy, The Court of Justice of the European Communities[132]

The reaction of the Court has been deliberately restrained and low-key apparently preferring to regard such incidents as temporary misunderstandings rather than as head to head conflicts. Its recent judgments have defined more clearly the limits upon the direct effect doctrine and the responsibilities of national courts in the context of the Article 177 procedure; judicial conferences have continued to bring national judiciary to Luxembourg to become better informed about the Court and to improve mutual understanding under the mellowing influence of wine and good cheer; and the great majority of national judges have loyally accepted the supremacy of Community law and its concomitant, the authority of the Court's rulings and decisions.

We have noted, with regard to the other political institutions, the dynamic character of their powers and functions. With respect to the Parliament, it has been a case of gradual expansion, while the position of the Commission and the Council have been more complex. Each institution has had varying periods of strength and weakness, and the position and powers of each are inextricably linked to those of the others. This institutional interconnectedness extends also to the Court of Justice, which has played its role in mediating between the institutions and defining the scope and limits of their powers, as well as mediating in the even more sensitive sphere between the Community and the Member States. Given the close relationship between the functioning of all of the institutions, it is not surprising that the Court, too, is seen to have had different 'phases' of activism, in response to events and to developments

[132] N. 78 above, 371.

within the other institutions and in the Member States. It had been suggested, after the revival of the political processes of integration which led up to the Single European Act, that the Court should adopt a 'minimalist' role.[133] However, as was noted earlier, it is difficult to develop over-arching theories about the role of the Court, since its decision-making is not necessarily consistently 'dynamic' in every area of adjudication. It may, for example, exercise a creative role in furthering the effectiveness of Community law by creating new remedies and methods of enforcement,[134] while simultaneously reducing its expansive role in an area of substantive law in which the institutions are becoming more active.[135]

The following comments, however, suggest a certain overall trend in the Court's decision-making which, after the TEU, seems to indicate a more modest role. The first is in the specific context of competition law, and the writer builds on Weiler's magisterial review of the entire period of Community development, including that of the Court, from its foundation until the 1990s.[136] He claims that the Court built a role for itself in the competition law system, which was based on 'intellectual leadership'.

D. Gerber, The Transformation of Community Competition Law[137]

Reflecting the centrality of the goal of integration, the Court made teleology the cornerstone of its interpretative strategy. As in its constitutional case law, the Court interpreted the treaty's competition law provisions in light of its own conception of what was necessary to achieve the integrationist goals of the Treaty. It conveyed a clear message that this goal-driven methodology was not merely to be one of many principles to be used in interpreting the Treaty, but rather the dominant interpretative method.

Having considered the dynamic phase of the Court during the Community's period of political lethargy, and then the post-Single European Act phase when it was argued that the Court should become less activist, he suggests that the Court's 'intellectual leadership' role has changed in response to altered circumstances:[138]

The Court's methodology has also evolved in accordance with this change in leadership role. The teleological reasoning that the Court relied on so heavily during earlier periods has become less evident, as the Court turns increasingly to the

[133] T. Koopmans, 'The Role of Law in the Next Stage of European Integration' (1986) 35 ICLQ 925.

[134] See Cases 106/89, *Marleasing SA* v. *La Comercial de Alimentacion SA* [1990] ECR I–4135, [1992] 1 CMLR 205 and C–6 and 9/90, *Francovich and Bonifaci* v. *Italy* [1991] ECR I–5357, [1993] 2 CMLR 66. See below, Chs. 4 and 5.

[135] Case 267–8/91, n. 100 above, could be seen as part of a trend showing the Court drawing back from a previously very wide jurisdictional role. See Ch. 14.

[136] J. Weiler, 'The Transformation of Europe', n. 115 above.

[137] [1994] Harvard Int.LJ 97.

[138] *Ibid.* 127, 130.

manipulation of narrower principles drawn largely from its own previous decisions. Teleology is an appropriate tool for an aggressive court, while reasoning that relies primarily on the authority of existing concepts and decisions comports more easily with a more cautious role.

. . .

Finally, the sheer growth of case law may tend to reduce the opportunities for the Court to exercise intellectual leadership. The notion here is that once the 'big' issues have been resolved and the basic conceptual framework has been established, a court has less room to play an aggressive role. There is simply more law, and this tends to restrict the Court's role.

The suggestion that the Court is playing a less proactive role in adjudication, not just in the competition law field, but more generally, has been echoed elsewhere. In its judgment on the constitutionality of Germany's ratification of the TEU, the Federal Constitutional Court sounded a warning note to the Court of Justice about its over-expansive methods of interpretation.[139] A commentator on that judgment, however, has suggested that the warning was unnecessary, and that the Court of Justice's dynamic approach to integration based on the notion of effectiveness or *effet utile* has been replaced 'by the more static notion of subsidiarity' and that 'all in all, the Federal Constitutional Court of Germany seems to have pulled the emergency brake at a moment when the integrationist train had already come to a halt'.[140] Whether these observations about the gradual shift in the Court's methodology, after the political activity of recent years, will be borne out through the rest of this decade, remains to be seen.

Others, however, have argued that the Court is likely, given that the era of unanimous decision-making in the Council of Ministers has passed, and given the newly added principle of subsidiarity in Article 3b, to be faced with the task of resolving difficult political disputes over the proper sphere of competence of the Community as against the Member States.[141]

J. Weiler, Journey to an Unknown Destination: A Retrospective and Prospective of the European Court of Justice in the Arena of Political Integration[142]

This era has now passed with the shift to majority voting in the post-SEA period. Governments of the Member States no longer have the 'veto guarantee' and thus have taken a new very hard look at the question. Limiting the competences of the Community has become one of the most sensitive issues of the Maastricht construct. The Treaty on European Union introduced formally not only the principle

[139] *Brunner* v. *The European Union Treaty* [1994] 1 CMLR 57. See Ch. 6.

[140] K. Meessen, 'Hedging European Integration: The Maastricht Judgment of the Federal Constitutional Court of Germany' [1994] Fordham Int.LJ 511, 529–30.

[141] See D. Curtin, 'The Constitutional Structure', n. 36 above, 62 and W. Robinson, 'The Court of Justice after Maastricht' in *Legal Issues of the Maastricht Treaty*, ed. D. O'Keeffe and P. Twomey (1994), 179, 186–92.

[142] (1993) 31 JCMS 417, 437.

of subsidiarity into the Community legal regime but also set severe limits on Community legislative action in some of the new fields such as culture, public health, and the like. Public opinion in the Member States has also become far more sensitive to this issue.

In this new climate the Court's earlier 'hands off' attitude to expansive Community competences will no longer work. Whether it likes it or not, it will be called upon, with increasing frequency, to adjudicate competence issues.

7. THE COURT OF AUDITORS

The Court of Auditors was established by the second Budgetary Treaty of 1975, and came into operation in 1977, replacing the previously existing Auditor of the ECSC and the Audit Board of the Communities.[143] Since the enactment of the TEU, the Court of Auditors occupies the status of the fifth Community institution in Article 4 of the EC Treaty. Its composition and functions are now governed by Articles 188a to 188c of the Treaty.

There are, after the new accessions, fifteen members of the Court of Auditors, one selected by each Member State, appointed unanimously by the Council after consulting the European Parliament. The Parliament has actively exercised its right of consultation at this stage, examining each of the proposed candidates thoroughly and not hesitating to express its disapproval of any candidate it considers to be unsuitable.[144] The term of office is six years, and the appointments are staggered. The auditors' qualifications are simply stated: they must belong or have belonged in their country to an external audit body, or they must be 'especially qualified for this office'. The most important feature, which is emphasized in Article 188b(1) and (4), seems to be that their independence must be beyond doubt, and this certainly seems to have been borne out by the sharp tone of some of the Court of Auditors' annual reports. The conditions of their office are strict: they may not engage in any other occupation whether paid or unpaid, and indeed even after leaving office they must 'behave with integrity and discretion as regards the acceptance . . . of certain appointments or benefits'.[145] A member of the Court of Auditors can only be removed from office by decision of the Court of Justice. The provisions of the Protocol on Privileges and Immunities which applies to the judges of the Court of Justice are also to apply to members of the Court of Auditors.

The task of the Court of Auditors is to scrutinize the finances of the Community and to ensure sound financial management, assisting the Parliament and the Council in their exercise of powers of control over the implementation of the budget. The Treaty provides that the Court is to 'examine the accounts of all revenue and expenditure of the Community', and of bodies set

[143] See Art. 22 of the Merger Treaty as amended by Art. 27 of the second Budgetary Treaty.

[144] M. Westlake, *A Modern Guide*, n. 35 above, 118–19.

[145] Art. 188b(5).

up by the Community, where that is permitted.[146] The Parliament and the Council are to be provided by the Court of Auditors with a statement of assurance as to the reliability of the accounts and the legality of transactions. The Court's audit is to be based on records but also, if necessary, it can be performed on the spot in the Community institutions and in the Member States, in liaison with the competent national audit body. These institutions and bodies must forward, at the Court's request, any necessary documentation.

The Court of Auditors may submit its observations on specific questions or may deliver opinions at the request of one of the other institutions. It also, at the end of each financial year, issues an annual report, which it must adopt by a majority of its members. This is sent to the other Community institutions and is published in the Official Journal together with the replies of the institutions.

By comparison with the other institutions the Court of Auditors has been, and will presumably continue to be, after the conferral of official status as an institution upon it, a low-key institutional player. Its annual report, however, with its often stinging criticism of the management and control of Community finances, leaves little doubt as to the independence and effectiveness of this fifth institution.[147]

8. OTHER COMMUNITY INSTITUTIONS

(a) The Economic and Social Committee

Article 4(2) of the EC Treaty makes provision for an Economic and Social Committee (ECOSOC) to assist the Council and Commission. It is an advisory body which represents various sectional interests, and the provisions which govern its existence are now contained in Articles 193 to 198 of the EC Treaty. Article 193 provides that ECOSOC is to consist of representatives of producers, farmers, carriers, workers, dealers, craftsmen, professional occupations, and the general public. As matters have worked out, the main components are workers, who are principally represented by trade unions, employers, and others, such as farmers, consumer groups, and the professions. ECOSOC had 189 members, and this number has now risen to 220 with the accession of the three new Member States.[148] Each country has a specified number of members, the largest being twenty-four and the smallest six. Members of ECOSOC are appointed by the Council for four years, this term being renewable.

The members of ECOSOC may not be bound by any mandatory instructions, must be completely independent in the performance of their duties, and

146 Art. 188c(1).
147 See e.g. the introduction to its recent report for 1993, [1994] OJ C327/5.
148 Art. 194.

must act in the general interest of the Community.[149] ECOSOC operates via a number of different committees. In certain instances the Treaty stipulates that ECOSOC must be consulted, and the Commission or Council may consult it on other matters.[150] The Council or Commission may set a time limit, of not less than one month, within which ECOSOC has to act, and if it does not do so then matters can proceed without its input.

(b) The Committee of the Regions

This Committee was established by the TEU to represent regional and local bodies,[151] in part to counter the idea that the Community was becoming too centralized. The total number of members is the same as for ECOSOC, as is the allocation between each Member State. Once again the Council appoints the members for a renewable four-year term. They must, like the members of ECOSOC, be independent and act in the Community's general interest. The Committee of the Regions must be consulted where the Treaty so specifies, and may be consulted in other instances.[152] Time limits, like those appertaining to ECOSOC, can be set within which the Committee of the Regions must function.

9. THE INTER-INSTITUTIONAL DIMENSION: THE BUDGET

(a) Introduction

The discussion thus far has focused on the separate roles of the respective Community institutions. In the next chapter we shall see how these institutions interrelate in the Community's legislative process. The object of this section is to provide a bridge between these two parts of the analysis, by focusing on the way in which the institutions interact in the context of budgetary issues.

There are a number of reasons why budgetary matters are of such interest when looked at in this manner. From an intra-Community perspective, there is the fundamental fact that control over the purse strings carries with it a degree of power over the more general direction of Community policy, *and* operates as a lever whereby pressure can be exerted by an institution to augment its own authority. Small wonder, then, that the three principal Community decision-makers have vied for control over this issue. From the perspective of the Member States themselves, budgetary disagreements as to the size of contributions and resultant benefits have proved to be a potent source of conflict and tension.[153]

[149] *Ibid.* [150] Art. 198. [151] Art. 198a. [152] Art. 198c.
[153] See above, Ch. 1.

(b) Community Revenue

The initial funding of the Community was based on contributions from the Member States. This was changed to some extent in 1970, with the decision by the Member States to provide the Community with its own resource base. Moneys coming from these sources would belong to the Community itself. The principal sources from which these Community funds were to be derived were: customs duties, agricultural levies, and a percentage of Value Added Tax (VAT), up to 1 per cent.

This was fine in principle, but in practice it proved to be less so, since the Community's expenditure outstripped its revenue base. It was, of course, open to the Member States to increase this by, for example, raising the amount which the Community took from VAT. This required agreement from the Member States and no such consensus was forthcoming. The United Kingdom used the budgetary impasse to vent its dislike of the amounts of Community revenue which were being expended on agriculture, on which more will be said below. The Community lurched from budgetary crisis to budgetary crisis, until a deal was brokered in the 1984 Fointainebleau Summit. This proved to be only a temporary respite. Almost as soon as the newly increased level of Community's own resources had been introduced, it was seen to be inadequate to meet its needs.

Intervention from the European Council was once again required. Reforms agreed to at the Brussels summit in 1988 were incorporated into an Inter-Institutional Agreement on Budgetary Discipline and Improvement of the Budgetary Procedure, which was signed by the Presidents of the Council, Commission, and the Parliament. This Agreement helped to engender financial stability both by setting a financial perspective for the period 1988–92, and by expanding the scope of the Community's own resources. Further meetings of the European Council have built upon the foundations laid in 1988. Notable in this regard is the Edinburgh summit in 1992, at which a financial perspective for 1993–9 was agreed.[154]

At present the Community's own resources consist of: customs duties and the like imposed on non-Member States; agricultural levies; a percentage of VAT; a budgetary resource which is based on each Member State's Gross National Product (GNP). VAT constitutes the largest component of Community revenue, about 50 per cent, but it is diminishing in relation to the second largest element, which is derived from the GNP resource. In total monetary terms the Community budget is not that large. The figure for 1994 was approximately £56 billion, which represents only 1.2 per cent of the Gross National Product of the Member States.[155]

[154] See above, 20.

[155] However it should be borne in mind that these figures do not take into account the costs which have to be borne by national governments or private undertakings in complying with Community norms.

(c) Community Expenditure

The tensions concerning the Community's revenue base have been matched by those concerning expenditure, the only difference being that, in relation to expenditure, the Member State versus Member State dimension is overlaid by intra-institutional strains as well. The rationale for these pressures can be stated quite simply. The key distinction is that between compulsory and non-compulsory expenditure. The former is approximately 55 per cent of the overall budget and most of this goes on supporting farm prices in one form or another. That so large a part of the budget is expended in this manner helps to explain the pressures mentioned above. In terms of conflict between the Member States, there is the fact that certain states regard the Common Agricultural Policy (CAP), which lies at the root of the agricultural expenditure, as wasteful. In intra-institutional terms, there is the equally important fact that Parliament has greater power over non-compulsory, than over compulsory, expenditure.[156] Hence the smaller the former in relation to the latter, the less freedom for manœuvre does the Parliament have. There has, therefore, been much pressure to reduce the cost of the CAP and to increase expenditure on other items, such as the structural funds.

The main items of expenditure for the 1993–9 period are: agriculture, the plan being to reduce this to 46 per cent of total budgetary expenditure by 1999; structural expenditure,[157] the plan being that this should rise to 35 per cent of total expenditure by 1999; internal policies, which consume only around 5 per cent of the budget; external policies; administrative expenses; and reserves.

(d) The Budgetary Procedure

Given the importance of the budget it is scarcely surprising that the procedures for its making and approval are complex. As will become apparent, they accord the three principal institutions a carefully balanced role in the budgetary process. Moreover, as with many areas of the Treaty, a bare reading of the relevant Treaty provision, Article 203, fails to convey the full reality of the way in which things actually happen. The description which follows will therefore draw on both the Treaty text itself and also on the actual workings of the budgetary procedures.

It is the Commission which has the principal responsibility for the preparation of the Preliminary Draft Budget (PDB).[158] The Community's financial year runs from 1 January to 31 December[159] and the Commission will begin to work on the budget about one year before it is due. Within the Commission, DGXIX, the Directorate General for Budgets, will do most of the initial work, with the Budget Commissioner having overall responsibility. This

[156] Art. 203.
[157] For the benefit of the poorer regions, to tackle unemployment, etc.
[158] Art. 203(2). [159] Art. 203(1).

Commissioner will present the PDB to the College of Commissioners for approval. The 1993 Inter-Institutional Agreement on the Budget provides for three-way discussions between delegations from Commission, Council, and Parliament before the PDB is approved by the Commission. We noted earlier that since 1988 there has been a financial perspective and this will constrain the detailed proposals which emerge in the PDB.

The PDB is then considered by the Council's Budget Committee, which is composed of national officials. From there it will proceed to COREPER. The object of both bodies is to secure agreement on as many items as possible before the Council itself meets. Voting in the Council is by qualified majority.[160] If it appears to be likely that there will be conflict between the Council and the Parliament over the division between compulsory and non-compulsory expenditure, the 1993 Inter-Institutional Agreement makes provision for a conciliation procedure involving representatives of both institutions plus the Commission.

Once the Council has approved the PDB it then passes to the Parliament for its first reading.[161] Although this is Parliament's first formal look at the budget, it will, as noted above, have already seen the PDB and begun work on it. The principal responsibility falls to the Committee on Budgets. The plenary session of Parliament can then either: accept the PDB; propose amendments to non-compulsory expenditure;[162] or propose modifications to compulsory expenditure. Once again the financial perspectives will constrain the changes which the Parliament is able to suggest, but, other things being equal, the Parliament has persistently sought to increase non-compulsory expenditure relative to compulsory expenditure.

The PDB then goes back to the Council for its second reading.[163] It has three options, each of which require a qualified majority: it can reject the Parliament's amendments;[164] it can reject modifications to compulsory expenditure proposed by Parliament which do not have the effect of increasing total expenditure, but if it does not do so then the modifications stand;[165] it can accept Parliament's proposed modifications to compulsory expenditure where these do increase total expenditure, but if it does not do so then the modifications fall.[166] If within fifteen days of receipt of the PDB the Council has not modified Parliament's amendments, and has accepted the latter's proposed modifications, then the budget will be deemed to be finally adopted.[167]

If this does not occur then the next turn of the wheel is for Parliament to have its second reading of the budget.[168] It then has fifteen days in which to exercise its options. It can, acting by a majority of its members and three-fifths of the votes cast, amend or reject the modifications to its amendments made by the Council. If it does not act within this period then the budget is deemed to have been adopted. The most potent weapon which the Parliament has is

[160] Art. 203(3). [161] Art. 203(4). [162] *Loc. cit.* [163] Art. 203(5).
[164] Art. 203(5)(a). [165] Art. 203(5)(b). [166] Art. 203(5)(c). [167] Art. 203(5).
[168] Art. 203(6).

to reject the entire budget and request a new PDB.[169] If matters appear to be heading in this direction then there will normally be feverish negotiations between the institutions at all levels.

(e) The Budget and the Institutional Division of Power

It is clear that both the Council and the Parliament have a real say in the budget. It is equally clear that the former is still pre-eminent. Developments since the late 1980s have redressed this balance of power to some extent by, for example, increasing the proportion of the budget which is devoted to non-compulsory expenditure and by providing a budgetary framework in the form of Inter-Institutional Agreements to which the Parliament is a party.

The budgetary process cannot, however, be separated from more general issues of institutional power within the Community. History is replete with examples of legislative bodies at national level which have used their power over the purse as a lever to improve their position in the overall constitutional hierarchy. The European Parliament is no different in this respect. As Nugent states, with 'the EP dissatisfied with its overall position in the EU system, it is only natural that it should have sought to use the budget to maximum advantage'.[170] To this end it has, on occasion, rejected the entire budget; interpreted the dividing line between compulsory and non-compulsory expenditure to the benefit of the latter; and attempted to exploit differences of opinion within the Council itself.[171] The conflicts which this has produced have sometimes ended up in the Court.[172] While the introduction of Inter-Institutional Agreements and financial perspectives are likely to reduce the incidence of conflicts of this nature, one can still expect Parliament to continue to use its budgetary powers to press for policies which it favours and to improve its own position in the Community's constitutional hierarchy.

10. FURTHER READING

BROWN, N., and KENNEDY, T., *The Court of Justice of the European Communities* (4th edn., Sweet & Maxwell, 1994)

BULMER, S., and WESSELS, W., *The European Council* (Macmillan, 1987)

GEORGE, S., *Politics and Policy in the European Community* (2nd edn., Oxford University Press, 1991)

KIRCHNER, E., *Decision-Making in the European Community: The Council Presidency and European Integration* (Manchester University Press, 1992)

JACOBS, F., CORBETT, R., and SHACKLETON M., *The European Parliament* (2nd edn., Longman, 1992)

[169] Art. 203(8). This requires a majority of its members and two-thirds of the votes cast.

[170] N. 4 above, 359.

[171] *Ibid.* 359–60.

[172] See e.g. Case 34/86, *Council* v. *European Parliament* [1986] ECR 2155; Case C–284/90, *Council* v. *European Parliament* [1992] ECR I–2277.

JENKINS, R., *European Diary 1977–1981* (Collins, 1981)
LODGE, J. (ed.), *The European Community and the Challenge of the Future* (2nd edn., Pinter, 1994)
NUGENT, N., *The Government and Politics of the European Union* (3rd edn., Macmillan, 1994)
O'KEEFFE, D., and TWOMEY, P. M. (ed.), *Legal Issues of the Maastricht Treaty* (Chancery, 1994)
SHACKLETON, M., *Financing the European Community* (Pinter, 1990)
TSOUKALIS, L., *The New European Economy: The Politics and Economics of Integration* (2nd edn., Oxford University Press, 1993)
TUGENDHAT, C., *Making Sense of Europe* (Viking, 1986)
WALLACE, W. (ed.), *The Dynamics of European Integration* (Pinter, 1990)
WESTLAKE, M., *A Modern Guide to the Europan Parliament* (Pinter, 1994)
—— *The Parliament and the Commission: Partners and Rivals in the European Policy-Making Process* (Butterworths, 1994)

3

Community Legislation and Policy-Making

1. INTRODUCTION

In the previous chapter we examined the differing institutional actors within the Community, and the powers which they possess. In this chapter we shall be considering the way in which Community policy is formulated and enacted. The discussion will be broken down into three broad parts.

First, there will be an analysis of the different forms which Community action can take, and the substantive and procedural conditions which must be satisfied if such action is to be legal, (sections 2 to 4).

Secondly, we shall consider the differing procedures which are established in the Treaty for the promulgation of legislation. These are, as will become apparent, complex, and reveal much that is of interest concerning the general balance of institutional competence in the EC (sections 5 to 7).

The final part of the chapter will address the reality of Community decision-making. The object of this part of the discussion is to convey both a more rounded view as to how the pattern of institutional competence which we now have has evolved; and also to explain the nature of the inter-institutional exchange which is such an important characteristic of the Community's policy making process, (sections 8 to 10).

2. THE TYPES OF COMMUNITY LEGISLATION

The Community legislative process is, as will be seen below, complex to say the least. Before tackling this difficult topic it is important to understand the different forms which Community legislation can assume. Article 189 is the foundational provision in this respect:

> In order to carry out their task and in accordance with the provisions of this Treaty, the European Parliament acting jointly with the Council, the Council and the Commission shall make regulations and issue directives, take decisions, make recommendations or deliver opinions.
>
> A regulation shall have general application. It shall be binding in its entirety and directly applicable in all Member States.

A directive shall be binding, as to the result to be achieved, upon each Member State to which it is addressed, but shall leave to the national authorities the choice of form and methods.

A decision shall be binding in its entirety upon those to whom it is addressed.

Recommendations and opinions shall have no binding force.

(a) Regulations

As Article 189 indicates, regulations are binding upon all the Member States and are regarded as directly applicable within all such states. Regulations have to be published in the Official Journal and come into force on the date which is specified in the particular regulation or, if no such date is specified, on the twentieth day following publication.[1]

In most instances the Treaty leaves open the choice whether to proceed by way of regulation, directive, or decision. Only rarely does it prescribe the necessity of legislating by way of regulation.[2]

The power to make regulations may be conferred on the Commission by a Council regulation. This issue will be considered more fully below.[3]

The issue whether a measure which is called a regulation really is one, as opposed to being a decision, arises not infrequently, most commonly in the context of challenges by individuals to annul a measure under Article 173. This is because Article 173 places limits on the ability of non-privileged applicants to challenge measures which are in the form of regulations. The Court has made clear that the test of whether a measure really is a regulation is one of substance and not form. The fact that the contested act is called a regulation will not therefore be conclusive. The details of this case law will be examined below.[4]

It is common to think of regulations as akin to either primary or secondary legislation made by Member States. In some respects this analogy has force. Regulations are measures of general application, applicable to all Member States. Moreover, as will be seen more fully later,[5] the Court has held that regulations are characterized as abstract normative measures which are not directed towards a particular named person or persons. While this reinforces the sense that regulations are analogous to domestic legislation, either primary or secondary, one should be cautious about pressing this analogy too far. Many measures which emerge as regulations, for example in the agricultural sphere, affect only a very small group of people, and may be operative for only a very short period of time. Such regulations may, in this sense, be indistinguishable from measures which would be regarded as administrative or executive acts within national legal systems.

While the definition of a regulation is readily accessible in most respects a

[1] Art. 191. Regs. which are made under the Art. 189b procedure must also be signed by the President of the European Parliament and by the President of the Council: Art. 191(1).

[2] See e.g. Art. 48(3)(d), Art. 94, concerning workers and state aids respectively.

[3] See below, 128–31. [4] See below, 461–5. [5] See below, 462–4.

word needs to be said concerning the meaning of the term 'directly applicable'. The precise meaning of this term has been the subject of debate among commentators.[6] The meaning which the authors of the Treaty intended the phrase to have cannot readily be discerned in the absence of any available *travaux préparatoires* indicating the Treaty-making process. It is in particular unclear whether the Treaty framers meant the phrase 'directly applicable' to connote the idea that individuals have rights which they can enforce in their own name through national courts. We shall see in the subsequent discussion that the ECJ has indeed interpreted directly applicable in this manner.[7] It is however important to understand that the term 'directly applicable' has another, albeit related, meaning which is concerned with the way in which international norms make their way into national legal systems.

This can be explained in the following manner. Regulations are norms made by an international body, the EC. Under general principles of international law it is necessary for such norms to enter a national legal system. This can be accomplished either by the national system transforming the measure in question into national law or by a shorter national act which adopts the relevant international act. A moment's thought will indicate that this can be a terribly cumbersome procedure, more particularly when the number of international measures which are to be transferred into national legal systems is large. The Community passes thousands of regulations, and if each one of these had to be separately incorporated into each national legal system before it could be effective then the Community would grind to a halt. The phrase 'directly applicable' within Article 189 obviates this difficulty by signifying that regulations are to be taken to become part of the national legal systems automatically without the need for separate national legal measures. In this sense regulations, once made, automatically become part of the legal orders of the Member States of the Community. Indeed the ECJ has gone further and signified that Member States should not pass any measure which purports to transform a Community regulation into national law: the regulation is part of the national legal order without the need for any such state action. This is forcefully demonstrated by the following case.

Case 34/73, Variola v. Amministrazione delle Finanze [1973] ECR 981

The ECJ was asked by a national court whether the provisions of a regulation could be introduced into the legal order of a Member State by internal measures which reproduced the contents of the Community provision 'in such a way that the subject-matter is brought under national law'.

[6] See e.g. J. Steiner, 'Direct Applicability in EEC Law—A Chameleon Concept' (1982) 98 LQR 229; A. Dashwood, 'The Principle of Direct Effect in European Community Law' (1978) 16 JCMS 229.

[7] See below, Ch. 4.

THE ECJ

10. The direct application of a Regulation means that its entry into force and its application in favour of those subject to it are independent of any measure of reception into national law.

By virtue of the obligations arising from the Treaty and assumed on ratification, Member States are under a duty not to obstruct the direct applicability inherent in Regulations and other rules of Community law.

Strict compliance with this obligation is an indispensable condition of simultaneous and uniform application of Community Regulations throughout the Community.

11. More particularly, Member States are under an obligation not to introduce any measure which might affect the jurisdiction of the Court to pronounce on any question involving the interpretation of Community law or the validity of an act of the institutions of the Community, which means that no procedure is permissible whereby the Community nature of a legal rule is concealed from those subject to it.

Under Article 177 of the Treaty in particular the jurisdiction of the Court is unaffected by any provisions of national legislation which purport to convert a rule of Community law into national law.

(b) Directives

Directives differ from regulations in two important ways: they can be addressed to any one Member State and do not have to be directed at all Members of the Community; and they are binding as to the end to be achieved while leaving some choice as to form and method open to the Member States.

All directives must be notified to the person to whom they are addressed.[8] There was, prior to the TEU, no duty to publish directives in the Official Journal, even though in practice many were. It is now the case that directives which apply to all Member States, and those which are passed pursuant to the Article 189b procedure, have to be published in the Official Journal.[9] The date of entry into force of directives is the same as that for regulations: either the date specified in the directive or, in the absence of any such date, the twentieth day following that of publication.[10]

The Community institutions generally have, as noted above, considerable choice whether to legislate by means of regulations or directives. There are however a number of Treaty Articles which state that directives must be used.[11]

The ability to legislate by means of directive as well as regulation gives the Community valuable flexibility as to the way in which Community policy is developed. The reason this is so important is as follows. Regulations have in one sense the most direct impact as a species of Community legislation. This derives from the fact that they are directly applicable within the legal systems of the Member States without any need for intervention by the national

[8] Art. 191(3). [9] Art. 191. [10] Art. 191(1) and (2).
[11] See e.g. Arts. 54, 56(2), 63, 69, 70, 100, 101, 113(3), 118(2).

legislatures. Indeed as we have seen from the *Variola* case such intervention is prohibited. This feature is clearly a strength of regulations. It does, however, also serve to limit the utility of this legislative device. Given that regulations are directly applicable, norms which are passed in this way have to be capable of being 'parachuted' into the legal systems of all the Member States just as they are. This means that normally every 't' must be crossed and every 'i' must be dotted in the regulation since the Member States are not to tamper with the norm in any way. It also means that the norm which is enacted in this manner must, in a more general sense, be suited to integration within all the legal systems of the Community just as it is.

Now if this were the only way in which Community policy could be developed, the legislative process would work very slowly. There might indeed be a number of areas where it was difficult to devise regulations which had the requisite specificity and which at the same time were suited to immediate impact into all of the Member States. It should be remembered in this respect that the Member States of the Community have differing legal systems, some being common law, some civil law, and that even within those systems which have a civil law base there are considerable differences in terms of detail. Add to differences of this nature the obvious fact that there are variations in the existing political, administrative, and social arrangements within the national regimes which make up the Community, and one can begin to realise the difficulty of developing all species of Community policy through regulations. Directives are a particularly useful device when the aim is to harmonize the laws within a certain area, rather then produce strict uniformity.

It is for this reason that directives have proved to be such a valuable legislative device for developing Community policy. The fact that the directive does not need to be addressed to all Member States and, more importantly, the fact that ends can be stipulated, while leaving choice as to form and method of implementation, means that directives provide a flexible method of furthering Community policy.

Having said this, one should not be under any misapprehension as to the degree of specificity which is to be found even within directives. These norms will often set out the ends which Member States are to meet in considerable detail. Notwithstanding this fact, directives have, for the reasons indicated above, provided an extremely valuable addition to the Community's legislative armoury.

The potency of this legislative device has been increased by important decisions of the ECJ. The Court has, as will be seen,[12] held that directives have direct effect, enabling individuals to rely on them, at least in actions against the state. This has enabled the Court itself to adjudicate on claims that, for example, the state has not been implementing the directive within the required time, or that the means of implementing the directive have not in fact achieved the ends specified therein. This branch of the Court's case law has more

[12] See below, 175–81.

recently been complemented by decisions holding the Member State liable in damages for non-implementation of a directive, even where the provision of the directive in question was not, at that time, directly effective.[13]

(c) Decisions

As Article 189 makes clear, decisions are binding in their entirety on those to whom they are addressed. They must be notified to the addressee and take effect when notified to those to whom they are addressed.[14] Decisions which are adopted pursuant to the Article 189b procedure must be published in the Official Journal; they take effect from the date specified therein or, in the absence of any such date, on the twentieth day following that of their publication.[15]

The Community institutions remain free to proceed by way of making decisions in many areas. It is, for example, common for the Commission to respond to requests concerning the detailed application of the CAP by issuing a decision on the matter. There are, however, a number of areas in which the Treaty stipulates that decisions should be the chosen method of policy-making. One of the most important of such areas concerns the infringement of the competition rules; breach of such rules will be recorded by the Commission in the form of a reasoned decision.[16] Another area in which decisions are specified as the chosen mode of denoting a breach of Community law concerns state aids; a decision will be made that an aid is not compatible with the Common Market.[17] The Treaty also indicates issues in relation to which the Council should proceed by way of decision. Thus Article 100b states that the Council may make a decision recognizing that measures which are in force in one Member State should be regarded as equivalent to those in force in another state for the purposes of completing the internal market.

It is open to the Council to delegate power to the Commission to take decisions which are within the competence of the Council itself.[18]

We have already noted that the ECJ will determine whether a measure which takes the form of a regulation is in substance to be classified in this way. The corollary of this is that measures which are labelled as regulations, but which the Court finds not to be regulations in substance, will be regarded as decisions. This issue is of particular importance in relation to actions for annulment under Article 173, and will be discussed in more detail below.[19]

(d) Recommendations and Opinions

Article 189 states clearly that recommendations and opinions are to have no binding force. While this precludes such measures from having direct effect, it does not mean that they are immune from the judicial process. It is, for

[13] See below, 224–6.
[14] Art. 191(3).
[15] Art. 191(1).
[16] Art. 89(2).
[17] Art. 93(2).
[18] Art. 145. See below, 128–31.
[19] See, 461–5.

example, open to a national court to make a reference to the ECJ concerning the interpretation or validity of such a measure.[20]

Article 155 imbues the Commission with a general power to formulate recommendations or deliver opinions on matters dealt with in the Treaty, either where it expressly so provides,[21] or where the Commission believes that it is necessary to do so.

(e) Other Methods of Developing Policy

The four categories considered above constitute the principal ways in which policy is developed within the Community. Whether the list is exhaustive is another matter. The Commission has, for example, issued a number of policy guidelines in the area of state aids, as a means of indicating how it will exercise its discretion within that area.[22] These are not, as such, recommendations for the purpose of Article 189, but they can, as we shall see later, have an important impact on the way in which the Commission chooses to exercise its discretion within a particular area.

There are in addition other ways in which the institutions can develop policy. One evolving technique is the Inter-Institutional Agreement. The place of such agreements within the Community scheme will be examined more fully below.[23] Suffice it to say for the present that these are agreements between the Council, Commission, and the Parliament, and that they have been made on topics of constitutional significance such as subsidiarity, transparency, and participation rights.

There is a connection between the methods of developing Community policy mentioned within this section, and recommendations and opinions. These measures taken as a whole constitute 'soft law', as opposed to the more formal measures such as regulations, decisions, and directives. The development of Community policy through various soft-law devices has become more important as of late[24] for reasons which will become apparent in the course of the ensuing analysis.

[20] Case C–322/88, *Grimaldi* v. *Fonds des Maladies Professionelles* [1989] ECR 4407.

[21] Express provision for making recommendations or opinions is to be found in e.g. Arts. 81, 102, 105, 113(3) and 128(5).

[22] See below, 1089–91.

[23] See below, 140–2.

[24] K. Wellens and G. Borchardt, 'Soft Law in European Community Law' (1989) 14 ELRev. 267; J. Klabbers, 'Informal Instruments before the European Court of Justice' (1994) 31 CMLRev. 997.

3. SUBSTANTIVE AND PROCEDURAL CONDITIONS FOR THE LEGALITY OF COMMUNITY ACTION: GENERAL PRINCIPLES

The general topic of review of Community action, whether by privileged or non-privileged parties, will be considered in detail below.[25] As will be seen all binding acts, and acts which produce legal effects, are capable of being reviewed by the ECJ or the CFI. Our present concern is related, but more limited, in nature. It is to examine the initial substantive and procedural requirements for the legality of Community legislation. These will be considered in turn.

(a) Substantive Requirements

The principal initial substantive requirement for the legality of Community legislation is that the legislation is properly based upon some particular Treaty Article. This may sound obvious, and so indeed it is. Normally this requirement will be unproblematic: the particular regulation will, for example, stipulate the Treaty Article on which it is based. Matters can, however, be more difficult for two reasons.

First, the institutions may claim that a particular Treaty Article contains an implied power to make the regulation in question. The notion of implied powers is well known in both domestic and international legal systems. The precise meaning of the phrase 'implied power' is a more contestable issue. It can, as Hartley notes, be given a narrow or a wide formulation:[26]

> According to the narrow formulation, the existence of a given power implies also the existence of any other power which is reasonably necessary for the exercise of the former; according to the wide formulation, the existence of a given *objective* or *function* implies the existence of any power reasonably necessary to attain it.

There is no doubt that the narrow sense of implied power has been long accepted within the Community.[27] It is now clear that the ECJ is also willing to embrace the wider formulation. This is exemplified by the following case on the immigration of non-Community workers. This decision provides a good example of the mode of reasoning adopted by the Court in relation to the legislative competence of the Community institutions.

[25] See below, Ch. 11.

[26] T. C. Hartley, *The Foundations of European Community Law* (3rd edn., Oxford, 1994), 110. Italics in the original.

[27] Case 8/55, *Fédération Charbonnière de Belgique* v. *High Authority* [1956] ECR 245, 280.

Cases 281, 283–285, 287/85, Germany v. Commission [1987] ECR 3203, [1988] 1 CMLR 11

The Commission made a decision pursuant to Article 118 which established a prior communication and consultation process in relation to migration policies affecting workers from non-EC countries. The Member States were to inform the Commission and other Member States of their draft measures concerning entry, residence, employment, equality of treatment, and the integration of such workers into the social and cultural life of the country. After notification to the Commission of such draft measures there would then be consultation with the Commission and other Member States. A number of states challenged this measure as being *ultra vires* the Commission. Article 118, which concerns collaboration in the social field, did not expressly give the Commission power to make binding decisions.

THE ECJ

15. The essence of the arguments put forward by the applicant Member States is that migration policy in relation to non-Member countries is not part of the social field envisaged by Article 118, or, alternatively, that it falls only partly within that field.

16. As regards the applicants' main argument it must be observed that the employment situation and, more generally, the improvement of living and working conditions within the Community are liable to be affected by the policies pursued by the Member States with regard to workers from non-Member countries. In the preamble to Decision 85/381/EEC the Commission rightly considers that it is important to ensure that the migration policies of Member States in relation to non-Member countries take into account both common policies and the actions taken at Community level, in particular within the framework of Community labour market policy, in order not to jeopardise the results.

17. As early as 1974, in its resolution of 21 January 1974 concerning a social action programme, the Council recognised that the migration policies pursued by the Member States affect the Community's social policy, in particular in view of their influence on the Community employment market and on Community workers' employment conditions . . .

18. It must therefore be held that the argument that migration policy in relation to non-Member States falls entirely outside the social field, in respect of which Article 118 provides for co-operation between the Member States, cannot be accepted.

[*The ECJ did find that the decision in question was partly* ultra vires *in so far as it sought to promote consultation in relation to cultural matters. It then proceeded to consider whether Article 118 could be construed to include a power to make binding decisions.*]

27. Since the contested decision falls only partly outside the social field covered by Article 118, it must be considered whether the second paragraph of Article 118, which provides that the Commission is to act, *inter alia*, by arranging consultations, gives it the power to adopt a binding decision with a view to the arrangement of such consultations.

28. In that connection it must be emphasised that where an Article of the EEC Treaty—in this case Article 118—confers a specific task on the Commission it

must be accepted, if that provision is not to be rendered wholly ineffective, that it confers on the Commission necessarily and *per se* the powers which are indispensable in order to carry out that task. Accordingly, the second paragraph of Article 118 must be interpreted as conferring on the Commission all the powers which are necessary in order to arrange the consultations. In order to perform that task of arranging consultation the Commission must necessarily be able to require the Member States to notify essential information, in the first place to identify the problems and in the second place in order to pinpoint the possible guidelines for any future joint action on the part of the Member States; likewise it must be able to require them to take part in consultation.

29. Indeed, the collaboration between Member States required by Article 118 is only possible within the framework of organised consultations. In the absence of any action to initiate it that collaboration might remain a dead letter, even though provision is made for it in the Treaty. Since the Commission was specifically given the task of promoting such collaboration and arranging it, it is entitled to initiate consultation procedures within the social field referred to in Article 118.

The second reason there can be difficulties concerning the legality of the chosen basis for legislation relates to Article 235 of the Treaty. Most of the Treaty Articles relate to a specific subject-matter area, whether this be workers, establishment, capital, or goods. The Treaty does, in addition, contain broader provisions on which legislative competence can be based, the most notable example being Article 100, which empowers the Council to issue directives for the approximation of such laws as directly affect the establishment or functioning of the common market. Article 235 is broader still. It provides that:

If action by the Community should prove necessary to attain, in the course of the operation of the common market, one of the objectives of the Community and this Treaty has not provided the necessary powers, the Council shall, acting unanimously on a proposal from the Commission and after consulting the European Parliament, take the appropriate measures.

Article 235 has proved to be a valuable residual legislative power, particularly when, at the relevant time, the Community did not possess more specific legislative authority in certain substantive areas. Thus the Article has been used to legitimate legislation on areas such as the environment and regional policy before these matters were dealt with through specific provisions in the Treaty introduced by the SEA or the TEU. Weiler captures the importance of this provision and the manner in which it was interpreted.

J. Weiler, The Transformation of Europe[28]

In a variety of fields, including, for example, conclusion of international agreements, the granting of emergency food aid to third countries, and creation of new

[28] (1991) 100 Yale LJ 2403, 2445–2446.

> institutions, the Community made use of Article 235 in a manner that was simply not consistent with the narrow interpretation of the Article as a codification of implied powers doctrine in its instrumental sense. Only a truly radical and 'creative' reading of the Article could explain and justify its usage as, for example, the legal basis for granting emergency food aid to non-associated states. But this wide reading, in which all the institutions partook, meant that it would become virtually impossible to find an activity which could not be brought within the objectives of the Treaty.

The Article has few limitations. It requires that the power should be used to attain one of the objectives of the Community, and that attainment of this objective must take place in the course of the operation of the Common Market. Given, however, the breadth of the Treaty objectives, especially after the TEU, and given also the ECJ's purposive mode of interpreting broad Community aims, these 'conditions' for the exercise of Article 235 hardly place any severe constraint on the Council.

The aspect of Article 235 which has given rise to more controversy concerns the condition that the Treaty has not 'provided the necessary powers'. It is clear that the mere fact that another, more specific, provision of the Treaty has given a power to make recommendations will not preclude the use of Article 235 to enact binding measures.[29] Nor, it seems, will Article 235 be excluded by the fact that the specific Treaty provisions could be interpreted broadly by using the implied-powers doctrine discussed above.[30]

Whether the Treaty has provided necessary powers elsewhere can, however, be of particular significance in two types of circumstance. One such situation is where the specific Treaty Articles provide for differing, and more extensive, involvement of other institutions than that which is provided for in Article 235 itself. One of the key differentiating features of the various legislative procedures which exist under the Treaty is, as we shall see, the differing degrees of participatory rights accorded to the European Parliament. Article 235 requires the Council to consult the Parliament, but other Treaty Articles stipulate that the Parliament should have greater rights in the legislative process, of the kind set out in Articles 189b and 189c. If the Council is able to proceed via Article 235, rather than by using other, more specific Treaty Articles which touch on the issue, there is a danger that this will diminish the role in the legislative process which the Parliament would otherwise have. The other type of situation in which the choice between Article 235 and some other more specific Treaty Article can be of significance is where there are differences in the voting rules under the respective Articles. Article 235 requires unanimity, whereas many other Treaty provisions demand only a qualified majority.

The institutions of the Community are not averse to resolving their intra-institutional disputes through recourse to the ECJ, and cases featuring the appropriate boundaries of Article 235 have numbered amongst these. Thus in

[29] Case 8/73, *Hauptzollamt Bremerhaven* v. *Massey-Ferguson* [1973] ECR 897.
[30] *Ibid.*, para. 4.

the *Tariff Preferences* case[31] the Commission sought the annulment of a Council regulation concerning tariff preferences for goods which came from developing countries. The Council argued that, since the purpose of the measures was in reality development aid, they could only be adopted by using Article 235; the Commission contended that Article 113, which concerned the common commercial policy, could be used, and that this only required qualified majority voting. In fact the Council did not specify any particular Article of the Treaty in the measures. The ECJ annulled the regulations both because of failure to state the legal basis of the measures; and because, on substantive grounds, they could have been adopted by using Article 113. The Court alluded to the fact that Articles 235 and 113 have different rules regarding the manner in which the Council may arrive at its decision.[32]

We shall have occasion to consider the legality of the chosen legislative basis for Community action when discussing other topics in EC law.[33] Suffice it to say for the present that this problem is a recurring one, the incidence of which is likely to increase, given the increase in the substantive areas over which the Community exercises some form of competence, combined with the differing voting rules and the varying participatory rights of the Parliament under these various provisions.

(b) Procedural Requirements

We have in the course of the preceding analysis touched on one procedural requirement which has to be satisfied by the Community institutions when enacting measures, this being the duty to publish and notify. Article 190 encapsulates one of the other important procedural conditions for the legality of Community norms, the giving of reasons. It reads as follows:

> Regulations, directives and decisions adopted jointly by the European Parliament and the Council, and such acts adopted by the Council or the Commission, shall state the reasons on which they are based and shall refer to any proposals or opinions which were required to be obtained pursuant to the Treaty.

This is an important provision which has implications for the scope and intensity of substantive as well as procedural review. We shall have occasion to consider these links in more detail when discussing the grounds of review under Article 173 of the Treaty.[34] For the present the discussion will be confined to the importance of reasons as a condition precedent to the legality of the measures listed in Article 190.

[31] Case 45/86, *Commission* v. *Council* [1987] ECR 1493.

[32] See also Case 165/87, *Commission* v. *Council* [1988] ECR 5545; Case C–295/90, *European Parliament* v. *Council* [1992] ECR I–4193, [1992] 3 CMLR 281.

[33] See below, 1131 for discussion in the context of the completion of the internal market.

[34] See below, 496–505.

We can begin this analysis by noting the *scope* of Article 190. It applies to regulations, decisions, and directives adopted either by the Council, Commission, and Parliament, or by the Council and Commission alone. The significance of this is worthy of comment. The duty to give reasons in national legal systems varies in scope as between the different Member States. In the United Kingdom, for example, the courts have recently expanded this duty in a series of important decisions.[35] The ambit of this obligation is none the less limited when compared to that contained within Article 190. This is in part because the Community obligation has been in place since the inception of the EEC Treaty, whereas that which exists in a number of the Member States has developed later. It is in part because the scope of the duty imposed by Article 190 is still broader than that which exists within many of the Member States. Thus Article 190 imposes a duty to give reasons not only in the context of administrative decisions, but also in relation to norms of a legislative nature, such as regulations or directives which apply to all the Member States. Many national legal systems either do not impose a reasons requirement on legislative acts at all, or do so only in limited circumstances. This important fact should be borne in mind when assessing complaints about 'Brussels bureaucracy' and the nature of the Community decision-making process. The reality is that Community policy-making is a good deal more transparent than that which exists within many of the Member States, and one of the important reasons this is so is the duty contained within Article 190.

The mention of transparency leads naturally on to a second line of inquiry, this being the *policy rationale for the existence of the duty to provide reasons*. The provision of reasons serves a number of purposes. From the perspective of affected parties, it makes the decision-making process more transparent, enabling those who are affected to know why a particular measure has been adopted. This facilitates participation in the process of decision-making since they will be better placed to be able to make representations to the deciding body, in the hope that it may alter its position. From the perspective of the decision-maker itself, an obligation to give reasons will help to ensure that this person or body has thought through the rationale for its action; having to explain oneself, and defend the rationality of one's choice, is always a salutary exercise. From the perspective of the ECJ, the existence of reasons facilitates the exercise of its review power. It enables the Court to determine whether, for example, the Commission was attempting to use a particular power for an improper purpose, or whether its decision was disproportionate. The relationship between the requirement to give reasons and the scope of substantive review will be examined more fully below.[36] The Court itself has recognized the range of benefits to be secured by a duty to give reasons. Thus it has stated that:[37]

[35] P. P. Craig, 'The Common Law, Reasons and Administrative Justice' (1994) 53 CLJ 282.
[36] See below, 496–505.
[37] Case 24/62, *Germany* v. *Commission* [1963] ECR 63, 69, [1963] CMLR 347, 367.

> In imposing upon the Commission the obligation to state reasons for its decisions, Article 190 is not taking mere formal considerations into account but seeks to give an opportunity to the parties defending their rights, to the court of exercising its supervisory functions and to Member States and to all interested nationals of ascertaining the circumstances in which the Commission has applied the Treaty.

What then of the *content* of the obligation to give reasons? How extensive is this? In answering these questions two factors should be taken into account.

One is that, as a matter of principle, the content of the obligation should relate back to the rationale for its initial existence. It should, in this sense, be sufficient to enable the policy rationales for the existence of the duty to be properly effectuated. This will normally require that the contested measure should at least specify the legal foundation in the Treaty on which it was based; the factual background to the measure; and the purposes or aims which the measure is striving to attain. Thus in the *Tariff Preferences* case[38] the ECJ annulled a Council measure in part because the legal basis of the measure had not been specified, while in *Germany* v. *Commission*[39] the Court held that it was sufficient to set out in a concise, but clear and relevant, manner the principal issues of law and fact upon which the action was based, such that the reasoning which led the Commission to its decision could be understood. On some occasions the Court will sanction the incorporation of reasons from another instrument. This will occur not infrequently in areas such as the CAP, where the Commission may have to make numerous decisions or pass many regulations within a short space of time. Where this is so the Court has accepted that the Commission can refer back to a previous decision or regulation setting out the considerations which shaped the Commission's action.[40] Where, however, a decision is in effect establishing a new principle, or applying it in a novel fashion, there will have to be sufficient reasons in the decision itself.[41]

The other factor to be borne in mind when considering the content of the duty under Article 190 is the very diversity of measures to which it applies. The fact that the Article 190 obligation applies to general legislative norms at one end of the spectrum, and to individualized decisions at the other, means that it is unsurprising that the content of the duty will vary in these differing instances. The degree of specificity which the Court demands will, therefore, depend upon the nature of the contested measure in question. This was explicitly recognized by the Court in the *Beus* case[42], where it stated that:

> The extent of the requirement laid down by Article 190 of the Treaty to state the reasons on which measures are based, depends on the nature of the measure in question.

[38] Case 45/86, n. 31 above. [39] Case 24/62, n. 37 above.

[40] See e.g. Case 16/65, *Schwarze* [1965] ECR 877.

[41] See e.g. Case 73/74, *Papiers Peints de Belgique* v. *Commission* [1975] ECR 1491.

[42] Case 5/67, *Beus* [1968] ECR 83, 95.

> It is a question in the present case of a regulation, that is to say, of a measure intended to have general application, the preamble to which may be confined to indicating the general situation which led to its adoption, on the one hand, and the general objectives which it intended to achieve on the other.
>
> Consequently, it is not possible to require that it should set out the various facts, which are often very numerous and complex, on the basis of which the regulation was adopted, or *a fortiori* that it should provide a more or less complete evaluation of those facts.

The Court may well demand greater specificity where the measure which is being challenged is of an individual, rather than general, legislative nature. Thus in *Germany* v. *Commission*[43] Germany produced an alcoholic drink called Brenwein, which was made from wine much of which was imported from outside the Community. The establishment of the common external tariff resulted in significant increases in the costs of this raw material, and therefore the German Government made a request to the Commission whereby 450,000 hectolitres of this wine could be imported at the old, lower rate of duty. The Commission acceded to this request in principle, but only for 100,000 hectolitres. The Commission justified this decision on the basis that there was ample production of wine in the Community, and on the ground that the grant of a quota of the volume suggested would lead to serious disturbances of the market in the product in question. This decision was challenged by the German Government, and the ECJ found that the reasoning of the Commission was insufficient. This was both because the Commission was insufficiently specific concerning the nature and size of any Community surplus in this area and because it had not made clear why serious disturbances in the market would in fact have resulted from the grant of this request.

The concern over the content of the duty to provide reasons relates not only to the relative specificity of this obligation. Another factor which is of importance is the extent to which the Court will require the Community institutions to respond to arguments which have been advanced by the parties, what has been termed the dialogue dimension.[44] The ECJ has been cautious in this respect. In the *Sigarettenindustrie* case[45] the Court held that, although Article 190 requires the Commission to state its reasons, including the factual and legal basis of its decision and the considerations which led it to adopt the measure, it was not required to discuss all the issues of fact and law raised by every party during the administrative proceedings. It therefore dismissed the claim that the Commission had ignored the applicants' arguments and that none of these arguments had featured in the decision.[46] Shapiro explains why

[43] Case 24/62, n. 37 above.

[44] M. Shapiro, 'The Giving Reasons Requirement' (1992) *UChic. Legal Forum* 179, 203–204.

[45] Cases 240–2, 261–2, 268–9/82, *Stichting Sigarettenindustrie* v. *Commission* [1985] ECR 3831, [1987] 3 CMLR 661, para. 88.

[46] See also Case 42/84, *Remia BV and Nutricia BV* v. *Commission* [1985] ECR 2545, [1987] 1 CMLR 1.

the ECJ has been reluctant to move in this direction, and also why, none the less, it may be pushed to do so.

M. Shapiro, The Giving Reasons Requirement[47]

The basic reason that the parties push and the ECJ resists dialogue lies in the difference between transparency and participation. Courts are likely to be initially hostile to demands for dialogue. Such requests are the last resort of regulated parties who have no substantive arguments left. Moreover, if dialogue claims are judicially accepted, they lead to a more and more cumbersome administrative process because the regulated parties will be encouraged to raise more and more arguments to which the agency will have to respond. If the only instrumental value for giving reasons is transparency, the courts will resist dialogue demands. One can discover an agency's actions and purposes without the agency rebutting every opposing argument.

. . .

If the ECJ sticks closely to transparency as the sole goal of Article 190, the ECJ is unlikely to move towards a dialogue requirement. Yet participation in government by interests affected by government decisions presents an increasingly compelling value in contemporary society, particularly where environmental matters are involved. The ECJ has already, however unintentionally, opened one avenue for linking participation to Article 190 by stating that the Council need not give full reasons to the Member States where they have participated in the decisions. To be sure, these ECJ opinions are transparency-based. They require that those Member States already know what was going on because they were there. Nevertheless they create an opening for counter-arguments from complainants who were not present and claim that, therefore, they need the Commission to be responsive. In short, full transparency can only be achieved through participation or through dialogue as a form of participation.

There is some indication of movements in this direction, albeit indirect rather than direct. *One* such indication is to be found in recent judicial decisions. The advent of the Court of First Instance (CFI) has been of significance in this respect. One of the reasons for the establishment of this Court was to reduce the burden on the ECJ itself, and to have it deal with cases within specialized fields where the facts are often complex, such as in competition matters. The CFI has passed judgment on Article 190 on a number of occasions. In one respect its decisions simply apply existing orthodoxy, in the sense of confirming that, for example, the Commission is under no obligation to respond to all the arguments adduced by the parties in support of their application. In another respect, however, these decisions signal a more intensive species of review. This has occurred through the emphasis which the CFI has placed on the principle that the reasons which have been given must be sufficient to enable the CFI properly to exercise its function of judicial review; *and* through the scrutiny which the CFI then brings to bear on the

[47] N. 44 above, 204–5.

reasoning which was actually employed by the Commission, annulling this reasoning if it does not withstand examination.[48] It is clear that the relationship between the giving of reasons and the judicial review function is an important one. We shall return to it later when considering Article 173. Suffice it to say for the present that judicial review is one device through which to ensure the reality of the reasons requirement, in the sense of preventing the Commission from 'dressing up' a measure by giving more acceptable reasons than those which it actually had in mind.[49]

The *other* indication of movement towards both greater transparency and participation rights is to be found in the important 1993 Inter-Institutional Declaration on Democracy, Transparency, and Subsidiarity. The content of this Declaration will be examined more fully below.[50] What is so significant about this Declaration is that it lays the foundation not only for more systematic transparency and freedom of information, but also for something akin to the notice and comment procedures which govern rulemaking in the USA. This stems from the fact that the Commission is to introduce a notification procedure, consisting of the publication in the Official Journal of a brief summary of the measure proposed by the Commission, combined with a deadline by which interested parties are invited to submit their comments. The implications which this may have for judicial review will be considered later.[51]

4. SUBSTANTIVE AND PROCEDURAL CONDITIONS FOR THE LEGALITY OF COMMUNITY ACTION: SUBSIDIARITY

The discussion thus far has focused on the general substantive and procedural conditions which affect the legality of Community action. One aspect of this topic does, however, merit separate treatment, and that is subsidiarity. The centrality of subsidiarity to the Maastricht negotiations is well known. For those who feared further movement to some species of federalist Community the concept of subsidiarity was the panacea designed to halt such centralizing initiatives. The 'S' concept was to be used to defeat those who hoped to increase the federalist leanings of the Community under the TEU. It was one of the symbols used to placate the Tory right wing during those long nights spent debating the new Treaty at Westminster.

But what exactly does the concept mean? How far will it in fact restrict the legislative powers of the Community? And what will be the role played by the ECJ in interpreting this concept? These are some of the questions which we

48 See e.g. Case T–44/90, *La Cinq SA* v. *Commission* [1992] 4 CMLR 449; Case T–7/92, *Asia Motor France SA* v. *Commission* [1994] 4 CMLR 30.

49 N. 26 above, 134.

50 See below, 140–2.

51 See below, 479–81.

will be examining within this section. Let us begin by being clear about the wording of Article 3b:

> The Community shall act within the limits of the powers conferred upon it by this Treaty and of the objectives assigned to it therein.
>
> In areas which do not fall within its exclusive competence, the Community shall take action, in accordance with the principle of subsidiarity, only if and in so far as the objectives of the proposed action cannot be sufficiently achieved by the Member States and can therefore, by reason of the scale or effects of the proposed action, be better achieved by the Community.
>
> Any action by the Community shall not go beyond what is necessary to achieve the objectives of this Treaty.

Article 3b can be broken down for ease of analysis into three parts.

(a) The Community Must Act within the Limits of its Powers

This requirement, which is derived from the first paragraph of Article 3b, need not detain us for long. It has always been recognized that the Community only has competence within the limited areas in which it has been given power. The extent to which this serves as a real limit to the sphere of Community competence has, however, been reduced by two developments. On the one hand, the range of areas in which the Community exercises some form of authority has expanded with each major revision of the Treaty. Thus the SEA and the TEU have both added significantly to the subject-matter competence of the Community. On the other hand, the ECJ has, as we have seen above, interpreted the Community's legislative competence broadly through recognition of the implied-powers doctrine and through the use of Article 235. The first paragraph of Article 3b will therefore be unlikely to be of significance in subsequent problems concerning subsidiarity.

(b) The Exclusive Competence of the Community

The same cannot be said for the second point of our inquiry, which is, in some ways, the most crucial aspect of subsidiarity: Article 3b is explicit that subsidiarity will only fall to be considered with respect to areas which do *not* fall within the exclusive competence of the Community. If an area is within the Community's exclusive competence then there is no legal obligation[52] to apply the subsidiarity concept.

So far so good. The problem is, of course, that there is no ready criterion for distinguishing between those areas which are, and those which are not, within the Community's exclusive competence. The Treaty itself is not

[52] The question whether there is a legal power, as opposed to a duty, to apply subsidiarity in such instances is another matter.

explicitly framed in these terms. Given that this is so it becomes a matter of interpretation of the meaning which should be given to this crucial phrase. The Commission has taken the view that an area falls within the exclusive competence of the Community if the Treaties impose on the Community a duty to act, in the sense that it has sole responsibility for the performance of a particular task.[53] It argues that there is a 'block' of exclusive powers which are joined by the thread of the internal market, including: free movement of goods, persons, services, and capital ; the Common Commercial Policy; competition; the Common Agricultural Policy (CAP); the conservation of fisheries; and transport policy.

Commentators who have examined the problem differ quite considerably on this issue. One can perceive both broad and narrow constructions of the term 'exclusive competence'. Toth provides the argument in favour of the broad view.

A.G. Toth, A Legal Analysis of Subsidiarity[54]

The Court has confirmed time and again . . . that in all matters transferred to the Community from the Member States, the Community's competence is, in principle, exclusive and leaves no room for concurrent competence on the part of the Member States. Therefore, where the competence of the Community begins, that of the Member States ends. From then on, Member States no longer have the power unilaterally to introduce legislation. They can act only within the limits of strictly defined management/implementing powers delegated back to the national authorities by the Community institutions. As the Court of Justice has stated: 'The existence of Community powers excludes the possibility of concurrent powers on the part of the Member States.'[55] Even the fact that during a certain period the Community fails to exercise a competence which has been transferred to it, does not create concurrent competence for the Member States during that period. This principle also follows from, or is closely related to, the doctrine of the supremacy of Community law, which of course is a basic tenet of Community law.

The central feature of this broad view is that the Community's exclusive competence exists in those areas in which the Member States have transferred power to the Community, *irrespective* of whether the Community has actually exercised this power. From this premise Toth concludes that subsidiarity cannot apply to any matter covered by the original EEC Treaty, including: the free movement of goods, services, persons, and capital; the Common Commercial Policy; competition; the Common Agricultural Policy; Transport Policy; and the common organization of the fisheries. Toth accepts that the Community does not possess exclusive competence within many of the newer

[53] Bull. EC 10–1992, 116. See now 1st Report of Commission on Subsidiarity, COM (94) 533.

[54] D. O'Keeffe and P. M. Twomey (eds.), *Legal Issues of the Maastricht Treaty* (1994), Ch. 3, 39–40.

[55] The quote comes from the *ERTA* case, Case 22/70, *Commission* v. *Council* [1971] ECR 263, 276.

areas in which it has been given some power, such as the environment, economic and social cohesion, education and vocational training, consumer protection, and Social Policy. This is quite simply because the relevant Treaty Articles are framed so as to give the Community more limited powers in these spheres. However, he rightly points out that policies can be designed to serve more than one function: Community legislation on the environment might also seek to facilitate the completion of the internal market. On the broad view of the term exclusive competence this would preclude the use of subsidiarity.[56]

> Since . . . the development of the internal market is within exclusive Community competence, at least those aspects of health, safety, environmental and consumer protection policies which are connected with the internal market must fall within the Community's exclusive competence and therefore outside the scope of application of subsidiarity.

This view of the term 'exclusive competence' has not gone unchallenged. Steiner adopts a narrower construction of this important phrase.

J. Steiner, Subsidiarity under the Maastricht Treaty[57]

> The EC, even at its beginnings, was not concerned with dividing competence between the Community and the Member States, but with sharing powers over a wide range of activity in order to achieve certain common and mutually beneficial objectives. Whilst it was clear that in some areas there would be little scope for action by Member States if the desired goal was to be achieved—a customs union is a necessary prerequisite to a single market—in most areas competence was concurrent. This did not mean that States and the Community could legislate on the same issue at the same time, nor that States' competence in these matters was unrestrained (since they are bound to comply with the rules of the EC Treaty), but that their action would be complementary or supplementary. Once the Community has exercised its powers under the Treaty, to regulate a particular matter within a certain area of activity, clearly States are not free to enact measures which conflict with those rules. As the volume and scope of Community law increase, so will States' powers diminish. But there are few areas of activity in which Member States do not retain some degree of competence. Thus it is not surprising that commentators have had difficulty in identifying areas in which the Community has exclusive competence, nor that the Heads of State refrained from doing so at Maastricht.
>
> One is forced to the conclusion that the only areas in which the Community has exclusive competence for the purposes of Article 3b are those in which it *has already legislated* . . . Surely the competence of Member States ends, not as Toth suggests, where the competence of the Community begins, but where its powers have been exercised . . . The fact that the competence to act, even to act comprehensively, has been granted to the Community by the Treaty does not, and surely

[56] A. G. Toth, 'A Legal Analysis of Subsidiarity', 41.
[57] D. O'Keeffe and P. M. Twomey (eds.), n. 54 above, Ch. 4, 57–8. Italics in the original.

> cannot mean that its competence to act in these areas cannot be subject to the subsidiarity principle. To allow whole areas of activity to escape scrutiny under paragraph 2, simply because the Community has potential competence in these areas, would surely undermine the very purpose for which this provision was intended.

The difference between this view and that advanced by Toth is readily apparent. On Steiner's hypothesis the subsidiarity principle will only be excluded where the Community has actually exercised its power; only in such areas will the Community have exclusive competence. Time will tell which of these two formulations most accurately captures the meaning of Article 3b. A decision of the ECJ will almost certainly be required before the matter is unequivocally settled.

There is however one crucial respect in which the Steiner formulation needs clarification. For Steiner the key idea is that the Community must have exercised the power in the relevant area. But the exercise of Community power can occur through the instrumentality of legislation enacted by the Council, Parliament, and Commission; or Community power can be exercised through judicial decisions made by the ECJ when interpreting the Treaty. For example, Community principles in relation to the free movement of goods can be implemented either by the legislative authorities passing a whole range of specific enactments which are designed to ensure that particular types of goods can move freely across borders; or the ECJ might give a judgment, as it has done,[58] which makes it clear that a broad category of national measures is inconsistent with the Treaty in so far as they inhibit the free movement of goods. It is clear that the Steiner approach would have to be construed to capture both of these modes of exercising Community power. Once one accepts that this must be so, then it becomes apparent that even the narrow formulation of the phrase 'exclusive competence' might not be as narrow as it appeared to be at first sight. This is particularly important, given the significance of the ECJ's contribution to many of the substantive areas of Community law, and given also the way in which the exercise of Community power by legislative and judicial means so often interacts.[59]

(c) The Subsidiarity Principle Itself

We are now in a position to examine the subsidiarity principle itself: the Community is to take action 'only if and in so far as the objectives of the proposed action cannot be sufficiently achieved by the Member States and can therefore by reason of the scale or effects of the proposed action, be better achieved by the Community'. Paragraph 3 of Article 3b then adds the further condition that 'any action by the Community shall not go beyond what is necessary to achieve the objectives of this Treaty'.

The sense of subsidiarity encapsulated in Article 3b embraces three separ-

[58] See below, 611–6. [59] See below, Chs. 4. and 25.

ate, albeit related, ideas: the Community is to take action only if the objectives of that action cannot be sufficiently achieved by the Member States; the action can therefore be better achieved by the Community because of the scale or effects of the proposed measure; if the Community is to take action then this should not go beyond what is necessary to achieve the objectives of the Treaty. It seems clear that the drafting of Article 3b was influenced by the experience of German law concerning the relationship of the Federal authorities and the Länder.[60]

The first two parts of this formulation entail what the Commission has termed a test of comparative efficiency:[61] is it better for the action to be taken by the Community or the Member States? If it is decided that action by the Community is warranted then the third part of the formulation comes into play. This entails the application of a proportionality test, requiring the Community to consider the intensity of the Community measures.

The 1993 Inter-Institutional Agreement on Procedures for Implementing the Principle of Subsidiarity requires all three institutions to have regard to the principle when devising Community legislation. The Commission must in particular provide in its explanatory memorandum concerning proposed legislation a justification for the measure in terms of the subsidiarity principle. Any amendment to the measure by the Council or the Parliament must likewise be accompanied by a justification in terms of subsidiarity if it entails more extensive Community intervention. In addition all three institutions are to check that both the choice of legal instrument and the content of the proposed measure are in accord with the subsidiarity principle.

Time will tell how subsidiarity in practice affects the scope and nature of Community legislation. Two comments are in order at this juncture.

On the one hand, it is reasonably clear that there will be many areas in which the comparative efficiency calculus comes out in favour of Community action. The idea that matters should be dealt with at the level closest to those who are to be affected is fine in principle. But the very *raison d'être* of the Community will, in many areas, demand Community action to ensure the uniformity of *general approach* which is of central importance to the realization of a common market. If we are to move towards a level playing field then centralized initiatives of some kind may be a necessary pre-condition for the attainment of this aim.

On the other hand, the very existence of Article 3b, and in particular paragraph 3 thereof, may have an impact on both the form and the intensity of Community action. The Community may, for example, choose to proceed through directives rather than regulations, on the ground that the former give some greater latitude to Member States. We may see a greater use of

[60] N. Emiliou, 'Subsidiarity: An Effective Barrier Against the "Enterprises of Ambition"?' (1992) 17 ELRev. 383 and 'Subsidiarity: Panacea or Fig Leaf?' in *Legal Issues of the Maastricht Treaty*, n. 54 above, Ch. 5.

[61] Commission Communication to the Council and the European Parliament, Bull. EC 10–1992, 116.

guidelines and codes of conduct. The idea of Community control with a 'lighter touch' fits in rather well with changes of approach which pre-date the TEU and Article 3b. Thus, as we shall see when considering the completion of the Single Market,[62] the new approach to harmonization entails a less detailed and less rigid form of Community oversight. One can expect the subsidiarity principle to encourage further developments of this kind.

(d) The Role of the Court

What then of the role of the ECJ with respect to Article 3b? As a matter of principle it is clear that the Article is a part of the EC Treaty and therefore that questions concerning its interpretation can come before the Court in the same way as with any other provision of Community law. Article 177 references would be a natural way for the issue to be brought before the ECJ.

The real issue is, therefore, as to the intensity of the judicial review process. We shall have occasion to see throughout the course of this book that the Court may decide to review the legality of Community action with varying degrees of intensity in different areas.[63] Much then will depend upon the intensity with which it decides to review, for example, a Commission assertion that, on grounds of comparative efficiency, Community action was required in a particular area. One should not underestimate the difficulties which the Court might face in this regard. If it decides to take a detailed look at the factual evidence underlying the Commission's claim it risks becoming embroiled in an issue which may have a heavy factual quotient, combined with a complex socio-economic calculus concerning the most effective level of government for different regulatory tasks. If, by way of contrast, the ECJ decides to be less intensive, and only to intervene if there is some manifest error, it may be open to the critique from Member States that it is effectively denuding the obligation in Article 3b of all content.

Either way there is the danger that the judicial process will become politicized. In the former instance of intensive review, the Court runs the risk of political clashes with other organs of the Community. On the latter hypothesis the clash is likely to be with the Member States themselves. It will be interesting to see whether the Court is able to tread a line which avoids the worst of both of these scenarios.

In 1992 Jacques Delors offered a prize to anyone who could define subsidiarity. Most of us can either gracefully decline the challenge, or proffer some definition secure in the knowledge that our chosen formula is unlikely to have dispositive effects. The Court may not be so fortunate. It may not have to provide a literal definition of the term. It will however have to interpret Article 3b. If, in doing so, it manages to tread the line indicated above, that will be prize enough.

[62] See below, 1136–43. [63] See below, 501–5.

5. THE LEGISLATIVE PROCESS: DEMOCRATIC LEGITIMACY AND POLITICAL PRAGMATISM

The discussion until now has focused on the ways in which the Community can act, through regulations, directives, decisions etc., and the general substantive and procedural conditions for the legality of that action. More detailed treatment of this latter issue will be given below.[64]

It is now time to consider the actual process by which Community legislation is enacted. Because of the complexity of these legislative procedures it is easy to lose sight of the very reasons for this intricacy. A word on this issue may well serve to render more comprehensible the procedures which will be described below.

The European Parliament is the Community institution with the greatest claim to political legitimacy because it is directly elected. The Council's democratic credentials are indirect: the Council representatives are, as we have seen, political appointees, but they are not directly elected at a European level. As for the Commission, it has no democratic legitimacy as such, since it is not elected at all.

The reasons for the complexity of the Community's legislative process have their roots in this simple fact: the body which has the greatest democratic claim to legislative power, the European Parliament, was given the smallest part to play in the legislative process in the original Rome Treaty. All of the subsequent Treaty modifications have been designed to increase the role of the European Parliament, but to do so in a way which is politically acceptable to the other players in the game. The ultimate goal from the European Parliament's perspective would be to have a right of legislative initiative itself, and to be accorded an equal status with the Council in the legislative process, in the sense that Community legislation would require the simple assent of both bodies. This has not yet been generally attained.

Why then has there been opposition to according the European Parliament a greater say in the Community's legislative process?

The answer to this is complex, but in essence it is because the other institutional players have differing reasons for being unenthusiastic about increasing the European Parliament's power in this way. National Parliaments, or at least some of them, fear that a fully empowered European Parliament would undermine their own authority, and give greater legitimacy to the Community. The Council is wary of the diminution in its own power if the European Parliament were to be accorded equal status. Increase in the power of the European Parliament would also have ramifications for the Commission. If the former were to have some right of legislative initiative it is doubtful whether the Commission's own independent right of legislative initiative could really survive in its present form. It would, at the very least, diminish the

[64] See below, Ch. 11.

extent to which the Commission and Council[65] were in control of the development of policy.

The paradox is, of course, that the Community as a whole has to try to bolster its own democratic credentials, the more so as it covers an ever wider range of subject-matter. It is already susceptible to attack on the grounds that important policy decisions are being made by a process which is, at best, only imperfectly democratic. It is for this reason, amongst others, that the European Parliament has been given greater powers than hitherto in order to try to meet this critique. With these thoughts in mind we can now consider the various legislative procedures which exist.

6. THE LEGISLATIVE PROCESS: SIX PROCEDURES

The legislative process which operates in the Community is complex, with different legislative procedures applicable in different contexts. This section will be concerned with the different procedures themselves. Subsequent sections will focus on the way in which the policy-making process actually works.

The distinguishing characteristic of these different procedures is, for the most part, the degree of power which the European Parliament has in each of these processes. There are two keys to preserving sanity when seeking to understand the Community's legislative procedures. One is to dispel any thought of identifying a single body as the 'legislature' for the Community as a whole; the players which comprise the legislature for the purpose of Community law vary in the different procedures described below. The other key to emerging mentally intact is to realize that there is no magic formula determining which of these procedures applies in any particular area of the Treaty. Do not search for one. Which of these procedures applies is dependent, in formal terms, simply upon what the EC Treaty specifies under any particular Treaty Article.[66] Each Article will indicate the legislative process to be applied in that context. In so far as there is any substantive criterion which determines this allocation it is political in the following sense. The European Parliament will seek to maximize its power by attempting to maximize the areas in which the Treaty stipulates that the procedures giving it the most say apply. Thus, as we shall see, a number of issues which were previously subject to the Article 189c procedure are now subject to that under Article 189b.

[65] Many legislative initiatives which emerge from the Commission have their origins in suggestions for action by the Council.

[66] A list of the areas which are subject to the differing legislative procedures can be found in S. Weatherill and P. Beaumont, *EC Law* (1993), 796–7, and in M. Westlake, *The Commission and the Parliament: Partners and Rivals in the European Policy-Making Process* (Butterworths, 1994), App. 7.

(a) Commission Acting Alone

This is quite rare. However the Treaty does accord the Commission itself a power to make legislation without any intervention from the other institutions in some areas. For example, the Commission has power under Article 90(3) of the Treaty to promulgate directives or decisions to ensure the application of the provisions of Article 90. This Article is concerned with the role of the state in relation to public undertakings, or those to whom it has granted special or exclusive rights. The Commission has exercised this power to enact a directive on the transparency of financial relations between Member States and public undertakings,[67] and a directive on competition as it relates to the telecommunications terminal market.[68] Both directives have been challenged by Member States, in part on substantive grounds, and in part because Commission legislation made under Article 90(3) excludes the states, as represented in the Council, from any formal role in the legislative process, and the Member States argued that a different Article of the Treaty should have been used, which would have given them such a role.[69] Another area in which the Commission can act on its own initiative is under Article 48(3)(d). This enables the Commission to pass regulations concerning the right of workers to remain in the territory of another Member State after having been employed there.[70]

(b) Council and Commission Acting Alone

There are a number of areas where the Council and the Commission can take action without any intervention by the European Parliament at all. In these areas the Council will act on a proposal from the Commission and take the decision in accordance with the voting requirement laid down in the relevant Treaty Article. The Council may choose to consult the Parliament, but does not have to do so.[71] It should not be thought that the areas in which this legislative procedure applies are of minor importance. It is used, for example, in relation to aspects of free movement of workers, capital, economic policy, and the common commercial policy.

(c) Council, Commission, and Consultation with Parliament

The legislative process in the original Treaty concentrated power upon the Commission and the Council: the former would propose a measure, and the latter would vote upon it. The only role for the European Parliament was a consultative one, where this was specified by a particular Treaty Article.

There are still a number of areas in which the role of Parliament is limited

67 Dir. 80/723, [1980] OJ L195/35.

68 Dir. 88/301, [1988] OJ L131/73.

69 For discussion of these cases, see below, 1078–80.

70 See e.g. Reg. 1251/70, [1970] OJ Spec.Ed. L142/24.

71 See e.g. Arts. 20, 28, 44–46, 51, 55, 59, 66, 73b–73g, 101, 103, 104c, 113, 228a.

in this manner. Failure to wait for its opinion before the Council adopts the measure can lead to the measure being annulled;[72] and Parliament may have to be reconsulted where there are important changes to the measure, not prompted by Parliament itself, after the initial consultation and prior to its adoption by the Council.[73] None the less, a bare requirement to consult with the European Parliament is all that is required, and the real legislative process is still dominated by the Council and the Commission in these areas. The Council is not therefore bound to adopt the opinion of the Parliament in the spheres to which this procedure applies.

The range of topics on which the Parliament has only a bare right to be consulted include, after the TEU: Article 8b, concerning rights to vote and stand in municipal elections; Article 8e, reinforcing citizenship rights; Article 94, state aids; Article 99, harmonization of indirect taxation; Article 100, approximation of laws for the functioning of the common market; Article 106(6), provisions relating to the Statute of the European System of Central Banks; and Article 130s(2), fiscal measures etc. relating to the environment.

(d) Council, Commission, and the Co-operation Procedure with the European Parliament

It was to be nearly thirty years before there was any real modification to allow the European Parliament a greater say in the legislative process. In so far as there was any attempted justification for the limited role accorded to the Parliament by the original Treaty it was based on the claim that, since this body was, at the inception of the Community, only indirectly elected, its claim to participate in the legislative process was thereby weakened. This argument was palpably flawed. The indirectly elected Parliament had as strong, or stronger, a democratic claim to participate in the legislative process as any of the other Community institutions. In any event the argument failed even in its own terms after the advent of direct elections. Notwithstanding this obvious fact there was no rush on the part of the other institutions to accord a greater democratic role to the Parliament. Quite the contrary. The attempts by the Parliament to secure for itself an equal role with the Council in the legislative process were studiously ignored, or side-lined, in the negotiations which led up to the SEA. What did emerge was a good deal less than equal status, although it did at least give the Parliament more power than it had hitherto.

The change which was brought about by the SEA is now, after the TEU, Article 189c of the EC Treaty. This procedure applies whenever the Treaty provides that the adoption of an act is to be in accordance with Article 189c.

[72] Case 138/79, *Roquette Frères* v. *Council* [1980] ECR 3333.

[73] Case C–388/92, *European Parliament* v. *Council* [1994] ECR I–2067. Where the changes are either technical or in accordance with Parliament's wishes reconsultation may not be necessary: Case 41/69, *ACF Chemiefarma* v. *Commission* [1970] ECR 661; Case 817/79, *Buyl* v. *Commission* [1982] ECR 245; Case C–331/88, *R.* v. *Minister of Agriculture, Fisheries and Food and Secretary of State for Health, ex p FEDESA* [1990] ECR I–4023.

(*a*) The Council acting on a proposal from the Commission, and after obtaining an Opinion from the European Parliament, adopts a common position.[74]

(*b*) This is then communicated to the European Parliament, (EP). The Council and the Commission are to inform the EP fully of the reasons which led the Council to adopt its common position and also of the Commission's position. If within three months the EP has either approved the common position or has not taken a decision then the Council shall definitively adopt the act in accord with the common position.[75]

(*c*) If the Parliament rejects the common position by an absolute majority of its component members then the Council can only adopt the act by unanimity. The Parliament may, alternatively, within three months, propose amendments by an absolute majority of its component members.[76]

(*d*) If the latter occurs, it is then for the Commission within one month to re-examine the original proposal in the light of the EP's amendments. The Commission then forwards the re-examined proposal to the Council, together with the amendments of the EP which it has not accepted, and shall express an opinion on these amendments. The Council may then adopt such amendments by unanimity.[77]

(*e*) The Council, acting by qualified majority, shall then adopt the proposal as re-examined by the Commission. Unanimity is required in the Council to amend the proposal as re-examined by the Commission. [78]

(*f*) The Council must act within three months in the situations covered by (c), (d), and (e) above. If no decision is made within this period then the Commission proposal will be deemed not to have been adopted.[79]

(*g*) The periods referred to in (b) and (f) may be extended by a maximum of one month by common accord between the Council and the EP.[80]

The procedure described above clearly gives the European Parliament a greater role in the legislative process than hitherto. The Article 189c process in effect creates two readings of the proposed measure: the first, as identified in paragraph (a), occurs when the EP gives an opinion on the measure before the Council adopts its common position; the second reading takes place after the Council has adopted its common position, at which point the EP has the options set out in paragraphs (b) and (c). The EP has rejected the Council's common position only on a limited number of occasions.[81] It has, however,

[74] Art. 189c(a). [75] Art. 189c(b). [76] Art. 189c(c). [77] Art. 189c(d).
[78] Art. 189c(e). [79] Art. 189c(f). [80] Art. 189c(g).

[81] D. Earnshaw and D. Judge, 'The European Parliament and the Sweeteners Directive: From Footnote to Inter-Institutional Conflict' (1993) 31 JCMS 1; R. Corbett, 'Testing the New Procedures: The European Parliament's First Experience with its New "Single Act" Powers' (1989) 27 JCMS 4.

tabled a large number of amendments, both at the first and the second reading stage. Until October 1993 the EP had tabled 4,397 amendments at first reading, of which 2,403 (54.65 per cent) were accepted by the Commission and 1,882 (42.8 per cent) by the Council. At the second reading the EP tabled 1,031 amendments, of which 452 (43.84 per cent) were accepted by the Commission, and 242 (23.47 per cent) by the Council.[82]

When it was originally introduced in the SEA it was used for many of the measures which were designed to implement the single market. For example, measures to achieve the internal market passed under Article 100a required the use of the co-operation procedure, as did directives designed to facilitate the mutual recognition of diplomas under Article 57, thereby enabling the self-employed more easily to work in other countries of the Community. The TEU has now changed this. It has upgraded the degree of participation by the EP by requiring the use of the stronger procedure of Article 189b described below. At the same time the TEU also upgraded the legislative process which is required in certain areas from the ordinary consultation procedure to the co-operation process of Article 189c.

The areas in which the Article 189c procedure now applies include: Article 75, transport; Articles 104a and 104b, aspects of economic policy; Article 118a, health and safety; Article 125, implementation of decisions relating to the European Social Fund; Article 130e, implementation of decisions relating to the European Regional Development Fund; and Article 130s(1), pursuit of basic objectives of environmental policy.

The impact of the Article 189c procedure comes out clearly from the following extract. When reading this bear in mind the way in which changes in the legislative process can have broader ramifications for inter-institutional relationships.

M. Westlake, The Commission and the Parliament: Partners and Rivals in the European Policy-Making Process[83]

The Single European Act in general, and the co-operation procedure in particular, represented a major constitutional innovation in the Community system . . .

First, it was immediately apparent that a badly-administered co-operation procedure could lead to blockages and delays. The Commission considered the potential stalling or loss of legislation to be the major risk of the new procedure, particularly in the field of the internal market, where the Single European Act had also introduced a 31 December 1992 deadline. The Commission's reaction was two-fold: internal reform, and increased inter-institutional co-operation, particularly with the Parliament.

Second, the procedure accords the Commission important gate-keeping functions at various stages in the procedure which frequently involve it in delicate political arbitration. It must draft its proposals with an eye to what will 'play' in Parliament, as well as in the Council. It is involved in the Council deliberations leading to the Common Position . . . It must give Parliament its opinion on the

[82] M. Westlake, n. 66 above, 39. [83] N. 66 above, 37–8.

Common Position. It must assist Parliament in its deliberations on the Common Position. Should amendments be carried, the Commission must decide whether to accept them (and which). The Commission frequently finds itself in the invidious position of regretfully refusing parliamentary amendments because they may upset the delicate balance of a Common Position qualified majority in the Council.

Third, both the Commission and the Parliament immediately recognised the fundamental importance of the first reading stage. At this point there is no majority requirement, nor any deadline, and Parliament can still hope to influence Council deliberations before a Common Position has coalesced. From the Commission's point of view, parliamentary emphasis on the first reading diminishes the risk of blockage at the second stage and reduces the number of situations where the Commission has to arbitrate between conflicting institutional desires. Clearly, emphasis on the first reading has given Parliament's power of delay fresh significance.

Fourth, and more generally, the co-operation procedure entailed a general change in institutional attitudes, particularly in the Commission and the Council. Parliament's powers in the legislative process were transformed from the weak and essentially unconstructive power of delay to a stronger and potentially constructive role in the drafting of legislation.

(e) *Council, Commission, and European Parliament: The Article 189b Procedure*[84]

The TEU has introduced yet another complex procedure which bolsters still further the powers of the European Parliament. This new procedure has been referred to as 'co-decision', both because it is designed to prevent a measure being adopted without the approval of the Council and the European Parliament, and because the procedure within the Article places emphasis on the reaching of a jointly approved text. The procedure is contained in Article 189b of the EC Treaty, and it applies whenever the Treaty refers to it for the adoption of an act.

(*a*) The process begins in the same way to that set out in Article 189c, with the qualification that the Commission's proposal is sent to both the Council and the European Parliament, (EP). The Council then, acting by qualified majority, adopts a common position after obtaining the opinion of the EP. The common position is then communicated to the EP and the Council informs the EP fully of the reasons which led it to adopt that position. The Commission is also obliged to inform the EP fully of its position.[85]

(*b*) If within three months of the common position being communicated to the EP it either approves of the common position, or does not take a decision, then the Council adopts the act in accord with the common position.[86]

[84] A. Dashwood, 'Community Legislative Procedures in the Era of the Treaty on European Union' (1994) 19 ELRev. 343.

[85] Art. 189b(2).

[86] Art. 189b(2).

(*c*) If the Parliament indicates by an absolute majority of its component members that it intends to reject the common position, then it must inform the Council, which may convene a meeting of the Conciliation Committee to explain further its position. The Parliament can then either confirm its rejection of the common position, in which case the proposed act shall be deemed not to have been adopted, or propose amendments by an absolute majority of the component members.[87]

(*d*) If the EP does propose amendments then the amended text is to be forwarded to the Council and Commission, which shall deliver an opinion on the amendments.[88]

(*e*) If, within three months of the matter being referred to it, the Council, acting by a qualified majority, approves of all the amendments of the EP, then it shall amend its common position accordingly and adopt the act in question. Unanimity is, however, required in relation to those amendments on which the Commission has delivered a negative opinion. If the Council does not approve the act in question then the Presidents of the Council and the EP convene a meeting of the Conciliation Committee.[89]

(*f*) The Conciliation Committee is composed of equal numbers of the Council and the European Parliament. Its task is to try to reach agreement on a joint text when there has been disagreement as to the original common position adopted by the Council. The Commission takes part in the Committee's work and will attempt to reconcile the disagreements between Council and the EP.[90]

(*g*) If within six weeks the Conciliation Committee approves a joint text, then there is a further period of six weeks in which the EP, by absolute majority of the votes cast, and the Council, by qualified majority, can adopt the act in accordance with the joint text. If one of the two institutions fails to do so then the act is deemed not to have been adopted.[91]

(*h*) There are then complex provisions which indicate what is to happen if the Conciliation Committee cannot agree upon a joint text.[92] In essence the proposed act is deemed not to have been adopted: *unless* the Council by qualified majority confirms, within six weeks of expiry of the period granted to the Conciliation Committee, the original common position (possibly with amendments proposed by the EP) to which it agreed before the conciliation procedure was initiated, in which case the act will be adopted; *unless* this is trumped by the Parliament rejecting the text by an absolute majority, within six weeks of the Council's confirmation, in which case the proposed act will be deemed not to have been adopted.[93]

[87] Art. 189b(2)(c). [88] Art. 189b(2)(d). [89] Art. 189b(3). [90] Art. 189b(4).
[91] Art. 189b(5). [92] Art. 189b(6).
[93] It is possible to extend the time limits in this Art.: see Art. 189b(7).

The complexity of this procedure is self-evident, and one can only wonder at the behind-the-scenes negotiations which went into the production of the 'finished Article'. In order to comprehend this legislative provision it may help to stand back from the details in order that its overall shape can be appreciated. In essence there are three readings in the Article 189b procedure. The first reading occurs when the EP gives its opinion to the Council before the latter adopts a common position (paragraph (a) above). The second reading takes place when the EP receives the communication from the Council of its common position, and the EP then has the option to approve, propose amendments, or reject the measure (paragraphs (b)–(e) above). It is at this stage that the Conciliation Committee can come into operation (paragraphs (e)–(g)). The third reading by the EP occurs when the Conciliation Committee fails to approve a joint text, and the matter can then go back to the EP once again (paragraph (h)).

The reason this procedure gives more power to the EP than that under Article 189c is this: the bottom line under Article 189b is that the Parliament can actually veto legislation of which it disapproves. It can in this sense exercise a negative block on such legislation. The limits of this power must, none the less, be borne in mind. The EP cannot actually force the Council to accept its amendments. Moreover, the very fact that the EP's power at the third-reading stage is essentially negative has led some to believe that if matters progress thus far the balance will tip in the Council's favour. This is both because the negative quality of the EP's intervention may mean that there is pressure not to use it too often, and because the veto power under Article 189b(6) requires an absolute majority which may not always be easy to muster.[94] Having said this, it should also be recognized that many of the points made in the extract from Westlake will apply in the context of the Article 189b procedure, including: the potential for delay and blockage of legislation, with the consequential need for inter-institutional co-operation; the gate-keeping and arbitration roles performed by the Commission; the importance of the first reading; and the change of institutional attitudes as a result of giving the EP a more constructive role in the legislative process.

This legislative procedure applies to a number of important areas including: Article 49, free movement of workers; Article 54, freedom of establishment, Article 57, mutual recognition of qualifications; Article 66, freedom to provide services; Article 100a, provisions concerned with the completion of the internal market; Article 128(5), incentive measures relating to culture; Article 129(4), incentive measures relating to public health; and Article 130s(3), certain aspects of environmental policy.

(f) Council, Commission, and the European Parliament: Assent

The assent procedure is simplicity itself as compared with those considered above: the Council acts after obtaining the assent of the European Parliament.

[94] Westlake, n. 66 above, 91.

This is a true form of co-decision, and the act can only be adopted if it has been approved by both the Council and the European Parliament. The assent procedure therefore 'grants Parliament an infinite power of delay and an absolute power of rejection'.[95] In order to render this power more discriminating Parliament's rules now provide for the possibility of an interim report with a draft resolution containing recommendations for modification or implementation of the proposal.[96] The Parliament has also unilaterally introduced a conciliation procedure with the Council.[97]

The assent procedure was introduced by the SEA for important matters such as the expansion of Community membership,[98] and association agreements.[99]

The areas in which the assent procedure applies after the TEU now include the following. Article O of the TEU, concerning membership of the European Union: any European state may apply for membership of the European Union; applications are addressed to the Council which shall act unanimously after consulting the Commission and receiving the assent of the EP, which shall act by an absolute majority of its component members. Article 8a(2) applies the assent procedure to provisions concerning the free movement of citizens within the Community. The Council acts unanimously on a proposal from the Commission after obtaining the assent of the EP; on this occasion assent only requires a simple majority in the EP. Various aspects of the functioning of a European Central Bank are made subject to the assent procedure under Article 105(6), as is amendment to the Statute of the European System of Central Banks under Article 106(5). And the assent procedure is stipulated for certain measures relating to economic and social cohesion under Article 130b.

This list of matters to which the assent procedure now applies may fail, in and of itself, to convey the significance of the changes brought about by the TEU in this area. The assent procedure has been extended in three ways. First, in the context of external relations it no longer only applies to accession and association agreements, but also to a wider range of agreements. Secondly, the procedure now applies to specific legislative areas, such as citizenship. Thirdly, the TEU has substituted a voting condition of simple majority in the EP in most instances, rather than one of absolute majority.[100]

(g) The Exercise of Delegated Legislative Power by the Commission

The discussion thus far has concentrated on the varying ways in which Community norms are enacted under the EC Treaty. Six such procedures have been considered, and in this sense we have exhausted the remit indicated by the title of this section. Our understanding of the Community legislative process would, however, be deficient if it did not take account of the way in which the Commission exercises delegated legislative power. It is to this issue that we should now turn.

[95] Westlake, n. 66 above, 96. [96] *Loc. cit.* [97] *Loc. cit.* [98] Art. 237.
[99] Art. 238. [100] Westlake, n. 66 above, 95–6.

We have already seen that the Commission possesses power to make legislation without the formal participation of the other institutions in certain limited areas. The Commission has also been delegated power to make regulations by the Council. A moment's thought will indicate why this has been necessary. There are certain areas of Community policy, such as that concerned with agriculture, which are highly regulated and which require numerous regulations, often passed quickly to cope with changing market circumstances. If the standard methods of enacting Community norms were to be applied in these areas the process would grind to a halt, both because of the number of such norms, and because they could not be enacted with sufficient expedition. This explains why the Council, through a 'parent' regulation, has authorized the Commission to enact more specific regulations within a particular area. It should not be thought that delegated power has been used by the Commission only to enact detailed regulations of the kind which are common in the agricultural area. It has also provided the basis for important Commission regulations in the competition sphere which exempt certain species of agreements from the reach of Article 85.[101]

However, the Council has not been willing to give the Commission carte blanche to legislate in this manner. It has made the exercise of this delegated legislative power subject to institutional constraints, in the form of committees through which Member State interests can be represented before the detailed norms are made. The rationale for these constraints can be explained quite straightforwardly here. The Member States, as represented in the Council, recognized the necessity for delegation of power to the Commission. A parent regulation would be passed, in one of the ways described above, and this would frame the general strategy for a particular area. The Member States wished for further input into the exercise of the power which had been delegated to the Commission for two complementary reasons.

On the one hand, there might be disagreements between the states themselves as to the content of the more detailed norms which should be made. It is common to think that Member States only ever disagree on points of general principle. This is quite mistaken. Often the Member States might agree on the general strategy which should be employed, but disagree on the nature of its detailed application. The committee structure which will be described below gave the Member States the opportunity for input into the detailed norms which would emerge pursuant to a delegation of power by the Council to the Commission.

On the other hand, the Council imposed conditions on the delegation of power to the Commission because of the real tensions which existed between these bodies at the time when the committee structure was invented. The Council was wary, to say the least, of the federalizing tendencies of the Commission. It is unsurprising, then, that at a time when the Council perceived the Community in inter-governmental terms, it should be unwilling to

[101] The empowering parent provision in this context is Reg. 19/65 [1965] OJ L66/35. See below, Ch. 19.

delegate power to the Commission without the existence of some institutional checks designed to ensure the *formal* representation of Member State interests.

The nature of these institutional checks can now be examined. What the Council essentially did was to condition the exercise of the delegated power on the approval of a committee which was composed of Member State representatives. There was no express warrant for the creation of such committees in the original Treaty, and the legality of the committee structure was challenged before the Court. The ECJ upheld the constitutional validity, in principle, of the committee system, reasoning that if the Council were enabled by the Treaty to delegate power to the Commission, then it could do so on terms.[102] Whether this argument really works in the context of the more general allocation of power within the Community is questionable, and the Court's decision may well have been influenced by the realization that to find the committee structure unconstitutional would have caused a major upset in the evolving pattern of Community decision-making.

The SEA modified Article 145 of the Treaty in order both to provide a more secure foundation for the existence of delegation subject to conditions, and an impetus for the more orderly organization of the committee structure. The third indent of Article 145 states that the Council can confer on the Commission, in the acts which the Council adopts, powers for the implementation of the rules which the Council lays down. It further stipulates that the Council may impose certain requirements on the exercise of these powers, and that it may reserve the right, in specific cases, itself to exercise directly implementing powers. The procedures which are imposed are to be consonant with principles and rules laid down in advance by the Council, acting unanimously on a proposal from the Commission after consulting the European Parliament. A framework decision establishing the principles and rules to be followed was adopted by the Council in 1987.[103] This decision did rationalize the committee structure, although both the Commission and the Parliament were unhappy with it, principally because it gave too much blocking power to the Council.[104] The adopted decision distinguishes between three differing procedures.

Under Procedure I the Commission is assisted by a committee of a purely advisory nature composed of representatives of the Member States and chaired by the Commission. The Commission submits a draft of the proposed measure to the committee, and the committee then delivers its opinion. The Commission is not bound by this opinion, although it shall take the 'utmost account of it'.[105]

Procedure II is known as the management committee procedure. The composition of the committee is the same as above. The Commission will submit

[102] Case 25/70, *Koster* [1970] ECR 1161.

[103] Dec. 87/373, [1987] OJ L197/33.

[104] For the earlier Commission draft, see [1986] OJ C70/6. The Parliament challenged the adopted decision, but the action was held to be inadmissible: Case 302/87, *European Parliament* v. *Council* [1988] ECR 5615.

[105] Dec. 87/373, n. 103 above, Art. 2.

a proposal to it, and the committee then delivers an opinion within a time limit set by the Commission chairman. The Committee votes in the same manner as the Council itself.[106] Under this procedure the Commission adopts measures which 'shall apply immediately',[107] *but* if the committee *votes against* the measure the Commission must then communicate this to the Council. The Commission itself has no vote on the committee. There are then two variants which determine what is to happen next.

Under variant (a) the Commission *may* defer application of the measure for one month, and the Council acting by qualified majority can take a different decision within the time limit which has been set by the Commission chairman of the committee.

Under variant (b) the Commission *is obliged* to defer application of the measure for a period specified in the act under which the power was originally delegated, provided that this does not exceed three months.

Procedure III is known as the regulatory committee procedure and is even more pro-Council in its orientation. Once again we have a committee chaired by a non-voting Commission representative, and a committee composed of representatives of the Member States. Once again the voting is in accordance with the same system as appertains in the Council. The sting in the tail of Procedure III is that the Commission can only adopt a measure *if it is in accord* with the opinion of the committee. If *it is not in accord* with the committee's opinion, or *if no opinion* is delivered, then the Commission must submit to the Council a proposal relating to the measures to be taken. There are then two variants as to what occurs next.

Under variant (a) if the Council does not act within the period specified in the act under which the power was originally delegated, which may not exceed three months, the proposed measure shall be adopted by the Commission.

Under variant (b) the position is the same, with the qualification that the Council has the option to reject the measure by simple majority.

The committee structure which has been formalized in the manner described above provides a means whereby Member State influence can continue to be brought to bear even when power has been delegated to the Commission. It is, of course, true that even if this structure did not exist, the Commission would consult Member State interests when enacting detailed norms. The management and regulatory committee system none the less institutionalizes this process, and formalizes the retention of Council power in the event that the representatives in the committee disagree with the Commission proposal. Moreover the fact that the number of occasions on which the committees actually reject or refuse to approve Commission measures is relatively low is of limited significance. It does not reveal how far the Commission has felt constrained to modify its proposals in order to prevent reference back to the Council.

[106] See below, 133–4. [107] Above, n. 103.

(h) The Seeds of Legislative Initiative for the Parliament: Article 138b

The procedures outlined above encapsulate the existing ways in which measures can be enacted in the Community. It should, however, be noted that the European Parliament can be the catalyst for the initiation of the legislative process by virtue of Article 138b. This provides that the European Parliament may, acting by a majority of its members, request the Commission to submit any appropriate proposal on matters on which it considers that a Community act is required for the purpose of implementing the Treaty. The proposal will then take the legislative route which is appropriate for measures of that kind as identified in a particular Treaty Article. While Article 138b does not vest the Parliament with any right of initiative as such, it does provide a means whereby it can be 'proactive' rather than simply being 'reactive'. The Commission, for its part, does not accept that it must automatically pursue a matter referred to it under Article 138b, although it recognizes that it will be an important political signal. Caution in this area also affects Parliament's view of the Article:[108]

> Parliament recognises that resort to this right must be sparing and realistic. To this end, it has introduced a series of filtering mechanisms into its rules. Such a resolution must result from an own-initiative report from the committee responsible, authorised by the Conference of Presidents. Before requesting authorisation, the committee must establish that no such proposal is under preparation. The resolution must indicate the appropriate legal basis and be accompanied by detailed recommendations and must respect the principle of subsidiarity and the fundamental rights of citizens.

(i) Legislative Initiative and the Council's Use of Article 152

The discussion of the legislative procedures within the Community would be incomplete if it did not take account of Article 152 of the Treaty. This is not a procedure for the enactment of legislation as such, but it is a mechanism whereby the Council can adopt a more proactive role in the initiation of the legislative process. Under this Article the Council may request the Commission to undertake any studies which the Council considers desirable for the attainment of the common objectives, and to submit to it any appropriate proposals. While the wording of this Article might suggest that the requests from Council to Commission would be couched in rather general terms this has not always proven to be so. The Council has not infrequently made use of this Article to give very specific instructions to the Commission concerning action which it, the Council, believes to be desirable. When this occurs the Commission will, at the very least, feel a strong pressure to bring forward legislation of the type suggested by the Council. The legislative

[108] Westlake, n. 66 above, 96.

procedure which is then to be used for this purpose will depend upon the subject-matter of the proposed norm.

7. THE VOTING REQUIREMENTS IN THE COUNCIL

The general principle is that voting in the Council is to be by majority.[109] The Treaty actually provides for three different rules on voting: on some occasions unanimity is required; in some instances a simple majority; and in most circumstances a qualified majority is stipulated. The figure specified for a qualified majority was fifty-four out of a possible seventy-six votes.[110] France, Germany, Italy, and the United Kingdom each have ten votes; Spain has eight; Greece, Belgium, Portugal, and the Netherlands have five; Denmark and Ireland each have three; and Luxembourg has two. The newest Member States to join the Community will alter the figure needed for a qualified majority. Sweden and Austria will have four votes each in the Council, while Finland will have three. This brings the total number of Council votes to eighty-seven.

In 1994 it was agreed that the blocking minority would be raised accordingly from twenty-three to twenty-seven votes. The United Kingdom wished to keep the blocking minority at twenty-three, and a compromise was worked out whereby if members of the Council representing a total of twenty-three to twenty-five votes indicated that they intended to oppose the adoption of an act by qualified majority, then a reasonable time should elapse in order to see if an agreement could be found before the new blocking minority was actually used. The original agreement had specified a margin of twenty-three to twenty-six votes. It has now been altered to twenty-five because of Norway's rejection of Community membership. Time will tell how well this compromise works.

Qualified-majority voting has been the formal legal norm in many areas where the Community acts since the end of the second stage of the transitional period in 1965. The range of issues which can be decided in this way was extended by the SEA, particularly through the addition of Article 100a which allows many matters concerned with the completion of the internal market to be determined in this manner. A requirement of unanimity now only applies to politically sensitive topics,[111] to decisions which are of particular importance for the character of the Community,[112] or in circumstances where the Council is seeking to depart from a proposal from one of the other Community institutions, as described above.

For some considerable time these formal legal powers were overshadowed

[109] Art. 148(1).

[110] Art. 148(2).

[111] e.g. harmonization of indirect taxes: Art. 99; grant of state aid in exceptional circumstances, Art. 93(2).

[112] e.g. accession of new Member States: Art. O TEU.

by the Luxembourg Compromise. This was the result of a political crisis in the Community in the mid-1960s, and coincided with the shift to qualified-majority voting in the Council.[113] In essence it provided that when majority voting applied to a topic which concerned the important interests of states, they should attempt to reach a solution acceptable to all, and France added the rider that discussion should continue until unanimity was attained. Suffice it to say for the present that the impact of the Compromise was to foster a climate in which majority voting prejudicial to the interests of a particular state tended to be avoided, and consensus decision-making fostered instead. The 'threat' that a Member State would exercise a *de facto* power of veto over proposals which it considered as threatening to its vital interests certainly did not enhance the speed of Community decision-making. While the Luxembourg Compromise has not been formally abolished, because it never formally existed in legal terms, the climate in the Community after the SEA and the TEU renders it less likely that states will attempt to use any explicit veto power.[114] Both the SEA and the TEU require a greater use of qualified-majority voting in order to effectuate the goals contained therein. Moreover, both of these modifications to the original Treaty reflect a shift in Member State perceptions about the nature of the Community as a whole, which renders it less likely that exclusively national interests will be regarded as a valid rationale for the exercise of a veto. The ability to invoke the veto will be further dependent on the perceptions of other states as to whether the state which is invoking it really does have very important interests at stake. Having said this it should also be noted that the very fact that use of the veto may now be less readily accepted[115] than hitherto will mean that Member States are more likely to exert pressure at other parts of the decision-making system so as to ensure that the measure which emerges is to their liking.

8. THE REALITY OF COMMUNITY DECISION-MAKING: THE TEMPORAL DIMENSION

The discussion thus far has focused on the types of Community norm and the ways in which they are enacted. To stop there would, however, give only an imperfect grasp of the way in which the Community legislative process operates. We need to press further to understand the way in which Community decision-making actually works. That is the object of the remainder of this chapter. There are a number of different dimensions to this inquiry, one of which is temporal in nature.

[113] See above, 12–14.

[114] Even before the SEA there were signs that the use of the veto would not be automatically accepted by the other states. Thus in 1982 an attempt to use the veto by the UK was ignored by enough of the other states to secure a qualified majority for the measure in question.

[115] The Luxembourg Compromise has, however, been invoked by Germany in 1985, by Ireland in 1986, and by Greece in 1988, in the context of the CAP.

By the temporal dimension we mean the following: the way in which decision-making within the Community has unfolded since its inception. To concentrate exclusively on the way in which decision-making currently operates is to miss significant aspects in the evolution of the Community institutions. The earlier discussion of the history of the Community has provided a framework within which to understand the development of the EC. We need now to consider more specifically the respective roles played by the Community institutions in the decision-making process and their evolution. What follows does not purport to be a thorough historical analysis, but rather a thematic one.

The theme which runs through this period is the development of institutional structures outside the strict letter of the Treaty, as a response to tensions which existed between the Council and Commission.

We have already seen that, prior to the SEA, the Parliament played only a minor role in Community decision-making. The Commission and the Council were the dominant forces. There were, however, tensions between these institutions, since they embodied differing conceptions of the Community.

The Council perceived it principally in inter-governmental terms, and this conception had both a substantive and a procedural dimension. In substantive terms the Council was unclear precisely how far it really did wish to travel down the road of European integration. In procedural terms inter-governmentalism connoted the idea both that Member State interests should not readily be sacrificed to the Community good; and that the Council, as representative of those interests, should retain control over the development of Community policy.

The Commission had a more federalist conception of the Community. This, too, had a substantive and a procedural component. In substantive terms it manifested itself in a commitment to proceed with the attainment of the Community goals as expeditiously as possible, then moving beyond these to other issues which would further the process of integration. In procedural terms the Commission vision naturally inclined to the use of majority voting, as dictated by the Treaty itself in many areas, with the necessary consequence that the interests of a particular Member State might have to be sacrificed to achieve the greater Community good.

The original Rome Treaty did, of course, split power between Council and Commission. But in many respects it placed the Commission in the driving seat as regards the development of Community policy. This is evident from the Commission's right of legislative initiative; from the plethora of other functions which it was given; and from the important fact that the voting rules, while requiring Council consent to a measure, also required unanimity for any modification of it by the Council. The message was that, while the Council had to consent to a proposed norm, it was not going to be easy for it to alter the measure drafted by the Commission.

The first twenty years or so of the Community were marked by *de facto* changes in the nature of Community decision-making, the unifying theme being the increased dominance of the Council over the Commission, and the limiting of the federalist tendencies within the Commission by the inter-governmental impulses of the Council. Institutional developments outside the strict letter of the Treaty were the vehicle through which this was achieved.

The Luxembourg Accords were one such development. They are the prime example of negative inter-governmentalism, in the sense that they gave the Member States the power to block measures they disliked which they felt touched on their vital interests. Statistics as to the number of occasions on which this power was actually used are, of course, only part of the story, since the threat of use of the power would shape the very policies which the Commission would put forward, and shape also the negotiations concerning them.[116] The Council's inter-governmental orientation also had a more positive side to it. The Luxembourg Accords were fine if the ultimate objective was to veto a measure. But the Member States also desired more finely tuned tools through which to be able to exercise an influence over legislation which they did wish to see enacted. The growing influence of COREPER, the establishment of management and regulatory committees, the increased use of Article 152, and the evolution of the European Council were all features of positive inter-governmentalism: they were all designed to increase and/or had the effect of increasing Member State influence over legislation which emerged from the Community. They did so in complementary ways. COREPER and the management/regulatory committees provided the means whereby the Council could have a more formalized input into the detail of the emergent legislation. The increased use of Article 152 became a useful vehicle whereby the Council could suggest Community action in particular areas. While the European Council became a mechanism which enabled Member States to discuss general issues of Community concern, outside the framework of the Council itself. The results of their deliberations were often 'binding', in the sense of laying down the parameters of future Community action, whether this be in relation to the size of the CAP budget, or the timetable for moves towards closer economic union.

These developments in the political decision-making structure of the Community did little to speed the enactment of Community norms. Quite the contrary. They were responsible in large part for the Euro-scelerosis which beset the Community during much of the 1970s. This had reverberations for the judicial role exercised by the ECJ. This story has been told most fully by Weiler.[117] He explains how the impediments to the attainment of Community objectives through the political process led to the growing importance of what he terms normative supranationalism: this is the relationship and hierarchy which exists between Community policies and measures on the one hand, and competing policies and legal measures of the Member States on the other.[118]

[116] See the important analysis by K. Neunreither, 'Transformation of a Political Role: Reconsidering the Case of the Commission of the European Communities' (1971–2) 10 JCMS 233.

[117] J. Weiler, 'The Community System: The Dual Character of Supranationalism' (1981) 1 YBEL 267. See also J. Weiler, 'The Transformation of Europe', n. 28 above, 2412–31.

[118] The precise causality/relationship between the inter-governmentalism which beset the political organs and the evolution of the legal devices is itself an interesting one, Weiler, n. 28 above.

The tools which mediated this relationship included the doctrines of direct effect, the supremacy of Community law, and pre-emption. These conceptual tools proved to be valuable devices through which areas of Community law could continue to be developed by the Court, notwithstanding the fact that the legislative process itself was not producing the required regulations etc. at all, or not with sufficient speed.[119]

Many of the institutional developments charted above which took place outside the strict letter of the Treaty have now been accorded *de jure* status by their express inclusion in subsequent Treaty revisions. Thus we have already seen how the management and regulatory committee structure attained a more secure footing by the revisions to Article 145 in the SEA. The European Council was also recognized by the SEA and now has its foundations in Article D of the TEU, while the existence of COREPER has, since the TEU, been accorded a more formal status in Article 151 of the EC Treaty.

The fact that this has now occurred is obviously of importance, but not only for an understanding of the present structure of Community decision-making. It serves to emphasize the fact that the very nature of the Community decision-making process is dynamic, not static. To concentrate wholly on the current Treaty provisions, and to 'freeze' them, means losing sight of the institutional dynamics which shaped the regime which we now have. The temporal dimension is then of crucial importance in enriching our understanding both of the reality of Community decision-making in the first twenty-five years of the Community's life; and also in helping us to comprehend the existing pattern of institutional competence.

9. THE REALITY OF COMMUNITY DECISION-MAKING: THE INTER-INSTITUTIONAL DIMENSION

(a) Institutional Co-operation: Planning the General Legislative Strategy

The institutional reforms enacted in the SEA had a mixed impact on the pattern of Community decision-making. In one respect these reforms expedited the decision-making process. In formal terms the SEA increased the number of areas in which qualified majorities could be used in the Council, the most important instance being Article 100a. In informal terms the climate which existed at the time when the SEA was passed meant that it was less likely that Member States would be able to employ the veto. These developments rendered it easier than hitherto for the Commission to get its proposals accepted. In another respect however the SEA served to make the decision-making

[119] P. P. Craig, 'Once Upon a Time in the West: Direct Effect and the Federalization of EEC Law' (1992) 12 OJLS 453.

process more complex than it had previously been. This was the result of according the Parliament greater power in the legislative process under what is now Article 189c of the EC Treaty. For the future there would be another institutional player in the legislative process whose views had to be accommodated in order to facilitate the passage of legislation. The nature of the change which this brought about has already been touched upon in the previous quotation from Westlake:[120] there were concerns about the effect of these changes on the speed of decision-making; the Commission would henceforth have to frame its legislative proposals with a greater sense of what would be acceptable to the Parliament; and the Commission's own arbitral role increased as it was forced to mediate between Council and Parliamentary views on any particular issue. This increase in Parliament's power led, as we have seen, both to a change in institutional attitudes as a consequence of the fact that Parliament could now play a more constructive role in the drafting of legislation, and to the realisation that there would have to be more inter-institutional co-operation. One important facet of this inter-institutional co-operation concerns the planning of the overall legislative programme. The nature of this process is brought out clearly by Westlake.

M. Westlake, The Commission and the Parliament: Partners and Rivals in the European Policy-Making Process[121]

Although only recently instigated and still evolving procedurally, the annual legislative programming exercise has already become a centre-piece of Commission–Parliament relations. The Single European Act greatly enhanced the importance of collaborative planning. It was in the Commission's interest first, to give Parliament advanced warning of its general intent in particular policy areas, enabling any general debate to precede specific proposals and, second, to give Parliament an overall view of the legislative calendar, enabling it to programme its work efficiently. Planning has taken on further practical importance with the implementation of the Maastricht Treaty, and political importance in the light of the Treaty's provisions on the nomination of the Commission and its President. As the procedure is still evolving, the schematic description given here is necessarily tentative, although the basic trend is clear.

In the autumn preceding each legislative year, the Commission President presents the Commission's Programme to the Parliament, and a debate then ensues. The Programme is not an exhaustive document but is intended to set out the main themes and political priorities of the Commission for the coming legislative year. Parliament is constantly considering ways of organising its work so as to gain maximum influence over the Programme, in particular by setting out its political priorities in advance, and continues to seek to exert influence thereafter, concluding with a plenary debate. Parliament has attempted to provide an additional dimension by drawing in the work programme of the Council Presidency-in-office. The December 1992 Edinburgh Council endorsed a Commission proposal that the annual work programme be produced in October of the preceding year, thereby providing Parliament (and, of course, public opinion) with more time to exert

[120] See above, 124–5. [121] N. 66 above, 19–21.

policy influence. In the longer term, the timing of the presentation of the work programme will be important in the context of the nomination of the Commission, Parliament's new rules already foreseeing that the incoming President should present a programme as part of the nomination process.

. . .

Together with its Programme, the Commission submits to Parliament a copy of its indicative legislative timetable. Although it cannot be exhaustive, the timetable sets out all major and important proposals for the forthcoming year. It includes all proposals related to the political priorities established in the Commission's Programme, but has in the past rarely extended beyond these to the broader range of Commission competences. However, at the December 1992 Edinburgh Council the Commission undertook, in line with a greater desire for transparency and broader consultation, to resort more frequently to green papers, and the 1993 legislative programme subsequently annexed a list of those topics where it was intending to draft green papers during the year in question.

A document of hybrid status, the Commission's indicative legislative timetable is divided into quarterly rolling programmes and is constantly updated. It serves as a concretisation of the Commission's Programme, is designed to involve the other Community institutions, and serves as the basis for co-ordination between them. Indeed, the indicative legislative timetable is the subject of considerable co-operation and co-ordination between Parliament and Commission services, and although the Commission retains some rights of authorship, the result is nevertheless a jointly-agreed programme.

Inter-institutional co-operation which is directed to the general nature of the legislative programme also takes forms other than those noted above. Thus there is an Inter-Institutional Co-ordination Group[122] (known as the Neunreither Group after the founder), which meets on a certain date preceding the plenary sessions in Strasbourg. Representatives from the Commission, the Economic and Social Committee, and the General Council secretariats are invited to attend, as are those from the Parliament's sessional services and from the *cabinet* of its President. The Group now considers a wide range of matters concerning the plenary agenda, and sets priorities for future plenary agendas in line with the joint annual legislative programme. Inter-institutional communications also take place through what is now the Conference of Presidents,[123] chaired by the President of the Parliament in a non-voting capacity, and composed of the leaders of the political groups, each of which has a vote which is weighted in accordance with the numerical strength of that group in the Parliament. This body will meet during the plenary session week in Strasbourg, and prepare the plenary session for the following month.[124] The Commission will normally attend, and it, as well as the Council, will have the opportunity to make suggestions as to the content of the agenda, in order, for example, to expedite the passage of urgent business.

[122] *Ibid.* 21.

[123] *Ibid.* 21–2.

[124] This is how the predecessor body to the Conference of Presidents functioned, and it seems as if the Conference of Presidents will do the same.

(b) Institutional Co-operation: Inter-Institutional Agreements

Institutional co-operation can assume a more formal mode than that described above. One of the increasingly important vehicles through which this now occurs is the Inter-Institutional Agreement or Declaration.[125] Such agreements or declarations form what has been termed 'a sort of constitutional glue'[126] to flesh out either particular Articles of the Treaty, or the framework provided by inter-governmental conferences. An example of the former is to be found in the 1993 Inter-Institutional Agreement on Subsidiarity; an example of the latter is the 1993 Inter-Institutional Declaration on Democracy, Transparency, and Subsidiarity. Agreements of this nature have also been made in relation to, for example, budgetary procedure and budgetary discipline. We have already had occasion to consider the agreement concerning subsidiarity itself. That which concerns democracy, transparency, and subsidiarity may be considered here as an example of the role which such agreements can play in developing general constitutional principles to govern Community decision-making.

The 1993 Inter-Institutional Declaration on Democracy, Transparency, and Subsidiarity was agreed to by the three institutions on the margins of the 1993 Brussels European Council. Each of the institutions was to adopt this text in accordance with its own internal procedures. Article 1 of the Declaration affirms the attachment of the three institutions to principles of democracy and transparency, within the framework of the existing legislative procedures. Article 2 states that the Council will, as soon as Parliament has adopted its resolution on the annual legislative programme proposed by the Commission, make its position clear in a declaration and undertake to implement as soon as possible the provisions to which it attaches priority, on the basis of formal Commission proposals and in compliance with the procedures laid down by the Treaties. Article 3 then brings together and formalizes a number of steps which the institutions have already taken, or are taking, in order to increase the transparency of the Community.

For the Parliament this means confirmation of the fact that its plenary sessions and its committee meetings are to be in public.

For the Council, it entails opening some of its debates to the public; publishing records and explanations of its voting; publishing the common positions adopted under Articles 189b and 189c, together with the reasons accompanying them; improving information for the press and the public on its work and decisions; simplifying and consolidating legislation in co-operation with the other institutions; and providing access to archives.

For the Commission it means, *inter alia*, making wider consultations before presenting proposals, in particular through Green or White Papers; flagging

[125] Such agreements can be found at various stages of the Community's development: J. Monar, 'Interinstitutional Agreements: The Phenomenon and its Dynamics after Maastricht' (1994) 31 CMLRev. 693.

[126] N. 66 above, 101.

those proposals in its legislative programme which are suited for wide-ranging consultation; the introduction of a notification procedure, consisting in the publication in the Official Journal of a brief summary of the proposed measure, plus a deadline by which interested parties can comment; publication of legislative and work programmes within the Official Journal to publicize action planned by the Commission; publication in the legislative programme of plans for the consolidation of Community legislation; provision of easier access to documents held by the Commission, with effect from the beginning of 1994; publication each week in the Official Journal of lists of documents on general topics, combined with wider public access to documents on specific topics; faster publication of Commission documents in all Community languages; adoption of additional measures to facilitate the general public's understanding of Commission business; and creation by the Commission of a database on special-interest groups to be used by the general public and Community officials. Both the Council and the Commission have already taken decisions which are designed to give more concrete expression to these principles, particularly in relation to access to information.[127]

This particular declaration is clearly of importance in itself, and we have already had occasion to comment on the relevance of the participatory provisions of the declaration, and will return to this issue once again later.[128] It is also of significance for the insights which it gives us on the way in which principles of constitutional significance evolve within the Community. The Inter-Institutional Agreement or Declaration provides the Community with a flexible tool to flesh out particular Treaty Articles or more general principles which are inherent within the Community's legal structure. In this sense, they constitute both a valuable form of 'constitutional glue' and a foundation for the development of more specific principles or rules designed to put into effect the general principles which have been agreed upon.

The emergence of agreements of this nature is also of more general interest for the light which it sheds on the politics of the Community. Thus Lodge argues that the very attention given by the Member States to ideas such as transparency as it related to the Commission was motivated in part by the desire to divert attention away from the secrecy of the Council itself, and in part to deflect attention away from broader issues concerning the balance of power within the Community.[129]

> As the Maastricht ratification process became increasingly tortuous, member governments, *inter alia*, began to insist that a democratic deficit existed also within the ranks of the Commission: its proposals were impenetrable; its practices and personnel were byzantine, inaccessible and an affront to the conduct of

[127] Council Dec. 93/731, [1993] OJ L340/43; Commission Dec. 94/90, [1994] OJ L46/58.

[128] See above, 111–12, and below, 479–81.

[129] J. Lodge, 'Transparency and Democratic Legitimacy' (1994) 32 JCMS 343, 345. As Lodge rightly notes the Commission has always been more rather than less accessible than most national governments.

democratic politics. If the EU were to close the democratic deficit, the Commission's alleged lack of openness needed to be rectified. Thus attention was diverted from interinstitutional relations and the relative position of the Council and the European Parliament to the Commission.

(c) Inter-Institutional Co-operation and Conflict-Resolution: The Making of Particular Policies

The discussion within this section has focused on the differing ways in which the institutions interact in the formulation of *general* legislative policy choices. It is now time to consider the ways in which these institutions interact in the making of a *particular* legislative norm.

We have already seen in this regard the detailed procedures which are used to enact such norms, and the varying roles played by the three major institutions in this process. An understanding of these procedures is a necessary precondition for comprehending the way in which Community policy evolves. It is not, however, sufficient. To focus exclusively on these procedures leaves much unstated about how legislation emerges within the Community, and the interaction between the institutions which this process entails. The object of this section is to fill this gap.

Legislative proposals on a particular issue do not emerge from the Commission out of thin air. They will be the result of a Commission initiative. If the issue is of any importance then it will normally have been flagged in the Commission's outline of legislation which has been submitted to the Parliament. Although the Commission has the right of initiative it should not be thought that the actual emergence of draft legislation will always be a one-directional process. The Council has, in recent years, made increasing use of its power under Article 152 of the Treaty to request the Commission to submit to it proposals on what are, in effect, detailed legislative initiatives which the Council wishes to see enacted.[130]

The *content of the Commission proposal* will be the result of interaction between the Commission, interest groups, national experts, and senior civil servants. Within the Commission itself the relevant Commissioner will assume overall responsibility for a proposal which comes within his or her area. It will have been fashioned by the relevant Directorate-General, and by the appropriate Directorates and Divisions which are part of that sphere. When all those who are directly involved with the proposed measure have given their approval, the draft will be sent to the *cabinet* of the Commissioner who is responsible for the subject. Once the Commissioner is satisfied with the draft it will then be submitted to the College of Commissioners. Legislative proposals, once formulated, require the endorsement of the whole Commission. The College of Commissioners will normally meet weekly. Legislative drafts which have been framed by those lower within the Commission hierarchy will pass up to higher levels, to be accepted, amended, or rejected as the case may

[130] Sir Leon Brittan, 'Institutional Development of the European Community' [1992] PL 567.

be. One should not, however, assume that the process works in only one way.[131]

> There is no single way in which decisions are taken. In practice teams of relevant commissioners can be delegated to act on behalf of the College; brain storming can be used; or a written procedure adopted whereby urgent and/or uncontroversial proposals are deemed adopted if no objection is lodged within a specified time to the dossier and draft proposal, normally a week . . . Only routine matters are delegated to individual commissioners who are then empowered to act within the confines of a very narrow remit on the Commission's behalf: recurrent agricultural regulations are adopted in this way.

The *role of groups of national experts, civil servants, and interest groups in this process of policy formation* is an interesting one. The framing of the proposal will, as just indicated, involve close collaboration and consultation with a wide variety of groups. It should be emphasised that this will occur *before* the proposal begins its legislative journey on one of the roads considered above, whether this be the Article 189b route, or the Article 189c route, etc. The following extract states one view about the relationship between national civil servants and the Community bureaucracy. It expresses the idea that bureaucracies at the national and the Community level may be becoming more interlocked, or *engrenagé*. On this view one can perceive a discourse taking place between the two bureaucratic levels.

W. Wessels, Administrative Interaction[132]

> By participating in Community decision-making the national civil servants gain 'access' to and 'influence' on EC decision-making and implementation, thus also increasing their weight inside their respective national systems. The same general cost-benefit calculation applies to Community officials who gain access and influence on 'national' domains by opening their policy cycles to the national colleagues—although traditional federalists and supranationalists would argue that this is an unacceptable loss in autonomy and independence of the EC bureaucracy. This cost-benefit analysis by civil servants (*mutatis mutandis* by heads of state, ministers and interest groups, but not by national parliamentarians) creates a major dynamic for European integration leading not to a transfer of loyalty by national officials to a new centre but to cooperation of officials into a new system of shared government. This stage of state evolution is characterized by an increasing degree of cooperation, in vertical terms between different governmental levels, and in horizontal terms, among several groups of actors. The 'multi-level' interactions of civil servants of several national and international administrations thus reinforce trends towards specific forms of the 'sharing' or 'fusion' of powers between 'bureaucrats and politicians' which non-EC-related studies have identified.

[131] J. Lodge, 'EC Policymaking: Institutional Dynamics' in J. Lodge (ed.), *The European Community and the Challenge of the Future* (2nd. edn., Pinter, 1993), 11.
[132] W. Wallace (ed.), *The Dynamics of European Integration* (RISIA/Pinter, 1990), Ch. 13, 230.

National civil servants are not the only group which has an input into the process of policy-formation. Interest groups have, not surprisingly, concentrated increasing resources on the Community decision-making process, quite simply because it has such an impact on their own areas of concern. Given that the maxim of lobbyists is to 'shoot where the ducks are' we should therefore expect interest groups to organize themselves at a European level to the extent to which that is the most efficient way to effectuate their goals. There is a growing body of literature documenting the way in which such groups operate within the Community.[133] Certain matters are reasonably clear. Successful lobbying is dependent upon developing good advance intelligence; watching the national agenda; maintaining good links with national administrations; maintaining close contacts with Commission officials; presenting rational arguments; being co-operative; developing a European perspective; not gloating when successful; and not ignoring the implementation process.[134] Perhaps the most significant factor is to begin the lobbying process as early as possible. The general consensus is that much lobbying activity comes too late, and that therefore it should begin when there is the merest hint of a future legislative initiative from the Commission. What is also apparent is that the very complexity of the decision-making processes within the Community renders it difficult for interest groups to know how best to expend their resources. Much time and effort is spent lobbying the Commission itself, since it will be the Commission which formulates the detailed legislative proposal. To this end many Euro-associations have been formed to foster this process. The attitude of the Commission to such associations is, however, somewhat ambivalent as the following extract demonstrates.

S. Mazey and J. Richardson, Pressure Groups and Lobbying in the EC[135]

There are many examples of the Commission helping to resource these associations and of individual officials 'massaging' the developmental process within the associations (via direct funding and via 'soft' money, for example financing conferences etc.). Thus much of the Commission's activity—particularly at the service level—is very supportive of Euro-associations. Yet, when faced with the day-to-day pressures of initiating and formulating policy proposals which will actually work in the twelve Member States, Commission officials regularly by-pass the Euro-associations. The reasons for this are two-fold. First . . . the associations are of necessity broad in their interests. Commonly, the national industries being represented by the associations have quite different traditions, different structures, and above all, different and *competing* interests. For example, the financial services sector is quite different in Britain and Germany. This means that a European-level regulatory regime which would suit the British would probably not

[133] See e.g. S. P. Mazey and J. J. Richardson, *Lobbying in the EC* (Oxford, 1992); R. H. Pedler and M. P. C. M. Van Schendelen (eds.), *Lobbying the European Union: Companies, Trade Associations and Issue Groups* (Dartmouth, 1994).

[134] S. P. Mazey and J. J. Richardson, 'Pressure Groups and Lobbying in the EC' in J. Lodge (ed.), n. 131 above, 44.

[135] *Ibid.* 38–9. Italics in the original.

> suit the Germans. As with governmental coalitions, the associations have to devise compromise policies—often referred to by the Commission as 'lowest common denominator policies'—which are so general as to be of little practical use to officials. Moreover, the associations often lack the necessary expertise so needed by Commission officials. Thus, it is very common for officials to develop links with individual national associations . . . and to develop links with individual firms as a means of securing reliable technical information quickly.

Interest-group pressure at the Community level is to be expected as a feature of political activity in the process of policy-formation. It is likely to increase further as a consequence both of the growing ambit of Community competence, and of the moves to improve transparency and participation in decision-making. This does not mean we should be complacent about the nature of the problems which it entails. The very complexity of the EC legislative process, and of the large number of interest groups seeking to influence Community decision-making, have lessened any risk of what administrative lawyers term 'agency capture'[136] by a particular prominent group. Having said this, it should also be noted that profit-making groups outnumber non-profit groups by a very significant margin, and that the resources of the former are commensurately much larger. The costs of organizing at the European level may be especially onerous for the voluntary/non-profit sector. The moves within the Community to develop more formal participation procedures which were discussed above are important in this respect. Powerful groups are likely to make their voices heard irrespective of whether formal participatory rights exist. This is less obviously so for those which have less financial muscle. The commitment to greater transparency and participation via notice and comment can help to ensure that those which are less powerful will, at least, have some specified means for making their views known.

Once a Commission proposal has been formulated *it will make its way to the Council*, and also to the European Parliament if the latter has a legislative role in the particular area in question. We shall consider first the way in which the proposal is handled by the Council.

COREPER is of crucial importance in this respect. The structure of this body has been considered in the previous chapter.[137] What we are concerned with here is the role played by COREPER in the legislative process. Before any measure is actually seen by the Council itself, it will have been thoroughly examined by one or more working groups which assist COREPER, as well as by COREPER I or II. These working groups are composed of national officials and experts from the Member States, plus a member of the Commission. They may be permanent or *ad hoc*. One estimate of the number

[136] This is the process whereby the regulator of a particular area comes to identify with the group which is being regulated, and fails to pursue the regulatory aims as objectively or as strenuously as it should otherwise do.

[137] See above, 50.

of such groups in 1989 put it at nearly 200.[138] These working groups will examine the Commission proposal and prepare a report. This will indicate the areas on which agreement has been reached ('Roman I points') and all other points ('Roman II points'). The latter will then be discussed within COREPER I or II depending on the topic. Points which have been agreed on in the working group will normally be accepted by COREPER, with debate focusing on those issues where consensus has not yet been attained. Reference back to the working group may occur.

COREPER continues to be of significance once proposed measures have actually been tabled before the Council itself. This is because of the agenda-setting function performed by COREPER. Issues on which there is agreement within COREPER will be placed on the 'A list' and will be adopted without discussion. If agreement within COREPER has not been possible then such issues will be placed on the 'B list', indicating that debate and decision by the Council is required. Members of COREPER will attend Council meetings as advisers to their national ministerial representatives.

The modifications in the decision-making process since the SEA have increased the importance of the Council Presidency. The Office of the Presidency will co-ordinate the meetings of the differing Councils. It should be remembered in this respect that the Council is fragmented, in the sense that the participants will vary depending upon the subject-matter in issue: on some occasions foreign ministers will attend, on others it will be the minister responsible for a particular sectoral problem. The President will also mediate conflicts between the Member States themselves, between the Member States and the Commission, and between the Council and the Parliament. The President of the Council will, in addition, be able to exert influence on the Commission in order that legislative initiatives which are of interest to the state which holds the Presidency are forthcoming.

The necessity for conflict mediation, both by the Council President and by the Commission, is particularly important in those areas in which the European Parliament has a greater say in the legislative process under Articles 189b and 189c, and, of course, in those areas where the assent procedure applies.

At the end of the day decisions on many matters within the Council will be reached by consensus. This should not, however, cause us to underestimate the importance of the shift to majority voting brought about by the SEA. Weiler captures this when stating that 'reaching consensus under the shadow of the vote is altogether different from reaching it under the shadow of the veto'.[139]

It is to the *role of the Parliament* in the passage of legislation that we should now turn. The detailed procedures have been set out above.[140] The main part of the Parliament's legislative work is, not surprisingly, undertaken by standing committees, the remit of which is largely determined by subject-

[138] F. Hayes-Renshaw, C. Lequesne and P. Mayor Lopez, 'The Permanent Representations of the Member States to the European Communities' (1989) 27 JCMS 119, 132.

[139] N. 28 above, 2461.

[140] See above, 120–34.

matter.[141] The appropriate committee will make the initial draft report on legislation which is submitted to the Parliament pursuant to Articles 189b or 189c. The responsibility for drawing up the report of the committee is given to a *rapporteur*. The *rapporteur* can seek assistance from the Parliament's secretariat, from the secretariat of his or her own political group, from the research services which each MEP possesses, and from research institutes. The *rapporteur* will present the draft report to the committee. It will normally have four parts: any amendments to the Commission proposal; a Draft Legislative Resolution; an Explanatory Statement; and any relevant Annexes. The committee will advise the MEPs as a whole how they should vote in the plenary session, and the *rapporteur* will usually act as the committee's spokesperson. Where the Article 189b and 189c procedures apply the same committee will examine the proposed legislation in the light of the common position adopted by the Council.

The Commission will, as indicated earlier,[142] often have an important arbitral role to play in such areas. This will be of particular significance when the European Parliament appears minded to reject the Council's common position, or when the Parliament suggests amendments to proposed legislation. In this latter circumstance the Commission will often have to 'juggle' matters in the attempt to find a legislative package which will be agreeable to the Parliament, the Council and to itself. As Nugent states:[143]

> The Commission has a more difficult task under the cooperation and co-decision procedures than it has under the consultation procedure, in exercising its judgment as to whether, and if so at what stage, it should amend its text so as to get proposals through in a reasonably acceptable form. At the second reading stage, in particular, a delicate balance may have to be struck: between, on the one hand, being sufficiently sympathetic to EP amendments so as not to upset MEPs too much, and, on the other hand, being aware that a revised text might break up a majority attained in the Council at first reading.

10. CONCLUSION

There is a story often told about the consequences of the Reform Act 1832 which modified the franchise in the United Kingdom. This legislation was not radical in its immediate impact. Even after its passage only 5 per cent of the population could vote. Its main impact was to enfranchise the better-off within the towns by giving the vote to the £10 householder. Its longer-term effects were greater. The previous franchise system was unjust and illogical, but it did have the weight of history behind it. The system post-1832 was based

[141] See above, 60.

[142] See above, 124–7.

[143] N. Nugent, *The Government and Politics of the European Union* (3rd edn., MacMillan 1994), 325.

on no real principle at all. If the £10 householder could vote, then why not the £5 householder too?

There are 'lessons' here for the distribution of political power within the Community. The existing regime of legislative competence is, as we have seen, the result of political compromise. The overall pattern of legislative authority has not proven to be stable, in large part because it, like the franchise in the United Kingdom post-1832, is not based on any principled criterion as such. The Parliament has pressed for greater legislative power, and obtained it, albeit only in small doses and not to the extent to which it would like. Each Treaty revision has witnessed further changes in the legislative process. The Parliament has won stronger powers for itself, and has negotiated also for an increase in the number of areas in which the Article 189b and assent procedures apply. And yet the status quo is neither principled nor stable. There are already murmurings that the Parliament will press for further legislative authority at the 1996 Inter-Governmental Conference, using its powers of approval for potential new members of the Community as the bargaining chip with the Council. It is, of course, true that the very definition of a 'principled' solution to the pattern of legislative authority within the Community is a contestable issue on which people will disagree. What is reasonably clear is that there are two key components in the resolution of this matter one way or another: the nature of Parliament's role in the legislative process and the right of legislative initiative.

As to the former, Parliament's aim is to have a true, co-equal status with the Council. In procedural terms this would entail the generalization of the assent procedure, or something akin thereto, to a much wider number of areas. The TEU has, as we have seen, made some modest, but important, steps in this direction. Future Treaty revisions are likely to see the Parliament attempting to build on this foundation.

As to the latter, the matter is, if anything, more problematic. In many respects the Commission and the Parliament have been allies in furthering integration within the Community. The Parliament has indeed, in its many blueprints for constitutional reform, been willing to accept that the Commission should be regarded as the executive in a Community in which the Parliament and the Council have co-equal legislative status. Much turns, however, on what one means by ascribing the label 'executive' to the Commission. This is demonstrated by the fact that the Parliament pressed hard in the 1990–1 Inter-Governmental Conference for a limited, but automatic, right of legislative initiative. The response of the Commission is captured by Westlake:[144]

> The Commission could not accept such an inroad, however circumscribed, believing its sole right of initiative to be a fundamental constitutional prerogative vital to the good functioning of the Community's institutional balance and its legislative machinery.

[144] N. 66 above, 79.

The idea that the Commission should be perceived as the executive is none the less problematic in the long term, in so far as this entails the Commission's retention of the right of legislative initiative. This is in part because of Parliament's opposition. It is in part because of the very status of the Commission itself. It is common in domestic political systems for the balance of power as between the legislative and executive branches to differ, in both *de jure* and *de facto* terms. One only has to compare countries such as the United Kingdom, France, Germany, and the United States for this to become apparent. But in none of these systems does the right of legislative initiative vest in an unelected institution. And the Commission is not elected. Nor is this fact altered by the greater say that the Parliament now has over the appointment of the Commission.

Now it might be argued by way of response that the Commission is merely giving effect to the policies contained in the Treaty itself. This may well be so in a general sense, but it provides no conclusive answer to the argument made above. The Treaty objectives are often set out at a high level of generality. How one chooses to flesh these out, both in terms of the priority accorded to the fulfilment of differing Treaty objectives and the content of those policies, involves real choices, which are unavoidably political in nature. To regard the Commission as a body of Platonic guardians, neutrally giving effect to Treaty objectives, is to miss the contentious, value-laden quality of the process of agenda-setting and legislative initiation.

A different response might be to contend that the retention of the legislative initiative by the Commission does not matter too much since it and the Parliament have commonly been on the same 'side' and of the same 'mind', in the sense that both institutions are pro-integrationist. This response may well have some empirical validity. But it is no more a conclusive answer than that considered above. This is in part because these two institutions have not in fact always been of the same mind. It is in part because the general ascription of the term pro-integrationist, or pro-federalist, to the Parliament and the Commission serves to conceal as much as it reveals. The reason is obvious once stated: it is perfectly possible for a number of people all to be pro-integrationist, or pro-federalist, in a general sense, but to differ markedly as to the best way to attain this end. A right-of-centre approach to the problems of regional policy in the Community may differ markedly from one which would be espoused by those of a more centrist or left-of-centre leaning. The proponents of each of these views may be pro-integrationist or pro-federalist, but they might disagree significantly as to what the best federal solution to a problem actually is. Difficulties of this nature are likely to increase as the scope of Community action encompasses yet broader areas, more particularly in the broadly social and political sphere. The potential for conflict between the Parliament and Commission as to the best way forward for the Community will be ever-present.

Time will tell how the pattern of legislative competence within the Community unfolds. The next round of Treaty revision will, in all probability, result in further, pragmatic political accommodation between the three institutions. If this 'works' then the fact that it does not accord with perfect principle may not matter too much. It will, however, be unlikely to be any more stable over the medium term than have the arrangements up until now. The European Parliament 'was born hungry and frustrated and has developed into an habitual struggler'.[145] It is not likely to cease striving and become quiescent. If it does succeed in attaining co-equal legislative status with the Council, then it will probably turn more of its firepower to the issue of the legislative initiative. If it were to prove successful on this then the implications for the overall balance of power within the Community would be significant indeed.

The danger is of course that a Parliament possessed of the legislative initiative might operate as a market for interest-group bargaining in a way which would be damaging to Community goals. It may well then be necessary for us to develop a political structure which allows the Commission to retain the legislative initiative while making the Commission both procedurally and substantively accountable for the exercise of such power.

11. FURTHER READING

GEORGE, S., *Politics and Policy in the European Community* (2nd ed., Oxford, 1991)

JACOBS, F., CORBETT, R., and SHACKLETON, M., *The European Parliament* (2nd edn., Longman, 1992)

LODGE, J. (ed.), *The European Community and the Challenge of the Future* (2nd edn., Pinter, 1993)

LOUIS, J.-V., and WAELBROECK, D. (eds.), *Le Parlement Européen dans L'Evolution Institutionelle* (1989)

MAZEY, S., and RICHARDSON, J. J. (eds.), *Lobbying in the European Community* (Oxford, 1993)

NUGENT, N., *The Government and Politics of the European Union* (3rd edn., Macmillan, 1994)

O'KEEFFE, D., and TWOMEY, P. M. (eds.), *Legal Issues of the Maastricht Treaty* (Chancery, 1994)

PEDLER, R. H., and VAN SCHENDELEN, M. P. C. M. (eds.), *Lobbying the European Union: Companies, Trade Associations and Issue Groups* (Dartmouth, 1994)

PRYCE, R. (ed.), *The Dynamics of European Union* (Croom Helm, 1987)

RAWORTH, M. P., *The Legislative Process in the European Community* (Kluwer, 1993)

WALLACE, W. (ed.), *The Dynamics of European Integration* (RIIA/Pinter, 1990)

WESTLAKE, M., *The Commission and the Parliament: Partners and Rivals in the European Policy-Making Process* (Butterworths, 1994)

—— *A Modern Guide to the European Parliament* (Pinter, 1994)

[145] M. Westlake, *A Modern Guide to the European Parliament* (Pinter, 1994), 28.

4

The Nature of EC Law: Direct and Indirect Effect

1. INTRODUCTION

One of the most remarkable features of European Community law, and the feature which has probably attracted most attention to the functioning of the Community legal system, is the impact it has had on the legal and political integration of the Member States. By way of contrast with other international organizations of states such as the Council of Europe or the United Nations, the European Community has created an organization of states with an autonomous legal system, a system of norms which bind each of the states and which have been internalized into the domestic systems of the different states as a uniform body of law. Much of this development has been brought about not by the express agreement of the states which founded the Community nor by means of a detailed blueprint for an integrated Community legal system, but through the interpretive practice and influence of the European Court of Justice. Through its case law, the Court has developed a bold theory of the nature of European Community law, attributing to it the characteristics and force which it considered necessary to carry through a set of profoundly altering and potentially far-reaching common goals within a group of politically and geographically distinct nations and historically sovereign states. The success of this development depended upon a very different approach from that which has governed the domestic treatment of norms of international law between states.

The domestic effect of an international agreement or treaty has traditionally been a matter to be determined in accordance with the constitutional law of each of the states which is party to that treaty. In countries like the United Kingdom which adopt a dualist approach to international law, international agreements and treaties do not of themselves give rise to rights or interests which citizens of the states which are party to such treaties can plead and have enforced before their national courts. Even if they are designed for the protection of individuals (as, for example, in the case of the European Convention on Human Rights) the provisions of these treaties bind only the states at an inter-governmental level, and in the absence of implementation, cannot be domestically invoked or enforced by citizens.[1]

[1] See D. Wyatt, 'New Legal Order or Old' (1982) 7 ELRev. 147.

The texts of the EC Treaties make no reference to the effect which their provisions are to have, and it is apparent from arguments made in the early cases before the Court that at least some of the Member States did not envisage that the provisions of these Treaties would be any different, in terms of their domestic effect, from other international treaties and conventions. The Court, however, took a rather different approach to the nature and effect of the EC Treaties, an approach which was based on the Court's vision of the kind of Community which those Treaties had set out to create, and the kind of legal system which the effective creation of such a Community would necessitate. This view became clear in one of its most important decisions—perhaps the most famous of all of the Court's decisions—in which it outlined the doctrine of what has become known as the 'direct effect' of Community law.

Case 26/62, N.V. Algemene Transporten Expeditie Onderneming van Gend en Loos v. Nederlandse Administratie der Belastingen [1963] ECR 1; [1963] CMLR 105.

The Van Gend en Loos company had imported a quantity of chemical substance from Germany into the Netherlands. It was charged by Customs and Excise with an import duty which the company alleged had been increased (by changing the tariff classification of the substance from one with a lower to a higher tariff-heading) since the time of coming into force of the EEC Treaty, contrary to Article 12 of that Treaty. An appeal against payment of the duty was brought before the Dutch Tariefcommissie, and Article 12 was raised in argument. The Tariefcommissie referred two questions to the Court of Justice under Article 177 of the Treaty, asking in the first 'whether Article 12 of the EEC Treaty has direct application within the territory of a Member State, in other words, whether nationals of such a State can, on the basis of the Article in question, lay claim to individual rights which the courts must protect'.

Observations in the case were submitted to the Court of Justice by the Belgian, German and Netherlands governments. The Belgian Government argued that the question was one of whether a national law ratifying an international Treaty would prevail over another law, and that this was a question of national constitutional law which lay within the exclusive jurisdiction of the Netherlands court. The Netherlands government also argued that the EEC Treaty was no different from a standard international Treaty, and that the concept of direct effect would contradict the intentions of those who had created the Treaty. It warned of the possibility of the states refusing to cooperate if the Court of Justice decided that a Treaty Article could indeed be invoked by individuals before national courts.

THE ECJ[2]

To ascertain whether the provisions of an international treaty extend so far in their effects it is necessary to consider the spirit, the general scheme and the wording of those provisions.

The objective of the EEC Treaty, which is to establish a Common Market, the functioning of which is of direct concern to interested parties in the Community,

[2] [1963] ECR 1, 12.

implies that this Treaty is more than an agreement which merely creates mutual obligations between the contracting states. This view is confirmed by the preamble to the Treaty which refers not only to governments but to peoples. It is also confirmed more specifically by the establishment of institutions endowed with sovereign rights, the exercise of which affects Member States and also their citizens. Furthermore, it must be noted that the nationals of the states brought together in the Community are called upon to cooperate in the functioning of this Community through the intermediary of the European Parliament and the Economic and Social Committee . . .

The conclusion to be drawn from this is that the Community constitutes a new legal order of international law for the benefit of which the states have limited their sovereign rights, albeit within limited fields, and the subjects of which comprise not only Member States but also their nationals. Independently of the legislation of Member States, Community law therefore not only imposes obligations on individuals but is also intended to confer upon them rights which become part of their legal heritage. These rights arise not only where they are expressly granted by the Treaty, but also by reason of obligations which the Treaty imposes in a clearly defined way upon individuals as well as upon the Member States and upon the institutions of the Community.

Van Gend en Loos was a ground-breaking judgment. The strong submissions made on behalf of the three governments which intervened in the case,(at the time there were, in all, only six Member States) indicate that the concept of direct effect—the immediate enforceability in national courts by individual applicants—of Treaty provisions, probably did not accord with the intention or understanding of those states of the obligations they had assumed when they became parties to the EEC Treaty. Compare with the Court's judgment the opinion of the Advocate General who, although he agreed that certain Treaty provisions could produce direct effects, concluded that Article 12 was not one of these. He evidently considered that to hold Article 12 to be directly effective could lead to a non-uniform application of that Article by different courts amongst the Member States.

ADVOCATE GENERAL ROEMER[3]

The effect of an international treaty depends in the first place on the legal force which its authors intended its individual provisions to have, whether they are to be merely programmes or declarations of intent, or obligations to act on the international plane or whether some of them are to have a direct effect on the legal system of Member States . . .

Very impressively, [the Commission] submitted that, judged by the international law of contract and by the general legal practice between States, the European Treaties represent a far-reaching legal innovation and that it would be wrong to consider them in the light only of the general principles of the law of nations . . .

Having regard to this situation it is in my opinion doubtful whether the authors,

[3] *Ibid.* 19, 20, 24.

when dealing with a provision of such importance to customs law, intended to produce the consequences of an uneven development of the law involved in the principle of direct application, consequences which do not accord with an essential aim of the Community.

It can be seen that the Court of Justice in the case reasoned in part by reference to the text of the Treaty itself, but most markedly by reference to a vision of the kind of legal Community that the Treaties seemed designed to create. *Van Gend en Loos* provides an early example of the Court of Justice's distinctive interpretive approach and methodology. Variously referred to as instrumentalist, purposive, or teleological, this method of interpretation involves the Court reading the text—and the gaps in the text—of the Treaty in such a way as to further what it sees as the underlying and continuing aims of the Community enterprise as a whole. Of course, one of the problems with this methodology is that so many aspects of that enterprise and its legitimate scope are neither articulated nor clearly expressed in the Treaties, and these matters continue to generate very heated debate and disagreement. Given that the actual provisions of the Treaty set out the Community's aims in very broad and general terms, the textual constraints on the Court's decision-making are often weak. Thus the teleological approach of the Court is controversial, and its decisions are not always well received in the Member States.

In *Van Gend* itself, the Court based its elaboration of the concept of direct effect principally upon the kind of legal order the Treaties were 'intended' to create, in the sense of looking to the kind of legal system which would be necessary to carry through in different Member States the political and legislative programme outlined in those documents. Pierre Pescatore, a former judge of the Court, has commented on the *Van Gend* ruling in the following way:

P. Pescatore, The Doctrine of 'Direct Effect': An Infant Disease of Community Law[4]

It appears from these considerations that in the opinion of the Court, the Treaty has created a Community not only of States but also of peoples and persons and that therefore not only Member States but also individuals must be visualised as being subjects of Community law. This is the consequence of a democratic ideal, meaning that in the Community, as well as in a modern constitutional State, Governments may not say any more what they are used to doing in international law: *L'Etat, c'est moi.* Far from it; the Community calls for participation of everybody, with the result that private individuals are not only liable to burdens and obligations, but that they have also prerogatives and rights which must be legally protected. It was thus a highly political idea, drawn from a perception of the constitutional system of the Community, which is at the basis of *Van Gend en Loos* and which continues to inspire the whole doctrine flowing from it.

[4] (1983) 8 ELRev. 155, 158.

Apart from its invocation of the 'spirit' of the Treaties, the Court in *Van Gend* also attempted to draw on the text—in particular on the Preamble and Article 177 of what was then the EEC Treaty—in support of the specific concept of direct effect, or direct applicability, as the Court termed it. The preamble makes reference to citizens as well as to states, and the Court concluded also that the preliminary-ruling procedure set out in Article 177 envisages that parties before national courts would be pleading and relying on points of EC law. The Court pointed also to the fact that citizens were envisaged as having a role to play under the Treaties through the medium of the European Parliament. None of this textual 'evidence' for direct effect is particularly strong, however, and the Court's elaboration of the aims of the Treaties provides a better explanation (if not a justification) of its decision to conclude that Article 12 could be invoked and enforced by Van Gend before the Dutch courts. The Court clearly considered that a strong enforcement method was needed to ensure that Member States did in practice comply with the provisions to which they had agreed. To this effect, automatic internalization of Treaty rules into national legal systems would strengthen the force and effectiveness of Community norms as well as aiding the Commission in its Article 169 enforcement function by involving individuals and all levels of the national court system directly in their implementation.

P. P. Craig, Once upon a Time in the West: Direct Effect and the Federalization of EEC Law[5]

Legal systems have two principal mechanisms through which to enforce the norms which comprise the system. They may choose to rely on public enforcement by the state or an organ thereof. To rely solely on this species of enforcement can, however, be inefficient, inefficacious, or both. The reasons for this may differ depending on the precise legal area which is in question . . . Notwithstanding these differences of detail, it is common for public enforcement *per se* to generate problems which cause a legal system to supplement it by allowing private actions brought by individuals. The experience within the EEC provides a particularly good example of this phenomenon. The particular problems with public enforcement in the EEC, and the way in which these were ameliorated or solved by the addition of private enforcement, are both interesting and instructive.

The various drawbacks of the public enforcement mechanism of the Community, and in particular its weakness in so far as the vindication or enforcement of an individual right is concerned, are considered in some detail in chapter 9. For present purposes, however, we need merely note that Commission proceedings against Member States for breach of Treaty obligations are often quite political in nature, they are beyond the control of aggrieved individuals, and until recently they lacked any formal legal sanction or 'bite'. Consequently, the Court presumably perceived a demand for a more

[5] (1992) 12 OJLS 453.

effective method of private enforcement in which individuals could play a role.

2. THE CONDITIONS FOR DIRECT EFFECT

If integration, effectiveness, and uniformity were amongst the essential motivating factors behind the attribution of direct effect to provisions of Community law, the Court recognized that there could be practical limitations to this approach. If the idea is that the same Community goals should be pursued similarly in all states, then national courts in all of the Member States must be capable of appreciating the exact scope and meaning of the provisions of Community law in question, so that they may be applied to the context of the case in which they are pleaded. If a provision is vague, if it sets out only a very general aim which needs further fleshing out or implementation to be made concrete and clear, then it is difficult to accord direct effect to that provision and to allow its direct application by a national court. In the first place, its interpretation and application by different national courts in different states would be likely to differ, thus undermining the uniform pursuit of the same goals. And in the second place, if the national courts were to flesh out a provision which clearly required further elaboration or discretion in its implementation, those courts would be usurping the role of whichever authority—be it the Member States or one of the Community institutions—was entrusted with the power of implementing that provision.

Probably in view of these concerns, and also perhaps to introduce the idea of direct effect in a manner more restrained and more palatable to those states which were opposed to it, the Court in *Van Gend en Loos* (see above) set out certain criteria for the direct effect of a Treaty provision:

> The wording of Article 12 contains a clear and unconditional prohibition which is not a positive but a negative obligation. This obligation, moreover, is not qualified by any reservation on the part of states which would make its implementation conditional upon a positive legislative measure enacted under national law. The very nature of this prohibition makes it ideally adapted to produce direct effects in the legal relationship between Member States and their subjects.
>
> The implementation of Article 12 does not require any legislative intervention on the part of the states. The fact that under this Article it is the Member States who are made the subject of the negative obligation does not imply that their nationals cannot benefit from this obligation . . .
>
> It follows from the foregoing considerations that, according to the spirit, the general scheme and the wording of the Treaty, Article 12 must be interpreted as producing direct effects and creating individual rights which national courts must protect.[6]

[6] N. 2 above, 13.

Thus the characteristics of Article 12 of the EC Treaty which satisfied the Court that it was capable of 'direct application' were that it was *clear, negative, unconditional, containing no reservation on the part of the Member State, and not dependent on any national implementing measure*. Pescatore has argued that these criteria in fact are simply conditions of justiciability, set out to ensure that national courts could apply the laws without undue uncertainty or complexity in cases arising before them.[7]

Pescatore, The Doctrine of 'Direct Effect': An Infant Disease of Community Law[8]

It appears thus in the last analysis that the prerequisite of the unconditional character and the sufficient degree of precision of Community provisions, in order to be recognised as having 'direct effect', boil down to a question of justiciability. A rule can have direct effect whenever its characteristics are such that it is capable of judicial adjudication, account being taken both of its legal characteristics and of the ascertainment of the facts on which the application of each particular rule has to rely. This means that 'direct effect' of Community rules in the last analysis depends less on the intrinsic qualities of the rules concerned than on the *possumus* or *non possumus* of the judges in the different Member States, on the assumption that they take these attitudes in a spirit of goodwill and with a constructive mind.

To this extent, direct effect appears to be in a way *l'art du possible*, as from the point of view of Community law it is to be expected that national courts are willing to carry the operation of the rules of Community law up to the limits of what appears to be feasible, considering the nature of their judicial function. Within these bounds a rule has direct effect, whereas beyond them this effect must be denied.

So, for example, if the terms of a provision are not clearly defined or are dependent upon the exercise of further discretionary power, national courts will face difficulties in attempting to apply that provision properly and in a manner consistent with the way in which it is being applied in other Member States. The arguments of the German Government in the later case of *Becker*, provide a good summary of the reasons for these conditions:

(g) If the provision in question of the directive leaves the Member State concerned a margin of discretion regarding its implementation, the existence of personal rights must be denied owing to the specific role of the courts, including both the Court of Justice and the national courts, which is to uphold the law. It would be incompatible with that role if they were to assume the political discretion of the Member States. Justification for the exclusion of personal rights may also be

[7] Van Gerven A.G. has suggested that the test for direct effect is whether a provision of Community law is 'sufficiently operational' in itself to be applied by a court: case C–128/92, *Banks* v. *British Coal* [1994] ECR I–1209, 1237, [1994] 5 CMLR 30.

[8] N. 4 above, 176–7.

found in the principle of legal certainty, which requires that the legal effects arising under a legal system should be clearly defined . . .

(j) The need for clear and unconditional rules overlaps with the requirement that it must no longer be necessary to adopt further provisions, of Community or national law, in as much as the rules laid down by the directive must disclose unambiguously their legal effects without the need for adaption of national law.[9]

However, as Pescatore's comments suggest, the Court's elaboration of these specific criteria for direct effect has not hindered its extension to a very wide range of Treaty provisions, and, as we shall see, to many other forms of Community law. Where Treaty provisions have seemed too broad or general, the Court has found ways of severing or considering separately the less precise parts. It has purported to interpret the unconditional and negative part of a Treaty provision, even where another part of that provision imposed on the states a general and less precise positive obligation, thus enabling the part which was deemed sufficiently clear and exact to be applied directly by the national court. This can be seen in the following case:

Case 6/64, Flaminio Costa v. Enel
[1964] ECR 585, [1964] CMLR 425

Costa was an Italian electricity consumer and a shareholder of an electricity company which had been affected by an Italian law nationalising the electricity industry. In legal proceedings before the Giudice Conciliatore in Milan, he claimed that this law infringed various provisions of the EEC Treaty, including Articles 37, 53, 93 and 102. Article 37(1) was a provision which did not impose a precise obligation on Member States to abolish commercial State monopolies, but which specified instead that they should be progressively adjusted over a period of time. A reference was made to the Court of Justice under Article 177, and although the Italian judge had not formulated its question appropriately, the Court of Justice held that the question being asked was whether the Treaty provisions in the case produced direct effects and created individual rights which national courts had to enforce.

THE ECJ[10]

Article 37(1) provides that Member States shall progressively adjust any State monopolies of a commercial character so as to ensure that no discrimination regarding the conditions under which goods are procured and marketed exists between nationals of Member States. By Article 37(2), the Member States are under an obligation to refrain from introducing any new measure which is contrary to the principles laid down in Article 37(1) . . .

Article 37(2) contains an absolute prohibition: not an obligation to do something but an obligation to refrain from doing something. This obligation is not accompanied by any reservation which might make its implementation subject to any positive act of national law. This prohibition is essentially one which is cap-

[9] Case 8/81, *Becker* v. *Finanzamt Münster-Innenstadt* [1982] ECR 53, [1982] CMLR 499, see the arguments of the German Government in the written observations submitted to the Court.
[10] [1964] ECR 585, 597.

able of producing direct effects on the legal relations between Member States and their nationals.

Such a clearly expressed prohibition which came into force with the Treaty throughout the Community, and so became an integral part of the legal system of the Member States, forms part of the law of those States and directly concerns their nationals, in whose favour it creates individual rights which national courts must protect.

We shall see that the criteria of precision, unconditionality, and the absence of a need for further implementing measures have not been closely adhered to by the Court. Article 52 of the EC Treaty, for example, provides that restrictions on freedom of establishment of Community nationals in states other than that of their nationality are to be abolished 'within the framework of the provisions set out below'. The framework in question was to have included a general programme and a set of directives adopted under Articles 54(2) and 57(1) to liberalize the categories of activities of employed and self-employed persons, but few of these had in fact been adopted by the time the *Reyners* case arose in 1973:

Case 2/74, Reyners v. Belgium
[1974] ECR 631, [1974] 2 CMLR 305

Jean Reyners was a Dutch national who obtained his legal education in Belgium, but was refused admission to the Belgian Bar (to the profession of *avocat*) solely on the ground that he was not of Belgian nationality. He challenged the relevant Belgian legislation before the Conseil d'Etat, which referred several questions to the Court of Justice under Article 177, including the question whether Article 52 was directly effective in the absence of implementing directives under Articles 54 and 57.

THE ECJ

24. The rule on equal treatment with nationals is one of the fundamental legal provisions of the Community.

25. As a reference to a set of legislative provisions effectively applied by the country of establishment to its own nationals, this rule is, by its essence, capable of being directly invoked by nationals of all the other Member States.

26. In laying down that freedom of establishment shall be attained at the end of the transitional period, Article 52 thus imposes an obligation to attain a precise result, the fulfilment of which had to be made easier by, but not made dependent on, the implementation of a programme of progressive measures.

27. The fact that this progression has not been adhered to leaves the obligation itself intact beyond the end of the period provided for its fulfilment . . .

. . .

29. It is not possible to invoke against such an effect the fact that the Council has failed to issue the directive provided for by Articles 54 and 57 or the fact that certain of the directives actually issued have not fully attained the objective of non-discrimination required by Article 52.

30. After the expiry of the transitional period the directives provided for by the

Chapter on the right of establishment have become superfluous with regard to implementing the rule on nationality, since this is henceforth sanctioned by the Treaty itself with direct effect.

31. These directives have however not lost all interest since they preserve an important scope in the field of measures intended to make easier the effective exercise of the right of freedom of establishment.

In this case the Court was determined to ensure that, despite the slow pace of harmonization of national laws in the field of freedom of movement and establishment of self-employed people, the Treaty itself could be invoked by individuals affected in order to claim equal treatment or to challenge obvious instances of nationality-discrimination in the state in which they were establishing themselves. Thus the principle of non-discrimination was held to be directly effective, even though the conditions for genuine freedom of establishment were far from being achieved. Whereas many cases on direct effect concern the enforcement of obligations against a defaulting Member State which has failed to properly implement Community requirements (*Van Gend*, *Costa* v. *Enel*, and *Defrenne No 2*[11]), the *Reyners* case on the other hand shows the Court employing the direct effect concept to compensate for insufficient activity on the part of the Community's legislative institutions. Quite obviously, as long as genuine disparities in professional qualifications and other legislative requirements in different Member States remain as a substantial barrier to freedom of establishment, the 'core principle' of non-discrimination in Article 52 will be of little practical use to non-nationals affected by such disparities, unless directives have been passed at Community level to harmonize the relevant requirements as between different Member States. Without such harmonizing legislation in place, it is difficult to allege that discrimination—a breach of Article 52—has in fact occurred. Indeed, four of the Member States argued in *Reyners* that the Court should not ignore the absence of directives and should not declare Article 52 of itself to be directly effective, since it was not 'for the courts to exercise a discretionary power reserved to the legislative institutions of the Community and the Member States'. Despite these arguments, however, the Court made clear that where there were no such disparities between the laws of two Member States, yet one of the states specifically treated non-nationals less favourably on grounds of nationality, then the principle of Article 52 could be directly invoked by the affected individual regardless of the absence of any implementing directives.

ADVOCATE GENERAL ROEMER[12]

Finally it is proper to enquire whether by inviting the Council to issue certain directives to implement Article 52, the draftsmen of the Treaty have given it a

[11] Case 43/75, *Defrenne* v. *Société Anonyme Belge de Navigation Aerienne* [1976] ECR 455, [1976] 2 CMLR 98.

[12] [1974] ECR 631, 663.

margin of discretionary power such that the effective fulfilment of the obligations which this Article imposes would have been possible only by means of these measures . . .

Article 52, however, imposed on it in any event an obligation to achieve a particular state of affairs by a particular date. The Council did not have the power either to escape this obligation or to alter its content.

The Member States had the same obligation to achieve this state of affairs, with the same conditions, and the failure of the Council to take certain prescribed implementing measures within the period specified did not in any way authorize them to set themselves against the principle which it contains.

P. P. Craig, Once Upon a Time in the West: Direct Effect and the Federalization of EEC Law[13]

The consequence of the ECJ's decision in *Reyners* is that the court is adopting a legislative role. The very nature of the divide between 'adjudicatory' functions and 'legislative' functions is, of course, fraught with definitional and conceptual difficulty . . .

The sense in which the ECJ can be said to be undertaking a legislative-type role is as follows. Article 52 enshrines a principle which is then to be further filled out by a plethora of legislation made by the Commission and the Council. This legislation has not in fact emerged by the designated date for reasons which will be examined below. The decision by the ECJ to accord Article 52 direct effect even though the legislation has not been promulgated requires the court to undertake a legislative function itself in the following manner. A 'visual metaphor' may help in understanding this. Let us imagine that the totality of the relevant rules on freedom of establishment is represented by a chess board. Article 52, the core principle of the area, is the boundary of the board, while the particular squares thereof represent the detailed rules which should be enacted by the Commission and the Council. These squares are however blank because the legislation has not emerged. The decision by the ECJ means that it will have the task of filling in the appropriate squares. Cases will come to the court from the national court under Article 177 as a result of Article 52 having been given direct effect. The questions posed will often refer to matters which should have, but have not, been resolved by Community legislation; the relevant square on our chess board is blank. The ECJ will provide an answer to such enquiries and will in that sense fill in the appropriate square. It functions as a surrogate legislature when the 'real' legislature is unable to perform the tasks assigned to it.

The use of direct effect to kick-start the proper implementation of a Treaty provision in respect of which both Community and states have been slow to act can also be seen in another Belgian case, *Defrenne* v. *Sabena* (the second *Defrenne* case),[14] which arose a few years after *Reyners*. The *Defrenne* ruling can be seen to relax further the criteria for direct effect originally set out by the Court in *Van Gend en Loos*. Whereas in *Reyners*, the Treaty Article in question seemed explicitly to envisage further implementing measures, the relevant Article in *Defrenne* appeared to lack sufficient precision to be relied on

[13] N. 5 above, 464–5. [14] Case 43/75, n. 11 above.

by an individual and directly enforced by a national court. The provision in dispute was Article 119, which requires Member States to ensure 'the application of the principle that men and women should receive equal pay for equal work'.[15] In contrast to the Treaty provisions in cases like *Van Gend* and *Costa*, Article 119 does not appear as a precise and straightforward negative obligation imposed on the Member States. For example, the term 'principle' is not very specific, nor are the terms 'pay' and 'equal work' defined. Indeed it appeared from a Commission recommendation of 20 July 1960 and a resolution of the Member States of 30 December 1961 concerning proposed methods of implementing Article 119 that neither the Commission nor the states considered that provision to be directly effective or legally complete.[16]

Case 43/75, Defrenne v. Société Anonyme Belge de Navigation Aerienne [1976] ECR 455, [1976] 2 CMLR 98

Gabrielle Defrenne brought an action for compensation against Sabena, the company which employed her as an air hostess, on the ground of discrimination in pay as compared with male colleagues who were doing the same job. Since the airline did not dispute that the work done by male stewards and female air hostesses was identical, or that there was discrimination in terms of pay, the question referred to the Court of Justice was whether Article 119 was directly effective.

ADVOCATE GENERAL TRABUCCHI[17]

Although the form of the words used: 'principle that men and women should receive equal pay' may seem too vague and the meaning of the word 'principle' itself not to be very specific, the purpose of the rule is nevertheless clear: to prohibit any discrimination to the detriment of women with regard to pay.

It can be argued that, even though Article 119 defines the concept of pay for the purposes of equality, the definition given of it is not so complete as to exclude all doubt about the precise meaning of the rule. Under the case law of the Court, however, the fact that the concepts relied upon in a provision require interpretation by the national court, which may, *inter alia*, avail itself of the procedure in Article 177 of the Treaty, constitutes no obstacle to recognition of its direct effect . . .

Apart from cases where work which is not identical has to be established as being of equal value, which could undoubtedly give rise to fairly complicated assessments on the part, in the first place, of the legislature, the application of Article 119 does not necessarily require the adoption of implementing legislation in circumstances . . . where work which is undoubtedly identical is differently rewarded on grounds of sex.

THE ECJ

7. The question of the direct effect of Article 119 must be considered in the light of the nature of the principle of equal pay, the aim of this provision and its place in the scheme of the Treaty . . .

18. For the purposes of the implementation of these provisions a distinction must be drawn within the whole area of application of Article 119 between, first,

[15] See further Ch. 18 on Equal Treatment of Women and Men.

[16] See Trabucchi A.G. in Case 43/75, n. 11 above, 485. [17] *Ibid.* 486–7.

direct and overt discrimination which may be identified solely with the aid of the criteria based on equal work and equal pay referred to by the article in question and secondly, indirect and disguised discrimination which can only be identified by reference to more explicit implementing provisions of a Community or national character.

19. It is impossible not to recognize that the complete implementation of the aim pursued by Article 119, by means of the elimination of all discrimination, direct or indirect, between men and women workers, not only as regards individual undertakings but also entire branches of industry and even of the economic system as a whole, may in certain cases involve the elaboration of criteria whose implementation necessitates the taking of appropriate measures at Community and national level . . .

. . .

28. First of all, it is impossible to put forward an argument against its direct effect based on the use in this article of the word 'principle', since, in the language of the Treaty, this term is specifically used in order to indicate the fundamental nature of certain provisions, as is shown, for example, by the heading of the first part of the Treaty which is devoted to 'Principles' and by Article 113, according to which the commercial policy of the Community is to be based on 'uniform principles' . . .

. . .

30. It is also impossible to put forward arguments based on the fact that Article 119 only refers expressly to 'Member States'.

31. Indeed, as the Court has already found in other contexts, the fact that certain provisions of the Treaty are formally addressed to the Member States does not prevent rights from being conferred at the same time on any individual who has an interest in the performance of the duties thus laid down . . .

What the Court did in *Defrenne*, then, was to isolate the principle of Article 119—that of equal pay for equal work—and to ignore the fact that there could be cases involving complex questions regarding 'work of equal value' in the context of jobs which are quite different in nature. In the latter sort of case there might well not be sufficient precision or clarity to enable the national court to apply Article 119 directly nor to afford a remedy to the worker in question, but that would not affect the direct effectiveness of the core principle of Article 119 in cases where the factual issues were clearly determined.

Clearly, the Court's concern in these direct effect cases was to ensure that the Community's aims were not ignored either by reluctant Member States or by politically sluggish Community institutions, during the years of legislative sclerosis which followed the Luxembourg Accords.[18] Out of broadly worded provisions, the Court derived binding 'core principles', and the absence of important harmonizing legislation or the presence of limitations on the precision of various measures did not deter it from extending the entitlement of individuals to rely in domestic litigation on an increasingly wide range of Treaty provisions. As can be seen from the comment of Advocate General Trabucchi above, if a national court was unsure as to the exact meaning of

[18] See Ch. 1.

the relevant provision, the Court would be more than willing to clarify its scope for that court in a preliminary ruling under Article 177. Occasionally, too, the Court would temper the effects of one of its particularly significant rulings to take account of the concerns of states which were responsible for a delay in the implementation of Community requirements. Thus in *Defrenne*, for example, in response to the concerns of the United Kingdom and Irish Governments about the financial implications of the equal pay ruling under Article 119, the Court limited the retroactivity of its ruling and held that Article 119 could only be relied upon by workers in legal proceedings already commenced prior to the date of its *Defrenne* ruling.[19]

And despite its apparent concern to advance the application and effectiveness of Treaty provisions which have not been properly implemented or followed, the Court has shown that there are limits to its willingness to find precision of purpose in the text of a very broadly phrased provision. In certain cases, even the Court with its integrationist bias will not require national courts to give content to a particularly vague or aspirational Treaty provision.[20] Quite apart from the lack of uniformity and uncertainty to which it could give rise, such a requirement, in the absence of some more specific implementing measures at Community level, would involve too great a transfer of political discretion and legislative power to the national courts.

Case 126/86, Zaera v. Institutio Nacionale de la Seguridad Social [1987] ECR 3697, [1989] 1 CMLR 827

Mr Zaera wished to challenge a rule of Spanish law which prohibited him from holding a post in the public service at the same time as being in receipt of a retirement pension. The Tribunal Central, to which he had appealed his case, referred several questions to the Court of Justice. One of the questions asked whether Articles 2, 117, and 118 of the Treaty prevented a state from introducing a national rule which prohibited the overlapping of a retirement pension with the emoluments of a public servant, and which accordingly reduced the income of the person concerned.

THE ECJ

10. Article 2 of the Treaty describes the task of the European Economic Community. The aims laid down in that provision are concerned with the existence and functioning of the Community; they are to be achieved through the establishment of the Common Market and the progressive approximation of the economic policies of Member States, which are also aims whose implementation is the essential object of the Treaty.

11. With regard to the promotion of an accelerated raising of the standard of living, in particular, it should therefore be stated that this was one of the aims

[19] See also Case C–262/88, *Barber* v. *Guardian Royal Exchange Assurance Group* [1990] ECR I–1889, [1990] 2 CMLR 513, discussed in detail in Ch. 18.

[20] See Case C–236/92, *Comitato di Coordinamento per la Difesa della Cava* v. *Regione Lombardia* [1994] ECR I–483 for an example of a dir. on waste disposal which was held by the Court not to be sufficiently precise or unconditional to give rise to direct effect.

which inspired the creation of the European Economic Community and which, owing to its general terms and its systematic dependence on the establishment of the Common Market and progressive approximation of economic policies, cannot impose legal obligations on Member States or confer rights on individuals.

ADVOCATE GENERAL MANCINI[21]

Article 2 provides that 'the Community shall have as its task, by establishing a common market and progressively approximating the economic policy of Member States, to promote . . . an accelerated raising of the standard of living'. It thus repeats the undertaking contained in the third recital in the preamble to the Treaty . . . and reaffirms it by upgrading the 'efforts' to be made to a 'task' and by stating the instruments by which that task is to be accomplished. However, it is impossible to say that such instruments are attributed any specific legal character, let alone binding force. As has been correctly stated, the rule 'contains expressions of intent, purpose and motive, rather than rules that are of direct operative effect' . . .

There is therefore no obligation on the states and, consequently, no right upon which individuals can rely against the states.

3. THE DIRECT EFFECT OF MEASURES OTHER THAN TREATY PROVISIONS

Apart from the provisions of the Treaties, which are seen as the foundational or constitutional basis of the Community,[22] there are various other sources of Community law. The specific forms of legislative action which the Community institutions may adopt are set out in Article 189 of the EC Treaty, the most important of these being regulations and directives. The Community also has external competence to enter into agreements with countries outside the EC[23] (such as association agreements under Article 238, or trade agreements such as those within the GATT and under Article 113) and with other international organizations, which then constitute Community acts forming part of its legal order. A further, and increasingly important, source of Community law is what the Court refers to as the 'general principles' and fundamental rights deriving from the common traditions and constitutional rules shared by the Member States,[24] and from international agreements and conventions to which they are all party.[25] So far, the direct effect of Treaty provisions has been discussed, but what of these other sources of Community law?

[21] [1987] ECR 3697, 3708–9.

[22] See para. 3 of the judgment in Case 294/83, *Parti Ecologiste 'Les Verts'* v. *Parliament,*[1986] ECR 1339, [1987] 2 CMLR 343 and para. 21 of Opinion 1/91 (Draft Treaty on a European Economic Area) [1991] ECR 6079, [1992] 1 CMLR 245.

[23] For further discussion see T. C. Hartley, *The Foundations of European Community Law* (3rd edn., Oxford, 1994), Ch. 6.

[24] See Chs. 7 and 8.

[25] See in particular Case 11/70, *Internationale Handelsgesellschaft* [1970] ECR 1125, [1972] CMLR 255.

(a) Regulations and Decisions

It has been seen that the textual basis in the EC Treaty for the conclusion that Treaty provisions could have direct effect was not strong. However, Article 189 of the Treaty provides that, in the case of a regulation, the measure 'shall be binding in its entirety and directly applicable in all Member States'. Policy considerations aside, this language seems to envisage that regulations, at least, will immediately become part of the domestic law of the Member States, and presumably that they are capable then of being relied upon by individuals in national courts, and subject to direct enforcement by those courts.[26]

Case 39/72, Commission v. Italy
[1973] ECR 101, [1973] CMLR 439

The Commission by a series of regulations instituted a system of premiums for slaughtering cows and for withholding milk products from the market. It considered that Italy was in breach of the regulations since Italy had not properly applied or given effect to the premium system in its territory. The Commission brought infringement proceedings against Italy under Article 169, claiming that both the delay and the eventual manner of giving effect to the system were in breach of Community obligations and of the Commission Regulations.

THE ECJ

17. By following this procedure, the Italian Government has brought into doubt both the legal nature of the applicable provisions and the date of their coming into force.

According to the terms of Article 189 and 191 of the Treaty, Regulations are, as such, directly applicable in all Member States and come into force solely by virtue of their publication in the *Official Journal* of the Communities, as from the date specified in them, or in the absence thereof, as from the date provided in the Treaty.

Consequently, all methods of implementation are contrary to the Treaty which would have the result of creating an obstacle to the direct effect of Community Regulations and of jeopardizing their simultaneous and uniform application in the whole of the Community . . .

20. According to the third paragraph of Article 43(2) of the Treaty, on which Regulation No 1975/69 is founded, Regulations are validly enacted by the Council as soon as the conditions contained in the Article are fulfilled.

Under the terms of Article 189, the Regulation is binding 'in its entirety' for Member States.

In consequence, it cannot be accepted that a Member State should apply in an incomplete or selective manner provisions of a Community Regulation so as to render abortive certain aspects of Community legislation which it has opposed or which it considers contrary to its national interests.

[26] There has been considerable discussion of the possible differences in meaning of the terms 'direct applicability' and 'direct effect', although the ECJ has used them interchangeably. See T. Winter 'Direct Applicability and Direct Effects' (1972) 9 CMLRev. 425 and see Warner A.G. in Case 131/79 *Santillo* [1980] ECR 1585, 1608–9, [1980] 2 CMLR 308.

In this case the Court emphatically confirmed the direct effect of regulations and strongly disapproved of any attempt by a Member State to alter or dilute the requirements of a Community regulation. This does not necessarily mean, however, that any national measure enacted with the intention of giving effect to a regulation will be invalid. It is only if the national measure alters, obstructs or obscures the nature of the Community regulation that it will constitute a breach of Community law.

Case 50/76, Amsterdam Bulb BV v. Produktschap voor Siergewassen [1977] ECR 137, [1977] 2 CMLR 218

A set of Community regulations on the common organization of the market in bulbs and other plants, provided in part for the introduction of a system of minimum prices for the export to third countries of bulbs. A Dutch company which exported bulbs to the United States objected to a Dutch Export Price Order under which it could apply for, but had been refused, an exemption from the application of minimum prices. The company argued before the national court that the national measure was incompatible with the Community regulations and a question was referred to the Court of Justice, asking whether one of the regulations forbade a Member State authority from adopting rules conforming only partly to that regulation but also containing provisions—such as the power to grant exemptions, and to impose sanctions for breach—which were not at all based on the Community measure.

THE ECJ

4. As the Court has already stated in other contexts, in particular in its judgment of 10 October 1973 (*Variola SpA* v. *Amministrazione Italiana delle Finanze* [1973] ECR 981), the direct application of a Community Regulation means that its entry into force and its application in favour of or against those subject to it are independent of any measure of reception into national law.

5. By virtue of the obligations arising from the Treaty the Member States are under a duty not to obstruct the direct effect inherent in regulations and other rules of Community law.

6. Strict compliance with this obligation is an indispensable condition of simultaneous and uniform application of Community regulations throughout the Community.

7. Therefore, the Member States may neither adopt nor allow national organizations having legislative power to adopt any measure which would conceal the Community nature and effects of any legal provision from the person to whom it applies.

The Court's concern here was that, by taking steps to transpose a regulation into national law, a Member State might obscure the fact that the provision was one of Community law. This could have adverse consequences for the Community, since the particular qualities of Community law—that it takes priority over conflicting national law, that there must be adequate remedies for breach, that it might be subject to different methods of interpretation from those traditionally used in the national context, etc.—may be ignored. Further, the Court was clearly concerned that Member States might alter or adversely affect the content of the regulation by adopting measures to transpose it into national law in a slightly different form. However, the Court in the *Amsterdam Bulb* case itself did accept that Member States could provide for appropriate sanctions in national legislation to assist in the enforcement of the regulation, and that the domestic legislation in that case could legitimately continue to regulate aspects of various bulb sizes which were not specifically covered in the regulation.

Another of the forms of Community act listed under Article 189 is that of a decision, which is to be 'binding in its entirety upon those to whom it is addressed'. Unlike a regulation, a decision will not be a general measure but an individual one which is directed to a specific addressee. The Court had little hesitation in holding that decisions, too, could be directly effective, despite the fact that, unlike in the case of regulations, Article 189 made no reference to their 'direct applicability'.

Case 9/70, Franz Grad v. Finanzamt Traunstein
[1970] ECR 825, [1971] CMLR 1

A German Finanzgericht in Munich referred a question to the Court of Justice under Article 177, asking whether various Council decisions on turnover taxes and VAT, in conjunction with a Council directive governing the date from which the tax systems were to apply, could be directly effective. The plaintiff had sought to rely directly on these provisions before the Finanzgericht in order to have a German law on transport tax declared incompatible with them.

THE ECJ

4. The German Government in its observations defends the view that by distinguishing between the effects of regulations on the one hand and of decisions and directives on the other, Article 189 precludes the possibility of decisions and directives producing the effects mentioned in the question, which are reserved to regulations.

5. However, although it is true that by virtue of Article 189, regulations are directly applicable and therefore by virtue of their nature capable of producing direct effects, it does not follow from this that other categories of legal measures mentioned in that article can never produce similar effects. In particular, the provision according to which decisions are binding in their entirety on those to whom they are addressed enables the question to be put whether the obligation created by the decision can only be invoked by the Community institutions against the addressee or whether such a right may possibly be exercised by all those who have an interest in the fulfilment of this obligation. It would be incompatible with the binding effect attributed to decisions by Article 189 to exclude in principle the possibility that persons affected may invoke the obligation imposed by a decision. Particularly in cases where, for example, the Community authorities by means of a decision have imposed an obligation on a Member State or all the Member States to act in a certain way, the effectiveness (*l'effet utile*) of such a measure would be weakened if the nationals of that State could not invoke it in the courts

and the national courts could not take it into consideration as part of Community law. Although the effects of a decision may not be identical with those of a provision contained in a regulation, this difference does not exclude the possibility that the end result, namely the right of the individual to invoke the measure before the courts, may be the same as that of a directly applicable provision of a regulation.

In that case the Court held that the obligation imposed in the decision in question was sufficiently unconditional, clear, and precise to be capable of giving rise to direct effect.

(b) International Agreements

By virtue of Articles 210 and 228 of the EC Treaty, the Community has legal personality and is empowered to enter into contractual relations with other persons and organizations. Further, specific Articles of the Treaty, such as Article 113 on commercial policy and Article 238 on 'association' agreements, expressly give the Community external powers to enter particular agreements with countries and organizations outside the Community itself. And in the famous *ERTA* case,[27] the Court of Justice held that, apart from the express powers given in the Treaty, the Community also had the power (the external competence), whenever this was necessary to fulfil one of the aims of the Treaty, to enter into international agreements across the entire field of 'internal' competence accorded to it by the Treaty. The question which followed from this was: what was to be the legal effect of such agreements? On the one hand, as Treaties concluded with other states or international organizations, they could be seen as traditional international agreements binding only the states or organizations which signed them and having no effect upon individuals. On the other hand, as acts of the Community, there could be attributed to them some of the specific characteristics of EC law, such as that they could be directly effective and enforceable at the suit of individual litigants whenever sufficiently precise and unconditional. Opting for the approach which would make the actions and agreements of the Community more effective and harmonious as between different Member States, the Court held that international agreements can, in certain circumstances, be directly effective.

Cases 21–24/72, International Fruit Company v. Produktschap voor Groenten en Fruit [1972] ECR 1219, [1975] 2 CMLR 1

The plaintiffs brought proceedings before a Dutch court seeking the annulment of the Dutch agency's rejection of their application for import licences for apples from third countries. They had been refused the relevant import certificates on the basis of several Community regulations which governed that area. The plaintiffs alleged, amongst other things, that the Community measures were incompatible

[27] Case 22/70, *Commission* v. *Council* [1971] ECR 263, [1971] CMLR 335.

with a particular provision of the General Agreement on Tariffs and Trade (GATT). This was an agreement to which all Member States were party prior to joining the European Community. The Dutch court asked the Court of Justice whether the impugned regulations were contrary to the provisions of GATT, and indeed whether the Court of Justice had jurisdiction under Article 177 to rule on the validity of a Community measure against a measure of international law.

ADVOCATE GENERAL MAYRAS[28]

It is therefore necessary to examine whether Article XI of GATT has direct effect in the Community system . . .
There are serious reasons for thinking that this is not the case . . .
I consider first that by the General Agreement the states undertook only to adopt a particular line of conduct in commercial policy, that they did not intend to establish directly applicable rules which the national courts must protect, even when it conflicts with a domestic law; secondly, that the procedures prescribed by GATT for the settlement of conflicts arising through its application also exclude the concept of direct effect.

THE ECJ

7. Before the incompatibility of a Community measure with a provision of international law can affect the validity of that measure, the Community must first of all be bound by that provision.

8. Before invalidity can be relied upon before a national court, that provision of international law must also be capable of conferring rights on citizens of the Community which they can invoke before the courts . . .

. . .

18. It therefore appears that, in so far as under the EEC Treaty the Community has assumed the powers previously exercised by Member States in the area governed by the General Agreement, the provisions of that agreement have the effect of binding the Community.

19. It is also necessary to examine whether the provisions of the General Agreement confer rights on citizens of the Community on which they can rely before the courts in contesting the validity of a Community measure.

20. For this purpose, the spirit, the general scheme and the terms of the General Agreement must be considered.

Following a similar line of reasoning to that of the Advocate General, the Court considered various aspects of GATT, including the 'great flexibility of its provisions', the possibilities of derogation, and the power of unilateral withdrawal from its obligations. Having done so, it concluded that the General Agreement 'is not capable of conferring on citizens of the Community rights which they can invoke before the courts'. The Court's reasoning can be understood in the following way. In Community law, it has held that provisions will have direct effect when they have a clear and binding aim, do not involve the exercise of broad discretionary powers, and are 'legally complete'. And although the Court wishes to show that it will ensure the observation and enforcement in

[28] [1972] ECR 1219, 1237–8.

national courts of the Community's international obligations, it takes the view that the provisions of GATT allow for too much flexibility and modification of obligations to be sufficiently concrete and unconditional in their content.[29] It is also worthy of note that in cases in which the direct effect of GATT provisions has been pleaded, these provisions have generally been invoked in order to argue that a provision of Community law was incompatible therewith, and this is not a conclusion which the Court will often be willing to reach.[30]

In a case decided some ten years after the *International Fruit Company* case, the Court was confronted with a similar question in the context of an international free trade agreement between the Community and Portugal, before that state had joined the Community.

Case 270/80, Polydor Ltd. and RSO Records Inc v. Harlequin Record Shops Ltd. and Simons Records Ltd [1982] ECR 329, [1982] 1 CMLR 677

The plaintiffs brought an action against Harlequin and Simons for infringement of copyright, seeking to restrain them from importing from Portugal and selling copies of certain records in the United Kingdom, where Polydor held the exclusive licence to sell and distribute the relevant recordings. Harlequin and Simons, in their defence, sought to rely on certain provisions of the agreement between Portugal and the Community which prohibited measures having an effect equivalent to quantitative restrictions. These provisions were similar to Articles 30 and 36 of the EEC Treaty on free movement of goods, but Harlequin and Simons argued that the interpretation of the EEC provisions should not be the same as those under the agreement with Portugal. A reference was made from the Court of Appeal to the Court of Justice for an interpretation of the relevant provisions of the agreement.

THE ECJ

18. The considerations which led to that interpretation of Articles 30 and 36 of the Treaty do not apply in the context of the relations between the Community and Portugal as defined by the Agreement. It is apparent from an examination of the Agreement that . . . it does not have the same purpose as the EEC Treaty, inasmuch as the latter, as has been stated above, seeks to create a single market reproducing as closely as possible the conditions of a domestic market.

. . .

29 See, however, J. Scott, 'The GATT and Community Law: Rethinking the Regulatory Gap' in *New Legal Dynamics of European Union*, ed. J. Shaw and G. More (forthcoming) who argues that after the conclusion of the 1994 GATT agreement and the establishment of the World Trade Organization with more effective means of enforcement, it may be difficult for the Court to continue to deny the direct effect of GATT provisions.

30 In Case C–69/89, *Nakajima* v. *Council* [1991] ECR 2069, the Court ruled that provisions of international agreements need not be directly effective, but need only be binding on the Community, in order for an applicant to argue that Community legislation is incompatible with them. Unsurprisingly, the Court ruled that the Community anti-dumping rules in issue did not conflict with the Anti-Dumping Code adopted under the provisions of GATT. See, however, case C–280/93, *Germany* v. *Commission*, judgment of 5 Oct. 1994, in which the Court held that a GATT rule could only be invoked in this way if the Community intended to implement that obligation, or if the Community measure being challenged expressly referred to the provision of GATT.

20. In the present case such a distinction is all the more necessary inasmuch as the instruments which the Community has at its disposal in order to achieve the uniform application of Community law and the progressive abolition of legislative disparities within the common market have no equivalent in the context of the relations between the Community and Portugal.

In this case, the difference between the free trade agreement with Portugal and the single-market system set up by the Community, with its legislative and executive institutions and its integrated legal system, led the Court to the conclusion that even similarly worded provisions in two such different agreements could not be given the same meaning or effect.

Despite such cases where the Court has denied the direct effect of specific international agreements or treaties, however, its recognition of the possibility of the direct effect of international agreements has not remained purely a matter of theory. In *Hauptzollamt Mainz* v. *Kupferberg*,[31] the Court held that a different provision of the free trade agreement with Portugal was directly effective, since the provision was unconditional, sufficiently precise, and its direct application was within the purpose of the agreement. It is worthy of note that, unlike in the GATT case discussed above, according direct effect to the agreement in *Kupferberg* had the effect of extending the scope of Community rules rather than challenging them.

The Court's extension of direct effect to international agreements has not gone without criticism. Several Member States have argued to the Court that the principle of reciprocity which applies to international agreements would be breached if Member States were required directly to enforce the provisions of such an agreement in national courts when the other party to the agreement need not do so. The Court in response ruled, somewhat unconvincingly, that although the principle of reciprocity required contracting parties to execute fully the commitments they had undertaken, this did not necessarily require direct application of the agreement in question since the parties remained free to decide how its aims should be achieved within their own legal systems. Other criticisms have been made of the Court's apparent readiness to extend direct effect to the realm of international law.

G. Bebr, Agreements concluded by the Community and their Possible Direct Effect: From International Fruit Company to Kupferberg[32]

Before analysing the very heart of the problem, [the Court] dealt with two ancillary points. First, it characterized, for the first time, the nature and scope of the obligations assumed by the Member States under an agreement concluded exclusively by the Community. In the Court's opinion, the Member States accepted, in such an instance, a double obligation: first an obligation towards the Community which is responsible for the proper execution of such an agreement; the other

[31] Case 104/81 [1982] ECR 3641, [1983] 1 CMLR 1.

[32] (1983) 20 CMLRev. 35, 60. Footnotes are omitted from the passage quoted.

towards the third State. Although the Court did not explicitly state so, the former obligation of the Member States could be viewed as a Community obligation resulting from the limited transfer of the treaty-making power by the Member States to the Community . . . Secondly, considering such an agreement to form an integral part of the Community legal order, the Court reaffirmed the vital need to ensure a uniform interpretation and application of Community agreements throughout the Community.

. . . The direct effect of a Community rule is the general rule in the Community legal order rather than the exception. This effect conferring enforceable Community rights on individuals is derived from the specificity of the Community legal order and developed in the light of its unprecedented objectives. It may, therefore, be doubtful whether one of the fundamental principles, as actually developed within this genuine, autonomous legal Community, could be transposed without any further restriction and qualification to the loose international legal system governed by different principles and concepts. Thus it could hardly be maintained that international law (despite its efforts to strengthen the status of individuals) or the practice of national courts recognize the self-executing nature of international agreements as a general rule as the Court does when interpreting Community rules.

. . . All that is suggested is that the differences between the Community legal order and the international legal system be recognized and the necessary consequences be drawn therefrom, not only for the meaning of a provision of a Community agreement but also for its effect.

The Court, however, has continued to recognize the direct effect of provisions of certain international agreements, in particular of the so-called association agreements concluded with countries which hope eventually to join the Community as a full member. The context and aim of these agreements are not necessarily so very different from those of the Treaties, since they usually represent a stage in the process of eventual accession to the Community by the state in question. Again, as in the case of *Polydor* and by contrast with the GATT case, the direct effect of the provisions adopted under the agreement in the following case was not pleaded in order to challenge Community law, but in order to extend the principles of Community law to cover a situation involving a national from a non-Member State.[33] Further, it was not even a provision of an international agreement to which the Community was party whose direct effect was pleaded in this case, but rather a decision which was adopted by a Council of Association which had been set up by the Turkey–EC Agreement.

Case C–192/89, S.Z. Sevince v. Staatsecretaris van Justitie [1990] ECR I–3461, [1992] 2 CMLR 57

Mr Sevince, a Turkish national living in The Netherlands, had appealed from a decision of the Staatsecretaris rejecting his application for a new residence permit.

[33] See also Cases C–237/91, *Kus* v. *Landeshauptstadt Wiesbaden* [1992] ECR I–6781, [1993] 2 CMLR 887 and C–355/93, *Eroglu* v. *Land Baden-Württemberg*, [1994] ECR I–5113.

Certain provisions of the Association Agreement between Turkey and the Community followed the principles set out in the chapter of the EEC Treaty on the free movement of workers, and the EEC–Turkey Association Council which was set up under the former Agreement had adopted certain decisions to implement its objectives. Sevince relied in his application upon two decisions of the Association Council, by virtue of which a Turkish worker was entitled, under certain conditions, to free access to any employment of his or her choice. On appeal, the Dutch court referred several questions to the Court of Justice.

THE ECJ

8. By way of a preliminary observation, it should be borne in mind that, as the Court has consistently held, the provisions of an agreement concluded by the Council under Articles 228 and 238 of the EEC Treaty form an integral part of the Community legal system as from the entry into force of that agreement . . .

9. The Court has also held that, since they are directly connected with the Agreement to which they give effect, the decisions of the Council of Association, in the same way as the Agreement itself, form an integral part, as from their entry into force, of the Community legal system . . .

. . .

15. In *Demirel* (Case 12/86 [1987] ECR 3719), the Court held that a provision in an agreement concluded by the Community with non-member countries must be regarded as being directly applicable when, regard being had to its wording and the purpose and nature of the agreement itself, the provision contains a clear and precise obligation which is not subject, in its implementation or effects, to the adoption of any subsequent measure. The same criteria apply in determining whether the provisions of a decision of the Council of Association can have direct effect.

However, although the Court has increasingly recognized the direct effect of provisions of such agreements and decisions, this did not always improve the position of the applicants—usually 'third country' workers—in such cases. In the earlier *Demirel* case, although the Court held that the provisions of the Agreement could be directly effective, the right of the applicant, who was a Turkish national, to remain in Germany with her family after expiration of her visa was held not to be covered by the provisions of the agreement.[34] In *Sevince*, by contrast, the decisions which had been adopted by the Council of Association did cover the right of access to employment claimed by the applicant, but the Court concluded that, if his residence permit had been revoked and he was no longer in 'legal employment', he could not avail of that right.[35]

[34] Case 12/86, *Demirel* v. *Stadt Schwäbisch Gmünd* [1987] ECR 3719, [1989] 1 CMLR 421, discussed further in Ch. 7. See also, however, Case C–355/93 n. 33 above.

[35] For cases in which migrant workers had more success in claiming directly effective rights, see Cases C–18/90, *Onem* v. *Kziber* [1991] ECR I–199 and 58/93, *Yousfi* v. *Belgium* [1994] ECR I–1353 on the EEC–Morocco Co-operation Agreement, and Cases C–237/91 and C–355/93, both n. 33 above, on decisions of the Council of Association of the EC–Turkey Agreement.

(c) Directives

The best argument supplied by the Court for the direct effect of Treaty provisions was that the fundamental aims of the Treaty would be seriously hampered if its clear provisions could not be domestically enforced by those it affected and governed. In the case of the provisions of international agreements, the explanation was that direct effect was important in order to ensure respect in every Member State for the commitments of the Community arising from agreements concluded with non-member countries. The explanation for the direct effect of regulations was less teleological and more straightforwardly textual: Article 189 specifically provided for their direct applicability, which the Court treated as being synonymous with direct effectiveness. In the case of decisions, the Court seemed to take the view that, since they were intended to be binding upon the addressee, then if the terms of a measure were sufficiently clear, there was no reason why that decision should not be directly relied upon and enforced before a national court.

The position of directives under the Treaty, however, is rather different. Under Article 189, a directive 'shall be binding as to the result to be achieved, upon each Member State to which it is addressed, but shall leave to the national authorities the choice of form and methods'. Unlike in the case of regulations or decisions, national implementation of directives is specifically envisaged and considered necessary by the Treaty. The provisions of a directive may represent a compromise which is the result of prolonged negotiations between Member States on a complex matter—often a matter of harmonizing divergent bodies of law in different Member States—and in respect of which certain discretionary options may be left open to the states. Eventual implementation may not and need not be uniform in every Member State, although the central and uniform aim of the directive must be properly secured in each. From this brief description, it would immediately appear that some of the Court's criteria for direct effect are missing. A directive may well leave some discretion to the Member States; it will always require further implementing measures according to the express terms of Article 189, and since it may only set out its aim in general terms, it may not be sufficiently precise to allow for proper national judicial enforcement.

These factors, however, did not deter the Court from considering whether directives might nevertheless give rise to direct effects. The policies which first prompted the Court to develop the idea of the direct effect of Treaty provisions were equally strong here: those of legal integration and effectiveness. Under the Treaty, many important areas of Community policy rely for their practical realization on the proper implementation of Community directives. If States are failing or refusing for any reason to implement such measures, those Community policies will suffer, and the overall progress of the Community's aims may be seriously undermined. Thus the Court's inclination is strong, especially at the suit of aggrieved individuals before a national court who have become aware of the favourable provisions of a directive, to encourage the national court to enforce the provisions of the directive directly, even in the absence of its domestic legislative implementation.

While it provides us with an explanation, however, the Court's policy of furthering the effectiveness of directives by declaring them to be capable of direct effect does not solve the question of how this policy can be reconciled with the Court's earlier criteria for direct effect—the requirements of precision, unconditionality, the absence of discretion, and the absence of a need for further implementing measures. This issue was faced in a case where the provisions of a directive left the Member States with a certain area of discretion as to what restrictive measures they could deem to be necessary in order to secure the interests of national public policy. The Court repeated many of the arguments it had made in support of the direct effect of decisions in its judgment in the *Grad* case, above,[36] adapting these somewhat to accommodate the specific character of directives.

Case 41/74, Van Duyn v. Home Office [1974] ECR1337, [1975] 1 C.MLR 1

Yvonne Van Duyn was a Dutch national who had come to the UK to take up an offer of employment with the Church of Scientology, an organization which was officially regarded by the British Government as socially harmful, although no legal restrictions were placed upon its practices. Van Duyn was refused leave to enter the UK on account of her plans to work for the Church of Scientology. She challenged this refusal on the basis of Article 48 of the EEC Treaty, Regulation 1612/68, and Directive 64/221, all of which regulate the freedom of movement of workers within the Community. The High Court referred several questions to the Court of Justice, asking amongst other things whether Directive 64/221, which governed the kinds of restrictions on the free movement of workers which Member States remained free to adopt, was directly effective.

THE ECJ

12 . . . It would be incompatible with the binding effect attributed to a directive by Article 189 to exclude, in principle, the possibility that the obligation which it imposes may be invoked by those concerned. In particular, where the Community authorities have, by directive, imposed on Member States the obligation to pursue a particular course of conduct, the useful effect of such an act would be weakened if individuals were prevented from relying on it before their national courts and if the latter were prevented from taking it into consideration as an element of Community law. Article 177, which empowers national courts to refer to the Court questions concerning the validity and interpretation of all acts of the Community institutions, without distinction, implies furthermore that these acts may be invoked by individuals in the national courts. It is necessary to examine, in every case, whether the nature, general scheme and wording of the provision in question are capable of having direct effects on the relations between Member States and individuals.

[36] Case 9/70, *Franz Grad* v. *Finanzamt Traunstein* [1970] ECR 825, [1971] CMLR 1, para. 5 of the judgment.

The thrust of the Court's argument in this passage is that, if directives are binding, then the possibility of relying on them directly before national courts cannot be ruled out, and each provision must be examined in its context to see whether the obligation it imposes or the right it creates is sufficiently clear and exact to be capable of being applied directly by a national court. The problem with Directive 64/221 was that it allowed Member States to take measures restricting the movement of non-nationals on the ground of public policy, and it did not define the permissible range of public policy concerns, leaving this for each Member State to regulate in accordance with its own cultural, social, and political traditions. But did this not leave too much discretion to the state for a national court to be able to say that the Directive prohibited a given state from adopting a particular restrictive national measure? The Court in *Van Duyn* did not think so:

> 23. By providing that measures taken on grounds of public policy shall be based on the personal conduct of the individual concerned, Article 3(1) of Directive No. 64/221 is intended to limit the discretionary power which national laws generally confer on the authorities responsible for the entry and expulsion of foreign nationals. First, the provision lays down an obligation which is not subject to any exception or condition and which, by its very nature, does not require the intervention of any act on the part either of the institutions of the Community or of Member States. Secondly, because Member States are thereby obliged, in implementing a clause which derogates from one of the fundamental principles of the Treaty in favour of individuals, not to take account of factors extraneous to personal conduct, legal certainty for the persons concerned requires that they should be able to rely on this obligation even though it has been laid down in a legislative act which has no automatic direct effect in its entirety.
>
> 24. If the meaning and exact scope of the provision raise questions of interpretation, these questions can be resolved by the courts, taking into account also the procedure under Article 177 of the Treaty.

Despite the fact that the concept of public policy within Article 48(3) of the Treaty, which the Directive was designed to implement, is a discretionary matter for Member States to decide, the Court found that the exercise of that discretion was restricted by a provision of the Directive which imposed a clear, precise, and 'complete' obligation. But again, what comes through most strongly in the judgment is the desire to make directives an effective form of Community law, to further their aims, and above all to enable persons affected by their provisions to avail themselves of their protection by having them enforced before national courts.

The case was not, however, a uniformly popular one, and some of the Member States felt that the Court had gone too far in advancing its conception of Community law at the expense of the clear language of the Treaty, and the obvious limitations on directives as a form of legislation. It was felt that directives were specifically intended to leave the Member States with choices as to how to enact a particular Community obligation, and that the Court should not allow this to be by-passed by individuals pleading the provisions of the directive itself.

From its general reasoning in *Van Duyn* that there was no reason in principle why directives could not have direct effect, the Court added a more specific line of reasoning in later cases. This was based on the argument that their refusal to fulfil the Treaty obligation to implement a directive properly or on time precluded the Member States from refusing to recognize its binding effect in cases where it was pleaded by an individual against them.

Case 148/78, Pubblico Ministero v. Tullio Ratti [1979] ECR 1629, [1980] 1 CMLR 96

Mr Ratti's Italian company had begun packaging and labelling its containers of solvents in accordance with two Council directives regulating the area. These directives had not yet been implemented in Italy, and the requirements of the Italian legislation on the matter were more stringent than those under the Directive, and provided for penalties for those who failed to comply. Criminal proceedings were instituted against Ratti under the domestic legislation in Milan, and he relied in his defence on the Community Directives. A preliminary reference was made to the Court of Justice asking whether the provisions of the Directive were directly effective.

ADVOCATE GENERAL REISCHL[37]

However, it is clear from the Treaty and has also been emphasized again and again in the case-law that a clear distinction must be drawn between regulations and directives, the latter creating obligations only for the Member States. So under no circumstances can one say—as the defendant in the main action has said—that directives may also have the content and effects of a regulation; at most directives may produce *similar* effects . . . The essence of such effects is that in certain cases, which however constitute the exception to the rule, Member States which do not comply with their obligations under the directive are unable to rely on provisions of the internal legal order which are illegal from the point of view of Community law, so that individuals become entitled to rely on the directives as against the defaulting State and acquire rights thereunder which national courts must protect.

The Court repeated much of what it said in the *Van Duyn* case about the possibility of direct effect for directives (see paragraph 12 of the judgment above), but proceeded then to emphasize the default of the Member States.

THE ECJ

22. Consequently a Member State which has not adopted the implementing measures required by the directive in the prescribed periods may not rely, as against individuals, on its own failure to perform the obligations which the directive entails.

[37] [1979] ECR 1629, 1650.

23. It follows that a national court requested by a person who has complied with the provisions of a directive not to apply a national provision incompatible with the directive not incorporated into the internal legal order of a defaulting Member State, must uphold that request if the obligation in question is unconditional and sufficiently precise.

The Italian court had also asked whether the Directive could be directly relied upon by an individual even before the time limit given to Member States for its implementation had expired. The Court answered as follows:

43. It follows that, for the reasons expounded in the grounds of the answer to the national court's first question, it is only at the end of the prescribed period and in the event of the Member State's default that the directive . . . will be able to have the effects described in the answer to the first question.

44. Until that date the Member States remain free in that field . . .

. . .

46. In conclusion, since a directive by its nature imposes obligations only on Member States, it is not possible for an individual to plead the principle of 'legitimate expectation' before the expiry of the period prescribed for implementation.

The argument runs that because the terms of each directive will give Member States a specific date by which implementation must be assured, the provisions of the directive cannot be pleaded directly by individuals before that date. Until then, the discretion of the Member State as to the 'choice of form and methods' which is provided for in Article 189 of the Treaty will be respected. But the direct effect of the directive comes about by virtue of the state's failure to implement the measure by that date, because by such failure the state forfeits the discretion granted to it under Article 189 and is 'estopped' from relying on conflicting provisions of national law as against individuals affected.

Ratti involved a situation in which the direct effect of the provisions of a directive were pleaded in defence of an individual who had been prosecuted by the state under conflicting provisions of national law—a defensive use of the estoppel argument. A few years later, the Court was asked to rule in a case where an individual had herself relied on the provisions of a directive in order to bring proceedings against the state—an active or offensive reliance on the estoppel argument.

Case 8/81, Becker v. Finanzamt Münster-Innenstadt [1982] ECR 53, [1982] 1 CMLR 499

Ursula Becker was a self-employed credit negotiator who requested, in her tax returns for a particular year, certain tax exemptions which were calculated in accordance with a Council directive on the harmonization of turnover taxes. Although the date for implementation of the directive had expired, it had not yet been implemented in Germany. The German Finanzamt argued that it was not directly effective, since it conferred a margin of discretion on the Member States with respect to the manner of implementing the tax exemptions, and that the court would be assuming the political discretion of the State if it purported to enforce the directive in a particular manner. The German Government argued further that since various provisions of the directive pleaded would not be favourable to certain individuals, that they could not have effect until the Member State clearly implemented them.

THE ECJ

19. It follows that wherever a directive is correctly implemented, its effects extend to individuals through the medium of the implementing measures adopted by the Member State concerned . . .

20. However, special problems arise where a Member State has failed to implement a directive correctly and, more particularly, where the provisions of the directive have not been implemented by the end of the period prescribed for that purpose . . .

. . .

25. Thus, wherever the provisions of a directive appear, as far as their subject-matter is concerned, to be unconditional and sufficiently precise, those provisions may, in the absence of implementing measures adopted within the prescribed period, be relied upon as against any national provision which is incompatible with the directive or in so far as the provisions define rights which individuals are able to assert against the State . . .

. . .

29. Whilst the Sixth Directive undoubtedly confers upon the Member States varying degrees of discretion as regards implementing certain of its provisions, individuals may not for that reason be denied the right to rely on any provisions which owing to their particular subject-matter are capable of being severed from the general body of provisions and applied separately. This minimum guarantee for persons adversely affected by the failure to implement the Directive is a consequence of the binding nature of the obligation imposed on the Member States by the third paragraph of Article 189 of the Treaty. That obligation would be rendered totally ineffectual if the Member States were permitted to annul, as the result of their inactivity, even those effects which certain provisions of a directive are capable of producing by virtue of their subject-matter.

The Court also delivered a sharp rebuke in response to the German Government's argument that 'it would be demanding too much of individuals, administrative authorities and national courts to take it upon themselves to disregard the national law and its penalties and to rely on personal rights arising from the Directive'.

47. As regards the administrative difficulties of a more general nature which are alleged to result from the application of the exemption provided for by the Directive, in a situation in which the tax legislation and administrative practice have not yet been adapted so as to take account of the new factors introduced by Community law, it is sufficient to point out that if such difficulties were to arise, they would be the consequence of the Member State's failure to implement the Directive in question within the period prescribed for that purpose. The consequences of that situation must be borne by the administrative authorities and may not be passed on to

> the tax-payers who rely on the fulfilment of a precise obligation which has been incumbent on the State under Community law since 1 January 1979.

This passage emphasizes the 'punitive' or reactive basis for the direct effect of directives inherent in the Court's approach. Article 189 does not declare directives to be directly applicable, as it does in the case of regulations, and so they do not automatically become part of national law as soon as the Community institutions adopt them. However, they may produce 'similar effects' to regulations (in other words they can have direct effect) when the time limit for their implementation has expired and the state has incorrectly implemented them or has failed altogether to implement them. The conditions of precision, unconditionality, and absence of discretion apparently must be met, but as we have seen the Court is very flexible in its treatment of these criteria. Clearly, for the Court, the concerns of effectiveness and timely, uniform, enforceablility of Community legislation in all states take precedence over concerns about political usurpation, legal certainty, and ease of application by national authorities and courts.

The expansion of direct effect did not, however, continue entirely unchecked. The Court continued to emphasize the distinction between regulations and directives, repeating that the 'direct applicability' of directives was not provided for under Article 189 and that direct effectiveness was a property which directives could acquire only when a Member State failed to comply with the method of implementation provided for under that Article. The distinction became quite stark after the 1986 decision in which the Court decided that the direct effectiveness of directives could only be pleaded by an individual against the state which had failed to implement it, and not against any non-state entity.

Case 152/84, Marshall v. Southampton and South-West Hampshire Area Health Authority (Teaching)
[1986] ECR 723, [1986] 1 CMLR 688

Miss Marshall, a dietician who worked for the respondent Health Authority for fourteen years, was dismissed in 1980 on the ground that she had passed the normal retiring age applicable to women. Under the written policy of the Authority, female employees were to retire at 60 and male employees at 65. Under national legislation, women became eligible for a state pension at 60, whereas men did not become eligible until the age of 65, but that did not impose any obligation to retire at 60, since payment of the state pension or occupational pension would be deferred until actual retirement. Although the 1975 Sex Discrimination Act appeared to exempt matters relating to retirement from its scope, Marshall complained before the Industrial Tribunal that her dismissal violated the provisions of the 1976 Equal Treatment Directive. On appeal, the Court of Appeal referred a question to the Court of Justice asking whether she could rely on the provisions of the Directive notwithstanding the apparent inconsistency between the Directive and the earlier Sex Discrimination Act.

ADVOCATE GENERAL SLYNN[38]

In my opinion the decision in [case 8/81 *Becker* v. *Finanzamt Münster-Innenstadt* [1982] ECR 53] is to be taken as limited to the situation before the Court—where a litigant was held entitled to say that a Member State could not rely on national provisions kept alive by its own failure to adopt a Community directive which would have conferred rights on the litigant. As against the State in default the litigant could assert those rights.

I remain . . . of the view expressed in my opinion in *Becker* that a directive not addressed to an individual cannot of itself impose obligations on him. It is, in cases like the present, addressed to Member States and not to the individual. The obligations imposed by such a directive are on the Member States. Such a directive does not have to be notified to the individual and it is only published in the *Official Journal* by way of information—in my view far too tenuous a link with the individual concerned to create a legal obligation . . .

To give what is called 'horizontal effect' to directives would totally blur the distinction between regulations and directives which the Treaty establishes in Articles 189 and 191 . . .

THE ECJ

48. With regard to the argument that a directive may not be relied upon against an individual, it must be emphasized that according to Article 189 of the EEC Treaty, the binding nature of a directive, which constitutes the basis for the possibility of relying on the directive before a national court, exists only in relation to 'each Member State to which it is addressed'. It follows that a directive may not of itself impose obligations on an individual and that a provision of a directive may not be relied upon as such against such a person.

Although they reached the same conclusion, the Advocate General and the Court differed in their reasoning. Advocate General Slynn seemed to be motivated by two separate concerns: in the first place, that to accord full direct effect to directives would destroy the distinction between directives and regulations; and in the second place, that directives were not required at that time (although it was nevertheless normal in practice) to be notified or published in the Official Journal.[39] The desire to maintain the distinction between regulations and directives may be due to the fact that, in areas of complexity or considerable divergence as between Member States, it can be useful to reach agreement on the basic principles to be achieved, thus avoiding laborious delay in the Community law-making process and leaving the bulk of detail, amendment of existing bodies of legislation, and the provision of appropriate procedures to be brought about through implementation by the Member States. The Advocate General's second reason was a 'rule of law' concern—that since directives, before the TEU, were not required to be notified or published other than to their addressees, individuals might not have known of their provisions and so might

[38] [1986] ECR 723, 734.

[39] Art. 191 was amended by the TEU to provide that dirs. as well as regs. are to be published in the OJ, thus formalizing the existing practice as a requirement.

not have been aware of possible legal obligations under a given directive.[40] While it is true that there are problems of legal certainty which could be created by the so-called 'horizontal' application of directives, these are problems which the Court has surmounted in the case of the direct effect of other kinds of Community law. Directives contain a time limit for their implementation, and this would have to be known to all persons subject to the measure, since up until that date the Member States have a certain discretion as to the means of implementation: however, the requirement of publication resolves this. Another argument has been that directives, even if their 'core principle' is clear and thus directly effective, often leave much to be fleshed out in the various national implementing measures, such as the setting-up of appropriate procedures and remedies for breach, and the adaptation or repeal of existing national legislation in the area. However, this is equally true of the 'vertical' direct effect of directives, and it has not stopped the Court pursuing its quest for effectiveness in the case of Treaty Articles which share similar characteristics.

By way of comparison with the Advocate General, the only reason offered by the Court against developing horizontal direct effect for directives was one based upon the text of Article 189, under which the binding effect of a directive is said to exist only as against the state or states to which it is addressed. This argument is weaker even than those of the Advocate General, especially given the fact the Court normally looks to the exact text of the Treaty simply as one (albeit important) factor in deciding on the interpretation of the relevant provision. There was no explicit weighing by the Court of the need to ensure the effectiveness of directives, as against the text of Article 189 and the fact that they are said to be binding only on the states to which they are addressed. It is interesting to compare the Court's emphasis on the addressee of directives in this context with its approach to the direct effectiveness of certain Treaty Articles which, like directives, are explicitly addressed only to the Member State. Article 119, as was seen above, is addressed to the Member States, providing that states are to apply the principle that men and women shall receive equal pay for equal work.

Case 43/75, Defrenne v. Sabena
[1976] ECR 455, [1976] 2 CMLR 98

ADVOCATE GENERAL TRABUCCHI[41]

A subsidiary argument contended for by the representative of the Commission is to the effect that, from a purely technical standpoint, Article 119 could enable individuals to bring an action which, although admissible, would be upheld only if it were based on discrimination for which, as the employer, the state was responsible, or at least, on systems of payment directly fixed by the national legislative or executive authorities in the country concerned.

[40] See also the Court in Case C–192/89, *Sevince* v. *Staatssecretaris van Justitie* [1990] ECR I–3461, [1992] 2 CMLR 57, para. 24.

[41] N. 11 above, 488.

The above-mentioned arguments seem to me to misconceive the principles of the Community legal order which have been developed by case-law covering more than twenty years.

To begin with, if we were to accept that the provision is directly applicable only against public employers, this would, as was emphasized by the agent of the Irish Government, constitute fresh and unacceptable discrimination between the public and private sectors. The legal status of Sabena and its relationship with the Belgian State have, therefore, no relevance to the present dispute.

THE ECJ

39. In fact, since Article 119 is mandatory in nature, the prohibition on discrimination between men and women applies not only to the action of public authorities, but also extends to all agreements which are intended to regulate paid labour collectively, as well as to contracts between individuals.

This has the effect of undermining some of the force of the Court's textual argument in *Marshall*, since the fact that Article 119 was addressed only to Member States did not affect its application to private employers and individuals as well to the state. More important, in the Advocate General's view, was the unacceptable discrimination between the private and the public sectors which would ensue from such a limitation.

4. GIVING EFFECT TO DIRECTIVES IN OTHER WAYS

However, having imposed this particular 'horizontal' limitation on the scope of the direct effect of directives, the Court nevertheless proceeded to enhance the domestic application of these measures in other ways, in the first place, by expanding the notion of a 'public body' and in the second place by developing a strong principle of interpretation to be applied by national courts.[42]

(a) Broadening the Concept of the State

Despite having introduced into the case this restriction on the direct effect of directives, both the Court and the Advocate General in *Marshall* concluded that the complainant could nevertheless rely on the provisions of the Directive as against the Health Authority, since that body could be regarded as an organ of the state.

[42] See Case 14/83, *Von Colson and Kamann* v. *Land Nordrhein-Westfalen* [1984] ECR 1891, [1986] 2 CMLR 430.

ADVOCATE GENERAL SLYNN[43]

What constitutes the 'State' in a particular national legal system must be a matter for the national court to decide. However . . . as a matter of Community law, where the question of an individual relying upon the provisions of a directive as against the State arises, I consider that the 'State' must be taken broadly, as including all the organs of the State . . .

I would thus reject the argument put to the Court that a distinction should be drawn between the State as employer and the State in some other capacity. For present purposes the State is to be treated as indivisible, whichever of its activities is envisaged.

THE ECJ

49. In that respect it must be pointed out that where a person involved in legal proceedings is able to rely on a directive as against the State he may do so regardless of the capacity in which the latter is acting, whether employer or public authority. In either case it is necessary to prevent the State from taking advantage of its own failure to comply with Community law . . .

51. The argument submitted by the United Kingdom that the possibility of relying on provisions of the directive against the respondent *qua* organ of the State would give rise to an arbitrary and unfair distinction between the rights of State employees and those of private employees does not justify any other conclusion. Such a distinction may easily be avoided if the Member State concerned has correctly implemented the directive into national law.

It is clear from decisions of the Court that the justification for allowing the 'vertical' direct effect of directives against organs of the state is not based upon the responsibility of the particular state organ in question for failure to implement the directive pleaded. Yet if the justification for giving direct effect to directives was a form of estoppel, based on the idea that since the state was responsible for failing properly to implement a directive it could not rely on this failure to resist the applicability of the measure, this justification is unconvincing in the case of a body which has no responsibility for implementing Community legislation.

Nevertheless, the Court has held that direct effect does not simply operate to give a legal argument to the affected individual before a national court, but that state organs, even those far removed from responsibility for implementing directives, are actually bound to apply the provisions of directives in practice.

Case 103/88, Fratelli Costanzo SpA v. Comune di Milano [1989] ECR 1839, [1990] 3 CMLR 239

The plaintiff, Costanzo, contested the procedure for the award of a public works contract in preparation for the 1990 World Cup for football in Italy. After its bid had been excluded by the Comune di Milano (Municipality of Milan) from the

[43] N. 38 above, 735.

tendering procedure under a provision of Italian law, Costanzo claimed that the Italian legislation which was intended to implement a 1971 Council Directive on the award of public-works contracts was in fact incompatible with that Directive. Amongst the questions referred to the Court of Justice by the Tribunale Amministrativo was whether, if the Italian law was found to be incompatible, the municipal authority was bound by the provisions of the Directive itself.

THE ECJ

30. It is important to note that the reason for which an individual may, in the circumstances described above, rely on the provisions of a directive in proceedings before the national courts is that the obligations arising under those provisions are binding upon all the authorities of the Member States.

31. It would, moreover, be contradictory to rule that an individual may rely upon the provisions of a directive which fulfil the conditions defined above in proceedings before the national courts seeking an order against the administrative authorities, and yet to hold that those authorities are under no obligation to apply the provisions of the directive and refrain from applying provisions of national law which conflict with them. It follows that when the conditions under which the Court has held that individuals may rely on the provisions of a directive before the national courts are met, all organs of the administration, including decentralized authorities such as municipalities, are obliged to apply those provisions.

This broad interpretation of what constitutes an organ of the state for the purposes of enforcement of directives has gone some of the way towards ensuring their wider effectiveness, despite the refusal to extend their direct enforceability to relations between individuals or non-state entities in *Marshall*. And even though it has persisted in this refusal throughout its case law, most recently in the *Dori* case,[44] the Court has nevertheless continued to adopt a very expansive concept of the state. One potential problem emerged from the opinion of the Advocate General in the *Marshall* case, when he suggested that it was for each of the Member States to determine what constitutes a public body. Clearly if each state is to apply its own conception of a public body, then the direct application of non-implemented directives is likely to differ very much from state to state, undermining the principles of uniformity and integration. Several commentators have criticized the Court for failing in its decisions to provide adequate guidance on this complex issue.

D. Curtin, The Province of Government: Delimiting the Direct Effect of Directives in the Common Law Context[45]

The basic problem engendered by this abstemious approach is the delimitation one about how widely the parameters of the State fall to be defined: is the split personality of States to be acknowledged or is a strict distinction to be drawn between the State acting in its regulatory capacity in the exercise of its imperium and the State acting in its entrepreneurial capacity as a market participant? In other words

[44] Case C–91/92, *Dori* v. *Recreb Srl* [1994] ECR I–3325. See further below.

[45] (1990) 15 ELRev. 195, 198–9.

can a public authority or a synonym be constituted by a so-called public undertaking or enterprise? If the answer is affirmative then must the public authorities carry out economic activities in a particular legal form such as a statutory corporation or is it also accepted that they can carry on their business activities by participating as a shareholder in a private company incorporated in accordance with the companies legislation? If the latter hypothesis is acceptable then what is the extent of the interest which the State must have? Is there any requirement as to the degree of control *de facto* or *de jure* which the State must be able to exert over the policies and business of the undertaking in question? Must a borderline be drawn between the economic or commercial activity of a public corporation or undertaking and those activities constituting the so-called 'public service' duties performed on behalf of the executive power of the state? . . .

Given the Community context in which the concept of 'public authority' and its synonyms was elaborated it is clear that a uniform meaning in the different Member States must emerge and that it should not be defined by reference to the different legal concepts of the national legal systems.

The Court of Justice addressed the question of what constitutes an 'organ of the state' more directly in a case which involved a nationalized industry.

Case C–188/89, A. Foster and Others v. British Gas plc [1990] ECR I–3313, [1990] 2 CMLR 833

The plaintiffs were employed by British Gas, whose policy it was to require women to retire at 60 and men at 65. Although privatized in 1986, British Gas was, at the time relevant to these proceedings, a nationalized industry with responsibility for and a monopoly of the gas-supply system in Great Britain. The plaintiffs sought to rely against British Gas on the provisions of the 1976 Equal Treatment Directive. Having agreed that the imposition of a discriminatory retirement age breached the Directive, the House of Lords referred a question to the Court of Justice, asking whether British Gas was a body of the kind against which the provisions of the Directive could be invoked.

THE ECJ

18. On the basis of those considerations, the Court has held in a series of cases that unconditional and sufficiently precise provisions of a directive could be relied on against organizations or bodies which were subject to the authority or control of the State or had special powers beyond those which result from the normal rules applicable between individuals.

19. The Court has accordingly held that provisions of a directive could be relied on against tax authorities (the judgments in Case 8/81 *Becker* [1982] ECR 53, Case 221/88 *ECSC* v. *Busseni* [1990] ECR I–495), local or regional authorities (judgment in Case 103/88 *Costanzo* [1989] ECR 1839), constitutionally independent authorities responsible for the maintenance of public order and safety (judgment in Case 222/84 *Johnston* v. *Chief Constable of the RUC* [1986] ECR 1651), and public authorities providing public health services (judgment in Case 152/84 *Marshall* [1986] ECR 723).

20. It follows from the foregoing that a body, whatever its legal form, which

has been made responsible, pursuant to a measure adopted by the State, for providing a public service under the control of the State and has for that purpose special powers beyond those which result from the normal rules applicable in relations between individuals, is included in any event among the bodies against which the provisions of a directive capable of having direct effect may be relied upon.

ADVOCATE GENERAL VAN GERVEN[46]

The point is not who is the State or an individual in the abstract but against whom the failure of a Member State to implement a directive correctly and in good time in its own legal system can be pleaded, having regard to the underlying reasons . . .

Nevertheless it appears from those cases that the concept of a public body must be understood very broadly and that all bodies which pursuant to the constitutional structure of a Member State can exercise any authority over individuals fall within the concept of the 'State'. In that respect it is immaterial how that authority . . . is organised and how the various bodies which exercise that authority are related . . .

The question in the case now before us is how much further the application of those judgments can extend, in particular with regard to undertakings, in this case public undertakings, which as such exercise no authority in the strict sense over individuals. I think the answer is this: it may extend as far as 'the State' (in the broad sense described in the preceding paragraph) has given itself powers which place it in a position to decisively influence the conduct of persons—whatever their nature, public or private, or their sphere of activity—with regard to the subject-matter of the directive which has not been correctly implemented . . .

It is for the national court to apply that criterion in specific cases.

It can be seen that the Advocate General here is attempting to connect the definition and scope of a 'public body' for the purposes of enforcement of directives, with the estoppel justification which was originally used by the Court to develop the direct effect of directives. He refers to the 'underlying reasons' for allowing the fact of failure to implement a directive to be pleaded against certain bodies, and suggests a definition which looks at whether the defaulting state has given itself power (through those bodies) over the conduct of persons with regard to the subject-matter of the non-implemented directive. Of course this definition, too, is problematic, since it does not indicate what kind of control over the body the state must have in order for it to be a body which represents the power of the state. Further, the estoppel argument remains weak, since British Gas could hardly have affected the state's decision as to how and when to implement the Equal Treatment Directive, yet the end result of the *Foster* case would be to allow the plaintiff to rely on the Directive in order to challenge discriminatory retirement ages.

Thus, despite the clear indication in paragraph 20 of the *Foster* ruling that the Court considered a company in the position of British Gas to be an organ

[46] [1990] ECR I–3313, 3333, 3339–40.

of the state, considerable uncertainty remains as to what other bodies and institutions will similarly be held responsible, on account of their connection with the state, for failure to comply with the provisions of non-implemented directives.[47]

E. Szyszczak, Foster v. British Gas[48]

It is now agreed that the question of which kind of public bodies are subject to the binding effects of directives is a question of Community law to be applied by the national courts. The difficulty with this approach is that the Court does not give any indication of the criteria to be applied by the national courts but instead has issued a general and arguably restrictive test. The indications from the Advocate General's Opinion are that it is not possible to formulate an exhaustive set of criteria to be applied uniformly across Community law and within the various legal systems of the Member States. Instead factors such as control, regulation, exercise of the 'classic functions' of the state, supply of public services are indicative, but not conclusive, evidence that a public authority should be bound in the same way as the government of a Member State by the obligations contained in Community law . . .

The question emerges, therefore, of how is a 'public service' to be defined in Community law? The Advocate General's test is much easier and more realistic, to apply in that it recognizes that the modern state has delegated a wide range of powers to bodies performing regulatory and funding functions . . .

Bodies funded by or only partially regulated by the state are more problematic . . . As the ruling in *Foster* stands a private undertaking controlled by the state in this way would be unlikely to be offering the requisite 'public service' within the *Foster* ruling. Universities are equally problematic. They act as employers and providers of the public service of education . . . In the United Kingdom universities are autonomous institutions but are largely reliant on public funding . . . As a result of the ruling in *Foster* it is clear that no definitive categorisation of universities can be given for the purposes of Community law. A university may be subject to the vertical direct effects of one directive but not of another . . .

The *Foster* ruling is remarkably silent upon the solution to the problem of categorizing the extent of state involvement in commercial life.

(b) 'Indirect Effect': Development of the Principle of Interpretation

The second way in which the Court of Justice has extended the application and effectiveness of directives, despite refusing to allow their direct enforcement in national courts against non-state entities or persons, is by developing a principle requiring the interpretation of national law in the light of directives. By encouraging national courts to read domestic law in such a way as to

[47] More recently, Case C–419/92, *Scholz* v. *Opera Universitaria di Cagliari* [1994] ECR I–505, [1994] 1 CMLR 873 proceeded on the 'common ground' that the University of Cagliari was an emanation of the state. See R. White, 'Equality in the Canteen' (1994) 19 ELRev. 308, pointing out that whether other universities are to be treated as 'emanations of the State' will depend on the organization and funding of the institution.

[48] (1990) 27 CMLRev. 859, 868.

conform with the provisions of directives, the Court attempted to ensure that directives would be given effect despite the absence of proper domestic implementation.

Case 14/83, Von Colson and Kamann v. Land Nordrhein-Westfalen [1984] ECR 1891, [1986] 2 CMLR 430

The plaintiffs had applied for two posts as social workers at a German prison. When two male candidates were appointed to the posts, the plaintiffs successfully brought legal proceedings against the prison administrators, claiming that they had been discriminated against on grounds of sex. They sought by way of remedy to be appointed to a post in the prison, or to be awarded six months salary in the alternative. The Arbeitsgericht which heard their case considered that under German law, which purported to implement the 1976 Equal Treatment Directive, it could allow only the claim for 'reliance loss'—i.e the reimbursement of one of the plaintiffs' travelling expenses. A preliminary reference was made to discover whether the Directive specifically required that discrimination be remedied by the appointment of the complainant to a post.

THE ECJ

26. However, the Member States' obligation arising from a directive to achieve the result envisaged by the directive and their duty under Article 5 of the Treaty to take all appropriate measures, whether general or particular, to ensure the fulfilment of that obligation, is binding on all the authorities of Member States including, for matters within their jurisdiction, the courts. It follows that, in applying the national law and in particular the provisions of a national law specifically introduced in order to implement Directive No 76/207, national courts are required to interpret their national law in the light of the wording and the purpose of the Directive in order to achieve the result referred to in the third paragraph of Article 189.

27. On the other hand, as the above considerations show, the directive does not include any unconditional and sufficiently precise obligation as regards sanctions for discrimination which, in the absence of implementing measures adopted in good time may be relied on by individuals in order to obtain specific compensation under the directive, where that is not provided for or permitted under national law.

28. . . . It is for the national court to interpret and apply the legislation adopted for the implementation of the directive in conformity with the requirements of Community law, in so far as it is given discretion to do so under national law.

ADVOCATE GENERAL ROZES[49]

In order to comply with the obligation thus incorporated in national law it is not however sufficient merely to adopt those procedural measures . . . Although the directive is silent on that point and leaves it to the national authorities to take the necessary measures, it does not follow that in this case it is possible to disregard the nature of the general obligations incumbent on those authorities in implementing all Community measures . . .

[49] N. 42 above, 1915, 1916.

National measures intended to implement a directive must actually serve to bring about the results that the Member States are required to achieve.

It can be seen that the Court went somewhat further than the Advocate General in this case, stating expressly that national courts, as organs of the state, are also responsible for the fulfilment of Community obligations, and not apparently restricting this responsibility specifically to their interpretation of national *implementing* legislation. This judgment is a very significant one from the point of view of enhancing the effectiveness of non-implemented or misimplemented directives. The German law had not provided for adequate sanctions when it sought to implement the Equal Treatment Directive, but the Court did not allow this to undermine the aim of the Directive. Instead it specifically called on the national court to supplement the task of the Member State's legislature in implementing the Directive, by reading the national legislation in conformity with its provisions. Not only is this a very useful way of enhancing the implementation of directives, but it does not seem to be subject to the more restrictive conditions for direct effect, i.e. of being clear, precise, unconditional, and requiring no further implementing measures.

A number of questions soon arose, however, as to the extent of the *Von Colson* interpretation requirement. First, how far were national courts permitted or required to go in their attempts to read the provisions of national law in conformity with a directive? Was the obligation to interpret 'sympathetically', as it is sometimes called, triggered only where there was a sufficient degree of uncertainty or ambiguity in the domestic legislation, or where the language clearly lent itself to more than one interpretation? Secondly, could those courts read national law 'horizontally' in the light of a directive rather than 'vertically' only, i.e. by reading it against an individual rather than against the state? Thirdly, from what date should the national court construe national law in the light of a directive: after adoption of the directive, after the adoption of inadequate national implementing provisions, or only after the expiry of the date for implementation? Fourthly, was the principle of interpretation one which was limited to the interpretation of national *implementing* legislation?[50]

The answers to some of these questions emerged through several later cases which were referred to the Court. The ruling in *Kolpinghuis* involved the first and the third questions, addressing the issue whether a national court could or should interpret national law in the light of a directive where this would retroactively increase the penal liability of an individual and touching on the question whether it mattered if the period for implementing the directive had not yet expired.

[50] See the doubts to which this latter question gave rise in the UK—compare *Pickstone* v. *Freemans* [1989] 1 AC 66 and *Litster* v. *Forth Dry Dock* [1990] 1 AC 546 with *Duke* v. *Reliance Systems Ltd* [1988] AC 618 and *Finnegan* v. *Clowney Youth Training Programme Ltd* [1990] 2 AC 407.

Case 80/86, Criminal proceedings against Kolpinghuis Nijmegen BV [1987] ECR 3969, [1989] 2 CMLR 18

The defendant, who stocked and sold bottles of 'mineral water' was charged with infringing a Dutch measure which regulated the sale of goods for human consumption. At the time of the alleged offence, the 1980 Council Directive on marketing of mineral waters had not yet been implemented in The Netherlands, but the Public Prosecutor was of the view that the Directive already had the force of law at that time. The case was referred to the Court of Justice, asking whether the provisions of a non-implemented Directive could be relied upon by the state against its nationals, and whether the national court was obliged or permitted to interpret its existing national law in the light of this non-implemented Directive. After repeating its ruling in *Von Colson* (see paragraph 26 of the *Von Colson* judgment above), the Court addressed itself to the specific issue raised.

THE ECJ

13. However, that obligation on the national court to refer to the content of the directive when interpreting the relevant rules of its national law is limited by the general principles of law which form part of Community law and in particular the principles of legal certainty and non-retroactivity. Thus the Court ruled in its judgment of 11th June 1987 in Case 14/86 *Pretore di Salo* v. *X* [1987] ECR 2545 that a directive cannot, of itself and independently of a national law adopted by a Member State for its implementation, have the effect of determining or aggravating the liability in criminal law of persons who act in contravention of the provisions of that directive.

14. The answer to the third question should therefore be that in applying its national legislation a court of a Member State is required to interpret that legislation in the light of the wording and the purpose of the directive in order to achieve the result referred to in the third paragraph of Article 189 of the Treaty, but a directive cannot, of itself and independently of a law adopted for its implementation, have the effect of determining or aggravating the liability in criminal law of persons who act in contravention of the provisions of that directive.

15. . . . As regards the third question concerning the limits which Community law might impose on the obligation or power of the national court to interpret the rules of its national law in the light of the directive, it makes no difference whether or not the period prescribed for implementation has expired.

The ruling in this case is not entirely clear, and although it indicates that there are limits—such as the need to respect the general principles of Community law—to the requirement of 'harmonious' or 'sympathetic' interpretation set out in *Von Colson*, it does not provide a direct answer to question three above, namely the date from which a national court should interpret national law in the light of a directive. In paragraph 32 the Court stated that, since the national court was not bound to be guided by the non-implemented directive in this case, it was irrelevant whether the period prescribed for implementation had expired. However, whether it would be equally irrelevant in a case in which a court was bound to be guided in its interpretation of national law by a non-implemented directive is not clear. It would seem likely, given that the Member States are entitled to choose the appropriate manner of implementation before the expiry of the period, that the national courts would not be obliged (although they might perhaps be permitted) in interpreting existing national law, to be guided by a non-implemented directive before the end of that period. However, if an implementing measure has been passed before the expiry of the time limit, but one which does not appear to implement the directive properly, it is more likely that the Court would require a national court, in interpreting that provision of national law, to be guided by the directive it was intended to implement. On the other hand the Court might not require this, given that, until the period for implementation has expired, the Member State should still have the choice as to how best to implement.

With regard to questions one and two above—concerning the limits of the interpretation principle and whether it applies horizontally, as between individuals—some inferences can be drawn from the Court's ruling. By contrast with the opinion of Advocate General Mischo in the case, the judgment did not expressly state that a directive cannot be used to aid in the interpretation of national law in a case between individuals. What it did state was that the obligation on the national court to construe domestic legislation in the light of non-implemented directives was limited by 'principles of certainty and non-retroactivity', which in the context of this case meant that the prosecutor could not use the directive to interpret national law in such a way as to determine or aggravate the individual's criminal liability. But what of cases not involving aggravated criminal liability? Can or must a national court refer to the provisions of a non-implemented directive in order to interpret pre-existing national law in a case between individuals?[51] And if it can, are there any limits on this permission or obligation?

If national law is not already in conformity with a directive, then the use of that directive to inform the interpretation of the national law will necessarily entail altering the meaning of the national law. And in a case between individuals where the provisions of the directive are at issue, this will almost inevitably mean reading national law differently to the disadvantage of one of the individuals. Would this contravene the principles of legal certainty and non-retroactivity, referred to in *Kolpinghuis*?

In the case of *Marleasing*[52] below, the Court answered some of these

[51] The UK Government intervened before the Court in various cases to argue that the *Von Colson* principle could only apply to the interpretation of national implementing legislation, and not to the interpretation of legislation which pre-dated the dir. See e.g. Case 125/88, *Nijman* [1989] ECR 3533, 3537, [1991] 1 CMLR 92. See the Opinion of Slynn A.G. in Case 80/86, *Criminal proceedings against Kolpinghuis Nijmegen BV* [1987] ECR 3969, [1989] 2 CMLR 18, at para. 22, and of Mischo A.G. in Case 152/84, *Marshall (No 1)* n. 38 above, 733 (ECR).

[52] See Case C–106/89, *Marleasing SA* v. *La Comercial de Alimentacion SA* [1990] ECR I–4135, [1992] 1 CMLR 305, confirmed in many cases since then, including Cases C–373/90, *Re Criminal Proceedings against X* [1992] ECR I–131, C–334/92, *Wagner-Miret* [1993] ECR I–6911, and C–271/91, *Marshall (no 2)* [1993] ECR I–4367, [1993] 3 CMLR 293. For comments on the case see G. de Búrca 'Giving Effect to European Community Dirs.' (1992) 55 MLR 215; P. Mead 'The Obligation to Apply European Law: Is *Duke* Dead?' [1991] ELRev. 490 and J. Stuyck and P. Wytinck (1991) 28 CMLRev. 205.

questions by ruling that a non-implemented directive could indeed be relied on to inform the interpretation of national law in a case between individuals, and that this was the case even where the national law predated the directive. The ruling, however, did not make clear what the exact limits to this interpretation obligation might be and various questions remain unanswered. First, when will a reading of national law in conformity with a directive (other than in criminal proceedings) infringe the principles of certainty and non-retroactivity? And secondly, how far must national courts go in their efforts to read unambiguous and clear provisions of national law so as to comply with the provisions of a directive, given that the obligation of interpretation of the national court, as outlined in *Von Colson*, was said to extend only 'in so far as it is given discretion to do so under national law'?

Case C–106/89, Marleasing SA v. La Comercial Internacionale de Alimentacion SA [1990] ECR I-4135, [1992] 1 CMLR 305

The plaintiff company brought an action against La Comercial in order to have the defendant company's articles of association declared void as having been created for the sole purpose of defrauding and evading creditors, including Marleasing. The provisions of the relevant Council Directive did not include this 'lack of cause' as a ground for the nullity of a company, whereas certain provisions of the Spanish Civil Code provided for the ineffectiveness of contracts for lack of cause. The Spanish court referred the case under Article 177 asking whether the Council Directive could have direct effect between private individuals so as to preclude the declaration of nullity of a company on grounds other than those set out in the Directive.

THE ECJ

7. However, it is apparent from the documents before the Court that the national court seeks in substance to ascertain whether a national court hearing a case which falls within the scope of Directive 68/151 is required to interpret its national law in the light of the wording and the purpose of that directive in order to preclude a declaration of nullity of a public limited company on a ground other than those listed in Article 11 of the directive.

8. In order to reply to that question, it should be observed that, as the Court pointed out in its judgment in case 14/83 *Von Colson and Kamann* v. *Land Nordrhein-Westfalen* [1984] ECR 1891, paragraph 26, the Member States' obligation arising from a directive to achieve the result envisaged by the directive and their duty under Article 5 of the Treaty to take all appropriate measures, whether general or particular, to ensure the fulfilment of that obligation, is binding on all the authorities of Member States including, for matters within their jurisdiction, the courts. It follows that, in applying national law, whether the provisions in question were adopted before or after the directive, the national court called upon to interpret it is required to do so, as far as possible, in the light of the wording and the purpose of the directive in order to achieve the result pursued by the latter and thereby comply with the third paragraph of Article 189 of the Treaty.

ADVOCATE GENERAL VAN GERVEN[53]

7. . . . That obligation on the part of the national courts to interpret their national law in conformity with a directive, which has been reaffirmed on several occasions, does not mean that a provision in a directive has direct effect in any way as between individuals. On the contrary, it is the national provisions themselves which, interpreted in a manner consistent with the directive, have direct effect.

8. The obligation to interpret a provision of national law in conformity with a directive arises whenever the provision in question is to any extent open to interpretation. In those circumstances the national court must, having regard to the usual methods of interpretation in its legal system, give precedence to the method which enables it to construe the national provision concerned in a manner consistent with the directive.

The obligation to give an interpretation in conformity with a directive is, it is true, restricted by Community law itself, of which the directive forms part, and in particular by the principles of legal certainty and non-retroactivity which also form part of Community law. In cases involving criminal proceedings, for example, such an interpretation cannot result in criminal liability unless such liability has been introduced by the national legislation implementing the directive. Nor, similarly, can a directive of itself—that is to say in the absence of national implementing legislation—introduce a civil penalty, such as nullity, in national law. However, that is not the issue here: this case is concerned with a provision of a directive which excludes certain grounds of nullity.

9. Furthermore, as part of Community law, the directive concerned in principle takes precedence over all provisions of national law. That is true in particular in the case of national provisions which, as in this case, relate to the branch of the law covered by the directive, even though they predate the directive and were thus not enacted for its implementation. [In the case of national provisions adopted previously, an interpretation in conformity with the directive is normally applicable only as from the expiry of the time-limit for implementation prescribed by the directive (or even as from the entry into force of the directive: see the judgment in *Kolpinghuis Nijmegen*, paragraphs 15 and 16). Events occurring prior to that date continue of course to be governed by the national provisions construed without regard to the directive. In this case, however, the company in question, La Comercial, was incorporated on 7 April 1987, that is to say at a time when the time-limit for the implementation of the First Directive by Spain had already expired.]

The Advocate General elaborated more than the Court did on what limits there might be to the interpretation obligation, suggesting that any interpretation of national law in the light of a directive, which would impose a criminal or a civil penalty upon an individual would contravene the principles of legal certainty and non-retroactivity. In his view, however, that problem did not exist in the *Marleasing* case, because the directive was not being used in such a way as to impose the civil penalty of annulment of a company's articles of association and instrument of incorporation: rather it was being used

[53] N. 52 above, 4146.

to prevent the company being declared void. But this raises another problem. The interpretation of Spanish contract law in the light of the non-implemented Company Directive worked to the disadvantage of Marleasing SA, which was a creditor of the defendant company, and presumably had entered into the agreement to lend money to La Comercial on the basis that it was a *bona fide* company which would repay the debt in the ordinary way. On the basis of Spanish contract law as argued by Marleasing, if a contract was made without cause, or for fraudulent purposes e.g. in order to evade creditors, then that contract would be declared void; thus it argued that if a company was incorporated purely as a means of evading creditors, its contract of association should be declared void, and the company, too, would be declared null and void, so that money could be recovered personally from the 'men of straw'. If Marleasing entered its credit agreement with La Comercial on this assumption, then the law was altered to its detriment by the use of the Directive, since arguably Marleasing might have taken other precautions if it were not already protected under Spanish law against a fraudulent company by means of having it declared void and being able to sue those responsible personally.[54]

Perhaps the Advocate General expressed his view as he did in *Marleasing* because the Spanish law was not actually clear on the grounds for nullity of a company, so that Marleasing could not have had any well-founded expectation that Spanish law would declare a company void if its contract of association was entered into 'without purpose' or for fraudulent purposes. In other words, he may have felt that the question whether the Spanish law (the Commercial Code) on nullity of contracts should be applied by analogy to company law was an open one, and since a real question of interpretation thus arose, that interpretation should not be at variance with the grounds of nullity set out in the Directive, since it would not retroactively affect anyone nor adversely affect the interests of anyone who might 'legitimately' have relied on the law being otherwise. On this assumption, there would have been no real detriment for Marleasing, given that it was not at all clear that a straight application of existing national law would have favoured it. What view the Court will take in cases in which the interpretation of national law in the light of a non-implemented directive would operate to an individual's disadvantage or detriment (not being one which involves criminal liability) remains to be seen.

The ruling in *Marleasing* was ambiguous as to the strength of the obligation to interpret in conformity with directives. What constraints will the relatively clear language of a national statute impose upon a national court which is faced with a relevant directive on the same subject matter?[55] The judgment in *Marleasing* states that national courts must 'in so far as possible' read

[54] See, for a contrary view, N. Maltby 'Marleasing: What is All the Fuss About?' (1993) 109 LQR 301.

[55] In Case C–271/91, *Marshall (no 2)*, n. 52 above, the Commission argued that the Court should not require an interpretation of the UK legislation in the light of Dir. 76/207 where that would override the clear limits of the legislation and offend the principle of legal certainty. The Court avoided this difficulty by finding the provision of the Dir. to be directly effective.

national law in conformity with a relevant directive, but in that case itself, the Court held that the Spanish court was precluded from interpreting national law in a way which did not comply with the provisions of the directive in question. The exact limits on the 'interpretive obligation' of national courts remain to be seen in the course of future case law, but it is unlikely that the Court would ever require national courts to override the language of a national measure which clearly conflicted with the provisions of a directive in whose light it was to be interpreted.[56] In *Wagner-Miret*, the Court accepted that the Spanish legislation in question in that case could not be interpreted in such a way as to give effect to the result sought by the applicants.[57] However, the reason for this conclusion on the interpretation of the Spanish legislation is not entirely clear. It may have been that the Court considered that the terms of the legislation were too clearly contrary to the requirements of the directive in question, or it may have been that the directive itself—Directive 80/987, which was also in issue in the earlier *Francovich* case[58]—did not require the exact result which the applicant claimed. The Directive permitted the states to set up different salary guarantee institutions for different classes of employee, to protect them in the event of the employer's insolvency. Such an institution had already been set up in Spain for a certain category of employees but not for the applicants, who were management staff. It was held that the applicant could neither rely directly on the Directive nor require the law setting up a guarantee institution for other employees to be read as if it included him, since, although the Directive required the salaries of all categories of employee to be protected, the Member States were permitted to set up different institutions for each category. This reasoning seems sensible, given that the guarantee institution which had already been set up might not have been adequately financed to cover the salary claims of groups of employees who had not been considered to be within its remit. If it was this factor which led the Court to conclude that the national law was not capable of being read in the way required by the Directive, then the scope of the interpretation principle was limited not so much by the language of the national law as by the fact that to read it in the way requested might actually undermine the effectiveness of the Directive's aims, given that the defendant institution might not be in a financial position to guarantee the salaries of all the claimants.

[56] See Van Gerven A.G. in Case C–262/88, n. 19 above, 1937 (ECR): 'Hence it would appear that Community law may set limits to certain methods of interpretation applied under a national legal system, without of course being able to compel the national court to give an interpretation *contra legem*'. See the same A.G. in Cases 63–64/91, *Jackson* v. *Chief Adjudication Officer* [1992] ECR I–4737, [1992] 3 CMLR 389, para. 29 of his opinion, and in Case C–271/91 *Marshall (No 2)*, n. 52 above, para. 10 of his opinion.

[57] See Case C–334/92 n. 52 above, para. 22. In Case C–91/92, n. 44 above, para. 27, the Court also acknowledges limits to the interpretation approach.

[58] See Cases C–6/90 and C–9/90, *Francovich and Bonifaci* v. *Italy* [1991] ECR I–5357, [1993] 2 CMLR 66. This ruling is discussed in detail in Ch. 5.

(c) State Liability in Damages for Non-implementation of a Directive

The applicants in *Wagner-Miret*, however, were not left without any means of enforcing the Directive since the Court, following its ruling in *Francovich*, suggested that the state could be liable to them in damages for failure to implement the Directive.[59] This third method of enforcement by means of state liability is likely to become increasingly important, and to be extended to cover breaches of provisions of Community law other than directives. Its significance will be discussed in fuller detail in the next chapter.

It can be seen, however, that the domestic effect to be given to directives remains a complex issue in Community law. Despite the fact that it has continued to enhance the effectiveness of directives in other, often problematic ways, by elaborating an expansive notion of the state, by requiring national courts under Article 5 of the Treaty to interpret national law in the light of non-implemented directives, and by making the state liable in damages for their non-implementation, the Court has repeatedly refused to extend the direct application of directives to cases between individuals. This was most recently reiterated in the *Dori* case, in which the Court was asked to rule that directives could have so-called horizontal direct effect.[60] Having heard submissions from a number of Member States—all but one of which opposed the extension of direct effect—as well as from the parties to the case, the Court stated that to rule as requested would be 'to recognize a power in the Community to enact obligations for individuals with immediate effect, whereas it has competence to do so only where it is empowered to adopt regulations'.[61]

This continued refusal by the Court, despite its other developments, to extend horizontal direct effect to directives is perhaps still best explained by reference to the reaction of the Member States who wish to retain the discretion left to them by Article 189. Reasons such as those put forward by the Advocate General in *Marshall (No 1)* (above) based on legal certainty and lack of publication are not convincing, given that there is now a requirement of publication, and considerable uncertainty already exists as to the scope of the state for the purposes of vertical direct effect and as to the limits of the *Von Colson/Marleasing* principle of interpretation.

However, the Court has, in its ruling in *Francovich*, provided a further sharp incentive for Member States to implement directives before the expiry of the time limit for implementation. And to judge from the ruling in *Wagner-Miret*,[62] it would seem that this indirect method of enforcement by means of an action for damages, although subject to specific conditions, may be more useful and give rise to fewer difficulties (other than for the Member States

[59] N. 52 above.

[60] Case C–91/92, n. 44 above. For a comment criticizing this case, and suggesting a strong theoretical justification for the horizontal direct effect of directives, see J. Coppel, 'Rights, Duties and the End of Marshall' (1994) 57 MLR 859.

[61] N. 60 above, para. 24 of the judgment.

[62] Case C–334/92, n. 52 above.

which must pay damages!) than the obligation of interpretation outlined in *Von Colson* and *Marleasing*.

5. FURTHER READING

BEBR, G., 'Agreements concluded by the Community and their Possible Direct Effect: From *International Fruit Company* to *Kupferberg*' (1983) 20 CMLRev. 35

COPPEL, J., 'Rights, Duties and the End of Marshall' (1994) 57 MLR 859

DE BURCA, G., 'Giving Effect to European Community Directives' (1992) 55 MLR 215

CRAIG, P. P., 'Once upon a Time in the West: Direct Effect and the Federalization of EEC Law' (1992) 12 OJLS 453

CURTIN, D., 'The Province of Government: Delimiting the Direct Effect of Directives in the Common Law Context' (1990) 15 ELRev. 195

MALTBY, N., 'Marleasing: What is All the Fuss About?' (1993) 109 LQR 301

MEAD, P., 'The Obligation to Apply European Law: Is Duke Dead?' (1991) 16 ELRev. 490

PESCATORE, P., 'The Doctrine of "Direct Effect": An Infant Disease of Community Law' 63 (1983) 8 ELRev. 155

WINTER, T., 'Direct Applicability and Direct Effects' (1972) 9 CMLRev. 425

WYATT, D., 'New Legal Order or Old' (1982) 7 ELRev. 147

5

The Application of EC Law: Remedies in National Courts

1. INTRODUCTION

Given that the driving force behind the development of direct effect was the concern to make Community law as effective as possible in all of the Member States, it gradually became clear that even the direct enforceability of that law before national courts would not necessarily ensure its proper observance throughout the Community. It was evident that the idea of effectiveness or *effet utile* of Community law, which was central to the development by the Court of Justice of the doctrine of direct effect, would be undermined by the absence of effective sanctions and remedies for breach of Community law. Neither the Treaty nor any specific Community legislation lays down a general scheme of procedures for the enforcement of EC law, nor any general system of remedies for its breach by the states. It will be seen in the following discussion how, from an initial approach which left the issue of remedies as a matter for national law rather than Community law, the Court over the years increasingly invoked and built upon Article 5 of the EC Treaty to develop the role of national courts, in particular, in providing remedies for breach of Community law.[1] Article 5 provides as follows:

> Member States shall take all appropriate measures, whether general or particular, to ensure fulfilment of the obligations arising out of this Treaty or resulting from action taken by the institutions of the Community. They shall facilitate the Community's tasks.
>
> They shall abstain from any measure which could jeopardise the attainment of the objectives of the Treaty.

(a) *The Principle of National Procedural Autonomy*

Early on in its case law, the Court ruled that it was for the national legal system to determine how the interests of a person adversely affected by an infringement of Community law were to be protected.[2] What, then, was a

[1] J.Temple Lang, 'Community Constitutional Law: Article 5 EEC Treaty' (1990) 27 CMLRev. 645.

[2] Case 6/60, *Humblet* v. *Belgium* [1960] ECR 559; Case 13/68, *Salgoil* v. *Italian Ministry for Foreign Trade* [1973] ECR 453, [1969] CMLR 181.

national court to do when an individual, who had been subject to national legal provisions, sought a remedy before it by pleading the direct effect of provisions of Community law to the contrary?

Case 33/76, Rewe-Zentralfinanz eG and Rewe-Zentral AG v. Landwirtschaftskammer für das Saarland [1976] ECR 1989, [1977] 1 CMLR 533

The applicant companies had paid charges in Germany for inspection costs associated with the import of fruit from France. These charges were subsequently held by the Court of Justice to be in breach of provisions of the EEC Treaty prohibiting measures having equivalent effect to customs duties. The companies applied to the Landwirtschaftskammer for annulment of the decisions to impose the charges and for a refund of the amounts paid including interest. On dismissal of the applications they appealed to the German Federal Administrative Court. Since under the rules of procedure of national law, the time limit for contesting the validity of national administrative measures had passed, the German court referred several questions to the Court of Justice to see whether Community law required that the applicants be granted the remedy sought.

THE ECJ[3]

Applying the principle of cooperation laid down in Article 5 of the Treaty, it is the national courts which are entrusted with ensuring the legal protection which citizens derive from the direct effect of the provisions of Community law.

Accordingly, in the absence of Community rules on this subject, it is for the domestic legal system of each Member State to designate the courts having jurisdiction and to determine the procedural conditions governing actions at law intended to ensure the protection of the rights which citizens have from the direct effect of Community law, it being understood that such conditions cannot be less favourable than those relating to similar actions of a domestic nature . . .

In the absence of such measures of harmonisation the right conferred by Community law must be exercised before the national courts in accordance with the conditions laid down by national rules.

The position would be different only if the conditions and time-limits made it impossible in practice to exercise the rights which the national courts are obliged to protect.

This is not the case where reasonable periods of limitation of actions are fixed.

ADVOCATE GENERAL WARNER[4]

I am, however, of the opinion, that it is for the national law of each Member State to determine the nature and extent of the remedies available in the courts of that State to give effect to those rights. There is ample authority in this Court for that proposition. As long ago as 1960, in case 6/60 *Humblet* v *Belgium* [1960] ECR 559 the Court held that, where a Member State had exacted income tax from an ECSC official in an amount incompatible with the Protocol on the Privileges and Immunities of that Community, it was for the internal legislation of that State to say whether or not he was entitled to have the excess tax refunded to him with

[3] [1976] ECR 1989, 1997. [4] *Ibid.* 2002–4.

> interest. In case 28/67 *Mölkerei-Zentrale Westfalen* v *Hauptzollamt Paderborn* [1968] ECR 148 and case 34/67 *Luck* v *Hauptzollamt Köln* [1968] ECR 245, the Court held that it was for the competent Court in each Member State to decide, according to the rules of its national law, what remedies were appropriate for the purpose of upholding the rights conferred on private persons by Article 95 of the EEC Treaty . . .
>
> The plaintiff submitted that to allow national law to apply in such circumstances was to allow it to override Community law. I do not think that that is a correct description of the situation. I see it as a situation in which Community law and national law operate in combination, the latter taking over where the former leaves off, and working out its consequences . . .
>
> I do not think that any such independent right of action was conferred on the plaintiffs by Community law: I think that it was for their national laws to lay down the remedies to which they were entitled in consequence of the invalidity of the fiscal legislation in question. But even if there were such an independent right of action created by Community law, the fact remains that there is no Community procedural law applicable to the exercise of such a right, and therefore no provision of Community law with which national procedural law could be held incompatible.

Both the Advocate General and the Court emphasized the responsibility of the Member State, where there are no relevant Community rules, for determining the procedural conditions under which Community rights are to be protected.[5] The Court, however, imposed two 'Community' requirements on any national procedural conditions: (i) that the remedies and forms of action available to ensure the observance of national law must be made available in the same way to ensure the observance of Community law, and (ii) that a certain minimum standard of protection had to be achieved, in that the applicable national conditions and procedures should not make the exercise of the right impossible in practice.

(b) The Absence of an Obligation to Create New Remedies

The main thrust of the Court's approach was that, where no such Community rules existed, the matter of remedies for breach of Community law and the procedures governing them was primarily for the Member States. In the absence of harmonization of such rules, Community law apparently did not require the states to alter their legal systems by developing remedies which would not be available under national law.

Case 158/80, Rewe-Handelsgesellschaft Nord mbH v. Hauptzollamt Kiel [1981] ECR 1805, [1982] 1 CMLR 449

German law permitted certain 'butter-buying cruises' to enable passengers to buy during the course of the cruise various goods which would be free of tax on their

[5] See also Case 45/76, *Comet BV* v. *Produktschap voor Siergewassen* [1976] ECR 2043, [1977] 1 CMLR 533 and Case 179/84, *Bozetti* v. *Invernizzi* [1985] ECR 2301, [1986] 2 CMLR 246.

importation back into Germany. The applicants had argued before the German Finanzgericht that these cruises adversely affected them as local retailers and wholesale businesses dealing in similar goods within Germany, and that the cruises were contrary to various provisions of EC regulations and directives governing customs duties and turnover taxes. Since the basis of their argument was that their economic interests were adversely affected through the non-application by the Member State of Community rules to third party competitors, they were seeking a remedy from the Finanzgericht which would effectively compel the national authorities to apply those Community rules or to refrain from breaching them.

THE ECJ

44. With regard to the right of a trader to request the courts to require the authorities of a Member State to compel a third party to comply with obligations arising from Community rules in a given legal situation in which that trader is not involved but is economically adversely affected by the failure to observe Community law, it must be remarked first of all that, although the Treaty has made it possible in a number of instances for private persons to bring a direct action, where appropriate, before the Court of Justice, it was not intended to create new remedies in the national courts to ensure the observance of Community law other than those already laid down by national law. On the other hand the system of legal protection established by the Treaty, as set out in Article 177 in particular, implies that it must be possible for every type of action provided for by national law to be available for the purpose of ensuring observance of Community provisions having direct effect, on the same conditions concerning the admissibility and procedure as would apply were it a question of ensuring observance of national law.

By this stage it was clear that Member States could apply their own procedural rules and conditions governing the grant of remedies for breach of Community provisions pleaded by individuals in national courts, without being required to create new national remedies. This, however, was apparently still subject to the two conditions set out above, i.e. equality with national remedies and the practical possibility of exercising the Community right. An example of a national rule or principle which would violate the second condition can be seen in the following case, where an applicant who had been overpaid under Community law sought to resist a claim for the return of the money by invoking the principle of legal certainty in national law.[6]

Case 265/78, Ferwerda v. Produktschap voor Vee en Vlees [1980] ECR 617, [1980] 3 CMLR 737

Ferwerda was a Dutch exporter of meat who had wrongly been granted export refunds by the respondent Dutch authority, pursuant to a mistaken application of

[6] See Case 309/85, *Barra* v. *Belgium* [1988] ECR 355, [1988] 2 CMLR 409 in which the Court considered that national legislation restricting repayment of a fee which had been charged in breach of Community law would render the exercise of Community rights impossible. See also Case 199/82, *Amministrazione delle Finanze dello Stato* v. *San Giorgio* [1983] ECR 3595, [1985] 2 CMLR 658.

a Commission Regulation. The authority, in accordance with a further provision of that Regulation, then sought repayment of the refund from Ferwerda, who argued that the claim for repayment would constitute a breach of the principle of legal certainty which is recognized in the legal system of The Netherlands. The Dutch court referred several questions to the Court of Justice asking whether the provisions of the Regulation would rule out the application of such a principle of national law, and whether the principle of legal certainty formed part of Community law.

THE ECJ

10. It follows, as the Court held in its judgment of 21 May 1976 in Case 26/74 *Roquette* [1976] ECR 677, that disputes in connexion with the reimbursement of amounts collected for the Community are thus a matter for the national courts and must be settled by them under national law in so far as no provisions of Community law are relevant. In those circumstances it is for the courts of Member States to provide, in pursuance of the requirement of cooperation embodied in Article 5 of the Treaty, the legal protection made available as a result of the direct effect of the Community provisions both when such provisions create obligations for the subject and when they confer rights on him. It is, however, for the national legal system of each Member State to determine the courts having jurisdiction and to fix the procedures for applications to the courts intended to protect the rights which the subject obtains through the direct effect of Community law but such procedures may not be less favourable than those in similar procedures concerning internal matters and may in no case be laid down in such a way as to render impossible in practice the exercise of the rights which the national courts must protect.

. . .

15. In this connexion it must be observed that no consideration whatever, which under one of the national legal systems of the Member States is or may be based on a principle of legal certainty, can in all cases constitute a defence against a claim for the recovery of Community financial benefits wrongly granted. It must in each case be considered whether such application does not jeopardize the very basis of the rule providing for such recovery and whether it does not result in practice in frustrating such recovery.

However, where a particular national rule would not operate so as to deny a remedy or to render the Community provision or right impossible to exercise in practice, then according to the Court's case law, national procedural and substantive rules could be applied despite the fact that this might give rise to fifteen differing methods of protection or enforcement in the Member States. As Advocate General Warner said in *Ferwerda*[7]:

It seems logical that it should be left to each Member State to determine, by its own laws, when and to what extent it ought to bear the loss.

To that one might object that, if so, there will be a lack of uniformity in the

[7] Case 265/78, *Ferwerda* v. *Produktschap voor Vee en Vlees* [1980] ECR 617, 640, [1980] 3 CMLR 737, 748.

> consequences of the application of Community law in the different Member States. The answer to that objection is . . . that this Court cannot create Community law where none exists: that must be left to the Community's legislative organs.

The problem of lack of uniformity to which the Advocate General adverted, however, was one which was bound to become more acute as the number of cases in which parties successfully pleaded the direct effect of Community law before national courts multiplied. The Court had made clear that, given the absence of a harmonized system of Community remedies and procedures, the enforcement of Community law before national courts was to be secured in accordance with national rules and procedures. And although the application of national rules to the enforcement of Community provisions was said by the Court to be subject to the two conditions listed above, it gradually became clear that full or even reasonable enforcement of Community law would not necessarily be ensured by these conditions.

(c) National Penalties and Remedies for Breach of Community Law: The Requirements of Proportionality, Adequacy, and Effectiveness

Several of the cases discussed above involved national procedures and rules governing the attempts by Member State authorities or individual applicants to recover, pursuant to Community measures, money wrongly paid in breach of those measures. But the issue of Member State remedies and procedural rules has also arisen in the context of national administrative or criminal sanctions which states impose upon those who derive rights from or are regulated by Community law. Some of these cases, such as *Sagulo* and *Heylens* below, questioned the compatibility with Community law of penalties imposed by a Member State for relatively minor administrative breaches by persons enjoying rights under Community law. Others, such as *Von Colson*, concerned the adequacy and deterrent effect of national penalties for serious breaches by companies or individuals of fundamental rules of Community law.[8] In these cases the Court elaborated on and extended the conditions under which Member States could apply national rules and procedures to remedy breaches within the field of Community law.

Case 8/77, Sagulo, Brenca, and Bakhouche
[1977] ECR 1495, [1977] 2 CMLR 585

Criminal proceedings were brought in Germany against two Italian nationals and a French national on the grounds that they had resided in Germany without the necessary residence permits and documentation, and without complying with the formalitites required to obtain these. The German Court referred several questions to the Court of Justice on the interpretation of Council Directive 68/360 and

[8] See also Case 68/88, *Commission* v. *Greece* [1989] ECR 2965.

Articles 7 and 48 of the EEC Treaty in order to establish whether the application of certain penal provisions of German law to the three accused was compatible with Community law.

THE ECJ

4. . . . Under the third paragraph of Article 189 of the Treaty it is for the Member States to choose the form and methods to implement the provisions of the directive in their territory either by the adoption of a special law or regulations or by the application of appropriate provisions of their general regulations on aliens. The Member States are also competent to lay down penalties or to apply the penalties provided for in their general regulations in order to secure observance in their territory of the formalities provided for in Directive No 68/360.

. . .

11. In so far as [Directive 68/360] imposes special obligations such as the possession of a passport or an identity card on the nationals of a Member State who enter the territory of another Member State or reside there, the persons affected thereby cannot simply be put on the same footing as nationals of the country of residence.

12. . . . In the absence of a criterion which in the present case might be based on the principle of national treatment contained in Article 7 of the Treaty it is nevertheless to be observed that although Member States are entitled to impose reasonable penalties for infringement by persons subject to Community law of the obligation to obtain a valid identity card or passport, such penalties should by no means be so severe as to cause an obstacle to the freedom of entry and residence provided for in the Treaty . . .

13. The answer to the question raised must therefore be that it is for the competent authorities of each Member State to impose penalties where appropriate on a person subject to the provisions of Community law who has failed to provide himself with one of the documents of identity referred to in Article 3 of Directive No 68/360 but that the penalties imposed must not be disproportionate to the nature of the offence committed.

This case does not concern someone seeking a remedy for the Member State's breach of a Community right, but rather the state seeking to impose national sanctions or penalties upon an individual who has not complied with a provision of Community law. The Court's response is that, although the Member State and the national court may impose national penalties in such circumstances, this is subject to the condition that the penalties must not be disproportionate,[9] and must not undermine a basic Community right such as freedom of movement. Determining what would 'undermine' a Community right is presumably similar to determining what conditions would render the exercise of a right 'practically impossible', as we have seen above.

In subsequent cases, the Court was asked about the compatibility with Community law of national sanctions, where those sanctions were intended to remedy breaches by the state (or an employer) of fundamental principles of Community law which had adversely affected the rights of individuals.

[9] See also Case 77/81, *Zuckerfabrik Franken* [1982] ECR 681.

Case 14/83, Von Colson and Kamann v. Land Nordrhein-Westfalen [1984] ECR 1891, [1986] 2 CMLR 430

The facts are set out in Chapter 4.[10] In addition to outlining the duty of national courts to interpret national law in the light of Community directives, the Court elaborated, in greater detail than before, on the obligation of national courts to provide remedies to ensure the enforcement of and to penalise breaches of Community law.

THE ECJ

12. The Danish Government considers that the directive deliberately left to Member States the choice of sanctions, in accordance with their national circumstances and legal systems. Member States should penalize breaches of the principle of equal treatment in the same way as they penalize similar breaches of national rules in related areas not governed by Community law.

13. The United Kingdom is also of the opinion that it is for Member States to choose the measures which they consider appropriate to ensure the fulfilment of their obligations under the directive. The directive gives no indication as to the measures which Member States should adopt and the questions referred to the Court themselves clearly illustrate the difficulties encountered in laying down appropriate measures.

. . .

23. Although . . . full implementation of the directive does not require any specific form of sanction for unlawful discrimination, it does entail that that sanction be such as to guarantee real and effective judicial protection.

. . .

28. It should, however, be pointed out to the national court that although Directive No 75/207/EEC, for the purpose of imposing a sanction for the breach of the prohibition of discrimination, leaves the Member States free to choose between the different solutions suitable for achieving its objective, it nevertheless requires that if a Member State chooses to penalize breaches of that prohibition by the award of compensation, then in order to ensure that it is effective and that it has a deterrent effect, that compensation must in any event be adequate in relation to the damage sustained and must therefore amount to more than purely nominal compensation such as, for example, the reimbursement only of the expenses incurred in connection with the application.

Consequently, in addition to the conditions previously imposed by the Court on the application of national remedies and procedural rules—i.e. (i) that they must not be discriminatory as compared with remedies for similar breaches of national law, (ii) that they must not render the exercise of a Community right in practice impossible, and (iii) that any penalties imposed for breaches of Community law must be proportionate—the issue of their *adequacy* and *effectiveness* in securing Community rights emerged from this case to become of central importance. This is evident from further decisions of the

[10] See 190.

Court, such as those in *Johnston*[11] and *Heylens*.[12] In the latter case, the applicant was a Belgian national who was engaged to work as a football trainer in France by the Lille Olympic Sporting Club. His Belgian trainer's diploma was refused recognition by the relevant French authorities, and he was prosecuted for continuing nevertheless to practise. The Court, drawing support from the right to an effective judicial remedy in Articles 6 and 13 of the European Convention on Human Rights, held that:

> since free access to employment is a fundamental right which the Treaty confers individually on each worker in the Community, the existence of a remedy of a judicial nature against any decision of a national authority refusing the benefit of that right is essential in order to secure for the individual effective protection for his right.[13]

According to the Court, the right to judicial review, if it was to be an effective remedy, had generally to require the giving of reasons for decisions which curtailed or denied a Community right, and must enable the person affected 'to defend that right under the best possible conditions'.[14]

(d) A Conflict Between the Principle of Effectiveness and the Principle that National Courts need not Create New Remedies?

But once the focus had shifted somewhat from the non-discriminatory nature of the application of national procedural rules and remedies and had moved to their adequacy in ensuring the effectiveness of Community law, it became clear that there was a certain tension in the Court's case law. In *Von Colson*, the reimbursement of the plaintiffs' travelling expenses would have been inadequate compensation for the refusal to employ them on grounds of sex, in breach of Council Directive 76/207. As it happened, German law other than the specific legislation which had purported to implement that Directive was capable of being read in a way which would provide for more substantial compensation, so that the requirements of adequacy and effectiveness of the remedy could be met. But what if national law had been very clear that the only available remedy was reimbursement of expenses, and no other reading had been possible? In such circumstances the application of the national provision could hardly be said to provide an adequate or effective remedy for the breach of Community law which had occurred. Yet the Court in *Rewe-Handelsgesellschaft Nord v Hauptzollamt Kiel* had held that there was no oblig-

[11] Case 222/84, *Johnston* v. *Chief Constable of the RUC* [1986] ECR 1651, [1986] 3 CMLR 240. See also Cases C–87–89/90 *Verholen* v. *Sociale Verzekeringsbank* [1991] ECR I–3757, [1994] 1 CMLR 157, para. 24, on the question of national rules of standing.

[12] Case 222/86, *UNECTEF* v. *Heylens* [1987] ECR 4097, [1989] 1 CMLR 901.

[13] *Ibid*., para. 14. See Chs. 7 and 16 for further discussion of the case.

[14] *Ibid*., para. 15.

ation on national courts to create new remedies,[15] but only to provide existing remedies under the same conditions which applied in the case of a breach of national law. If the German legislation in *Von Colson* had not been capable of being interpreted so as to provide a more adequate remedy, would the German court have been obliged to ignore the national measure and to provide an effective remedy beyond that which was explicitly set out in the relevant national legislation? This question was not clearly addressed by the Court, and the tension between the two propositions—(a) that national courts are not obliged to create new remedies and that existing national rules and procedures may be applied so long as they are non-discriminatory and do not render the exercise of a Community right impossible; and (b) that the sanctions imposed and remedies granted by national courts for breaches of Community law must be adequate and effective—was neither addressed nor resolved.

However, in the later case of *Factortame*, the Court emphasized again the importance of the effectiveness principle, and clearly gave that principle priority over rules of national law. And although this might seem to be no more than what the Court had previously ruled in *Ferwerda*,[16] where if a national rule rendered the exercise of a Community right impossible that rule could not be applied, the results in *Factortame* were rather more dramatic. The national rule in question was not one like the principle of legal certainty in issue in *Ferwerda*, which could operate in particular cases to bar an available legal remedy. Rather, the national rule was one which, according to the House of Lords, prohibited absolutely the grant of the particular remedy sought. It followed that in this case, the result of requiring the principle of effectiveness of Community law to be given priority over the national rule was to require the grant of a remedy in novel circumstances, where such a remedy would not be available in a comparable situation involving purely national law.

Case C-213/89, R. v. Secretary of State for Transport, ex parte Factortame Ltd and Others
[1990] ECR I–2433, [1990] 3 CMLR 1

Factortame Ltd and several other companies, most of the directors and shareholders of which were Spanish nationals, were incorporated under UK law and were owners or operators of fishing vessels registered in the register of British vessels under the Merchant Shipping Act 1894. The 1988 Merchant Shipping Act was introduced in Britain in order to prevent so-called 'quota-hopping', whereby British fishing quotas were alleged to have been misappropriated by vessels which flew the British flag but which had no genuine link with the UK. The 1988 Act required all fishing vessels to register anew, but the applicants did not satisfy the new conditions for registration. They sought to challenge these conditions, which included a nationality requirement for 75 per cent of directors and shareholders of company-owned vessels, by way of judicial review before the High Court,

[15] Case 158/80, *Rewe-Handelsgesellschaft Nord mbH* v. *Hauptzollamt Kiel* [1981] ECR 1805, [1982] 1 CMLR 449, para. 44.

[16] Case 265/78, n. 7 above.

arguing that the conditions were in breach of Community law. They also sought interim relief until such time as final judgment was given in the judicial review action. When the matter reached the House of Lords it was held that the grant of interim relief was precluded both by the common law rule prohibiting the grant of an interim injunction against the Crown and by the presumption that an Act of Parliament is in conformity with Community law until a decision on its compatibility with Community law has been given. However, several questions were referred to the Court of Justice to determine whether Community law empowered or obliged national courts to give interim protection in these circumstances.

THE ECJ

13. The House of Lords . . . found in the first place that the claims by the appellants in the main proceedings that they would suffer irreparable damage if the interim relief which they sought were not granted and they were successful in the main proceedings were well founded. However, it held that, under national law, the English courts had no power to grant interim relief in a case such as the one before it. More specifically, it held that the grant of such relief was precluded by the old common law rule that an interim injunction may not be granted against the Crown . . . in conjunction with the presumption that an Act of Parliament is in conformity with Community law until such time as a decision on its compatibility with that law has been given.

. . .

17. It is clear from the information before the Court, and in particular from the judgment making the reference and, as described above, the course taken by the proceedings in the national courts before which the case came at first and second instance, that the preliminary question raised by the House of Lords seeks essentially to ascertain whether a national court which, in a case before it concerning Community law, considers that the sole obstacle which precludes it from granting interim relief is a rule of national law, must disapply that rule.

. . .

19. In accordance with the case-law of the Court, it is for the national courts, in application of the principle of cooperation laid down in Article 5 of the EEC Treaty, to ensure the legal protection which persons derive from the direct effect of provisions of Community law . . .

20. The Court has also held that any provision of a national legal system and any legislative, administrative or judicial practice which might impair the effectiveness of Community law by withholding from the national court having jurisdiction to apply such law the power to do everything necessary at the moment of its application to set aside national legislative provisions which might prevent, even temporarily, Community rules from having full force and effect are incompatible with those requirements, which are the very essence of Community law (judgment of 9 March 1978 in Case 106/77 *Simmenthal* [1978] ECR 629).

21. It must be added that the full effectiveness of Community law would be just as much impaired if a rule of national law could prevent a court seised of a dispute governed by Community law from granting interim relief in order to ensure the full effectiveness of the judgment to be given on the existence of the rights claimed under Community law. It follows that a court which in those circumstances would grant interim relief, if it were not for a rule of national law, is obliged to set aside that rule.

It is interesting that the Court chose to concentrate in its judgment on the issue of effectiveness, and on the need for national courts to set aside rules of national law which render Community provisions ineffective. This is a different emphasis from that which was evident in earlier cases dealing with the issue of national procedural rules and remedies. The Court in *Factortame* did not begin by reiterating the principle that it is for the Member States to lay down the conditions and rules which govern the enforcement of Community measures, nor did it repeat its previous statement that there was no obligation on the national court to create new remedies for this purpose. Instead it focused on the effectiveness principle and on the obligation of national courts under Article 5 of the Treaty to ensure its observance by setting aside obstructive national rules which precluded or limited the grant of an appropriate remedy. It did not go so far as to specify the conditions under which a national remedy such as interim relief should be granted in a given case,[17] leaving this to the House of Lords to decide in accordance with national principles, but it made clear that a rule which prohibited absolutely the grant of interim relief would contradict the principle of effectiveness.

Although *Factortame* can be explained on the basis of the Court's previous rulings that national rules governing the grant of remedies should not be such as to render the exercise of a Community right (albeit only a putative right) ineffective, it seems to fit less well with the Court's other statement that, in the absence of harmonization, national courts are not obliged, by virtue of Community law, to create new remedies. Article 5 in this case was given a more dynamic role by the Court. According to the House of Lords, the remedy of interim relief against the Crown was not available under national law, yet the effect of setting aside the 'rule of national law' which prohibited the grant of relief would be to provide for this very remedy to ensure the effectiveness of Community law. Indeed, this point was argued by the United Kingdom and Ireland in their submissions to the Court in the case:[18]

> 30. According to the United Kingdom, the concept of the direct effect of certain Treaty provisions cannot create new remedies in national law. It emphasizes that this position was confirmed by the Court in its judgment in [*Rewe* v *Hauptzollamt Kiel*] . . .
>
> 31. The Court therefore acknowledges by implication that the scope of the protection of directly effective rights will vary from one Member State to another pending harmonization by Community legislation. The only requirement of Community law is that existing remedies should not be emasculated to the point at which there is, in practice, no remedy at all.
>
> . . .

[17] Contrast the willingness of the ECJ to specify the precise conditions under which interim relief against a provision of national law which implemented Community law (which, by contrast with the situation in *Factortame*, was effectively interim relief against the application of Community law) should be available in Cases C–143/88 and C–92/89, *Zuckerfabrik Suderdithmarschen* [1991] ECR I–415, [1993] 3 CMLR 1.

[18] Case C–213/89 [1990] ECR I–2433, 2440–2.

39. Finally, Ireland submits that it would be wholly inappropriate to require the creation of new remedies in national law. Divergences between the national systems as to the right to interim protection can be removed only by legislation on the part of the Council. In the absence of a Community measure of that kind, any problem raised in that regard by national law may be dealt with in the context of a direct action brought by the Commission against the Member State in question.

However, it seems that the Court did not accept the force of these arguments in reaching its decision, nor did it expressly address them in the case.

M. Ross, Refining Effective Enjoyment[19]

Prima facie, the assertion that national courts must make interim relief accessible may appear to be a back-door creation of a Community remedy, in contradiction to the usual premise (specifically repeated by the Advocate General in *Factortame*) that Community law does not impose remedies or judicial procedures different from those already provided by the domestic law of Member States. However, it would seem clear from the Court's ruling that the appropriate distinction to be drawn is between the national courts' primary obligation and the manifestation of compliance. The former is a matter of Community law, by virtue of Article 5, whereas the latter is an adjustment of national law. At its most extreme, this means that if a Member State had no domestic system of interim relief at all, its courts would be required to invent one. That system could still be different from those pertaining in other Member States, pending the creation of any harmonised Community regime, but its *existence* would be demanded as a matter of Community law. It is at this point that *Factortame* may well represent a development of previous rulings on supremacy, rather than just a restatement . . .

It is therefore necessary to consider whether the European Court has changed its stance regarding the jurisdiction of the Community to create new remedies . . .

The greatest radicalism of the *Factortame* decision may yet prove not to be the direct assault on Parliamentary sovereignty as perceived in the popular press, but the more stealthy creation of a Community obligation on national courts to create remedies . . . The Court's judgment in *Factortame* seems to confirm that the availability of proper remedies is part of, not a result of, the doctrine of direct effect. In other words, direct effect is not just a *locus standi* rule but a matter of substantive enjoyment of rights.

Factortame thus indicates that the principle of effectiveness, and Article 5 in particular, requires national courts to set aside any national rule which forms the sole obstacle to the grant of a remedy to protect what may be directly effective Community rights, and to grant such relief as is necessary to ensure the practical effect of the Community measure.

[19] (1990) 15 ELRev. 476, 478.

(e) A Conflict Between the Principle of Effectiveness and the Application of National Procedural and Jurisdictional Rules?

What, then, of national procedural rules which do not form an absolute obstacle to the grant of a remedy, but which nevertheless detract from the adequacy or effectiveness of the remedy? In other words, what of national rules which do not render the exercise of the Community right impossible in practice, but rather which impose restrictions upon it. On the one hand, the Court has said that in the absence of Community harmonization, the Member States may apply national rules of procedure so long as they do not apply them differently to national situations, and so long as they do not render the exercise of the right impossible in practice. Yet on the other hand, the Court in *Von Colson* has stated that the obligation on national courts under Article 5 of the Treaty includes the obligation to provide adequate and effective remedies for breach of Community rights. Again there is a tension between these two principles—the pre-eminence of national rules in the absence of Communuity harmonization on the one hand, and the principle of effectiveness of Community law on the other.

The Court has had to address this issue in the course of several cases in which it was confronted with the application of national rules of procedure and substance which imposed specific limitations—although not absolute barriers to a certain kind of remedy, as in *Ferwerda* and *Factortame*—on the grant of a remedy for breach of Community law.

Case C–177/88, Dekker v Stichting voor Jong Volwassenen (VJV) Plus [1990] I–ECR 3941

The applicant, Dekker, was refused a job with the defendants on the ground that she was pregnant. She sought an order for damages before the Dutch courts and questions were referred to the Court of Justice to ask whether in such circumstances there would be discrimination on grounds of sex in breach of Community law. Having ruled that there would be such discrimination, the Court of Justice addressed the question whether national law could require an applicant to prove fault on the part of the employer before the applicant's claim for judicial redress would succeed.

THE ECJ

23. Article 6 of the Directive recognizes the existence of rights vesting in the victims of discrimination which can be pleaded in legal proceedings. Although full implementation of the Directive does not require any specific form of sanction for unlawful discrimination, it does entail that that sanction be such as to guarantee real and effective judicial protection (judgment in case 14/83 *Von Colson* [1984] ECR 1891, paragraph 23). It must, furthermore, have a real deterrent effect on the employer.

24. It must be observed that, if the employer's liability for infringement of the principle of equal treatment were made subject to proof of a fault attributable to him and also to there being no ground of exemption recognized by the applicable

> national law, the practical effect of those principles would be weakened considerably.
>
> . . .
>
> 26. Accordingly, the answer must be that, although Directive 76/207 gives the Member State, in penalizing infringments of the prohibition of discrimination, freedom to choose between the various solutions appropriate for achieving its purpose, it nevertheless requires that, where a Member State opts for a sanction forming part of the rules on civil liability, any infringement of the prohibition of discrimination suffices in itself to make the person guilty of it fully liable, and no regard may be had to the grounds of exemption envisaged by national law.

Thus, although it held that the remedy was to be determined in accordance with national law, the Court held that the provisions of national law governing civil liability could not be applied in the case where they would subject the claim for redress for breach of a directly effective prohibition against discrimination to a requirement of fault or to a defence of justification.[20] The judgment marks a further departure from the principle of national autonomy in the absence of harmonization of Community procedural rules and remedies, especially since the national rule did not discriminate between situations involving Community law and those involving purely domestic law, and the requirement of fault would probably not render the exercise of the Community right impossible in practice. Further, the requirement of fault and the availability of a defence were not procedural requirements which were to be ignored or overridden, but were in fact substantive provisions relating to national remedies. Advocate General Darmon's comments on the desirability of uniformity form an interesting contrast with the passage from Advocate General Warner's opinion in *Ferwerda*, cited above,[21] where Warner accepted the inevitability of a lack of uniformity in the absence of action by the Community's legislative organs to bring about harmonization:

> Similarly, it would greatly weaken the practical effect of the Community principle of equality of treatment, as well as the uniform application of Community rules, if it were possible to rely on grounds of exemption which necessarily differ between the legal systems of the Member States. Once a female worker has established that she has been discriminated against and has shown the injury caused by that discrimination, it is not, in my opinion, open to the employer to plead any exemption under national law, and the national court will then have the task of imposing sanctions on the discriminatory conduct in accordance with national law, since the Directive leaves that to the discretion of the Member States subject to the proviso laid down by the Court that sanctions shall be 'sufficiently effective to achieve the objective of the directive'.[22]

[20] For further discussion of remedies in the context of sex discrimination, see Ch. 18, pt. 5.

[21] See n. 7 above and text.

[22] Case C–177/88, *Dekker* [1990] ECR I–3941, 3963.

A further weakening in the basic principle that national procedural rules may be applied to the grant of remedies for breach of Community law can be seen in various cases in which individuals brought claims for redress for a state's breach of a directive which had not yet been implemented.

Case C–377/89, Cotter and McDermott v. Minister for Social Welfare and Attorney General
[1991] ECR I–1155, [1991] 3 CMLR 507

The two applicants had sought an order before the Irish High Court to quash the decisions of the Minister for Social Welfare refusing to pay them certain social welfare benefits which had been made available to men who were similarly situated. The applicants had previously obtained a ruling from the Court of Justice that the provisions of Council Directive 79/7 prohibiting all discrimination on grounds of sex in matters of social security were directly effective, and that as long as the Directive remained unimplemented in Ireland they were entitled to have the same national rules applied to them as were applied to men. The rules in question in the case had operated in such a way that married men automatically received increased social welfare payments to provide for dependants, whether or not they actually had any dependents. When the two applicants sought a similar benefit for the same period, the Supreme Court considered that it would offend against the principle of unjust enrichment for them to receive increases for dependants if their husbands had received such increases during the period in question. However, several questions were referred to the Court of Justice to determine whether the applicants would be entitled to the increases even if 'double payment' would occur.

THE ECJ

20. According to the Irish Government, to grant such a right to married women could, in certain circumstances, result in double payment of the same increases to the same families, in particular where both spouses received social security benefits during the period at issue. Such payments would be manifestly absurd and would infringe the prohibition on unjust enrichment laid down by national law.

21. To permit reliance on that prohibition would enable the national authorities to use their own unlawful conduct as a ground for depriving Article 4(1) of the directive of its full effect.

22. The reply to the first question must therefore be that Article 4(1) of the directive must be interpreted as meaning that if, after the expiry of the period allowed for implementation of the directive, married men have automatically received increases in social security benefits in respect of a spouse and children deemed to be dependants without having to prove actual dependency, married women without actual dependants are entitled to those increases even if in some circumstances that will result in double payment of the increases.

Thus the principle of national law could not operate as an obstacle which would prevent the applicants from receiving redress for the breach of the prohibition against sex discrimination.[23] The fact that the principle would have

[23] On the substance of this case, see further Ch. 18. p. 879.

enabled the state to profit from or to rely on its own wrong seems indeed to have played as strong a part in the Court's conclusion that it could not apply, as did the fact that it would have undermined or negated the effectiveness of the Directive by preventing the applicants from receiving any remedy for the breach.[24]

Case C–208/90, Emmott v. Minister for Social Welfare [1991] ECR I–4269, [1991] 3 CMLR 894

The applicant had received disability benefit at a reduced rate which was applicable to all married women pursuant to Irish social security law at the time. She now sought retrospective payment for the period of time during which Council Directive 79/7 had remained unimplemented, and the lower payment had been made to her in breach of the equal treatment principle. Before commencing her case she had corresponded with the Department of Social Welfare seeking the benefit of the Directive, but she had been told that no decision could be made in relation to her until the outcome of the proceedings in the case of *Cotter and McDermott* (above). When she did finally apply for judicial review of the decisions of the authorities in relation to her social security payments, the respondent pleaded that her delay in initiating the claim constituted a bar to the claim. The High Court referred questions to the Court of Justice asking whether it was contrary to Community law for the relevant authorities to rely against the applicant upon a national time limit so as to restrict or to refuse her compensation.

THE ECJ

16. As the Court has consistently held . . . in the absence of Community rules on the subject, it is for the domestic legal system of each Member State to determine the procedural conditions governing actions at law intended to ensure the protection of the rights which individuals derive from the direct effect of Community law, provided that such conditions are not less favourable than those relating to similar actions of a domestic nature nor framed so as to render virtually impossible the exercise of rights conferred by Community law.

17. Whilst the laying down of reasonable time-limits which, if unobserved, bar proceedings, in principle satisfies the two conditions mentioned above, account must nevertheless be taken of the particular nature of directives.

. . .

21. So long as a directive has not been properly transposed into national law, individuals are unable to ascertain the full extent of their rights. That state of uncertainty for individuals subsists even after the Court has delivered a judgment finding that the Member State in question has not fulfilled its obligations under

[24] Contrast Case 68/79, *Hans Just I/S* v. *Danish Ministry for Fiscal Affairs* [1980] ECR 501, [1981] 2 CMLR 714, in which the state was not obliged to repay taxes it had imposed in breach of Community law, if that would unjustly enrich a trader who had passed on the cost of the tax to third parties. Is the difference between the cases explicable on the basis that the applicant in *Cotter* might not have been 'enriched' by the benefits received by the male in respect of the same dependants, or on the basis that the state's breach of Community law as regards taxes in *Just* was a less important 'mistake' than the sex discrimination in social security benefits in Cotter? Or is neither explanation convincing?

> the directive and even if the Court has held that a particular provision or provisions of the directive are sufficiently precise and unconditional to be relied upon before a national court.
>
> . . .
>
> 23. It follows that, until such time as a directive has been properly transposed, a defaulting Member State may not rely on an individual's delay in initiating proceedings against it in order to protect rights conferred upon him by the provisions of the directive and that a period laid down by national law within which proceedings must be initiated cannot begin to run before that time.

In this case the Court clearly decided that, although the procedural rule of national law satisfied its two previous conditions of non-discrimination and not rendering the exercise of the right impossible, it could nevertheless not be applied against an applicant seeking to rely on the provisions of a directive until that directive had been implemented into national law. As with its reasoning in *Cotter and McDermott*, the Court relied to a considerable extent on the concept of 'estoppel', i.e. the idea of preventing the state from relying upon its own default. In *Emmott*, what that meant was that the state should not be able to benefit from a national time limit to bar an action, until such time as it has given individuals clear knowledge of their right to bring such an action by properly implementing the Social Security Directive. Thus the national rule here did not have to yield to the principle of adequacy or effectiveness, as, for example, was the case in *Dekker* and *Factortame*, but instead to the prior obligation of the state to implement directives before time could start running to bar the rights arising under them.

After *Factortame*, *Cotter*, and *Emmott*, the approach of the Court to the requirement that remedies for breach of Community law be adequate and effective had made considerable inroads into the principle of national procedural autonomy. Although in principle, where no specific Community provisions existed, remedies were to be governed by national substantive rules and procedures, this initial deference to national law could quickly be displaced by the Community requirements of adequacy and effectiveness, which required of the national courts a degree of creativity. These requirements, however, could also give rise to a considerable amount of uncertainty about what a national court, faced with an 'inadequate' remedy and a non-implemented directive, should do. This was evident in the second *Marshall* case in which, having succeeded in establishing a directly effective right in the first series of litigation, the complainant was faced with a domestic statutory provision limiting her right to obtain damages for past discrimination. Should the national court override the statutory limit on damages and decide that she had a right to 'adequate compensation' for the breach, or, in the absence of a sufficiently specific Community provision on remedies for sex discrimination, should it apply the national provision which did not, after all, render the exercise of her right 'practically impossible'?

Case C–271/91, Marshall v. Southampton and South West Area Health Authority (No. 2) [1993] ECR I-4367, [1993] 3 CMLR 293

Following the judgment in case 152/84 *Marshall (No 1)* [1986] ECR 723, in which the Court of Justice held that Marshall could rely directly on Directive 76/207 against her public employer to challenge the termination of her employment at age 62, while men could continue to work until age 65, the case was remitted to the national court for compensation to be assessed. It was assessed by the Industrial Tribunal at £18,405 including a sum of £7,710 by way of interest. Under the United Kingdom Sex Discrimination Act 1975, however, the maximum amount of compensation which could be awarded at the relevant time was £6,250, and it was not clear whether the Industrial Tribunal had power under national law to award interest on such an award of compensation. The House of Lords referred several questions to the Court of Justice, asking in essence whether a victim of sex discrimination on the part of an authority which is an emanation of the state is entitled to full reparation for the loss sustained, and whether Article 6 of Directive 76/207 could be relied on by the victim as against national legislation which was intended to give effect to the Directive but which set limits to the amount of compensation which could be awarded.

THE ECJ

19. The purpose of the Directive is to put into effect in the Member States the principle of equal treatment for men and women as regards the various aspects of employment, in particular working conditions, including the conditions governing dismissal.

. . .

21. As the Court held in Case 152/84 *Marshall*, cited above, since Article 5(1) prohibits generally and unequivocally all discrimination on grounds of sex, in particular with regard to dismissal, it may be relied upon as against a State authority acting in its capacity as an employer, in order to avoid the application of any national provision which does not conform to that article.

22. Article 6 of the Directive puts Member States under a duty to take the necessary measures to enable all persons who consider themselves wronged by discrimination to pursue their claims by judicial process. Such obligation implies that the measures in question should be sufficiently effective to achieve the objective of the directive and should be capable of being effectively relied upon by the persons concerned before national courts.

23. As the Court held in Case 14/83, *Von Colson and Kamann* v. *Land Nordrhein-Westfalen* [1984] ECR 1891, paragraph 18, Article 6 does not prescribe a specific measure to be taken in the event of a breach of the prohibition of discrimination but leaves Member States free to choose between the different solutions suitable for achieving the objective of the Directive, depending on the different situations which may arise.

24. However, the objective is to arrive at real equality of opportunity and cannot therefore be attained in the absence of measures appropriate to restore such equality when it has not been observed. As the Court stated in paragraph 23 in *Von Colson*, cited above, those measures must be such as to guarantee real and effective judicial protection and have a real deterrent effect on the employer.

25. Such requirements necessarily entail that the particular circumstances of each breach of the principle of equal treatment should be taken into account. In the event of discriminatory dismissal contrary to Article 5(1) of the Directive, a situation of equality could not be restored without either reinstating the victim of discrimination or, in the alternative, granting financial compensation for the loss and damage sustained.

26. When financial compensation is the measure adopted in order to achieve the objective indicated above, it must be adequate, in that it must enable the loss and damage actually sustained as a result of the discriminatory dismissal to be made good in full in accordance with the applicable national rules.

. . .

30. It also follows from that interpretation that the fixing of an upper limit of the kind at issue in the main proceedings cannot, by definition, constitute proper implementation of Article 6 of the directive, since it limits the amount of compensation *a priori* to a level which is not necessarily consistent with the requirement of ensuring real equality of opportunity through adequate reparation for the loss and damage sustained as a result of discriminatory dismissal.

31. With regard to the second part of the second question relating to the award of interest, suffice it to say that full compensation for the loss and damage sustained as a result of discriminatory dismissal cannot leave out of account factors, such as the effluxion of time, which may in fact reduce its value. The award of interest, in accordance with the applicable national rules, must therefore be regarded as an essential component of compensation for the purposes of restoring real equality of treatment.

. . .

34. It follows from the considerations set out above as to the meaning and scope of Article 6 of the Directive, that that provision is an essential factor for attaining the fundamental objective of equal treatment for men and women, in particular as regards working conditions, including the conditions governing dismissal, referred to in Article 5(1) of the Directive, and that where, in the event of discriminatory dismissal, financial compensation is the measure adopted in order to restore that equality, such compensation must be full and may not be limited *a priori* in terms of amount.

35. Accordingly, the combined provisions of Article 6 and Article 5 of the Directive give rise, on the part of a person who has been injured as a result of discriminatory dismissal, to rights which that person must be able to rely upon before the national courts as against the State and authorities which are an emanation of the State.

36. The fact that Member States may choose among different solutions in order to achieve the objective pursued by the directive depending on the situations which may arise, cannot result in an individual's being prevented from relying on Article 6 in a situation such as that in the main proceedings where the national authorities have no discretion in applying the chosen solution.

. . .

38. Accordingly, the reply to be given to the third question is that a person who has been injured as a result of discriminatory dismissal may rely on the provision of Article 6 of the Directive as against an authority of the State acting in its capacity as employer in order to set aside a national provision which imposes limits on the amount of compensation recoverable by way of reparation.

This case represents an interesting change in approach by the Court, given that it had decided in *Von Colson* that Article 6 of the Equal Treatment Directive was not sufficiently precise to give rise to a right to any specific remedy. The terms of the 1975 Act were clearly not capable of 'interpretation in the light of' the requirements of access to an adequate remedy in the Directive,[25] and if the remedial provision (Article 6) of the Directive was not sufficiently precise to be capable of direct effect, it seemed as though the applicant would be left without an adequate remedy. However, the Court decided that, although Article 6 did not specify any precise remedy, it did require that whatever remedy the state chose to provide should be adequate and effective. Thus, once the state provided a form of remedy, an applicant could rely directly on Article 6 of the Directive to ensure the adequacy and effectiveness of that particular remedy. Given that the remedy chosen by the United Kingdom here was damages, both the imposition of a statutory ceiling on damages and the possible refusal to award interest on those damages were contrary to the principle of adequacy and effectiveness embodied in Article 6.

Following on from *Factortame*, *Emmott*, and *Cotter*, here then were two more national remedial rules, one substantive and one jurisdictional—a ceiling on damages and a lack of power to award interest—which were to be ignored or overridden by the national court in favour of providing an effective remedy for a past breach of a fundamental rule of Community law. However, it is interesting to compare the conclusion in *Marshall (No 2)* with the earlier case law of the Court which is cited in some of the extracts quoted above, in particular the cases of *Humblet*[26] and *Roquette*.[27] We have seen that in these cases the Court ruled that the question whether or not to award interest on the reimbursement of sums which were wrongly levied under Community law was for the Member States to decide.[28] In *Marshall*, however, it was clearly not for the Member State to decide whether or not to award interest on damages which represent compensation for a breach of Community law. Whether breach of the Community prohibition on sex discrimination was considered by the Court to be more serious or more fundamental than the wrongful imposition of a tax or levy in pursuance of Community law, or whether the *Roquette* and *Humblot* cases would be differently decided today is not clear.

The first noticeable brake imposed by the Court on this progressive development of the 'effective national remedy' requirement came, however, with the case of *Steenhorst-Neerings*. In what seemed like a similar case to that of

[25] See Case C–106/89, *Marleasing SA* v. *La Comercial de Alimentacion SA* [1990] ECR I–4135, [1992] 1 CMLR 205.

[26] Case 6/60, n. 2 above.

[27] Case 26/74, *Société Roquette Frères* v. *Commission* [1976] ECR 677.

[28] See also a recent case in which the Court ruled that where a Member State sought to recover sums which were due under Community law but which, through a mistake of the national authorities, had not been charged, it was for national law to decide whether or not a demand for payment of the sums would be barred: C–31–44/91, *Lageder* v. *Amministrazione delle Finanze dello Stato* [1993] ECR I–1761.

Emmott, the Court was asked to rule on the compatibility with Community law of a national law restricting the right to retroactive payment of damages for sex discrimination.

Case C–338/91, Steenhorst-Neerings v. Bestuur van de Bedrijfsvereniging voor Detailhandel, Ambachten en Huisvrouwen [1993] ECR I–5475

Under the Dutch Act (AAW), men and unmarried women were entitled to benefits after the first year of incapacity for work up to the age of 65. This entitlement was extended in 1979 to married women, with the exception of those whose incapacity for work arose before October 1975. The Higher Social Security Court held that this exception was discriminatory on the ground of sex and thus invalid, since it applied only to married women. The AAW also provided that benefits should not be payable retroactively for more than one year before the date on which they were claimed. Following the ruling of the Higher Social Security Court, Steenhorst-Neerings in 1988 applied for benefits on the basis of incapacity for work with effect from one year earlier than her claim, that is from 1987. She was granted those benefits, but at the same time they were withdrawn as from 1989 when she became entitled to a widow's pension. When she challenged that decision, several questions were referred to the Court of Justice as to the compatibility of the various provisions of the AAW with Directive 79/7.

THE ECJ

14. By virtue of Article 4(1) of Directive 79/7 Member States may not maintain beyond 23 December 1984, the expiry date for transposition of the Directive, any inequality of treatment which is attributable to the previously applicable conditions for entitlement to benefit (Case 80/87, *Dik and Others* v. *College van Burgemeester en Wethouders* [1988] ECR 1601); if the Directive has not been implemented that provision may be relied on by individuals after the date in order to preclude the application of any national provision inconsistent with the Directive (Case 71/85, *Netherlands* v. *Federatie Nederlandse Vakbeweging* [1986] ECR 3855).

15. The right to claim benefits for incapacity for work under the same conditions as men, conferred on married women by the direct effect of Article 4(1) of Directive 79/7, must be exercised under the conditions determined by national law, provided that, as the Court has consistently held, those conditions are no less favourable than those relating to similar domestic actions and that they are not framed so as to render virtually impossible the exercise of rights conferred by Community law (see, *inter alia*, Case C–208/90 *Emmott* [1991] ECR I–4269, paragraph 16).

16. The national rule restricting the retroactive effect of a claim for benefits for incapacity for work satisfies the two conditions set out above.

17. However, the Commission considers that according to the judgment in *Emmott* (paragraphs 21, 22 and 23) the time-limits for proceedings brought by individuals seeking to avail themselves of their rights are applicable only when a Member State has properly transposed the Directive and that that principle applies in this case.

18. That argument cannot be upheld.

. . .

21. It should be noted first that, unlike the rule of domestic law fixing time-limits for bringing actions, the rule described in the question referred for a preliminary ruling in this case does not affect the right of individuals to rely on Directive 79/7 in proceedings before the national courts against a defaulting Member State. It merely limits the retroactive effect of claims made for the purpose of obtaining the relevant benefits.

22. The time-bar resulting from the expiry of the time-limit for bringing proceedings serves to ensure that the legality of administrative decisions cannot be challenged indefinitely. The judgment in *Emmott* indicates that that requirement cannot prevail over the need to protect the rights conferred on individuals by the direct effect of provisions in a directive so long as the defaulting Member State responsible for those decisions has not properly transposed the provisons into national law.

23. On the other hand, the aim of the rule restricting the retroactive effect of claims for benefits for incapacity for work is quite different from that of a rule imposing mandatory time-limits for bringing proceedings. As the Government of the Netherlands and the defendant in the main proceedings explained in their written observations, the first type of rule, of which examples can be found in other social security laws in the Netherlands, serves to ensure sound administration, most importantly so that it may be ascertained whether the claimant satisfied the conditions for eligibility and so that the degree of incapacity, which may well vary over time, may be fixed. It also reflects the need to preserve financial balance in a scheme in which claims submitted by insured persons in the course of a year must in principle be covered by the contributions collection during that same year.

It is clear that the national rule in *Steenhorst-Neerings* restricting the retroactivity of a claim for benefit, when that benefit could not have been claimed in previous years owing to the existence then of a national provision which was incompatible with the Social Security Directive, very seriously undermines the effectiveness of the Directive. The applicant in this case had been effectively prevented, until the judgment of the domestic court in 1988, from claiming the benefit to which she was entitled under the Directive, yet she was now, in the interests of the state's administrative convenience and financial balance, to be debarred from claiming that benefit with retroactive effect. There is no doubt that the administrative convenience and financial concerns of the state in *Emmott* would equally well have been served by a ruling that a time limit on judicial review proceedings did not undermine the effectiveness of the applicant's remedy, but the Court did not rule in this way. Yet the circumstances in *Steenhorst-Neerings* are very similar to those in *Emmott*, given the existence of a plaintiff who had in the past been prevented by national provisions from claiming a right under Community law, and who now found herself confronting a restriction which seriously reduced the effectiveness of the remedy available to her. Although it is true that in *Emmott* the effect of the time limit for judicial review would have been to bar the applicant's claim completely before the Directive was implemented, whereas in *Steenhorst-Neerings* it merely reduced her remedy to a back-claim of one year only, it is clear that the ruling in the latter case represents a distinct change in judicial approach. Where an applicant is prevented from realizing the extent of her rights under Community law on account of inadequate implementation or non-implementation of a directive, the principle underlying *Emmott* would point to a conclusion that a Member State could not rely on a procedural rule such as a limit on the retroactivity of a claim for benefit, until it had made clear what rights the applicant had by implementing the directive properly.

Further, if a ceiling on damages or a lack of power to award interest was contrary to the principle of effectiveness in *Marshall (No 2)*, it is difficult to see how the restriction of the retroactive effect of a claim for a benefit in *Steenhorst-Neerings* was not equally contrary to that principle. The emphasis of the Court in paragraphs 14 to 15 of the latter decision is on the two conditions seen in its early case law—that there is equality with domestic remedies and that the exercise of the right is not impossible in practice—with no mention of the stronger requirements of adequacy and effectiveness which had emerged in more recent case law. *Steenhorst-Neerings* is a poorly reasoned judgment which fits ill with the Court's conclusions in many previous decisions and with the philosophy of effectiveness which underlies them. However, it has since been extended and reinforced by the subsequent ruling in *Johnson (No 2)*, in which the Court ruled that, even if the concerns of the state to ensure administrative convenience and financial balance were not in issue, a similar rule restricting to one year the retroactive effect of a claim for a non-contributory incapacity benefit was compatible with Community law.[29] The Court took the view that the rule satisfied the two conditions for national procedural autonomy, since it applied to national causes of action and Community causes of action alike, and it did not render the exercise of the right impossible. Again, there was no reference to the requirement of effectiveness or adequacy, and the principles on which the rulings in *Von Colson*, *Emmott*, and *Marshall (No 2)* were based, were abandoned.

2. A DIFFERENT APPROACH? THE EXPRESS CREATION OF A 'UNIFORM' REMEDY BY THE COURT OF JUSTICE

Given the continued absence of a uniform system of Community procedural rules and conditions governing the enforcement of Community law and the grant of remedies for breach, a considerable volume of litigation of the kind exemplified above which seeks a ruling from the Court on the compatibility of particular national procedural and substantive rules with the principles of adequacy and effectiveness is likely to arise. But the Court, in a decision of

[29] Case C–410/92, *Johnson* v. *Chief Adjudication Officer*, 6 Dec. 1994. For further discussion, see Ch. 18. p. 883.

considerable constitutional significance for the Community, added a new dimension to its jurisprudence concerning remedies for breach of EC law by requiring the uniform provision amongst the Member States of at least one important form of remedy: a claim in damages for breach of Community law. And significantly, too, the Court ruled that this remedy should be available for the failure to comply with Community measures which are not themselves directly effective.

Cases C–6/90 and C–9/90, Francovich and Bonifaci v. Italy [1991] ECR I–5357, [1993] 2 CMLR 66

The applicants brought separate domestic actions in this case arising out of the failure by the Italian government to implement Directive 80/987 on the protection of employees in the event of the insolvency of their employer. Both were owed wages from their employers after insolvency, but since no steps had been taken pursuant to the Directive to guarantee the employees payment of the outstanding claims, they brought proceedings against the Italian state claiming that it was liable to pay them the sums owed, either by way of having the guarantees in the Directive enforced against the state, or by way of an action in damages against the state. Upon receiving references in identical terms from the two Italian courts, the Court of Justice held that, although the provisions of the Directive in question lacked sufficient precision to be directly effective and to enable individuals to rely on them against the state, the Directive nevertheless clearly intended to confer rights of which these individuals had been deprived through the state's non-implementation of the Directive.

THE ECJ

29. The national court thus raises the issue of the existence and scope of a State's liability for harm resulting from the breach of its obligations under Community law . . .

(a) *The existence of State liability as a matter of principle*

30. It must be recalled first of all that the EEC Treaty has created its own legal system which is an integral part of the legal systems of the Member States and which their courts are bound to apply; the subjects of that legal system are not only the Member States but also their nationals. Just as it imposes obligations on individuals, Community law is also intended to create rights which become part of their legal patrimony; those rights arise not only where they are expressly granted by the Treaty but also by virtue of obligations which the Treaty imposes in a clearly defined manner both on individuals and on the Member States and the Community institutions: see Case 26/62 *Van Gend en Loos* and Case 6/64 *Costa v. ENEL.*

. . .

32. Furthermore, it has been consistently held that the national courts whose task it is to apply the provisions of Community law in cases within their jurisdiction must ensure that those rules have full effect and protect the rights which they confer on individuals: see in particular Case 106/77 *Simmenthal* and Case C–213/89 *Factortame*.

33. It must be held that the full effectiveness of Community rules would be

impaired and the protection of the rights which they grant would be weakened if individuals were unable to obtain compensation when their rights are infringed by a breach of Community law for which a Member State can be held responsible.

34. The possibility of compensation by the Member State is particularly indispensible where, as in this case, the full effectiveness of Community rules is subject to prior action on the part of the State and consequently individuals cannot, in the absence of such action, enforce the rights granted to them by Community law before the national courts.

35. It follows that the principle of State liability for harm caused to individuals by breaches of Community law for which the State can be held responsible is inherent in the system of the Treaty.

36. Further foundation for the obligation on the part of Member States to pay compensation for such harm is to be found in Article 5 EEC, under which the Member States are required to take all appropriate measures, whether general or particular, to ensure fulfilment of their obligations under Community law. Among these is the obligation to nullify the unlawful consequences of a breach of Community law . . .

37. It follows from all the foregoing that it is a principle of Community law that the Member States are obliged to pay compensation for harm caused to individuals by breaches of Community law for which they can be held responsible.

There is no doubt that *Francovich* is a very important judgment, although it left many questions about the shape and scope of the Community damages remedy unanswered. Some of these questions will be addressed below. But it is interesting first to consider to what extent it represents a departure from the Court's previous approach to the provision of remedies at national level for breach of Community law.

We have seen that the Court had stated that it did not require the creation of new remedies, although in *Factortame* it had required something very close to the creation of a new national remedy—the availability of interim relief against the Crown, which according to the House of Lords was prohibited under national law. It might be argued that *Factortame* was, like many of the other cases cited above, simply an example of the Court requiring the removal of a national barrier to the grant of an existing national remedy or requiring the application of an existing national remedy to a new situation. This analysis seems to collapse the distinction between the creation of a new remedy and the provision of an existing national remedy in a new situation. But if the analysis is correct and the Court in *Factortame* was merely requiring the grant of an existing remedy in a novel situation, then it is hard to understand what sort of situation the Court had in mind when it stated in earlier judgments that Community law did not require the creation of new national remedies. There are very few genuinely 'new' remedies, since most states provide standard remedies such as damages, a mandatory or prohibitory injunction, or a declaration, although they do so in varying situations and under varying conditions of national law. On this analysis, it is hard to think of an example of a wholly new remedy which the Court might have required, and its reassurance to national courts that the creation of new remedies is not demanded by Community law would seem empty of substance. On the other hand, if what the Court meant was that it would not require the application in aid of Community law of a national remedy in circumstances or under conditions in which it could *never* have been available purely under national law (e.g. requiring specific performance of a contract of employment) then, as was argued earlier, the ruling in *Factortame* would seem to contradict this. Indeed in *Francovich*, Advocate General Mischo expressly argued at paragraph 53 of his opinion:

> Since Case 213/89 *Factortame*, there can no longer, I think, be any doubt that in certain cases Community law may itself directly confer on national judicial authorities the necessary powers in order to ensure effective judicial protection of those rights, even where similar powers do not exist in national law.

This leads one to question what was so novel about the approach in *Francovich*, given that the Court seems already effectively to have required the 'creation of new remedies' in national law. *Francovich* does indeed mark a break from the previous case law on the provision of remedies for breach of Community law. It is clear from the Court that the principle of state liability in damages is to be applicable nationally as a *Community* remedy and not merely as a national remedy. As a consequence of the fundamental requirements of supremacy and effectiveness, it ruled, the principle of state liability in damages is inherent in Community law as an actual principle of *Community* law, and not merely by virtue of the adaptation of a national remedy to Community circumstances.

There has been considerable comment on the novelty and significance of the *Francovich* decision in this regard:

G. Bebr, *Francovich* v *Italy*, *Bonifaci* v *Italy*[30]

The non-contractual liability of the Member States for a breach of Community law has hardly been questioned. However, the legal ground for such liability has remained controversial. The jurisprudence of the Court has been generally understood as implying that such liability is subject to national law—which is neither a satisfactory nor a reliable solution as it presupposes the existence of a national legal system of public tort liability.

In the absence of any Treaty provision on the liability of the Member States, the Court faced once more a difficult task in closing the gap . . . Even this time, the Court closed this gap availing itself of the general system of the Treaty and of its underlying principles. *Van Gend en Loos* and *Costa* are the classic examples for such creative jurisprudence. Following these constitutional rulings, the Court placed the liability of the Member States under Community law . . .

For this purpose the Court turned to Article 5 EEC, under which the Member

[30] (1992) 29 CMLRev. 559, 572.

States are committed to a loyal cooperation in executing their Community obligations. The Court has increasingly invoked this Treaty provision and practically elevated it to a constitutional principle.

M. Ross, Beyond *Francovich*[31]

The position as clarified by *Factortame* would seem to have been that there is a Community law right to an appropriate remedy inherent in any directly effective right, but still leaving the national court to discern or create the remedy in question. By extending liability in *Francovich*, the Court has invented a Community law remedy for for a particular type of breach of obligation by a Member State, but this does not mean that it supersedes the obligations on national courts that already exist . . .

Thus, insofar as *Francovich* would demand the specific remedy of damages for breach of Article 30, it represents a development of individual protection. Plaintiffs are no longer at the mercy of national courts as to what qualifies as 'effective' protection . . .

A more fundamental result and reappraisal of the regime of Community law is achieved if *Francovich* is interpreted as travelling at least some way down the path towards establishing and entrenching an individual right to have Member States observe their Community obligations . . . On the narrower view, the case refines what is meant by *effective* (in the form of a new remedy in Community law) whereas the more radical interpretation emphasises its effect on *protection* (by adding to the rights which can give rise to a remedy) . . .

Thus, in the longer term, it is suggested that the likeliest contribution of *Francovich* to the framework of Community law is constitutional in character.

P.P. Craig, *Francovich*, Remedies and the Scope of Damages Liability[32]

The language used by the Advocate General throws the issue of Community law involvement with the remedies available under national law into sharp relief . . .

Now it may be contended that the most difficult aspect of this issue did not have to be faced squarely in *Francovich* itself, since the case was not concerned with the situation where the relevant national law had to create a wholly new type of remedy. After all the actual relief at stake was a damages remedy against the state, and most legal systems recognise an action of this kind.

The reasoning conceals as much as it reveals. The crucial issue is the meaning to be accorded to phrases such as 'type of remedy' or 'kind of action'. It is readily apparent that the broader the construction given to these phrases, the less often will it appear to be the case that Community law is requiring the Member State to create a new remedy. Thus, while most, if not all, legal systems will recognise some species of damages action against the state, there will be significant differences as to the more precise conditions of that liability . . . If Community law requires a Member State to adopt, for example, a damages action which is subject to very different criteria from that which existed hitherto then in reality that state is being required to create what amounts to a new remedy.

[31] (1993) 56 MLR 55, 60–61, 71. [32] (1993) 109 LQR 595, 600.

Thus it can be seen that, while commentators agree on the fundamental constitutional significance of the *Francovich* decision for the Community, there are differing views as to why this is. One view is that the requirement that the states provide a damages remedy is not in itself so significant, since an award of damages is not a remedy unknown to any of the Member States. Thus *Francovich* did not necessarily involve the creation of an entirely new kind of remedy by the Court and, besides, the Court in *Factortame* had already effectively required the provision of remedies which were unavailable in national law. Another view is that what is important about the case is the fact that it expressly held that the principle of state liability—the requirement of a damages remedy for breach of Community law—was inherent in *Community* law, and was not simply a matter of protecting Community rights by means of some existing national remedy.

A further view, which will be examined first, is that the primary significance of the judgment lies in the fact that it requires the provision by national courts of a damages remedy for breach of Community measures which lack direct effect, thus enhancing the effectiveness of such laws without their first having to satisfy the criteria (precision, etc.) for direct effect. As was seen earlier in this chapter, the Court, in response to the failure of states to implement EC law properly, had done much to ensure the enforcement of Community law through its elaboration of the principle of direct effect. But this principle had its own limitations, and the Court also began to develop ways—through the cases of *Von Colson* and *Marleasing*[33]—to further the domestic enforcement of Community law which was not directly effective. *Francovich* represents an important additional move in this direction, by providing individuals who are affected by the failure of states to comply with measures which lack direct effect to obtain a remedy in damages.

D.Curtin, State Liability under Private Law: A New Remedy for Private Parties[34]

It can be said that the Court is being more than a little creative. The case law it cites has always been premised on the duty of national courts to ensure the effective protection of *directly effective* rights . . . The Court in its judgment in *Francovich* simply refers to 'rights' thereby deciding the point that it is not only rights which are capable of being categorised as 'directly effective' which must be afforded judicial protection by the national courts but also those rights which are not directly effective. *Sotto voce*, therefore, the Court has taken a significant step forward in its reasoning.. . . .

The Court's judgment in *Francovich* has considerably boosted the enforcement of Community law by vigilant individuals, strengthening the possibility of being awarded damages against a State because of its failure to legislate is a considerable incentive for individuals to turn to national courts.

[33] Case 14/83, *Von Colson and Kamann* v. *Land Nordrhein-Westfalen* [1984] ECR 1891, [1986] 2 CMLR 430 and Case 106/89, n. 25 above.

[34] (1992) 21 ILJ 74, 78.

J. Steiner, From Direct Effects to Francovich[35]

The breakthrough in *Francovich* lay not so much in the fact that individuals were entitled to claim damages against the State—in the context of actions based on directly effective Community law against 'public' bodies, that had long been possible—but that their claim to compensation was independent of the principle of direct effects . . .

A principle of State liability as applied in *Francovich* is arguably more legitimate as a means of enforcement of Community law than the principle of direct effects. Under the latter principle, Treaty provisions, the scope of which may not be clear (for example Art 119), may be enforced against the legitimate expectations of private parties. The majority of 'public' bodies, against which directives may be invoked, can hardly be seen as responsible for non-implementation . . .

The principles of direct and indirect effect have done much to enable citizens to assert their Community rights, and obtain an appropriate remedy, in the individual case. But neither principle . . . rectifies the primary failure of Member States adequately to implement Community law. Thus a remedy by way of damages for individuals deprived of their Community rights as a result of the State's failure to implement Community law is necessary to ensure the full effectiveness of Community law.

3. *FRANCOVICH* AND REMEDIES IN THE FUTURE

Apart from the variety of views as to the most important aspects of the *Francovich* ruling, one matter which was common to most commentators was a criticism of the absence of adequate guidance by the Court as to the conditions for the grant of the damages remedy. If it is indeed a Community remedy, why did the Court not lay down uniform conditions beyond the three minimal conditions it specified for cases involving the non-implementation of a directive—i.e. the existence of a right, whose content is clearly defined by the directive, and a causal link between the individual's loss and the breach of Community law? Why did the Court continue to refer to national law to determine the substantive and procedural conditions governing the grant of this remedy?:

38. Although State liability is thus required by Community law, the conditions under which that liability gives rise to a right to compensation depend on the nature of the breach of Community law giving rise to the harm.

39. Where, as in this case, a Member State fails to fulfil its obligations under Article 189(3) EEC to take all measures necessary to achieve the result prescribed by a directive, the full effectiveness of that rule of Community law requires that there should be a right to compensation where three conditions are met.

[35] (1993) 18 ELRev. 3, 9–10, 21.

> 40. The first of those conditions is that the result prescribed by the directive should entail the grant of rights to individuals. The second condition is that it should be possible to identify the content of those rights on the basis of the provisions of the directive. Finally, the third condition is the existence of a causal link between the breach of the State's obligation and the harm suffered by the injured parties.

Apart from these three prerequisites, the Court specified no more precise or detailed conditions under which the remedy should be made available. Nor did it give any indication of the conditions which might apply to state breaches other than the non-implementation of or failure to comply with a directive. Instead, the Court continued as in its earlier case law to point in the direction of national procedural autonomy, even while requiring the uniform provision among the Member States of a damages remedy as a matter of Community law:

> 42. Subject to that reservation, it is in accordance with the rules of national law on liability that the State must make reparation for the consequences of the harm caused. In the absence of any Community legislation, it is a matter for the internal legal order of each Member State to determine the competent courts and lay down the detailed procedural rules for legal proceedings intended fully to safeguard the rights which individuals derive from Community law: see Case 60/75, *Russo* v. *Aima*, Case 33/76, *Rewe* v. *Landwirtschaftskammer Saarland* and Case 158/80, *Rewe* v. *Hauptzollamt Kiel*.
>
> 43. It must also be pointed out that the substantive and procedural conditions laid down by the national law of the various Member States on compensation for harm may not be less favourable than those relating to similar internal claims and may not be so framed as to make it virtually impossible or excessively difficult to obtain compensation.

Given its emphasis on the requirement of state liability for breach as a principle of Community law, it is curious that the Court did not lay down more detailed guidelines for the development of the Community damages remedy, since leaving to national substantive and procedural rules the task of determining the scope and shape of the remedy was likely to undermine the very reasons for the Court's establishment of the remedy, by leading to differing standards of effectiveness of protection for the Community measure from state to state. Advocate General Mischo in the case took the view that the *substantive* conditions relating to the availability of the new remedy should be for the Court to lay down, but that the procedural rules should be left to be determined by national law. But the Court did not seem to distinguish between substantive and procedural conditions (apart from the three substantive conditions laid down above for failure to comply with a directive), and instead indicated that all such conditions and rules should be primarily for Member States to lay down. The *Francovich* decision provoked a great deal of comment and divergent views were expressed regarding the likely future scope of the damages remedy and the conditions under which it may be available.

G. Bebr, Francovich v. Italy, Bonifaci v. Italy[36]

As the liability of the Member States is based on Community law, so are of course also the conditions required for it which the Court had to state . . . [The writer then sets out and discusses the three conditions specified by the Court of Justice.]

The Court unequivocally stated that these conditions were 'sufficient' for incurring the liability of the Member States, thus implying that these conditions were exhaustive. It may, therefore, safely be assumed that neither a fault nor negligence on the part of the defaulting Member State is required for engaging its liability . . .

Curiously enough, the Court did not state any criteria for assessing the damage inflicted. Is a general damage sufficient or must it be a special one? Must the damage be already actual or does it suffice if the damage is determined later on? And is there a relation, if any, between the nature of the breach of a Community obligation and the damage suffered or, to state it differently, does any breach of a Community obligation by a Member State incur its liability?

M. Ross, Beyond Francovich[37]

On the surface, therefore, the *Francovich* judgment appears to open up a host of possible breaches by Member States of Treaty obligations which might lead to claims for damages by individuals. There is no mention of any need for breach by the State to be deliberate, so that even merely 'accidental' failures to transpose directives accurately would create liability. However, this is consistent with the primary importance attached by the Court to the 'inherent' principle of State liability. Similarly, there is no indication of any defences which might be recognised by the Court . . .

This typically paradoxical judgment, combining terseness of expression with expansiveness of principle, thus raises a wide range of controversial and complicated issues. For example, is the application of the *Francovich* principle of liability the same for all sources of Community law obligations which might be infringed? Is the doctrine permissible in the context of directly effective rights as well as those which are not? Is it a remedy of last resort where other options are unproductive or impossible for the plaintiff, or is it an independent and inalienable right? Against which arms or organs of the State does the principle operate?

It should be noted at this point that, although it is true that the Court in *Francovich* did not mention the need for deliberate failure on the part of the Member State, it was dealing in the case with a failure to implement a directive on time, which in itself is a knowing breach of Community law. Thus what remained to be answered, and what the Court was to be asked in further preliminary references, was whether it would require other conditions in cases not involving non-implementation of directives. Anticipating such questions, several commentators set out the arguments against a standard of absolute or

[36] N. 30 above, 569, 579, 583. [37] N. 31 above, 60–61, 71.

strict Member State liability for any breach of Community law. Both the principles of fairness and a comparison with the standard of *Community* liability for unlawful acts under Article 215 were suggested as reasons for restricting the scope of state liability.

J. Steiner, From direct effects to Francovich[38]

Moreover, given the dual purpose of *Francovich*, that of protecting individuals' Community rights and ensuring the full effect of Community law there seems no reason in principle why *Francovich* should not apply to a failure by a Member State to fulfil *any* binding obligation of Community law . . .

Secondly, if Member States are to be liable for breach of any binding Community obligation, under what circumstances will they be liable? . . .

A failure to fulfil a Community obligation can take many forms, embracing a broad spectrum of culpability . . . Such failures may be deliberate, knowing, negligent or innocent . . .

Clearly a deliberate or knowing breach of Community law should attract liability . . . There are no reasons of policy for denying liability in respect of such breaches; . . . But there is also a need for a less rigorous standard . . .

The 'special characteristics' and 'particular difficulties' of Community law lie in its lack of precision and uncertainty of scope. The precise nature of a State's obligation may not be clear until elucidated by the Court of Justice. A ruling under Article 169 or Article 177 will undoubtedly clarify matters, not only for the parties concerned but for all Member States. But where a decision of the Court of Justice breaks new ground and makes 'new' law . . . a State should not be liable for acts or omissions which are found to be wrongful as a result of that decision until it has had time to rectify the failure . . .

In the following extract, after discussing the opinion of Advocate General Mischo, the author concludes that he envisaged that Member States would be subjected to a wider liability and on different conditions from that to which the Community is subject under Article 215—and indeed that he envisaged a form of strict liability, not only for non-implementation but also possibly for misimplementation of a Directive.[39]

P. P. Craig, Francovich, Remedies and the Scope of Damages Liability[40]

In the *Francovich* case itself the ECJ made it clear . . . that the conditions of liability would depend upon the nature of the breach of Community law which was in issue. The Advocate General devoted more consideration to this general issue, and considered the relevance of Article 215 as a guide in this respect . . .

The reasons for being wary of imposing some form of strict liability can also be appreciated by reverting to three of the examples given above.

[38] N. 35 above, 11, 17–20.

[39] See also the opinion of Van Gerven A.G.in Case C–128/92, *Banks* v. *British Coal* [1994] ECR I–1209, 1256, [1994] 5 CMLR 30, 79 on the issue of damages for breach of the ECSC Treaty.

[40] N. 32 above, 605, 614, 620–621.

The first concerns the situation in which the Member State incorrectly implements a directive. As has been seen, Advocate General Mischo regards this as an instance in which the requirements of liability fashioned in the context of proceedings under Article 215(2) should not apply: the State is only left with choice as to form and method by which to implement a directive, and these are not choices of economic policy, nor do they involve wide discretionary power. Some stricter species of liability, which involves a more extensive state liability in damages, appears to be envisaged.

This is surely too simple. There may well be no justifiable excuse for a state which has taken no measures to implement a directive within the requisite period. The 'step' from non-implementation to incorrect implementation is much more problematic precisely because the latter phase can cover a wide variety of situations. At one end of the spectrum is the case where the state has, in reality, done almost nothing to fulfil its obligations under the directive . . . At the other end of the spectrum there may be instances in which the scope of the obligations imposed by the directive only become clear in the light of later decisions by the ECJ. In this situation the state may well have passed bona fide measures to apply the directive within national law, but it may simply be unclear until these later decisions of the ECJ that the directive was meant to cover a particular fact situation. In between the two previous examples we can perceive a third. A Member State makes a bona fide attempt to implement the directive. It enacts legislation, or passes certain administrative measures, with this objective in mind. These do not, however, work perfectly, in the sense that they do not in fact wholly succeed in fulfilling the ends stipulated in the Community norm. Other things being equal, this type of problem is more likely to arise the broader is the remit of the directive, and the less specific are the ends stipulated therein. To impose liability in damages in the second and third of these instances for incorrect implementation of the directive *per se* is far from self-evidently desirable or justifiable . . .

One of the central arguments of this paper is that we should think long and hard before assuming that such a strict standard of liability is warranted in relation to many of the other breaches of Community law which might be committed by a state. The paradigm case presented in *Francovich* itself, non-implementation of a directive, is distinctive. The state knows that it is meant to implement the directive within a certain period and it has not done so. The availability of damages in these circumstances is warranted on the conditions laid down in *Francovich* . . . The Advocate General has, however, already signalled that strict conditions of liability might well be applicable against the state in other spheres . . . The arguments against such a development have been presented above. This is not to suggest that there should be no liability for other breaches of Community law by Member States. Rather that the nature and standard of such liability must be carefully thought through. In some circumstances strict liability may be warranted; in others a species of fault-based responsibility may be more appropriate. One thing is clear. If strict liability for illegality per se does become the norm, then the business of government will become risky indeed.

Given the uncertainty left in the wake of *Francovich*, and the wide variety of views expressed in relation to the potential future scope of this principle of state liability, further references to the Court were both desirable and inevitable. In two joined cases, *Brasserie du Pêcheur SA* v. *Germany* and *Factortame (No 3)*,[41] the Court was asked to clarify several questions arising out of the *Francovich* decision. In summary, these questions are (1) whether the principle of state liability is applicable to legislative measures which infringe Community law, (2) whether equivalent domestic limitations and conditions on the right to compensation are applicable in the case of state failure to comply with Community law, (3) whether compensation may be made conditional upon fault on the part of the state in question, (4) whether the national legal system may restrict recovery to property damage only, or whether financial loss including items such as expenses, loss of income, loss of profits, and exemplary damages must also be recoverable, and (5) from which date such damages ought to be assessed. The answers to these questions should go a considerable way towards clarifying the nature of the new damages remedy, and should help to ascertain the extent to which it really involves the creation of a 'new' remedy, as opposed to the application of existing national remedies.

As Craig commented above, the more precisely the Court defines the conditions for the grant of a particular remedy in a way which differs from the national conditions governing the grant of that remedy, the more readily can it be said to be creating new remedies. Given that, in *Francovich*, it had clearly required the provision of a damages remedy in all Member States as a matter of Community law, why did the Court hesitate to outline the shape and scope of this remedy in any more detail? Why did it invoke its earlier case law concerning national procedural autonomy? Was the Court still reluctant to appear to be creating a wholly new remedy which national courts must provide in the precise and uniform circumstances laid down by the Court? Would its elaboration of new remedies really be any more innovative or radical or objectionable to the Member States than was its earlier development of the concepts of direct effect and supremacy?

P. P. Craig, Francovich, Remedies and the Scope of Damages Liability[42]

Why should Community law not be able to direct Member States to develop new remedies, or new species of existing remedies, where these are needed to effectuate Community rights? After all, it is accepted that Community law can lead to the introduction of new rights which might not have previously existed in a Member State, so why not new remedies to give effect to those rights? Two objections are possible.

One is that it might be said that this would infringe upon the division of competence between the ECJ and national courts. In Article 177 actions the former interprets Community law while the latter applies that interpretation to the case at hand when it returns to the national forum. This objection is misplaced. In so far as the ECJ does indicate the type of remedies which are necessary to give effect to Community rights, it *is* interpreting Community law. The fact that this will

[41] Case C–46/93 [1993] OJ C92/4 and C–48/93 [1993] OJ C94/13.

[42] N. 32 above, 600–601.

have an impact at the national level is both obvious and intended, but it does not involve any transgression of function by the ECJ. It will continue to be for national law to determine the more precise conceptual label to be attached to this cause of action, and the procedural conditions under which the remedy can be sought, in the manner described below.

The other objection to the Court demanding new remedies within Member States is that this may necessitate domestic legislative action, if the new remedies cannot be developed by the national courts themselves. But this cannot, in reality, be an objection to any such ECJ rulings. The method by which any particular Member State fulfils its Community law obligations is a purely contingent issue which is dependent on the detailed constitutional arrangements within that state. It cannot, of itself, affect the actual legitimacy of the ECJ ruling in this respect.

It may be that where the Court really does leave to the Member States the decision as to what legislative changes to make in order to comply with Community law, including the substantive and procedural conditions which will shape the availability of a particular Community remedy, it is content that it will not be perceived to be taking on a substantive legislative role. Cases like *Van Gend en Loos*[43] and *Simmenthal*[44] are examples of this, since the Court specified what the required result must be, but left it to the Member States to take whatever national action would be necessary to achieve that. All that was required was to demand that Member States give effect to existing Community measures, by whatever *national* means were appropriate. Where the Community law to which direct effect was 'given' by the Court was fairly clear and sufficiently detailed, the legislative role of the Court then was not so explicit. The same could also be said of its rulings which required Member States to ensure that Community provisions were made effective by the application of existing national remedies to breaches of Community law. But if the Court were to outline not just the effect which was to be given to an existing Community measure but also the details of the exact scope and form of remedy by which the state's breach of Community law should be made good, this would evidently involve a more substantial legislative role on the part of the Court. And although the Court has always been concerned with effectiveness, with the practical realization of the Community's aims at a national level, and has played a considerable role in fleshing out these objectives and in specifying the required result, it has generally left to the Member States the choice of how to implement these aims. This approach seems to embody a recognition that in the case of each Member State, there may be a distinct legal and constitutional system which will have its own way of fulfilling Community obligations and of domestically enforcing and incorporating Community law. The Court has not been concerned with the national mechanisms for enforcement and compliance, but simply with the end result, and

[43] Case 26/62, *Van Gend en Loos* [1963] ECR 1, [1963] CMLR 105.

[44] Case 106/77, *Amministrazione delle finanze dello Stato* v. *Simmenthal SpA* [1978] ECR 629, [1978] 3 CMLR 263. See Ch. 6 for further discussion of this case.

so it has avoided specifying precise legislative alterations to be carried out by all Member States. Thus, as we have repeatedly seen in its case law on remedies, the Court has held that it is for the states to provide remedies for breaches of Community measures, but that in the absence of harmonized Community legislation this can be done in accordance with existing national legal remedies subject to certain threshold conditions. It is interesting to consider again in this light the argument made by Ireland in its submission to the Court in *Factortame*, in support of the argument of the United Kingdom.

> The Irish government emphasises that, if it were otherwise, there would be an unwarranted interference by the court in the manner in which national courts apply Community law according to internal procedures . . .
>
> Finally, Ireland submits that it would be wholly inappropriate to require the creation of new remedies in national law. Divergences between the national systems as to the right to interim protection can be removed only by legislation on the part of the Council.[45]

But the changing approach in *Factortame*, and in cases such as *Emmott*, *Dekker*, *Cotter*, and *Marshall*, demonstrated what was perhaps an increasing impatience on the part of the Court with the pace and weakness of national enforcement of Community law, and the inadequacies of existing systems of national remedies for this purpose. Thus, just as in *Reyners*, in the absence of required Community legislation harmonizing national requirements which restricted freedom of establishment, the Court required national courts to enforce Article 52 directly, in *Francovich* the Court seems to have decided, in the absence of Community legislation providing for harmonized remedies for breach of Community rights, to require national courts to provide a specific remedy as a matter of Community law. If the Court had spelt out at that stage the precise conditions for the grant of the remedy, in the absence of a Community legislative standard by which to proceed, it would be making its own legislative role very clear. Yet in not doing so, it gave rise to a host of questions, some of which inevitably returned very soon to the Court in the *Brasserie du Pêcheur* and *Factortame (No 3)* cases. It may be that the Court prefers to develop the scope of the damages remedy gradually and incrementally, according as cases are referred to it. In this way, its casuistic development of principles and conditions of state liability may be less open to the charge of blatant and detailed law creation by the Court, or of judicial alteration of the existing system of remedies in the Member States, which many would argue should only be done by Community legislation after careful consideration by the relevant political institutions.

The Court very gradually developed principles on the application of national remedies in aid of Community rights from the time of *Rewe-*

[45] See paras. 37 and 39 of the report for the hearing in Case C–213/89, *Factortame Ltd* v. *Secretary of State for Transport* [1990] ECR I–2433, [1990] 3 CMLR 1.

Handelsgesellschaft Nord v. *Hauptzollamt Kiel*,[46] where the only conditions were that the national remedies must be applied in a non-discriminatory manner which did not render the exercise of the Community right impossible, to its ruling in *Factortame* where the condition of effectiveness required any national rule which formed an obstacle to the enforcement of the Community rule to be set aside. The rulings in *Steenhorst-Neerings* and *Johnson (No 2)* seem to indicate a shift back towards national procedural autonomy and away from the central Community requirement of effectiveness, and it remains to be seen whether or not they represent part of a broader pattern. The approach which the Court takes with regard to specifying the substantive and procedural conditions governing the new 'Community remedy'—the *Francovich* principle of state liability—and the role it accords to national provisions in this respect should help in assessing whether or not there is in fact a general trend towards a form of 'judicial subsidiarity' in the area of remedies.

The development by the Court of strong legal requirements in the area of national remedies for breach of Community law has generally been welcomed as a significant contribution to the effectiveness of Community law, at least through the medium of judicial intervention by national courts. However, the welcome has not been unconditional, and many commentators have called on the legislative institutions and political players in the Community legal process to take appropriate action, rather than to leave this area of law for the Court to develop through the inevitably haphazard process of litigation. In part, the concern is that the Court cannot address the issue of remedies on a case-by-case basis as comprehensively or coherently as the political institutions could, and in part it is that the Court is not the most legitimate or appropriate institution for the task of creating a harmonized or co-ordinated system of Community remedies. The following writer has aptly summed up many of the disadvantages of excessive reliance on judicial strategies for ensuring the effectiveness of Community law. His comments are about the role of the Court in enhancing the effectiveness of EC law in general and, although they are not restricted to the issue of remedies, they are very pertinent in this context.

F.Snyder, The Effectiveness of European Community Law[47]

The use of a judicial liability system to ensure the effectiveness of Community law has several disadvantages . . . The first disadvantage stems from the judicial origins of the system. The system has been developed by means of the process of adjudication, that is, by the judiciary in response to *ad hoc* claims. Consequently, almost by definition, it is likely to be less normatively coherent and less comprehensive than a legislative scheme.

A pertinent example concerns the judicial harmonization of national remedies. The general principles of law, elaborated by the Court of Justice on the basis of Articles 164, 173 and 215 EEC, surely include the right to an effective remedy. Differences in national remedies affect the extent to which individuals can rely in

[46] Case 158/80, n. 15 above. [47] (1993) 56 MLR 19, 50–53.

practice on rights derived from Community law. It is, however, open to question whether the institutions, processes, tools and techniques which are currently being used to harmonise remedies are entirely adequate for this purpose. Achieving a harmonisation of national remedies sufficient to ensure effective enforcement of Community rights, while simultaneously respecting the legitimate differences amongst the Member States, is a difficult task. The judiciary, litigation, Article 5 EEC and treaty interpretation all have inherent limits . . .

In the Community context, moreover, the structure of the judicial liability system has broader implications for institutional development. By breathing new life into the form of judicial cooperation envisaged by Article 177 it strengthens the vertical relations of collaboration within the judicial branch at two levels of government. However, it does not directly involve any other national institutions such as parliaments. In addition, it does not necessarily strengthen existing relations between Community institutions, nor does it create any new horizontal links between them, as might have been the case if, for example, the judicial liability system had been enacted by the Council, following a Commission proposal and in cooperation with the Parliament . . .

A second shortcoming of the judicial liability system with regard to ensuring the effectiveness of Community law derives from the fact that it relies on *ad hoc* claims. On the one hand, in general, there is a real question whether the effectiveness of law can be ensured adequately by a system triggered solely by individual claims. This deficiency is accentuated by the absence of framework legislation. On the other hand, a judicial liability system of the Community is inevitably more complex than in any national system. For example, litigation rates throughout the Community are influenced by diverse legal cultures and, for this reason among others, they differ substantially among the different Member States. This alone would make it unlikely that individual litigation by itself could result in the uniform effectiveness of Community law. More generally, however, we simply know too little about the sociological features of Community law or litigation involving Community law to rely heavily on a judicial liability system as a principal means for ensuring effectiveness.

Third, any judicial liability system is only a very diffuse, extensive form of supervision. It represents one end of a continuum, the other end of which is occupied by direct regulation. In developing the judicial liability system, it may be suggested the Court of Justice so far has been concerned more with ensuring the formal enactment of national transposing legislation and less with guaranteeing any particular legislative content . . . Symbolic action is significant, but it may fail to make any real impact on the effectiveness of Community law, especially if by 'effectiveness' we refer to effects in addition to the elaboration of legal doctrine.

Fourth, the European Community system involves complex and delicate relations, not only among Community institutions, but also between the Community and the Member States. Some room for manœuvre for Member States is essential. It may be suggested that if one means of preserving such a political space is denied, others will be found. Therein lies the difficulty of an increasingly extensive interpretation of Article 5 EEC. The Court of Justice has increasingly deduced specific practical duties from its general words. In these circumstances, it would not be surprising if Member States were to seek other strategies. Such strategies may be illegal, such as various forms of non-compliance, or they may be legal, such as systematic recourse to subsidiarity, creative compliance with the letter but not necessarily the spirit of the law, or opting out. In addition, Member States may resort to devices which can play a role analagous to that of directives, as originally intended; that is, to encourage, facilitate or permit decentralised decision-making. Such devices include techniques of statutory interpretation, national legal remedies or instances in which central governments take refuge behind national constitutional structures to preserve regional or local decision-making.

In this context the use by the Court of Justice of Article 5 is a double edged sword. It tends to restrict or close off some of these avenues, but at the same time it suggests the existence of underlying problems which currently cannot be dealt with by the Community by any other means. As part of the process of enforcing Community law, it may be effective both in elaborating legal doctrine and in stimulating changes in specific cases. At the same time, however, when used as a tool to achieve major institutional changes, such as the harmonisation of national remedies, the increasingly broad interpretation of Article 5 may have reached its limits. Its further extension may jeopardise the legitimacy of the Court of Justice without necessarily achieving more general social and political results. Adjudication and a judicial liability system may be less adequate than other processes and tools, whether at Community level, through the European Council, by intergovernmental means, or by the Community in conjunction with the other Member States.

4. FURTHER READING

CRAIG, P. P., '*Francovich*, Remedies and the Scope of Damages Liability' (1993) 109 LQR 595

LEWIS, C., and MOORE, S., 'Duties, Directives and Damages in European Community Law' [1993] Pub.L 151

ROSS, M., 'Refining Effective Enjoyment' (1990) 15 ELRev 476

—— 'Beyond *Francovich*' (1993) 56 MLR 55

STEINER, J., 'From direct effects to *Francovich*' (1993) 18 ELRev. 3

SNYDER, F., 'The Effectiveness of European Community Law' (1993) 56 MLR 19

TEMPLE LANG, J., 'Community Constitutional Law: Article 5 EEC Treaty' (1990) 27 CMLRev. 645

6

The Relationship Between EC Law and National Law: Supremacy

1. INTRODUCTION

We have seen, in examining the concept of direct effect, how the Court of Justice contrasted the novel character of the European Community with that of other international organizations of states, and how this emphasis led to the Court's development of certain unique features of the EC legal order. The fact that the EC was established to achieve a set of ambitious common goals amongst its Member States, and that new political and legal institutions were created for this purpose was evidence, in the Court's view, of the fact that the Community represented a departure from the traditionally 'intergovernmental' nature of the international legal order.

2. THE FIRST DIMENSION: SUPREMACY OF COMMUNITY LAW FROM THE COURT OF JUSTICE'S PERSPECTIVE

According to its reasoning in *Van Gend en Loos*,[1] the subjects and participants in this new legal order were to be not only the Member States but also their citizens. However, the directly effective nature of Community law was not the only dramatic consequence of the Court's conception of this new legal order. The Court reasoned further that if the far-reaching goals set out in the Treaties—the creation of a genuinely common market and 'ever closer union' among the Member States—were to be realized, then the laws of this single Community would have to apply to the same extent and with equal force in each Member State. States could not introduce unilateral change where that was not contemplated by Community law, and Community measures could not be subjected to the varying requirements of the respective national laws of each Member State. Thus the principle of the *supremacy* of Community law over national law was first established by the Court.

[1] Case 26/62, *NV Algemene Transporten Expeditie Ovderneming van Gend en Loos* v. *Nederlandse Administratie der Belastingen* [1963] ECR 1, [1963] CMLR 105.

Case 26/62, NV. Algemene Transporten Expeditie Onderneming van Gend en Loos v. Nederlandse Administratie der Belastingen [1963] ECR 1, [1963] CMLR 105.

The facts are set out in Chapter 4.[2] In the observations submitted in the case, the Belgian Government argued that the Court of Justice should not answer the first question submitted to it, since the matter fell exclusively within the jurisdiction of the Dutch court from which the reference was made:

> That court is confronted with two international treaties both of which are part of national law. It must decide under national law . . . which Treaty prevails over the other or more exactly whether a prior national law of ratification prevails over a subsequent one. This is a typical question of national constitutional law which has nothing to do with the interpretation of an Article of the EEC Treaty and is within the exclusive jurisdiction of the Netherlands court because it can only be answered according to the constitutional principles and jurisprudence of the national law of the Netherlands.

THE ECJ[3]

> The objective of the EEC Treaty, which is to establish a Common Market, the functioning of which is of direct concern to interested parties in the Community, implies that this Treaty is more than an agreement which merely creates mutual obligations between the contracting states . . . It is also confirmed more specifically by the establishment of institutions endowed with sovereign rights . . .
>
> The conclusion to be drawn from this is that the Community constitutes a new legal order of international law for the benefit of which the states have limited their sovereign rights, albeit within limited fields, and the subjects of which comprise not only Member States but also their nationals.

The reasoning of the Court in the case is brief, and apart from its elaboration of the concept of direct effect, where it stressed the need for direct enforcement by national courts of Community norms, little more was said about the need for national courts to accord *primacy* to Community law over conflicting national law. The Court's focus in the *Van Gend* case was on whether Article 12 could give rise to so-called direct effects, so that an individual could rely on and have that Article enforced before domestic courts. Little, if any, express consideration was given to the problem this might create for a domestic court—particularly a domestic court which was not at the highest level of the national court system—which was faced with a clearly conflicting provision of national law.

However, the Advocate General in the case, who did not agree with the Court's conclusion on the direct effect of Article 12, did make mention of the constitutional difficulties which national courts could face.

[2] At 152. [3] N. 1 above, 12.

ADVOCATE GENERAL ROEMER[4]

Even if these arguments alone provide sufficient reasons for rejecting the view that Article 12 has direct internal effect, the following additional arguments must be mentioned.

The position of the constitutional laws of the Member States, above all with regard to the determination of the relationship between supranational or international law and subsequent national legislation is far from uniform.

If Article 12 is deemed to have a direct internal effect, the situation would arise that breaches of Article 12 would render the national customs laws ineffective and inapplicable in only a certain number of Member States. That appears to me to be the case in the Netherlands, the Consitution of which (Article 66) gives international agreements containing generally binding and directly applicable provisions a superior status to that of national law; in Luxembourg . . . and, it may be, in France . . .

On the other hand, it is certain that the Belgian Constitution does not include any provision dealing with the legal effect of international treaties in relation to national law. They seem, according to the case law of the country, to have the same status as national laws.

Similarly there is no provision in the text of the Italian Constitution from which the supremacy of international law over national law can be inferred . . .

Finally, with regard to German constitutional law, Article 24 of the Basic Law provides that the Federation may by legislation transfer sovereign rights to international institutions . . . However, contrary to the views of certain authors, it cannot be inferred from case law that international treaties have supremacy over later national laws.

Clearly the Advocate General felt that the differing constitutional positions of the Member States with regard to the effect of international treaties on national law meant that uniformity of Community law amongst the Member States would not be achieved through the doctrine of direct effect.

On the other hand, the Court of Justice chose to avoid the problem of Member States' differing constitutional approaches to international treaties by describing the legal order created by the Member States under the EEC Treaty as an entirely new system which was different in nature from international law. The Court argued not from the specific perspective of the constitutional law of any individual Member State, but instead spoke broadly of a constitutional transfer of power from the Member States. In the Court's view, the novel nature of the EEC Treaty and of the legal order it had created was to be understood on the basis that the states had limited their sovereign rights and had established new political institutions which they had endowed with sovereign rights. Beyond this major and controversial constitutional claim, the Court concentrated in its judgment in *Van Gend* on the specific legal nature of the Treaty Article in question, and on whether it was capable of conferring rights on individuals which they could invoke before national courts.

[4] N. 1 above, 23.

In a second important case two years later, however, the Court expanded on its constitutional theory of the Community, declaring again that the states had created a sovereign Community by limiting their own sovereign rights, and spelling out this time the precise implications for a provision of national law which was in conflict with a provision of EC law.

Case 6/64, Flaminio Costa v. Enel
[1964] ECR 585, [1964] CMLR 425, 593.

The facts have been set out in Chapter 4.[5]

THE ECJ

The Italian Government submits that the request of the Giudice Conciliatore is 'absolutely inadmissible', in as much as a national court which is obliged to apply a national law cannot avail itself of Article 177.

By contrast with ordinary international treaties, the EEC Treaty has created its own legal system which, on the entry into force of the Treaty, became an integral part of the legal systems of the Member States and which their courts are bound to apply.

By creating a Community of unlimited duration, having its own institutions, its own personality, its own legal capacity and capacity of representation on the international plane and, more particularly, real powers stemming from a limitation of sovereignty or a transfer of powers from the States to the Community, the Member States have limited their sovereign rights, albeit within limited fields, and have thus created a body of law which binds both their nationals and themselves.

The integration into the laws of each Member State of provisions which derive from the Community, and more generally the terms and the spirit of the Treaty, make it impossible for the states, as a corollary, to accord precedence to a unilateral and subsequent measure over a legal system accepted by them on the basis of reciprocity. Such a measure cannot therefore be inconsistent with that legal system. The executive force of Community law cannot vary from one State to another in deference to subsequent domestic laws, without jeopardizing the attainment of the objectives of the Treaty set out in Article 5(2) and giving rise to the discrimination prohibited by Article 7.

The obligations undertaken under the Treaty establishing the Community would not be unconditional, but merely contingent, if they could be called into question by subsequent legislative acts of the signatories . . .

The precedence of Community law is confirmed by Article 189, whereby a regulation 'shall be binding' and 'directly applicable in all Member States'. This provision, which is subject to no reservation, would be quite meaningless if a State could unilaterally nullify its effects by means of a legislative measure which could prevail over Community law.

It follows from all these observations that the law stemming from the Treaty, an independent source of law, could not, because of its special and original nature, be overridden by domestic legal provisions, however framed, without being deprived of its character as Community law and without the legal basis of the Community itself being called into question.

[5] At 158.

> The transfer by the states from their domestic legal system to the Community legal system of the rights and obligations arising under the Treaty carries with it a permanent limitation of their sovereign rights, against which a subsequent unilateral act incompatible with the concept of the Community cannot prevail.

It is worth looking individually at each of the arguments made by the Court in support of its conclusion that Community law had to be given primacy by national courts over any incompatible national law.[6] Just as in the case of the principle of direct effect, the EC Treaty is silent on the question of the relationship between national law and Community law, and certainly makes no reference to the supremacy of Community law. The first two arguments are in fact assertions by the Court, giving its interpretation of what the spirit and aims of the Treaty require and of how the Member States brought this about.

First is the statement that the Treaty created its own legal order which immediately became 'an integral part' of the legal systems of the Member States. *Secondly*, and perhaps more contentiously, is the Court's statement on how, in constitutional terms, the Member States created this legal order: i.e. by conferring on the new Community institutions 'real powers stemming from a limitation of sovereignty or a transfer of powers from the states to the Community'. As in the case of *Van Gend*, the Court made no reference to the constitution of any particular Member State to see whether such a transfer or limitation of sovereignty was contemplated or even was possible in accordance with that constitution.

In its *third* argument, the Court drew on the spirit and the aims of the Treaty to conclude that it was 'impossible' for the Member States to accord primacy to domestic laws. The 'spirit' of the Treaty required that they all act with equal diligence to give full effect to Community laws which they had accepted on the basis of 'reciprocity'—meaning presumably that since each state was equally bound by laws passed for the Community as a whole, they had all agreed that no one of them would unilaterally derogate from Treaty obligations. And since the 'aims' of the Treaty were those of integration and of co-operation (express reference being made by the Court to Article 5 of the Treaty[7]), their achievement would be undermined by one Member State refusing to give effect to a Community law which, it had been agreed, should uniformly bind all. This, again, was a pragmatic and purposive argument rather than a textual one, and an argument which is to be seen over and over again in the case law of the Court: that securing the uniformity and effectiveness of

[6] Several of these arguments were later used by the Procureur Général before the Belgian Cour de Cassation in the case of *Minister for Economic Affairs* v. *SA Fromagerie Franco-Suisse 'Le Ski'* [1972] 2 CMLR 330, where he successfully persuaded the court that the supremacy of Community law over Belgian should be acknowledged.

[7] That Art. provides that 'Member States shall take all appropriate measures, whether general or particular, to ensure fulfilment of the obligations arising out of this Treaty or resulting from action taken by the institutions of the Community' and that they shall 'abstain from any measure which could jeopardise the attainment of the objectives of the Treaty'.

Community law is necessary if the concrete aims of the Community, as set out in the Treaties, are to be realized.

The *fourth* argument was again a practical one—that the obligations undertaken by the Member States in the Treaty would be 'merely contingent' rather than unconditional if they were to be subject to later legislative acts on the part of the states. The only genuinely textual evidence used by the Court was in its *fifth* argument: that the language of direct applicability in Article 189 would be meaningless if states could negate the effect of Community law by passing subsequent inconsistent legislation. Yet this textual argument is weak, since Article 189 refers only to the direct applicability of regulations, while on the other hand the Court in *Costa* v. *Enel* was seeking to establish a general principle of the supremacy of *all* binding Community law, and specifically the supremacy of an Article of the Treaty. Further, direct applicability refers to the way in which Community law becomes part of the national legal system without the need for implementing measures, but it does not resolve the question of priority between this law and other forms of law within the national legal system.

Above all, what comes across most strongly in the judgment is the teleology of the Court's approach. The judgment continually emphasizes the aims of the Community and the spirit of the Treaties and, without much concrete support from the actual text, rules that Community law has a 'special and original nature' of which it would be deprived if subsequent domestic laws were to prevail. Of course, the Court's opinion is not 'neutral' in any legal or political sense, nor does it purport to be so. The Court is quite open about its interpretation of the kind of Community created by the Treaties, and about the fact that the aim of integration requires the supremacy of Community law. It was a bold step for the Court to support its conception of the Community legal order by declaring that the states had limited their own powers and had transferred sovereignty to the Community institutions. The Advocate General in the case was clearly aware of the political significance of the Court's ruling, but strove to present the transfer of sovereignty as a necessary and inevitable *effect* of the creation of new legislative institutions by the Member States, rather than as an express and deliberate action on their part.

ADVOCATE GENERAL LAGRANGE[8]

Without recourse to legal theory upon the nature of the European Community (which is too open to controversy) and without taking sides between 'Federal Europe' and 'the Europe of Countries' or between the 'supranational' and the 'international', the court (and indeed such is its function) can only consider the Treaty as it is. But—and it is indeed a simple observation—the Treaty establishing the European Economic Community, as well as the other two 'European Treaties', creates its own *legal system* which, although distinct from the legal system of each of the Member States, by virtue of certain precise provisions of the

[8] [1964] ECR 585, 602–3, 606.

Treaty, which bring about a *transfer of jurisdiction* to the Community institutions, partly replaces the internal legal system . . .

If it happened that the constitutional court of one of the Member States, possessed of its full jurisdiction, felt bound to acknowledge . . . that ordinary national laws, contrary to the Treaty, might prevail against the Treaty itself without any court (not even the constitutional court) having the power to stop their application, so that they could only be repealed or modified by Parliament such a decision would create an insoluble conflict between the two legal systems and would undermine the very foundations of the Treaty.

In *Van Gend en Loos* and *Costa* v. *Enel*, then, the Court set out its theoretical basis for the principle of supremacy of Community law. The force and practical application of the principle became clearer still in its later decisions. In the following case, the Court made clear that the legal status of a conflicting national measure was not relevant to the question whether Community law should take precedence: not even a fundamental rule of national constitutional law could, of itself, be invoked to challenge the supremacy of a directly applicable Community law.

Case 11/70, Internationale Handelsgesellschaft mbH v. Einfuhr- und Vorratsstelle für Getreide und Futtermittel [1970] ECR 1125, [1972] CMLR 255

The facts are set out in Chapter 7.[9]

THE ECJ

3. Recourse to the legal rules or concepts of national law in order to judge the validity of measures adopted by the institutions of the Community would have an adverse effect on the uniformity and efficacy of Community law. The validity of such measures can only be judged in the light of Community law. In fact, the law stemming from the Treaty, an independent source of law, cannot because of its very nature be overridden by rules of national law, however framed, without being deprived of its character as Community law and without the legal basis of the Community itself being called into question. Therefore the validity of a Community measure or its effect within a Member State cannot be affected by allegations that it runs counter to either fundamental rights as formulated by the constitution of that State or the principles of a national constitutional structure.

As will be seen below, this decision gave rise for some time to a potentially serious deadlock in relations between the German Constitutional Court, which held that the Community deposit system breached a fundamental provision of the national legal order, and the Court of Justice, which denied that national constitutional principles could have any effect on the domestic applicability of Community law.[10] The eventual resolution of the conflict contains a

[9] At 290. [10] See n. 28 below and text.

certain tension which is also present in the relationship between the constitutional position of many other Member States on the one hand, and the constitutional claim to supremacy of Community law on the part of the Court on the other. But far from backing off from its claims, the Court continued to emphasize the importance of ensuring that the supremacy of Community law was not simply a matter of principle or of theory only, but was given practical effect by all national courts in cases arising before them.

Case 106/77, Amministrazione delle Finanze dello Stato v. Simmenthal SpA [1978] ECR 629, [1978] 3 CMLR 263

The respondent company, which had imported beef from France into Italy, brought an action before the Pretore claiming repayment of the fees which had been charged to it for a vetinary and public health inspection at the frontier. The company argued that the fees were incompatible with Community provisions on the free movement of goods and requested a reference to the Court of Justice. After the Court had ruled that the fees would be contrary to the Treaty, the Pretore ordered repayment of the amounts with interest. The Italian fiscal authorities objected to this order and claimed that the national court could not simply fail to apply a national law which conflicted with Community law, but that it must first bring the matter before the Italian Constitutional Court which could declare the Italian law unconstitutional. The Pretore accordingly stayed proceedings and for a second time referred several questions to the Court of Justice asking whether in these circumstances the national law would have to be disregarded forthwith without waiting until it was set aside by the appropriate constitutional authority.

THE ECJ

17. Furthermore, in accordance with the principle of the precedence of Community law, the relationship between provisions of the Treaty and directly applicable measures of the institutions on the one hand and the national law of the Member States on the other is such that those provisions and measures not only by their entry into force render automatically inapplicable any conflicting provision of current national law but—in so far as they are an integral part of, and take precedence in, the legal order applicable in the territory of each of the Member States—also preclude the valid adoption of new national legislative measures to the extent to which they would be incompatible with Community provisions.

18. Indeed any recognition that national legislative measures which encroach upon the field within which the Community exercises its legislative power or which are otherwise incompatible with the provisions of Community law had any legal effect would amount to a corresponding denial of the effectiveness of obligations undertaken unconditionally and irrevocably by Member States pursuant to the Treaty and would thus imperil the very foundations of the Community.

. . .

21. It follows from the foregoing that every national court must, in a case within its jurisdiction, apply Community law in its entirety and protect rights which the latter confers on individuals and must accordingly set aside any

provision of national law which may conflict with it, whether prior or subsequent to the Community rule.

22. Accordingly any provision of a national legal system and any legislative, administrative or judicial practice which might impair the effectiveness of Community law by witholding from the national court having jurisdiction to apply such law the power to do everything necessary at the moment of its application to set aside national legislative provisions which might prevent Community rules from having full force and effect are incompatible with those requirements which are the very essence of Community law.

23. This would be the case in the event of a conflict between a provision of Community law and a subsequent national law if the solution of the conflict were to be reserved for an authority with a discretion of its own, other than the court called upon to apply Community law, even if such an impediment to the full effectiveness of Community law were only temporary.

24. The first question should therefore be answered to the effect that a national court which is called upon, within the limits of its jurisdiction, to apply provisions of Community law is under a duty to give full effect to those provisions, if necessary refusing of its own motion to apply any conflicting provision of national legislation, even if adopted subsequently, and it is not necessary for the court to request or await the prior setting aside of such provision by legislative or other constitutional means.

Simmenthal is an interesting and an important case, since it spells out the practical implications for the Community legal order of the principles of supremacy and direct effect. According to the Court, all national courts are obliged to enforce directly and immediately a clear and unconditional provision of Community law even where there is a directly conflicting national law. Although this much had been made clear in *Costa* v. *Enel* and *Internationale Handelsgesellschaft*, the facts of *Simmenthal* highlighted a further problem for national courts: what if the national court was one which had no jurisdiction in the domestic legal system to question or to set aside national legislative acts? In the Italian legal system, this is the function of the Constitutional Court, and for this reason the Italian tax authorities in *Simmenthal* questioned the order of the Pretore di Susa awarding the repayment of fees which had been charged under an existing national law. The clear implication of the Court's response was that, even if the only national court empowered to pronounce on the constitutionality of a national law is the Constitutional Court, nevertheless if such a case arises before any other national court, that court is bound to give immediate effect to the Community law without awaiting the ruling of the Constitutional Court. Advocate General Reischl in *Simmenthal* put it in the following way:

Community law is not in any way concerned to eliminate, as it were, from Italian law the procedures designed to obtain a declaration that a national law is unconstitutional. What matters as far as Community law is concerned is only that its application—in those cases where direct applicability is intended—does not encounter any kind of obstacle under national law.[11]

Thus the case was an early example of what we have seen in the chapter on remedies, i.e. how Community law has 'conferred' on domestic courts—indeed how it has *required* them to exercise—powers and jurisdiction which they did not have under national law. The key emphasis in these decisions is on the principle of effectiveness. The Court, as was apparent also in its decisions on remedies, does not wish to be seen to create new areas of jurisdiction for national courts, and so it frames its judgments in a negative way: that national courts must ignore or must not apply national rules which form an obstacle to the immediate applicability or effectiveness of Community law.[12] It is clear from the outcome of these cases, however, that they result in a change and an increase in the jurisdiction and function of many national courts—even where the national jurisdictional limitations are of a constitutional nature. This certainly became clear in the United Kingdom after the ruling in the well-known *Factortame* litigation, on the question of interim relief against a provision of national law which appeared to conflict with one of Community law. Having repeated much of its ruling in *Simmenthal* on the need for effectiveness and for the automatic precedence of Community law over national law, the Court addressed the issue of interim relief.

Case C–213/89, R. v. Secretary of State for Transport, ex parte Factortame Ltd and Others [1990] ECR I–2433, [1990] 3 CMLR 1

The facts are set out in Chapter 5.[13]

THE ECJ

21. It must be added that the full effectiveness of Community law would be just as much impaired if a rule of national law could prevent a court seised of a dispute governed by Community law from granting interim relief in order to ensure the full effectiveness of the judgment to be given on the existence of the rights claimed under Community law. It follows that a court which in those circumstances would grant interim relief, if it were not for a rule of national law, is obliged to set aside that rule.

The overriding requirement that priority be given to directly effective Community law over conflicting national law meant that, even if the

[11] Case 106/77, [1978] ECR 629, 655–6.

[12] Art. 234 EC provides a limited exception to the obligation of Member States to ensure the supremacy of EC law, in the case of conflicting state obligations arising from agreements concluded with non-Member States before the entry into force of the EC Treaty: see Cases C-158/91, *Ministère Public and Direction du Travail et de l'Emploi* v. *Levy* [1993] ECR I–4287 and C-13/93, *Office Nationale de l'Emploi v. Minne* [1994] ECR I–371 and the discussion in Ch. 18.

[13] At 209.

Community law were only allegedly or putatively directly effective, a national rule which absolutely barred domestic courts from giving interim relief in any such circumstance should be set aside or ignored by those domestic courts. In the United Kingdom, where the principle of parliamentary sovereignty is a fundamental tenet of constitutional law, this ruling—despite being based on the same reasoning as the earlier well-established *Simmenthal* judgment—had a sharp impact. The Court, however, did not spend any time in its judgment repeating the basis for the principle of supremacy, but simply spelt out the practical consequences for the national judicial system. Advocate General Tesauro, too, brushed aside the need for a justification of this latest manifestation of the consequences of the supremacy principle:

> I do not consider it useful, and even less so in this context, to enter into a sterile dialectical discussion on the theoretical basis of such a firmly established principle. What matters, in so far as is relevant in this case, is that the national court is obliged to afford judicial protection to the rights conferred by a Community provision as from the entry into force of that provision and for so long as it continues in force.[14]

Thus, in so far as the Court was concerned, by 1989 the principle of supremacy of Community law, the requirement of securing its practical effectiveness among the Member States, and the resulting necessary changes in the legal systems and jurisdiction of the courts of Member States were established beyond question. Nevertheless, the supremacy of Community law is neither a simple nor a unilateral matter. For although the Court may have elaborated and propounded such a theory and repeatedly emphasized its requirements, its normativity and its practical application are ultimately dependent on the internal acceptance and adaptation of the legal and constitutional orders of the Member States. And, as Advocate General Roemer noted in *Van Gend en Loos*, the constitutional orders of some of the Member States do not easily accomodate the principle of supremacy.

J. Weiler, The Community System: the Dual Character of Supranationalism[15]

As in the case of 'direct effect' the derivation of supremacy from the Treaty depended on a 'constitutional' rather than international law interpretation. The Court's reasoning that supremacy was enshrined in the Treaty was contested by the governments of Member States in this case and others. Acceptance of this view amounts in effect to a quiet revolution in the legal orders of the Member States . . .

It follows that the evolutionary nature of the doctrine of supremacy is necessarily bi-dimensional. One dimension is the elaboration of the parameters of the doctrine by the European Court. But its full reception, the second dimension,

[14] Case C-213/89, [1990] ECR I–2433, 2454.

[15] (1981) 1 YBEL 267, 275–6.

> depends on its incorporation into the constitutional orders of the Member States and its affirmation by their supreme courts. It is relatively easy to trace the evolution of the Community dimension of the doctrine . . .
>
> As regards the second dimension, the evolutionary character of the process is more complicated. It should be remembered that in respect of the original Member States there was no specific consitutional preparation for this European Court inspired development . . . In some Member States the reception of the principle caused no major problems (Benelux), in others the Courts accepted the doctrine with reservations regarding either the procedural implications of the doctrine (Italy) or the possible incompatibility of Community law with fundamental human rights enshrined in their Constitutions (Italy, Germany) . . . In others still, the judiciary split, with one branch accepting the doctrine and the other refusing it (France).

The evolutionary nature of the process of acceptance of supremacy, in Weiler's terms, is indeed still evident. The tension between national accounts of the character of Community law and the Court of Justice's account continues, and not simply as a matter of theory. Conflicts continue to arise in specific cases, in particular when issues of national constitutional importance are affected, and it is ultimately for the national court to resolve a case which comes before it and which involves a conflict between a provision of Community law and one of national law. Even if the courts of a Member State accept that, within its proper sphere, Community law should take precedence over national law, there may not be agreement on the prior question of competence—in other words, on the question whether it is in fact the proper sphere of Community law. Given the lack of any clear delimitation of spheres of competence in the Treaty, the question of *Kompetenz-Kompetenz*—that is, of who is to determine the allocation of competence as between the Community and the Member States—remains a contentious one. As we have seen in Chapter 3, the principle of subsidiarity recently added in Article 3b of the EC Treaty, although it purports to set some sort of standard for judging the appropriateness of Community action in a given field, does not provide very clear guidance and awaits political and judicial construction.

The accomodation so far reached by the courts of various Member States on the issue of the primacy of Community law will now be examined—focusing in particular detail on the position of the United Kingdom—in order to complete this second half of the supremacy story. For reasons of space, only a certain number of the Member States will be discussed, although every state has its own interesting constitutional perspective to offer.

3. THE SECOND DIMENSION: SUPREMACY OF COMMUNITY LAW FROM THE PERSPECTIVE OF THE MEMBER STATES

(a) France

The French judicial system is divided between the administrative courts and the ordinary courts, and the 'split' referred to by Weiler occurred when the supremacy of Community law over French law was accepted in 1975 by the Cour de Cassation,[16] the highest of the ordinary judicial courts, but was rejected in practice by the Conseil d'Etat, the supreme administrative court, until as late as 1989.[17] In the case of *Semoules*,[18] the problem was expressed as a jurisdictional one: the Conseil d'Etat ruled that, since it had no jurisdiction to review the validity of French legislation, it could not find such legislation to be incompatible with Community law nor could it accord priority to the latter. And although the French Constitution provided for the primacy of certain international treaties over domestic law, in the view of the Conseil d'Etat, decisions on the constitutionality of legislation were matters for the Conseil Constitutionnel—the Constitutional Council—to make before the legislation was promulgated.

However, in the *Cafe Jacques Vabres* case in 1975, when faced with a conflict between Article 95 of the EC Treaty and a later domestic provision—article 265 of the French Customs Code—, the Cour de Cassation took a different view of its jurisdiction. Following the suggestion of the Procureur Général, the Cour de Cassation held that the question was not whether it could review the constitutionality of a French law. In the view of the court, when a conflict existed between an 'internal law' and a properly ratified 'international act' which had thus entered the internal legal order, the Constitution itself accorded priority to the latter. Respect for the principle of the primacy of international treaties should not be left to the Conseil Constitutionnel to secure, since it was the duty of the ordinary courts before which such problems actually arose to respond and to do justice in the case. However, the court based its decision on Article 55 of the French Constitution, rather than adopting the *communautaire* or 'global' approach urged by Procureur Général Adolphe Touffait, who argued that the Article 55 approach could have damaging effects as regards those Member States whose constitutions did not contain a similar provision:

[16] Decision of 24 May, 1975 in *Administration des Douanes v. Société 'Cafés Jacques Vabre' et SARL Weigel et Cie.* [1975] 2 CMLR 336.

[17] For a discussion of the attitude of the Conseil d'Etat to EC law during this period, see T. C. Hartley, *Foundations of European Community Law* (3rd edn., Oxford, 1994) 247–56, and D. Pollard, (1990) 15 ELRev. 267, 268–70.

[18] Decision of 1 Mar., 1968 in *Syndicat Général de Fabricants de Semoules de France* [1970] CMLR 395.

It would be possible for you to give precedence to the application of Article 95 of the Rome Treaty over the subsequent statute by relying on Article 55 of our Constitution, but personally I would ask you not to mention it and instead to base your reasoning on the very nature of the legal order instituted by the Rome Treaty.

Indeed, so far as you restricted yourselves to deriving from Article 55 of our Constitution the primacy in the French internal system of Community law over national law you would be explaining and justifying that action as regards our country, but such reasoning would let it be accepted that it is on our Constitution and on it alone that depends the ranking of Community law in our internal legal system.

In doing so you would impliedly be supplying a far from negligible argument to the courts of the Member States which, lacking any affirmation in their constitutions of the primacy of the Treaty would be tempted to deduce therefrom the opposite solution, as the Italian Constitutional Court did in 1962 when it claimed that it was for internal constitutional law to fix the ranking of Community law in the internal order of each Member State.[19]

It was not until 1989, however, that the Conseil d'Etat finally abandoned its so-called 'splendid isolation' and decided, in its capacity as an electoral court, to adopt the same position as the Conseil Constitutionnel and the Cour de Cassation.[20]

Raoul Georges Nicolo [1990] 1 CMLR 173

The applicants were two French citizens who brought an action for the annulment of the European Parliament elections in France in 1989, on the grounds that the right to vote and to stand had been given to French citizens in the non-European overseas departments and territories of France. One of the grounds pleaded was that the French statutory rule under challenge—Act 77–729—was contrary to the EEC Treaty. The case came before the French Administrative Court, the Conseil d'Etat, where the Commissaire du Gouvernement in his opinion concluded that the applications should be dismissed.

Commissaire Frydman[21]

However, the whole difficulty is then to decide whether, in conformity with your settled case law, you should dismiss this second argument by relying on the 1977 Act alone, without even having to verify whether it is compatible with the Treaty of Rome, or whether you should break fresh ground today by deciding that the Act is applicable only because it is compatible precisely with the Treaty.

[19] N. 16 above, 363–4.

[20] Decision of 20 Oct., 1989 in *Nicolo*. It has been suggested that earlier decisions of the French Constitutional Court—the Conseil Constitutionnel—which indicated that it was for the other French courts to ensure that international treaties were applied, acted as a spur to the Conseil d'Etat to reverse its original position. See P. Oliver 'The French Constitution and the Treaty of Maastricht' (1994) 43 ICLQ 1, 10.

[21] [1990] 1 CMLR 173, 177, 178.

In this connection we know that you held, in the famous divisional decision of 1 March 1968, *Syndicat Général des Fabricants de Semoules de France* that an administrative court cannot accord treaties precedence over subsequent legislation which conflicts with them and that this case law applies to Community rules just as much as to ordinary international conventions . . .

The theoretical foundation of these decisions, which clearly does not take the form of an objection to the principle of the superiority of treaties over statutes, which is expressly stated by Article 55, should rather be sought in your wish to uphold the principle that it is not for the administrative courts to review the validity of legislation . . .

On the other hand I believe it is possible to take the view that . . . Article 55 of itself necessarily enables the courts, by implication, to review the compatibility of statutes with treaties. Indeed, we must attribute to the authors of the Constitution an intention to provide for actual implementation of the supremacy of treaties which they embodied in that provision . . . In truth, in the terms in which it is worded this constitutional provision, which has the sole object of laying down a system of priority for different rules, seems to me to be addressed primarily to the courts . . .

On this basis, therefore, I propose that you should agree to give treaties precedence over later statutes.

. . . France cannot at one and the same time accept restrictions on sovereignty and uphold the supremacy of its own law before the courts; there is an element of illogicality here which, it seems to me, your 1968 decision may have underestimated . . .

So far as foreign courts are concerned, and I shall confine myself to the framework of European law, all I would say is that your Court is now the last which formally refuses to apply Community measures which are contradicted by later laws.

. . . I am aware that the Court of Justice of the European Communities—which, as we know, gives Community law absolute supremacy over the rules of national law, even if they are constitutional—has not hesitated for its part to affirm the obligation to refuse to apply in any situation laws which are contrary to Community measures.

I do not think you can follow the European Court in this judge-made law which, in truth, seems to me at least open to objection. Were you to do so, you would tie yourself to a supranational way of thinking which is quite difficult to justify, to which the Treaty of Rome does not subscribe expressly and which would quite certainly render the Treaty unconstitutional, however it may be regarded in the political context . . ..

I therefore suggest that you should base your decision on Article 55 of the Constitution and extend its ambit to all international agreements.

Although it did not expressly adopt the view expressed by the Commissaire, the Conseil d'Etat in its decision appeared to accept the premises on which that view was based. Although it held that the French statutory rules were not invalid, the Conseil did so on the ground that they were 'not incompatible with the clear stipulations of the above mentioned Article 227(1) of the Treaty of Rome'.

D. Pollard, The Conseil d'Etat is European—Official[22]

The *Semoules* decision and subsequent case law resulted in treaties repudiated by subsequent statutes having no force within the French internal legal system while at the same time continuing to bind France on the international legal plane; the existence of two lines of case law, one by the Conseil d'Etat and one by the Cour de Cassation, led to absurd practical consequences for the citizen and there was no logic in one jurisdiction applying the treaty and one the statute; it was a scandal that the ordinary citizens could not rely before the French administrative courts on a rule which they would be allowed to invoke in other Member States, for the sole reason that in France the rule had been abrogated by a subsequently enacted statute; . . .

The decision's legal basis is significant. The Conseil d'Etat could have rejected M. Nicolo's action simply on the combination of the electoral statute and Articles 2 and 72 of the Constitution. In one sense it was unnecessary to invoke the compatibility of the electoral statute with the EEC Treaty. However, the traditional case law of the Conseil d'Etat was seen as being increasingly at variance with France's obligations under the EEC Treaty and it was a useful decision to make during the French Presidency of the Council of Ministers and at a time of strident calls for ever closer European integration.

It is interesting, however, to note that Commissaire Frydman discouraged the Conseil d'Etat from subscribing entirely to the 'supranational way of thinking' of the Court of Justice in its exposition of the principle of supremacy of Community law. The *Nicolo* case certainly does not represent an unqualified acceptance by the Conseil d'Etat of the supremacy of EC law on the Court's terms—rather, it relies primarily on the interpretation of Article 55 of the French Constitution which provides for the superiority of international treaties over national law. The Conseil d'Etat has also, since that decision, recognized the priority of both Community regulations and directives over French statutes, without discussing the theoretical basis for that supremacy.[23] The French Constitution has since been amended to give effect to changes made by the TEU, so that 'the Community is now placed on a clearer constitutional footing in France',[24] but whether or not reliance will continue to be placed on Article 55 as a basis for the supremacy of Community law in France remains to be seen.[25]

The caution displayed by the French Conseil d'Etat in its approach to the supremacy of Community law is evident in the case law of many other Member States. The Court of Justice's view that national law can never take

[22] Pollard, n. 17 above, 271, 273–4.

[23] See *Boisdet* [1991] 1 CMLR 3, on a reg. which was adopted after the French law, and *Rothmans and Philip Morris* and *Arizona Tobacco and Philip Morris* [1993] 1 CMLR 253 on a dir. adopted before the French law. For comment on *Boisdet*, see H. Cohen (1991) 16 E.L.Rev. 144.

[24] P. Oliver, n. 20 above, 24.

[25] See P. Roseren, 'The Application of Community Law by French Courts From 1982 to 1993' (1994) 31 CMLRev. 315, 342 who argues that Art. 55 cannot explain the primacy of Community *secondary* legislation over French law in cases such as *Boisdet* and *Rothmans*.

precedence over directly effective EC law on account of a transfer of sovereignty by the Member States and the 'spirit of the EC Treaties' is not unconditionally accepted by the courts of Member States. Neither is there agreement over the extent of the powers which have been transferred by the Member States to the Community, nor that the Court and the Community institutions, rather than the Member States, should decide the question of competence.

In France, the main obstacle to the recognition of supremacy of EC law was the jurisdictional limitation of the French courts. In other Member States, in particular in Germany, the difficulties which arose related to the fundamental constitutional nature of the national legislation which appeared to contravene Community law.

B. De Witte, Community Law and National Constitutional Values[26]

> Yet, the thesis of the absolute supremacy of Community law, even over national constitutional provisions, is not fully accepted by all national supreme courts. First of all, those courts tend to recognize the privileged position of Community law, not by virtue of the inherent nature of Community law as the Court of Justice would have it, but under the authority of their own national legal order. This does not matter so much for the relation between Community law and ordinary legislation, because all national courts have found the legal resources to ensure, by and large, the supremacy of Community law in those cases. But when it becomes a matter of deciding a conflict between Community law and a norm of constitutional rank, the theoretical basis matters very much. If the courts (and other national authorities) think that Community law ultimately derives its validity in the domestic order from the authority of the constitution, then they are unlikely to recognize that Community law might prevail over the very foundation from which its legal force derives. More precisely, the typical constitutional provision allowing for the transfer of powers to international organizations (or to the Community specifically) is seen as allowing *a priori* implicit amendments to other provisions of the constitution, but not as allowing alterations to basic principles of the constitution.

(b) Germany

Article 24 of the German Constitution allows for the transfer of legislative power to international organizations, but in litigation which arose over apparent conflicts between Community legislation and provisions of the German Constitution, the extent of power which could be transferred in accordance with this Article was questioned. In particular, the focus of the case law was on whether Article 24 permitted the transfer, to an organization outside the German constitutional structure, of a power to contravene certain basic principles protected under the Constitution itself.

[26] (1991) 2 LIEI 1, 4.

Internationale Handelsgesellschaft mbH v. Einfuhr und- Vorratstelle für Getreide und Futtermittel [1972] CMLR 177

The facts are those as set out in Case 11/70 before the European Court of Justice.[27] After the ruling of the Court of Justice in that case was received by the German Administrative Court, the following decision was given.

VERWALTUNGSGERICHT (Administrative Court)[28]

This Chamber agrees with those who wish to test Community law against the fundamental principles of the Constitution, since a critical appraisal of the views set out above shows that the view that Community law takes precedence cannot be based on any legal foundation. The integration powers contained in Article 24 enable the Federal legislature to alienate its legislative monopoly in certain spheres in favour of international institutions. The Community organs have thereby obtained the power to enact law directly effective within the territorial scope of the Constitution without a separate writ of enforcement. However, since the effect of Article 24 cannot be equated with an amendment of the Constitution the Federal legislature could not, when ratifying the EEC Treaty, disclaim the observance of elementary basic rights in the Constitution, within the scope of Article 24.

This chamber believes that it has found the real reason for the contradictory views in the various, purely politically conditioned attitudes to the Community. Some . . . see in too rigid an adherence to the traditional legal structures and claims to sovereignty a considerable obstacle to the necessary progress within the Community, which was conceived by its founders as the preliminary stage of a European federal state and regarded as a method for achieving the national and political unification of Europe. Others . . . do not wish to renounce completely the safeguards that accrue to citizens from the existing 'traditional' institutions, unless new written constitutional guarantees are provided . . .

However, if Community law, for this reason, is given precedence over any divergent constitutional provisions, and this European legal system is exempt from the obligations contained in Articles 19(2) and 79(3) of the Constitution, it would lead to a constitutional and legal vacuum. For constitutional law would be eliminated as the highest national check on a European legislation that is becoming increasingly more expansive without the institution of equivalent legal safeguards. The democratic constitutional state guaranteed by the Constitution will itself only be able with difficulty to remain faithful to its basic decisions in constitutional law if as a result of particular advancing integration processes crucial spheres are withdrawn from its jurisdiction and, with the constant decline in the standing of the national legislature, placed under a supranational 'purely executive regime' which does not have to observe the fundamental principles laid down in Articles 19(2) and 79(3) of the Constitution in its measures.

It is evident from this passage that the German court was worried about several things. On the one hand, it was concerned that Germany would be deemed to have already transferred greater powers to the Community than it was capable, under its Constitution, of exercising let alone transferring, and

[27] At 290. [28] [1972] CMLR 177, 184.

on the other hand it was concerned that the continuing process of integration might gradually withdraw crucial spheres from national jurisdiction. The consequences were not only that Germany would be held to have given away power which it was not constitutionally permitted to give, but also that in so doing it would be empowering a supranational executive which was not bound by the same guarantees as those of the German Constitution. With these concerns in mind, the Administrative Court ruled, in the face of the conflicting judgment of the Court of Justice, that the Community deposit system breached basic principles of German constitutional law, and it requested a ruling on the matter from the Bundesverfassungsgericht (Federal Constitutional Court). This ruling was given by the Constitutional Court in 1974:[29]

> This Court—in this respect in agreement with the law developed by the European Court of Justice—adheres to its settled view that Community law is a component part neither of the national legal system nor international law, but forms an independent system of law flowing from an autonomous legal source; for the Community is not a state, in particular not a federal state, but a '*sui generis* community in the process of progressive integration'; an 'inter-State institution' within the meaning of Article 24 (1) of the Constitution . . .
>
> Article 24 of the Constitution deals with the transfer of sovereign rights to inter-state institutions. This cannot be taken literally . . . That is, it does not open the way to amending the basic structure of the Constitution, which forms the basis of its identity, without a formal amendment to the Constitution, that is, it does not open any such way through the legislation of the inter-state institution. Certainly, the competent Community organs can make law which the competent German constitutional organs could not make under the law of the Constitution and which is nonetheless valid and is to be applied directly in the Federal Republic of Germany. But Article 24 of the Constitution limits this possibility in that it nullifies any amendment of the Treaty which would destroy the identity of the valid constitutional structure of the Federal Republic of Germany by encroaching on the structures which go to make it up . . .
>
> The part of the Constitution dealing with fundamental rights is an inalienable essential feature of the valid Constitution of the Federal Republic of Germany and one which forms part of the constitutional structure of the Constitution. Article 24 of the Constitution does not without reservation allow it to be subjected to qualifications. In this, the present state of integration of the Community is of crucial importance. The Community still lacks a democratically legitimated Parliament directly elected by general suffrage which possesses legislative powers and to which the Community organs empowered to legislate are fully responsible on a political level. It still lacks in particular a codified catalogue of fundamental rights, the substance of which is reliably and unambiguously fixed for the future in the same way as the substance of the Constitution . . .
>
> Provisionally, therefore, in the hypothetical case of a conflict between Community law and . . . the guarantees of fundamental rights in the Constitution, there arises the question of which system of law takes precedence, that is, ousts the other. In this conflict of norms, the guarantee of fundamental rights in the

[29] [1974] 2 CMLR 540, 549–50.

Constitution prevails as long as the competent organs of the Community have not removed the conflict of norms in accordance with the Treaty mechanism.

This refusal by the highest German court—the Federal Constitutional Court—to recognize the unconditional supremacy of Community law constituted a considerable blow to the smooth development by the Court of Justice of the relationship between national law and Community law and of the Court's own important relationship with the courts of the Member States. The major objection of the Federal Constitutional Court to recognizing the supremacy of Community law was not merely, as in the case of the French Conseil d'Etat, a jurisdictional concern, but rather a concern over the possible impact on basic rights enshrined in the German Constitution of conflicting measures of Community law. For this reason it held that the clause in the German Constitution which allowed for the transfer of legislative power to international organizations could not cover a transfer of power to alter or amend an 'inalienable essential feature' of the German constitutional structure, such as its express protection for fundamental rights. The Constitutional Court was not prepared to abandon its jurisdiction to rule on which transfers of legislative power are permissible and which would purport to alter an unalterable feature of the Constitution. For this reason it concluded by saying that the protection for fundamental rights in the German Constitution would have to prevail in the event of any conflict.

By 1986, however, in a decision arising out of a further set of domestic proceedings in which the applicant challenged the EC Commission's system of import licences for mushrooms, despite an earlier Court of Justice ruling to the contrary,[30] the Federal Constitutional Court found against the appellant and in so doing, gave a judgment which revised considerably its earlier 1974 decision. This decision is known as the '*Solange II*' case, the 1974 decision being the first '*Solange*' case. Literally translated, this means the 'so long as' case, and it refers to the statement of the German Constitutional Court that so long as the Community had not removed the possible 'conflict of norms' between provisions of Community law and national constitutional rights, the German court would ensure that those rights took precedence over Community law.

Having considered various changes in Community law since the time of the 1974 decision, including the development by the Court of Justice of a doctrine of protection for fundamental rights, the various declarations on fundamental rights and democracy in the EC by the Community institutions,[31] and the fact that all Member States of the EC had by this stage acceded to the European Convention on Human Rights, the German Court in *Solange II* gave the following ruling:[32]

[30] The ECJ had upheld the validity of the licence system in case 345/82, *Wünsche Handelsgesellschaft* v. *Germany* [1984] ECR 1995.

[31] See Ch. 7.

[32] *Re Wünsche Handelsgesellschaft*, Dec. of 22 Oct. 1986 [1987] 3 CMLR 225, 265.

In view of these developments, it must be held that, *so long as* the European Communities, and in particular the case law of the European Court, generally ensure an effective protection of fundamental rights as against the sovereign powers of the Communities which is to be regarded as substantially similar to the protection of fundamental rights required unconditionally by the Constitution, and in so far as they generally safeguard the essential content of fundamental rights, the Federal Constitutional Court will no longer exercise its jurisdiction to decide on the applicability of secondary Community legislation cited as the legal basis for any acts of German courts or authorities within the sovereign jurisdiction of the Federal Republic of Germany, and it will no longer review such legislation by the standard of the fundamental rights contained in the Constitution.

J. Fröwein, Solange II[33]

As the Court points out, its finding leads to the result that the Federal Constitutional Court will no longer exercise jurisdiction over the applicability of secondary Community law in the Federal Republic of Germany and will no longer control such law on the basis of the fundamental rights in the basic law. It is clear that the Federal Constitutional Court did not give up its jurisdiction or come to the conclusion that no such jurisdiction exists. It only states that it will not exercise the jurisdiction as long as the present conditions as to the protection of fundamental rights by the European Court of Justice prevail. One may ask whether the court could have gone further. However, at least for practical purposes this could hardly be expected after the decision of 1974 had clearly claimed jurisdiction on this question.

Moreover, it seems doubtful whether one should not accept the great wisdom which exists in constructing a rather careful balance with eventual safeguards on the national level. There is no dispute under British constitutional law that the House of Commons could, by an Act of Parliament, immediately stop the applicability of European Community law on British soil. The Italian Constitutional Court has reserved a final position for extreme cases. Under German law the legislature cannot intervene in Community matters because of the acceptance of the priority of Community law. The Federal Constitutional Court wanted to preserve its final authority to intervene where real problems concerning the protection of fundamental rights in Community law could arise. As long as the Community system has not developed into a federal structure, questions of sovereignty or final priority as to sources of law have to be kept in suspense. Only where the rules concerning conflict between European Constitutional Law and National Constitutional Law lead to the same result can a harmonious development take place.[34]

More recently, the Federal Constitutional Court has had again to consider the constitutional relationship between European Community law and German law, on the occasion of the ratification of the TEU. This time, the issue which gave rise to the litigation was not a human rights issue, but a basic

[33] (1988) 25 C.M.L.Rev 201, 203–4. See also W. Roth, 'The Application of Community law in West Germany: 1980–1990' (1991) 28 CMLRev. 137.

[34] See further the cases discussed by W. Roth, *ibid.* 144–5.

question of the competence of the German state, under its Constitution, to ratify the new Treaty. Germany had completed the legislative part of the process of ratification of the TEU in December 1992, amending its Constitution, but before the Federal President signed the formal instrument of ratification, constitutional complaints were lodged alleging that ratification would breach the Constitution. The second chamber of the Federal Constitutional Court gave judgment on 12 October 1993, ruling that ratification was compatible with the Constitution. The Federal Court took the opportunity to rule not just on Germany's constitutional competence at that moment in time to ratify the Treaty, but also on what the future position would be if the European Community attempted to exercise powers which were not clearly provided for in the TEU. There are several interesting statements about the constitutional relationship between the Union, the Community, and the German state, which show that the concept of the sovereignty of the German state is still very important, and that the Federal Court clearly has no intention of relinquishing its power to decide on the validity and compatibility of Community law with the German Constitution. The fundamental question, not just of the compatibility of a specific provision of Community law with German law, but of the competence of the Community to enact laws in certain spheres, is confronted in the judgment. It will be seen that the *Kompetenz-Kompetenz* question is directly addressed, and that the Constitutional Court asserts and clearly intends to exercise a power of review over the scope of Community competence.

Brunner v. The European Union Treaty
[1994] 1 CMLR 57

THE FEDERAL CONSTITUTIONAL COURT

13. . . . The Federal Constitutional Court by its jurisdiction guarantees that an effective protection of basic rights for the inhabitants of Germany will also generally be maintained as against the sovereign powers of the Communities and will be accorded the same respect as the protection of basic rights acquired unconditionally by the Constitution, and in particular the Court provides a general safeguard of the essential content of the basic rights. The Court thus guarantees this essential content as against the sovereign powers of the Community as well . . .

48. There is . . . a breach of Article 38 of the Constitution if an Act that opens up the German legal system to the direct validity and application of the law of the (supra-national) European Communities does not establish with sufficient certainty the intended programme of integration. If it is not clear to what extent and degree the German legislature has assented to the transfer of the exercise of sovereign powers, then it will be possible for the European Community to claim functions and powers that were not specified. That would be equivalent to a general enablement and would therefore be a surrender of powers, something against which Article 38 of the Constitution provides protection.

49. . . . What is decisive is that Germany's membership and the rights and duties that follow therefrom (and especially the immediately binding legal effect within the national sphere of the Communities' actions) have been defined in the

Treaty so as to be predictable for the legislature and are enacted by it in the Act of Acccession with sufficient certainty . . . Thus, if European institutions or agencies were to treat or develop the Union Treaty in a way that was no longer covered by the Treaty in the form that is the basis for the Act of Accession, the resultant legislative instruments would not be legally binding within the sphere of German sovereignty. The German state organs would be prevented for constitutional reasons from applying them in Germany. Accordingly the Federal Constitutional Court will review legal instruments of European institutions and agencies to see whether they remain within the limits of the sovereign rights conferred on them or transgress them.

. . .

55. The Federal Republic of Germany, therefore, even after the Union Treaty comes into force, will remain a member of a federation of States, the common authority of which is derived from the Member States and can only have binding effects within the German sovereign sphere by virtue of the German instruction that its law be applied. Germany is one of the 'Masters of the Treaties' which have established their adherence to the Union Treaty concluded 'for an unlimited period' (Article Q) with the intention of long-term membership, but could ultimately revoke that adherence by a contrary act. The validity and application of European law in Germany depends on the application-of-law instruction of the Accession Act. Germany thus preserves the quality of a sovereign state in its own right.

. . .

99. Inasmuch as the Treaties establishing the European Communities, on the one hand, confer sovereign rights applicable to limited factual circumstances and, on the other hand, provide for Treaty amendments . . . this distinction is also important for the future treatment of the individual powers. Whereas a dynamic extension of the existing Treaties has so far been supported on the basis of an open-handed treatment of Article 235 of the EEC Treaty as a 'competence to round off the Treaty' as a whole, and on the basis of considerations relating to the 'implied powers' of the Communities, and of Treaty interpretation as allowing maximum exploitation of Community powers (*effet utile*), in future it will have to be noted as regards interpretation of enabling provisions by Community institutions and agencies that the Union Treaty as a matter of principle distinguishes between the exercise of a sovereign power conferred for limited purposes and the amending of the Treaty, so that its interpretation may not have effects that are equivalent to an extension of the Treaty. Such an interpretation of enabling rules would not produce any binding effects for Germany.

This is a powerful judgment, and a warning to the Community institutions and to the Court of Justice that Germany's acceptance of the supremacy of Community law is not an unquestioning acceptance of every measure and every judgment that emanates from those institutions. In particular, the Constitutional Court has emphasized its intention to ensure that the Community does not stray beyond the powers which have expressly been conferred upon it by the Member States in the various Treaties. Whereas the *Solange* cases concerned a challenge to a specific Community measure which allegedly breached fundamental constitutional rights, the *Brunner* judgment focused on the bigger question of challenging the competence of the

Community to legislate at all in a particular field. Even if the German courts have now accepted that within its proper sphere of application, Community law should be given precedence over national law, the Constitutional Court in *Brunner* has made clear that it will continue to review the actions of European 'institutions and agencies'—which presumably includes the Court —to ensure that they remain within the proper limits of their acquired powers.[35] Thus, even if the Court were to give an interpretation of the concept of subsidiarity in Article 3b in the context of a disputed matter of state/Community competence, it does not appear that the German Constitutional Court would necessarily accept this interpretation as definitive. The critical tone of paragraph 99 of its judgment, in which it refers to the 'open-handed treatment of Article 235' and the difference between interpretation and amendment of the Treaty, suggests that the Constitutional Court will not readily defer to the Court of Justice on such questions.

(c) Italy

Article 11 of the Italian Constitution permits such limitations of sovereignty as are necessary to an organization which ensures peace and justice between nations, and it encourages international organizations which promote such ends. This has formed the basis for the Italian courts' acceptance of the supremacy of Community law, although, as in the case of other Member States, this acceptance has not been unconditional.

Frontini v. Ministero delle Finanze
[1974] 2 CMLR 372

The plaintiff, who had been subjected under a Community regulation to increased agricultural levies on the import of meat into Italy, brought proceedings before the Italian courts challenging the applicability of the levies. The plaintiff argued that the Community regulation was inapplicable in Italy, and the case was transmitted to the Italian Constitutional Court to determine the constitutional legitimacy of the Italian EEC Treaty Ratification Act 1957. That Act made Article 189 of the EEC Treaty, which provides for the direct applicability of Community regulations, effective in Italy.

THE COURT[36]

The EEC Treaty Ratification Act 1957, whereby the Italian Parliament gave full and complete execution to the Treaty instituting the EEC, has a sure basis of validity in Article 11 of the Constitution whereby Italy 'consents, on condition of reciprocity with other states, to limitations of sovereignty necessary for an arrangement which may ensure peace and justice between the nations' and then 'promotes and favours the international organizations directed to such an aim'. That provision, which not by chance is included in the 'fundamental principles' of

[35] See M. Herdegen, 'Maastricht and the German Constitutional Court: Constitutional Restraints for an Ever Closer Union' (1994) 31 CMLRev. 235.

[36] [1974] 2 CMLR 372, 384.

the Constitution, indicates a clear and precise political aim: the makers of the Constitution referred, in the preamble, to the adherence of Italy to the United Nations Organization, but were inspired by policy principles of general validity, of which the European Community and the other European regional organizations constitute a concrete actualisation . . .

It should, on the other hand, be mentioned that the legislative competence of the organs of the EEC is laid down by Article 189 of the Rome Treaty as limited to matter concerning economic relations . . . so that it appears difficult to form even abstractly the hypothesis that a Community regulation can have an effect in civil, ethico-social, or political relations through which provisions conflict with the Italian Constitution. It is hardly necessary to add that by Article 11 of the Constitution limitations of sovereignty are allowed solely for the purpose of the ends indicated therein, and it should therefore be excluded that such limitations of sovereignty, concretely laid out in the Rome Treaty, signed by countries whose systems are based on the principle of the rule of law and guarantee the essential liberties of citizens, can nevertheless give the organs of the EEC an unacceptable power to violate the fundamental principles of our constitutional order or the inalienable rights of man. And it is obvious that if ever Article 189 had to be given such an aberrant interpretation, in such a case the guarantee would always be assured that this Court would control the continuing compatibility of the Treaty with the above mentioned fundamental principles.

While accepting the direct effectiveness of Community law, and confirming the competence of Italy to join the Community and to ratify the Treaties, the Constitutional Court in this judgment expressed similar reservations to those voiced by the German Federal Constitutional Court. In particular, although it appeared to accept the effectiveness of Community law within its proper field of application, the Italian court confirmed that it would continue to review the exercise of power by the 'organs of the EEC' to ensure that there was no infringement of fundamental rights nor of the basic principles of the Italian constitutional order.

The *Frontini* decision was followed in 1984 by the case of *Grantial*,[37] in which the Italian Constitutional Court accepted that, in order to give effect to the supremacy of Community law, Italian courts must be prepared in the case of a clash to apply Community law and to disregard the conflicting national law. However, this acceptance by the Constitutional Court was not unreserved, and its reservations have left open various questions concerning the supremacy of Community law in Italy.

R. Petriccione, Italy: Supremacy of Community Law over National Law[38]

In *Granital* the Constitutional Court restates its firm belief that Community law and national law must be kept conceptually distinct. However, the practical

[37] Dec. 170 of 8 June 1984 in *SpA Granital* v *Amministrazione delle Finanze*. For an unofficial translation see G. Gaja (1984) 21 CMLRev. 756.

[38] (1986) 11 ELRev. 320.

implications which it draws from this theoretical premise are meant to be the same as those which would derive from a 'unitary' approach, such as that followed by the European Court . . . Given the separation between the two legal systems, Community rules and national ones have separate fields of application, so that no problem of temporal order arises between them. Since the division of competence between Community institutions and the national legislature has been given a constitutional foundation, the result is that once a matter is governed by a Community regulation, that regulation alone applies as it must under Article 189 EEC. In this way there is no question of the abrogation, or nullity, of national law: it must simply be ignored, because the field in which it is supposed to operate has been pre-empted by the intervention of Community institutions, whose competence, in the areas provided for by the Treaty, prevails over that of the national legislature. The national provisions survive, and they still govern the subject-matter in all the aspects which are beyond the scope of the relevant Community act . . .

However, the problems which the *Granital* case has left unsolved are of no little relevance. First, the Constitutional Court has reserved to itself not only the question of conflicts between Community provisions and basic constitutional principles or the inalienable rights of the human being, but also the question of national law which challenges the very division of competence established by the Treaties, on the grounds, obviously, that such a division draws constitutional force from Article II of the Constitution. Should this be the case, an ordinary judge is not allowed to disregard the national legislation but is bound to refer it to the Constitutional Court. More generally, this is a consequence of the markedly different approach to the issue of the supremacy of Community law adopted by the Court when contrasted with the view taken by the European Court: a difference which could still lead, in the future, to further conflicts.

That the prospect of such conflicts arising is more than a theoretical possibility has since been demonstrated. In the case of *Fragd*,[39] the Italian Constitutional Court reiterated its ruling that a provision of Community law would not be applied in Italy if it contravened a fundamental principle of the Italian Constitution relating to the protection for human rights, even where the Court of Justice had upheld the validity of the rule under Community law.

G. Gaja, New Developments in a Continuing Story: The Relationship between EEC Law and Italian Law[40]

While the *Frontini* decision by the Constitutional Court has often been viewed as a significant example of the willingness on the part of national courts to subject EEC legislation to constitutional rules concerning the protection of fundamental rights, little has happened so far to justify this evaluation. While the German Constitutional Court, after finding in *Frontini* one of its sources of inspiration for allowing EEC legislation to be checked in its application in Germany, radically changed its attitude in *Solange II*, the Italian Constitutional Court has given some

[39] *Spa Fragd* v *Amministrazione delle Finanze*, Dec. 232 of 21 Apr. 1989, (1989) 72 RDI.
[40] (1990) 27 CMLRev. 83, 93–4.

indication that it intends to persist in its approach in this regard and also that it may wish to go further.

In *Spa Fragd* v. *Amministrazione delle Finanze*, the Court examined whether a system, such as that applying to preliminary rulings on validity of Community acts, whereby a declaration of invalidity may not produce any effect in the proceedings before the referring court, is consistent with the constitutional principles on judicial protection. The Constitutional Court came to the conclusion that in the case in hand the question could not be raised because the proceedings before the national court had been started after the Court of Justice had given a ruling on the validity of the relevant regulation. However, the Constitutional Court took the opportunity of adddressing the question of the temporal effects of rulings on validity by the Court of Justice, especially in relation to the proceedings before the referring court. The Constitutional Court's main aim was to try and support the view that, as a matter of Community law, rulings should always have some effects in those proceedings. Possibly as a way of persuading the Court of Justice of the need to accept this solution, the Constitutional Court also viewed the problem from the perspective of the constitutional protection of fundamental rights. The Court said:

> If a judgment (by the Court of Justice) went as far as ruling out that the effects of a declaration of invalidity cover the act or acts which are the object of the dispute that led to the preliminary reference by the national court, serious doubts would arise about the consistency of the rule that allows this type of judgment with the essential elements of the right to judicial protection . . .
>
> In substance, everyone's right to have a court and judicial proceedings for each dispute would be emptied of its essential content if, when a court doubts the validity of a rule which should be applied, the answer came from the court to whom the question has to be referred, that the rule is in fact void, but that this should not be relevant for the dispute before the referring court, which should nevertheless apply the rule that is declared to be void.
>
> Contrary to the State Attorney's view, one could not invoke the primary need for the uniform application of Community law and for certainty of law against the possible violation of a fundamental right.

. . . Unlike *Frontini*, the *Fragd* decision shows that the Constitutional Court is willing to test the consistency of individual rules of Community law with the fundamental principles for the protection of human rights that are contained in the Italian Constitution. This significantly widens the way for the exercise by the Constitutional Court of a control which has hitherto been only theoretical.

This concern on the part of the Italian court that EC law might infringe fundamental principles of the national constitution—such as the right of access to court and to effective judicial proceedings—are clearly shared by several other Member States. And indeed in Fröwein's view, even if it does not accord with the view of the Court of Justice as to the primacy of Community law, there is considerable wisdom in maintaining, at this stage of European integration, ultimate safeguards at the national level with regard to fundamental constitutional norms.

In his comments, above, Petriccione noted that the Italian Constitutional Court was prepared to adjudicate not simply on questions of conflict between specific Community measures and fundamental rights in the Italian Constitution, but also on the basic question of the division of competence between national law and Community law. As was seen also in the judgment of the German court in the *Brunner* case, the Italian court is not prepared to accept the final word of the Community institutions or the European Court of Justice on this fundamental question of competence.

Petriccione also noted that it had not been easy to persuade national authorities to accept the supremacy of Community law when that law had been introduced without a constitutional amendment to guarantee its supremacy—as indeed was the case in France until the recent amendment to facilitate the TEU changes, and in Germany and Italy whose constitutions already contained provisions which contemplated the transfer of legislative power to an international organization. However, even a specific constitutional amendment cannot be a failsafe way of securing the recognition by the national judiciary of the unconditional supremacy of Community law. Consider, for example, the comments of Walsh J in the Irish Supreme Court, when the argument was made that Article 59 of the EC Treaty required Ireland not to restrict freedom of information or the freedom to travel to obtain an abortion in another Member State.[41] In response to the argument that Article 29 of the Irish Constitution had specifically been amended in 1972 to provide for the supremacy of Community law, Walsh J suggested that this constitutional provision might have been qualified by a later constitutional amendment guaranteeing the right to life of the unborn.[42] Although the potential crisis was defused in that case by the fact that the Court of Justice avoided giving a substantive ruling on the issue raised, it does indicate that where fundamental aspects of a Member State's constitution or its national identity are felt to be threatened, no formal, legal mechanism or amendment can guarantee with certainty the continuing supremacy of Community law.

(d) The United Kingdom

The acceptance of the supremacy of Community law within the United Kingdom has certainly not been unproblematic. Since the British Constitution is largely unwritten it is difficult to speak of 'amending' it. What are known as constitutional conventions in United Kingdom law cannot be formally created, but rather they evolve or emerge over a considerable period of time. No special mechanism exists for amending rules or conventions of a constitutional nature, in the way that the Irish Constitution was amended, other than by an ordinary Act of Parliament. The central obstacle to acceptance by the United Kingdom of the supremacy of EC law is the fundamental constitutional principle of the sovereignty of Parliament. According to this principle, Parliament

[41] *Society for the Protection of the Unborn Child* v. *Grogan* [1989] IR 753.

[42] *Ibid.* 768.

has the power to do anything other than to bind itself for the future.[43] A fundamental principle of this nature clearly made it very difficult, constitutionally, for the United Kingdom to transfer to the European Community institutions a sphere of exclusive legislative power.

Further, on its dualist approach to international law—which in contrast to a monist approach treats domestic law and international law as two entirely different and separate systems of law—international treaties signed and ratified by the United Kingdom are not part of the domestic law of the United Kingdom. Consequently, in order to be enforceable and to bind at the domestic level, such treaties must be domestically incorporated in an Act of Parliament. But the principle of absolute Parliamentary sovereignty then seems to make it very difficult for the supremacy of Community law over later Parliamentary legislation to be guaranteed in the United Kingdom. If the Treaties are made domestically binding and enforceable through an Act of Parliament, such incorporation of EC law would seem vulnerable to any later Act of Parliament which contravened or contradicted it. This is because the principle of Parliamentary sovereignty would not allow the earlier statute to bind the powers of the Parliament, which might well wish to contradict its earlier measure in a later statute. The courts would be obliged, as their constitutional role apparently dictates, to give effect to the latest expression of the will of Parliament in its legislation and to treat the earlier Act as having been repealed by implication.

With those problems in mind, it was nevertheless decided, after the EC Treaties were signed and ratified by the United Kingdom in 1972, to give internal legal effect to Community law by means of an Act of Parliament: the European Communities Act 1972. The central provision of the Act is section 2(1) which provides as follows:

> All such rights, powers, liabilities, obligations and restrictions from time to time created or arising by or under the Treaties, and all such remedies and procedures from time to time provided for by or under the Treaties, as in accordance with the Treaties are without further enactment to be given legal effect or used in the United Kingdom shall be recognised and available in law, and be enforced, allowed and followed accordingly; and the expression 'enforceable Community right' and similar expressions shall be read as referring to one to which this subsection applies.

Section 2(2) provides for the implementation of Community obligations—even when they are intended to replace national legislation and Acts of Parliament—by means of Order in Council or statutory instrument rather than by primary legislation only. Section 2(4) follows, providing rather obscurely:

[43] For a discussion of the meaning of Parliamentary sovereignty, see P. P. Craig, 'United Kingdom Sovereignty after *Factortame*' (1991) 11 YBEL 221.

> The provision that may be made under subsection (2) above includes, subject to Schedule 2 to this Act, any such provision (of any such extent) as might be made by Act of Parliament, and any enactment passed or to be passed, other than one contained in this Part of this Act, shall be construed and have effect subject to the foregoing provisions of this section; but, except as may be provided by any Act passed after this Act, Schedule 2 shall have effect in connection with the powers conferred by this and the following sections of this Act to make Orders in Council and regulations.

The Schedule to which the provision refers sets out a number of powers—such as increasing taxation or legislating retroactively—which cannot be exercised by Order in Council or by delegated legislation, even if they are necessary to comply with a Community obligation. For these powers, presumably, an Act of Parliament will be needed. But the part of section 2(4) which has received most attention is the middle clause of the provision, beginning 'any enactment passed or to be passed', which became prominent when the courts sought a way to reconcile new obligations under Community law with the traditional approach to statutory interpretation.

Section 3 of the Act then provides:

> For the purposes of all legal proceedings any question as to the meaning or effect of any of the Treaties, or as to the validity, meaning or effect of any Community instrument, shall be treated as a question of law (and, if not referred to the European Court, be for determination as such in accordance with the principles laid down by and any relevant decision of the European Court or any court attached thereto).

What this provision appears to do is to make the decisions of the Court of Justice on the meaning and effect of EC law authoritative in United Kingdom courts—giving them, to use domestic legal language, the force of precedent.

However, it is section 2(1) which aims to make the concept of direct effect a part of the United Kingdom legal system. It states that law which under the EC Treaties is to be given immediate legal effect is to be directly enforceable in the United Kingdom Thus the United Kingdom courts, which on the domestic approach to international law could not enforce a provision of an international treaty or a measure passed thereunder, are directed by section 2(1) to enforce any measures which, in accordance with the EC Treaties, are to be directly effective. This means that from the point of view of the United Kingdom courts, there need not be a fresh act of incorporation in order to enable them to enforce each EC Treaty provision, regulation, or directive which according to EC law has direct effect. As in the cases of France, Germany, and Italy, it is apparent that the supremacy of EC law is thus recognized in the United Kingdom by virtue of *domestic* legal processes and legal theory, rather than by what Petriccione calls the monist view urged by the European Court of Justice. Unlike in those three countries, there is no special constitutional provision in the United Kingdom which can legitimate the transfer of legislative power to an international organization, but instead the channel for the reception into its domestic constitutional order of Community law is a simple Act of Parliament.

But again, just as in the case of those other Member States, the existence of a domestic constitutional channel for the incorporation of European Community law did not prevent judicial difficulties from arising over the practical recognition of the supremacy of EC law over national law. As in the case of the Conseil d'Etat, which for many years repeatedly held that it had no jurisdiction to rule upon the constitutionality or validity of French legislation, the English courts traditionally have no constitutional jurisdiction to review Acts of Parliament, their role in relation to such primary legislation being limited to its interpretation and enforcement.

What remained to be seen, then, was what the courts would do when faced with a provision of national law which appeared to conflict with a directly effective provision of Community law. Despite earlier judicial comments to the contrary,[44] the English Master of the Rolls, Lord Denning, in the case of *Shields* v. *Coomes* demonstrated a willingness to accept the principle of supremacy of Community law.[45]

> Long before the United Kingdom joined the European Community, the European Court had laid down two principles of great importance to all member states and their citizens. When we joined the Community, our Parliament enacted that we should abide by those principles laid down by the European Court: see s. 3(1) of the European Communities Act 1972 . . .
>
> The first is the principle of 'direct applicability' . . .
>
> The second is the principle of 'the supremacy of Community law'. It arises whenever there is a conflict or inconsistency between the law contained in an article of the EEC Treaty and the law contained in the internal law of one of the member states, whether passed before or after joining the Community. It says that in any such event the law of the European Community shall prevail over that of the internal law of the member state . . . It seems to me that when the Parliament of the United Kingdom sets up a tribunal to carry out its treaty obligations, the tribunal has jurisdiction to apply Community law, and should apply it, in the confident expectation that this is what Parliament intended. If such a tribunal should find any ambiguity in the statutes or any inconsistency with Community law, then it should resolve it by giving the primacy to Community law.

Thus Lord Denning avoided the problem of implied repeal by giving such weight to the European Communities Act and to Parliament's presumed intention in enacting it that in his view a United Kingdom court should not enforce a later conflicting Act of Parliament—either if the domestic statute was

[44] *Felixstowe Dock and Railway Company* v. *British Transport and Docks Board* [1976] 2 CMLR 655.

[45] See *Shields* v. *E Coomes (Holdings) Ltd* [1979] 1 All ER 456, 461.

ambiguous or if it was inconsistent with Community law. He did not, however, say that national courts should give primacy to Community law even if the statute expressly showed that Parliament intended to contradict Community law on that matter. However, on the facts of the *Shields* case, there was no actual conflict between national law and Community law, and it was not until a later case that a genuine conflict appeared to arise between Article 119 of the EC Treaty concerning equal pay and section 1 of the Equal Pay Act 1970 in the United Kingdom.

Macarthys v. Smith
[1979] 3 All. ER 325

LORD DENNING[46]

Under s. 2(1) and (4) of the European Communities Act 1972 the principles laid down in the Treaty are 'without further enactment' to be given legal effect in the United Kingdom; and have priority over 'any enactment passed or to be passed' by our Parliament . . . In construing our statute, we are entitled to look to the Treaty as an aid to its construction; but not only as an aid but as an overriding force. If on close investigation it should appear that our legislation is deficient or is inconsistent with Community law by some oversight of our draftsmen then it is our bounden duty to give priority to Community law. Such is the result of s 2(1) and (4) of the European Communities Act 1972.

I pause here, however, to make one observation on a constitutional point. Thus far I have assumed that our Parliament, whenever it passes legislation, intends to fulfil its obligations under the Treaty. If the time should come when our Parliament deliberately passes an Act with the intention of repudiating the Treaty or any provision in it or intentionally of acting inconsistently with it and says so in express terms then I should have thought that it would be the duty of our courts to follow the statute of our Parliament.

Here, then, is the judicial reconciliation of Parliamentary sovereignty with the supremacy of European Community law. A provision of domestic legislation which appears to contravene Community law is presumed to be an accidental contravention, and in such circumstances section 2(1) and (4) direct the courts to construe the domestic law in conformity with EC law, or if necessary, to override the conflicting domestic provision. But the overriding of the Act of Parliament is to be seen as a fulfilment of true Parliamentary intention—the intention to comply with directly effective Community law—and if it is made clear that the legislative contravention of Community law was intentional, then domestic law must prevail. In other words, the supremacy of Community law is assured in the United Kingdom only in so far as Parliament intends it to be, and the courts have no power to undermine the clear will of Parliament, whether or not it represents a breach of Community law.[47]

[46] [1979] 3 All ER 325, 329.

[47] See T. Allan, 'Parliamentary Sovereignty: Lord Denning's Dexterous Revolution' (1983) 3 OJLS 22.

However, Lord Denning's view on how the courts should proceed when there was an 'accidental' conflict between Community law and national law was not entirely shared by the other two judges in *Macarthys*. They felt that the meaning of the English Act was fairly clear, and that if there was indeed a conflict between Article 119 and the Act, there would have to be a choice between the two provisions, rather than a 'construction' of the Equal Pay Act in the light of the Treaty provision. In the words of Cumming-Bruce LJ:

> I do not think that it is permissible, as an aid to construction, to look at the terms of the Treaty. If the terms of the Treaty are adjudged in Luxembourg to be inconsistent with the provisions of the Equal Pay Act 1970, European Law will prevail over that municipal legislation. But such a judgment in Luxembourg cannot affect the meaning of the English statute.[48]

On the return of the case from the Court of Justice, whose interpretation of Article 119 did indeed contradict the English court's reading of the Equal Pay Act, the Court of Appeal ruled that Article 119 should be directly applied in the case.[49] Thus it appeared that the English court, unlike the Conseil d'Etat in France, was quite prepared to take on the new role of reviewing an Act of Parliament and of giving priority to a conflicting Community measure—but in the confidence that this reflected the true intention of Parliament as expressed in the European Communities Act.

Shortly afterwards, in *Garland* v. *British Rail Engineering Ltd* before the House of Lords, Lord Diplock cited section 2(4) of the European Communities Act and reverted to the approach favoured by Lord Denning in *Macarthys*, stating that where an apparently conflicting provision of English law was capable of being read in conformity with Community law, that this was the proper approach for the English courts to take.[50] Lord Diplock, in addition to referring to 'the express direction as to the construction of enactments to be passed which is contained in s. 2(4)' also drew on an already well-established principle of construction of English statutes:

> My Lords, even if the obligation to observe the provisions of Article 119 were an obligation assumed by the United Kingdom under an ordinary international treaty or convention and there were no question of the treaty obligation being directly applicable as part of the law to be applied by the courts in this country without need for any further enactment, it is a principle of construction of United Kingdom statutes, now too well established to call for citation of authority, that the words of a statute passed after the treaty has been signed and dealing with the subject matter of the international obligation of the United Kingdom are to be construed, if they are reasonably capable of bearing such a meaning, as intended to carry out the obligation and not to be inconsistent with it. A fortiori is this the

[48] N. 46 above, 335–6. [49] [1981] 1 QB 180, 199. [50] [1983] 2 AC 751.

case where the treaty obligation arises under one of the Community treaties to which s. 2 of the European Communities Act 1972 applies.[51]

However, the *Garland* approach to securing the supremacy of Community law over national law—i.e. by 'harmonious construction' of national law rather than the Macarthys method of direct application of EC law—led to some later difficulties. The approach implied in section 2(4) and approved by Lord Diplock in *Garland* advocates not the direct application of directly effective Community law, but the interpretation of national law in conformity with it.[52] The approach of the Court of Justice to the Member States' obligations to secure the primacy of Community law, however, is rather different and requires national courts, as the ruling in *Simmenthal* above shows, to ensure the immediate and direct enforcement of directly effective EC law.

The situation became more complex when the Court of Justice began to direct its attention beyond the role of national courts in ensuring the supremacy and immediate enforcement of directly effective Community law, to their role in remedying the failure of Member States to implement non-directly effective Community law. As has been seen in the chapter on direct effect, directives require national implementation, and they are not fully directly effective in that they can only ever be directly enforced against the state. Consequently, in cases between two non-state parties, national courts were under no obligation to accord supremacy to an EC directive over national law—indeed they could not, under Community law, enforce a directive against a private litigant.[53] However, in the cases of *Von Colson*[54] and *Marleasing*,[55] we saw that the Court of Justice elaborated further on the role of national courts in these circumstances, ruling that Article 5 of the EC Treaty imposed an obligation on their part to ensure the effectiveness of EC law by interpreting national law in the light of the wording and purpose of directives. This encountered some initial problems in the United Kingdom courts which had adopted the interpretation approach to section 2(4) of the European Communities Act, as suggested by Lords Denning and Diplock. Interpretation of national law in the light of Community law was the method they had advocated to give effect to the supremacy of directly effective EC law, as required by the ECJ in cases such as *Van Gend* and *Simmenthal*. The Court of Justice, on the other hand, required national courts to ensure the supremacy of *directly effective* Community law by directly enforcing it, and

[51] Ibid. 771.

[52] Contrast the ruling of the CA in *Pickstone* v. *Freemans plc* [1989] AC 66 where Art. 119 EC was applied directly in preference over s. 1(2)(c) of the Equal Pay Act, with the ruling of the HL on appeal in the same case [1989] AC 66, 109, that s. 1(2)(c) should be construed in conformity with Art. 119.

[53] Case 152/84, *Marshall* v. *Southampton and South West Hampshire Area Health Authority (Teaching)* [1986] ECR 723, [1986] 1 CMLR 688.

[54] Case 14/83, *Von Colson* v. *Land Nordrhein-Westfalen* [1984] ECR 1891, [1986] 2 CMLR 430.

[55] Case C-106/89, *Marleasing SA* v. La Comercial Internacional de Alimentacion SA [1990] ECR I–4135, [1992] 1 CMLR 305.

required those courts to assist in the enforcement of *non-directly effective* Community law (mainly directives[56]) by interpreting national law in conformity with it. The difference between the two respective approaches can be seen in the following case, where the House of Lords was unwilling to adopt the interpretive approach in order to give effect to the Community measure.

Duke v. GEC Reliance Ltd
[1988] AC 618

Mrs Duke claimed that her employer, the respondent GEC Reliance Ltd, had unlawfully discriminated against her contrary to the 1975 Sex Discrimination Act by requiring her to retire at the age of 60, whereas male employees were not forced to retire until the age of 65. The respondent relied upon section 6(4) of the 1975 Act, which provided that the prohibition on discrimination did not apply to 'provision in relation to . . . retirement'. Council Directive 76/207 on Equal Treatment, which was enacted after the 1975 Act, was later held by the Court of Justice to prohibit discrimination with regard to retirement, but the United Kingdom did not amend section 6(4) of the Act until 1986, some years after Mrs Duke was dismissed. It was argued on her behalf that the court now ought to construe the Sex Discrimination Act 1975, as from the time of its enactment, in accordance with the Court of Justice's later interpretation of the Equal Treatment Directive, and that she ought consequently to recover damages for unlawful discrimination.

LORD TEMPLEMAN[57]

Of course a British court will always be willing and anxious to conclude that United Kingdom law is consistent with Community law. Where an Act is passed for the purpose of giving effect to an obligation imposed by a directive or other instrument a British court will seldom encounter difficulty in concluding that the language of the Act is effective for the intended purpose. But the construction of a British Act of Parliament is a matter of judgment to be determined by British courts and to be derived from the language of the legislation considered in the light of the circumstances prevailing at the date of enactment . . . The Acts were not passed to give effect to the Equal Treatment directive and were intended to preserve discriminatory retirement ages . . .

On the hearing of this appeal, your Lordships have had the advantage . . . of full argument, which has satisfied me that the Sex Discrimination Act 1975 was not intended to give effect to the equal treatment directive as subsequently construed in *Marshall's case* and that the words of s. 6(4) are not reasonably capable of being limited to the meaning ascribed to them by the appellant. Section 2(4) of the European Communities Act 1972 does not in my opinion enable or constrain a British court to distort the meaning of a British statute in order to enforce against an individual a Community directive which has no direct effect between individuals. Section 2(4) applies and only applies where Community provisions are directly applicable . . .

[56] See also Case 322/88, *Salvatore Grimaldi* v. *Fonds des Maladies Professionelles* [1989] ECR 4407, [1991] 2 CMLR 265, for the obligation on national courts to take into account other non-directly effective EC laws such as recommendations, when interpreting national implementing laws.

[57] [1988] AC 618, 638–41.

> The submission that the Sex Discrimination Act 1975 must be construed in a manner which gives effect to the equal treatment directive as construed by the European court in *Marshall's case* is said to be derived from the decision of the European court in *Von Colson* . . .
>
> The *Von Colson* case is no authority for the proposition that . . . a court of a member state must distort the meaning of a domestic statute so as to conform with Community law which is not directly applicable.

Lord Templeman's view of section 2(4) here was that it was the method chosen by Parliament to ensure the supremacy of directly effective Community law, and that the direction in section 2(4) to construe domestic law in accordance with Community law has no application to a case involving a directive as between private parties. He took the view that the ruling in the *Von Colson* case would make no difference, since it did not require national courts to 'distort' the words of a national statute. The decision in *Duke* was followed in several other cases,[58] but the House of Lords subsequently took a different approach in the cases of *Litster* v. *Forth Dry Dock Co Ltd*[59] and *Pickstone* v. *Freemans*.[60] In these cases, the House of Lords demonstrated that it was prepared to construe the words of domestic statutes in conformity with EC law which was not directly effective, even where that construction was not in accordance with the literal meaning of the statutes. The difference between *Litster* and *Pickstone* on the one hand, and *Duke* on the other, was that the domestic statutes in the former two cases were introduced specifically in order to give effect to the non-directly effective EC law. Thus the United Kingdom courts could conform with the *Von Colson* ruling of the ECJ (as section 3 of the 1972 Act would require them to do) and at the same time could more comfortably claim to be carrying out the intention of Parliament in reading an undeniably 'implementing' domestic measure in compliance with the Community directive in question.

After the case of *Marleasing*, however, it became clear that from the Court of Justice's point of view, the national courts' obligation to construe domestic legislation in accordance with directives was *not* restricted to legislation designed to implement those directives. Thus to follow *Marleasing*, although the national courts would be acting in accordance with the intention of Parliament in one sense by complying with section 3 of the European Communities Act, they would have to ignore the specific intention of Parliament represented by the particular domestic law which they were construing against its *prima facie* literal interpretation, and in accordance with a later Community directive. And although the United Kingdom courts have been quite prepared to do this in the case of directly effective Community law (as shown in *Macarthys* and *Factortame*), they have been considerably more reluctant to ensure supremacy in the case of non-directly effective Community

[58] See the HL decision in *Finnegan* v. *Clowney Youth Training Ltd.* [1990] 2 AC 407, the CA in *Marshall* v. *Southampton and South West Hampshire Area Health Authority (Teaching)* [1991] ICR 136 and in *Webb* v. *EMO Cargo* [1992] 2 All ER 43.

[59] [1990] 1 AC 546.

[60] N. 52 above.

directives. It is understandable that the 1972 Act appeared to provide in section 2(1) and (4) for the supremacy of directly effective Community law, since that was all the Court of Justice in 1972 had required. But by now the Court has required national courts to ensure, in so far as they can by means of interpretation of any relevant national law, to secure the effectiveness of non-directly effective EC law. And since section 3 of the 1972 Act directs United Kingdom courts to accept the rulings of the Court of Justice as to the meaning and effect of EC law, the courts are driven in two ways. They are directed to give effect to EC law which is directly effective, but they are also directed to accept the rulings of the Court of Justice as to the effect of Community law.

This dilemma was faced by the Court of Appeal in *Webb* v. *EMO*,[61] where the provisions of the 1975 Sex Discrimination Act were alleged by the applicant to conflict with the Court of Justice's interpretation of the 1976 Equal Treatment Directive. Although the Court of Appeal accepted that it should read a domestic law in the light of a non-directly effective directive even where the domestic measure was not designed to implement the directive, it held, citing *Duke*, that to read the 1975 Act in the manner contended for by the applicant would distort the natural meaning of the British statute and that the *Marleasing* ruling did not require national courts to do this. Interestingly, although it agreed that national courts were not required by the ruling in *Marleasing* to 'distort' the meaning of a domestic statute, the House of Lords, on appeal, referred the case to the Court of Justice for a ruling as to the meaning of the relevant provision of the Equal Treatment Directive.[62] The interpretation given by the Court of Justice supported the claim of the applicant, so that, in the circumstances, her dismissal on grounds of unavailability for work due to her pregnancy constituted direct sex discrimination. However, this did not accord with the interpretation given by the Court of Appeal or the House of Lords of the 1975 Sex Discrimination Act. It now remains to be seen whether, in view of this apparent conflict between the Directive and the 1975 Act as interpreted by the Court of Appeal and the House of Lords, the House of Lords will be prepared to depart from that interpretation and to read it instead in compliance with the Court of Justice's ruling. In the view of the Court of Appeal—and perhaps of House of Lords, although it did not explicitly say so—such a reading would amount to a distortion of the words of the British Act. The willingness of the House of Lords nevertheless to make a reference on the meaning of the Directive could indicate one of several things: either that the House of Lords does not consider that the interpretation of the Directive given by the Court would be a distortion of the words of the British statute; or that it is prepared to alter what it originally considered to be the clear meaning of the statutory language and to read it in accordance with the ruling of the Court; or that it considers that the interpretation given by the Court would require a distortion of the national statute and that

[61] [1992] 2 All ER 43. [62] [1993] 1 WLR 49.

amending legislation is required before effect can be given to the Directive against a non-state employer.

The supremacy drama is certainly not yet over. But the United Kingdom courts have changed their approach considerably since the enactment of the European Communities Act 1972. The 'construction' approach to section 2(4) has been supplemented by a willingness to enforce directly effective provisions of Community law directly, even where it involves suspending or setting aside an inconsistent Act of Parliament. And the construction or interpretation approach has been extended, in accordance with the rulings in *Von Colson* and *Marleasing*, so that where a Community directive lacks direct effect in a case, national statutes which were not introduced in order to implement that directive may nevertheless be read in conformity with the directive, possibly even (depending on the outcome of the *Webb* case in the House of Lords) where that does not conform with the literal meaning favoured by the national court.

As far as directly effective Community law is concerned, the clearest recent statement of the national courts' approach was made by Lord Bridge in the course of the *Factortame* litigation. His language shows that, although an equilibrium may now have been reached in the relationship between the United Kingdom courts and the Court of Justice as to the requirements of supremacy of EC law, in so far as the United Kingdom courts are concerned, their obligations do not stem directly from the Treaties but from the express will of the Parliament, and their responsibility is not to the Court of Justice but to the United Kingdom Parliament. The first excerpt below is from Lord Bridge's judgment before the case was referred to the Court of Justice, and the second is from his judgment after its return.

Factortame Ltd v. Secretary of State for Transport [1990] 2 AC 85

LORD BRIDGE[63]

If the applicants fail to establish the rights they claim before the European Court, the effect of the interim relief granted would be to have conferred on them rights directly contrary to Parliament's sovereign will and correspondingly to have deprived British fishing vessels, as defined by Parliament, of the enjoyment of a substantial proportion of the United Kingdom quota of stocks of fish protected by the common fisheries policy. I am clearly of the opinion that, as a matter of English law, the court has no power to make an order which has these consequences.

It follows that this appeal must fall to be dismissed unless there is, as the applicants contend, some overriding principle derived from the jurisprudence of the European Court which compels national courts of Member States, whatever their own law may provide, to assert, and in appropriate cases to exercise, a power to provide an effective interlocutory remedy to protect putative rights in Community law.

[63] [1990] 2 AC 85, 143.

After the Court of Justice gave its ruling in the case, to the effect that a national rule which was the sole obstacle to the national court's grant of interim relief in a case concerning directly effective Community rights should be set aside by the national court, Lord Bridge summarized, in response to some of the adverse public comment which this ruling attracted, what he understood to be the constitutional position of the United Kingdom:

Factortame Ltd v. Secretary of State for Transport (No 2)
[1991] 1 AC 603

LORD BRIDGE[64]

Some public comments on the decision of the Court of Justice, affirming the jurisdiction of the courts of member states to override national legislation if necessary to enable interim relief to be granted in protection of rights under Community law, have suggested that this was a novel and dangerous invasion by a Community institution of the sovereignty of the United Kingdom Parliament. But such comments are based on a misconception. If the supremacy within the European Community of Community law over the national law of member states was not always inherent in the EEC Treaty it was certainly well established in the jurisprudence of the Court of Justice long before the United Kingdom joined the Community. Thus, whatever limitation of its sovereignty Parliament accepted when it enacted the European Communities Act 1972 was entirely voluntary. Under the terms of the 1972 Act it has always been clear that it was the duty of a United Kingdom court, when delivering final judgment, to override any rule of national law found to be in conflict with any directly enforceable rule of Community law. Similarly, when decisions of the Court of Justice have exposed areas of United Kingdom statute law which failed to implement Council directives, Parliament has always loyally accepted the obligation to make appropriate and prompt amendments. Thus there is nothing in any way novel in according supremacy to rules of Community law in those areas to which they apply and to insist that, in the protection of rights under Community law, national courts must not be inhibited by rules of national law from granting interim relief in appropriate cases is no more than a logical recognition of that supremacy.

In his comment on the *Factortame* case, Craig contrasts two differing views of parliamentary sovereignty: the 'traditional view', according to which limitations on the subject-matter and form of legislation by Parliament can only come about by virtue of a constitutional revolution and the 'new view', according to which Parliament itself can change the rules which determine the appropriate form and manner of its legislation. In discussing how proponents of each respective view would explain the means by which supremacy is accorded to Community law, he writes as follows:

64 [1991] 1 AC 603, 658.

P. P.Craig, United Kingdom Sovereignty after *Factortame*[65]

[Lord Bridge's] reasoning is, by way of contrast, explicitly grounded on the idea that the decision concerning sovereignty was made by Parliament, and not the courts. The decision on membership of the EEC was made by Parliament, and carried into effect by the European Communitites Act 1972. This decision to join the Community must, said Lord Bridge, have been based on the assumption of the supremacy of Community law, both because the case law of the European Court of Justice was clear on this, even prior to 1972, and because it was inherent in the very nature of membership of the EEC. The reasoning of Lord Bridge does not therefore fit very well with that articulated by the traditional theory. The reason for this is not hard to find. The courts do not wish to be seen as making a 'political choice' at the 'boundary of the legal system'. They would prefer to express the matter as one in which the essential choice has been made by the legislature, in this instance the legislature of the early 1970's. This mode of reasoning accords, in substance, better with that advanced by the new view. A Parliament is perceived as having made a choice, to join the Community in 1972. The implications of this choice have repercussions for later Parliaments, in the sense that the consequence of membership is, for the reasons given by Lord Bridge, to afford supremacy to Community law. This 'consequence' can of course be changed by later Parliaments, either by withdrawing from the EEC, or perhaps by expressly stating in a certain context that national law is departing from Community norms . . .

The possible future implications of the developments considered thus far can only be guessed at. It can none the less be considered highly likely that the courts will continue to accord priority to Community law, unless either the United Kingdom withdraws from the EEC, which is very unlikely, or Parliament explicitly states its intent to depart from Community law in a particular area. In the latter eventuality the courts might follow the national statute, but they might also state that this form of 'partial compliance' with Community law is not possible; that while the United Kingdom remains in the EEC it cannot pick and choose which norms of EEC law to comply with.

In the most recent phase of its acceptance of the supremacy of Community law, the House of Lords has stated that there is no constitutional barrier to an applicant before the United Kingdom courts directly seeking judicial review of primary legislation, which is alleged to be in breach of Community law. As in the *Factortame* case, although this is presented by the House of Lords as a natural extension of its earlier case law and, by implication, based on the will of Parliament as expressed in the 1972 Act, the impact of the ruling is nonetheless quite dramatic.

Equal Opportunities Commission v. Secretary of State for Employment [1994] 1 WLR 409

The Equal Opportunities Commission (EOC) took the view that the provisions of the Employment Protection (Consolidation) Act of 1978 on part-time workers

[65] N. 43 above, 252.

resulted in indirect discrimination against women, and thus was contrary to Community law. In a letter from the Secretary of State for Employment to the Commission, the Secretary refused to accept that the UK was in breach of EC law. The EOC sought judicial review of the Secretary of State's decision, and also sought a declaration and an order of mandamus requiring the Secretary to introduce legislation to provide equal pay for equal work for men and women, and to amend the 1978 Act so as to provide certain protection for part-time workers. The Secretary of State argued that the English court had no jurisdiction to declare that the UK of the Secretary of State was in breach of any obligations under Community law.

LORD KEITH[66]

The question is whether judicial reivew is available for the purpose of securing a declaration that certain United Kingdom primary legislation is incompatible with Community law . . . In the *Factortame* series of cases . . . the applicants for judicial review sought a declaration that the provisions of Part II of the Merchant Shipping Act 1988 should not apply to them on the ground that such application would be contrary to Community law, in particular Articles 7 and 52 of the EEC Treaty . . . The Divisional Court, under Article 177 of the Treaty, referred to the Court of Justice of the European Communities a number of questions, including the question whether these restrictive conditions were compatible with Articles 7 and 52 of the Treaty. The European Court . . . answered that question in the negative, and although the final result is not reported, no doubt the Divisional Court in due course granted a declaration accordingly. The effect was that certain provisions of United Kingdom primary legislation were held to be invalid in their purported application to nationals of Member States of the European Community, but without any prerogative order being available to strike down the legislation in question, which of course remained valid as regards nationals of non-member States. At no stage in the course of the litigation, which included two visits to this House, was it suggested that judicial review of legislation was not available for obtaining an adjudication upon the validity of the legislation in so far as it affected the applicants.

The *Factortame* case is thus a precedent in favour of the EOC's recourse to judicial review for the purpose of challenging as incompatible with Community law the relevant provisions of the 1978 Act. It also provides an answer to the third procedural point taken by the Secretary of State, which maintains that the Divisional Court had no jurisdiction to declare that the United Kingdom or the Secretary of State was in breach of obligations under Community law. There is no need for any such declaration. A declaration that the threshold provisions of the 1978 Act are incompatible with Community law would suffice for the purposes sought to be achieved by the EOC and is capable of being granted consistently with the precedent afforded by *Factortame*.

[66] [1994] 1 WLR 409, 418–19.

4. CONCLUSION

The bi-dimensional picture of the supremacy of Community law presented by Weiler, above, has clearly not lost its relevance. Despite the fact that all of the Member States and their courts by now accept the practical requirement of giving priority to Community law over national law, few, if any, would be prepared to abandon their supervision of the Community institutions—and indeed of the Court of Justice—to ensure that the Community does not attempt to extend the powers it has been given. In other words, where Community law has been adopted within its proper sphere, the Member States are generally willing to accord it priority over conflicting national law. However, on the more difficult *Kompetenz-Kompetenz* issue, they are not prepared to relinquish jurisdiction to examine the exercise of Community powers in order to ascertain whether the Community has exceeded the limits of the powers specifically granted to it under the Treaties in accordance with the constitutional system of each Member State. This is particularly evident from the decision of the German Constitutional Court in *Brunner*, in which that Court referred somewhat cryptically to the previous tendency of the Court of Justice to extend the scope of Community powers on an open-handed reading of the Treaty, and in which it stressed that, in the future, a clear distinction would have to be drawn between the interpretation of existing powers and an actual amendment or extension of the Treaty. In view of the difficulty in giving any concrete meaning to the term, it is not clear whether the concept of subsidiarity will have much effect in averting potential legal and political clashes over issues of supremacy in the future.

It is perhaps appropriate to end with the comments of one commentator encouraging a less polarized approach to the constitutional relationship between the Member States and the European Community than that which is often adopted, and calling instead for recognition of and building upon the constructive dialogue which has existed between the national and the Community perspectives.

B. De Witte, Community Law and National Constitutional Values[67]

The gradual acceptance of the principles of direct effect and supremacy of Community law has been sustained by a continuous dialogue between the European Court of Justice and the national courts. The recognition by the European Court of the existence of an unwritten Bill of Rights was, to a large extent, the result of a direct challenge by the German Constitutional Court against the supremacy of Community law over the national constitution. The relationship between Community law and the national constitutions is not to be settled according to unilateral principles of hierarchy, and national courts should not be torn between loyalty to their own constitution and loyalty to their Community duties.

[67] N. 26 above, 22.

Both the Court of Justice and the national constitution and supreme courts could recognize that the relationship can be seen from two different, but equally legitimate, perspectives and that there is now a plurality of 'supreme' texts in Europe. The dialogue might be facilitated by the fact that, on substance, there has probably never before been such a community of values among European States. The challenge ahead is to make out of the national constitutions building blocks of European Unity rather than bulwarks of sovereignty.

5. FURTHER READING

CRAIG, P. P., 'United Kingdom Sovereignty after Factortame' (1991) 11 Y.B.E.L. 221

DE WITTE, B., 'Community Law and National Constitutional Values' (1991) 2 LIEI 1

GAJA, G., 'New Developments in a Continuing Story: The Relationship between EEC Law and Italian Law' (1990) 27 CMLRev. 83

HERDEGEN, M., 'Maastricht and the German Constitutional Court: Constitutional Restraints for an Ever Closer Union' (1994) 31 CMLRev. 235

OLIVER, P., 'The French Constitution and the Treaty of Maastricht' (1994) 43 ICLQ 1

PETRICCIONE, R., 'Italy: Supremacy of Community Law over National Law' (1986) 11 ELRev. 320

POLLARD, D., 'The Conseil d'Etat is European—Official' (1990) 15 ELRev. 267

ROSEREN, P., 'The Application of Community Law by French Courts From 1982 to 1993' (1994) 31 CMLRev. 315

ROTH, W., 'The Application of Community law in West Germany: 1980–1990', (1991) 28 CMLRev. 137

WEILER, J., 'The Community System: the Dual Character of Supranationalism' (1981) 1 YBEL. 267

7

General Principles I: Fundamental Rights

1. INTRODUCTION

It is perhaps appropriate to begin a chapter of this nature by posing the question which many students of Community law ask: why do the EC Treaties contain no charter of rights nor any express reference to the need for protection of basic human rights and other such values in the conduct of Community affairs? The Community is, after all, a large and powerful bureaucracy responsible for an immense amount of regulatory legislation affecting many aspects of people's lives. Given the Court of Justice's frequent rhetoric relating to respect for the 'rule of law' in the Community and its reference to the Treaties as the constitution of the Communities,[1] how is it that these documents contain no clause limiting or directing the exercise of institutional power by reference to the requirement of protection for human rights? Why is there no reference even to very basic traditional civil and political rights, to values such as human dignity, freedom of expression, and privacy? These are values which are generally considered to be of both practical and symbolic importance in modern, liberal, democratic, or would-be-democratic political systems, as indeed are the more controversial social and economic rights. Several answers have been suggested to explain this omission in the original three European Community Treaties.

One view is that the absence can be explained by reference to the history and background to the signing of the original three Treaties, in particular leading up to the signing of the European Economic Community Treaty in 1957. The Treaty establishing a European Defence Community had been signed by the six original Member States in 1952 at a time when there were great hopes for European integration.[2] More ambitious proposals for a European Political Community were then drawn up in 1953, and presented in a document entitled the 'Draft Treaty embodying the Statute of the European Community'.[3] This draft Treaty set out as one of its primary aims the protection of human rights and fundamental freedoms, and proposed incorporating the rights provisions of the European Convention on Human Rights

[1] See Case 294/83, *Parti Ecologiste 'Les Verts'* v. *European Parliament* [1986] ECR 1339 and C–2/88, *Zwartveld* [1990] ECR I–3365, [1990] 3 CMLR 457.

[2] See Ch. 1.

[3] See for a discussion A. H. Robertson 'The European Political Community' (1952) XXIX BYIL 383.

and Fundamental Freedoms into the new Treaty. In 1954, however, the French National Assembly failed to ratify the European Defence Treaty, and with that the proposals for European Political Union also fell.[4] It is likely that considerable restraint was exercised when it came to the drafting of the EEC Treaty, lest this, too, would suffer the same fate as the earlier draft treaties. It is certainly clear that, after the failure by the French Parliament to ratify the Defence Community Treaty, plans for the negotiation of a treaty to achieve closer integration in Europe were scaled down. The 1957 EEC Treaty was restricted to the aims of economic integration and no mention of political union or of human rights was included. In the words of one commentator 'the original euphoria gave way to very sober utilitarian considerations and sight of a general concept of fundamental and human rights was lost'.[5] The stated aims of the EEC and Euratom Treaties were thus limited in their field of application, and the only express reference to anything nobler or more aspirational than the aim of economic progress was to be found in the preambles to the Treaties. The preamble to the earlier ECSC Treaty, for example, contains the following recitals, which posit economic integration as a means to a better end rather than as the sole end in itself:

> *Considering* that world peace can be safeguarded only by creative efforts commensurate with the dangers that threaten it, . . .
>
> *Resolved* to substitute for age-old rivalries the merging of their essential interests; to create, by establishing an economic community, the basis for a broader and deeper community among peoples long divided by bloody conflicts;

And in the preamble to the EEC Treaty, similarly, are the following recitals:

> *Resolved* to ensure the economic and social progress of their countries by common action to eliminate the barriers which divide Europe, . . .
>
> *Resolved* by thus pooling their resources to preserve and strengthen peace and liberty, and calling upon the other peoples of Europe who share their ideal to join in their efforts;

Nevertheless, these references to a broader ideal are only to be found in the preambles, and the concrete provisions of the Treaties made no specific mention of human rights protection.

A second possible explanation for this omission derives from the first: that since the Treaties, and particularly the EEC Treaty, were necessarily focused on and limited primarily to economic matters, it may not have been immediately apparent that the regulation envisaged could encroach on traditionally

[4] See A. H. Robertson, *European Institutions* (2nd edn., Stevens & Sons, 1966), 19–21.

[5] M. Dauses, 'The Protection of Fundamental Rights in the Community Legal Order' (1985) 10 ELRev. 398, 399. See also P. Pescatore, 'The Context and Significance of Fundamental Rights in the Law of the European Communities' (1981) 2 HRLJ 295.

protected fundamental human rights—at least not on negative civil and political rights, such as freedom of speech, religion, and association, nor even on more positive social and economic rights, such as social security, housing, and healthcare. No doubt it seemed that those who were likely to be adversely affected by European Economic Community legislation would mostly be economic actors—commercial entities and industries which generally enjoy a concentration of economic power, rather than the traditional subjects of civil liberties and rights. However, in view of the extremely wide authority which was conferred on its institutions under the EEC Treaty, the Community quickly became a very powerful entity whose actions had considerable impact on many political and social matters, as well as upon interests in the economic and commercial sphere. And indeed, as the Community legal order has continued to develop and to expand, it has shown itself to be capable of affecting many other interests and rights in areas which were probably not originally foreseen. Its spheres of competence have continued to expand into areas such as the environment, consumer protection, culture, education, and research, both through the addition of new Treaties such as the Single European Act and the TEU, as well as through the case law of the Court of Justice.

However, it was in respect of economic and commercial interests that the area of so-called fundamental rights protection was first developed by the European Court of Justice. And although such interests may not represent values which are as important as, for example, the right to life or to self-determination, they are nevertheless interests which are accorded a degree of legal or constitutional protection in many Member States: rights to property, freedom to pursue a trade or profession, the right to a livelihood, and so on.

Much attention has been focused on the way in which the Court gradually declared fundamental rights to be a part of the Community legal order. The initial trigger for this development was the challenge to the supremacy of Community law from Member States which felt that Community legislation was encroaching upon important rights and interests which were protected under national law. The development had the full support of the Member States, given that fundamental rights were being introduced into Community law as a restraint and a limit upon powers of the Community institutions. But more than two decades later, there are very different reasons for, and very different consequences of, the continued expansion of the role of fundamental rights by the Court.

The powers of the Community have grown considerably, and the evolution of an economic community into a broader social and political union has continued apace. The Court has played a substantial role in the process of integration and incremental federalization of the legal systems of the Member States. If a supranational Court in a quasi-federal legal and political system such as the European Community is to maintain its authority and status, it is virtually inevitable that it will begin to exercise a 'rights' jurisdiction. Even if the challenge to the supremacy of Community law had not come when it did, there is little doubt but that the Court would eventually have declared respect for fundamental rights and general principles of law to be part of the law of the Community.[6]

Further, the consequences of the initial 'incorporation' of fundamental rights into the Community legal order have also changed as the case law of the Court has developed. The Member States did not object to the degree of judicial creativity which this involved, since it appeared to be done primarily in order to limit rather than to expand the Community's powers. But now that the jurisprudence of the Court relating to human rights and general principles is well established, it has become apparent that the Court considers that the actions of the Member States within the field of EC law, and not just the actions of the Community, should be in compliance with those values. The similarities between the process of development and expansion of the jurisdiction of the United States Supreme Court and the EC Court have often been cited, suggesting that just as the U.S. Supreme Court declared the federal Bill of Rights to be applicable also to the actions of the states, so has the Court of Justice declared that the fundamental rights which are part of Community law are binding, to an ever-increasing extent, on the Member States. Had this prospect, with its potential to further the role of the Court of Justice as a sort of federal supreme court, been foreseen by the Member States at the time of the Court's earlier case law, they might not have accepted the initial development with such ready approval.

2. THE DEVELOPMENT OF FUNDMENTAL RIGHTS AND GENERAL PRINCIPLES AS STANDARDS BINDING ON THE COMMUNITY

(a) The Court's Initial Resistance

It was as a direct result of the insistence of one Member State in particular, that the Court of Justice acknowledged the existence and the relevance of unwritten general principles of law, including protection for certain fundamental rights, as part of the Community legal order. The Court initially had resisted attempts by litigants to invoke such principles, and certain basic legal values recognized in domestic law, as part of the Community's legal order. Only after its refusal, in several cases, to consider the application of rights and principles which were not specifically set out in the Treaties, did the Court decide to change its approach and to declare that they did form part of Community law. The more benevolent interpretation of the Court's early approach is not that it was unconcerned about basic human rights and recognized consitutional and legal principles, but that it objected to the specific

[6] See Ch. 8 for discussion of some of the 'general principles of law'.

source of the principles invoked. Most litigants relied on fundamental principles recognized in their domestic law, such as protection for vested rights, legitimate expectations, proportionality, and natural justice. Perhaps the Court felt that, had it accepted these, it would have appeared that Community law was to be subordinated to the general legal principles and values as recognized by different Member States, and that it could neither be supreme nor applicable equally in every Member State.

Thus, in the initial cases which were brought under the ECSC Treaty the Court refused to consider, as a ground for annulment of a Community measure, the fact that it infringed a principle of a Member State's legal system. In *Stork*,[7] in which a coal wholesaler complained of a decision of the High Authority (now the Commission of the Coal and Steel Community) governing the sale of coal, the Court refused to consider the argument that the decision breached basic rights which were protected under German law. According to the Court, 'the High Authority is not empowered to examine a ground of complaint which maintains that, when it adopted its decision, it infringed principles of German constitutional law'.[8]

The concern raised in *Stork* was that Community law was apparently riding roughshod over principles which had an important place in national law, particularly principles of a fundamental constitutional nature. Yet despite the potential constitutional dispute brewing over the supremacy of Community law, in the event of a conflict between protected rights in the national legal order and specific Community measures, the Court continued to declare that it was not for it, when considering the legality of Community acts, to ensure that the constitutional rules of the Member States were respected. In *Geitling*,[9] another case concerning a challenge by coal wholesalers to a High Authority decision which prevented them from selling coal directly, the Court not only rejected the relevance of a fundamental right in German constitutional law, but also went on to dismiss the suggestion that Community law might of itself protect such a right: 'Community law, as it arises under the ECSC Treaty, does not contain any general principle, express or otherwise, guaranteeing the maintenance of vested rights'.[10]

In the case of *Sgarlata*,[11] some five years later, the Court stated that it could not allow the express provisions of the Treaty to be overridden by a plea which was founded upon other principles, even if those were fundamental principles which were common to the legal systems of all the Member States.[12]

[7] Case 1/58, *Stork* v. *High Authority* [1959] ECR 17.

[8] *Ibid*., para. 4 of the judgment.

[9] Cases 36, 37, 38, and 40/59, *Geitling* v. *High Authority* [1960] ECR 423.

[10] *Ibid.* 438.

[11] Case 40/64, *Sgarlata and others* v. *Commission* [1965] ECR 215, [1966] CMLR 314.

[12] Note, however, that the Court did not deny the existence in Community law of any general principles of law other than those written in the Treaty: see Case 35/67, *Van Eick* v. *Commission* [1968] ECR 329, 342 where the Court held that the Disciplinary Board under the Community staff regulations was bound to exercise its powers in accordance with 'the fundamental principles of the law of procedure'. However, unlike in the case of *Sgarlata*, there was no question of these general principles overriding specific Treaty provisions.

(b) A More Receptive Approach

Some years after *Sgarlata*, however, the Court's attitude to these arguments began to change, and it responded more positively to an applicant's claim that the implementation of a Community scheme constituted an infringement of his human rights. The Commission in the case argued that, although only Community law and not national law could be considered, Community law itself did protect fundamental rights, both expressly in certain Articles of the Treaty, and in its unwritten law which was derived from legal principles of the Member States.

Case 29/69, Stauder v. City of Ulm
[1969] ECR 419, [1970] CMLR 112

In order to reduce the surplus of butter in the Community, the Commission authorized Member States to make subsidized butter available to categories of social security recipients, who would present the national trader with a coupon issued in their name. Stauder was a beneficiary of the scheme who objected to the requirement that the names and addresses of beneficiaries be revealed to the trader. He challenged the scheme before the Stuttgart Administrative Court on the ground that it infringed fundamental rights enshrined in the German Basic Law, and the case was referred to the Court of Justice.

THE ECJ

3. When a single decision is addressed to all the Member States the necessity for uniform application and accordingly for uniform interpretation makes it impossible to consider one version of the text in isolation but requires that it be interpreted on the basis of both the real intention of its author and the aim he seeks to achieve, in the light in particular of the versions in all four languages.

. . .

6. It follows that the provision in question must be interpreted as not requiring—although it does not prohibit—the identification of beneficiaries by name. The Commission was thus able to publish on 29 July 1969 an amending decision to this effect. Each of the Member States is accordingly now able to choose from a number of different methods by which the coupons may refer to the person concerned.

7. Interpreted in this way the provision at issue contains nothing capable of prejudicing the fundamental human rights enshrined in the general principles of Community law and protected by the Court.

It is instructive to observe the methodology of the Court in this case. Unlike the earlier cases in which general principles of law or nationally protected human rights were invoked in order to challenge a Community measure, the Court did not reject the applicability of principles of this nature. Neither did the Court, however, accept the claim that the Commission's butter scheme infringed any such right. Rather, it held, looking at versions of the Commission decision in other Community languages, that it was not necessary to identify a recipient of subsidized butter by name. Any possibility of discrimination or any potential infringement of the right to human dignity could be avoided by interpreting the measure in this way. From the point of view of the development of human-rights protection within Community law, however, the most telling part of the Court's decision is the short phrase in the final paragraph of the judgment where it declared, without any reference to its previous and apparently contrary case law, that fundamental human rights are a part of the general principles of Community law and are protected by it. Although the Court went no further than this in explaining the nature or extent of these general principles, nor their positive or other sources, Advocate General Roemer elaborated a little more on the matter, putting it into the context of the Court's previous case law.

> In the present case the Court is not, contrary to what one might think at first sight, being asked about the compatibility of a Community measure with national constitutional law. In fact in view of your previous case-law, examination of such a question would be impossible. The court making the reference is asking for a decision on the legal validity of the Commission's decision in the light of 'the general legal principles of Community law in force'. As the grounds of the order making the reference show, the Verwaltungsgericht thus thinks that it must be *guided by reference* to the fundamental principles of national law. This is in line with the view taken by many writers that general qualitative concepts of national constitutional law, in particular fundamental rights recognized by national law, must be ascertained by means of a comparative evaluation of laws, and that such concepts, which form an unwritten constituent part of Community law, must be observed in making secondary Community law. Applying this test, there is accordingly every justification for seeking to test the validity of the Commission decision.[13]

Although academic literature has focused on the restrictive attitude of the Court of Justice to the role of human rights in the earlier cases, and on the sudden change of approach in *Stauder*, it has also been argued that the Court in fact did not, prior to that case, take quite such a restrictive and positivist view of the sources of Community law.

U. Scheuner, Fundamental Rights in European Community law and in National Constitutional Law[14]

If one looks back at the previous, rather negative, pronouncements on fundamental liberties, this (i.e. the *Stauder* case) seems a turning point in the jurisprudence. In fact, the Court had from the outset given much attention to the development of general principles destined to protect individual rights in the exercise of its functions of review of the actions of Community organs. The Treaties themselves provided some useful elements for the elaboration of such principles . . . (misuse of power in Article 33 ECSC, and non-discrimination in Article 7 EEC) . . . The Court has further made use of two principles which probably stem

[13] [1969] ECR 419, 428. [14] (1975) 12 CMLRev. 171, 180–1.

from German sources: it gives protection to justifiable reliance of interested parties on the consistence of Community measures (*Vertrauensschutz*) and upholds in that manner the principle of legal security. The Court has also declared, that measures of the Community organs must be proportional to the objectives pursued (principle of proportionality). Finally, the Court applies general principles guaranteeing due process such as the double jeopardy rule (*ne bis in idem*) and the rule of a fair hearing of the interested parties.

However, although it may indeed have begun of its own accord to develop and apply principles of law which had their source in the legal systems of the Member States, the Court had certainly responded negatively in some early cases to the specific attempts of applicants to have particular general principles of law, other than those expressed in the Treaties, accepted as part of Community law, and to this extent *Stauder* represented a noticeable change in approach.[15]

(c) The Court's Development of Fundamental Rights as Grounds for Annulment of Community Laws

Stauder was a relatively easy case for the Court to decide, given the fact that the impugned Community measure could, without difficulty, be interpreted in conformity with the principle invoked in the reference of the national court. But the potential which was anticipated by some of the earlier cases, of a conflict between a Community measure and a right protected within a Member State's law which could not so easily be resolved through interpretation, was soon to be realized. In a case which again concerned an alleged infringement of basic principles of German constitutional law by a Community measure, an outright conflict between the interpretation of the German Constitutional Court and that of the Court of Justice occurred. Clearly this time, an adequate response by the Court of Justice was essential, since the applicant was effectively asking the German Constitutional Court to disapply or to 'strike down' a Community provision.[16]

Case 11/70, Internationale Handelsgesellschaft v. Einfuhr- und Vorratstelle für Getreide und Futtermittel [1970] ECR 1125, [1972] CMLR 255

The applicant, a German import–export company, obtained an export licence in respect of 20,000 metric tons of maize meal, the validity of which expired on 31

[15] For a discussion of the 'fundamental rights' explicit within the Treaty itself, and which gradually were described as fundamental principles of Community law by the Court, see Shachor-Landau, 'Reflections on the Two European Courts of Justice' in Y. Dinstein *et al.* (eds.), *International Law at a Time of Perplexity* (Martinus Nijhoff, 1989), 792: 'The skeleton of rights modestly specified in these scattered Treaty provisions has acquired flesh and blood through Community secondary legislation and through the consistent and coherent case law of the Community Court'.

[16] See Ch. 6.

December 1967. Council Regulation 120/67 had set up a system for the common organization of the cereal market whereby a licence could be obtained by lodging a deposit, and that deposit would be forfeit if the goods in question were not exported within the period of time set. A part of the applicant company's deposit was forfeit when the licence expired without all of the maize having been exported. The company then brought an action before the administrative court in Frankfurt claiming the return of this sum and questioning the validity of the deposit system. The national court considered that the deposit system was contrary to principles of national constitutional law, including the principles of freedom of action and of disposition, of economic liberty and of proportionality, and it referred the question of the system's validity to the Court of Justice.

THE ECJ

3. Recourse to the legal rules or concepts of national law in order to judge the validity of measures adopted by the institutions of the Community would have an adverse effect on the uniformity and efficacy of Community law. The validity of such measures can only be judged in the light of Community law. In fact, the law stemming from the Treaty, an independent source of law, cannot because of its very nature be overridden by rules of national law, however framed, without being deprived of its character as Community law and without the legal basis of the Community itself being called into question. Therefore the validity of a Community measure or its effect within a Member State cannot be affected by allegations that it runs counter to either fundamental rights as formulated by the constitution of that State or the principles of a national constitutional structure.

4. However, an examination should be made as to whether or not any analagous guarantee inherent in Community law has been disregarded. In fact, respect for fundamental rights forms an integral part of the general principles of Community law protected by the Court of Justice. The protection of such rights, whilst inspired by the constitutional traditions common to the Member states, must be ensured within the framework of the structure and objectives of the Community. It must therefore be ascertained, in the light of the doubts expressed by the Verwaltungsgericht, whether the system of deposits has infringed rights of a fundamental nature, respect for which must be ensured in the Community legal system.

The Court examined the grounds of infringement alleged, and it concluded that there had been no infringement of the rights claimed in the case, since the restriction on the freedom to trade was not disproportionate to the general interest which the deposit system sought to advance. When the case returned to the German Constitutional Court, however, a different conclusion was reached from that of the Court of Justice, to the effect that the principle of proportionality as protected within German constitutional law had indeed been violated by the Community deposit system. The prolonged adverse effect of this case on the constitutional relationship between Community law and German law is discussed in Chapter 6, but in itself the case provides an interesting illustration of the difficulties which face the Court of Justice if it wishes to assimilate the 'common constitutional principles' of the Member States as part of the Community legal order. If its interpretation of the requirements of these principles differs from the interpretation of the Member States which also claim to guarantee their protection, the legitimacy of the Court of Justice's adjudication might be called into question and its decisions on human rights matters, especially where it finds impugned Community measures to be compatible with human rights standards, might be disregarded by the national courts.

3. THE SOURCES OF FUNDAMENTAL RIGHTS DERIVED BY THE COURT

Despite the outcome of the *Handelsgesellschaft* litigation, the Court of Justice nevertheless continued to emphasize the autonomy of Community 'general principles' from the specific principles protected within the constitutional law of individual Member States. At the same time, however, the Court repeatedly stressed that the source of the general principles of law and human rights protected within Community law were certainly not independent of the legal culture of the Member States, but were to be found in their common constitutional traditions and also in international agreements to which all were party.[17]

Case 4/73, Nold v. Commission [1974] ECR 491, [1974] 2 CMLR 338

The applicant company had been a coal wholesaler which was seeking the annulment of a decision of the Commission authorizing the Ruhr coal-selling agency to adopt certain restrictive criteria for its supply of coal, which had the effect of withdrawing from Nold its status as a direct wholesaler. Nold claimed that the Commission Decision discriminated against it and breached its fundamental rights.

THE ECJ

13. As the Court has already stated, fundamental rights form an integral part of the general principles of law, the observance of which it ensures.

In safeguarding these rights, the Court is bound to draw inspiration from constitutional traditions common to the Member States, and it cannot therefore uphold measures which are incompatible with fundamental rights recognized and protected by the Constitutions of those States.

Similarly, international treaties for the protection of human rights on which the Member States have collaborated or of which they are signatories, can supply guidelines which should be followed within the framework of Community law.

[17] See Case 17/74, *Transocean Marine Paint* v. *Commission* [1974] ECR 1063, [1974] 2 CMLR 459, para. 17 where the Court, after a survey of the administrative law of several of the Member States by the A.G., recognized 'the general rule that a person whose interests are perceptibly affected by a decision taken by a public authority, must be given the opportunity to make his point of view known'.

Having clearly established the autonomous nature of the Community's general principles of law, the Court continued to make reference to particular 'sources of inspiration' for these, thereby giving a somewhat more concrete foundation to the development. In the case of *Rutili*, for example, even though the various rights invoked by the applicant were contained in express provisions of Community legislation, the Court nevertheless described these provisions as specific manifestations of more general fundamental principles of Community law which could be found elsewhere:

> Taken as a whole, these limitations placed on the general powers of Member States in respect of control of aliens are a specific manifestation of the more general principle, enshrined in Articles 8, 9, 10 and 11 of the Convention on Human Rights and Fundamental Freedoms, signed in Rome on 4 November 1950 and ratified by all the Member States, and in Article 2 of Protocol No.4 of the same Convention, signed in Strasbourg on 16 September 1963, which provide in identical terms, that no restrictions in the interests of national security or public safety shall be placed on the rights secured by the above-quoted articles other than such as are necessary for the protection of those interests 'in a democratic society'.[18]

Thus, the Court reasoned that the particular limits imposed by Community legislation on the powers of Member State authorities to limit the free movement and residence of Community citizens were specific manifestations of general principles which were contained in the European Convention on Human Rights. It would appear that the Court wished to emphasize the link between fundamental rules of European Community law and the law of the European Convention on Human Rights, and to indicate that some specific Community legislative measures had their source in internationally recognized human-rights principles, as it had earlier suggested in *Nold*. This reference to the Convention by the Court prompted comments at the time on whether the Convention had now been effectively incorporated into Community law as a formal and directly effective source of law. However, Advocate General Trabucchi in the subsequent case of *Watson and Belmann*, in which the right to privacy in Article 8 of the Convention on Human Rights was invoked, argued that such comments were misconceived:

> On the basis of this analogy between rules of Community law and rules of international law accepted by all the Member States, some learned writers have felt justified in concluding that the provisions of the said Convention must be treated as forming an integral part of the Community legal order, whereas it seems clear to me that the spirit of the judgment did not involve any substantive reference to the provisions themselves but merely to the general principles of which, like the Community rules with which the judgment drew an analogy, they are a specific expression.

[18] Case 36/75, *Rutili* v. *Minister for the Interior* [1975] ECR 1219, [1976] 1 CMLR 140, para. 32.

> In fact, in that judgment, the Court substantially reaffirmed the principle which had already emerged from its previous decisions that the fundamental human rights recognized under the constitutions of the Member States are also an integral part of the Community legal order.
>
> The extra-Community instruments under which those States have undertaken international obligations in order to ensure better protection for those rights can, without any question of their being incorporated as such in the Community order, be used to establish principles which are common to the States themselves.[19]

This passage effectively summarized the Court of Justice's approach to the source of 'Community fundamental rights', by stressing that the importance of international declarations of rights such as the European Convention lay not in their character as a positive source of Community law, but in the fact that they represented basic principles of law to which all of the Member States which were signatories to the Convention had subscribed. Thus they could be seen as an important expression of common values shared by the Member States of the Community, which in turn made them a valuable indicator of the Community's general principles of law and of human rights. In this way, the Court could maintain the supremacy of Community law over national legal principles, and could try to avoid the charge of having judicially incorporated the Convention and other international agreements into Community law without the consent of the Member State signatories, while at the same time using these sources to suggest a strong basis of consensus among the states for the general principles of Community law.

The number of cases in which particular fundamental rights were invoked gradually increased, and the Court's approach was given more concrete affirmation and official legitimacy in a declaration of the three political institutions of the Community. On 5 April 1977, the Parliament, Council, and Commission issued the following joint declaration on fundamental rights:[20]

> THE EUROPEAN PARLIAMENT, THE COUNCIL AND THE COMMISSION,
>
> Whereas the Treaties establishing the European Communitites are based on the principle of respect for the law;
>
> Whereas, as the Court of Justice has recognized, that law comprises, over and above the rules embodied in the Treaties and secondary Community legislation, the general principles of law and in particular the fundamental rights, principles and rights on which the constitutional law of the Member States is based;
>
> Whereas, in particular, all the Member States are Contracting Parties to the European Convention for the Protection of Human Rights and Fundamental Freedoms signed in Rome on 4 November 1950.
>
> HAVE ADOPTED THE FOLLOWING DECLARATION:
>
> 1. The European Parliament, the Council and the Commission stress the prime importance they attach to the protection of fundamental rights, as derived in par-

[19] Case 118/75, *Watson and Belmann* [1976] ECR 1185, 1207, [1976] 2 CMLR 552, 563–4.
[20] [1977] OJ C103/1.

ticular from the constitutions of the Member States and the European Convention for the Protection of Human Rights and Fundamental Freedoms.

2. In the exercise of their powers and in pursuance of the aims of the European Communities they respect and will continue to respect these rights.

Although a declaration is of little practical effect and is not a legally binding instrument, this joint declaration was of some symbolic importance in indicating that the political institutions of the Community supported the Court's derivation of rights from the European Convention and from principles shared by the Member States, and that they were prepared to say they would respect these rights in the exercise of their powers.

In subsequent case law, the Court continued its comparative approach to the sources of these Community fundamental rights by referring not just to the European Convention, but also to the specific constitutional provisions of particular Member State constitutions:

Case 44/79, Hauer v. Land Rheinland-Pfalz
[1979] ECR 3727, [1980] 3 CMLR 42

The applicant had applied to Land Rheinland-Pfalz for authorization to undertake the new planting of vines on a plot of land which she owned. She was refused authorization on the ground that the land was unsuitable for wine-growing, and upon her objection to this refusal, she was told that the Council had in the meantime passed a regulation prohibiting the new planting of vines for the administrative unit in which her land was situated. She appealed to the German court against the decision, pleading the incompatibility of the Council regulation with the German Basic Law (the Constitution), and a reference was made to the European Court of Justice.

THE ECJ

13. In its order making the reference, the Verwaltungsgericht states that if Regulation No 1162/76 must be interpreted as meaning that it lays down a prohibition of general application, so as to include even land appropriate for wine growing, that provision might have to be considered inapplicable in the Federal Republic of Germany owing to doubts existing with regard to its compatibility with the fundamental rights guaranteed by Articles 14 and 12 of the Grundgesetz concerning, respectively, the right to property and the right freely to pursue trade and professional activities.

14. As the Court declared in its judgment of 17 December 1970, *Internationale Handelsgesellschaft* [1970] ECR 1125, the question of a possible infringement of fundamental rights by a measure of the Community institutions can only be judged in the light of Community law itself. The introduction of special criteria for assessment stemming from the legislation or constitutional law of a particular Member State would, by damaging the substantive unity and efficacy of Community law, lead inevitably to the destruction of the unity of the Common Market and the jeopardizing of the cohesion of the Community.

15. The Court also emphasized in the judgment cited, and later in the judgment

of 14 May 1974, *Nold* [1974] ECR 491, that fundamental rights form an integral part of the general principles of the law, the observance of which it ensures; that in safeguarding those rights, the Court is bound to draw inspiration from constitutional traditions common to the Member States, so that measures which are incompatible with the fundamental rights recognized by the Constitutions of those States are unacceptable in the Community, and that, similarly, international treaties for the protection of human rights on which the Member States have collaborated or of which they are signatories, can supply guidelines which should be followed within the framework of Community law. That conception was later recognized by the joint declaration of the European Parliament, the Council and the Commission of 5 April 1977, which, after recalling the case law of the Court, refers on the one hand to the European Convention for the Protection of Human Rights and Fundamental Freedoms of 4 November 1950.

16. In these circumstances, the doubts evinced by the Verwaltungsgericht as to the compatibility of the provisions of Regulation No 1162/76 with the rules concerning the protection of fundamental rights must be understood as questioning the validity of the regulation in the light of Community law. In this regard, it is necessary to distinguish between, on the one hand, a possible infringement of the right to property and, on the other hand, a possible limitation upon the freedom to pursue a trade or profession.

The Court then referred to the right to property as protected within the First Protocol to the European Convention on Human Rights, and to the restrictions on the exercise of the right which were envisaged by that provision. It also made specific reference, mirroring the opinion of Advocate General Capotorti, to provisions of the German, Italian, and Irish Constitutions, and to the fact that in all Member States there were legislative provisions restricting the use of real property in order to promote various public interests.

Apart from the Convention on Human Rights and national consitutional provisions, the Court has also drawn on other international instruments on which the Member States have agreed or collaborated. In *Defrenne* v. *Sabena* (the third *Defrenne* case),[21] the Court ruled that 'the elimination of discrimination based on sex forms part of those fundamental rights' which were to be protected within Community law.[22] In support of its inclusion of this concept within the general principles of Community law, the Court added that 'the same concepts are recognized by the European Social Charter of 18 November 1961 and by Convention No 111 of the International Labour Organization of 25 June 1958 concerning discrimination in respect of employment and occupation'.[23]

[21] Case 149/77, *Defrenne* v. *Sabena* [1978] ECR 1365, [1978] 3 CMLR 312.

[22] Contrast the argument made by Roemer A.G.in the earlier *Sabbatini* case, Case 20/71 [1972] ECR 345, [1972] CMLR 945 that the legal systems of the Member States did not recognize any general principle of equality of treatment as between men and women.

[23] [1978] ECR 1365, para. 26 of the judgment. See also Case 6/75, *Horst* v. *Bundesknappschaft* [1975] ECR 823, 836, [1975] 2 CMLR 424, 436 where Reischl A.G. drew on an 'internationally recognized principle of social security as set out in Art. 22(2) of International Labour Convention No 48 on the Maintenance of Migrants' Pension Rights of 1935'.

The fact that the Court frequently draws on certain international agreements like the European Social Charter and the Convention on Human Rights as sources for the rights protected within Community law has not, however, precluded it from requiring protection for a right which may not be protected under those agreements. In the *A.M. & S.* case, Advocate General Warner drew attention to the fact that the Convention on Human Rights made no mention of a principle of lawyer/client confidentiality, yet the Court held that it was a part of Community law:

Case 155/79, A.M. & S. Europe Ltd. v. Commission [1982] ECR 1575, [1982] 2 CMLR 264

The applicant company brought an action for the annulment of a Commission decision. This decision had required the company to produce various documents to assist the Commission's investigation, under Council Regulation 17/1962, into suspected breaches by the company of Community competition law. The principal objection of A.M. & S. was that the documents required by the decision to be disclosed contained confidential communications between lawyer and client, which it claimed should be protected from disclosure on the ground of legal professional privilege. The company argued that written submissions between lawyer and client were protected by virtue of a principle common to all Member States, even though the scope of the protection might vary somewhat from country to country.

THE ECJ

18. However, the above rules do not exclude the possibility of recognizing, subject to certain conditions, that certain business records are of a confidential nature. Community law, which derives from not only the economic but also the legal interpenetration of the Member States, must take into account the principles and concepts common to the laws of those States concerning the observance of confidentiality, in particular, as regards certain communications between lawyer and client. That confidentiality serves the requirements, the importance of which is recognized in all the Member States, that any person must be able, without constraint, to consult a lawyer whose profession entails the giving of independent legal advice to all those in need of it.

19. As far as the protection of written communications between lawyer and client is concerned, it is apparent from the legal systems of the Member States that, although the principle of such protection is generally recognized, its scope and the criteria for applying it vary.

. . .

21. Apart from these differences, however, there are to be found in the national laws of the Member States common criteria inasmuch as those laws protect, in similar circumstances, the confidentiality of written communications between lawyer and client provided that, on the one hand, such communications are made for the purposes and in the interests of the client's rights of defence, and on the other hand, they emanate from independent lawyers, that is to say, lawyers who are not bound to the client by a relationship of employment.

22. Viewed in that context Regulation No 17 must be interpreted as protecting, in its turn, the confidentiality of written communications between lawyer and

client subject to those two conditions, and thus incorporating such elements of that protection as are common to the laws of the Member States.

Here the Court can be seen deriving a principle from the 'legal interpenetration' of the Member States, extracting common elements from the degree of protection given for the confidentiality of lawyer–client communications in different legal systems, and building a Community principle out of these.

4. THE TYPES OF RIGHTS RECOGNISED AND THEIR USE BY THE COURT

The Court's endeavour to lay firm and acceptable foundations for its development of fundamental rights in Community law, however, has not been unproblematic. Despite its intention to ground these unwritten Community rights in positive legal sources, in common constitutional traditions, and in contemporary international instruments, the identification of such apparently shared underpinnings is only a first step.

Indeed, even the express agreements to which all Member States are party might represent only a lowest common denominator, and may not provide a very satisfactory standard of protection for rights which certain Member States claim to hold dear, in the face of the very considerable and intrusive executive and legislative powers of the Community institutions. The view was put some years ago, in fact, that the European Convention would not provide a suitable charter for the Community in protecting fundamental rights and general principles of law, on the ground that the Convention provided too low a standard of protection.

U. Scheuner, Fundamental Rights in European Community law and in National Constitutional Law[24]

Legal opinion recognizes that today some sort of a common European law is taking shape in certain areas of common concern . . . During the debate in the Federal Republic [of Germany] on the guarantees of human rights (or the lack of such safeguards), the recommendation was given to the Court to derive such general rules of individual protection from a comparative survey of the legal orders of the Member States, as neither the human rights formulated within the framework of the United Nations nor the European Convention on Human Rights could be directly applied. The latter could provide guidance but one had to take into consideration that this Convention tended at protecting only a basic or minimal standard of human rights.

[24] N. 14 above, 181.

The comparison between the position of fundamental rights and the standard of their protection in Community law and under the Convention was made also by Advocate General Lenz in the case of *Mutsch*,[25] which concerned the right of Community workers in a Member State other than that of their nationality, to require that criminal proceedings against them take place in a language other than that normally used in the Court in question, if nationals of the host Member State had that right:

> Nor can I agree with the view that it is sufficient to place an interpreter at the disposal of the accused, as is required by the European Convention on Human Rights. In the area of fundamental rights the Court has certainly drawn guidelines from the Convention, in the sense that it has treated the Convention as supplying common minimum standards.
>
> It is not contrary to the European Convention on Human Rights for Community law to grant more extensive protection to individual rights. Indeed the Court has held that Community law takes precedence over other agreements concluded within the framework of the Council of Europe in so far as it is more favourable for individuals.[26]

However, even if all of the Member States were agreed about what specific rights should be protected, that would not be the same as being in agreement on how those rights should be protected. All of the states agree in the abstract that there should be protection for freedom of expression, yet they are likely to differ very much on how, in a particular context, it should be protected. The legal systems of Member States vary widely, for example, in the degree to which they regulate the nature and content of broadcasting. Some will accept greater restrictions than others on the scope of individual rights and freedoms in the pursuit of other public interests, as seen in *Hauer*,[27] above. It is not clear that human rights will necessarily be a unifying or an integrationist force, even amongst Member States which are signatories to the same international human rights instruments. Indeed, to take the example of lawyer–client confidentiality which, according to the Court in the *A.M. & S.* case, emerged from the 'legal interpenetration' of the Member States, it will be seen below that not all of the Member States were in agreement as to the result.

Even if the Court accepts the argument of a party that a given right should be recognized as part of Community law, the way in which the Court determines the scope of that right and the way in which it then utilizes the right in the context of the case before it may not be at all what that party had in mind. Despite the fact that in *Nold*[28], the Court moved beyond its ruling in *Stauder*[29] and declared that these 'general principles of law' would take precedence, in the event of conflict, over specific Community measures, the cases

[25] Case 137/84, *Ministère Public* v. *Mutsch* [1985] ECR 2681, [1986] 1 CMLR 648.

[26] *Ibid.*, 2690 (ECR).

[27] Case 44/79 [1979] ECR 3727, [1980] 3 CMLR 42.

[28] Case 4/73, *Nold* v. *Commission* [1974] ECR 491, [1974] 2 CMLR 338.

[29] Case 29/69, *Stauder* v. *City of Ulm, Sozialamt* [1969] ECR 419, [1970] CMLR 112.

in which Community legislation or action has been impeded by human rights claims are very few.

In the case of *Hauer*,[30] as also in Handelsgesellschaft,[31] the Court's recognition of the existence within Community law of specific rights—the principle of protection for property rights and the right to trade—did not result in an interpretation of those rights along the lines pleaded by the applicant, or even in accordance with the law of any particular Member State.[32] In *Nold*, the Court explained why the invocation of a right protected under Community law in any given case would not necessarily guarantee success for the claimant, and why in particular it did not guarantee success for Nold in the instant case.

> 14. If rights of ownership are protected by the constitutional laws of all the Member States and if similar guarantees are given in respect of their right freely to choose and practise their trade or profession, the rights thereby guaranteed, far from constituting unfettered prerogatives, must be viewed in the light of the social function of the property and activities protected thereunder.
>
> For this reason, rights of this nature are protected by law subject always to limitations laid down in accordance with the public interest.
>
> Within the Community legal order it likewise seems legitimate that these rights should, if necessary, be subject to certain limits justified by the overall objectives pursued by the Community, on condition that the substance of these rights is left untouched.
>
> As regards the guarantees accorded to a particular undertaking, they can in no respect be extended to protect mere commercial interests or opportunities, the uncertainties of which are part of the very essence of economic activity.
>
> 15. The disadvantages claimed by the applicant are in fact the result of economic change and not of the contested decision.[33]

It appears from these cases that the Court's formal recognition of fundamental rights as a source of Community law, and as a ground for the annulment of Community measures, had little practical impact on the outcome of cases brought in reliance on such claims.[34] Yet, despite the lack of success on the part of applicants before the Court, the number of cases in which pleas based on the infringement of general principles of law and fundamental rights were made continued to increase, and the Court continued to assert that they had a role in guiding the conduct of Community institutions.

In *Prais*, the applicant relied specifically on Article 9 of the European Convention on Human Rights, concerning freedom of religion, as a ground for the annulment of a decision of the Council.[35] The impugned decision had

[30] Case 44/79, *Hauer* v. *Land Rheinland-Pfalz* [1979] ECR 3727, [1980] 3 CMLR 42.

[31] Case 11/70, *Internationale Handelsgesellschaft* v. *Einfuhr- und Vorratstelle für Getreide und Futtermittel* [1970] ECR 1125, [1972] CMLR 255.

[32] N. 14 above, 184–7.

[33] N. 28 above.

[34] See e.g. A. Clapham, 'A Human Rights Policy for the European Community' (1990) 10 YBEL 309, 331, and J. Coppel and A. O'Neill 'The European Court of Justice: Taking Rights Seriously?' (1992) 12 *Legal Studies* 227, 237.

fixed the date of an open competition for a post for which the applicant had applied, which was to take place on a Jewish feast-day during which she could neither travel nor write. Although, as in so many other cases, the Court did not annul the Council's decision, its reasoning implied that the Council should 'take steps' to respect the requirements of a candidate's religion so long as it was given sufficient notice of these requirements by the candidate:

> If it is desirable that an appointing authority informs itself in a general way of dates which might be unsuitable for religious reasons, and seeks to avoid fixing such dates for tests, nevertheless, for the reasons indicated above, neither the Staff Regulations nor the fundamental rights already referred to can be considered as imposing on the appointing authority a duty to avoid a conflict with a religious requirement of which the authority has not been informed.[36]

Without rejecting the applicant's argument based on the Convention, or denying that freedom of religion should be protected within the operation of Community law, the Court nevertheless upheld the action of the Council in the case at hand.

Similarly, in *Hauer*, where the applicant claimed that the refusal of permission to grow vines on her land infringed her rights to trade and to property, the Court simultaneously acknowledged these rights as part of Community law, and denied that they had been impermissibly infringed in this case:

> Thus it may be stated, taking into account the constitutional precepts common to the Member States and consistent legislative practices, in widely varying spheres, that the fact that Regulation No 1162/76 imposed restrictions on the new planting of vines cannot be challenged in principle. It is a type of restriction which is known and accepted as lawful, in identical or similar forms, in the constitutional structure of all the Member States.[37]

Having identified the objectives of the Community's structural policy in the area of vine-growing as being the prevention of continued surpluses in wine production and the encouragement of high quality wine production, the Court concluded that, although the challenged regulation restricted the right to property, that restriction was not disproportionate to the aim of the measure and it did not infringe the 'substance' of the right.

The Court's careful justification of its conclusion that the rights invoked and recognized as part of Community law had not been disproportionately restricted contrasts markedly with its early decisions such as *Geitling* and *Sgarlata*.[38] Despite the fact that the Community measure was held to be justified in *Hauer*, the Court clearly wished to keep the constitutional

[35] Case 130/75, *Prais* v. *Council* [1976] ECR 1589, [1976] 2 CMLR 708.
[36] *Ibid.*, para. 18. [37] [1979] ECR 3727, para. 22. [38] At 287.

problems raised by the *Handelsgesellschaft* case at bay. The comments of Advocate General Capotorti in *Hauer* show that the potential threat to the supremacy of Community law and to the jurisdiction of the Court in matters of human rights protection, was not far from the Court's thoughts:

> In accordance with these premises it is necessary to reject the idea that it is permissible to appeal to the highest national courts, rather than to this Court, in order to secure the protection of fundamental rights as against the Communities, in particular when infringements as a result of the legislative activity of the Communities are alleged. It is the exclusive task of the Community Court to guarantee such protection, within the scope of its jurisdiction: the uniform application of Community law and its primacy over the legal orders of the Member States must not be endangered by the intervention of national courts, when it is a question of ascertaining whether or not Community provisions are in conformity with the principles concerning human rights.[39]

Despite the failure of the applicants in cases such as these to have Community legislation annulled for breach of fundamental rights, however, it is not true to say that there have been no beneficial results for those who have invoked such rights against Community measures to which they objected. The judicial successes of applicants are to be found more in cases concerning specific administrative acts than in cases involving legislation in, for example, the sphere of economic policy. Examples of the latter are particularly numerous in the area of the CAP, where the principles of proportionality, equality, and legitimate expectations are often invoked to challenge Community legislation, but seldom succeed. The following judgment concerned an administrative decision of the Commission in relation to a particular number of individuals, where the Court was prepared to require the Commission to alter its practice in a way which would respect certain rights of the applicant journalists:

Case 100/88, Oyowe and Traore v. Commission [1989] ECR 4285

The applicants were journalists employed by the European Co-operation Agency (ECA) to work on a publication concerning the relationship between the African-Caribbean-Pacific states and the Community. They were two of the only three staff members of the ECA which had not been appointed as officials of the Commission, and they objected to the Commission about the adverse effect which this had on their pension rights. When the Commission rejected their request to establish them as officials, they sought a declaration from the Court that they were members of staff of the Commission or an order that the Commission should appoint them as officials, on the grounds of breach of the principles of fairness, equality, and non-discrimination.

[39] N. 30 above.

THE ECJ

13. The Commission considers that the fact that it has not established the applicants is justified objectively by the consideration that the status of Community official is not compatible with the role of representing the perspective of the African, Caribbean and Pacific States (ACP States) fulfilled by the applicants within the joint editorial team of the Courier. The original reason for the applicants' recruitment is evidence of the special role which they fulfil. The duty of allegiance to the Community imposed on all officials under the Staff Regulations of Officials of the Communities cannot be reconciled with the duties which Mr Oyowe and Mr Traore are called upon to carry out within the Courier's editorial team.

. . .

16. . . . It must be borne in mind that in any event the duty of allegiance to the Communities imposed on officials in the Staff Regulations cannot be interpreted in such a way as to conflict with freedom of expression, a fundamental right which the Court must ensure is respected in Community law, which is particularly important in cases, such as the present, concerning journalists whose primary duty is to write in complete independence of the views of either the ACP States or the Communities.

The Court consequently annulled the Commission's decision to reject the applicants' complaint, on the ground that there was no justification for refusing to grant their request, and it stressed that the Commission must take steps to implement the judgment.[40] It seems odd, however, that the Court chose to emphasize the potential restriction on the applicants' freedom of expression, which was not expressly raised by them in their claim, yet not to address the principles of equality and non-discrimination which they specifically pleaded nor the issues of race which would appear to underlie the case.[41]

Apart from challenges to administrative decisions of this nature, the Court has appeared willing to recognize and give effect to a specific legal right, when to guarantee respect for that right would not interfere too much with the substance of a Community policy, but instead, perhaps, would require observance of procedural protection within the implementation of a substantive Community policy. In *Al-Jubail*, the Court was asked to declare provisions of an anti-dumping regulation void in its application to the plaintiffs, who argued that they had been denied the right to a fair hearing in the process leading to the adoption of the measure.[42] The Court stressed the importance of the right to a fair hearing and ruled that it should be taken into account in interpreting the regulation in question. Ultimately, it found that there had indeed been an infringement of the right to a fair hearing in the case at hand, and declared the impugned provision of the regulation void in so far as it imposed an anti-dumping duty on the applicants.

[40] See also Case C–404/92P, *X* v. *Commission,* [1994] ECR I–4737, discussed below.

[41] Darmon A.G. did, however, address the discrimination claim.

[42] Case C–49/88, *Al-Jubail Fertilizer Co and Saudi Arabian Fertilizer Co* v. *Council* [1991] ECR I–3187, [1991] 3 CMLR 377.

Another more fertile source of litigation, in which general principles of law and fundamental rights have been invoked with some success to challenge Community action, is that involving challenges to the Commission's enforcement powers in competition proceedings.[43] This is an area in which the complaints generally concern administrative or executive action rather than discretionary powers in the creation of legislative policy. The Commission's powers in competition proceedings are very wide, including the authority to investigate and make searches, as well as to impose severe financial penalties, and affected parties have repeatedly called upon the Court to limit and control their exercise by reference to fundamental legal principles.[44]

Cases 46/87 and 227/88, Hoechst AG v. Commission [1989] ECR 2859, [1991] 4 CMLR 410.

The applicant company brought an action for the annulment of various Commission decisions which had ordered an investigation into its affairs, in the context of suspected anti-competitive practices, and which had subsequently imposed periodic penalty payments upon it for refusing to permit the carrying out of this investigation. The applicant argued, amongst other things, that the decisions in question had violated fundamental rights protected within Community law, including various procedural rights and the right to inviolability of the home.

THE ECJ

12. It should be noted, before the nature and scope of the Commission's powers of investigation under Article 14 of Regulation No 17 are examined, that that article cannot be interpreted in such a way as to give rise to results which are incompatible with the general principles of Community law and in particular with fundamental rights.

13. The Court has consistently held that fundamental rights are an integral part of the general principles of law the observance of which the Court ensures, in accordance with constitutional traditions common to the Member States, and the international treaties on which the Member States have collaborated or of which they are signatories . . . The European Convention for the Protection of Human Rights and Fundamental Freedoms is of particular significance in that regard . . .

14. In interpreting Article 14 of Regulation No 17, regard must be had in particular to the rights of the defence, a principle whose fundamental nature has been stressed on numerous occasions in the Court's decisions (see in particular the judgment of 9 November 1983 in Case 322/81 *Michelin* v. *Commission* [1983] ECR 3461 paragraph 7).

15. In that judgment, the Court pointed out that the rights of the defence must be observed in administrative procedures which may lead to the imposition of

[43] See Ch. 22.

[44] See e.g. Cases 17/74, n. 17 above, 209–215/78 *Van Landewyck* v. *Commission* [1980] ECR 3125, [1981] 3 CMLR 134; 136/79, *National Panasonic* v. *Commission* [1980] ECR 2033, [1980] 3 CMLR 169; 100–103/80, *Musique Diffusion Française* v. *Commission* [1983] ECR 1825, [1983] 3 CMLR 221; 5/85, *AKZO Chemie* v. *Commission* [1986] ECR 2585, [1987] 3 CMLR 716; 374/87, *Orkem* v. *Commission* [1989] ECR 3283, [1991] 4 CMLR 502; T–11/89, *Shell* v. *Commission* [1992] ECR II–757. See D. Edward, 'Constitutional Rules of Community Law in EEC Competition Cases' (1989–90) 13 Fordham ILJ 111.

penalties. But it is also necessary to prevent those rights from being irremediably impaired during preliminary inquiry procedures including, in particular, investigations which may be decisive in providing evidence of the unlawful nature of conduct engaged in by undertakings for which they may be liable.

16. Consequently, although certain rights of the defence relate only to the contentious proceedings which follow the delivery of the statement of objections, other rights, such as the right to legal representation and the privileged nature of correspondence between lawyer and client . . . must be respected as from the preliminary inquiry stage.

17. Since the applicant has also relied on the requirements stemming from the fundamental right to the inviolability of the home, it should be observed that, although the existence of such a right must be recognized in the Community legal order as a principle common to the laws of the Member States in regard to the private dwellings of natural persons, the same is not true in regard to undertakings, because there are not inconsiderable divergences between the legal systems of the Member States in regard to the nature and degree of protection afforded to business premises against intervention by the public authorities.

18. No other inference is to be drawn from Article 8(1) of the European Convention on Human Rights which provides that: 'Everyone has the right to respect for his private and family life, his home and his correspondence'. The protective scope of that article is concerned with the development of man's personal freedom and may not therefore be extended to business premises. Furthermore, it should be noted that there is no case law of the European Convention on Human Rights on that subject.

19. None the less, in all the legal systems of the Member States, any intervention by the public authorities in the sphere of private activities of any person, whether natural or legal, must have a legal basis and be justified on the grounds laid down by law, and, consequently, those systems provide, albeit in different forms, protection against arbitrary or disproportionate intervention. The need for such protection must be recognized as a general principle of Community law. In that regard, it should be pointed out that the Court has held that it has the power to determine whether measures of investigation taken by the Commission under the ECSC Treaty are excessive . . .

Yet despite this ruling, the Court, on the facts, found no breach by the Commission of any of the principles invoked by the applicants in the case. The decision has been criticized on the ground that the Court too rapidly dismissed the argument that the Commission's power of search contravened the right to privacy of the dwelling which is protected in the Convention on Human Rights. It was pointed out by one commentator that later case law of the Court of Human Rights had suggested that Article 8 of the Convention could perhaps apply to business premises.[45] This commentator, like others, expressed concern that the Community should ensure the Commission's wide powers in competition proceedings remained within acceptable limits,

[45] See A. Clapham, n. 33 above, 337–8, referring to the European Commission on Human Rights Report in the *Chappell* case, App. no. 10461/83. The judgment of the Court of Human Rights in the case did not directly resolve the issue: Series A, No 152A.

respecting the rights of other parties.[46] Since that time, it has become clear that the ruling of the Court of Justice on this matter does not correspond with the current view of the Court of Human Rights. In the case of *Niemietz*,[47] the Court of Human Rights ruled that the right to respect for private life in Article 8 of the Convention did extend to business premises, stating that 'to interpret the words 'private life' and 'home' as including certain professional or business activities or premises would be consonant with the essential object and purpose of Article 8, namely to protect the individual against arbitrary interference by the public authorities'.[48] The scope of protection afforded by Article 8 as defined in that judgment is thus broader than the ruling of the Court in *Hoechst* allowed, and it will be interesting to see whether that court alters its view of Article 8 accordingly in future cases concerning the scope of the Commission's investigative powers.[49] Similarly in regard to the right to a fair trial in Article 6(1) of the Convention, it would seem that the decision of the Court in *Orkem*,[50] in which it ruled that Article 6 did not confer the right 'not to give evidence against oneself', is at odds with the subsequent ruling of the Court of Human Rights in the case of *Funke*, in which that court indicated that Article 6 did protect the right 'to remain silent and not to contribute to incriminating [oneself]'.[51] The cases certainly provide a good illustration of the point made at the beginning of this section, that the fact that the Court draws on recognized and shared sources for the rights which are protected within Community law does not mean that there will be agreement on the scope and practical application of any given right in a specific context. If the Court of Human Rights and the Court of Justice can reach different conclusions on their interpretation of the same Articles of the Convention in factually similar cases, it is certain that individual Member States will have very different interpretations and conceptions of many other such rights in Community law.

It has been noted that in the *A.M. & S.* case, the Court of Justice derived a principle of confidentiality between lawyer and client from a comparative survey of the laws of the Member States. Yet, as is evident from the comments of Advocate General Warner in the case, not all of the Member States were happy with the conclusion of the Court as to this supposedly common principle:

[46] Clapham, n. 34 above, 335–8. See also (1990) 27 CMLRev. 355 and (1990) 15 ELRev. 326.

[47] *Niemietz* v. *Germany*, Series A, No 251.

[48] *Ibid*., para. 31.

[49] Although of course the right protected by Art. 8 of the Convention is by no means absolute and can be limited or restricted in so far as is 'necessary in a democratic society' for the pursuit of various listed public interests. See the opinion of Mischo A.G. in *Hoechst* [1989] ECR 2859, para. 112.

[50] Case 374/87, n. 44 above, para. 30 of the judgment. However, the Court did go on to rule that by virtue of the 'rights of the defence' in investigative procedures, the Commission could not compel a company to provide it with answers which might involve an admission of a breach which it was incumbent on the Commission to prove. See also Case C–60/92, *Otto* v. *Postbank* [1993] ECR I–5683.

[51] *Funke* v. *France*, Series A, No 256A, para. 44 of the judgment. See W. Van Overbeek 'The Right to Remain Silent in Competition Investigations' (1994) 15 ECLR 127.

> The French Government bore alone the burden of arguing that there was no principle of Community Law restricting the powers of the Commission under Article 14 of Regulation 17 . . . that the relevant laws of the Member States were too disparate for there to be derived from them any general principle that might apply. The French Government went so far as to suggest that the present case represented an attempt to foist on the Community what was no more than a domestic rule of English law.[52]

However, he concluded despite these objections that a general principle could be distilled from among the various states even if the 'conceptual origin' of that principle and 'the scope of its application in detail differ from Member State to Member State'.[53] Further, the lawyer–client confidentiality principle was not in his view a 'fundamental human right' such as to prevail over any legislation which infringed it, but rather a right which was 'not lightly to be denied'.

This case clearly highlights the difficulty inherent in attempting to ascertain the degree of protection for a particular right or principle amongst twelve or more different Member States. Evidently neither the Advocate General nor the Court thought that the differences in the scope of the lawyer–client confidentiality principle from state to state was a barrier to the derivation of a common principle which would represent the appropriate level of Community protection. France, on the other hand, suspected that there was an attempt to foist a particular English legal principle on all of the Member States through the medium of Community law.[54] Similar issues will inevitably arise again, given the differences between the legal systems of the Member States.[55]

It is apparent that the Court is concerned to acknowledge respect for any legal principle which is of administrative or constitutional significance in one of the Member States, and its comment in *Al-Jubail*, in relation to the need to protect the right to a fair hearing, shows that it is conscious of the dangers of failing to do this:

> It should be added that, with regard to the right to a fair hearing, any action taken by the Community institutions must be all the more scrupulous in view of the fact

[52] Case 155/79, *A.M. & S. Europe Ltd* v. *Commission* [1982] ECR 1575, 1631.

[53] *Ibid.*

[54] The derivation of a general principle of Community law from the legal system of one or of a few Member States only is not unusual, nor is the subsequent expansion of such principles into the domestic law of other Member States. The principle of proportionality in EC law, which is thought to have been derived principally from German law, is increasingly being pleaded in the UK courts as a general principle of Community law which should also be domestically applied. See e.g. Lord Browne-Wilkinson, 'The impact of European Law on English Human Rights and Public Law' in B. Markesinis (ed.), *The Gradual Convergence: Foreign Ideas, Foreign Influences and English Law on the Eve of the 21st Century* (Clarendon Press, 1994) 202.

[55] Case 17/74, n. 17 above, provides another example of the recognition by the Court of a general principle of Community law where some but not all of the Member States afford protection to the particular right or principle.

> that, as they stand at present, the rules in question do not provide all the procedural guarantees for the protection of the individual which may exist in certain national legal systems.[56]

Clearly the Court does not wish to be seen to fall below the level of protection given to a right which is important in the legal systems of various Member States, although, as noted at the outset of this chapter, the concern to recognize any principle or right protected in the Member States is probably no longer motivated solely by fear of challenge to the supremacy of Community law from the Member States. It is likely that the Court also considers that if it is to function as the supreme court of an increasingly federalized Community, whose political and legal system is to maintain legitimacy, it requires a developed constitutional and administrative structure which must include internationally recognized legal rights and principles, and in particular an accepted system of protection for recognized human and fundamental rights. And since the Community is not a member of the Council of Europe and not within the European Convention system for protecting human rights, the Court of Justice is left to take on this role.

The following comment of Advocate General Darmon in *Al-Jubail* illustrates awareness of the need to be *perceived* by the Member States and others to be providing an adequate level of protection for rights of the kind in issue, especially since they are often also principles protected under the Convention on Human Rights.

> If the European Commission of Human Rights declares inadmissible applications directed against national decisions enacted pursuant to a Community act (Application No 13528/87 *M & Co.* v. *Federal Republic of Germany*—decision of 9 February 1990) the main reason is that, through its successive judgments, the Court [of Justice] has established the principle that it reviews the Community institutions' observance of fundamental rights. It is therefore far from unimportant to avoid conspicuous discrepancies between the construction this Court puts on the right to a fair trial and the requirements already laid down by the European Court of Human Rights[57]

It is particularly interesting that these comments draw attention to the fact that, far from providing too low a level of protection, as was suggested by Scheuner above, the European Convention on Human Rights as interpreted by the Court of Human Rights has come to represent a standard against which the Community institutions and indeed the Court of Justice measure their 'fundamental rights' performance. A sceptical observer might conclude that the Court of Justice often seems as much or more concerned with the public perception of its decisions on human rights, and with maintaining a profile of concern for such rights and principles, than it is with ensuring that

[56] N. 42 above, para. 16. [57] *Ibid.*, 3230–1.

they actually constrain the powers of the Community institutions or have any practical and beneficial impact on those affected by Community measures. This criticism will be discussed further below.

5. ARE THE GENERAL PRINCIPLES OF COMMUNITY LAW AND FUNDAMENTAL RIGHTS BINDING ON THE MEMBER STATES?

In most of the cases so far considered, the Court of Justice was asked to examine the compatibility of Community measures with, or to interpret Community measures in the light of, the requirements of protection for fundamental rights or other general principles of law. The more controversial development mentioned earlier, however, has been the extension of this approach so that these principles are also to be applied to acts of the Member States. Clearly, this goes a considerable step beyond reviewing Community measures for compatibility with human rights and other general principles of law. It is true that even in the absence of any written Bill or Charter of Rights, the derivation by the Court of Justice of such rights and principles from the constitutional systems of Member States and from international agreements, and their application to constrain the powers of the Community instruments, was a development which Member States might initially have welcomed. To apply this unwritten and uncertain cluster of legal rights and principles to the actions of the Member States, however, is a different matter.

It could, of course, be argued that, if the fundamental rights and general principles of Community law really are derived from the constitutional traditions of the Member States and from international agreements signed by them all, there should not be too much objection to the review of state action for compliance with those shared legal standards and values. However, as seen in the discussion above, not only is the interpretation of the meaning and scope of such rights certain to vary from state to state, but it is far from clear that all general principles of Community law will be shared by all states, nor that, even if they were, the Member States would want the Court of Justice to be the interpreter of those principles by reference to which Member State action is judged. And, further, the Court's express jurisdiction in relation to acts of the Member States under the Treaties is much more limited than its jurisdiction in relation to acts of the Community institutions. It can interpret Community law in the context of Article 177 references in such a way that it becomes obvious that a particular national law is in breach of the Treaty, and it can declare in enforcement proceedings brought by the Commission or a Member State that a Member State is failing to fulfil its obligations under the Treaty. But the Community 'law' with which the states must comply, and the Community 'obligations' which they must fulfil were understandably considered by the states to be those specific obligations expressly set out in the Treaties and in the legislation adopted by the Community institutions in which those Member States participate. It is unlikely that the consequences of membership of the European Community were understood by the Member States to include the partial incorporation of an unwritten and non-exhaustive 'Bill of Rights' against which their actions could be reviewed by the Court of Justice.[58] So how did the extension of a form of 'human rights review' by the Court of Justice to Member State action come about? One answer to this question is that it came about incrementally and very gradually.

(a) Member States Applying Provisions of Community Law which are based on Protection for Human Rights

In the *Rutili* case in 1975, discussed above, the Court of Justice had described provisions of Directive 64/221, which set limits on the restrictions which Member States could apply to the free movement of workers, as specific expressions of the more general principles enshrined in the European Convention on Human Rights. Thus, the restrictive measures adopted by France in that case would have to be examined for compliance with the provisions of the Directive, which in turn reflected provisions of the Human Rights Convention. Although the acknowledgment that provisions of Community law restricting state action were based on human rights principles was quite some way from declaring that the Court would require the assessment of Member State action for compliance with all of the Community's general principles and fundamental rights, nevertheless this aspect of the *Rutili* case attracted considerable attention.

The following year, Advocate General Trabucchi in the *Watson and Belmann* case outlined his view of the implications of the *Rutili* judgment for fundamental rights in the Community legal order.[59]

> The conclusion can be drawn that respect for the fundamental principles governing the protection of the rights of man as they have been embodied in international instruments binding all the Member States as well as in the constitutions of the countries concerned may, within the sphere of application of Community law, also be of importance in determining the legality of a State's conduct in relation to a freedom which the Treaty accords to individuals.
>
> Of course, in contrast to what happens in the case of acts of the Community executive, the acts of the States are subject to review by their own national courts

[58] Much has been written about the merits and demerits of the Community acceding to the Human Rights Convention, or adopting its own Bill or Charter of Rights. For some relatively recent comments, see K. Lenaerts 'Fundamental Rights to be Included in a Community Catalogue' (1991) 16 ELRev. 367, M. F. Dominick 'Towards a Community Bill of Rights: The European Community Charter of Fundamental Social Rights' (1990–1) 14 Fordham ILJ 639. and P. Twomey, 'The European Union: Three Pillars without a Human Rights Foundation' in D. O'Keeffe and P. Twomey (eds.), *Legal Issues of the Maastricht Treaty* (Chancery, 1994), 121, 128.

[59] Case 118/75, n. 19 above, 1207–8 (ECR).

which, together with the European Court of Human Rights, already provide effective protection for fundamental rights. However, without impinging upon the jurisdiction of other courts, this Court too, can look into an infringement of a fundamental right by a State body, if not to the same extent to which it could do so in reviewing the validity of Community acts, at least to the extent to which the fundamental right alleged to have been infringed may involve the protection of an economic right which is among the specific objects of the Treaty . . .

The protection of the rights of man accordingly forms part of the Community system, even as against the States, in as much as the fundamental right relied upon involves a relationship or a legal situation the regulation of which is among the specific objects of the Treaty.

The Court of Justice in *Watson*, however, chose to make no reference to the Convention on Human Rights, nor did it refer to any specific right or principle other than the requirement deriving directly from the Treaty—the basic principle of freedom of movement. Thus it did not consider whether the Member States might be bound, in areas to which Community law applied, by more general fundamental principles of law other than those specific principles of Community law expressly stated in the Treaty—or in a directive, as was the case in *Rutili*.[60]

However, the increasing reference to human rights principles in the context of Member States' laws became gradually more evident in later decisions of the Court.

Case 222/84, Johnston v. Chief Constable of the Royal Ulster Constabulary [1986] ECR 1651, [1986] 3 CMLR 240

The applicant challenged the decision of the Chief Constable of the RUC in 1980, which was taken on the ground that female reserves could not thenceforth be armed, not to renew her contract as a full-time reserve. She argued before the Industrial Tribunal that she had suffered unlawful discrimination under the 1976 Northern Ireland Sex Discrimination Order. The Chief Constable produced a certificate issued by the Secretary of State under Article 53 of the Sex Discrimination Order, certifying that the refusal to renew the applicant's contract was done for the purpose of safeguarding national security and protecting public safety and public order. The applicant relied on the prohibition on sex discrimination in the Equal Treatment Directive 76/207, Article 6 of which provides that those who consider themselves wronged by discrimination must be able to pursue their claims by judicial process, to challenge the compatibility of this certificate with the Directive.

THE ECJ

17. As far as this issue is concerned, it must be borne in mind first of all that Article 6 of the Directive requires Member States to introduce into their internal

[60] Note that the Court has been criticized for using the same term 'fundamental principle' to refer to instrumental integration-oriented requirements of Community law such as free movement of workers, goods, and services, as well as to refer to fundamental human rights principles and other important principles of adminstrative and constitutional law. See further 329–32.

legal systems such measures as are needed to enable all persons who consider themselves wronged by discrimination 'to pursue their claims by judicial process'. It follows from that provision that the Member States must take measures which are sufficiently effective to achieve the aim of the Directive and that they must ensure that the rights thus conferred may be effectively relied upon before the national courts by the persons concerned.

18. The requirement of judicial control stipulated by that article reflects a general principle of law which underlies the constitutional traditions common to the Member States. That principle is also laid down in Articles 6 and 13 of the European Convention for the Protection of Human Rights and Fundamental Freedoms of 4 November 1950. As the European Parliament, Council and Commission recognized in their joint Declaration of 5 April 1977 and as the Court has recognized in its decisions, the principles on which that Convention is based must be taken into consideration in Community law.

19. By virtue of Article 6 interpreted in the light of the general principle stated above, all persons have the right to obtain an effective remedy in a competent court against measures which they consider to be contrary to the principle of equal treatment for men and women laid down in the directive. It is for the Member States to ensure effective judicial control as regards compliance with the applicable provisions of Community law and of national legislation intended to give effect to the rights for which the directive provides.

The Court ruled ultimately that the national measure providing that a certificate of this kind would be conclusive evidence was an infringement of the principle of effective judicial control. As in *Rutili*, the Court, when interpreting a particular provision of Community legislation—in this case Article 6 of the Equal Treatment Directive—treated it as a specific manifestation of a recognized general principle of law—the requirement of access to a judicial remedy. The Community provision was therefore to be read 'in the light of' the corresponding principle in the European Convention (and that 'underlying the constitutional traditions common to the Member States') dealing with access to court and an effective judicial remedy. The use of the Convention as a standard against which domestic law would have to be assessed was again indirect. It was used as an interpretive aid to the written provisions of Community law against which a Member State's derogation was to be tested. Thus it could not quite be said that a provision of the European Convention was directly enforced against the United Kingdom. Instead it was a provision of Community law, although the scope and application of that provision in relation to the conclusive certificate was informed by the general principle of judicial control common to the Member States and enshrined in the European Convention.[61] The Court's indirect method of requiring a rule of national law to be reviewed for conformity with a principle embodied in the Convention might in this way be made more palatable to a Member State like the United Kingdom, which has not incorporated the Convention, by being presented as

[61] See also Case 222/86, *UNECTEF* v. *Heylens* [1987] ECR 4097, [1989] 1 CMLR 901.

no more than the application of a principle which is part of the Member State's own constitutional tradition.

(b) Member States Enforcing Community Policy and Interpreting Community Rules

Rutili and *Johnston* were cases referred to the Court under Article 177, so the ultimate question of the compatibility of the state measure with the particular right concerned was for the referring domestic court to decide when the case returned. But in a later case in which the Commission brought Article 169 proceedings against Germany, the Court of Justice had to rule directly on whether Germany was in breach of Community law on account of its implementation of Regulation 1612/68 on migrant workers.[62] In this case, the issue turned on whether there was an obligation on the state, in interpreting and implementing a Community provision, to read it in a way which complied with human rights requirements such as those in the European Convention. Article 10 of Regulation 1612/68 permits members of a migrant Community worker's family to install themselves with the worker in the host Member State, provided that the worker has available for the family housing 'considered as normal for national workers' in that region. Germany had implemented this provision in a way which made renewal of a family member's residence permit conditional upon the family living in appropriate housing, not merely at the time of their arrival in Germany, but for the entire period of residence. The Court ruled that the German legislation in question was incompatible with Community law:

> Regulation No 1612/68 must also be interpreted in the light of the requirement of respect for family life set out in Article 8 of the Convention for the Protection of Human Rights and Fundamental Freedoms. That requirement is one of the fundamental rights which, according to the Court's settled case-law, restated in the preamble to the Single European Act, are recognized by Community law.[63]

Here, then, was a case in which the legislation of a Member State was challenged, and in which the Court of Justice required the state, when interpreting and implementing Community law, to act in a way which would respect the rights set out in the European Convention on Human Rights.

In several other cases of this nature, involving the domestic implementation of Community measures, the Court has been willing to require Member States to alter their implementing rules and practices so as to protect the rights claimed by the applicants. Unlike the Community provisions in *Rutili* and *Johnston*, these Community measures did not themselves embody the

[62] Case 249/86, *Commission* v. *Germany* [1989] ECR 1263, [1990] 3 CMLR 540. See further Ch. 15 n. 99.

[63] *Ibid.*, para. 10.

particular right claimed, yet the Court required the Member State to respect that right. It has been suggested that in these circumstances the Member States must act in conformity with the requirements of human rights because they are acting as agents or delegates of the Community in implementing its policies.[64]

Case 63/83, R. v. Kent Kirk [1984] ECR 2689, [1984] 3 CMLR 522

The defendant was the master of a Danish fishing vessel who was convicted in the United Kingdom of an offence contrary to a 1982 Sea Fish Order, which prohibited Danish-registered fishing boats from fishing within twelve miles of the United Kingdom coast. The Court of Justice was asked whether the United Kingdom had the right under Community law to bring the 1982 Order into force, since the transitional period during which Member States could derogate from the principle of non-discrimination had earlier expired. However, in the interim between the expiry of that period and the adoption of a comprehensive fish conservation system by the Council, the Member States had been given the right to adopt certain temporary measures. When the Council finally enacted legislation governing the Community fisheries regime, it retroactively authorized the interim arrangements which Member States had maintained, but the defendant argued that the retroactive effect of the Council Regulation was not justified in the case of the Sea Fish Order, since it did not respect the legitimate expectations of those concerned.

THE ECJ

21. Without embarking upon an examination of the general legality of the retroactivity of Article 6(1) of that Regulation, it is sufficient to point out that such retroactivity may not, in any event, have the effect of validating *ex post facto* national measures of a penal nature which impose penalties for an act which, in fact, was not punishable at the time at which it was committed. That would be the case where at the time of the act entailing a criminal penalty, the national measure was invalid because it was incompatible with Community law.

22. The principle that penal provisions may not have retroactive effect is one which is common to all the legal orders of the Member States and is enshrined in Article 7 of the European Convention for the Protection of Human Rights and Fundamental Freedoms as a fundamental right; it takes its place among the general principles of law whose observance is ensured by the Court of Justice.

23. Consequently the retroactivity provided for in Article 6(1) of Regulation No. 170/83 cannot be regarded as validating *ex post facto* national measures which imposed criminal penalties, at the time of the conduct at issue, if those measures were not valid.

The defendant in this case did not question the validity of the Council regulation which had retroactively authorised certain Member State measures, but instead challenged the power of the United Kingdom to adopt, at the time it did, the order restricting Danish vessels from fishing. What the Court ulti-

[64] See J. Temple Lang, 'The sphere in which Member States are obliged to comply with the general principles of law and Community fundamental rights principles' [1991] LIEI 23.

mately ruled was that the *domestic effect* of applying the retroactive provision of Council Regulation 170/83 to the 1982 United Kingdom Sea Fish Order was impermissible, since it would violate the principle enshrined in Article 7 of the European Convention on Human Rights. Such an application of the Regulation would approve a breach by the United Kingdom of the principle of non-retroactivity of penal liability. The Court's ruling makes it clear that a national measure in the sphere of Community law, which purports to be an application of Community law but which breaches a fundamental right, will be invalid.

Some years later in the case of *Klensch*,[65] the Court ruled that where provisions relating to the CAP leave Member States to choose between various methods of implementation, the Member States must comply with the principle of non-discrimination stated in Article 40(3), which 'is merely a specific enunciation of the general principle of equality which is one of the fundamental principles of Community law'.[66]

The *Klensch* case was followed by that of *Wachauf*, which made it quite clear that the Member States were bound, in implementing Community law, by all of the same principles and rights which bound the Community in its actions.

Case 5/88, Wachauf v. Germany
[1989] ECR 2609, [1991] 1 CMLR 328

The applicant was a tenant farmer in Germany who, upon the expiry of his tenancy, requested compensation under German law for the discontinuance of milk production. The German law was based on a power contained in Council Regulation 857/84, and it provided for compensation for the discontinuance of milk production, on condition that where the application was made by a tenant farmer, the lessor must give written consent. Since the landlord of Wachauf's farm, who had never engaged in milk production nor contributed to the setting up of a dairy farm, had withdrawn consent, the Federal Office refused Wachauf compensation. He challenged the refusal before the Administrative Court in Frankfurt, and a reference was made to the Court of Justice for an interpretation of the Council Regulation.

THE ECJ

17. The Court has consistently held, in particular in its judgment in Case 44/79 *Hauer*, that fundamental rights form an integral part of the general principles of law, the observance of which is ensured by the Court. In safeguarding those rights, the Court has to look to the constitutional traditions common to the Member States, so that measures which are incompatible with the fundamental rights recognized by the constitutions of those states may not find acceptance in the Community. International treaties concerning the protection of human rights on which the Member States have collaborated or to which they have acceded can also supply guidelines to which regard should be had in the context of Community law.

. . .

[65] See also Cases 201 & 202/85, *Klensch* v. *Secrétaire d'Etat à l'Agriculture et à la Viticulture* [1986] ECR 3477, [1988] 1 CMLR 151.

[66] *Ibid.* para. 9.

19. Having regard to those criteria, it must be observed that Community rules which, upon the expiry of the lease, had the effect of depriving the lessee, without compensation, of the fruits of his labour and of his investments in the tenanted holding would be incompatible with the requirements of the protection of fundamental rights in the Community legal order. Since those requirements are also binding on the Member States when they implement Community rules, the Member States must, as far as possible, apply those rules in accordance with those requirements.

Thus far, we have seen that the Court of Justice would consider the compatibilty of Member States' laws with fundamental rights in two contexts: first, as in *Rutili* and *Johnston*, where it was considering the compatibility of state laws with provisions of Community law which reflected certain legal rights and principles, in particular rights protected within the Convention on Human Rights. And the second context, seen in *Commission* v. *Germany*, *Kirk*, *Klensch*, and *Wachauf*, was where the Member States were implementing a Community law or scheme, and thus in some sense acting as agent on the Community's behalf. Neither of these developments in itself involves a particularly serious or wide intrusion into the sphere of legislative and administrative action of the Member States. But the Court has gradually gone further in its extension of the general principles of Community law into spheres of Member State action.

(c) Member States Derogating from Community Law Requirements

Consider the situation in which a Member State, far from implementing Community law, seeks to derogate from its provisions or to justify a restriction on Community rules in the interests of some conflicting national policy. *Rutili* provides one example of such a situation, but in that case an EC directive, which defined the scope of the derogation, actually required the Member States to protect certain rights which are included within the Convention on Human Rights. In other cases, however, in which there were no such Community measures restricting the scope of the Member State's derogation, it was argued before the Court that the Member States were nevertheless bound, in creating an exception from the operation of Community rules, to respect the fundamental rights of the applicant. In other words, it was argued that, by creating a national exception to the operation of Community rules, the Member States were acting within the field of Community law and thus should be bound to respect such rights. It did not at first seem as though the Court would accept this argument.

Cases 60 & 61/84, Cinéthèque v. Fédération Nationale des Cinémas Français [1985] ECR 2605, [1986] 1 CMLR 365

These proceedings concerned a French law which provided that no film shown in cinemas could simultaneously be exploited in the form of videos for sale or hire until the expiration of a twelve month period. The applicant, Cinéthèque, had been granted a licence to produce and sell videos of a particular film before the expiry of the twelve-month period, but after it had begun to do so, the National Federation of French Cinemas obtained an interim order for the seizure of all video recordings of the film. The applicant and the producer of the film brought an action before the French courts, claiming that the French law in question was, amongst other things, contrary to Articles 30 and 36 of the EEC Treaty in creating an obstacle to the free movement of goods.

THE ECJ

24. The reply to the questions referred to the Court is therefore that Article 30 of the EEC Treaty must be interpreted as meaning that it does not apply to national legislation which regulates the distribution of cinematographic works by imposing an interval between one mode of distributing such works and another by prohibiting their simultaneous exploitation in cinemas and in video-cassette form for a limited period, provided that the prohibition applies to domestically produced and imported cassettes alike and any barriers to intra-Community trade to which its implementation give rise do not exceed what is necessary for ensuring that the exploitation in cinemas of cinematographic works of all origins retains priority over other means of distribution.

25. The plaintiffs and the interveners in the main action also raised the question whether Article 89 of the French law on audio-visual communication was in breach of the principle of freedom of expression recognized by Article 10 of the European Convention for the Protection of Human Rights and Fundamental Freedoms and was therefore incompatible with Community law.

26. Although it is true that it is the duty of this Court to ensure observance of fundamental rights in the field of Community law, it has no power to examine the compatibility with the European Convention of national law which concerns, as in this case, an area which falls within the jurisdiction of the national legislator.

ADVOCATE GENERAL SLYNN[67]

It is clear from Case 4/73 *Nold*, and Case 44/79 *Hauer* that the Convention provides guidelines for the Court in laying down those fundamental rules of law which are part of Community law, though the Convention does not bind, and is not part of the law of the Community as such . . .

In my opinion it is right, as the Commission contends, that the exceptions in Article 36 and the scope of 'mandatory requirements' taking a measure outside Article 30 should be construed in the light of the Convention.

It is clear that the Court rejected the proposal from Advocate General Slynn that it should construe any national measures which would breach Article 30 of the Treaty were it not for the existence of an exception in Article 36 or in the Court's case law on 'mandatory requirements',[68] in the light of the European Convention. Instead, the Court ruled that although the French law

[67] [1985] ECR 2605, 2616.

[68] See Case 120/78, *Rewe-Zentrale AG* v. *Bundesmonopolverwaltung fur Branntwein (Cassis de Dijon)* [1979] ECR 649, [1979] 3 CMLR 494, discussed in Ch. 14.

constituted a *prima facie* restriction on the free movement of goods within Article 30, the fact that it could be justified as a 'mandatory requirement' of the public interest (the promotion of the cinematographic industry in France) brought it 'within the jurisdiction of the national legislator'. And if it was within the jurisdiction of the national legislator, the Court ruled, it could not be examined for compliance with the Convention on Human Rights.

In the later case of *Demirel*,[69] the Court restated this point in a slightly different way, ruling that it would not examine the compatibility of national law with fundamental rights or general principles of law where the national law lay outside the jurisdiction of the Community. The case involved a Turkish woman who had come to Germany and who was ordered to leave the country when her visa expired.[70] Questions about the interpretation of the EC–Turkey Association Agreement were referred to the Court from the administrative court where she challenged the order. The Court ruled that rights to family reunification were not at that time covered by the provisions of the Agreement.[71] In response to the invocation on behalf of the applicant of Article 8 of the European Convention on Human Rights on the right to family life, the Court ruled as follows:

> As to the point whether Article 8 of the European Convention on Human Rights has any bearing on the answer to that question, it must be observed that, as the Court ruled in its judgment of 11 July 1985 in Joined Cases 60 and 61/84 *Cinéthèque* v. *Fédération Nationale des Cinémas Français* [1985] ECR 2605 at 2618 although it is the duty of the Court to ensure observance of fundamental rights in the field of Community law, it has no power to examine the compatibility with the European Convention on Human Rights of national legislation lying outside the scope of Community law. In this case, however, as is apparent from the answer to the first question, there is at present no provision of Community law defining the conditions in which Member States must permit the family reunification of Turkish workers lawfully settled in the Community. It follows that the national rules at issue in the main proceedings did not have to implement a provision of Community law. In those circumstances, the Court does not have jurisdiction to determine whether national rules such as those at issue are compatible with the principles enshrined in Article 8 of the European Convention on Human Rights.[72]

[69] Case 12/86, *Demirel* v. *Stadt Schwäbisch Gmünd* [1987] ECR 3719, [1989] 1 CMLR 421.

[70] On the protection of human rights of non-Community nationals, see J. Weiler, 'Thou Shalt not Oppress a Stranger: On the Judicial Protection of the Human Rights of Non-Community Nationals—a Critique' [1992] EJIL 65. From subsequent cases like Cases C–237/91, *Kus* v. *Landeshauptstadt Wiesbaden* [1992] ECR I–6781, [1993] 2 CMLR 887 and C–355/93, *Eroglu* v. *Land Baden-Württemberg*, [1994] ECR I–5113, however, it is clear that non-Community nationals will in certain circumstances fall within the scope of Community law and, on the reasoning of *Demirel*, it would seem that Member States in such circumstances will be obliged to respect their rights.

[71] There are now decisions of the EC–Turkey Council of Association which cover family members: see *Eroglu*, *ibid.*

[72] N. 69 above, para. 28..

The language used by the Court in *Demirel*—that the Court would not examine the compatibility with the European Human Rights Convention of national measures 'lying outside the scope of Community law'—indicates that the Court will examine the compatibility of any measures which lie *within* the scope of EC law. Of course, there are many areas in which the Community and the Member States share competence, and it seems on this wording that the Court would be prepared to consider the compatibility with the Convention of national measures, even where those measures also concern matters which fall partly within the jurisdiction of the Member States. In this way, *Demirel* may represent a move on from *Cinéthèque*, and, as has been noted with dismay by certain commentators, may represent an increase by the Court in its jurisdiction to promote its own conception of Community fundamental rights in the face of conflicting Member State legislation and conflicting state conceptions of national fundamental principles and rights.[73]

Some years later, in a case which was in many ways similar to *Cinéthèque*, involving the invocation by a Member State of a derogation in the Treaty from the principle of free movement, the Court took a different approach, holding that it was for it to ensure that the Member State had adequately respected the fundamental rights which were part of Community law:

Case C–260/89, Elliniki Radiophonia Tileorassi AE v. Dimotiki Etairia Pliroforissis and Sotirios Kouvelas
[1991] ECR I–2925, [1994] 4 CMLR 540

The applicant, ERT, was a Greek radio and television company to which the Greek state had granted exclusive rights under statute in carrying out its activities. It had sought an injunction from the Regional Court of Thessaloniki against the two respondents, an information company and the Mayor of Thessaloniki, who had set up a television station and had begun to broadcast programmes in defiance of the applicants' exclusive statutory rights. The respondents in their defence relied mainly on the provisions of Community law relating to the free movement of goods and to the rules on competition and monopolies, as well as on the provisions of the European Convention on Human Rights relating to freedom of expression.

THE ECJ

41. With regard to Article 10 of the European Convention on Human Rights, referred to in the ninth and tenth questions, it must first be pointed out that, as the Court has consistently held, fundamental rights form an integral part of the general principles of law, observance of which it ensures. For that purpose the Court draws inspiration from the constitutional traditions common to the Member States and from the guidelines supplied by international treaties common to the Member States and from the guidelines supplied by international treaties for the protection of human rights on which the Member States have collaborated

[73] See the views of J. Coppel and A. O'Neill, that the change in wording between *Cinéthèque*, n. 67 above, and *Demirel*, n. 69 above, was crucial in expanding the Court's influence over national legislation which would be required to comply with the Community's interpretation of fundamental rights: 'The European Court of Justice: Taking Rights Seriously?' (1992) 12 *Legal Studies* 227.

or of which they are signatories (see in particular Case C–4/73 *Nold* v. *Commission*, paragraph 13). The European Convention on Human Rights has special significance in that respect (see in particular Case C-222/84 *Johnston* v. *CC of the RUC*, paragraph 18). It follows that, as the Court held in its judgment in Case 5/88 *Wachauf* v. *Federal Republic of Germany*, paragraph 19, the Community cannot accept measures which are incompatible with observance of human rights thus recognized and guaranteed.

42. As the Court has held (see Cases C–60 & 61/84 *Cinéthèque*, paragraph 25 and Case C–12/86 *Demirel* v. *Stadt Schwäbisch Gmünd*, paragraph 28), it has no power to examine the compatibiity with the European Convention on Human Rights of national rules which do not fall within the scope of Community law. On the other hand, where such rules do fall within the scope of Community law, and reference is made to the Court for a preliminary ruling, it must provide all the criteria of interpretation needed by the national court to determine whether those rules are compatible with the fundamental rights the observance of which the Court ensures and which derive in particular from the European Convention on Human Rights.

42. In particular, where a Member State relies on the combined provisions of Articles 56 and 66 in order to justify rules which are likely to obstruct the exercise of the freedom to provide services, such justification, provided for by Community law, must be interpreted in the light of the general principles of law and in particular of fundamental rights. Thus the national rules in question can fall under the exceptions provided for by the combined provisions of Article 56 and 66 only if they are compatible with the fundamental rights, the observance of which is ensured by the Court.

44. It follows that in such a case it is for the national court, and if necessary, the Court of Justice to appraise the application of those provisions having regard to all the rules of Community law, including freedom of expression, as embodied in Article 10 of the European Convention on Human Rights, as a general principle of law the observance of which is ensured by the Court.

45. The reply to the national court must therefore be that the limitations imposed on the power of the Member States to apply the provisions referred to in Articles 66 and 56 of the Treaty on grounds of public policy, public security and public health must be appraised in the light of the general principle of freedom of expression embodied in Article 10 of the European Convention on Human Rights.

Contrasting with the judgment of the Court is the opinion in the same case of Advocate General Lenz who, citing the earlier *Cinéthèque* judgment, expressed a considerably more cautious view as to the role of the Court of Justice in considering the compatibility of national measures with the European Convention on Human Rights:

It is however also clear that it is not primarily the Court of Justice which is called upon to judge alleged or actual infringements by the Member States of the human rights protected by that Convention (that is a matter for the institutions designated by the Convention on Human Rights); in particular, it does not fall to the

Court to examine the compatibility of the rules of the Member States with the Convention on Human Rights (this has been clearly established in the case-law; see the judgment in joined cases C–60 and C–61/84 *Cinéthèque*).[74]

The Court in *ERT*, however, clearly made a decision to extend its jurisdiction to ensure compliance with fundamental rights by the Member States when they rely upon derogations from fundamental Treaty rules, incorporating important Community rights. Whether this case represents a departure from the *Cinéthèque* ruling is not clear, since there are at least formal grounds for arguing that the two cases are distinct. *ERT* involved reliance by a Member State on the express provision of Article 56 of the Treaty allowing for a 'public-policy' exception to Community rules. Such express reliance on a Community provision would seem to bring the national measure 'within the scope of Community law', so that the requirement that the measure, in order to avail itself of the derogation, must also be in compliance with Community fundamental rights, applies.[75] Given the similarities between the express exceptions in Article 56 and those in Article 48(3), this ruling does not, on its face, seem so far from the reasoning of the *Rutili* case.[76] However, the 'derogation' relied on by the Member State in *Cinèthèque* was not an express provision of the Treaty such as Article 36 or 56, but instead a Court-developed test for determining when national measures which obstructed inter-state trade would fall outside the scope of the Article 30 prohibition.[77] But even if the *Cinéthèque* ruling survives, it is clear that the Court's affirmation in *ERT* of its jurisdiction to consider the compatibility of national derogating laws with the Community's requirements for protection of fundamental rights represents a further extension of the Court's jurisdiction and a further encroachment by the principles of the European Convention and other general principles of law into the legal systems of the Member States. One of those who has commented on the significance of the *ERT* ruling was a judge of the Court, who remarked that 'anyone who reflects for a moment about how intimately some of those derogations are bound up with fundamental notions governing the relationship between States and their citizens cannot fail to appreciate the potential incidence of that judgment on national sovereignty'.[78]

[74] Case C–260/89, *E.R.T.* v. *D.E.P.* [1991] ECR I–2925, 2948.

[75] See also Case C–62/90, *Commission* v. *Germany* [1992] ECR I–2575, [1992] 2 CMLR 549, concerning the obligation on the Member States to respect fundamental rights, including the right to privacy, when invoking Art. 36 EC.

[76] Case 36/75, n. 18 above. See above 293, 310.

[77] See the opinion of Van Gerven A.G. in Case C–159/90, *SPUC* v. *Grogan* [1991] ECR I–4685, [1991] 3 CMLR 849 and see G. de Búrca, 'Fundamental Human Rights and the Reach of EC law' (1993) 13 OJLS 283.

[78] D. Mancini and D. Keeling, 'From *CILFIT* to *ERT*: The Constitutional Challenge facing the European Court' (1991) 11 YBEL 1, 11–12.

(d) A New Approach? Member States' Treatment of Nationals of other Member States who are Exercising Community Rights

Since the ruling in *ERT*, Advocate General Jacobs has made a suggestion for a further extension of the sphere in which Member States could be held to account by the Court for their failure to respect fundamental rights, but the Court did not take up his suggestion. This case involved a self-employed Greek masseur working in Germany, who complained that the German authorities were infringing his Community rights in their official mistranslation of his name. The referring court, the Amtsgericht, Tübingen, considered that there might be an infringement of the applicant's right of personal identity, as well as a possible breach of the principle of non-discrimination on the ground of nationality in the context of an employed or self-employed person. Having surveyed the law of the various Member States on the point, as well as the Convention on Human Rights, Advocate General Jacobs concluded that Article 8 of the Convention did protect an individual's right to oppose unjustified interference with his name. He then went on to examine whether the action of the German authorities fell within the scope of Community law, so that the Court of Justice could examine the compatibility of the action with the protection required by the Convention.

Case C–168/91 Konstantinidis v. Stadt Altensteig, Standesamt, and Landratsamt Calw, Ordnungsamt [1993] ECR I–1191, [1993] 3 CMLR 401

ADVOCATE GENERAL JACOBS[79]

44. First, it cannot be said that the regulations at issue in this case lie entirely outside the scope of Community law since they are, when applied to migrant workers, capable of having a particularly adverse effect on the nationals of one Member State. Secondly, there are now at least two situations in which Community law requires national legislation to be tested for compliance with fundamental rights: namely (a) when the national legislation implements Community law (paragraph 19 of the *Wachauf* judgment) and (b) when a Treaty provision derogating from the principle of free movement is invoked in order to justify a restriction on free movement (paragraph 43 of the *ERT* judgment) . . .

46. In my opinion, a Community national who goes to another Member State as a worker or self-employed person under Articles 48, 52 or 59 of the Treaty is entitled not just to pursue his trade or profession and to enjoy the same living and working conditions as nationals of the host State; he is in addition entitled to assume that, wherever he goes to earn his living in the European Community, he will be treated in accordance with a common code of fundamental values, in particular those laid down in the European Convention on Human Rights. In other words, he is entitled to say 'civis europeus sum' and to invoke that status in order to oppose any violation of his fundamental rights.

. . .

[79] [1993] ECR I–1191, 1211–12.

48 . . . When a breach of fundamental rights is in issue, I do not see how the non-discriminatory nature of the measure can take it outside the scope of Article 52. Indeed, the proposition that a Member State may violate the fundamental rights of nationals of other Member States, provided that it treats its own nationals in the same way, is untenable.

The position argued for by Advocate General Jacobs is clearly novel and wider than any suggested in previous case law, either by the Court or by an Advocate General. His contention is that whenever an EC national goes to another Member State in reliance on one of the rights of free movement in Article 48, 52, or 59, any failure to respect a fundamental human right of that national, whether or not it is connected with his or her work, should constitute an infringement of EC law. Implicit in his reasoning would seem to be the argument that such failure might dissuade the national from exercising Community rights of movement. This is clearly a very broad argument indeed, to the effect that any time an EC national is lawfully present in another Member State and exercising Community rights, he or she is entitled under Community law to protection against any infringement of his or her human rights.[80] The Court could monitor the level of protection afforded by means of the Article 177 procedure. And, according to Advocate General Jacobs, it would be irrelevant that this requirement might lead to favourable treatment for non-nationals in a Member State, and to discrimination against nationals. In other words, national authorities and courts in a Member State like the United Kingdom would be obliged to protect the fundamental rights of nationals of other Member States exercising Community rights within that Member State, even though such protection is traditionally not available to its own nationals, given the absence of a written Bill of Rights or of legislative incorporation of the European Convention.

The Court, however, made no reference to fundamental rights in the *Konstantinidis* case, nor to the argument of the Advocate General on this point, and gave a ruling in favour of the applicant on narrower grounds.[81] Its reasoning was based on settled EC law relating to the right of self-employed people to establish themselves in a Member State, without direct or indirect discrimination on grounds of nationality. If the German authorities required the spelling of the applicant's name in such a way as to misrepresent its pronunciation, said the Court, 'such distortion exposes him to a risk of confusion of identity on the part of his potential clients'.

However, although the Court may have rejected this particular invitation further to extend the scope of the Community's human rights jurisdiction over acts of the Member States, it is clear from the trend of its case law, in

[80] See the discussion in Ch. 15 pp. 708–9 of the 1990 'Residence Dirs.' and the new provisions of the EC Treaty on citizenship, which appear to extend rights of residence to Community nationals who are not economically active.

[81] See the comments of Gulman A.G. in Case C–2/92, *R.* v. *Ministry of Fisheries, Agriculture and Food, ex parte Bostock* [1994] ECR I–955, 971, where he disagrees with the arguments of Jacobs A.G. in *Konstantinidis* and notes that the Court did not adopt the same reasoning.

particular from the *ERT* ruling, that the range of state action over which the Court purports to exercise what may be called 'human-rights review' has expanded considerably.

6. THE POLITICAL IMPACT OF THE COURT'S DEVELOPMENT OF FUNDAMENTAL RIGHTS WITHIN EC LAW

To continue in what is perhaps a sceptical vein, it might be asked whether these judicial and legal developments have had any real political or practical impact within the Community. Whether or not the Court's case law has had any practical impact on events and policies within the Member States, it is clear that the dialogue which is often evident between the judicial and the political institutions of the Community has been continuing in the area of human rights. As has sometimes surprisingly occurred in the context of some of the Court's more creative case law,[82] the political institutions have confirmed the substance of its decisions, through a series of measures of increasing legal significance. After the 1977 Joint Declaration of the three political institutions (set out above), several other such non-binding political initiatives were taken. These include a Joint Declaration of the three institutions in 1986, various Declarations and Resolutions on Racism and Xenophobia by the European Council,[83] a Declaration of Fundamental Rights and Freedoms by the European Parliament in 1989,[84] and a Community Charter of Fundamental Social Rights, signed by eleven of the then twelve Member States in 1989.[85] These statements and resolutions, in themselves of little effect beyond their symbolic force, were given further backing in the Preamble to the Single European Act in which the Member State signatories declare themselves to be:

> *Determined* to work together to promote democracy on the basis of the fundamental rights recognized in the constitutions and laws of the Member States, in

[82] See e.g. the amended Art. 173 EC after the TEU, which confirmed the Court's case law on the *locus standi* of Parliament in Case C–70/88, *European Parliament* v. *Council* [1990] ECR I–2041, [1992] 1 CMLR 91, despite the fact that the Member States during negotiations on the earlier SEA had chosen not to make such a change. See further Chs. 2 and 11. See also the 'Students' Residence' Dir. 90/366 and its replacement, Dir. 93/96, tracking the Court's rulings in cases like Case 293/83, *Gravier* v. *City of Liège* [1985] ECR 593, [1985] 3 CMLR 1, discussed further in Ch. 15, pp. 708–9.

[83] See e.g. [1986] OJ C158/1, Bull. EC 5–1990, 1.2.247., Bull. EC 6–1991, I.45, and Bull. EC 12–1991, I.19.

[84] [1989] OJ C120/51.

[85] COM(89)471 Final. See Bull. EC 12–1989, 2.1.104.

the Convention for the Protection of Human Rights and Fundamental Freedoms and the European Social Charter, notably freedom, equality and social justice.

Since then, Article 130u of the Treaty, which was added to the EC Treaty by the TEU, provides that Community policy in the area of development co-operation:

> shall contribute to the general objective of developing and consolidating democracy and the rule of law, and to that of respecting human rights and fundamental freedoms.

We have already seen, in Chapter 2, that the European Parliament has chosen to exercise its right to withhold assent to certain international agreements, including development aid agreements, in order to call for the insertion of a clause concerning respect for democracy and human rights in the country in question.[86]

Significantly, too, Article F of the common provisions of the TEU (which do not, however, amend the provisions of the EC Treaty and are not in themselves justiciable) provides:

> 1. The Union shall respect the national identities of its Member States, whose systems of government are founded on the principles of democracy.
> 2. The Union shall respect fundamental rights, as guaranteed by the European Convention for the Protection of Human Rights and Fundamental Freedoms signed in Rome on 4 November 1950 and as they result from the constitutional traditions common to the Member States, as general principles of Community law.

Protection and respect for human rights and fundamental freedoms are also mentioned in the two other 'pillars' of the Maastricht Treaty, in Article J.1(2), as being amongst the objectives of the common foreign and security policy and, in Article K.2(1), in the context of justice and home affairs, which covers matters such as immigration and asylum policy.

It is interesting to look back, at this stage, at the failure of the European Political Community in 1953, with its attempt to incorporate the Convention on Human Rights, and to observe the way in which the European Community has travelled a much more gradual path since then, but a path which nevertheless has led to a Community which is considerably broader than the Economic Community originally designed in the ECSC, EEC, and Euratom Treaties. Following the Single European Act and the TEU, the Community

[86] The European Parliament also has a Committee on Legal Affairs and Citizens' Rights, a Committee on Women's Rights, a Committee on Civil Liberties and Internal Affairs, and a sub-committee on Human Rights.

has acquired new and broader areas of competence, while co-ordination on political action is undertaken still outside the framework of the Community, but within the framework of the Union. And most significantly, for the purposes of this chapter, although the Community has not formally incorporated the Convention on Human Rights as was envisaged in 1952, the Court has developed a substantial case law in this area which has been approved, through declarations and amendments, by the Member States and the political institutions of the Community.[87]

7. SOME CRITICAL COMMENTS ON THE COURT'S CASE LAW

Even if they have received the official imprimatur of the Member States as evidenced in these various instruments, however, are the Court of Justice's judicial pronouncements in the human rights sphere simply an endeavour, as some have claimed, to increase the Court's own power to require Member States, and in particular their national courts, to further particular Community goals and principles in the guise of 'fundamental rights'? Is the Court cynically manipulating the rhetorical force of the language of rights while in reality merely furthering commercial goals of the common market? Or even if the accusation is not taken this far, is the Court extending the jurisdiction of the Community, and hence of itself, into the sphere of human rights protection in which it is not the most competent or legitimate body to adjudicate? And is it attempting to extend the influence of Community law over areas which remain the primary concern of the Member States, given the considerable political, cultural, and ideological divergences between the Member States?

These questions have been raised by various commentators over the years. *The first concern* is that the Court may be engineering the intrusion of Community law and influence into spheres of national law which are controversial where there is little agreement between Member States and where the goals of uniformity of Community law and harmonization among the states are likely to be sharply challenged. *A second concern* of some observers, already noted earlier, is that the kinds of rights and principles which the Court requires Member States to observe are biased towards 'market rights' and those rights which further specific Community aims, instead of protecting values which are genuinely fundamental to the human condition. And finally, *a third concern* is that the Court of Justice may be setting itself up as another European Human Rights Court, when its primary purpose and function were originally quite different, and when another Court has specifically been entrusted by the Member States of the Council of Europe with that jurisdiction and role.

[87] See L. Krogsgaard, 'Fundamental Rights in the EC after Maastricht' [1993] LIEI 99.

Writing some years ago, one scholar, raising the first concern, questioned whether the Community commanded the allegiance, and the sense of cohesion and political integration among the states and their peoples, which would be required for the development of shared standards of common values, and a common human rights foundation.

M. Cappelletti, The Judicial Process in Comparative Perspective[88]

The tremendous difficulties of the path undertaken by the European Court of Justice in the attempted implementation of its 'great design' are obvious. Everybody appreciates that Europe is not like the United States. The differences are profound; they involve cultures and languages as well as political and social mores, religious attitudes, and, not least, economic structures and conditions. Developing a common bill of rights for over a quarter of a billion Europeans is indeed an awesome task . . .

This is not to say that a uniform standard of human rights among the member states, enforced by judicial review at the Community level, will never be realized. Rather it is to say that at this point in the Community's socio-political development it is at best speculative (and probably pointless) to predict the likelihood of the Court of Justice alone developing and enforcing such standards. Judging from the American experience, the prospect of the Court of Justice sitting in judgment of member state legislation on the basis of vague concepts of fundamental justice will remain a faint one until the Community reaches a higher level of integration, on the political and social levels as well as on the level of the Court's jurisprudence, than it has reached today. And enforcement of such rights would, quite probably, require a system of Community courts with ample jurisdiction and powers to enforce these Community rights in cases when they are violated by the member states and ignored by their courts. Even then, though, American history suggests that a great degree of legal integration may still leave much room for disagreement and diversity on questions of fundamental rights. What was important in the American integrationist experience was the ability to agree initially on a basic charter of rights and to create institutions capable of interpreting that charter through time. Ironically enough, while Europeans could probably agree on the components of such a charter, they would not at all likely be willing at the present time to endow a European Court with the power to interpret and directly apply its provisions in the member states. The necessary change in attitude will have to await the day when the French, the English and all the others regard themselves as being citizens of the Community, with rights as such. This revolution is obviously not within the powers of the Court of Justice alone to produce.

A more optimistic view has also been expressed about the ability and competence of the Court of Justice to forge, under the influence of national courts and the European Convention organs, a 'common identity' for Europe through the creation of a shared body of fundamental rights and principles.

[88] (Clarendon Press, 1989), 175, 381.

J. Fröwein, The ECHR as the Public Order of Europe[89]

While up until about 1975 only the Court of Justice of the European Communities had gained a profile of transnational legal integration in Europe, the Convention organs more and more came to occupy such a position. In fact, it may be that the transnational influence of doctrines on the interpretation and application of human and fundamental rights is more visible today as far as the Convention organs are concerned. The creation of a common understanding of fundamental rights throughout Europe is taking place.

. . . It may be possible to point to a few basic doctrines which the Convention system has helped to clarify throughout Europe, sometimes in a dialectical process between national constitutional courts, the Court of Justice of the European Communities, and the Convention organs. Those doctrines are for example the need for a clear legal basis for an interference with fundamental rights, the rule of proportionality concerning an interference, the prohibition for authorities to use a legal rule for a purpose not really within the aims of the law. In other words, very basic elements of the rule of law have been confirmed by the Convention system.

One can only hope that this shaping of a European identity in the protection of human and fundamental rights will continue successfully.

But the unifying force of human rights as a common foundation for the European Community legal system, even given the supposed adherence of all the Member States to the principles declared in the Convention on Human Rights, has also been doubted. The Convention is in some ways quite a loose declaration of rights, hedged about with exceptions, and leaving to its signatory states a measure of diversity and discretion. If the Court of Justice is to take on the interpretation and application of those provisions in concrete situations arising from Member State action, it has been seen from the earlier discussion that the Court's conclusion will not always accord with that of the Member State in question, as reflected in that state's culture, practices, and legal and constitutional system.[90]

A. Clapham, A Human Rights Policy for the European Community[91]

Talking about human rights may sometimes bestow identity on Community citizens . . .

Clearly, rights have an important role to play in the process of European Integration, but, it must be said that they may well operate as a double edged sword. Not only are they a cohesive force but they may well be divisive. Should the Community move to tackle issues such as divorce, contraception, abortion, blasphemy, surrogacy, etc., rights might no longer be handy tools for integration

[89] *Collected Courses of the Academy of European Law*, ed. A. Clapham and Emmert (Martinus Nijhoff, 1990) i–ii. 357–8.

[90] See also T. F. O' Higgins, 'The Constitution and the Communities—Scope for Stress?' in *Human Rights and Constitutional Law*, ed. J. O'Reilly (Round Hall Press, 1992), 227, 237–40.

[91] (1990) 10 YBEL 309, 311.

but vehicles of division and disintegration. Furthermore, not only will moral diversity have to be tolerated in the move towards unity, but it is clear that effective rights to challenge Community decisions or provisions could well slow up or completely ensnare new initiatives or progress at the Community level.

Both these disadvantageous side effects of promoting human rights in the Community tend to be exaggerated. The Community is unlikely to attempt a unification of moral values. It will continue to leave a 'margin of appreciation' to Member States on certain issues.

The second concern mentioned above, however, reflects a greater level of scepticism about the Court's ability to forge a satisfactory policy of human rights protection for the Community. This concern has been voiced by some of those who feel that the Court has manipulated the language of human rights to pursue the primarily economic goals of integration. Some of the most critical comments were prompted by the case of *Grogan*,[92] in which Advocate General van Gerven suggested that the prohibition in Ireland on the provision of information about abortion facilities in other Member States should be tested for compliance with other human rights, including freedom of information and expression. Although the Court did not follow the Advocate General's opinion, and ruled that the restriction on information did not fall within the scope of Community law on freedom to provide and receive services, this ruling was narrowly based on the fact that there was no commercial link between the providers of the medical service (abortion) in one Member State, and the providers of the information in the other Member State.[93]

J. Coppel and A. O' Neill, The European Court of Justice: Taking Rights Seriously?[94]

From the terms of the *Heylens* decision it appears that the four freedoms of workers, services, goods and capital enshrined in the Treaties can be translated into individuals' fundamental rights. It would seem, then, that there is no distinction and hence no hierarchical relationship being posited by the European Court between the basic human rights outlined, for example, in the European Convention on Human Rights and the free market rights arising out of the Treaties of the European Community.

. . . Such a procedure can be seen in the opinion of the Advocate General in *Grogan*. Ultimately, he balances freedom of information (seen as a corollary of the Community freedom to provide services) against the right to life of the unborn child. The result of this equality in practical terms can only be that the court will find it easier to subordinate a fundamental human right to a Community economic freedom . . .

[92] Case C–159/90, n. 77 above. See also Ch. 16. pp. 760–1.

[93] For an attempt by the Irish government (which it subsequently sought to qualify by means of a Declaration) to insulate the Irish constitutional prohibition on abortion, and on information and referral services, from the possible impact of Community law: see Prot. 17 of the TEU.

[94] (1992) 14 *Legal Studies* 227, 243–5.

Evidently it is economic integration, to be achieved through the acts of Community institutions, which the court sees as its fundamental priority. In adopting and adapting the slogan of protection of human rights the court has seized the moral high ground. However, the high rhetoric of human rights protection can be seen as no more than a vehicle for the court to extend the scope and impact of European law.

D. R. Phelan, Right to Life of the Unborn v. Promotion of Trade in Services: The European Court of Justice and the Normative Shaping of the European Union[95]

However, the concept of the protection of fundamental rights in Irish constitutional law has characteristics in common with other Member States: the protection of fundamental rights forms part of the foundation legal theory of justification, is an end in itself and helps achieve the realisation of an idea of the person which is one of the objectives of society. Where the rights conflict with economic interests, those interests give way, since economics is regarded as a means. Fundamental rights and social goals are in harmony. In contrast, by virtue of the application of the EC law techniques analysed above, where a human right and an economic objective conflict, it is the right, not the objective, which is modified to complement fundamental economic principles . . .

The direction of the ECJ's jurisprudence dealing with the effects of national fundamental rights appears from the Grogan case to be subject to an internal independent rationale and momentum towards objectives drawn from essentially economic Treaties between national governments. Under this rationale, the promotion of trade by the Court stands to override the promotion of life by a national constitution, Bunreacht na hEireann. Under this rationale, fundamental rights are shaped according to a market actor's economic role in the transnational society under construction; fundamental rights are not implied by a person's human and moral nature . . .

Others have taken a less sceptical view of the Court's strategy in promoting the field of application of human rights within EC law, criticizing the Court not because the rights which it favours in the case of conflicting national law are essentially market rights rather than human rights, but because it has stopped short of requiring Member States to observe human-rights principles in certain areas touched on by Community law, such as in the *Cinéthèque* case:

J. H. Weiler, The European Court at a Crossroads: Community Human Rights and Member State Action[96]

All this goes to show that the extension of Community human rights review to Member State measures would have to rest on a convincing rationale. I believe that such a rationale exists . . .

Only in those cases where *but for* a recognised Community exception to a fun-

[95] (1992) 55 M.L.R. 670, 686.

[96] *Du Droit International au Droit de l'Intégration*, ed. F. Capotorti *et al.* (Nomos, 1987), 839–41.

damental Community prohibition, a Member State measure would be in violation of Community law, should the Court also review the compatibility of the national measure with Community human rights . . .

There is another more dramatic and symbolic way of putting this argument. By refusing to scrutinize the derogations in the But/For situation for violation of human rights, while insisting on scrutinising them for, say, proportionality, is not the Court signalling that all that interests it is the economic integrity of the Common Market and not the individuals that make it up? Are not, in this fashion, individuals really turned into factors of production?

. . . The Supreme Court of the United States, on a much larger scale, took the plunge—and in the final analysis, despite some groans, triumphed. Here we are asking the European Court to take a much smaller step: to extend protection only to measures which already come up for European judicial scrutiny.

It can also be argued that there is not such a coherent design on the part of the Court to promote Community economic goals over conflicting national interests, and that the pattern of case law is more complex and less strategic. Although it has certainly appeared to promote these 'market rights' in some cases at the expense of important national concerns, there is also evidence of some recognition by the Court of the moral rather than the purely economic dimension of the 'fundamental rights' it may be called on by an applicant to protect. Rather than elevating every so-called market right into a fundmental legal right capable of 'trumping' competing rights protected under national law, it can be argued that the Court in some of its case law has recognized that rights created by the Treaty do not attach only to individuals as 'factors of production', as Weiler puts it, but to individuals as human beings. And these human rights may at times be required to prevail even over the Member State's conception of the public interest or the competing human right.

G. de Búrca, Fundamental Human Rights and the Reach of EC Law[97]

Phelan refers to the 'confusion between market rights and human rights' of those who consider freedom of movement of persons to be part of the cultural richness of the Community, rather than merely as another economic right. However, although the Community's aims and 'freedoms' did initially derive principally from a Treaty which is concerned with economic integration, they do have substantial moral and social importance beyond their economic significance, given that those aims involve, amongst other things, the creation of a fairer, more peaceful and democratic society. The principle of free movement of workers, for example, is not simply a means of enhancing the overall industrial efficiency and economic prosperity of the Community, but is intended to provide a means for each person to raise his or her standard of living, to provide for a family, and to enhance the quality of his or her life . . .

Human rights concerns have been asserted by the ECJ, and more recently in

[97] (1993) 13 O.J.L.S. 283.

> Community legislative instruments, as an independent concern rather than merely a functional means of promoting EC economic aims, even though their protection will often restrict these latter aims. The Advocate General's conclusion (in *Grogan*) that Irish restrictions on women's right to travel or on their freedom from unsolicited physical examinations *would* be disproportionate can be seen as reflecting the view that such measures would unacceptably undermine values and freedoms which have an independent moral content in Community law. Such measures would not simply restrict trade, since individual freedom of movement within the Community has more than a commercial value . . . Rather than the Community's preference for economic aims over fundamental national interests, this conclusion may represent his (and possibly that of the ECJ and the Court of Human Rights) substantive reconciliation within Community law of competing moral choices and human rights.

However, even if it is accepted that the Court is not always cynical or instrumental in the 'rights' it promotes nor concerned only to protect the economic interests of market actors, the third concern which was mentioned above questions the appropriateness of the Court as the European forum for human rights review, given the existence of the European Court of Human Rights (ECtHR), an international court set up precisely for that purpose.[98] True, the ECtHR cannot require the direct enforcement of its interpretations of human-rights standards as could the Court of Justice, but it is nevertheless a court set up by its signatories with that express jurisdiction, and it has acquired expertise and a moral status which the Court of Justice does not share. And there is also a concern that the Court of Justice's extension of the Community's competence to require national laws to comply with human rights and with general principles of law has created the possibility of overlap and potential conflict between the pronouncements of the two courts. Since the Community is not at present a member of the Council of Europe nor a signatory to the Convention, are the two European Courts likely to contradict one another in their rulings on similar or identical issues?[99] A possible further complication is that Article 27(1)(b) of the Convention on Human Rights provides that: 'The application must not be substantially the same as a matter which has already been examined by the Commission or has already been submitted to another procedure of international investigation or settlement unless it contains relevant new information.' The problem of overlap or conflict has been raised by several commentators.

[98] See the argument of the UK Government in Case 118/75, n. 19 above, 1191 (ECR).

[99] The EC Com. proposed, both in 1979 and again in 1990, that the Community should accede to the Convention on Human Rights, but no action was taken pursuant to these proposals. However, following the conclusions of the European Council at Copenhagen in 1993, the Council of Ministers, under Art. 228 EC, has referred to the ECJ the question whether accession to the Convention is compatible with the Treaty: see Bull. EC 4–1994, 1.1.4, [1994] OJC 174/8.

F. Jacobs, The European Convention on Human Rights[100]

While the existence of two separate European systems, in the Communities and in the Council of Europe, for the protection of fundamental rights may not ultimately be satisfactory, there are unlikely in the short term to be many cases of conflict, or even of overlap, between the two systems. In the first place, now that all the Member States of the European Communities have ratified the Human Rights Convention, the material provisions of the Convention can reasonably be considered as part of the law common to the Member States of the Communities, even though not all of them recognize the Convention as part of their domestic law. Of more practical importance, there are likely to be few situations where the procedures under the two systems will overlap. Even where the same factual situation arises both before the organs of the Convention in Strasbourg and before the Court of Justice in Luxembourg, the issues of legal principle are likely to differ. Thus in a case concerning the Italian cable television monopoly, which came before both instances, the Luxembourg Court dealt with the questions of State monopolies under Article 37 of the EEC Treaty, and with the possible abuse of a dominant position under Article 86. The Human Rights Commission, on the other hand, was concerned with the quite separate question of the right to freedom of expression under Article 10 of the Convention. There could be no question of the Commission rejecting the application under Article 27(1)(b) of the Convention as having 'already been submitted to another procedure of international investigation or settlement' for even if the procedure before the Luxembourg Court could correctly be described as international, the substance of the complaint before the Commission was quite different. In fact the correct view would seem to be that a reference for a preliminary ruling by the Court of Justice of the European Communities is not an international procedure but forms an integral part of proceedings before the national court making the reference.

While it is difficult to predict the future relations between the different European systems, it seems likely that any further development of European integration will lead to new measures to strengthen the protection of human rights in Europe.

Several decades later the same commentator, now an Advocate General of the Court of Justice, made similar remarks in the *Konstantinidis* case which came before the Court:[101]

The danger of an overlap between the jurisdiction of the Court of Justice and the European Court of Human Rights would not in fact be great. The latter has always stressed that its jurisdiction is subsidiary, in the sense that it is primarily for the national authorities and the national courts to apply the Convention . . . Thus if the Court of Justice were to extend the circumstances in which the Convention may be invoked under Community law, the result would simply be to

[100] (Clarendon Press, 1975), 279.

[101] Case C–168/91, n. 79 above, paras. 50–51 of the Opinion. See also F. Jacobs, 'The Protection of Human Rights in the Member States of the European Community' in *Human Rights and Constitutional Law*, n. 90 above, 243.

increase the likelihood of a remedy being found under domestic law, without the need for an application to the organs established by the Convention.

As for the possibility of conflicting rulings on the interpretation of the Convention, that has existed ever since the Court of Justice recognized that the Convention may be invoked under Community law. Such a possibility does not seem to have caused serious problems. It would in any event be paradoxical if the existence of the Convention and the system established under the Convention were to reduce the protection available in national law or in Community law.

A similar view about the unlikely prospect of any serious conflict between the interpretation and role of the ECtHR and that of the ECJ in this context was expressed by commentators on the Convention system.

P. Van Dijk and G. Van Hoof, Theory and Practice of the European Convention on Human Rights[102]

1. So far no decision of the Commission has been published in which an application was declared inadmissible on the ground of the fact that a matter had already been submitted to another international body for investigation or settlement . . .

2. Such a case might also occur in connection with a matter which has been submitted to the Court of Justice of the European Communities. Indeed, as appears from its case-law, this Court is prepared to review the acts and omissions of the Member States of the Communities and of the Community Institutions for their conformity with fundamental human rights on the ground that they form part of the general principles of Community law. The chances of such a coincidence, however, are not very great. Indeed, if, in connection with the same factual situation, a case were to be brought before the Courts both in Strasbourg and in Luxembourg, in the two procedures different legal issues will probably be involved . . . Moreover, even if the two cases are identical, the fact that a case has already been submitted to another judicial organ does not bar its admissibility under the European Convention if relevant information that is new to the Commission is put forward which is not or has not been examined by that other organ.

A less sanguine view of the harmonious relationship between the two European Courts has, however, been expressed elsewhere:

A. Clapham, A Human Rights Policy for the European Community[103]

At this point it is suggested that there should be closer cooperation between the two Courts. Although there have already been several meetings, there are quite a few divergences in approach. This is to be expected—the one Court being charged with furthering the objectives of the Community and the other being solely concerned with the protection of human rights. If, however, the Court of Justice is serious about protecting human rights in the Community legal order then it should

[102] (2nd edn., Kluwer, 1990), 71–2. [103] N. 91 above, 338.

show more deference to the Strasbourg case-law. A number of initiatives have been suggested to avoid disharmony between the two systems. These include: exchanges of documentation, the Human Rights Commission offering opinions to Community organs, a special human rights chamber within the Court of Justice, and an advisory scheme so that 'the Court of Justice should be able to consult the Human Rights Court on any matter concerning the Human Rights Convention, whereas the European Commission on Human Rights should be able to ask the Court of Justice for preliminary rulings (similar to the proceedings of Article 177, EEC Treaty) on any matter for which that Court is competent'. Finally, we should mention the idea put forward by the late Judge Max Sørensen who was a judge in both Courts, namely, that they should be merged so that the 'very ideal of human rights may in this way be harnessed to future moves for the reform of European Institutions'.

Although they appear to be prepared to hold Member States liable for actions which infringe the Human Rights Convention, even where the states were pursuing or implementing Community law, the Convention organs have not shown any inclination to admit applications where the case has already been decided by the Court of Justice. Some years ago, the Commission on Human Rights declared inadmissible an application brought against Germany, where the applicant complained that the issuing of a writ of execution by the Federal Minister of Justice of a judgment of the European Court of Justice was in breach of Article 6 of the Convention on Human Rights.[104] The complainant alleged that its constitutional rights had been violated by the Court of Justice, and that accordingly the writ of execution was wrongfully ordered by the Minister. The Commission on Human Rights dismissed the application with the following comments:

> The Commission first recalls that it is in fact not competent *ratione personae* to examine proceedings before or decision of organs of the European Communities, the latter not being a party to the European Convention on Human Rights (see No. 8030/77 *CFDT* v. *EC*, Dec. 10.7.78, D.R. 13 p.231; No. 13539/88 *D* v. *EC*, Dec. 19.1.89). This does not mean, however, that by granting executory power to a judgment of the European Court of Justice the competent German authorities acted *quasi* as Community organs and are to that extent beyond the scope of control exercised by the Convention organs. Under Article 1 of the Convention the Member States are responsible for all acts and omissions of their domestic organs allegedly violating the Convention regardless of whether the act or omission in question is a consequence of domestic law or regulations or of the necessity to comply with international obligations . . .
>
> The Commission considers that a transfer of powers does not necessarily exclude a State's responsibility under the Convention with regard to the exercise of the transferred powers. Otherwise the guarantees of the Convention could wantonly be limited or excluded and thus be deprived of their peremptory character . . .
>
> The Commission notes that the legal system of the European Communitites not

[104] App. no 13258/87 *Melcher* (M) v. *Germany*, 64 D & R 138.

> only secures fundamental rights but also provides for control of their observance. It is true that the constituent treaties of the EC did not contain a catalogue of such rights. However, the Parliament, the Council and the Commission of the European Communitites have stressed in a joint declaration of fundamental rights, as derived in particular from the Constitutions of the Member States and the European Convention for the Protection of Human Rights and Fundamental Freedoms. They pledged that, in the exercise of their powers and in pursuance of the aims of the European Communities, they would respect and continue to respect these human rights . . . In addition the Court of Justice of the ECs has developed a case law according to which it is called upon to control Community acts on the basis of fundamental rights, inluding those enshrined in the European Convention on Human Rights. In accordance with this reasoning the Court of Justice underlined in the present case that the right to a fair hearing is a fundamental principle of Community law . . . However, it came to the conclusion that this complaint was unfounded.

Although the relationship between the two European Courts, and the case law of each, remains as yet largely harmonious, it is clear that the Court of Justice has expanded its jurisdiction over issues which involve the observance of the so-called general principles of law and human rights by the Member States, in areas which it deems to fall within Community law. Conflicts in the application and understanding of such human rights principles are quite likely to arise, even if not deliberately, between the Court of Justice and the Court of Human Rights, just as conflicts arise between the interpretation given by national supreme courts and that given by the Court of Human Rights to particular rights in specific contexts. This may be somewhat more problematic in the case of the Court of Justice since, unlike in the case of Member States' courts, there is no mechanism for recourse to the Court of Human Rights against a judgment of the Court of Justice. The potential for differences in interpretation and different conclusions on the same issues can be seen by contrasting decisions like that of the Court of Human Rights in *Open Door Counselling*[105] with the opinion of the Advocate General in *Grogan*,[106] the ECJ in *Hoechst*[107] with the ECtHR in *Niemietz*,[108] the ECJ in *Orkem*[109] with the ECtHR in *Funke*,[110] and the approach of the ECJ in *ERT*[111] with that of the ECtHR in *Lentia* v. *Austria*.[112] But these are only examples, and the possibility of conflict may be exaggerated, especially since the Court of Justice is likely to want to follow or to parallel the jurisprudence of the Court of Human

[105] *Open Door Counselling Ltd and Dublin Well Woman Centre* v. *Ireland*, Series A no 246.

[106] Case C–159/90, n. 77 above.

[107] Cases 46/87 and 227/88, *Hoechst AG* v. *Commission* [1989] ECR 2859, [1991] 4 CMLR 410.

[108] *Niemietz* v. *Germany*, n. 47 above.

[109] Case 374/87, n. 44 and 50 above.

[110] *Funke* v. *France*, n. 51 above.

[111] Case C–260/89, *Elliniki Radiophonia Tileorassi AE* v. *Dimotiki Etairia Pliroforissis and Sotirios Kouvelas*, n. 74 above.

[112] *Informationsverein Lentia* v. *Austria*, Series A no 276. In this case the ECtHR found that the radio and television monopoly of the Austrian Broadcasting Corporation constituted a violation of Art. 10 of the Convention, whereas the ECJ in Case C–260/89, n. 111 above, left the Art. 10 issue to be decided by the national court, thus risking national variations in the application of the proportionality test.

Rights. Further, the Court of Justice is likely, in particular in Article 177 cases, to leave it to the national court to decide whether a particular national measure which falls within the scope of Community law is compatible with fundamental rights,[113] unless it is specifically asked for a ruling on that point.[114]

However, as the number of cases before the Court of Justice involving fundamental rights issues grows, litigants will increasingly argue not only that acts of the national legal system within the field of Community law but also acts of the Community institutions are in breach of Convention standards, and the Court of Justice will be required to consider these claims in a manner very similar to the way in which the Commission and Court of Human Rights would consider the same issues. The issue of Aids testing has arisen recently before the Court of First Instance and the Court of Justice, not in the form of claims of discrimination on grounds of sexual orientation, but in the form of privacy claims against the Community institutions under the Convention on Human Rights. And although the CFI has shown itself ready to dismiss these claims quickly,[115] the Court of Justice has been somewhat more cautious. In proceedings brought against the Commission by a staff member who argued that an Aids test had effectively been carried out without his consent, the Court found for the applicant and annulled the contrary decision of the CFI.[116] The Court ruled that there had in fact been a breach of the applicant's right to respect for private life which was 'embodied in Article 8 of the ECHR and deriving from the common constitutional traditions of the Member States'.[117] The fact that an application against the EC Commission would not be accepted by the Commission on Human Rights may have been a factor in the Court of Justice's decision in the case, given that the applicant would otherwise be seen to be left without any remedy against the Community for what was evidently a serious violation of his human rights—something which would not reflect well on a Community and a Union which loudly claims to protect fundamental rights.[118]

113 See *ERT*, n. 111 above.

114 See Case C–23/93, *TV10 SA* v. *Commissariaat voor de Media*, [1994] ECR I–4795, concerning Dutch broadcasting restrictions, in which the Court referred to its conclusion in an earlier case, Case C–353/89, *Commission* v. *Netherlands* [1991] ECR I–4069, that the maintenance of the pluralism which the broadcasting policy sought to safeguard was precisely what the European Convention on Human Rights was designed to protect. See the similar conclusion of the Commission on Human Rights in its Dec. of 11 Jan. 1994, App. no 21427/93, *X* v. *The Netherlands*, 76A D & R 129.

115 See Cases T–121/89, T–13/90, *X* v. *Commission* [1992] ECR II–2195 and T–10/93, *A* v. *Commission* [1994] ECR II–179, [1994] 3 CMLR 242. In the first case the CFI ruled that no Aids test had in fact taken place, and in the second it ruled that a decision on the applicant's medical unfitness for a post, based on the results of a voluntary HIV screening test, was legally made and that such a test was not in itself a breach of Art. 8 of the ECHR.

116 Case C–404/92P, n. 40 above, annulling the judgment in Cases T–121/89 and T–13/90, n. 115 above. The ECJ has not yet heard an appeal from Case T–10/93, n. 115 above. See also the app. in Case T–176/94, *K* v. *Commission* [1994] OJ C161/13, recently registered with the CFI.

117 Case C–404/92P, n. 40 above, para. 17.

118 Community law has been surprisingly silent on the issue of gay and lesbian rights, which is an important issue in general human rights law. See on this, *Homosexuality: A European Community Issue*, ed. K. Waaldijk and A. Clapham (Martinus Nijhoff, 1993).

As we have seen, the issue of legal enforcement of standards of fundamental rights against Member States by the Court of Justice raises still other problems. And as the field of substantive competence of the European Community within the European Union grows, it will be interesting to see whether the divergence in cultural and social norms among the Member States can adequately be accommodated or whether the State/Community conflict over fundamental rights, which was first seen in the *Handelsgesellschaft* case, will emerge again as a serious concern.

8. FURTHER READING

(a) Books

CASSESE, A., CLAPHAM, A., and WEILER, J., (eds.), *European Union: The Human Rights Challenge* (Nomos, 1991)

O'REILLY, J., (ed.), *Human Rights and Constitutional Law* (Round Hall Press, 1992)

(b) Articles

CLAPHAM, A., 'A Human Rights Policy for the European Community' (1990) 10 YBEL 309

COPPEL J., and O'NEILL A., 'The European Court of Justice: Taking Rights Seriously?' (1992) 12 *Legal Studies* 227

DAUSES, M., 'The Protection of Fundamental Rights in the Community Legal Order' (1985) 10 ELRev. 398

DE BURCA, G., 'Fundamental Human Rights and the Reach of EC law' (1993) 13 OJLS 283

KROGSGAARD, L., 'Fundamental Rights in the EC after Maastricht' [1993] LIEI 99

LENAERTS, K., 'Fundamental Rights to be Included in a Community Catalogue' (1991) 16 ELRev. 367

PESCATORE, P., 'The Context and Significance of Fundamental Rights in the Law of the European Communities' (1981) 2 HRLJ. 295

PHELAN, D. R., 'Right to Life of the Unborn v Promotion of Trade in Services: The European Court of Justice and the Normative Shaping of the European Union' (1992) 55 MLR 670

TEMPLE LANG, J., 'The sphere in which Member States are obliged to comply with the general principles of law and Community fundamental rights principles' [1991] LIEI 23

TWOMEY, P., 'The European Union: Three Pillars without a Human Rights Foundation' in D. O'Keeffe and P. Twomey (eds.), *Legal Issues of the Maastricht Treaty* (1994) 121

WEILER, J., 'Thou Shalt not Oppress a Stranger: On the Judicial Protection of the Human Rights of Non-Community Nationals—a Critique' (1992) EJIL 65

8

General Principles of Community Law II: Proportionality, Legitimate Expectations, and Non-Discrimination

1. INTRODUCTION

In the previous chapter we considered the role played by fundamental rights in Community law. We now move to discuss other general principles which have featured prominently within the Court's jurisprudence: proportionality, legitimate expectations, and non-discrimination. The dividing line between these two chapters should not be thought of in too absolute terms: there are certain principles, such as the right to a fair hearing, or legal and professional privilege, which some might classify as fundamental rights,[1] while others would characterize them as principles of administrative legality.

The treatment afforded to the principles considered within this chapter will be somewhat briefer than the discussion of fundamental rights. This should not be taken to signify that these principles are somehow less important in absolute terms. It is rather because the general principles which are analysed here will also be focused on in other parts of the book.[2]

Moreover, when reading the material within this chapter do not forget the earlier evaluation of subsidiarity.[3] This is in certain respects a general principle of Community law, albeit one which goes principally to the initial legality of Community conduct. Nor should the earlier discussion of transparency be forgotten in this context.[4] Transparency is itself a principle of good administration. The fact that the catalyst for the more detailed treatment of this issue came from the political organs of the Community, rather than the Court, should not cause us to lose sight of its emerging status within Community law.

[1] Both of these principles have been considered in the previous chap.
[2] See below, Chs. 11, 12, 15, 16, 18.
[3] See above 112–18. [4] See above 140–1.

2. PROPORTIONALITY

(a) The Role of Proportionality and Its Meaning

The EC Treaty does not possess an explicit, detailed set of principles against which to test the legality of Community or state action within the sphere covered by Community law. It has therefore largely fallen to the Court of Justice to fashion principles of administrative legality. In undertaking this task the ECJ has reasoned partly from specific provisions of the Treaty which justify Community action only where it is 'necessary' or 'required' in order to reach a certain end. It has also inevitably drawn upon principles which exist within the legal systems of the Member States and, as in many other contexts, it has then fashioned these principles to suit the needs of the Community itself.

The concept of proportionality is most fully developed within German law. It appeared initially in the context of policing, as a ground for challenging measures on the basis that they were excessive or unnecessary in relation to the objective which was being pursued.[5] In its modern formulation within Germany the consensus appears to be that proportionality involves the evaluation of three factors: the suitability of the measure for the attainment of the desired objective; the necessity of the disputed measure, in the sense that the agency has no other option at its disposal which is less restrictive of the individual's freedom; the proportionality of the measure to the restrictions which are thereby involved. Some notion of proportionality also features within the legal systems of other Member States such as France, although one should be cautious about ascribing the same meaning to the concept whenever the word 'proportionality' is to be found in any guise within differing legal systems.[6]

Proportionality is now well established as a general principle of Community law. It can be used to challenge Community action itself. It has also proved to be an important means of determining the legality of state action in areas where the Treaty permits exceptions to Community norms on the ground that they are justified on grounds of public policy, public security, and the like.

Examples of the Court's use of proportionality within both of these categories will be given below. But before doing so we must explore a little further the meaning of the concept itself. Clearly, proportionality entails some idea of balance, and of a proper relationship between means and ends. We can however be a little more precise than this.

Various linguistic formulations of proportionality are to be found. They include the following tests:

> is the disputed measure the least restrictive which could be adopted in the circumstances?
> do the means adopted to achieve the aim correspond to the importance of the aim, and are they necessary for its achievement?[7]

[5] J. Schwarze, *European Administrative Law* (1992), 685–6. [6] *Ibid.* 680–5.
[7] Case 66/82, *Fromançais SA* v. *F.O.R.M.A.* [1983] ECR 395, [1983] 3 CMLR 453.

is the challenged act suitable and necessary for the achievement of its objective, and one which does not impose excessive burdens on the individual?[8]

what are the relative costs and benefits of the disputed measure?

These particular tests must, however, be fitted into a broader framework. Or, putting the same point in a different way, the application of any one of these tests requires us to address a set of both prior and subsequent issues in order that we can reach a meaningful answer to the proportionality inquiry. The stages in a proportionality inquiry can then be presented as follows.

(i) The relevant interests must be identified;

(ii) There must be some ascription of weight or value to those interests, since this is a necessary condition precedent to any balancing operation;

(iii) Some view must be taken about whether certain interests can be traded off to achieve other goals at all;

(iv) A decision must be made on whether the public body's decision was indeed proportionate or not on the facts of the case in the light of the above considerations. Differing criteria can be used when answering this question. The test could be formulated in any of the ways identified above. As will be seen different formulations tend to be used in the context of different types of case. For example, the first version (is the measure the least restrictive which could be adopted in the circumstances?) will commonly be used in cases where the measure in question is in conflict with a right granted by the Treaty.

(v) The court will have to decide how intensively it is going to apply any one of the tests mentioned above. It is important to realize that all of these tests can be applied more or less intensively, as will become apparent.

What does it mean, then, to say that any of these tests can be applied more or less intensively? This is not difficult to explain. In any system of administrative law the courts will have to decide not only which tests to apply to determine the legality of administrative action, but also the rigour or intensity with which to apply them. In some legal systems, such as France, this differentiation is worked out to a high degree. But it is present to varying degrees in all such systems, including that in the United Kingdom.[9] The issue of the relative intensity of judicial review is therefore just as much a live question in relation to proportionality, as it is in relation to any other tool of judicial oversight. This can best be appreciated by reflecting on the differing types of administrative action which may be subject to challenge on grounds of proportionality. We can distinguish at least three broad types of case.

[8] This is very close to the test used in Germany: Schwarze, n. 5 above, 687.

[9] P. P. Craig, *Administrative Law* (3rd edn., 1994), Ch. 11.

One common scenario is for an individual to argue that his or her rights have been unduly restricted by administrative action. A second type of case is one in which the attack is on the penalty which has been imposed, the claim being once again that it is excessive. A third form which the action can assume is where the individual argues that the very policy choice made by the administration is disproportionate, in the sense either that the costs are excessive in relation to the benefits, or that the measure which has been adopted is not suitable or necessary to achieve the end in view.

A moment's thought will reveal why the Court may feel inclined to review these differing types of case with varying degrees of intensity. In the first type of case, where the clash is between administrative action and rights, the courts are more likely to engage in vigorous scrutiny. The very denomination of those interests as important Community rights means that any invasion of them should be kept to the minimum. Society may well accept that these rights cannot be regarded as absolute and that some limitations may be warranted in certain circumstances. Nonetheless there is a presumption that any inroad should interfere with the right as little as possible and no more than is merited by the occasion. In this sense the recognition of some idea of proportionality is a natural and necessary adjunct to the regard for such rights. Moreover, courts regard it as a natural and proper part of their legitimate function to adjudicate on the boundary lines between state action and individual rights, even though this line may be controversial.

Courts are also apt to be reasonably searching, when the claim is of the second kind, i.e. that the penalty is excessive. This is in part because penalties can, although they do not have to, impinge on personal liberties. It is in part also because a court can normally strike down a particular penalty without thereby undermining the entirety of the administrative policy with which it is connected.

The judiciary is likely to be more circumspect in cases of the third kind, where the essence of the proportionality challenge is to the very policy itself and where neither rights nor excessive penalties are at stake. The reasons are not hard to find. Policy choices are made by the administrative/political arm of government and it is generally recognized that the courts should not overturn these merely because they believe that a different way of doing things would have been better. They should not substitute their judgment for that of the administration. Now, this does not mean that proportionality is ruled out in such instances. It does mean that the courts are likely to apply this concept less intensively than in the previous two categories of case and will only overturn the policy choice if it is clearly or manifestly disproportionate.

What this means is that the crucial question in reality is the intensity with which the Court will apply the proportionality test in any particular case as the following extract reveals:

G. de Búrca, The Principle of Proportionality and its Application in EC Law[10]

It becomes apparent that in reaching decisions, the Court of Justice is influenced not only by what it considers to be the nature and the importance of the interest or right claimed by the applicant, and the nature and importance of the objective alleged to be served by the measure, but by the relative expertise, position and overall competence of the Court as against the decision-making authority in assessing those factors. It becomes apparent that the way the proportionality principle is applied by the Court of Justice covers a spectrum ranging from a very deferential approach, to quite a rigorous and searching examination of the justification for a measure which has been challenged.

. . . Courts are generally prepared to adjudicate on issues involving traditionally categorized individual rights, where interference with a discretionary policy decision can be explained not on the ground that it is not the most sensible or effective measure, but on the ground that it unjustifiably restricts an important legally recognized right, the protection of which is entrusted to the court. Courts are accepted as having a legitimate role in deciding on civil liberties and personal rights even in controversial contexts such as euthanasia, abortion and freedom of speech. But in certain specific political contexts, in the case of measures involving, for example, national security, economic policy or national expenditure concerns, courts tend to be considerably more deferential in their review. They are more reluctant to adjudicate if the interest affected is seen as a collective or general public interest rather than an individual right, and if the interest of the State is a mixed and complex one, e.g. in an area involving national economic and social policy choices. Where a measure of this nature is challenged, it may be that it does not appear to affect any traditionally characterized right, but rather indirectly affects the interests and welfare of many people. Or even if it does affect a recognized right, it also concerns many other interests, both individual and general, over which the policy-maker has presumably deliberated at length in coming to a decision . . . The ways in which a court may defer in such circumstances range from deeming the measure to be non-justiciable, to refusing to look closely at the justification for the restrictive effects of the measure, to placing the onus of proof on the challenger who is claiming that the measure is disproportionate. Courts tend to be deferential in their review in cases which highlight the non-representative nature of the judiciary, the limited evidentiary and procedural processes of adjudication, and the difficulty of providing a defined individual remedy in contexts which involve complex political and economic policies.

(b) Proportionality and Challenges to Community Action

The differing ways in which proportionality is applied, depending upon the type of case which is before the Court, can be demonstrated by considering challenges to Community action.

The general interrelationship between proportionality and fundamental rights was considered in the previous chapter. The *Hauer* case[11] provides a suitable

[10] [1993] YBEL 105, 111–12

[11] Case 44/79, *Hauer* v. *Land Rheinland-Pfalz* [1979] ECR 3727.

example of the way in which the Court applies proportionality in this type of case. It will be remembered that the applicant sought to challenge a Community regulation which placed limitations on the planting of new vines. The Court found that this did not, in itself, constitute an invalid restriction on property rights. It then proceeded to determine whether the planting restrictions were disproportionate, 'impinging upon the very substance of the right to property'.[12] The Court found that they were not. In reaching this conclusion the Court did, however, carefully examine the purpose of the general scheme within which the regulation in question fell. The objects of this scheme were to attain a balanced wine market, with fair prices for consumers and a fair return for producers; the eradication of surpluses; and an improvement in the quality of wine. The Regulation in dispute, 1162/76, which prohibited new plantings, was part of this overall plan. It was not disproportionate in the light of the legitimate, general Community policy for this area: it was designed to deal with an immediate problem of surpluses, while at the same time laying the foundation for more permanent measures to facilitate a balanced wine market.

Let us now consider the other two categories of cases, those concerning penalties and those concerning more general challenges to Community policy.

One of the most common areas from which cases of this nature arise is the CAP. The CAP is characterized by two features. On the one hand, there is the fact that the objectives to be achieved by the CAP are set out at a high level of generality in Article 39 of the Treaty. On the other hand, it is clear that these objectives can clash *inter se*, with the result that the Commission and Council will have to make difficult discretionary choices, often under fairly extreme exigencies of time, in order to decide how best to balance and attain these aims in any given concrete setting. Actions seeking the annulment of regulations and decisions made pursuant to the CAP have been very common. Cases of this kind have indeed established some of the main precedents for standing under Article 173.[13] They also provide insights into how the Court applies the principles of substantive review in particular subject-matter areas.[14]

There has been a regular stream of such cases in which the essence of the proportionality argument is that a penalty which has been imposed is excessive in relation to the aim of the measure in question. The Court has found in favour of the individual on a number of occasions. In *R.* v. *Intervention Board, ex parte E. D. & F. Man (Sugar) Ltd.*[15] The applicant was required to give a security deposit to the Board when seeking a licence to export sugar outside the Community. The applicant was then late, but only by four hours, in completing the relevant paperwork. The Board, acting pursuant to a Community regulation, declared the entire deposit of £1,670,370 to be forfeit. Not surprisingly the company was aggrieved. The Court held that the automatic forfeiture of the entire deposit in the event of any failure to fulfil the time requirement was too drastic, given the function performed by the system of

[12] Case 44/79, *Hauer* v. *Land Rheinland-Pfalz* [1979] ECR 3727, para. 23.
[13] See below 456–65.
[14] See below 476–8.
[15] Case 181/84, [1985] ECR 2889.

export licences.[16] In addition to cases dealing with penalties *stricto sensu* the Court has applied proportionality in the field of economic regulation, scrutinizing the level of charges which have been imposed by the Community institutions. Thus in *Bela-Mühle*[17] the Court held that a scheme whereby producers of animal feed were forced to use skimmed milk in their product, in order to reduce a surplus, rather than soya, was unlawful because, *inter alia*, skimmed milk was three times more expensive than soya: the obligation to purchase the milk, therefore, imposed a disproportionate burden on the animal feed producers.

The *Fedesa* case provides a good example of a challenge to a more general policy-choice of the Community authorities within the context of the CAP. The Court has emphasized on a number of occasions that the Community institutions possess a wide discretion in the operation of the CAP, and that review will not therefore be intensive.[18] Some of these authorities will be examined in more detail within the general context of substantive review under Article 173.[19] What the following case shows is that this more deferential approach is likely to carry across to applications based on proportionality:

Case C–331/88, R. v. Minister for Agriculture, Fisheries and Food, ex parte Fedesa [1990] ECR 4023, [1991] 1 CMLR 507

Council Directive 81/602 provided that the Council would take a decision as soon as possible on the prohibition of certain hormone substances for administration to animals, but that in the meantime, any arrangements made by Member States in relation to such substances would continue to apply. In 1988 Council Directive 88/146 was adopted as an approximating measure, prohibiting the use in livestock farming of certain of these hormonal substances. An earlier identical Directive adopted in 1985 had been declared void by the Court of Justice on grounds of an infringement by the Council of an essential procedural requirement. The applicants were manufacturers and distributors of veterinary medicine who brought proceedings before the United Kingdom High Court to challenge the validity of the national legislative measure implementing the 1988 Directive, on the ground that the Directive itself was invalid. The High Court stayed the proceedings and referred the matter to the Court of Justice, asking among other things whether the Directive infringed the principles of legal certainty, proportionality, equality, and non-retrospectivity. The following extract considers the ECJ's reasoning on proportionality.[20]

[16] *Ibid.*, para. 29; Case 240/78, *Atalanta Amsterdam BV* v. *Produktschap voor Vee en Vlees* [1979] ECR 2137; Case 122/78, *Buitoni SA* v. *Fonds d'Orientation et de Régularisation des Marchés Agricoles* [1979] ECR 677, [1979] 2 CMLR 665.

[17] Case 114/76, *Bela-Mühle Josef Bergman KG* v. *Grows-Farm GmbH & Co KG* [1977] ECR 1211, [1979] 2 CMLR 83.

[18] See e.g. Case 138/78, *Stolting* v. *Hauptzollamt Hamburg-Jonas* [1979] ECR 713, [1979] 3 CMLR 588; Case 265/87, *Schräder* v. *Hauptzollamt Gronau* [1989] ECR 2237.

[19] See below 477–8.

[20] For consideration of the aspects of the case concerning legal certainty and legitimate expectations, see below 351–2.

THE ECJ

12. It was argued that the Directive infringes the principle of proportionality in three respects. In the first place, the outright prohibition on the administration of the five hormones in question is inappropriate in order to attain the declared objectives, since it is impossible to apply in practice and leads to the creation of a dangerous black market. In the second place, outright prohibition is not necessary because consumer anxieties can be allayed simply by the dissemination of information and advice. Finally, the prohibition in question entails excessive disadvantages, in particular considerable financial losses on the part of the traders concerned, in relation to the alleged benefits accruing to the general interest.

13. The Court has consistently held that the principle of proportionality is one of the general principles of Community law. By virtue of that principle, the lawfulness of the prohibition of an economic activity is subject to the condition that the prohibitory measures are appropriate and necessary in order to achieve the objectives legitimately pursued by the legislation in question; when there is a choice between several appropriate measures recourse must be had to the least onerous, and the disadvantages caused must not be disproportionate to the aims pursued.

14. However, with regard to judicial review of compliance with those conditions it must be stated that in matters concerning the common agricultural policy the Community legislature has a discretionary power which corresponds to the political responsibilities given to it by Articles 40 and 43 of the Treaty. Consequently, the legality of a measure adopted in that sphere can be affected only if the measure is manifestly inappropriate having regard to the objective which the competent institution is seeking to pursue. (See in particular the judgment in Case 265/87, *Schräder* [1989] ECR 2237, paras. 21 and 22).

The Court went on to conclude that there had been no infringement of the principle of proportionality since the Council had made no manifest error and the prohibition, even though it might have caused some financial loss to certain traders, could not be regarded as manifestly inappropriate. The Court's application of the proportionality principle in this case contrasts with the more rigorous application of the principle in other cases, in which it is not Community action but Member State action that is being challenged.[21] In paragraph 13 of the judgment the Court described the concept of proportionality, stating that, when there is a choice between several appropriate measures, recourse must be had to the least onerous. Yet it dismissed the suggestions of the applicants on the less onerous measures which could have been taken, and ruled that the Commission has a wide discretion in the field of the CAP, and that a measure would only fall if it were 'manifestly

[21] See e.g. Case 5/88, *Wachauf v. Germany* [1989] ECR 2609, [1991] 1 CMLR 328. See further the case law involving state restrictions on freedom of movement in the Community, where the proportionality test applied by the Court to such measures generally involves a search for less restrictive alternatives: Case 104/75, *Officer van Justitie* v. *de Peijper* [1976] ECR 613, [1976] 2 CMLR 271; Case 261/81, *Walter Rau Lebensmittelwerke* v. *De Smedt, Pvba* [1982] ECR 3961, [1983] 2 CMLR 496; Case 33/74, *Van Binsbergen* v. *Bestuur van de Bedrijfsvereniging Metaalnijverheid* [1974] ECR 1299, [1975] 1 CMLR 298.

inappropriate', rather than merely that there was a less restrictive way of achieving the same aim.

(c) Proportionality and Challenges to Member State Action

There have been a number of cases which deal with proportionality in the context of rights granted by the Community Treaties and Member State action which seeks to restrict the ambit of those rights. In these types of cases the Court tends to engage in fairly intensive review, in order to determine whether the restriction which the Member State has imposed on a right granted by the Treaties really is necessary or warranted. This same theme can be seen throughout the Court's case law when dealing with free movement, whether of persons, services, or goods. These cases will commonly arise when Member States seek to argue that a restriction on the right in question is justified on grounds of public policy, public health, or one of the other limits which are, in principle, recognized by the Treaty.

Thus the Court has insisted that derogation from the fundamental principle of Article 48 can only be sanctioned in cases which pose a genuine and serious threat to public policy, and even then the measure must be the least restrictive possible in the circumstances.[22] The same principle is evident in cases on freedom to provide services, which is a protected right under Article 59. In *Van Binsbergen*[23] the Court held that residence requirements limiting this freedom might be justified, but only where they were strictly necessary to prevent the evasion, by those outside the territory, of professional rules which were applicable to the activity in question. We can see the same approach at work in cases concerned with the free movement of goods. Thus in the famous *Cassis de Dijon* case[24] the Court considered whether a German rule which prescribed the minimum alcohol content for a certain alcoholic beverage could constitute an impediment to the free movement of goods under Article 30 of the Treaty. Having decided that the rule could constitute such an impediment the Court assessed the defence that the rule was necessary in order to protect consumers from being misled. The Court rejected that defence, because the interests of consumers could be safeguarded in other, less restrictive ways, by displaying the alcohol content on the packaging of the drinks.

It is clear, then, that the Court will scrutinize carefully Member State claims that measures derogating from the rights granted by Articles such as Articles 30, 48, or 59 are justified on grounds of public policy, public security, public health, or any of the other recognized grounds of derogation provided for in the Court's case law. *How intensive* this review will be will, however, vary. This is unsurprising, given the variety of types of factual claims which can be

[22] Case 36/75, *Rutili* v. *Ministre de l'Intérieur* [1975] ECR 1219, [1976] 1 CMLR 140; Case 30/77, *R.* v. *Bouchereau* [1977] ECR 1999, [1977] 2 CMLR 800. See Chapter 17.

[23] Case 33/74, n. 21 above; Case 39/75, *Coenen* v. *Social Economische Raad* [1975] ECR 1547, [1976] 1 CMLR 30.

[24] Case 120/78, *Rewe Zentrale* v. *Bundesmonopolverwaltung für Branntwein* [1979] ECR 649, [1979] 3 CMLR 494.

advanced by Member States in this respect. These claims will be examined in detail within later chapters of this book.[25] Suffice it to say for the present that four variables appear to affect the intensity of the Court's review in this type of case.

First, other things being equal, the Court has tended to be more intensive in its review as time has gone on. Cases which have come before the Court involving similar facts, or raising similar principles, have tended to be subjected to more rigorous scrutiny, with the result that Member State action which was regarded as lawful in the earlier case has been held not to be so in the later instance.[26]

Secondly, the intensity of the Court's review will also be a function of how seriously it regards the Member State's argument that measures really were necessary in order to protect, for example, public health. If the Court feels that these measures were really a 'front' for a national protective policy, designed to insulate its own producers from the effects of foreign competition, then it will be inclined to subject the Member State's argument to close scrutiny. This is exemplified by the decision in *Commission* v. *United Kingdom*.[27] In this case the Court considered a claim by the United Kingdom Government that a ban on the import of poultry could be justified on grounds of public health under Article 36 of the Treaty. A reading of the Court's judgment leaves one in little doubt that it was suspicious, to say the least, of the motives for the United Kingdom action. The Court felt that the measures were, in reality, aimed at protecting United Kingdom poultry producers from the effects of French imports in the run up to Christmas. The Court accordingly rejected the United Kingdom's defence.

A third factor which will influence the intensity of review in cases involving Member State action will be the nature of the subject-matter. Thus in those instances where a Member State raises genuine concerns relating to public health,[28] in circumstances where there is scientific uncertainty about the effects of certain foodstuffs, the Court has been more willing to accept that limitations on free movement are warranted.[29] However, one should be cautious about characterizing such cases as involving less intensive review.[30] They may equally well be regarded as instances where the Court, *having surveyed the evidence*, believes that Member State action of the type under scrutiny is

[25] See below, Chs. 14, 15, 16, 17.

[26] Compare e.g. Case 41/74, *Van Duyn* v. *Home Office* [1974] ECR 1337, [1975] 1 CMLR 1, with Cases 115 and 116/81, *Adoui and Cornuaille* v. *Belgian State* [1982] ECR 1665, [1982] 3 CMLR 631. Compare Case 34/79, *R.* v. *Henn and Darby* [1979] ECR 3975, [1980] 1 CMLR 246, with Case 121/85, *Conegate* v. *Customs and Excise Commissioners* [1986] ECR 1007, [1986] 1 CMLR 739.

[27] Case 40/82 [1982] ECR 2793, [1982] 3 CMLR 497.

[28] See below 605.

[29] Case 174/82, *Officier van Justitie* v. *Sandoz BV* [1983] ECR 2445, [1984] 3 CMLR 43; Case 97/83, *Melkunie* [1984] ECR 2367, [1986] 2 CMLR 318.

[30] See the different views expressed by J. Schwarze, n. 5 above, 790 and Lord Slynn, 'The Concept of Free Movement of Goods and the Reservation for National Action under Art. 36 EEC' in *Discretionary Powers of the Member States in the Field of Economic Policies and their Limits under the EEC Treaty*, ed. J. Schwarze (1988).

warranted for the present. There are, moreover, certainly examples of claims based upon public health grounds where the Court, while accepting that some scientific uncertainty did exist, none the less concluded that a less restrictive way of achieving the Member State's aim could be found.[31]

The final variable which affects the intensity of the proportionality inquiry is rather different from those considered above. It may be explained as follows. In some instances the Court will pass the application of the proportionality issue back to the national courts. We shall have occasion to see this in later discussions of, for example, the free movement of goods.[32] This should not, however, be taken to mean that the Court is necessarily being more deferential in the application of proportionality in such circumstances. Whether it is in fact so will depend crucially on the conditions, or guidelines, which the Court lays down by way of indication to the national courts on how the proportionality inquiry should be determined in any particular area.[33]

3. LEGAL CERTAINTY AND LEGITIMATE EXPECTATIONS

The connected concepts of legal certainty and legitimate expectations are to be found in all the legal systems of the Member States which make up the Community, although their precise legal content may vary from one system to another.[34] These concepts are applied in a number of different ways and it is important to distinguish these in order to avoid confusion.

(a) *Legal Certainty and Actual Retroactivity*

One of the most obvious applications of legal certainty is in the context of rules which have an actual retroactive effect. Following Schwarze,[35] 'actual retroactivity' covers the situation where a rule is introduced and applied to events which have already been concluded. Retroactivity of this nature may occur either where the date of entry into force precedes the date of publication or where the regulation applies to circumstances which have actually been concluded before the entry into force of the measure.

The arguments against allowing measures of this nature to have legal effect are simple and compelling. A basic tenet of the rule of law is that people ought to be able to plan their lives, secure in the knowledge of the legal consequences of their actions. This fundamental aspect of the rule of law is violated by the application of measures which were not in force at the time that the actual

[31] Case 178/84, *Commission* v. *Germany* [1987] ECR 1227, [1988] 1 CMLR 780.

[32] See below 621–3.

[33] G. de Búrca, 'The Principle of Proportionality and its Application in EC Law' [1993] YBEL 105.

[34] J. Schwarze, n. 5 above, Ch. 6.

[35] *Ibid.* 1120.

events took place. Our concerns about retrospective norms are particularly marked in the context of criminal penalties, where the effect of the application of the norm may be to criminalize activity which was lawful when it was undertaken. The application of retrospective rules may also be extremely damaging to the individual in commercial circumstances, upsetting the presuppositions on which important transactions may have been based.

Small wonder, then, that legal systems have tended to take a very dim view of attempts by legislators or administrators to apply their rules in this manner. The Community is no different in this respect. The basic principle was enunciated in *Racke*.[36] In this case the Commission had introduced monetary compensatory amounts for a certain product by a regulation, and then in two further regulations altered the amounts. Each of the relevant regulations provided that they would apply fourteen days before they were published. The Court held that it was a fundamental principle of the Community legal order that a measure adopted by the public authorities shall not be applicable to those concerned before they have the opportunity to make themselves acquainted with it.[37] The Court then drew out the implications for retroactive measures, stating that:[38]

> Although in general the principle of legal certainty precludes a Community measure from taking effect from a point in time before its publication, it may exceptionally be otherwise where the purpose to be achieved so demands and where the legitimate expectations of those concerned are duly respected.

The Court has, in accordance with the proviso in this quotation, upheld the validity of retroactive measures in some cases, particularly in the agricultural sphere where such measures were necessary to ensure market stability. The normal presumption is, however, against the validity of retroactive measures. This manifests itself in both procedural and substantive terms.

In procedural terms, the Court has made it clear that it will interpret norms as having retroactive effect only if this clearly follows from their terms, or from the objectives of the general scheme of which they are a part. The general principle of construction is, therefore, against giving rules any retroactive impact.[39]

In substantive terms, the Court will strike down measures which do have a retroactive effect where there is no pressing Community objective which demands this temporal dimension, or where the legitimate expectations of those affected by the measure cannot be duly respected.[40] The following case provides a strong example of this.

[36] Case 98/78, *Firma A. Racke* v. *Hauptzollamt Mainz* [1979] ECR 69. See also Case 99/78, *Weingut Gustav Decker KG* v. *Hauptzollamt Landau* [1979] ECR 101.

[37] *Ibid.* 84.

[38] *Ibid.* 86.

[39] Cases 212–217/80, *Salumi* [1981] ECR 2735.

[40] Case 224/82, *Meiko-Konservenfabrik* v. *Federal Republic of Germany* [1983] ECR 2539.

Case 63/83, Regina v. Kent Kirk
[1984] ECR 2689, [1984] 3 CMLR 522

Criminal proceedings were brought in the United Kingdom on the ground of infringement of fisheries legislation. During the course of these proceedings the question arose whether Council Regulation 170/83 of 25 January 1983, by which, with retroactive effect from 1 January 1983, national measures contravening Community law prohibitions on discrimination were approved by way of transitional arrangements, could also retroactively validate national penal provisions. The ECJ said no, firmly.

THE ECJ

20. The Commission . . . contends that the Member States were empowered to adopt measures such as the Sea Fish Order 1982 by Article 6(1) of Regulation 170/83 of 25 January 1983 which authorises retroactively, as from 1 January 1983, the retention of the derogation regime defined in Article 100 of the 1972 Act of Accession for a further ten years, and which extends the coastal zones from six to twelve nautical miles. In the Commission's view, the Sea Fish Order 1982 constituted a proper exercise of the authorisation under Regulation 170/83 in view of the particular circumstances prevailing at that time.

21. Without embarking upon an examination of the general legality of the retroactivity of Article 6(1) of that Regulation, it is sufficient to point out that such retroactivity may not, in any event, have the effect of validating *ex post facto* national measures of a penal nature which impose penalties for an act which, in fact, was not punishable at the time at which it was committed. That would be the case where at the time of the act entailing a criminal penalty, the national measure was invalid because it was incompatible with Community law.

22. The principle that penal provisions may not have retroactive effect is one which is common to all the legal orders of the Member States and is enshrined in Article 7 of the European Convention for the Protection of Human Rights and Fundamental Freedoms as a fundamental right; it takes its place among the general principles of law whose observance is ensured by the Court of Justice.

23. Consequently the retroactivity provided for in Article 6(1) of Regulation 170/83 cannot be regarded as validating *ex post facto* national measures which imposed criminal penalties, at the time of the conduct at issue, if those measures were not valid.

24. It follows from the foregoing considerations that Community law regarding fishing did not authorise a Member State, at the time of the adoption of the Sea Fish Order 1982, to prohibit vessels registered in another Member State from fishing within a coastal zone specified by that Order and not covered by conservation measures.

Where there is a pressing Community objective and where the legitimate expectations of those concerned are duly respected, then retroactivity may, *exceptionally*, be accepted by the Court in the non-criminal context. This is exemplified by *Fedesa*.[41] The applicants argued that the Directive was in breach of the principle of non-retroactivity, on the ground that it was adopted

[41] Case C–331/88 [1990] ECR 4023, [1991] 1 CMLR 507.

on 7 March 1988 and stipulated that it was to be implemented by 1 January 1988 at the latest. The Court drew a distinction between the retroactive effect of penal provisions and retroactive effect outside the criminal sphere.

As to the former, the Court affirmed *Kent Kirk*, but held that the Directive in the *Fedesa* case would not impose any criminal liability as such.

On the latter, the Court ruled that the Directive did not contravene the principle of non-retroactivity. It had been adopted to replace an earlier Directive which was annulled, and in order to avoid a temporary legal vacuum where there would be no Community legislation to back up the Member States' existing implementing provisions, the date of the earlier Directive was maintained by the Council when it passed the later Directive.[42]

(b) Legal Certainty, Legitimate Expectations, and Apparent Retroactivity

Apparent retroactivity covers the situation where legislative acts are applied to events which have occurred in the past, but which have not yet been definitively concluded.[43] In many ways the problems which this type of case poses are greater than those within the previous section. It is not difficult to see why this is so. The moral arguments against allowing laws to have actual retroactive effect are powerful and straightforward. The category of apparent retroactivity is more problematic because the administration must obviously have the power to alter its policy for the future, even though this may have implications for the conduct of private parties which has been planned on the basis of the pre-existing legal regime. How then has the Court responded to this problem?

First, it is clear that the mere fact that a trader is disadvantaged by a change in the law will not, in and of itself, give any cause for complaint based upon disappointment of legitimate expectations.[44] As Schwarze states:[45]

> the Court has emphasised the essential freedom enjoyed by the legislature to alter for the future the fundamental legal conditions in which traders operate, even if the changes made work to the disadvantage of all firms in a certain industrial sector. In particular, the plea of infringement of fundamental rights or of the principle of legitimate expectations has been rejected where the actions in question are based only on the circumstance that the trading position of the firms in question has deteriorated as a result of changes in the legal position.

[42] The Court held that there was no infringement of the legitimate expectations of any individual, because the earlier Dir. was clearly only annulled because of a procedural defect, and people affected by the national implementing legislation could not expect the Council to change its attitude on the substance of the matter in the Dir. during the short time between the annulment of the first Dir. and the notification of the second dir.: *ibid.*, para. 47.

[43] Schwarze, n. 5 above, 1121.

[44] See e.g. Case 52/81, *W. Faust* v. *Commission* [1982] ECR 3745, 3762; Case 245/81, *Edeka* v. *Federal Republic of Germany* [1982] ECR 2745, 2758.

[45] *Ibid.* 1131.

Secondly, it is also clear that a claim will fail where the Court adjudges that the applicant's expectations were not legitimate, in that the Community activity which was complained of was seeking to close a legal gap in order to prevent traders from making a speculative profit.[46] Or that they were not legitimate, in the sense that they were not reasonable in all the circumstances. This may be because the action which was being complained of should have been foreseen by the applicants.[47] It may alternatively be because the Court simply disagrees with the basis on which the applicants claim that their expectations have been disappointed. Thus in the *Fedesa* case, considered above, the Court felt that the traders could not have had a reasonable expectation that the substances in question would not be banned in the absence of conclusive scientific findings as to their dangers.[48]

Thirdly, what more is required in order for an individual to have a legitimate expectation which must be taken into account when policy alters? The case law of the Court indicates that the individual must be able to point either to a bargain of some form which has been entered into between the individual and the authorities, or to a course of conduct or assurance on the part of the authorities which can be said to generate the legitimate expectation. The *Mulder* case illustrates the first of these situations.

Case 120/86, Mulder v. Minister van Landbouw en Visserij [1988] ECR 2321, [1989] 2 CMLR 1

The Community had an excess of milk. In order to reduce this excess it passed Regulation 1078/77, under which producers could cease milk production for a certain period in exchange for a premium for non-marketing of the milk. The applicant made such an arrangement in 1979 for five years. In 1984 he began to plan a resumption of his production and applied to the relevant Dutch authorities for a reference quantity of milk which he would be allowed to produce without incurring the payment of any additional levy. He was refused on the ground that he could not prove milk production during the relevant reference year, which was 1983. This was of course impossible for Mulder since he did not produce at all during that period, because of the bargain struck in 1979. He challenged Regulation 857/84, which was the basis of the Dutch authorities' denial of his quota, arguing, *inter alia*, that it infringed his legitimate expectations. The Court found in his favour.

THE ECJ

23. It must be conceded . . . that a producer who has voluntarily ceased production for a certain period cannot legitimately expect to be able to resume production under the same conditions as those which previously applied and not to be subject to any rules of market or structural policy adopted in the meantime.

24. The fact remains that where such a producer, as in the present case, has

[46] Case 2/75, *Einfuhr- und Vorratsstelle für Getreide und Futtermittel* v. *Firma C. Mackprang* [1975] ECR 607, [1977] 1 CMLR 198.

[47] E. Sharpston, 'Legitimate Expectations and Economic Reality' (1990) 15 ELRev. 103.

[48] Case C–331/88, n. 41 above, para. 10.

been encouraged by a Community measure to suspend marketing for a limited period in the general interest and against payment of a premium he may legitimately expect not to be subject, upon the expiry of his undertaking, to restrictions which specifically affect him precisely because he availed himself of the possibilities offered by the Community provisions.

25. However, the regulations on the additional levy on milk give rise to such restrictions for producers who, pursuant to an undertaking entered into under Regulation 1078/77, did not deliver milk during the reference year . . . Those producers may in fact be denied a reference quantity under the new system precisely because of that undertaking if they do not fulfil the specific conditions laid down in Regulation 857/84 or if the Member States have no reference quantity available.

26. . . . There is nothing in the provisions of Regulation 1078/77 or in its Preamble to show that the non-marketing undertaking entered into under that Regulation might, upon its expiry, entail a bar to resumption of the activity in question. Such an effect therefore frustrates those producers' legitimate expectations that the effect of the system to which they had rendered themselves would be limited.

Two illustrations can be given of the second type of situation, where the legitimacy of the applicant's expectation is based upon some course of conduct by the administration, or on an assurance which it has given to a person such as the applicant. In the *Sofrimport* case[49] the applicant sought to import apples from Chile into the Community. A licence was required in accordance with Regulation 346/88. By a later Regulation, 962/88, the Commission took protective measures and suspended all such licences for Chilean apples. The parent Regulation, 2707/72, which gave the Commission power to adopt protective measures, specifically stated in Article 3 that account should be taken of the special position of goods in transit, for the obvious reason that such measures could have a particularly harmful effect on traders. The applicant's goods were already in transit when Regulation 962/88 was introduced, but they were refused entry to the Community. In an action for annulment the Court held that the failure of the Commission to make any special provision for goods in transit as required by the parent Regulation was an infringement of the applicant's legitimate expectations. A similar theme is apparent in the *CNTA* case.[50] The case centred on monetary compensation amounts (mcas), which were payments designed to compensate for fluctuations in exchange rates. The applicant was a firm which had made export contracts on the supposition that mcas would be payable. After these contracts had been made, but before they were to be performed, the Commission passed a regulation abolishing mcas in that sector. The applicant suffered loss, since it had made the contracts on the assumption that the mcas would be payable. The Court held that, while mcas could not be said to insulate exporters from all

[49] Case C–152/88, *Sofrimport Sàrl* v. *Commission* [1990] ECR I–2477, [1990] 3 CMLR 80.
[50] Case 74/74, *CNTA SA* v. *Commission* [1975] ECR 533, [1977] 1 CMLR 171.

fluctuations in exchange rates, they did have the effect of shielding them from such risks, with the consequence that even a prudent exporter might choose not to cover himself against it. The Court then stated:[51]

> In these circumstances, a trader might legitimately expect that for transactions irrevocably undertaken by him because he has obtained, subject to a deposit, export licences fixing the amount of the refund in advance, no unforeseeable alteration will occur which could have the effect of causing him inevitable loss, by re-exposing him to the exchange risk.

In the absence of some overriding public interest, the Commission should have adopted transitional measures to protect those in the position of the applicant.[52]

Finally, there is still considerable uncertainty about the possible application of the doctrine of legitimate expectations when an applicant seeks to found the expectation on a Commission guideline or notice. The cases considered thus far have centred on the extent to which an individual can or cannot claim a legitimate expectation where the basis of the expectation is normally a pre-existing Community regulation or decision which has been altered to the applicant's detriment. We have already had occasion to note that Community policy may be developed through various 'soft-law' devices, such as guidelines, notices, and the like.[53] These are particularly prevalent in areas such as state aids. How far an applicant can claim that such provisions generate legitimate expectations is unclear, and the Community's case law in this area is still evolving.[54]

The Court has sought to balance the need of the Community to alter its policy for the future with the impact that such alteration might have on traders who have based their commercial bargains on pre-existing norms. This is a problem which all legal systems have to face.[55] One point which is worthy of note is that the Court is willing to accept that legitimate expectations can have a substantive and not just a procedural impact. Thus in the cases considered above in which the Court has found in favour of the applicant, the result is that the applicant obtains the substantive benefit which was being sought, in the absence of any overriding public interest to the contrary. This does not always mean that the applicant will succeed in a damages action against the Community.[56] It does mean, for example, in *Mulder* that the Community regulation denying the applicant his milk quota is actually struck down, with the Court making it clear that it is invalid for the Community institutions to deny him the opportunity to re-enter the milk market.

[51] *Ibid.*, para. 42. [52] *Ibid.*, para. 43. [53] See above 102. [54] See below Ch. 24.

[55] For the analogous problem in UK law, see P. P. Craig, *Administrative Law* (3rd edn., 1994), 432, 672–5.

[56] See below, Ch. 12.

(c) Legal Certainty, Legitimate Expectations, and Revocation of Unlawful Acts

The cases considered thus far have all been concerned with changes of policy by the Community institutions in circumstances which can have a deleterious impact on the individual. The policy choice in these cases was, however, not itself unlawful. What, then, of the situation in which the Community has passed an illegal act and then seeks to revoke it? For students of administrative law in the United Kingdom the appropriate analogy is with the problem of representations or decisions made by public bodies which are *ultra vires*, and the extent to which such matters may none the less be relied on by the individual.

The Community's case law on this issue is complex, being mainly derived from decisions concerning the functioning of the ECSC. This case law is, however, instructive, especially for those in the United Kingdom who are faced with the analogous problem. Detailed treatment can be found elsewhere,[57] but two of the central aspects of the Court's approach can be sketched briefly here.

First, unreasonable delay by the administration can operate as a bar to the revocation of an unlawful administrative act.[58]

Secondly, in deciding whether to allow revocation at all it may be necessary to balance the public interest in legality and the private interest in legal certainty. The former does not always trump the latter.[59]

This latter point is of particular interest in the United Kingdom where we are still generally wedded to the idea that the illegal nature of a decision or representation precludes any reliance on it by an individual. We could have much to learn from the more nuanced approach of the Court.[60]

4. NON-DISCRIMINATION

Although it is a universally recognized principle of considerable importance, the concept of discrimination is also not unproblematic. Identifying a difference in treatment between two people who appear to be similarly placed is only the first step in considering whether a breach of the principle of non-discrimination has taken place. The second step is to determine whether that difference in treatment was justified on any ground, given all of the circumstances. We will see some of the difficulties in identifying what constitutes

[57] Schwarze, n. 5 above, 991–1025; T. C. Hartley, *The Foundations of European Community Law* (3rd edn., 1994), 454–8.

[58] Case 15/85, *Consorzio Cooperative d'Abruzzo* v. *Commission* [1987] ECR 1005, [1988] 1 CMLR 841.

[59] Cases 42, 49/59, *SNUPAT* v. *High Authority* [1961] ECR 53; Case 14/61, *Hoogovens* v. *High Authority* [1962] ECR 253.

[60] For suggestions of a similar balancing approach in the UK, see Craig, n. 55 above, Ch. 18.

impermissible discrimination in later chapters dealing with the free movement of persons, services, and goods, as well as with sex discrimination.[61]

The non-discrimination principle in Community law is relevant in several distinct contexts. There are three major areas in which it arises and in which the Treaty makes specific reference to it, although it is also of broader application—hence its status as a 'general principle' of Community law. The three main areas are (1) the field of non-discrimination on grounds of nationality as expressed in Articles 6 (formerly 7), 48, 52, and 59–60 of the Treaty; (2) equal treatment of men and women as expressed chiefly in Article 119 and in secondary legislation; and (3) non-discrimination as between producers or consumers in the field of agriculture, in accordance with Article 40(3). There are also specific provisions such as Article 95, which prohibits the imposition of taxes which discriminate as between domestic products and those imported from other Member States and which is discussed in more detail in Chapter 13.

However, given its recognition by the Court as a general principle, the non-discrimination principle is not only applicable in the specific areas of Community policy in which the Treaty makes reference to it, but it may be applicable more generally where there is arbitrarily or unjustifiably unequal treatment of two persons within an area of Community competence. Examples of this are to be found in the context of staff policy, where the Court has held that the Community institutions are bound by the principle of equal treatment of the sexes, and that this is not restricted to equal pay or to what is specifically provided for in Article 119 and in the relevant secondary legislation.[62]

An area of considerable importance for the non-discrimination principle, given the numbers of 'guest workers' and visible minorities and the rise of the extreme right in the European Community, yet on which Community law has been virtually silent, is that of race. Apart from the work of the European Parliament, in setting up committees of inquiry into racism and xenophobia, and within its Committee on Civil Liberties, the Community has taken little action in this field. Various declarations against racism and xenophobia have been adopted by the Parliament and the other Community institutions and the European Council, but no other action has been taken to prevent or to deter racial discrimination within the scope of Community law.[63] Thus, the Community has never actually stated that the elimination of race discrimination constitutes a 'fundamental principle' of Community law, as it has said of sex discrimination.[64]

[61] See Chs. 13–18.

[62] Case 75, 117/82, *Razzouk and Beydoun* v. *Commission* [1984] ECR 1509, paras. 16–17. See also Case 20/71, *Sabbatini* [1972] ECR 345; [1972] CMLR 945, para. 3, and Case 149/77, *Defrenne* v. *Sabena* [1978] ECR 1365, [1978] 3 CMLR 312, paras. 26–7.

[63] However in its White Paper on Social Policy, COM(94)333, Pt. IV, the Commission has stated that it will press for special powers to combat racial discrimination to be included in the Treaty. Further, the European Council established a Consultative Committee in 1994 to consider matters relating to intolerance and racism in the European Union.

[64] See C. Docksey, 'The Principle of Equality between Women and Men as a Fundamental Right under Community Law' [1991] ILJ 258, for an argument that the Community's approach to sex discrimination should also be applicable to race. On sexual orientation discrimination see the European Parliament's resolution, [1994] OJ C61/40.

To discriminate means to treat things or people differently, which in itself seems innocuous enough. In Community law it becomes impermissible, however, when it is done without adequate justification on the basis of a prohibited ground, such as sex or nationality, or when there is no relevant difference between two persons (e.g. similar members of staff, or producers of competing goods) which would justify a difference in their treatment. This in itself is not necessarily an easy criterion to apply, since it is not always clear what factors may be taken into account to determine whether or not two persons are 'similarly situated'. Nor is it clear whether, if differences in situation are taken into account to justify discriminatory treatment, this should be seen as a form of justified 'positive discrimination' or should in fact be seen as not discriminatory at all.[65]

A straightforward example of discrimination on grounds of sex would be where a woman was paid a lower wage than a man for doing exactly the same job, and a simple example of discrimination on grounds of nationality would be where a United Kingdom employer refused to hire any employee who was not British. The more difficult situations arise where the discrimination is not clear and direct, as in the examples given, but is either indirect and disguised, or is entirely unintentional but discriminatory in its impact. Indirect and disguised discrimination would occur if, for example, a United Kingdom employer claimed to hire workers of any nationality so long as they had received their education in the United Kingdom, since in practice this requirement would not be fulfilled by most non-United Kingdom nationals.[66] A form of unintentional and indirect sex discrimination may occur if, for example, an employer pays part-time workers less per hour than full-time workers, where the overwhelming majority of part-time workers are women.[67]

In Community law, direct or deliberate disguised discrimination on grounds of sex or nationality is prohibited, subject to fairly limited grounds of exception,[68] whereas indirect and unintentional discrimination may be justified on a variety of non-exhaustive grounds.[69] Thus in the context of nationality discrimination, a language requirement which is indirectly discriminatory may be justified if it is proportionate and genuinely required for the job to be undertaken.[70] Similarly in the context of sex discrimination, the payment of a higher hourly wage to full-time than to part-time workers may, even where it indirectly discriminates against women, be 'objectively justified' on grounds

[65] See case C–132/92, *Roberts* v. *Birds Eye Walls Ltd* [1993] ECR I–5579 and the discussion in Ch. 18.

[66] An example of indirect discrimination can be found in Case 152/73, *Sotgiu* v. *Deutsche Bundespost* [1974] ECR 153, where the difference in pay was based on the country or place of recruitment, rather than the nationality of the worker.

[67] See below 801–14.

[68] See Chs. 15 and 16 on the subject of justifications for direct discrimination in the context of free movement of persons and services. See Ch. 18 on the subject of direct sex discrimination, for which limited grounds of exception are provided in some of the secondary legislation.

[69] See Chs. 15–18.

[70] See Chapter 15 and Art. 3(1) of Reg. 1612/68 on freedom of movement for workers.

relating to the needs of the employer.[71] Discrimination on grounds of nationality and on grounds of sex will be discussed in fuller detail in Chapters 15 to 18.

Like other legal concepts which have the status of 'general principles' of Community law, the principle of non-discrimination may be relevant in many different ways. It can be pleaded as a ground for the annulment of a Community measure under Article 173, or in the context of a declaration of invalidity or as an aid to interpretation of Community law under Article 177, or in an action for damages against a Community institution under Article 215. It can also be pleaded against Member State authorities when they are acting within the field of Community law, such as in the implementation of a Community scheme or the operation of a Community policy.[72]

An illustration of the principle's application and usefulness (or otherwise) in different kinds of legal proceedings can be found in a series of agricultural cases which arose in the 1970s. In the *Quellmehl and Gritz* cases actions in damages were brought against the Community. Producers of maize products objected that the Community had caused them loss by subsidizing starch, a direct competitor to the maize products, which had had their subsidy withdrawn.[73] The Court agreed that there had been a breach of the principle of non-discrimination and awarded them damages for the loss they had suffered. Thus the non-discrimination principle has the status of a 'superior rule of law' for the purposes of an action in damages against the Community under Article 215. However, it has at times been easier to convince the Court to annul a Community measure for violation of the discrimination principle than it has been to obtain damages as a result of such violation. In the *Skimmed Milk* and *Isoglucose* cases, the Court also acknowledged that there was impermissible discrimination by the Council in its treatment of particular producers as compared with its treatment of the producers of competing products, but for varying reasons it found the criteria for an award of damages to the 'victims' of discrimination were not satisfied.[74]

[71] e.g. Case 96/80, *Jenkins* v. *Kingsgate (Clothing Productions) Ltd* [1981] ECR 911, [1981] 2 CMLR 24. See further Ch. 18.

[72] See e.g. Case 207/86, *APESCO* v. *Commission* [1988] ECR 2151, para. 23 and Cases 201 and 202/85, *Klensch* v. *Secrétaire d'Etat à l'Agriculture et à la Viticulture* [1986] ECR 3477, [1988] 1 CMLR 151.

[73] Cases 241, 242, 245–250/78, *D.G.V.* v. *Council and Commission* [1979] ECR 3017; Cases 64, 113/76, 167, 239/78, 27, 28, and 45/79, *Dumortier* v. *Council* [1979] ECR 3091; Case 238/78, *Ireks-Arcady* v. *Council and Commission* [1979] ECR 2955, Cases 261 and 262/78 *Interquell* v. *Council and Commission* [1979] ECR 3045. For further discussion see Ch. 12.

[74] See *e.g.* Cases 116 and 124/77, *Amylum and Tunnel Refineries* v. *Council and Commission* [1979] ECR 3497 in the context of isoglucose, and Case 114/76, n. 17 above; Cases 83 and 94/76, 4, 15 & 40/77, *Bayerische HNL Vermehrungsbetriebe GmbH & Co KG* v. *Council and Commission* [1978] ECR 1209, [1978] 3 CMLR 566, in the context of skimmed milk.

5. FURTHER READING

ARNULL, A., *General Principles of EEC Law and the Individual* (Leicester University Press/Pinter, 1990)

SCHWARZE, J., *European Administrative Law* (Office for Official Publications of the European Communities/Sweet and Maxwell, 1992)

9

Enforcement Actions against Member States: Articles 169 and 170

1. INTRODUCTION

Among the tasks entrusted to the Commission by Article 155 of the EC Treaty is that of ensuring the proper application of Community law. The first part of that Article provides:

> In order to ensure the proper functioning and development of the common market, the Commission shall:—ensure that the provisions of this Treaty and the measures taken by the institutions pursuant thereto are applied;

This general function of the Commission is fleshed out by other specific Treaty provisions which indicate the nature of the action the Commission must take in fulfilment of its responsibility. Although, clearly, the institutions of the Community must comply with the Treaty and with provisions of secondary legislation, the Commission's primary task in ensuring the application of Community law is to see that the Member States observe and implement it properly. The Treaty provides for various enforcement mechanisms which involve judicial proceedings against the Member States, which are brought either by the Commission or by another Member State.[1] In particular, the procedure set out in Article 169 gives the Commission a broad power to bring enforcement proceedings against Member States which it considers to be in breach of their obligations under Community law.[2] Article 169 provides as follows:

[1] Some of the specific enforcement procedures provided for in the Treaty other than the general procedure in Art. 169 are dealt with elsewhere: see Ch. 24 on Art. 93(2) and Ch. 25 on Art. 100a(4). Further, under Art. 180 the Board of the European Investment Bank and the Council of the European Central Bank have powers similar to those of the Commission under Art. 169. Art. 225 also provides for an enforcement procedure where Member States have relied on Art. 224 to derogate from fundamental Community rules: see e.g. Case C–120/94R, *Commission* v. *Greece*, [1994] ECR I–3037.

[2] Under the similar enforcement provision of Art. 88 ECSC, the High Authority is empowered to record the failure of a state to fulfil its obligations, without first bringing the case before the ECJ. Following such a finding, however, the state affected may itself bring the matter before the Court. The parallel Euratom provisions are Arts. 141–2, which mirror Arts. 169–70 of the EC.

> If the Commission considers that a Member State has failed to fulfil an obligation under this Treaty, it shall deliver a reasoned opinion on the matter after giving the State concerned the opportunity to submit its observations.
>
> If the State concerned does not comply with the opinion within the period laid down by the Commission, the latter may bring the matter before the Court.

This procedure envisages that an apparent breach of Community law by a Member State should, if possible, be resolved or remedied after consultation between the Commission and the Member State concerned, without the need for immediate recourse to litigation before the Court. Clearly, repeated rulings by the Court that Member States have failed or refused to give effect to European Community law do not present a picture of an integrated, harmonious, or thriving Community. The Article 169 procedure thus aims to resolve potential Community–state confrontations in the first instance by political means.[3] Consequently the Commission is required, if it considers a Member State to be in breach of Treaty requirements, to give that state an opportunity to make its position on the alleged breach known to the Commission.

(a) The Procedure under Article 169 and its Function

The Commission initiates Article 169 proceedings either in response to a complaint from someone in a Member State, or on its own initiative from information gained, for example through the press, or from Parliamentary questions, or in discussions with national officials. The Commission has stated that complaints from citizens constitute the main source for the detection of infringements, and has expressed the view that the Article 169 procedure can, in this way, contribute towards creating a more participatory Community in which citizens can play a role in the enforcement of law.

> The large number of complaints is accounted for mainly by the growing awareness among ordinary people of the Commission's importance and, in some cases, by the limited means of redress at national level or the tendency to appeal to the Community when all national remedies have been exhausted. The Commission's complaints procedure is easily accessible, as it involves no formalities or expense. The Commission has tried to encourage its use with the aim of improving the application of Community law and at the same time fostering a real people's Europe. The success of the campaign has surpassed expectations, in particular on the environmental front.[4]

[3] See the *8th Annual Report* to the European Parliament on Commission Monitoring of the Application of Community Law 1990, [1991] OJ C338/6–7, where the Commission stressed its attempts to develop and support measures other than solely Art. 169 proceedings, to improve the application of Community law.

[4] *10th Annual Report* (1992) [1993] OJ C233/7. See also the *11th Annual Report* (1993), [1994] OJ C154/6.

However, despite this optimistic assessment of the value of Article 169 for individuals, we shall see that the individual in fact plays no role in the proceedings themselves and, indeed, has no say in determining whether or not the Commission initiates proceedings against a Member State.[5] The procedure is seen as something of an opportunity for political dialogue between the Commission and the states, with litigation as a last resort, and the participation of individual or even corporate complainants is not envisaged. Thus it may be a cheap and informal method of complaint, but the Commission ultimately has complete discretion as to whether or how it chooses to deal with the complaint.

(i) Negotiations at the initial *pre-contentious stage* give the Member State the occasion to explain its position and preferably to reach an accommodation with the Commission.

(ii) If the matter is not clarified or resolved informally between the two at this stage, the state will be *formally notified* of the specific infringement alleged by means of a letter from the Commission. The state is usually given two months to reply, except in cases of urgency, and the Commission normally decides within a year either to close a case or to proceed.

(iii) If, after negotiation with the state, the matter has not been resolved, the Commission may proceed to the stage of issuing a *reasoned opinion*. The reasoned opinion sets out clearly the grounds on which the alleged infringement rests, and marks the beginning of the two-month time period within which the Member State must comply, if it is to avoid stage

(iv) which is *referral* of the matter by the Commission *to the Court of Justice*.

In its *Eighth Report* to the European Parliament on Commission monitoring of the application of Community law 1990,[6] the Commission emphasized the sharp increase in the number of letters of formal notice which it sent to Member States—an increase from 664 in 1989 to 960 in 1990.[7] However, the proportionate increase in the number of reasoned opinions subsequently issued was considerably lower and the overall number of actions brought before the Court was down from ninety-four in 1989 to seventy-seven in 1990.

A year later in its *Ninth Annual Report*, the Commission this time noted that the number of reasoned opinions had risen sharply from 1990 to 1991, and it attributed this to the fact that in many cases its new and stricter procedure of issuing formal notices had not produced any response from the Member State concerned.[8] However, the number of cases initiated before the Court had fallen again from seventy-eight to sixty-five,[9] which the Commission took to highlight the fact 'that despite the sharp increase in reasoned opinions, infringements are being terminated before the final stage of the procedure is

[5] See Case 247/87, *Star Fruit* v. *Commission* [1989] ECR 291, [1990] 1 CMLR 733.
[6] [1991] OJ C338/6.
[7] *Ibid.*
[8] *9th Annual Report* (1991) [1992] OJ C250/6–7.
[9] *11th Annual Report*, n. 4 above.

reached'.[10] A similar pattern showed itself over 1992 and 1993, with an initial drop followed by an increase in the number of reasoned opinions, but a decline in the number of cases actually referred to the Court.[11] This number remained at sixty-four in 1992 and dropped to forty-four in 1993. According to the Commission, this ultimate drop in the number of cases reaching the Court highlights 'the effectiveness of action by the Commission, which succeeds in most cases in persuading Member States to observe Community law without having to go so far as a referral to the Court'[12], and it reflects the Commission's objective 'of using the Article 169 procedure to settle infringement cases rather than to sanction them at all costs'.[13] The Commission evidently values the opportunity which the pre-contentious stage gives it to spur the Member States into compliance without having to have recourse to more formal methods of enforcement, and has said that its 'contacts with government departments play a real part in increasing Member States' awareness and rallying them to action'.[14]

Clearly, then, although the Article 169 procedure is vital to help the Commission in monitoring the performance of Community obligations by the Member States, its value lies as much in the process of negotiation and settlement of differences between the states and the Community, as in the opportunity it provides for the Court to give a firm judicial ruling that certain state action constitutes a breach of Treaty obligations.

Further, the public, centralized Community enforcement mechanism provided by Article 169 is simply one mechanism for ensuring the application of EC law, and it is not by any means the best or the most effective method. In the first place, the Commission has neither the time nor the resources to detect and follow through every instance of national infringement of Community law. Secondly, there are pragmatic and political reasons why the Commission, even if it possessed the capacity to monitor all such infringements, might not want to pursue to judgment every alleged breach by a Member State.

Thirdly, until the ratification of the TEU, although it could cause political embarrassment and impose additional pressure on a Member State to comply, a judgment of the Court under Article 169 carried no sanction and was of declaratory effect only. Since November 1993, however, Article 171 has been amended to confer power on the Court to impose fines upon Member States which have been found to be in breach but which have failed to comply with the judgment.

[10] *9th Annual Report*, n. 8 above.

[11] *10th Annual Report*, and *11th Annual Report*, both n. 4 above.

[12] *11th Annual Report*, n. 4 above.

[13] *8th Annual Report*, n. 3 above.

[14] *10th Annual Report*, n. 4 above.

(b) Sharpening Article 169 as an Enforcement Procedure: The Pecuniary Penalty

Article 171 now provides:

> 1. If the Court of Justice finds that a Member State has failed to fulfil an obligation under this Treaty, the State shall be required to take the necessary measures to comply with the judgment of the Court of Justice.
>
> 2. If the Commission considers that the Member State concerned has not taken such measures it shall, after giving that State the opportunity to submit its observations, issue a reasoned opinion specifying the points on which the Member State concerned has not complied with the judgment of the Court of Justice.
>
> If the Member State concerned fails to take the necessary measures to comply with the Court's judgment within the time-limit laid down by the Commission, the latter may bring the case before the Court of Justice. In so doing it shall specify the amount of the lump sum or penalty payment to be paid by the Member State concerned which it considers appropriate in the circumstances.
>
> If the Court of Justice finds that the Member State concerned has not complied with its judgment it may impose a lump sum or penalty payment on it.
>
> This procedure shall be without prejudice to Article 170.

For the first time, the Court has jurisdiction under the Treaty to impose a pecuniary penalty on a Member State which has failed to comply with a previous judgment of the Court finding that state to be in breach of the Treaty. No upper limit is provided in the Article,[15] and guidance on an appropriate sum is left to the Commission, although the Court is clearly not to be bound by such suggestion or guidance. The efficiency and effectiveness of this new power has been questioned, given that there is no real mechanism for 'collection' should a Member State refuse to comply, and given the absence of injunctive powers.[16]

D. Curtin, The Constitutional Structure of the Union: A Europe of Bits and Pieces[17]

> The terms of Article 171, as amended, only envisage the imposition of administrative sanctions and not sanctions in the form of conferring the Commission, for example, with the power to seek an injunction against the State concerned, either before the Court itself, or, alternatively, before the appropriate national court. It would, however, have been possible, in the interests of maximum efficiency, to envisage a more far-reaching and open-ended wording, which could have left it to

[15] Art. 172, which provides for the imposition of penalties by the Court under regs. adopted by the Council and the Parliament, also specifies that the Court's jurisdiction under such legislation may be unlimited.

[16] Although the Court has power to order injunctive measures in interim proceedings under Art. 186, it does not have these powers under Art. 171 when giving judgment in Art. 169 proceedings. See below for discussion of Art. 186.

[17] (1993) 30 CMLRev. 17, 33.

the discretion of the Court to tailor the 'sanction' to the actual default in question, for example by ordering the Member State concerned to take certain very specific measures (other than a lump sum payment).

The language used in Article 171 EC is in the singular ('a lump sum payment') and may be interpreted as meaning that the Court cannot impose sanctions on an on-going or periodic basis until it has been quite satisfied that the infringement of Community law in question has indeed been terminated. If this is in fact the case, then the only remedy in such circumstances against a persistingly recalcitrant Member State, it seems, would be for the Commission to restart the Article 171 procedure. It may in any event prove exceedingly difficult in practice to arrive at a figure which will have a real deterrent effect. In the event that a Member State does not actually pay the prescribed lump sum or penalty payment, it may be crucial that some withholding method is developed for Community money earmarked for a particular Member State. No explicit power is conferred on the Court to order the suspension of payment of sums due from the Community to such recalcitrant Member State.

The Commission, on the other hand, despite its acknowledgment of serious delay in complying with adverse judgments,[18] seems concerned to emphasize the more conciliatory methods of ensuring compliance with Community law, and to look to the 'penalty payment' as a supplementary tool rather than as its most important enforcement method. In 1994 the Commission commented on Article 171 as a new instrument to 'strengthen its hand', but stressed that its enhanced powers would not lead it to neglect more co-operative forms of negotiation with Member States over the enforcement of Community law:

Thought is now being given to how this new instrument should be implemented in practice. It must be said that, at present, there are often long delays before Court judgments are implemented.

However, the Commission's tougher legal powers must not undermine its pursuit of cooperation and dialogue with national government departments, as this method very often leads to cases being settled at an early stage of proceedings.

The Commission therefore intends to encourage the holding of 'package meetings' and, in view of the success of the meetings on directives, to increase their frequency and extend them to other Member States, according to specific needs. It also intends to lay greater emphasis, in its contacts with national authorities, on the quality of national implementing measures, i.e. compliance with the requirements of directives. This is an aspect which is sometimes neglected, especially in certain areas of the internal market where all the implementing measures have not yet produced their full effect as they fail to meet all the objectives of the relevant directive.

Through this combination of tougher infringement procedures and sustained

[18] See Case C–291/93, *Commission* v. *Italy* [1994] ECR I–859, para. 6, in which the Court ruled that, although Art. 171 did not specify the period within which a judgment must be complied with, the interest in the immediate and uniform application of Community law required compliance as soon as possible.

administrative cooperation, the Commission will continue to play an effective role as guardian of the Treaties.[19]

2. THE RELATIONSHIP BETWEEN ARTICLE 169 AND THE 'PRIVATE ENFORCEMENT' MECHANISM OF ARTICLE 177

It is apparent from the early rulings of the Court of Justice, which established the principle of direct effect, that the institutional or state enforcement procedures under Article 169 and Article 170 are but one mode provided for ensuring the proper application of Community law. That the EC Treaty provides for other means of monitoring the enforcement of Community law was made clear by the Court in the case of *Van Gend en Loos*:

Case 26/62, Van Gend en Loos
[1963] ECR 1, [1963] CMLR 105

The facts of the case are set out in Chapter 6.[20] The Belgian, Dutch, and German Governments had argued before the Court that the reference was inadmissible under Article 177. It was claimed that if a Member State's failure to fulfil its Community obligations could be brought before the Court by a procedure other than those under Articles 169 and 170, the legal protection of that state would be unacceptably diminished.

THE ECJ[21]

In addition the argument based on Articles 169 and 170 of the Treaty put forward by the three Governments which have submitted observations to the Court in their statements of case is misconceived. The fact that these Articles of the Treaty enable the Commission and the Member States to bring before the Court a State which has not fulfilled its obligations does not mean that individuals cannot plead these obligations, should the occasion arise, before a national court, any more than the fact that the Treaty places at the disposal of the Commission ways of ensuring that obligations imposed upon those subject to the Treaty are observed, precludes the possibility, in action between individuals before a national court, of pleading infringements of these obligations . . .

The vigilance of individuals concerned to protect their rights amounts to an effective supervision in addition to the supervision entrusted by Articles 169 and 170 to the diligence of the Commission and of the Member States.

Advocate General Roemer explained further the difference between the procedure under Articles 169 to 170 and the application under Article 177 in this case:[22]

[19] *11th Annual Report*, n. 4 above.
[20] At 241.
[21] [1963] ECR 1, 13.
[22] *Ibid.* 25.

As regards the doubts which have arisen concerning the relation between the present proceedings and the procedure under Articles 169 and 170 of the Treaty, and the danger of circumventing that procedure, the following must be noted: Article 169 governs the judicial finding of an infringement of the Treaty by Member States. It can be invoked by the Commission if the Member State concerned does not comply with the opinion of the Commission. Article 170 provides an analogous procedure, which is initiated by an application to the Court by another Member State, and indeed, in certain circumstances, without a previous reasoned opinion by the Commission.

In this case, if the Court deals with the second question within the limits of its jurisdiction, it can give only a general interpretation of Article 12, of its meaning and purpose, leaving it to the national court to draw the necessary conclusions from it. There must not be any finding that its conduct is compatible with the Treaty, or that it constitutes an infringement of it.

The distinction outlined by Advocate General Roemer in *Van Gend* was that, in an application under Article 177, the Court will give only a ruling on the interpretation of Community law, leaving it for the national court to spell out the practical implications of that ruling in the particular case; whereas in proceedings under Article 169 or 170 the Court will actually pronounce directly on the compatibility of a Member State's conduct with Community law. In *Mölkerei-Zentrale* the Court ruled that proceedings by an individual were intended to protect individual rights in a specific case, whereas Commission proceedings were intended to ensure the general and uniform observance of Community law.[23] This meant, in the Court's view, that the two kinds of proceedings 'have different objects, aims and effects, and a parallel may not be drawn between them'.[24]

The importance of the distinction between the two kinds of proceedings was also emphasized by Advocate General Lagrange in a case where the Italian Government had argued in effect that to allow an individual to plead the direct effect of Community law through the mechanism of Article 177 would simply get around the fact that individuals had no right to bring an enforcement action under Article 169. Italy clearly wanted to avail itself of the safeguards of an action under Article 169 with its pre-litigation procedure, where the Court's decision would be of declaratory effect only, and where national law would not change until the Italian legislature chose to adopt measures to comply with that judgment of the Court. If an individual succeeded in pleading the direct effect of the Community provision in Article 177 proceedings, on the other hand, the Community provision would have to be given immediate effect over the national law by the national court which had referred the case.

[23] Case 28/67, *Mölkerei-Zentrale Westfalen* v. *Hauptzollamt Paderborn* [1968] ECR 143, 153.
[24] *Ibid.*

Case 6/64, Costa v. ENEL
[1964] ECR 585, [1964] CMLR 425

The facts of the case are set out in Chapter 4.[25]

ADVOCATE GENERAL LAGRANGE[26]

What must be avoided—and this is a danger which becomes apparent as cases under Article 177 multiply—is that this Court, under the guise of interpretation, might more or less substitute itself for the national court, which, let us not forget, retains jurisdiction to apply the Treaty and the regulations of the Community . . .

I must first dispose of the second objection, that infringement of the Treaty by a subsequent domestic law which conflicts with the Treaty can only be pleaded under the procedure for a finding of default by a Member State as laid down in Articles 169 to 171, a procedure which is not open to individuals and which does not affect the validity of the impugned law until it has been finally repealed following a judgment of the Court declaring its incompatibility with the Treaty.

However, despite the Advocate General's concern to emphasize the distinction between the interpretation of Community law and the application of that interpretation to the facts of a case involving national law, it is clear from *Van Gend en Loos* and from many subsequent decisions that the Court in Article 177 rulings on interpretation often performs a similar function to that in its Article 169 rulings on compatibility with Community law.[27]

The most common ground for enforcement proceedings against Member States is their failure to implement directives correctly or at all. This helps to explain the Court's development of the direct effect doctrine, since the result is to bypass the problem of national non-implementation of directives by encouraging their direct enforcement at the national judicial level. In this way it is a supplementary and considerably more effective method of enforcement than the direct enforcement action provided for in Article 169.

In *Van Gend* and *Costa* v. *Enel*, of course, the Member States were seeking to resist a Court ruling on the direct effect of Community law, and so they argued that the proper method of seeking compliance by a state with Community law was for the Commission to bring public enforcement proceedings under Article 169. Ironically, over two decades later, the German government made effectively the opposite argument by way of defence to an enforcement action brought against it under Article 169 by the Commission.

Case 29/84, Commission v. Germany
[1985] ECR 1661, [1986] 3 CMLR 579

Germany contended that the action brought against it for failure to implement the so-called 'nurses' directive' should be dismissed, on the ground that the administrative practice and constitutional principles of German law were adequate to 'implement' the directive without the need for specific legislative enactment. The

[25] At 158 [26] [1964] ECR 585, 601–2. [27] See Ch. 10, 442–4

Commission argued that Germany was in fact contending not that the directive had been properly transposed, but that it did not need transposition.

THE ECJ

21. Even if it is conceded that the administration is bound by its own practice to the extent indicated by the German Government, the Commission denies that that is sufficient to provide the legal certainty, clarity and transparency sought by the directives. In particular a Member State cannot rely on the direct effect of the principle of non-discrimination on grounds of nationality in order to evade the obligation to incorporate into domestic law a directive which is intended precisely to give that principle practical effect.

. . .

29. . . . As the Commission has pointed out, the direct effect of that Community principle may not be used in order to evade the obligation to implement a directive providing for specific measures to facilitate and secure the full application of that principle in the Member States.

The Court thus underlined the difference in function and effect of a plea of direct effect under Article 177 on the one hand and an enforcement ruling under Article 169 on the other. It made clear that the direct effectiveness of a Community provision, and thus the ability of individuals to enforce the provision before national courts, would not be accepted as a defence or an answer to a Commission action under Article 169 for failure to implement that provision.[28]

3. THE COMMISSION'S DISCRETION IN BRINGING ARTICLE 169 PROCEEDINGS

There has been considerable debate over the extent of the Commission's discretion to bring proceedings under Article 169. On the one hand, this discretion may be problematic if it leads the Commission to be less than strict with defaulting Member States, thus possibly undermining the effectiveness of Article 169 as an enforcement mechanism. But on the other hand, the breadth of its discretion could equally lead to an unfair or oppressive use of Article 169 proceedings, if there are too few constraints of time and procedure on the Commission in its exercise.

To begin with the first concern, given the role the Commission plays and the various functions it exercises as a Community institution, it has been argued that there may be political and other reasons leading it to exercise its discretion against bringing proceedings, even where it is clear that a Member State is in breach of the Treaty.

[28] See also Cases 102/79, *Commission* v. *Belgium* [1980] ECR 1473, [1981] 1 CMLR 282 and 168/85, *Commission* v. *Italy* [1986] ECR 2945, [1988] 1 CMLR 580.

P. P. Craig, Once upon a Time in the West: Direct Effect and the Federalization of EEC Law[29]

The Commission possesses a wide range of powers, including those of a legislative as well as a judicial nature. This can lead to tension which manifests itself in the exercise of prosecutorial discretion. An important legislative initiative may be under consideration in the Council, with the consequence that the Commission may be wary of pursuing an action against a Member State lest the latter should manifest its displeasure by rendering the passage of legislation more protracted. If the legislation is of importance, and the wrongdoing is of less significance, the temptation to ignore the latter, or to pursue it less vigorously, may be great, even though the breach may be of import to the particular group affected by it.

It seems reasonably clear from the terms of paragraph two of Article 169 that, once it has issued a reasoned opinion indicating that a Member State is in breach, the Commission has complete discretion as to whether or not to bring the matter before the Court ('the Commission . . . *may*'), but there has been some debate over whether it has the same discretion in respect of issuing a reasoned opinion in the first place. In other words, if the Commission considers that a Member State has failed to fulfil a Treaty obligation, is it *obliged* to issue a reasoned opinion to that effect? Whereas paragraph 2 states that the Commission 'may' bring the matter before the Court, paragraph 1 states that the Commission 'shall' deliver a reasoned opinion where it considers that a state has failed to fulfil a Treaty obligation. It has been suggested that this language nevertheless leaves the Commission with discretion whether and when to issue a reasoned opinion:

A. Evans, The Enforcement Procedure of Article 169 EEC: Commission Discretion[30]

First, no such obligation can arise, unless the Commission 'considers' that a breach has occurred. Hence a subjective and undefined power of appreciation is given to the Commission. Technically such a power may not constitute discretion but the effective distinction is slight. Secondly, no time-limits are laid down in paragraph one. As a result, the Commission seems free to select the date for delivery of a reasoned opinion.

Apart from the concern about insufficient exercise by the Commission of its discretion to bring proceedings, the second concern mentioned above was that the Commission may not be sufficiently constrained in the way it exercises its discretion under Article 169 in bringing proceedings. It has been argued before the Court that, despite the relatively open language of Article 169, the Commission's discretion is not unlimited. In particular it has been argued that there are certain constraints on the Commission's decision whether and why

[29] (1992) 12 OJLS 453, 456. [30] (1979) 4 ELRev. 442, 445.

an action should be brought, as well as certain constraints on the time at which proceedings should be brought.

In response to a challenge to enforcement proceedings on the ground of the Commission's motives for bringing the action, the Court has emphasized that the Article 169 proceedings are entirely 'objective'. This apparently means that the Court will examine only whether the infringement alleged by the Commission does in fact exist, and will not look into the Commission's motives for bringing the action.[31]

Case 416/85, Commission v. United Kingdom [1988] ECR 3127, [1988] 3 CMLR 169

The Commission brought an action alleging that that United Kingdom's continued zero-rating of VAT on certain products and services was in breach of a Council Directive on harmonization of turnover taxes. The United Kingdom challenged the admissibility of the Commission's action, claiming that it was attempting to evade the procedures set up under a different provision of the Directive.

THE ECJ

8. The United Kingdom contends that there is a political motive behind the Commission's application to the Court and that such a motive is not a proper basis for an action pursuant to Article 169 EEC. The Commission's action is intended in fact to attain by means of judicial proceedings an objective which can be achieved only by a decision of the Community legislature. It is clear from the Commission's reply that its intention in bringing these proceedings is to bypass the procedural requirements of Article 28 of the Sixth Directive, under which it is for the Council, acting unanimously, to decide to abolish the exemptions permitted by that article. The United Kingdom therefore submits that it is not the task of the Court 'to substitute itself for the political procedures envisaged by Article 28 of the Sixth Directive and to substitute an immediate obligation upon a Member State for the progressive compliance envisaged by Article 28'.

9. That argument cannot be upheld. In the context of the balance of powers between the institutions laid down in the Treaty, it is not for the Court to consider what objectives are pursued in an action brought under Article 169 of the Treaty. Its role is to decide whether or not the Member State in question has failed to fulfil its obligations as alleged. As the Court held in Case 7/68 *Commission* v. *Italy* [1968] ECR 423, an action against a Member-State for failure to fulfil its obligations, the bringing of which is a matter for the Commission in its entire discretion, is objective in nature.

It has also been argued that there are restrictions on the time at which proceedings should be brought, and limits to the length of time the Commission can take in bringing proceedings against a Member State on the basis of a

[31] See also Case C–200/88, *Commission* v. *Greece* [1990] ECR I–4299, [1992] 2 CMLR 151, para. 9, where the Court repeated that it was not for it to decide whether the Commission's discretion under Art. 169 had been 'wisely exercised'.

specific infringement. An attempt to make the first of these arguments was rejected by the Court in an early case:

Case 7/68, Commission v. Italy [1968] ECR 423, [1969] CMLR 1

The Commission brought an action against Italy for allegedly breaching Article 16 of the Treaty by continuing to impose a tax on the export of art treasures. In the course of the proceedings, the Italian Government complained to the Court that the Commission had not acted in accordance with the spirit of Article 2 of the EEC Treaty, since it had brought the enforcement action before the Court just as it was practically certain that the Italian Parliament was about to dissolve. On this ground the Italian Government felt that the Court should declare the Commission's action inadmissible.

THE ECJ[32]

It is for the Commission, under Article 169 of the Treaty, to judge at what time it shall bring an action before the court; the considerations which determine its choice of time cannot affect the admissibility of the action, which follows only objective rules.

Initially, the Court appeared to take a similarly 'hands-off' approach to the question of the length of time the Commission took to bring proceedings in respect of a particular infringement.

Case 7/71, Commission v. France [1971] ECR 1003, [1972] CMLR 453

The Commission brought an action against France under Article 141 of the Euratom Treaty, which is the equivalent of Article 169 of the EEC Treaty. France claimed that the Commission had known of the conduct constituting the alleged infringement for six years, and thus that its enforcement action against France should be deemed inadmissible on the ground that it was too late.

THE ECJ

5. The action for a declaration that a State has failed to fulfil an obligation provided for by Article 141 does not have to be brought within a predetermined period, since, by reason of its nature and its purpose, this procedure involves a power on the part of the Commission to consider the most appropriate means and time-limits for the purposes of putting an end to any contraventions of the Treaty.

6. The fact that the Commission only commenced its action after a lengthy period of time cannot have the effect of regularizing a continuing contravention.

ADVOCATE GENERAL ROEMER[33]

Article 141 of the Euratom Treaty does not provide any limitation period for the execution of proceedings to establish an infringement of the Treaty. This is certainly deliberate and is perfectly justified . . .

[32] [1968] ECR 423, 428. [33] [1971] ECR 1003, 1026.

> It would not be reasonable to initiate [the action for enforcement] immediately on every occasion. To invoke it excessively may in fact detract from its efficacy which is in any case limited because of the absence of any sanctions. Moreover, this procedure naturally puts in issue to a certain extent the prestige of the Member State concerned, even though it is merely an objective procedure intended to clarify the legal situation, without any moral judgement. For these reasons it seems proper to rule out any automatic application, any compulsion to initiate it, and instead to leave to the Commission a discretionary power to decide whether and when the procedure should be initiated.

However, in more recent proceedings against The Netherlands, the Court has indicated that the Commission's discretion when to bring proceedings is not entirely unfettered, and that the Treaty may place certain substantive limits upon its exercise. The Commission in this case had decided to wait until the Court had given judgment in another case before going ahead with these infringement proceedings:

Case C–96/89, Commission v. Netherlands
[1991] ECR 2461

THE ECJ

14. The Netherlands Government considers, in the first place, that the application is inadmissible owing to the delays attributable to the Commission in these proceedings. While the first letter sent by the Commission to The Netherlands Government regarding the matters in question dates from 1 February 1984, the Commission did not bring its action until 21 March 1989, that is to say, more than five years later . . .

15. In that regard, it is sufficient to point out that, as the Court ruled in its judgment of 10 April 1984 in Case 324/82 *Commission* v. *Belgium* [1984] ECR 1861, the rules of Article 169 of the Treaty, unlike those of Article 93 which derogate expressly therefrom, must be applied and the Commission is not obliged to act within a specific period. In the present case, the Commission has explained that it had decided to await the Court's judgment . . . in the *Krohn* case, as well as the reactions of the Netherlands Government to that judgment before bringing this action. In doing that the Commission has not exercised the discretion which it has under Article 169 in a way that is contrary to the Treaty.

16. It is true that in certain cases the excessive duration of the pre-litigation procedure laid down by Article 169 is capable of making it more difficult for the Member State concerned to refute the Commission's arguments and of thus infringing the rights of the defence. However, in the instant case, the Netherlands Government has not proved that the unusual length of the procedure had any effect on the way in which it conducted its defence.

It is clear from this judgment that, although there are no specific rules requiring the Commission to act within a given period of time under Article 169, an excessive delay in the period before bringing a case before the Court might prejudice the rights of the Member State's defence to such an extent that the Commission's action could be deemed inadmissible by the Court.

Restrictions are also imposed on the Commission's discretion when to refer a matter to the Court after the issuing of a reasoned opinion, rather than on its discretion in commencing the litigation procedure in the first place. Clearly, excessive haste in requiring a response to a reasoned opinion is just as likely or even more likely to affect the ability of a Member State to exercise its rights of defence than is delay in commencing proceedings. In an action against Ireland, the Court referred to the Commission's 'regrettable behaviour' and reprimanded it for the short length of time it allowed the State for compliance with the reasoned opinion. However, the Commission's action was nevertheless admissible since, despite the short time period, the Commission in the case had in fact awaited Ireland's reply before referring the matter to the Court:

> The Court is compelled to state its disapproval of the Commission's behaviour in this regard. It is indeed unreasonable, as Ireland has pointed out, to allow a Member State five days to amend legislation which has been applied for more than 40 years and which, moreover, has not give rise to any action on the part of the Commission over the period which has elapsed since the accession of the Member State in question. Furthermore, it is clear that there was no particular urgency.[34]

In proceedings against Belgium, the Court actually declared the Commission's action inadmissible on account of the shortness of the time allowed for responding to the letter of formal notice and the reasoned opinion.[35] The Court ruled that a reasonable period must be allowed, although very short periods could be justified in circumstances of urgency or where the Member State was fully aware of the Commission's views long before the procedure started.[36]

However, the Court's unwillingness to require the Commission, apart from a case in which the rights of the defence may be prejudiced, to initiate Article 169 proceedings within a reasonable time contrasts with its approach to the action under Article 175 of the EC Treaty or Article 35 of the ECSC Treaty.[37] Proceedings under Articles 175 and 35 are the converse of the action under Article 169, in that they can be brought against one of the Community institutions for failure to take action required by the Treaty, rather than against a Member State. In the case of proceedings against a Community institution, the Court has held that the party bringing the action is required to do so within a reasonable period, even though Article 175 and Article 35 make no mention of any time limit. In an early action against the Commission,[38] The

34 Case 74/82, *Commission* v. *Ireland* [1984] ECR 317, para. 12.

35 Case 293/85, *Commission* v. *Belgium* [1988] ECR 305, [1989] 2 CMLR 527.

36 *Ibid.*, para. 14 of the judgment. See also Case C–56/90, *Commission* v. *U.K.* [1993] ECR I–4109, [1994] 1 CMLR 769.

37 See also Art. 148 Euratom.

38 Case 59/70, *Netherlands* v. *Commission* [1971] ECR 639, paras. 14–18 of the judgment.

Netherlands attempted to require the Commission to bring enforcement proceedings against France, but failed on the grounds that the action under Article 35 of the ECSC Treaty had not been brought within a reasonable period of time. Although the Court did not discuss Article 175, its reasoning would be equally applicable to that provision.

The desire of the Court not to place too many fetters on the Commission's discretion under Article 169 is further revealed by the Court's response to actions for 'failure to act' brought by *non-privileged* parties against the Commission under Article 35 of the ECSC Treaty or Article 175 of the EC Treaty, which have attempted to require the Commission to initiate infringement proceedings under Article 169. Even where they have in fact been brought against the Commission within a reasonable period of time, the Court has refused to admit such actions.[39] In *Star Fruit* v. *Commission*, the Court rejected an attempt by the company to use Article 175 so as to require the Commission to commence infringement proceedings against France:

> It is clear from the scheme of Article 169 of the Treaty that the Commission is not bound to commence the proceedings provided for in that provision but in this regard has a discretion which excludes the right for individuals to require that institution to adopt a specific position.[40]

Although the lack of a role for individuals in the initiation and conduct of enforcement proceedings has provoked adverse comment,[41] various reasons have been offered to explain the scope of the Commission's discretion in relation to the commencement of such proceedings.

J. Weiler, The Community System: The Dual Character of Supranationalism[42]

In the first place, the decision of the Commission and/or Member States to bring an action against an alleged violation by another Member State will often be influenced by political considerations; the Commission, for example, might not wish to prejudice delicate negotiations with a Member State. Secondly, effective supervision will depend on the ability of the Commission to monitor the implementation of Community law. Given the vast range of Community measures, this becomes an impossible task . . . Even if alleged violations were brought to the attention of the Commission, it is unrealistic to expect them to take up all but the most flagrant violations.

[39] By way of contrast, an action for failure to act under Art. 35 ECSC will lie against the Commission for failure to bring enforcement proceedings under Art. 88 ECSC. See the discussion in T. C. Hartley, *Foundations of European Community Law* (3rd edn., Oxford University Press, 1994), 319–20.

[40] Case 247/87, n. 5 above, para. 11 of the judgment.

[41] See E. Szyszczak, 'L'Espace Sociale Européenne: Reality, Dreams, or Nightmares?' [1990] *German Yearbook of International Law* 284, 300.

[42] (1981) 1 YBEL 267, 299.

F. Snyder, The Effectiveness of European Community Law[43]

The main form of dispute settlement used by the Commission is negotiation, and litigation is simply a part, sometimes inevitable but nevertheless generally a minor part, of this process. The Commission's view of litigation thus differs substantially from that of the European Court. In order to understand why this is so, we need to consider the role of the Commission in the Community litigation system.

Put simply, it is a distinctive role. The Commission has complete discretion in bringing infringement proceedings against Member States under Article 169; it is a necessary intermediary in actions by one Member State against another under Article 170; it will . . . be entitled under the amended Article 171 to request the Court to impose a lump sum or penalty payment on Member States which have failed to comply with a previous judgment by the Court; . . . Consequently the Commission can use litigation as an element in developing longer-term strategies. Instead of simply winning individual cases, it is able to concentrate on establishing basic principles or playing for rules.

Despite this discretion in bringing Member States before the Court, in its *Seventh Annual Report* to the European Parliament on Commission monitoring of the application of Community law 1989,[44] the Commission nevertheless stated that its approach to monitoring the compliance of Member States with EC law would henceforth entail the bringing of immediate infringement proceedings against a defaulting state as soon as the time limit for implementation of directives had passed. In its *Annual Report* a year later, the Commission stated that a further new procedure had been established, and that 'it now routinely (every two months) issues letters of formal notice when Member States have not notified national measures implementing Directives which are due for implementation'.[45] As noted at the outset, however, the effect of these letters may be to reduce rather than to increase the number of infringement proceedings which the Commission needs to initiate before the Court, since the Commission uses Article 169, where possible, as a tool to secure state compliance with Community law, rather than as a means of bringing the states before the Court.

4. THE REASONED OPINION

The reasoned opinion which the Commission is required to issue and to notify to a Member State forms an important part of the pre-judicial procedure under Article 169, and provides the Member State concerned with a measure of protection.[46] It is the formal means by which the Commission communicates to

[43] (1993) 56 MLR 19, 30.

[44] [1990] OJ C232/6.

[45] *8th Annual Report*, n. 3 above, at 7(e).

[46] Under Art. 88 ECSC, the Commission does not issue an opinion, but a reasoned decision which, unlike an opinion, is binding and reviewable.

the state the substance of the complaint against it, and specifies a time period within which the violation of Community law must be remedied. Effectively, it is aimed to provide the Member State with a clear statement of the case against it.

A. Evans, The Enforcement Procedure of Article 169 EEC: Commission Discretion[47]

The Court, therefore, regards the provisions of the first paragraph of Article 169 and, in particular, the requirement that a reasoned opinion be delivered, as being designed to ensure that the Member State concerned is given an adequate chance to answer the allegations brought against it. The paragraph seems to be an elaborate means of ensuring respect for the *audi alteram partem* principle of natural justice. It is to be interpreted not as obliging the Commission to act against a Member State 'considered' to be in breach of Community law, but rather as laying down certain procedural conditions which must be fulfilled before the Commission may invoke the jurisdiction of the Court against a defaulting Member State.

(a) Challenging the Reasoned Opinion

The obligation to provide reasons is one of general importance in Community law, and Article 191 of the Treaty specifically requires regulations, directives, and decisions to state the reasons on which they are based.[48] Article 169 then extends this requirement to opinions issued by the Commission under the enforcement procedure of that Article. Although the reasoning requirement in EC law constitutes an 'essential procedural requirement', breach of which constitutes a ground for annulment of a measure under Article 173, the Commission's opinion under Article 169 is not subject to an action for annulment because it does not have binding effect.[49] According to Advocate General Lagrange in an early case:

> The jurisdiction conferred on the Court by Article 171 is very clearly defined: it is to find that a Member State has failed to fulfil an obligation under the Treaty, and not to pronounce on the validity of the reasoned opinion . . .
>
> No formalism must be demanded of this document, since, as I have said, the reasoned opinion is not an administrative act subject to review by the Court of its legality.[50]

However, although it may not be subject to a direct action for annulment, a Member State which is the subject of a reasoned opinion under Article 169 can contest the lack of adequate reasoning in a different way, by raising the

[47] (1979) 4 ELRev. 442, 446.

[48] See Ch. 3.

[49] Case 48/65, *First Lütticke Case* (*Alfons Lütticke GmbH* v. *Commission*) [1966] ECR 19, [1966] CMLR 378.

[50] Case 7/61, *Commission* v. *Italy* [1961] ECR 317, 334, 336, [1962] CMLR 39.

matter before the Court if and when the enforcement proceedings reach that stage. It has been argued, however, that if the Commission fails to bring a case before the Court or fails to bring it soon enough, the Member State to whom the reasoned opinion has been addressed could seek to challenge it before the Court.[51] The basis for this argument is that the reasoned opinion might affect the state's legal position and create a situation of legal uncertainty, and that, even if the state believed it to be legally incorrect, there would be no opportunity for the Court to consider it without allowing that state a direct challenge.

Member States have, however, indirectly challenged the legality of the reasoned opinion when proceedings under Article 169 were brought against them before the Court of Justice.

Case 7/61, Commission v. Italy
[1961] ECR 317, [1962] CMLR 39

The Italian Government claimed that a letter written to it by the Commission could not constitute a reasoned opinion, since it was not in due legal form. It was claimed that the letter lacked adequate reasoning since it had not examined whether Italy had been justified in taking the measures of which the Commission was complaining.

THE ECJ[52]

The opinion referred to in Article 169 of the Treaty must be considered to contain a sufficient statement of reasons to satisfy the law when it contains—as it does in this case—a coherent statement of the reasons which led the Commission to believe that the State in question has failed to fulfil an obligation under the Treaty.

This means that the Commission is not obliged in its reasoned opinion to address or to answer every argument made by the Member State at the pre-litigation stage. Nor is the Commission obliged to indicate in the reasoned opinion what steps should be taken by the state to remedy the alleged breach.[53] So long as it sets out clearly the grounds on which it has relied in concluding that the state has violated Community law, the reasoning requirement will be satisfied.

(b) Can the Commission Change the Subject Matter of its Action After it has Issued a Reasoned Opinion?

If the reasoned opinion is intended to operate as some form of procedural protection for the Member State, in that it contains a precise statement of the Commission's case against the state, it would seem that the Commission

[51] See H. Schermers and D. Waelbroeck, *Judicial Protection in the European Community* (5th edn., Kluwer, 1992), 296–7.

[52] [1961] ECR 317, 327.

[53] See Case C–247/89, *Commission v Portugal* [1991] ECR I–3659, para. 22.

should not be entitled to change or amend the content of its submission when the case comes to be heard before the Court. But what if both the Commission and the Member State in question wish the Court to consider other aspects of the state's conduct which took place after the date of the reasoned opinion?

Case 7/69, Commission v. Italy
[1970] ECR 111, [1970] CMLR 97

After the date of a reasoned opinion issued by the Commission, informing Italy that it was considered to be in breach of Commmunity law, the Italian Government issued a law in order to remedy the alleged violation. The Commission, however, was not satisfied that the new law had entirely cured the alleged violation, and so did not withdraw proceedings from before the Court. Both parties now wished the Court to take the impact of this new law into account in its judgment.

THE ECJ

5. Because of the importance which the Treaty attaches to the action available to the Community against Member States for failure to fulfil obligations, this procedure in Article 169 is surrounded by guarantees which must not be ignored, particularly in view of the obligation imposed by Article 171 on Member States to take as a consequence of this action the necessary measures to comply with the judgment of the Court. Accordingly the Court cannot give judgment in the present case on the failure to fulfil an obligation occurring after legislation has been amended during the course of the proceedings without thereby adversely affecting the rights of the Member State to put forward its arguments in defence based on complaints formulated according to the procedure laid down by Article 169.

The Court therefore refused to consider whether Italy was in breach of Community law after it had taken remedial action in response to the Commission's reasoned opinion, and it declared the application of the Commission to be inadmissible. Its reason for doing so was that the subject matter of the Commission's complaint had changed significantly since it had issued the reasoned opinion, which is a compulsory part of the preliminary procedure set up under Article 169 of the Treaty. In the Court's view, there are guarantees inherent in this procedure for the protection of the Member State in question. If the subject matter of the Commission's allegation against a Member State changed after having issued its reasoned opinion, then, in order to provide proper procedural safeguards for the state, the Court felt that the entire process under Article 169 should be initiated again. This requirement that the content of the reasoned opinion be essentially the same as the submissions in the Commission's application to the Court has been reiterated many times.[54] However, it will not be sufficient for the Commission when the matter comes

[54] See e.g. Cases 232/78, *Commission* v. *France* [1979] ECR 2729, [1980] 1 CMLR 418; 193/80, *Commission* v. *Italy* [1981] ECR 3019; 211/81, *Commission* v. *Denmark* [1982] ECR 4547, [1984] 1 CMLR 278; 124/81, *Commission* v. *UK* [1983] ECR 203, [1983] 2 CMLR 1; 166/82, *Commission* v. *Italy* [1984] ECR 459, [1985] 2 CMLR 615.

before the Court simply to refer in its application to 'all the reasons set out in the letter of formal notice and the reasoned opinion'—rather the application itself must contain a statement of the grounds on which it is based.[55]

5. WHY IS AN ENFORCEMENT ACTION ADMISSIBLE AFTER THE BREACH IS REMEDIED?

Article 169 sets out the conditions which must be satisfied before the Commission may initiate enforcement proceedings in the Court. If the Commission has not issued a reasoned opinion nor given the Member State concerned a period of time within which to cure the alleged infringement, the action will not be admissible. On the other hand, once those conditions have been fulfilled and the period laid down by the Commission for compliance has expired without any action being taken by the Member State, it is no answer for that state to assert, when the case is heard before the Court, that the breach has since been remedied. The issue for the Court is whether the Member State was in breach at the time the Commission found it necessary to initiate proceedings before the Court. As in its attitude to delay in initiating proceedings,[56] this approach of the Court can be contrasted with its approach to actions brought against one of the Community institutions for failure to act. In a case where proceedings were brought against the European Parliament under Article 175 for failure to act, the Court held that the action was devoid of purpose once the institution in question had acted to remedy its default.[57] Where proceedings have been brought under Article 169 by the Commission against Member States on the other hand, such actions have been declared admissible by the Court even thought the state in question had remedied its breach by that time. Several reasons have been offered to explain why enforcement actions may be admissible after the infringement has been cured.

(a) The Commission's Continued Interest In Bringing the Action

Case 7/61, Commission v. Italy [1961] ECR 317, [1962] CMLR 39.

THE ECJ[58]

It is true that the second paragraph of Article 169 gives the Commission the right to bring the matter before the Court only if the State concerned does not

[55] Case C–43/90, *Commission* v. *Germany* [1992] ECR I–1909, paras. 7–8. See also Case C–52/90, *Commission* v. *Denmark* [1992] ECR I–2187.

[56] See n. 37 above and text.

[57] Case 377/87, *Council* v. *Parliament* [1988] ECR 4017, [1989] 3 CMLR 870. The position, however, might be different if it were likely that some party might later wish to seek redress from the institution in question for loss caused by the illegal failure to act.

[58] N. 50 above, at 326.

comply with the Commission's opinion within the period laid down by the Commission, the period being such as to allow the State in question to regularize its position in accordance with the provisions of the Treaty.

However, if the Member State does not comply with the opinion within the prescribed period, there is no question that the Commission has the right to obtain the Court's judgment on that Member State's failure to fulfil the obligations flowing from the Treaty.

ADVOCATE GENERAL LAGRANGE[59]

The purpose of the action is to obtain the Court's finding that a Member State has failed to fulfil an obligation under the Treaty . . . If, subsequent to the making of the application, the State concerned took the measures necessary to bring the infringement to an end, it is possible that the action may no longer have very much practical effect, but, so the Commission argues, it still has the highest interest in having the Court settle the issue whether the failure indeed occurred . . . the opposite argument would allow a State which so desired to denude the action of its purpose by bringing its illegal conduct to an end just before the judgment, thereafter remaining safe to carry on with its improper conduct in the absence of any judgment finding that it was in breach of its obligations.

(b) The Need to Rule on the Legality of Short Breaches

Case 240/86, Commission v. Greece
[1988] ECR 1835, [1989] 3 CMLR 578

ADVOCATE GENERAL LENZ[60]

It follows from the second paragraph of Article 169 of the EEC Treaty that an action may be brought before the Court if the alleged breach of the Treaty is not discontinued within the period laid down in the reasoned opinion . . .

Otherwise, in view of the length of the pre-litigation procedure, it would in many cases be impossible for the Court to exercise its jurisdiction with regard to breaches of the Treaty of short duration. Since the duration of conduct which is contrary to the Treaty is no indication of the gravity of the infringement it must be possible to bring proceedings even in relation to a breach of the Treaty which is limited in time.

However, if the effects of a specific infringement, which is the subject matter of Commission proceedings, have actually come to an end before the expiry of the period set out in the reasoned opinion, the action before the Court will be inadmissible even if the Commission fears that a similar such breach is likely to occur again in the future.[61]

[59] N. 50 above, at 334. [60] [1988] ECR 1835, 1844.
[61] Case C–362/90, *Commission* v. *Italy* [1992] ECR I–2353.

(c) Establishing the Liability of a Defaulting Member State

Case 240/86, Commission v. Greece
[1988] ECR 1835, [1989] 3 CMLR 578

THE ECJ

14. As the Court has consistently held (see most recently the judgment in Case 103/84, *Commission* v. *Italy* [1986] ECR 1759) the subject-matter of an action brought under Article 169 is established by the Commission's reasoned opinion and even where the default has been remedied after the period laid down pursuant to the second paragraph of that article has elapsed, an interest still subsists in pursuing the action. That interest may consist in establishing the basis for a liability which a Member State may incur, by reason of its failure to fulfil its obligations, towards those to whom rights accrue as a result of that failure.

The series of judgments which this decision follows suggests that, as a result of a Member State's default, some party which has suffered loss or damage in consequence of that default may be able to establish a right to redress and to enforce it at a national level, in damages or otherwise, against the state. Clearly, an action for redress before the national courts could derive considerable assistance from a prior finding of the Court that the Member State in question had acted in violation of Community law. Indeed now, after the case of *Francovich and Bonifaci*,[62] it is clear that in certain circumstances, when a state fails to implement a directive which was intended to benefit individuals, Community law will render the state liable in damages to those individuals who have suffered loss as a result. A finding by the Court of an infringement under Article 169 may constitute an important means, albeit not a necessary one, of showing the illegality of state action when damages are sought for loss caused by that action. Hence the fact that the infringement or illegality has been remedied by the time the Article 169 proceedings are heard by the Court does not reduce the importance of securing a ruling on the legality of the past conduct of the state.[63]

6. TYPES OF BREACH BY MEMBER STATES OF COMMUNITY LAW

Article 169 is very general in its description of a Member State violation for the purposes of enforcement proceedings. The Commission must simply

[62] Cases C–6/90 and C–9/90, *Francovich and Bonifaci* v. *Italy* [1991] ECR I–5357, [1993] 2 CMLR 66. See Chapter 5.

[63] Note that A. Arnull in 'Refurbishing the Judicial Architecture of the European Community' (1994) 43 ICLQ 296, 306 suggests that the Court should hold, as one means of reducing its case load, that the subject matter of the action has ceased to exist if the Member State has complied with the judgment before the case comes to court, even if after the expiry of the reasoned opinion.

consider that a state 'has failed to fulfil an obligation under this Treaty'. Clearly this may include actions as well as omissions on the part of states, failure to implement directives, breaches of specific Treaty provisions or of other secondary legislation, or of any rule or standard which is a binding or effective part of Community law. Certain kinds of breach are far more often the subject of Article 169 proceedings than others. The following cases provide a sample of some of the kinds of breaches which may be the subject of Article 169 proceedings.

(a) Breach of the Obligation of Co-operation under Article 5 of the EC Treaty

Case 96/81, Commission v. Netherlands
[1982] ECR 1791

The Commission brought infringement proceedings against The Netherlands, alleging that the state had failed properly to implement certain directives on the pollution of bathing water. As part of its submission, the Commission claimed that the Dutch Government had failed to provide the Commission with information on its compliance with the provisions of one directive. The obligation to provide such information and to report to the Commission was imposed by the directive itself. The Commission's argument was to the effect that, since The Netherlands had failed to provide the required information, the Commission was entitled to presume that the respondent state had failed to implement the necessary national measures which would give effect to the directive. However, the subject matter of the breach claimed by the Commission was not 'failure to comply with the duty to provide information' but rather 'failure to fulfil the obligation to implement the directive'.

THE ECJ

6. It should be emphasized that, in proceedings under Article 169 of the EEC Treaty for failure to fulfil an obligation, it is incumbent upon the Commission to prove the allegation that the obligation has not been fulfilled. It is the Commission's responsibility to place before the Court the information needed to enable the Court to establish that the obligation has not been fulfilled, and in doing so the Commission may not rely on any presumption.

However, although the Commission cannot rely on a presumption of breach where a Member State fails to provide information on compliance, the Court has ruled that once the Commission has produced sufficient evidence to show that the Member State appeared to be violating Community law it is incumbent on the state not simply to deny the allegations, but to contest substantively the information produced.[64] In the bathing water case above, the Court went on to say that all Member States had, under Article 5 of the EC Treaty, an obligation to facilitate the achievement of the Commission's tasks, including that of

[64] Case 272/86, *Commission* v. *Greece* [1988] ECR 4875, para. 21.

monitoring compliance with the Treaty. The Court described Article 12 of the bathing water directive which imposed the obligation to provide information on compliance,[65] as a specific instance of the general obligation in Article 5 of the EC Treaty.

This particular mode of infringement, i.e. the breach of the obligation under Article 5 of the EC Treaty, has been increasingly invoked by the Commission in Article 169 enforcement procedings:

Case 240/86, Greece v. Commission
[1988] ECR 1835, [1989] 3 CMLR 578

The Commission was involved in a continuing dispute with Greece over whether Greece was in breach of certain Treaty provisions on the free movement of goods, and requested the Greek authorities to furnish it with certain information in this regard. When the authorities failed to respond to this request, the Commission brought an action under Article 169 claiming, among other things, that Greece was in breach of Article 5 of the Treaty by its failure to co-operate with the Commission. Although the Court did not find a breach of the substantive free movement provisions of the Treaty, it nevertheless held that Greece was in breach of Article 5.

ADVOCATE GENERAL LENZ

38. The first paragraph of Article 5 of the EEC Treaty lays down the Member States' duty to cooperate as a general principle. That provision can be relied on when no provisions of the Treaty expressly define the obligations of the Member States . . . The purpose of the pre-litigation procedure in actions for failure to fulfil obligations is to enable disputes to be settled without court proceedings, which implies that the Member State in question has an obligation to cooperate. Without active cooperation it cannot be determined whether a breach of the Treaty has been committed, nor, *a fortiori*, can such a breach be eliminated.

In this case, the Commission was complaining of a violation of the obligation to co-operate, which took place in the course of a preliminary investigation by the Commission into the existence of a separate breach of a specific Community obligation by the same Member State. Clearly, if a Member State is not willing to respond at the pre-litigation stage of an investigation by the Commission for the purposes of Article 169 proceedings, it will be difficult for the Commission to ascertain whether or not there has been a breach by the state. The Commission's attempt to find a way around this is to initiate separate enforcement proceedings on the basis of a breach of the obligation of co-operation. It seems a circuitous and rather time-consuming way for the Commission to monitor and ensure the application of Community law, but it may impress upon the states the importance to the Community of their duty to co-operate with the institutions in the achievement of Community goals. Its

[65] Dir. 76/160, 8 Dec. 1975, [1976] OJ L31/1.

importance to the Court, as well as to the legislative institutions, has been made obvious in many of its decisions.[66]

Case 272/86, Commission v. Greece
[1988] ECR 4875

THE ECJ

30. The Member States are under a duty, by virtue of Article 5 of the EEC Treaty, to facilitate the achievement of the Commission's tasks, which consist in particular, pursuant to Article 155 of the EEC Treaty, in ensuring that the provisions of the Treaty and the measures taken by the institutions pursuant thereto are applied. It was for those purposes that the Commission asked for information.

31. The Greek Government's refusal to cooperate with the Commission prevented the latter from obtaining information about an administrative practice and from determining whether it gave rise to barriers to trade in olive oil. That lack of cooperation was particularly serious because it persisted before the Court. The Court cannot accomplish the task entrusted to it by Article 164 of the Treaty, namely ensuring that in the interpretation and application of the Treaty the law is observed, where a government does not comply with its requests. The conduct of the Greek Government has therefore constituted in the present case a serious impediment to the administration of justice.

(b) Inadequate Implementation of Community Law

In many cases, the cause of the Commission's complaint is not the complete failure to implement Community legislation, but rather its inadequate implementation. The Commission has stressed in its recent *Annual Reports* to the Parliament that this is an area of particular concern on which it intends to focus in its contacts with the Member State authorities.

Case 167/73, Commission v. France
[1974] ECR 359, [1974] 2 CMLR 216

The French legislature had failed to repeal a provision of the French Code du Travail Maritime under which a certain proportion (roughly 3:1) of the crew of a ship was required to be of French nationality. This nationality requirement was contrary to Community law. However, the French Government claimed that directions had been given verbally to the naval authorities to treat Community nationals as French nationals, and that this was sufficient to comply with the requirements of Community law.

THE ECJ

40. It appears both from the argument before the Court and from the position adopted during the parliamentary proceedings that the present state of affairs is

[66] For other cases on Art. 5, see e.g. Cases C–35/88, *Commission* v. *Greece* [1990] ECR I–3125, [1992] 1 CMLR 548; C–48/89 *Commission* v. *Italy* [1990] ECR I–2425; and C–374/89, *Commission* v. *Belgium* [1991] ECR I–367, [1992] 3 CMLR 787.

that freedom of movement for workers in the sector in question continues to be considered by the French authorities not as a matter of right but as dependent on their unilateral will.

41. It follows that although the objective legal position is clear, namely, that Article 48 and Regulation No 1612/68 are directly applicable in the territory of the French Republic, nevertheless the maintenance in these circumstances of the wording of the Code du Travail Maritime gives rise to an ambiguous state of affairs by maintaining, as regards those subject to the law who are concerned, a state of uncertainty as to the possibilities available to them of relying on Community law.

42. This uncertainty can only be reinforced by the internal and verbal character of the purely administrative directions to waive the application of the national law.

In the case of directives, which are not in themselves directly applicable, it is clearly incumbent on the Member States to implement them fully. Even where directives are vertically directly enforceable—i.e. against the state—or where they can be given indirect domestic effect in another way, this does not reduce the obligation on the state to implement them properly. Article 189 provides that the manner and form of implementation of directives are a matter for each Member State to decide, but this does not mean that the Court will not review and, if necessary, declare insufficient the method of implementation chosen by a state.

Case 96/81, Commission v. Netherlands [1982] ECR 1791

THE ECJ

12. It is true that each Member State is free to delegate powers to its domestic authorities as it considers fit and to implement the directive by means of measures adopted by regional or local authorities. That does not however release it from the obligation to give effect to the provisions of the directive by means of national provisions of a binding nature. The directive in question, adopted *inter alia* pursuant to Article 100 of the EEC Treaty, is intended to approximate the applicable laws, regulations and administrative provisions in the Member States. Mere administrative practices, which by their nature may be altered at the whim of the administration, may not be considered as constituting the proper fulfilment of the obligation deriving from that directive.

In subsequent proceedings, the Court outlined a further objection to a Member State's reliance on such 'whimsical' administrative practices, namely that, quite apart from their uncertainty and alterability, they lacked the appropriate publicity to constitute adequate implementation.[67]

[67] Case 160/82, *Commission* v. *Netherlands* [1982] ECR 4637, [1984] 1 CMLR 230, para. 4.

However, the Court has not always found against a Member State where it has failed to adopt any specific measures to implement a directive.[68]

Case 29/84, Commission v. Germany
[1985] ECR 1661, [1986] 3 CMLR 579

The Commission brought enforcement proceedings against Germany for failure to implement Directives 77/452 and 77/453 governing the right of establishment and freedom to provide services for nurses.

THE ECJ

17. The German Government does not deny that mere administrative practices, which by their nature can be modified as and when the administration pleases and which are not publicized widely enough, cannot be regarded as a proper fulfilment of the obligation imposed on the Member States by Article 189 of the Treaty, as the Court has consistently held. However, the government claims that that principle cannot be applied in this instance because the administrative practice in question cannot be changed as and when the administration pleases and it has been given sufficient publicity.

After summarizing the Commission's counter-argument, the Court ruled as follows:

22. Faced with those conflicting views, the Court considers it necessary to recall the wording of the third paragraph of Article 189 of the Treaty, according to which a directive is binding, as to the result to be achieved upon each Member State to which it is addressed, but leaves to the national authorities the choice of form and methods.

23. It follows from that provision that the implementation of a directive does not necessarily require legislative action in each Member State. In particular the existence of general principles of constitutional or administrative law may render implementation by specific legislation superfluous, provided however that those principles guarantee that the national authorities will in fact apply the directive fully and that, where the directive is intended to create rights for individuals, the persons concerned are made fully aware of their rights and, where appropriate, afforded the possibility of relying on them before the national courts.

(c) Failure to Give Proper Effect to Community Law

In furtherance of its policy of encouraging Member States to take steps to ensure the effectiveness of Community law, the Court has also stated that

[68] On a related issue, see Case C–338/91, *Steenhorst-Neerings* v. *Bestuur van de Bedrijfsvereniging voor Detailhandel, Ambachten en Huisvrouwen* [1993] ECR I–5475, in which the Court ruled that where a Member State had not implemented a directive properly, the national courts were not precluded by Community law from reading inconsistent national legislation in way which conformed with the non-implemented dir.. This, however, would not absolve the Member State from the obligation to implement properly.

Article 5 of the EC Treaty will be breached if a Member State fails to penalize those who infringe Community law in the same way as it penalizes those who infringe national law.[69]

Case 68/88, Commission v. Greece
[1989] ECR 2979, [1991] 1 CMLR 31

THE ECJ

23. It should be observed that where Community legislation does not specifically provide any penalty for an infringement or refers for that purpose to national laws, regulations and administrative provisions, Article 5 of the Treaty requires the Member States to take all measures necessary to guarantee the application and effectiveness of Community law.

24. For that purpose, whilst the choice of penalties remains within their discretion, they must ensure in particular that infringements of Community law are penalised under conditions, both procedural and substantive, which are analogous to those applicable to infringements of national law of a similar nature and importance and which, in any event, make the penalty effective, proportionate and dissuasive.

(d) Action by the Courts of a Member State

A failure of a Member State's judiciary to comply with Community law has never formed the basis of Article 169 proceedings against that state. Does this mean that a national court's judgment cannot be the subject of infringement proceedings by the Commission under Article 169? Certainly, the Court has said that the Member State is responsible even for actions and inaction on the part of constitutionally independent organs of the state. And, given the central role played by national courts in the implementation and enforcement of Community law domestically, their failure to comply with Community obligations could have very serious consequences for Community law. Although the Court has not directly addressed the question whether a national court could be the subject of infringement proceedings, an Advocate General has expressed a view on the matter:[70]

Case 30/77, R. v. Bouchereau
[1977] ECR 1999, [1977] 1 CMLR 269

ADVOCATE GENERAL WARNER[71]

No doubt the constitutionally independent institution whose action, or rather inaction, in each of those cases lay at the root of the default of the Member State

[69] See also Case 143/83, *Commission* v. *Denmark* [1985] ECR 427, [1986] 1 CMLR 144, paras. 8–10 of the judgment. Indeed, as can be seen in Ch. 5, the Court has gone further than this and indicated that the same penalties which are available for infringements of national law might not be adequate or effective penalties for infringements of Community law.

[70] See also the discussion in T. C. Hartley, n. 39 above, 308–9.

[71] [1977] ECR 1999, 2020.

concerned was its Parliament, but the relevant principle, as there stated, is wide enough to apply also to the Judiciary of a Member State. Indeed it must logically do so. I am reminded that, in case 9/75 *Meyer-Burckhardt* v. *Commission* [1975] ECR 1171 at 1187, I felt no hesitation about that.

It is obvious on the other hand that a Member State cannot be be held to have failed to fulfil an obligation under the Treaty simply because one of its courts has reached a wrong decision. Judicial error, whether due to the misapprehension of facts or to misapprehension of the law, is not a breach of the Treaty. In the judicial sphere, Article 169 could only come into play in the event of a court of a Member State deliberately ignoring or disregarding Community law.

7. STATE ATTEMPTS TO RAISE DEFENCES IN ENFORCEMENT PROCEEDINGS

Although Member States have not lacked ingenuity or resourcefulness in providing reasons to justify their failure to fulfil Treaty obligations, the Court has not been very receptive to such arguments. There are many examples of 'defences' which have unsuccessfully been pleaded by the States in response to proceedings under Article 169.

(a) Force Majeure

Case 77/69, Commission v. Belgium
[1970] ECR 237, [1974] 1 CMLR 203

Belgium had drafted and put before Parliament a law designed to amend a national tax provision to comply with EC requirements, but the draft legislation had lapsed owing to the dissolution of Parliament. In response to infringement proceedings brought by the Commission, Belgium attempted to claim *force majeure*. It was argued that, on account of the separation-of-powers doctrine in Belgian constitutional law, the Government could not require the necessary measure to be passed in order to comply with EC law.

THE ECJ

15. The obligations arising from Article 95 of the Treaty devolve upon States as such and the liability of a Member State under Article 169 arises whatever the agency of the State whose action or inaction is the cause of the failure to fulfil its obligations, even in the case of a constitutionally independent institution.

Similar arguments were made by Italy in proceedings brought against it for breach of Article 171 in its failure to comply with a previous judgment of the Court.[72] It argued that difficulties had been encountered in the parliamentary

[72] See Cases 48/71, *Commission* v. *Italy* [1972] ECR 527, [1972] CMLR 699 and 7/68, *Commission* v. *Italy* [1968] ECR 423. For more recent Art. 169 proceedings against Italy claiming a further breach of Art. 171 see Case C–101/91, *Commission* v. *Italy* [1993] ECR I–191.

procedures which were required to abolish the offending measure, and which were outside its control. The Court, however, rejected the argument that the breach of Community law was beyond the control of the national authorities, ruling that any other conclusion would subject the application of Community law to the varying laws of the different Member States in this regard. Similar attempts by Member State governments to disclaim responsibility for infringements of Community law have been dismissed by the Court, which has repeatedly ruled that 'a Member State may not plead provisions, practices or circumstances existing in its internal legal system in order to justify a failure to comply with obligations and time limits laid down in Community directives'.[73] The overall responsibility of each state for any failure to comply with Community law thus precludes the argument that the breach was brought about by another organ or institution of the state which is independent of the government. The one situation which the Court agreed could constitute *force majeure* was where a bomb attack presented 'insurmountable difficulties', rendering compliance with the Treaty impossible.[74]

(b) There was No Inertia or Opposition to the Application of EC Law

Case 301/81, Commission v. Belgium
[1983] ECR 467, [1984] 2 CMLR 430

The Commission brought an action against Belgium under Article 169 for failure to implement Directive 77/780 concerning credit institutions. In its submission to the Court, Belgium emphasized difficulties of a technical, instiutitional, and political nature to explain why, despite the efforts of the Belgian Government, a bill incorporating the directive into national law had not yet been lodged before the Parliament. It was argued that the Commission's reasoned opinion contained no evidence to show any degree of inertia or opposition by the Belgian State to the application of Community law within the periods prescribed by the Commission, and that the period allowed was too short.

THE ECJ

8. In that respect it must be observed that the admissibility of an action based on Article 169 of the Treaty depends only on an objective finding of a failure to fulfil obligations and not on proof of any inertia or opposition on the part of the Member State concerned.

9. Finally, the Directive allowed the Member States a period of twenty-four months for the adoption of implementing measures. The period of two months laid down in the reasoned opinion merely constitutes an additional period in which the Member State is invited to put an end to the failure with which it is

[73] See Case 280/83, *Commission* v. *Italy* [1984] ECR 2361, para. 4. Also Cases 160/82, *Commission* v. *Netherlands* [1982] ECR 4637, [1984] 1 CMLR 230; 215/83, *Commission* v. *Belgium* [1985] ECR 1039, [1985] 3 CMLR 624.

[74] Case 33/69, *Commission* v. *Italy* [1970] ECR 93, [1971] CMLR 466, para. 16 of the judgment. However, the Court was not satisfied in the case that the bomb attack did render compliance excessively difficult by the time proceedings were brought. See also Case C–334/87, *Greece* v. *Commission* [1990] ECR I–2849, para. 11, for a definition of *force majeure* in other circumstances.

charged. Further, the Commission waited almost two years after sending the reasoned opinion before bringing the matter before the Court. It is therefore futile for the Kingdom of Belgium in those circumstances to challenge the period of two months laid down in the reasoned opinion.

This further underlines the point emphasized in various rulings of the Court that Article 169 proceedings are 'objective' in nature. The Court looks only to see whether or not the infringement has taken place as alleged, and the breach in question need not involve deliberate infringement or moral wrongdoing on the part of the Member State.[75]

(c) The Community Measure on Which the Infringement Proceedings are Based is Illegal

Case 226/87, Commission v. Greece
[1988] ECR 3611, [1989] 3 CMLR 569

The Commission in 1985 adopted a decision declaring certain Greek legislation relating to public-sector insurance to be incompatible with Article 90(1) of the EEC Treaty. Almost a year later, when no action had been taken to amend the legislation, the Commission commenced proceedings against Greece under Article 169. In the course of the proceedings before the Court, the Greek Government contested the lawfulness of the Commission's decision of 1985.

THE ECJ

14. The system of remedies set up by the Treaty distinguishes between the remedies provided for in Articles 169 and 170, which permit a declaration that a Member State has failed to fulfil its obligations, and those contained in Articles 173 and 175, which permit judicial review of the lawfulness of measures adopted by the Community institutions, or the failure to adopt such measures. Those remedies have different objectives and are subject to different rules. In the absence of a provision of the Treaty expressly permitting it to do so, a Member State cannot therefore plead the unlawfulness of a decision addressed to it as a defence in an action for a declaration that it has failed to fulfil its obligations arising out of its failure to implement that decision.

It would appear from this ruling that it is not possible for a Member State to plead the illegality of a decision which was addressed to it in order to resist judgment against it in Article 169 proceedings for failure to comply with that decision. The rationale seems to be that, had the Member State objected to the decision, it had had the opportunity to bring a direct action for its annulment under Article 173. It seems, however, that a plea of illegality might be a

[75] See, however, Case 146/89, *Commission* v. *UK* [1991] ECR 3533, [1991] 3 CMLR 649 in which, although the Court rejected the UK's attempt to justify its breach by pointing to the failure by other Member States to fulfil their similar obligations, it was sufficiently impressed by the 'exemplary conduct' of the UK in later voluntarily remedying its breach to order each party to bear its own costs, rather than ordering the UK to bear all.

defence to an action under Article 169 where the earlier measure was not a decision addressed to the Member State in question, but a regulation the illegality of which might reasonably not have been apparent to the Member State until the Commission brought enforcement proceedings, or where the Community measure was so gravely flawed as to be legally 'non-existent'.[76] It may also be possible for the illegality of the decision to be pleaded in an extreme case where the decision infringes a principle of a constitutional nature.[77]

(d) Other Member States are also in Breach

This ground has been pleaded many times by Member States, without success. The idea that the obligation to comply with Community law is a reciprocal one, dependent on full compliance by other Member States, has long been rejected by the Court. The Court has been determined since *Van Gend en Loos*[78] to distinguish Community law clearly from traditional forms and principles of international law.[79] However, this has not deterred Member States from continuing to raise the concept of reciprocity in their defence in infringement proceedings.

Case C–146/89, Commission v. United Kingdom [1991] ECR 3533, [1991] 3 CMLR 649

THE ECJ

47. It must first be pointed out in this regard that, according to the well-established case-law of the Court (see in particular the judgment of 26 February 1976 in Case 52/75 *Commission* v. *Italy* [1976] ECR 277) a Member State cannot justify its failure to fulfil obligations under the Treaty by pointing to the fact that other Member States have also failed, and continued to fail, to fulfil their own obligations. Under the legal order established by the Treaty, the implementation of Community law by Member States cannot be made subject to a condition of reciprocity. Article 169 and 170 of the Treaty provide a suitable means of redress for dealing with the failure by Member States to fulfil their obligations under the Treaty.

[76] See Mancini A.G. in Case 204/86, *Commission* v. *Greece* [1988] ECR 5323, 5343–5, [1990] 1 CMLR 481, 493–6 and Case 226/87, *Commission* v. *Greece* [1988] ECR 3611, 3617, [1989] 3 CMLR 569. For an unsuccessful attempt to plead the illegality of a *dir.* (rather than a dec. addressed to it) which the state had failed to implement, see case C–74/91 *Commission* v. *Germany* [1992] ECR I–5437.

[77] Cases 6 and 11/69, *Commission* v. *France* [1969] ECR 523, [1970] CMLR 43; 70/72, *Commission* v. *Germany* [1973] ECR 813, [1973] CMLR 741; and 156/77, *Commission* v. *Belgium* [1978] ECR 1881.

[78] Case 26/62, *NV Algemene Transporten Expeditie Onderneming van Gend en Loos* v. *Nederlandse Administratie der Belastingen* [1963] ECR 1, [1963] CMLR 105.

[79] See Case 52/75, *Commission* v. *Italy* [1976] ECR 277, [1976] 2 CMLR 320, para. 11.

8. ARTICLE 170

Apart from the enforcement action which the Commission may bring under Article 169, the EC Treaty also provides a means for any Member State to initiate an action against another state which it considers to be in breach of the Treaty.[80]

To that effect, Article 170 provides as follows:

> A Member State which considers that another Member State has failed to fulfil an obligation under this Treaty may bring the matter before the Court of Justice.
>
> Before a Member State brings an action against another Member State for an alleged infringement of an obligation under this Treaty, it shall bring the matter before the Commission.
>
> The Commission shall deliver a reasoned opinion after each of the States concerned has been given the opportunity to submit its own case and its observations on the other party's case both orally and in writing.
>
> If the Commission has not delivered an opinion within three months of the date on which the matter was brought before it, the absence of such opinion shall not prevent the matter from being brought before the Court.

Unlike under Article 169, the Member State bringing the action under Article 170 does not first have to contact the Member State which is the subject of the complaint. Rather, as can be seen, the matter must first be brought by the complainant state before the Commission. The procedure thereafter is similar to that under Article 169, except that both states in the case of Article 170 must be heard and given a chance to make oral and written submissions before the Commission gives its reasoned opinion. Given that Article 170 provides a mechanism for Member States rather than the Commission to bring a state before the Court, it would appear that the complainant state may bring the case to Court even where the Commission takes the view that there is no breach.

Article 170 has very rarely been used, no doubt because of the degree of political ill-will this would occasion between Member States.[81] However, in 1978 France brought an action against the United Kingdom under Article 170, after a French trawler was searched and its Master convicted of breaching a 1977 United Kingdom Fishing Nets Order.[82] France claimed that the United Kingdom Order was in breach of a Council regulation on the common structural policy for the fishing industry, and in breach of the duty of

[80] See also Art. 142 Euratom. The ECSC Treaty does not provide for this possibility.

[81] The procedure was set in motion by the Commission in response to a complaint from France against The Netherlands, which led to a reasoned opinion by the Commission finding The Netherlands in breach. The case was not, however, brought before the Court under Art. 170: see Case 169/84, *Cofaz* v. *Commission* [1986] ECR 391, [1986] 3 CMLR 385, para. 6 of the judgment.

[82] Case 141/78, *France* v. *UK* [1979] ECR 2923, [1980] 1 CMLR 6.

co-operation under Article 5 of the EEC Treaty. The Commission in its reasoned opinion had supported France's position, and when the United Kingdom refused to comply the matter was brought before the Court, which ruled that it was in fact in breach.

9. INTERIM MEASURES

Under Articles 185 and 186, the Court has the power to prescribe interim measures which it considers to be necessary in a case which has been brought before it.[83] Although they may be sought in any case before the Court,[84] they may be particularly useful for the Commission to seek at the same time as proceedings under Article 169.[85]

When in Article 169 proceedings a breach is found, the Court simply declares that the Member State has failed to fulfil its obligations, and its ruling does not have any effect on the impugned national rule or provision. The Treaty makes clear that, in general, actions before the Court—and not only actions under Article 169—do not have suspensory effect. Article 185 provides:

> Actions brought before the Court of Justice shall not have suspensory effect. The Court of Justice may, however, if it considers that circumstances so require, order that application of the contested act be suspended.

Article 186 then provides:

> The Court of Justice may in any cases before it prescribe any necessary interim measures.

Article 83(2) of the Court's Rules of Procedure specifies that such interim measures may not be ordered unless there are circumstances giving rise to urgency, as well as factual and legal grounds which establish a *prima facie* justification for granting the measures sought. The effect of the urgency requirement is that the interim measures requested must be of such a nature as to prevent the injury which is alleged.

[83] See also Art. 39 ECSC, 157–8 Euratom. See C. Gray, 'Interim Measures of Protection in the European Court' (1979) 4 ELRev. 80; G. Borchardt, 'The Award of Interim Measures by the ECJ' (1985) 22 CMLRev. 203.

[84] See e.g. the Court's dismissal of Greece's objection to an application for interim measures in the context of Art. 225 enforcement proceedings against it: Case C–120/94R, n. 1 above.

[85] To take a sample of 3 years: in 1991, 9 applications for interim measures were made to the ECJ, 4 in 1992 and 13 in 1993. For the same 3 years in the CFI the numbers were 10, 7, and 20 respectively.

A fairly recent example of such measures being sought by the Commission in the context of Article 169 proceedings was in an action brought against the United Kingdom.[86]

Case 246/89R, Commission v. United Kingdom [1989] ECR 3125, [1989] 3 CMLR 601

The Commission applied for interim measures against the United Kingdom on account of its rules concerning nationality requirements for the owners of British-registered fishing vessels. The United Kingdom contended that the condition of urgency was not satisfied, claiming that the fishing vessels which had been adversely affected by the nationality requirement would in any case not satisfy the other conditions for registration as fishing vessels, even if the Court suspended the nationality requirement. The Court rejected the factual basis for this claim and made some observations on the question of the irreparability of harm which needs to be established.

THE ECJ

37. It must be held in the first place that for fishing vessels which until 31 March 1989 were flying the British flag and fishing under a British fishing licence the loss of the flag and the cessation of their activities entails serious damage. There is no ground for believing that, pending delivery of the judgment in the main proceedings, these vessels can be operated in the pursuit of alternative fishing activities. The aforesaid damage must also, should the application in the main proceedings be granted, be regarded as irreparable.

10. CONCLUSION

Thus it can be seen that the enforcement procedures provided by the Treaty play a significant part in the remedial scheme of Community law. In particular, Article 169 provides the Commission with a very useful instrument for ensuring the effectiveness of Community law. It is clear that litigation is by no means the most important or most effective aspect of the procedure. Rather it is the opportunity which the pre-litigation and pre-contentious procedure gives the Commission to maintain a dialogue with the national authorities about the nature and extent of their obligations under Community law. Further, although individual complainants have no control over the commencement of proceedings against a Member State, their role in bringing potential infringements to the attention of the Commission is evidently very important to it. Even if the hope that it will create 'a people's Europe' may be an optimistic one, it is certainly the case that the ability to bring a complaint about a Member State to the Commission—as could also be said about the new procedure for making a complaint about the Community institutions to

[86] This action was brought prior to the reference to the ECJ from the HL in the well-known case arising from the same legislation, C–213/89, *R.* v. *Secretary of State for Transport, ex parte Factortame* [1990] ECR I–2433, [1990] 3 CMLR 1.

the Ombudsman[87]—adds a valuable dimension to the remedial provisions of Community law.

11. FURTHER READING

(a) Books

BEBR, G., *Development of Judicial Control in the European Communities* (2nd edn., Martinus Nijhoff, 1981), Ch. 6

HARTLEY, T. C., *The Foundations of European Community Law* (3rd edn., Oxford University Press, 1994)

SCHERMERS, H., and WAELBROECK, D., *Judicial Protection in the European Communities* (5th edn., Kluwer, 1992), Ch. 2, III

(b) Articles

BORCHARDT, G., 'The Award of Interim Measures by the European Court' (1985) 22 CMLRev. 203

DASHWOOD, A., and WHITE, R., 'Enforcement Actions Under Articles 169 and 170 EEC' (1989) 14 ELRev. 388

EVANS, A., 'The Enforcement Procedure of Article 169 EEC: Commission Discretion' (1979) 4 ELRev. 442

GRAY, C., 'Interim Measures of Protection in the European Court' (1979) 4 ELRev. 80

[87] See Ch. 2.

10

Preliminary Rulings and the Building of a European Judicial System

1. INTRODUCTION

Article 177, which contains the preliminary ruling procedure, is one of the most interesting provisions of the Treaty. There would have been few commentators, at the inception of the Treaty, who could have guessed at the importance which this Article would have had in shaping both Community law and the relationship between the national and Community legal systems. The importance of preliminary rulings has already been apparent from the discussion in previous chapters. It is now time to consider this matter in its own right. Article 177 reads as follows:

> The Court of Justice shall have jurisdiction to give preliminary rulings concerning:
>
> (a) the interpretation of the Treaty;
> (b) the validity and interpretation of acts of the institutions of the Community and of the ECB;
> (c) the interpretation of the statutes of bodies established by an act of the Council, where those statutes so provide.
>
> Where such a question is raised before any court or tribunal of a Member State, that court or tribunal may, if it considers that a decision on the question is necessary to enable it to give judgment, request the Court of Justice to give a ruling thereon.
>
> Where any such question is raised in a case pending before a court or tribunal of a Member State, against whose decision there is no judicial remedy under national law, that court or tribunal shall bring the matter before the Court of Justice.

We are now in a position to appreciate why Article 177 has been of importance in shaping both Community law itself and the relationship between national and Community legal systems. These can be considered in turn.

Article 177 has been of such significance to the *development of Community law* because it has been the vehicle through which seminal Community concepts, such as direct effect and supremacy, have been developed. This is graphically captured by Mancini and Keeling:[1]

> If the doctrines of direct effect and supremacy are . . . the 'twin pillars of the Community's legal system', the reference procedure laid down in Article 177 must surely be the keystone in the edifice; without it the roof would collapse and the two pillars would be left as a desolate ruin, evocative of the temple at Cape Sounion—beautiful but not of much practical utility.

It is through the device of preliminary rulings that the scope of, for example, direct effect has been delineated and expanded. Individuals would assert in national courts that a Community provision had been broken by their *Member States*, and that this provision gave them rights which they could enforce in their national courts. The national court would seek a ruling from the ECJ whether the particular Community provision really did have direct effect, and the ECJ was thereby enabled to develop the concept. It has been through Article 177 that the national courts and the ECJ have engaged in a *discourse* and *dialogue* on the appropriate substantive reach of Community law when it has come into conflict with national legal norms. Article 177 has also come to be increasingly relied on by individuals who wish to assert that the *Community institutions* are themselves in breach of Community law. The paradigm situation is one in which the individual believes himself to be wronged by a regulation or decision. A direct action against the Community is difficult, because the narrow-standing rules which pertain under Article 173 mean that an action under this Article will often never reach the substance of the case at all.[2] Individuals therefore sought to utilize Article 177 as a vehicle through which to challenge Community regulations and decisions which would otherwise be out of their reach. In these actions the Commission itself would not be the defendant. The action would, rather, be brought against, for example, a national intervention board, which was applying the Community norms at the national level. The reality of the situation was, none the less, often that the individual would be seeking to challenge a norm which could not otherwise be attacked.

Article 177 has also been one of the principal vehicles through which the *very relationship between the national and Community legal systems has been fashioned.* What then is the nature of this relationship?

In formal terms it is not an appellate one. No individual has a right of appeal as such to the ECJ; it is for the national court to make the decision to refer. Moreover, the ruling given by the ECJ is not normally an appeal on a point already decided by the national court. It is, rather, the first and often final hearing on the particular issue which has been referred, with the matter

[1] 'From *CILFIT* to *ERT*: the Constitutionl Challenge Facing the European Court' (1991) 11 YBEL 1, 2–3.

[2] For the reasons why this is so, see below, Ch. 11.

then being sent back to the national courts, which will apply the Community law to the case at hand.

To repeat the question posed above, what then is the nature of the relationship? It has changed over the years and is still evolving. The nature of this change can be described as follows.

The original conception was both *horizontal* and *bilateral*. The former trait connoted the idea that the ECJ and the national courts were separate but equal. They had differing functions, which each performed within its own appointed sphere. It was for the national court to decide whether to refer a matter to the ECJ, which the ECJ would then interpret. This interpretation of Community law would then be applied by the national court to the case at hand. The latter trait connoted the idea that, in principle at least, the rulings of the ECJ were delivered to the particular national court which made the request. In this sense, there was a series of bilateral relationships between the ECJ and each of the national courts.

This picture of the relationship between the ECJ and the national courts may always have been over-idealized and not readily sustainable. In any event, the passage of time has altered its nature. It will be seen that the relationship has become steadily more *vertical* and *multilateral*. It has become more vertical in the sense that a number of developments, both separately and together, have served to emphasize the fact that the ECJ sits in a superior position to that of the national courts. The verticality of the relationship also manifests itself in a less obvious, but equally important, manner. The ECJ has, in effect, enrolled the national courts as enforcers and appliers of Community law. They are to be perceived as part of a Community-wide judicial hierarchy in which the ECJ sits at the apex, but in which the national courts also have a role to play in the application and enforcement of Community law itself. The relationship has become more multilateral in that judgments given in response to the request for a ruling from one Member State are increasingly held to have either a *de facto* or *de jure* impact on all other national courts.

The developments which have brought about these changes will be considered in the course of the subsequent discussion. Taken together they serve to lay the foundations for the ECJ to assume the role of a more 'superior court', within a Community which is in transition to a closer social and political union.

2. THE PROVISIONS WHICH CAN BE REFERRED

Article 177 expressly envisions references being made concerning three types of subject matter.

First, references may be made concerning the interpretation of the Treaty: Article 177(1)(a). This includes all Treaties amending or supplementing the EC

Treaty. Particular subsidiary conventions may provide for references to be made to the ECJ. It should be noted, as stated at the beginning of this Chapter, that it is through Article 177(1)(a) that the Court has given many of its seminal judgments concerning direct effect. The 'interpretation' of the Treaty will, therefore, cover the issue of whether a Treaty Article is capable of generating rights for individuals.

Article 177(1)(b) allows for preliminary references to be made which relate to the validity and interpretation of acts of the institutions of the Community. The former will embrace situations such as that in the *ICC* and *Foto-Frost* cases, to be considered below,[3] in which the validity of, for example, a Community decision or regulation may arise in proceedings before a national court. The latter will cover, *inter alia*, those cases, such as *Slaughtered Cow*,[4] in which an individual argues that a Community regulation is capable of giving rise to rights which can be enforced in national courts. However, it should be made clear that references can be made under Article 177(1)(b) irrespective of whether the Community provision is directly effective. A reference may be required in such circumstances in order to clarify the interpretation of the provision in question. Non-binding acts such as recommendations and opinions may also be the subject-matter of a reference.[5] It has also been held that Article 177(1)(b) gives the ECJ jurisdiction to make a ruling in respect of certain agreements with non-member states.[6]

The precise ambit of Article 177(1)(c), which embraces the interpretation of statutes of bodies established by an act of the Council, is not so clear. The word 'statute' in Community law normally connotes an instrument which governs the operation of an institution, such as the statute of the ECJ. Such statutes will be acts of the Council, and will therefore fall within Article 177(1)(b). It may well be that, as Hartley suggests, Article 177(1)(c) is designed to limit the scope of Article 177(1)(b) in relation to such statutes.[7]

The ECJ has also held that a preliminary reference may be made in circumstances in which a provision of national law is based on or makes some reference to Community law, even if the consequence is that the ambit of Community law is extended by the national provisions.[8]

In practice it is Articles 177(1)(a) and (b) which provide the foundation for the great bulk of references which are made. This will become evident in the

[3] Case 66/80, *International Chemical Corporation* v. *Amministrazione delle Finanze dello Stato* [1981] ECR 1191, [1983] 2 CMLR 593; Case 314/85, *Firma Foto-Frost* v. *Hauptzollamt Lübeck-Ost* [1987] ECR 4199, [1988] 3 CMLR 57.

[4] Case 93/71, *Leonesio* v. *Italian Ministry of Agriculture and Forestry* [1972] ECR 287.

[5] Case 322/88, *Salvatori Grimaldi* v. *Fonds des Maladies Professionnelles* [1989] ECR 4407.

[6] Case 181/73, *Haegeman* v. *Belgium* [1974] ECR 449, [1975] 1 CMLR 515. See also, Cases 267–269/81, *Amministrazione delle Finanze dello Stato* v. *Società Petrolifera Italiana SpA and SpA Michelin Italia* [1983] ECR 801, [1984] 1 CMLR 354. For critical comment see, T. C. Hartley, *The Foundations of European Community Law* (3rd edn., Clarendon 1994), 271–4.

[7] Hartley, n. 6 above, 268–9.

[8] Cases C–297/88 and 197/89, *Dzodzi* v. *Belgium* [1990] ECR I–3763; Case C–231/89, *Gmurzynska-Bscher* v. *Oberfinanzdirektion Köln* [1990] ECR I–4003; Arnull, Note (1993) 18 ELRev. 129.

discussion which follows throughout the course of this Chapter, and in other chapters in which Article 177 is of relevance.

3. THE COURTS OR TRIBUNALS TO WHICH ARTICLE 177 APPLIES

Article 177(2) and (3) is framed in terms of courts or tribunals of a Member State, which may or must make a reference. It is clear that it is a matter for the ECJ to decide whether a body is a court or tribunal for the purposes of Article 177, and that the categorization of that body under national law is not conclusive.[9] This is demonstrated by the *Broekmeulen* case:

Case 246/80, C. Broekmeulen v. Huisarts Registratie Commissie [1981] ECR 2311, [1982] 1 CMLR 91

The case concerned a Dutch body called the Appeals Committee for General Medicine. It heard appeals from another body, which was responsible for registering those who wished to practise medicine in The Netherlands. Both these bodies were established under the auspices of the Royal Netherlands Society for the Promotion of Medicine. Although this was a private association, it was indirectly recognized in other parts of Dutch law, and in reality it was not possible to practise without registration. The Appeals Committee was not a court or tribunal under Dutch law, but it did follow an adversarial procedure and allow legal representation. Broekmeulen was of Dutch nationality, but had qualified in Belgium. He sought to establish himself as a doctor in the Netherlands and his application to be registered was refused. The question arose whether the Appeals Committee was a court or tribunal for the purposes of Article 177.

THE ECJ

12. The Netherlands Government stated that, in its opinion, the Appeals Committee cannot be considered a court or tribunal under Netherlands law. However, it pointed out that that fact is not decisive for the interpretation of Article 177 of the Treaty and suggested that the question whether a body such as the Appeals Committee is entitled to refer a case to the Court under that provision should be determined in the light of the function performed by that body within the system of remedies available to those who consider that their rights under Community law have been infringed.

13. In this regard, the order for reference mentions a Royal Decree of 1966, the decree concerning benefits (*Verstreckingenbesluit*), adopted under the Sickness Fund Law; for the purposes of that decree the term 'general practitioner' refers exclusively to a doctor enrolled on the register of general practitioners maintained by the Society. The practice of a doctor who is not enrolled on the register would thus not be recognised by the sickness insurance schemes. Under those circum-

[9] Case 43/71, *Politi* v. *Italy* [1971] ECR 1039.; Case C–24/92, *Corbiau* v. *Administration des Contributions*, [1993] ECR I–1277.

stances a doctor who is not enrolled on the register is unable to treat, as a general practitioner, patients covered by the social security system. In fact, private practice is likewise made impossible by the fact that private insurers also define the term 'general practitioner' in their policies in the same way as the provisions of the decree concerning benefits.

14. A study of the Netherlands legislation and of the statutes and internal rules of the Society shows that a doctor who intends to establish himself in the Netherlands may not in fact practise either as a specialist, or as an expert in social medicine, or as a general practitioner, without being recognised and registered by the organs of the Society. In the same way it may be seen that the system thus established is the result of close cooperation between doctors who are members of the Society, the medical faculties and the departments of State responsible for higher education and health.

15. It is thus clear that both in the sector covered by the social security system and in the field of private medicine the Netherlands system of public health operates on the basis of the status accorded to doctors by the Society and that registration as a general practitioner is essential to every doctor wishing to establish himself in the Netherlands as a general practitioner.

16. Therefore a general practitioner who avails himself of the right of establishment and the freedom to provide services conferred upon him by Community law is faced with the necessity of applying to the Registration Committee established by the Society, and, in the event of his application's being refused, must appeal to the Appeals Committee. The Netherlands Government expressed the opinion that a doctor who is not a member of the Society would have the right to appeal against such a refusal to the ordinary courts, but stated that the point had never been decided by the Netherlands courts. Indeed all doctors, whether members of the Society or not, whose application to be registered as a general practitioner is refused, appeal to the Appeals Committee, whose decisions to the knowledge of the Netherlands Government have never been challenged in the ordinary courts.

17. In order to deal with the question of applicability in the present case of Article 177 of the Treaty, it should be noted that it is incumbent upon Member States to take the necessary steps to ensure that within their own territory the provisions adopted by the Community institutions are implemented in their entirety. If, under the legal system of a Member State, the task of implementing such provisions is assigned to a professional body acting under a degree of governmental supervision, and if that body, in conjunction with the public authorities concerned, creates appeal procedures which may affect the exercise of rights granted by Community law, it is imperative, in order to ensure the proper functioning of Community law, that the Court should have an opportunity of ruling on issues of interpretation and validity arising out of such proceedings.

18. As a result of all the foregoing considerations and in the absence, in practice, of any right of appeal to the ordinary courts, the Appeals Committee, which operates with the consent of the public authorities and with their cooperation, and which, after an adversarial procedure, delivers decisions which are recognised as final, must, in a matter involving the application of Community law, be considered as a court or tribunal of a Member State within the meaning of Article 177 of the Treaty. Therefore, the Court has jurisdiction to reply to the question asked.

In order for a court or tribunal to be entitled to make a reference under Article 177, the body seeking to make the reference must be one which has an obligation to resolve the matter brought before it, as opposed to, for example, making a declaration relating to a dispute concerning one of the parties before it and the courts or tribunals of another Member State.

It is, moreover, necessary that the body making the reference be a court or tribunal of a Member State.[10] This can be problematic in, for example, the context of arbitration. The ECJ has held that whether an arbitral court or tribunal can be regarded as an emanation of a Member State will depend on the nature of the arbitration in question. The fact that the arbitral body gives a judgment according to law, and that the award is binding between the parties, will not, however, be sufficient. There must be a closer link between the arbitration procedure and the ordinary court system in order for the former to be considered as a court or tribunal of a Member State.[11]

Article 177 draws a distinction between courts or tribunals which have a discretion to refer to the ECJ, which are covered by Article 177(2), and courts or tribunals 'against whose decisions there is no judicial remedy under national law', which are dealt with in Article 177(3). In this latter instance the body is under an obligation to refer, provided that a decision on a question is necessary to enable the court or tribunal to give judgment. Whether this obligation to refer can be affected by, for example, the existence of an ECJ decision on the matter will be considered below. However, it must first be determined which courts or tribunals are within the ambit of Article 177(3).

Two views have been posited as to the type of bodies covered by the phrase 'against whose decisions there is no judicial remedy under national law'. According to the abstract theory, the only bodies which come within Article 177(3) are those whose decisions are never subject to appeal. According to the concrete theory, the real test is whether the court or tribunal's decision is subject to appeal in the type of case in question.

The case law on this issue is not entirely clear. The ruling of the ECJ in *Costa* v. *ENEL* would suggest that the ECJ favours the concrete theory. In that case the *giudice conciliatore*, magistrate, made a reference to the ECJ. Although the decisions of the *giudice conciliatore* were appealable in some instances, there was no such right of appeal in the particular case, because the sum involved was relatively small. Notwithstanding this fact, the ECJ treated the national court as one against whose decision there was no judicial remedy in the actual case at hand.[12]

[10] Case C–355/89, *DHSS (Isle of Man)* v. *Barr and Montrose Holdings Ltd* [1991] ECR I–3479, establishes that this includes territories to which the general institutional provisions of the EC Treaty apply, even if not all the substantive provisions of Community law are equally applicable. Jacobs A.G. was of the opinion that Art. 177 could also be used in relation to the courts etc. of territories to which any part of the Treaty applies, by virtue of Art. 227, even if it is only in part. See also Case C–100/89, *Kaefer and Procacci* v. *France* [1990] ECR I–4647.

[11] Case 102/81, *Nordsee Deutsche Hochseefischerei GmbH* v. *Reederei Mond Hochseefischerei Nordstern AG and Co KG* [1982] ECR 1095.

[12] Case 6/64, [1964] ECR 585, 592, [1964] CMLR 425.

If the concrete theory is correct, the application of that theory in the context of the United Kingdom might still be problematic. Court of Appeal decisions can be appealed to the House of Lords only if the leave of either the Court of Appeal or the House of Lords is granted. If the Court of Appeal does grant leave to appeal it would clearly not be within Article 177(3), since it would not be a body against whose decisions there was no appeal under national law. The position where it refuses leave to appeal to the House of Lords is more difficult. This is put succinctly by Hartley:[13]

> Assuming that the concrete theory is correct, there are two possible solutions: on the one hand, it could be argued that, if a reference is appropriate, the Court of Appeal is obliged *either* to make the reference *or* to grant leave to appeal to the House of Lords. If it does neither, it would be in breach of Article 177(3). On the other hand, the position could be saved if the House of Lords itself granted leave. In other words, if the Court of Appeal both refuses to make a reference and refuses leave, the House of Lords would be obliged—if the concrete theory is correct—to grant leave to appeal.

Difficulties may also arise in circumstances where the judgment in question can be reconsidered in other proceedings. This issue arose in *Hoffmann-La Roche* v. *Centrafarm*.[14] The plaintiff sought an interim order from the German courts to prevent the defendant from marketing certain goods with a particular trade mark. The defendant responded by asserting that it had a right to market the products, given the Community law on the issue. The interim order was, nonetheless, made. The judgment of the relevant German court could not be appealed within interlocutory proceedings, but it was capable of being reviewed in the subsequent main action. A ruling made by the German court on Community law could, therefore, be contested in the main action. It was held by the ECJ that there was no obligation to make a reference in such a case, even though there was no appeal from the finding in the interlocutory proceedings themselves, provided that the decision was subject to review in the main action, and provided also that the main action could be initiated by either party.

4. THE EXISTENCE OF A QUESTION: THE DEVELOPMENT OF PRECEDENT

It is clear that Article 177 is designed to be used only if there is a question to be answered which falls into one of the categories mentioned in Article 177(1).

[13] N. 6 above, 282, italics in the original. See *R.* v. *Henn and Darby* [1978] 1 WLR 1031 (CA), [1980] 2 WLR 597 (HL) for an example of this situation arising. For a discussion of the issues arising from this type of case, see Hartley, *ibid.* 282–3, and F. Jacobs, 'Which Courts and Tribunals Are Bound to Refer to the European Court?' (1977) 2 ELRev. 119.

[14] Case 107/76, [1977] ECR 957, [1977] 2 CMLR 334.

There may be a number of different reasons why a 'question' which is posed by the national court does not necessitate a ruling by the ECJ. One obvious instance is that in which the ECJ has already given a ruling on the matter. This is exemplified by the following decision.

Cases 28–30/62, Da Costa en Schaake NV, Jacob Meijer NV and Hoechst-Holland NV v. Nederlandse Belastingadministratie [1963] ECR 31, [1963] CMLR 224

The facts in the case were materially identical to those in Case 26/62, *Van Gend en Loos* v. *Nederlandse Administratie der Belastingen* [1963] ECR 1. The questions asked were also materially identical to those posed in the *Van Gend* case.

THE ECJ

The regularity of the procedure followed by the Tariefcommissie in requesting the Court for a preliminary ruling under Article 177 of the EEC Treaty has not been disputed and there is no ground for the Court to raise the matter of its own motion.

The Commission . . . urges that the request be dismissed for lack of substance, since the questions on which an interpretation is requested from the Court in the present cases have already been decided . . . in Case 26/62, which covered identical questions raised in a similar case.

This contention is not justified. A distinction should be made between the obligation imposed by the third paragraph of Article 177 upon national courts or tribunals of last instance and the power granted by the second paragraph of Article 177 to every national court or tribunal to refer to the Court of the Communities a question on the interpretation of the Treaty. Although the third paragraph of Article 177 unreservedly requires courts or tribunals of a Member State against whose decisions there is no judicial remedy under national law—like the Tariefcommissie—to refer to the Court every question of interpretation raised before them, the authority of an interpretation under Article 177 already given by the Court may deprive the obligation of its purpose and thus empty it of its substance. Such is the case especially when the question raised is materially identical with a question which has already been the subject of a preliminary ruling in a similar case.

When it gives an interpretation of the Treaty in a specific action pending before a national court, the Court limits itself to deducing the meaning of the Community rules from the wording and spirit of the Treaty, it being left to the national court to apply in the particular case the rules which are thus interpreted. Such an attitude conforms with the function assigned to the Court of ensuring unity of interpretation of Community law within the six Member States . . .

It is no less true that Article 177 always allows a national court, if it considers it desirable, to refer questions of interpretation to the Court again. This follows from Article 20 of the Statute of the Court of Justice, under which the procedure laid down for the settlement of preliminary questions is automatically set in motion as soon as such a question is referred by a national court.

The Court must, therefore, give a judgment on the present application.

The interpretation of Article 12 of the EEC Treaty, which is here requested, was given in the Court's judgment . . . in Case 26/62.

[*The Court then repeated the judgment it had given in the case of* Van Gend en Loos. *It continued as follows.*]

The questions of interpretation posed in this case are identical with those settled as above and no new factor has been presented to the Court.

In these circumstances the Tariefcommissie must be referred to the previous judgment.

The approach of the ECJ appears clearly in this extract. The ability of a national court to refer a matter to the ECJ is, in formal terms, preserved, even if a ruling on the issue has been given by the Court. However, it is clear that an application in such instances must raise some new factor or argument. If it does not do so, then the Court will be strongly inclined to restate the substance of the earlier case. Moreover, the Court makes it evident that the existence of a ruling on the point can deprive the obligation of a national court to refer 'of its purpose and thus empty it of its substance'. The *Da Costa* case, therefore, indicates the beginnings of, what is in effect a system of precedent. These seeds have been developed by the ECJ in later cases:

Case 283/81, Srl CILFIT and Lanificio di Gavardo SpA v. Ministry of Health
[1982] ECR 3415, [1983] CMLR 472

The plaintiffs were textile firms who alleged that certain duties which they were obliged to pay under Italian law were in breach of Regulation 827/68. The Italian Ministry of Health urged the Italian Court of Cassation, against whose decisions there was no judicial remedy under national law, not to refer the matter to the ECJ, on the ground that the answer to the substantive question was so obvious as to obviate the need for a reference. The Court of Cassation decided that this contention was itself an issue of Community law. It therefore requested a ruling from the ECJ on whether the obligation to refer imposed in Article 177(3) was unconditional, or whether it was premised on the existence of reasonable interpretive doubt about the answer which should be given to a question. The ECJ's response to the *acte clair* point will be examined in detail below. The ECJ also gave guidance on the relevance of its prior decisions.

THE ECJ

8. In this connection, it is necessary to define the meaning for the purposes of Community law of the expression 'where any such question is raised' in order to determine the circumstances in which a national court or tribunal against whose decisions there is no judicial remedy under national law is obliged to bring a matter before the Court of Justice.

9. In this regard, it must in the first place be pointed out that Article 177 does not constitute a means of redress available to the parties to a case pending before a national court or tribunal. Therefore the mere fact that a party contends that the dispute gives rise to a question concerning the interpretation of Community law does not mean that the court or tribunal concerned is compelled to consider that a question has been raised within the meaning of Article 177. On the other

hand, a national court or tribunal may, in an appropriate case, refer a matter to the Court of Justice of its own motion.

10. Secondly, it follows from the relationship between paragraphs (2) and (3) of Article 177 that the courts or tribunals referred to in paragraph (3) have the same discretion as any other national court or tribunal to ascertain whether a decision on a question of Community law is necessary to enable them to give judgment. Accordingly, those courts or tribunals are not obliged to refer to the Court of Justice a question concerning the interpretation of Community law raised before them if that question is not relevant, that is to say, if the answer to that question, regardless of what it may be, can in no way affect the outcome of the case.

11. If, however, those courts or tribunals consider that recourse to Community law is necessary to decide a case, Article 177 imposes an obligation on them to refer to the Court of Justice any question of interpretation which may arise.

12. The question submitted by the Corte di Cassazione seeks to ascertain whether, in certain circumstances, the obligation laid down by paragraph (3) of Article 177 might nonetheless be subject to certain restrictions.

13. It must be remembered in this connection that in its judgment of 27 March 1963 in Joined Cases 28–30/62 (*Da Costa* v. *Nederlandse Belastingadministratie*) the Court ruled that: 'Although paragraph (3) of Article 177 unreservedly requires courts or tribunals of a Member State against whose decision there is no judicial remedy under national law . . . to refer to the Court every question of interpretation raised before them, the authority of an interpretation under Article 177 already given by the Court may deprive the obligation of its purpose and thus empty it of its substance. Such is the case especially when the question raised is materially identical with a question which has already been the subject of a preliminary ruling in a similar case.'

14. The same effect, as regards the limits set to the obligation laid down by paragraph (3) of Article 177, may be produced where previous decisions of the Court have already dealt with the point of law in question, irrespective of the nature of the proceedings which led to those decisions, even though the questions at issue are not strictly identical.

15. However, it must not be forgotten that in all such circumstances national courts and tribunals, including those referred to in paragraph (3) of Article 177, remain entirely at liberty to bring a matter before the Court of Justice if they consider it appropriate to do so.

The above extract contains a number of important observations concerning the relationship between the national courts and the ECJ. Some of these concern the degree of discretion possessed by the former in deciding whether to refer a case to the latter. These will be considered in detail below.[15] For the present, attention will be concentrated on that part of the judgment which is concerned with the effect of prior decisions.

The *CILFIT* case adds to the earlier decision in *Da Costa* by stating that a case can be relied on even if the ruling did not emerge from the same type of proceedings, and even though the questions at issue are not strictly identical.

[15] See below, 420–6.

Provided that the point of law has already been determined by the ECJ, this can be relied on by a national court in a later case and obviates the need for a reference. This is qualified by the last paragraph in the extract, in which the ECJ leaves it open to the national court to refer in such circumstances if it really wishes to do so. The message from the ECJ is none the less clear. There is a clear encouragement to national courts to rely on prior rulings of the ECJ, in instances where the substance of the legal point has already been adjudicated. Those earlier ECJ rulings will, in that sense, be regarded as precedents for the national courts.

This development of a system of precedent has implications for the more general relationship between national courts and the ECJ touched on in the introduction. It modifies the original conception of a horizontal and bilateral relationship. The reasons are clear. In so far as ECJ rulings do have precedential value, they place the Court in a superior position to the national courts. The very existence of a system of precedent is indicative of a shift to a vertical hierarchy between the Community and national court regimes, since it is the former which will be laying down the authoritative interpretation of a legal point, which will then be adopted by the latter. The creation of a body of precedent serves also to render that relationship less bilateral, and more multilateral, since an earlier ECJ ruling can be relied on by any national court which is faced with the point of law which has already been decided by the ECJ.

Both of the cases discussed thus far have concerned the impact of an earlier ECJ ruling when it has been Member State action which has been alleged to be in breach of the Treaty. The ECJ has been even more forceful when the impact of its own previous decisions on the validity of Community legislation has been in issue. This is exemplified by the *ICC* case:

Case 66/80, International Chemical Corporation v. Amministrazione delle Finanze dello Stato [1981] ECR 1191, [1983] 2 CMLR 593

Council Regulation 563/76 was designed to reduce the stocks of skimmed-milk powder. The Regulation made the grant of certain Community aid dependent on proof that the recipient had purchased a certain quantity of such skimmed-milk held by an intervention agency. Compliance with this obligation was secured, *inter alia*, by the payment of security which was forfeited if the skimmed-milk was not in fact bought. The plaintiff received the Community aid and paid the security, but it did not comply with the obligation to buy the skimmed-milk powder, and hence the national intervention agency did not release the security. In an earlier case the ECJ had found that Regulation 563/76 was invalid, because the price at which the milk powder was to be bought was regarded as disproportionately high.[16] The plaintiff, therefore, took the view that the security could not be forfeited, since it only served to ensure compliance with an obligation (to buy the

[16] See Case 116/76, *Granaria* v. *Hoofdproduktschap voor Akkerbouwprodukten* [1977] ECR 1247, [1979] 2 CMLR 83.

milk powder) which was itself invalid. The Italian court requested a ruling on whether the earlier judgment, holding the regulation to be null and void, was effective in any subsequent litigation, or whether such a finding was only of relevance in relation to the court which had originally sought the ruling.

THE ECJ

11. The main purpose of the powers accorded to the Court by Article 177 is to ensure that Community law is applied uniformly by national courts. Uniform application of Community law is imperative not only when a national court is faced with a rule of Community law the meaning and scope of which is to be defined; it is just as imperative when the Court is confronted by a dispute as to the validity of an act of the institutions.

12. When the Court is moved under Article 177 to declare an act of one of the institutions to be void there are particularly imperative requirements concerning legal certainty in addition to those concerning the uniform application of Community law. It follows from the very nature of such a declaration that a national court may not apply the act declared to be void without once more creating serious uncertainty as to the Community law applicable.

13. It follows therefrom that although a judgment of the Court given under Article 177 of the Treaty declaring an act of an institution, in particular a Council or Commission regulation, to be void is directly addressed only to the national court which brought the matter before the Court, it is sufficient reason for any other national court to regard that act as void for the purposes of a judgment which it has to give.

14. That assertion does not however mean that national courts are deprived of the power given to them by Article 177 of the Treaty and it rests with those courts to decide whether there is a need to raise once again a question which has already been settled by the Court where the Court has previously declared an act of a Community institution to be void. There may be such a need in particular if questions arise as to the grounds, the scope and possibly the consequences of the invalidity established earlier.

15. If that is not the case national courts are entirely justified in determining the effect on the cases brought before them of a judgment declaring an act void given by the Court in an action between other parties.

16. It should further be observed, as the Court acknowledged in its judgments of 19 October 1977 in Joined Cases 117/76 and 16/77 *Ruckdeschel and Diamalt*,[17] and Joined Cases 124/76 and 20/77, *Moulins de Pont-à-Mousson* and *Providence Agricole*,[18] that as those responsible for drafting regulations declared to be void the Council or the Commission are bound to determine from the Court's judgment the effect of that judgment.

17. In the light of the foregoing considerations and in view of the fact that by its second question the national court has asked, as it was free to do, whether Regulation 563/76 was void, the answer should be that that is in fact the case for the reasons already stated in the judgments of 5 July 1977.

The decision of the ECJ in the *ICC* case provides further evidence of the attitude of the Court to the issue of precedent. The national court is left with

[17] [1977] ECR 1753, [1979] 2 CMLR 445.

[18] [1977] ECR 1795, [1979] 2 CMLR 445.

the discretion to refer a matter to the Court, even if the latter has already given judgment on the issue. However, the ECJ makes it patently clear that, although such a judgment is addressed primarily to the court which requests the original ruling, it can and should be relied on by other national courts before which the matter arises. The original ruling will, in this sense, have a multilateral and not merely a bilateral effect. A decision of the ECJ will, therefore, have a precedential impact on all national courts within the Community, and this serves to enhance the status of the ECJ itself as the supreme court within the Community system.

While a ruling by the ECJ on the validity of a Community regulation will have an *erga omnes* effect, the Court has made it clear that national courts cannot themselves find a Community norm to be invalid. This emerges from the *Foto-Frost* case:

Case 314/85, Firma Foto-Frost v. Hauptzollamt Lübeck-Ost [1987] ECR 4199, [1988] 3 CMLR 57

A national court inquired whether it had the power to declare invalid a Commission decision, on the ground that it was in breach of a Community regulation on a certain issue.

THE ECJ

13. In enabling national courts against whose decisions there is a judicial remedy under national law to refer to the Court for a preliminary ruling questions on interpretation or validity, Article 177 did not settle the question whether those courts themselves may declare that acts of Community institutions are invalid.

14. Those courts may consider the validity of a Community act and, if they consider that the grounds put forward before them by the parties in support of invalidity are unfounded, they may reject them, concluding that the measure is completely valid. By taking that action they are not calling the existence of the Community measure into question.

15. On the other hand, those courts do not have the power to declare acts of the Community institutions invalid. As the Court emphasised in the judgment of 13 May 1981 (Case 66/80, *International Chemical Corporation* v. *Amministrazione delle Finanze* [1981] ECR 1191), the main purpose of the powers accorded to the Court by Article 177 is to ensure that Community law is applied uniformly by national courts. That requirement of uniformity is particularly imperative when the validity of a Community act is in question. Divergences between courts in the Member States as to the validity of Community acts would be liable to place in jeopardy the very unity of the Community legal order and detract from the fundamental requirement of legal certainty.

. . .

17. Since Article 177 gives the Court exclusive jurisdiction to declare void an act of a Community institution, the coherence of the system requires that where the validity of a Community act is challenged before a national court the power to declare the act invalid must also be reserved to the Court of Justice.

18. It must also be emphasised that the Court of Justice is in the best position to decide on the validity of Community acts. Under Article 20 of the Protocol on

the Statute of the Court of Justice of the EEC, Community institutions whose acts are challenged are entitled to participate in the proceedings in order to defend the validity of the acts in question. Furthermore, under the second paragraph of Article 21 of that Protocol the Court may require the Member States and institutions which are not participating in the proceedings to supply all information which it considers necessary for the purpose of the case before it . . .

19. It should be added that the rule that national courts may not themselves declare Community acts to be invalid may have to be qualified in certain circumstances in the case of proceedings relating to an application for interim measures; however, that case is not referred to in the national court's question.[19]

20. The answer to the first question must therefore be that national courts have no jurisdiction to declare that acts of Community institutions are invalid.

5. THE EXISTENCE OF A QUESTION: THE 'ACTE CLAIR' DOCTRINE

A national court may well feel that, even though one of the parties to the case before it has argued that there is a question of Community law to be considered, this claim is misconceived. The national court may believe that the answer to the issue is so clear that no reference to the ECJ is warranted. National courts have, in the past, refused to make a reference for this reason.[20] The conditions in which it is legitimate for a national court to take this course were considered in the *CILFIT* case:

Case 283/81, Srl CILFIT and Lanificio di Gavardo SpA v. Ministry of Health [1982] ECR 3415, [1983] CMLR 472

The facts of this case have been set out above. In reading what follows, it is important to realize that the conditions which the ECJ stipulates may operate independently from the situation in which there is a precedent stemming from a prior decision of the ECJ. Where a precedent does actually exist, then the relationship of the ECJ and the national court is as set out in the preceding section. The *acte clair* doctrine may apply in circumstances where no such prior decision of the ECJ on this point currently exists. The extract which is given below follows on immediately from that given above.

THE ECJ

16. Finally, the correct application of Community law may be so obvious as to leave no scope for any reasonable doubt as to the manner in which the question

[19] On this point see now Cases C–143/88 and 92/89, *Zuckerfabrik Süderdithmarschen AG* v. *Hauptzollamt Itzehoe* [1991] ECR I–415, [1993] 3 CMLR 1, in which the ECJ developed principles for the granting of interim relief by national courts where the validity of a national measure which is implementing a Community norm is challenged on the basis that the Community norm is itself invalid.

[20] See e.g. *Re Société des Pétroles Shell-Berre* [1964] CMLR 462.

raised is to be resolved. Before it comes to the conclusion that such is the case, the national court or tribunal must be convinced that the matter is equally obvious to the courts of the other Member States and to the Court of Justice. Only if those conditions are satisfied may the national court or tribunal refrain from submitting the question to the Court of Justice and take upon itself the responsibility for resolving it.

17. However, the existence of such a possibility must be assessed on the basis of the characteristic feature of Community law and the particular difficulties to which its interpretation gives rise.

18. To begin with, it must be borne in mind that Community legislation is drafted in several languages and that the different language versions are equally authentic. An interpretation of a provision of Community law thus involves a comparison of the different language versions.

19. It must also be borne in mind, even where the different language versions are entirely in accord with one another, that Community law uses terminology which is peculiar to it. Furthermore, it must be emphasised that legal concepts do not necessarily have the same meaning in Community law and in the law of the various Member States.

20. Finally, every provision of Community law must be placed in its context and interpreted in the light of the provisions of Community law as a whole, regard being had to the objectives thereof and to its state of evolution at the date on which the provision in question is to be applied.

21. In the light of all those considerations, the answer to the question submitted by the Corte Suprema di Cassazione must be that paragraph (3) of Article 177 of the EEC Treaty is to be interpreted as meaning that a court or tribunal against whose decisions there is no judicial remedy under national law is required, where a question of Community law is raised before it, to comply with its obligation to bring the matter before the Court of Justice, unless it has established that the question raised is irrelevant or that the Community provision in question has already been interpreted by the Court or that the correct application of Community law is so obvious as to leave no scope for any reasonable doubt. The existence of such a possibility must be assessed in the light of the specific characteristics of Community law, the particular difficulties to which its interpretation gives rise and the risk of divergences in judicial decisions within the Community.

The implications of the ECJ's decision in the *CILFIT* case have been considered by a number of commentators. Two different views of the case will be presented.

(a) *CILFIT as Part of a Discourse with, and Constraint on, National Courts*

G. F. Mancini and D. T. Keeling, From CILFIT to ERT: The Constitutional Challenge Facing the European Court[21]

CILFIT has many detractors. They accuse the Court of having capitulated in the face of the resistance that its role under Article 177 encountered in the late 1960s

[21] N. 1 above, 4.

and early 1970s on the part of some of Europe's great courts. Like Shakespeare's shrew, Katherine, the Court surrendered, at the end of a long and painful taming process, having verified its evident inability to 'seek for rule, supremacy and sway'.

Such criticism is misconceived. It fails to appreciate the subtlety displayed by the Court in *CILFIT*, together with an acute understanding of judicial psychology. It is true that at least three supreme courts—the French Conseil d'Etat, the equivalent Greek organ, and the German Bundesfinanzhof—blatantly defied the authority of the Court of Justice. It is equally certain that, without reaching that extremity the supreme courts of all the other Member States simply ignored the obligation imposed by Article 177 on at least one or two occasions. But the Court of Justice was not 'tamed' by such conduct, nor can it be said to have rendered more than lip service to the argument—the so-called doctrine of *acte clair*—with which the national courts sought to justify their attitude. For proof of that one need only look at the most notorious instance of a breach of the third paragraph of Article 177: namely, the French Conseil d'Etat's refusal to make a reference in the *Cohn-Bendit* case. Such a refusal would clearly not have been justified under the *CILFIT* guidelines, no matter how liberally they are construed.

The correct analysis of *CILFIT* was given by a Danish scholar, Professor Hjalte Rasmussen,[22] who maintains that the judgment was based on an astute strategy of 'give and take'. The Court, recognizing that it could not in any case coerce the national courts into accepting its jurisdiction, concedes something—a great deal in fact, nothing less than the right not to refer if the Community measure is clear—to the professional or national pride of the municipal judge, but then, as we have just seen, restricts the circumstances in which the clarity of the provision may legitimately be sustained to cases so rare that the nucleus of its own authority is preserved intact (or rather consolidated because it voluntarily divested itself of a part of its exclusive jurisdiction). The objective of the Court is plain: by granting supreme courts the power to do lawfully that which they could in any case do unlawfully, but by subjecting that power to stringent conditions, the Court hoped to induce the supreme courts to use willingly the 'mechanism for judicial co-operation' provided by the Treaty. The result is to eliminate sterile and damaging conflicts and to reduce the risk that Community law might be the subject of divergent interpretations.

For Mancini and Keeling *CILFIT* is then to be seen as a necessary dialogue between the ECJ and the national courts, the intent being to rein in the latter. On this view the give and take of *CILFIT* involved the ECJ in accepting the *acte clair* doctrine in principle, but placing significant constraints on its exercise in the hope that national courts would play the game and only refuse to refer when matters really were unequivocally clear.

(b) *CILFIT as a Flexible Tool which can be Manipulated by National Courts*

Not all writers have, however, perceived the *CILFIT* ruling as a successful instance of the ECJ curbing the discretion of national courts. Compare the views of Mancini and Keeling with those of Arnull:

[22] H. Rasmussen, 'The European Court's *Acte Clair* Strategy in *CILFIT*' (1984) 9 ELRev. 242.

A. Arnull, The Use and Abuse of Article 177[23]

The effect of the *CILFIT* decision, it was argued,[24] would be to enable national judges to justify any reluctance they might feel to ask for a preliminary ruling by reference to a decision of the European Court. Of the factors to be borne in mind by national courts before they concluded that the meaning of a provision of Community law was clear, only the requirement that the different language versions be compared, it was submitted, had any teeth. However, even this requirement was less onerous than it seemed, as comparison of the different language versions would usually be carried out by reference to the version in the judge's own tongue. Moreover, the extension of the *da Costa* principle noted above risked opening the way for extensive examinations by national courts of the European Court's case law in order to elicit the answer to a particular question. In short, the overall effect of *CILFIT* would be to encourage national courts to decide points of Community law for themselves. This could only jeopardise the uniform application of the Treaty.

Arnull then examines the practice of the United Kingdom courts which have cited the *CILFIT* decision. He concludes in the following vein:[25]

The English cases in which *CILFIT* has been cited and a reference made seem to support Rasmussen's view that the effect of that decision, despite appearances to the contrary, would be to make national courts wary of deciding points of Community law for themselves. However, the English cases where *CILFIT* was mentioned but no reference made show that sometimes the outcome of that ruling has been far less beneficial. They illustrate how it can be used to justify refusing to make a reference where the national court has formed a view as to how the points of Community law at issue should be resolved. Courts in the United Kingdom make far fewer references than courts in other Member States of comparable size and even some smaller ones, as the results of a project co-ordinated by the European University Institute in Florence show. It is therefore a serious matter when a decision of the European Court is used by the English Courts as a reason for failing to take a step which it might otherwise have been more difficult to avoid.

6. PRECEDENT, ACTE CLAIR, AND SECTORAL DELEGATION: THE DEVELOPMENT OF A MORE HIERARCHICAL JUDICIAL SYSTEM

Opinions will doubtless continue to differ on the rationale for, and success of, the ECJ's strategy in *CILFIT*. The doctrine of precedent, the *acte clair*

[23] (1989) 52 MLR 622, 626.

[24] Arnull is referring to an earlier piece, 'Reflections on Judicial Attitudes at the European Court' (1985) 34 ICLQ 168, 172.

[25] N. 23 above, 636–7.

concept, and sectoral delegation of functions to national courts do, however, have broader ramifications for the development of the judicial system in the Community as a whole. The reasons this is so will be considered within this section.

Let us begin by considering the *doctrine of precedent* itself. The *Da Costa* decision, which introduced a *de facto* system of precedent into Community law, can be seen as a rational step for the ECJ to have taken. Rasmussen is surely correct in pointing out the advantages which this tactic has for Community law.[26] The *authority* of the Court's decisions is thereby enhanced, in the sense that those decisions can be seen by national courts as authoritative rulings on the issues contained therein. The fact that this may have altered the original conception of the relationship between national courts and the ECJ, from one which was essentially bilateral, in which rulings were only of relevance to the national court which requested them, to one which was essentially multilateral, in which ECJ rulings would have an impact on all national courts, is undeniable. It might also have been expected, since it affords the ECJ the basis from which to construct a more truly authoritative and federal system of Community law.

The decision of the ECJ in the *CILFIT* case to reinforce this doctrine, and to expand it to embrace past decisions which might have been given in different proceedings, and to cover also previous cases which have dealt with the same point of law, even if the question posed was somewhat different, was surely not unintentional. The ECJ would have been aware of the use made by national courts of the *Da Costa* ruling. The ECJ's determination to expand the precedential impact of past cases, notwithstanding this evidence, is also explicable. The explanation is of the same type as that given above. By expanding the precedential impact of past decisions in this manner, the ECJ thereby increased the authoritative scope of its past rulings. Those rulings were now to have authority for situations in which the point of law at stake is the same, even though the exact questions posed in earlier cases were different, and even though the proceedings in which the issue originally arose differed.

It may be objected that this legitimation of the system of precedent leaves open the possibility that national courts may misinterpret past ECJ authority, and even refuse to make a reference on mistaken assumptions about the existing state of Community law on an issue. There are two answers to this objection.

On the one hand, it can be accepted that national courts may make mistakes of this nature, but this does not undermine the rationality of having a system of precedent. The development of such a system is still perfectly sensible, provided that it leads *in aggregate* to a more effective regime of Community law. This point requires explanation. Let us accept that a system of precedent entails certain 'error costs', in terms of the possibility of mistakes

[26] N. 22 above, 249–50.

by national courts. The acceptance of precedent does, however, also have 'benefits'. The benefits are substantial and important. At the most fundamental level these reside in the fact that the national courts now become enforcers of Community law in their own right. Once an issue of Community law has been determined by the ECJ, national courts can then apply that law without further resort to the ECJ. The national courts are, in this sense, 'enrolled' as part of a network of courts adjudicating on Community law, with the ECJ at the apex of that network. National courts are no longer to be seen as courts which only apply national law. They become 'delegates' in the enforcement of EC law, and part of a broader Community judicial hierarchy. The amount of work that can be processed through this enlarged judicial regime is thereby increased. The costs of precedent must therefore be weighed against the benefits which ensue therefrom. These benefits include both the increased volume of Community law which can be litigated, mostly correctly, at any one time, and also the important symbolic advantage which flows from the recognition that the national courts are part of a real Community judicial hierarchy.

On the other hand, the legitimation of precedent by the ECJ, notwithstanding the possibility that mistakes may occur, can be defended on the ground that there was not, in reality, any other step for the ECJ to take. Let it be accepted for the sake of argument that the original conception of the relationship between the ECJ and national courts really was bilateral; that rulings by the Court were only meant to be of relevance for the national court which requested them. This bilateral conception was certain to be placed under severe strain, precisely because it was always unrealistic. Taken literally it would mean that a ruling would have to be given, even if the inquiry sought by a national court replicated exactly the inquiry in an earlier decision made by the ECJ. The Court would be 'forced' solemnly to hear the matter, only to reach the same conclusion as it had done previously, with this conclusion being a precise carbon copy of the original finding on the matter. A judicial system could not be supposed to exist on such terms. It would come under severe strain from both directions. The ECJ would quickly tire of the waste of time and resources thereby entailed. The national courts would not see the sense of a system which placed pressure on them to allow issues to be litigated again, in circumstances in which the ECJ had already given a considered judgment.

It is, therefore, not surprising that the ECJ took the step it did in *Da Costa*, of allowing a national court to refer a matter again if it so wished, but making it clear that this would not be needed unless the national court really did believe that there was some aspect of the matter which had not been properly considered or was novel. The expansion of this idea in *CILFIT* marks an extension of the same reasoning.

Let us now move to *acte clair*. How does the ECJ's treatment of this concept fit in with the preceding analysis? How does it fit in with a general strategy in which the ECJ assumes a more federal appellate role within the Community judicial hierarchy? For the sake of clarity the *acte clair* doctrine will be taken in the following sense: to cover instances in which there has as yet been no direct ECJ ruling on the actual issue which arises before the national court.

The argument would be as follows. The Court in *CILFIT* was faced with a choice. It could have chosen to deny any place for the *acte clair* doctrine in Community law. This was the view espoused by Advocate General Capotorti.[27] The Court chose not to follow this approach, and instead gave the doctrine the limited support evident from the preceding extract. Now it might be contended, as seen above, that the real objective was to deal a death blow to the concept, by hedging it around with a plethora of restrictions. Or, to extend the discourse metaphor employed earlier, that the Court's purpose in legitimating the concept was to convince national courts to be more responsible when using it.

We must, however, distinguish cause and effect. Even accepting the Mancini/Keeling thesis on the Court's overall purpose, the effect of the decision is to leave any cases which do fall within these conditions to be decided by the national courts. For such clear-cut cases, then, the national courts operate once again as the delegates of the ECJ for the application of Community law. The ECJ itself can then utilize its time in the resolution of more problematic cases. The strict conditions which the ECJ sets for the application of the concept help to ensure that national courts will not readily regard cases as coming within this sphere unless they really are free from interpretive doubt. It is doubtless true that national courts could still manipulate these criteria, should they be minded to do so, and thereby avoid the need to make a reference. Notwithstanding this possibility of misuse by the national courts, the qualified approval given to the concept by the ECJ can still be regarded as rational for the following reasons.

One such reason is that the cost/benefit analysis discussed above in the context of precedent would apply equally here. The fact that a national court might, on occasion, misapply the criteria, intentionally or unintentionally, does not render the exercise a failure. These costs would have to be balanced against the benefits which would be gained. These would consist of the more expeditious discharge of straightforward cases in the national courts; and also the fact that this method of dealing with such case law would further emphasize the role of national courts as but one part of a broader judicial hierarchy which has the ECJ at the apex.

The other reason the qualified acceptance of the *acte clair* idea can be regarded as rational is that there are 'safety' devices built into the system as a whole, quite independently of the conditions mentioned in *CILFIT* itself. The type of case which is of concern to us is that in which a national court refuses to make a reference, even though the conditions in *CILFIT* are not present. This is clearly a danger, as the preceding discussion makes clear. However, even should this transpire the matter might, if it is of more general

[27] [1982] ECR 3415, 3439.

importance, still come before the ECJ via a different legal system: if an issue is of significance it might well arise in other Member States, and hence a referral from such an alternative route would be possible. Moreover, even if this should not transpire, it would still be open to the ECJ to correct aberrant interpretations by national courts, in the context of a case on a related point which has come before it. The danger of incorrect constructions made by national courts becoming embedded or ossified, while possible, should not, therefore, be over-stated. The dangers which are inherent within the *CILFIT* strategy are further alleviated by the fact that the ECJ has made it clear that national courts have no jurisdiction to declare acts of the Community institutions to be invalid. This is demonstrated by the *Foto-Frost* case considered above.[28]

This discussion would be incomplete if it did not take into account what is in effect *sectoral delegation of responsibility* from the Community judicial institutions to the national courts. One of the themes which we have sought to emphasize throughout this book is the interconnection between the institutional and substantive law of the Community. It is of particular importance in this context. By the phrase 'sectoral delegation of responsibility' we mean a conscious choice made by the Community judicial institutions to devolve and delegate certain application and enforcement functions to the national courts. The most notable instance where this has occurred is in the context of competition policy.[29] The rationale for this devolution is instructive. The Commission is charged with the initial role in the enforcement of competition policy. It does not possess anything like the resources needed effectively to police even a fraction of all possible competition violations. The resolution of this resourcing problem has been to call in aid the national courts. These have always played a role in the enforcement of competition law, but there has now been a move to generalize this, whereby straightforward competition violations are dealt with at national level. The Commission, the CFI, and the ECJ will deal with more difficult cases, or those which raise new issues of principle.

There is a very real connection between this aspect of the topic, precedent, and the *acte clair* doctrine. Sectoral delegation of responsibility feeds off these concepts. The cases which the national courts will deal with are rendered easier both because of the accumulated weight of Community precedent in this area, and because, even where no precedent actually exists, the matter may none the less be evident within the sense of the *acte clair* doctrine.

Now it would, of course, be mistaken to pretend that there are no difficulties with the application of this regime.[30] But then few choices are ever problem-free. The willingness of the Community to persist with this approach bears testimony to the themes explored throughout this section. There may, of course, be mistakes made by the national courts, and in that sense error costs. Yet the benefits are equally undeniable and compelling: the more expeditious discharge of large numbers of cases, the consequential improvement in the enforcement of

[28] See above, 411–12 [29] See below, Ch. 22. [30] See below, 1024–5

Community principles, and the further development of a Community judicial hierarchy in which the national courts play an increased role as Community, and not just national, judicial institutions.

7. THE DECISION TO REFER: THE NATIONAL COURT'S PERSPECTIVE

The discussion thus far has touched on a number of factors which can influence the national court's decision whether to refer a matter to the ECJ, in particular the existence of an ECJ ruling on the issue and the *acte clair* doctrine. The more general factors which a national court may or should take into account when making this decision must now be considered. Article 177(2) posits two criteria which must be satisfied before a reference may be made.

The first is that the question must be raised before the court or tribunal of the Member State. However, it has been seen that the Court in the *CILFIT* case held that a national court may none the less raise a matter of its own motion, even if this has not been done by the parties.

The second general criterion is that the national court must consider that a decision on the question is necessary to enable it to give judgment. The ruling in the *CILFIT* case makes it clear that even a national court which is covered by Article 177(3) must believe that a decision on the question is necessary, as a condition precedent to the obligation to make a reference. It should also be pointed out that Article 177 does not provide that the reference must be necessary, but that a decision on the question be necessary, to enable the national court to give judgment. The danger of confusing these two issues is brought out in the *Bulmer* case, which is of further, general interest for the light which it sheds on the way in which courts in the United Kingdom exercise the discretion accorded to them:

H. P. Bulmer Ltd v. J. Bollinger SA
[1974] 2 WLR 202, [1974] 2 CMLR 91

Bollinger made champagne and claimed that the use of the word champagne by makers of cider, in the form of champagne cider, should be prohibited. As part of its claim, Bollinger alleged that the use of the word champagne to describe products other than those which came from the Champagne region in France was contrary to Community law. Bollinger asked that this question of Community law should be referred to the ECJ. The judge at first instance refused to make the reference, and Bollinger appealed to the Court of Appeal.

COURT OF APPEAL: LORD DENNING MR

The impact of the Treaty on English Law

The first and fundamental point is that the Treaty concerns only those matters which have a European element, that is to say, matters which affect people or property in the nine countries of the Common Market besides ourselves. The Treaty does not touch any of the matters which concern solely the mainland of England and the people in it. These are still governed by English law. They are not affected by the Treaty. But when we come to matters with a European element, the Treaty is like an incoming tide. It flows into estuaries and up the rivers. It cannot be held back. Parliament has decreed that the Treaty is henceforward to be part of our law. It is equal in force to any statute . . .

[*His Lordship then quoted section 2(1) of the European Communities Act 1972 and continued as follows:*]

The statute is expressed in forthright terms which are absolute and all-embracing. Any rights or obligations created by the Treaty are to be given legal effect in England without more ado . . . In future, in transactions which cross the frontiers, we must no longer speak or think of English law as something on its own. We must speak and think of community law, of community rights and obligations, and we must give effect to them . . .

By what Courts is the Treaty to be Interpreted?

It is important to distinguish between the task of interpreting the Treaty—to see what it means—and the task of *applying* it—to apply its provisions to the case in hand. Let me put on one side the task of *applying* the Treaty. On this matter in our courts, the English judges have the final word. They are the only judges who are empowered to decide the case itself. They have to find the facts, to state the issues, to give judgment for one side or the other, and to see that the judgment is enforced.

Before the English judges can apply the Treaty, they have to see what it means and what is its effect. In the task of *interpreting* the Treaty, the English judges are no longer the final authority. They no longer carry the law in their breasts. They are no longer in a position to give rulings which are of binding force. The supreme tribunal for *interpreting* the Treaty is the European Court . . .

. . .

The Discretion to Refer or Not to Refer

Short of the House of Lords, no other English court is bound to refer a question to the European Court at Luxembourg. Not even a question on the *interpretation* of the Treaty. Article 177(2) uses the permissive word 'may' in contrast to 'shall' in Article 177(3). In England the trial judge has complete *discretion*. If a question arises on the interpretation of the Treaty, an English judge can decide it for himself. He need not refer it to the Court at Luxembourg unless he wishes. He can say: 'It will be too costly', or 'It will take too long to get an answer', or 'I am well able to decide it for myself'. If he does decide it for himself, the European Court cannot interfere . . . The European Court would not listen to any party who went moaning to them. The European Court take the view that the trial judge has complete discretion to refer or not to refer: see *Rheinmühlen Düsseldorf (Firma)* v. *Einfuhr- und Vorratsstelle für Getreide und Futtermittel*, January 16, 1974—with which they cannot interfere: see *Milchwerke Heinz Wohrmann & Sohn KG* v. *Commission* [1963] CMLR 152. If a party wishes to challenge the decision of the trial judge in England—to refer or not to refer—he must appeal to the Court of Appeal of England . . . The judges of the Court of Appeal, in their turn, have complete discretion . . . If a party wishes to challenge the decision of the Court of Appeal—to refer or not to refer—he must get leave to go to the House of Lords and go there. It is only in that august place that there is no discretion. If the point of interpretation is one which is 'necessary' to give a ruling, the House *must* refer it to the European Court at Luxembourg. The reason behind this imperative is this. The cases which get to the House of Lords are substantial cases of the first importance. If a point of interpretation arises there, it is assumed to be worthy of a reference . . . Whereas the points in the lower courts may not be worth troubling the European Court about . . .

The Condition Precedent to a Reference: It must be 'Necessary'

Whenever any English court thinks it would be helpful to get the view of the European Court—on the interpretation of the Treaty—there is a *condition precedent* to be fulfilled. It is a condition which applies to the House of Lords as well as to the lower courts. It is contained in the same paragraph of Article 177(2) of the Treaty and applies in Article 177(3) as well. It is this. An English court can only refer the matter to the European Court '*if it considers* that a decision on the question is necessary to enable it to give judgment'. Note the words 'if *it* considers'. that is, 'if the *English court* considers'. On this point again the opinion of the English courts is final, just as it is on the matter of discretion. An English judge can say either: 'I consider it necessary', or 'I do not consider it necessary'. His discretion in that respect is final. Let me take the two in order.

(i) If the English judge considers it *necessary* to refer the matter, no one can gainsay it, save the Court of Appeal. The European Court will accept his opinion. It will not go into the grounds on which he based it. The European Court so held in *Van Gend en Loos, NV* [1963] CMLR 105, 128, 129 . . . It will accept the question as he formulates it: *Fratelli Grassi* [1973] CMLR 332, 335. It will not alter it or send it back. Even if it is a faulty question, it will do the best it can with it: see *Deutsche Grammophon* [1971] CMLR 631, 656 . . .

(ii) If the English judge considers it 'not *necessary*' to refer a question of interpretation to the European Court—but instead decides it itself—that is the end of the matter. It is no good a party going off to the European Court. They would not listen to him. They are conscious that the Treaty gives the final word in this respect to the English courts . . . They never do anything to trespass on any ground which is properly the province of the national courts.

The Guide Lines

. . .

(1) *Guide lines as to whether a decision is necessary*

(i) *The point must be conclusive.*

The English court has to consider whether 'a decision on the question is *necessary* to enable it to give *judgment*'. That means judgment in the very case which is before the court. The judge must have got to the stage when he says to himself: 'This clause of the Treaty is capable of two or more meanings. If it means *this,* I give judgment for the plaintiff. If it means *that*, I give judgment for the defendant.' In short, the point must be such that, whichever way the point is decided, it is conclusive of the case. Nothing more remains but to give judgment . . .

(ii) *Previous ruling.*

In some cases, however, it may be found that the same point—or substantially the same point—has already been decided by the European Court in a previous case. In that event it is not necessary for the English court to decide it. It can follow the previous decision without troubling the European Court. But . . . the European Court is *not* bound by its previous decisions. So if the English court thinks that a previous decision of the European Court may have been wrong—or if there are new factors which ought to be brought to the notice of the European Court—the English court may consider it *necessary* to re-submit the point to the European Court. In that event, the European Court will consider the case again. It was so held . . . in the *Da Costa* case [1963] CMLR 224 . . .

(iii) *Acte claire.*

In other cases the English court may consider the point is reasonably clear and free from doubt. In that event there is no need to interpret the Treaty but only to apply it: and that is the task of the English court . . .

(iv) *Decide the facts first.*

It is to be noticed that the word is 'necessary'. This is much stronger than 'desirable' or 'convenient' . . . As a general rule you cannot tell whether it is necessary to decide a point until all the facts are ascertained. So in general it is best to decide the facts first.

(2) *Guidelines as to the exercise of discretion.*

Assuming that the condition about 'necessary' is fulfilled, there remains the matter of discretion . . .

(i) *The time to get a ruling.*

The length of time which may elapse before a ruling can be obtained from the European Court. This may take months and months . . . Meanwhile, the whole action in the English court is stayed until the ruling is obtained. This may be very unfortunate, especially in a case where an injunction is sought or there are other reasons for expedition . . .

(ii) *Do not overload the Court.*

The importance of not overloading the European Court by references to it. If it were overloaded, it could not get through its work . . .

(iii) *Formulate the question clearly.*

The need to formulate the question clearly. It must be a question of *interpretation only* of the Treaty. It must not be mixed up with the facts. It is the task of the national courts to find the facts and apply the Treaty. The European Court must not take that task on themselves. In fairness to them, it is desirable to find the facts and state them clearly before referring the question . . .

(iv) *Difficulty and importance.*

The difficulty and importance of the point. Unless the point is really difficult and important, it would seem better for the English judge to decide it himself. For in so doing, much delay and expense will be saved . . .

(v) *Expense.*

The expense of getting a ruling from the European Court . . .

(vi) *Wishes of the parties.*

The wishes of the parties. If both parties want the point referred . . . the English court should have regard to their wishes, but it should not give them undue weight. The English court should hesitate before making a reference against the wishes of one of the parties, seeing the expense and delay which it involves.

On the facts of the case, Lord Denning MR decided that a reference was not needed. His Lordship reached this decision for a number of reasons, *inter alia*: the time and expense involved; that the facts had not been fully found; and that the point was not a difficult one to determine.[31] Stephenson LJ, with

[31] [1974] 3 WLR 202, 216–17.

whom Stamp LJ concurred, held that a reference should only be made if it was necessary, as opposed to being convenient or desirable, for the purposes of giving judgment in the case before the court. On the facts it was held that there was, as yet, no such necessity.[32]

Lord Denning's judgment is not uncontroversial. The relevant issue is whether a decision on the question posed is necessary to enable the court to give judgment; and not, as suggested at one stage in the judgment, whether a reference is necessary. Moreover, the guidelines given can be criticized in certain respects. The following extract from Jacobs exemplifies this latter point. It begins by critically considering what Lord Denning had to say concerning the relevance of cost and delay:

F. G. Jacobs, When To Refer To The European Court[33]

Lord Denning refers to these matters as grounds for refusing to exercise the discretion to refer; but there will be many situations . . . where both time and costs will be saved by an early reference. Indeed *Bulmer* v. *Bollinger* is the best illustration, since the time and costs incurred by a reference from the judge at first instance, resulting in a ruling from the European Court on the point at issue, will hardly be greater than those incurred by a fruitless appeal to the Court of Appeal against the refusal to make a reference . . .

Closely connected with this is another factor mentioned by Lord Denning, the difficulty and importance of the point . . . Clearly this is a matter which it is proper for the court to consider in exercising its discretion. But in Community law, as in English law, points of the first importance have often arisen in cases where little is at stake between the parties. *Costa* v. *ENEL* is the classic example, but there are many others.

Later national courts which have considered the issue of whether to refer have acknowledged the 'authority' of Lord Denning's judgment in the *Bulmer* case, but have, none the less, tended to be more ready to refer than was the Master of the Rolls. This can be seen from the following two cases:

Customs and Excise Commissioners v. ApS Samex (Hanil Fiber Industrial Co. Ltd, third party) [1983] 1 All ER 1042, [1983] 3 CMLR 194

An EC regulation allowed Member States to impose quantitative limits on the import of textiles from certain countries outside the Community. The implementation of the import scheme was left to the Member States, who were to issue import licences up to the quota for each year. The defendant made a contract to buy goods from a non-Member State, and obtained a licence which stipulated that the goods had to be shipped by a certain date. The Customs authorities discovered that the goods had been shipped outside the relevant dates, and imposed penalties on the defendant. The latter responded by arguing that the Customs

[32] [1974] 3 WLR, 218–19. [33] (1974) 90 LQR 486, 492.

authorities were in breach of the Community regulation, and sought a reference to the ECJ. Bingham J considered the guidelines set out by Lord Denning MR in *Bulmer*. He then continued as follows.

HIGH COURT: BINGHAM J

In endeavouring to follow and respect these guidelines I find myself in some difficulty, because it was submitted by counsel on behalf of the defendant that the issues raised by his client should be resolved by the Court of Justice as the court best fitted to do so, and I find this a consideration which does give me some pause for thought. Sitting as a judge in a national court, asked to decide questions of Community law, I am very conscious of the advantages enjoyed by the Court of Justice. It has a panoramic view of the Community and its institutions, a detailed knowledge of the treaties and of much subordinate legislation made under them, and an intimate familiarity with the functioning of the Common Market which no national judge denied the collective experience of the Court of Justice could hope to achieve. Where questions of administrative intention and practice arise the Court of Justice can receive submissions from the Community institutions, as also where relations between the Community and non-Member States are in issue. Where the interests of Member States are affected they can intervene to make their views known . . . Where comparison falls to be made between Community texts in different languages, all texts being equally authentic, the multinational Court of Justice is equipped to carry out the task in a way which no national judge, whatever his linguistic skills, could rival. The interpretation of Community instruments involves very often not the process familiar to common lawyers of laboriously extracting the meaning from words used but the more creative process of supplying flesh to a spare and loosely constructed skeleton. The choice between alternative submissions may turn not on purely legal considerations, but on a broader view of what the orderly development of the Community requires. These are matters which the Court of Justice is very much better placed to assess and determine than a national court.

Bingham J went on to make a reference to the ECJ.

R. v. Plymouth Justices, ex parte Rogers
[1982] 3 WLR 1, [1982] 2 All ER 175, [1982] 3 CMLR 221

The defendant was charged with using fishing nets which had a device attached to them, the object of which was to reduce the size of the nets' mesh. This was contrary to Community and national law. The defendant admitted all the evidence, except for the evidence that the device had in fact reduced the size of the nets. At the end of the case the defendant claimed that the Community regulations and the national law were both in breach of the Treaty, and sought a reference to the ECJ. The magistrates decided to make the reference. The prosecution sought judicial review of the magistrates' decision, on the ground that as there was an issue of fact still to be determined (*viz.* the issue whether the device had reduced the size of the nets), therefore a reference was not necessary at this stage. In making this argument, reliance was placed on Lord Denning MR in *Bulmer*, who had stressed that the facts should be found before a reference was to be made.

COURT OF CRIMINAL APPEAL: LORD LANE CJ

Applying these arguments to the facts of the present case, counsel for the applicant submits that if the answer to the questions were in favour of the prosecution, that would not be the end of the case, it would still be necessary for the justices to give an opportunity to the respondent to deal with the issue which he did not admit. He conceded that if the answer was in favour of the respondent, that would be the end of the case, but this, he contends, is not sufficient.

Taking the argument of counsel for the applicant to its logical conclusion, it means that no court or tribunal can refer questions to the European Court under Article 177 unless all the facts have been admitted or found on all the issues in the case. It must be a situation where, subject to argument as to the effect of the answers given by the European Court, it is in a position to give final judgment . . . This involves giving an extremely narrow interpretation to the word 'necessary' in Article 177.

Such an interpretation is not in accord with the general approach to Article 177 adopted by the European Court . . .

[*Lord Lane CJ then quoted from the* Rheinmühlen *case [1974] ECR 33, 38, and from the decision of the Court of Appeal in* Polydor *[1980] 2 CMLR 413, 426, 428.*]

Having regard to these authorities, it is not right to say that the magistrates' court in this case had no jurisdiction to agree to refer questions to the European Court at the stage which the case which was then before them had reached. The validity of the regulations was the substantive issue before the court. As counsel for the respondent correctly pointed out, in a criminal case a defendant was entitled to have a decision whether there was a case to answer before he was called on to lead evidence in support of his defence. To rule on the submission, a decision on the questions of Community law raised by the respondent was necessary, since if the decision was in the respondent's favour he would be acquitted and if it was not, he would have to decide whether to contest further the one issue of fact which remained.

Thus while United Kingdom courts continue to make reference to the guidelines in *Bulmer* they also tend to be more ready to make a reference than his Lordship was in that case. The more modern approach is encapsulated in another ruling by Bingham MR, where His Lordship stated that, once the facts have been found the Community law issue being critical to the final decision of the national court, then the normal course is to refer to the ECJ, unless the national court has real confidence that it can resolve the issue itself.[34]

[34] *R.* v. *International Stock Exchange, ex p. Else* [1993] QB 534. See also *Polydor Ltd* v. *Harlequin Record Shops Ltd* [1980] 2 CMLR 413; *R.* v. *Pharmaceutical Society of Great Britain, ex p. The Association of Pharmaceutical Importers* [1987] 3 CMLR 951; *R.* v. *HM Treasury, ex p. Daily Mail and General Trust plc* [1987] 2 CMLR 1.

8. THE REFERENCE TO THE ECJ: THE INITIAL APPROACH, COME ONE, COME ALL

In the preceding section we have considered the factors which the national court takes into account in deciding whether to refer a matter to the ECJ. This section and the two which follow will be concerned with the reverse side of the same coin: the way in which the ECJ perceives its role when an issue is referred to it by a national court. The discussion within this section will take the following form. Litigants have made a number of different objections to the exercise of the ECJ's jurisdiction, when a reference has been made to it under Article 177. The materials set out below will address the way in which the ECJ has responded to these arguments. In addition, the discussion will also focus on the extent to which the case law contains insights which are of relevance to the more general inquiry outlined at the beginning of the chapter: the extent to which the ECJ's role in relation to national courts has been changing, to become more appellate and federal in nature. When reading the materials within these sections it will become apparent that the approach of the ECJ has altered since the inception of the Community and more particularly within its more recent jurisprudence.

(a) The Correction of Improperly Framed References

A not uncommon objection to the jurisdiction of the ECJ to give a preliminary ruling is that the questions framed by the national court are, in some sense, incorrect. The approach of the ECJ, particularly in the early days of the Community, was, wherever possible, to read the references in such a way as to preserve its ability to pass judgment on the substance of the case. This is exemplified by the *Schwarze* and *Costa* cases:

Case 16/65, Firma C. Schwarze v. Einfuhr- und Vorratsstelle für Getreide und Futtermittel
[1965] ECR 877, [1966] CMLR 172

Schwarze obtained import licences from the Einfuhr- und Vorratsstelle für Getreide und Futtermittel (the EVSt) to import barley. The EVSt fixed the rate of levy which should be paid, pursuant to a Council regulation. The rate of levy was fixed on the basis of a Commission decision. Schwarze argued that the levy rate was too high, and that the Commission decision was both procedurally and substantively illegal. The Finanzgericht therefore submitted a number of detailed questions to the ECJ. Written comments were submitted by France, which argued that many of these questions were not within the scope of Article 177. The French argument was that the questions being asked were really concerned not with the interpretation of the Treaty, but rather with the validity of Community acts; and that the proper way of challenging such acts was via Article 173.

THE ECJ

It appears from the wording of the questions submitted that the Hessisches Finanzgericht is concerned not so much with the interpretation of the Treaty or of an act of a Community institution, as with a preliminary ruling on the validity of such an act under Article 177(1)(b) . . .

In its comments, the government of the French Republic complains that several of the questions submitted call for more than just an interpretation of the Treaty. The Court of Justice would, in answering these alleged questions of interpretation, actually be ruling on points involving not the interpretation of the Treaty but the validity of acts of the EEC institutions.

The contention of the French Republic that Article 177 cannot be used to obtain from the Court a ruling that such an act is null and void is pertinent. That provision does, however, expressly give the Court power to rule on the validity of such an act. Where it appears that the real object of the questions submitted by a national court is a review of the validity of Community acts rather than an interpretation thereof, the Court of Justice must nevertheless decide the questions immediately, instead of holding the referring court to a strict adherence to form which would only serve to prolong the Article 177 procedure and be incompatible with its true nature. Such a strict adherence to form is conceivable in actions between parties whose respective rights must be determined according to strict rules. It would not, however, be appropriate in the very special area of judicial cooperation provided for in Article 177, where the national court and the Court of Justice—each within its own jurisdiction and with the purpose of ensuring a uniform application of Community law—must together and directly contribute to the legal conclusions. Any other procedure would have the result of letting the national courts rule on the validity of acts of the Community.

Case 6/64, Costa v. ENEL [1964] ECR 585, [1964] CMLR 425

The facts of the case have been set out above.[35] It will be remembered that Costa alleged that the nationalization of electricity in Italy infringed certain Articles of the Treaty. The Giudice Conciliatore in Milan sought a ruling on these arguments from the ECJ. The Italian Government objected that the questions posed by the Italian court were not confined to an interpretation of the Treaty, but also asked the ECJ to determine whether certain Italian laws were compatible with the Treaty; the Government argued that the only procedure by which this type of issue could be litigated was Articles 169 and 170.

THE ECJ

The complaint is made that the intention behind the question posed was to obtain, by means of Article 177, a ruling on the compatibility of a national law with the Treaty.

By the terms of this Article, however, national courts against whose decisions, as in the present case, there is no judicial remedy, must refer the matter to the Court of Justice so that a preliminary ruling may be given upon the 'interpretation of the Treaty' whenever a question of interpretation is raised before them. This provision gives the Court no jurisdiction either to apply the Treaty to a

[35] See above, 158.

specific case or to decide upon the validity of a provision of domestic law in relation to the Treaty, as it would be possible for it to do under Article 169.

Nevertheless, the Court has power to extract from a question imperfectly formulated by the national court those questions which alone pertain to the interpretation of the Treaty. Consequently a decision should be given by the Court not upon the validity of an Italian law in relation to the Treaty, but only upon the interpretation of the above mentioned Articles in the context of the points of law stated by the Giudice Conciliatore.

(b) Challenging the Reasons for Making a Reference or the Facts on Which it is Based

Litigants who do not wish the ECJ to make a ruling have often sought to argue that it should reassess either the reasons for making the reference, and/or the facts on which the reference was based. It has already been seen that Lord Denning MR in the *Bulmer* case was forthright in his views about the division of power between the national courts and the ECJ: it was for the former to determine whether a reference was required.[36] This view has, subject to what will be said below, been echoed by the ECJ itself. Three examples can be given of this approach.

In the *Costa* case a further objection to the ECJ giving a preliminary ruling was that the ruling was not necessary for the solution of the dispute before the national court. The Court responded by stating that Article 177 'is based on a clear separation of functions between national courts and the Court of Justice', and that the latter is not empowered to 'investigate the facts of the case or to criticise the grounds and purpose of the request for interpretation'.[37]

Case 35/76, Simmenthal SpA v. Ministero delle Finanze [1976] ECR 1871, [1977] 2 CMLR 1

Simmenthal had imported meat into Italy from France. The meat was inspected at the border, and the costs of the inspection were levied on Simmenthal. It was argued by Simmenthal that the charges were equivalent to customs duties on trade between Member States, that they were contrary to the Treaty and that it should be entitled to recover the money paid. Proceedings were begun in the Italian court, which referred certain questions to the ECJ.

THE ECJ

2. The plaintiff in the main action takes the view that the fees have been charged unlawfully, on the one hand because the organisation of compulsory and systematic veterinary and public health inspections . . . since the implementation of the veterinary and public health directives of 26 June 1964 has been a measure having an effect equivalent to a quantitative restriction prohibited by the Treaty, which is the reason why the imposition of fees on this occasion was unlawful and, on the other hand because, in any event, the charging of fees for such inspections

[36] See above, 420–3. [37] N. 12 above, 593.

> is an infringement of Articles 9 and 13 of the Treaty which prohibit the imposition of any charges having an effect equivalent to a customs duty on imports . . .
>
> 3. The Government of the Italian Republic has denied that the veterinary and public health inspections of the products referred to in the directives which it organised were carried out systematically and produces documents in support of its view that this is not the case. Consequently it has expressed doubts as to the relevance of the questions referred.
>
> 4. Article 177 of the EEC Treaty is based on a distinct separation of functions between national courts and tribunals on the one hand and the Court of Justice on the other hand and it does not give the Court jurisdiction to take cognisance of the facts of the case, or to criticise the reasons for the reference.

The ruling of the ECJ in the *Pierik* case[38] provides the third in the trilogy of cases exemplifying the point. In that case, which concerned the application of social security schemes to workers and their families within the Community, the Commission took the view that the question posed by the Dutch court was not relevant to the case at hand. The ECJ reiterated that Article 177 was based on a clear division of function, and that this precluded the ECJ from judging the relevance of the questions asked, or from determining whether those concepts of Community law really were applicable to the case before the national court.

The approach of the ECJ during the Community's early development was therefore an open and flexible one. The Court clearly did not wish to discourage litigants from having recourse to Community law. This was especially important precisely because, as we saw at the beginning of this Chapter, it was through Article 177 that the Court was able to develop the fundamental doctrines of direct effect and supremacy. Nor did the ECJ wish to place obstacles in the path of national judiciaries who were minded to make use of Article 177 by refusing to answer questions unless they were perfectly framed. This would not have encouraged national judges to make use of novel legal machinery.

9. THE REFERENCE TO THE ECJ: THE FOUNDATIONS OF THE COURT'S AUTHORITY OVER THE CASES REFERRED TO IT

Notwithstanding the authorities considered in the previous section, the ECJ has, on occasion, considered the reasons for the making of a reference, and has also declined to give a ruling where it believed that it would be inappropriate to do so. The best known early example of this is the decision in the *Foglia* case:

[38] Case 117/77, *Bestuur van het Algemeen Ziekenfonds, Drenthe-Platteland* v. *G. Pierik* [1978] ECR 825, [1978] 3 CMLR 343.

Case 104/79, Pasquale Foglia v. Mariella Novello [1980] ECR 745, [1981] 1 CMLR 45

Foglia made a contract to sell wine to Novello, and the contract stated that Novello would not be liable for various charges, including any taxes levied by the French or Italian authorities which were contrary to Community law. The goods were carried by Danzas, a general transporter. The contract of carriage also contained a clause stipulating that Foglia would not be liable for charges which were contrary to Community law. Danzas in fact paid a French tax, and this was included in the bill submitted to Foglia, who paid the bill including the amount of the disputed tax, notwithstanding the clause in the contract of carriage which would have entitled him not to pay that portion of the total bill. Foglia then sought to recover this amount from Novello in an action before an Italian court. The latter refused to pay, relying on the clause in her contract with Foglia which stipulated that she would not be liable for any unlawful charge. Novello argued that the charge was contrary to Article 95 of the Treaty. The Italian court sought a preliminary ruling whether the French tax was in fact contrary to Community law.

THE ECJ

9. In their written observations submitted to the Court of Justice the two parties to the main action have provided an essentially identical description of the tax discrimination which is a feature of the French legislation concerning the taxation of liqueur wines; the two parties consider that that legislation is incompatible with Community law. In the course of the oral procedure before the Court Foglia stated that he was participating in the procedure before the Court in the view of the interest of his undertaking as such and as an undertaking belonging to a certain category of Italian traders in the outcome of the legal issues involved in the dispute.

10. It thus appears that the parties to the main action are concerned to obtain a ruling that the French tax system is invalid for liqueur wines by the expedient of proceedings before an Italian court between two private individuals who are in agreement as to the result to be attained and who have inserted a clause in their contract in order to induce the Italian court to give a ruling on the point. The artificial nature of this expedient is underlined by the fact that Danzas did not exercise its rights under French law to institute proceedings over the consumption tax although it undoubtedly had an interest in doing so in view of the clause in the contract by which it was also bound and moreover of the fact that Foglia paid without protest that undertaking's bill which included a sum paid in respect of that tax.

11. The duty of the Court of Justice under Article 177 of the EEC Treaty is to supply all courts in the Community with the information on the interpretation of Community law which is necessary to enable them to settle genuine disputes which are brought before them. A situation in which the Court was obliged by the expedient of arrangements like those described above to give rulings would jeopardise the whole system of legal remedies available to private individuals to enable them to protect themselves against tax provisions which are contrary to the Treaty.

12. This means that the questions asked by the national court, having regard to the circumstances of this case, do not fall within the framework of the duties of the Court of Justice under Article 177 of the Treaty.

13. The Court of Justice accordingly has no jurisdiction to give a ruling on the questions asked by the national court.

The judge in the Italian court then referred certain further questions to the ECJ, the essence of which was to ask whether the judgment set out above was consistent with the principle that it was for the national judge to determine the facts and the need for a reference. These issues were dealt with by the ECJ in the second *Foglia* case:

Case 244/80, Pasquale Foglia v. Mariella Novello (No 2) [1981] ECR 3045, [1982] 1 CMLR 585

THE ECJ

12. In his first question the Pretore requested clarification of the limits of the power of appraisal reserved by the Treaty to the national court on the one hand and the Court of Justice on the other with regard to the wording of references for a preliminary ruling and of the appraisal of the circumstances of fact and law in the main action, in particular where the national court is requested to give a declaratory judgment.

. . .

14. With regard to the first question it should be recalled, as the Court of Justice has had occasion to emphasise in very varied contexts, that Article 177 is based on cooperation which entails a division of duties between the national courts and the Court of Justice in the interest of the proper application and uniform interpretation of Community law throughout all the Member States.

15. With this in view it is for the national court—by reason of the fact that it is seised of the substance of the dispute and that it must bear the responsibility for the decision to be taken—to assess, having regard to the facts of the case, the need to obtain a preliminary ruling to enable it to give judgment.

16. In exercising that power of appraisal the national court, in collaboration with the Court of Justice, fulfils a duty entrusted to them both of ensuring that in the interpretation and application of the Treaty the law is observed. Accordingly the problems which may be entailed in the exercise of its power of appraisal by the national court and the relations which it maintains within the framework of Article 177 with the Court of Justice are governed exclusively by the provisions of Community law.

17. In order that the Court of Justice may perform its task in accordance with the Treaty it is essential for national courts to explain, when the reasons do not emerge beyond any doubt from the file, why they consider that a reply to their question is necessary to enable them to give judgment.

18. It must in fact be emphasised that the duty assigned to the Court by Article 177 is not that of delivering advisory opinions on general or hypothetical questions but of assisting in the administration of justice in the Member States. It accordingly does not have jurisdiction to reply to questions of interpretation which are submitted to it within the framework of procedural devices arranged by the parties in order to induce the Court to give its view on certain problems of Community law which do not correspond to an objective requirement inherent in

the resolution of a dispute. A declaration by the Court that it has no jurisdiction in such circumstances does not in any way trespass upon the prerogatives of the national court but makes it possible to prevent the application of the procedure under Article 177 for purposes other than those appropriate for it.

19. Furthermore, it should be pointed out that, whilst the Court of Justice must be able to place as much reliance as possible upon the assessment by the national court of the extent to which the questions submitted to it are essential, it must be in a position to make any assessment inherent in the performance of its own duties in particular in order to check, as all courts must, whether it has jurisdiction. Thus the Court, taking into account the repercussions of its decisions in this matter, must have regard, in exercising the jurisdiction conferred upon it by Article 177, not only to the interests of the parties to the proceedings but also to those of the Community and of the Member States. Accordingly it cannot, without disregarding the duties assigned to it, remain indifferent to the assessments made by the courts of the Member States in the exceptional cases in which such assessments may affect the proper working of the procedure laid down by Article 177.

. . .

21. The reply to the first question must accordingly be that whilst, according to the intended role of Article 177, an assessment of the need to obtain an answer to the questions of interpretation raised, regard being had to the circumstances of fact and law involved in the main action, is a matter for the national court it is nevertheless for the Court of Justice, in order to confirm its own jurisdiction, to examine, where necessary, the conditions in which the case has been referred to it by the national court.

. . .

25. The reply to the fourth question must accordingly be that in the case of preliminary questions intended to permit the national court to determine whether provisions laid down by law or regulation in another Member State are in accordance with Community law the degree of legal protection may not differ according to whether such questions are raised in proceedings between individuals or in an action to which the State whose legislation is called in question is a party, but that in the first case the Court of Justice must take special care to ensure that the procedure under Article 177 is not employed for purposes which were not intended by the Treaty.

It will be seen from the cases set out below[39] that the ECJ did not immediately build upon the discretion which it arrogated to itself in the *Foglia* ruling. Claims that preliminary rulings should be refused because the case was hypothetical, or the opinion sought was arbitrary, did not fare well before the ECJ.

Case 261/81, Walter Rau Lebensmittelwerke v. De Smedt PvbA [1982] ECR 3961, [1983] 2 CMLR 496

Belgian law required that margarine should be retailed only in blocks which were cube-shaped. An action was brought in the German courts between a German

[39] See also Case C–150/88, *Eau de Cologne and Parfumerie-Fabrik Glockengasse No 4711 KG* v. *Provide Srl* [1989] ECR 3891, [1991] 1 CMLR 715.

seller and a Belgian buyer of margarine which was packaged in cone-shaped tubs. In the course of these proceedings, the German court referred to the ECJ a question on the compatibility of the Belgian law with Article 30 of the Treaty.

THE ECJ

8. The Belgian Government points out that the importation of the margarine into Belgium by the defendant in the main action is already the subject of criminal proceedings in Belgium and that the Court should therefore inquire whether a dispute which gave rise to the request for a preliminary ruling is a genuine dispute. In this regard the Belgian Government recalls the judgment . . . in Case 244/80 *Foglia* [1981] ECR 3045.

9. In this instance there is nothing in the file on the case which provides grounds for doubting that the dispute is genuine. Therefore there is no reason for concluding that the Court has no jurisdiction.

Case 46/80, Vinal SpA v. Orbat SpA [1981] ECR 77, [1981] 3 CMLR 524

Vinal, who was an Italian importer of alcohol, made a contract with Orbat to supply the latter with certain synthetic alcohol from France. Orbat accepted the basic price charged, but contended that the imposition of a revenue charge by the Italian Government was contrary to Article 95 of the Treaty. The Italian court made a reference seeking the correct interpretation of Article 95 in these circumstances.

THE ECJ

5. The Italian Government has put in issue the admissibility of the request for a preliminary ruling submitted by the Pretura, Casteggio. It raises the question whether the action brought before the national court is not really a fictitious dispute and whether the procedure under Article 177 has not been employed in this case to impeach the Italian State in the absence of any dispute giving rise to questions of Community law as between the parties. In these circumstances the Italian Government asks whether the situation should not be compared to that which formed the subject-matter of the judgment . . . in Case 104/79 *Foglia* v. *Novello* [1980] ECR 745 in which the Court held that it had no jurisdiction to give a ruling on the questions put to it by the national court.

6. In view of that contention, which the Italian Government set out in its written observations, the Court requested the parties to supply it with additional information.

7. Having studied the replies to those questions the Court considers that in this case it is possible to set aside the doubts expressed by the Italian Government and to broach the substance of the case.

What view should then be taken of the *Foglia* case in the light of the reasoning employed therein, and in the light of the later case law touching on the same issue? The case generated a considerable amount of comment when it first appeared. Bebr expresses the argument against the *Foglia* ruling:

G. Bebr, The Existence of a Genuine Dispute: An Indispensable Precondition for the Jurisdiction of the Court under Article 177 EEC Treaty?[40]

In its well-established case law the Court of Justice has always viewed Article 177 as establishing a method of co-operation between the national courts and the Court, based on jurisdictional exclusivity rather than on a hierarchical superiority. Moreover it has systematically refused to review the grounds for questions raised and their relevance to the pending litigation, being obviously anxious to demonstrate that its function is limited to an interpretation of Community rules or to a review of validity of Community acts . . .[41]

The Court refrained from reviewing the relevance of questions raised even in such instances in which a referring national court admitted that the question referred was not relevant to the litigation but that its clarification would be helpful for future cases . . . Thus in *Rewe-Zentrale* v. *Hauptzollamt Emmerich*, the referring national court itself stated in its reference that one of the questions raised was not relevant to the litigation. Yet it considered the question appropriate because the litigation was a test case for a great number of similar forthcoming cases . . .

. . . In this case it took note of several factors from which it inferred that the dispute was fabricated and that, therefore, it lacked jurisdiction. It is difficult to imagine how otherwise the Court could have reached such a conclusion. In a sense it went even further than merely reviewing the relevance of the questions raised. It reviewed the very nature of the dispute. Thus it noted the ambivalent stand of the plaintiff or, to cite another example, it viewed the failure of the carrier to challenge the legality of the imposed charges before the French courts as another indication of the fabricated nature of the litigation . . .

The fabricated nature of a dispute as a precondition for the admissibility of a referral is a slippery concept, not without dangerous pitfalls. The French government which participated in the preliminary proceedings did not, it may be noted, even contest the jurisdiction of the Court. The Court did so of its own motion. Of course, there may be various shades and degrees to which litigation may appear fabricated. The situation may seldom be clear cut. Litigation in which a private party seeks to obtain a ruling in a test case in which it invokes a directly effective Community rule against a Member State before its own national courts may raise a similar problem; it may also lack the character of a genuine dispute. Who may say with any certainty that the plaintiff entertained the action seriously or whether he merely sought to obtain a decision in a test case which although of negligible interest to him, raised a question of principle? Of course, such litigation may, at first, appear less suspicious as to its genuine character than that which arises between private parties—simply because it may be easier in this instance to fabricate such a dispute.[42]

40 (1980) 17 CMLRev. 525, 530–2.

41 The author quotes examples of this approach including cases such as *Costa*.

42 Bebr also objected to the *Foglia* ruling because of the difficulties which it would thereby create for the judge in the national courts, and for the implications which it might have for the ambit of direct effect.

Not all were however opposed to the Court's decision in *Foglia*. Wyatt expresses the argument in favour of the ruling:

D. Wyatt, Foglia (No.2): The Court Denies it has Jurisdiction to Give Advisory Opinions[43]

Where Member States are alleged to have infringed the Treaty . . . actions may be initiated by the Commission or by other Member States to establish that fact under Articles 169 and 170 EEC. Both Articles contain pre-trial safeguards for Member States. Actions under either Article may be subjected to preliminary objections as to admissibility, which the Court will examine to consider whether or not the action in question is capable of securing its intended purpose, i.e. whether or not the Court's jurisdiction has been properly invoked.

. . . At bottom the controversy over the Court's decision in *Foglia* v. *Novello* . . . turns on the simple question whether or not references to the European Court from national courts are subject, before the European Court, to the same preliminary objections as to admissibility as any other claim upon the part of private parties, Member States, or Community institutions, to invoke the Court's jurisdiction. If they are not, then the guardians of the European Court's judicial functions, indeed of its very jurisdiction, within the framework of Article 177 EEC, are national courts, rather than the Court itself. It is not impossible that the draftsmen of the Treaty should have ordained such a thing. Simply improbable, in view of the departure from principle which it would involve: superior courts are invariably entrusted with the competence to determine their own jurisdiction.

[*Wyatt then demonstrates,* inter alia, *differing ways in which the ECJ would itself determine various jurisdictional issues, such as whether the body making the reference really was a court or not. At a later point in the article he refers to the reasoning in* Foglia (No 2)*, in which the ECJ emphasizes that it has no jurisdiction to give advisory opinions, and that it must not be compelled to answer questions which are only submitted to it as the result of procedural devices arranged between private parties. He then continues as follows:*]

While the Court must be able to place as much reliance as possible upon assessments by national courts of questions referred, it must, it insisted, be in a position to make *itself* any assessment inherent in the performance of its own duties, in particular in order to *check*, as all *courts* must, whether it *had jurisdiction.* In exercising its jurisdiction under Article 177, the Court was bound to consider, not only the interests of the parties to the proceedings, but also the interests of the Community, and of the Member States . . .

The Court's reasoning is convincing. It affirms its right to determine its own jurisdiction, and contrasts its own essentially judicial functions, with the delivery of advisory opinions. The distinction between a judgment and an advisory opinion is that the former affects the legal position of the parties to a dispute; the latter has no such effect. The capacity to give a *judgment* itself characterises the organ in question as a *court*. The capacity to give legal advice of course has no such corollary; indeed, the constitutional objection to courts giving advisory opinions in the United States has from early times been rationalised as a facet of the separation of powers between the executive and the judiciary. It will be noted that

[43] (1982) 7 ELRev. 186, 187–8, 190, italics in the original.

the preliminary rulings are binding on national courts which seek them—a feature rather at odds with the capacity to give advisory opinions (the International Court of Justice's jurisdiction to give Advisory Opinions is discretionary, and such Opinions—in contrast with its judgments in contentious proceedings—are not binding).

10. THE REFERENCE TO THE ECJ: DEVELOPING CONTROL OVER THE ARTICLE 177 PROCEDURE

The principle in *Foglia* lay dormant for some considerable time. Attempts to invoke it did not, as we have seen above, prove markedly successful. This served to fuel the belief that the case was a one-off, justified by the particular circumstances and unlikely to be repeated. It was business as usual, with the ECJ's 'come one, come all' strategy operating as before.

This view obscured the important point of principle which the ECJ had indelibly imprinted on the law reports in *Foglia*: it, the ECJ, would be the ultimate determinor of the scope of its own jurisdiction. Due regard would, of course, be paid to the views of the national courts on whether a response was required to a question, but the ultimate decision rested with the ECJ itself. If, in order to resolve this issue, further and better particulars were required from the national courts, then these must be forthcoming. When understood in this sense *Foglia* was not simply, or even primarily, about hypothetical cases and the like. It was about the primacy of control over the Article 177 procedure and about the shape of the judicial hierarchy, involving Community and national courts, which operates through this Article. The original division of function between national courts and the ECJ may have been separate but equal, as manifested in the idea that the former decide whether to refer and on what grounds, while the latter gives the ruling on the matter placed before it. *Foglia* represented a reshaping of that conception. The ECJ was not simply to be a passive receptor, forced to adjudicate on whatever was placed before it. It was to assert control over the suitability of the reference. The decision in the case itself, concerning the allegedly hypothetical nature of the proceedings, was simply one manifestation of this assertion of jurisdictional control.

The reasons the ECJ wishes to have ultimate control over the Article 177 procedure are readily apparent. As a matter of principle, as Wyatt has correctly pointed out, superior courts do, and should have, the capacity to determine the limits to their own jurisdiction. Within the context of the EC this must mean that the ECJ is the ultimate determinor of whether, for example, a body seeking a reference really is a court or tribunal. It should also mean, as the ECJ stated in *Foglia (No 2)*, that the ECJ can 'make any assessment inherent in the performance of its own duties in particular in order to check, as all courts must, whether it has jurisdiction'.

If this constitutes the general rationale for ultimate ECJ control over the Article 177 procedure, there are other more specific reasons why the ECJ may wish to decline to hear a case presented to it. The ECJ will normally be in a better position to make an assessment of whether a case falls within one of these categories than would a national court which is less familiar with the intricacies of Community law.

The hypothetical nature of the question provides one example. The reasons for refusing to give rulings in such cases are varied. They are, in part, of a practical nature, in the sense that it would be a waste of judicial resources to give a ruling in a case which was hypothetical, because the putative problem may never in fact transpire. There are also problems of a more conceptual nature. If a case really is hypothetical it may be unclear precisely who should be the appropriate parties to the action, and there is the connected difficulty that the relevant arguments for and against the point being argued may not be put. Moreover, if the hypothetical problem does actually become 'concrete', it may not do so in exactly the form envisaged by the court's judgment, thereby giving rise to problems concerning the relevance of the original judgment in the light of what has subsequently transpired.

While there may, therefore, be sound reasons for refusing to give opinions in hypothetical cases, there is also a fine line dividing that type of case from test cases.[44] One function of all legal systems is to enable people to plan their lives with the knowledge of the legal implications of the choices they make. Test cases enable individuals to gain such knowledge. That the line between advisory opinions/hypothetical judgments and test cases can be a fine one is exemplified by the facts of the *Foglia* case itself.[45]

The hypothetical nature of the claim before the Court is not the only reason it may decline to hear it. It may wish to do so because the questions raised are not indeed relevant to the resolution of the substantive action which

[44] Case C–412/93, *Leclerc-Siplec* v. *TFI Publicité and M6 Publicité*, Jacobs A.G., 24 Nov. 1994.

[45] It is far from self-evident that the *Foglia* case on its facts was a hypothetical case of the kind which the ECJ should have declined. The facts certainly did not represent a request for an advisory opinion concerning a hypothetical case, as that phrase is normally understood. The case was concerned with an actual seller of wine, whose business was being affected by a current French tax, which he believed to be contrary to Community law. The issues were sharply defined and current. The arguments utilized by the Court to suggest that the issue could and should have been resolved by a different route will not withstand examination. Danzas, the general carrier, would have no incentive to press the claim in France, even though it initially paid the tax. The company was a general carrier, and it would make no commercial sense for it to start an expensive suit which was of no specific concern to its business. There is also an explanation for Foglia's decision to pay Danzas, even though it could have resisted payment under the terms of its contract. If Foglia had resisted payment then one of two outcomes would have been likely. Either Danzas would have accepted this, swallowed the loss, and still not have pursued the claim in France because it would not be worthwhile; and/or it would have accepted this, but increased the cost of carriage by the amount of the tax for subsequent journeys and thence passed it on to Foglia. In either eventuality the legality of the tax under Community law might have remained uncontested, because both of the preceding outcomes would probably have been reached without formal litigation. Even if, contrary to the above, Danzas had resorted to formal litigation with Foglia, there is every reason to believe that this suit would have been initiated in Italy, since it would have been an ordinary contract suit the governing law of which would probably have been Italian.

has been started in the national court. Given the complexity of Community law this may not be evident to the referring court.

A third rationale for refusing to take a case may be that the questions are not articulated clearly enough for the ECJ to be able to give any meaningful legal response. It would not be a sensible or proper use of the ECJ's time to attempt to elicit the 'real' question from a reference which was very badly framed. This should be contrasted with the situation in which the ECJ does tease out the real question from a reference which has been imperfectly formulated.

Closely allied to this third rationale is a fourth, which covers the situation in which the facts are insufficiently clear for the Court to be able to apply the relevant legal rules. It is often mistakenly thought that the ECJ merely responds in an abstract manner to very generally framed questions under Article 177. This is not so. The Court will normally only be able to characterize the nature of the relevant legal issue if it is presented with a reference which has an adequate factual foundation.

In recent years[46] the ECJ has shown itself to be more willing to decline to take a case on one of the grounds articulated above.

The *Meilicke*[47] case has many of these features. The action was brought by a German lawyer who had spent a considerable amount of time and energy attacking a particular theory of non-cash contributions of capital as it had been developed by the German courts. He held a single share in a German company and the company sought to raise capital. He put a number of questions to the German company in order to determine whether the method of raising capital involved the issue of non-cash subscriptions. Being dissatisfied with the result he then began an action in the German courts and a question was referred to the ECJ on the compatibility of the theory of disguised non-cash subscriptions with the Second Banking Directive.

The ECJ declined to give a ruling. It referred to the duty of co-operation between national courts and the ECJ, accepting in principle that when the national court asked a question it should give an answer. However, it then went on to cite *Foglia (No 2)*, drawing from that case the principle that the ECJ may, if necessary, have to examine the circumstances of the reference in order to determine whether the Court's jurisdiction had been properly invoked. The ECJ emphasized that the national court should find the facts first and deal with any issues of national law, and that it was not for the Court to deliver advisory opinions on hypothetical issues. On the facts of the case it declined to give a ruling because the questions which were raised were hypothetical: it had not been shown that the issue of non-cash subscriptions was really at stake in the main substantive action, and therefore the possible compatibility of that theory with the banking directive was a hypothetical issue.

[46] For earlier case law, Case 126/80, *Salonia* v. *Poidomani and Giglio* [1981] ECR 1563; Case C–368/89, *Crispoltini* v. *Fattoria Autonoma Tabacchi di Città di Castello* [1991] ECR I–3695.

[47] Case C–83/91, *Wienand Meilicke* v. *ADV/ORGA F.A. Meyer AG* [1992] ECR I–4871.

Similar reasoning is to be found in the *Dias* case.[48] Dias was a van driver who was prosecuted for modifying his imported vehicle in a manner which altered its categorization for tax purposes, without having paid the extra tax. The ECJ was presented with a number of questions from the national court concerning the compatibility of the relevant national rules with Article 95. The ECJ used exactly the same reasoning as in *Meilicke* to describe the relationship between national courts and the ECJ under Article 177, adding only that it was essential for national courts to explain the reasons why a ruling was necessary in order to resolve the dispute before them. This addition was not fortuitous: the ECJ decided that six of the eight questions posed by the national court had manifestly no connection with the substantive action, and that this was so on the facts as stated by the referring court. These questions were not relevant and were not answered. This filtering approach was apparent once again in the *Corsica Ferries* case[49] where the Court reiterated that it had no jurisdiction to rule on questions which bore no relation to the facts or the subject-matter of the main action and were therefore not required to be answered in order to settle the dispute. It decided that only four of the possible eight questions met this criterion. The same concern with relevance is evident in the *Monin* case[50] where the ECJ held that it lacked jurisdiction to answer questions which did not involve an interpretation of Community law which was objectively required for the decision to be taken by the national court. It therefore declined to answer questions placed before it by an insolvency judge, given that this judge would not have to deal with these issues in the insolvency itself.

The ECJ has also had occasion to insist in *Telemarsicabruzzo*[51] that the need to give a practical interpretation of Community law required the national courts to define the factual and legal framework in which the questions had arisen, or at the very least to explain the factual assumptions on which those questions were based. In the absence of such information the ECJ declined to hear the case. The Court has, however, held that these requirements are less pressing where the questions relate to specific technical points and the file contains sufficient information even though it does not provide an exhaustive description of the legal and factual situation.[52]

[48] Case C–343/90, *Lorenco Dias* v. *Director da Alfandega do Porto* [1992] ECR I–4673.

[49] Case C–18/93, *Corsica Ferries Italia Srl* v. *Corpo dei Piloti del Porto di Genova* [1994] ECR I–1783.

[50] Case C–428/93, *Monin Automobiles-Maison du Deux-Roues* [1994] ECR I–1707.

[51] Cases C–320–322/90, *Telemarsicabruzzo SpA* v. *Circostel, Ministero delle Poste e Telecommunicazioni and Ministerio della Difesa* [1993] ECR I–393. See also Case C–157/92, *Banchero* [1993] ECR I–1085; Case C–386/92, *Monin Automobiles* v. *France* [1993] ECR I–2049.

[52] Case C–316/93, *Vaneetveld* v. *Le Foyer SA* [1994] ECR I–763.

11. THE REFERENCE TO THE ECJ: CASE-LOAD, DOCKET CONTROL, AND THE EMERGING AGENDA

The rhetoric in the cases just considered will often be phrased in traditional terms: the judgment will speak of the co-operation between national courts and the ECJ and of the fact that it is for the national court to decide whether to refer or not. This form of language *is* still meaningful. The relationship under Article 177 is a co-operative one. It is, however, now common for the traditional formula to be supplemented by appropriately drawn caveats which make it clear that the ECJ will not adjudicate if the questions are not relevant, or if they are hypothetical etc.[53] With changes in the rhetoric have come changes in reality. The co-operation between national courts and the ECJ still exists, but the latter is no longer the passive receptor of anything thrust before it. It has begun to exercise more positive control over its own jurisdiction in the manner redolent of most other superior courts.

We have already seen why the Court would wish as a matter of principle to have this greater degree of control. Practical pressures are driving the ECJ in the same direction. The 1961 volume of the European Court Reports had 350 pages. The 1993 volume contained 7,066 pages for the ECJ and another 1,500 for the CFI. It does not take a mathematical wizard to realize that the 'come one, come all' strategy would lead to practical problems of work-load for the ECJ. This is without the additional burdens which flow from increased membership of the Community, and from the expansion of its competence after the SEA and the TEU. The establishment of the CFI has done something to alleviate the workload, but not enough in the longer term.

What, then, are the options for the ECJ in such circumstances? One option would be to obviate the problem by creating what are in effect a series of lower Community courts which operate in regions of the EC.[54] These courts would, for example, be able to deliver preliminary rulings to national courts. The ECJ would then be the highest Community court taking certain types of cases itself and hearing appeals from the Regional courts.[55] A second possibility would be for the ECJ to be able to filter all requests for preliminary rulings with the object of taking only those cases which are of significance for the development of Community law. Other superior courts, such as the Supreme Court in the United States, exercise this type of control over their case-load. Most such courts have some form of filtering to ensure that the case is worth the time of

[53] See e.g., Cases C–332, 333, and 335/92, *Eurico Italia Srl* v. *Ente Nazionale Risi* [1994] ECR I–711, [1994] 2 CMLR 577.

[54] J. P. Jacque and J. Weiler, 'On the Road to European Union—A New Judicial Architecture: An Agenda for the Intergovernmental Conference' (1990) 27 CMLRev. 185.

[55] Although this looks like a federal court system on the US model, there are still real differences which flow from the fact that the structure preserves the centrality of the idea of a reference from a national court, as opposed to an appeal which is in the hands of the individual.

the country's top court.[56] Yet another option would be to fast-track some cases, so that they could be dispensed with expeditiously should the ECJ decide that the matter was really covered by its existing case law.[57] Changes of this nature may not be adopted in the foreseeable future. Kennedy points to the consequences for the ECJ which will continue to be pressed by an increasing workload:

T. Kennedy, First Steps Towards a European Certiorari?[58]

> In those circumstances the Court may therefore be thrown back on its own resources and be forced to use, more actively, the means which it already has at its disposal to decline jurisdiction under Article 177 which it has so far used most sparingly. These measures are likely to include on the one hand stricter checking that all the necessary elements for the Court to provide a useful interpretation of Community law are available to it and on the other hand a more careful examination of the relevance of the questions asked.
>
> For a case to pass both of these tests before the relevant issues of Community law can be dealt with by the Court of Justice will require a greater awareness on the part of national judges of *their* role in the Article 177 procedure. It is hard to escape the conclusion that in *Meilicke* and *Lourenço Dias* the Court of Justice, by spelling out in identical and categorical terms the nature of that role, has made a start towards ensuring that cases submitted to it under the preliminary ruling procedure raise issues which it is appropriate to deal with at that level and that such cases should be presented in such a way as to enable the Court of Justice to give a useful reply to the questions which they raise.

12. INTERPRETATION VERSUS APPLICATION

Article 177 gives the ECJ power to interpret the Treaty, but does not specifically empower it to apply the Treaty to the facts of a particular case. Indeed the very distinction between interpretation and application is meant to be one of the characteristic features of the division of authority between the ECJ and national courts. The former interprets the Treaty, the latter apply that interpretation to the facts of a particular case. This distinction is, moreover, perceived to be a further reason for differentiating the relationship between national courts and the ECJ from that which exists in a more truly federal, appellate structure. In a more fully developed federal appellate system, the superior court may well decide the actual case, on fact and/or law, including

[56] The difficulty with such an option at present is that, whereas in a country such as the US, a lower federal court could resolve the matter, the absence of such a judicial hierarchy in the EC means that this is not possible. It would be more feasible if there were to be regional Community courts as per option one.

[57] T. Kennedy, 'First Steps Towards a European *Certiorari*?' (1993) 18 ELRev. 121, 128–9.

[58] N. 57 above, 129.

the precise remedy available; it will often make the decision and apply it to the actual case.

As with many other aspects of Community law the theory and the reality have not always marched hand in hand. The dividing line which separates interpretation and application can be perilously thin. Other things being equal, the more detailed is the interpretation provided by the ECJ the closer does it approximate to application. The line between the two ideas is rendered more problematic by the fact that many of the questions submitted to the Court are, by their nature, very detailed, and are only capable of answer at all through a specific response by the ECJ.

From the very inception of the Court's jurisdiction under Article 177, litigants have attempted to argue that the Court should decline to give a ruling because the question posed was not asking for an interpretation of the Treaty, but necessitated rather an application of it. The ECJ has not been deterred by such objections. Thus in the *Van Gend en Loos* case[59] itself it was argued that the question presented concerning the tariff classification of urea-formaldehyde required, not an interpretation of the Treaty, but rather an application of the relevant Dutch customs legislation. The Court rejected the objection, stating that the question did relate to interpretation, the point at stake being in essence the meaning to be attributed to the notion of duties existing before the coming into force of the Treaty.

A willingness to respond in detailed terms can be perceived in, for example, *Cristini* v. *SNCF*.[60] The case was concerned with the meaning of Article 7(2) of Regulation 1612/68, which provides that a Community worker who is working in another Member State should be entitled to the same 'social advantages' as workers of that state. The question put by the French court was whether this meant that a provision which allowed large French families to have reduced rail fares was a social advantage within the ambit of Article 7(2). Although the ECJ denied that it had power to determine the actual case, in reality it did just that, and responded to the question by stating that the concept of a social advantage did indeed include the very type of fare reduction offered by the French rail authorities.[61]

A more recent example of the detailed nature of the ECJ's rulings can be found in the *Marleasing* case.[62] The case has already been considered above in the context of direct effect.[63] The relevance of the ruling in the present context is that it exemplifies once again how detailed the rulings of the Court can be, even if there is, in formal terms, no direct effect. The ECJ, in essence, produced a detailed response to the question whether Article 11 of Directive 68/151 was exhaustive of the types of case in which the annulment of the registration of a company could be ordered. Spanish law held contracts to be void

[59] Case 26/62, [1963] ECR 1.

[60] Case 32/75, [1975] ECR 1085.

[61] *Ibid.*, para. 19.

[62] Case C–106/89, *Marleasing SA* v. *La Comercial Internacional de Alimentacion SA* [1990] ECR 4135, [1992] 1 CMLR 305.

[63] See above, 194–6.

if they were made without cause or where the cause was unlawful, and these grounds did not exist under Article 11. It was held by the Court that, even though the Directive did not have horizontal direct effect, the national court should none the less take it into account when interpreting their national law, and endeavour to ensure that the national law was in conformity with it. The ECJ then engaged in a detailed analysis of whether Article 11 should be regarded as exhaustive, and decided that it was. Grounds of annulment of the type existing in Spanish law could not co-exist with the grounds mentioned in the Directive. Now it is, of course, the case that the Spanish courts still had some 'choice' as to how far they should take account of the Directive when interpreting their law. This is, however, no more than to say that national courts have a volitional choice whether to comply with Community norms. Assuming that the national court does wish to comply, the ECJ in the *Marleasing* case furnished it with a very specific answer to the question asked and one which would require no more of the Spanish court than to execute the ruling of the ECJ.

As stated at the outset of this section, the willingness of the ECJ to provide very specific answers to questions serves to blur the line between interpretation and application. It also serves to render the idea of the ECJ and the national courts being separate but equal, each having their own assigned roles, more illusory. The more detailed the ruling given by the ECJ, the less there is for the national court to do, other than literally apply that ruling to the case at hand, in the sense of executing an issue-specific judgment of the Court.

There is much, however, which is of interest for us even in those many situations in which the ECJ does leave an important issue of application to the national courts. What is becoming increasingly clear is that in many such cases the ECJ is in effect delegating an important aspect of Community law to be decided by the national courts. One of many examples will suffice for the present. The ECJ might decide that, as a matter of principle, the idea of collective dominance can apply within Article 86 of the Treaty.[64] It will lay down the general criteria by which the existence of this concept is to be judged and then pass the matter back to the national courts to determine whether these criteria exist on the facts of the case. In cases of this nature it is misguided to perceive the national courts as simply applying Community law, in the sense of executing a decision which has already been arrived at by the ECJ. Their role is more important and creative than this. They will be helping in the articulation, development, and application of Community law itself under the guidance of the principles set out by the ECJ itself.

[64] See below, 973–5.

13. CONCLUSION: A GLIMPSE OF THE FUTURE

The ECJ is not a fully developed federal, appellate supreme court in either a procedural or an institutional sense. In procedural terms, individuals still have no right of appeal to the ECJ and the national court can decide whether a reference is necessary; the Court's judgments are still, in theory at least, only given on points of interpretation and validity; and much play continues to be made of the division of responsibilities between national courts and the ECJ. In institutional terms, notwithstanding the creation of the Court of First Instance, the EC does not yet have the judicial hierarchy characteristic of federal systems. In countries such as the United States, there is a system of federal courts which subsist below the Supreme Court, and these federal courts will exercise jurisdiction over a particular circuit which embraces a geographical area of the country. No such regime has yet been instituted in the Community, and something of this order may well be necessary in the medium term.

Having said all this, it should also be said that the original conception of the relationship between national courts and the ECJ no longer represents reality. As stated at the outset of this Chapter, that relationship was characterized as one which was *horizontal* and *bilateral*. The former connoted the idea that the ECJ and the national courts had separate but equal functions; the latter captured the notion that a ruling by the Court was only of relevance to the national court which requested it. Many of the developments which have been discussed in this Chapter have served to transform the relationship into one which is more *vertical* and *multilateral*. These include: the assertion of the supremacy of Community law over national law; the development of a system of *de facto* precedent; the qualified support for the *acte clair* doctrine; the sectoral devolution of responsibility to national courts; the desire of the ECJ to exercise control over the types of case which it will hear; and the blurring of the line between interpretation and application. All these changes serve to emphasize the evolution of a Community judicial hierarchy in which the ECJ sits at the apex, as the ultimate Constitutional Court for the Community, assisted by national courts which are also to play a role as interpreters and appliers of Community law. The increasing emphasis which the ECJ places on Article 5 of the Treaty, rendering it applicable to national courts as well as to the political arm of Member States, is merely one further and important manifestation of this process in operation.

There are, of course, modern judicial statements which continue to extol the relationship between the ECJ and the national courts in terms redolent of the original model. This is in part because aspects of the original model still remain, and in part because it may make political sense to express the judicial relationship in these terms, in order not to offend the judiciary in national legal systems. This should not, however, serve to mask reality. The Community as a whole is in a state of transition, and it would be surprising if the relationship between the ECJ and the national courts were to remain immune from these wider changes. As the Community moves towards a closer social and political union, one could well expect the ECJ to cement its position at the apex of the judicial hierarchy.

14. FURTHER READING

(a) Books

SCHERMERS, H., TIMMERMANS, C., KELLERMAN, A., and STEWART WATSON, J., *Article 177 EEC: Experiences and Problems* (North Holland, 1987)

(b) Articles

ARNULL, A., 'The Use and Abuse of Article 177 EEC' (1989) 52 MLR 622

——'Does the Court of Justice Have Inherent Jurisdiction?' (1990) 29 CMLRev. 683

—— 'References to the European Court' (1990) 15 ELRev. 375

—— 'The Evolution of the Court's Jurisdiction under Article 177 EEC' (1993) 18 ELRev. 129

BARAV, A., 'Preliminary Censorship? The Judgment of the European Court in *Foglia* v. *Novello*' (1980) 5 ELRev. 443

BEBR, G., 'The Possible Implications of *Foglia* v. *Novello II*' (1982) 9 CMLRev. 421

—— 'Arbitration Tribunals and Article 177 of the EEC Treaty' (1985) 22 CMLRev. 489

DASHWOOD, A., and ARNULL, A., 'English Courts and Article 177 of the EEC Treaty' (1984) 4 YBEL 225

JACOBS, F. G., 'When to Refer to the European Court' (1974) 90 LQR 486

JACQUE, J. P., and WEILER, J., 'On the Road to European Union—A New Judicial Architecture: An Agenda for the Intergovernmental Conference' (1990) 27 CMLRev. 185

KENNEDY, T., 'First Steps Towards a European *Certiorari*?' (1993) 18 ELRev. 121

MAHER, I., 'National Courts as European Community Courts' (1994) 14 LS 226

MANCINI, F., and KEELING, D., 'From *CILFIT* to *ERT*: The Constitutional Challenge Facing the European Court' (1991) 11 YBEL 1

RASMUSSEN, H., 'The European Court's *Acte Clair* Strategy in *CILFIT*' (1984) 9 ELRev. 242

WYATT, D., '*Foglia (No 2)*: The Court Denies it has Jurisdiction to give Advisory Opinions' (1982) 7 ELRev. 186

11

Review of Legality

1. INTRODUCTION

It is readily apparent from the materials considered thus far that the Community has power to advance policy through the promulgation of regulations, directives, and decisions. A great number of such norms are in fact made each year. It would be surprising if some of these were not challenged by those who felt that they were either substantively or procedurally invalid. Any developed legal system must have a mechanism whereby those who harbour such feelings have a legal avenue through which they can test the legality and validity of the governmental norms on the substantive and procedural grounds indicated above. At its most fundamental, therefore, this topic is concerned with access to justice, and the consequential substantive review of legality by the ECJ.

One of the principal methods for such challenge is to be found in Article 173 of the Treaty, but, as will be seen below, other provisions can also be used to attack Community norms. Article 173 reads as follows:

> The Court of Justice shall review the legality of acts adopted jointly by the European Parliament and the Council, of acts of the Council, of the Commission, and of the ECB other than recommendations and opinions, and acts of the European Parliament intended to produce legal effects *vis-à-vis* third parties.
>
> It shall for this purpose have jurisdiction in actions brought by a Member State, the Council or the Commission on the grounds of lack of competence, infringement of an essential procedural requirement, infringement of this Treaty or of any rule of law relating to its application, or misuse of powers.
>
> The Court shall have jurisdiction under the same conditions in actions brought by the European Parliament and by the ECB for the purpose of protecting their prerogatives.
>
> Any natural or legal person may, under the same conditions, institute proceedings against a decision addressed to that person or against a decision which, although in the form of a regulation or decision addressed to another person, is of direct and individual concern to the former.
>
> The proceedings provided for in this Article shall be instituted within two months of the publication of the measure, or of its notification to the plaintiff, or, in the absence thereof, of the day on which it came to the knowledge of the latter, as the case may be.

It is evident from the structure of Article 173 that four broad conditions have to be satisfied before an act can successfully be challenged: the act has to be of a kind which is open to challenge at all; the institution or person making the challenge must have standing to do so; there must be a procedural or substantive illegality of a type mentioned in Article 173(1); and the challenge must be brought within the time limit indicated in Article 173(5).

As will become apparent from the ensuing discussion, the interpretation of each of these conditions has proven to be problematic, particularly the extent to which private individuals have standing to contest the legality of Community acts. The analysis which follows will attempt to unravel some of these complexities and will also seek to address the policy issues concerning why the Court appears to have been restrictive in its interpretation of Article 173(4).

The discussion will also focus on a number of different interrelationships which are at play within this important area. One is that between Article 173 and other methods of challenging Community acts, for example through Article 177 of the Treaty. A second point of connection which will be highlighted is the link between standing and other aspects of citizen-involvement in the decision-making process. What connection is there, and what connection should there be, between participation in the making of the original decision or regulation, and standing to challenge the resultant act before the Court? What is the link between standing and the ability to intervene in proceedings before the Court? These are relatively neglected issues but ones which are, as will be seen, of growing importance. Finally, there is the relationship between the intensity of substantive review which the Court engages in if it does allow an applicant to enter its doors and the nature of the subject-matter which is at stake in the action.

2. ARTICLE 173 EC: THE RANGE OF REVIEWABLE ACTS

It is apparent from the wording of Article 173 that it allows the Court to review the legality of acts other than recommendations and opinions. This clearly covers regulations, decisions, and directives, which are listed in Article 189 of the Treaty. The ECJ has, however, also held that this list is not exhaustive, and that other acts which are *sui generis* can also be reviewed, provided that they have binding force or produce legal effects. This is evident from the *ERTA* case:

Case 22/70, Commission v. Council
[1971] ECR 263, [1971] CMLR 335

The Member States acting through the Council adopted a Resolution on 20 March 1970, the object of which was to coordinate their approach to the negotiations for a European Road Transport Agreement (ERTA/AETR). The Commission disliked the negotiating procedure established in the Resolution, and sought to challenge it before the ECJ under Article 173.

THE ECJ

48. As regards negotiating, the Council decided, in accordance with the course of action decided upon at its previous meetings, that the negotiations should be carried on and concluded by the six Member States, which would become contracting parties to the AETR.

49. Throughout the negotiations and at the conclusion of the agreement, the States would act in common and would constantly coordinate their positions according to the usual procedure in close association with the Community institutions, the delegation of the Member State currently occupying the Presidency of the Council acting as spokesman.

50. It does not appear from the minutes that the Commission raised any objections to the definition by the Council of the objective of the negotiations.

51. On the other hand, it did lodge an express reservation regarding the negotiating procedure, declaring that it considered that the position adopted by the Council was not in accordance with the Treaty, and more particularly with Article 228.

52. It follows from the foregoing that the Council's proceedings dealt with a matter falling within the power of the Community, and that the Member States could not therefore act outside the framework of the common institutions.

53. It thus seems that in so far as they concerned the objective of the negotiations as defined by the Council, the proceedings of 20 March 1970 could not have been simply the expression or the recognition of a voluntary coordination, but were designed to lay down a course of action binding on both the institutions and the Member States, and destined ultimately to be reflected in the tenor of the regulation.

54. In the part of its conclusions relating to the negotiating procedure, the Council adopted provisions which were capable of derogating in certain circumstances from the procedure laid down by the Treaty regarding negotiations with third countries and the conclusion of agreements.

55. Hence, the proceedings of 20 March 1970 had definite legal effects both on relations between the Community and the Member States and on the relationship between institutions.

Whether a particular act does in fact produce legal effects may sometimes be controversial.[1] The *IBM* case furnishes a good example of this point:

Case 60/81, International Business Machines Corporation v. Commission [1981] ECR 2639, [1981] 3 CMLR 635

IBM sought the annulment of a Commission letter notifying it of the fact that the Commission had initiated competition proceedings against it, in order to determine whether it was in breach of Article 86 of the Treaty. The letter was

[1] T. C. Hartley, *The Foundations of European Community Law* (3rd edn., Clarendon Press, 1994), 346–53.

accompanied by a statement of objections, with a request that the company reply to it within a specified time. The Commission objected that the impugned letter was not an act challengeable for the purposes of Article 173.

THE ECJ

9. In order to ascertain whether the measures in question are acts within the meaning of Article 173 it is necessary, therefore, to look to their substance. According to the consistent case-law of the Court any measure the legal effects of which are binding on, and capable of affecting the legal interests of, the applicant by bringing about a distinct change in his legal position is an act or decision which may be the subject of an action under Article 173 for a declaration that it is void. However, the form in which such acts or decisions are cast is, in principle, immaterial as regards the question whether they are open to challenge under that article.

10. In the case of acts or decisions adopted by a procedure involving several stages, in particular where they are the culmination of an internal procedure, it is clear from the case-law that in principle an act is open to review only if it is a measure definitively laying down the position of the Commission or the Council on the conclusion of that procedure, and not a provisional measure intended to pave the way for the final decision.

11. It would be otherwise only if acts or decisions adopted in the course of the preparatory proceedings not only bore all the legal characteristics referred to above but in addition were themselves the culmination of a special procedure distinct from that intended to permit the Commission or the Council to take a decision on the substance of the case.

12. Furthermore, it must be noted that whilst measures of a purely preparatory character may not themselves be the subject of an application for a declaration that they are void, any legal defects therein may be relied upon in an action directed against the definitive act for which they represent a preparatory step.

On the facts of the case the applicant failed.[2] The letter was merely the initiation of the competition procedure, a preparatory step leading to the real decision at a later stage; and the statement of objections did not, in itself, alter the legal position of IBM, although it might indicate, as a matter of fact, that it was in some real danger of being fined at a later juncture.[3] By way of contrast the Court held in the *SFEI* case[4] that in an area, such as competition policy, where the Commission has power to investigate and impose fines pursuant to a complaint from an individual, a letter from the Commission indicating that it did not intend to pursue the matter was reviewable as an act producing legal consequences.[5]

[2] See also Cases C–133 and 150/87, *Nashua Corporation* v. *Commission and Council* [1990] ECR I–719.

[3] Compare Case 53/85, *AKZO Chemie BV* v. *Commission* [1986] ECR 1965, [1987] 1 CMLR 231.

[4] Case C–39/93P, *Syndicat Français de l'Express International (SFEI)* v. *Commission* [1994] ECR I–2681.

[5] See also Cases T–10–12, 15/92, *SA Cimenteries CBR* [1992] ECR II–2667, [1993] 4 CMLR 259; Case C–25/92R, *Miethke* v. *European Parliament* [1993] ECR I–473; Case T–83/92, *Zunis Holding SA* v. *Commission* [1994] 5 CMLR 154.

Article 173 now refers to review of the legality of: acts adopted jointly by the European Parliament and the Council; acts of the Council;[6] acts of the Commission; acts of the European Central Bank; and acts of the European Parliament. Prior to the TEU, Article 173 only formally applied to the Council and the Commission, but the ECJ held that the acts of the European Parliament were also susceptible to review by the ECJ.[7] Moreover, as Hartley states, if a Community institution which has the power to take reviewable decisions delegates that power to another institution, the Court will not be prevented from reviewing the acts of such a delegate.[8]

The general principle is that an act which is reviewable will have legal effect until it is set aside by the ECJ or the CFI,[9] and the challenge must be brought within the time limit specified in Article 173(5). The exception to this general rule is for acts which are tainted by particularly serious illegality, which are deemed to be 'non-existent'. Three consequences flow from the ascription of this label. One is that the normal time limits for challenge do not apply, since such an act can never be cloaked with legality by the effluxion of time. A second is that such acts do not have any provisional legal effects. The final consequence is that, odd although it may seem, non-existent acts are not actually susceptible to annulment as such, because there is no 'act' to annul. A judicial finding that an act is non-existent will, however, have the same effect in practice as if it had been annulled. Thus in the *BASF* case[10] the CFI found that a decision of the Commission in competition proceedings against the PVC cartel was non-existent on the grounds that: the Commission could not locate an original copy of the decision which had been duly authenticated in the manner required by the Rules of Procedure; it appeared that the Commissioners had not agreed on the precise text of the decision; and it had been altered after it had been formally adopted. The non-existence of a measure should, said the CFI, be raised by the Court of its own motion at any time during the proceedings. The matter was appealed from the CFI to the ECJ,[11] which took a different view. It held that the defects were not so serious as to make the act non-existent, but it did, however, find that the decision was tainted by sufficient irregularity for it to be annulled.

[6] The Court may review acts of the Council which are intended to have legal effects irrespective of whether they have been passed pursuant to Treaty provisions: Case C–316/91, *European Parliament* v. *Council* [1994] ECR I–625, [1994] 3 CMLR 149. However, decisions adopted by representatives of the Member States acting not as the Council, but as representatives of their governments, and thus collectively exercising the powers of the Member States, are not reviewable under Art. 173: Cases C–181 and 248/91, *European Parliament* v. *Council and Commission* [1994] 3 CMLR 317. It will be for the Court to decide whether a measure really was an act of the institutions or whether it was an act of the Member States acting independently, *ibid.*

[7] Case 294/83, *Parti Ecologiste 'Les Verts'* v. *European Parliament* [1987] 2 CMLR 343. The case is considered below, 471.

[8] Hartley, n. 1 above, 359–60. This assumes that the delegation itself is legal.

[9] Case C–137/92P, *Commission* v. *BASF AG* [1994] ECR I–2555.

[10] Cases T–79, 84–86, 89, 91–92, 94, 96, 98, 102, 104/89, *BASF AG* v. *Commission*, [1992] ECR II–315.

[11] Case C–137/92P, n. 9 above.

3. ARTICLE 173 EEC: STANDING FOR PRIVILEGED APPLICANTS

Article 173(2) states that the action may be brought by a Member State, the Council, or the Commission. It appears from this that these applicants are always to be allowed to bring an action, even where the decision is in fact addressed to some other person or body.

Whether the Parliament should be accorded the status of a privileged applicant has proven to be more contentious. We have already had occasion to consider Parliament's role as a litigant and reference should be made to that discussion when reading this section.[12] Prior to the passage of the TEU it was not accorded any formal privileged status. Article 173 was re-drafted in the TEU and Article 173(3) now reflects the legal position which the ECJ had arrived at even before the TEU's passage: the Parliament does have standing to defend its own prerogatives. The saga may be briefly described as follows.

In the '*Comitology*' case the Court's finding had not placed the Parliament in a strong position,[13] the ECJ rejecting the Parliament's argument that it should have the same unlimited standing as other privileged applicants. The issue was considered again in the '*Chernobyl*' case, and the Court took a different view.

Case C–70/88, European Parliament v. Council [1990] ECR I–2041

The case arose out of a Council regulation adopted after the Chernobyl incident. The regulation sought to establish the maximum level of radioactive contamination of food and feedingstuffs. This regulation was adopted under Article 31 of the Euratom Treaty, but the Parliament argued that it should be based on Article 100A of the EC Treaty instead. The rationale for this was that Parliament has greater rights under the latter, since the co-operation procedure allows it more involvement in the legislative process.

THE ECJ

15. In the judgment in Case 302/87, after having stated the reasons why the Parliament did not have capacity to bring an action under Article 173 of the EEC Treaty, the Court pointed out that various legal remedies were available to ensure that the Parliament's prerogatives were defended. As was observed in that judgment, not only does the Parliament have the right to bring an action for failure to act, but the Treaties provide means for submitting for review by the Court acts of the Council or the Commission adopted in disregard of the Parliament's prerogatives.

16. However, the circumstances and arguments adduced in the present case show that the various legal remedies provided for both in the Euratom Treaty and

[12] See above, 65–9.

[13] Case 302/87, *European Parliament* v. *Council* [1988] ECR 5615.

in the EEC Treaty, however effective and diverse they may be, may prove to be ineffective or uncertain.

17. First, an action for failure to act cannot be used to challenge the legal basis of a measure which has already been adopted.

18. Secondly, the submission of a reference for a preliminary ruling on the validity of such an act or the bringing of an action by Member States or individuals for the annulment of the act are mere contingencies, and the Parliament cannot be sure that they will materialize.

19. Finally, while the Commission is required to ensure that the Parliament's prerogatives are respected, that duty cannot go so far as to oblige it to adopt the Parliament's position and bring an action for annulment which the Commission itself considers unfounded.

20. It follows from the foregoing that the existence of those various legal remedies is not sufficient to guarantee, with certainty and in all circumstances, that a measure adopted by the Council or the Commission in disregard of the Parliament's prerogatives will be reviewed.

21. Those prerogatives are one of the elements of the institutional balance created by the Treaties. The Treaties set up a system for distributing powers among the different Community institutions, assigning to each institution its own role in the institutional structure of the Community and the accomplishment of the tasks entrusted to the Community.

22. Observance of the institutional balance means that each institution must exercise its powers with due regard for the powers of the other institutions. It also requires that it should be possible to penalize any breach of that rule which may occur.

23. The Court, which under the Treaties has the task of ensuring that in the interpretation and application of the Treaties the law is observed, must therefore be able to maintain the institutional balance and, consequently, review the observance of the Parliament's prerogatives when called upon to do so by the Parliament, by means of a legal remedy which is suited to the purpose which the Parliament seeks to achieve.

24. In carrying out that task the Court cannot, of course, include the Parliament among the institutions which may bring an action under Article 173 of the EEC Treaty or Article 146 of the Euratom Treaty without being required to demonstrate an interest in bringing an action.

25. However, it is the Court's duty to ensure that the provisions of the Treaties concerning the institutional balance are fully applied and to see to it that the Parliament's prerogatives, like those of the other institutions, cannot be breached without it having available a legal remedy, among those laid down in the Treaties, which may be exercised in a certain and effective manner.

26. The absence in the Treaties of any provision giving the Parliament the right to bring an action for annulment may constitute a procedural gap, but it cannot prevail over the fundamental interest in the maintenance and observance of the institutional balance laid down in the Treaties establishing the European Communities.

27. Consequently, an action for annulment brought by the Parliament against an act of the Council or the Commission is admissible provided that the action seeks only to safeguard its prerogatives and that it is founded only on submissions alleging their infringement. Provided that condition is met, the Parliament's action

for annulment is subject to the rules laid down in the Treaties for actions for annulment brought by the other institutions.

28. In accordance with the Treaties, the Parliament's prerogatives include participation in the drafting of legislative measures, in particular participation in the cooperation procedure laid down in the EEC Treaty.

29. In the present case, the Parliament claims that the contested Regulation is based on Article 31 of the Euratom Treaty, which provides only that the Parliament is to be consulted, whereas it ought to have been based on Article 100a of the EEC Treaty, which requires implementation of the procedure for cooperation with the Parliament.

30. The Parliament infers from that that the Council's choice of legal basis for the contested Regulation led to a breach of its prerogatives by denying it the possibility, which the cooperation procedure offers, of participating in the drafting of the measure more closely and actively than it could in the consultation procedure.

31. Since the Parliament claims that its prerogatives were breached as a result of the choice of legal basis for the contested measure, it follows from all the foregoing that the present action is admissible. The Council's objection of inadmissibility must therefore be dismissed and the proceedings must be continued with regard to the substance of the case.

Article 173(3) now enshrines this ruling. This still leaves open the precise scope of the Court's judgment. Which matters touch on the Parliament's prerogatives?

K. Bradley, Sense and Sensibility: Parliament v. Council Continued[14]

In *Chernobyl*, the Court did not indicate the limits of the parliamentary prerogatives which merit judicial protection, other than specifying that it is *qua* element of the institutional balance created by the Treaty that such protection can be justified in the absence of an express jurisdictional clause in the Treaty. The principal prerogative Parliament enjoys is its participation in the legislative process to the correct extent (assent, cooperation or consultation). In one pending case, introduced before the Court's judgment, Parliament is arguing that this also includes the right of reconsultation on a proposal substantially modified after the adoption of its opinion. An extensive definition of Parliament's prerogatives could include the obligation on the Council to await its opinion following a voluntary consultation, and respect for interinstitutional agreements, while it has even been suggested that a Parliamentary delaying power would not be 'so extraordinary in a system in which both the Commission . . . and the Council itself are able to prevent decisionmaking'.

If the general limitation the Court has imposed on Parliament's right of action, that such action may only seek to safeguard its prerogatives, might be justified as being the maximum required by the necessity to ensure respect for the institutional balance, the limitation on the grounds Parliament may rely upon, those which are

[14] (1991) 16 ELRev. 245, 251–4. See also J. Weiler, 'Pride and Prejudice—*Parliament* v. *Council*' (1989) 14 ELRev. 334; G. Bebr, 'The Standing of the European Parliament in the Community System of Legal Remedies: A Thorny Jurisprudential Development' (1990) 10 YBEL 171.

based on violation of its prerogatives, may prove anomalous in practice. While Parliament will, for example, be able to rely on the infringement of an essential procedural requirement, such as the obligation to consult it where the Treaty so requires, would it be unable to argue before the Court that a legislative measure infringes the Treaty or constitutes a violation of the fundamental rights of the citizen and (voter) whose respect the Court is pledged to guarantee? . . .

It has been suggested that limitations on Parliament's right of action could constitute a safeguard against political forces leading Parliament to use Article 173 in a 'judicially inappropriate manner', and that the judges in *Comitology* may have thought that recognising a right of action to Parliament would be 'unleashing a loose cannon ball'. This appears to assume that Parliament would be less capable than the other institutions of self-restraint in the matter of recourse to judicial proceedings, a question to which the brevity of the period elapsed since *Chernobyl* does not permit a response.

There are some indications that the ECJ will take a broad reading of what is now Article 173(3). Thus in *European Parliament* v. *Council*[15] the Court held that the right to be consulted in accordance with a provision of the Treaty was part of Parliament's prerogatives. In such circumstances the adoption of an act on an incorrect legal basis which did not provide for consultation was liable to infringe Parliament's prerogatives, even if there had been optional consultation.

4. ARTICLE 173 EC: A CRITICAL ANALYSIS OF THE GENERAL STANDING RULES FOR NON-PRIVILEGED APPLICANTS

In many of the cases considered below the Court may refer to Article 173(2), which was the provision on standing for non-privileged applicants prior to the TEU. The matter is now governed by Article 173(4), but there has been no change in the wording of this part of the Article. Article 173(4) clearly does not give non-privileged applicants unfettered access to the ECJ. Review proceedings can only be brought in three types of case. The first is straightforward, and is the situation where there is a decision addressed to the applicant. In these circumstances the addressee may challenge the decision before the ECJ. The second situation is that in which there is a decision addressed to a another person, and the applicant claims that it is of direct and individual concern. The third type of case which can arise is where there is a decision in the form of a regulation, and the applicant claims that it is of direct and individual concern. Not surprisingly, litigation has been primarily concerned with categories two and three, and it is these which will be considered in turn.

[15] Case C–316/91, n. 6 above. See also Case C–187/93, *European Parliament* v. *Council* [1994] ECR I–2855.

(a) Decisions Addressed to Another Person

The seminal case on this type of situation is the decision in *Plaumann*:

Case 25/62, Plaumann & Co. v. Commission
[1963] ECR 95, [1964] CMLR 29

In 1961 the German Government requested the Commission to authorize it to suspend the collection of duties on clementines imported from third countries. The Commission refused the request, and addressed its answer to the German Government. The applicant in the case was an importer of clementines, who sought to contest the legality of the Commission's decision. The ECJ adopted the following test to determine whether the applicant was individually concerned by the decision addressed to the German Government.

THE ECJ

Persons other than those to whom a decision is addressed may only claim to be individually concerned if that decision affects them by reason of certain attributes which are peculiar to them or by reason of circumstances in which they are differentiated from all other persons and by virtue of these factors distinguishes them individually just as in the case of the person addressed. In the present case the applicant is affected by the disputed Decision as an importer of clementines, that is to say, by reason of a commercial activity which may at any time be practised by any person and is not therefore such as to distinguish the applicant in relation to the contested Decision as in the case of the addressee

For these reasons the present action for annulment must be declared inadmissible.

The test in the *Plaumann* case has been cited in many later cases where an applicant has sought to challenge a decision which has been formally addressed to another.[16] Some of these will be considered below. Because the test has proved to be of such importance, it is worth dwelling a little on the essence of the test itself and its application to the facts of the case. By doing so one can understand why private applicants have found it so difficult to succeed under the *Plaumann* formula. The preceding quotation from *Plaumann* can be neatly divided into two parts, the test itself and the application of the test to the facts of the case.

The *test itself* is encompassed by the first sentence in the paragraph. This serves to emphasize that applicants who claim to be individually concerned by a decision addressed to another can only do so if they are in some way differentiated from all other persons, and by reason of these distinguishing features singled out in the same way as the initial addressee. The test does, however, recognize that it is perfectly possible for there to be more than one applicant who is individually concerned in the above sense.

[16] For a recent example not concerning agriculture, see Case T–83/92, n. 5 above.

The *application of the test* to the facts of the case is contained in the second sentence of the quotation: the applicant in the instant case failed because it practised a commercial activity which could be carried on by any person at any time. The reason for rejecting the claim can be criticized on both pragmatic and conceptual grounds.

In *pragmatic terms* the application of the test can be criticized as being economically unrealistic. If there are, for example, only a very limited number of firms pursuing a certain trade this is not fortuitous, nor is the number of those firms likely to rise overnight. The presently existing range of such firms is established by the ordinary principles of supply and demand: if there are two or three firms in the industry this is because they can satisfy the current market demand. Even if there should be a sudden surge of desire for clementines, the result will normally be that the existing firms will import more of the produce. The argument that the activity of importing clementines can be undertaken by any person, that the number might alter significantly, and that therefore the applicant is not individually concerned, is thus unconvincing.

The reasoning of the ECJ is also open to criticism in *conceptual terms*. Put shortly, the reasoning of the Court renders it literally impossible for an applicant *ever* to succeed, except in a very limited category of retrospective cases. This can be demonstrated as follows. The test in the first sentence of the quotation has to be applied at some point in time. There are only three choices. One could ask the relevant question at the time that the determination being challenged was made; one could pose that test at the time of the challenge itself; or one could pose the test at some future, undefined date. Intuitively one would imagine that choices one or two would represent the most appropriate juncture at which to ask the question contained in the first sentence of the *Plaumann* case: was the applicant singled out in the requisite manner at one of these dates? In actual fact the ECJ applied choice three: the applicant failed because the activity of clementine-importing could be carried out by anyone at any time. On this reasoning the applicant would fail even if there were only one such importer at the time the challenged decision was made, since it would always be open to the Court to contend that others could enter the industry. On this reasoning no applicant could ever succeed, subject to the caveat considered below, since it could *always* be argued that others might engage in the trade at some juncture. The 'possibility' of *locus standi* for an applicant would be like a mirage in the desert, ever-receding and never capable of being grasped. Even if our sole trader were to return to the Court and protest that it was still the only firm affected by the decision, it would still be greeted by the invocation of the same reasoning as on its first foray into the judicial arena. It would still be argued that it had not demonstrated the necessary individuality because others might engage in the activity in question.[17] As Advocate General Roemer stated in the *Eridania* case, it must be mistaken to take such account of the future effect of a decision, since otherwise it would

[17] In reality such reported forays would not be possible since there would be time-limit problems.

never be possible to claim individual concern in relation to a measure which had a permanent effect, even though at the time it was made the decision affected only one firm.[18]

The argument advanced in the previous paragraph might be opposed by contending that the applicant in the *Plaumann* case was properly rejected since he was a member of an open rather than closed category of applicants, and hence was not individually concerned. Thus Hartley remarks that since anyone can import fruit, and the measure would apply to anyone who commenced operations after the decision came into effect, the category was an open one and the applicant was not individually concerned by it.[19] Open categories are regarded as those in which the membership is not fixed at the time of the decision; a closed category is one in which it is thus fixed. This reasoning, however, does not serve to dispel the concerns expressed above. Quite the contrary. It reinforces those concerns. There are two problems with this reasoning.

On the one hand, in practical terms, the language of open categories is employed to rule out standing for any applicant, even if there is only a very limited number presently engaged in that trade, on the ground that others might undertake the trade thereafter. If the presence of such notional, future traders is to render the category open, and not determinate at the date on which the decision comes into force then, as indicated previously, this ignores the practical economics which determine the number of those who supply a particular commodity.

On the other hand, in conceptual terms, the sense in which a category is said to be open at the time of the contested decision is questionable. To regard any category as open merely because others might notionally undertake the trade in issue is not self-evident. It would mean, of course, that any decision which had any future impact would be unchallengeable because the category would be regarded as open. The first half of the *Plaumann* quotation, which contains the test itself, is based on the assumption that some people have attributes which distinguish them from others, and that they possess these attributes at the time the contested decision is made. The fact that others might acquire these attributes *later*, by joining that trade, does not, of course, mean that they are presently part of the same category as those who already do work in that sphere, let alone that somehow they are to be regarded retrospectively as part of the limited group which initially operated in that area. The matter may be put quite simply. The fact that I might wish to become striker for England, a great pianist, or a clementine importer, does not mean that I currently have the attributes associated with any of these roles in life.

[18] Cases 10 and 18/68, *Società 'Eridania' Zuccherifici Nazionali* v. *Commission* [1969] ECR 459, 492. Roemer A.G. did not believe that the *Plaumann* test intended to limit applicants in this manner, but it is difficult to read the application of the test in *Plaumann* itself and in later cases in any other way.

[19] Hartley, n. 1 above, 366, 375–6.

The argument that the Court's test is unduly restrictive is reinforced when one realizes the reality of the situation in cases such as *Plaumann*. The applicants in this case were in effect objecting to a decision which affected them directly. The fact that the decision was addressed to and through the German Government should not serve to mask this point. The reason this was so was due to the structure of decision-making within this area of Community law: traders would request that a certain duty should be lowered, the request would be dealt with initially by the national authorities, who would then pass it on to the Commission. The Commission decision would then be given to the German Government, but the real addressees were the clementine importers themselves. The same point can be made about the *Piraiki-Patraiki* case: the decision to allow France to impose a quota on yarn coming from Greece was in reality also a decision prohibiting the Greek yarn producers from exporting to France during the relevant period. It is to this case that we should now turn.

Case 11/82, A.E. Piraiki-Patraiki v. Commission [1985] ECR 207, [1985] 2 CMLR 46

The applicants were seven Greek cotton undertakings who sought to challenge a decision authorizing the French government to impose a quota system on imports into France of yarn from Greece between November 1981 and January 1982. Some of the undertakings had already entered into contracts to export cotton yarn to France, which were to be fulfilled during the quota period and which were for amounts of yarn in excess of that allowed by the quota. The Court quoted the test from the *Plaumann* case, and then reasoned as follows.

THE ECJ

12. The applicants argue that they fulfil the conditions set out above since they are the main Greek undertakings which produce and export cotton yarn to France. They argue that they therefore belong to a class of traders individually identifiable on the basis of criteria having to do with the product in question, the business activities carried on and the length of time during which they have been carried on. In that regard the applicants emphasize that the production and export to France of cotton yarn of Greek origin requires an industrial and commercial organization which cannot be established from one day to the next, and certainly not during the short period of application of the decision in question.

13. That proposition cannot be accepted. It must first be pointed out that the applicants are affected by the decision at issue only in their capacity as exporters to France of cotton yarn of Greek origin. The decision is not intended to limit the production of those products in any way, nor does it have such a result.

14. As for the exportation of those products to France, that is clearly a commercial activity which can be carried on at any time by any undertaking whatever. It follows that the decision at issue concerns the applicants in the same way as any other trader actually or potentially finding himself in the same position. The mere fact that the applicants export goods to France is not therefore sufficient to establish that they are individually concerned by the contested decision.

As will be seen below, certain of the applicants were given standing, but notwithstanding this fact the decision in the *Piraiki-Patraiki* case provides a fitting example of the difficulties which applicants face in this area. The applicants contended that they should be regarded as individually concerned, being those firms which would be affected by the quota introduced by the contested decision. Let us ignore the basic economics of supply and demand. Let us assume, even though there was no evidence whatsoever for the assumption, that there might be an incentive for new yarn traders to enter the market. None the less, it was quite clear that no other firm could plausibly set up production in this area during the limited period of validity of the decision in question. It would take considerably longer than three months to adapt any factory to this line of business, let alone establish any new factory. The applicants' argument that they were a limited group was therefore forceful, but it was rejected by the Court in the manner set out above.[20]

In the preceding discussion it was indicated that applicants had been successful in one type of case. This is where the decision concerns a completed set of past events. The *Toepfer* case provides a fitting example of this:

Cases 106 and 107/63, Alfred Toepfer and Getreide-Import Gesellschaft v. Commission[21]
[1965] ECR 405, [1966] CMLR 111

The applicants were dealers in grain who applied for import licences from the German authorities on 1 October 1963. On that date the levy for the relevant imports was zero. Because of changes in market conditions the German authorities realized that the dealers would make large profits, and therefore rejected their applications until the levy had been increased. The importers were told that their applications would be rejected, and the Commission was asked to confirm this decision. The Commission then raised the levy from 2 October, and on 3 October confirmed the ban with regard to the period from 1–4 October inclusive. The dealers sought to have this decision annulled.

THE ECJ

It is clear from the fact that on 1 October 1963 the Commission took a decision fixing new free-at-frontier prices for maize imported into the Federal Republic as from 2 October, that the danger which the protective measures retained by the Commission were to guard against no longer existed as from this latter date.

Therefore the only persons concerned by the said measures were importers who had applied for an import licence during the course of the day of 1 October 1963. The number and identity of these importers had already become fixed and ascertainable before 4 October, when the contested decision was made. The

[20] Other restrictive examples of the application of *Plaumann* can be found in Case 1/64, *Glucoseries Réunies* v. *Commission* [1964] CMLR 596; Case 38/64, *Getreide-Import Gesellschaft* v. *Commission* [1965] CMLR 276; Case 97/85, *Union Deutsche Lebensmittelswerke GmbH* v. *Commission* [1987] ECR 2265; Case 34/88, *CEVAP* v. *Council* [1988] ECR 6265; Case 191/88, *Co-Frutta SARL* v. *Commission* [1989] ECR 793; Case 206/87, *Lefebvre Frère et Sœur SA* v. *Commission* [1989] ECR 275.

[21] See also Case 62/70, *Bock* v. *Commission* [1971] ECR 897.

Commission was in a position to know that its decision affected the interests and the position of the said importers alone.

The factual situation thus created differentiates the said importers, including the applicants from all other persons and distinguishes them individually just as in the case of the person addressed.

Therefore the objection of inadmissibility which has been raised is unfounded and the applications are admissible.

Case 11/82, A.E. Piraiki-Patraiki v. Commission [1985] ECR 207, [1985] 2 CMLR 46

The facts have been set out above. Some of the applicants had made contracts to supply cotton yarn to French buyers prior to the contested decision.

THE ECJ

15. The applicants argue however that their situation may be distinguished from that of any other exporter to France of cotton yarn of Greek origin inasmuch as they had entered into a series of contracts of sale with French customers, to be performed during the period of application of the decision and covering quantities of cotton yarn in excess of the quotas authorized by the Commission. The applicants state that those contracts could not be carried out because of the quota system applied by the French authorities. They take the view that in those circumstances their individual interests were affected by the decision in question.

16. According to the applicants the Commission was in a position, and even under an obligation, to identify the traders who, like the applicants, were individually concerned by its decision. In failing to obtain information in that regard it did not comply with the conditions of application of Article 130 of the Act of Accession . . .

17. It should first be observed that if that argument were held to be well founded it would only avail those applicants who could show that before the date of the contested decision they had entered into contracts with French customers for the delivery of cotton yarn from Greece during the period of application of that decision.

[*The applications of certain firms were therefore ruled out since they had not made such contracts.*]

19. With regard to the other applicants, it must be held that the fact that, before the adoption of the decision at issue, they had entered into contracts which were to be carried out during the months to which the decision applied constitutes a circumstance which distinguishes them from any other person concerned by the decision, in so far as the execution of their contracts was wholly or partly prevented by the adoption of the decision.

(b) Decisions in the Form of Regulations

The other type of case which has proven to be problematic is that in which an individual asserts that, although the challenged measure is in the form of a regulation, it is in reality a decision which is of direct and individual concern to him or her. Applications of this type have not proven to be notably successful, and the ECJ has not always adopted the same approach to the issue. Two tests can be identified in the case law on this topic: the closed category test, and the abstract terminology test. As will be seen, the latter is, in essence, stricter than the former, and it is this latter test which now constitutes the general rule applied by the Court. The *Calpak* case is one of the best examples of the abstract terminology test in operation, and the test has been used in many other judgments:[22]

Cases 789 and 790/79, Calpak SpA and Società Emiliana Lavorazione Frutta SpA v. Commission [1980] ECR 1949, [1981] 1 CMLR 26

The applicants were producers of William pears, and they complained that the calculation of production aid granted to them was void. Under the terms of an earlier regulation, production aid was to be calculated on the basis of the average production over the previous three years, in order to avoid the risk of over-production. The applicants alleged that the Commission had in fact abandoned this method of assessing aid, and had based its aid calculation on one marketing year, in which production was atypically low. The applicants also claimed that they were a closed and definable group, the members of which were known to, or identifiable by, the Commission.

THE ECJ

6. The Commission's main contention is that as the disputed provisions were adopted in the form of regulations their annulment may only be sought if their content shows them to be, in fact, decisions. But in the Commission's view the provisions in question, which lay down rules of general application, are truly in the nature of regulations within the meaning of Article 189 of the Treaty . . .

7. The second paragraph of Article 173 empowers individuals to contest, *inter alia*, any decision which, although in the form of a regulation, is of direct and individual concern to them. The objective of that provision is in particular to prevent the Community institutions from being in a position, merely by choosing the form of a regulation, to exclude an application by an individual against a decision which concerns him directly and individually; it therefore stipulates that the choice of form cannot change the nature of the measure.

8. By virtue of the second paragraph of Article 189 of the Treaty the criterion for distinguishing between a regulation and a decision is whether the measure is of general application or not . . .

9. A provision which limits the granting of production aid for all producers in respect of a particular product to a uniform percentage of the quantity produced by them during a uniform period is by nature a measure of general application within the meaning of Article 189 of the Treaty. In fact the measure applies to

[22] See also Cases 103–109/78, *Beauport* v. *Council and Commission* [1979] ECR 17, [1979] 3 CMLR 1; Case 162/78, *Wagner* v. *Commission* [1979] ECR 3467; Case 45/81, *Alexander Moksel Import-Export GmbH & Co Handels KG* v. *Commission* [1982] ECR 1129; Cases 97, 99, 193, 215/86, *Asteris AE and Greece* v. *Commission* [1988] ECR 2181, [1988] 3 CMLR 493; Case 160/88R, *Fédération Européenne de la Sainté Animale* v. *Council* [1988] ECR 4121; Case C–298/89, *Gibraltar* v. *Council* [1993] ECR I–3605, [1994] 3 CMLR 425; Case C–308/89, *Codorniu SA* v. *Council* [1994] ECR I–1853.

objectively determined situations and produces legal effects with regard to categories of persons described in a generalized and abstract manner. The nature of the measure as a regulation is not called in question by the mere fact that it is possible to determine the number or even identity of the producers to be granted the aid which is limited thereby.

10. Nor is the fact that the choice of reference period is particularly important for the applicants, whose production is subject to considerable variation from one marketing year to another as a result of their own programme of production, sufficient to entitle them to an individual remedy. Moreover, the applicants have not established the existence of circumstances such as to justify describing that choice . . . as a decision adopted specifically in relation to them and, as such, entitling them to institute proceedings under the second paragraph of Article 173.

11. It follows that the objection raised by the Commission must be accepted as regards the applications for the annulment of the provisions in the two regulations in question.

The abstract terminology test places those who wish to challenge an act which is in the form of a regulation in a difficult position. The nature of this difficulty can be presented as follows.

The purpose of allowing any challenges to acts which are in the form of regulations is, as the ECJ made clear in the *Calpak* case, to prevent the Community institutions from immunizing matters from attack by the form of their classification. Thus, if regulations were never open to challenge the institutions could classify matters in this way, safe in the knowledge that they could never be annulled by private individuals. Article 173(4) seeks to prevent this from happening by permitting a challenge when the regulation is in reality a decision which is of direct and individual concern to the applicant. As the ECJ made clear in the *Calpak* case, this requires the Court to look behind the *form* of the measure, in order to determine whether in *substance* it really is a regulation or not.

The problem with the abstract terminology test is that, rather than looking behind form to substance, it comes perilously close to looking behind form to form. The reason is the nature of the test. A regulation will be accepted as a true regulation if, as stated in *Calpak*, it applies to 'objectively determined situations and produces legal effects with regard to categories of persons described in a generalized and abstract manner'. However, it is always possible to draft norms in this manner, and thus to immunize them from attack, more especially as the Court makes it clear that knowledge of the number or identity of those affected will not prevent the norm from being regarded as a true regulation. If the Commission wishes, therefore, to ensure that its measures are rendered safe from challenge under Article 173(4), it can frame them as regulations drafted in the abstract and generalized manner described above.

It is, moreover, quite clear that many measures which are regarded as 'true' regulations, and are in this sense characterized as 'legislative' in nature, are short-lived in terms of time and apply only to a very limited group. They do not differ from many measures which in domestic legal systems would be classified as administrative in nature.

The Court has, however, adopted a closed-category approach in cases which deal with a completed set of past events, where the regulation relates to a fixed, closed category of traders. In this type of case the category is closed in the sense that the disputed regulation applies to past events, and does not have a future impact. Thus in *International Fruit*[23] importers of apples from non-Member States applied in advance to the relevant national authorities for an import licence. The national authorities would pass the information to the Commission, and the Commission would then enact a regulation which laid down rules for deciding on such applications. Thus the regulation applied to a closed category of persons, those who had made import applications in the previous week. The Court held that an action to challenge the regulation was admissible, and it characterized the measure as being a bundle of individual decisions.[24]

The abstract terminology test then provides the general criterion which the ECJ will apply in this area, with the closed-category test being used to admit applicants only when the case concerns a completed set of past events.

There are, however, some cases where the ECJ will admit an applicant even though on the facts neither of the preceding criteria is met. Thus in *Codorniu*[25] the applicant challenged a regulation which stipulated that the term *cremant* should be reserved for sparkling wines of a particular quality coming from France or Luxembourg. The applicant made sparkling wine in Spain and held a trade mark which contained the word *cremant*. However, other Spanish producers also used this term. The Council argued vigorously that the measure was a regulation within the *Calpak* test, and that it could not be challenged irrespective of whether it was possible to identify the number or identity of those affected by it. The ECJ agreed with this general test and accepted that it formed the criterion which the Court would normally employ.[26] It also agreed that the contested measure was a true regulation in substance as well as form under this test: it was of a legislative nature and applied to traders in general.[27] It held none the less that this did *not* prevent it from being of individual concern to some of them.[28] The Court then found that the applicant was individually concerned in this manner, largely it seems because it possessed a trade mark containing the word *cremant*.[29] It will be interesting to see how often the Court is willing to make exceptions of this nature.

The reason the Court has been restrictive in its construction of Article 173(4) has been the subject of academic discussion which will be considered below. Before doing so, it is necessary to consider certain types of case in

[23] Cases 41–44/70, *International Fruit Company BV* v. *Commission* [1971] ECR 411.

[24] See also Case 100/74, *Société CAM SA* v. *Commission* [1975] ECR 1393; Case C–354/87, *Weddel* v. *Commission* [1990] ECR I–3487.

[25] Case C–309/89, *Codorniu SA* v. *Council* [1994] ECR I–1853.

[26] *Ibid.*, para. 18.

[27] *Ibid.*, para. 19.

[28] *Ibid.*

[29] For another example of a case where the Court applied a more liberal approach see Case C–152/88, *Sofrimport* v. *Commission* [1990] ECR I–2477.

which the ECJ has adopted a more liberal attitude to standing by private parties.

5. ARTICLE 173 EC: THE MORE LIBERAL CASE LAW ON THE STANDING OF NON-PRIVILEGED APPLICANTS

The ECJ has been more liberal in according standing in four main types of case. These cases will be examined, and this examination will be followed by an analysis of the policy reasons which have coloured the Court's case law in these areas and in the 'mainline' cases considered in the previous section.

(a) *Anti-dumping Cases*

One of the areas in which the Court has been more liberal is in the context of dumping. The Community has passed dumping regulations, with the object of preventing those outside the Community from selling goods within the Community at too low a price, to the detriment of traders within the EC. The Community response is to impose an anti-dumping duty on the firm or firms in question. Whether a firm is in fact dumping, and the consequential issues concerning the calculation of its 'normal' production costs and prices of sale, are often very controversial.

Three types of applicant may wish to challenge an anti-dumping duty: the firm which initiated the complaint about dumping, the producers of the product which is subject to the anti-dumping duty, and the importers of the product on which the duty is imposed.[30] In deciding whether to accord standing to such applicants the Court is placed in a difficult position since, as will be seen below, dumping duties must be imposed by regulation, as opposed to decision. If, therefore, the Court holds that the regulation is not in fact a regulation at all, then it is arguable that the Commission had no power to impose the measure. If, however, the Court holds, without more, that it is a true regulation, then this may preclude any challenge by any applicant. This conundrum serves to explain the reasoning of the ECJ in the cases examined below, in which it formally recognizes the measure as a regulation, but then seeks to determine whether the applicant is individually concerned by it.

The *Timex* case provides an example of the first category of applicant: a company which initiated the complaint, but is unhappy with the resultant regulation:

[30] A. Arnull, 'Challenging EC Anti-Dumping Regulations: The Problem of Admissibility' [1992] 2 ECLR 73.

Case 264/82, Timex Corporation v. Council and Commission [1985] ECR 849, [1985] 3 CMLR 550

The Community had imposed, through the form of a regulation, an anti-dumping duty on watches from the USSR. It had done so at the instigation of Timex, which had initiated the proceedings, and the duty had explicitly stated that it had taken account of the injury caused to Timex by the dumped imports. However, Timex sought to challenge the regulation, arguing that the duty was too low, and thus that it was still being injured by the imports. An initial issue was whether Timex had standing to challenge the regulation. The Council and Commission argued that Timex was not named in the regulation, and that it was not individually concerned by it, since it affected all watchmakers in the Community alike. Timex argued by way of response that the regulation was in reality a decision which was of individual concern to it, since it had initiated the proceedings, and since the duty was fixed with reference to its economic situation.

THE ECJ

12. Article 13(1) of Regulation 3017/79 provides that 'Anti-dumping or countervailing duties, whether provisional or definitive, shall be imposed by regulation'. In the light of the criteria set out in Article 173(2) the measures in question are, in fact, legislative in nature and scope, inasmuch as they apply to traders in general; nevertheless, their provisions may be of direct and individual concern to some of those traders. In this regard it is necessary to consider in particular the part played by the applicant in the anti-dumping proceeding and its position on the market to which the contested legislation applies.

. . .

14. The complaint which led to the opening of the investigation procedure . . . owes its origin to the complaints originally made by Timex. Moreover, it is clear from the preamble to Council Regulation 1882/82 that Timex's views were heard during that procedure.

15. It must also be remembered that Timex is the leading manufacturer of mechanical watches and watch movements in the Community and the only remaining manufacturer of those products in the United Kingdom. Furthermore, as is also clear from the preambles to Regulation 84/82 and 1882/82, the conduct of the investigation procedure was largely determined by Timex's observations and the anti-dumping duty was fixed in the light of the effect of the dumping on Timex. More specifically, the preamble to Regulation 1882/82 makes it clear that the definitive anti-dumping duty was made equal to the dumping margin which was found to exist 'taking into account the extent of the injury caused to Timex by the dumped imports'. The contested regulation is therefore based on the applicant's own situation.

16. It follows that the contested regulation constitutes a decision which is of direct and individual concern to Timex within the meaning of Article 173(2) of the EEC Treaty. As the Court held in its judgment of 4 October 1983 in Case 191/82, *EEC Seed Crushers'and Oil Processors' Federation (Fediol)* v. *Commission*, the applicant is therefore entitled to put before the Court any matters which would facilitate a review as to whether the Commission has observed the procedural guarantees granted to complainants by Regulation 3017/79 and whether or not it has committed manifest errors in its assessment of the facts, has omitted to take

any essential matters into consideration or has based the reason for its decision on considerations amounting to a misuse of its powers. In that respect, the Court is required to exercise its normal powers of review over a discretion granted to a public authority, even though it has no jurisdiction to intervene in the exercise of the discretion reserved to the Community authorities by the aforementioned regulation.

17. Since the action is therefore admissible, the objection of inadmissibility raised by the Council and the Commission must be dismissed.

In the *Timex* case it was the complainant who was accorded standing in order to challenge the level of the anti-dumping duty. The next case indicates the Court's approach when the applicant is the exporter affected by the relevant duty:

Cases 239/82 and 275/82, Allied Corporation v. Commission [1984] ECR 1005, [1985] 3 CMLR 572

Representatives of the European fertilizer industry had complained to the Commission about the import of fertiliser from the United States of America. This led to the imposition of anti-dumping duty on the relevant products. The applicant companies who were affected by the regulation agreed to raise their prices in 1981, but withdrew these undertakings in 1982. The Commission, therefore, reimposed an anti-dumping duty on the products, and it was this regulation which was challenged by the applicants.

THE ECJ

11. Article 13(1) of Regulation 3017/79 provides that 'anti-dumping or countervailing duties, whether provisional or definitive, shall be imposed by regulation'. Although it is true that, in the light of the criteria set out in Article 173(2), such measures are, in fact, as regards their nature and scope, of a legislative character, inasmuch as they apply to all the traders concerned, taken as a whole, the provisions may none the less be of direct and individual concern to those producers and exporters who are charged with practising dumping. It is clear from Article 2 of Regulation 3017/79 that anti-dumping duties may be imposed only on the basis of the findings resulting from investigations concerning the production prices and export prices of undertakings which have been individually identified.

12. It is thus clear that measures imposing anti-dumping duties are liable to be of direct and individual concern to those producers and exporters who are able to establish that they were identified in the measure adopted by the Commission or the Council or were concerned by the preliminary investigations.

13. As the Commission has rightly stated, to acknowledge that undertakings which fulfil those requirements have a right of action, in accordance with the principles laid down in Article 173(2), does not give rise to a risk of duplication of means of redress since it is possible to bring an action in the national courts only following the collection of the anti-dumping duty which is normally paid by an importer residing within the Community. There is no risk of conflicting decisions in this area since, by virtue of the mechanism of the reference for a preliminary

ruling under Article 177 of the EEC Treaty, it is for the Court of Justice alone to give a final decision on the validity of the contested regulations.

14. It follows that the applications lodged by Allied, Kaiser and Transcontinental are admissible. All three applicants gave an undertaking under Article 10 of Regulation 3017/79, they were accordingly referred to individually in Article 2 of Regulation 349/81 and, after withdrawing their undertakings, their individual circumstances formed the subject matter of the two regulations contested in the applications.

There is, as stated above, a third category of applicant who may wish to contest the legality of an anti-dumping regulation: this is the importer of the product against which the anti-dumping duty has been imposed. The position would appear to be as follows. The mere fact that the importer is an agent for one of the companies affected by the regulation is insufficient. Such an importer must be referred to in the contested measures, in the sense of, for example, the level of the duty being established partly by reference to the resale prices charged by the importer; or the importer may qualify as individually concerned if other factors single it out, such as the fact that it is the most important importer of the product, the ultimate consumer of it, and particularly dependent on the imported product for its business.[31] In rejecting applications by importers under Article 173 in circumstances other than these, the ECJ has been influenced by the fact that importers can make use of Article 177 as a method of contesting a regulation. They are able to raise their objections in a legal action brought against the agency which collects the duty, and the national court can then refer the matter to the ECJ.

(b) Competition Cases

A second area in which the ECJ has been more liberal in its construction of the criteria for standing concerns competition policy, which is regulated by Articles 85 and 86 of the Treaty. Under Article 3(2) of Regulation 17, a Member State, or any natural or legal person who claims to have a legitimate interest, can make an application to the Commission, putting forward evidence of a breach of Articles 85 and 86. The Commission is also empowered to investigate matters of its own initiative.

Case 26/76, Metro-SB-Großmärkte GmbH & Co KG v. Commission [1977] ECR 1875, [1978] 2 CMLR 1

Metro argued that the distribution system operated by SABA was in breach of Article 85 of the Treaty. It initiated a complaint under Article 3(2) of Regulation 17. The Commission decided that certain aspects of the distribution system were

[31] Cases 239 and 275/82, *Allied Corporation* v. *Commission* [1984] ECR 1005, [1985] 3 CMLR 572, para. 15; Cases C–133 and 150/87, n. 2 above; Case C–358/89, *Extramet Industrie SA* v. *Council* [1991] ECR I–2501, [1993] 2 CMLR 619. Cf. Case C–323/88, *Sermès SA* v. *Directeur des Services des Douanes de Strasbourg* [1992] 2 CMLR 632.

not in fact in breach of Article 85, and it was this decision, addressed to SABA, that Metro sought to annul. The question arose whether Metro could claim to be individually concerned by a decision addressed to another.

THE ECJ

The contested decision was adopted in particular as the result of a complaint submitted by Metro and that it relates to the provisions of SABA's distribution system, on which SABA relied and continues to rely as against Metro in order to justify its refusal to sell to the latter or to appoint it as a wholesaler, and which the applicant had for this reason impugned in its complaint.

It is in the interests of a satisfactory administration of justice and of the proper application of Articles 85 and 86 that natural or legal persons who are entitled, pursuant to Article 3(2)(b) of Regulation No 17, to request the Commission to find an infringement of Articles 85 and 86 should be able, if their request is not complied with wholly or in part, to institute proceedings in order to protect their legitimate interests.

In those circumstances the applicant must be considered to be directly and individually concerned, within the meaning of the second paragraph of Article 173, by the contested decision and the application is accordingly admissible.

The more liberal attitude of the Court in this case is apparent by contrasting it to the approach which is evident in the case law interpreting the *Plaumann* test. If the 'normal' interpretation of individual concern had been adopted then Metro would almost certainly have failed. The decision addressed to SABA would have been held to affect an open category—all those who were self-service wholesalers and who wished to handle the products of SABA. Given the special circumstances of competition policy, the Court was, however, willing to accord standing to Metro in the instant case.

The willingness of the Court to review competition decisions pursuant to a complaint under Article 3 of Regulation 17 is further exemplified by the *BEUC* case.[32] In this case a number of public-interest groups submitted a complaint to the Commission about an agreement between British and Japanese motor manufacturers which sought to restrict imports of Japanese cars into the Community. The Commission declined to take up the complaint for a number of reasons. The CFI reviewed and annulled the Commission's decision.

(c) *State Aid*

The provision of state aid to industry is a matter regulated by the Treaty in Articles 92 to 94. The principal objective is to prevent the conditions of competition from being distorted, which would be the case if the firms in one state could obtain aid or subsidies from their government.[33] The Commission will investigate state aid in order to determine whether it is compatible with the

[32] Case T–37/92, *Bureau Européen des Unions des Consommateurs* v. *Commission*, 18 May 1994.
[33] See below, Ch. 24.

Treaty, and will address a decision to the relevant state. That state could clearly challenge the decision under Article 173, but the Treaty is less clear on whether a complainant may also do so. Such complainants are not afforded the same recognition as they are in the context of competition proceedings, but the ECJ has shown itself to be liberal in its construction of the standing criteria in this area.

Case 169/84, Compagnie Francaise de l'Azote (COFAZ) SA v. Commission [1986] ECR 391, [1986] 3 CMLR 385

Three French fertilizer companies complained to the Commission that The Netherlands was granting a preferential tariff for the supply of natural gas to its own Dutch producers of fertilizer. The Commission instituted an investigation under Article 93(2), in which the applicant companies played a full part. The Dutch Government then modified its pricing policy for gas, and the Commission decided that the procedure under Article 93(2) could be halted. The applicants disagreed and sought to have the decision of the Commission annulled. Did they have standing to challenge it? The Court quoted the *Plaumann* test and then proceeded as follows.

THE ECJ

23. More particularly, as regards the circumstances referred to in that judgment, the Court has repeatedly held that where a regulation accords applicant undertakings procedural guarantees entitling them to request the Commission to find an infringement of Community rules, those undertakings should be able to institute proceedings in order to protect their legitimate interests (judgments in Cases 26/76, *Metro* v. *Commission*, 181/82, *Fediol* v. *Commission*, and 210/81, *Demo-Studio Schmidt* v. *Commission*).

24. In its judgment in Case 264/82 (*Timex Corporation* v. *Commission*) the Court pointed out that it was necessary to examine in that regard the part played by the undertaking in the administrative proceedings. The Court accepted as evidence that the measure in question was of concern to the undertaking, within the meaning of Article 173(2) EEC, the fact that the undertaking was at the origin of the complaint which led to the opening of the investigation procedure, the fact that its views were heard during that procedure and the fact that the conduct of the procedure was largely determined by its observations.

25. The same conclusions apply to undertakings which have played a comparable role in the procedure referred to in Article 93 EEC provided, however, that their position on the market is significantly affected by the aid which is the subject of the contested decision. Article 93(2) recognises in general terms that the undertakings concerned are entitled to submit their comments to the Commission but does not provide any further details.

We shall examine the ability of a complainant and/or competitor to challenge Commission decisions in the field of state aid in more detail within the subsequent discussion.[34]

[34] See below, 1102–3.

(d) Reinforcing the Democratic Nature of the Community

The last type of case in which there is evidence of a more lenient approach to standing concerns the institutional structure of the Community itself, and the extent to which this can be perceived as a democratic community open to all parties across the political spectrum.

Case 294/83, Parti Ecologiste 'Les Verts' v. Parliament [1986] ECR 1339, [1987] 2 CMLR 343

The Parliament made an allocation of funds to cover the costs incurred by political parties who had participated in the 1984 European elections. The manner of allocating the funds was biased towards those parties which had been represented in Parliament before the election, and was less favourable to those seeking representation for the first time. The allocation was challenged by a party in this latter category.

THE ECJ

35. This action concerns a situation which has never before come before the Court. Because they had representatives in the institution, certain political groupings took part in the adoption of a decision which deals both with their own treatment and with that accorded to rival groupings which were not represented. In view of this, and in view of the fact that the contested measure concerns the allocation of public funds for the purpose of preparing for elections and it is alleged that those funds were allocated unequally, it cannot be considered that only groupings which were represented and which were therefore identifiable at the date of the adoption of the contested measure are individually concerned by it.

36. Such an interpretation would give rise to inequality in the protection afforded by the Court to the various groupings competing in the same elections. Groupings not represented could not prevent the allocation of the appropriations at issue before the beginning of the election campaign because they would be unable to plead the illegality of the basic decision except in support of an action against the individual decisions refusing to reimburse sums greater than those provided for. It would therefore be impossible for them to bring an action for annulment before the Court prior to the decisions or to obtain an order from the Court under Article 185 of the Treaty suspending application of the contested basic decision.

37. Consequently, it must be concluded that the applicant association, which was in existence at the time when the 1982 Decision was adopted and which was able to present candidates at the 1984 elections, is individually concerned by the contested measures.

38. In the light of all those considerations, it must be concluded that the application is admissible.

6. ARTICLE 173 EC: THE POLICY ARGUMENTS CONCERNING STANDING OF NON-PRIVILEGED APPLICANTS

It is apparent from the preceding analysis of the case law that applicants, other than those who fall within the categories considered in the previous section, have not readily been accorded standing under Article 173(4). Why the ECJ has adopted a generally restrictive construction of standing is the issue which will be addressed in this section. As will be seen, commentators have given differing answers to this question. Any such answer must fulfil two conditions if it is to be effective: it must furnish a convincing explanation why the Court has been restrictive in the general run of cases and it must provide an acceptable explanation for the Court's greater willingness to allow standing in areas such as dumping, competition, and the like.

(a) The Appellate Court Argument

In the following extract Rasmussen addresses the first of these questions. He considers, and rejects, a number of possible rationales for the Court's restrictive approach under Article 173(4), some of which will be addressed below. Rasmussen then proffers his own preferred explanation:

H. Rasmussen, Why is Article 173 Interpreted against Private Plaintiffs?[35]

It is the contention of this paper that . . . a comprehensive pattern does exist. The suggestion is that the Court arguably has a long term interest in reshaping the judiciary of the Community to allow itself to act more like a high court of appeals of Community law, with the courts and tribunals of the Member States, and any administrative and other Community courts which might be established, acting as courts of first instance. This interest outweighs the citizen's interest in direct access to the Court. The remaining part of this paper is concerned with relating the empirical evidence which supports this hypothesis.

[*Three types of evidence are adduced by Rasmussen to support his argument.*]

First, the Court not only restricts the citizen's access to judicial review of administrative acts. It also restricts the right of private individuals under Article 175(3), to seek an injunction against an institution which disregards an obligation to act under Community law. Several individuals have sought such an injunction, but the Court has dismissed the actions, primarily on the ground that the parties did not satisfy the Article's requirements on standing . . .

For many years the Court was equally unsympathetic to actions for damages brought under Article 178, generally on the ground that they attempted to circumvent Article 173's narrow standing requirements. In the early 1970s the Court ostensibly shifted its position, interpreting more liberally the provisions that allow

[35] (1980) 5 ELRev. 112, 122–7.

private persons to sue the Community for damages. Despite this apparent shift, the Court has, for two reasons, clearly disappointed the expectations of private plaintiffs. First, the Court defined the conditions for Community liability so narrowly that no private party has yet been awarded damages. Secondly, the Court has found alternative means to inhibit private actions . . .

The denial of a remedy under Article 173 is thus paralleled by the unavailability of remedies under Articles 175 and 178. This parallelism strongly supports, in my opinion, the validity of the hypothesis that these denials are but elements of the Court's policy to establish itself as . . . a high appellate Court on matters of Community law.

[*The second piece of evidence adduced by Rasmussen is the existence of a Court memorandum from 1978, in which the ECJ sought to persuade the Council of the need for changes in the ECJ's structure, through the introduction of a Court of First Instance. The object was to relieve the ECJ itself of certain cases, such as those concerning staff, and more generally to allow it to concentrate on matters of law. The third strand of the argument draws on the development of direct effect. On this Rasmussen argues as follows.*]

A last brick should be put into place. It is this. If the restriction of the citizen's access to the Court was not to amount to a pure denial of justice or rather a denial of remedies, it was necessary simultaneously to enlarge the responsibility of the national courts and tribunals to provide the citizen with an effective protection of his Community rights. To that effect the Court's continuous expansion of the applicability of Community law must be understood, an expansion which the Court has been promoting from the earliest days of the Common Market. If the framers of the EEC Treaty intended the law of the Community to be directly applicable (and there are indications in the Treaty that they did), it is fair to say that in the hands of the Court direct applicability has been extended far beyond their intentions.

In sum, injured parties have no choice but to bring actions before the national courts. In turn, these courts should, in the opinion of the European Court, seek preliminary rulings under Article 177 in all instances where an interpretation of Community law is desirable or required by law, or where doubt about its validity is aired before the national judge.

In theory, then, the national courts will try the cases on their merits with the European Court serving as the ultimate arbiter of questions of interpretation of Community law and its validity. It is no secret, however, that in practice, when making preliminary rulings the Court has often transgressed the theoretical borderline between mere interpretation and fact evaluation. The court does so when it provides the national judge with an answer in which questions of law and of fact are sufficiently interwoven as to leave the national judge with only little discretion and flexibility in making his final decision . . . It should not, therefore, be a surprise that one commentator has seen the Court's way of going about its business as a '[demonstration of] the ease with which Article 177 could be turned into a vehicle of appellate review'.

The thesis advanced by Rasmussen is interesting, and may well have played some part in the approach of the Court. There are, however, two difficulties in accepting it as the main motivating force behind the Court's case law.

First, as Harding has argued,[36] it is hard to explain the early, restrictive case law as being based on a desire by the ECJ to assert itself as an appellate court. This case law was developed in the 1960s at a time when the Court was not faced with severe work-load problems.

Secondly, although the ECJ may well have aspirations to become a 'federal appellate court' for the Community, the contention that this is the prime reason it has 'closed down' Article 173, with the objective of forcing applicants to proceed via Article 177 instead, is problematic for the following reason. The ECJ clearly wishes to limit the range of applicants who can, in general, challenge decisions or regulations within Article 173. However, under Article 177 references can be made at the behest of a wide range of individuals who are affected by a Community norm, even if the norm is substantively a true regulation. The individual will, in such a case, base the claim on the fact that, for example, the norm in question is contrary to a provision of the Treaty itself, which Treaty Article has direct effect and gives the applicant rights which can be utilised through the national courts.[37] The idea, then, that the ECJ intended to limit Article 173 very restrictively, with the intention of forcing claims through Article 177, when it would have very little control over the range of applicants using the latter Article, or the types of norm challenged thereby, is not wholly convincing. The 'causality' in this area may well have been otherwise: the ECJ restricted Article 173 for reasons to be considered below, and applicants who sought to challenge Community norms were forced to do so through the mechanism of Article 177.

(b) Restrictive Access and the Language of the Treaty

A different explanation for the ECJ's case law in this area is that it is explicable simply on the ground that the Treaty itself did not countenance any broader grounds of challenge.

C. Harding, The Private Interest In Challenging Community Action[38]

It has perhaps been easy, amid the welter of technical and difficult discussion of 'direct and individual concern' under Article 173(2), to lose sight of a relatively simple message that is forcefully sent out from some of the earlier instances of private challenge of the legality of Community action: that Article 173(2) itself, taken together with Article 189, does not, and was probably never intended to hold out much hope to private plaintiffs in the case of measures not actually addressed to them. From the Treaty, it is unequivocally clear that true regulations cannot be challenged by individuals, that there is a difference between regulations and decisions and that decisions not addressed to the complainant can only be challenged by him if he has a special interest in the matter—that is, he is directly and individually concerned. The purport of Article 173(2) would appear to be that in

[36] C. Harding, 'The Private Interest in Challenging Community Action' (1980) 5 ELRev. 354, 355.

[37] See below, 492–4.

[38] N. 35 above, 355.

> practice only rarely should a private party be able to challenge directly a Community measure which is more than an administrative act concerned simply with the person's case. More specifically, regulations and decisions addressed to Member States ought not in principle to be susceptible to private challenge . . . If an explanation is sought for this apparently restrictive view of Article 173(2), the answer is perhaps disarmingly simple: that provision is based on the assumption that it would not be a good policy to allow private parties to challenge measures such as regulations and decisions addressed to Member States. It should also be remembered that the Court . . . emphasised that for private persons the action under Article 173(2) was in some respects more restrictive than the corresponding earlier procedure under Article 33 of the Coal and Steel Community Treaty. This difference could be justified on account of the wider legislative competence of the Community institutions under the EEC Treaty, which may be viewed as a '*traité-cadre*' rather than a '*traité-loi*'.

While it is true that the Treaty clearly imposes limits on the extent to which individuals may contest the legality of matters under Article 173(4), the explanation proffered by Harding is, none the less, contestable. It is, of course, the case that the Treaty does not readily countenance challenges to decisions which are addressed to others; and it is equally true that 'real' regulations are not to be challengeable at all. However, it is equally the case that the Treaty does contemplate some challenges in the former instance; and it is also within the express intent of the Treaty that the ECJ should be able to determine whether a regulation really is a regulation, as opposed to a decision. The crucial issue is, therefore, not whether the Treaty imposes limits on standing, but whether the interpretation of those limits is on the right lines, or whether it could be considered to be overly restrictive and, if the latter, the policy reasons for this degree of restriction. What is apparent from the tests, and their manner of application, in the *Plaumann* type of case, and in the *Calpak* type of case, is that it is virtually impossible for an individual to succeed in any case which does not involve some completed set of past events. The judicial reasoning which is used to reach such conclusions is, as seen above, open to criticism, *even given* the language of Article 173(4) itself. Indeed, the conclusions which are reached may, as the discussion of the abstract terminology test revealed, serve to undermine the rationale for allowing this species of challenge at all. The idea that the Court's case law in this area is simply an application of the intent of the Treaty, and that this renders further evaluation of the policy issues underlying this case law unnecessary, does not, therefore, suffice.

Moreover, whatever the intent of the original framers of the Treaty, we have now moved on. The Community is not the same now as it was in 1958 or 1968. The EC has long since ceased to be a Community in which the states were the sole significant members. The control of illegality by and through individual actions is as important in the Community context as it is within any national legal system. The Court has shown itself quite capable of fashioning Treaty

Articles to meet the current needs of the Community, even where it has considerably less to work with than in the case of Article 173(4).

(c) The Nature of the Subject Matter: Discretionary Determinations and the CAP

An understanding of the Court's reluctance to allow standing to individuals in the mainline cases may be best appreciated by focusing on the nature of the subject matter involved. Hartley has correctly observed that the ECJ appears to be more reluctant to afford standing where the norm which is contested is of a discretionary nature.[39] The reasons for this reluctance can be appreciated by focusing more closely on the subject matter in such cases.

Virtually all the cases considered in section 4 above concern challenges to norms which have been made pursuant to the Common Agricultural Policy (CAP). The type of substantive challenge made to these norms is, for example, that there has been a breach of Article 40(3). This Article provides that the common organization of agricultural markets shall be limited to pursuit of the objectives contained in Article 39, and shall exclude discrimination between producers or consumers within the Community. An allegation of a breach of Article 40(3) may well, therefore, require the Court to consider whether Article 39 has itself been breached. Article 39 is the foundational provision of the CAP, and is of a broad discretionary nature. This discretion is manifest in two complementary ways. On the one hand, the Article sets out a broad range of objectives which the CAP is to advance, which are themselves set at a high level of generality. They include the increase in agricultural productivity, with the object, *inter alia*, of ensuring a fair standard of living for the agricultural community; the stabilization of markets; assuring the availability of supplies; and reasonable prices for consumers. On the other hand, it is apparent that these objectives can clash with each other,[40] and therefore that the Commission and Council when making particular norms will have to make difficult discretionary choices. Whether the resultant choices do discriminate between producers may be contentious, since it may be arguable whether a particular norm is only placing one producer group on the same footing as another, or whether it is advantaging one group at the expense of another, and hence discriminating against the latter.[41] As Wyatt and Dashwood state:[42]

[39] N. 1 above, 383.

[40] See e.g. Case 34/62, *Germany* v. *Commission* [1963] ECR 131; Case 5/67, *Beus* v. *Hauptzollamt München* [1968] ECR 83.

[41] See e.g. Case 8/82, *KG in der Firma Hans-Otto Wagner GmbH Agrarhandel* v. *Bundesanstalt für Landwirtschaftliche Marktordnung* [1983] ECR 371; Case 283/83, *Firma A. Racke* v. *Hauptzollamt Mainz* [1984] ECR 3791.

[42] *The Substantive Law of the EEC* (2nd edn., 1987), 300–1 (the topic is not dealt with in the most recent edition). The decision referred to in the quotation is that in Cases 197–200, 243, 245, 247/80, *Ludwigshafener Walzmühle Erling KG* v. *Council* [1981] ECR 3211.

> Both the Council and the Commission enjoy wide discretionary powers in fulfilling their functions under the common agricultural policy. The Court has stressed that the Council must be recognised as having a discretionary power in this area which corresponds to the political responsibilities which Articles 40 and 43 impose upon it. In the case of both the Commission and the Council, this discretion extends to assessment of the factual basis of the measures they adopt, as well as to the purpose and scope of those measures. As the court declared in *Ludwigshafener*:
>
> > 'It should be remembered that, in determining their policy in this area, the competent Community institutions enjoy wide discretionary powers regarding not only establishment of the factual basis of their action, but also definition of the objectives to be pursued, within the framework of the provisions of the Treaty, and the choice of the appropriate means of action.'

It is not surprising that the regulations or decisions which result will not always please all those concerned. The very nature of the choices which have to be made pursuant to Articles 39, 40, and 43, will often mean that there are certain winners and losers from any specific aspect of the regulatory process: certain groups will be content with, for example, the aid or subsidies granted to them; others will feel that they have been harshly treated; in other areas a particular group may feel that the levy imposed upon it has been unduly harsh. Countless claims of this kind are possible, given the plethora of regulations and decisions made by the Community in the context of the CAP.

The ECJ, as is evident from the preceding quotation, does not wish to be placed in a position whereby it is being constantly asked to second-guess the discretionary choices made by the other Community institutions. This would swamp the Court with cases of this kind. It would also be inappropriate for the Court simply to substitute its view on the 'correct' balance between the objectives set out in Article 39 for that of the Commission and the Council. Given that this is so, the ECJ has two techniques at its disposal to prevent it being placed in this position.

One approach is to adopt a restrictive standard of review, whereby it will only overturn choices reached by the original decision-makers if there is some manifest error. Challenges are possible on the basis that the norm is disproportionate, or that it is discriminatory, but the Court will not lightly annul the discretionary choice which has been made. This approach is evident in the following extract from Wyatt and Dashwood:[43]

> The Court has held that where the Commission is charged with evaluation of a complex economic situation, it enjoys a wide measure of discretion, and that in reviewing the legality of such discretion, the Court must confine itself to examining whether it contains a manifest error or constitutes a misuse of power or whether the administration has clearly exceeded the bounds of its discretion.

[43] N. 42 above, 301. For a discussion of the way in which the Court limits the intensity of its review in such instances, see below, 501–5.

The other approach is to employ very strict tests of standing, as a mechanism to limit the number of cases of this type that the Court hears pursuant to Article 173. The advantage of this second approach over the first is that it far less demanding upon the Court's time. The first technique of limited review still requires the Court to hear the entire substance of the case, even if it ultimately finds that the applicant has failed to show the required level of error to justify annulling the challenged norm. If the applicant is excluded at the standing level, then an in-depth analysis of the substantive claim is obviated.

The very strict requirements for standing in the mainline cases may, therefore, be explained to a significant degree by the desire of the Court not to become enmeshed in large numbers of cases in which applicants seek to challenge the way that the Commission and Council have exercised their discretion to make policy choices pursuant to the CAP.

A similar judicial wariness about according standing is evident in other areas in which the Commission makes complex discretionary and evaluative choices, such as when deciding whether a corporate change falls within the Merger Regulation.[44]

The way in which applicants have sought to circumvent these limits, by channelling their actions through Article 177, will be considered below.

(d) The Nature of the Subject Matter: Quasi-Judicial Determinations and the More Liberal Case Law

What explanation can then be proffered for the more liberal stance of the ECJ, in the context of dumping, state aids, and competition? Two features of this case law serve to distinguish it from the mainline cases considered above.

One feature is that the *procedure* in these areas does explicitly or implicitly envisage a role for the individual complainant, who can alert the Commission to the breach of Community law. Moreover, as is evident from the cases on this topic, the complainant may then play a prominent role in the assessment of whether the alleged breach has actually occurred. The nature of this assessment has been properly described as quasi-judicial.[45]

The other distinguishing feature relates to the *substantive* nature of the subject-matter in these cases. A common feature in the areas where the ECJ has been more liberal is that the nature of the subject-matter is such that the interests of the Community can be stated less equivocally. State aids can be taken as an example. The provision of such aid is contrary to the Community's interest, since it places the recipient firms at a competitive advantage as compared with firms in other countries. The Court is, therefore, likely to be receptive to an argument, such as that put in the *COFAZ* case, that the Commission has been mistaken in thinking that the transgressing state has corrected its past illegal behaviour.[46] A similar point can be made about dumping. The

[44] Case T–83/92, n. 5 above.

[45] Hartley, n. 1 above, 378–83.

[46] It should, however, be noted that the Court will not normally engage in intensive review of Commission decisions in the field of state aids: see below, Ch. 24.

Community has a clear interest in ensuring that goods from outside the Community are not sold within it at too low a price. The Court is, therefore, once again likely to be willing to listen to an argument, put forward in a case such as *Timex*, that the Commission has set the dumping duty too low, with the consequence that firms within the Community are still being harmed. This is particularly so when the applicant firm is well placed to make an assessment of the pricing and cost issues which are involved.[47]

The situation in these areas can be contrasted with that in the mainline cases on the CAP. In these cases the paradigm is one in which there are conflicting claims within the Community. Discretionary choices will be made, pursuant to Articles 39, 40, and 43, and it may not be possible to satisfy all those affected by the choice on every occasion. For the reasons given above, the ECJ is reluctant to become engaged in an extensive process of second-guessing the precise nature of the discretionary choice made in a particular instance.

The rationale for the more liberal approach in the *Les Verts* case must be sought on yet other grounds. The most likely explanation is that the Court wished to emphasize the fact that the Community was open to all shades of political party, and in that sense representative of European opinion. It did not wish to be seen supporting a regime in which those currently represented within the Parliament could weight the financial system in their own favour. To borrow from the language of Ely, the Court was willing to use its own power to ensure that the democratic system was not used by the 'ins' to exclude or prejudice the 'outs'.[48]

(e) *Standing, Participation, and Intervention: A Glimpse of the Future?*

Predicting future developments is never easy. It may well be foolish even to try. There have, however, been certain developments in other areas of Community law which will certainly have some impact on this area, although the precise nature of the impact remains unclear at present.

Public lawyers will immediately recognize the connection between three related matters: standing to seek judicial review; participation in the original decision which is now being challenged; and intervention rights for third parties, whether before the body which is making the initial decision or before the reviewing court itself.[49]

[47] The rationale for allowing the firms on which the dumping duty is imposed to have standing is obviously different. The explanation here is probably a combination of two connected ideas. The first is that, while the dumping duty must, as seen above, be imposed by regulation, it is in reality often closer to a decision addressed to specific firms. The second is that the whole issue of the existence of dumping, and the calculation of the costing and pricing factors, is very controversial. To allow the affected firms to contest the regulation may well, therefore, be a political judgment on the part of the Court.

[48] J. H. Ely, *Democracy and Distrust: A Theory of Judicial Review* (Cambridge, Mass., 1980). Case 294/83, *Partie Ecologiste 'Les Verts'* v. *Parliament* [1986] ECR 1339, [1987] 2 CMLR 343, is set out above, 471.

[49] R. Stewart, 'The Reformation of American Administrative Law' (1975) 88 Harv.LR 1667.

The nature of this connection can be explained quite simply: the greater the participation or intervention rights which are afforded to parties when the initial decision is being made, the greater is the likelihood that such parties will also be afforded standing to challenge the resultant decision before the Court via judicial review. The reason is obvious. If parties are granted the ability to have an input into the making of the initial decision then it makes sense for them to be able to challenge that decision in judicial review proceedings. They may wish to argue, for example, that their views, although listened to in a formal sense, were in fact disregarded; that the decision-maker had in effect reached a decision which was biased towards certain interests; and that the substantive decision should therefore be overturned.

These links are already apparent in the jurisprudence of the ECJ. We have already seen that the Court's willingness to accord standing to seek judicial review in areas such as competition and state aids was directly premised on the fact that the applicant was afforded a role in the initial decision-making of, or complaint to, the Commission.

The reason this connection is of potential significance is because of the important recent developments in the field of participation and Community decision-making which have occurred. We have already mentioned this when discussing the Community's legislative process.[50] The 1993 Inter-Institutional Declaration on Democracy, Transparency, and Subsidiarity provides, as the title suggests, for greater access to documentation and files etc. in the Community's possession. It also provides for a notification procedure which is to consist of the publication in the Official Journal of a brief summary of any measure planned by the Commission, with the setting of a deadline by which interested parties may submit their comments. Even if we assume that the term 'any measure' is not taken literally, and that procedural and internal management rules are excluded, the implications of this reform may be far-reaching. Some will recognize the clear analogy between the formulation of the Community's notification procedure, and that which applies in the United States. In the USA the Administrative Procedure Act established a notice and comment procedure whereby rules have to be published in the Federal Register and the agency has to allow a period of time for notice and comment. The 1993 Declaration appears to have borrowed directly from the American experience. Anyone familiar with that experience will also know that United States courts have regularly been faced with actions in which participants in the notice and comment procedure are granted standing to seek judicial review, the substance of the complaint being that the agency did not listen to the applicant's views and that the weight of evidence was against the rule which the agency finally produced.[51]

Now it may be that the ECJ will resist this move. It may decide that the mere fact that individuals or groups have exercised their right to proffer their views when the original decision was being made does not suffice to give them

[50] See above, Ch. 3, 140–2.

[51] A. Aman, *Administrative Law and Process* (Matthew Bender, 1993), Chs. 4 and 6.

standing to challenge that decision via judicial review. It may take this view. Fear of the practical consequences may drive it to this conclusion.

Yet the arguments the other way are forceful. There is the fact that the Court does recognize the link between participation/complaint rights and standing to seek review in areas such as competition and state aids. Given that this is so, there would have to be some reasoned argument about why this connection did not operate in relation to the participation rights accorded pursuant to the 1993 Declaration. Doubtless a Court so minded could produce some explanation, but how convincing it would be is another matter.[52] Moreover, even if it might be contended that participation does not *always* lead to standing rights, could it plausibly be argued that the participation provisions resulting from the 1993 Declaration *never* do so?

There is also the fact that participation is increasingly recognized as a value in modern society. It is perceived as a valuable way of making decision-making more accessible to those affected by it, and of enabling such parties to have some direct participatory input into the decision which is reached. This may be of particular importance in the Community context where the decisions are taken at a more distant level from those who are affected by them. There is, moreover, as Shapiro correctly notes, a connection between transparency and participation: 'full transparency can only be achieved through participation or through dialogue as a form of participation'.[53] Given that this is so, it might well prove difficult for the Court to set its face against any connection between participation and standing. To do so would run the risk of being seen to undermine or undervalue the very worth of participation which had been approved by the three other institutions in the 1993 Declaration.

Our discussion thus far has focused on the possible implications for standing of the recent developments in participatory rights. We should not, however, forget that intervention rights in judicial review actions can be important in themselves as a means of facilitating public-interest litigation before the ECJ.[54] Intervention rights are governed by Article 37 of the Statute of the Court of Justice: Member States and Community institutions can intervene as of right; private parties can do so only in cases between private parties and only where they can establish an interest. Intervention rights clearly cannot be a substitute for standing, in the sense that someone must be granted standing before others can intervene. There is, however, much to be said for using such rights to enable interest groups to make their views known when a case does come before the Court. It obviates the need for separate action on the same point; facilitates class actions; and makes it easier for interest groups to proffer their opinions.

[52] It might, e.g. be argued that there is a more proximate connection between the complainant/intervenor and the subject matter of the Commission decision in the cases of state aids and competition than there is in some other areas in which participation rights might be accorded.

[53] M. Shapiro, 'The Giving Reasons Requirement' (1992) UChic. Legal Forum 179, 205.

[54] C. Harlow, 'Towards a Theory of Access for the European Court of Justice' (1992) 12 YBEL 213.

7. ARTICLE 173 EC: DIRECT CONCERN

Even if an applicant succeeds in proving individual concern, it will also have to show that the decision was of direct concern to it, if it is to be successful in claiming standing. This can be problematic, particularly if there is some autonomous exercise of will interposed between the original decision and its implementation.

Cases 41–44/70, NV International Fruit Company v. Commission [1971] ECR 411, [1975] 2 CMLR 515

The case was concerned with the importation of apples from non-member countries. The Community had adopted a regulation which limited the import of such apples from third countries during the period from 1 April 1970 to 30 June 1970. The regulation provided for a system of import licences, which were granted to the extent to which the Community market allowed. Under this system, a Member State would notify the Commission, at the end of each week, of the quantities for which import licences had been requested during the preceding week. The Commission would then decide on the issue of licences in the light of this information. The challenge was to a regulation applying this scheme to a particular week. The ECJ held that the applicant was individually concerned: the number of those applications affected by this regulation was fixed and known when the regulation was adopted, and the Court held that the Regulation should be treated as a bundle of individual decisions. Was it of direct concern to the applicant?

THE ECJ

23. Moreover, it is clear from the system introduced by Regulation No 459/70, and particularly from Article 2(2) thereof, that the decision on the grant of import licences is a matter for the Commission.

24. According to this provision, the Commission alone is competent to assess the economic situation in the light of which the grant of import licences must be justified.

25. Article 1(2) of Regulation No 459/70, by providing that the 'Member States shall in accordance with the conditions laid down in Article 2, issue the licence to any interested party applying for it', makes it clear that the national authorities do not enjoy any discretion in the matter of the issue of licences and the conditions on which applications by the parties concerned should be granted.

26. The duty of such authorities is merely to collect the data necessary in order that the Commission may take its decision in accordance with Article 2(2) of that regulation, and subsequently adopt the national measures needed to give effect to that decision.

27. In these circumstances as far as the interested parties are concerned, the issue of or refusal to issue the import licences must be bound up with this decision.

28. The measure whereby the Commission decides on the issues of the import licences thus directly affects the legal position of the parties concerned.

29. The applications thus fulfil the requirements of the second paragraph of Article 173 of the Treaty, and are therefore admissible.

The decision in the *International Fruit* case can be compared to the following judgment by the Court:[55]

Case 222/83, Municipality of Differdange v. Commission [1984] ECR 2889, [1985] 3 CMLR 638

The Commission authorized Luxembourg to grant aid to steel firms, on the condition that they undertook reductions in capacity. The applicant municipality argued that it was directly and individually concerned by this decision, *inter alia*, on the ground that the reduction in production capacity and closure of factories would lead to a reduction in local taxes.

THE ECJ

10. In this case the contested measure, which is addressed to the Grand Duchy of Luxembourg, authorizes it to grant certain aids to the undertakings named therein provided that they reduce their production capacity by a specified amount. However, it neither identifies the establishments in which the production must be reduced or terminated nor the factories which must be closed as a result of the termination of production. In addition, the Decision states that the Commission was to be notified of the closure dates only by 31 January 1984 so that the undertakings affected were free until that date to fix, where necessary with the agreement of the Luxembourg government, the detailed rules for the restructuring necessary to comply with the conditions laid down in the Decision.

11. That conclusion is, moreover, confirmed by Article 2 of the Decision according to which the capacity reductions may also be carried out by other undertakings.

12. It follows that the contested Decision left to the national authorities and undertakings concerned such a margin of discretion with regard to the manner of its implementation and in particular with regard to the choice of factories to be closed, that the Decision cannot be regarded as being of direct and individual concern to the municipalities with which the undertakings affected, by virtue of the location of their factories, are connected.

13. Since the action is therefore inadmissible also to the extent to which it is based on the provisions of the EEC Treaty, it must be dismissed.

8. ARTICLE 175 EC: FAILURE TO ACT

The Community Treaties provide an action for a wrongful failure to act. The relevant provision of the EC Treaty is Article 175, which states:

Should the European Parliament, the Council or the Commission, in infringement of this Treaty, fail to act, the Member States and the other institutions of

[55] See also Case 69/69, *Alcan Aluminium Raeren* v. *Commission* [1970] ECR 385; Case 62/70, *Bock* v. *Commission* [1971] ECR 897.

the Community may bring an action before the Court of Justice to have the infringement established.

The action shall be admissible only if the institution concerned has first been called upon to act. If, within two months of being so called upon, the institution concerned has not defined its position the action may be brought within a further period of two months.

Any natural or legal person may, under the conditions laid down in the preceding paragraphs, complain to the Court of Justice that an institution of the Community has failed to address to that person any act other than a recommendation or an opinion.

The Court of Justice shall have jurisdiction, under the same conditions, in actions or proceedings brought by the ECB in the areas falling within the latter's field of competence and in actions or proceedings brought against the latter.

(a) The Range of Reviewable Omissions

There is clearly a close relationship between Articles 173 and 175 of the EC Treaty. This should be reflected in the range of omissions which are reviewable under Article 175. On principle, it would seem that the only failures to act which should come within Article 175 are failures to adopt a reviewable act, in the sense of an act which has legal effects. Article 175(1) does, however, simply refer to failure to act, without any more specific delineation of the scope of this phrase. An argument could, therefore, be made that this allows the action to be used in relation to the failure to adopt a non-binding act, such as a recommendation or an opinion.[56] There are, however, conceptual and practical objections to this view, which would serve to create an odd distinction between the action for annulment and that for failure to act.[57] Notwithstanding this the Court stated in the *Comitology* case[58] that the Parliament could bring an Article 175 action for failure to adopt a measure that was not itself a reviewable act. If this is indeed so it will only apply in the context of Article 175(1), since Article 175(3) makes it clear that the action cannot be brought by private individuals with respect to recommendations or opinions.[59]

The interrelationship between Articles 173 and 175, and the scope of reviewable omissions, is also evident in the *Eridania* case considered below:

Cases 10 and 18/68, Società 'Eridania' Zuccherifici Nazionali v. Commission
[1969] ECR 459

The applicants sought the annulment of decisions whereby the Commission had granted aid to certain sugar refineries in Italy. They claimed that their competitive position on the sugar market would be deleteriously affected by the grant of such aid. The Court rejected this action on the ground that the applicants were not

[56] A. G. Toth, 'The Law as it Stands on the Appeal for Failure to Act' (1975) 2 LIEI 65, 79–80.
[57] Hartley, n. 1 above, 400–2.
[58] Case 302/87, n. 13 above.
[59] For further comment on this point, see Hartley, n. 1 above, 402–3.

individually concerned by the decision in question: the fact that their competitive position on the relevant market might be affected was not sufficient to show individual concern. The same applicants also brought an action under Article 175, arguing that there had been a failure to act, this being the failure to revoke the decisions in question.

THE ECJ

15. This application concerns the annulment of the implied decision of rejection resulting from the silence maintained by the Commission in respect of the request addressed to it by the applicants seeking the annulment or revocation of the three disputed decisions for illegality or otherwise because they are inappropriate.

16. The action provided for in Article 175 is intended to establish an illegal omission as appears from that Article, which refers to a failure to act 'in infringement of this Treaty' and from Article 176 which refers to a failure to act declared to be 'contrary to this Treaty'.

Without stating under which provision of Community law the Commission was required to annul or revoke the said decisions, the applicants have confined themselves to alleging that those decisions were adopted in infringement of the Treaty and that this fact alone would thus suffice to make the Commission's failure to act subject to the provisions of Article 175.

17. The Treaty provides, however, particularly in Article 173, other methods of recourse by which an allegedly illegal Community measure may be disputed and if necessary annulled on the application of a duly qualified party.

To admit, as the applicants wish to do, that the parties concerned could ask the institution from which the measure came to revoke it and, in the event of the Commission's failing to act, refer such failure to the Court as an illegal omission to deal with the matter would amount to providing them with a method of recourse parallel to that of Article 173, which would not be subject to the conditions laid down by the Treaty.

18. This application does not therefore satisfy the requirements of Article 175 of the Treaty and must thus be held to be inadmissible.

The reference in the ECJ's judgment to the use of Article 175 to evade limits placed on Article 173, includes, *inter alia*, the ability to bypass the time limits for contesting an action under Article 173.[60] On the facts of the case it was indeed argued that the applicants were out of time to challenge the legality of two of the relevant decisions under Article 173, although the Court preferred to rule against the entirety of the nullity action on the ground that the applicants had no individual concern.

(b) The Procedure

Article 175 requires the applicant to call upon the institution to act in order for the action for failure to act to be admissible. Hartley explains the purpose of this requirement:[61]

[60] See also Cases 21–26/61, *Meroni* v. *High Authority* [1962] ECR 73, 78.
[61] Hartley, n. 1 above, 408.

What is the purpose of this special procedure? In answering this question it must be remembered that an important difference between an act and an omission is that while one can say exactly what the contents of an act are and when it came into existence, this is not always so easy in the case of an omission. The function of the special procedure is to make good this deficiency: the omission is deemed to have taken place at the end of the first two-month period and its contents are defined by the terms of the request. The purpose of the procedure is, therefore, formally to put the respondent in default.

The Treaties do not specify any time limit within which the procedure for failure to act should be initiated. The Court has, however, specified that this procedure must be initiated within a reasonable time.[62]

Once the request to act has been made, the institution concerned has a period of two months within which to define its position. If it has not done this, the applicant has a further two months within which to bring the action under Article 175.[63]

(c) Standing

Article 175, like Article 173, draws a distinction between privileged and non-privileged applicants. The former are identified in Article 175(1): the Member States and other institutions of the Community. This has been held to cover the European Parliament.[64] The latter are covered by Article 175(3). The wording of this Article allows a natural or legal person to complain of a failure to address an act, other than a recommendation or an opinion, to that person. Whether this places the individual in a worse position under Article 175 than under Article 173 is unclear, as the following discussion reveals:

A. G. Toth, The Law As It Stands on the Appeal For Failure To Act[65]

As regards the destination of the measure, two different opinions have been put forward . . . The first view is based on the assumption that unlike the E.C.S.C. Treaty, the E.E.C./Euratom Treaties created two distinct legal remedies in the form of action for annulment and action for failure to act. While a private party can bring annulment proceedings against measures which, although adopted in the form of a regulation or a decision addressed to another person, affect him directly and individually, he can use the action for failure to act only to obtain an act which by its very nature and destination must be addressed to him. He cannot institute this action if he is not the addressee of the measure requested, even if the measure affects him directly and individually. In other words, the addressee of the

[62] Case 59/70, *Netherlands* v. *Commission* [1971] ECR 639. For a critique of the reasoning therein, see Hartley, n. 1 above, 408–11.

[63] The construction of these provisions is contestable. Contrast the views of Toth, n. 56 above, 81–82, with those of Hartley, n. 1 above, 407–8.

[64] Case 13/83, *European Parliament* v. *Council* [1985] ECR 1513. For discussion of the issues involved see G. Bebr, n. 14 above, 173–81.

[65] N. 56 above, 85–6.

> measure requested can only be the person making the request. According to a second view, the action for annulment and action for failure to act form one and the same legal remedy and, therefore, the concept of an 'act' that can be the subject of an appeal is necessarily the same for the purposes of both actions. An action for failure to act is, therefore, available in respect of all acts which are subject to annulment, even if not formally addressed (if taken) to the person bringing the action provided they concern him directly and individually. Should this not be so, the undesirable situation might arise in certain cases that the existence or absence of a judicial remedy would depend on the (arbitrary) conduct of the institution to which a request was submitted. If the institution responds by a formal act (either granting or refusing the request), an action for annulment would be available whether or not the applicant is the addressee of that act as long as it affects him directly and individually. Should, however, the institution fail to respond at all, the applicant would be deprived of any legal remedy if he is not the addressee of the measure requested even if it affects him directly and individually . . . It would seem that while the first view is supported by a strict interpretation of the Treaty text, the second is more in accordance with the logic of the system of remedies open to private parties under the E.E.C./Euratom Treaties.

As the author states, the second, broader view is preferable in principle, and this view has the support of Advocate General Dutheillet de Lamothe.[66] The matter has now been resolved by the ECJ, which ruled in the *ENU* case[67] that standing under Article 148 of the Euratom Treaty, which is the equivalent of Article 175, would be available to an applicant provided that it would be directly and individually concerned: it was not necessary for the applicant to be the actual addressee of the decision.[68]

9. ARTICLE 184 EC: THE PLEA OF ILLEGALITY

Article 184 of the EEC Treaty provides:

> Notwithstanding the expiry of the period laid down in the fifth paragraph of Article 173, any party may, in proceedings in which a regulation adopted jointly by the European Parliament and the Council, or a regulation of the Council, of the Commission or of the ECB is at issue, plead the grounds specified in the second paragraph of Article 173, in order to invoke before the Court of Justice the inapplicability of that regulation.

66 Case 15/71, *Mackprang* v. *Commission* [1971] ECR 797, 807–8. Cf. Case 246/81, *Lord Bethell* v. *Commission* [1982] ECR 2277, 2295–6, Slynn A.G.

67 Case C–107/91, *ENU* v. *Commission* [1993] ECR I–599.

68 An individual would still not be able to use Art. 175(3) to challenge a failure to act where the act in question was a regulation or a directive, since this would not be addressed to him at all. A challenge of this nature would only be possible if the individual could show that the act which was omitted, although it might have taken the form of a regulation, would in substance have been a decision addressed to him; or would have been a decision which directly and individually concerned him.

(a) The Range of Acts which can be Challenged

The essence of the idea covered by Article 184 is as follows. An individual may wish, in the course of proceedings which have been initiated for a different principal reason, to call into question the legality of some other measure. Thus, for example, the principal foundation for the action may be a challenge to a decision, in the course of which the applicant wishes to raise the legality of a more general measure on which the particular decision is based.

Under Article 184 the legality only of regulations can be contested in this way. Moreover, there must be some real connection between the individual decision which is the subject matter of the action, and the general measure the legality of which is being contested.[69] However, in this, as in other areas of Community law, it is the substance of the measure, and not its form, which is decisive. The mere fact that an act is expressed to be in the form of a decision will not, therefore, preclude a challenge if the Court decides that in substance it is a regulation. This is demonstrated by the *Simmenthal* case:

Case 92/78, Simmenthal SpA v. Commission
[1979] ECR 777, [1980] 1 CMLR 25

The applicant sought to annul a Commission Decision concerning the minimum selling prices for frozen beef. In support of its claim, the applicant wished to use Article 184 to challenge the legality of certain regulations and notices which formed the legal basis of the contested decision. The ECJ held that the applicant was directly and individually concerned by the primary decision, even though it was actually addressed to the Member State. The Court then considered the arguments concerning Article 184.

THE ECJ

34. While the applicant formally challenges Commission Decision No 78/258 it has at the same time criticized, in reliance on Article 184 of the EEC Treaty, certain aspects of the 'linking' system in the form in which it has been implemented pursuant to the new Article 14 of Regulation No 805/68, by Regulation No 2900/77 and No 2901/77 and also by the notices of invitations to tender of 13 January 1978.

. . .

36. There is no doubt that this provision (Article 184) enables the applicant to challenge indirectly during the proceedings, with a view to obtaining the annulment of the contested decision, the validity of the measures laid down by Regulation which form the legal basis of the latter.

37. On the other hand there are grounds for questioning whether Article 184 applies to the notices of invitations to tender of 13 January 1978 when according to its wording it only provides for the calling in question of 'regulations'.

38. These notices are general acts which determine in advance and objectively

69 A. Barav, 'The Exception of Illegality in Community Law: A Critical Analysis' (1974) 11 CMLRev. 366, 373–4.

the rights and obligations of the traders who wish to participate in the invitations to tender which these notices make public.

39. As the Court in its judgment . . . in Case 15/57, *Compagnie des Hauts Fourneaux de Chasse* . . . , and in its judgment . . . in Case 9/56, *Meroni* . . . , has already held in connexion with Article 36 of the ECSC Treaty, Article 184 of the EEC Treaty gives expression to a general principle conferring upon any party to proceedings the right to challenge, for the purpose of obtaining the annulment of a decision of direct and individual concern to that party, the validity of previous acts of the institutions which form the legal basis of the decision which is being attacked, if that party was not entitled under Article 173 of the Treaty to bring a direct action challenging those acts by which it was thus affected without having been in a position to ask that they be declared void.

40. The field of application of the said article must therefore include acts of the institutions which, although they are not in the form of a Regulation, nevertheless produce similar effects and on those grounds may not be challenged under Article 173 by natural or legal persons other than Community institutions and Member States.

41. This wide interpretation of Article 184 derives from the need to provide those persons who are precluded by the second paragraph of Article 173 from instituting proceedings directly in respect of general acts with the benefit of judicial review of them at the time when they are affected by implementing decisions which are of direct and individual concern to them.

42. The notices of invitations to tender of 13 January 1978 in respect of which the applicant was unable to initiate proceedings are a case in point, seeing that only the decision taken in consequence of the tender which it had submitted in answer to a specific invitation to tender could be of direct and individual concern to it.

43. There are therefore good grounds for declaring that the applicant's challenge during the proceedings under Article 184, which relates not only to the above-mentioned regulations but also to the notices of invitations to tender of 13 January 1978, is admissible, although the latter are not in the strict sense measures laid down by Regulation.

The basis of the Court's reasoning in the *Simmenthal* case could also lead to the conclusion that individuals should be able to use Article 184 to challenge individual acts which would not be challengeable under Article 173, where the absence of relief under the latter Article is because the individual cannot show direct and individual concern.

By way of contrast, it now appears to be the case that where it is clear that the individual would be able to bring a direct challenge under Article 173, then an indirect action seeking to use Article 184 will not be possible.[70] This aspect of the matter will be considered more fully below.[71]

[70] Case C–188/92, *TWD Textilwerke Deggendorf GmbH* v. *Germany* [1994] ECR I–833.
[71] See below, 495–6.

(b) The Forum in which Article 184 can be Used

Article 184 does not specify the court or courts in which the plea of illegality may be raised. The ECJ has, however, held that Article 184 cannot be used in proceedings before a national court, but can only be raised in proceedings before the ECJ itself.

Cases 31 and 33/62, Milchwerke Heinz Wohrmann & Sohn KG and Alfons Lütticke GmbH v. Commission [1962] ECR 501, [1963] CMLR 152

The applicants wished to challenge a decision by which the Commission had authorized Germany to impose certain duties on the import of powdered milk. They could not use Article 173 itself, since they were out of time. The question which arose was whether they could invoke Article 184 before the ECJ as an ancillary device to the action placing in issue a regulation before a national court.

THE ECJ

Before examining the question whether the contested measures are of their nature decisions or regulations, it is necessary to examine whether Article 184 empowers the Court to adjudicate upon the inapplicability of a regulation when this is invoked in proceedings—as in the present case—before a national court or tribunal.

Article 184 enables any party, notwithstanding the expiry of the period laid down in the third paragraph of Article 173, to invoke before the Court of Justice, for the purpose of making an application for annulment, the inapplicability of a regulation in proceedings in which it is at issue and to plead the grounds specified in the first paragraph of Article 173.

Because Article 184 does not specify before which court or tribunal the proceedings in which the regulation is at issue must be brought, the applicants conclude that the inapplicability of that regulation may in any event be invoked before the Court of Justice. This would mean that there would exist a method of recourse running concurrently with that available under Article 173.

This is however not the meaning of Article 184. It is clear from the wording and the general scheme of this Article that a declaration of the inapplicability of a regulation is only contemplated in proceedings brought before the Court of Justice itself under some other provision of the Treaty, and then only incidentally and with limited effect.

More particularly, it is clear from the reference to the time limit laid down in Article 173 that Article 184 is applicable only in the context of proceedings brought before the Court of Justice and that it does not permit the said time limit to be avoided.

The sole object of Article 184 is thus to protect an interested party against the application of an illegal regulation, without thereby in any way calling in issue the regulation itself, which can no longer be challenged because of the expiry of the time limit laid down in Article 173.

. . .

Although, therefore, Article 184 does not provide sufficient grounds to enable the Court of Justice to give a decision at the present stage, Article 177 does empower the Court to give a ruling if a national court or tribunal were to refer proceedings instituted before it to the Court.

In the light of all these considerations, the Court must declare that it has no jurisdiction to consider the present applications, both insofar as they seek the annulment of the contested measures and insofar as they seek to have them declared inapplicable. It is unnecessary therefore to decide upon the question of the Court's jurisdiction with regard to the exact nature of the measures of the Commission which are challenged by the applicants.

It is clear from the above case that Article 184 can only be used before the ECJ itself, and then only when the primary challenge is based on some other provision of the Treaty. The nature of the proceedings in which the Article 184 plea can be raised must, therefore, be considered.

(c) The Types of Proceedings in which Article 184 can be Raised[72]

The most common usage of Article 184 is an additional, incidental challenge in an annulment action brought under Article 173, as exemplified by the *Simmenthal* case.[73]

It is less clear whether Article 184 can be used as an incident to enforcement proceedings brought under Article 169 against a Member State. There are cases which reject Article 184 in the context of an Article 169 action. However, the rationale for this stance appears to be that the state was attempting to use Article 184 in the context of resisting a decision addressed to it; to have allowed the state to rely on Article 184 in such circumstances would have allowed it to circumvent the time limits laid down under Article 173.[74]

(d) The Parties who are Allowed to use Article 184

It is clear that private parties can utilize Article 184. More contentious is the issue whether it can be used by privileged applicants, the Community institutions, and the Member States. Bebr is against privileged applicants being able to use Article 184, on the ground, *inter alia*, that such applicants can challenge any binding act of Community law under Article 173 within the time limit.[75] However, as Barav has noted,[76] the irregularities in a general act may appear only after the relevant implementation measures have been adopted, and hence the state may not have realized the necessity for challenging the general act until after the time limit under Article 173 has passed. The observations

[72] Barav, n. 69 above, 375–81.

[73] It has also been used in the context of failure to act under Art. 35 ECSC: Cases 32 and 33/58, *SNUPAT* v. *High Authority* [1959] ECR 127.

[74] Barav, n. 69 above, 378–9; Hartley, n. 1 above, 424.

[75] G. Bebr, 'Judicial Remedy of Private Parties against Normative Acts of the European Communities: The Role of the Exception of Illegality' (1966) 4 CMLRev. 7.

[76] N. 69 above, 371.

of Advocate General Roemer suggest that Article 184 should be available to Member States,[77] both for the reason advanced by Barav, and because the wording of the Article refers to 'any party'. The ECJ did not deal with the point, deciding the case on other grounds.

10. ARTICLE 177 EC: PRELIMINARY RULINGS AS A MECHANISM FOR CONTESTING THE LEGALITY OF COMMUNITY MEASURES

(a) *The Rationale for Using Article 177*

More important in practice than Article 184 as a method of indirect challenge to the legality of Community action is the use of preliminary rulings. Article 177(1)(b) of the EC Treaty allows national courts to refer to the ECJ questions concerning the 'validity and interpretation of acts of the institutions of the Community'. This provision has assumed an increased importance for private applicants in the light of the Court's narrow construction of the standing criteria under Article 173. Often a reference under Article 177 is the only mechanism whereby such parties may contest the legality of Community norms. The object of this section will be to explain the way in which preliminary rulings function in this context, and their relationship with more direct forms of attack under Article 173. The following extract from Harding provides a succinct summary of the reasons why individuals wish to use Article 177:

C. Harding, The Impact of Article 177 of the EEC Treaty on the Review of Community Action[78]

It should perhaps be borne in mind at this point why a request for a ruling under Article 177(b) is likely to take place in certain kinds of case rather than a direct action . . . A direct claim may not be a feasible course for a number of reasons. Firstly, the time limit (two months) may well have passed before the alleged illegality or indeed the private party's wish or need to litigate has become apparent. In the second place, the individual may lack locus standi: he may not challenge true regulations or directives and may only attack decisions disguised as regulations or addressed to other persons if directly and individually concerned, which itself presents an insurmountable hurdle in many cases. There is, finally, a related point. It would be misleading to picture the private plaintiff as a disinterested legal watchdog, alert to identify as soon as may be any possibly illegal Community activity. In practice, the individual's interest is likely to arise when his own activities are affected by Community action—usually through the instrumentality of

[77] Case 32/65, *Italy* v. *Commission* [1966] ECR 389, 414.

[78] (1981) 1 YBEL 93, 96. See also C. Harding, 'Who Goes to Court in Europe? An Analysis of Litigation against the European Community' (1992) 17 ELRev. 105.

Member State authorities and not necessarily very soon after the inception of the Community measure. If the individual's interest is seen in this light, then Article 177(b) appears as an equally if not more natural avenue of review than Article 173. Consequently, in a period of more intensive Community activity which is likely to provoke enquiries into the legality of the action taken, it would not be surprising to discover a sharp increase in the number of applications under Article 177(b).

(b) *The Mechanism for Testing Community Legality via the National Courts*

How, then, does an individual who is unable to raise a matter directly under Article 173 actually do so under Article 177? Who are the parties to the action in the national court from which the reference to the ECJ is then made? The answer is that this varies depending upon the factual situation which is in issue. However, a common type of situation would be as follows. Imagine that there is a regulation made pursuant to the CAP which cannot be contested under Article 173, either because the applicant lacks standing, or because it is outside the time limit. Regulations of this nature will normally be applied at a national level by a national intervention agency, which will be responsible for collecting the appropriate levies, applying the rules concerning security deposits and the like, which are demanded by the relevant Community norms. This provides the factual setting for the Article 177 action. The national intervention agency will apply the regulation passed by the Community institutions. This may, for example, require in certain circumstances the forfeiture of a deposit which has been given by a trader. The trader believes that this forfeiture, and the regulation on which it is based, are contrary to Community law. The allegation may be that there has been a breach of general principles of Community law, such as proportionality or legitimate expectations; or the allegation may be that there has been a breach of the Treaty itself, in the sense that the regulation is in violation of the principle of non-discrimination contained in Article 40(3). If the security is forfeited the trader may then institute judicial review proceedings in the national courts, claiming that the regulation is invalid for one of the reasons described above. It will then be for the national court to decide whether to refer the matter to the ECJ under Article 177(1)(b). In other instances the matter may arise somewhat differently. Thus, if a regulation contains a demand for a levy which the trader believes to be in breach of Community law for one of the reasons set out above, then the trader's strategy might be to resist payment, be sued by the national agency, and then raise the alleged invalidity of the regulation on which the demand is based by way of defence. Once again, it would then be for the national court to decide whether to refer the matter to the ECJ.

Brief examples can be given of these strategies at work. In *R.* v. *Intervention Board for Agricultural Produce, ex parte E. D. & F. Man (Sugar) Ltd*,[79] Man, a sugar trader, submitted to the intervention board a tender for the export of

[79] Case 181/84, [1985] ECR 2889, [1985] 3 CMLR 759.

sugar to non-member countries. Security sums had to be lodged. The relevant Community legislation provided that the export licences had to be applied for by a certain time. Man was four hours late in his application owing to internal staff difficulties. The security deposit was forfeited by the intervention board. This was a sizeable sum: £1,670,370. Man, therefore, brought judicial review proceedings in the national court and argued that the forfeiture was disproportionate and hence that the relevant regulation was invalid. This was referred to the ECJ, and the Court held that the particular Article in the regulation was invalid, in so far as it demanded forfeiture of the entire deposit for late licence application. The *ICC* case, considered above in the context of preliminary rulings,[80] provides a further example of the same type of situation. In that case the grant of certain Community aid was made dependent on proof that the recipient of the aid had purchased a certain quantity of skimmed-milk powder held by an intervention agency. Compliance with this obligation was enforced by the deposit of a security which was forfeit if the skimmed-milk was not in fact bought. The applicant received the aid, deposited the security, but did not buy the milk, and hence the agency refused to release the deposit. In an earlier case the ECJ had held that the regulation was invalid, because the price at which the milk powder was to be bought was disproportionately high. The applicant, therefore, took the view that the deposit could not be forfeited, since it only served to ensure compliance with an obligation which was itself invalid. The Italian court made a reference to the ECJ, asking whether the judgment in the earlier case, holding the regulation to be invalid, was also of relevance in subsequent litigation involving the same issue, albeit that it arose from a different national court. The response of the ECJ was to hold that the national court could rely on the previous ruling on the issue.

(c) The Acts which can be Challenged under Article 177

Article 177(1)(b) allows a challenge to be made to the validity of acts of the Community institutions. It is apparent from the preceding examples that this countenances challenges to regulations via the national courts.

The problem with respect to individual decisions is more complex. A person who is *not* the addressee of an individual decision may, it seems, contest this decision through the national courts, in much the same way as in the context of challenging a regulation. Thus, if a decision is addressed to a Member State or state agency which requires that certain action should be taken, then an individual affected by this can contest the validity of the decision on which the action is based through the national courts.[81] This is exemplified by the *Universität Hamburg* case.[82] In that case the Commission had issued a decision to all Member States refusing to allow an exemption from customs duty in relation to scientific equipment which had been imported from the United

[80] See above, 409–11.

[81] Case C–188/92, n. 70 above.

[82] Case 216/82, *Universität Hamburg* v. *Hauptzollamt Hamburg-Kehrwieder* [1983] ECR 2771.

States.[83] The German authorities applied this decision, refusing the customs exemption, and the applicant sought to contest this before the national court. The ECJ held that the case could be brought via Article 177. It was influenced in this decision by the fact that the Commission decision in question did not have to be published, and that it did not have to be notified to the person applying for the tax exemption. Both of these factors would have rendered any challenge within the time limit under Article 173 virtually impossible. The Court pronounced more generally on the point in the following case:

Case 133–136/85, Walter Rau Lebensmittelwerke v. Bundesanstalt für Landwirtschaftliche Marktordnung [1987] ECR 2289

The applicants, who were margarine producers, wished to contest the legality of a scheme whereby the Community sold cheap butter on the German market to test consumer reaction. Could a challenge be made through Article 177?

THE ECJ

11. It must be emphasised that there is nothing in Community law to prevent an action from being brought before a national court against a measure implementing a Decision adopted by a Community institution where the conditions laid down by national law are satisfied. When such an action is brought, if the outcome of the dispute depends on the validity of that Decision the national court may submit questions to the Court of Justice by way of a reference for a preliminary ruling, without there being any need to ascertain whether or not the plaintiff in the main proceedings has the possibility of challenging the Decision directly before the Court.

12. The answer to the first question must therefore be that the possibility of bringing a direct action under the second paragraph of Article 173 of the EEC Treaty against a Decision adopted by a Community institution does not preclude the possibility of bringing an action against a measure adopted by a national authority for the implementation of that Decision on the ground that the latter Decision is unlawful.

This decision must, however, now be seen in the light of the Court's holding in the *TWD* case.[84] In this case the Commission declared aid which Germany had granted to a firm to be incompatible with the common market. The aid had, therefore, to be repaid. The German Government informed the company of this and told it also that the Commission's decision could be challenged under Article 173. The company did not do so, but instead sought to raise the legality of the Commission's decision in an action in the German courts. The ECJ held that no indirect challenge was possible in this instance, given that the company had been informed of its right to challenge under

[83] The rationale being that the Commission claimed that equipment of equivalent scientific value was being manufactured in the Community itself.

[84] Case C–188/92, n. 70 above.

Article 173, and given also that it would 'without any doubt'[85] have had standing to do so.[86]

It seems therefore that a challenge under Article 177 will not be possible if the matter could have been raised by a person who had standing under Article 173, and who knew of the matter within the time limits for a direct action. Where it is unclear whether the applicant would have standing for an Article 173 action the ECJ is likely to be more willing to admit the indirect action. The ECJ is also likely to be more receptive to actions under Article 177 where the applicant would not have known of the relevant measure in time to challenge it under Article 173.[87]

11. THE GROUNDS OF REVIEW

Once the applicant has established standing, and has also overcome the other hurdles such as time limits for the bringing of an action, it will still have to show the existence of some reason for the act of the Community to be annulled, or declared invalid. Four grounds are specified in Article 173 of the EC Treaty: lack of competence; infringement of an essential procedural requirement; infringement of the Treaty or any rule of law relating to its application; and misuse of power.[88]

(a) Lack of Competence

The Community institutions must be able to point to a power within the Treaty which serves to authorize their action. If they are not able to do so then the act in question will be declared to be void for lack of competence. This ground of review is, however, used relatively rarely. There are two connected reasons for this.

On the one hand, the ECJ has interpreted the powers of the Community institutions broadly and purposively, in order to facilitate the attainment of the objectives of the Community. This approach to Treaty interpretation has itself been complemented by the implied-powers doctrine, under which the Commission has been held impliedly to have the powers which are necessary to enable it to carry out the tasks expressly conferred on it by the Treaty.[89]

On the other hand, there are provisions of the Treaty which confer broader

[85] Case C–188/92, n. 70 above, para. 24.

[86] The ECJ distinguished *Rau* on the ground that the applicants in that case had in fact brought an annulment action before the ECJ, and that therefore the issue of the time bar under Art. 173 and the effect of this on a possible Art. 177 action did not arise.

[87] See the ground on which the Court distinguished the *Universität Hamburg* case in *TWD*, n. 70 above, para. 23.

[88] The same grounds appear to be of relevance in challenges brought under Art. 177: Hartley, n. 1 above, 424–5.

[89] Cases 281, 283–285, 287/85, *Germany* v. *Commission* [1987] ECR 3203, [1988] 1 CMLR 11.

legislative power, notably Articles 100 and 235.[90] Thus, it will be rare for the Community's action to be struck down on this ground.

One of the instances in which this might be utilized is where the claimant alleges that there has been an unlawful delegation of power. This is exemplified by the *Meroni* case,[91] in which the High Authority had delegated certain powers to outside agencies in connection with the administration of a scrap equalization scheme. The Court held that it was legitimate to delegate clearly defined executive powers which were subject to objective criteria set by the delegating authority. It was not, however, permissible to delegate broad, discretionary powers which entailed the exercise of considerable freedom of judgement for the delegee.

Another reason why it might well be argued that the Community had no competence to act is subsidiarity. The meaning of this term was examined earlier.[92] A claim by a Member State that Community legislation had infringed the subsidiarity principle could be framed in terms of the Community's lack of competence to adopt the measure in question.

(b) Infringement of an Essential Procedural Requirement

The Treaty does not regard all failures to comply with procedural requirements as grounds for annulling the act in question. The defect must relate to an essential procedural requirement. What counts as essential for these purposes is a matter of construction for the ECJ. The following are examples of procedural requirements which have been held to be essential for these purposes: the requirement to give a hearing;[93] the duty to provide reasons;[94] and the duty to consult. The following case provides an example of the Court's reasoning in this context:

Case 138/79, Roquette Frères SA v. Council
[1980] ECR 3333

The applicant and the Parliament claimed that a regulation had been adopted without regard to the consultation procedure of Article 43(2) of the Treaty.

THE ECJ

32. The applicant and the Parliament in its intervention maintain that since Regulation No 1111/77 as amended was adopted by the Council without regard to the consultation procedure provided for in the second paragraph of Article 43 of the Treaty it must be treated as void for infringement of essential procedural requirements.

33. The consultation provided for in the third subparagraph of Article 43(2), as

[90] See above, 104–7.
[91] Case 9/56, *Meroni and Co Industrie Metallurgiche SpA* v. *ECSC* [1957–8] ECR 133.
[92] See above, 112–18.
[93] Case 17/74, *Transocean Marine Paint* v. *Commission* [1974] ECR 1063, [1974] 2 CMLR 459.
[94] Case 24/62, *Germany* v. *Commission* [1963] ECR 63, [1963] CMLR 347; Case 5/67, *Beus GmbH & Co* v. *Hauptzollamt München* [1968] ECR 83, [1968] CMLR 131.

in other similar provisions of the Treaty, is the means which allows the Parliament to play an actual part in the legislative process of the Community. Such power represents an essential factor in the institutional balance intended by the Treaty. Although limited, it reflects at Community level the fundamental democratic principle that the peoples should take part in the exercise of power through the intermediary of a representative assembly. Due consultation of the Parliament in the cases provided for by the Treaty therefore constitutes an essential formality disregard of which means that the measure concerned is void.

34. In that respect it is pertinent to point out that observance of that requirement implies that the Parliament has expressed its opinion. It is impossible to take the view that the requirement is satisfied by the Council's simply asking for the opinion. The Council is, therefore, wrong to conclude in the references in the preamble to Regulation No 1293/79 a statement to the effect that the Parliament has been consulted.

(c) Infringement of the Treaty or of any Rule of Law Relating to its Application

It is readily apparent that this third ground of review is capable of overlapping with the other grounds mentioned above. It is, therefore, not surprisingly pleaded in almost all cases.

Infringement of the Treaty embraces all the provisions of the constitutive treaties, the EEC, ECSC, and Euratom, as well as Treaties which amend or supplement these.

The phrase 'any rule of law relating to its application' covers all those rules of Community law other than those which exist in the Treaties themselves. Two of the most common types of rules which are pleaded in this respect are general principles of Community law,[95] and the fact that one Community act is in breach of another Community act which is hierarchically superior to it. These two categories of illegality are exemplified in the following cases:

Case 4/73, Nold KG v. Commission [1974] ECR 491, [1974] 2 CMLR 338

The full facts of the case have been set out above.[96] It will be remembered that Nold sought the annulment of a Commission decision which meant that it could only purchase coal from a supplier on conditions which were burdensome. As a result it suffered loss because it could no longer buy direct from its supplier.

THE ECJ

12. The applicant asserts finally that certain of its fundamental rights have been violated, in that the restrictions introduced by the new trading rules authorized by the Commission have the effect, by depriving it of direct supplies, of jeopardizing both the profitability of the undertaking and the free development of its business activity, to the point of endangering its very existence.

In this way, the Decision is said to violate, in respect of the applicant, a right

[95] See above, Chs. 7 and 8. [96] See above, 292.

akin to a proprietary right, as well as its right to the free pursuit of business activity, as protected by the Grundgesetz of the Federal Republic of Germany and by the Constitutions of other Member States and various international treaties, including in particular the Convention for the Protection of Human Rights and Fundamental Freedoms of 4 November 1950 and the Protocol to that Convention of 20 March 1952.

13. As the Court has already stated, fundamental rights form an integral part of the general principles of law, the observance of which it ensures.

In safeguarding these rights, the Court is bound to draw inspiration from constitutional traditions common to the Member States, and it cannot therefore uphold measures which are incompatible with fundamental rights recognized and protected by the Constitutions of those States.

Similarly, international treaties for the protection of human rights on which the Member States have collaborated or of which they are signatories, can supply guidelines which should be followed within the framework of Community law.

The submissions of the applicant must be examined in the light of these principles.

14. If rights of ownership are protected by the constitutional laws of all the Member States and if similar guarantees are given in respect of their right freely to choose and practise their trade or profession, the rights thereby guaranteed, far from constituting unfettered prerogatives, must be viewed in the light of the social function of the property and activities protected thereunder.

For this reason, rights of this nature are protected by law subject always to limitations laid down in accordance with the public interest.

Within the Community legal order it likewise seems legitimate that these rights should, if necessary, be subject to certain limits justified by the overall objectives pursued by the Community, on condition that the substance of these rights is left untouched.

As regards the guarantees accorded to a particular undertaking, they can in no respect be extended to protect mere commercial interests or opportunities, the uncertainties of which are part of the very essence of economic activity.

15. The disadvantages claimed by the applicant are in fact the result of economic change and not of the contested Decision.

It was for the applicant, confronted by the economic changes brought about by the recession in coal production, to acknowledge the situation and itself carry out the necessary adaptations.

16. This submission must be dismissed for all the reasons outlined above.

The decision in *CNTA SA* v. *Commission*[97] provides a good example of an attempt to found the illegality of one Community norm on the fact that it was in breach of a more basic, but still secondary, norm of Community law. The case will be more fully considered in the context of a damages action.[98] It will be seen that the applicant argued that the withdrawal of monetary compensatory amounts (mcas), which were designed to compensate traders for fluctuations in exchange rates, was in breach of the basic regulation governing the payment of such sums. The applicant contended that this basic regulation did

[97] Case 74/74, [1975] ECR 533, [1977] 1 CMLR 171. [98] See below, 519–21.

not allow the withdrawal of mcas once instituted, and that in any event, if this were to be done it could only be done on the basis of monetary factors, to the exclusion of broader economic factors. This claim was rejected on the construction of the relevant basic regulation, but claims of this type are commonplace.

The phrase 'any rule of law relating to its application' can also cover other matters in addition to infringement of general principles of Community law, and breach of higher Community secondary norms. Thus, as we have seen,[99] an individual can base a claim on a breach of an international agreement with non-member states, provided that the agreement is binding on the Community and provided also that it has direct effect.[100]

(d) *Misuse of Powers*

The concept of misuse of powers covers the situation in which a power is used for a purpose other than that for which it was granted. All systems of public law possess a doctrine similar, if not identical, to this. Thus, in the administrative law of the United Kingdom it is commonplace for challenges to be based on the fact that the administration has used its power for improper purposes. Challenges of this sort are less commonplace within the EC, principally because applicants base their claims on one of the other heads of review. There is, moreover, a close connection between claims based on misuse of powers and those based on proportionality. The distinguishing feature, in principle, is that in the former instance the object or purpose which is sought to be achieved will itself be improper, whereas in the latter instance the objective will be legitimate, and the issue will be whether it was achieved in a disproportionate manner.

There are, however, examples of successful claims based on misuse of power, as the case of *Franco Giuffrida* v. *Council*[101] demonstrates. The applicant sought the annulment of a decision appointing Martino to a higher grade in the Community service, pursuant to a competition in which he and Martino were the two contestants for the post. He claimed that the competition was in reality an exercise to appoint Martino to the job, the rationale being that Martino had already been performing the duties associated with the higher grade. The Court quashed the appointment, stating that the pursuit of such a specific objective was contrary to the aims of the recruitment procedure, and was, therefore, a misuse of power. Internal promotions should be based on selecting the best person for the job, rather than pre-selecting a particular candidate to whom the job would be given.

[99] See above, 169–74.

[100] For the possibility of using a subsidiary convention to attack a Community act, see Hartley, n. 1 above, 432–3.

[101] Case 105/75, [1976] ECR 1395.

(e) The Intensity of Review

The discussion thus far has concentrated on the heads of review which are available under the Treaty. To stop there would, however, be to give only an incomplete view of the subject. Anyone familiar with public law systems will be aware that there is another aspect of the matter which is relevant to the enquiry. This concerns the intensity of the review. How far will the Court go in reassessing decisions made by the Commission and Council? To what extent will the Court be ready to accept determinations made by the institutions relating to the balancing of competing aims within the Community's objectives, and will the ECJ's attitude differ from one area to another? These questions will be considered within this section.

Article 33 of the ECSC Treaty contains certain explicit dictates on the matter.[102] There is no provision in the EC Treaty which performs the same function as Article 33. However, the intensity of review has, not surprisingly, also been an issue under the EC Treaty. Many of the cases in which applicants seek to have Community acts annulled or declared illegal concern determinations made pursuant to the CAP. The question of the intensity of the Court's review of the impugned Community act has arisen at a number of different levels.

First, it can arise in the context of a challenge to the *very choice of objective to be pursued, and the appropriate means by which this should be done*. We have already seen that the foundational provisions of the Treaty in this area, Articles 39, 40, and 43, contain a number of objectives which are set out at a relatively high level of generality.[103] This necessitates the making of discretionary choices by the Commission and the Council. In evaluating the chosen option the Court has held that the competent Community institutions enjoy wide discretionary power concerning, *inter alia*, the definition of the objectives to be pursued and the choice of the appropriate means of action.[104] A similar recognition of the discretion of the Community institutions is to be found in the *Balkan-Import-Export* case, in which the Court stated that:[105]

> Article 39 of the EEC Treaty sets out various objectives of the common agricultural policy. In pursuing these objectives, the Community Institutions must secure the permanent harmonization made necessary by any conflict between these aims taken individually and, where necessary, allow any one of them temporary priority in order to satisfy the demands of the economic factors or conditions in view of which their decisions are made.

[102] It provides that the Court may not examine the evaluation of the situation resulting from economic facts or circumstances in the light of which the High Authority made its decisions or recommendations, except where the High Authority is alleged to have misused its powers or has manifestly failed to observe the provisions of the Treaty or any rule of law relating to its application. Although the Art. only applies to the evaluation of economic facts, the Court has shown a similar restraint in other instances where the Community institutions possess particular expertise or knowledge.

[103] See above, 476–8.

[104] Cases 197–200, 243, 245 and 247/80, n. 42 above.

[105] Case 5/73, *Balkan-Import-Export GmbH* v. *Hauptzollamt Berlin Packhof* [1973] ECR 1091, 1112.

The *Biovilac* case provides a further good illustration of the same theme.[106] In that case the applicant argued that Community regulations on skimmed-milk powder were illegal for a number of reasons, one of which was that they disregarded the object of stabilizing markets set out in Article 39(1)(c). The Court rejected the claim. It stated that even if the object of stabilizing markets and that of ensuring a fair return to the agricultural community (enshrined in Article 39(1)(b)) were only partially reconciled by the regulations in question, it could not be said that these were illegal as being in breach of Article 39: the legality of such measures could only be affected if they were *manifestly unsuitable* for achieving the aim pursued.

A second, related context in which the intensity of review can arise concerns the *interpretation of regulations or decisions* made pursuant to the CAP. These may often contain terms which premise Community action on the basis that there are 'serious disturbances' on the relevant market, or where 'economic difficulties' might be caused by a certain change in prices, or currency values. There is no doubt that, as a matter of principle, the Court could undertake an extensive re-evaluation of the factual and legal issues, in order to determine whether such circumstances exist, and that on occasion it has engaged in quite close scrutiny of the data.[107] To adopt this approach on a broad scale would, however, be time-consuming; it would encourage applicants to ask the Court to second-guess evaluations made by the Community institutions; and it would involve intensive review of measures which are often adopted under severe time constraints, or in situations where there is an urgent need for measures to combat a temporary problem in the market. The presence of these reasons for a less intensive species of review is evident in the following extract. Lord Mackenzie Stuart considers the problems posed for the Community institutions and the Court by the currency fluctuations of the 1970s:

Lord Mackenzie Stuart, The European Communities and the Rule of Law[108]

It is difficult to give a short and up-to-date account of the various currency crises since 1971 and I make no attempt. It would, I fear, be out of date before the ink dried on the page and of only antiquarian interest by the time these lectures are delivered.

In any case, you might ask, what is the relevance of this to the work of the Court? It could be said that I have just described a series of economic emergencies requiring a political rather than a legal solution. This is true. Nonetheless commerce continues and must continue in good times as in bad. Moreover, economic storms can sometimes bring fortune to those who can ride with them provided they can still steer a course when driven under bare poles. At any rate, the economic climate of the Community is ever reflected in the disputes, claims and

[106] Case 59/83, *SA Biovilac NV* v. *European Economic Community* [1984] ECR 4057.

[107] See e.g. Cases 106 and 107/63, *Alfred Toepfer and Getreide-Import Gesellschaft* v. *Commission* [1965] ECR 405.

[108] (Stevens, 1977), 91, 96.

grievances of those whose commercial transactions have been affected. Accordingly the Court has been compelled, in spite of the obvious difficulties, to apply the discipline of legal analysis to measures whose impetus has been the necessity of finding an immediate response to unacceptable economic pressures.

That is to say, the Court has had to consider the actions of the Community institutions taken, of necessity, at speed against a background of rapidly changing pressures, when almost every aspect has been under fire from those whose interests have been affected.

Lord Mackenzie Stuart illustrated these problems by reference to a number of cases, including *Balkan-Import-Export*[109] and *Merkur*, the latter of which will be considered more fully below. Lord Mackenzie Stuart then continued as follows:

What do these instances demonstrate? First, I think, that the Court has had and is having to deal with a series of cases—I could extend the list many times without difficulty—arising in circumstances not only never envisaged by the Treaty of Rome but in circumstances running counter to one of its basic premises. Secondly, they show that the Court appreciates that in moments of economic stress when contingency measures have to be taken the Community authorities must be allowed some lee-way. That with hindsight it may appear that the measures chosen were not necessarily the best is not sufficient to annul what has been done. Even so, and this is the third and most important point, 'the law' must be applied to protect the administered if, no doubt with the best motives imaginable, the Council or Commission, as the case may be, has failed to protect their legitimate interest.

The predominant approach of the Court has, therefore, not been one of complete substitution of judgment, or of a complete rehearing of issues of fact or mixed fact and law, at least not within the context of cases arising from the CAP, which accounts for many of the actions brought against the Community under either Article 173 or Article 177.

Brief examples can be given of the ECJ's approach in this area. In the *CNTA* case,[110] considered above, the applicant complained of the withdrawal of monetary compensatory amounts, and also contested the criteria on which such sums should be given. Mcas can be given to compensate for certain exchange-rate movements, in circumstances where those movements might otherwise disturb trade in agricultural products. The Court held that the Commission possessed a large degree of discretion in determining whether alterations in monetary values as a result of exchange-rate movements might lead to such disturbances in trade and, therefore, whether mcas were warranted. In reaching this conclusion, the Court also held that the Commission could properly take account of broader economic factors, and was not

[109] Case 5/73, n. 105 above. See also n. 116 below.

[110] Case 74/74, *CNTA SA* v. *Commission* [1975] ECR 533, [1977] 1 CMLR 171.

confined to considering only monetary values. A similar approach can be perceived in the *Deuka* case.[111] The applicant sought, through Article 177, to test the legality of a particular regulation under which premiums payable on wheat were modified. It was argued that this was illegal, on the ground that the basic regulation on these matters only permitted adjustments 'where the balance of the market in cereals is likely to be disturbed'. The Court rejected the claim. It stated that the Commission had a 'significant freedom of evaluation' in deciding on both the existence of a disturbance, and the method of dealing with it:[112]

> When examining the lawfulness of the exercise of such freedom, the courts cannot substitute their own evaluation of the matter for that of the competent authority, but must restrict themselves to examining whether the evaluation of the competent authority contains a patent error or constitutes a misuse of power.

This approach was confirmed, albeit with some modification, in the *Racke* case.[113] Once again the case arose through Article 177. Once again the applicant claimed that certain particular regulations, this time on mcas, were in violation of the more basic regulation governing the area. The latter only permitted such mcas to be granted or charged where changes in the exchange rates of currencies could bring about disturbances to trade in agricultural products. The respective roles of the Commission and the Court were clearly delineated by the ECJ: it was for the Commission to decide on the existence of a risk of disturbance to trade, and in this evaluation of a complex economic situation it possessed a wide discretion:[114]

> In reviewing the legality of the exercise of such discretion, the Court must examine whether it contains a manifest error or constitutes a misuse of power or whether the authority did not clearly exceed the bounds of its discretion.

The third context in which the question of the intensity of review can arise concerns the *application of principles such as legitimate expectations, proportionality, and non-discrimination.*[115] It is quite clear that these principles can be used in the context of the CAP to strike down regulations or decisions. It is also clear that the Court will not readily find that these principles have been violated in the agricultural sphere, from which many of the cases concerned with the legality of Community action arise. This is apparent from both the primary and secondary literature. For example, in the *Merkur* case the applicant complained that the Commission had failed to fix compensatory

[111] Case 78/74, *Deuka, Deutsche Kraftfutter GmbH, B. J. Stolp* v. *Einfuhr- und Vorratsstelle für Getreide und Futtermittel* [1975] ECR 421.

[112] *Ibid.* 432. See also Case 57/72, *Westzucker GmbH* v. *Einfuhr- und Vorratsstelle für Zucker* [1973] ECR 321.

[113] Case 98/78, *Firma A. Racke* v. *Hauptzollamt Mainz* [1979] ECR 69, [1979] 1 CMLR 552.

[114] *Ibid.* 81.

[115] See above, Ch. 8.

payments for certain products in line with a basic regulation on this issue, and that this constituted discrimination since others in a similar position had received such payments. The Court rejected the claim. It was influenced by the fact that the basic Community regulation was an emergency measure, and that the rules for its implementation to particular product categories had to be devised within a very short space of time.[116]

> Since the assessment which the Commission had to make was perforce an overall one, the possibility that some of the decisions it made might subsequently appear to be debatable on economic grounds or subject to modification would not in itself be sufficient to prove the existence of a violation of the principle of non-discrimination, once it was established that the considerations adopted by it were not manifestly erroneous.

Space precludes any detailed analysis of the application of these principles in the agricultural sphere, but it is clear that the Court will be similarly reluctant to find, for example, a breach of the proportionality principle unless there was some manifest disproportionality in the decision in question.[117] This is borne out by the secondary literature which attests to the difficulty of successfully utilizing such principles. Thus, Vajda comments that the Court's reluctance to involve itself in economic-policy considerations makes it hesitant to question the Commission's exercise of discretion on the grounds of proportionality, unless the charge in question was really disproportionate.[118] Sharpston is equally clear on the difficulties which face applicants who wish to plead legitimate expectations. Relatively few such cases succeed in the agricultural sphere, and the 'general rule appears to be that the European Court will usually be prepared to back the Council and/or the Commission and to hold that they are entitled to have a fairly wide margin of manœuvre in market management, even where the chosen scheme has been subjected to fairly heavy criticism'.[119]

It should not be thought that the issue concerning the intensity of judicial review is only of relevance in the context of the CAP. That would be mistaken. A similar judicial reluctance to engage in intensive review is also apparent in other areas in which the Commission is possessed of discretionary power requiring it to make complex evaluative choices, as in the case of state aids,[120] and the application of rules relating to mergers.[121]

[116] Case 43/72, *Merkur GmbH* v. *Commission* [1973] ECR 1055, 1074.

[117] Case C–331/88, *R.* v. *Minister of Agriculture, Fisheries and Food and the Secretary of State for Health, ex. p. FEDESA* [1990] ECR I–4023, 4061; Case C–8/89, *Vincenzo Zardi* v. *Consorzio Agrario Provinciale di Ferrara* [1990] ECR I–2515, 2532–3. For more general discussion, see above, Ch. 8.

[118] C. Vajda, 'Some Aspects of Judicial Review within the Common Agricultural Policy—Part II' (1979) 4 ELRev. 341, 347–8.

[119] E. Sharpston, 'Legitimate Expectations and Economic Reality' (1990) 15 ELRev. 103, 108.

[120] See below, Ch. 24.

[121] See below, Ch. 21.

12. THE CONSEQUENCES OF ILLEGALITY AND INVALIDITY

The EC Treaty has two principal provisions which are of relevance in determining the consequences of illegality. Article 174 provides that if the action under Article 173 is well founded, the Court shall declare the act concerned to be void. This is then modified by Article 174(2) which states that, in the case of a regulation, the Court shall, if it considers it necessary, state which of the effects of the regulation which it has declared void shall be considered as definitive. Article 176 complements this by stating that the institution whose act has been declared void, or whose failure to act has been declared contrary to the Treaty, shall be required to take the necessary measures to comply with the judgment of the Court.

The general principle of Community law is that nullity is retroactive, in the sense that once the illegal act is annulled under Article 173 it is void *ab initio*. Such a ruling has an effect *erga omnes*. The precise meaning of this phrase is, however, open to question. Some writers interpret it to mean that the effects of the original ruling apply equally to persons who were not party to the original annulment proceedings.[122] Others adopt a rather more restrictive construction. Thus, Toth argues that:[123]

> the scope of these *erga omnes* effects is not as wide as it might seem at first sight or might be implied from the literal meaning of the term ('affecting everyone'). The true meaning of the phrase, as stated by the Court above,[124] is that a measure 'which has already been annulled cannot compromise the rights or interests' of others. It follows that annulment affects only those persons whose rights or interests could have been compromised in the first place. Since, as a general rule, it is only law making measures, such as ECSC general decisions and EEC/Euratom regulations, that can, by definition, affect the rights or interests of the general public (since only those have *erga omnes* binding effects), it is only the annulment of such law-making measures that can produce genuine *erga omnes* effects, affecting the public at large. Annulment of individual measures, such as decisions, produces only a 'limited' *erga omnes* effect, affecting, apart from the parties in the case, only such persons as are directly affected by the measures themselves.

Normally an act will have to be challenged for its invalidity to be established, but there are certain limited instances in which the acts will be treated as absolutely void or non-existent, in which instances the act may be treated as if it were never adopted.[125] In general, however, proceedings will be

[122] Hartley, n. 1 above, 449.

[123] A. G. Toth, 'The Authority of Judgments of the European Court of Justice: Binding Force and Legal Effects' (1984) 4 YBEL 1, 49.

[124] Referring to Case 3/54, *ASSIDER* v. *High Authority* [1955] ECR 63.

[125] See above, 451.

required to establish the illegality of the act in question. The principle of retroactive nullity can cause hardship, particularly in those instances in which the measure is a regulation which has been relied on by many, and which may be the basis of other measures adopted at a later date. This is the rationale for Article 174(2), which allows the Court to qualify the extent of the nullity.[126] This Article has been used to limit the temporal effect of the Court's ruling. Thus, in *Commission* v. *Council*[127] the Court annulled part of a regulation concerning staff salaries. However, if the regulation were annulled retroactively then the staff would not be entitled to any salary increases until a new regulation had been adopted. The Court, therefore, used Article 174(2), ruling that the regulation in question should continue to have effect until a new regulation which was in accord with the Court's judgment had been promulgated. In addition to the power to limit the temporal effect of its rulings, the Court may also find that the illegality affects only part of the measure in question.

A finding of invalidity pursuant to Article 177 is, in theory, different from a decision made pursuant to Article 173. The former is addressed only to the national court which requested the ruling. However, as has been seen in the discussion of preliminary rulings,[128] the Court has held that its rulings on Article 177 references concerning validity do have an *erga omnes* effect, and such rulings provide a sufficient reason for any other national court to treat that act as void for the purpose of a judgment which it has to give.[129] Moreover, the Court has applied the principles of Articles 174 and 176, which technically only operate in the context of Articles 173 and 175, by analogy to cases arising under Article 177. This has further eroded any distinction between the effects of a judgment given under Articles 173 and 177. This is exemplified by the following case:[130]

Case 112/83, Société de Produits de Maïs v. Administration des Douanes [1985] ECR 719

The case concerned the effects of a ruling by the ECJ on the validity of a regulation, following a reference from the French courts under Article 177.

THE ECJ

16. It should in the first place be recalled that the Court has already held in its judgment of 13 May 1981 (Case 66/80, *International Chemical Corporation* [1981] ECR 1191) that although a judgment of the Court given under Article 177 of the Treaty declaring an act of an institution, in particular a Council or Commission Regulation, to be void is directly addressed only to the national court which

[126] The ECJ has extended the principle of Art. 174(2) to dirs.: Case C–295/90, *European Parliament* v. *Council*, [1992] ECR I–4193.

[127] Case 81/72, [1973] ECR 575, [1973] CMLR 639.

[128] See above, 409–11.

[129] Case 66/80, *International Chemical Corporation* v. *Amministrazione delle Finanze dello Stato* [1981] ECR 1191, [1983] 2 CMLR 593. The national court may make a reference on the same point if it is unclear about the scope, grounds, or consequences of the original ruling.

[130] See also Cases C–38, 151/90, *R.* v. *Lomas* [1992] ECR I–1781, [1992] 2 CMLR 653.

brought the matter before the Court, it is sufficient reason for any other national court to regard that act as void for the purposes of a judgment which it has to give.

17. Secondly, it must be emphasised that the Court's power to impose temporal limits on the effects of a declaration that a legislative act is invalid, in the context of preliminary rulings under indent (b) of the first paragraph of Article 177, is justified by the interpretation of Article 174 of the Treaty having regard to the necessary consistency between the preliminary ruling procedure and the action for annulment provided for in Articles 173, 174 and 176 of the Treaty, which are two mechanisms provided by the Treaty for reviewing the legality of acts of the Community institutions. The possibility of imposing temporal limits on the effects of the invalidity of a Community Regulation, whether under Article 173 or Article 177, is a power conferred on the Court by the Treaty in the interest of the uniform application of Community law throughout the Community. In the particular case of the judgment of 15 October 1980, referred to by the Tribunal [Case 145/79], the use of the possibility provided for in the second paragraph of Article 174 was based on reasons of legal certainty more fully explained in paragraph 52 of that judgment.

18. It must be pointed out that where it is justified by overriding considerations the second paragraph of Article 174 gives the Court discretion to decide, in each particular case, which specific effects of a Regulation which has been declared void must be maintained. It is therefore for the Court, where it makes use of the possibility of limiting the effect of past events of a declaration in proceedings under Article 177 that a measure is void, to decide whether an exception to that temporal limitation of the effect of its judgment may be made in favour of the party which brought the action before the national court or of any other trader which took similar steps before the declaration of invalidity or whether, conversely, a declaration of invalidity applicable only to the future constitutes an adequate remedy even for traders who took action at the appropriate time with a view to protecting their rights.

In addition to the discretion to limit the temporal effects of a ruling given under Article 177, the Court has held that the principle underlying Article 176 is also applicable in the context of Article 177. This enables the Court to order remedial action which it considers to be appropriate instead of a simple declaration of invalidity.[131]

13. CONCLUSION

It is apparent from the preceding discussion that there are a number of avenues through which to test the legality of Community action, and that the ECJ has a considerable range of review powers against which this test can be conducted. It is also apparent that the interpretation of these latter powers

[131] See Cases 4, 109, 145/79, *Société Co-opérative 'Providence Agricole de la Champagne'* v. *ONIC* [1980] ECR 2823.

leaves a considerable discretion to the Court in deciding whether in fact to strike down a Community norm. In reaching this decision the nature of the subject-matter under scrutiny will, not surprisingly, play an important part both in determining whether to accord standing and in determining the standard or intensity of review which is adopted. This has been exemplified in the preceding discussion, in the approach adopted by the ECJ in agricultural cases, which form a large percentage of the challenges brought under Articles 173 and 177. The reasons for the Court's reluctance to grant standing in such instances have been examined above.[132] The connection between this reluctance, and the standard of review adopted if the Court does hear the substance of the case was outlined at that stage. This connection can now be better appreciated. It is, of course, the case that differing considerations may well apply in other areas, in which the Court may be more willing to grant standing and to engage in more intensive review. It is also the case that there are areas, such as state aids, in which the ECJ is more willing to grant standing, for the reasons examined earlier, even though it does not engage in extensive review. The breadth of subject matter covered by Community law renders this diversity of judicial approach highly likely. Any assessment of Community law must always be evaluated against the backdrop of the substantive issues involved before the Court. In this way a richer understanding can be gained of the Court's decisions concerning review of legality, whether these relate to procedural or substantive aspects of the topic.

14. FURTHER READING

(a) On Locus Standi

ARNULL, A., 'Challenging EC Anti-Dumping Regulations: The Problem of Admissibility' [1992] 2 ECLR 73

BARAV, A., 'Direct and Individual Concern: An Almost Insurmountable Barrier to the Admissibility of Individual Appeal to the EEC Court' (1974) 11 CMLRev. 191

BEBR, G., 'The Standing of the European Parliament in the Community System of Legal Remedies: A Thorny Jurisprudential Development' (1990) 10 YBEL 170

BRADLEY, K., 'Sense and Sensibility: *Parliament* v. *Council* Continued' (1991) 16 ELRev. 245

CRAIG, P. P., 'Legality, Standing and Substantive Review in Community Law' (1994) 14 OJLS 507

DINNAGE, J., '*Locus Standi* and Article 173 EEC' (1979) 4 ELRev. 15

GREAVES, R. M., '*Locus Standi* under Article 173 EEC when Seeking Annulment of a Regulation' (1986) 11 ELRev. 119

HARDING, C., 'The Private Interest in Challenging Community Action' (1980) 5 ELRev. 354

HARLOW, C., 'Towards a Theory of Access for the European Court of Justice' (1992) 12 YBEL 213

[132] Above, 476–8.

RASMUSSEN, H., 'Why is Article 173 Interpreted against Private Plaintiffs?' (1980) 5 ELRev. 112

SCHERMERS, H., 'The Law as it Stands on the Appeal for Annulment' (1975) 2 LIEI 92

STEIN, P., and VINING, J., 'Citizen Access to Judicial Review of Administrative Action in a Transnational and Federal Context' (1976) 70 Am.JComp.L 219

WEILER, J., 'Pride and Prejudice—*Parliament* v. *Council*' (1989) 14 ELRev. 334

(b) On Failure to Act

TOTH, A. G., 'The Law as it Stands on the Appeal for Failure to Act' (1975) 2 LIEI 65

(c) On the Exception of Illegality

BARAV, A., 'The Exception of Illegality in Community Law: A Critical Analysis' (1974) 11 CMLRev. 366

BEBR, G., 'Judicial Remedy of Private Parties against Normative Acts of the European Communities: The Role of the Exception of Illegality' (1966) 4 CMLRev. 7

(d) On the Use of Article 177

BEBR, G., 'Preliminary Rulings of the Court of Justice: Their Authority and Temporal Effect' (1981) 18 CMLRev. 475

—— 'The Reinforcement of the Constitutional Review of Community Acts Under Article 177 EEC Treaty' (1988) 25 CMLRev. 667

HARDING, C., 'The Impact of Article 177 of the EEC Treaty on the Review of Community Action' (1981) 1 YBEL 93

(e) On the Consequences of Illegality

BEBR, G., 'Preliminary Rulings of the Court of Justice: Their Authority and Temporal Effect' (1981) 18 CMLRev. 475

HARDING, C., 'The Impact of Article 177 of the EEC Treaty on the Review of Community Action' (1981) 1 YBEL 93

TOTH, A. G., 'The Authority of Judgments of the European Court of Justice: Binding Force and Legal Effects' (1984) 4 YBEL 1

WAELBROECK, M., 'May the Court of Justice Limit the Retrospective Operation of its Judgments?' (1981) 1 YBEL 115

12

Damages Actions and Money Claims

1. INTRODUCTION

In any developed legal system there must be a mechanism whereby losses caused by governmental action may be recovered in an action brought by an individual. The precise standard or criterion of liability which should be applied is, however, a subject of some considerable difficulty. Compensation within the EEC is governed by Article 215(2), which provides:

> In the case of non-contractual liability, the Community shall, in accordance with the general principles common to the laws of the Member States, make good any damage caused by its institutions or by its servants in the performance of their duties.

The Article leaves the ECJ with considerable room for interpretation regarding the more particular circumstances in which damages may be claimed and, as we shall see, the Court has modified the criterion for such recovery. The Article directs the ECJ to consider the general principles common to the laws of the Member States. Certain types of case emerged. The analysis will begin with a discussion of the tort liability of the Community.

2. TORT LIABILITY

(a) Acts for which the Community is Responsible

It is readily apparent that loss may be caused to an individual by the action of the Community. Article 215 allows for loss to be claimed either where it has been caused by the Community institutions or by the acts of its servants 'in the performance of their duties'. It is also clear that not every act performed by a servant will be deemed to be an act in the performance of his or her duties, and therefore Community law, like any other legal system, will have to draw distinctions concerning the boundaries of a servant's duties.

The matter is rendered more complex by the fact that Article 12 of the Protocol on the Privileges and Immunities of the European Communities states that:

officials and other servants of the Community shall . . . be immune from legal proceedings in respect of acts performed by them in their official capacity.

The interrelationship between these provisions will be considered in the subsequent discussion. Before doing so the leading case in this area must be analysed:

Case 9/69, Sayag v. Leduc
[1969] ECR 329

Sayag was an engineer employed by Euratom. He was instructed to take Leduc, a representative of a private firm, on a visit to certain installations. He decided to drive him there in his own car, and he obtained a travel order which enabled him to claim the expenses for the trip from the Community. An accident occurred and Leduc claimed in the Belgian courts damages against Sayag for the injuries which he had suffered. It was argued that Sayag was driving the car in the performance of his duties, and that therefore the action should have been brought against the Community. The Belgian Cour de Cassation sought a preliminary ruling on the meaning of the phrase 'in the performance of their duties' in Article 188(2) of the Euratom Treaty, which is equivalent to 215(2) of the EEC Treaty.

THE ECJ

By referring at one and the same time to damage caused by the institutions and to that caused by the servants of the Community, Article 188 indicates that the Community is only liable for those acts of its servants which, by virtue of an internal and direct relationship, are the necessary extension of the tasks entrusted to the institutions.

In the light of the special nature of this legal system, it would not therefore be lawful to extend it to categories of acts other than those referred to above.

A servant's use of his private car for transport during the course of his duties does not satisfy the conditions set out above.

A reference to a servant's private car in a travel order does not bring the driving of such car within the performance of his duties, but is basically intended to enable any necessary reimbursement of the travel expenses involved in this means of transport to be made in accordance with the standards laid down for this purpose.

Only in the rare case of *force majeure* or in exceptional circumstances of such overriding importance that without the servant's using private means of transport the Community would have been unable to carry out the tasks entrusted to it, could such use be considered to form part of the servant's performance of his duties, within the meaning of the second paragraph of Article 188 of the Treaty.

It follows from the above that the driving of a private car by a servant cannot in principle constitute the performance of his duties within the meaning of the second paragraph of Article 188 of the EAEC Treaty.

The range of acts done by its servants for which the Community will accept responsibility is therefore narrow, and more limited than that which exists in the laws of most of the Member States.[1] No real justification for the limited nature of this liability is provided by the ECJ.

If the Community is not liable then an action can be brought against the servant in his personal capacity, and any such action is brought in national courts and is governed by national law. However, as seen above, the Protocol on the Privileges and Immunities of the European Communities provides that servants have immunity from suit in national courts in relation to 'acts performed in their official capacity'. The language of this provision differs from that of Article 215(2), which speaks in terms of servants acting in 'performance of their duties'. Normally one would expect that, where the Community is liable under Article 215(2) because the servant is held to be acting in the performance of his duties, then it would also follow that the servant would not be personally liable, since he would be deemed to be acting in an official capacity. The interrelationship between these two provisions may, nonetheless, be more problematic, and the ECJ has held that the servant's personal immunity and the scope of the Community's liability for the acts of the servant are separate issues.[2] The matter is considered by Schermers, who addresses the relationship between the two provisions in the following way:

H. G. Schermers, Official Acts of Civil Servants[3]

Claiming immunity involves liability. Whenever the Community invokes immunity of jurisdiction for a particular act of a civil servant it implicitly accepts that the act is an act of the Community, because it has no right to invoke immunity for any other act. The reverse is not necessarily true. By accepting liability for an act of one of its civil servants the Community does not necessarily imply that the act is a Community act. There is no legal prohibition on the Community from accepting liability for private acts of its staff. In practice, however, the Community accepts liability only for acts which it considers as official acts. Otherwise, problems would arise in the field of budgetary control.

Schermers proceeds to argue that, although it would be possible to give a different meaning to 'in their official capacity' and 'in the performance of their duties', the two phrases are so close that it would be misleading to give them a substantially different connotation. He points out that the immunity which a servant possesses for acts done in an official capacity may be waived by the Community under Article 18(2) of the Protocol whenever the relevant Community institution believes that such a waiver is not contrary to the interests of the Communities. He continues in the following vein:

[1] See the survey made by Gand A.G. in Case 9/69, *Sayag* v. *Leduc*, [1969] ECR 329, 340–1.
[2] Case 5/68, *Sayag* v. *Leduc* [1968] ECR 395, 408.
[3] H. G. Schermers, T. Heukels, and P. Mead (eds.), *Non-Contractual Liability of the European Communities* (Martinus Nijhoff, 1988), Ch. 6, 79–80.

> This makes it possible to use a wide definition for both cases: all acts performed by an official in the exercise of his duties and having some relationship with his professional activities may be seen as 'official acts', provided that immunity from jurisdiction is waived in any case where the Community considers that the waiver is not contrary to the interests of the Community.

It has been assumed thus far that the Community will be liable for the acts of its institutions, and for the acts of its servants, subject to the limitations of the *Sayag* case. Hartley points out that there may in fact be a third category of acts for which the Community is also responsible. This category covers acts performed by bodies to which the Communities have delegated certain governmental functions. Drawing on case law concerning the ECSC,[4] Hartley states:[5]

> From this it may be concluded that, where a Community institution delegates governmental powers to some other body, the acts of that body in the exercise of those powers may be imputed to the Community; but where such a body carries out functions which are not of a governmental nature, its acts will not be imputable to the Community.

(b) The Nature of the Community's Liability

Article 215(2) states that the Community shall make good losses in accordance with the general principles common to the laws of the Member States. There is no specific mention of a fault requirement, which is by way of contrast to Article 40(1) and (2) of the ECSC Treaty. These provisions of the ECSC Treaty require the applicant to show a wrongful act or omission on the part of the Community, or a personal wrong by a servant of the Community in the performance of his duties.[6] These phrases draw directly upon concepts in French law, *faute de service* and *faute personnelle.*

The degree of difference between the two systems should not, however, be overstated. The Court is instructed, under Article 215, to consider the general principles common to the laws of the Member States. In many countries fault is one of the principal grounds of establishing the liability of a public body, even if other, non-fault-based grounds of liability also exist. The possible application of non-fault-based grounds of liability will be examined later within this Chapter. In general, the Court has, however, demanded proof of some wrong before imposing liability on the Community.

The precise meaning of fault is not always clear, and it should not necessarily be assumed that the connotation given to this word will be the same in

[4] Case 18/60, *Worms* v. *High Authority* [1962] ECR 195.

[5] T. C. Hartley, *The Foundations of European Community Law* (3rd edn., Clarendon Press, 1994), 475–6.

[6] A useful comparison between the provisions of the EC and the ECSC Treaties can be found in Hartley, *ibid.* 468.

different types of case. Thus, as will be seen in the next section, the sense in which the Community must be found to have committed some wrong when an individual claims to have suffered loss as a result of a legislative norm being held to be illegal, will not always be the same as in cases which are closer to the paradigm of an ordinary tort action.

Moreover, it is clear that the existence of some mistake by the Community institutions will not, in and of itself, suffice to establish liability under Article 215(2). Thus, while it is possible to list a variety of errors which *might* lead to liability (for example, failure to gather the facts before reaching a decision, taking a decision based on irrelevant factors, failure to accord appropriate procedural rights to certain individuals before making a decision, and inadequate supervision of bodies to whom power has been delegated), the mere proof of the existence of such an error will not always ensure success in a damages action. This is aptly demonstrated by the next case:

Cases 19, 20, 25, 30/69, Denise Richez-Parise and Others v. Commission [1970] ECR 325

The applicants were Community officials who had been given incorrect information concerning their pensions. This information was supplied as a consequence of a request by the Commission to the officials concerned that they should contact the relevant department in order to obtain information concerning their financial provisions on termination of employment. The information which was given was based on an interpretation of the relevant regulation which was believed to be correct at the time at which it was given. The department which gave the information later had reason to believe that its interpretation of the regulation was incorrect, but no immediate steps were taken to inform the applicants of this. This was done only at a later stage, by which time the applicants had already committed themselves on the form in which they would take their pension entitlements. The applicants sought, *inter alia*, to obtain compensation for losses which they had suffered.

THE ECJ

36. Apart from the exceptional instance, the adoption of an incorrect interpretation does not constitute in itself a wrongful act.

37. Even the fact that the authorities request those concerned to obtain information from the competent departments does not necessarily involve those authorities in an obligation to guarantee the correctness of the information supplied and does not therefore make them liable for any injury which may be occasioned by incorrect information.

38. However, whilst it may be possible to doubt the existence of a wrongful act concerning the supply of incorrect information, the same cannot be said of the department's delay in rectifying the information.

39. Although such rectification was possible as early as April 1968 it was deferred without any justification until the end of 1968.

. . .

41. A correction made shortly before or after 16 April, that is to say, before the time when those concerned had to make their decision, would have certainly enabled the defendant to avoid all liability for the consequences of the wrong

information. The failure to make such a correction is, on the other hand, a matter of such a nature as to render the Communities liable.

The case furnishes a good illustration of the nature of a wrongful act for the purposes of liability under Article 215. An incorrect interpretation of a regulation will not necessarily, in and of itself, suffice for the establishment of liability in a damages action. Such regulations are often complex and are open to more than one construction. To render the Communities liable in damages on any occasion on which one such construction was proved to be incorrect would be too harsh. It would, in effect, open the Community to a form of strict liability, where the only condition for recovery would be proof that the interpretation adopted was incorrect, even if that interpretation was plausible, and even if the decision-maker had taken due care in reaching it. It is not surprising that the ECJ has declined to adopt such a test, and that it has required some further element of wrongdoing before being willing to impose monetary liability on the Community.[7]

The wrong which is the subject matter of a damages action may also take the form of an error on the part of a particular official, as opposed to a wrong on the part of the institution as such. This is exemplified by the tragic facts of the next case:

Case 145/83, Stanley George Adams v. Commission [1985] ECR 3539, [1986] 1 CMLR 506

In 1973 Adams sent a letter to the Commission indicating that his employer in Switzerland was engaged in a number of anti-competitive practices. He stated in the letter that he was about to leave the company, and that he would then be prepared to give evidence in court. The Commission investigated the company and made a decision against it. The company believed that Adams was the informant and had him arrested for economic espionage when he returned to Switzerland in 1974. He was held in solitary confinement and not allowed to communicate with his family. His wife committed suicide. Early in 1975 the Commission confirmed that he was the informant. Adams was eventually given a one year suspended sentence. He claimed damages on the ground that the Commission had wronged him by disclosing his identity to the company. The Court stated that information supplied in circumstances such as these did give rise to a duty of confidentiality, more especially since the informant had requested that his identity should be kept secret. It continued as follows.

THE ECJ

35. As regards the case before the Court, it is quite clear from the applicant's letter of 25 February 1973 that he requested the Commission not to reveal his identity. It cannot therefore be denied that the Commission was bound by a duty

[7] The same type of problem can occur in domestic law, where an agency construes a statute incorrectly and losses are caused to individuals: see P. P. Craig, *Administrative Law* (3rd edn., 1994), Ch. 17.

of confidentiality to the applicant in that respect. In fact the parties disagree not so much as to the existence of such a duty but as to whether the Commission was bound by a duty of confidentiality after the applicant had left his employment with Roche.

36. In that respect it must be pointed out that the applicant did not qualify his request by indicating a period upon the expiry of which the Commission would be released from its duty of confidentiality regarding the identity of its informant. No such indication can be inferred from the fact that the applicant was prepared to appear before any court after he had left Roche . . .

37. It must therefore be inferred that the Commission was under a duty to keep the applicant's identity secret even after he had left his employer.

. . .

53. It must therefore be concluded that in principle the Community is bound to make good the damage resulting from the discovery of the applicant's identity by means of the documents handed over to Roche by the Commission. It must however be recognised that the extent of the Commission's liability is diminished by reason of the applicant's own negligence.

In addition to proving that the Community has taken action which will found a claim under Article 215, the applicant will also have to show that this action caused his loss, and that the type of loss is recoverable. Issues concerned with causation and the types of losses which are recoverable will be considered below, since many of the relevant cases are of the kind to be considered in the next section.

3. LIABILITY FOR LEGISLATIVE ACTS

(a) The General Test

The cases considered in this section are those in which the individual is seeking compensation for a general norm, usually of an economic character, which has caused loss. The norm may not have been annulled; the restrictive interpretation of the provisions on *locus standi* have meant that only a small number of actions for annulment have succeeded. The cases normally arise out of the CAP, and are concerned with complaints that, for example, a certain section of the agricultural community has been discriminated against, or that its commercial expectations have been upset by Commission action. The ECJ has been faced with numerous such cases.

The early approach of the ECJ did not augur well for individuals, for it was held in the *Plaumann* case[8] that annulment of the offending norm was a necessary condition precedent to the ability to use Article 215. If this requirement had been adhered to Article 215 would have been of little use, given the difficulty an individual faces in satisfying the *locus standi* conditions for

[8] Case 25/62, *Plaumann* v. *Commission* [1963] ECR 95, [1964] CMLR 29.

annulment. The necessity for annulment was, however, discarded in later cases, and the action for damages came to be regarded as an independent, autonomous cause of action.[9] It was the decision in the *Schoppenstedt* case which laid down the test for recovery:

Case 5/71, Aktien-Zuckerfabrik Schöppenstedt v. Council [1971] ECR 975

The applicant claimed that Regulation 769/68, concerning the sugar market, was in breach of Article 40(3), in that it was discriminatory in the way in which it established the pricing policy for the product.

THE ECJ

11. In the present case the non-contractual liability of the Community presupposes at the very least the unlawful nature of the act alleged to be the cause of the damage. Where legislative action involving measures of economic policy is concerned, the Community does not incur non-contractual liability for damage suffered by individuals as a consequence of that action, by virtue of the provisions contained in Article 215, second paragraph, of the Treaty, unless a sufficiently flagrant violation of a superior rule of law for the protection of the individual has occurred. For that reason the Court, in the present case, must first consider whether such a violation has occurred.

The ECJ decided that no breach of a superior rule of law could be proven on the facts of the case, and therefore that the applicant's claim failed. The test laid down in the case has been taken to establish the general conditions for liability in this area, and later cases have further developed the meaning of the specific conditions mentioned in the *Schöppenstedt* case.

(b) The Meaning of Superior Rule of Law

The case law of the ECJ has indicated that three differing types of norms can, in principle, qualify as superior rules of law for the protection of the individual.

First, it is clear that certain Treaty provisions fall within this category. One of the most commonly cited grounds in cases under Article 215(2) is the ban on discrimination contained in Article 40(3) of the Treaty, which is concerned with the CAP. This is not surprising, given that many of the damages actions are brought pursuant to regulations made under the CAP.[10]

A second ground of claim is that a regulation is in breach of a hierarchically superior regulation. This requires a brief explanation. The regulations which

[9] Case 5/71, *Aktien-Zuckerfabrik Schöppenstedt* v. *Council* [1971] ECR 975; Cases 9 and 11/71, *Compagnie d'Approvisionement de Transport et de Crédit SA et Grands Moulins de Paris SA* v. *Commission* [1972] ECR 391

[10] See e.g. Case 43/72, *Merkur-Aussenhandels-GmbH* v. *Commission* [1973] ECR 1055; Case 153/73, *Holtz und Willemsen GmbH* v. *Commission* [1974] ECR 675.

are made pursuant to, for example, the CAP, may be 'one-off' provisions, but they may also relate to a prior network of regulations on the same topic. There may therefore be regulations which are made pursuant to more general regulations on the same topic. A claim that a regulation is in breach of a more general regulation is clearly admissible in principle under Article 215.[11]

A third ground which has been held capable of sustaining the claim in damages is where the Community legislation is held to infringe certain general principles of law such as proportionality, legal certainty, or legitimate expectations.

The ECJ does not articulate *why* the above might constitute superior rules of law, nor *what* other matters might be added to the list. It is often left to the Advocate General to question the wisdom of adding to the list of such rules.[12] Superior sometimes seems to be equated with 'important', and sometimes with a more formalistic conception of one rule being higher than another, as in the case of the regulation being in breach of a parent regulation. These various possible grounds of claim can be exemplified by considering the *CNTA* case:

Case 74/74, Comptoir National Technique Agricole (CNTA) SA v. Commission [1975] ECR 533, [1977] 1 CMLR 171

The applicant claimed that it had suffered loss by the withdrawal of monetary compensatory amounts (mcas) by Regulation 189/72. The system of mcas was designed to compensate traders for fluctuations in exchange rates. Regulation 189/72, which entered into force on 1 February 1972, abolished these mcas in so far as they had been applicable to colza and rape seeds, because the Commission decided that the market situation had altered, thereby rendering the mcas unnecessary. The applicant had, however, entered into contracts before the Regulation was passed, even though these contracts were to be performed after the ending of the scheme. It argued that it had made these contracts on the assumption that the mcas would still be payable, and that it had set the price on that hypothesis. The sudden termination of the system in this area, without warning, was said by the applicant, to have caused it loss. The ECJ began by citing the general principle from the *Schöppenstedt* case and then continued in the following vein.

THE ECJ

17. In this connexion the applicant contends in the first place that by abolishing the compensatory amounts by Regulation 189/72 the Commission has infringed basic Regulation 974/71 of the Council.

18. That Regulation, it contends, while conferring on the Commission the power to ascertain that the conditions for the application of the compensatory amounts are met, does not allow it to take a decision withdrawing compensatory amounts once instituted and it requires in any event that the Commission's decision be taken on the basis of an assessment of solely monetary factors to the

[11] Case 74/74, *Comptoir National Technique Agricole (CNTA) SA* v. *Commission* [1975] ECR 533, [1977] 1 CMLR 171.

[12] See e.g. Trabbuchi A.G. in the *CNTA* case, n. 11 above, 560–1.

exclusion of economic factors which in this case the Commission has taken into consideration.

19. It follows from the last sentence of Article 1(2) of Regulation No 974/71 that the option for Member States to apply compensatory amounts may only be exercised where the monetary measures in question would lead to disturbances to trade in agricultural products.

20. As the application of compensatory amounts is a measure of an exceptional nature, this provision must be understood as enunciating a condition not only of the introduction but also of the maintenance of compensatory amounts for a specific product.

21. The Commission has a large measure of discretion for judging whether the monetary measure concerned might lead to disturbances to trade in the product in question.

22. In order to judge the risk of such disturbances, it is permissible for the Commission to take into account market conditions as well as monetary factors.

23. It has not been established that the Commission exceeded the limits of its power thus defined when it considered towards the end of January 1972 that the situation on the market in colza and rape seeds was such that the application of compensatory amounts for those products was no longer necessary.

[*The ECJ then considered whether the withdrawal of the compensatory amounts violated certain general principles of law. It held that Regulation 189/72 was not retroactive, as had been claimed by the applicants. The Court then proceeded to consider whether this withdrawal had violated the principle of legitimate expectations. It held that the object of the regime for the fixing of refunds in advance on export orders could not be regarded as tantamount to a guarantee for traders against the risk of movements in exchange rates. It continued as follows.*]

41. Nevertheless the application of the compensatory amounts in practice avoids the exchange risk, so that a trader, even a prudent one, might be induced to omit to cover himself against such a risk.

42. In these circumstances, a trader may legitimately expect that for transactions irrevocably undertaken by him because he has obtained, subject to a deposit, export licences fixing the amount of the refund in advance, no unforeseeable alteration will occur which could have the effect of causing him inevitable loss, by re-exposing him to the exchange risk.

43. The Community is therefore liable if, in the absence of an overriding matter of public interest, the Commission abolished with immediate effect and without warning the application of compensatory amounts in a specific sector without adopting transitional measures which would at least permit traders either to avoid the loss which would have been suffered in the performance of export contracts, the existence and irrevocability of which are established by the advance fixing of the refunds, or to be compensated for such loss.

44. In the absence of an overriding matter of public interest, the Commission has violated a superior rule of law, thus rendering the Community liable, by failing to include in Regulation 189/72 transitional measures for the protection of the confidence which a trader might legitimately have had in the Community rules.

The ECJ stated, however, that the Community was not liable to pay the full cost of the relevant mcas which would have been applicable to the transactions, but rather that the extent of the applicant's legitimate expectation was merely that of not suffering loss by reason of the withdrawal of the mcas. In later proceedings it was held that the applicant had not in fact suffered such losses.[13]

(c) The Meaning of Flagrant Violation: The Early Case Law

It is evident from the extract taken from the *Schöppenstedt* case that the individual must prove not only that there has been a breach of a superior rule of law which is for the protection of the individual, but also that the breach was flagrant. It is the meaning of this term which must now be considered.

Cases 83, 94/76, 4, 15, 40/77, Bayerische HNL Vermehrungsbetriebe GmbH & Co KG v. Council and Commission [1978] ECR 1209, [1978] 3 CMLR 566

The Community was experiencing a surplus of milk which took the form of large stocks of skimmed-milk powder. In order to reduce these stocks Council Regulation 563/76 was passed. This Regulation imposed an obligation to purchase skimmed-milk powder for use in certain feedingstuffs. The applicant claimed that this had rendered the costs of feeding its animals more expensive. In a series of earlier cases the ECJ had held that the Regulation was null and void, on the ground that it had imposed the obligation to purchase at such a disproportionate price that it was equivalent to a discriminatory distribution of the burden of the costs between the various agricultural sectors, which was not justified by the objective in view, namely the disposal of stocks of skimmed-milk powder.[14] The present action was concerned with the applicants' claim for damages.

THE ECJ

3. The finding that a legislative measure such as the Regulation in question is null and void is however insufficient by itself for the Community to incur non-contractual liability for damage caused to individuals under the second paragraph of Article 215 of the EEC Treaty. The Court of Justice has consistently stated that the Community does not incur liability on account of a legislative measure which involves choices of economic policy unless a sufficiently serious breach of a superior rule of law for the protection of the individual has occurred.

[*The ECJ held that a breach of Article 40(3) was such a superior rule of law, and that it had been broken in this case. The Court stated, however, that more was required before the Community could be liable, and that the laws of the Member States indicated that it was only 'exceptionally and in special circumstances' that a public authority would be liable for losses resulting from a legislative measure which involved choices of economic policy. The Court continued as follows:*]

4. . . . This restrictive view is explained by the consideration that the legislative authority, even where the validity of its measures is subject to judicial review, cannot always be hindered in making its decisions by the prospect of applications for

[13] Case 74/74 [1976] ECR 797.

[14] See e.g. Case 116/76, *Granaria BV* v. *Hoofdproduktschap voor Akkerbouwprodukten* [1977] ECR 1247.

damages whenever it has occasion to adopt legislative measures in the public interest which may adversely affect the interests of individuals.

5. It follows from these considerations that individuals may be required, in the sectors coming within the economic policy of the Community, to accept within reasonable limits certain harmful effects on their economic interests as a result of a legislative measure without being able to obtain compensation from public funds, even if that measure has been declared null and void. In a field such as the one in question, in which one of the chief features is the exercise of a wide discretion essential for the implementation of the Common Agricultural Policy, the Community does not therefore incur liability unless the institution concerned has manifestly and gravely disregarded the limits on the exercise of its powers.

6. This is not so in the case of a measure of economic policy such as that in the present case, in view of its special features. In this connection it is necessary to observe first that this measure affected very wide categories of traders, in other words all buyers of compound feeding-stuffs, so that its effects on individual undertakings were considerably lessened. Moreover, the effects of the Regulation on the price of feeding-stuffs as a factor in the production costs of those buyers were only limited since that price rose by little more than 2 per cent. This price increase was particularly small in comparison with the price increases resulting, during the period of application of the Regulation, from the variations in the world market prices of feeding-stuffs containing protein, which were three or four times higher than the increase resulting from the obligation to purchase skimmed-milk powder introduced by the Regulation. The effects of the Regulation on the profit-earning capacity of the undertakings did not ultimately exceed the bounds of economic risks inherent in the activities of the agricultural sectors concerned.

It is apparent from the ECJ's judgment that the breach was held not to be manifest and grave because its *effects* were not regarded as serious enough to warrant recovery under Article 215. The factors which the Court considers when it discusses the facts of the *Bayerische* case relate primarily to this issue. Whether this ought to be a criterion for recovery will be discussed below. Before doing so it is necessary to analyse another important decision in this area, in order to decide whether the effect of the breach is the only issue which the Court will take into account.

Cases 116 and 124/77, Amylum NV and Tunnel Refineries Ltd v. Council and Commission
[1979] ECR 3497

The applicants were manufacturers of isoglucose, which was a sweetener made from starch. The product could not, at the time, be crystallized. It was however possible to use it in liquid form, and in this form it was in competition with sugar. There was a surplus of sugar on the market and sugar was subject to production constraints. The producers of isoglucose were therefore perceived as having an economic advantage, and it was decided that they too should be subject to a production levy. The system for levies was introduced by Council Regulation 1111/77 and Commission Regulation 1468/77. In an earlier case arising under Article 177 the ECJ had held that Regulation 1111/77 was invalid because the particular production levy which was imposed was in breach of Article 40(3), although the Court had added that the Council could nonetheless devise appropriate measures to ensure that the market in sweeteners functioned properly.[15] The applicants sought compensation for losses suffered, as a result of the reduction in profits due to the fact that the companies replaced sales of isoglucose with less profitable sales of starch, and because of lost production in their factories. The Court began its judgment in the damages action by quoting the principle laid down in the *Bayerische* case set out above. It then proceeded to consider whether there had been a manifest and grave disregard of the limits of their power by the Council and Commission.

THE ECJ

17. In this respect it must be recalled that the Court did not declare invalid any isoglucose production levy, but only the method of calculation adopted and the fact that the levy applied to the whole of the isoglucose production. Having regard to the fact that the production of isoglucose was playing a part in increasing sugar surpluses, it was permissible for the Council to impose restrictive measures on such production.

. . .

19. In fact, even though the fixing of the isoglucose production levy at 5 units of account per 100 kg. of dry matter was vitiated by errors, it must nevertheless be pointed out that, having regard to the fact that an appropriate levy was fully justified, these errors were not of such gravity that it may be said that the conduct of the institutions in this respect was verging on the arbitrary and was thus of such a kind as to involve the Community in non-contractual liability.

20. It must also be pointed out that Regulation No 1111/77 was adopted in particular to deal with an emergency situation characterized by growing sugar surpluses and in circumstances which, in accordance with the principles set out in Article 39 of the Treaty, permitted a certain preference to be given to sugar beet, Community production of which was in surplus, while Community production of maize was in deficit.

The ECJ decided therefore that the applicants had not shown that the Community had manifestly and gravely disregarded the limits of its power so as to render the Community institutions liable in damages. It is readily apparent that the reasons for the applicants' failure in the *Amylum* case are not the same as in the *Bayerische* decision. In the *Amylum* case the applicants did not fail because their losses were deemed to be insufficient to warrant recovery; they did not lose because the *effects* of the breach were insufficiently serious. This is not the reasoning of the Court, and it would not have been plausible on the facts of the case, since the losses were severe. The reasoning of the ECJ focuses rather upon the *manner* of the breach. The action of the institutions is said not to be arbitrary, in the following sense. The *general end* being

[15] Cases 103 and 145/77, *Royal Scholten-Honig (Holdings) Ltd* v. *Intervention Board for Agricultural Produce*; *Tunnel Refineries Ltd* v. *Intervention Board for Agricultural Produce* [1978] ECR 2037, [1979] 1 CMLR 675.

pursued by the Community, that of stabilizing and rationalizing the market in sweeteners, was a legitimate one for the Community to pursue. Mistakes had occurred in the *particular way* in which this end was achieved, namely in the calculation of the levy. This was not, however, enough to render the decision arbitrary, especially given the fact that this was an emergency situation.

The result of *Bayerische* and *Amylum* would therefore appear to be as follows. An applicant will have to show both that the *effects* of the breach were serious, in terms of the quantum of loss suffered, and also that the *manner* of the breach was arbitrary, in the sense articulated above. These hurdles will not be easy to surmount, particularly the second. It will be rare for the Community institutions to promulgate a regulation which is wholly unrelated to the general ends which they are entitled to advance under the powers of Article 39. The breadth of this Article has been discussed above.[16] The mistakes are likely to be made precisely in the carrying out of general, legitimate policies in an erroneous manner. The broader policy arguments that are raised by the current approach of the Court will be discussed below. Before doing so it will be useful to consider one case in which the applicants actually succeeded:

Cases 64, 113/76, 167, 239/78, 27, 28, 45/79 Dumortier Frères SA v. Council [1979] ECR 3091

Certain Council regulations provided that production refunds should be payable for maize starch, but that they should be abolished in the case of maize groats and meal (gritz), which were used in the production of beer. This differential treatment had been held to be in breach of Articles 39 and 40,[17] and the applicants now claimed damages for the losses suffered. The subsidies had been restored in the light of the ECJ's decision, but only for the future, and therefore losses had still been suffered in the intervening period. The Court cited the principle from the *Bayerische* case, and found that there had been a manifest and grave breach by the Community. It reasoned as follows.

THE ECJ

11. In the first place, it is necessary to take into consideration that the principle of equal treatment, embodied in particular in the second paragraph of Article 40(3) of the EEC Treaty, which prohibits any discrimination in the common organisation of the agricultural markets, occupies a particularly important place among the rules of Community law intended for the protection of the individual. Secondly, the disregard of that principle in this case affected a clearly defined group of commercial operators . . . Further, the damage alleged by the applicants goes beyond the bounds of the economic risks inherent in the activities of the sector concerned. Finally, equality of treatment with the producers of maize starch,

[16] See above, 476–8.

[17] Cases 124/76, 20/77, *SA Moulins et Huileries de Pont-à-Mousson and Société Cooperative 'Providence Agricole de la Champagne'* v. *Office National Interprofessionnel des Céréals* [1977] ECR 1795, [1979] 2 CMLR 445.

which had been observed from the beginning of the common organization of the market in cereals, was ended by the Council in 1975 without sufficient justification.

12. The Council's disregard of the limits imposed upon its discretionary power is rendered all the more manifest by the fact that, as the Court pointed out in its judgment of October 19, 1977, the Council has not acted on a proposal made by the Commission in June 1975 to reintroduce the refunds for maize gritz on the ground that the absence of such refunds could upset the balance between the breweries' raw material costs in maize gritz and maize starch.

There are two ways in which one might reconcile the decisions in *Amylum* and *Dumortier*. On the one hand, it could be contended that the decision in the latter case was explicable because the *general* objective being pursued in *Dumortier* was not justifiable within the terms of the CAP; that there was no reason for the differential treatment of maize gritz and maize starch. On the other hand, it is clear from the judgment that the Court was particularly 'annoyed' by the fact that the Council had impeded corrective measures being taken by the Commission. The latter had realized the error that had been made in the *Dumortier* case and had attempted to pass correcting legislation, the passage of which had been held up by the Council. Thus Member State interests in the Council had prevented the realization of Community objectives. The willingness of the ECJ to grant damages may well have been intended as a signal to the Council that the 'cost' of this behaviour could take the form of a greater risk of damages being given to individuals.

(d) The Meaning of Flagrant Violation: More Recent Developments

There have been more recent cases on the meaning of flagrant violation which evince a less restrictive approach to the interpretation of this important element in the Article 215(2) action. These cases have modified the conditions for success under Article 215(2) in two ways.

On the one hand, the Court has signalled in the *Stahlwerke* case[18] that it is no longer necessary to show that the conduct of the Community authorities was verging on the arbitrary. It should not, however, be assumed from this that illegality *per se* will suffice for liability. There are differing degrees of fault between arbitrariness at one end of the spectrum and simple negligence at the other. Moreover, the Court has not acceded to the argument that illegality *per se* will suffice for liability. Thus in the *Stahlwerke* case itself the CFI, whose decision was being reviewed by the ECJ, had found fault, examined whether this fault was the result of an excusable or an inexcusable error, and decided on the facts that there was fault of such a nature as to render the Community liable. The ECJ held that fault in the nature of arbitrariness was not required for liability. It did not hold that liability could be established without any

[18] Case C–220/91–P, *Stahlwerke Peine-Salzgitter AG* v. *Commission* [1993] ECR I–2393. See also Case T–120/89, *Stahlwerke Peine-Salzgitter* v. *Commission* [1991] ECR II–279.

showing of fault at all. Similarly, in *Vreugdenhil*[19] the applicants argued that in a case such as the present one in which the illegality resided in an excess of power by the Commission, it was sufficient for them to show this excess of power, and that they did not have to prove the *Bayerische* test, that there had been a sufficiently serious breach of a superior rule of law for the protection of the individual. The Court found that the rule which was broken was not one designed for the protection of individuals. But it also went out of its way to state that the 'mere fact that a legislative measure . . . is found to be invalid is insufficient by itself for the Community to incur non-contractual liability under Article 215(2)'.[20] Such liability still required proof of the *Bayerische* test, including the necessity of proving that the breach was sufficiently serious.[21]

On the other hand, the ECJ also appears to be more liberal, in the sense that the potential of a large number of claimants for damages will not, in itself, rule out an Article 215(2) action. This is evident from the *Mulder* case.[22] This case was a sequel to the earlier *Mulder* case which we considered when discussing legitimate expectations.[23] It will be remembered that in the first *Mulder* case the ECJ held that a Community regulation which precluded Mulder from being qualified for a milk quota was invalid. Mulder had ceased milk production for a limited period pursuant to an agreement with the Community authorities and to deny him a milk quota at the end of that period constituted a breach of legitimate expectations. As a result the Council then adopted another regulation which allowed farmers in this position a special quota of 60 per cent of the quantity which they had marketed in the year preceding the agreement to cease production. This, too, was challenged and found to be illegal, the Court holding that the 60 per cent quota was too low. A further regulation was then adopted which gave the farmers a higher quota. Mulder brought a damages action for the losses sustained in the interim period. The question before the ECJ was whether the illegality found in the earlier cases was sufficiently serious to render the Community liable. In this respect the ECJ drew the following distinction.

With reference to the regulation which totally denied the farmers any quota at all, a damages action could lie. This regulation constituted a breach of the farmers' legitimate expectations, and there was no countervailing, higher public interest justifying this action.[24]

With reference to the illegality of the later regulation imposing a 60 per cent quota, the ECJ reached the opposite conclusion. The Court accepted that this, too, infringed the legitimate expectations of the applicants, but this illegality was not sufficiently serious. It was not sufficiently serious *because* there was a

[19] Case C–282/90, *Industrie- en Handelsonderneming Vreugdenhil BV* v. *Commission* [1992] ECR I–1937, [1994] 2 CMLR 803, paras. 17–19.

[20] *Ibid.* para. 19.

[21] *Ibid.*

[22] Cases C–104/89 & 37/90, *Mulder* v. *Council and Commission* [1992] ECR I–3061.

[23] Case 120/86, *Mulder* v. *Minister van Landbouw en Visserij* [1988] ECR 2321, [1989] 2 CMLR 1.

[24] See also Case C–152/88, *Sofrimport Sarl* v. *Commission* [1990] ECR I–2477, [1990] 3 CMLR 80.

higher public interest at stake here: the 60 per cent quota was a choice of economic policy made by the Council, seeking to balance the need to avoid excess production in this area with the interest of the farmers who had entered the earlier scheme.

Mulder does represent a loosening up of the criteria for an action under Article 215(2), in the sense that the existence of a large number of claimants in a similar position will not, by itself, defeat the claim. However, as with respect to the Court's more liberal attitude to arbitrariness mentioned above, one should be wary of reading too much into *Mulder*. The case shows forcefully that it is still necessary to prove the existence of a serious breach. It also shows that a breach may not be deemed to be sufficiently serious precisely because there is a higher public interest being sought by the Community institutions.

(e) The Present Law: An Assessment

The current law can be summarized in the following way. For an applicant to succeed it will be necessary to show that there has been a manifest and grave, or sufficiently serious, violation of a superior rule of law for the protection of individuals. In order to show the existence of the serious violation it is no longer fatal to a claim that there is a large number of potential applicants, nor does the manner of the breach have to be arbitrary. However, some species of fault over and beyond the mere existence of the illegality will be required; in some circumstances at least, the illegality will be deemed not to be sufficiently serious because the Community was attempting to give effect to a higher public interest;[25] and the applicant will have to show that the loss suffered was serious and outside the normal risks which are inherent in that activity.

Notwithstanding the Court's more liberal stance, it is clear that the stumbling-block to successful actions is the interpretation accorded to the term 'serious breach', and it is this which will be analysed in the ensuing discussion. It is clear that there can be differences of view on whether the ECJ's present approach is still too restrictive, whether it is too liberal, or whether it is just about right. What, then, should the test of liability be and does the ECJ's current approach strike the correct balance? The matter may be approached in the following manner.

(i) There *are* valid reasons for limiting liability under Article 215(2). Most of the major cases arise out of the CAP, under which the Community institutions have to make difficult discretionary choices of a legislative nature. This will often entail a complex balancing process designed to balance the conflicting variables identified in

[25] This line of reasoning is to be found in cases where the illegality resides in a breach of one of the general principles of Community law, such as legitimate expectations. Whether it could ever be invoked in cases where the illegality takes the form of a breach of a Treaty Art. is unclear. In such a case the Court would be more likely to fashion its judgment by saying that the breach of the relevant Treaty Art. *per se* did not give rise to a cause of action under Art. 215(2).

Article 39. A finding of illegality *per se* should not suffice as the basis for any subsequent damages action. Such a strict standard of liability would render the decision-makers susceptible to a potentially wide liability, and would run the risk that the Court might be 'second-guessing' the decisions made by the Council and Commission as to how the variables within Article 39 should be balanced in any particular instance.[26] The only circumstances in which it would be feasible to regard illegality *per se* as the appropriate test under Article 215(2), is if such illegality were only to be taken as proven where the conduct of the Community institutions was particularly flagrant. Such a test would, in effect, be building an element of fault into the definition of illegality which was to operate in this area.

(ii) Should *seriousness of the loss* be of relevance? Where loss has been caused by illegal action it is difficult to see why the applicant should have to prove that the loss was particularly serious. The applicant will have to show that the illegality *caused* the loss, but there should be no requirement over and above this. In any event, the ordinary 'economics of litigation' should ensure that claims are, in general, only pursued when it is economically worthwhile to do so. Thus, a potential plaintiff will normally have to have suffered a loss large enough to make litigation a sensible option, *and* will also have to discount the value of the claim to take account of the possibility that it might fail. There is much to be said for Advocate General Capotorti's view on this point. He argued against the need to show seriousness of loss for two reasons.[27] One was that proof of serious losses was not normally required in the laws of the Member States when a claim was based on illegal conduct by the administration; it was normally only required when the claim was based on a lawful measure which was alleged to have placed a particularly burdensome obligation on an individual. The other major reason for disapproving of this criterion is that it is difficult to apply. Small losses for a large undertaking may be large losses for a small firm, and it would not be feasible or fair for the Court to make separate assessments for each applicant involved in each case.

(iii) *Should fault be of relevance*? The answer to this question has been given above. If one believes that illegality *per se* is too strict a test for liability then some species of fault will be required. There are two possible responses to this.

One would be to argue that fault should not be required since it is already present in the finding of illegality. An argument of this nature has been advanced by Advocate General Capotorti in *Bayerische*,

[26] Cf. Capotorti A.G. in Cases 83 and 94/76, 4, 15 and 40/77, *Bayersiche HNL Vermehrungsbetriebe GmbH & Co KG* v. *Council and Commission* [1978] ECR 1209, 1223–4, [1978] 3 CMLR 566, 577.

[27] *Ibid.* 1233–4 (ECR), 580 (CMLR).

who stated that 'the undoubtedly voluntary nature of the acts adopted by the institutions is sufficient and that nature gives rise to a presumption of blame when an unlawful measure is enacted'.[28] This argument is questionable at the very least. In one sense any illegal act connotes blame, but this sense of the word blame is not terribly helpful. It would mean that any and every time that a person does something illegal there is blame, even if the wrong committed is based on strict liability. This sense of the word blame or fault is therefore of limited utility. A different sense of fault or blame would be something much more akin to a finding that there has been a breach of a duty of care, in the ordinary sense of negligence. Used in this way there is no necessary relationship between a finding of illegality and the presence of fault. An administrator may well have taken reasonable care in interpreting and applying the relevant rules, but nonetheless he may be held to have misconstrued the ambit of his power and to have acted illegally.[29] Moreover, the fact that an act is 'voluntary' tells one nothing in itself about whether a consequential unlawful measure is blameworthy in this narrower sense. Whether fault in this narrower sense should feature as a condition of liability will be considered below.

The other response would be to contend that the ECJ's test in cases such as *Bayerische* is specifically geared to situations in which it is a legislative, discretionary power in the economic sphere which is at issue; that the test devised in that case may not be appropriate in cases where there is less discretion, and/or where the measure is of a more administrative than legislative nature; and that a stricter standard of liability might be warranted in such circumstances. There are three points to be made in this regard.

One is that many administrative measures may involve discretionary choices which are just as difficult as those which have to be made in the context of legislative action. The very line between the two is difficult to draw, as attested to by the fact that many of the Community measures which are regarded as regulations, and hence legislation, are no different in nature from many matters which would be characterized as administrative choices in domestic legal systems.

The second point follows from the first: many of those who do argue that a different test from that in *Bayerische* should be applied outside the discretionary, economic sphere, also make it clear that they are not advocating liability being based on illegality alone.[30]

The final point which is of relevance in this respect is that, as we have seen above, the ECJ has been markedly reluctant to impose

[28] *Ibid.* 1233 (ECR), 578 (CMLR).

[29] For an illustration of this in a domestic context, see P. P. Craig, n. 7 above, Ch. 17.

[30] See e.g. Darmon A.G. in *Vreugdenhil*, n. 19 above, 821–2.

non-fault-based strict liability in instances outside the legislative sphere, where, for example, losses have been caused by misconstruction of the relevant Community legislation.[31]

(iv) In so far as it is of relevance, *what meaning should the term fault bear*? It is clear from the preceding discussion that arbitrariness is no longer actually required to sustain an action. It is still, however, necessary to consider the meaning which the term 'fault' should bear.

One possible meaning of the term is *result-oriented*, in that it relates to the issue of whether the measure was adequately justified. This is the view taken by some commentators.[32] On this view the illegality in *Amylum* was held not to be actionable in damages because an appropriate levy was justified, and because the particular levy established was set during an emergency situation. The idea appears to be that, if the general end being pursued is legitimate, then errors of calculation in the measures designed to attain this end will not found a damages claim.

A different meaning of the term fault is however possible. It could be accorded a more *procedural orientation* in the following sense. The applicants in *Amylum* were injured in part at least because the particular levy was fixed at the wrong level. *If* they could establish that this was because of some fault or error in calculation, some 'operational negligence',[33] then why in principle should a claim be denied? Now it may well be difficult to prove such fault, especially when the measure under attack was adopted in an emergency situation. However, why should this approach be precluded in principle? The word 'fault' is capable of bearing this meaning, which may indeed be a more natural linguistic interpretation than the alternative considered above. It is, moreover, clear that a measure may be found to be illegal even though there was no fault in the second sense considered here.

The interpretation of the word 'fault' considered in the previous paragraph is procedural in the sense that it relates to the *manner* in which a Community policy has been executed. Most, if not all, legal systems allow actions against public bodies where there has been some fault in this sense, and it is not readily apparent why the Community should be treated differently in this respect.

This would not, of course, preclude the possibility of an action where there was fault in the result-oriented sense outlined above. The two foundations for a damages action could co-exist. To countenance an action *only* where there has been fault in the result-oriented

[31] See above, 515–16.

[32] E. Grabitz, 'Liability for Legislative Acts' in *Non-Contractual Liability of the European Communities*, n. 3 above, Ch. 1, 10.

[33] For a general discussion of the idea of operational negligence in domestic law, see Craig, n. 7 above, Ch. 17.

sense would mean, however, that few applicants would have very much chance of success. This would be so even if, as is now the case, fault in this result-oriented sense could be proven without having to show something as extreme as arbitrariness.

(v) Finally, we should be aware of the connection between the scope of the Community's damages liability under Article 215(2) and the potential scope of Member States' liability in damages pursuant to *Francovich*.[34] The latter has been considered above.[35] The point of connection can be stated quite simply. In so far as the Community itself is not liable in damages for illegality *per se* it is, at the very least, incumbent on those wishing to do so to justify imposing any form of stricter regime on the Member States.[36]

4. LIABILITY FOR VALID LEGISLATIVE ACTS

(a) The Nature of the Problem

Individuals may well suffer loss flowing from lawful acts of the Community, as well as from acts which are tainted with some form of illegality. This problem can occur in any legal system, but the potential for its occurrence in the Community is particularly marked, as the following extract demonstrates:

H. J. Bronkhorst, The Valid Legislative Act as a Cause of Liability of the Communities[37]

There are many reasons why private individuals have a particular interest in the existence of a clearly defined principle concerning Community liability for legal acts which result in damage to them. In the first place, the Common Agricultural Policy, which in the beginning existed as a price support mechanism, has been transformed for several sectors into a means for imposing quantitative production limits. In this respect, the Community has had recourse to various instruments, such as production quotas, for example. At the same time, other instruments have been applied to reduce over-production: in the field of common fisheries, the EEC Council has reduced the length of beams to be used for catching certain species of fish in defined fishery zones. Does a fisherman, who, on very short notice, has to make very important changes to his vessel, thus incurring substantial financial costs, have an action for compensation even if the Community measures as such cannot be challenged on the ground of illegality?

In the second place, private individuals, operating in the field of the Common Agricultural Policy, may easily suffer financial injury because of the fact that

[34] Cases 6 and 9/90, *Francovich* v. *Italian State* [1991] ECR I–5357, [1993] 2 CMLR 66.

[35] See above, 224–6.

[36] P. P. Craig, '*Francovich*, Remedies and the Scope of Damages Liability' (1993) 109 LQR 595.

[37] H. G. Schermers, T. Heukels, and P. Mead, n. 3 above, Ch. 2, 13.

competing producers are favoured by Community measures. Producers of vegetable fats may very well undergo the effects of (uneven) competition if producers of butter or milk powder are able to dispose of large quantities of their products on the European markets with the help of Community subsidies.

As indicated above, the problem of loss being caused by lawful governmental action is not peculiar to the Community. Thus, French law recognizes a principle of *égalité devant les charges publiques*, and German law has the concept of *Sonderöpfer*. Under these principles loss caused by lawful governmental action can be recovered, albeit in limited circumstances.[38] While there is hardship for individuals in the situations postulated by Bronkhorst, the difficulties of deciding when to grant such compensation should not be underestimated. That this is so can be appreciated from the following passage:

P. P. Craig, Compensation in Public Law[39]

Legislation is constantly being passed which is explicitly or implicitly aimed at benefiting one section of the population at the expense of another. It is a matter of conscious legislative policy. This may be in the form of tax changes or in a decision to grant selective assistance to one particular type of industry rather than another. Any incorporation of state liability arising out of legislation as part of a risk theory would necessitate the drawing of a difficult line. It would be between cases where the deleterious effect on a firm or group was the aim of the legislation or a necessary correlative of it, and where legislation is passed which incidentally affects a particular firm in a serious manner, but where there is no legislative objection to compensating the firm for the loss suffered.

The drawing of such a line in the context of the EC is particularly problematic, given that within, for example, the CAP there will often be 'winners and losers' as the result of the institutions' attempts to give effect to the often conflicting objectives which lie at the heart of that policy.[40] At the very least, it serves to explain why the Community is reluctant to admit such claims. It is to the relevant case law that we should now turn.

(b) The Case Law

Cases 9 and 11/71, Compagnie d'Approvisionnement de Transport et de Credit SA and Grands Moulins de Paris SA v. Commission [1972] ECR 391, [1973] CMLR 529

The applicants claimed losses resulting from a wrongful act of the Commission, in that, under the terms of Regulations 1670/69 and 1505/70 it had fixed at too low a level the import subsidies on wheat and spelt corn from non-member states,

[38] See Bronkhorst, in n. 3 above, 17–20. [39] (1980) 96 LQR 413, 450.
[40] See above, Ch. 11 for discussion of this issue.

which were to be granted by France following the devaluation of the French franc in 1969. The ECJ found that there was in fact no such wrongful act. The applicants claimed in the alternative that they should be compensated even in the absence of such illegality.

THE ECJ

45. The applicants claim that the Community incurs liability even in the absence of illegality because the applicants have suffered 'unusual and special damage' owing to the fact that they were treated less favourably than, first, importers from Member States other than France and, secondly, than German and Netherlands exporters.

46. Any liability for a valid legislative measure is inconceivable in a situation like that in the present case since the measures adopted by the Commission were only intended to alleviate, in the general economic interest, the consequences which resulted in particular for all French importers from the national decision to devalue the franc.

47. Consequently, the submission is unfounded.

Cases 54–60/76, Compagnie Industrielle et Agricole du Comté de Loheac v. Council and Commission [1977] ECR 645

The applicants were sugar producers in the French departments of Martinique and Guadaloupe, and claimed to have suffered loss as a result of the Community not taking into account the fact that, when the intervention price for sugar was fixed, there was a discrepancy between the harvesting and selling periods in Europe and in the French territories. The Court found that there had been no wrongful act by the Community, and then considered whether there could be liability even in the absence of illegality.

THE ECJ

19. Finally the complaint of having suffered direct, special and abnormal damage cannot be substantiated, particularly since the damage is alleged to result not from a loss but from a failure to make a profit, the existence of which is difficult to prove within the framework of commercial contracts outside the sphere of the Community arrangements.

Applicants have not been notably successful in more recent cases. Thus in the *Biovilac* case,[41] the Court stated that an Article 215 action based on unlawful legislative action would require proof that the damage alleged by the applicant exceeded the limits of the economic risk inherent in the area in question; and that this test would have to be applied *a fortiori* if the concept of liability without fault were to be accepted as part of Community law. The applicants made feedingstuffs for animals and began their trade at a time when regulations for the sale of competing products (skimmed-milk powder for use in feed for pigs and poultry) had been temporarily suspended. The regulations were

[41] Case 59/83, *SA Biovilac NV* v. *EEC* [1984] ECR 4057, 4080–1.

reintroduced in 1982 and the applicant suffered a serious reduction in sales. On the facts of the case, the ECJ found that the limits of economic risk had not been exceeded because the applicant ought to have anticipated that the measure causing the damage would be adopted by the Commission. It should have anticipated that the Commission would reintroduce the regulations complained of should market conditions require this.[42]

It appears, therefore, to be the case that, if liability for lawful action causing loss is recognized in Community law, an action will only succeed if the measure affects only a limited and clearly defined group and if the damage exceeds the economic risks inherent in the area in question. It also appears to be the case that the Court will not find the latter element to be proven if the Community measure which causes the damage could have been foreseen. Successful actions of this type will, therefore, be rare.

5. CAUSATION AND DAMAGE

(a) Causation

A. G. Toth, The Concepts of Damage and Causality as Elements of Non-Contractual Liability[43]

The establishment of the necessary causality may give rise to difficult problems in practice. This is particularly so in the field of economic and commercial relations where the cause of an event can usually be traced back to a number of factors, objective as well as subjective, operating simultaneously or successively and producing direct as well as indirect effects. Broadly speaking, it may be said that there is no causality involving liability where the same result would have occurred in the same way even in the absence of the wrongful Community act or omission in question. The converse proposition, *i.e.*, that the requisite causality exists whenever it can be shown that the damage would not have occurred without the Community action, is, however not always correct. Although in theory it is true that any circumstance, near or remote, without which an injury would not have been produced may be considered to be its cause, the fact that a Community act or omission is one only of several such circumstances may not in itself be sufficient to establish a causal connection entailing non-contractual liability. For that purpose, the causality must be 'direct, immediate and exclusive' which it can be only if the damage arises directly from the conduct of the institutions and does not depend on the intervention of other causes, whether positive or negative.

The difficulties which applicants may have in proving that it was the Community's action which caused them loss can be exemplified by a further reference to the *Dumortier* case:

[42] See also Case 265/85, *Van den Bergh & Jurgens BV and Van Dijk Food Products (Lopik) BV v. EEC* [1987] ECR 1155.

[43] H. G. Schermers, T. Heukels, and P. Mead n. 3 above, Ch. 3, 31.

Cases 64, 113/76, 167, 239/78, 27, 28, 45/79, Dumortier Frères SA v. Council [1979] ECR 3091

The facts have been given above. Some of the applicants claimed that they should be compensated because they were forced to close their factories.

THE ECJ

21. . . . The Council argued that the origin of the difficulties experienced by those undertakings is to be found in the circumstances peculiar to each of them, such as the obsolescence of their plant and managerial or financial problems. The data supplied by the parties in the course of the proceedings are not such as to establish the true cause of the further damage alleged. However, it is sufficient to state that even if it were assumed that the abolition of the refunds exacerbated the difficulties encountered by those applicants, those difficulties would not be a sufficiently direct consequence of the unlawful conduct of the Council to render the Community liable to make good the damage.

It will be necessary for an applicant to show not only that the Community action caused the loss being claimed, but also that the chain of causation has not been broken by the action either of the Member State or of the applicant himself.

The ECJ has held that where the loss arises from an independent/autonomous act by the Member State, the Community is no longer liable.[44] If, however, this conduct has been made possible by an illegal failure of the Commission to exercise its supervisory powers, then it will be this failure which will be considered to be the cause of the damage.[45] There may be instances where both the Community and the Member State are responsible. This complex issue will be considered below.

Precisely what type of conduct by the individual will serve to break the chain of causation is not entirely clear. Negligence, or contributory negligence, will suffice either to defeat the claim or to reduce the award of damages.[46] It has also been held, as seen above, that if the individual ought to have foreseen the possibility of certain events which might cause loss, then the possibility of claiming damages will be diminished.[47] Moreover, an individual who believes that a wrongful act of the Community has caused loss has been encouraged by the Court to challenge the measure in proceedings under Article 177. Thus, in the *Amylum* case the ECJ stated that this was a course

[44] Case 132/77, *Société pour l'Exportation des Sucres SA* v. *Commission* [1978] ECR 1061, 1072–3.

[45] Cases 9 and 12/60, *Vloeberghs* v. *High Authority* [1961] ECR 197, 240, [1963] CMLR 44; Case 4/69, *Alfons Lütticke GmbH* v. *Commission* [1971] ECR 325, 336–8.

[46] See Case 145/83, *Adams* v. *Commission* [1985] ECR 3539, 3592, [1986] 1 CMLR 506 where the Court believed that Adams had been negligent in, e.g., returning to Switzerland.

[47] See Case 59/83, n. 41 above.

open to an individual, particularly in those areas where the implementation of the measure was in the hands of national authorities.[48]

(b) Damage

Although Article 215 speaks of the duty of the Community to make good 'any damage', it is clear from the case law of the Court that losses will only be recoverable if they are certain and specific, proven and quantifiable.[49] These requirements will be examined in turn.

While the damage claimed must in general be *certain*, the Court has held in *Kampffmeyer* that it is possible to maintain an Article 215 action 'for imminent damage foreseeable with sufficient certainty even if the damage cannot yet be precisely assessed'. The rationale for this was that it might be necessary to pursue an action immediately in order to prevent even greater damage.[50]

The idea that the damage suffered must be *specific*, in the sense that it affects the applicant's interests in a special and individual way, is to be found in various guises in a number of ECJ decisions. Thus, in the *Bayerische* case, considered above, it will be noted that, in denying recovery to the applicants the Court emphasized that the effects of the regulation did not exceed the bounds of economic risk inherent in the activity in question.[51] Similar themes concerning the special nature of the burden imposed on a particular trader, or group of traders, can be found in the case law concerning the possible recovery for lawful governmental action.[52] The question whether an applicant should have to prove abnormal or special damage in a case concerning unlawful Community action has already been discussed.

The injured party will have the onus of *proving* that the damage occurred. In general the individual will have to show that the injury was actually sustained.[53] This may not be easy, and it is not uncommon for cases to fail for this reason.[54]

As stated above, the damage must also be *quantifiable* if the applicant is to succeed. In order to decide whether the loss is indeed quantifiable, one needs to know what *types* of damage are recoverable. Advocate General Capotorti has put the matter in the following way:[55]

> It is well known that the legal concept of 'damage' covers both a material loss *stricto sensu*, that is to say, a reduction in a person's assets, and also the loss of an increase in those assets which would have occurred if the harmful act had not taken place (these two alternatives are known respectively as *damnum emergens*

[48] Cases 116, 124/77, *Amylum NV and Tunnel Refineries Ltd* v. *Council and Commission* [1979] ECR 3497.

[49] Toth, n. 43 above, 23–31.

[50] Cases 56–60/74, *Kampffmeyer* v. *Commission and Council* [1976] ECR 711, 741.

[51] See above, 521–2.

[52] See above, 532–4.

[53] Case 26/74, *Roquette Frères* v. *Commission* [1976] ECR 677, 694, *per* Trabucchi A.G.

[54] See e.g. Case 26/68, *Fux* v. *Commission* [1969] ECR 145, 156.

[55] Case 238/78, *Ireks-Arkady* v. *Council and Commission* [1979] ECR 2955, 2998–9.

and *lucrum cessans*) . . . The object of compensation is to restore the assets of the victim to the condition in which they would have been apart from the unlawful act, or at least to the condition closest to that which would have been produced if the unlawful nature of the act had not taken place: the hypothetical nature of that restoration often entails a certain degree of approximation . . . These general remarks are not limited to the field of private law, but apply also to the liability of public authorities, and more especially to the non-contractual liability of the Community.

While the ECJ has been prepared to grant damages for losses which were actually sustained, and while it is willing in principle to give damages for lost profits, recovery of the latter sums will often prove more difficult than the former. Thus, in the *Kampffmeyer* case, while the Court admitted that lost profit was recoverable, it did not grant such damages to traders who had abandoned their intended transactions because of the unlawful act of the Community, even though these transactions would have produced profits.[56] In the *CNTA* case it was held that lost profits were not recoverable where the claim was based on the concept of legitimate expectations, the argument being that that concept only served to ensure that losses were not suffered owing to an unexpected change in the legal position; it did not serve to ensure that profits would be made.[57] However, in *Mulder*[58] the ECJ was prepared to compensate for lost profit, although it held that any such sum must take into account the income which could have been earned from alternative activities, applying the principle that there is a duty to mitigate loss.

In quantifying the loss suffered by the applicant the Community institutions have argued that damages should not be recoverable if the loss has been passed on to the consumers. This was accepted in principle by the ECJ in the *Quellmehl and Gritz* litigation.[59] This aspect of the reasoning has been justly criticized by Toth, who argues that whether a firm could pass on a cost increase to consumers would depend upon a whole range of variables, which may operate differently for different firms and which would be difficult to assess; and, moreover, that such an idea is wrong in principle, since it would mean that losses would be borne by consumers, rather than by the institutions which had committed the wrongful act.[60]

6. JOINT LIABILITY OF THE COMMUNITY AND THE MEMBER STATES

Questions of some considerable complexity can arise concerning the joint liability of the Community and the Member States for losses caused to

[56] Cases 5, 7, 13–24/66, *Kampffmeyer* v. *Commission* [1967] ECR 245, 266–7.
[57] Case 74/74, n. 11 above, 550.
[58] Cases C–104/89 and 37/90, [1992] ECR I–3061.
[59] See Case 238/78, n. 55 above, 2974.
[60] See above, n. 43, 29–30.

individuals. These issues can only be dealt with in outline here, and more detailed treatment can be found elsewhere.[61] The approach of Oliver, which distinguishes between procedural and substantive issues, will be adopted here.[62]

(a) Procedural Issues

In procedural terms it is not possible to bring an action for the non-contractual liability of the Community in the courts of the Member States. Article 178 of the EEC Treaty confers this jurisdiction on the ECJ and, while it does not state that this jurisdiction is exclusive, this is implied by Article 183.[63] Conversely, it is not possible for an individual to bring an action against a Member State before the ECJ, since there is no provision for this in the Treaty.

When an action is brought before the ECJ under Article 215(2), it is clear that Community law is applied. An action brought against a Member State in the national court will be governed by national law. This will, however, include Community law, in the sense that the national courts will be under an obligation to provide an effective remedy for the enforcement of directly effective Community provisions; and the rights against the state in such suits must be no less favourable than those which exist in domestic matters.[64]

(b) Substantive Issues

Joint liability of the Community and the Member States can arise in different situations. Two such will be explored here.

The first is where the Community has taken inadequate steps to prevent a breach of Community law by national authorities. This issue arose in the *Lütticke* case where the Court appeared to accept that, in principle, such an action was possible.[65] However, there are considerable obstacles in the path of any such action. It is, for example, doubtful whether the Commission has a duty to bring an action under Article 169 against a Member State which is in breach of Community law.[66] The position may well be different where the Commission has adopted a more formal measure, which approves of the illegal national action. This was the situation in the *Kampffmeyer* case:

[61] See e.g. A. Durand, 'Restitution or Damages: National Court or European Court?' (1975–6) 1 ELRev. 431; Hartley, n. 5 above, 498–507; T. C. Hartley, 'Concurrent Liability in EEC Law: A Critical Review of the Cases' (1977) 2 ELRev. 249; W. Wils, 'Concurrent Liability of the Community and a Member State' (1992) 17 ELRev. 191.

[62] P. Oliver, 'Joint Liability of the Community and the Member States', in *Non-Contractual Liability of the European Communities*, n. 3 above, Ch. 10.

[63] Art. 183: 'save where jurisdiction is conferred on the Court by this Treaty, disputes to which the Community is a party shall not on that ground be excluded from the jurisdiction of the courts or tribunals of the Member States.'

[64] See Oliver, n. 62 above, 127.

[65] Case 4/69, *Alfons Lütticke GmbH* v. *Commission* [1971] ECR 325. See above, Ch. 9.

[66] See Oliver, n. 62 above, 134.

Cases 5, 7, 13–24/66, Kampffmeyer v. Commission [1967] ECR 245

The case arose from the gradual establishment of a common market in cereals. On 1 October 1963 the German intervention board issued a notice stating that the levy for the import of such products would be set at zero. On that same day, the applicants applied for import licences for the import of maize from France, with the levy having been set at zero for January 1964. Some of the applicants had actually bought maize from France. The German government, on the same day, 1 October 1963, then suspended the zero-rated import licences for maize. Under Article 22 of Regulation 19 the German Government could only refuse such applications if there was a threat of a serious disturbance to the market in question. Such a decision had to be confirmed by the Commission, and the Commission on 3 October, duly authorized this to remain in force until 4 October. This decision was annulled in an action before the ECJ.[67] The applicants then sought compensation from the Commission under Article 215. Some of them had paid the duties imposed by the German authorities and imported the maize on these terms; others had repudiated their contracts to buy the maize, after the German Government had refused to issue the zero-rated licences. These are the two categories of applicants referred to by the ECJ in the following extract. Referring to the Commission decision authorizing the protective measures, the ECJ reasoned as follows.

THE ECJ

As is clear, moreover, from the judgment of the Court of 1 July, 1965, this decision constituted an improper application of Article 22 of Regulation No 19 . . . On October 3 1963 the Commission applied Article 22(2) of Regulation No 19 in circumstances which did not justify protective measures in order to restore the situation resulting from the fixing by it of a zero levy. As it was aware of the existence of applications for licences, it caused damage to the interests of importers who had acted in reliance on the information provided in accordance with Community rules. The Commission's conduct constituted a wrongful act or omission capable of giving rise to liability on the part of the Community.

In trying to justify itself by the assertion that in view of the economic data at its disposal on 3 October 1963 a threat of serious disturbance was not to be excluded and that consequently its mistaken evaluation of the data is excusable, the defendant misjudges the nature of the wrongful act or omission attributed to it, which is not to be found in a mistaken evaluation of the facts but in its general conduct which is shown clearly by the improper use made of Article 22, certain provisions of which, of a crucial nature, were ignored.

[*The ECJ then proceeded to determine the appropriate forum in which the issue of compensation should be decided.*]

However, with regard to any injury suffered by the applicants belonging to the first and second categories above-mentioned, those applicants have informed the Court that the injury alleged is the subject of two actions for damages, one against the Federal Republic of Germany before a German court and the other against the Community before the Court of Justice. It is necessary to avoid the applicants' being insufficiently or excessively compensated for the same damage by the

[67] Cases 106 and 107/63, *Toepfer* v. *Commission* [1965] ECR 405.

different assessment of two different courts applying different rules of law. Before determining the damage for which the Community should be held liable, it is necessary for the national court to have the opportunity to give judgment on any liability on the part of the Federal Republic of Germany. This being the case, final judgment cannot be given before the applicants have produced the decision of the national court on this matter, which may be done independently of the evidence asked of the applicant in the first category to the effect that they have exhausted all possible methods of recovery of the amounts improperly paid by way of levy. Furthermore, if it were established that such recovery was possible, this fact might have consequences bearing upon the calculation of the damages concerning the second category. However, the decisive nature of the said evidence required does not prevent the applicants from producing the other evidence previously indicated in the meantime.

It is clear from the *Kampffmeyer* case that the Community can, therefore, be liable when it has authorized a measure taken by a national body, where that authorization was wrongfully given. The procedural aspect of the case has, however, been the subject of widespread criticism. It has been argued that there was no reason to require the applicants to proceed initially in the German courts, and that the ECJ's rationale for doing so was based implicitly on the assumption that the German authorities were primarily liable, with the Community bearing only a residual liability.[68]

This criticism may be overstated, and it may be necessary to distinguish the claim for the return of the levies paid from the more general tort action. As regards the former, the idea that the primary liability rested with Germany may well have substance, given that it was Germany which imposed the levy and it was Germany to which the funds were paid. As regards the latter, there is no particular reason why the liability of the Community should be seen as somehow secondary to that of the Member State.

The second situation in which the issue of joint liability may arise is that in which the Member State applies unlawful Community legislation. This can arise, for example, in the context of the CAP, in which area relevant Community regulations will often be applied by national intervention boards. The general rule here is that it is the national intervention boards, and not the Commission, which are responsible for the application of the CAP, and that an action must normally be commenced in the national courts. The next case illustrates this in relation to the recovery of charges which an individual believes to have been wrongfully levied:

Case 96/71, R. and V. Haegeman Sprl v. Commission [1972] ECR 1005, [1973] CMLR 365

Haegeman was a Belgian trading company which imported wine from Greece which was at the time outside the Community. It alleged that it had suffered loss

[68] See Oliver, n. 62 above, 126–7.

because of a countervailing charge which was imposed on the import of wine from Greece to Belgium. This charge was imposed by a Council regulation and was levied by the Belgian authorities.

THE ECJ

7. Disputes concerning the levying on individuals of the charges and levies referred to by this provision must be resolved, applying Community law, by the national authorities and following the practices laid down by the law of the Member States.

8. Issues, therefore, which are raised during a procedure as to the interpretation and validity of regulations establishing the Communities' own resources must be brought before the national courts which have at their disposal the procedure under Article 177 of the Treaty in order to ensure the uniform application of Community law.

. . .

14. The applicant maintains further that by reason of the defendant's behaviour it has suffered exceptional damage as a result of loss of profit, unforeseen financial outlay and losses on existing contracts.

15. The question of the possible liability of the Community is in the first place linked with that of the legality of the levying of the charge in question.

16. It has just been found that, in the context of the relationship between individuals and the taxation authority which has levied the charge in dispute, the latter question comes under the jurisdiction of the national courts.

17. Accordingly, at the present stage the claim for compensation for possible damage must be dismissed.

The decision in the *Haegeman* case might well be criticized, since the moneys levied went into the Community's funds. The mere fact that the sums were collected by national authorities should make no difference, given that these sums were imposed by the Community and were collected on behalf of the Community by the Member State.[69] It does, however, appear to be the case that an action to recover such a charge must be commenced in the national courts and that this is also so where a trader is seeking payment of a sum to which he believes himself to be entitled under Community law. The next case illustrates this situation:

Case 99/74, Société des Grands Moulins des Antilles v. Commission [1975] ECR 1531

The applicants were claiming export refunds and carry-over payments which were due under the relevant Community legislation in relation to cereals exported from or stocked in French overseas departments. The national authorities had refused to pay principally because the European Agriculture Guidance and Guarantee Fund (EAGGF), a Community organization, had itself refused to fund such payments to overseas departments.

[69] See Hartley, n. 5 above, 502.

THE ECJ

16. The refusal by a Community institution to pay a debt which may be owed by a Member State under Community law is not a matter involving the non-contractual liability of the Community.

17. For an action involving non-contractual liability to lie it is necessary that an injury arising from an act or omission of the Community be alleged.

. . .

22. The provisions of Community law, especially Article 10 of Regulation No 1041/67 and Article 3 of Regulation No 1554/73, leave no doubt that payment or refusal of payment are measures appropriate to the national authorities.

23. It is thus for the national courts having jurisdiction in the matter to give a ruling on the legality of such measures, in pursuance of Community law, within the forms laid down by national law, following recourse, where necessary, to Article 177 of the Treaty.

24. Consequently, it is impossible to accept the applicant's attempt to disregard the precise wording of the implementing regulations, providing that the national authorities have the requisite powers, the more so since any rights which it might have against those authorities cannot depend upon a prior financial authorization by the Community.

25. Since the applicant has failed to allege an injury arising from an act or omission of the Community capable of affecting it adversely, its application is inadmissible under Article 178 of the Treaty.

It has also been held that this principle applies even where the Commission has sent telexes to the national board setting out its interpretation of the relevant regulations.[70] The authorities of a Member State may, however, be able to recover from Community funds where they have paid for losses which are the responsibility of the Community.[71]

There are, however, a number of situations in which it is possible to proceed against the Community directly. First, if the Commission sends a telex which is interpreted, in the context of the relevant legislation, as an instruction to the national agency to act in a particular manner, then an action may be brought against the Commission for damages.[72] A second situation in which it is possible to proceed against the Community is where no action could conceivably be brought against any national authority and hence there would be no remedy available in the national courts. Thus, in the *Unifrex* case, an applicant sought damages before the ECJ by reason of the failure of the Commission to pass a regulation which would have granted the applicant a subsidy for exports to Italy at the time the Italian lira was devalued. It was

[70] Case 133/79, *Sucrimex SA and Westzucker GmbH* v. *Commission* [1980] ECR 1299, [1981] 2 CMLR 479; Case 217/81, *Compagnie Interagra SA* v. *Commission* [1982] ECR 2233.

[71] This may be possible in the context of the CAP. The basis for shifting the loss to the Community is to be found in Council Reg. 729/70, and is bound up with the operation of the EAGGF. For discussion of this issue, see Oliver, n. 62 above, 142–3; J. A. Usher, *Legal Aspects of Agriculture in the European Community* (Oxford University Press, 1988), 104–6, 150–2.

[72] Case 175/84, *Krohn & Co Import-Export GmbH & Co KG* v. *Commission* [1986] ECR 753, [1987] 1 CMLR 745.

held that the action could proceed before the ECJ, since proceedings in the national court would not have helped the applicant: even if the relevant Community rules had been declared illegal pursuant to an Article 177 action, 'that annulment could not have required the national authorities to pay higher monetary compensatory amounts to the applicant, without the prior intervention of the Community legislature'.[73] The third situation in which it is possible to bring a claim in the ECJ is where the substance of the claim is that the Community has committed a tortious wrong to the applicant, as exemplified by the *Dietz* case:[74]

Case 126/76, Firma Gebrüder Dietz v. Commission [1977] ECR 2431

Dietz was a German firm which had made a contract to sell sugar to Italy. After the formation of the contract, but prior to its performance, a levy was introduced on imports into Italy. Dietz suffered a loss and argued that the imposition of the charge was a breach of the principle of legitimate expectations.

THE ECJ

5. According to the applicant, the damage suffered does not result from measures adopted by the national authorities but from an omission on the part of the Commission within the context of the Regulations issued in implementation of Article 6 of Regulation No 974/71.

The Court has only stated that it has no jurisdiction in cases in which the application was in fact directed against measures adopted by the national authorities for the purpose of applying provisions of Community law.

Even if the Court, within the context of proceedings for a preliminary ruling, considered that the rules applicable were such as to cause damage because of the absence of appropriate transitional measures, the national court would not be empowered to adopt those measures itself, with the result that a direct application to the Court on the basis of Article 215 of the Treaty would still be necessary.

6. The matter has been brought before the Court within the bounds of its jurisdiction and it is therefore under a duty to examine whether the alleged omission in the Community Regulations issued in implementation of Article 6 of Regulation No 974/71 constitutes an infringement of the law such as to incur the liability of the Community.

7. The application is therefore admissible.

7. LIABILITY IN CONTRACT

The discussion thus far has focused on the liability of the Community arising under Article 215(2) of the EEC Treaty, which deals with non-contractual

[73] Case 281/82, *Unifrex* v. *Commission and Council* [1984] ECR 1969.

[74] The application of the principle in the *Dietz* case, which allows the action to proceed in the ECJ, may not operate if the national authorities themselves were partially to blame for the loss caused to the individual: see e.g. the first *Kampffmeyer* case, 539–40 above.

liability. The Community will obviously also make contracts, and the ECJ is given jurisdiction over this area by Article 181 of the EC Treaty, which states:

> The Court of Justice shall have jurisdiction to give judgment pursuant to any arbitration clause contained in a contract concluded by or on behalf of the Community, whether that contract be governed by public or private law.[75]

Article 215(1) then determines the law which should be applied to the contract in question:

> The contractual liability of the Community shall be governed by the law applicable to the contract in question.

The meaning of this phrase requires explanation. Contracts are often made between parties in different countries, and therefore it is necessary to determine which law should govern the contract. The answer to this question will often be of considerable importance, since the contractual rules in different countries may differ significantly as regards a whole range of matters including, for example, the place of formation of the contract and the types of damages which are recoverable in the event of a breach of contract. The body of law which deals with this issue is known as the conflict of laws or private international law. Contracts often have choice-of-law clauses, which specify the law which is to be applied to the contract in the event of a dispute. The Commission always inserts such a clause in its contracts, and it has been held that this clause prevails and cannot be displaced by arguments that the contract was more closely connected with a different country from that specified in the choice-of-law clause.[76]

It would of course be possible in principle for a choice-of-law clause to specify Community law as that which is applicable to the contract. It is true that Article 215(1), in contrast to Article 215(2), does not state that the Community is to develop a system of law by drawing on the relevant general principles which are common to the laws of the Member States. The implication of this might be that the Community is not to develop its own Community contract law. However, such a development may well be necessary in the future, as an adjunct of the expansion of Community competence into novel areas.

A development of this nature can be seen, albeit indirectly, in staff cases which have come before the ECJ. The Court has characterized contracts of employment of certain Community officials as public-law contracts, emphasizing that the work performed was of a governmental nature. One

[75] Although Art. 181 talks of the ECJ giving judgment pursuant to an arbitration clause, it is clearly not simply an arbitrator in the normal sense of that term.

[76] Case 318/81, *Commission* v. *CODEMI* [1985] ECR 3693.

consequence of this characterization was that the contracts were governed by administrative law, and the Court did not state that any system of national administrative law was to be applied.[77]

8. LIABILITY TO MAKE RESTITUTION

In addition to liability based on tort and contract, most legal systems also recognize some species of liability in restitution or quasi-contract. The precise nature of this liability is an issue which continues to divide academics in this area, but the better view is that it is distinct from both contract and tort. The reasons for this cannot be examined in detail here, but the essence of this reasoning can be conveyed at a general level. Restitution is not based upon the existence of a promise, but rather on the existence of unjust enrichment on the part of the defendant; hence its difference from contractual liability. Restitution does not normally require the proof of a wrongful act by the defendant, in the sense of some fault or breach of a duty of care, and the measure of recovery is normally determined by the extent of the defendant's unjust enrichment rather than the extent of the loss to the plaintiff; hence its difference from most forms of tort liability.

One type of restitutionary claim which is common within national systems concerns payments made to public bodies in circumstances where the public body has no right to claim the money. It is readily apparent that this species of claim is of considerable importance in the context of the EC. It can arise in two types of situation. On the one hand, there can be cases where a Member State has, for example, imposed a levy which it is not entitled to impose because of Community rules which prohibit the imposition of such charges. Many of the cases on direct effect have arisen from such factual situations, including *Van Gend en Loos* itself. In such cases, the matter will be remitted to the national court, once the ECJ has found that the levy was in breach of Community law. It will then be for the national court to devise a remedy which gives effect to the Community right, and this will often take the form of a return of the sum which has been paid over to the national authority.[78] On the other hand, there may be instances which arise under, for example, the CAP in which money is paid into Community funds, pursuant to an obligation imposed by Community law, where there may be no legal obligation to pay the sum in question. It is this latter issue which concerns us here.

Principles of restitution have been applied by the ECJ in some instances in which unjust enrichment by an individual against the Community has been found.[79] It would clearly be correct in principle that a remedy should be

[77] Case 1/55, *Kergall* v. *Common Assembly* [1955] ECR 151; Cases 43, 45, 48/59, *Von Lachmüller* v. *Commission* [1960] ECR 463.

[78] See above, Ch. 5.

[79] See e.g. Case 18/63, *Wollast* v. *EEC* [1964] ECR 85; Case 110/63, *Willame* v. *Commission* [1965] ECR 649.

available in favour of an individual, where the Community has been unjustly enriched at his or her expense, as in the instance in which a charge has been imposed by the Community, where the charge was unwarranted under Community law. If a levy imposed by a Member State, which is unlawful because it is in breach of the Treaty, should be recoverable, so too should a charge levied by the Community itself, where that charge is in breach of the Treaty. The matter is, however, complicated in two different ways.

First, there is case law of the ECJ, outlined above, which has insisted that, in many such instances, the action should be commenced in the national court against the national collecting agency, even where the funds are treated as Community funds.[80]

Secondly, there is the difficulty of locating restitutionary claims within the Treaty itself. It could be argued that such claims may be based on Article 215(2), but, as has been pointed out,[81] the wording of the Article which requires the Community to 'make good any damage caused' by its institutions, does not fit perfectly with the idea of a restitutionary action. The Article is, however, framed in terms of 'non-contractual liability', and this is clearly wide enough to cover restitutionary relief. Moreover, if the ECJ were to find that it had no jurisdiction over such actions, then Article 183 would mean that relief could be sought in an action against the Community in national courts. It is doubtful whether the ECJ would wish to be in a position where it had 'no control' over the development of appropriate restitutionary principles which involved Community liability.

9. FURTHER READING

(a) Books

SCHERMERS, H. G., HEUKELS, T., and MEAD, P. (eds.), *The Non-Contractual Liability of the European Communities* (Martinus Nijhoff, 1988)

(b) Articles

DURAND, A., 'Restitution or Damages: National Court or European Court?' (1975–6) 1 ELRev. 431

HARDING, C., 'The Choice of Court Problem in Cases of Non-Contractual Liability under EEC Law' (1979) 16 CMLRev. 389

HARTLEY, T. C., 'Concurrent Liability in EEC Law: A Critical Review of the Cases' (1977) 2 ELRev. 249

JONES, M. L., 'The Non-Contractual Liability of the EEC and the Availability of an Alternative Remedy in the National Courts' (1981) 1 LIEI 1

LEWIS, A. D. E., 'Joint and Several Liability of the European Communities and National Authorities' [1980] CLP 99

[80] See above, 538–41.

[81] Hartley, n. 5 above, 465.

Oliver, P., 'Enforcing Community Rights in the English Courts' (1987) 50 MLR 881
Wils, W., 'Concurrent Liability of the Community and a Member State' (1992) 17 ELRev. 191

13

Free Movement of Goods: Duties, Charges, and Taxes

1. INTRODUCTION: FORMS OF ECONOMIC INTEGRATION

The discussion in the previous chapters has focused on the institutional law of the EC. The analysis within the remainder of the book will be concerned with what is known as the substantive law of the EC, although we will be stressing the links between the two parts of Community law throughout the chapters which follow, in much the same way as we have already done in the preceding discussion.

This Chapter and that which follows will be concerned with the free movement of goods. This is one of the 'four freedoms' guaranteed by the original Rome Treaty, the others being free movement of workers, freedom of establishment, and the provision of services, and free movement of capital. In order to understand the importance of these provisions and their place within the overall fabric of the Treaty it is necessary to take a step back before moving forward. We need therefore to begin by understanding what a common market actually is, how it differs from other forms of economic integration, and how the provisions on the free movement of goods fit within this framework. Swann provides a succinct description of the different forms of economic integration.

D. Swann, The Economics of the Common Market[1]

Economic integration can take various forms and these can be ranged in a spectrum in which the degree of involvement of participating economies, one with another, becomes greater and greater. The *free trade area* is the least onerous in terms of involvement. It consists in an arrangement between states in which they agree to remove all customs duties (and quotas) on trade passing between them. Each party is free, however, to determine unilaterally the level of customs duty on imports coming from outside the area.The next stage is the *customs union*. Here tariffs and quotas on trade between members are also removed but members agree to apply a *common* level of tariff on goods entering the union from without. The latter is called the common customs, or common external, tariff. Next comes the

[1] (7th edn., Penguin, 1992), 11–12, italics in the original.

common market and this technical term implies that to the free movement of *goods* within the customs union is added the free movement of the *factors of production*—labour, capital and enterprise. Finally there is the *economic union*. This is a common market in which there is also a complete unification of monetary and fiscal policy. There would be a common currency which would be controlled by a central authority and in effect the member states would become regions within the union.

Part Three of the Treaty contains many of the fundamental principles which are of importance in the establishment of a *customs union and common market*.[2] This part of the Treaty sets out, *inter alia*, the 'four freedoms' which are of central importance in realizing the goals of the Community.

Title I of Part Three is concerned with Free Movement of Goods. This is designed to ensure the removal of duties, quotas, and other quantitative restrictions on the movement of goods within the Community: Articles 12 to 17, and 30 to 37. These rules are complemented by those contained in Articles 18 to 29, which deal with the establishment of a Common Customs Tariff. The fundamental objective of these provisions is to ensure that competition between goods coming from different Member States is neither prevented nor distorted by the existence of government provisions which limit the amount of such goods which can be imported (quotas), or increase their price (tariffs).

Other Treaty Articles contained within Title III of Part Three specify the rules for the free movement of labour, capital, and enterprise.

A brief explanation will be of help in understanding the relationship between these provisions and those on the free movement of goods, and also in conveying the economic objectives of these Articles taken as a whole.

The provisions on the free movement of goods are designed to establish the basic principles of a customs union: the prohibition of tariffs etc. on trade between Member States, and the existence of a common tariff. The object is to ensure that goods themselves can move freely, with the consequence that those which are most favoured by consumers will be most successful, irrespective of the country in which they were made. Consumer choice is thereby enhanced and the firms which make the most desirable goods from the consumer's perspective will be most successful on a Community-wide basis, which will serve to maximize wealth-creation in the Community as a whole.

The provisions of Title III, which are concerned with free movement of workers, establishment, services, and capital reflect the same idea. These Articles have, as will be seen below,[3] social as well as economic objectives. It is with the basic economic aims that we are concerned here. Labour and capital are two of the economic factors of production, i.e. the elements which go

[2] Prior to the TEU the provisions on free movement of goods were contained within what was labelled Part Two of the Treaty, entitled Foundations of the Community. After the TEU Part Two of the Treaty deals with Citizenship of the Union and Part Three of the Treaty now has the name Community Policies. The provisions on free movement of goods constitute one such policy of the Community.

[3] See below, Chs. 15–18.

to make a product. The essential idea is to ensure the optimal allocation of resources within the Community, by enabling factors of production to move to the area where they are most valued. This is not a complex idea and can be explained as follows. Labour is one of the factors of production, one of the elements which is used to make goods. Now it may well be the case that this factor of production is valued more highly in some areas than in others. This would be so if, for example, there were an excess of supply over demand for labour in southern Italy, and an excess of demand over supply in certain parts of Germany. In this situation labour is worth more in Germany than it is in Italy. The value of labour within the Community as a whole will, therefore, be maximized, or at least come closer to being so, if workers are free to move within the Community to the area where they are most valued. Take another example, this time of a business which is based in Holland and is thinking of setting up in France. The idea is that if a firm which is established in Holland believes that it could capture part of the French market, but only if it were allowed to set up in business there, then it should not be prevented from so doing by rules of French law which discriminate on grounds of nationality. The economic theme of optimal allocation of resources underlies this area too, albeit in a slightly different manner than in the case of workers. Once again the argument can be put quite simply. If the Dutch firm is correct, and it is more efficient than its French counterpart, then the latter may either lose part of its trade to the former or be forced out of business altogether. In either eventuality the resources of the Community as a whole will be better utilized. If, to take the extreme instance, the French firm is forced to close because its Dutch competitor is more efficient, then the economic resources hitherto used by the French firm will be reallocated by the market mechanism to some other usage where they are more valuable. In that sense, the resources of the Community as a whole will be enhanced.[4]

2. THE BASIC STRUCTURE OF THE PROVISIONS CONCERNING FREE MOVEMENT OF GOODS

In this Chapter and that which follows we will be considering the jurisprudence of the ECJ as it relates to those provisions of the Treaty which are primarily concerned with the free movement of goods. A moment's reflection will cause the reader to realize that the free movement of goods can be impeded

[4] The discussion in the text is, of course, a simplified one. There may, for example, be cogent reasons why a political system wishes to preserve domestic industry in a particular region, and there may also be circumstances in which the firm which 'wins' is not unequivocally the more efficient. It should also be noted that there have been difficulties in realizing the free movement of capital. This is, in essence, because capital movements can have a dramatic effect on the exchange rates of differing currencies, and can thus have broader ramifications for domestic economic policy within a particular state.

in a number of different ways, each of which is dealt with by particular provisions of the Treaty.

The most obvious form of protectionism will occur when a state attempts to erect customs duties or charges which have an equivalent effect, with the object of rendering foreign goods more expensive than their domestic counterparts. This problem is dealt with by Articles 9 to 16 of the Treaty. Closely related to this species of protection is that which exists when a state attempts to treat domestic goods more favourably than imports by discriminatory taxes which benefit the former. Articles 95 to 99 are designed to cope with this problem. Both of these issues will be considered within this Chapter and the relationship between the two sets of Treaty Articles will be discussed in detail below.[5]

A state may, however, seek to preserve advantages for its own goods by imposing quotas, or measures which have an equivalent effect on imports, thereby reducing the quantum of imported products. This aspect of free movement is dealt with in Articles 30 to 37 of the Treaty. There has, as will be seen in the next chapter, been an extensive jurisprudence on the meaning of Article 30 which is still evolving.

The third of the chapters which deals directly with free movement of goods concerns the legislative and judicial techniques for the completion of the single market. As we shall see, this area of substantive law provides a particularly good example of the way in which the Court and the legislature have combined to attain this fundamental objective of the Community. The discussion of the completion of the Single Market will, however, be delayed until the end of the book, since it has ramifications for topics other than free movement of goods.[6]

What this and the following chapter have in common is that it is state action creating barriers to trade which is being controlled. Such action, which can prevent the existence of a level playing field for all Community products, can in addition come about as a result of aid granted by a state to a specific industry. This will obviously have the effect of disadvantaging competing products from other Member States, and Community law therefore closely regulates the granting of such aid through Articles 92 to 94. The law on this topic will be analysed fully below.[7]

It should not, however, be forgotten that private parties may also take action which can have the effect of partitioning the market along national lines and hence impede the realization of the Single Market. This can occur when private parties use industrial property rights to divide the Community on the basis of existing national divisions, or when firms agree among themselves not to compete in each other's markets. Community law has to address both of these issues in order to prevent private action from recreating barriers to trade analogous in their effect to duties or quotas. The way in which EC law has tackled both of these problems will be considered in later chapters.[8]

[5] See below, 576–80. [6] See below, Ch. 25. [7] See below, Ch. 24.
[8] See below, Chs. 19, 20, 21, 23.

The discussion of the various Treaty provisions which impinge on the free movement of goods must perforce proceed by considering the relevant Treaty Articles individually. When reading the materials which follow do not, however, forget that these Articles should be seen as a whole. They interrelate, with the consequence that the ECJ's case law under any one of these Treaty Articles will be affected by the way in which it perceives that particular Article to fit into the broader aim of creating and preserving a single market for goods within the Community.

3. ARTICLES 9–17: DUTIES AND CHARGES

Article 9(1)[9] is the foundational provision of this part of the Treaty:

> The Community shall be based upon a customs union which shall cover all trade in goods and which shall involve the prohibition between Member States[10] of customs duties on imports and exports and of all charges having an equivalent effect, and the adoption of a common customs tariff in their relation with third countries.[11]

It is important to understand the structure of the other provisions which make up this part of the Treaty. This is as follows. Article 12 is a standstill provision which imposes an obligation on states not to introduce *new* customs duties or charges equivalent thereto. This provision has direct effect, and it was indeed Article 12 which was in issue in the famous *Van Gend* case which laid the foundations for the concept of direct effect within Community law.[12] The ECJ, in this area as in many others, has made a notable contribution to the interpretation of this Article.

> Member States shall refrain from introducing between themselves any new customs duties on imports or exports or any charges having equivalent effect, and from increasing those which already apply in their trade with each other.

[9] Art. 9 will almost always be used in conjunction with one of the other Treaty Arts. in this area. When it is employed in this manner it will have direct effect: see e.g. Case 18/71, *Eunomia di Porro & Co.* v. *Italian Ministry of Education* [1971] ECR 811.

[10] The ECJ has interpreted Art. 9 to prohibit customs duties etc. even when they are applied within a Member State and are imposed on goods which enter one particular region of that state: Cases C–363, 407, 409, 411/93, *René Lancry SA* v. *Direction Générale des Douanes*, 9 Aug. 1994.

[11] The goods which benefit from the provisions on free movement contained in Arts. 9–17 and 30–36 are those which originate in a Member State and those which come from outside the Community, but are in free circulation within the Member States: Art. 9(2). The criteria for goods which come from outside the Community to be in free circulation within the Community are contained in Art. 10(1): the goods must have complied with import formalities, and any customs duties and charges must have been paid by the trader and not have been reimbursed.

[12] See above, 152–3.

Article 13[13] complements Article 12. It provides that Member States shall progressively abolish *existing* customs duties and charges having an equivalent effect on imports during the transitional period.[14]

Article 16[15] relates to duties and charges concerning exports. It stipulates that these must be abolished by the end of the first stage.[16]

Having examined the general structure of the Treaty Articles which make up this area we are now in a position to examine the Court's case law.

(a) Duties and Charges: Effect, Not Purpose

In its early case law the Court made it clear that whether Article 12 would bite would depend upon the effect of the duty or charge, and not on its purpose. This comes out clearly from the *Italian Art* case:

Case 7/68, Commission v. Italy
[1968] ECR 423

Italy imposed a tax on the export of artistic, historical and archæological items. The Commission brought an action under Article 169 alleging that this was in breach of Article 16 which prohibits duties and charges on exports. Italy argued that the items should not be regarded as goods for the purpose of the rules on the customs union and that the purpose of the tax in question was not to raise revenue, but to protect the artistic etc. heritage of the country. The Court rejected these arguments in the following terms.

THE ECJ

1. *The Scope of the Disputed Tax*

. . .

Under Article 9 of the Treaty the Community is based on a customs union 'which shall cover all trade in goods'. By goods, within the meaning of that provision, there must be understood products which can be valued in money and which are capable, as such, of forming the subject of commercial transactions.

The articles covered by the Italian law, whatever may be the characteristics which distinguish them from other types of merchandise, nevertheless resemble the latter, inasmuch as they can be valued in money and so be the subject of commercial transactions. That view corresponds with the scheme of the Italian law itself, which fixes the tax in question in proportion to the value of the articles concerned.

It follows from the above that the rules of the Common Market apply to these goods subject only to the exceptions expressly provided by the Treaty.

2. *The Classification of the Disputed Tax Having Regard to Article 16 of the Treaty*

In the opinion of the Commission the tax in dispute constitutes a tax having an effect equivalent to a customs duty on exports and therefore the tax should have

[13] Art. 13(2) was held to be directly effective in Case 33/70, *SACE* v. *Italian Ministry of Finance* [1970] ECR 1213.

[14] The details of this progressive abolition are contained in Arts. 14 and 15 EC.

[15] This has direct effect when read in conjunction with Art. 9 EC, Case 18/71, n. 9 above.

[16] 31 Dec. 1961.

been abolished, under Article 16 of the Treaty, no later than the end of the first stage of the common market, that is to say, from 1 January 1962. The defendant argues that the disputed tax does not come within the category, as it has its own particular purpose which is to ensure the protection and safety of the artistic, historic and archaeological heritage which exists in the national territory. Consequently, the tax does not in any respect have a fiscal nature, and its contribution to the budget is insignificant.

Article 16 of the Treaty prohibits the collection in dealings between Member States of any customs duty on exports and of any charge having an equivalent effect, that is to say, any charge which, by altering the price of an article exported, has the same restrictive effect on the free circulation of that article as a customs duty. That provision makes no distinction based on the purpose of the duties and charges the abolition of which it requires.

It is not necessary to analyse the concept of the nature of the fiscal system on which the defendant bases its argument upon this point, for the provisions of the section of the Treaty concerning the elimination of customs duties between the Member States exclude the retention of customs duties and charges having an equivalent effect without distinguishing in that respect between those which are and those which are not of a fiscal nature.

The disputed tax falls within Article 16 by reason of the fact that export trade in the goods in question is hindered by the pecuniary burden which it imposes on the price of the exported articles.

Once a tax is deemed to be caught by Article 12 or 16 as a duty or charge which is of equivalent effect then it is in effect *per se* unlawful. Thus, attempts by Italy in the preceding case to argue that its tax could be defended on the basis of Article 36 were rejected by the Court: Article 36 can only be used as a defence in relation to quantitative restrictions which are caught by Article 30; it cannot serve to validate fiscal measures which are prohibited by Articles 9 to 17.

The emphasis in the *Italian Art* case on effect as opposed to purpose is clearly justifiable. The peremptory force of Articles 9 to 17 would be significantly weakened if it were open to a state to argue that a duty or charge should not be regarded as being within the reach of these Articles because its purpose was in some sense non-fiscal in nature. Had the Court proved receptive to this species of argument it would, moreover, have meant that the judiciary would have had to adjudicate on which types of social policy should be regarded as possessing a legitimate purpose sufficient to take them outside the Treaty.

The ECJ has reaffirmed its emphasis on effect rather than purpose in other cases. It has also made it clear that the provisions of the Treaty in this area can be applicable even if the state measure in question was not designed with protectionism in mind. Thus in *Diamantarbeiders*[17] the Court considered the legality of a Belgian law requiring 0.33 per cent of the value of imported

[17] Cases 2 and 3/69, *Sociaal Fonds voor de Diamantarbeiders* v. *SA Ch. Brachfeld & Sons* [1969] ECR 211, [1969] CMLR 335.

diamonds to be paid into a social fund for workers in the industry. The fact that the purpose of the fund was neither to raise money for the exchequer, nor to protect domestic industry,[18] did not save the charge in question: that the charge was imposed on goods by reason of the fact that they had crossed a border sufficed to bring it within Article 12.

(b) Charges Having an Equivalent Effect: General Principles[19]

The text of Articles 9, 12, and 16, which are the key provisions in this area, prohibits not only customs duties but also charges having an equivalent effect (CEE). The reason is obvious. Member States are not stupid. If this phrase had been omitted from the Treaty then it would have been open to those who were minded not to play the Community system fairly to comply with the abolition of customs duties *stricto sensu*, but to reach the same protectionist goal through measures which created, in economic terms, a similar barrier against imported goods. Small wonder, then, that the idea of CEEs should have been included within these Treaty Articles, and that an analogous phrase is to be found within Article 30.[20] Nor is it surprising that the ECJ should have interpreted the term expansively to ensure that it could catch the many forms which such charges can assume.

Case 24/68, Commission v. Italy
[1969] ECR 193, [1971] CMLR 611

Italy imposed a levy on goods which were exported to other Member States with the ostensible purpose of collecting statistical material for use in discerning trade patterns. The Court reiterated its holding that customs duties were prohibited irrespective of the purpose for which the duties were imposed, and irrespective of the destination of the revenues which were collected. It then continued as follows.

THE ECJ

8. The extension of the prohibition of customs duties to charges having an equivalent effect is intended to supplement the prohibition against obstacles to trade created by such duties by increasing its efficiency.

The use of these two complementary concepts thus tends, in trade between Member States, to avoid the imposition of any pecuniary charge on goods circulating within the Community by virtue of the fact that they cross a national border.

9. Thus, in order to ascribe to a charge an effect equivalent to a customs duty, it is important to consider this effect in the light of the objectives of the Treaty, in the Parts, Titles and Chapters in which Articles 9, 12, 13 and 16 are to be found, particularly in relation to the free movement of goods.

Consequently, any pecuniary charge, however small and whatever its designation

[18] Belgium did not produce diamonds.
[19] R. Barents, 'Charges Having an Equivalent Effect to Customs Duties' (1978) 15 CMLRev. 415.
[20] See below, Ch. 14.

and mode of application, which is imposed unilaterally on domestic or foreign goods by reason of the fact that they cross a frontier, and which is not a customs duty in the strict sense, constitutes a charge having equivalent effect within the meaning of Articles 9, 12, 13 and 16 of the Treaty, even if it is not imposed for the benefit of the State, is not discriminatory or protective in effect and if the product on which the charge is imposed is not in competition with any domestic product.

10. It follows from all the provisions referred to and from their relationship with the other provisions of the Treaty that the prohibition of new customs duties or charges having equivalent effect, linked to the principle of the free movement of goods, constitutes a fundamental rule which, without prejudice to the other provisions of the Treaty, does not permit of any exceptions.

The clear message from the Court in this case was repeated once again in *Diamantarbeiders*.[21] The ECJ reproduced the broad definition of a CEE and made it clear that this would bite whether those affected by the charge were all the citizens of the Community, those from the importing state, or only the nationals from the state which was responsible for passing the measure under scrutiny.

These judgments signalled the Court's intent that the Articles of the Treaty concerned with customs duties and CEEs were to be taken seriously.[22] They were not to be circumvented by the form in which the charge was imposed; they were applicable whether the duty/charge was discriminatory or not; they had an impact irrespective of whether the product on which the charge was imposed was in competition with domestic goods; and they admitted of no exceptions.

This strident approach by the ECJ is unsurprising and entirely warranted, given the centrality of abolishing customs duties and CEEs to the very notion of a single Community market. The realization of a single market will, of course, require the legal control and prohibition of other measures which can impede intra-Community trade. The abolition of customs duties and CEEs does, however, go to the very heart of this Community ideal. It was a necessary first step in the attainment of market integration. Eradicating customs duties and the like was vital if the broader aims of the common market were to be fulfilled. Had the Court faltered at this juncture this could well have had profound and negative ramifications, rendering it more difficult to put into effect other provisions of the Treaty concerned with different types of barriers to Community trade.

[21] Cases 2 and 3/69, n. 17 above.

[22] See also Case 29/72, *Marimex SpA* v. *Italian Finance Administration* [1972] ECR 1309, [1973] CMLR 486; Case 39/73, *Rewe Zentralfinanz* v. *Direktor der Landwirtschaftskammer Westfalen-Lippe* [1973] ECR 1039.

(c) Charges Having an Equivalent Effect: Inspections and the 'Exchange Exception'

One common argument which has been advanced by states is that the charge imposed on imported goods is justified on the ground that it is merely payment for a service which the state has rendered to the importer and that therefore it should not be regarded as a CEE for the purposes of Article 12. While the Court has been willing to accept this argument in principle, it has been equally alert to the fact that a state might present a charge in this way when in reality it was actually seeking to impede imports, or in circumstances where there was in reality no commercial exchange at all. The Court has therefore closely scrutinized such claims from states and has not readily accepted them.

Thus in *Commission* v. *Italy*,[23] considered above, the Italian Government argued that the charge in question should be seen as consideration for the statistical information which it collected; that this information 'affords importers a better competitive position in the Italian market whilst exporters enjoy a similar advantage abroad';[24] and that therefore the charge should be viewed as consideration for a service rendered, as a *quid pro quo*, and not as a CEE. The Court was unconvinced. It held that the statistical information was beneficial to the whole economy and to the administrative authorities. It then continued in the following vein:[25]

> Even if the competitive position of importers and exporters were to be particularly improved as a result, the statistics still constitute an advantage so general, and so difficult to assess, that the disputed charge cannot be regarded as the consideration for a specific benefit actually conferred.

The same theme is to be found in other ECJ decisions. In *Cadsky*[26] the Court refused to accept that charges for quality checks performed on certain vegetables exported from Italy could be legitimated on the basis that they constituted consideration for the performance of a commercial transaction. There was, said the Court, no specific and direct benefit to the relevant traders. The fact that the reputation of Italian vegetables might be enhanced, and that this would benefit such vegetable growers, was not sufficient in this respect.

Even when the charge *is* more directly related to some action taken by the state with respect to specific imported goods the Court has still been reluctant to accept that the charge can be characterized as consideration for a service rendered. This is apparent from the *Bresciani* case:

[23] Case 24/68 [1969] ECR 193, [1971] CMLR 611, paras. 15–16. [24] *Ibid.*, para. 15.
[25] *Ibid.*, para. 16.
[26] Case 63/74, *W. Cadsky SpA* v. *Istituto Nazionale per il Commercio Estero* [1975] ECR 281, [1975] 2 CMLR 246.

Case 87/75, Bresciani v. Amministrazione Italiana delle Finanze [1976] ECR 129, [1976] 2 CMLR 62

The Italian authorities imposed a charge for the compulsory veterinary and public-health inspections which were carried out on imported raw cowhides. Was this to be regarded as a CEE or not?

THE ECJ

6. The national court requests that the three following considerations be taken into account:

First, the fact that the charge is proportionate to the quantity of the goods and not to their value distinguishes a duty of the type at issue from charges which fall within the prohibition under Article 13 of the EEC Treaty. Second, a pecuniary charge of the type at issue is no more than the consideration required from individuals who, through their own action in importing products of animal origin, cause a service to be rendered. In the third place, although there may be differences in the method and time of its application, the duty at issue is also levied on similar products of domestic origin.

. . .

8. The justification for the obligation progressively to abolish customs duties is based on the fact that any pecuniary charge, however small, imposed on goods by reason of the fact that they cross a frontier constitutes an obstacle to the free movement of such goods.

The obligation progressively to abolish customs duties is supplemented by the obligation to abolish charges having equivalent effect in order to prevent the fundamental principle of the free movement of goods within the common market from being circumvented by the imposition of pecuniary charges of various kinds by a Member State.

The use of these two complementary concepts thus tends, in trade between Member States, to avoid the imposition of any pecuniary charge on goods circulating within the Community by virtue of the fact that they cross a national frontier.

9. Consequently, any pecuniary charge, whatever its designation and mode of application, which is unilaterally imposed on goods imported from another Member State by reason of the fact that they cross a frontier, constitutes a charge having an effect equivalent to a customs duty. In appraising a duty of the type at issue it is, consequently, of no importance that it is proportionate to the quantity of the imported goods and not to their value.

10. Nor, in determining the effects of the duty on the free movement of goods, is it of any importance that a duty of the type at issue is proportionate to the costs of a compulsory public health inspection carried out on entry of the goods. The activity of the administration of the State intended to maintain a public health inspection system imposed in the general interest cannot be regarded as a service rendered to the importer such as to justify the imposition of a pecuniary charge. If, accordingly, public health inspections are still justified at the end of the transitional period, the costs which they occasion must be met by the general public which, as a whole benefits from the free movement of Community goods.

11. The fact that the domestic production is, through other charges, subjected to a similar burden matters little unless those charges and the duty in question are

applied according to the same criteria and at the same stage of production, thus making it possible for them to be regarded as falling within a general system of internal taxation applying systematically and in the same way to domestic and imported products.

The ECJ's judgment in *Bresciani* indicates clearly its reluctance to accede to arguments which will take pecuniary charges outside the reach of this part of the Treaty. In paragraph 9 it rejects the first of the Italian arguments: the fact that the charge is proportionate to the quantity of imported goods makes no difference, since Articles 12, 13, etc. prohibit *any* charge imposed by reason of the fact that goods cross a frontier.[27] The rejection of the second of the Italian arguments in paragraph 10 is equally significant, both in and of itself and because of the reasoning which the ECJ employs. On the face of it the state's argument has plausibility: if you wish to import a type of product which has health implications necessitating an inspection, then you, the importer, should bear the cost. The Court's response is, however, unequivocal: the cost of inspections to maintain public health should be borne by the general public. Whether this makes sense in micro-economic terms is doubtful, to say the least.[28] The conclusion which the ECJ reaches on this point is indicative of its belief that the free movement of goods should be enhanced by limiting the ambit of any escape routes from the reach of Articles 9 to 17. This is equally apparent in the way in which the Court disposes of the state's third contention. The ECJ's response is to be found in paragraph 11 of its judgment and requires a strict equivalence between the charges levied on domestic and imported goods in order that the charge in question can be held lawful under this part of the Treaty. Other attempts to employ the exchange argument have not generally proven more successful than in *Bresciani*.[29]

(d) Charges Having an Equivalent Effect: Inspections and Fulfilment of Mandatory Legal Requirements

Where Community legislation *permits* an inspection to be undertaken by a state, the national authorities cannot recover any fees charged from the traders.[30] The Court has, however, accepted that a charge imposed by a state will escape the prohibition contained in Articles 9 to 17 when it is levied to cover the cost of a *mandatory* inspection required by Community law.[31]

[27] A charge will be deemed to be a CEE if it is a flat-rate charge which is based on the value of the goods: Case 170/88, *Ford España* v. *Spain* [1989] ECR 2305.

[28] For the obvious reason that by placing the cost on the general public it means that the importer of the product will not have to bear what is in reality one of the costs of making that product.

[29] See e.g. Case 43/71, *Politi SAS* v. *Italian Ministry of Finance* [1971] ECR 1039; Case 132/82, *Commission* v. *Belgium* [1983] ECR 1649, [1983] 3 CMLR 600; Case 340/87, *Commission* v. *Italy* [1989] ECR 1483, [1991] 1 CMLR 437; Case C–209/89, *Commission* v. *Italy* [1991] ECR I–3533, [1993] 1 CMLR 155.

[30] Case 314/82, *Commission* v. *Belgium* [1984] ECR 1543, [1985] 3 CMLR 134.

[31] Case 46/76, *Bauhuis* v. *Netherlands* [1977] ECR 5; Case 1/83, *IFG* v. *Freistaat Bayern* [1984]

Case 18/87, Commission v. Germany
[1988] ECR 5427

German regional authorities charged certain fees on live animals which were imported into the country. These charges were to cover the cost of inspections undertaken pursuant to Directive 81/389. The question arose whether they should be regarded as CEEs. The ECJ began by stating the now orthodox proposition that any pecuniary charge imposed as a result of goods crossing a frontier was caught by the Treaty, either as a customs duty or as a CEE. It then recognized an exception to this basic principle.

THE ECJ

6. However, the Court has held that such a charge escapes that classification if it relates to a general system of internal dues applied systematically and in accordance with the same criteria to domestic products and imported products alike (. . . Case 132/78, *Denkavit* v. *France* [1979] ECR 1923), if it constitutes payment for a service in fact rendered to the economic operator of a sum in proportion to the service (. . . Case 152/82, *Commission* v. *Denmark* [1983] ECR 3573), or again, subject to certain conditions, if it attaches to inspections carried out to fulfil obligations imposed by Community law (. . . Case 46/76, *Bauhuis* v. *Netherlands* [1977] ECR 5).

7. The contested fee, which is payable on importation and transit, cannot be regarded as relating to a general system of internal dues. Nor does it constitute payment for a service rendered to the operator, because this condition is satisfied only if the operator in question obtains a definite specific benefit (see . . . Case 24/68, *Commission* v. *Italy* [1969] ECR 193), which is not the case if the inspection serves to guarantee, in the public interest, the health and life of animals in international transport (see . . . Case 314/82, *Commission* v. *Belgium* [1984] ECR 1543).

8. Since the contested fee was charged in connection with inspections carried out pursuant to a Community provision, it should be noted that according to the case law of the Court (. . . in *Bauhuis* . . . ; judgment of 12 July 1977 *Commission* v. *Netherlands* [1977] ECR 1355; . . . in Case 1/83, *IFG* v. *Freistaat Bayern* [1984] ECR 349) such fees may not be classified as charges having an effect equivalent to a customs duty if the following conditions are satisfied:

(a) they do not exceed the actual costs of the inspections in connection with which they are charged;
(b) the inspections in question are obligatory and uniform for all the products concerned in the Community;
(c) they are prescribed by Community law in the general interest of the Community;
(d) they promote the free movement of goods, in particular by neutralizing obstacles which could arise from unilateral measures of inspection adopted in accordance with Article 36 of the Treaty.

ECR 349, [1985] 1 CMLR 453. The costs of checks carried out pursuant to mandatory obligations imposed by international conventions to which all the Member States are party are treated in the same way: Case 89/76, *Commission* v. *Netherlands* [1977] ECR 1355.

9. In this instance these conditions are satisfied by the contested fee. In the first place it has not been contested that it does not exceed the real cost of the inspections in connection with which it is charged.

10. Moreover, all the Member States of transit and destination are required, under, *inter alia*, Article 2(1) of Directive 81/389/EEC . . . to carry out the veterinary inspections in question when the animals are brought into their territories, and therefore the inspections are obligatory and uniform for all the animals concerned in the Community.

11. Those inspections are prescribed by Directive 81/389/EEC, which establishes the measures necessary . . . for the protection of live animals during international transport, with a view to the protection of live animals, an objective which is pursued in the general interest of the Community and not a specific interest of individual states.

12. Finally, it appears in the preambles to the . . . directives that they are intended to harmonize the laws of the Member States regarding the protection of animals in international transport in order to eliminate technical barriers resulting from disparities in the national laws . . . In addition, failing such harmonization, each Member State was entitled to maintain or introduce, under the conditions laid down in Article 36 of the Treaty, measures restricting trade which were justified on grounds of the protection of the health and life of animals. It follows that the standardization of the inspections in question is such as to promote the free movement of goods.

13. The Commission has claimed, however, that the contested fee is to be regarded as a charge having equivalent effect to a customs duty because, in so far as fees of this type have not been harmonized, such harmonization, moreover, being unattainable in practice—their negative effect on the free movement of goods could not be compensated or, consequently, justified by the positive effects of the Community standardization of inspections.

14. In this respect, it should be noted that since the fee in question is intended solely as the financially and economically justified compensation for an obligation imposed in equal measure on all the Member States by Community law, it cannot be regarded as equivalent to a customs duty; nor, consequently, can it fall within the ambit of the prohibition laid down in Articles 9 and 12 of the Treaty.

15. The negative effects which such a fee may have on the free movement of goods in the Community can be eliminated only by virtue of Community provisions providing for the harmonization of fees, or imposing the obligation on the Member States to bear the costs entailed in the inspections or, finally, establishing that the costs in question are to be paid out of the Community budget.

While the fee exacted in this case was therefore accepted as legitimate under Community law, the conditions which the ECJ lays down in paragraph 8 are strict. As already noted fees levied pursuant to inspections which are permitted, but not demanded, by Community legislation will not be recoverable from traders, and the other conditions mentioned in paragraph 8 serve to limit further the circumstances in which state authorities can pass on the costs of inspections to private undertakings.

4. ARTICLES 95–99: DISCRIMINATORY TAX PROVISIONS

The preceding discussion has focused on Articles 9 to 17 of the Treaty and the way in which they are central to the establishment of a customs union. It is necessary now to shift our focus to the provisions on discriminatory taxes, to understand the importance of these Articles and the way in which they relate to those concerning customs duties and charges having an equivalent effect.

Article 95 is the central provision in this area. It has been directly effective since January 1 1962.[32]

> No Member State shall impose, directly or indirectly, on the products of other Member States any internal taxation of any kind in excess of that imposed directly or indirectly on similar domestic products.
>
> Furthermore, no Member State shall impose on the products of other Member States any internal taxation of such a nature as to afford indirect protection to other products.
>
> Member States shall, not later than at the beginning of the second stage, repeal or amend any provisions existing when this Treaty enters into force which conflict with the preceding rules.

(a) The Purpose of Article 95

The aim of Article 95 can be stated quite simply: it is to prevent the objectives of Articles 9 to 17 from being undermined by discriminatory internal taxation. This is easily explained. We have already seen that Articles 9 to 17 are designed to prevent financial measures, whether in the form of customs duties or charges equivalent thereto, from impeding the free flow of goods. While national measures which seek to levy charges etc. at the border do not, as we have seen, have to be protectionist to be caught by Articles 9 to 17 they often are. The Treaty therefore outlaws such measures, whatever legal form they assume, when they are imposed as a result of a product *crossing a frontier*. These provisions would, however, be to little avail if it were open to a state to prejudice foreign products once they were *inside* its own territory by levying discriminatory taxes, thereby disadvantaging those imported products which were in competition with domestic goods. Article 95 is designed to prevent this from happening and this has been recognized by the ECJ.[33]

[32] Case 57/65, *Alfons Lütticke GmbH* v. *Hauptzollamt Saarlouis* [1966] ECR 205; Case 28/67, *Mölkerei-Zentrale Westfalen/Lippe GmbH* v. *Hauptzollamt Paderborn* [1968] ECR 143, [1968] CMLR 187; Case 74/76, *Ianelli & Volpi* v. *Meroni* [1977] ECR 557.

[33] Cases 2 and 3/62, *Commission* v. *Belgium and Luxembourg* [1962] ECR 425, 431; Case 252/86, *Gabriel Bergandi v. Directeur Général des Impôts* [1988] ECR 1343, 1374.

(b) Article 95(1): Direct Discrimination

Article 95(1) does not stipulate that a Member State must adopt any particular regime of internal taxation. It only requires that whatever system is chosen should be applied without discrimination to similar imported products.

Thus in *Commission* v. *Italy*[34] the Italian Government charged lower taxes on regenerated oil than on ordinary oil. The policy was motivated by ecological considerations, but imported regenerated oil did not benefit from the same advantage. In its defence Italy argued that it was not possible to determine whether imported oil was regenerated or not. This argument was rejected by the ECJ which held that it was for the importers to show that their oil came within the relevant category, subject to reasonable standards of proof, and that a certificate from the state of export could be employed to identify the nature of the oil. Similarly in the *Hansen* case[35] the ECJ insisted that a German rule making tax relief available to spirits made from fruit by small businesses and collective farms must be equally applicable to spirits which were in the same category coming from elsewhere in the Community.[36]

The rules relating to non-discrimination with respect to the payment of taxes will also be broken if the procedure for collection of the tax treats domestic goods and those which come from another Member State unequally. This is demonstrated by *Commission* v. *Ireland*.[37] In this case, although the tax itself applied to all goods irrespective of origin, domestic producers were treated more leniently as regards payment, being allowed a number of weeks before payment was actually demanded, whereas importers had to pay the duty directly on importation.

(c) Article 95(1): Indirect Discrimination

The discussion thus far has focused on cases of direct discrimination under Article 95(1). The measures in question explicitly treated domestic goods and imports differently to the detriment of the latter. It is, however, clear that indirect discrimination may equally be caught by this Article. There may well be tax rules which do not on their face differentiate between the tax liability of goods based on the country of origin, but which none the less do place a greater burden on commodities coming from another Member State. The *Humblot* case provides a clear example of this.

Case 112/84, Humblot v. Directeur des Services Fiscaux [1985] ECR 1367, [1986] 2 CMLR 338

French law imposed an annual car tax. The criterion for the amount of tax to be paid was the power rating of the car. Below a 16CV rating the tax increased

[34] Case 21/79, [1980] ECR 1, [1980] 2 CMLR 613.

[35] Case 148/77, *H. Hansen* v. *Hauptzollamt Flensburg* [1978] ECR 1787, [1979] 1 CMLR 604.

[36] See also Case 196/85, *Commission* v. *France* [1987] ECR 1597, [1988] 2 CMLR 851.

[37] Case 55/79, [1980] ECR 481, [1980] 1 CMLR 734.

gradually to a maximum of 1,100 francs. For cars above 16CV in power there was a flat rate of 5,000 francs. There was no French car which was rated above 16CV, and therefore the higher charge was borne only by those who had imported cars. Humblot was charged the 5,000 francs on a 36CV imported vehicle, and argued that this tax violated Article 95.

THE ECJ

12. It is appropriate in the first place to stress that as Community law stands at present the Member States are at liberty to subject products such as cars to a system of road tax which increases progressively in amount depending on an objective criterion, such as the power rating for tax purposes, which may be determined in various ways.

13. Such a system of domestic taxation is, however, compatible with Article 95 only in so far as it is free from any discriminatory or protective effect.

14. That is not true of a system like the one at issue in the main proceedings. Under that system there are two distinct taxes: a differential tax which increases progressively and is charged on cars not exceeding a given power rating for tax purposes and a fixed tax on cars exceeding that rating which is almost five times as high as the highest rate of the differential tax. Although the system embodies no formal distinction based on the origin of the products it manifestly exhibits discriminatory or protective features contrary to Article 95, since the power rating determining liability to the special tax has been fixed at a level such that only imported cars, in particular from other Member States, are subject to the special tax whereas all cars of domestic manufacture are liable to the distinctly more advantageous differential tax.

15. In the absence of considerations relating to the amount of the special tax, consumers seeking comparable cars as regards such matters as size, comfort, actual power, maintenance costs, durability, fuel consumption and price would naturally choose from among cars above and below the critical power rating laid down by French law. However, liability to the special tax entails a much larger increase in taxation than passing from one category of car to another in a system of progressive taxation embodying balanced differentials like the system on which the differential tax is based. The resultant additional taxation is liable to cancel out the advantages which certain cars imported from other Member States might have in consumers' eyes over comparable cars of domestic manufacture, particularly since the special tax continues to be payable for several years. In that respect the special tax reduces the amount of competition to which cars of domestic manufacture are subject and hence is contrary to the principle of neutrality with which domestic taxation must comply.

16. In the light of the foregoing considerations the question raised by the national court for a preliminary ruling should be answered as follows: Article 95 of the EEC Treaty prohibits the charging on cars exceeding a given power rating for tax purposes of a special fixed tax the amount of which is several times the highest amount of the progressive tax payable on cars of less than the said power rating for tax purposes, where the only cars subject to the special tax are imported, in particular from other Member States.

The *Humblot* case provides a good example of the ECJ's determination to catch indirect as well as direct discrimination. The reasoning of the Court is cogent, demonstrating as it does the way in which such tax provisions can distort the competitive process in the car market. The French authorities duly revised the tax rules in the light of the Court's decision, but the new scheme was itself challenged and found to be in breach of Community law. Under this new regime the French authorities replaced the 5,000 franc tax for cars above 16CV with nine more specific tax bands the application of which was dependent on the power of the car. Although this scheme was less obviously discriminatory than that which had been condemned in *Humblot* it was still the case that the tax rate increased sharply above 16CV. This new tax system was therefore condemned in *Feldain*.[38]

(d) Article 95: National Autonomy and Fiscal Choices

While the Treaty will therefore stop indirect as well as direct discrimination under Article 95(1) it may be necessary to determine which species of partiality is in issue in any particular case. The reason for care in this respect is that while direct discrimination on the grounds of nationality cannot be justified, tax rules of a Member State which tend none the less to favour the national producers may be saved if there is some *objective justification* for the conduct complained of. This idea of objective justification is, as we shall see, one which recurs throughout many areas of Community substantive law, whether in relation to other Articles concerning free movement of goods, or those which regulate free movement of workers or competition policy.[39] The basic theme is that the Court will allow Treaty rules to be ameliorated by enabling the defence to plead that there was some objective policy reason, which is acceptable to the Community, to justify the state's action. In this way such Treaty Articles are prevented from becoming too harsh or draconian in their application. The *Chemial* case exemplifies this judicial approach.

Case 140/79, Chemial Farmaceutici v. DAF SpA
[1981] ECR 1, [1981] 3 CMLR 350[40]

Italy taxed synthetic ethyl alcohol more highly than ethyl alcohol obtained from fermentation. This was so even though the products could be used interchangeably. Italy was not a major producer of the synthetic product. The object behind the tax policy was to favour the manufacture of ethyl alcohol from agricultural products, and to restrain the processing into alcohol of ethylene, a petroleum derivative, in order to reserve that raw material for more important economic uses. The Court makes the following observations on this policy choice.

THE ECJ

13. . . . It accordingly constitutes a legitimate choice of economic policy to which effect is given by fiscal means. The implementation of that policy does not

[38] Case 433/85, *Feldain* v. *Directeur des Services Fiscaux* [1987] ECR 3536; Case 76/87, *Seguela* v. *Administration des Impôts* [1988] ECR 2397, [1989] 3 CMLR 225.

[39] See below, Chs. 15, 19.

[40] See also Case 46/80, *Vinal SpA* v. *Orbat SpA* [1981] ECR 77, [1981] 3 CMLR 524.

lead to any discrimination since although it results in discouraging imports of synthetic alcohol into Italy, it also has the consequence of hampering the development in Italy itself of production of alcohol from ethylene, that production being technically perfectly feasible.

14. As the Court has stated on many occasions . . . in its present stage of development Community law does not restrict the freedom of each Member State to lay down tax arrangements which differentiate between certain products on the basis of objective criteria, such as the nature of the raw materials used or the production process employed. Such differentiation is compatible with Community law if it pursues economic policy objectives which are themselves compatible with the requirements of the Treaty and its secondary law and if the detailed rules are such as to avoid any form of discrimination, direct or indirect, in regard to imports from other Member States or any form of protection of competing domestic products.

15. Differential taxation such as that which exists in Italy for denatured synthetic alcohol on the one hand and denatured alcohol obtained by fermentation on the other satisfies these requirements. It appears in fact that that system of taxation pursues an objective of legitimate industrial policy in that it is such as to promote the distillation of agricultural products as against the manufacture of alcohol from petroleum derivatives. That choice does not conflict with the rules of Community law or the requirements of a policy decided within the framework of the Community.

16. The detailed provisions of the legislation at issue before the national court cannot be considered as discriminatory since, on the one hand, it is not disputed that imports from other Member States of alcohol by fermentation qualify for the same tax treatment as Italian alcohol produced by fermentation and, on the other hand, although the rate of tax prescribed for synthetic alcohol results in restraining the importation of synthetic alcohol originating in other Member States, it has an equivalent economic effect in the national territory in that it also hampers the establishment of profitable production of the same product in Italian industry.

It is true that the Court in the *Chemial* case predicates its acceptance of the Italian policy on the basis that it does not result in any discrimination, whether direct or indirect. Notwithstanding this the ECJ's reasoning bears testimony to its willingness to accept objective justifications where the national policy is acceptable from the Community's perspective, even if this benefits domestic traders more than importers. It is clear, as the Court points out, that the Italian policy would hamper an Italian producer which wished to make synthetic ethylene alcohol, but on the facts of the case there was little domestic production of this product, and in this sense the Italian tax rule hit importers harder than it did firms based in Italy itself. The same reasoning as in *Chemial* can be seen in other decisions.

Thus in *Commission* v. *France*[41] the Commission alleged that a French rule which taxed sweet wines produced in a traditional manner at a lower rate than liqueur wines was contrary to Article 95. The Court disagreed. It found that

[41] Case 196/85, [1987] ECR 1597, [1988] 2 CMLR 851.

there was no direct discrimination on grounds of origin or nationality. Sweet wines made in the natural manner tended to be produced in areas where the growing conditions were less than optimal; there would often be poor soil and low rainfall. The rationale for the French policy was to provide some fiscal incentives for production in these areas. The Court was willing to accept that this species of regional aid could constitute an objective justification which was legitimate under Article 95.

It would, moreover, be possible to imagine circumstances in which differential tax rates on cars would, the *Humblot* case notwithstanding, escape the prohibition of Article 95.

S. Weatherill and P. Beaumont, EC Law[42]

If a state is able to show that it taxes particular types of car at punitively high rates in order to encourage the use of more environmentally friendly models, which are given substantial tax concessions, then the Court would be prepared to hear submissions that the state's system is lawful even if it were shown that most of the models subjected to higher rates were imported. If the heavy burden felt especially by importers is seen to be purely incidental to the primary lawful purpose of environmental protection, then no breach of Article 95 has occurred: it is not unlawful to discriminate according to the capacity to pollute. Of course, this would not be so if the state exempted its own polluters from the regime; the system must be based on quality, not nationality.

That this is indeed so can be seen from the decision in *Commission* v. *Greece*.[43] The ECJ was once again faced with a national fiscal measure which imposed a progressively higher tax based on the cylinder capacity of the car. It held that this would not constitute a breach of Article 95 unless it was discriminatory, and this would not be the case unless it both discouraged customers from buying highly taxed imported cars and encouraged them to buy domestic cars instead. The mere fact that all cars in the highest tax bracket were imported was not sufficient to establish a violation of Article 95. EC law did not therefore prohibit the use of tax policy to attain social ends, provided that the tax was based on an objective criterion, was not discriminatory, and did not have a protective effect.

(e) The Relationship between Article 95(1) and 95(2)

Article 95(1) prohibits the imposition of internal taxes on products from other Member States which are in excess of those levied on *similar* domestic products. Thus once the two relevant products are judged to be similar then Article 95(1) bites, with the consequence that excessive taxes levied on the imported goods are banned.

[42] *EC Law* (Penguin, 1993), 346.
[43] Case C–132/88, [1990] ECR I–1567, [1991] 3 CMLR 1.

The dividing line between Article 95(1) and 95(2) may be problematic since it will obviously be a contestable issue whether goods are deemed to be similar or not. This issue will be addressed below. The object of Article 95(2) is, however, to deal with the state which applies differential tax rates to products which need not be similar in the sense connoted by Article 95(1). Article 95(2) is designed to catch national tax provisions which apply unequal tax ratings to goods which may not be strictly similar, but which may nonetheless be in competition with each other. The object is to prevent these differential tax ratings from affording indirect protection to the domestic goods. An example will serve to make this idea clearer. Wine and beer may not be adjudged to be similar goods as such, but there may, notwithstanding this fact, be a degree of competition between them. Economists term this relationship cross-elasticity of demand. As the price of one product rises in relation to another, so consumers will to some extent switch their consumption to the product which retains the lower price. How much consumer demand will switch to the lower-priced goods will depend upon a number of factors which go to determine how high or low the cross-elasticity of demand is between the two commodities. These factors will include the extent of the price difference between the two products, and the degree to which consumers perceive them to be interchangeable. Thus, if a state which produces little wine but much beer chooses to tax the former at a considerably higher rate than the latter, then it is clear that wine sellers will be relatively disadvantaged and beer producers afforded a measure of indirect protection. Article 95(2) is designed to catch such situations. This relationship between Articles 95(1) and (2) is brought out in the following case:

Case 168/78, Commission v. France
[1980] ECR 347, [1981] 2 CMLR 631

France had higher tax rates for spirits which were based on grain such as whisky, rum, gin, and vodka, than those which were based on wine or fruit, such as cognac, calvados, and armagnac. France produced very little of the former category of drinks, but was a major producer of fruit-based spirits. The Commission brought an Article 169 action alleging that the French tax regime violated Article 95. The ECJ began by emphasizing the connection between Article 95 and Articles 9 to 17: Article 95 was to supplement the provisions on customs duties and charges by prohibiting internal taxation which discriminated against imported products. It continued as follows.

THE ECJ

5. The first paragraph of Article 95, which is based on a comparison of the tax burdens imposed on domestic products and on imported products which may be classified as 'similar', is the basic rule in this respect. This provision, as the Court has had occasion to emphasize in its judgment . . . in Case 148/77, *H. Hansen* v. *Haupzollamt Flensburg* [1978] ECR 1787, must be interpreted widely so as to cover all taxation procedures which conflict with the principle of the equality of treatment of domestic products and imported products; it is therefore necessary to

interpret the concept of 'similar products' with sufficient flexibility. The Court specified in the judgment . . . in the *Rewe* case (Case 45/75 [1976] ECR 181) that it is necessary to consider as similar products those which 'have similar characteristics and meet the same needs from the point of view of consumers'. It is therefore necessary to determine the scope of the first paragraph of Article 95 on the basis not of the criterion of the strictly identical nature of the products but on that of their similar and comparable use.

6. The function of the second paragraph of Article 95 is to cover, in addition, all forms of indirect tax protection in the case of products which, without being similar within the meaning of the first paragraph, are nevertheless in competition, even partial, indirect or potential, with certain products of the importing country. The Court has already emphasized certain aspects of that provision in . . . Case 27/77, *Firma Fink-Frucht GmbH* v. *Hauptzollamt München-Landsbergerstrasse* [1978] ECR 223, in which it stated that for the purposes of the application of the first paragraph of Article 95 it is sufficient for the imported product to be in competition with the protected domestic production by reason of one of several economic uses to which it may be put, even though the condition of similarity for the purposes of the first paragraph of Article 95 is not fulfilled.

7. Whilst the criterion indicated in the first paragraph of Article 95 consists in the comparison of tax burdens, whether in terms of the rate, the mode of assessment or other detailed rules for the application thereof, in view of the difficulty of making sufficiently precise comparisons between the products in question, the second paragraph of that Article is based upon a more general criterion, in other words the protective nature of the system of internal taxation.

(f) Article 95(1) and (2): The Determination of Similarity

It is clear from the preceding discussion that the first step for the ECJ is therefore to determine whether the relevant products are similar. If they are then Article 95(1) applies; if they are not then the tax rules might still be caught by Article 95(2). This issue has arisen in a number of cases. As might be predicted the state authorities who are seeking to defend their tax will seek to argue that the two products are sufficiently dissimilar to render Article 95(1) inapplicable; while the Commission or the private party bringing the action will contend that the two commodities are sufficiently similar for Article 95(1) to bite.

In one of its relatively early judgments the ECJ held that products would be regarded as similar if they came within the same tax classification.[44]

However, in some instances the response of the ECJ has been to condemn the tax without too detailed an analysis of whether this is because of Article 95(1) or (2). This approach is particularly apparent in the early 'spirits cases' in which the Commission brought a number of Article 169 actions against Member States, alleging that their tax rules on spirits infringed Article 95. The action in *Commission* v. *France*, discussed above, was one such case.[45] The

[44] Case 27/67, *Fink-Frucht GmbH* v. *Hauptzollamt München-Landsbergerstrasse* [1968] ECR 327.

[45] See also Case 169/78, *Commission* v. *Italy* [1980] ECR 385; Case 171/78, *Commission* v. *Denmark* [1980] ECR 447.

reason the ECJ did not trouble unduly whether the condemnation should be based on Article 95(1) or (2) is apparent in the further extract from this judgment:

Case 168/78, Commission v. France
[1980] ECR 347, [1981] 2 CMLR 631

The facts have been set out above. The Commission argued that all spirits constituted a single market. France responded by contending that they should be broken down into a number of more specific markets, depending on their composition, physical characteristics and consumer usages. The ECJ, having considered the characteristics of the spirits, decided, on the one hand, that they possessed certain generic features (such as high alcohol content); and on the other hand, that they were made from differing materials, and were consumed in different ways.

THE ECJ

12. Two conclusions follow from this analysis of the market in spirits. First, there is, in the case of spirits considered as a whole, an indeterminate number of beverages which must be classified as 'similar products' within the meaning of the first paragraph of Article 95, although it may be difficult to decide this in specific cases, in view of the nature of the factors implied by distinguishing criteria such as flavour and consumer habits. Secondly, even in cases in which it is impossible to recognize a sufficient degree of similarity between the products concerned, there are nevertheless, in the case of all spirits, common characteristics which are sufficiently pronounced to accept that in all cases there is at least partial or potential competition. It follows that the application of the second paragraph of Article 95 may come into consideration in cases in which the relationship of similarity between the specific varieties of spirits remains doubtful or contested.

13. It appears from the foregoing that Article 95, taken as a whole, may apply without distinction to all the products concerned. It is sufficient therefore to examine whether the application of a given national tax system is discriminatory or, as the case may be, protective, in other words whether there is a difference in the rate or the detailed rules for levying the tax and whether that difference is likely to favour a given national production.

[*The Court then considered various arguments adduced by the French authorities which were designed to show that the spirits in question differed in terms of taste, use, and the like.*]

39. After considering all these factors the Court deems it unnecessary for the purposes of solving this dispute to give a ruling on the question whether or not the spiritous beverages concerned are wholly or partially similar products within the meaning of the first paragraph of Article 95 when it is impossible reasonably to contest that without exception they are in at least partial competition with the domestic products to which the application refers and that it is impossible to deny the protective nature of the French tax system within the second paragraph of Article 95.

40. In fact, as indicated above, spirits obtained from cereals have, as products obtained from distillation, sufficient characteristics in common with other spirits to constitute at least in certain circumstances an alternative choice for consumers . . .

41. As the competitive and substitution relationships between the beverages in question are such, the protective nature of the tax system criticized by the Commission is clear. A characteristic of that system is in fact that an essential part of domestic production, . . . spirits obtained from wine and fruit, come within the most favourable tax category whereas at least two types of product, almost all of which are imported from other Member States, are subject to higher taxation under the 'manufacturing tax'.

What these early 'spirits' cases demonstrate is that the Court will not be overly concerned whether a case is characterized as relating to Article 95(1) or 95(2) if, on the one hand, the nature of the products renders any such classification difficult (paragraph 12 above); and if, on the other hand, the Court feels sure that the tax in question should be condemned whether the goods are classified as similar or not, because they are, in any event, in competition to some degree and the tax is protective (paragraph 39 above).

While one can understand the reasons for this judicial stance it is not without problems. The most important consequence of 'globalizing'[46] Article 95(1) and (2) in this manner is that it 'obscures the proper response of the infringing state'[47] in the following sense. A breach of Article 95(1) means that the offending state has to equalize the taxes which it imposes on domestic and imported goods. However, if there is a finding that Article 95(2) has been violated then it is incumbent on the state to remove the protective effect, but this may not necessitate equalization of the tax burdens on the respective goods. A second difficulty with the globalizing approach is that it will obviously be less convincing the greater is the difference between the goods which have been subject to the distinct tax liabilities.

It is for these reasons that later courts which have been faced with the need to adjudicate on the line between Article 95(1) and (2) have been more careful to determine whether the analysis should proceed under one provision or the other. This is exemplified by the ECJ's approach in *John Walker* v. *Ministeriet for Skatter*.[48] In that case the issue was whether liqueur fruit wine was similar to whisky for the purposes of Article 95(1) of the Treaty. The ECJ analysed the objective characteristics of the products, including their respective alcoholic contents and methods of manufacture, as well as consumer perceptions of the nature of the product. On the basis of these criteria the Court decided that the goods were not similar for the purposes of Article 95(1): they did not possess the same alcohol content, nor was the process of manufacture the same, since whisky was produced by distillation rather than fermentation. Any further scrutiny of the tax would therefore have to take place within the confines of Article 95(2).[49] The same approach can be perceived in

[46] A. Easson, 'Fiscal Discrimination: New Perspectives on Art. 95 of the EEC Treaty' (1981) 18 CMLRev. 521, 535.

[47] Weatherill and Beaumont, n. 42 above, 354.

[48] Case 243/84, [1986] ECR 875.

[49] Cf. Case 106/84, *Commission* v. *Denmark* [1986] ECR 833.

Commission v. *Italy*.[50] In that case the Commission brought an action against Italy claiming that its consumption tax on fruit was discriminatory under Article 95. Italy produced large amounts of fruit, such as apples, pears, peaches, plums, and oranges, but almost no bananas which were imported from France. Italy imposed a consumption tax on bananas which amounted to almost half the import price; other fruit were not subject to the tax. The Court began its analysis by considering whether bananas and other fruit were similar for the purposes of Article 95(1). It found that they were not, taking account of the objective characteristics of the products, including their organoleptic properties and the extent to which they could satisfy the same consumer need.[51] Any further examination of the Italian tax should, said the Court proceed under Article 95(2).

(g) Article 95(2): The Determination of Protective Effect

One of the original 'spirits' cases brought by the Commission was against the United Kingdom for discriminatory taxation of wine with respect to beer. This was clearly a more difficult case than the others within this category, since there is undoubtedly a greater difference between wine and beer than there is between two spirits. It is for this reason that the ECJ initially declined to rule that the United Kingdom provisions were in breach of Article 95, and required further information as to the nature of the competitive relationship between the two products. Its judgment was finally delivered some years later, and provides insights in to the way in which the Court approaches the difficult adjudicatory problems presented by Article 95(2):

Case 170/78, Commission v. United Kingdom
[1983] ECR 2265, [1983] 3 CMLR 512

The United Kingdom levied an excise tax on certain wines which was roughly five times that which was levied on beer. The tax on wine represented about 38 per cent of the sale price of the product, as compared to the tax on beer which was 25 per cent of the product's price. As is well known, the United Kingdom produces considerable amounts of beer, but very little wine. The Commission brought an Article 169 action, claiming that the differential United Kingdom excise tax was in breach of Article 95.

THE ECJ

8. As regards the question of competition between wine and beer, the Court considered that, to a certain extent at least, the two beverages in question were capable of meeting identical needs, so that it had to be acknowledged that there was a degree of substitution for one another. It pointed out that, for the purpose of measuring the possible degree of substitution, attention should not be confined

[50] Case 184/85, [1987] ECR 2013.

[51] Bananas do not have the same water content as other fruit and therefore their thirst-quenching qualities are not the same; and bananas were perceived to have a nutritional value in excess of other fruit: *ibid.*, para. 10.

to consumer habits in a Member State or in a given region. Those habits, which were essentially variable in time and space, could not be considered to be immutable; the tax policy of a Member State must not therefore crystallize given consumer habits so as to consolidate an advantage acquired by national industries concerned to respond to them.

9. The Court nonetheless recognized that, in view of the substantial differences between wine and beer, it was difficult to compare the manufacturing processes and the natural properties of those beverages, as the Government of the United Kingdom had rightly observed. For that reason, the Court requested the parties to provide additional information with a view to dispelling the doubts which existed concerning the nature of the competitive relationship between the two products.

. . .

11. The Italian Government contended in that connection that it was inappropriate to compare beer with wines of average alcoholic strength or, *a fortiori*, with wines of greater alcoholic strength. In its opinion, it was the lightest wines with an alcoholic strength in the region of 9, that is to say the most popular and cheapest wines, which were genuinely in competition with beer. It therefore took the view that those wines should be chosen for purposes of comparison where it was a question of measuring the incidence of taxation on the basis of either alcoholic strength or the price of the products.

12. The Court considers that observation by the Italian Government to be pertinent. In view of the substantial differences in the quality and, therefore, in the price of wines, the decisive competitive relationship between beer, a popular and widely consumed beverage, and wine must be established by reference to those wines which are the most accessible to the public at large, that is to say, generally speaking the lightest and cheapest varieties. Accordingly, that is the appropriate basis for making fiscal comparisons by reference to the alcoholic strength or to the price of the two beverages in question.

[*The Commission, Italy, and the United Kingdom differed as regards the criteria which should be used to determine whether the tax on the two products was discriminatory. The Commission argued that assessment of the tax burden should be based on volume plus alcohol content; Italy contended that volume alone should be determinative; while the United Kingdom argued that the true basis of comparison was product price net of tax. The ECJ held that none of these tests was sufficient in itself, but that all three could provide 'significant information for the assessment of the contested tax system'.*]

19. It is not disputed that comparison of the taxation of beer and wine by reference to the volume of the two beverages reveals that wine is taxed more heavily than beer in both relative and absolute terms. Not only was the taxation of wine increased substantially in relation to the taxation of beer when the United Kingdom replaced customs duty with excise duty . . . , but it is also clear that during the years to which those proceedings relate, namely 1976 and 1977, the taxation of wine was, on average, five times higher, by reference to volume, than the taxation of beer; in other words wine was subject to an additional tax of 400% in round figures.

20. As regards the criterion for comparison based on alcoholic strength . . .

21. In the light of the indices which the Court has already accepted, it is clear that in the United Kingdom during the period in question wine bore a tax burden

which, by reference to alcoholic strength, was more than twice as heavy as that borne by beer, that is to say an additional tax burden of at least 100%.

22. As regards the criterion of the incidence of taxation on the price net of tax, the Court experienced considerable difficulty in forming an opinion, in view of the disparate nature of the information provided by the parties . . .

26. After considering the information provided by the parties, the Court has come to the conclusion that, if a comparison is made on the basis of those wines which are cheaper than the types of wine selected by the United Kingdom and of which several varieties are sold in significant quantities on the United Kingdom market, it becomes apparent that precisely those wines which, in view of their price, are most directly in competition with domestic beer production are subject to a considerably higher tax burden.

27. It is clear, therefore, following the detailed inquiry conducted by the Court—whatever criterion for comparison is used, there being no need to express a preference for one or the other—that the United Kingdom's tax system has the effect of subjecting wine imported from other Member States to an additional burden so as to afford protection to domestic beer production, inasmuch as beer production constitutes the most relevant reference criterion from the point of view of competition. Since such protection is most marked in the case of the most popular wines, the effect of the United Kingdom tax system is to stamp wine with the hallmarks of a luxury product which, in view of the tax burden which it bears, can scarcely constitute in the eyes of the consumer a genuine alternative to the typically produced domestic beverage.

28. It follows from the foregoing considerations that, by levying excise duty on still light wines made from fresh grapes at a higher rate, in relative terms, than on beer, the United Kingdom has failed to fulfil its obligations under the second paragraph of Article 95 of the EEC Treaty.

The decision in the United Kingdom *Wine/Beer* case throws interesting light on the Court's methodology when adjudicating on Article 95(2). Its judgment proceeds in two stages.

At the first stage the ECJ is concerned to establish that there is some competitive relationship between the two products in order to render Article 95(2) applicable at all (paragraphs 8 to 12). In determining the existence of this relationship the Court will take account of the extent to which the goods are substitutable for each other. However, as the ECJ notes in paragraph 8 of its judgment, the degree to which consumers currently perceive the two products to be substitutable will not be regarded as fixed for all time. This is in part because consumer preferences are not immutable and in part because the very shape of those preferences will themselves be affected by, *inter alia*, the relative tax rates of the two products. If the varying taxes levied on the commodities serve to place them artificially within separate categories in consumers' eyes, this will correspondingly reduce the significance of the extent to which the buying public currently perceives the products to be substitutable. It is this which the Court has in mind when castigating the United Kingdom tax policy for stamping wine with the hallmark of being a luxury product which is in a different category from beer (paragraph 27). This part of the ECJ's judgment also attests to the importance of accurately defining the nature of the two allegedly competing products. It would, as the Court recognized, not have been plausible to suggest any meaningful competitive association between beer and expensive, quality wine. Hence the Court's acceptance of the Italian Government's contention that the real comparison was between beer and the cheaper end of the wine market.

Having established that there is some competitive relationship between the respective goods, the Court then moves on to determine whether the tax system was in fact protective of beer. Its judgment on this aspect of the case demonstrates its willingness to listen to and apply varying criteria suggested by the parties in order to decide whether a protective effect has been established or not. It is readily apparent that the criteria which were used by the Court in this case may or may not be of relevance when dealing with two different products. On the facts of the actual dispute it is, however, difficult to contest the conclusion that the United Kingdom tax was indeed discriminatory. In circumstances where the disparity in tax rates between the two products is less dramatic than that between wine and beer, more finely tuned analysis may well be required to determine whether there is any protective effect. Thus it may, for example, be necessary to determine the degree of cross-elasticity between the two products. If this is low, then only a 'large difference in tax burdens will have a protective tendency'.[52] Similarly, if the level of tax is low with respect to the final selling price of the goods, then it will take a very significant tax differential to have any protective impact.[53]

The same two stages can be perceived in other ECJ decisions under Article 95(2). Thus in *Commission* v. *Italy*[54] the ECJ proceeded to consider whether the Italian consumption tax imposed on bananas was protective or not. It began by noting that, although bananas and other fruit were not similar, they were in partial competition, since bananas did afford consumers some further choice in the fruit market. This was, however, only the case with respect to fresh and not dried bananas, since there was no competitive relation between the latter and table fruit. Having established the existence of some form of competition between the two products, the Court proceeded to the second stage of deciding whether the Italian tax had a protective effect. It found that it did. The imposition of a consumption tax which was equivalent to half the import price of bananas, while no such tax applied at all to most Italian table fruit, was clear evidence of protectionism.

The existence of a tax differential between a domestic and an imported product will not, however, always suffice to establish protectionism for the purposes of Article 95(2). In *Commission* v. *Belgium*[55] it was held that a 6 per cent difference in the tax levied on beer, which was a domestic product, and wine, which was largely imported, with the latter being taxed at a higher rate, was not sufficient to demonstrate a protective effect under Article 95(2). This

[52] A. Easson, n. 46 above, 539. [53] *Ibid.*

[54] Case 184/85, n. 50 above, paras. 11–15.

[55] Case 356/85, [1987] ECR 3299, [1988] 3 CMLR 277.

was principally because the cost of the two products differed substantially and the Court concluded that the relatively minor difference in the tax rates would not serve to protect the Belgian beer producers.

5. THE BOUNDARY BETWEEN ARTICLES 9–17 AND 95–99

The relationship between Articles 9 to 17 and Articles 95 to 99 has been touched on in the preceding analysis. It is now time to consider this issue in a little more detail.

The general principle is that the two sets of Articles are mutually exclusive.[56] They both concern the imposition of fiscal charges by the state. Articles 9 to 17 bite on those duties or charges which are levied as a result of goods crossing a border; the duty or charge is exacted at the time of or on account of the importation and is borne specifically by the imported product to the exclusion of similar domestic products.[57] Articles 95 to 99, by way of contrast, are designed to catch fiscal policy which is internal to the state, in the sense of preventing discrimination against goods from other Member States once they have come into the territory of one particular country of the Community. As might be expected the Court has construed both sets of provisions so as to ensure that there is no gap between them.

The decision on which set of Treaty Articles is at stake is however of importance, since the result of this characterization can be of significance for the legal test which is applied.[58] If a state fiscal measure is held to be caught by Article 12 then it will be unlawful. This reflects the importance of breaking down trade barriers. Customs duties or charges are the quintessential barriers to the establishment of a customs union and hence the Treaty's insistence that they should be removed. If, by way of contrast, a fiscal measure falls within Article 95 then the obligation on the state is different. The existence of taxation levels which are set by the state is not unlawful under the Treaty, and thus the inquiry will be whether the tax discriminates against the importer under Article 95(1) or has a protective effect under Article 95(2).

In most circumstances there will be little difficulty in determining whether the issue should fall under Article 12 or under Article 95. There are, however, certain fact patterns which present more difficulty. Three are worthy of mention here.

The first type of case which may present problems of characterization is that

[56] Case 10/65, *Deutschmann* v. *Federal Republic of Germany* [1965] ECR 469; Case 57/65, n. 32 above; Case 105/76, *Interzuccheri SpA* v. *Ditta Rezzano e Cavassa* [1977] ECR 1029.

[57] Case 193/85, *Cooperative Co-Frutta Srl* v. *Amministrazione delle Finanze dello Stato* [1987] ECR 2085, para. 8.

[58] Case 105/76, n. 56 above, para. 9.

in which a state imposes a levy on an importer. Now such a case would normally be decided on the basis of Article 12, the levy would be deemed to be a CEE, and the state would be condemned unless it could show that the levy was consideration for a service which it had given to the importer or that it was imposed pursuant to mandatory requirements of Community law.[59] Attempts to argue that the levy should be considered under Article 95 instead, because domestic producers also had to pay, have not been notably successful, as the *Bresciani* case discussed earlier demonstrates.[60] In exceptional circumstances the Court may, however, decide that although the charge or levy is taken at the border it is not to be characterized as a CEE within Article 12, but as a tax the legality of which will be tested under Article 95. In *Denkavit*[61] the applicant was an importer of feedingstuffs from Holland into Denmark. Danish law required, *inter alia*, that the importer obtain an authorization from the Ministry of Agriculture and charged an annual levy to meet the costs of checking samples of the goods. The ECJ held that the requirement of an authorization was caught by Article 30 of the Treaty,[62] but that it could be justified under Article 36.[63] The Court then proceeded to the question whether the levy was itself lawful. This levy was imposed on all those engaged in the feedingstuffs trade, whether importers or domestic producers. But should the levy be considered under Articles 9 and 12 or under Article 95?[64]

> the Court has consistently held that the prohibition laid down in Article 9 of the Treaty . . . covers any charge levied on the occasion or by reason of importation specifically affecting an imported product to the exclusion of a similar domestic product. Such a charge however does not fall within that classification if, as in the present case, it relates to a general system of internal dues applied systematically and in accordance with the same criteria to domestic products and imported products alike, in which case it does not come within the scope of Article 9 but within that of Article 95 of the Treaty.

The second type of case in which there can be boundary line problems between Articles 12 and 95 is that in which the importing state does not make the imported product, but imposes a tax on it none the less. Should this be considered to be a charge within Article 12 or a tax within Article 95? On the face of it one might have thought that the ECJ would choose the former characterization, since there are no similar domestic goods. This will not always be so as demonstrated by *Co-Frutta*:

[59] See above, 553–61.
[60] See above, 558–9.
[61] Case 29/87, *Dansk Denkavit ApS* v. *Danish Ministry of Agriculture* [1988] ECR 2965.
[62] As a measure having equivalent effect to a quantitative restriction, on which see below, Ch. 14.
[63] On the basis that although there was a Community dir. relevant to the case, which would normally render recourse to Art. 36 impossible, the dir. did not extend to the situation in the instant case. For the relationship between a Community dir. and the ability of states to use Art. 36 EC, see below, 608–10.
[64] *Denkavit*, n. 61 above, para. 33. See also Case C–130/93, *Lamaire NV* v. *Nationale Dienst voor Afzet van Land- en Tuinbouwprodukten (NDALTP)*, 7 July 1994.

Case 193/85, Cooperative Co-Frutta Srl v. Amministrazione delle Finanze dello Stato
[1987] ECR 2085

This was another case which arose from the imposition by Italy of a consumption tax on bananas even though no such tax was levied on other fruit produced in Italy. It will be remembered from the earlier discussion that Italy produced only a negligible number of bananas itself. This action was brought by a banana importer via Article 177 to test the legality of the tax. One of the initial questions which the Court addressed was whether the tax should be viewed as a CEE within Article 12 or as a tax to be assessed under Article 95.

THE ECJ

8. According to established case law of the Court, the prohibition laid down by Articles 9 and 12 of the Treaty in regard to charges having an equivalent effect covers any charge exacted at the time of or on account of importation which, being borne specifically by an imported product to the exclusion of the similar domestic product, has the result of altering the cost price of the imported product, thereby producing the same restrictive effect on the free movement of goods as a customs duty.

9. The essential feature of a charge having an effect equivalent to a customs duty which distinguishes it from an internal tax therefore resides in the fact that the former is borne solely by an imported product as such whilst the latter is borne both by imported and domestic products.

10. The Court has however recognized that even a charge which is borne by a product imported from another Member State, when there is no identical or similar domestic product, does not constitute a charge having equivalent effect but internal taxation within the meaning of Article 95 of the Treaty if it relates to a general system of internal dues applied systematically to categories of products in accordance with objective criteria irrespective of the origin of the products.

11. Those considerations demonstrate that even if it were necessary in some cases, for the purpose of classifying a charge borne by imported products, to equate extremely low domestic production with its non-existence, that would not mean that the levy in question would necessarily have to be regarded as a charge having an effect equivalent to a customs duty. In particular, that will not be so if the levy is part of a general system of internal dues applying systematically to categories of products according to the criteria indicated above.

12. A tax on consumption of the type at issue in the main proceedings does form part of a general system of internal dues. The 19 taxes on consumption are governed by common tax rules and are charged on categories of products irrespective of their origin in accordance with an objective criterion, namely the fact that the product falls into a specific category of goods. Some of those taxes are charged on products intended for human consumption, including the tax on the consumption of bananas. Whether those goods are produced at home or abroad does not seem to have a bearing on the rate, the basis of assessment or the manner in which the tax is levied. The revenue from those taxes is not earmarked for a specific purpose; it constitutes tax revenue identical to other tax revenue and, like it, helps to finance State expenditure generally in all sectors.

13. Consequently, the tax at issue must be regarded as being an integral part of

> a general system of internal dues within the meaning of Article 95 of the Treaty and its compatibility with Community law must be assessed on the basis of that Article rather than Articles 9 and 12 of the Treaty.

The reasoning of the ECJ makes good sense. If any charge imposed by a state on a product which it did not make at all, or only in negligible quantities, was to be classified as a CEE under Article 12 then two consequences would follow. The charge would be automatically unlawful.[65] And it would mean that the state of import could not tax goods which it did not produce itself, since any such tax would be condemned under Article 12. This draconian conclusion would have made little social, economic, or political sense and it is not therefore surprising that the Court should have avoided this result.[66] There may be perfectly good reasons why a state should choose to tax, for example, a luxury item even if there is no domestic production of this item. The criterion adopted by the ECJ provides a sensible and workable resolution of this problem. If the test propounded by the ECJ is met the charge will not necessarily be regarded as lawful; it will still fall to be assessed under Article 95 of the Treaty. In the instant case the tax was in fact held to be in breach of Article 95(2) for the same reasons as were given in the action brought against Italy by the Commission.[67]

The third type of case which can produce problems of classification arises when a state chooses to make a selective refund of a tax. The position would appear to be as follows. If the money derived from a tax flows into the national exchequer and is then used for the benefit of a particular domestic industry, the most appropriate line of challenge would be to use the Treaty provisions on state aid contained in Articles 92 to 94.[68] Classification problems as between Articles 12 and 95 arise when the money which has been refunded can be linked to that which has been levied pursuant to a specific tax. The correct classification will then depend upon whether the refund to the national producers wholly or partially offsets the tax. If the former, then the tax will be treated under Article 12, the rationale being that what in effect exists is a charge which is only being levied on the imported product. If, however, the refund is only partial the matter will fall to be assessed under Article 95, the rationale here being that the partial refund in effect means that there could be a discriminatory tax. Barents, summarizing the early case law,[69] finds that there are three conditions in order for a charge to be considered under Article 12 rather than Article 95:[70]

[65] Assuming of course that it could not be saved on the ground that it represented consideration for a service etc.

[66] See also Case 90/79, *Commission* v. *France* [1981] ECR 283.

[67] See above, 571–2.

[68] Cases C–78–83/90, *Compagnie Commerciale de l'Ouest* v. *Receveur Principal des Douanes de la Pallice Port* [1992] ECR I–1847, [1994] 2 CMLR 425.

[69] Case 77/76, *Fratelli Cuchi* v. *Avez* [1977] ECR 987; Case 94/74, *Industria Gomma Articoli Vari* v. *Ente Nazionale per la Cellulosa e per la Carta* [1975] ECR 699; Case 105/76, n. 56 above.

[70] N. 19 above, 430.

> Firstly, the charge must be destined exclusively for financing activities which very largely benefit the taxed domestic product; secondly, there must exist identity between the taxed product and the domestic product benefiting from the charge; and thirdly, the charges imposed on the domestic product must be completely compensated.

This approach is exemplified by the recent decision in *Scharbatke*.[71] In that case there was a challenge to mandatory contributions levied in Germany when slaughtered animals were presented for inspection. The contribution was applied under the same conditions to national and imported products, and the money was assigned to a marketing fund for agricultural, forestry, and food products. The ECJ held that the mandatory contribution constituted a parafiscal charge.[72] Where the resulting revenue benefited solely national products, so that the advantages accruing *wholly* offset the charge imposed on the products, then the charge would be regarded as a CEE within Article 12.[73] If the advantages which accrued only *partially* offset the charges imposed on national products, then the charge would constitute discriminatory internal taxation under Article 95.[74]

6. CONCLUSION

The original Rome Treaty left a considerable degree of autonomy to Member States in the fiscal field, albeit subject to the constraints imposed by Articles 9 to 17 and 95. Many of the problems concerning divergences between national taxation systems can only ever be fully resolved when harmonization occurs. It should, however, be noted that in this area as in many others there is often a link between judicial doctrine and legislative initiatives. The very fact that a challenged national tax policy will, according to the ECJ's decisions in *Chemial* and the *French Sweet Wines* case,[75] only be upheld if the Court accepts it in general terms and deems it to be compatible with the Treaty itself has paradoxical results as Lonbay notes:[76]

> The absence of harmonization in this field has, it seems, led to the ironical result whereby the Commission, abetted by the European Court, has managed to wield perhaps more influence over Member State tax policies, and thus their economic

[71] Case C–72/92, *H. Scharbatke GmbH* v. *Federal Republic of Germany*, [1993] ECR I–5509 See also Cases C–78–83/90, n. 68 above.

[72] The ECJ held that the charge which was levied might also constitute state aid under Art. 92.

[73] It is not entirely clear whether *Scharbatke* is intended to modify earlier cases which had held that in order for the charge to be regarded as a CEE within Art. 12 there must, *inter alia*, be a strict coincidence between the product which was being taxed and that which was receiving the benefit, Case 105/76, n. 56 above.

[74] See also Case 73/79, *Commission* v. *Italy* [1980] ECR 1533.

[75] See above, 565–7.

[76] (1989) 14 ELRev. 48, 50.

and social policies, than would be the case if the Council of Ministers could agree on a uniform tax regime.

There is little doubt that the decisions of the ECJ in this area have, as we have seen above, made a significant contribution to the effective realization of a single market. The Court's jurisprudence has consistently looked behind the form of a disputed measure to its substance, and the ECJ has interpreted the relevant Articles in the manner best designed to ensure that the Treaty objectives are achieved. It must, however, also be admitted that the cases do not always sit easily together. This should not come as a surprise, given the plethora of ways in which disputes about fiscal matters can arise, and given also the necessity for the Court to draw a line between the allowable limits of fiscal autonomy and the demands of the Treaty. The following extract demonstrates the nature of some of these difficulties. Easson discusses the ECJ's decisions in the spirits cases and in *Chemial*:

A. Easson, Fiscal Discrimination: New Perspectives on Article 95 of the EEC Treaty[77]

It was implicit, in all the 'Spirits' cases, that Article 95 may be infringed notwithstanding that the provisions in question are applied in an identical manner to imported products. In those cases, the fact that domestic production of the more heavily taxed products was minimal was taken to be an indication of the discriminatory nature of the tax systems, rather than the reverse. The Court moreover appeared to endorse the view, expressed by the Commission and Advocate General Reischl, that regard cannot be had only to the state of the national market in question and to local consumer habits, since these may be the result of the very fiscal discrimination which it ought to eliminate. Yet the Court (in *Chemial*) now seems to be saying that if the absence of domestic production of the more heavily taxed category is due to fiscal discrimination, rather than to some other factor such as climatic conditions or consumer preferences, Article 95 is not infringed!

To summarise, it appears that to distinguish, for fiscal purposes, between different categories of products, even though these may be similar or competing from the point of view of the consumer, is a legitimate exercise of national fiscal sovereignty. To do so with the *intention* of protecting domestic production is not. In the 'Spirits' cases, this intention was inferred from the state of the national markets in question: this the Court declined to do in the 'denatured alcohol' cases. That, it is suggested, is the real distinction between the two groups of cases. In reality, the issue is determined not simply by an analysis of market conditions and the respective proportions of domestic and imported products in the lower and higher-taxed categories, but rather by an attempt to evaluate the purpose of the discrimination in question. Though the result may be to tilt the balance in favour of national fiscal autonomy, this nevertheless is a potentially contentious role for the Court to play.

[77] (1981) 18 CMLRev. 521, 546, italics in the original.

7. FURTHER READING

BARENTS, R., 'Charges of Equivalent Effect to Customs Duties' (1978) 15 CMLRev. 415

—— 'Recent Case Law on the Prohibition of Fiscal Discrimination Under Article 95' (1986) 23 CMLRev. 641

DANUSSO, M., and DENTON, R., 'Does the European Court of Justice Look for a Protectionist Motive Under Article 95?' [1990] 1 LIEI 67

EASSON, A., 'The Spirits, Wine and Beer Judgments: A Legal Mickey Finn?' (1980) 5 ELRev. 318

—— 'Fiscal Discrimination: New Perspectives on Article 95 of the EEC Treaty' (1981) 18 CMLRev. 521

GRABITZ, E., and ZACKER, C., 'Scope for Action by the EC Member States for the Improvement of Environmental Protection Under EEC Law: The Example of Environmental Taxes and Subsidies' (1989) 26 CMLRev. 423

LONBAY, J., 'A Review of Recent Tax Cases' (1989) 14 E.L.Rev 48

SCHWARZE, J., 'The Member States' Discretionary Powers under the Tax Provisions of the EEC Treaty' in Schwarze, J. (ed.), *Discretionary Powers of the Member States in the Field of Economic Policies and their Limits under the EEC Treaty* (Nomos, Baden-Baden, 1988).

14

Free Movement of Goods: Quantitative Restrictions

1. INTRODUCTION

The discussion in the previous chapter focused on the limits placed by Community law on duties, taxes, and the like. This is, however, only part of the overall Community strategy for the building of an integrated Single Market. The free movement of goods within the Community has been profoundly affected by the Court's jurisprudence under Articles 30 to 36 of the Treaty. Article 30 is the central provision within this Chapter of the Treaty. It states that:

> Quantitative restrictions on imports and all measures having equivalent effect shall, without prejudice to the following provisions, be prohibited between Member States.

Article 34 contains similar provisions relating to exports, while Article 36 provides an exception for certain types of case in which a state is allowed to place restrictions on the movement of goods. Before examining the case law under this Chapter of the Treaty it may be helpful to understand some of the more general themes which underlie this area.

(a) *The Place and Importance of Articles 30–36*

Let us begin with the *way in which Articles 30 to 36 fit into the more general strategy concerning the free movement of goods*. Articles 9 to 29 lay the foundations for a customs union by providing for the elimination of customs duties between Member States and by establishing a Common Customs Tariff. If matters rested there free movement would be only imperfectly attained since it would still be open to states to place quotas on the amount of goods which could be imported, and to restrict the free flow of goods by measures which do not constitute quotas as such, but which have an equivalent effect. The object, then, of Articles 30 to 36 is to prevent Member States from engaging in either of these strategies.

This bare description of the interrelationship between the provisions on free movement of goods does not, however, serve to convey the *importance of Articles 30 to 36 in the process of achieving single market integration*. We have to press further in order to understand this. There are two reasons why the ECJ's construction of these Articles has had such a marked impact.

On the one hand, it has given a broad interpretation to the phrase 'measures having equivalent effect' to a quantitative restriction (MEQR).

On the other hand, it has held that Article 30 can be breached not only when there has been discrimination in the way in which a state treats its own goods and those coming from outside; it has also made it clear, in the famous *Cassis de Dijon* case,[1] that Article 30 can bite, subject to certain exceptions, when the same rule applies to both domestic goods and imports in circumstances where the relevant rule can inhibit the free flow of goods across borders within the Community. Discrimination is therefore a sufficient, but not necessary, condition for the invocation of Article 30. A moment's reflection will indicate why this step was of such significance. Many states will possess trade rules which apply to all goods of a certain kind wherever they are made. A rule may, for example, require a drink of a particular kind to possess a stipulated level of alcohol. This same drink may be made in a different country and have a lower level of alcohol. Yet if State *A* can prohibit the importation of the drink from State *B* because it does not comply with the rule on alcohol levels then trade between the states in this commodity will not occur. The fact that indistinctly applicable rules, that is rules which apply to all goods irrespective of their origin, can be caught by Article 30 constituted a major contribution by the ECJ to the attainment of a real single market for goods.

The ECJ's jurisprudence has not, however, been unproblematic. The decisions of the ECJ which have rendered Article 30 applicable to trade rules even where they do not discriminate between goods on the basis of country of origin have led to difficulties about the outer boundaries of this area of Community law. It has become difficult to determine where the reach of this branch of EC law 'stops'. We shall see in the course of the subsequent analysis that the ECJ itself has experienced problems in this respect and that it has recently taken the unusual step of explicitly going back on some of its own earlier case law.

Moreover, as will also become apparent in the following discussion, the impact of Article 30 will be to render inapplicable national regulatory measures on a particular subject. The relationship between the desire for integration, and the need for governmental regulation is brought out well by Wils:

W. P. J. Wils, The Search for the Rule in Article 30 EEC: Much Ado About Nothing?[2]

Article 30 is one of the Treaty articles concerning *the integration of national markets for goods*. This same purpose is served by the whole of Part I, Title I of the Treaty, and also, in part by Articles 100 and 100A.

[1] Case 120/78, *Rewe-Zentrale AG* v. *Bundesmonopolverwaltung für Branntwein* [1979] ECR 649, [1979] 3 CMLR 494.

[2] (1993) 18 ELRev. 475, 476–8, italics in the original.

Integration can best be looked at from the negative side. The Community's efforts to integrate national markets are basically attempts to limit the influence of national governments on production and consumption activities throughout the Community. The desire to limit the influence of national governments stems from economic as well as political concerns. National measures restrict people in their economic activities throughout the Community, often at the expense of common welfare. As national governments regulate according to the desires of their constituencies alone, many national measures contain some protectionist bias. But even in the absence of this problem, the mere existence of a geographical patchwork of different regulations may impose a substantial economic burden . . .

Although integration constitutes the specific concern of Article 30, it is only one among society's many objectives, with which it has to be reconciled. Given society's various objectives of efficiency and distributional justice, *a need for government regulation* is felt in many instances. This regulation will often have to be national regulation, either for practical reasons, Community regulation being unavailable, or for reasons of principle. Differences in societal preferences, or divergent natural or cultural characteristics may militate in favour of national regulation . . .

Partial integration is the pragmatic solution reconciling the desire for integration with the desire for government intervention, translated—for the reasons just mentioned—into a desire for national regulation. In the Community's partially integrated market, national governments can influence people's activities, but only to some limited extent.

Partial integration is inherently unstable, however. Over time, opinions on the desirable scope of integration (and thus, conversely, on the scope of national government) will fluctuate. Historically, the tendency has always been towards more integration, but at varying speeds. The current concern with 'subsidiarity' may herald a change of direction, although a shift to a lower gear may be as likely an outcome . . . National governments are allowed, and supposed, to influence people's activities, but only to a limited extent. There is thus a continuous need to identify and police the border between legitimate and illegitimate national regulation. Inevitably, some national government measures will overstep that boundary . . . Article 30 is the tool for *policing the borderline between legitimate and illegitimate national regulation.*

(b) The Attainment of a Single Market: The Interconnection between Judicial and Legislative Initiatives

There is, however, a more general and interesting story involved in this area of the law which can be missed if one concentrates solely on the case law of the Court. The Court's approach to this part of Community law sheds interesting light on the relationship between judicial and legislative means of attaining Community goals. One of the themes which we have stressed throughout this book is the need to see the links between the Community's institutional and substantive law, and also between the actions of the Court and other Community institutions. The case law on Articles 30 to 36 provides an excellent example of these connections.

The reasons are not hard to find. One way of dealing with trade rules which differ between Member States is for these rules to be harmonized through Commission legislative initiatives. Such initiatives have led to Community legislation in various areas. The process of such harmonization has, however, been slow. This was in part due to the difficulties which the Commission had in getting legislation through the Council in the period when the latter was proving less than perfectly co-operative, from the mid-1960s until the early 1980s;[3] it was in part due to the fact that the legislative process for the promulgation of such norms was more difficult prior to the introduction of Article 100A in the SEA; and it was in part simply a reflection of the problem of attaining agreement between twelve states on important technical issues.

The decision by the ECJ to make Article 30 applicable to such trade rules constituted an alternative means for bringing about the free flow of goods even in the absence of legislation which harmonized the relevant rules. As will be seen, the Court's approach was to hold that such rules could not hinder the free movement of goods, even in the absence of harmonization measures, unless they could be justified on certain specific grounds, such as consumer protection. The message was clear: attainment of this central part of Community policy was not to be held up indefinitely by the absence of harmonization legislation.

What is particularly interesting is the consequence of this reasoning by the ECJ. The relationship between Community institutions is seldom a one-dimensional process. Judicial reactions to a problem will often produce responses from other institutions which cause those other institutions to modify their own approach. We can see this process in action in this area. The Court's decisions on Article 30 were welcomed by the Commission, *and* it led the Commission to the view that harmonization through legislation was less necessary than hitherto. The Commission made it clear that its own scarce resources should be best directed towards achieving harmonization in respect of those rules which were still to be allowed under the *Cassis de Dijon* formula, on the grounds that, for example, they were necessary to protect consumers or safeguard public health. The judicial approach, therefore, caused the Commission to reorient its own legislative programme.

The implications of this interrelationship between Court and legislature do, however, go further, and affect the very nature of what we mean by the free movement of goods and harmonization. The approach of the ECJ in *Cassis de Dijon* leads to what has accurately been termed 'negative harmonization': indistinctly applicable rules will be rendered unenforceable when they hinder cross-border trade unless they come within one of the exceptions. Harmonization is essentially negative and deregulatory in the sense that the result is that national rules are held not to apply. This can be contrasted with 'positive harmonization' which results from the promulgation of Community legislative measures, stipulating which rules can apply across the Community

[3] See above, 12–14, 137–9.

as a whole. There are, as will be seen below, important consequences which flow from developing Community policy by these differing strategies.

These matters will be explored more fully in due course. Before doing so we must examine the Court's case law.

2. DIRECTIVE 70/50 AND *DASSONVILLE*

Article 30 will catch quantitative restrictions and all measures which have an equivalent effect (MEQR). The notion of a quantitative restriction was defined broadly in the *Geddo* case[4] to mean 'measures which amount to a total or partial restraint of, according to the circumstances, imports, exports or goods in transit'. MEQRs are more difficult to define, and will, by their very nature, be more varied. Both the Commission and the Court have taken a broad view of such measures.

Guidance on the Commission's view on this issue can be found in Directive 70/50. This Directive was only formally applicable during the Community's transitional period, but it continues to furnish some idea of the scope of MEQRs. The list of matters which can constitute an MEQR are specified in Article 2 and include:[5] minimum or maximum prices specified for imported products; less favourable prices for imported products; lowering the value of the imported product by reducing its intrinsic value or increasing its costs; payment conditions for imported products which differ from those for domestic products; conditions in respect of packaging, composition, identification, size, weight, etc. which only apply to imported goods or which are different and more difficult to satisfy than in the case of domestic goods; the giving of a preference to the purchase of domestic goods as opposed to imports, or otherwise hindering the purchase of imports; limiting publicity in respect of imported goods as compared with domestic products; prescribing stocking requirements which are different from and more difficult to satisfy than those which apply to domestic goods; and making it mandatory for importers of goods to have an agent in the territory of the importing state. Article 2, therefore, lists a number of ways in which the importing state can discriminate against goods coming from outside. It should be noted that, even as early as 1970, the Commission was thinking of the potential reach of Article 30 to indistinctly applicable rules, since Article 3 of the Directive, which will be considered below, regulates such rules to some degree.

The seminal judicial decision on the interpretation of MEQRs is to be found in *Dassonville*:

[4] Case 2/73, *Geddo* v. *Ente Nazionale Risi* [1973] ECR 865, [1974] 1 CMLR 13.
[5] Dir. 70/50, Art. 2(3).

Case 8/74, Procureur du Roi v. Dassonville [1974] ECR 837, [1974] 2 CMLR 436

Belgian law provided that goods bearing a designation of origin could only be imported if they were accompanied by a certificate from the government of the exporting country certifying their right to such a designation. Dassonville imported Scotch whisky into Belgium from France without being in possession of the requisite certificate from the British authorities. Such a certificate would have been very difficult to obtain in respect of goods which were already in free circulation in a third country, as in this case. Dassonville was prosecuted in Belgium and argued by way of defence that the Belgian rule constituted an MEQR.

THE ECJ

5. All trading rules enacted by Member States which are capable of hindering, directly or indirectly, actually or potentially, intra-Community trade are to be considered as measures having an effect equivalent to quantitative restrictions.

6. In the absence of a Community system guaranteeing for consumers the authenticity of a product's designation of origin, if a Member State takes measures to prevent unfair practices in this connection, it is however subject to the condition that these measures should be reasonable and that the means of proof required should not act as a hindrance to trade between Member States and should, in consequence, be accessible to all Community nationals.

7. Even without having to examine whether such measures are covered by Article 36, they must not, in any case, by virtue of the principle expressed in the second sentence of that Article, constitute a means of arbitrary discrimination or a disguised restriction on trade between Member States.

8. That may be the case with formalities, required by a Member State for the purpose of proving the origin of a product, which only direct importers are really in a position to satisfy without facing serious difficulties.

9. Consequently, the requirement by a Member State of a certificate of authenticity which is less easily obtainable by importers of an authentic product which has been put into free circulation in a regular manner in another Member State than by importers of the same product coming directly from the country of origin constitutes a measure equivalent to a quantitative restriction as prohibited by the Treaty.

Certain aspects of the ECJ's reasoning in *Dassonville* should be noted. It is clear from the definition in paragraph 5 that the crucial element in proving the existence of a MEQR is its *effect*: a discriminatory intent is not required. The ECJ signals that it will take a very broad view of measures which may hinder the free flow of goods within the Community. Indeed on its face this definition does not even require that the rules actually discriminate between domestic and imported goods. In this sense *Dassonville* sowed the seeds which bore fruit in the later *Cassis de Dijon* case where the ECJ formally decided that Article 30 could apply to rules which were not in themselves discriminatory.

Another aspect of *Dassonville* which is of importance is to be found in paragraph 6 of the judgment. Here the ECJ indicates that reasonable restraints may not be caught by the prohibition of Article 30. Herein lies the origin of the idea which has become known as the 'rule of reason'. The precise meaning of this concept will be examined more fully below.

In the discussion which directly follows we shall consider some examples of the breadth of Article 30 in cases involving discrimination.

3. DISCRIMINATORY BARRIERS TO TRADE

There are numerous examples of instances where the Court has struck down national rules which directly or indirectly discriminate between domestic and imported goods. These cases occur in a variety of areas.

(a) Import and Export Restrictions

One common scenario is where a state applies discriminatory rules in the form of import or export restrictions. The ECJ has always been particularly harsh on such measures. Thus import or export licences are caught by Article 30.[6] So, too, are provisions which subject imported goods to requirements which are not imposed on domestic products. This is exemplified by *Commission* v. *Italy*,[7] in which the ECJ held that procedures and data requirements for the registration of imported cars, making their registration longer, more complicated, and costly than that of domestic vehicles were prohibited by Article 30. While in *Rewe*[8] phyto-sanitary inspections on imports of plants were caught by Article 30 where no similar examination was made of domestic products. The same approach is apparent with respect to discriminatory export rules. Thus in *Bouhelier*[9] a French rule which imposed quality checks on watches for export, but not on those intended for the domestic market, was in breach of Article 34 of the Treaty.

(b) Promotion or Favouring of Domestic Products

Another form of discrimination which is caught by Article 30 is that in which a state promotes or favours domestic products to the detriment of competing imports. This can occur in a number of different ways.

The most obvious form which this type of discrimination can assume is where a *state engages in a campaign to promote the purchase of domestic as opposed to imported goods*. The 'Buy Irish' case provides a clear example of this:

[6] Cases 51–54/71, *International Fruit Company* v. *Produktschap voor Groenten en Fruit (No 2)* [1971] ECR 1107; Case 68/76, *Commission* v. *French Republic* [1977] ECR 515, [1977] 2 CMLR 161.

[7] Case 154/85, [1987] ECR 2717, [1988] 2 CMLR 951.

[8] Case 4/75, *Rewe-Zentralfinanz* v. *Landwirtschaftskammer* [1975] ECR 843, [1977] 1 CMLR 599.

[9] Case 53/76, *Procureur de la République Besancon* v. *Bouhelder* [1977] ECR 197, [1977] 1 CMLR 436.

Case 249/81, Commission v. Ireland [1982] ECR 4005, [1983] 2 CMLR 104

The Irish government sought to promote sales of Irish goods, the object being to achieve a switch of 3 per cent in consumer spending from imports to domestic products. To this end it adopted a number of measures including: an information service indicating to consumers which products were made in Ireland and where they could be obtained (the Shoplink Service); exhibition facilities for Irish goods; the encouragement of the use of the 'Buy Irish' symbol for goods made in Ireland; and the organization of a publicity campaign by the Irish Goods Council in favour of Irish products, designed to encourage consumers to buy Irish products. The first two of these activities were subsequently abandoned by the Irish Government, but the latter two strategies continued to be employed. The Commission brought Article 169 proceedings, alleging that the campaign was a MEQR. Ireland responded by arguing that it had never adopted 'measures' for the purpose of Article 30 and that any financial aid given to the Irish Goods Council should be judged in the light of Articles 92 to 93 and not Article 30. The members of the Irish Goods Council were appointed by an Irish Government minister and its activities were funded in proportions of about six to one by the Irish Government and private industry respectively.

THE ECJ

15. It is thus apparent that the Irish government appoints the members of the Management Committee of the Irish Goods Council, grants it public subsidies which cover the greater part of its expenses and, finally, defines the aims and the broad outline of the campaign conducted by that institution to promote the sale and purchase of Irish products. In the circumstances the Irish government cannot rely on the fact that the campaign was conducted by a private company in order to escape any liability it may have under the provisions of 104 the Treaty.

. . .

21. The Irish government maintains that the prohibition against measures having an effect equivalent to quantitative restrictions in Article 30 is concerned only with 'measures', that is to say, binding provisions emanating from a public authority. However, no such provision has been adopted by the Irish government, which has confined itself to giving moral support and financial aid to the activities pursued by the Irish industries.

22. The Irish government goes on the emphasise that the campaign has had no restrictive effect on imports since the proportion of Irish goods to all goods sold on the Irish market fell from 49.2% in 1977 to 43.4% in 1980.

23. The first observation to be made is that the campaign cannot be likened to advertising by private or public undertakings . . . to encourage people to buy goods produced by those undertakings. Regardless of the means used to implement it, the campaign is a reflection of the Irish government's considered intention to substitute domestic products for imported products on the Irish market and thereby to check the flow of imports from other Member States.

24. It must be remembered here that a representative of the Irish government stated when the campaign was launched that it was a carefully thought-out set of initiatives constituting an integrated programme for promoting domestic products; that the Irish Goods Council was set up at the initiative of the Irish government

a few months later; and that the task of implementing the integrated programme as it was envisaged by the government was entrusted, or left, to that Council.

25. Whilst it may be true that the two elements of the programme which have continued in effect, namely the advertising campaign and the use of the 'Guaranteed Irish' symbol, have not had any significant success in winning over the Irish market to domestic products, it is not possible to overlook the fact that, regardless of their efficacy, those two activities form part of a government programme which is designed to achieve the substitution of domestic products for imported products and is liable to affect the volume of trade between Member States.

. . .

27. In the circumstances the two activities in question amount to the establishment of a national practice, introduced by the Irish government and prosecuted with its assistance, the potential effect of which on imports from other Member States is comparable to that resulting from government measures of a binding nature.

28. Such a practice cannot escape the prohibition laid down by Article 30 of the Treaty solely because it is not based on decisions which are binding upon undertakings. Even measures adopted by the government of a Member State which do not have binding effect may be capable of influencing the conduct of traders and consumers in that State and thus of frustrating the aims of the Community as set out in Article 2 and enlarged upon in Article 3 of the Treaty.

29. That is the case where, as in this instance, such a restrictive practice represents the implementation of a programme defined by the government which affects the national economy as a whole and which is intended to check the flow of trade between Member States by encouraging the purchase of domestic products, by means of an advertising campaign on a national scale and the organization of special procedures applicable solely to domestic products, and where those activities are attributable as a whole to the government and are pursued in an organized fashion throughout the national territory.

30. Ireland has therefore failed to fulfil its obligations under the Treaty by organizing a campaign to promote the sale and purchase of Irish goods within its territory.

The ECJ's reasoning in this case provides an excellent example of its more general strategy under Article 30. Its whole approach is to look to substance, not form. This is manifested in the way in which it treats the involvement of the Irish government with the Irish Goods Council (paragraph 15); with the way in which it rebuts the Irish argument that only formally binding measures are caught by Article 30 (paragraphs 21 and 28); and in its rejection of the argument that, as the campaign appeared to have failed, therefore EC law should be unconcerned with it (paragraph 25).[10]

A second type of case in which Article 30 will bite is related to, but distinct from, the first. This where *a state has rules on the origin-marking of certain*

[10] It is of course the case that the campaign may have had some impact, since the diminution in sales of Irish goods might have been even greater had the campaign not been mounted.

goods. The intent of the ECJ to prohibit measures which favour domestic goods, or inhibit the penetration of the market by imports, is equally apparent in this type of case, even though the discriminatory effect on imports is more indirect.

Case 207/83, Commission v. United Kingdom
[1985] ECR 1201, [1985] 2 CMLR 259

The Commission brought an Article 169 action against the United Kingdom, arguing that United Kingdom legislation which required that certain goods should not be sold in retail markets unless they were marked with their country of origin was in breach of Article 30 as a MEQR. The United Kingdom argued that the legislation applied equally to imported and national products, and that this information was of importance to consumers since they regarded origin as an indication of the quality of the goods. The following extract relates to the first of these arguments.

THE ECJ

17. . . . it has to be recognised that the purpose of indications of origin or origin-marking is to enable consumers to distinguish between domestic and imported products and that this enables them to assert any prejudices which they may have against foreign products. As the Court has had occasion to emphasise in various contexts, the Treaty, by establishing a common market and progressively approximating the economic policies of the Member States, seeks to unite national markets in a single market having the characteristics of a domestic market. Within such a market, the origin-marking requirement not only makes the marketing in a Member State of goods produced in other Member States in the sectors in question more difficult; it also has the effect of slowing down economic interpenetration in the Community by handicapping the sale of goods produced as the result of a division of labour between Member States.

18. It follows from those considerations that the United Kingdom provisions in question are liable to have the effect of increasing the production costs of imported goods and making it more difficult to sell them on the United Kingdom market.[11]

Member State legislation which contains rules on origin-marking will normally only be acceptable if the origin implies a certain quality in the goods, that they were made from certain materials or by a particular form of manufacturing, or where the origin is indicative of a special place in the folklore or tradition of the region in question.[12] Thus in the 'Irish Souvenirs' case[13] the

[11] The ECJ also rejected the second argument advanced by the UK to the effect that origin-marking was related to consumer protection. The Court held that the origin-marking rules were only equally applicable to domestic and imported products as a matter of form: in reality they were intended to enable consumers to give preference to national goods, Case 207/83 above, para. 20.

[12] Case 12/74, *Commission* v. *Germany* [1975] ECR 181, [1975] 1 CMLR 340; Case 113/80, *Commission* v. *Ireland* [1981] ECR 1625, [1982] 1 CMLR 706.

[13] Case 113/80, n. 12 above, para. 15.

Court held that Irish legislation which prohibited the importation of certain souvenirs such as shamrocks, wolfhounds, etc. unless they had an indication of the country of origin, or the word 'foreign' attached to them, was a MEQR within Article 30. The origin-marking in this case did not come within the acceptable criteria mentioned above because the essential characteristic of the souvenirs was that they constituted a pictorial reminder of the place which had been visited; this did not mean that the souvenirs had to have been manufactured in the country of origin.

Not all measures which promote domestic goods will, however, be caught by the Treaty. The preceding decisions should be compared with the case which follows:

Case 222/82, Apple and Pear Development Council v. K. J. Lewis Ltd [1983] ECR 4083, [1984] 3 CMLR 733

The Apple and Pear Development Council was established in the United Kingdom by statutory instrument by the relevant minister. Membership was mandatory for most growers of fruit who paid a certain sum per hectare of land towards its running. The objects of the Council were, *inter alia*, to promote the marketing of the goods. It brought actions against certain fruit growers who had not paid the required sums. They resisted payment, claiming that its functions were contrary to the Treaty. The ECJ reiterated its judgment in the '*Buy Irish*' case, and then continued as follows.

THE ECJ

18. . . . such a body [as the Council] is under a duty not to engage in any advertising intended to discourage the purchase of products of other Member States or to disparage those products in the eyes of consumers. Nor must it advise consumers to purchase domestic products solely by reason of their national origin.

19. On the other hand, Article 30 does not prevent such a body from drawing attention, in its publicity, to the specific qualities of fruit grown in the Member State in question or from organising campaigns to promote the sale of certain varieties, mentioning their particular properties, even if those varieties are typical of national production.

The Court's clear intent to stamp firmly on national measures which favour domestic over imported products is equally apparent in a third type of case. Thus it has held that *public procurement* cannot be structured so as to favour domestic producers. This was confirmed in the *Du Pont* case[14] in which the ECJ held that the reservation by a Member State of a proportion of its public supplies to products which were processed in a particular depressed region of the country *ipso facto* impeded imports contrary to Article 30 and was not excused by the rule of reason, nor by Article 36. While in *Campus Oil*[15] an

[14] Case C–21/88, *Du Pont de Nemours Italiana SpA* v. *Unità Sanitaria Locale No 2 Di Carrara* [1990] ECR I–889, [1991] 3 CMLR 25.

[15] Case 72/83, *Campus Oil Ltd* v. *Minister for Industry and Energy* [1984] ECR 2727, [1984] 3 CMLR 544.

obligation on importers into Ireland to buy a certain proportion of their supplies of oil from a national supplier was held to fall within Article 30. The insistence that public procurement should be decided without preference for domestic tenderers is clearly evident in the *Dundalk Water Supply* case:

Case 45/87, Commission v. Ireland
[1988] ECR 4929, [1989] 1 CMLR 225

Dundalk Council put out to tender a contract for water supply. One of the clauses of the contract specification (4.29) was that tenderers had to submit bids based on the use of certain pipes which complied with a particular Irish standard (IS 188: 1975). One of the bids was based on the use of a piping which had not been certified by the Irish authorities, but which did comply with international standards. The Council refused to consider it for this reason. The Commission brought an Article 169 action claiming a breach of Article 30.

THE ECJ

19. . . . it must first be pointed out that the inclusion of such a clause (as 4.29) in an invitation to tender may cause economic operators who produce or utilize pipes equivalent to pipes certified with Irish standards to refrain from tendering.

20. It further appears . . . that only one undertaking has been certified by the IIRS[16] to IS 188: 1975 to apply the Irish Standard Mark to pipes of the type required for the purposes of the public works contract at issue. That undertaking is located in Ireland. Consequently, the inclusion of Clause 4.29 had the effect of restricting the supply of the pipes needed for the Dundalk scheme to Irish manufacturers alone.

21. The Irish government maintains that it is necessary to specify the standards to which materials must be manufactured, particularly in a case such as this where the pipes utilized must suit the existing network. Compliance with another standard, even an international standard such as ISO 160:1980, would not suffice to eliminate technical difficulties.

22. That technical argument cannot be accepted. The Commission's complaint does not relate to compliance with technical requirements but to the refusal of the Irish authorities to verify whether those requirements are satisfied where the manufacturer of the materials has not been certified by the IIRS to IS 188. By incorporating in the notice in question the words 'or equivalent' after the reference to the Irish standard, as provided for by Directive 71/305 where it is applicable, the Irish authorities could have verified compliance with the technical conditions without from the outset restricting the contract to tenderers proposing to utilize Irish materials.

. . .

24. The Irish government further maintains that protection of public health justifies the requirement of compliance with the Irish standard in so far as that standard guarantees that there is no contact between the water and the asbestos fibres in the cement pipes, which would adversely affect the quality of the drinking water.

25. That argument must be rejected. As the Commission has rightly pointed

[16] Institute for Industrial Research and Standards.

out, the coating of the pipes, both internally and externally, was the subject of a separate requirement in the invitation to tender.

It is clear that in all the types of case discussed above the ECJ will, in line with the letter and spirit of *Dassonville*, look to the substance or effect of the domestic practice and not merely its legal form, when deciding whether a state has favoured domestic products over competing imports from another Member State. This is apparent in the next case concerning the import of franking machines into France:

Case 21/84, Commission v. France
[1985] ECR. 1356

French law had discriminated against postal franking machines from other countries. This law had been changed, but a British company claimed that, notwithstanding this formal change in the law the French authorities had repeatedly refused to approve its machines. The Commission brought an action alleging a breach of Article 30 by the French authorities.

THE ECJ

11. The fact that a law or regulation such as that requiring prior approval for the marketing of postal franking machines conforms in formal terms to Article 30 of the EEC Treaty is not sufficient to discharge a Member State of its obligations under that provision. Under the cloak of a general provision permitting the approval of machines imported from other Member States, the administration might very well adopt a systematically unfavourable attitude towards imported machines, either by allowing considerable delay in replying to applications for approval or in carrying out the examination procedure, or by refusing approval on the grounds of various alleged technical faults for which no detailed explanations are given or which prove to be inaccurate.

12. The prohibition on measures having an effect equivalent to quantitative restrictions would lose much of its useful effect if it did not cover protectionist or discriminatory practices of that type.

13. It must however be noted that for an administrative practice to constitute a measure prohibited under Article 30 that practice must show a certain degree of consistency and generality. That generality must be assessed differently according to whether the market concerned is one on which there are numerous traders or whether it is a market, such as that in postal franking machines, on which only a few undertakings are active. In the latter case, a national administration's treatment of a single undertaking may constitute a measure incompatible with Article 30.

14. In the light of those principles it is clear from the facts of the case that the conduct of the French postal administration constitutes an impediment to imports contrary to Article 30 of the EEC Treaty.

15. It must therefore be concluded that by refusing without proper justification to approve postal franking machines from another Member State, the French Republic has failed to fulfil its obligations under Article 30 of the EEC Treaty.

(c) Price-Fixing

There are diverse ways in which a state can treat imported goods less favourably than domestic products. Price fixing regulations imposed by a state may have this effect by rendering it more difficult for importers to market their goods within the territory of the state which is imposing the restrictions.

If the price fixing is discriminatory it is clearly caught by Article 30. Thus in the *Roussel* case[17] the ECJ held that maximum selling prices for certain drugs which were fixed according to different criteria for domestic and imported goods were discriminatory and infringed Article 30.[18] However, Article 30 can catch pricing rules even where they are not, on their face, discriminatory. This is demonstrated by the *Van Tiggele* case:

Case 82/77, Openbaar Ministerie v. Van Tiggele [1978] ECR 25, [1978] 2 CMLR 528[19]

Dutch legislation laid down minimum selling prices for certain spirits. A seller was accused in criminal proceedings of selling them below the stipulated price. The question before the ECJ was whether the minimum selling prices were a MEQR within Article 30.

THE ECJ

12. For the purposes of this prohibition it is sufficient that the measures in question are likely to hinder, directly or indirectly, actually or potentially, imports between Member States.

13. Whilst national price-control rules applicable without distinction to domestic products and imported products cannot in general produce such an effect they may do so in certain specific cases.

14. Thus imports may be impeded in particular when a national authority fixes prices or profit margins at such a level that imported products are placed at a disadvantage in relation to identical domestic products either because they cannot profitably be marketed in the conditions laid down or because the competitive advantage conferred by lower cost prices is cancelled out.

On the facts of the case the ECJ found that the Dutch rule did contravene Article 30. It seems that rules which fix prices by reference to a maximum percentage profit will, by way of contrast, be found to be more readily compatible with Article 30. Such rules may take account of differences in production cost between domestic goods and imports.[20]

[17] Case 181/82, *Roussel Labaratoria BV* v. *The State of the Netherlands* [1983] ECR 3849, [1985] 1 CMLR 834.

[18] See also Case 56/87, *Commission* v. *Italy* [1988] ECR 2919, [1989] 3 CMLR 707.

[19] See also Case 65/75, *Riccardo Tasca* [1976] ECR 291, [1977] 2 CMLR 183.

[20] Case 78/82, *Commission* v. *Italy* [1983] ECR 1955.

(d) Measures which make Imports more Difficult or Costly

There are numerous ways in which rules of one Member State can render it more difficult for importers to break into that market. We have touched upon this idea already in the preceding analysis. The ECJ has used Article 30 to ensure that rules of this nature are prohibited unless they can be saved by reliance on Article 36. The *Schloh* case provides a good example of this:

Case 50/85, Schloh v. Auto Contrôle Technique
[1986] ECR 1855

Schloh bought a car in Germany and obtained from a Ford dealer in Belgium a certificate of conformity with vehicle types in Belgium. Under Belgian law he was required to submit his car to two roadworthiness tests; fees were charged for these tests. He challenged the tests, arguing that they were a MEQR. The extract which follows concerns the first roadworthiness test.

THE ECJ

12. Under the terms of Article 30 of the Treaty, quantitative restrictions on imports and all measures having equivalent effect are prohibited between Member States. Roadworthiness testing is a formality which makes the registration of imported vehicles more difficult and more onerous and consequently is in the nature of a measure having an effect equivalent to a quantitative restriction.

13. Nevertheless, Article 36 may justify such a formality on grounds of the protection of human life and health, provided that it is established, first, that the test at issue is necessary for the attainment of that objective and, secondly, that it does not constitute a means of arbitrary discrimination or a disguised restriction on trade between Member States.

14. As far as the first condition is concerned, it must be acknowledged that roadworthiness testing required prior to the registration of an imported vehicle may . . . be regarded as necessary for the protection of human health and life where the vehicle in question has already been put on the road. In such cases roadworthiness testing performs a useful function inasmuch as it makes it possible to check that the vehicle has not been damaged and is in a good state of repair. However such testing cannot be justified on those grounds where it relates to an imported vehicle carrying a certificate of conformity which has not been placed on the road before being registered in the importing Member State.

15. As far as the second condition is concerned, it must be stated that the roadworthiness testing of imported vehicles cannot, however, be justified under the second sentence of Article 36 of the Treaty if it is established that such testing is not required in the case of vehicles of national origin presented for registration in the same circumstances. If that were the case it would become apparent that the measure in question was not in fact inspired by a concern for the protection of human health and life but in reality constituted a means of arbitrary discrimination in trade between Member States. It is for the national court to verify that such non-discriminatory treatment is in fact ensured.

The ECJ therefore held that the Belgian rule was contrary to Article 30, save in relation to cars which were already on the road, provided that in this type of case the rules were applied in a non-discriminatory fashion.

(e) National Measures versus Private Action

One further point should be addressed before proceeding to consider possible defences based on Article 36 of the Treaty: this concerns the scope of Article 30. It is clear that the prohibition contained in Article 30 applies only to measures which have been adopted by the state as opposed to those taken by private parties. Other Articles of the Treaty, notably Articles 85 and 86, will apply to actions by private parties which restrict competition and have an impact on inter-state trade. The ambit of these provisions will be considered in due course.[21]

This does, of course, mean that the issue of what is a state entity will have to be faced within the context of proceedings under Article 30. The ECJ has addressed the matter on a number of occasions. Thus in the '*Buy Irish*' case[22] we have already seen that the ECJ rejected the argument that the Irish Goods Council was a private body and therefore immune from the application of Article 30; the Irish Government's involvement with the funding of the organization and the appointment of its members was sufficient to render it public for these purposes.[23] While in the *Apple and Pear Development Council* case[24] the existence of a statutory obligation on growers of fruit to pay certain levies to the Council sufficed to render the body public for these purposes.

It is clear that institutions such as those concerned with trade regulation may come within the definition of the state for these purposes even if they are nominally private, provided that they receive a measure of state support or 'underpinning'. Thus in *R.* v. *The Pharmaceutical Society, ex parte API*[25] the Society was an independent body responsible for the regulation of standards among United Kingdom pharmacists. A pharmacist had to appear on its register in order to be able to practise. Certain functions were, however, conferred on the Society by statute; its disciplinary functions had a statutory basis in the Pharmacy Act 1954; and removal from its register would effectively prevent a pharmacist from continuing to practise. In these circumstances the Court held that the Society was bound by Article 30 of the Treaty.

[21] See below, Chs. 19–23.
[22] Case 249/81, *Commission* v. *Ireland* [1982] ECR 4005, [1983] 2 CMLR 104.
[23] See above, 590–1.
[24] Case 222/82, *Apple and Pear Development Council* v. *K. J. Lewis Ltd* [1983] ECR 4083, [1984] 3 CMLR 733.
[25] Case 266/87, [1989] ECR 1295, [1989] 2 CMLR 751.

4. JUSTIFYING DISCRIMINATORY BARRIERS TO TRADE: ARTICLE 36

If trade rules are found to be discriminatory[26] then they can only be saved through Article 36 which provides that:

> The provisions of Articles 30 to 34 shall not preclude prohibitions or restrictions on imports, exports or goods in transit justified on grounds of public morality, public policy or public security; the protection of health and life of humans, animals or plants; the protection of national treasures possessing artistic, historic or archaeological value; or the protection of industrial and commercial property. Such prohibitions or restrictions shall not, however, constitute a means of arbitrary discrimination or a disguised restriction on trade between Member States.

It will not come as a surprise to learn that the Court has construed Article 36 strictly. National rules which do discriminate against goods from other Member States will be closely scrutinized before the Court accepts that they can be saved on one of the grounds listed above. In addition to showing that the challenged rule comes within one of the listed categories, the ECJ has also insisted that it should pass a test of proportionality: given that Article 36 is an exception to one of the important rights safeguarded by the Treaty the Court demands that the discriminatory measure sought to be justified under that Article is the least restrictive possible to attain the end in view. With these preliminary remarks we can now focus more specifically on the Court's case law under the particular heads of Article 36.

(a) *Public Morality*

Two of the main precedents on this issue have emerged from cases concerning the United Kingdom. Both cases concerned challenges to laws dealing with pornography.

In *Henn and Darby*[27] the defendants were convicted of fraudulently evading the prohibition on the importation of indecent or obscene articles, contrary to United Kingdom law.[28] They had imported pornography into England from Rotterdam. Their defence was that the relevant United Kingdom laws were contrary to Article 30. The United Kingdom Government

[26] There may of course be a question whether a rule really is discriminatory or not, and therefore whether it is caught by Art. 30, and requires justification under Art. 36. A good example of the difficulty which can be caused in this respect can be seen in Case C–2/90, *Commission* v. *Belgium* [1992] ECR I–4431, noted by L. Hancher and H. Sevenster (1993) 30 CMLRev. 351, and D. Geradin (1993) 18 ELRev. 144.

[27] Case 34/79, *R.* v. *Henn and Darby* [1979] ECR 3795, [1980] 1 CMLR 246.

[28] As contained in the Customs Consolidation Act 1876, s. 42 and the Customs and Excise Act 1952, s. 304.

relied on Article 36. The ECJ found that the import ban was indeed within Article 30 and then proceeded to consider whether it could be saved by the public morality exception found in Article 36. It reasoned as follows. It was, said the Court, for each Member State to determine the standards of public morality which prevailed in its territory, and it did not matter in this respect that somewhat different laws applied within different parts of the United Kingdom. The ECJ then proceeded to consider whether such national laws could constitute a disguised restriction on trade or a means of arbitrary discrimination within the terms of Article 36. The rationale for examining this issue was that United Kingdom law imposed an absolute ban on the import of pornography, even though domestic law did not ban absolutely the possession or even dissemination of such material. Notwithstanding this fact the ECJ found that the United Kingdom import ban was not a disguised restriction on trade or a means of arbitrary discrimination. The Court held that while domestic United Kingdom law was not absolute in this respect, its purpose, taken as a whole, was to restrain the manufacture and marketing of pornography. From this the ECJ concluded that there was no lawful trade in such goods within the United Kingdom. The United Kingdom could therefore rely on Article 36 with the consequence that the criminal convictions were upheld. However, a different result was reached in the *Conegate* case:

Case 121/85, Conegate Ltd v. Commissioners of Customs and Excise [1986] ECR 1007, [1986] 1 CMLR 739

Conegate imported life-size inflatable dolls from Germany into the United Kingdom. The invoice for the dolls claimed that they were for the purpose of window display, but the Customs officials were unconvinced, particularly when they found items described as 'love love dolls'. They seized the goods, and magistrates ordered them to be forfeit. Conegate argued that the seizure and forfeiture were in breach of Article 30. The national court asked whether a prohibition on imports could be justified even though the state did not ban the manufacture or marketing of the same goods within the national territory. The ECJ repeated its reasoning from *Henn and Darby* that it was for each Member State to decide upon the nature of public morality for its own territory. It continued as follows.

THE ECJ

15. However, although Community law leaves the Member States free to make their own assessments of the indecent or obscene character of certain articles, it must be pointed out that the fact that goods cause offence cannot be regarded as sufficiently serious to justify restrictions on the free movement of goods where the Member State concerned does not adopt, with respect to the same goods manufactured or marketed within its territory, penal measures or other serious and effective measures intended to prevent the distribution of such goods in its territory.

16. It follows that a Member State may not rely on grounds of public morality to prohibit the importation of goods from other Member States when its legislation contains no prohibition on the manufacture or marketing of the same goods on its territory.

17. It is not for the Court, within the framework of the powers conferred on it by Article 177 . . . to consider whether, and to what extent, the United Kingdom legislation contains such a prohibition. However, the question whether or not such a prohibition exists in a State comprised of different constituent parts which have their own internal legislation can be resolved only by taking into consideration all the relevant legislation. Although it is not necessary, for the purposes of the application of the above-mentioned rule, that the manufacture and marketing of the products whose importation has been prohibited should be prohibited in the territory of all the constituent parts, it must at least be possible to conclude from the applicable rules, taken as a whole, that their purpose is, in substance, to prohibit the manufacture and marketing of those products.

18. In this instance . . . the High Court took care to define the substance of the national legislation the compatibility of which with Community law is a question which it proposes to determine. Thus it refers to rules in the importing Member State under which the goods in question may be manufactured freely and marketed subject only to certain restrictions . . . namely an absolute prohibition on the transmission of such goods by post, a restriction on their public display and, in certain areas of the Member States concerned, a system of licensing of premises for the sale of those goods to customers aged 18 years and over. Such restrictions cannot however be regarded as equivalent in substance to a prohibition on manufacture and marketing.

Conegate therefore recovered its goods, given that the United Kingdom defence based on Article 36 failed. It is interesting to reflect on the difference between *Conegate* and *Henn and Darby*. It is clear that the crucial distinction resides in the ECJ's evaluation of whether imported goods which were subject to an absolute ban were being treated more harshly than similar domestic goods manufactured and marketed in the United Kingdom. In *Henn and Darby* the ECJ was willing to find that United Kingdom law did restrain the manufacture and marketing of pornography sufficiently to enable it to conclude that there was no lawful trade in such goods within the United Kingdom. In *Conegate*, by way of contrast, the ECJ examined the relevant national rules more closely and reached the opposite conclusion: the restrictions which existed could not be said to amount to a prohibition on domestic manufacture or marketing.

It is clear, then, that while Member States are free to determine the sense of public morality which should pertain within their own territory, they cannot seek to place markedly stricter burdens on goods coming from outside than those which are applied to equivalent domestic goods. In this respect the Court's reasoning in *Conegate* is in line with its jurisprudence in other areas, such as free movement of workers: claims that workers should be excluded on grounds of public policy have foundered in circumstances where there is no proscription on domestic workers undertaking the same job as that which the foreign workers are seeking to do.[29]

[29] See below, Ch. 15.

(b) Public Policy

Public policy constitutes a separate head of justification within Article 36. The phrase is potentially broad, but the ECJ has resisted attempts to interpret it in a manner which would lead to a significant inroad on the principle in Article 30 itself. The Court has, for example, rejected arguments that the term public policy can embrace concerns for consumer protection, on the ground that, since Article 36 derogates from a fundamental rule of the Treaty enshrined in Article 30, it must be interpreted strictly and cannot be extended to objectives which are not expressly mentioned therein.[30]

A public policy justification must, therefore, be made in its own terms, and cannot be used as a vehicle through which to advance what amounts to a separate ground for defence. It is for this reason that relatively few cases contain any detailed examination of the public policy argument. One case which does consider the issue is *Centre Leclerc*:

Case 231/83, Cullet v. Centre Leclerc
[1985] ECR 305, [1985] 2 CMLR 524

French legislation imposed minimum retail prices for fuel fixed primarily on the basis of French ex-refinery prices and French refinery costs. The Court found that this constituted a MEQR within Article 30, since imports could not benefit fully from lower cost prices in the country of origin. The French Government sought to justify its action on the basis, *inter alia*, of public policy within Article 36. It argued that, in the absence of the pricing rules there would be civil disturbances, blockades, and violence. Both the Advocate General and the ECJ rejected this argument, but the reason for doing so differed. Let us consider the views of the Advocate General first. He considered that the case law of the ECJ did not support such a wide conception of public policy, and then continued as follows.

ADVOCATE GENERAL VERLOREN VAN THEMAAT[31]

However, I would add that the acceptance of civil disturbances as justification for encroachments upon the free movement of goods would, as is apparent from experiences of last year (and before, during the Franco–Italian 'wine war') have unacceptably drastic consequences. If roadblocks and other effective weapons of interest groups which feel threatened by the importation and sale at competitive prices of certain cheap products or services, or by immigrant workers or foreign businesses, were accepted as justification, the existence of the four fundamental freedoms of the Treaty could no longer be relied upon. Private interest groups would then, in the place of the Treaty and Community (and, within the limits laid down by the Treaty, national) institutions, determine the scope of those freedoms. In such cases, the concept of public policy requires, rather, effective action on the part of the authorities to deal with such disturbances.

[30] Case 113/80, n. 12 above; Case 177/83, *Kohl* v. *Ringelhan* [1984] ECR 3651, [1985] 3 CMLR 340; Case 229/83, *Leclerc* v. *Sàrl Au Blé Vert* [1985] ECR 1, [1985] 2 CMLR 286.

[31] [1985] ECR 305, [1985] 2 CMLR 524, 534.

THE ECJ

32. For the purpose of applying Article 36, the French Government has invoked the disturbances to law and order (*ordre public*) and public security caused by violent reactions which should be expected from retailers affected by unrestricted competition.

33. On this point it is sufficient to observe that the French Government has not shown that an amendment of the regulations in question in conformity with the principles set out above would have consequences for law and order (*ordre public*) and public security which the French Government would be unable to meet with the resources available to it.

Thus, while the Advocate General rejected the French arguments on principle, the ECJ appeared ready to accept that they could be pleaded under Article 36, while rejecting them on the facts. The approach adopted by the ECJ might well have been simply a more diplomatic way of disposing of the point, but the analysis of the Advocate General is more convincing as a matter of first principle. If interest–group pressure leading to potential violence could provide the grounds for justification under Article 36, and the analogous Treaty Articles concerned with workers and services, then fundamental Community freedoms would be placed in jeopardy. This is more particularly so given that certain issues, such as workers from Member States taking jobs within another country, can generate real tensions, especially during periods of recession and unemployment.

(c) *Public Security*

Claims to justify trade rules based upon public security are often found alongside those based on public policy. This was so in *Centre Leclerc*, to which we shall revert once again below. The leading authority on this point is, however, the *Campus Oil* case:

Case 72/83, Campus Oil Ltd v. Minister for Industry and Energy [1984] ECR 2727, [1984] 3 CMLR 544

Irish law required importers of petrol into Ireland to buy 35 per cent of their requirements from a state-owned oil refinery at prices fixed by the Irish government. This rule was held to constitute a MEQR within Article 30. In defence Ireland sought to rely on public policy and security within Article 36. The argument was that the importance of oil for the life of the country meant that it was vital for Ireland to be able to maintain refining capacity of its own, and the challenged rule was the means of ensuring that the products of its refinery could be marketed.[32] The ECJ held that recourse to Article 36 would not be possible in

[32] The applicants who challenged the Irish system countered by arguing that the real issue was not whether Ireland should maintain an independent refining capacity, but whether such a refinery should operate at a profit or loss; this was they claimed an economic issue which could not come within the ideas of public policy or security.

such a case if there were Community rules providing the necessary protection for oil supplies. Certain Community measures did exist, but they were not comprehensive. The Court continued as follows.

THE ECJ

31. Consequently, the existing Community rules give a Member State whose supplies of petroleum products depend totally or almost totally on deliveries from other countries certain guarantees that deliveries from other Member States will be maintained in the event of a serious shortfall in proportions which match those of supplies to the market of the supplying State. However, this does not mean that the Member State concerned has an unconditional assurance that supplies will in any event be maintained at least at a level sufficient to meet its minimum needs. In those circumstances, the possibility for a Member State to rely on Article 36 to justify appropriate complementary measures at national level cannot be excluded, even where there exist Community rules on the matter.

[*The Court then considered whether the term 'public security' could cover this situation.*]

34. It should be stated in this connection that petroleum products, because of their exceptional importance as an energy source in the modern economy, are of fundamental importance for a country's existence since not only its economy but above all its institutions, its essential public services and even the survival of the inhabitants depend upon them. An interruption of supplies of petroleum products, with the resultant dangers for the country's existence, could therefore seriously affect the public security that Article 36 allows States to protect.

35. It is true that, as the Court has held on a number of occasions, most recently in . . . (Case 95/81, *Commission* v. *Italy*), Article 36 refers to matters of a non-economic nature. A Member State cannot be allowed to avoid the effects of measures provided for in the Treaty by pleading the economic difficulties caused by elimination of barriers to intra-Community trade. However, in the light of the seriousness of the consequences that an interruption in supplies of petroleum products may have for a country's existence, the aim of ensuring a minimum supply of petroleum products at all times is to be regarded as transcending purely economic considerations and thus as capable of constituting an objective covered by the concept of public security.

36. It should be added that to come within the ambit of Article 36 the rules in question must be justified by objective circumstances corresponding to the needs of public security . . .

37. As the Court has previously stated . . . Article 36, as an exception to a fundamental principle of the Treaty, must be interpreted in such a way that its scope is not extended any further than is necessary for the protection of the interests which it is intended to secure and the measures taken pursuant to that Article must not create obstacles to imports which are disproportionate to those objectives. Measures adopted on the basis of Article 36 can therefore be justified only if they are such as to serve the interest which that Article protects and if they do not restrict intra-Community trade more than is absolutely necessary.

While the ECJ, therefore, accepts the public security argument in principle in *Campus Oil*, the circumstances to which it will be applicable are likely to be factually limited.[33] There is little enthusiasm for extending the reasoning, and in *Centre Leclerc* Advocate General Verloren van Themaat devoted time in his opinion to distinguishing *Campus Oil* from the situation in *Centre Leclerc*.[34]

It should not, however, be forgotten in this respect that Member States can take certain measures relating to national security pursuant to Articles 223 to 225 of the Treaty.

(d) Protection of Health and Life of Humans, Animals, or Plants

There have been a number of cases in which states have attempted to defend measures on this ground under Article 36. That such a ground of justification should exist is not surprising. Nor, however, should it come as a surprise that the Court will look closely at such claims before accepting that they can come within this provision. One can perceive a number of differing ways in which the Court will scrutinize cases of this kind.

First, the Court will subject such claims to close scrutiny in order to determine whether the protection of public health is the real purpose behind the Member States' action, or whether it was designed to protect domestic producers. This is exemplified by the decision in *Commission* v. *United Kingdom*.[35] In this case the United Kingdom in effect banned poultrymeat imports from most other Member States, justifying this on the ground that it was necessary to protect public health, by preventing the spread of Newcastle disease which affected poultry. The ECJ rejected the argument. It found that imports of poultry into the United Kingdom from other states had increased markedly; that this had resulted in pressure from domestic producers, who were concerned at the subsidies available to foreign producers of poultry, and who insisted that the government should do something to protect their interests; that the ban was imposed so as to maximize its impact on the import of turkeys for Christmas consumption; that the French authorities had in any event imposed controls directed towards preventing Newcastle disease; and that the United Kingdom ban was introduced with haste and with little in the way of consultation. From these factors the Court concluded that the import ban was motivated more by commercial reasons, to block French poultry, than by considerations of public health.[36]

The ECJ will also closely examine the cogency of arguments concerning public health to determine whether they make sense on the facts, as is apparent from *Commission* v. *United Kingdom*[37]. The ECJ considered the legality of

[33] See also Case C–367/89, *Criminal Proceedings against Richardt and Les Accessoires Scientifiques suc* [1991] ECR I–4621.

[34] N. 31 above, 312 (ECR), 535–6 (CMLR).

[35] Case 40/82, [1982] ECR 2793, [1982] 3 CMLR 497.

[36] The ECJ also noted that less stringent measures could have been taken to reach the same end as that desired by the UK Government: *ibid.* para. 41. See also Case 42/82, *Commission* v. *France* [1983] ECR 1013, [1984] 1 CMLR 160.

[37] Case 124/81, [1983] ECR 203, [1983] 2 CMLR 1.

United Kingdom measures requiring ultra-heat-treated (UHT) milk to be imported only with a licence, and to be marketed only by licensed dealers who had packed the milk in a local dairy. The rules effectively rendered imports of UHT milk wholly uneconomic. In rejecting the United Kingdom's claim that the marketing system was necessary to protect public health the Court took account of the following factors: UHT milk was in fact made according to very similar rules in the different Member States; very similar machines were used in the productive process; and the nature of UHT milk obviated the need for control over the whole production cycle of the product, provided that proper precautions were taken at the time of the heat treatment.

Secondly, the ECJ may have to decide whether a public health claim is sustainable in circumstances where there is no perfect consensus on the scientific or medical impact of particular substances. The approach of the Court to cases of this kind is exemplified by the *Sandoz* decision:

Case 174/82, Officier van Justitie v. Sandoz BV
[1983] ECR 2245, [1984] 3 CMLR 43

Authorities in Holland refused to allow the sale of muesli bars which contained added vitamins, on the ground that the vitamins were dangerous to public health. The muesli bars were readily available in Germany and Belgium. It was accepted that vitamins could be beneficial to health, but it was also acknowledged that excessive consumption of vitamins could be harmful to health. Scientific evidence was not, however, certain as regards the point at which consumption of vitamins became excessive, particularly because vitamins consumed in one source of food might be added to those eaten from a different food source. There had been some Community legislation which touched on the general issue of food additives.

THE ECJ

15. The abovementioned Community measures clearly show that the Community legislature accepts the principle that it is necessary to restrict the use of food additives to the substances specified, whilst leaving the Member States a certain discretion to adopt stricter rules. The measures thus testify to great prudence regarding the potential harmfulness of additives, the extent of which is still uncertain in respect of each of the various substances, and leave a wide discretion to the Member States in relation to such additives.

16. As the Court found in its judgment . . . in Case 272/80 (*Frans-Nederlandse Maatschappij voor Biologische Producten* [1981] ECR. 3277), in so far as there are uncertainties at the present state of scientific research it is for the Member States, in the absence of harmonization, to decide what degree of protection of the health and life of humans they intend to assure, having regard however for the requirements of the free movement of goods within the Community.

17. Those principles also apply to substances such as vitamins which are not as a general rule harmful in themselves but may have special harmful effects solely if taken to excess as part of the general nutrition, the composition of which is unforeseeable and cannot be monitored. In view of the uncertainties inherent in the scientific assessment, national rules prohibiting, without prior authorization, the marketing of foodstuffs to which vitamins have been added are justified on

principle within the meaning of Article 36 of the Treaty on the grounds of the protection of human health.

18. Nevertheless the principle of proportionality which underlies the last sentence of Article 36 of the Treaty requires that the power of the Member States to prohibit imports of the products in question from other Member States should be restricted to what is necessary to attain the legitimate aim of protecting public health. Accordingly, national rules providing for such a prohibition are justified only if authorizations to market are granted when they are compatible with the need to protect health.

19. Such an assessment is, however, difficult to make in relation to additives such as vitamins the above mentioned characteristics of which exclude the possibility of foreseeing or monitoring the quantities consumed as part of the general nutrition and the degree of harmfulness of which cannot be determined with sufficient certainty. Nevertheless, although in view of the present stage of harmonization of national laws at the Community level a wide discretion must be left to the Member States, they must, in order to observe the principle of proportionality, authorize marketing when the addition of vitamins to foodstuffs meets a real need, especially a technical or nutritional one.

20. The first question must therefore be answered to the effect that Community law permits national rules prohibiting without prior authorization the marketing of foodstuffs marketed in another Member State to which vitamins have been added, provided that the marketing is authorized when the addition of the vitamins meets a real need, especially a technical or nutritional one.

The approach of the Court in *Sandoz* is finely tuned: the ECJ will decide whether the public-health claim is sustainable in principle; if there is then uncertainty as to the precise medical implications of some substance it will,[38] in the absence of Community harmonization measures, be for the Member States to decide upon the appropriate degree of protection to assure to their citizens; this will, however, be subject to the principle of proportionality, as applied by the ECJ in paragraph 18 of its judgment. A similar approach is apparent in other cases on this topic.[39]

Issues concerning public health as a defence to Article 30 can also arise in a third way. A state may not impose an outright ban on goods which come from other states, but it may subject them to checks which render import more difficult, and it may do so even though the goods in question were subject to checks in the state of origin. This problem of double-checking has come before the ECJ on a number of occasions. As can be imagined the ECJ has been duly suspicious of checks imposed by the state of import where the goods have already been checked in the state of export. The Court has, on the whole, become stricter with respect to this matter in its more recent case law.

[38] See, however, Case 178/84, *Commission* v. *Germany* [1987] ECR 1227, discussed below, 637–8.

[39] Case 53/80, *Officier van Justitie* v. *Koniklijke Kaasfabriek Eyssen BV* [1981] ECR 409, [1982] 2 CMLR 20; Case 94/83, *Officier van Justitie* v. *Albert Heijn BV* [1984] ECR 3263; Case 304/84, *Ministère Public* v. *Mueller* [1986] ECR 1511, [1987] 2 CMLR 469; Case C–62/90, *Commission* v. *Germany*, [1992] ECR I–2575, [1992] 2 CMLR 549.

The early approach in *Denkavit*[40] was to urge national authorities to co-operate in order to avoid dual burdens, and to impose an obligation on the national authorities to ascertain whether the documents from the state of export raised a presumption that the goods complied with the demands of the importing state. The Court did, however, admit that a second set of checks in the state of import might nonetheless be lawful, provided that the requirements were necessary and proportionate. Even at this early juncture the Court would strike down such requirements if it felt that a less restrictive method of achieving the Member State's objective could be devised.[41]

Although a second set of checks may still be lawful on some occasions the Court's more recent case law exhibits a healthy scepticism regarding whether such controls are really required. This is evident from the decision in *Commission* v. *United Kingdom*[42] concerning UHT milk which was considered above. In the course of its judgment the ECJ held that the United Kingdom's concerns about the product could be met by less restrictive means than the import ban and marketing system which it had instituted. The United Kingdom could, said the Court, lay down requirements that imported milk had to meet, and could demand certificates from the authorities of the exporting state.[43] However, if such certificates were produced then it would be for the authorities within the importing state to ascertain whether these certificates raised a presumption that the imported goods complied with the demands of domestic legislation. In fact the ECJ itself concluded that the conditions for such a presumption existed in this case,[44] a conclusion which was rendered easier by the fact that the milk was sealed and not tampered with between export and import. An unwillingness to subject goods to a second set of checks can also be seen in the *Biologische Producten* case[45]. While accepting that dual checks may be required, the ECJ placed strict limits on when checks within the importing state would be lawful. They would not be so where they unnecessarily imposed technical tests which had already been carried out in the state of origin, nor where the practical effect of the tests in the exporting state met the demands of the importing state.[46]

The final way in which public-health defences can arise is closely related to, but distinct from, the type of case which has just been discussed. This is where Community harmonization measures *have been* passed. The general rule is that the existence of such measures renders recourse to the public-health exception within Article 36 inadmissible. Thus in *Moormann*[47] the ECJ held that the

[40] Case 251/78, *Denkavit Futtermittel* v. *Minister für Ernährung, Landwirtschaft und Forsten* [1979] ECR 3369, [1980] 3 CMLR 513.

[41] Case 132/80, *United Foods* v. *Belgium* [1981] ECR 995, [1982] 1 CMLR 706.

[42] Case 124/81, *Commission* v. *United Kingdom* [1983] ECR 203, [1983] 2 CMLR 1.

[43] *Ibid.*, paras. 27–8.

[44] *Ibid.*, para. 30.

[45] Case 272/80, *Frans-Nederlandse Maatschappij voor Biologische Producten* [1981] ECR 3277, [1982] 2 CMLR 497.

[46] *Ibid.*, paras. 14–15.

[47] Case 190/87, *Oberkreisdirektor* v. *Moormann BV* [1988] ECR 4689, [1990] 1 CMLR 656. See also Case 5/77, *Tedeschi* v. *Denkavit Commerciale Srl* [1977] ECR 1555, [1978] 1 CMLR 1; Cases C–277, 318, and 319/91, *Ligur Carni Srl* v. *Unità Sanitaria Locale No XV di Genova* [1993] ECR I–6621; Case C–294/92, *Commission* v. *Italy* 20 Sept. 1994.

existence of Community measures harmonizing certain health inspections for poultry meant that a state could no longer resort to defences based on Article 36 in an attempt to legitimate national rules on the matter. Problems may, however, occur when the ambit of the Community harmonization measure is more limited, as demonstrated by the next case:

Case 4/75, Rewe-Zentralfinanz GmbH v. Landwirtschaftskammer [1975] ECR 843, [1975] 1 CMLR 599

The German authorities imposed checks on imported apples. There was a Council Directive 69/466 which laid down provisions relating to harmful organisms in fruit etc. (including San José scale), but it was clear from the recitals to the Directive that the measure was intended to supplement and not to replace national laws of the Member States.

THE ECJ

7. . . .

By authorizing those states to adopt such additional or stricter provisions as may be required to control San Jose scale or to prevent it from spreading, Article 11 reserves to them the power to maintain such measures in force to the extent necessary.

In the light of the current Community rules in this matter, a phytosanitary inspection carried out by a Member State on the importation of plant products constitutes, in principle, one of the restrictions on imports which are justified under the first sentence of Article 36 of the Treaty.

8. However, the restrictions on imports referred to in the first sentence of Article 36 cannot be accepted under the second sentence of that Article if they constitute a means of arbitrary discrimination.

The fact that plant products imported from another Member State are subject to a phytosanitary inspection although domestic products are not subject to an equivalent examination when they are despatched within the Member State might constitute arbitrary discrimination within the meaning of the above mentioned provision.

Therefore, the phytosanitary inspection of imported products which are shown to originate in areas other than those referred to in Article 3 of Council Directive No. 69/466/EEC may constitute an additional or stricter measure which is not justified by Article 11 of that Directive and should be regarded as a means of arbitrary discrimination within the meaning of the second sentence of Article 36 of the Treaty.

The different treatment of imported and domestic products, based on the need to prevent the spread of the harmful organism could not, however, be regarded as arbitrary discrimination if effective measures are taken in order to prevent the distribution of contaminated domestic products and if there is reason to believe, in particular on the basis of previous experience, that there is a risk of the harmful organism's spreading if no inspection is held on importation.

It is clear, then, that, as the process of Community harmonization increases, so the ability of Member States to rely on Article 36 will correspondingly diminish. Such harmonization measures are designed to provide Community-wide standards for a particular area which both serve to enshrine appropriate protections for public health etc., and also to facilitate the attainment of the Single Market by preventing states from relying upon their own national rules which may impede the free flow of goods. The difficulties which beset the Community legislative endeavours in this area will be discussed more fully below.[48]

(e) Other Grounds for Validating Discriminatory Measures?

How far can a Member State seek to justify a discriminatory measure on grounds other than those listed in Article 36? The general answer to this is that it cannot. A state is not able to raise possible justifications which do not appear within Article 36, even if they are to be found in the list which may be invoked in the case of indistinctly applicable measures.[49]

It is questionable whether the decision in *Commission* v. *Belgium*[50] is to be seen as an exception to this proposition. In that case the Commission challenged a Belgian regional decree, the effect of which was to ban the importation of all waste into that area. The decree was in a sense discriminatory, in that it did not cover disposal of locally produced waste. Notwithstanding this fact the Court allowed environmental protection to be taken into account when considering the legality of the regional decree. On one reading, therefore, the case could be seen as allowing justifications to be pleaded which are not to be found in Article 36. However, this interpretation of the case is almost certainly mistaken for the following reason. The ECJ in effect held that the decree was not in fact discriminatory, notwithstanding appearances to the contrary in the challenged instrument. This was because of the special nature of the subject matter, waste. There were strong arguments, the Court said, for disposing of such material locally, and each area had the responsibility for disposing of its own waste. Thus, although the decree only applied to imports it was not discriminatory.

Now one may well disagree with the ECJ in this respect, but given that this was the Court's reasoning the case does not stand as authority for the ability to use justifications which are not to be found in Article 36. Moreover, given the Court's general hostility to discriminatory state measures, there is very little likelihood that the ECJ will be willing to expand the range of exceptions to be found in Article 36.

[48] See below, Ch. 25. [49] See below, 636–7. [50] Case C–2/90, [1992] ECR I–4431.

5. INDISTINCTLY APPLICABLE RULES: *CASSIS DE DIJON*

If the reach of Article 30 had been confined to the types of case considered within the previous sections it would still have made a notable contribution to the creation of a single market. The removal of discriminatory trade barriers is undoubtedly a *necessary* condition for the attainment of single-market integration. It is not, however, *sufficient*. There are many rules which do not discriminate as such between goods dependent upon the country of origin, but which nevertheless can create real barriers to the passage of products between Member States.

That this was so was appreciated by the Commission in Directive 70/50. Article 2 of this Directive was concerned with discriminatory measures which impeded inter-state trade and has been considered above.[51] However, Article 3 signalled the intent of the Commission to go further. It provides that the Directive also covers measures governing the marketing of products which deal, *inter alia*, with shape, size, weight, composition, presentation, and identification, where the measures are equally applicable to domestic and imported products, and where the restrictive effect of such measures on the free movement of goods exceeds the effects intrinsic to such rules. This is said to be the case in particular where the restrictive effects on the free movement of goods are out of proportion to their purpose or where the same objective can be attained by other means which are less of a hindrance to trade.

The possibility that Article 30 could be applied to indistinctly applicable rules is also apparent from the decision of the ECJ in *Dassonville*. The definition of a MEQR provided in paragraph 5 of that case does not actually require a measure to be discriminatory in order for it to be caught by Article 30.

The seeds which were sown in Directive 70/50 and in *Dassonville* came to fruition in the seminal *Cassis de Dijon* case:

Case 120/78, Rewe-Zentrale AG v. Bundesmonopolverwaltung für Branntwein [1979] ECR 649, [1979] 3 CMLR 494

The applicant intended to import the liqueur 'Cassis de Dijon' into Germany from France. The relevant German authorities refused to allow the importation because the French drink was not of sufficient alcoholic strength to be marketed in Germany: under German law such liqueurs had to have an alcohol content of 25 per cent, whereas the French drink had an alcohol content of between 15 and 20 per cent. The applicant argued that the German rule was a MEQR, since it prevented the French version of the drink from being lawfully marketed in Germany.

[51] See above, 587.

THE ECJ

8. In the absence of common rules relating to the production and marketing of alcohol . . . it is for the Member States to regulate all matters relating to the production and marketing of alcohol and alcoholic beverages on their own territory.

Obstacles to movement within the Community resulting from disparities between the national laws relating to the marketing of the products in question must be accepted in so far as those provisions may be recognised as being necessary in order to satisfy mandatory requirements relating in particular to the effectiveness of fiscal supervision, the protection of public health, the fairness of commercial transactions and the defence of the consumer.

9. The Government of the Federal Republic of Germany . . . put forward various arguments which, in its view, justify the application of provisions relating to the minimum alcohol content of alcoholic beverages, adducing considerations relating on the one hand to the protection of public health and on the other to the protection of the consumer against unfair commercial practices.

10. As regards the protection of public health the German Government states that the purpose of the fixing of minimum alcohol contents by national legislation is to avoid the proliferation of alcoholic beverages on the national market, in particular alcoholic beverages with a low alcohol content, since, in its view, such products may more easily induce a tolerance towards alcohol than more highly alcoholic beverages.

11. Such considerations are not decisive since the consumer can obtain on the market an extremely wide range of weakly or moderately alcoholic products and furthermore a large proportion of alcoholic beverages with a high alcohol content freely sold on the German market is generally consumed in a diluted form.

12. The German Government also claims that the fixing of a lower limit for the alcohol content of certain liqueurs is designed to protect the consumer against unfair practices on the part of producers and distributors of alcoholic beverages.

This argument is based on the consideration that the lowering of the alcohol content secures a competitive advantage in relation to beverages with a higher alcohol content, since alcohol constitutes by far the most expensive constituent of beverages by reason of the high rate of tax to which it is subject.

Furthermore, according to the German Government, to allow alcoholic products into free circulation wherever, as regards their alcohol content, they comply with the rules laid down in the country of production would have the effect of imposing as a common standard within the Community the lowest alcohol content permitted in any of the Member States, and even of rendering any requirements in this field inoperative since a lower limit of this nature is foreign to the rules of several Member States.

13. As the Commission rightly observed, the fixing of limits to the alcohol content of beverages may lead to the standardization of products placed on the market and of their designations, in the interests of a greater transparency of commercial transactions and offers for sale to the public.

However, this line of argument cannot be taken so far as to regard the mandatory fixing of minimum alcohol contents as being an essential guarantee of the fairness of commercial transactions, since it is a simple matter to ensure that suitable information is conveyed to the purchaser by requiring the display of an indication of origin and of the alcohol content on the packaging of products.

14. It is clear from the foregoing that the requirements relating to the minimum

alcohol content of alcoholic beverages do not serve a purpose which is in the general interest and such as to take precedence over the requirements of the free movement of goods, which constitutes one of the fundamental rules of the Community.

In practice, the principal effect of requirements of this nature is to promote alcoholic beverages having a high alcohol content by excluding from the national market products of other Member States which do not answer that description.

It therefore appears that the unilateral requirement imposed by the rules of a Member State of a minimum alcohol content for the purposes of the sale of alcoholic beverages constitutes an obstacle to trade which is incompatible with the provisions of Article 30 of the Treaty.

There is therefore no valid reason why, provided that they have been lawfully produced and marketed in one of the Member States, alcoholic beverages should not be introduced into any other Member State; the sale of such products may not be subject to a legal prohibition on the marketing of beverages with an alcohol content lower than the limits set by the national rules.

The significance of the *Cassis de Dijon* decision can hardly be overstated and it is therefore worth dwelling upon both the result and the reasoning which the Court employs.

In terms of *result* the Court's ruling in *Cassis* affirms and develops the *Dassonville* judgment. It *affirms* paragraph 5 of *Dassonville* in the sense of making it clear that Article 30 can indeed apply to national rules which do not discriminate against imported products as such, but which inhibit trade nonetheless merely because they are different from the trade rules which apply in the country of origin. The *Cassis* ruling also *builds* upon paragraph 6 of *Dassonville*. It will be recalled that in that paragraph the ECJ had introduced the idea of the rule of reason: in the absence of Community harmonization on a particular topic reasonable measures could be taken by a state to prevent unfair trade practices. Paragraph 8 of the *Cassis* judgment develops this idea. Four matters (fiscal supervision, etc.) are listed which may prevent a trade rule which inhibits the free movement of goods from being caught by Article 30.[52] It should be emphasized that, as will be seen below, this list is not exhaustive; it can be and has been added to by the ECJ. It should also be emphasized that obstacles to the free movement of goods which are in this sense reasonable will be held not to fall within Article 30: the mandatory requirements which constitute the rule of reason are taken into account *within* the fabric of Article 30 and are separate from any analysis based upon Article 36. Notwithstanding the extended list of mandatory requirements which serve to take a case outside Article 30, the broad impact of the decision is captured by paragraph 14(4) of the ECJ's judgment: the presumption is that, once goods have been lawfully marketed in one Member State, they should be admitted into any other state without restriction, unless the state of import can successfully

[52] In one way this extended list of mandatory requirements can be seen as a *quid pro quo* for the affirmation that Art. 30 will indeed catch indistinctly applicable rules. This point will be developed more fully below: see 634–6.

invoke one of the mandatory requirements. In this sense the *Cassis* judgment encapsulates a principle of *mutual recognition*, in that Member States must respect the trade rules of other states and not seek to impose their own rules on goods which have been lawfully marketed in another territory of the Community. Small wonder, then, that Lord Mackenzie Stuart regarded the *Cassis* case as the most important decision made by the Court during his tenure of office.[53]

The *reasoning* employed in the *Cassis* case is just as significant as the result. This is often so with seminal ECJ decisions, and the *Cassis* case is no exception. The core of the reasoning is to be found in paragraph 8 of the judgment. This is a paragraph to be savoured, and we can learn a lot about the Court's style of judicial discourse by focusing upon its dynamics. The ECJ begins by affirming the right of the states to regulate all matters which have not yet been the subject of Community harmonization. Yet within half a dozen lines the whole balance has shifted: state regulation of such areas must be accepted together with any obstacles to trade which may follow from disparities in national laws, *but* only in so far as these trade rules can be justified by one of the mandatory requirements listed in paragraph 8. What began by an assertion of states' rights is transformed into a legal conclusion which places the state on the defensive, having to justify the indistinctly applicable rules under one of the heads of the rule of reason. The reasoning in the remainder of the judgment bears testimony to how closely the ECJ will scrutinize assertions that one of the mandatory requirements applies to the instant case. Now to be sure the German Government's claim in paragraph 10 is risible, and the Court is, if anything, more polite in its response than the argument warrants. The substance of the main claim in paragraph 12 is little better, and is properly countered in paragraph 13. The one point of real substance raised by the German Government is to be found in paragraph 12(3) and this elicits no direct response from the Court. This is a point which was touched upon in the introduction: the effect of *Cassis* is deregulatory, in the sense of rendering inapplicable trade rules which prevent goods lawfully marketed in one state from being imported into another state. Yet, as the argument in paragraph 12(3) makes clear, the result of this process may be to end up with no rules at all on a particular issue, or with a common standard which would reflect the rule pertaining in the country with the lowest rules on alcohol levels, what is often referred to as the 'regulatory race to the bottom'.[54] Now it may be felt that this result is either desirable, or at the least not something which we should be overly concerned about. This may be so on the facts of *Cassis*, but, as we shall see below, matters are not always so simple.

[53] Interview by one of the authors in 1993.

[54] This will not always be so: see Ch. 25..

6. INDISTINCTLY APPLICABLE RULES: THE POST-*CASSIS* JURISPRUDENCE

There have been numerous cases applying the *Cassis* doctrine to varying types of trade rules. In *Deserbais*[55] an importer of Edam cheese from Germany into France was prosecuted for unlawful use of a trade name: in Germany such cheese could be lawfully produced with a fat content of only 34.3 per cent, whereas in France the name Edam was restricted to cheese which had a fat content of 40 per cent. The importer relied on Article 30 by way of defence to the criminal prosecution. On a preliminary reference to the ECJ the Court held that the French rule was incompatible with Article 30. It was true that there were no Community rules governing the issue, but the French rule constituted a restriction on trade in relation to goods which had been lawfully marketed in another Member State. This rule could only be saved if it came within one of the mandatory requirements of *Cassis*. This was not so on the facts of the case, since the consumer could be provided with adequate information on the relative fat content of different Edam cheeses. The ECJ acknowledged that there might be cases where a product presented under a particular name was so different in terms of its content from products generally known by that name that it could not be regarded as falling within the same category. This was not so on the facts of the instant case. In *Gilli and Andres*[56] the importers of apple vinegar from Germany into Italy were prosecuted for fraud, on the ground that they had sold vinegar in Italy which was not made from the fermentation of wine. Once again the importers relied on Article 30 by way of defence. Once again there was no Community harmonization on the issue. The ECJ adopted the same reasoning as in *Cassis* itself: in the absence of such harmonization the state could regulate the matter, *provided* that such regulation did not constitute an obstacle, actually or potentially, to intra-Community trade. The rule in this case did hamper Community trade and could, therefore, only be saved if it came within one of the mandatory requirements. On the facts the Italian rule could not be saved on this ground, since the imported apple vinegar was not harmful to health and proper labelling on the bottle could alert consumers to the nature of the product, thereby avoiding any consumer confusion.

The same approach is apparent in the *Rau* case[57] which was concerned with national rules on packaging rather than content. Belgian law required all margarine to be marketed in cube-shaped packages. This rule applied to all margarine, irrespective of where it had been made, but it was clearly more difficult for non-Belgian manufacturers to comply without incurring cost increases

[55] Case 286/86, *Ministère Public* v. *Déserbais* [1988] ECR 4907, [1989] 1 CMLR 516.

[56] Case 788/79, *Italian State* v. *Gilli and Andres* [1980] ECR 2071, [1981] 1 CMLR 146. See also Case C–17/93, *J. J. J. van der Veldt*, 14 July 1994.

[57] Case 261/81, *Walter Rau Lebensmittelwerke* v. *de Smedt Pvba* [1982] ECR 3961, [1983] 2 CMLR 496.

since they would not normally have packaged their goods in this way. The ECJ held that the Belgian rule was caught by Article 30 and that it could not be justified on the basis of consumer protection: consumer confusion about the nature of the product could be avoided by means which were less inhibiting on intra-Community trade, such as by the obligation to label products clearly. More recently, in *Commission* v. *Germany*[58] the Court held that a German rule which restricted the expiry dates for medicinal products which could be shown on a package to two a year was caught by Article 30, since it would require importers to alter the expiry dates on their products. While in *Piageme*[59] a national law which required the exclusive use of a specific language for the labelling of foodstuffs was held to infringe Article 30, unless it allowed for the use of another language which would also be understood by purchasers or left open the possibility that purchasers could be informed in some other way.

7. INDISTINCTLY APPLICABLE RULES AND ARTICLE 34

Article 34 of the Treaty prohibits quantitative restrictions and MEQRs in relation to exports in the same manner as does Article 30 in relation to imports. The ECJ has, however, held that there is a difference in the scope of the two provisions. Whereas Article 30 will apply to discriminatory provisions and also to indistinctly applicable measures in the manner described above, Article 34 will, it seems, only apply if there is discrimination. An exporter faced with a national rule on, for example, quality standards which have to be met for a product to be marketed in that state cannot use Article 34 to argue that compliance with such a rule renders it more difficult for that exporter to penetrate other Community markets. This was established in the *Groenveld* case[60]. Dutch legislation prohibited all manufacturers of meat products from having in stock or processing horsemeat. The purpose was to safeguard the export of meat products to countries which prohibited the marketing of horseflesh. It was impossible to detect the presence of horsemeat within other meat products, and therefore the ban was designed to prevent its use by preventing meat processors from having such horsemeat in stock at all. The sale of horsemeat was not actually forbidden in the Netherlands. Nonetheless the Court held that the Dutch rule did not infringe Article 34. It stated that the purpose of

[58] Case C–317/92, [1994] ECR I–2039.

[59] Case C–369/89, *Groupement des Producteurs, Importeurs et Agents Généraux d'Eaux Minérales Etrangères (Piageme) Asbl* v. *Peeters Pvba* [1991] ECR I–2971, [1993] 3 CMLR 725.

[60] Case 15/79, *P. B. Groenveld BV* v. *Produktschap voor Vee en Vlees* [1979] ECR 3409, [1981] 1 CMLR 207. See also Case 237/82, *Jongeneel Kaas* v. *The State (Netherlands) and Stichting Centraal Orgaan Zuivelcontrole* [1984] ECR 483, [1985] 2 CMLR 53; Case 98/86, *Ministère Public* v. *Mathot* [1987] ECR 809, [1988] 1 CMLR 411.

Article 34 concerned national measures which have as their specific object or effect the restriction of patterns of exports and thereby the establishment of a difference in treatment between the domestic trade of a Member State and its export trade in such a way as to provide a particular advantage for national production at the expense of the trade of other Member States. This was not the case here, said the Court, since the prohibition in the instant case applied to the production of goods of a certain kind without drawing a distinction depending on whether such goods were intended for the national market or for export.[61]

The justification for defining the ambit of Articles 30 and 34 differently has been defended on the ground that the rationale for making Article 30 applicable to measures which do not discriminate is that they impose a dual burden on the importer who will have to satisfy the relevant rules in his or her own state and also the state of import; whereas in a case such as *Groenveld* the rule applied to all goods, both those for the domestic and the export market, and the goods were subject to no further rule at all at that stage of production or sale.[62] One could, however, imagine instances where a dual burden might exist.

8. INDISTINCTLY APPLICABLE RULES: THE LIMITS OF ARTICLE 30

(a) *The Nature of the Problem:* Cinéthèque *and* Torfaen

It would be easy to give many examples of cases in which the *Cassis* doctrine has been applied,[63] and indeed further instances will be discussed below when considering in detail the ECJ's interpretation of the mandatory requirements. It is, however, necessary at this juncture to focus on an important issue which is raised by *Cassis*: the limits or outer boundaries of Article 30.

The problem can be presented as follows. *Cassis* signalled the willingness of the ECJ to extend Article 30 to catch indistinctly applicable rules which inhibited trade in some manner. The difficulty is that all rules which concern trade, directly or indirectly, could be said to affect the free movement of goods in various ways. Are all such measures within Article 30, with the consequent need to show a distinct justification for the relevant rule? In the words of Weatherill and Beaumont:[64]

61 N. 60 above, para. 7.

62 R. Barents, 'New Developments in Measures Having Equivalent Effect' (1981) 18 CMLRev. 271; Weatherill and Beaumont, *EC Law* (Penguin, 1993), 465.

63 See e.g. Case 298/87, *Smanor SA* [1988] ECR 4489; Case 407/85, *Drei Glocken GmbH* v. *USL Centro-Sud and Provincia Autonomafeti Bolzano* [1988] ECR 4233; Case C–362/88, *GB-INNO-BM* v. *Confédération du Commerce Luxembourgeois Asbl* [1990] ECR I–667, [1991] 2 CMLR 801.

64 N. 62 above, 467–8.

> Consider building regulations that restrict the erection of shops where imported goods might be sold; rules requiring the owner of a firearm, which might be imported, to hold a licence; or spending limits imposed on a government department that reduce its capacity to purchase imported goods. All these rules have the potential to reduce sales opportunities for imported products.

As the authors note it might be thought to be absurd to bring such rules within Article 30, and yet the *Dassonville* principle is broad enough to render the Treaty applicable in such instances, particularly when that principle is seen in the light of *Cassis* itself.

Having said that, one can nonetheless perceive a distinction between the type of case which *Cassis* is intended to catch and the type of rule exemplified in the above quotation. One way of expressing the distinction is, as Weatherill and Beaumont note,[65] between what may be termed dual-burden rules and equal-burden rules.

Cassis, and many of the cases decided after it, concerns dual-burden rules. State *A* imposes certain rules on the content of goods, and these rules are applied to goods imported from state *B*, even though the goods produced in state *B* would already have had to comply with the relevant trade rules from that state. The impact of *Cassis* is to render such rules incompatible with Article 30 unless they can be saved by one of the mandatory requirements.

Equal-burden rules are those applying to all goods, irrespective of origin, which regulate trade in some manner, which are not designed to be protectionist, which may have an impact on the overall volume of trade, but which have no greater impact in this respect on imports than they do on domestic products.

The crucial question is whether rules of this latter nature should be held to fall within Article 30, subject to a possible justification, or whether they should be deemed to be outside Article 30 altogether. Although the result of these two strategies may be the same in a particular case, in that the rule may be held lawful through either strategy, the choice between them is nonetheless of real importance. On the former view the rule is *prima facie* subject to Article 30. This fact can be relied upon in any relevant litigation, and the burden will be on those seeking to uphold the rule to bring it within an objective justification. On the latter view, the rule will be outside Article 30 *in toto*.

The attitude of the ECJ towards this issue has not always been uniform. In a number of cases the ECJ held that rules which did not relate to the *characteristics* of the goods and did not impose a dual burden on the importer, but only concerned the conditions on which all goods were *sold*, were outside Article 30. Thus in *Oebel*[66] the Court held that a rule which prohibited the delivery of bakery products to consumers and retailers (but not wholesalers) at night was not caught by Article 30, since trade between the Member States was possible at all times and the rule prohibiting delivery applied in the same

[65] N. 62 above, 468–76.

[66] Case 155/80, [1981] ECR 1993, [1983] 1 CMLR 390.

way to all producers wherever they were established.[67] Similarly in *Forest*[68] the ECJ decided that a French law imposing quotas for the milling of flour for human consumption did not affect the possibility of importing flour from other Member States, and consequently that the measure had no impact on wheat imports and would not be likely to affect trade between Member States.[69] While in *Blesgen*[70] the ECJ considered that a national rule restricting the sale of drinks above a certain strength on premises used for consumption by the public had no connection with the import of such products and was not, in its nature, such as to affect trade between Member States. And in *Quietlynn*[71] the Court found that a rule of United Kingdom law which restricted the sale of lawful sex articles to shops which had been licensed for the purpose was not in breach of Article 30, since it merely regulated the distribution of the products without discrimination against imported goods.

In a number of other cases the Court has, however, held that Article 30 can apply to rules which are not dissimilar to those in the preceding paragraph. The *Cinéthèque* case provides a good illustration of the problem posed by equal-burden rules. More recently the ECJ in the *Keck* case[72] has departed from some of its previous case law. It is, however, impossible to understand the significance of this finding without an appreciation of the Court's earlier case law.

Cases 60 and 61/84, Cinéthèque SA v. Fédération Nationale des Cinémas Français [1985] ECR 2605, [1986] 1 CMLR 365

French law banned the sale or hire of videos of films during the first year in which the film was released, the objective being to encourage people to go to the cinema and hence protect the profitability of cinematographic production. The rule applied equally to domestic and imported videos. The law was challenged by a distributor of videos as being in breach of Article 30. The ECJ noted that most Member States had some provisions akin to those in France, that they had the same objective, and that the Treaty left it to the states to determine the need for and form of such a system. It continued as follows.

THE ECJ

21. In that connection it must be observed that such a system, if it applies without distinction to both video-cassettes manufactured in the national territory and to imported video-cassettes, does not have the purpose of regulating trade patterns; its effect is not to favour national production as against the production of other Member States, but to encourage cinematographic production as such.

[67] *Ibid.*, para. 20.

[68] Case 148/85, *Direction Générale des Impôts and Procureur de la République* v. *Forest* [1986] ECR 3449, [1988] 2 CMLR 577.

[69] *Ibid.*, para. 11.

[70] Case 75/81, *Belgian State* v. *Blesgen* [1982] ECR 1211, [1983] 1 CMLR 431.

[71] Case C–23/89, *Quietlynn Ltd.* v. *Southend-on-Sea BC* [1990] ECR I–3059, [1990] 3 CMLR 55.

[72] Cases C–267 and 268/91, *Criminal Proceedings against Keck and Mithouard* [1993] ECR I–6097.

22. Nevertheless, the application of such a system may create barriers to intra-Community trade in video-cassettes because of the disparities between the systems operated in the different Member States and between the conditions for the release of cinematographic works in the cinemas of those States. In those circumstances a prohibition of exploitation laid down by such a system is not compatible with the principle of free movement of goods provided for in the Treaty unless any obstacle to intra-Community trade thereby created does not exceed that which is necessary in order to ensure the attainment of the objective in view and unless that objective is justified with regard to Community law.

23. It must be conceded that a national system which, in order to encourage the creation of cinematographic works irrespective of their origin, gives priority, for a limited initial period, to the distribution of such works through the cinema, is so justified.

24. The reply to the questions referred to the Court is therefore that Article 30 of the EEC Treaty must be interpreted as meaning that it does not apply to national legislation which regulates the distribution of cinematographic works by imposing an interval between one mode of distributing such works and another by prohibiting their simultaneous exploitation in cinemas and in video-cassette form for a limited period, provided that the prohibition applies to domestically produced and imported cassettes alike and any barriers to intra-Community trade to which its implementation may give rise do not exceed what is necessary for ensuring that the exploitation in cinemas of cinematographic works of all origins retains priority over other means of distribution.

The Court's reasoning in *Cinéthèque* can be summarized in the following manner: the rule was *prima facie* within Article 30, but it might be regarded as lawful if there was an objective justification for it which was acceptable with regard to Community law, and provided also that the method of attaining the objective was proportionate. This emerges from paragraph 22. In paragraph 23 the ECJ accepts the objective of the French rule, the enhancement of cinema distribution, and then reiterates the proportionality idea in paragraph 24. Viewed in this way the decision regards equal-burden rules as being within Article 30, and appears merely to add to the *Cassis* list of mandatory requirements a further ground for objective justification based on the protection or enhancement of artistic works.

The approach adopted by the ECJ in *Cinéthèque* can be contrasted with that taken by Advocate General Slynn. He defined the ambit of Article 30 to cover three types of case: import restrictions, discriminatory barriers to trade, and indistinctly applicable rules which require 'a producer or distributor to take steps additional to those which he would normally and lawfully take in the marketing of goods, which thereby render importation more difficult, so that imports may be restricted and national producers be given protection in practice'.[73] This last category represented the *Cassis* doctrine, but Advocate General Slynn believed that it should be distinguished from the type of case before the ECJ in *Cinéthèque*:[74]

[73] Cases 60 and 61/84, *Cinéthèque* [1985] ECR 2605, 2611.

[74] *Ibid.*

On the other hand, in an area in which there are no common Community standards or rules, where a national measure is not specifically directed at imports, does not discriminate against imports, does not make it any more difficult for an importer to sell his products than it is for a domestic producer, and gives no protection to domestic producers, then in my view, *prima facie*, the measure does not fall within Article 30 even if it does in fact lead to a restriction or reduction of imports.

On the facts of the case Advocate General Slynn felt that the French rule was of the type described in this quotation: it was not designed to protect the French video market, it did not have this effect, and importers of videos were in no worse position than their French counterparts.

It is clear then that the approach adopted by the ECJ and by Advocate General Slynn was markedly different: on the Court's view the French rule was prima facie within Article 30, albeit capable of being justified in the above manner; on the Advocate General's approach the French rule was not within the reach of Article 30 at all.

The difficult question of the outer limits of Article 30, and whether it should be interpreted to catch equal burden rules, came before the ECJ once again in the *Sunday Trading* cases:

Case 145/88, Torfaen BC v. B & Q plc
[1989] ECR 385, [1990] 1 CMLR 337

B & Q was prosecuted for violation of the Sunday trading laws which prohibited retail shops from selling on Sundays, subject to exceptions for certain types of products. B & Q claimed that these laws constituted a MEQR. The effect of the laws was to reduce total turnover by about 10 per cent, with a corresponding diminution of imports from other Member States. But imported goods were, in this respect, in no worse a position than domestic goods: the reduction in total turnover would affect all goods equally.

THE ECJ

10. By its first question the national court seeks to establish whether the concept of measures having an equivalent effect to quantitative restrictions within the meaning of Article 30 of the Treaty also covers provisions prohibiting retailers from opening their premises on Sunday if the effect of the prohibition is to reduce in absolute terms the sales of goods in those premises, including imported goods from other Member States.

11. The first point which must be made is that national rules prohibiting retailers from opening their premises on Sunday apply to imported and domestic products alike. In principle, the marketing of products imported from other Member States is not therefore made more difficult than the marketing of domestic products.

12. Next, it must be recalled that in its judgment . . . in Joined Cases 60 and 61/84 (*Cinéthèque*) the Court held, with regard to a prohibition of the hiring of video-cassettes applicable to domestic and imported products alike, that such a

prohibition was not compatible with the principle of the free movement of goods provided for in the Treaty unless any obstacle to Community trade thereby created did not exceed what was necessary in order to ensure the attainment of the objective in view and unless that objective was justified with regard to Community law.

13. In those circumstances it is therefore necessary in a case such as this to consider first of all whether rules such as those at issue pursue an aim which is justified with regard to Community law. As far as this question is concerned the Court has already stated in its judgment . . . in Case 155/80 (*Oebel* [1981] ECR 1993) that national rules governing the hours of work, delivery and sale in the bread and confectionery industry constitute a legitimate part of economic and social policy, consistent with the objectives of public interest pursued by the Treaty.

14. The same consideration must apply as regards national rules governing the opening hours of retail premises. Such rules reflect certain political and economic choices in so far as their purpose is to ensure that working and non-working hours are so arranged as to accord with national or regional socio-cultural characteristics, and that, in the present state of Community law, is a matter for Member States. Furthermore such rules are not designed to govern the patterns of trade between Member States.

15. Secondly, it is necessary to ascertain whether the effects of such national rules exceed what is necessary to achieve the aim in view. As is indicated in Article 3 of Commission Directive 70/50 . . . the prohibition laid down in Article 30 covers national measures governing the marketing of products where the restrictive effect of such measures on the free movement of goods exceeds the effects intrinsic to trade rules.

16. The question whether the effects of specific national rules do in fact remain within that limit is a question to be determined by the national court.

17. The reply to the first question must therefore be that Article 30 of the Treaty must be interpreted as meaning that the prohibition which it lays down does not apply to national rules prohibiting retailers from opening their premises on Sunday where the restrictive effects on Community trade which may result therefrom do not exceed the effects intrinsic to rules of that kind.

The approach in *Torfaen* was therefore conceptually identical to that which the Court had adopted in *Cinéthèque*: the rule was *prima facie* caught by Article 30, but it could escape prohibition provided that the objective behind the rule was justified from the perspective of Community law, and provided also that the effects of the rule were proportionate, in the sense that they were not excessive in relation to the objective sought to be achieved.

One of the problems with this approach was that it was for national courts to determine whether the proportionality criterion was met or not. Subsequent case law within the United Kingdom courts attested to the difficulty which was felt by these courts in applying the test laid down by the ECJ, some courts finding that the Sunday trading laws were compatible with Article 30, while others reached the opposite conclusion.[75]

[75] *Stoke City Council* v. *B & Q plc* [1990] 3 CMLR 31; *Wellingborough BC* v. *Payless* [1990] 1 CMLR 773; *B & Q plc* v. *Shrewsbury BC* [1990] 3 CMLR 535; *Payless* v. *Peterborough CC* [1990] 2 CMLR 577. See generally A. Arnull, 'What Shall We Do On Sunday?' (1991) 16 ELRev. 112.

Subsequent decisions by the ECJ on related issues can be seen as attempting to make life easier for national courts. Thus in cases concerning the legality of national rules which restricted the employment of staff on Sundays the ECJ applied the *Torfaen* test, but then made it clear that these measures did not create restrictive effects which were disproportionate to their objectives.[76] In the context of Sunday trading rules the ECJ has now also held in the *Stoke CC* case[77] that such rules are indeed proportionate and lawful.

Notwithstanding these more recent decisions by the ECJ which were designed to give clearer guidance to national courts on the legality of equal-burden rules, the fundamental approach remained the same: such rules were *prima facie* within Article 30, but could be upheld provided that the objective was justified under Community law, and provided also that they were proportionate in the sense described above. The post-*Torfaen* case law simply made things easier for national courts by providing guidance on the application of the proportionality part of this overall criterion.

It is now clear that the ECJ has had second thoughts on whether this general strategy for dealing with equal burden rules is really correct. The *Keck* case signals a change of attitude towards such rules, and the adoption of a position which is more redolent of that taken by Advocate General Slynn in *Cinéthèque*.

(b) Academic Opinion Prior to Keck

As might be expected, the ECJ's case law provided academics with a rich source of material for discussion, and a number of articles emerged devoted to considering the proper boundaries of Article 30. Not surprisingly opinions differed.

Some saw little wrong with the ECJ's approach in *Cinéthèque* and *Torfaen*: the relevant measures could be held to be *prima facie* within Article 30, and it would then be incumbent on the parties to seek to take the rule out of that Article in the manner described in the Court's jurisprudence.

Others were less happy with the Court's approach. A variety of possible criteria were suggested for demarcating the proper limits of Article 30. Steiner argued that the Court should focus on whether a challenged rule constituted a hindrance to trade.[78] White on the other hand proposed a different test. The author was a member of the Commission's legal service, and had been the Commission's representative in the *Torfaen* case. The criterion which he proposed for the limits of Article 30 did not find immediate favour with the Court, but, as will be seen below, the ECJ's judgment in *Keck* has now adopted a similar approach to that advocated by White. The essence of this approach is captured in the following extract:

[76] Case C–312/89, *Union Département des Syndicats CGT de l'Aisne* v. *SIDEF Conforama* [1991] ECR I–997; Case C–332/89, *Ministère Public* v. *Marchandise* [1991] ECR I–1027.

[77] Cases C–306/88, C–304/90, C–169/91, *Stoke-on-Trent CC* v. *B & Q plc* [1992] ECR I–6457, 6493, 6635, [1993] 1 CMLR 426.

[78] J. Steiner, 'Drawing the Line: Uses and Abuses of Art. 30 EEC' (1992) 29 CMLRev. 749.

E. White, In Search of the Limits to Article 30 of the EEC Treaty[79]

The different legal and economic environment of the Member State of origin finds its expression in the different *characteristics* of an imported product compared with the national product. Consequently, as the judgment of the Court in *Cassis de Dijon* clearly shows, Member States are not entitled to require that imported products have the same *characteristics* as are required of, or are traditional in, domestic products unless this is strictly necessary for the protection of some legitimate interest. There is not, however, the same need to require the rules relating to the *circumstances* in which certain goods may be *sold or used* in the importing Member State to be overridden for this purpose as long as imported products enjoy *equal access* to the market of the importing Member State compared with national goods. In such a case the imported product is not deprived of any advantage it derives from the different legal and economic environment prevailing in the place of production. In fact, any reduction of total sales (and therefore imports) which may result from restrictions on the circumstances in which they may be sold does not arise from *disparities* between national rules but rather out of the *existence* of the rules in the importing Member State.

. . . The proposed definition of a measure of equivalent effect to a quantitative restriction on imports for indistinctly applicable measures based on *Cassis de Dijon* case law is therefore *the application by a Member State to products legally produced and marketed in another Member State of its national rules relating to the characteristics required of such products on its territory (which therefore prevents this product from benefiting in the importing Member State from the advantages arising out of its production in the different legal and economic environment prevailing in the other Member State)*. The *Cassis de Dijon* case law shows that the term 'characteristics' includes the composition, size, shape, and weight of goods as well as their presentation, denomination and labelling. State measures which are entirely neutral in their effect on goods legally produced and marketed in other Member States, because they only regulate the circumstances in which all goods of the same kind may be sold or used, should not be regarded as falling under Article 30.

Mortelmans was in sympathy with the general approach adopted by White, but believed that White's definition allowed too many national rules to escape from Article 30. He accepted that rules relating to the characteristics of the product should be within Article 30, but argued that some national rules concerned with market circumstances, i.e. the terms on which the goods were sold, should also be caught.

K. Mortelmans, Article 30 of the EEC Treaty and Legislation Relating to Market Circumstances: Time to Consider a New Definition?[80]

In my view, apart from product rules which are in all cases governed by Article 30 EEC, the scope of this Treaty Article remains restricted to two categories of

[79] (1989) 26 CMLRev. 235, 246–7, italics in the original.
[80] (1991) 28 CMLRev. 115, 130.

market circumstances rules. First the rules which apply distinctly to national and imported products and secondly the indistinctly applicable rules without a territorial element. These last rules, which do not relate to activities situated in a fixed location, could pose a real threat to the completion of the internal market, because they actually assume free circulation of persons and/or goods. The door-to-door selling legislation (*Buet* case), the limiting of promotional gifts (*Oosthoek*—Belgian connection—case) therefore continue to fall under Article 30 EEC. However, rules on market circumstances relating to a fixed location (pub, shop, shopping centre, petrol station, bakery) and where the good or service is only a secondary consideration, fall outside the scope of Article 30 EEC (or Article 59 EEC). This includes the trading hours law (*Torfaen* case and others), the Van der Velde Act (*Blesgen* case), the prohibition on baking at night (*Oebel* case), sex shop legislation (*Quietlynn* case), and town and country planning regulations (*Gauchard* case). These measures do not pose any real threat to the completion of the internal market. Furthermore, in some cases (*Oosthoek*—Dutch connection—case and *Gauchard* case) there were no links with Community law: the so- called 'internal situation' rule.

The range of academic opinion must now be seen in the light of the ECJ's judgment in the *Keck* case, in which the Court took the opportunity to reconsider its previous case law on this topic.

(c) The Judgment in Keck

Cases C–267 and 268/91, Criminal Proceedings against Keck and Mithouard [1993] ECR I–6097

Keck and Mithouard (K & M) were prosecuted in the French courts for selling goods at a price which was lower than their actual purchase price (resale at a loss), contrary to a French law of 1963 as amended in 1986. The law did not ban sales at a loss by the manufacturer. K & M claimed that the law was contrary to Community law concerning free movement of goods, persons, services and capital, and also that it was contrary to the principles of free competition within the Community. The case was referred to the ECJ under Article 177. The ECJ dismissed the claim in so far as it related to free movement of persons, services, and capital, and then focused on the argument concerning free movement of goods.

THE ECJ

11. By virtue of Article 30, quantitative restrictions on imports and all measures having equivalent effect are prohibited between Member States. The Court has consistently held that any measure which is capable of directly or indirectly, actually or potentially, hindering intra-Community trade constitutes a measure having equivalent effect to a quantitative restriction.
12. It is not the purpose of national legislation imposing a general prohibition on resale at a loss to regulate trade in goods between Member States.
13. Such legislation may, admittedly, restrict the volume of sales, and hence the

volume of sales of products from other Member States, in so far as it deprives traders of a method of sales promotion. But the question remains whether such a possibility is sufficient to characterize the legislation in question as a measure having equivalent effect to a quantitative restriction on imports.

14. In view of the increasing tendency of traders to invoke Article 30 of the Treaty as a means of challenging any rules whose effect is to limit their commercial freedom even where such rules are not aimed at products from other Member States, the Court considers it necessary to re-examine and clarify its case law on this matter.

15. In '*Cassis de Dijon*' . . . it was held that, in the absence of harmonization of legislation, measures of equivalent effect prohibited by Article 30 include obstacles to the free movement of goods where they are the consequence of applying rules that lay down requirements to be met by such goods (such as requirements as to designation, form, size, weight, composition, presentation, labelling, packaging) to goods from other Member States where they are lawfully manufactured and marketed, even if those rules apply without distinction to all products unless their application can be justified by a public-interest objective taking precedence over the free movement of goods.

16. However, contrary to what has previously been decided, the application to products from other Member States of national provisions restricting or prohibiting certain selling arrangements is not such as to hinder directly or indirectly, actually or potentially, trade between Member States within the meaning of the *Dassonville* judgment . . . provided that those provisions apply to all affected traders operating within the national territory and provided that they affect in the same manner, in law and fact, the marketing of domestic products and of those from other Member States.

17. Where those conditions are fulfilled, the application of such rules to the sale of products from another Member State is not by nature such as to prevent their access to the market or to impede access any more than it impedes the access of domestic products. Such rules therefore fall outside the scope of Article 30 of the Treaty.

18. Accordingly, the reply to be given to the national court is that Article 30 of the EEC Treaty is to be interpreted as not applying to legislation of a Member State imposing a general prohibition on resale at a loss.

The decision in *Keck* clearly signals a re-thinking by the ECJ about the outer limits of Article 30. It constitutes one of those rare occasions on which the Court explicitly states not only that it is re-examining its own previous jurisprudence, but that it is also departing from some of its earlier case law (paragraphs 14 and 16).

Three central issues are raised by the decision: what does the case actually decide, what is the rationale for the Court's approach, and what problems is the decision likely to generate? These questions will be addressed in turn.

(d) Keck: *The Legal Effect of the Decision*

The difficulty of answering the first of these questions is readily apparent from the ECJ's judgment set out above: the Court indicates that it is departing from its previous case law, but does not state explicitly which cases fall within this category. One can nonetheless draw certain conclusions from its reasoning.

It is clear that the touchstone of the Court's judgment is the distinction between *rules which relate to the goods themselves* in terms of composition, packaging, presentation, and the like, which are properly held to fall within Article 30 under the *Cassis* doctrine (paragraph 15); and *rules relating to selling arrangements* which, although they may affect the total volume of goods sold (paragraph 13), are not thought to be within the reach of Article 30, *provided* that the conditions mentioned in the second part of paragraph 16 are met. Rules which fall within this latter category are outside Article 30 both because their *purpose* is not to regulate trade as such (paragraph 12), and because their *effect and nature* are not such as to prevent access to the market, or at least not to impede access to the market for importers any more than they do for domestic products (paragraph 17). If, however, the proviso expressed in paragraph 16 of *Keck* is thought to apply then a case would be brought back within the ambit of Article 30.

The reference to the earlier case law which was being reassessed by *Keck* (paragraph 16) is unclear, in part because the Court does not name specific cases, and in part because of uncertainty about the meaning of the term 'selling arrangement'. The Court's re-thinking would appear to encompass decisions such as *Torfaen* and probably *Cinéthèque*.[81] In both of these cases the challenged rule concerned selling arrangements, which affected importers no more than domestic producers; in both the effect on intra-Community trade resided in a reduction in the total volume of sales; in both cases the ECJ held that the rule was, nonetheless, caught by Article 30, subject to the possibility that it could be legitimated in the manner described above. We have already seen that Advocate General Slynn in *Cinéthèque* would have preferred to regard such rules as outside Article 30[82], and the ECJ in *Keck* adopts an approach which is close to that put forward by him. On the view adopted in *Keck* such rules will be deemed to be outside the remit of Article 30. It will no longer be necessary to inquire whether the object pursued by rules of this nature was legitimate from a Community perspective, nor will it be necessary to determine whether the attainment of this objective was proportionate or not. National provisions relating to selling arrangements will be regarded as outside Article 30, provided that the conditions mentioned in paragraph 16 are met: the provisions must apply to all traders operating within the national territory, and they must affect in the same manner, in law and fact, the

[81] The reason for the greater hesitation about whether *Cinéthèque* was included in the ECJ's reassesment of previous authority is that the ban on sales in that case was absolute for the relevant period of one year. Whether, therefore, the ECJ would wish to subject such cases to closer supervision than allowed by the *Keck* judgment remains to be seen. However, in Cases C–401 and 402/92, *Criminal Proceedings against Tankstation 't Heustke vof and J. B. E. Boermans* [1994] ECR I–2199, 2220 Van Gerven A.G. felt that *Cinéthèque* would be decided differently now in the light of *Keck*.

[82] See above, 620–1.

marketing of domestic goods and imports. Community law will then intrude on such provisions only if there are harmonization measures present.

Thus in the *Tankstation* case[83] the Court held that national rules which provided for the compulsory closing of shops, in this instance petrol stations, were not caught by Article 30. The ECJ repeated the essence of its ruling in *Keck* and concluded that the rules related to selling arrangements which applied equally to all traders without distinguishing between the origin of the goods; while in *Punto Casa SpA*[84] the Court reached the same conclusion in relation to Italian legislation on the closure of retail outlets on Sundays: provided that the rules on selling arrangements applied equally to domestic and imported products, in the sense of affecting them in the same manner in law and fact, they were outside the scope of Article 30. The same theme is apparent in *Hunermund*[85]. In that case the ECJ held that a rule which prohibited pharmacists from advertising para-pharmaceutical products which they were allowed to sell was not caught by Article 30. Using language drawn from the *Keck* opinion the Court observed that the rule was not directed towards intra-Community trade; that it did not preclude traders other than pharmacists from advertising such goods; that the rule applied evenly as between all traders; and that although it might have some impact on the overall volume of sales this was not enough to render it a MEQR for the purpose of Article 30.

Problems concerning the ambit of the term 'selling arrangements' do, however, undoubtedly exist and will be examined further below.[86]

(e) Keck*: The Rationale for the Court's Approach*

It is apparent from the ECJ's judgment that the motivation behind the rethinking of the law in *Keck* was the tendency for traders to challenge any rules which limit their commercial freedom even where such rules were not aimed at imports (paragraph 14).

In answering the question posed in this section it may be helpful to begin by asking whether *Keck* can be rationalized on the basis of the dichotomy drawn above between dual-burden rules and equal-burden rules? It is clear that this distinction plays some part in the Court's judgment, as is evident from the reasoning in paragraphs 15 to 17.

Cassis-type rules relating to the goods themselves are properly regarded as within Article 30, in part because these rules will have to be satisfied by the importer in addition to any such provisions existing within his or her own state (paragraph 15). They impose a dual burden on the importer, even if the challenged rule in the importing state applies indistinctly to all goods of a

[83] Cases C–401 and 402/92, n. 81 above.

[84] Cases C–69 and 258/93, *Punto Casa SpA* v. *Sindaco del Commune di Capena* [1994] ECR I–2355.

[85] Case C–292/92, *R. Hunermund* v. *Landesapothekerkammer Baden-Württemburg* [1993] ECR I–6787.

[86] See below, 629–30.

certain kind. In this sense such rules are by their very nature[87] likely to impede access to the market for imported goods.

Rules concerning selling arrangements by way of contrast simply impose an equal burden on all those seeking to market goods in a particular territory (paragraph 17). Such rules do not normally demand any adaptation of the imported product, and hence do not impose extra costs on the importer.[88]

It may be helpful in this respect to focus on the ECJ's own reasoning in *Keck*. The distinction which the Court draws is, as we have seen, between rules which relate to the *characteristics of the goods* as opposed to those *rules which concern selling arrangements for the goods*. The latter are deemed to be outside Article 30 for a number of connected reasons: the purpose of the relevant legislation is not to regulate trade (paragraph 12), it only affects the overall volume of trade (paragraph 13), and any effect on sales is equal as between domestic and imported goods (paragraphs 16–17). It is readily apparent that the test adopted by the Court in *Keck* is very similar to that advocated by White in the quotation set out above.

(f) Keck*: Future Problems*

While one can appreciate the desire of the ECJ to limit Article 30, the distinction which the Court draws is nonetheless problematic in certain respects. Two such problems may be addressed here.

On the one hand, the distinction drawn by the Court in *Keck* will, like all distinctions, leave grey areas where it is uncertain how one should characterize the rule in question, whether as one which goes to the nature of the product itself or to the selling arrangements for that product. The problem resides ultimately in the ambiguity as to the meaning of the term 'selling arrangements'. This could connote only what may be termed static selling arrangements: rules relating to the hours at which shops may be open, the length of time for which people may work, or the type of premises in which certain goods may be sold. Non-static or dynamic selling arrangements include the ways in which a manufacturer chooses *to market this specific product*, through a certain form of advertising, free offers, and the like. The objection to taking all rules of this latter kind out of Article 30 is that they can relate much more closely to the very definition of the product itself; they may form an integral aspect of the goods, in much the same way as do rules relating to composition, labelling, or presentation. Yet it is clear from *Keck* that the Court appears to regard some such rules as akin to selling arrangements and outside Article 30. Thus in paragraph 13 of its judgment it admits that a rule prohibiting sales at a loss deprives traders of a method of sales-promotion and hence reduces the volume of sales, and yet treats this rule as a selling arrangement which is outside Article 30 for the reasons given above. While in

[87] Cases 401 and 402/92, n. 81 above, 2215. [88] *Ibid.*

Hunermund[89] a limited ban on advertising was characterized as a method of sales-promotion and held to be outside Article 30.

On the other hand, in addition to these problems of characterization there are bound to be continuing difficulties with the application of the proviso in paragraph 16. The effect of this proviso is that, even if a rule is categorized as one which goes to selling arrangements rather than being expressive of a characteristic of the goods themselves, it will still remain within Article 30 if, for example, the effect of the rule on domestic traders and importers is not the same. There can be national provisions which restrict selling opportunities which may not have an equal impact on domestic and imported goods alike. This is exemplified by *Oosthoek*[90]. In that case the ECJ held that national rules which prohibited the offer of free gifts to buyers of encyclopædias were within Article 30. The reasoning was that legislation which restricted certain forms of advertising or sales-promotion might limit intra-Community trade, even if the rules were indistinctly applicable: it might force a producer to adopt sales-promotion or advertising schemes which differed as between states, or to discontinue a scheme which was thought to be particularly effective.[91] Now we have already seen in the preceding paragraph that some such rules may still be within the ambit of Article 30 even after *Keck*.[92] However, even if rules of this nature were *prima facie* to be outside Article 30 because they were held to constitute selling arrangements, they could still be brought within Article 30 if the case was felt to come within the proviso to paragraph 16 of the judgment.

(g) Keck *and the Scope of Article 30: 'Full Tests v. Simplified Rules or Simplified Standards'*

Notwithstanding the problems with the rationale for the *Keck* judgment, and notwithstanding also some of the difficulties which will remain to be resolved in the light of the decision, it can nonetheless be regarded as a broadly sensible step for the Court to have taken. The case law prior to *Keck* had exemplified the difficulties in defining the outer boundaries of Article 30. The ECJ in its pre-*Keck* jurisprudence was being asked to apply Article 30 to an ever-wider range of rules, the effect of which on trade was marginal. Even if such rules were ultimately held to be legitimate on the basis of the reasoning in *Cinéthèque* and *Torfaen* this strategy had a number of disadvantages: it meant that such rules were *prima facie* within Article 30, which had important consequential implications for the parties; it meant that scarce judicial resources of the ECJ were taken up with adjudicating on the legality of such rules, and

[89] Case C–292/92 n. 85 above.

[90] Case 286/81, *Oosthoek's Uitgeversmaatschappij BV* [1982] ECR 4575, [1983] 3 CMLR 428. See also Case 382/87, *Buet* v. *Minstère Public* [1989] ECR 1235.

[91] On the facts of the case the rule benefited from the objective justification founded on consumer protection, since consumers could be misled as to the real prices of certain products.

[92] This is probably still the case notwithstanding *Hunermund*, since the advertising ban in that case was very limited in its scope, but see now *Leclerc-Siplec*, 632–3.

that national courts might have to apply the proportionality part of this test, with all the consequential complications which became apparent in the Sunday Trading cases. Small wonder then that the Court in *Keck* felt that the time was ripe for a reappraisal of the outer limits of Article 30.

There is another, more formal, method of expressing the conclusion of the previous paragraph. It can be presented as follows. In many contexts legal systems will be faced with choices concerning how best to give effect to the objectives of any particular legal norm.

At one end of the scale lies the choice of a *'full test'*, signifying that on each and every occasion the Court should engage in a complex balancing exercise to determine the result which will best give effect to the purpose behind the norm in question. Wils expresses this approach in the following way:[93]

> The borderline between legitimate and illegitimate national regulation under Article 30 should reflect the balance between the desire for integration, that is, the desire to limit the influence of national governments on people's activities throughout the Community, and the desire for government intervention, translated—for practical reasons or reasons of principle—into a desire for national regulation. It follows that those national measures should be struck down under Article 30 which are more harmful than beneficial, in that their obstructive effect on the integration of national markets outweighs their valued regulatory contribution. The test is thus essentially a balancing test.

On this view, then, it would be for the ECJ to weigh on each occasion the anti-integrationist effect of a measure, with the valued regulatory effect of the national provision.[94] The administrative costs of operating such a test are, however, considerable, both for the ECJ and for national courts, particularly if the latter are given the task of applying the proportionality part of any such criterion. Any calculation of administrative costs would also have to take account of costs for private parties, who would be relatively uncertain about the legality of their planned conduct.

It is for these reasons that legal systems often forego such complex tests and replace them with *simpler rules or standards* which are designed to reduce public and private costs and to provide clearer guidance to the parties on the limits of legitimate trading activity. To quote Wils once again:[95]

> Among the judgments in which the Court used a simplified standard, are the *Oebel*, *Blesgen*, *Krantz* and *Quietlynn* decisions. Each of these cases concerned a national measure the valued regulatory effect of which most obviously exceeded its anti-integrationist effect . . . In these judgments the Court did not go the whole way of applying the full balancing test, by analysing the obviously negative anti-integrationist effect, enumerating the regulatory objectives, demonstrating their

[93] W. P. J. Wils, 'The Search for the Rule In Art. 30 EEC: Much Ado About Nothing?' (1993) 18 ELRev. 475, 478.

[94] *Ibid.* 478–9.

[95] *Ibid.* 483.

Community value, and confirming the effectiveness of the national measure, so as to reach the anyway obvious conclusion that the valued regulatory effect outweighed the anti-integrationist effect. Instead, the Court wrote down, in varying words, its sufficiently clear first-sight impression that the anti-integrationist effect of the measure was no match for its valued regulatory effects, and that the measure should thus withstand the prohibition of Article 30.

Viewed in this way the decision in *Keck* can be regarded as a further shift to a *formal, general rule* which is designed to give broader guidance than had been forthcoming from decisions such as *Oebel* or *Quietlynn*. Whereas the Court had made it clear that Article 30 was inapplicable on the *facts of those cases* without any complex balancing exercise, the ECJ continued to be faced with challenges to similar national trade rules, in part at least because of its own decisions in cases such as *Cinéthèque* and *Torfaen*, indicating that Article 30 could bite in such instances. *Keck*, then, represents a choice by the ECJ to draw a more formal and general line as to the types of rule which will be held to fall within Article 30. To be sure, this choice may result in some increase in error costs, in the sense that selling rules may be held to be legitimate even though the anti-integrationist impact exceeds the valued national regulatory benefit.[96] To be sure, there will also be some grey areas in which it will be difficult to determine whether trade rules should be classified as relating to product characteristics or selling arrangements. Yet these are the inevitable consequences of a more rule-based regime. You cannot have finger-tip precision in the application of this type of legal norm, *and also* a relatively high degree of certainty plus relatively low administrative costs. There will always be trade-offs to be made in this respect.[97] Given the problems encountered by the ECJ[98] when it applied a fuller, *ad hoc* balancing approach to each possible Article 30 case, the general approach in *Keck* is not unreasonable, in the light of the difficult nature of the problem.[99]

(h) Keck *and the Scope of Article 30: Fine-Tuning the Nature of the Rule?*

While one can therefore appreciate the rationale for the ECJ's choice of a 'general rule' strategy, the fact that the judgment may serve to exclude selling arrangements which really could have an impact on trade may be a cause for disquiet. An interesting suggestion has been made by Advocate General Jacobs in *Leclerc-Siplec*[100] for a way in which *Keck* could be modified to accommodate these concerns.

[96] The proviso to para. 16 of the *Keck* judgment will in any event be a safeguard in this situation.

[97] For a different view that the certainty aimed at by *Keck* is illusory, and that the Court should have persisted with a case-by-case approach see N. Reich, 'The "November Revolution" of the European Court of Justice: *Keck*, *Meng* and *Audi* Revisited' (1994) 31 CMLRev. 459.

[98] And national courts.

[99] Wils, writing before the *Keck* decision, favours a more open-textured, less rule-based approach to Art. 30: n. 93 above, 488–491.

[100] Case C–412/93, *Leclerc-Siplec* v. *TFI Publicité and M6 Publicité* 24 Nov. 1994.

The case concerned a prohibition on television advertising imposed by French law on the distribution sector, the purpose being to protect the regional press by forcing the sectors in question to advertise through that medium. Advocate General Jacobs was clear that the rule would not fall within Article 30 as interpreted in *Keck* and *Hunermund*. He was equally clear that advertising could play a very important part in breaking down barriers to inter-state trade, and was therefore unhappy with the idea that it should always be outside Article 30.

In this sense he was against an approach which drew a rigid distinction between rules relating to selling arrangements and those concerning the products themselves. If one paused there one might get the impression that the Advocate General was favouring a return to the pre-*Keck* 'full test' regime, which was 'non-rule'-based in the sense discussed above. This would be mistaken. His preferred approach represents a subtle modification of the *Keck* formula.

Advocate General Jacobs' basic starting point is that all undertakings which engage in legitimate economic activity should have unfettered access to the market. If there is a *substantial* restriction on that access then it is caught by Article 30. When the measure affects the goods themselves, as in *Cassis*-type cases, then it will be *presumed* to have this substantial impact. If, however, the contested measure affects selling arrangements and is not discriminatory the substantiality of the impact will depend on a number of factors, including the range of goods affected, the nature of the restriction, whether the impact is direct or indirect, and the extent to which other selling arrangements are available. If there is no substantial impact, or the effect on trade is *de minimis*, then measures of this nature will not be within Article 30.

This approach deserves serious consideration. It is not the 'general-rule'-based strategy of *Keck*, but neither is it a return to the pre-*Keck* 'full-test' approach. The division between measures which pertain to the goods themselves and those which concern selling arrangements is maintained. The former are deemed by their nature to have a substantial impact on trade. The latter require closer analysis in order to decide whether this is so on the facts of a particular case, with the express recognition of a *de minimis* exception. This strategy will not be as clear cut as that in *Keck* itself, but that is simply a consequence of the move away from the general-rule approach adopted in that case. The ECJ has however declined to follow the suggestions of the Advocate General and has applied *Keck* in an unaltered way to the case.[101]

[101] Case C-412/93, *Leclerc-Siplec* v. *TFI Publicité SA and M6 Publicité SA*, 9 February 1995. There is an interesting analogy here with competition law which in effect treats certain types of cartel behaviour as unlawful in and of themselves, while other types of activity are subjected to a market analysis to determine whether they do impede competition: see below, Ch. 19.

9. INDISTINCTLY APPLICABLE RULES: THE MANDATORY REQUIREMENTS

(a) The Rationale for the Mandatory Requirements

In the description of the post-*Cassis* case law we have already come across some examples of the way in which the ECJ treats possible justifications for rules which inhibit intra-Community trade. It is now time to focus more closely upon this issue. Before addressing the case law of the Court on the specific mandatory requirements it may be helpful to consider two more general questions: the rationale for the existence of these requirements; and the reason for dealing with them separately from Article 36.

Let us begin by considering the first of these questions, the *rationale for the mandatory requirements*. This is not hard to find and may be summarized as follows: *many rules which in some way regulate trade are also capable of restricting trade, yet some of these rules may serve objectively justifiable purposes*. This will be so even in respect of those rules which remain within the ambit of Article 30 after *Keck*. The two parts of this proposition can be explained quite easily.

If a country stipulates that certain goods should be packed in a particular manner, that they should have a prescribed content, or that they should be subject to checks of varying kinds, then such rules may render it more difficult for importers of such goods from other Member States to compete in the country which is imposing the conditions. The production and marketing processes of manufacturers from other Member States will not have been geared up to meet such criteria, and the goods produced will already have had to comply with any rules prescribed by the country in which they were made. It is clear, then, that indistinctly applicable rules which do not discriminate on the basis of country of origin may nonetheless impede intra-Community trade. This is the conceptual rationale for bringing them within Article 30, and provides the explanation for the first limb of the proposition set out above.

Yet the very fact that very many such rules which regulate trade may also inhibit it in the manner just described means that it would be inappropriate to render *all* such rules illegal *per se*. Trade rules of the above kind may serve justifiable purposes, as exemplified by the list of mandatory requirements in the *Cassis* case, and this is the justification for the second limb of the proposition mentioned earlier. Whether they in fact do so will be for the ECJ to determine in the manner to be described below.

As we have already seen, the 'list' of mandatory requirements mentioned in *Cassis* is sometimes referred to as the rule of reason, drawing upon the earlier hint in *Dassonville* that, in the absence of Community measures on an issue, reasonable trade rules would be accepted in certain circumstances. The term 'rule of reason' has its origins in the competition law of the United States and, as will be seen below, there is a lively debate whether the concept and/or the phrase itself should form part of the language of Community competition policy.[102] The details of this debate need not detain us now, but we should at least understand why the term has been taken across into the law on free movement of goods. The reason is an underlying similarity of problem faced by the legal regulation of competition and free movement of goods. One branch of competition law proscribes agreements or arrangements in which the parties restrict or distort competition. Now the paradigm type of case which such legal rules is designed to catch is, for example, a price-fixing agreement between manufacturers the effect of which is to raise price and limit output to the detriment of consumers. The problem is that most systems of competition policy have generally worded provisions, which prohibit agreements etc. affecting trade which distort competition. The origin of the 'rule of reason' is to be found in the early jurisprudence of the United States' courts at the turn of this century. They correctly perceived that in some ways all contracts restrain trade or limit competition by, for example, preventing *A* from agreeing to sell the same goods to *C* if *A* has already made a contract to sell them to *B*. Yet it would be absurd if all contracts which are the 'life blood' of commerce were to be caught by competition law. Hence the creation of the juristic device of the rule of reason through which the United States' courts limited the reach of competition policy to those agreements which were not reasonable.

We can now perceive the connection between the use of that phrase in the sphere of competition and its utilization to describe the *Cassis* reasoning. In the same way that one might regard all contracts as restraining trade for the purposes of competition policy, so, too, might one regard all rules regulating trade as inhibiting trade for the purposes of free movement. It is the unacceptability of such a draconian solution which has led the courts in both areas to fashion an exception for rules which can be justified on specified grounds.[103] A similar approach can be seen in other areas of Community law, such as those dealing with the freedom to provide services, or freedom of establishment: national rules which limit such freedoms have on occasion been upheld where the Court feels that they serve some objectively justifiable goal.[104] This function of the rule of reason is brought out clearly by Advocate General Verloren van Themaat,[105] who regarded it as a general principle of interpretation designed to mitigate the effects of strict prohibitions laid down in the Treaty, whether these be found in Article 30 or in the context of freedom of establishment or the provision of services.

[102] See below, Ch. 19.

[103] The precise nature of the grounds of justification is itself an interesting issue. Broadly speaking one might use the term to capture the idea that although the contract/trade rules restrain competition or inhibit trade there is some objective justification, in the form of some other policy aim, which serves to outweigh the limitation on competition or inhibition on trade. Alternatively the term could be used as descriptive of the conclusion that the contract/trade rules really do not distort competition or impede trade at all, because, for example, the impact of the contract/trade rules is too remote, minimal or indirect; or because, for example, any diminution of competition in one area is outweighed by an increase in competition in a different sphere.

[104] See below, Ch. 16..

[105] Case 286/81, n. 90 above, n. 3.

What, then, of the second of the questions posed above? *Why are the* Cassis *mandatory requirements treated separately from other Member State justifications which must fall within Article 36?* In answering this question it should be emphasized that the *Cassis* exceptions may only be used in respect of rules which are not discriminatory; it is only indistinctly applicable rules which can take advantage of the mandatory requirements. This has been made clear by the ECJ on more than one occasion. Thus in *Gilli and Andres*[106] the Court stated that it was only where national rules applied without discrimination to both national and imported products that they could be justified by using the mandatory requirements derived from *Cassis*. The point emerges once again from the *Irish Souvenirs* case[107]. The Irish Government sought to defend its policy in relation to origin-marking of souvenirs by pleading that this was necessary to protect consumers and for the fairness of commercial transactions. It sought to plead these matters under Article 36, but the Court responded by stating that those issues were not dealt with in Article 36 at all, and therefore could not be pleaded under that Article. The ECJ then proceeded to consider whether the matters which the Irish Government sought to raise could be taken into account on the basis of the *Cassis* decision. It concluded that this was not possible since the Irish rules in question were discriminatory, and *Cassis* only applied to indistinctly applicable rules.[108] Given that the *Cassis* mandatory requirements can only be used in relation to rules which are not discriminatory,[109] there would appear to be two complementary reasons why this aspect of the ECJ's case law was developed outside Article 36.

On the one hand, the *Cassis* list of mandatory requirements clearly includes matters, such as the protection of consumers and the fairness of commercial transactions, which are not mentioned within Article 36. It would therefore have been difficult, albeit not impossible, to have read Article 36 so as to cover such matters. The *Cassis* list is also not exhaustive and the Court has added other objective justifications which might have been difficult to fit within the framework of Article 36.

On the other hand, the very willingness of the ECJ to create a broader category of possible justifications for indistinctly applicable rules than those which exist for rules which are deliberately discriminatory is explicable by the difference between the two types of rule. Such discriminatory rules strike at the very heart of what the Community is intended to abolish. It is unsurprising that they are viewed with suspicion by the Court, and that any possible justifications should be narrowly confined. The extension of Article 30 to catch indistinctly applicable rules which inhibit trade, in the absence of any relevant harmonization measures, represented a bold move by the ECJ. We have already seen why it would have been overly harsh to regard all such rules as *per se* illegal. Exceptions or defences were therefore required, and the Court was willing to cast these in broader terms than Article 36 to reflect the differ-

[106] Case 788/79, n. 56 above, para. 6.

[107] Case 113/80, n. 12 above, paras. 5–8.

[108] *Ibid.*, para. 11.

[109] For consideration of Case C–2/90, n. 50 above, see above, 610.

ences between discriminatory and non-discriminatory rules. The articulation of these justifications separately from Article 36 represented a judicial desire to construct appropriate qualifications which were geared to the nature of indistinctly applicable rules, and to do so independently of Article 36 in order not to confuse the narrow application of that provision as it applied to discriminatory rules.[110]

(b) The Mandatory Requirements

(i) Consumer Protection One of the best known decisions which deals with this topic is the *German Beer* case:

Case 178/84, Commission v. Germany
[1987] ECR 1227, [1988] 1 CMLR 780

German law prohibited the marketing of beer which was lawfully manufactured in another Member State unless it complied with sections 9 and 10 of the Biersteuergesetz (Beer Duty Act 1952). Under this law only drinks which complied with the German Act could be sold as '*Bier*', and this meant that the term could only be used in relation to those drinks which were made from barley, hops, yeast, and water. The German Government sought to defend its rule by arguing that the reservation of the term '*Bier*' to beverages made only from the substances mentioned in the German legislation was necessary to protect consumers who associated the term '*Bier*' with beverages made from these ingredients. It also argued that its legislation was not protectionist in aim, in that any trader who made beer from such ingredients could market it freely in Germany. The ECJ cited the principles from *Dassonville* and *Cassis*; it found that the German rule did constitute an impediment to trade and then proceeded to consider whether the rule was necessary to protect consumers.

THE ECJ

31. The German Government's argument that section 10 of the Biersteuergesetz is essential in order to protect German consumers because, in their minds, the designation *'Bier'* is inseparably linked to the beverage manufactured solely from the ingredients laid down in section 9 . . . must be rejected.

32. Firstly, consumers' conceptions which vary from one Member State to the other are also likely to evolve in the course of time within a Member State. The establishment of the Common Market is, it should be added, one of the factors that may play a major contributory role in that development. Whereas rules protecting consumers against misleading practices enable such a development to be taken into account, legislation of the kind contained in section 10 . . . prevents it from taking place. As the Court has already held in another context (Case 170/78, *Commission* v. *United Kingdom*), the legislation of a Member State must not 'crystallize given consumer habits so as to consolidate an advantage acquired by national industries concerned to comply with them'.

110 For the possibility that the list of exceptions in Art. 36 might not be closed, see above, 610 for the discussion of Case C–2/90, n. 50 above.

33. Secondly, in the other Member States of the Community the designations corresponding to the German designation *'Bier'* are generic designations for a fermented beverage manufactured from barley, whether malted barley on its own or with the addition of rice or maize. The same approach is taken in Community law as can be seen from heading 22.03 of the Common Customs Tariff. The German legislature itself utilises the designation *'Bier'* in that way in section 9(7) and (8) of the Biersteuergesetz in order to refer to beverages not complying with the manufacturing rules laid down in section 9(1) and (2).

34. The German designation *'Bier'* and its equivalents in the languages of the other Member States may therefore not be restricted to beers manufactured in accordance with the rules in force in the Federal Republic of Germany.

35. It is admittedly legitimate to seek to enable consumers who attribute specific qualities to beers manufactured from particular raw materials to make their choice in the light of that consideration. However, as the Court has already emphasised (Case 193/80, *Commission* v. *Italy*) that possibility may be ensured by means which do not prevent the importation of products which have been lawfully manufactured and marketed in other Member States and, in particular, 'by the compulsory affixing of suitable labels giving the nature of the product sold'. By indicating the raw materials utilised in the manufacture of beer 'such a course would enable the consumer to make his choice in full knowledge of the facts and would guarantee transparency in trading and in offers to the public'. It must be added that such a system of mandatory consumer information must not entail negative assessments for beers not complying with the requirements of section 9 of the Biersteuergesetz.

The ECJ therefore held the German law to be in breach of Article 30. The way in which it dealt with the argument concerning consumer protection is instructive and characterizes the Court's approach in cases of this kind. The argument is closely scrutinized to determine whether it really 'works' at all on the facts of the case. Even if there is some substance to the claim the ECJ will then assess whether the interests of consumers could be safeguarded by means which were less restrictive for the free movement of goods. Thus in the instant case the Court in paragraph 35 counters the German Government's contention by stating that consumer interests could adequately be met through rules on the provision of information, rather than through an outright ban on marketing beer which did not comply with German law.

The same approach of closely scrutinizing claims concerning consumer protection is apparent in other cases.[111] The *De Kikvorsch* case[112] proves that arguments about beer cut both ways. Dutch law contained indistinctly applicable rules which impeded the import of beer from Germany. This was in part because German beer exceeded the level of acidity permitted by Dutch law. The purpose behind this rule was to protect the 'sour' taste of beer to which the Dutch were accustomed. The ECJ dismissed the argument that the Dutch

[111] See e.g. Case 261/81, n. 57 above.

[112] Case 94/82, *De Kikvorsch Groothandel-Import-Export BV* [1983] ECR 947, [1984] 2 CMLR 323.

rule could be justified on the ground of consumer protection: consumers should not be prevented from trying beers which were brewed according to a different tradition, and proper labelling could alert the consumer that the beer was of a different kind from that to which he was accustomed.[113] The import of German beer was also impeded by the fact that Dutch law prohibited the printing on the label of the original wort strength of the beer. The purpose behind this rule was that Dutch law required the strength of the beer to be indicated on the bottle in terms of alcohol percentages, and the Dutch felt that the inclusion of references to the wort strength would confuse consumers. The ECJ dealt with this aspect of the case somewhat differently: national rules limiting the amount of information available to consumers might be defensible on the ground that the limit was necessary to prevent consumers from being misled, but it must be shown that there really was a risk of consumer confusion and this was a matter for the national courts to determine.[114] A similar approach is evident in *Neeltje*[115] where the ECJ held that, while national legislation concerning the hallmarking of precious metals was in principle defensible in terms of consumer protection, a particular state had to accept the method of hallmarking in another state, even if it differed in detail, provided that it was intelligible to consumers of the importing state.

It is apparent from the cases considered above that the ECJ has often rejected justifications based on consumer protection for rules relating to the content of goods, by stating that adequate labelling requirements can achieve the desired national aims with less impact on intra-Community trade. However, even labelling requirements themselves may not escape Article 30. Thus in *Fietje*[116] the ECJ held that the obligation to use a certain name on a label could make it more difficult to market goods coming from other Member States. Such a rule would therefore have to be justified on the ground of consumer protection. Labelling requirements which demanded that the purchaser was provided with sufficient information on the nature of the product, in order to prevent confusion with similar products, could, said the Court, be justified, even if the effect was to make it necessary to alter the labels of some imported goods.[117] However, such protection would not be necessary or justifiable if the details given on the original labels of the goods contained the same information as required by the state of import, and that information was just as capable of being understood by consumers. Whether there was such equivalence was for the national court to determine.[118] Similarly in the *Clinique* case[119] the ECJ held that a German law forbidding the use of the name 'Clinique' on cosmetic products imported from other states was caught

[113] *Ibid.*, para. 8.

[114] *Ibid.*, para. 12.

[115] Case C–293/93, *Ludomira Neeltje* v. *Barbara Houtwipper*, 15 Sept. 1994.

[116] Case 27/80, *Fietje* [1980] ECR 3839, [1981] 3 CMLR 722.

[117] *Ibid.*, para. 11.

[118] *Ibid.*, para. 12. See also Case 76/86, *Commission* v. *Germany* [1989] ECR 1021, [1991] 1 CMLR 741.

[119] Case C–315/92, *Verband Sozialer Wettbewerb eV* v. *Clinique Laboratoires SNC* [1994] ECR I–317.

by Article 30. The argument that the German rule could be defended on the ground that it was to protect consumers from being misled into believing that the product had medicinal properties was rejected by the Court: the goods were only sold in perfumeries and cosmetic departments of stores, not in pharmacies, and there was no indication of consumer confusion in the countries where the goods were marketed under the name 'Clinique'.

Justifications based on consumer protection can arise from varying factual situations. The *Oosthoek* case,[120] which was considered above,[121] provides an example of a rule which the ECJ thought could be protective of consumers. It will be remembered that Dutch law forbad the offer of free gifts to those who purchased encyclopædias. The ECJ found that such a law could impede intra-Community trade, because it could force a producer to discontinue a marketing scheme which was thought to be particularly effective. However, because the offering of free gifts could mislead the consumer about the real price of goods, such a law as that in issue could contribute to consumer protection and fair trading.

(ii) Fairness of Commercial Transactions There is clearly an overlap between consumer protection and the fairness of commercial transactions. Both may well be pleaded in order to save a national rule from condemnation under Article 30. This was so in, for example, the *Oosthoek* case, considered above.

This particular mandatory requirement has also been used to justify national rules which seek to prevent unfair marketing practices, such as the selling of imported goods which constitute precise imitations of familiar domestic goods. It would seem, however, that in order to be justified on this ground the national rule must not prohibit the marketing of goods which have been made according to fair and traditional practices in state *A*, merely because they are similar to goods which have been made in state *B*.[122]

(iii) Public Health We have already noted that it is only indistinctly applicable rules which can take advantage of the mandatory requirements. However, when the ECJ comes to consider possible justifications for such rules it may, on occasion, not be too concerned about whether it treats this justification within Article 36 or within the list of mandatory requirements, *provided* that the justification pleaded by the state comes within both lists. Public health finds a place both in the list of *Cassis* mandatory requirements and in Article 36, and although the Court should, on logical grounds, use the former in the context of indistinctly applicable rules, it may reason the case instead on the basis of Article 36. It may be inclined to do so particularly where it is unclear

[120] Case 286/81, n. 90 above.

[121] See above, 630.

[122] Case 58/80, *Dansk Supermarked* v. *Imerco* [1981] ECR 181, [1981] 3 CMLR 590; Case 16/83, *Karl Prantl* [1984] ECR 1299, [1985] 2 CMLR 238.

whether the impugned rule is discriminatory or not. The following extract from the *German Beer* case provides an apt example of this:[123]

Case 178/84, Commission v. Germany
[1987] ECR 1227, [1988] 1 CMLR 780

A second rule of German law was challenged in the *German Beer* case which was discussed above. Under the German Foodstuffs Act 1974 there was an absolute ban on the marketing of beer which contained additives. In essence this Act prohibited non-natural additives on public-health grounds. The Commission in an Article 169 action challenged this rule. It was accepted that the German rule did constitute a barrier to the import of beer lawfully marketed in other states which contained additives. The question before the ECJ was whether the rule could come within Article 36 on public-health grounds.

THE ECJ

41. The Court has consistently held (in particular in Case 174/82, *Criminal Proceedings Against Sandoz BV*) that 'in so far as there are uncertainties at the present state of scientific research it is for the Member States, in the absence of harmonization, to decide what degree of protection of the health and life of humans they intend to assure, having regard to the requirements of the free movement of goods within the Community.'

42. As may also be seen from the decision of the Court (and especially the *Sandoz* case, cited above, in Case 247/84, *Motte*, and in Case 308/84, *Ministère Public* v. *Muller*), in such circumstances Community law does not preclude the adoption by Member States of legislation whereby the use of additives is subjected to prior authorisation granted by a measure of general application for specific additives, in respect of all products, for certain products only or for certain uses. Such legislation meets a genuine need of health policy, namely that of restricting the uncontrolled consumption of food additives.

43. However, the application to imported products of prohibitions on marketing products containing additives which are authorised in the Member State of production but prohibited in the Member State of importation is permissible only in so far as it complies with the requirements of Article 36 of the Treaty as it has been interpreted by the Court.

44. It must be borne in mind, in the first place, that in its judgments in *Sandoz*, *Motte* and *Muller*, the Court inferred from the principle of proportionality underlying the last sentence of Article 36 of the Treaty that prohibitions on the marketing of products containing additives authorised in the Member State of production but prohibited in the Member State of importation must be restricted to what is actually necessary to secure the protection of public health. The Court also concluded that the use of a specific additive which is authorised in another Member State must be authorised in the case of a product imported from that Member State where, in view, on the one hand, of the findings of international scientific research, and in particular the work of the Community's Scientific Committee for Food, the Codex Alimentarius Committee of the Food and

[123] See also Case 53/80, n. 39 above; Case 97/83, *Criminal Proceedings against Melkunie BV* [1984] ECR 2367, [1986] 2 CMLR 318.

Agriculture Organisation of the United Nations (FAO) and the World Health Organisation, and, on the other, of the eating habits prevailing in the importing Member State, the additive in question does not present a risk to public health and meets a real need, especially a technical one.

45. Secondly, it should be remembered that, as the Court held in *Muller*, by virtue of the principle of proportionality, traders must also be able to apply, under a procedure which is easily accessible to them and can be concluded within a reasonable time, for the use of specific additives to be authorised by a measure of general application.

[*The Court then pointed out that the German rule prohibited all additives; that there was no procedure whereby traders could obtain authorization for a specific additive; and that additives were permitted by German law in beverages other than beer. The German Government then argued that such additives would not be needed in the manufacture of beer if it were made in accordance with section 9 of the Biersteuergesetz. The ECJ responded as follows:*]

51. It must be emphasised that the mere reference to the fact that beer can be manufactured without additives if it is made from only the raw materials prescribed in the Federal Republic of Germany does not suffice to preclude the possibility that some additives may meet a technological need. Such an interpretation of the concept of technological need, which results in favouring national production methods, constitutes a disguised means of restricting trade between Member States.

52. The concept of technological need must be assessed in the light of the raw materials utilised and bearing in mind the assessment made by the authorities of the Member States where the product was lawfully manufactured and marketed. Account must also be taken of the findings of international scientific research and in particular the work of the Community's Scientific Committee for Food, the Codex Alimentarius Committee of the FAO and the World Health Organisation.

53. Consequently, in so far as the German rules on additives in beer entail a general ban on additives, their application to beers imported from other Member States is contrary to the requirements of Community law as laid down in the case law of the Court, since that prohibition is contrary to the principle of proportionality and is therefore not covered by Article 36 of the EEC Treaty.

(iv) Other Mandatory Requirements The list of mandatory requirements in *Cassis* is not exhaustive. This is evident from the case itself, in which the ECJ stated that the mandatory requirements included *in particular* those mentioned in the judgment.[124] The non-exhaustive character of the *Cassis* list has been confirmed by later cases. That the protection of the environment can come within the rule of reason was confirmed by the following case:

Case 302/86, Commission v. Denmark
[1988] ECR 4607, [1989] 1 CMLR 619

Danish law required that containers for beer and soft drinks should be returnable and that a certain proportion should be re-usable. A national environmental

[124] [1979] ECR 649, para. 8.

agency had to approve containers to ensure compliance with these criteria. There was also a deposit-and-return system for empty containers. The Danish government argued that the rule was justified by a mandatory requirement related to the protection of the environment.

THE ECJ

8. The Court has already held in . . . Case 240/83, *Procureur de la République* v. *Association de Défense des Brûleurs d'Huiles Usagées* . . . that the protection of the environment is 'one of the Community's essential objectives', which may as such justify certain limitations of the principle of free movement of goods. That view is moreover confirmed by the Single European Act.

9. In view of the foregoing, it must therefore be stated that the protection of the environment is a mandatory requirement which may limit the application of Article 30 of the Treaty.

[*The Commission argued that the Danish laws were disproportionate.*]

12. It is therefore necessary to examine whether all the restrictions which the contested rules impose on the free movement of goods are necessary to achieve the objectives pursued by those rules.

13. First of all, as regards the obligation to establish a deposit-and-return system for empty containers, it must be observed that this requirement is an indispensable element of a system intended to ensure the re-use of containers and therefore appears necessary to achieve the aims pursued by the contested rules. That being so, the restrictions which it imposes on the free movement of goods cannot be regarded as disproportionate.

14. Next it is necessary to consider the requirement that producers and importers must use only containers approved by the National Agency for the Protection of the Environment.

[*The Danish Government argued that the number of approved containers had to be limited because otherwise retailers would not take part in the system. This meant that a foreign producer might have to manufacture a type of container already approved, with consequent increases in costs. To overcome this problem the Danish law was amended to allow a producer to market up to 3,000 hectolitres a year in non-approved containers, provided that a deposit-and-return system was established. The Commission argued that the limit of 3,000 hectolitres was unnecessary to achieve the objectives of the scheme.*]

20. It is undoubtedly true that the existing system for returning approved containers ensures a maximum rate of re-use and therefore a very considerable degree of protection of the environment since empty containers can be returned to any retailer of beverages. Non-approved containers, on the other hand, can be returned only to the retailer who sold the beverages, since it is impossible to set up such a comprehensive system for those containers as well.

21. Nevertheless, the system for returning non-approved containers is capable of protecting the environment and, as far as imports are concerned, affects only limited quantities of beverages compared with the quantity of beverages consumed in Denmark owing to the restrictive effect which the requirement that containers should be returnable has on imports. In those circumstances, a restriction of the quantity of products which may be marketed by importers is disproportionate to the objective pursued.

22. It must therefore be held that by restricting . . . the quantity of beer and

soft drinks which may be marketed by a single producer in non-approved containers to 3,000 hectolitres a year, the Kingdom of Denmark has failed, as regards imports of those products from other Member States, to fulfil its obligations under Article 30 of the EEC Treaty.

23. The remainder of the application must be dismissed.

It is clear, then, that in the absence of Community harmonization measures national provisions on environmental protection can constitute a further mandatory requirement to be added to the *Cassis* list.

Nor is environmental protection the only new addition to this catalogue. The decisions in *Cinéthèque* and *Torfaen* provide evidence of other possible grounds which would come within the rule of reason. Thus in *Cinéthèque*[125] the ECJ was willing to recognize that the fostering of certain forms of art could constitute a justifiable objective within the context of Community law; while in *Torfaen*[126] it accepted that rules governing the opening hours of premises pursued an aim which was justifiable with regard to the EC, in that such rules reflected certain social and political choices which might differ between Member States. We have already seen that the precise status of these decisions post-*Keck* is in doubt: both factual situations would probably now be held to fall outside Article 30.[127] These cases are nonetheless of continuing relevance in this context. In part this is because factual situations of this kind may still fall within Article 30 if the impact of the relevant national rules on domestic and imported goods is uneven. And in part it is because the recognition of these possible grounds of objective justification may well be of relevance in cases which do indubitably fall within the province of Article 30 even after *Keck*. This would be the case where the national rule related to characteristics of the goods rather than selling conditions, and the state sought to defend it on one of the grounds mentioned above.

10. THE ADVANTAGES AND DISADVANTAGES OF *CASSIS* AND THE INTERRELATIONSHIP BETWEEN JUDICIAL AND LEGISLATIVE INITIATIVES

(a) The Advantages of the Court's Jurisprudence and the Commission's Response to Cassis de Dijon

The Court's judgment in *Cassis* was, in part, a response to the difficulties faced by the Commission in securing acceptance by the Member States of harmonization measures. This difficulty was itself partly due to the technically complex nature of many harmonization measures, which might therefore not prove easy to draft; it was in part because the Member States might not read-

[125] Cases 60 and 61/84, [1985] ECR 2605, [1986] 1 CMLR 365.
[126] Case 145/88, [1989] ECR 3851. [127] See above, 627–8.

ily reach agreement on the substantive content of a proposed harmonization measure; and it was in part a result of the fact that harmonization measures, even if they were passed, would result, to some degree, in the standardization of the rules applicable to an area, with the result that national diversity might be stifled or lost, being replaced by one Community concept of beer, cheese, sausage, and the like. The ECJ's judgment in *Cassis* had the effect, as we have seen, of rendering indistinctly applicable rules which impeded trade incompatible with Article 30, unless they could be saved by one of the mandatory requirements. This was so even in the absence of relevant harmonization provisions. In this sense the judgment had the advantageous consequence of fostering single market integration by breaking down barriers to trade which resulted from the existence of indistinctly applicable national trade rules and obviating the need for specifically Community harmonization provisions.

In the introduction to this Chapter it was argued that the ECJ's jurisprudence under Article 30 could not be viewed in isolation. It has had an impact upon how the other institutions of the Community perceive their role. The Commission was not slow to respond to the Court's initiative in this area. It published a Communication setting out its interpretation of the *Cassis* decision, which also provided insights into how the Commission perceived its legislative role in this area:

Commission Communication
3 October 1980, [1980] OJ C256/2

Whereas Member States may, with respect to domestic products and in the absence of relevant Community provisions, regulate the terms on which such products are marketed, the case is different for products imported from other Member States.

Any product imported from another Member State must in principle be admitted to the territory of the importing Member State if it has been lawfully produced, that is, conforms to rules and processes of manufacture that are customarily and traditionally accepted in the exporting country, and marketed in the territory of the latter.

This principle implies that Member States, when drawing up commercial or technical rules liable to affect the free movement of goods, may not take an exclusively national viewpoint and take account only of requirements confined to domestic products. The proper functioning of the common market demands that each Member State also gives consideration to the legitimate requirements of the other Member States.

Only under very strict conditions does the Court accept exceptions to this principle; barriers to trade resulting from differences between commercial and technical rules are only admissible:

—if the rules are necessary, that is appropriate and not excessive, in order to satisfy mandatory requirements . . .;

—if the rules serve a purpose in the general interest which is compelling enough to justify an exception to a fundamental rule of the Treaty such as the free movement of goods;

—if the rules are essential for such a purpose to be attained, i.e. are the means which are the most appropriate and at the same time least hinder trade.

[*The Commission then set out a number of guidelines in the light of the Court's judgment.*]

—The principles deduced by the Court imply that a Member State may not in principle prohibit the sale in its territory of a product lawfully produced and marketed in another Member State even if the product is produced according to technical or quality requirements which differ from those imposed on its domestic products. Where a product 'suitably and satisfactorily' fulfils the legitimate objective of a Member State's own rules (public safety, protection of the consumer or the environment, etc.), the importing country cannot justify prohibiting its sale in its territory by claiming that the way it fulfils the objective is different from that imposed on domestic products.

In such a case, an absolute prohibition of sale could not be considered 'necessary' to satisfy a 'mandatory requirement' because it would not be an 'essential guarantee' in the sense defined in the Court's judgment.

The Commission will therefore have to tackle a whole body of commercial rules which lay down that products manufactured and marketed in one Member State must fulfil technical or qualitative conditions in order to be admitted to the market of another and specifically in all cases where the trade barriers occasioned by such rules are inadmissible according to the very strict criteria set out by the Court.

The Commission is referring in particular to rules covering the composition, designation, presentation and packaging as well as rules requiring compliance with certain technical standards.

—The Commission's work of harmonization will henceforth have to be directed mainly at national laws having an impact on the functioning of the common market where barriers to trade to be removed arise from national provisions which are admissible under the criteria set out by the Court.

The Commission will be concentrating on sectors deserving priority because of their economic relevance to the creation of a single internal market.

To forestall later difficulties, the Commission will be informing Member States of potential objections, under the terms of Community law, to provisions they may be considering introducing which come to the attention of the Commission.

It will be producing suggestions soon on the procedures to be followed in such cases.

Two themes are apparent in the Commission's Communication. Both are important.

The first is what has become known as the principle of *mutual recognition*. Goods which have been lawfully marketed in one state should, in principle, be admitted to the market of any other state. Commercial or technical rules cannot be drawn up by a particular state solely from a national perspective. Legitimate consideration must be given to the demands of other states. Provided that the product from state *A* 'suitably and satisfactorily' fulfils the legitimate objectives of state *B's* own rules, the latter cannot justify prohibiting an import on the ground that the way state *A* fulfils those objectives is different from that imposed on domestic goods by state *B*.

The second theme which emerges from the Communication concerns the Commission's enforcement and legislative strategy for trade rules post-*Cassis*. This was to be double-edged. On the one hand, it would tackle those rules which were *inadmissible* in the light of the criteria set down by the ECJ, by using its powers under Article 169 to bring Member States to the Court where they refused to abandon the application of such rules to imports. On the other hand, the harmonization process would be directed towards those trade rules which were *admissible* under the *Cassis* test.

The twin aspects of the Commission's policy possess a certain symmetry: rules which would not survive the *Cassis* test would be struck down through the judicial process, or through negotiation against the backdrop of received judicial doctrine; rules which survived that criterion on the basis of the mandatory requirements, and therefore still posed a problem for market integration, would be dealt with through harmonization, since the *Cassis* exceptions only operated on the condition that no harmonization provisions were in place.

The effect of the *Cassis* doctrine was thus to induce the Commission to re-orient the direction of its own legislative programme, by causing it to concentrate on those national rules which were still valid under the Court's case law. This is a theme to which we will return later when we consider the Commission's strategy for completion of the internal market and the New Approach to harmonization.[128]

The Commission's Communication was important not only for what it said, but because its publication ensured that the *Cassis* decision received more attention from the Member States than it might otherwise have done. The combined effect of *Cassis* and the Communication drew a variety of responses from states and interest groups within the Community.

K. J. Alter and S. Meunier-Aitsahalia, Judicial Politics in the European Community: European Integration and the Pathbreaking Cassis de Dijon Decision[129]

The Member States reacted with apprehension and discontent to the broad policy implications of the *Cassis* decision drawn by the Commission. As relatively high standard countries, France, Germany and Italy were the most vigorously opposed to the new policy. They repeated the German government's argument that the principle of mutual recognition of goods would lead to a lowering of safety and quality standards. Even the British government had some reservations, although the United Kingdom was generally favourable to the principle of market liberalization and opposed to the excess of legislation in the EC.

. . .

The publication of the Communication also triggered the mobilization of various interest groups. Consumer groups were torn between welcoming and rejecting the

[128] See below, Ch. 25. We shall see that the Commission's strategy for harmonization has been further modified since its Communication on the effect of the *Cassis* case.

[129] (1994) 26 *Comparative Political Studies* 535, 542, 544.

Commission's interpretation of the *Cassis* ruling. Although looking forward to the greater diversity and lower prices of products implied by a common market, consumer groups were worried that trade liberalization could have negative consequences on consumer safety and jeopardize the gains previously made in consumer legislation on the national front. The EC consumer group argued that 'it is necessary to maintain a balance between the securing of free trade, which should afford consumers a broad range of products, and the need to protect the health, safety and economic interests of consumers. We are concerned that the Commission interpretation of the *Cassis* ruling may jeopardize that balance' . . . Consumer groups also denounced the use of the judicial process rather than legislative harmonization because such a process prevents groups from having an impact on the eventual directives.

Notwithstanding its mixed reception, the *Cassis* decision had the advantage of fostering single-market integration, and facilitating the task of the Commission in this general area. It would, however, be over-simplistic to suggest that the results of this approach were all unequivocally positive. It is to the problems generated by *Cassis*, and the Commission's response thereto, that we must now turn.

(b) Problems Flowing from Cassis *and the Commission's Response Thereto*

There is no doubt that *Cassis* represented a welcome development for the Commission. No longer would it have to attempt to promulgate a mass of harmonization measures to cover all spheres of trade policy. It could restrict its initiatives to those areas in which national rules were still valid under *Cassis*. We can thus perceive a method of developing Community policy in this area through a mixture of adjudication and rule-making. *Adjudication* pursuant to the *Cassis* principle would be used to evaluate trade rules and declare them incompatible with Article 30 unless they could be saved by one of the mandatory requirements. *Rule-making* would be employed for at least some of those national provisions which survived the adjudicative process, in the sense that the Commission would try to draft appropriate regulations to harmonize the differing national laws on a topic.[130]

A further consequence of this overall method of developing policy should be noted at this juncture, one which was touched on at the beginning of this Chapter. The impact of the *adjudicative limb* of this overall strategy was essentially *deregulatory* or resulted in *negative regulation*: those trade rules which could not be legitimated under the *Cassis* doctrine would be declared incompatible with Article 30, either totally or partially.[131] The importing state

[130] As we shall see in Ch. 25, the Commission has in fact modified its approach to harmonization. Under what has become known as the New Approach to Harmonization the Commission no longer attempts to lay down all the details on any particular product, but rather restricts itself to legislating on essential requirements concerning matters such as safety which a product must meet.

[131] In the sense that the Court would conclude that the object of the importing state's policy could be met by a rule which was less restrictive on intra-Community trade than the one being challenged before the Court.

could not therefore rely on the offending rule against imports from other Member States. By way of contrast the impact of the *rule-making limb* of the general strategy resulted in *positive regulation*. Rules which survived the *Cassis* test because of one of the mandatory requirements could obviously still constitute a barrier to intra-Community trade and, as the above Communication makes clear, the Commission would then see whether harmonization measures could be enacted on such topics. Where a harmonization measure could be passed successfully then the result would be positive regulation, in that there would be a set of rules on the issue which all states would have to comply with. There are, however, three problems with this general strategy.

The first problem is that the strategy is dependent upon agreement with the outcome of the adjudicative process. If the challenged rules failed the *Cassis* test then they would have to be removed from the national statute book, and, provided that this was done, the Commission would probably leave the matter there. This conclusion would be fine provided that one agreed that the rules ought to fall in this manner. The result would be less satisfactory if one disagreed with the ECJ's judgment, on the ground that it should have found certain trade rules to be saved by one of the mandatory requirements, with the consequence that the Commission would attempt to enact harmonization provisions on that issue.

The force of this point can be demonstrated by focusing on the ECJ's judgments concerning food standards. We have already seen that its general approach towards this issue has been to find that such rules are not saved by the mandatory requirements, because it believes that the policy of the importing state can be given effect to by less restrictive rules on product labelling.[132] Lasa has contested this assumption.[133] He shows that food standards have a dual purpose: to preclude economic adulteration of the product, by preventing the manufacturer substituting inferior ingredients; and to provide a yardstick against which inferior or superior quality can be measured. He then argues that labelling requirements, as opposed to food standards, may not adequately protect the consumer for the following reasons:

H.-C. von Heydebrand u.d. Lasa, Free Movement of Foodstuffs, Consumer Protection and Food Standards in the European Community: Has the Court of Justice Got it Wrong?[134]

First of all, the Court might simply not be right that consumers are adequately informed through labels. After all, the majority of the consumers apparently do not pay much attention to the information given on the label. How does the Court know that for example German consumers will not be misled by the traditional champagne-type bottles with a wired stopper which a French importer used for the marketing of partially fermented grape juice having an alcoholic strength below 3 per cent? . . .

[132] See above, 606–9. [133] See n. 134 below.

[134] (1991) 16 ELRev. 391, 409–13. See also O. Brouwers, 'Free Movement of Foodstuffs and Quality Requirements: Has the Commission Got it Wrong?' (1988) 25 CMLRev. 237.

Secondly, the Court's approach can confer an unfair competitive advantage on the importer. For example, the use of the designation jenever by a Dutch importer for a beverage which does not meet the Dutch standard for jenever, the similarity of the French fermented grape juice bottles with the German sparkling wine bottles . . . amount to a marketing advantage for which the importer does not pay. The consumer associates with the name or presentation of the product a familiar domestic product of a certain quality which is not met by the imported product, and will therefore perhaps be misled . . .

Fourthly, the Court's case law, if implemented strictly in the long run, may well result in a 'labelling jungle' which even judges would find difficult to penetrate. The yardstick function of food standards . . . is put at risk, if labelling is substituted for standards on a large scale . . .

Fifthly, while administrative resources are saved by foregoing harmonization, authorities of the Member States have to struggle with the food standards of the various Member States, since the imported product must still be 'lawfully produced and marketed' in the Member States of export. Mutual recognition of official inspections has its difficulties too, especially where the product designated for export is not at all or less carefully examined than the product which is sold on the home market.

Sixthly, depending on the market of the foodstuff in question, mutual recognition can lead to discrimination against manufacturers situated in the importing Member State, if that Member State does not timely adjust the food standard. For example, an obligation on Member States to allow the importation of milk substitutes lawfully produced and marketed in another Member State does not affect the obligation of their domestic manufacturers to comply with the standard which bans or restricts the sale of these products . . .

More important . . . the Member State of export can by way of the economic damage caused by inverse discrimination impose *de facto* its food standard or standard free food law on the Member State of import. Relocation of production to the exporting Member State in an effort to secure market share at home has already occurred in practice . . .

Seventhly, the preference of the Court for labelling is not sufficiently responsive to the local needs of the people of the importing Member State to define and classify the food they eat according to their conceptions, expectations and habits. It is not clear why the creation of a common market should require the strong disregard of these needs as reflected in the case law of the Court of Justice . . .

. . . The attitude of the Court of Justice towards food standards makes it *de facto* impossible for the people of a Member State to enforce requirements about the quality, composition, designation and presentation of their food when their views are not shared by the people in the Member State of export . . .

The second problem with the strategy set out above is related to, but distinct from, the first. Community legislative initiatives may well be required in order to ensure that the protective function played by many trade rules is not lost sight of in the desire to enhance single market integration.[135] We have

[135] See, however, Case C–320/93, *Lucien Ortscheit GmbH* v. *Eurim-Pharm Arzneimittel GmbH*, 10 Nov. 1994, for a judicial recognition of this problem and the way in which it affects the Court's reasoning.

already seen in the earlier discussion the way in which Article 30 mediates between the objective of integration and the legitimate protective concerns underlying many national rules.[136] While it is true that safety and the like can be taken into account under the *Cassis* mandatory requirements, there is, as Weatherill and Beaumont note,[137] a risk inherent in the *Cassis* line of authority 'that the Court has introduced a legal test that tends to tip the balance away from legitimate social protection towards a deregulated (perhaps unregulated) free market economy in which standards of, *inter alia*, consumer protection will be depressed'.

The final problem can be presented as follows. Even if one does agree that certain national trade rules should be regarded as incompatible with Article 30, this species of negative regulation may still require supplementation with more positive regulation which can only be produced through Community legislative action. The essence of this point is captured well by Weatherill and Beaumont:[138]

> the essential concern about *Cassis* resides in the fear that it has promoted free trade but that the terms on which such trade will ensue are thoroughly uncertain. *Cassis* may have deregulated the market by eliminating many national technical barriers to trade, but it remains questionable whether the removal of national barriers without accompanying positive Community regulations is sufficient to secure the realization of a true common market. At a more fundamental level of policy, one must address the question of the extent to which the Community *ought* to regulate the market in a positive sense.

This important theme will be returned to when we consider in detail the Community's policy for the completion of the internal market. For the present it should merely be emphasized once again that judicial developments can never be analysed in isolation from the context in which they occur. There will always be interaction between judicial strategies directed towards the attainment of central Treaty objectives, and those of the other Community institutions. Understanding the way in which they connect is one of the interesting aspects of Community law; understanding the way in which they ought to connect one of the most challenging.

[136] See above, 584–5. [137] N. 62 above, 461.
[138] *Ibid.* 459–60, italics in the original.

11. FURTHER READING

(a) Books

BURROWS, F., *Free Movement in European Community Law* (Oxford University Press, 1987)

GORMLEY, L. W., *Prohibiting Restrictions on Trade within the EEC* (Elsevier/North Holland, 1985)

GREEN, N., HARTLEY, T. C., and USHER, J. A., *The Legal Foundations of the Single European Market* (Oxford University Press, 1991)

OLIVER, P., *Free Movement of Goods in the EEC* (2nd. edn., European Law Centre, 1988)

(b) Articles

ALTER, K. J., and MEUNIER-AITSAHALIA, S., 'Judicial Politics in the European Community: European Integration and the Pathbreaking *Cassis de Dijon* Decision' (1994) 26 *Comparative Political Studies* 535

BARENTS, R., 'New Developments in Measures Having Equivalent Effects' (1981) 18 CMLRev. 271

GORMLEY, L. W., '*Cassis de Dijon* and the Communication from the Commission' (1981) 6 ELRev. 454

—— 'Actually or Potentially, Directly or Indirectly? Obstacles to the Free Movement of Goods' (1989) 9 YBEL 197

—— 'Recent Case Law on the Free Movement of Goods: Some Hot Potatoes' (1990) 27 CMLRev. 825

LASA, H.-C. VON HEYDEBRAND u.d., 'Free Movement of Foodstuffs, Consumer Protection and Food Standards in the European Community: Has the Court of Justice Got it Wrong?' (1991) 16 ELRev. 391

MATTERA, A., 'L'Arrêt "*Cassis de Dijon*": Une Nouvelle Approche pour la Réalisation et le Bon Fonctionnement du Marché Interieur' [1980] *Revue du Marche Commun* 505

MORTELMANS, K., 'Article 30 of the EEC Treaty and Legislation Relating to Market Circumstances: Time to Consider a New Definition?' (1991) 28 CMLRev. 115

OLIVER, P., 'A Review of the Case law of the Court of Justice on Articles 30 to 36 EEC in 1984' (1985) 22 CMLRev. 301

—— 'A Review of the Case Law of the Court of Justice on Articles 30 to 36 EEC in 1985' (1986) 23 CMLRev. 325

REICH, N., 'The "November Revolution" of the European Court of Justice: *Keck*, *Meng* and *Audi* Revisited' (1994) 31 CMLRev. 459

STEINER, J., 'Drawing the Line: Uses and Abuses of Article 30 EEC' (1992) 29 CMLRev. 749

VAN RIJN, T., 'A Review of the Case Law of the Court of Justice on Articles 30 to 36 EEC in 1986 and 1987' (1988) 25 CMLRev. 593

WHITE, E., 'In Search of the Limits to Article 30 of the EEC Treaty' (1989) 26 CMLRev. 235

WILS, W. P. J., 'The Search for the Rule in Article 30 EEC: Much Ado About Nothing?' (1993) 18 ELRev. 475

15

Free Movement of Workers and Beyond

1. INTRODUCTION

The Treaty provisions on freedom of movement for workers, which form the first chapter within the policy on free movement of persons, services, and capital, form an essential part of one of the earliest, central aims of the Community, namely the establishment of a common market.

Broadly speaking, the aim of setting up a common market was to increase wealth, to strengthen the economies of the Member States, and to bring them closer together. From this point of view, a flexible, mobile, and well-trained labour force would contribute to the overall economic empowerment and expansion of the EEC's Member States. However, in addition to this function of the policy of free movement of workers, and to some extent in tension with it, was the aspiration of integration of the peoples of Europe. In 1961, Levi-Sandri, a Commission member, after discussing the central economic importance of the free movement of workers, commented that:

> this, in the last analysis, must be and will be the most important political and social result of the liberalisation of the labour market: to the extent to which it is attained, we shall all be made to appreciate the effective range of European solidarity and the progress of the idea of unity in the minds of our peoples.[1]

The same commentator, seven years later, by then Vice-President of the Commission, said that the Community was 'not intended to be an inward-looking body, a rich man's club, deaf to the requirements of the rest of the world',[2] and referred to the free movement of workers as an embryonic form of European citizenship.[3] It will be seen below that this concept of citizenship was, thirty-five years after the signing of the EEC Treaty, and thirty-eight years after the failure of the proposed European Political Community, made explicit in European Community law by the amendments of the TEU in 1992: According to the Commission, this development placed the general right to

[1] Levi-Sandri, 'The Free Movement of Workers in the countries of the European Economic Community', Bull. EC 6–1961, 5.

[2] Levi-Sandri, 'Address to the XVIth World Congress of the I.F.C.T.U.', Bull. EC 11–1968, 53.

[3] Levi-Sandri, 'Free Movement of Workers in the European Community', Bull. EC 11–1968 5. See also Plender, 'An Incipient Form of European Citizenship' in *European Law and the Individual*, ed. F. Jacobs (North-Holland, 1976), 39.

move freely and reside within the Member States 'on a new conceptual basis, by enshrining it in the Treaties themselves'.[4]

This change is clearly of symbolic importance, since citizenship indicates a political and a social status rather than merely an economic right, and it is not expressly tied to any other occupation or status such as that of a worker, a retired worker, a tourist, or an economically independent person. However, whether it really adds much more than a symbolic veneer to the previously existing rights of workers and other specific categories of persons within Community law is open to question. These issues will be discussed in more detail below.[5] However, looking back to 1957, it is certainly the case that the conferral of rights, even within the context of an initially limited economic community, to move freely to take up employment in the different Member States was in itself of social and political, and not just of economic significance, when the EEC Treaty was originally drafted.

A distinct tension between these different aspects of the provisions on free movement of persons is reflected in the case law of the Court, just as it is in other areas of Community law, in particular in the area of sex discrimination.[6] This tension is evident in the arguments made to the Court over the interpretation of Treaty provisions and secondary legislation, by the Member States, the Commission, and the various parties. The image of the Community worker as a mobile unit of production, contributing to the creation of a single market and to the economic prosperity of Europe, vies with the image of the worker as human being, exercising a right to move and to live in another state and to take up employment there without discrimination, to improve the standard of living of his or her family. As it has done with most of the central or foundational Community rules, the Court has declared the provisions on free movement of workers to be fundamental to the Community's aims, and hence deserving of a wide interpretation, while it has, on the whole, restrictively read and curbed those provisions which allow for exceptions and derogations on the part of the Member States.

2. THE EFFECT OF ARTICLE 48

The basic provision is set out in Article 48 of the Treaty, which provides as follows:

> 1. Freedom of movement of workers shall be secured within the Community by the end of the transitional period at the latest.
>
> 2. Such freedom of movement shall entail the abolition of any discrimination based on nationality between workers of the Member States as regards employment, remuneration and other conditions of work and employment.

[4] See the Commission Report on the Citizenship of the Union, COM(93)702.

[5] At 707–11.

[6] See Ch. 18.

3. It shall entail the right, subject to limitations justified on grounds of public policy, public security or public health:
   (a) to accept offers of employment actually made;
   (b) to move freely within the territory of Member States for this purpose;
   (c) to stay in a Member State for the purpose of employment in accordance with the provisions governing the employment of nationals of that State laid down by law, regulation or administrative action;
   (d) to remain in the territory of a Member State after having been employed in that State, subject to conditions which shall be embodied in implementing regulations to be drawn up by the Commission.

4. The provisions of this Article shall not apply to employment in the public service.

The central importance of the principle of freedom of movement and non-discrimination on grounds of nationality in Article 48 has repeatedly been emphasized by the Court in its case law, and particularly in those cases in which it has pronounced on the general applicability of the provision. Article 48 represents an application, in the specific context of workers, of the general principle in Article 6 (formerly 7) of the Treaty that 'within the scope of application of this Treaty . . . any discrimination on grounds of nationality shall be prohibited'. In proceedings brought by the Commission against France for failing to repeal provisions of the French Maritime Code, which had required a certain proportion of the crew of a ship to be of French nationality, the Court ruled that Article 48 was 'directly applicable in the legal system of every Member State' and would render inapplicable all contrary national law.[7] The Court also made clear, in the case of *Walrave and Koch*,[8] that the provisions of Article 48 were not just of 'vertical' direct effect. The rules under challenge, which required 'pacemakers' in world cycling championships to be of the same nationality as the 'stayers', were made by an international cyclists association which was not a public or a state body. However, the Court ruled that this did not exempt them from the application of Article 48:

> Prohibition of such discrimination does not only apply to the action of public authorities but extends likewise to rules of any other nature aimed at regulating in a collective manner gainful employment and the provision of services . . .
>
> Since, moreover, working conditions in the various Member States are governed sometimes by means of provisions laid down by law or regulations and sometimes by agreements and other acts concluded or adopted by private persons, to limit the prohibitions in question to acts of a public authority would risk creating inequality in their application.[9]

[7] Case 167/73, *Commission* v. *French Republic* [1974] ECR 359, [1974] 2 CMLR 216. See Ch. 9 at 386.

[8] Case 36/74, *Walrave and Koch* v. *Association Union Cycliste Internationale* [1974] ECR 1405, [1975] 1 CMLR 320.

[9] *Ibid.*, paras. 17–19.

The Court also made clear that Article 48 would apply even if the work was done outside the Community, so long as the legal relationship of employment was entered within the Community.

Indirect as well as direct discrimination on grounds of nationality is prohibited by Article 48, so that a condition of eligibility for a benefit which is far more easily satisfied by national than by non-national workers is likely to fall foul of the Treaty. In *Ugliola*, an Italian worker in Germany challenged a German law under which a worker's security of employment was protected by having periods of military service taken into account in calculating the length of employment.[10] The law in question applied only to those who had done their military service in the Bundeswehr, although the nationality of the worker was irrelevant. The Court stressed that Article 48 allowed for no restrictions on the principle of equal treatment other than as provided for in paragraph (3), and concluded that the German law had created an unjustifiable restriction by 'indirectly introducing discrimination in favour of their own nationals alone'. It did not directly discriminate, since nationality was not a relevant factor in deciding whose military service should count, but the requirement that the service be done in the Bundeswehr was indirectly discriminatory since it would clearly be satisfied by a far greater number of nationals than non-nationals.

A similar issue arose in *Sotgiu*, where the German Post Office increased the separation allowance paid to workers employed away from their place of residence within Germany.[11] This increase was not to be paid to workers whose residence at the time of their initial employment was situated abroad and Sotgiu, an Italian employee, argued that this was in breach of Community law on equal treatment in conditions of work and remuneration of non-nationals. As in *Ugliola*, the discrimination was not direct, given that Italian nationals could have been initially recruited in Germany, and German nationals in other Member States. However, the rule in practice was likely to favour German nationals, and thus according to the Court, was covered by the Treaty prohibition:

> The rules regarding equality of treatment, both in the Treaty and in Article 7 of Regulation No 1612/68, forbid not only overt discrimination by reason of nationality but also all covert forms of discrimination which, by the application of other criteria of differentiation, lead in fact to the same result.
>
> This interpretation, which is necessary to ensure the effective working of one of the fundamental principles of the Community, is explicitly recognised by the fifth recital of the preamble to Regulation No 1612/68 which requires that the equality of treatment of all workers shall be ensured 'in fact and in law'.
>
> It may therefore be that criteria such as place of origin or residence of a worker may, according to circumstances, be tantamount, as regards their practical effect,

[10] Case 15/69, *Würtemmbergische Milchverwertung-Südmilch-AG* v. *Salvatore Ugliola* [1970] ECR 363, [1969] CMLR 194.

[11] Case 152/73, *Sotgiu* v. *Deutsche Bundespost* [1974] ECR 153.

to discrimination on the grounds of nationality, such as is prohibited by the Treaty and the Regulation.[12]

It is notable, too, that the Court did not conclude that the separation allowance in question must be contrary to Community law, but rather allowed for the possibility that the difference in treatment between nationals and non-nationals could be explained on the basis of objective differences in their situations, e. g. if the payment of the allowance to those resident in Germany was coupled with an obligation to transfer residence to the new place of work, whereas those resident outside Germany were not subject to such an obligation.

An obvious form of indirect discrimination is the imposition of a language requirement for certain posts, since it is likely that a far higher proportion of non-nationals than nationals will be affected by it. However, since such a requirement might well be legitimate, Article 3(1) of Regulation 1612/68 allows for the imposition of 'conditions relating to linguistic knowledge required by reason of the nature of the post to be filled'. The scope of this exception was examined by the Court in a case concerning a linguistic condition attached to a post, in circumstances where the post in question would never actually require the use of that language:

Case 379/87, Groener v. Minister for Education [1989] ECR 3967, [1990] 1 CMLR 401

Groener was a Dutch national working in Ireland as a part-time art teacher at a state vocational college, who applied after two years for a permanent full-time post at the college. Despite being recommended for appointment, she was not appointed because she failed a special oral test in the Irish language. This was a requirement for appointment to the post which applied both to nationals and non-nationals, even though lessons would not have to be given in Irish. Her request to the Minister for Education to waive the requirement was refused, on the ground that this could only be done where no other fully qualified applicants had applied for the post. She argued that these conditions were contrary to Article 48 of the Treaty and Article 3 of Regulation 1612/68.

THE ECJ

15. According to the documents before the Court, the teaching of art, like that of most other subjects taught in public vocational education schools, is conducted essentially or indeed exclusively in the English language. It follows that, as indicated by the terms of the second question submitted, knowledge of the Irish language is not required for the performance of the duties which teaching of the kind at issue specifically entails.

16. However, that finding is not in itself sufficient to enable the national court to decide whether the linguistic requirement in question is justified 'by reason of

[12] *Ibid.*, para. 11.

the nature of the post to be filled' within the meaning of the last subparagraph of Article 3(1).

. . .

18. As is apparent from the documents before the Court, although Irish is not spoken by the whole Irish population, the policy followed by Irish governments for many years has been designed not only to maintain but also to promote the use of Irish as a means of expressing national identity and culture. It is for that reason that Irish courses are compulsory for children receiving primary education and optional for those receiving secondary education. The obligation imposed on lecturers in public vocational education schools to have a certain knowledge of the Irish language is one of the measures adopted by the Irish Government in furtherance of that policy.

19. The EEC Treaty does not prohibit the adoption of a policy for the protection and promotion of a language of a Member State which is both the national language and the first official language. However, the implementation of such a policy must not encroach upon a fundamental freedom such as that of the free movement of workers. Therefore, the requirements deriving from measures intended to implement such a policy must not in any circumstances be disproportionate in relation to the aim pursued and the manner in which they are applied must not bring about discrimination against nationals of other Member States.

The Court concluded that the role of teachers in the educational process was an important one in the implementation of a state policy of this kind, and that so long as the language requirement was not disproportionate (e. g. in the level of knowledge demanded, or the denial of an opportunity to retake the test, or by requiring the linguistic knowledge to be obtained within the national territory), it could fall within the exception set out in Article 3(1) of Regulation 1612/68. The Court obviously took a broad view of the 'nature of the post' within Article 3(1), and was clearly influenced by the wider policy concerns raised by the Commission, the intervening French Government, and the Advocate General in the case, about the importance of cultural diversity and identity and the protection of minority languages within the Community. For this reason the language requirement, which was clearly indirectly discriminatory, could be justified.[13]

However, it is not only when the Member State invokes a specific exception set out in the Treaty or in a provision like Article 3 of Regulation 1612/68, that indirect discrimination contrary to Article 48 can be justified. This much is clear from several recent decisions concerning provisions of Belgian tax law. In *Commission* v. *Belgium*[14] and *Bachmann*,[15] the Court held that although national rules, which allowed the deductibility from income tax of various insurance and pension contributions only if those contributions were paid in

[13] For an example of indirect discrimination which was not justifiable, see Cases C–259/91, 331–332/91 *Allué and Coonan* [1993] ECR I–4309, in which the Member State had imposed restrictions on the contracts of foreign language teaching assistants.

[14] Case C–300/90, *Commission* v. *Belgium* [1992] ECR I–305, [1993] 1 CMLR 785.

[15] Case C–204/90 *Bachmann* v. *Belgium* [1992] ECR I–249, [1993] 1 CMLR 785.

Belgium, were indirectly discriminatory contrary to Article 48, they could be justified by the need to ensure the cohesion of the Belgian tax system. The Court accepted that contributions paid in Belgium were permitted to be deducted under the law because these deductions were offset by the tax imposed on sums paid out by insurers in Belgium, whereas there could be no such certainty that the sums paid out by insurers not based in Belgium had been taxed.[16] These indirectly discriminatory measures were held by the Court to be justified, without the need for the state to invoke the special grounds of exception in Article 48(3), which are discussed in detail below. It will be seen in Chapter 16 that the Court's approach to the justification of discrimination under Article 59 on the freedom to provide services seems somewhat more restrictive than its approach to the justification of discrimination under Article 48, since only the Treaty grounds of exception in Article 56 can be pleaded as justification for deliberate discrimination in the context of services. However, this conclusion depends on whether the tax rules in *Bachmann* are considered to be intentionally or unintentionally discriminatory. If they are viewed as being unintentionally discriminatory, then, just as in the context of free movement of services, Member States should be able to plead grounds other than those set out in Article 48(3) to justify the restrictive effects.

The Court has ruled on several occasions that Article 48 does not prohibit discrimination in a so-called 'wholly internal' situation. This has been referred to by writers and others as a situation of 'reverse discrimination' since its effect is that national workers cannot claim rights in their own Member State which workers who are nationals of other Member States could claim there. The Court made clear in the case of *Saunders*—in which it differed from the more generous conclusion of Advocate General Warner—that since there was 'no factor connecting' the defendant 'to any of the situations envisaged by Community law', she could not rely on Article 48 to challenge a 'binding over' order which effectively excluded her from part of the national territory.[17] This approach by the Court has given rise to some particularly invidious results in the context of the rights of workers and their families, which will be discussed in more detail below.[18]

[16] Contrast the opinion of Mischo A.G., *ibid.* 260, who concluded that the Belgian legislation was disproportionately restrictive, since there were other means available to obviate the risk of tax evasion. See also Case C–175/88, *Biehl* v. *Luxembourg* [1990] ECR I–1779, [1990] 3 CMLR 143.

[17] Case 175/78, *R.* v. *Saunders* [1979] ECR 1129, [1979] 2 CMLR 216. See also Case 298/84, *Pavlo Iorio* v. *Azienda Autonomo delle Ferrovie dello Stato* [1986] ECR 247, [1986] 3 CMLR 665. In Case 180/83, *Hans Moser* v. *Land Baden-Württemberg* [1984] ECR 2539, [1984] 3 CMLR 720, the prospect of a national being disadvantaged in his possible future search for employment abroad was not a sufficient 'connecting factor' to attract Art. 48. See now Case C–229/94, *R.* v. *Secretary of State for the Home Department, ex p. Adams*, referred on 29 July 1994 to the ECJ by the Div. Ct., where, relying on his European citizenship in Art. 8a, the applicant in Northern Ireland challenged an exclusion order prohibiting him from entering Britain.

[18] See in particular Cases 35 and 36/82, *Morson and Jhanjan* v. *Netherlands* [1982] ECR 3723, [1983] 2 CMLR 221 at 698, below.

3. WHO IS PROTECTED BY ARTICLE 48?

Article 49 of the Treaty provides for the making of secondary legislation by the Council to bring about, by progressive stages, the freedoms set out in Article 48. Several directives and regulations have been passed in order to implement Article 48, governing the conditions of entry, residence, and treatment of EC workers and their families. The most important of these are Directive 64/221, which governs the main derogations or exceptions to the rules on free movement;[19] Directive 68/360, which regulates the formalities and conditions of entry and residence of workers and the self-employed; and Regulation 1612/68, which elaborates on the equal-treatment principle and sets out many of the substantive rights and entitlements of workers and their families.

Regulation 1251/70 protects the right of the worker and those members of the worker's family listed in Regulation 1612/68 to remain in the territory of a Member State, mainly in the event of retirement, permanent incapacity to work, or death, after having been employed in that state for a period of time and subject to certain conditions.[20] In brief, the principal conditions to be satisfied are: (a) that the person should have reached pensionable age, should have worked in that state for a least a year preceding that time, and should have resided there continuously for over three years; or (b) that the person should have resided continuously in the state for over two years and have ceased to work there due to permanent incapacity (there is no length of residence requirement if the incapacity is due to certain accidents at work or occupational illness), or (iii) that the person, who now works in the territory of another Member State but resides in the first state and returns there weekly, should have resided and worked continuously in the first state for three years.[21]

Despite the existence of the various measures of secondary legislation, however, the basic terms which determine the scope of these provisions are not defined either in the Treaty or in the secondary legislation, but have been left to be shaped by the Court. The key term, of course, which establishes the actual scope and impact of these provisions in the Member States is the term 'worker'. The discussion and argument over who is the proper subject of these rights created by the Treaty can be seen from the earliest judgments of the Court right up until its very recent decisions.

One matter which is not immediately apparent from Article 48 is whether 'workers of the Member States' in paragraph (2) is intended to refer only to nationals of the Member States, or whether it includes non-EC nationals who

[19] Dir. 64/221 is discussed in detail in Ch. 17.

[20] [1970] II OJ spec. Ed. 402, [1970] JO L142/24.

[21] *Ibid.*, Art. 2. Art. 3 governs the rights of family members. Art. 8 also provides that Member States shall 'facilitate re-admission' of workers who had left the state after having resided and worked there for a long period.

are living and working in the Community.[22] One commentator has suggested that the contrast between Article 69 of the ECSC Treaty, which mentions 'workers who are nationals of the Member States', and Article 48 of the EEC Treaty, which makes no reference to nationality, implies that 'the draftsmen of the EEC Treaty intended to establish a common policy for all workers in the Community, irrespective of their nationality'.[23] However, the secondary legislation subsequently passed to implement Article 48, in particular Regulation 1612/68, specifically restricts its application to workers who are nationals of the Member States, and that has been the interpretation of Article 48 adopted by the Court. The status of non-EC nationals who are residents and workers within the Community will be discussed further below, in the context of the provisions on citizenship added by the TEU.

The 'package' of rights and benefits created by the Treaty and by secondary legislation for the group of EC nationals who qualify as 'workers' is quite considerable and, as a result, the definition of the scope of the term is important. Because Article 48 is concerned with workers (despite the reference in the Title III to free movement of 'persons'), it is clear that economic status of some kind is necessary, but what exactly that status must be, and who should control its interpretation, has been the subject of continued debate.

Case 75/63, Hoekstra (neé Unger) v. Bestuur der Bedrijfsvereniging voor Detailhandel en Ambachten [1964] ECR 177, [1964] CMLR 546

The applicant, Hoekstra, who had been employed in The Netherlands, had the benefit of voluntary insurance with the defendant vocational association. She became ill while visiting her parents in Germany, and, on returning to the Netherlands, was refused insurance payments in respect of medical expenses incurred while she had been away. A reference was made to the ECJ from the Dutch social security court for a ruling on the meaning of the term 'wage-earner or assimilated worker' in Council Regulation No 3 on social security.

THE ECJ[24]

The reply to the question put thus depends essentially upon the scope, whether Community or otherwise, of the provisions of the Treaty from which the concept of 'wage-earner or assimilated worker' in so far as they affect the field of social security, was drawn by the said regulation . . .

The establishment of as complete a freedom of movement for workers as possible, which thus forms part of the 'foundations' of the Community, therefore constitutes the principal objective of Article 51 and thereby conditions the interpretation of the regulations adopted in implementation of that Article.

Articles 48 to 51 of the Treaty, by the very fact of establishing freedom of movement for 'workers', have given Community scope to this term.

[22] See F. Burrows, *Free Movement in European Community Law* (Clarendon Press, 1987), 124.
[23] R. Plender, 'Competence, European Community Law and Nationals of Non-Member States' (1990) 39 ICLQ 599. See also Plender, n. 3 above.
[24] [1964] ECR 177, 184.

If the definition of this term were a matter for the competence of national law, it would therefore be possible for each Member State to modify the meaning of the concept of 'migrant worker' and to eliminate at will the protection afforded by the Treaty to certain categories of person.

Moreover nothing in Articles 48 to 51 of the Treaty leads to the conclusion that these provisions have left the definition of the term 'worker' to national legislation.

On the contrary, the fact that Article 48(2) mentions certain elements of the concept of 'workers', such as employment and remuneration, shows that the Treaty attributes a Community meaning to that concept.

Articles 48 to 51 would therefore be deprived of all effect and the above-mentioned objectives of the Treaty would be frustrated if the meaning of such a term could be unilaterally fixed and modified by national law . . .

The Treaty and Regulation No 3 thus did not intend to restrict protection only to the worker in employment but tend logically to protect also the worker who, having left his job, is capable of taking another.

Two things are clear from this judgment: first, that the Court requires the term worker to be a Community concept—in other words, it is claiming ultimate authority to define its meaning and scope. In the words of Mancini, a former Advocate General and now Judge of the Court, it conferred on itself a 'hermeneutic monopoly' to counteract possible unilateral restrictions of the application of the rules on freedom of movement by the different Member States.[25] And, secondly, the Court will construe the term generously so that not only a current worker, but also one who has just been a worker may also be covered. These two themes, that the authority to define most of the key concepts is to be the Court's rather than the Member States', and that the right-conferring terms of Articles 48, 51, and their implementing legislation are to be construed broadly, are recurrent in the Court's case law.

Although *Hoekstra* established that the Court would determine who was a worker for the purposes of Community law, it did not go much further in clarifying that concept. A clearer definition gradually emerged from a series of subsequent cases, some of which reveal the tension between what might be called the economic aspects and the social or human aspects of the policy on free movement of workers. In discussing the question of the Court's 'activism' in this area, Mancini has commented:

It is true that in the field of labour-related matters, such activism has frequently been motivated by a desire to consolidate the jurisdiction of the Court and at the same time to ensure the full and effective functioning of the Common Market. It is, however, also true that the judges of the Court have approached the human problems associated with the free movement of workers in a very sensitive

[25] See G. F. Mancini, 'The Free Movement of Workers in the Case-Law of the European Court of Justice' in *Constitutional Adjudication in European Community and National Law*, D. Curtin and D. O' Keeffe (eds.), (Butterworths, 1992), 67.

manner. If it can be said to be a good thing that our Europe is not merely a Europe of commercial interests, it is the judges who must take much of the credit.[26]

Whether or not this somewhat self-congratulatory statement is true can be reflected upon in reading this Chapter.

In the case of *Levin*, the issue of part-time workers was raised, and the Court was asked whether they were covered by Article 48 and the related secondary legislation:

Case 53/81, Levin v. Staatssecretaris van Justitie [1982] ECR 1035, [1982] 2 CMLR 454

The appellant was a British citizen living in The Netherlands and married to a non-EC national. She was refused a residence permit there on the ground that she had not been in work for over a year preceding the date of refusal of the permit. She argued that she had sufficient income for her and her husband's maintenance, and that she had also taken up part-time employment as a chambermaid in the meantime. The Staatssecretaris van Justitie had submitted that she was not a 'favoured EC citizen' since her employment did not provide sufficient means for her support, equal at least to the minimum legal wage prevailing in The Netherlands. A reference was made from the Dutch court to the ECJ, where the appellant argued that this 'minimum-wage' argument would place other Member State nationals in a less favourable position than nationals of the host country who have the option of working part-time for an income below the subsistence level.

THE ECJ

9. Although the rights deriving from the principle of freedom of movement for workers and more particularly the right to enter and stay in the territory of a Member State are thus linked to the status of a worker or of a person pursuing an activity as an employed person or desirous of so doing, the terms 'worker' and 'activity as an employed person' are not expressly defined in any of the provisions on the subject. It is appropriate, therefore, in order to determine their meaning, to have recourse to the generally recognized principles of interpretation, beginning with the ordinary meaning to be attributed to those terms in their context and in the light of the objectives of the Treaty.

[*The Court then referred to the* Hoekstra *judgment and to its argument that Member States could not unilaterally restrict the scope and meaning of the term worker.*]

12. Such would, in particular, be the case if the enjoyment of the rights conferred by the principle of freedom of movement for workers could be made subject to the criterion of what the legislation of the host State declares to be a minimum wage, so that the field of application *ratione personae* of the Community rules on this subject might vary from one Member State to another. The meaning and the scope of the terms 'worker' and 'activity as an employed person' should thus be clarified in the light of the principles of the legal order of the Community.

[26] *Ibid.*

13. In this respect it must be stressed that these concepts define the field of application of one of the fundamental freedoms guaranteed by the Treaty and, as such, may not be interpreted restrictively.

Here again, as in *Hoekstra*, the Court makes it clear that, since the rules on free movement of persons are fundamental to the Community, they are to be broadly and inclusively interpreted. While the Member States clearly would prefer to exclude non-nationals who are not earning enough to support themselves from the protection offered by Community law, the Court focused not on the financial self-sufficiency of workers, nor on their overall contribution to the economy of the host Member State, but on the benefits and usefulness to them of being able to engage in part-time work:

14. In conformity with this view the recitals to Regulation No 1612/68 contain a general affirmation of the right of all workers in the Member States to pursue the activity of their choice within the Community, irrespective of whether they are permanent, seasonal or frontier workers or workers who pursue their activities for the purpose of providing services. Furthermore, although Article 4 of Directive 68/360 grants the right of residence to workers upon the mere production of the document on the basis of which they entered the territory and of a confirmation of engagement from the employer or a certificate of employment, it does not subject this right to any condition relating to the kind of employment or to the amount of income derived from it.

15. An interpretation which reflects the full scope of these concepts is also in conformity with the objectives of the Treaty which include, according to Articles 2 and 3, the abolition, as between Member States, of obstacles to freedom of movement for persons, with the purpose *inter alia* of promoting throughout the Community a harmonious development of economic activities and a raising of the standard of living. Since part-time employment, although it may provide an income lower than what is considered to be the minimum required for subsistence, constitutes for a large number of persons an effective means of improving their living conditions, the effectiveness of Community law would be impaired and the achievement of the objectives of the Treaty would be jeopardized if the enjoyment of rights conferred by the principle of freedom of movement for workers were reserved solely to persons engaged in full-time employment and earning, as a result, a wage at least equivalent to the guaranteed minimum wage in the sector under consideration.

What the Court emphasized here was the freedom to take up employment in Article 48, not just as a means towards the creation of a single market for the benefit of the economies of the states, but as a right for the worker to raise her or his standard of living by whatever means available, even if this was not sufficient to reach the minimum level of subsistence in a particular state. The fact that the worker had additional means, such as family support or private property, to supplement this income would not affect his or her status as a protected 'worker' within Community law:

17. It should however be stated that whilst part-time employment is not excluded from the field of application of the rules on freedom of movement for workers, those rules cover only the pursuit of effective and genuine activities, to the exclusion of activities on such a small scale as to be regarded as purely marginal and ancillary. It follows both from the statement of the principle of freedom of movement for workers and from the place occupied by the rules relating to that principle in the system of the Treaty as a whole that those rules guarantee only the free movement of persons who pursue or are desirous of pursuing a genuine economic activity.

Finally, in response to the suggestion that Levin may only have sought work in order to obtain a residence permit to remain in the country, the Court ruled that the purpose or motive of the worker was immaterial, once he or she was pursuing or wishing to pursue a genuine and effective economic activity.

It is evident, then, that the criteria by which the Court will judge whether or not someone qualifies as a worker for the purposes of Article 48 will depend, not on the reason for taking up employment, nor the amount earned, but on the genuineness of the economic activity undertaken. Once it constitutes 'effective' work, then the worker will come within the scope of Community law. This requirement that the work be undertaken as a genuine economic activity probably responds to the concerns of Member States that their social security and social assistance schemes would become overburdened as a result of the arrival of migrants from other countries whose systems of social benefits are less generous, and who do not really intend to engage in effective work. However, although this concern was acknowledged by Advocate General Slynn in the case, he also pointed out the impact which the exclusion of part-time workers from the scope of the Treaty would have on particular groups:

> The issues raised are thus important to the individual, particularly in a time of extensive unemployment and of an increasing dependence on part-time work; and to the Member State which wishes to prevent the rights being abused by someone who is not in any real or genuine sense a worker. . .
>
> . . . I find it impossible to accept the argument that a part-time worker as such is not a worker within the meaning of Article 48. Such a result would in present circumstances exclude a very large, and probably increasing number of persons from the rights conferred by Article 48 and the Regulation and Directives to which reference has been made. The group includes not only women, the elderly and disabled who, for personal reasons might wish only to work part-time, but also women and men who would prefer to work full time but are obliged to accept part-time work.

The *Levin* judgment thus clarified that part-time workers were covered by Community law on free movement of workers, and that it did not matter if workers chose to supplement their income from other sources, such as from family or private funds. In the subsequent case of *Kempf*,[27] however, the issue was taken a step further. A German national who was living and working in The Netherlands as a music teacher, giving approximately twelve lessons a week, was refused a residence permit. The Dutch and Danish Governments argued that work providing an income below the minimum means of subsistence in the host state could not be regarded as genuine and effective work if the person doing the work claimed social assistance from public funds. The Court disagreed, ruling that when a genuine part-time worker sought to supplement earnings below the subsistence level, it was:

> irrelevant whether those supplementary means of subsistence are derived from property or from the employment of a member of his family, as was the case in *Levin*, or whether, as in this instance, they are obtained from financial assistance drawn from the public funds of the Member State in which he resides.[28]

Again, Advocate General Slynn addressed the concerns of the Member States about the possible abuse of the provisions on free movement of workers by those who were simply seeking a Member State with better social provision in which to reside. However, he concluded that these concerns did not justify the exclusion of part-time workers in Kempf's position from the scope of Article 48 since, 'if a person deliberately and for no good reason took a part-time job when he could do a full-time job, that might under national law affect his rights to public funds. It does not prevent him from being a worker'.[29]

This extensive reading of the scope of Article 48 and the term 'worker' is characteristic of the Court's case law in this area. It has ruled that the practice of sport may fall within Community law in so far as it constitutes an economic activity, although the composition of teams, and in particular national teams, was said by the Court to be a question of purely sporting and not of economic interest.[30] It has also ruled that fishermen who are paid a share of the proceeds of sale of their catches could be considered to be 'workers', despite the irregular nature of their remuneration.[31]

Despite the guidance given by the Court on the need for 'genuine and effective work' and the exclusion of 'marginal and ancillary activities', questions on the concrete application of these terms to specific cases in the Member States have repeatedly been referred to the Court for resolution. In *Lawrie-Blum*,[32] the Court was asked to rule on the compatibility of German rules restricting access for non-nationals to the preparatory service stage which was necessary

[27] Case 139/85, *Kempf* v. *Staatssecretaris van Justitie* [1986] ECR 1741, [1987] 1 CMLR 764.

[28] *Ibid.*, para. 14.

[29] [1986] ECR 1741, 1744.

[30] Case 36/74, n. 8 above, and Case 13/76, *Donà* v. *Mantero* [1976] ECR 1333, [1976] 2 CMLR 578.

[31] See Case 3/87, *R.* v. *Ministry of Agriculture, Fisheries and Food, ex p. Agegate Ltd* [1989] ECR 4459, [1990] 1 CMLR 366, paras. 33–36.

[32] Case 66/85, *Lawrie-Blum* v. *Land Baden-Württemberg* [1986] ECR 2121, [1987] 3 CMLR 389.

for qualification as a secondary school teacher. Addressing the question whether a trainee teacher participating in the preparatory service course would qualify as a worker within Article 48, the Court provided a more elaborate three-part definition of a 'worker' within Community law:

> That concept must be defined in accordance with objective criteria which distinguish the employment relationship by reference to the rights and duties of the persons concerned. The essential feature of an employment relationship, however, is that for a certain period of time a person performs services for and under the direction of another person in return for which he receives remuneration.[33]

The Court ruled that a trainee teacher did qualify as a worker since, during the period of preparatory service, the three conditions would be fulfilled: she would perform services of economic value, under the direction of the school in question, and would receive a measure of remuneration in return. The fact that the pay received was less than the full salary for a teacher was immaterial, in the Court's view, for the same sorts of reasons given in *Levin* and *Kempf*—what mattered was the genuinely economic nature of the work and the receipt of some remuneration, and not the amount of the pay.

In the subsequent case of *Steymann*, the Court pushed the concept of remuneration, and hence of economic activity, a little further than before:

Case 196/87, Steymann v. Staatsecretaris van Justitie [1988] ECR 6159, [1989] 1 CMLR 449

Steymann was a German national who lived in The Netherlands, where he had worked for a short time as a plumber. He then joined the Bhagwan Community, a religious community which provided for the material needs of its members. He participated in the life of the community by performing plumbing work, general household duties and other commercial activity on the community's premises. His application for a residence permit to pursue an activity as an employed person was refused, and on his application for review of this, a reference was made to the Court.

THE ECJ

9. It must be observed *in limine* that, in view of the objectives of the European Economic Community, participation in a community based on religion or another form of philosophy falls within the field of application of Community law only in so far as it can be regarded as an economic activity within the meaning of Article 2 of the Treaty.

. . .

11. As regards the activities in question in this case, it appears from the documents before the Court that they consist of work carried out within and on behalf of the Bhagwan Community in connection with the Bhagwan Community's commercial activities. It appears that such work plays a relatively important role in

[33] *Ibid.*, para. 17.

the way of life of the Bhagwan Commuity and that only in special circumstances can the members of the community avoid taking part therein. In turn, the Bhagwan Community provides for the material needs of its members, including pocket-money, irrespective of the nature and the extent of the work which they do.

12. In a case such as the one before the national court it is impossible to rule out *a priori* the possibility that work carried out by members of the community in question constitutes an economic activity within the meaning of Article 2 of the Treaty. In so far as the work, which aims to ensure a measure of self-sufficiency for the Bhagwan Community, consitutes an essential part of participation in that community, the services which the latter provides to its members may be regarded as being an indirect *quid pro quo* for their work.

The fact that the work might be seen, in conventional terms, as being unpaid, did not mean that it was not effective economic activity. Since he provided services of value to the Bhagwan Community which would otherwise have to be performed by someone else, and since his material needs were provided for in return, he fell within the scope of the Treaty.

A year later, the Court was asked to rule in *Bettray* on the application of Article 48 to someone who was undertaking therapeutic work as part of a drug-rehabilitation programme under Dutch social employment law.[34] The aim of the programme was to reintegrate people who were temporarily incapacitated into the workforce. They would be paid a certain amount, and treated, in so far as possible, in accordance with normal conditions of paid employment. The Court began by noting that a job was being carried out under supervision and in return for remuneration, and that the low pay from public funds and the low productivity of the worker would not in themselves prevent the application of Article 48. However, the Court then (unlike in its judgment in *Levin* where the reason for undertaking work was said not to be relevant) examined the purpose of the work performed, and reached a different conclusion:

However, work under the Social Employment Law cannot be regarded as an effective and genuine economic activity if it constitutes merely a means of rehabilitation or reintegration for the persons concerned and the purpose of the paid employment, which is adapted to the physical and mental possibilities of each person, is to enable those persons sooner or later to recover their capacity to take up ordinary employment or to lead as normal as possible a life.

It also appears from the order for reference that persons employed under the Social Employment Law are not selected on the basis of their capacity to perform a certain activity; on the contrary, it is the activities which are chosen in the light of the capabilities of the persons who are going to perform them in order to maintain, re-establish or develop their capacity for work. Finally, the activities involved

[34] Case 344/87, *Bettray* v. *Staatssecretaris van Justitie* [1989] ECR 1621, [1991] 1 CMLR 459.

> are pursued in the framework of undertakings or work associations created solely for that purpose by local authorities.[35]

Clearly the purpose for undertaking the work was crucial to the decision which was reached by the Court here. The fact that the main or even sole purpose of the work was to rehabilitate the person, to find work which would suit that person's needs and capabilities rather than to meet a genuine economic need (as was the case in *Steymann*), resulted in a ruling against Bettray. The case may be criticized, partly because ensuring the mobility of a well-trained workforce would seem to be an important part of the Treaty scheme, and to retrain and reintegrate people back into the workforce through sheltered employment should be a part of this. Further, it is not clear whether the *Bettray* ruling would apply to the case of sheltered employment for disabled people, something which was mentioned by the Advocate General in the case. Is all sheltered employment now outside the scope of the Treaty rules on free movement of workers, or is it only when the *sole* purpose of the work is to reintegrate someone who is temporarily incapacitated back into employment? Organizations such as the Rehabilitation Institute create and support projects which provide sheltered employment for disabled people on a longer-term basis, and although productivity may be lower than that performed by able-bodied workers, the work generally is of some commercial value. Such workers should equally have the benefit of the Treaty rules on freedom of movement, and it may be that the fact that the activities would not be solely therapeutic, but partly for therapeutic and partly for commercial purposes, would be sufficient to distinguish them from the programme in *Bettray*.

Bettray, however, is one of the few judgments in which the Court adopted a limiting approach to the concept of worker in Article 48. The more usually expansive approach was taken by the Court in the cases of *Raulin*[36] and *Bernini*.[37] In *Bernini*, the Court drew on its ruling in *Lawrie-Blum*[38] to conclude that an Italian national who was employed for ten weeks as a paid trainee as part of her occupational training was not precluded from being a worker either by the fact that her productivity was low, or that she worked only a small number of hours a week and received limited wages. This ruling was not entirely unqualified, however, since the national court was nonetheless entitled, 'when assessing the genuine and effective nature of the services in question, to examine whether in all the circumstances the person concerned has completed a sufficient number of hours in order to familiarize himself with the work'.[39] If the worker voluntarily left employment in order to take up a course of full-time study, the Court held, the status of worker would be

[35] *Ibid.*, paras. 17–19.

[36] Case C–357/89, *Raulin* v. *Minister van Onderwijs en Wetenschappen* [1992] ECR I–1027, [1994] 1 CMLR 227.

[37] Case C–3/90, *Bernini* v. *Minister van Onderwijs en Wetenschappen* [1992] ECR I–1071.

[38] Case 66/85, n. 32 above.

[39] [1992] ECR I–1071, para. 16.

retained so long as there was a link between the previous employment and the study undertaken.[40]

Raulin concerned a French national who was employed in The Netherlands as a waitress under an on-call contract (*oproepcontract*), which gave no guarantee of the hours to be worked, but under which she had worked for sixty hours in all over an eight-month period. The Court held, again, that she was not precluded, by virtue of the conditions of the on-call contract, from being considered a worker within Article 48. But, as in *Bernini*, the question whether the woman would qualify as a worker was, with the aid of certain guidelines, ultimately left to the national court to determine as a matter of fact:

> The national court may, however, when assessing the effective and genuine nature of the activity in question, take account of the irregular nature and limited duration of the services actually performed under a contract for occasional employment. The fact that the person concerned worked only a very limited number of hours in a labour relationship may be an indication that the activities exercised are purely marginal and ancillary. The national court may also take account, if appropriate, of the fact that the person must remain available to work if called upon to do so by the employer.[41]

Phrasing its ruling in *Bernini* in a negative light, the Court held that, with the exception of someone who became involuntarily unemployed, a migrant worker who left work to begin a course of full-time study without any link with the previous employment would not retain the status of a migrant worker for the purposes of Article 48 of the EC Treaty.

Does this mean that so long as a migrant registers for a course which is linked with employment previously held in that Member State, he or she remains a protected 'worker' and is entitled to all of the advantages and benefits assured to such under Article 48 and Regulation 1612/68? The case of *Brown* indicates that, although someone who has engaged in genuine and effective work prior to a course of study will be considered to be a 'worker' within Article 48, the fact that the work was undertaken purely in order to prepare for the course of study, rather than to prepare for an occupation or employment, would mean that not all of the advantages provided for workers within Community law may be claimed.[42] This is an interesting, if somewhat difficult, notion introduced by the Court, of a semi-status between worker and non-worker, which may be held when someone is engaged in genuine and effective work, but purely as a means to become a student rather than as a means in itself of preparing for an occupation. Brown was a dual national, relying on his French nationality in the United Kingdom , who had worked for nine months for a company in Scotland as a form of 'pre-university indus-

[40] [1992] ECR I–1071, para. 21. See further below.
[41] [1992] ECR I–1027, para. 14.
[42] Case 197/86, *Brown* v. *Secretary of State for Scotland* [1988] ECR 3205, [1988] 3 CMLR 403.

trial training', before beginning an electrical engineering degree at Cambridge University. The Court ruled that he was to be regarded as a 'worker', but that he was not entitled to the advantage of a maintenance grant since his employment was merely 'ancillary' to the course of study he wished to undertake. The case is rather a difficult one because the Court is clearly making rather fine distinctions based on the purpose for which work is undertaken. It appeared from earlier cases such as *Levin* that the purpose of undertaking work was irrelevant to the genuineness of the employment, and yet the purpose of the work (i.e. to gain pre-University experience) was taken into account in Brown's case. However, the Court did not rule that this purpose disqualified him as a 'worker' under Article 48 (since he had clearly engaged in eight months of effective, full-time economic activity, satisfying the three criteria of *Lawrie-Blum*), but concluded that it meant that he could not benefit from all of the social rights and advantages which, it will be seen below, workers are normally entitled to enjoy under Community law. This conclusion, as will be seen in the discussion of educational rights, below, represents a response by the Court to concerns voiced by the Member States about the abuse of the provisions on free movement of workers by those who merely wished to avail themselves of the generous educational provision in a particular Member State. But the Court nevertheless ruled in *Bernini*, by contrast with *Brown*, that where an EC national in a Member State other than his or her own is engaged in genuine, effective, 'non-ancillary' work, which is later given up in order to pursue a related course of study, that person will retain the full status of worker with all the material and social advantages which go with it. Both Brown and Bernini would be workers within Article 48, but whereas a worker in Brown's situation would enjoy this status only to a limited extent, a worker in Bernini's situation would enjoy all of the benefits associated with the full status.

Other examples of something like the 'semi-status' of worker seen in *Brown* can be found in cases where the Court separates the formal status of worker protected under Article 48 from the bundle of material advantages which would normally attach to that status under provisions of Community law. One such case is that of *Antonissen*,[43] in which the Court ruled that persons not yet employed but seeking work were covered by Article 48, although their rights would not necessarily be the same as those of others who had obtained employment in the host Member State.

The *Antonissen* case provides a very clear example of the Court's purposive interpretive approach, in suggesting a wider scope for Article 48 than the words of the Article might convey. In *Levin*, the Court had referred in passing to the rules relating to freedom of movement for persons 'who wish

[43] Case C–292/89, *R.* v. *Immigration Appeal Tribunal, ex p. Antonissen* [1991] ECR I–745, [1991] 2 CMLR 373. See also Case 316/85, *Centre public d'aide sociale de Courcelles* v. *Lebon* [1987] ECR 2811, [1989] 1 CMLR 337, for a similar illustration of the more limited status accorded by the Court to an EC national who is unemployed, but who claims to be moving in search of work.

to pursue an activity as an employed person',[44] and in *Royer* to the right 'to look for or pursue an occupation',[45] but these comments had not been fully reasoned by the Court, nor was the apparent discrepancy between the assumption that non-nationals had a right to enter and search for work and the narrower wording of Article 48 explained.

Case C–292/89, R v. Immigration Appeal Tribunal, ex parte Antonissen [1991] ECR I–745, [1991] 2 CMLR 373

Antonissen was a Belgian national who had arrived in the United Kingdom in 1984, and had attempted unsuccessfully to find work. In 1987, after he had been convicted of and imprisoned for a drug-related offence, the Secretary of State decided to deport him. He applied for judicial review of the dismissal of his appeal against deportation, and the case was referred to the Court. One of the arguments made before the Court was that only the nationals of Member States in possession of a confirmation of engagement of employment were entitled to a right of residence in another Member State.

THE ECJ

9. In that connection it has been argued that, according to the strict wording of Article 48 of the Treaty, Community nationals are given the right to move freely within the territory of the Member States for the purpose only of accepting offers of employment actually made (Article 48(3)(a) and (b)) whilst the right to stay in the territory of a Member State is stated to be for the purpose of employment (Article 48(3)(c)).

10. Such an interpretation would exclude the right of a national of a Member State to move freely and to stay in the territory of the other Member States in order to seek employment there, and cannot be upheld.

. . .

12. Moreover, a strict interpretation of Article 48(3) would jeopardize the actual chances that a national of a Member State who is seeking employment will find it in another Member State, and would, as a result, make that provision ineffective.

13. It follows that Article 48(3) must be interpreted as enumerating, in a non-exhaustive way, certain rights benefiting nationals of Member States in the context of the free movement of workers and that that freedom also entails the right for nationals of Member States to move freely within the territory of the other Member States and to stay there for the purposes of seeking employment.

The technique of the Court is to examine the Article and to identify its purpose: in this case, to ensure the free movement of workers. It then concludes that a literal—and hence restrictive—interpretation of the terms of Article 48 would hinder and make ineffective that purpose. In other words, if nationals could only move to another Member State when they already had an offer of employment, the number of people who could move would be very small

[44] Case 53/81, *Levin* v. *Staatssecretaris van Justitie* [1982] ECR 1035, [1982] 2 CMLR 454, para. 16.

[45] Case 48/75, *Royer* [1976] ECR 497, [1976] 2 CMLR 619, para. 31.

indeed, and many workers who could well seek and find employment on arrival in a Member State would be prevented from so doing. The Court did not, however, rule that the right to remain in search of work was unlimited, nor that the status of an EC national searching for work in a Member State was the same as that of an EC national who was actually employed in the Member State.[46] Further, Member States retain the power to expel someone who is searching for work, but who has not found work after a period of time, even without invoking one of the grounds of exception under Article 48(3). This is discussed in further detail below.

A particularly interesting feature of the *Antonissen* judgment is the comment of the Court about the rights which are specifically listed in Article 48. In paragraph 13 the Court states that these are non-exhaustive, in other words that Article 48 may confer many rights on Member State nationals within the context of free movement of workers, other than those listed therein. This open-ended approach leaves the Court with the power to adapt and even extend Article 48 through interpretation, in accordance with the changing social, economic, and political climate in the Community.

4. THE ARTICLE 48(4) EXCEPTION

It is evident from the discussion so far that the approach of the Court to the definition of worker in Article 48 has been an expansive one, the parameters being determined by the Court and not by the Member States. Conversely, its approach to the limiting clause in Article 48(4), which provides that the rest of Article 48 shall not apply to 'employment in the public service', has been a restrictive one, designed to ensure that the scope of the exception does not go further than is necessary to fulfil the purpose for which it was put into the Treaty. This, of course, requires an analysis of why the exception is in the Treaty, and the case law on this point provides a nice example of the contrast between a kind of 'original intent' interpretation argued for by the Member States, based on what the statess intended when they agreed to the inclusion of that clause in the Treaty, and the less historically rooted 'purposive' interpretation employed by the Court. The Court does not confine its 'hermeneutic monopoly' to the right-conferring terms in Article 48, such as 'worker', but extends it also to the public-service derogation: it is the Court and not the Member State which decides what constitutes employment in the public service.

The battle over the scope of the public-service exception has been hard-fought, perhaps even more strongly than that over the scope of the term worker. An explanation for this is offered by Mancini, Judge on the Court

46 See Case 316/85, n. 43 above, in which the Court held that many of the social and tax advantages guaranteed to workers within Community law were not available to those who were moving in search of work.

and former Advocate General, who attributes it to 'the widespread view that the functioning of the public service is an exercise of full State sovereignty'.[47] The issue arose in the case of *Sotgiu*, discussed above, where the Court did not define exactly what was meant by 'employment in the public service', but rather clarified in what way the Member States could use that exception. Germany had invoked Article 48(4) in an attempt to justify its provisions on separation allowances, which worked to the disadvantage of non-nationals, and this gave the Court the opportunity to comment on the underlying purpose of the exception:

> Taking account of the fundamental nature, in the scheme of the Treaty, of the principles of freedom of movement and equality of treatment of workers within the Community, the exceptions made by Article 48(4) cannot have a scope going beyond the aim in view of which this derogation was included.
>
> The interests which this derogation allows Member States to protect are satisfied by the opportunity of restricting admission of foreign nationals to certain activities in the public service.
>
> On the other hand this provision cannot justify discriminatory measures with regard to remuneration or other conditions of employment against workers once they have been admitted to the public service.
>
> The very fact that they have been admitted shows indeed that those interests which justify the exceptions to the principle of non-discrimination permitted by Article 48(4) are not at issue.[48]

Here the Court made clear that the use of Article 48(4) was confined to restricting the admission of non-nationals into the public service, whereas if they were deemed to be sufficiently trustworthy or loyal to the state to be admitted to such employment, there could then be no grounds for paying them less or treating them differently on account of their nationality.

The other point emphasized by the Court in *Sotgiu* was that which was first made in *Hoekstra* (above) in relation to workers, namely that the authority to define the scope of the exception must lie with the Court and not with the Member States:

> It is necessary to establish further whether the extent of the exception provided for by Article 48(4) can be determined in terms of the designation of the legal relationship between the employee and the employing administration.
>
> In the absence of any distinction in the provision referred to, it is of no interest whether a worker is engaged as a workman (*ouvrier*), a clerk (*employé*), or an official (*fonctionnaire*) or even whether the terms on which he is employed come under public or private law.
>
> These legal designations can be varied at the whim of national legislatures and cannot therefore provide a criterion for interpretation appropriate to the requirements of Community law.[49]

[47] G. F. Mancini, n. 25 above, 77. [48] Case 152/73, Sotgiu n. 11 above, para. 4.
[49] *Ibid.*, para. 5.

The Court makes it quite clear here that the Member States cannot deem a particular post to be 'in the public service' by the name or designation they give to that post, or by the mere fact that the terms of the post are regulated by public law. Germany had argued before the Court that, because the Community was founded upon the state organizations of the Member States, the concept of the public service could only be interpreted in the light of these national concepts. However, given that the Court had already ruled that the scope of the Article 48(4) exception would be exhausted by the admission of Sotgiu to the post in the first place, it did not need to go on to say what it was about a particular post that would bring it within the exception. This was left to be done in subsequent cases, in which the Commission brought enforcement proceedings against various Member States for breach of Article 48.

Case 149/79, Commission v. Belgium
[1980] ECR 3881; [1981] 2 CMLR 413

Possession of Belgian nationality was required as a condition of entry for posts with Belgian local authorities and public undertakings, regardless of the nature of the duties to be performed. Examples of such posts were those of unskilled railway workers, hospital nurses, and night-watchmen. The Commission brought proceedings against Belgium under Article 169, arguing that the scope of Article 48(4) could only cover posts implying actual participation in the exercise of official authority by those occupying them. The Belgian Government in response argued that, when the Treaties were drafted, there was no Community concept of the objectives and scope of public authorities and that the Member States' governments wished the conditions of entry to public office to remain their preserve.

THE ECJ

10. That provision [Article 48(4)] removes from the ambit of Article 48(1) to (3) a series of posts which involve direct or indirect participation in the exercise of powers conferred by public law and duties designed to safeguard the general interests of the State or of other public authorities. Such posts in fact presume on the part of those occupying them the existence of a special relationship of allegience to the State and reciprocity of rights and duties which form the foundation of the bond of nationality.

11. The scope of the derogation made by Article 48(4) to the principles of freedom of movement and equality of treatment laid down in the first three paragraphs of the article should therefore be determined on the basis of the aim pursued by that article. However, determining the sphere of application of Article 48(4) raises special difficulties since in the various Member States authorities acting under powers conferred by public law have assumed responsibilities of an economic and social nature or are involved in activities which are not identifiable with the functions which are typical of the public service yet which by their nature still come under the sphere of application of the Treaty. In these circumstances the effect of extending the exception contained in Article 48(4) to posts which, whilst coming under the States or other organizations governed by public law, still do not involve any association with tasks belonging to the public service properly so called, would be to remove a considerable number of posts from the ambit of the

principles set out in the Treaty and to create inequalities between Member States according to the different ways in which the State and certain sectors of economic life are organized.

The Court here confirmed what it said in *Sotgiu*, that simply including certain activities, perhaps of a social or economic kind, within the scope of the public law of the State, and taking responsibility for their performance, would not bring those activities within the Article 48(4) exception. The argument based on the states' intentions at the time of drafting the Treaty was ignored by the Court, and it focused instead on the aim of the provision in the context of the Treaty and the Chapter as a whole. This was, in the Court's view, to permit Member States, should they so wish, to reserve for nationals those posts which would require a specific bond of allegiance and mutuality of rights and duties between state and employee. The Court's description of the posts which could be said to require such allegiance and to depend upon the bond of nationality was twofold: they must involve participation in the exercise of powers conferred by public law, and they must entail duties designed to safeguard the general interests of the state. The notion of 'powers conferred by public law' is rather a vague one, given the difficulties inherent in defining the scope of public law, but the idea of 'safeguarding the general interests of the state' is somewhat more concrete. Different views have been expressed on this point, but it would seem from the *Lawrie-Blum* case[50] that the two requirements are cumulative rather than alternative, i. e. that a post will only benefit from the derogation in Article 48(4) if it involves *both* the exercise of power conferred by public law *and* the safeguarding of the general interests of the state.[51]

The Court dismissed the arguments of the French and Belgian Governments to the effect that the idea of nationality as a necessary condition for entry to any post in the public service of the state actually had constitutional status in certain states. In response, the Court emphasized the need for the 'unity and efficacy' of Community law, and repeated its view that the interpretation of limiting concepts such as public service employment could not be left to the discretion of Member States—presumably even if the state's rules were of a constitutional nature.[52]

However, the Court ruled that it did not have enough information in the case to be able to identify which of the specified posts fell outside Article 48(4), and it invited Belgium and the Commission to re-examine and resolve the issue in the light of its judgment, and to report any solution to the Court. When they failed to agree on certain of the posts, the case came back to the Court two years later, where it ruled that, with the exception of a limited number of posts—including certain supervisory posts, night watchman and architect with

[50] Case 66/85, n. 32 above, para. 27.

[51] See D. O'Keeffe, 'Judicial Interpretation of the Public Service Exception to the Free Movement of Workers' in n. 25 above, 89, 96.

[52] [1980] ECR 3881, paras. 18–19.

the municipality of Brussels—none of the other posts satisfied the criteria for the application of Article 48(4).[53]

These decisions, however, were not well received in the Member States. The Belgian Government had argued in the proceedings against it that Article 48(4) differed from Article 55, which provides a somewhat similar derogation in the context of freedom of establishment and freedom to provide services, when the activity in question involved the 'exercise of official authority'. This difference, according to the Belgian Government, was deliberately reflected in the respective wording of each: Article 55 specifically mentions the exercise of official authority, which implies a functional concept, whereas Article 48(4) refers to 'employment in the public service' which is an institutional concept. This argument, which was supported in the case by the interventions of the United Kingdom, German, and French governments, maintains that what is important for the application of Article 48(4) is the institution within which the worker is employed, rather than the characteristics or the nature of the work itself.

Given the strength of feeling on the part of some of the Member States about the meaning of the public service exception, it is unsurprising that, despite the lack of success in the *Belgium* cases, they did not abandon the attempt to alter and expand the interpretation given to Article 48(4) by the Court. It is evident from the very critical and trenchant opinion of Advocate General Mancini in subsequent Article 169 proceedings involving public nursing posts in France, that various states still felt strongly that the definition should be one for the Member States and not for the Community, and that the concept should be an 'organic or institutional' one, rather than the functional one adopted by the Court in the two *Belgium* cases:

> The decisions to which I have referred gave rise to severe criticisms from academic lawyers and, what is more important, they have not been 'taken in' by numerous governments. Such resistance is not surprising if it is borne in mind how deep-rooted is the conviction that the public service is an area in which the State should exercise full sovereignty and how wide-spread is the tendency, in times of high unemployment, to see the public service as a convenient reservoir of posts. Such resistance is a matter for concern and should be tackled head-on before cases similar to the present one multiply . . .
>
> . . . In short, in order to be made inaccessible to nationals of another State, it is not sufficient for the duties inherent in the post at issue to be directed specifically towards public objectives which influence the conduct and action of private individuals. Those who occupy the post must don full battle dress: in non-metaphorical terms, the duties must involve acts of will which affect private individuals by requiring their obedience or, in the event of disobedience, by compelling them to comply. To make a list . . . is practically impossible; but certainly the first examples which come to mind are posts relating to policing, defence of the State, the administration of justice and assessments to tax.

[53] Case 149/79, *Commission* v. *Belgium (No 2)* [1982] ECR 1845, [1982] 3 CMLR 539.

> . . . It is a fact that an extremist disciple of Hegel might truly think that access to posts like the ones at issue here [nursing] should be denied to foreigners. But anyone who does not regard the State as 'the march of God in the world' must of necessity take the contrary view.[54]

A further argument made by the four governments who were represented in the *Belgium* cases, was that certain posts which may not at the outset involve participation in the powers conferred by public law require a certain flexibility of character, in that the duties and responsibilities of the post may change, or the holders of such initial posts may subsequently become eligible for careers at a higher grade with duties involving the exercise of public powers. This, too, was rejected by the Court as a reason for treating the initial post as being within the public service exception, since that exception 'allows Member States to reserve to their nationals, by appropriate rules, entry to posts involving the exercise of such powers and such responsibilities within the same grade, the same branch, or the same class'.[55] The argument made by the United Kingdom that this would be burdensome for the states, since it would require them to re-examine the position of a non-national employee at all stages of his or her career, did not impress the Court.

The point was made again by the Court in enforcement proceedings brought by the Commission against Italy, concerning laws protecting the security and tenure of researchers at the National Research Council (CNR) which were not applied to non-nationals.[56] Italy's argument was twofold: first, that the work undertaken by the CNR involved satisfying the general interests of the state and was financed out of public funds, and secondly, that if researchers became established members of staff, they could be promoted to higher managerial positions which would entail participation in the exercise of public power. The Court rejected the first argument in the following terms:

> Simply referring to the general tasks of the CNR and listing the duties of all its researchers is not sufficient to establish that the researchers are responsible for exercising powers conferred by public law or for safeguarding the general interests of the State. Only the duties of management or of advising the State on scientific and technical questions could be described as employment in the public service within the meaning of Article 48(4).[57]

The second argument was equally summarily dismissed, with reference being made to the Court's ruling in the *Belgium* cases:

[54] Case 307/84, *Commission* v. *France* [1986] ECR 1725, 1727–33, [1987] 3 CMLR 555. For criticism of the Court's ruling in this case, see D. O'Keeffe, n. 51 above, 89, 101–103.

[55] N. 52 above, para. 21.

[56] Case 225/85, *Commission* v. *Italy* [1987] ECR 2625, [1988] 3 CMLR 635.

[57] *Ibid.*, para. 9.

It is sufficient to point out that Community law does not prohibit a Member State from reserving for its own nationals those posts within a career bracket which involve participation in the exercise of powers conferred by public law or the safeguarding of the general interests of the State.[58]

Yet repeated failure to get the Court to adopt a looser approach to Article 48(4), and to accept the Member States' categorizations of public-service employment, has not deterred Member States from making fresh arguments to widen the scope of the exception. In the case of *Lawrie-Blum*, discussed above, which concerned the reservation of places for trainee school teachers to nationals, the German Government argued that Article 48(4) applied because state schoolteachers were entrusted with the discharge of public functions. The Court simply repeated its ruling in the two *Belgium* cases and said that these 'very strict conditions' could not be fulfilled in the case of a trainee teacher.[59]

More recently in the *Scholz* case, which touched on the public service in a broader context but in which the Member State sensibly did not attempt to invoke Article 48(4), a German woman challenged the rejection of her application for a canteen job in an Italian university.[60] Points had been awarded to applicants for previous employment in the public service (not necessarily in canteen-related work), but only in the Italian public service, so that Scholz's experience in the German public service was not taken into account. The Court held that, if the rules of recruitment for a post provide for the taking into account of previous employment in the public service, even that which did not fall under Article 48(4) and which was unconnected with the duties of canteen staff, then the refusal to take into account previous employment in the public service of another Member State would constitute unjustified indirect discrimination. The case is similar to that of *Ugliola*, where the Court held that, if periods of military service were to be taken into account, then this should apply to periods of military service done in any Member State. If the public service employment was not such as would fall within Article 48(4), so that the 'allegiance factor' would not apply, then, according to Advocate General Jacobs, the probable reason for taking such employment into account was the different ethos: lower pay in return for prospects of security, and possibly a desire to perform a public service. This was a reason which should apply regardless of the country in which the employment was carried out.

Given the continued debate and dissent over the scope of the public service exception, it may seem surprising that, unlike the public policy and other

58 *Ibid.*, para. 10.

59 Case 66/85, n. 32 above, para. 28. See also Cases 33/88, *Allué and Coonan* v. *Università degli Studi di Venezia* [1989] ECR 1591, [1991] 1 CMLR 283, C–213/90, *ASTI* v. *Chambre des Employés Privés* [1991] ECR I–3507; and C–4/91 *Bleis* v. *Ministère de l'Education Nationale* [1991] ECR I–5627, [1994] 1 CMLR 793, in which Art. 48(4) was held to be inapplicable.

60 Case 419/92, *Scholz* v. *Opera Universitaria di Cagliari* [1994] ECR I–505, [1994] 1 CMLR 873.

derogations under Article 48(3), there is no secondary legislation which attempts to clarify the concept. This point was made rather testily by the Belgian Government in the first *Belgium* case:

> The attitude of the Commission to this is paradoxical and contradictory . . . When urged to clarify this largely unworkable concept by means of a regulation or directive it refuses to do so yet sets itself up as a judge over the application of the concept by the Member States.[61]

In contrast with this argument, it has been commented that, although the Commission did at one stage propose to draft legislation to clarify Article 48(4), that proposal was opposed by those who thought that the Member States might take advantage of detailed legislation to undermine the established case law, and also that such legislation could ossify the process of creating a 'citizens' Europe'.[62] The Commission instead, in 1988, published a document in the Official Journal relating to the scope of Article 48(4), and providing some guidance on the sorts of state functions which it considered to fall within that provision, and those which it considered would not.[63] Those functions which it categorized as falling within the exception included the armed forces, police, judiciary, tax authorities, and certain public bodies engaged in preparing or monitoring legal acts. Posts which were unlikely to be within the exception were nursing, teaching, and non-military research in public establishments.

It can be seen from the discussion of Article 48(4) that the area is still fraught with ideological tensions, the underlying debate being one about the concept of nationality and about when it is legitimate for the Member States to require nationality as a condition for employment. The efforts of the Member States to define Article 48(4) in terms of the 'public sector'—the institutional appproach—have failed, and the Court has adhered to a rather more difficult but narrower 'functional' approach, which examines closely the character of posts which might be said to require the reciprocal bond of allegiance which is said to be characteristic of nationality. The debate provides an excellent example of the federal tensions, which emerge in many areas of Community law, over the proper scope of national as opposed to Community jurisdiction and competence, and in particular where such a sensitive political issue as nationality is concerned.

A final, optimistic thought on Article 48(4) considers whether the new provisions in the EC Treaty on citizenship, which were added by the TEU, could undermine the thinking behind, and reduce the importance of, the public service exception:

[61] Case 149/79, n. 53 above. [62] Mancini, n. 25 above. [63] [1988] OJ C72/2.

D. O'Keeffe, Judicial Interpretation of the Public Service Exception to the Free Movement of Workers[64]

There is an inherent conflict between Article 48(4) on the one hand and the creation of the internal market and increased European integration on the other. The public service exception is geared to a conception of the State performing certain essential activities related to its function as the State, where the legitimate interests of the State can best be served and protected by the recruitment of the State's own nationals to perform certain tasks on its behalf.

However, this view of the public service exception is founded on a conception of nationality which may face increasing strain. It is based on a very traditional notion of loyalty to the State and finds its parallel in the denial to foreigners of political rights . . .

It is clear that these provisions [of the Treaty on European Union on citizenship] will alter the perceptions of Member States concerning nationals of other Member States. They blur the distinction between the State's own nationals and nationals of other Member States in several ways which go to the heart of the concept of nationality. Previously, Community law, and in particular the case-law of the Court of Justice, had concentrated on the economic and social integration of Community migrants (viewed as economic actors by the Treaty) in order to create a Community citizenship. As Community nationals are now to enjoy political rights deriving from Community law, it will become progressively more difficult to justify a different treatment of them as regards employment in the public service, which is founded upon political considerations.

5. DIRECTIVE 68/360

The second legislative measure of importance in the context of free movement of workers is Directive 68/360, which was adopted under Article 49, so that, unlike Directive 64/221, it is applicable only to the employed and not also to the self-employed. Directive 68/360 sets out to facilitate freedom of movement and the abolition of restrictions, in part by clarifying certain formal requirements relating to the right of entry and residence of non-nationals. This measure specifies what documents an EC worker will require on entering a Member State other than his or her own, and it provides for the issuing of residence permits to workers and their families.

Article 1 is a straightforward provision requiring the abolition of restrictions on movement and residence of nationals and their families. The family members covered are those to whom Regulation 1612/68 applies. This Regulation is discussed in further detail below. Article 2 requires Member States to grant such persons the right to leave their territory to go and work in other Member States, simply on producing an identity card or passport which their Member State must provide for them and which will be valid throughout the Community. No visa requirement may be imposed. Article 3

[64] See n. 25 above, 105.

to enter another Member State—all that is required is a valid identity card or passport and a visa requirement is impermissible, save for family members who are not EC nationals. Articles 4 and 9 provide for the issuing of five-year, automatically renewable, residence permits free of charge to those persons listed in Article 1, as proof of their right of residence. Article 6 provides for temporary residence permits for temporary and seasonal workers who work for more than three months but less than a year. To obtain a permit, the worker must produce the document with which he or she entered the territory and proof of engagement from an employer. Family members must produce the document with which they entered the country, as well as proof of their relationship with the worker, and evidence of dependency or co-habitation if required under Regulation 1612/68. For family members who are non-EC nationals, a residence document co-extensive with that of the worker must be issued. The Directive makes clear in Article 5 that the rights to reside and work are not conditional upon initial satisfaction of the formalities for which it provides. Article 7 deals partly with unemployment, and Article 8 with those short-term (less than three months), seasonal, and so-called 'frontier' workers whose right of residence must be recognized without the need for residence permits. Article 10 ties in with Directive 64/221 by providing that Member States shall not derogate from the provisions of this Directive, 68/360, save on grounds of public policy, public security, or public health, and Article 11 distinguishes the provisions on workers of the ECSC and Euratom Treaties.

The Court has been at pains to point out that the provisions of Directive 68/360 are not limiting measures, in the sense that they are neither conditions which, if unfulfilled, will justify deporting the non-national, nor measures which confer rather than confirm the rights of the worker. Instead they elaborate on or give substance to existing rights which are inherent or express in the EC Treaty, and provide various formal and procedural protections to ensure the full exercise and benefit of those rights.

There are many instances in the case law of Member States unsuccesssfully attempting to impose additional requirements which are not provided for in the Directive, or attempting to use the non-fulfilment of one of the formal requirements for entry against a worker, either as a means of refusing entry to or deporting that worker.

Case 48/75, Royer
[1976] ECR 497, [1976] 2 CMLR 619

Royer, who was a tradesman of French nationality residing in Belgium with his wife, was ordered by the Belgian police to leave the country on the ground that he was unlawfully resident there. On arrival in Belgium, he had not completed the administrative formalities of entry on the population register. After complying with the order to leave, Royer subsequently re-entered the country in breach of the prohibition on returning, and was convicted and sentenced for this breach. At a later Tribunal hearing concerning his continued unauthorized residence, questions were referred to the Court asking whether the right of residence was independent of the possession of a permit, and whether failure to comply with administrative requirements for a permit could constitute a ground for deportation. The Court began by setting out the various rights conferred by the Treaty, and by considering the relevant provisions of secondary legislation.

THE ECJ

28. These provisions show that the legislative authorities of the Community were aware that, while not creating new rights in favour of persons protected by Community law, the regulation and directives concerned determined the scope and detailed rules for the exercise of rights conferred directly by the Treaty.

29. It is therefore evident that the exception concerning the safeguard of public policy, security and public health contained in Articles 48(3) and 56 (1) of the Treaty must be regarded not as a condition precedent to the acquisition of the right of entry and residence but as providing the possibility, in individual cases where there is sufficient justification, of imposing restrictions on the exercise of a right derived directly from the Treaty.

. . .

33. The grant of this [residence] permit is therefore to be regarded not as a measure giving rise to rights but as a measure by a Member State serving to prove the individual position of a national of another Member State with regard to the provisions of Community law.

. . .

38. The logical consequence of the foregoing is that the mere failure by a national of a Member State to complete the legal formalities concerning access, movement and residence of aliens does not justify a decision ordering expulsion.

However, the Court in *Royer* also ruled that Community law would not prevent the states from adopting provisions to control non-nationals, backed up with appropriate sanctions other than expulsion. The principle of proportionality of sanctions for administrative breaches, which requires that sanctions should not impose excessive restrictions on freedom of movement, is central to the case law in this area.

Case 118/75, Watson and Belmann [1976] ECR 1185, [1976] 2 CMLR 552

A British national, who had stayed with an Italian family apparently as an *au pair*, was charged, along with one of the family, with failure to report the presence of a foreign national, within three days, to the police. The penalty for non-performance of this obligation was a maximum of three months' detention or a fine of up to 80,000 lire, or, in the case of a foreign national, possible deportation from the state. A reference was made to the Court from the Pretura di Milano.

The Court ruled that Member States were not prevented from adopting measures to enable the national authorities to have an exact knowledge of population movements within the territory, so that an obligation to report to the police did not infringe the rules on free movement of persons. But it went on to say that the formalities required might infringe those rules if they were unduly restrictive.

THE ECJ

19. In particular as regards the period within which the arrival of foreign nationals must be reported, the provisions of the Treaty are only infringed if the period fixed is unreasonable.

20. Among the penalties attaching to a failure to comply with the prescribed declaration and registration formalities, deportation, in relation to persons protected by Community law, is certainly incompatible with the provisions of the Treaty since, as the Court has already confirmed in other cases, such a measure negates the very right conferred and guaranteed by the Treaty.

21. As regards other penalties, such as fines and detention, whilst the national authorities are entitled to impose penalties in respect of a failure to comply with the terms of provisions requiring foreign nationals to notify their presence which are comparable to those attaching to infringement of provisions of equal importance by nationals, they are not justified in imposing a penalty so disproportinate that it becomes an obstacle to the free movement of persons.

In *Pieck*, in which a Dutch worker in Britain was prosecuted for outstaying his leave, the Court ruled that the prohibition, in Article 3(2) of Directive 68/360, on Member States demanding an entry visa or similar requirement applied to the stamp of 'leave to enter for six months' which had been placed on his passport when re-entering the United Kingdom.[65] All that the Directive permitted the states to require was the production of a valid identity card or passport. Similarly in *Sagulo*, the Court made it clear that there could be no penalty imposed for failure to have a residence permit other than the permit provided for under Directive 68/360.[66] But the Court did, perhaps surprisingly, hold that non-nationals who fail to show the documents required by that Directive need not be treated in the same way, for example, as nationals whose identity card ceased to be valid:

> There is therefore no objection to such persons being subject to different penal provisions from those applying to nationals who infringe an obligation, possibly having its origin in a law of regulation, to obtain certain identity documents . . . It is nevertheless to be observed that although Member States are entitled to impose reasonable penalties for infringement by persons subject to Community law of the obligation to obtain a valid identity card or passport, such penalties should by no means be so severe as to cause an obstacle to the freedom of entry and residence provided for in the Treaty.[67]

[65] Case 157/79, *R.* v. *Pieck* [1980] ECR 2171, [1980] 3 CMLR 220.

[66] Case 8/77, *Sagulo, Brenca and Bakhouche* [1977] ECR 1495, [1977] 2 CMLR 585. See also Case C–363/89, *Roux* [1991] ECR I–273, [1993] 1 CMLR 3, where the Court ruled that the issuing of a residence permit could not be made dependent on prior registration with a social security scheme, or on any factor other than being engaged in effective economic activity.

[67] *Ibid.*, paras. 10–11. See also Case C–265/88, *Lothar Messner* [1989] ECR 4209, [1991] 2 CMLR 545.

In a subsequent case brought by the Commission against Belgium, challenging that state's practice of sometimes asking non-Belgian EC nationals at the border to produce their residence permit in addition to their passport or identity card, the Court showed its more usual concern that any differences in treatment between nationals and non-nationals be minimized as far as possible.[68] The Commission argued that only exceptional public order or security concerns could justify such checks, which went beyond what was provided for in Directive 68/360, whereas Belgium argued that it was not frontier control but a general police check applicable to all inhabitants. The Court ruled that the only precondition a state could impose on those covered by the Directives was the possession of a valid identity card or passport, but that that did not necessarily mean the Belgian measures were impermissible:

> The controls at issue are not a condition for the exercise of the right of entry into Belgian territory and it is undisputed that Community law does not prevent Belgium from checking, within its territory, compliance with the obligation imposed on persons enjoying a right of residence under Community law to carry their residence or establishment permit at all times, where an identical obligation is imposed upon Belgian nationals as regards their entry card.[69]

Unlike in the case of *Sagulo*, the emphasis on equal treatment as between nationals and non-nationals here is clear. Interestingly, there is also a suggestion in the judgment that, even given such equal treatment, checks of this kind could fall foul of the requirement of freedom of movement if they were not simply carried out on an occasional basis, but in a 'systematic' or 'unnecessarily restrictive' manner.[70] This is also a theme which runs through the law relating to free movement of goods and services, i. e. that even non-discriminatory restrictions on freedom of movement may be in breach of the Treaty if they constitute an excessive or unnecessary hindrance to freedom of movement. But it is a theme which is not usually seen in the area of free movement of workers, in which direct or indirect discrimination on grounds of nationality has generally been a key requirement for intervention by the Community or the Court under Article 48.[71]

6. DIRECTIVE 68/360 AND THOSE WHO MOVE IN SEARCH OF WORK

It is clear that, if a Community national has a right of residence in a host Member State, either through being a worker or a family member of a worker

[68] Case 321/87, *Commission* v. *Belgium* [1989] ECR 997, [1990] 2 CMLR 492.

[69] *Ibid.*, para. 12.

[70] *Ibid.*, para. 15.

[71] For a recent example see Case C–165/91, *Van Munster* v. *Rijksdienst voor Pensionen*, 5 Oct., 1994, para. 19.

(or by falling within one of the 1990 residence Directives, or Article 8 of the Treaty, discussed below), failure to possess or produce a residence permit cannot justify expulsion by the Member State. It is less clear what is to happen to a worker who leaves a job or otherwise becomes unemployed, or to someone of limited resources who has been seeking employment for a period of time, but who has not been able to find work.

The only mention of unemployment in Directive 68/360 is in Article 7, paragraph 1 of which provides that a residence permit cannot be withdrawn solely on the ground that the worker is unemployed either involuntarily or through incapacity due to illness or accident, provided that the unemployment office confirms this. Paragraph 2 provides that, where involuntary unemployment has continued for more than twelve consecutive months, the period of residence may be restricted, if the residence permit is being renewed for the first time, to not less than twelve months. Nothing is said in the Directive about unemployment which is voluntary or which is due to something other than the stated causes of incapacity, and the inference could be drawn that Member States are permitted to refuse to renew a residence permit, or perhaps to revoke a permit, in such circumstances.[72] On the other hand, if someone voluntarily leaves employment due to dissatisfaction with that post and is actively seeking other employment, the inference above may well be unjustified. This is suggested by the judgment in *Antonissen*, which raised the question not of voluntary unemployment, but of the status of someone who is unemployed yet actively seeking work.[73] Although the Court ruled, as was seen above, that Article 48 also protects the right to enter in *search* of work, the United Kingdom argued that this right was not unlimited, and that a Member State could, compatibly with Article 48 and Directive 68/360, deport a non-national who had not yet found work after a certain period of time. It was argued that this period should be three months (although the United Kingdom legislation provided for six months), since that was the period provided for in a Council directive relating to the receipt of social security in a host Member State, and since the minutes of a Council meeting revealed that that was the period intended by the Council when it adopted Directive 68/360.

Case C–292/89, Antonissen
[1991] ECR I–745, [1991] 2 CMLR 373

The facts are set out above.

THE ECJ

16. In that regard, it must be pointed out in the first place that the effectiveness of Article 48 is secured in so far as Community legislation or, in its absence, the legislation of a Member State gives persons concerned a reasonable time in which to apprise themselves, in the territory of the Member State concerned, of offers of

[72] See D. Wyatt and A. Dashwood, *European Community Law* (3rd edn., Sweet & Maxwell, 1993), 248 and J. Steiner, *Textbook on EEC Law* (4th edn., Blackstones, 1994), 214.
[73] Case C–292/89, n. 43 above.

employment corresponding to their occupational qualifications and to take, where appropriate, the necessary steps in order to be engaged.

As regards the declaration in the minutes of the Council meeting during which Directive 68/360 was adopted, referring to a three-month period in which to seek work, the Court was dismissive, indicating clearly its preference for a broad purposive interpretation over one based even on the stated intention of the legislator which adopted the measure:[74]

18. However, such a declaration cannot be used for the purpose of interpreting a provision of secondary legislation where, as in this case, no reference is made to the content of the declaration in the wording of the provision in question. The declaration therefore has no legal significance.

The Court also dismissed the argument of the United Kingdom based on the three-month entitlement to unemployment benefit provided for in another directive, ruling that there was no necessary connection between unemployment benefit and the right to remain in a Member State. It concluded by ruling that a six-month period was probably not too short, but added a *caveat* which seemed to leave the period, during which a non-national may search for work, potentially open-ended:[75]

21. In the absence of a Community provision prescribing the period during which Community nationals seeking employment in a Member State may stay there, a period of six months, such as that laid down in the national legislation at issue in the main proceedings, does not appear in principle to be insufficient to enable the persons concerned to apprise themselves, in the host Member State, of offers of employment corresponding to their occupational qualifications and to take, where appropriate, the necessary steps in order to be engaged and, therefore, does not jeopardize the effectiveness of the principle of free movement. However, if after the expiry of that period the person concerned provides evidence that he is continuing to seek employment and that he has genuine chances of being engaged, he cannot be required to leave the territory of the host Member State.

In a comment on *Antonissen*, which recalls Judge Mancini's statement that it is thanks to the Court that the European Community is not just a Europe of commercial interests, O'Keeffe has suggested that 'when confronted with the free movement of persons, which it sees as the way to an embryonic

[74] For a similar dismissal of the relevance of a declaration which preceded the adoption of a Dir., see Case 306/89, *Commission* v. *Greece* [1991] ECR 5863, [1994] 1 CMLR 803, paras. 6 and 8. But contrast Case 136/78, *Ministère Public* v. *Auer* [1979] ECR 437, [1979] 2 CMLR 373, paras. 25–6.

[75] See, however, Case C–171/91, *Tsiotras* v. *Landeshauptstadt Stuttgart* [1993] ECR I–2925, for an example of a situation where the length of the period of unemployment would justify a decision by a Member State to deport.

Community citizenship, the Court's vision is now informed by human rights principles, rather than by the strict imperatives of socio-economic law promoted by the Treaty'.[76] However, other commentators, quoted below, have doubted whether the Member States share the same vision of the free movement of persons throughout the Community.

7. CONTROLS ON FREEDOM OF MOVEMENT IN THE FUTURE

It is evident from the case law that Directive 68/360 has been carefully interpreted by the Court to ensure that, on the one hand, its provisions are not used by the Member States as grounds for expelling non-nationals who do not fulfil its administrative or formal requirements, yet, on the other hand, to enable Member States to retain certain controls over population movements. This represents a recognition by the Court that Member States may have legitimate reasons for wishing to keep account of the flow of persons within their territories.

In 1987, however, the Single European Act introduced into the Treaty Article 8a, which was renamed Article 7a by the TEU. This Article provides that the Community shall progressively establish 'the internal market' (which was, optimistically, to be accomplished by the end of 1992 at the latest), and which 'shall comprise an area without internal frontiers in which the free movement of goods, persons, services and capital' is to be ensured.[77] It would appear that border controls within the Community would be incompatible with this provision, but unsurprisingly, given the concerns of Member States over security and their desire to control the flow of immigrants from outside the Community, there has been disagreement over the question of passport controls.[78] Matters of immigration from outside the Community are now covered,[79] and to be dealt with on an inter-governmental basis, under the provi-

[76] D. O'Keeffe 'Trends in the Free Movement of Persons' in *Human Rights and Constitutional Law*, ed. J. O'Reilly (Round Hall Press, Dublin, 1992) 262, 274.

[77] In a separate attempt, outside the Community institutional structure, to abolish checks at their shared borders and to co-operate on matters of visa policy, 9 of the Member States signed the Schengen Convention of 1985 and the Schengen Implementing Convention of 1990. The coming into force of the Convention has, however, been repeatedly delayed: see the European Parliament Res. of 10 Feb. 1994, [1994] OJ C61/185. See also D. O' Keeffe, 'The Schengen Convention: A Suitable Model for European Integration' (1991) 11 YBEL 185.

[78] See the communication of the Commission on 6 May 1992 on Art. 8a (now 7a) EC, to the effect that there were to be no more border controls: Bull. EC 5–1992 1.1.7. The European Parliament has brought proceedings under Art. 175 against the Commission for failure to present the necessary proposals for legislation under Art. 7a: Case C–445/93, [1994] OJ C1/24. See also Parliament's Res. of 28 Mar. 1994, on the incompatibility of passport checks with Art. 7a: [1994] OJ C91/316.

[79] See also the earlier 'non-Community workers' case, in which the Court ruled that the Community had the power to adopt measures in the area of social policy, even where those measures had some impact on immigration policy, which was not of itself within Community

visions on Justice and Home Affairs in the TEU (Articles K to K.9), which in principle fall outside the scope of the European Community.[80] Visa policy on non-Community nationals after the TEU, however, falls within the scope of Article 100c of the EC Treaty, and indeed matters falling under the Justice and Home Affairs title can also be brought within Article 100c by unanimous decision of the Council, in accordance with Article K.9 of the TEU.[81]

In a sceptical review of the difficulties encountered in the attempt to abolish the internal frontiers between the Member States, and to co-operate on matters relating to visa and asylum policy, one writer has commented:

> One cannot but think that the difficulties . . . show unambiguously that of the four fundamental freedoms the freedom of movement of persons is the lesser one in an organisation which does not stop telling us that this is citizens' Europe. The European Community seems to fear its citizens as much as it fears uncontrolled migration, and makes clear again that, whatever the name, it is still an overwhelmingly economic enterprise.[82]

8. WORKERS AND THEIR FAMILIES: SOCIAL ADVANTAGES AND OTHER RIGHTS

(a) Regulation 1612/68

The main focus thus far has been on the negative effects of Article 48 and the secondary legislation: the prohibition on discrimination and on barriers to freedom of movement, the prohibition on demanding entry visas or similar restrictions. The other side of this coin is that, in imposing restrictions and prohibitions on the Member States, Article 48 of the Treaty confers on workers positive, substantive rights of freedom of movement and equality of treatment. The substantive nature of these rights is, to some extent, given shape and flesh by the secondary legislation, and in particular by Regulation 1612/68.[83] It was seen in the context of Directive 68/360 that the Court wished to emphasize that the Directive did not confer rights, but gave concrete

competence: Cases 281, 283–5, 287/85, *Germany and Others* v. *Commission* [1987] ECR 3203, [1988] 1 CMLR 11.

[80] See the proposal for a dec. under Art. K3 of the TEU to establish a Convention on the crossing of external frontiers of the Member States: [1994] OJ C11/6, and Parliament's amendments: [1994] OJ C128/346, 350, 358. The Commission has also issued a communication concerning immigration and asylum policy to the Council and to Parliament: see COM(94)23.

[81] See the proposal for a Council Reg. on visa policy under Art. 100c: [1994] OJ C11/15, and a Reg. on a uniform format for visas: [1994] OJ C238. See K. Hailbronner, 'Visa Regulations and Third Country Nationals' (1994) 31 CMLRev. 969.

[82] H. D'Oliveira, 'Expanding External and Shrinking Internal Borders: Europe's Defence Mechanisms in the Areas of Free Movement, Immigration and Asylum' in O'Keeffe and Twomey (eds.), *Legal Issues of the Maastricht Treaty* (Chancery, 1994) 261, 278.

[83] [1968] OJ L257/2, [1968] OJ Spec. Ed. 475.

protection to and facilitated the exercise of the primary rights conferred by the Treaty. The same is true of the Court's approach to Regulation 1612/68, and although the principle of equal treatment forms the backbone of the legislation, its degree of detail and specificity goes beyond what is express in the Treaty, and requires the Member States to ensure that Community workers enjoy a considerable range of the substantive benefits available to nationals. In particular, the Regulation covers the families of workers, which are nowhere mentioned in the Treaty. According to the Regulation's preamble, the elimination of obstacles to the free movement of workers will require ensuring 'the worker's right to be joined by his family and the conditions for the integration of that family into the host country'.

There are three titles within Part I of the Regulation, Title I (Articles 1 to 6) on eligibility for employment, Title II (Articles 7 to 9) on equality of treatment within employment, and Title III (Articles 10 to 12) on workers' families. Part II of the Regulation contains detailed provisions which require co-operation amongst the relevant employment agencies of the Member States, and between the Member State agencies, the Commission, and the European Co-ordination Office, on applications for employment and the clearance of vacancies. Part III of the Regulation sets up an Advisory Committee and a Technical Committee made up of Member State representatives, to ensure close co-operation on matters concerning free movement of workers and employment. Parts II and III of the Regulation, which have been amended several times over the years, have attracted comparatively little legal attention. However, although they have not been the subject of litigation before the Court at the suit of individual workers, as have many of the provisions of Part I, it can be seen from examining the structures set up to facilitate the clearance of vacancies that these are of considerable significance for a worker who is seeking to move to another Member State to find employment. The Member State authorities are required to provide detailed information on vacancies, working conditions, and the state of the national labour market, and to co-operate with the Commission in conducting studies on various matters.

However, it is Part I of the Regulation which has been the subject of most comment and analysis, and its provisions have generated a large amount of litigation. Article 1 of the Regulation sets out the right of Member State nationals to take up employment in another Member State under the same conditions as its nationals and Article 2 prohibits discrimination against such workers or employees in concluding and performing contracts of employment. Articles 3 and 4 prohibit certain directly or indirectly discriminatory administrative practices, such as reserving a quota of posts for national workers, restricting advertising or applications, or setting special recruitment or registration procedures for other Member State nationals, but with an exception for genuine linguistic requirements. Article 5 guarantees the same assistance from employment offices to non-nationals as well as to nationals, and Article 6 prohibits discriminatory vocational or medical criteria for recruitment and appointment. Article 7 fleshes out Article 48(2) of the Treaty, providing in particular for the same social and tax advantages for nationals and non-nationals, equal access to vocational training, and it declares void any discriminatory provisions of collective or individual employment agreements. Article 8 provides for equality of trade-union rights with nationals,[84] and Article 9 for the same access to all rights and benefits in matters of housing. Article 10 sets out the family members who have the right to install themselves with a worker who is employed in another Member State, so long as the worker has adequate housing available: these are the spouse and their descendants who are either under 21 or dependent, and dependent relatives in the ascending line of the worker and spouse. Member States are also required to 'facilitate the admission' of other family members who are either dependent on the worker or living under the worker's roof in the Member State of origin. Article 11 gives the spouse and children mentioned in Article 10 the right to take up activity as employed persons in the host Member State, and Article 12 provides for equal access for the children of a resident worker to the state's educational courses.

There has, predictably, been a considerable amount of litigation over the provisions of the Regulation. It will be seen that many of the cases, in particular those concerning the meaning of 'social advantages' in Article 7(2), are concerned also with distinguishing a social advantage under this Regulation from a social security benefit under Regulation 1408/71, since the latter is more restrictive than the concept of a social advantage in Article 7(2). Indeed, Article 7 has probably been the most fruitful provision for workers and their families, and it raises interesting questions about when, if at all, Member States are entitled to treat their own nationals more favourably than other EC nationals. Clearly, there are some advantages enjoyed by citizens of a state which are not available to others, such as the right to vote in national elections, and Article 7 of Regulation 1612/68 focuses attention on the permissible limits of these advantages. The evolving interpretation by the Court of this Article and its related provisions illustrates very well the inevitable social and political consequences of economic integration, and shows how the initial conferral of limited rights on economic actors has developed—even before the 'citizenship' amendments made by the TEU—into something more substantial.

(b) Article 7(2) of Regulation 1612/68

Initially, in *Michel S*, the Court read Article 7(2) in a more limited way, ruling that it concerned only benefits connected with employment.[85] Thus the disabled son of an Italian employee who had worked in Belgium until he died could not invoke Article 7(2) to obtain specific benefits which were available

[84] See Cases C–213/90, n. 59 above, and C–118/92, *Commission* v. *Luxembourg* I–1891, on the right to vote and stand in elections in national occupational guilds.

[85] Case 76/72, *Michel S.* v. *Fonds National de Reclassement Handicapés* [1973] ECR 457.

under Belgian legislation, to enable disabled Belgian nationals recover their ability to work. The applicant, however, succeeded on other grounds. The Court, drawing on the references in the Regulation's preamble to freedom and dignity, ruled that the list of educational arrangements (general educational, apprenticeship, and vocational training courses) for workers' children in Article 12 was not exhaustive, so that it could also cover the Belgian disability benefit. Subsequently in *Casagrande*, the Court continued its expansive reading of Article 12 by ruling that, although it specified only that the children of non-national workers should be 'admitted to courses', the fact that Member States are exhorted to encourage them to attend 'under the best possible conditions' meant that that provision would also cover any 'general measures intended to facilitate educational attendance', including an educational grant for secondary school in Germany.[86] This was clearly a controversial interpretation, since strong submissions were made to the Court that the areas of educational and cultural policy in Germany were specifically reserved to the Länder, and that this would be viewed as an encroachment on those powers by Community law.[87] The increasingly blurred boundary between state and Community competence in the field of education will be discussed further below.

In keeping with its expansive interpretation of Article 12, the Court soon departed silently from its more restrictive interpretation of Article 7(2) in *Michel S.* In *Cristini* v. *SNCF*, the Italian widow of an Italian worker in France was refused a reduction card for rail fares for large families on the ground of her nationality.[88] It was argued that the benefits in Article 7 were restricted to those connected with the contract of employment itself, but the Court ruled that in the light of other provisions of the measure, the term 'social advantages' in Article 7(2) could not be interpreted restrictively:

> It therefore follows that, in view of the equality of treatment which the provision seeks to achieve, the substantive area of application must be delineated so as to include all social and tax advantages, whether or not attached to the contract of employment, such as reductions in fares for large families.[89]

The Court held that this right to equality of treatment was applicable not just to workers, but also, by virtue of Regulation 1251/71, which governs the right of workers and their families to remain in a Member State after having been employed there, to those surviving family members who had been residing with the deceased worker.

In *Inzirillo*, where an Italian worker in France was refused a disability allowance for his adult son, it was argued to the Court that Article 7 of the

[86] Case 9/74, *Casagrande* v. *Landeshauptstadt München* [1974] ECR 773, [1974] 2 CMLR 423.
[87] Warner A.G., *ibid.* 783–4 (ECR).
[88] Case 32/75, *Fiorini (neé Cristini)* v. *Société Nationale des Chemins de Fer Français* [1975] ECR 1085, [1976] 1 CMLR 573.
[89] *Ibid.*, para. 13.

Regulation was not applicable, since the allowance would not be a social advantage to the worker, as provided in the Article, but rather to his son.[90] The Court, however, ruled that adult dependant offspring were covered by Article 10(1) of the Regulation, and that an allowance for handicapped adults which a Member State awarded to its own nationals would indeed constitute a social advantage to a non-national worker in a case like this. The Court made clear in a subsequent case that the notion of dependency in Article 10 was a matter of fact, i. e. that a 'dependant' would be a member of the family who is in fact supported by the worker, whatever the reason for the support.[91]

Thus Article 7(2) has been held to cover all social and tax advantages, not just those which are linked to employment, and even when they are of indirect rather than of direct benefit to the worker herself or himself.[92] On the other hand, the Court has set limits to this wider reading of Article 7(2) by ruling, in the case of *Lebon*, that it can only be invoked where the advantage claimed is actually of some direct or indirect benefit to the worker, and not just to a family member.

> However, the members of a worker's family, within the meaning of Article 10 of Regulation No 1612/68 qualify only indirectly for the equal treatment accorded to the worker himself by Article 7 of Regulation No 1612/68. Social benefits such as the income guaranteed to old people by the legislation of a Member State (see the judgment of 12 July 1984 in case 261/83 *Castelli* v. *ONPTS* [1984] ECR 3199) or guaranteeing in general terms the minimum means of subsistence operate in favour of members of the worker's family only if such benefits may be regarded as a social advantage, within the meaning of Article 7(2) of Regulation No 1612/68, for the worker himself.[93]

Are there limits to the rights which may be claimed by a worker under Article 7(2)? The right to vote in national elections, which is central to the concept of nationality, was mentioned above, but is there anything short of this which may be enjoyed by nationals and denied to non-national EC workers?

Case 207/78, Ministère Public v. Even and ONPTS
[1979] ECR 2019, [1980] 2 CMLR 71

Even was a French worker in Belgium, who received an early retirement pension from the Belgian national pension office. A percentage reduction in the size of the pension per year of early payment was made for all workers except Belgian nationals who were in receipt of a Second World War service invalidity pension granted by an Allied nation. Even was in receipt of a war service pension under French

[90] Case 63/76, *Inzirillo* v. *Caisse d'Allocations Familiales de l'Arondissement de Lyon* [1976] ECR 2057, [1978] 3 CMLR 596.
[91] Case 316/85, n. 43 above.
[92] See also Case 94/84, *Office National de l'Emploi* v. *Joszef Deak* [1985] ECR 1873.
[93] Case 316/85, n. 43 above, para. 12.

legislation, and he pleaded the principle of equality of treatment between nationals and non-nationals to claim the benefit of an early retirement pension without any deduction. On a reference to the Court, Regulation 1612/68 was considered.

THE ECJ

22. It follows from all its provisions and from the objective pursued that the advantages which this regulation extends to workers who are nationals of other Member States are all those which, whether or not linked to a contract of employment, are generally granted to national workers primarily because of their objective status as workers or by virtue of the mere fact of their residence on the national territory and the extension of which to workers who are nationals of other Member States therefore seems suitable to facilitate their mobility within the Community.

23. . . . The main reason for a benefit such as that granted by the Belgian national legislation in question to certain categories of national workers is the services which those in receipt of the benefit have rendered in wartime to their own country and its essential objective is to give those nationals an advantage by reason of the hardships suffered for that country.

24. Such a benefit, which is based on a scheme of national recognition, cannot therefore be considered as an advantage granted to a national worker by reason primarily of his status of worker or resident on the national territory and for that reason does not fulfil the essential characteristics of the 'social advantages' referred to in Article 7(2) of Regulation No 1612/68.

Three factors are mentioned by the Court in determining whether workers are entitled, under Article 7(2), to a particular benefit in a host Member State: their status as workers, their residence on the national territory, and the suitability of the benefit in facilitating their mobility within the Community. Of course this is an inconclusive test, since arguably any kind of benefit available in a Member State, including indeed the right to vote, could be said to encourage workers from other Member States to move to the former state to reside and work there with their families.

The *Even* case is not very different on its facts from that of *Ugliola*,[94] yet the Court found that there was impermissible discrimination in *Ugliola* but not in *Even*. *Ugliola* concerned the taking into account of military service in calculating seniority at work, and it may be that carrying out military service during peacetime is not as closely linked to notions of patriotism and nationalism as are services performed for a country during wartime, but this is not a very convincing distinction.

The decision in *Even* also contrasts in an interesting way with the subsequent ruling in *Reina*, on the issue of what benefits could be said to flow from citizenship, so that they are excluded from the scope of Article 7(2) of Regulation 1612/68. In *Reina*, an interest-free 'childbirth loan' granted under German law to German nationals in order to stimulate the birth-rate of the population was held to be a social advantage within Article 7(2), so that an

[94] See n. 10 above.

Italian couple in Germany, one of whom was a worker, was also entitled to eligibility for the loan.[95] The Court reached this conclusion despite the defendant bank's arguments that the refusal to grant a loan in no way hindered the mobility of workers within the Community and, that being principally a matter of demographic policy, such a discretionary loan fell within the area of political rights linked to nationality. The Court's response to this was to hold that the loan was a social advantage since its main aim was to alleviate the financial burden on low-income families, and the fact that it touched on the Member State's pursuance of demographic policy did not rule out the application of Community law. The Court chose not to address the fact that the demographic policy being pursued by the state was to boost the birth-rate of German nationals.

(c) Rights of Families as Parasitic on the Workers' Rights

Generous though the interpretation of 'social advantages' may be, however, it is only workers and those family members specifically listed in the Regulation who may avail themselves of them. This was made clear by the Court in *Lebon*, where it ruled that, once the child of a worker reached the age of 21 and was no longer dependent on the worker, benefits to that child could not be construed as an advantage to the worker.[96] The Court went on to consider the position of such an adult child—or indeed of any EC national—who was seeking work but not yet employed:

> It must be pointed out that the right to equal treatment with regard to social and tax advantages applies only to workers. Those who move in search of employment qualify for equal treatment only as regards access to employment in accordance with Article 48 of the EEC Treaty and Articles 2 and 5 of Regulation No 1612/68.[97]

The *Lebon* judgment makes clear the importance of being a full worker, or a specifically included family member of such a worker, in order to benefit from the substantive rights described in the secondary legislation. And if the rights of someone who is unemployed but searching for work are limited as indicated in *Lebon*, so too, presumably, are the rights of the family members of such a person.[98] The Court has not had occasion to rule on what difference, if any, there might be between Article 10(1) and Article 10(2) of

[95] Case 65/81, *Reina* v. *Landeskredit Bank Baden-Württemberg* [1982] ECR 33, [1982] 1 CMLR 744. See also Case C–111/91, *Commission* v *Luxembourg* [1993] ECR I–817, [1994] 2 CMLR 781.

[96] Case 316/85, n. 43 above. For a restrictive reading of Art. 7(2) in relation to a spouse who was not an EC national, see Case C–243/91, *Belgium* v. *Taghavi* [1992] ECR I–4401.

[97] *Ibid.*, para. 26.

[98] See, however, Cases C–3/90, n. 37 above and C–357/89, n. 36 above, which suggest that a worker who becomes involuntarily unemployed and takes up a course of study retains the right to educational benefits under Art. 7 of Reg. 1612/68.

Regulation 1612/68. Article 10(2) provides that Member States shall 'facilitate the entry' of dependent relatives and those who were living under the same roof as the worker in the Member State of origin. This is more restrictively worded than Article 10(1), which guarantees to the worker the right to have specified family members installed with him or her, subject to the availability of suitable housing.[99] However, the difference may not be significant in the light of the broad reading the Court has given to Article 7(2), by virtue of which a benefit to a dependent or co-resident relative of the worker may well be considered an advantage to the worker.

An inventive use of Article 7(2) can be seen in the case of *Reed*, in which the interpretation of the term 'spouse' arose.[100] The case concerned the denial of a right of residence to an unemployed British national who had come to The Netherlands to live with her long-term partner, who was a British national employed there. In contrast to its approach in giving a clear Community meaning to terms such as 'worker' and 'public service' in Article 48 of the Treaty, the Court ruled that the term 'spouse' referred only to a marital relationship. A wider reading would be unjustifiable, in the Court's view, given the absence of consensus and the lack of a 'general social development' amongst all Member States towards treating unmarried companions as spouses. However, although the effect of this reasoning was to deny Reed an independent right of residence under Article 10(1), the Court followed the suggestion of the Commission and ruled that Article 7(2) could nevertheless be of assistance in the case. The Netherlands, as part of its policy on aliens, treated a person who had a stable relationship with a worker of Dutch nationality as that worker's spouse. Accordingly:

> it must be recognised that the possibiltiy for a migrant worker of obtaining permission for his unmarried companion to reside with him, where that companion is not a national of the host Member State, can assist his integration in the host State and thus contribute to the achievement of freedom of movement for workers. Consequently, that possibility must also be regarded as falling within the concept of a social advantage for the purposes of Article 7(2) of Regulation 1612/68.[101]

Cases such as *Lebon* and *Reed* highlight the derivative nature of families' rights, and make clear the importance of the requisite—traditionally defined—family link, whether it be that of a dependent child, a spouse, or as otherwise provided for in Regulation 1612/68. The significance of a specific and continuing family link can be seen in the case of *Diatta*, where a non-EC national had married an EC national, but divorce proceedings had been initiated:

[99] The Court has ruled that the housing requirement could only apply at the initial stage of entry of the family, and could not constitute a ground for refusing to renew residence permits if housing conditions subsequently deteriorated: Case 249/86, *Commission* v. *Germany* [1989] ECR 1263, [1990] 3 CMLR 540. For further discussion see Ch. 7, 313.

[100] Case 59/85, *Netherlands* v. *Reed* [1986] ECR 1283, [1987] 2 CMLR 448.

[101] *Ibid.*, para. 28.

Case 267/83, Diatta v. Land Berlin
[1985] ECR 567, [1986] 2 CMLR 164

The applicant was a Senegalese national who had married a French national, and both were resident and working in Berlin. After some time together, she separated from her husband with the intention of divorcing him, and moved into separate accommodation. She was then refused an extension of her residence permit on the ground that she was no longer a family member of an EC national. The Court was asked whether a migrant worker's family must live permanently with that worker in order to qualify for a right of residence, or whether Article 11 gave it an independent right of residence.

THE ECJ

18. In providing that a member of a migrant worker's family has the right to install himself with the worker, Article 10 of the Regulation does not require that the member of the family in question must live permanently with the worker, but, as is clear from Article 10(3), only that the accomodation which the worker has available must be such as may be considered normal for the purpose of accommodating his family. A requirement that the family must live under the same roof permanently cannot be implied.

19. In addition, such an interpretation corresponds to the spirit of Article 11 of the Regulation, which gives the member of the family the right to take up any activity as an employed person throughout the territory of the Member State concerned, even though that activity is exercised at a place some distance from the place where the migrant worker resides.

20. It must be added that the marital relationship cannot be regarded as dissolved so long as it has not been terminated by the competent authority. It is not dissolved merely because the spouses live separately, even where they intend to divorce at a later date.

However, the Court made it clear that the worker's family did not have any independent right of residence, either under Article 11 of the Regulation or under any provision of the Treaty or otherwise.[102] Rather, the spouse's right of residence is conditional on the right of residence of the worker and on the satisfaction of the housing requirement in Article 10, although there is no obligation to live together.[103] The Court was probably influenced by the argument made on behalf of Mrs Diatta that, if cohabitation was mandatory, a worker could at any moment cause the expulsion of a spouse by depriving that spouse of a roof. However, although the ruling makes clear that neither living apart nor the likelihood of divorce affects the rights of a spouse under Community law, the Court did not state what the position would be after divorce. The same question arose again in the case of *Singh*, where, despite the existence of a decree *nisi* of divorce, the Court ruled that the right of

[102] For criticism of the case, see J. Weiler, 'Thou Shalt not Oppress a Stranger: On the Judicial Protection of the Human Rights of Non-Community Nationals—a Critique' [1992] EJIL 65, 85.

[103] On the right of the spouse of a worker under Art. 11 of Reg. 1612/68 to access to employment see Case 131/85, *Gül* v. *Regierungs-präsident Düsseldorf* [1986] ECR 1573, [1987] 1 CMLR 501.

residence of a spouse who is a non-Community national was not affected.[104] The judgment suggests that the marriage must be *bona fide*, since the Court specifically commented that there was no suggestion of a sham.

(d) Family Members in an 'Internal Situation'

Like *Diatta*, the *Singh* case provides a good illustration of the importance of the requisite family link to a non-Community national or to a non-working Community national. However, it is also important in that it highlights some of the invidious results and curious distinctions which arise as a result of the Court's approach to the so-called 'wholly internal situation'. It was seen that in *Saunders*,[105] the Court ruled that a national could not rely on Article 48 in his or her own Member State to challenge a restriction on freedom of movement, since there was no factor connecting the situation with Community law. This was rather more harshly illustrated in the cases of *Morson and Jhanjan*, where it was held that two Dutch nationals working in The Netherlands had no right under Community law to bring their parents, of Surinamese nationality, into the country to reside with them.[106] Had they been nationals of any other Member State working in The Netherlands, they would have been covered by Article 10 of Regulation 1612/68, but because they were nationals working in their own Member State 'who had never exercised the right to freedom of movement within the Community', they had no rights under Community law.[107] In *Singh* the situation was slightly different. An Indian national had married a British national, and had travelled with her to Germany where they had both worked for some years before returning to the United Kingdom. Despite the United Kingdom's argument that the British spouse's right to re-enter the United Kingdom derived from national law and not from Community law, the Court clearly considered that the period of working activity in another Member State made all the difference, and enabled Singh now to claim rights as the spouse of a Community worker.

Case4 C–370/90, R v. Immigration Appeal Tribunal and Surinder Singh, ex parte Secretary of State for the Home Department [1992] ECR I–4265, [1992] 3 CMLR 358

THE ECJ

119. A national of a Member State might be deterred from leaving his country of origin in order to pursue an activity as an employed or self-employed person as envisaged by the Treaty in the territory of another Member State if, on returning to the Member State of which he is a national in order to pursue an activity there as an employed or self-employed person, the conditions of his entry and residence were not at least equivalent to those which he would enjoy under the Treaty or secondary law in the territory of another Member State.

[104] C–370/90, *R.* v. *Immigration Appeal Tribunal, ex p. Secretary of State for the Home Department* [1992] ECR I–4265, [1992] 3 CMLR 358.

[105] N. 17 above.

[106] Cases 35 and 36/82, n. 18 above.

[107] *Ibid.*, para. 17.

20. He would in particular be deterred from so doing if his spouse and children were not also permitted to enter and reside in the territory of his Member State of origin under conditions at least equivalent to those granted them by Community law in the territory of another Member State.

Quite apart from the slim and rather arbitrary distinction between *Morson and Jhanjan* and *Singh*, the latter ruling has also attracted criticism on account of its ambiguity over whether the rights of nationals returning with their spouses to their own Member State are dependent on the spouses' continued economic activity. It has been suggested that, on one reading of the judgment, Singh's right of residence in the United Kingdom as the spouse of a Community national would terminate if his wife ceased to work, and that, if her entry was to be governed by Community rather than national law, her status in her own country could be reduced to that of an 'alien'.[108]

9. EDUCATION

Until the amendments made by the TEU, there was no reference in the EEC Treaty to education, but only to 'vocational training' in what was formerly Article 128. As a result of the amendments, Articles 3(p) and Article 126 of the EC Treaty now specifically refer to the development of education, thus bringing it expressly within the competence of the Community.

However, even before the new Treaty provisions on education were adopted, the competence of the Community already extended in various circumstances to cover aspects of education. Legislation was adopted—with the approval of the Court[109]—to establish Community schemes in areas such as vocational training, foreign languages, educational exchange, and educational mobility, such as Erasmus,[110] Commett,[111] and Lingua,[112] and to set up a European Training Foundation.[113]

Further, there are three principal ways in which 'educational rights', as such, were previously guaranteed as part of Community law.[114] Two of these are specifically set out in the secondary legislation relating to workers, and the third has largely been developed by the Court in the context of persons who did not satisfy the criteria for workers, but who had moved throughout the

[108] P. Watson, 'Free Movement of Workers: A one-way ticket?' (1993) 22 ILJ 68.

[109] See e.g. Cases C–51/89, 90/89, 94/89, *UK* v. *Council* [1991] ECR I–2757, [1992] 1 CMLR 40.

[110] Dec. 87/327: [1987] OJ L166/20.

[111] Decs. 86/365: [1986] OJ L22/17 and 89/27, [1989] OJ L13/28.

[112] Dec. 89/489: [1989] OJ L239. See also the Tempus Programme, Dec. 90/233, and the recent proposal on Socrates, [1994] OJ C244, and Leonardo da Vinci, [1994] OJ C244.

[113] Reg. 90/233, [1990]OJ L131.

[114] Note also the Community has always had competence under Art. 57 EEC in relation to the mutual recognition of qualifications. This is discussed further in Ch. 16.

Community in order to study, rather than simply in order to work. Each of these three categories guarantees a slightly different range of educational rights, although the third has probably now been transformed by the amended Article 126.

(a) Children (and Family Members) of Workers

The first and the most generous of the categories within which educational rights can be claimed under Community law is that of the children of a worker. Although they are not mentioned in the Treaty, Article 12 of Regulation 1612/68 provides that 'the children of a national of a Member State, who is or has been employed in the territory of another Member State, shall be admitted to courses of general education, apprenticeship and vocational training under the same conditions as the nationals of that State, if those children reside in its territory' and that Member States are to encourage 'steps allowing such children to follow the above mentioned courses under the best conditions'.[115] It has been seen from the discussion above that Article 12 has been generously interpreted by the Court, both in the kinds of educational courses and arrangements it covers,[116] and in terms of the broad meaning given to the phrase 'admitted to courses' so that grants and other such facilitative measures are included.[117] Essentially, Article 12 places the children of EC workers residing in a Member State in the same position as the children of nationals of that Member State in so far as education of any kind is concerned. It has been held to protect the right to educational assistance even where the working parent has returned to his or her state of nationality, if the child is obliged by reason of the non-compatiblity of educational systems to remain and to complete his or her education in the host state.[118] Article 12 has also been held to require that, where grants are available to the children of nationals to study abroad, these must also be made available to the children of migrant EC workers, even if the studies abroad are to be in the Member State of the child's nationality.[119]

Further, although Regulation 1612/68 does not make specific provision for the education of other family members of the worker, it is likely that the Court's interpretation of 'social advantages' to the worker in Article 7(2) includes at least some educational benefits for the protected family members of that worker, even if not the full range of benefits which are available to children who are dependent or under 21.

[115] See also the provisions of Dir. 77/486 on language teaching for the children of migrant workers: see [1977] OJ L199/32.

[116] Case 76/72, n. 85 above.

[117] Case 9/74, n. 86 above.

[118] Cases 389 and 390/87, *Echternach and Moritz* [1989] ECR 723, [1990] 2 CMLR 305.

[119] Case C–308/89, *Di Leo* v. *Land Berlin* [1990] ECR I–4185.

(b) Workers

The second category of persons who have been able to claim educational rights under Community law is that of workers themselves. As in the case of the children of workers, these rights are not mentioned in the Treaty but are set out in Article 7(3) of Regulation 1612/68 as part of the substantive equality of treatment with nationals to which EC workers are entitled. Article 7(3) provides that the worker shall 'by virtue of the same right and under the same conditions as national workers, have access to training in vocational schools and retraining centres'.

This provision has, however, been quite restrictively interpreted by the Court. Thus, although it is has indicated that training must be available to non-national workers on exactly the same conditions as nationals, including tuition fees, maintenance grants, and any other such facilities as are available, a narrow reading was given to the institutions and courses covered by Article 7(3) in the case of *Lair*:

> In that regard, it should be noted that in order for an educational institution to be regarded as a vocational school for the purposes of that provision, the fact that some vocational training is provided is not sufficient. The concept of a vocational school is a more limited one and refers exclusively to institutions which provide only instruction either alternating with or closely linked to an occupational activity, particularly during apprenticeship. That is not true of universities.[120]

However, as though to compensate to some extent for the narrowness of Article 7(3), the Court went on to hold that workers could also invoke the 'social advantages' provision of Article 7(2) to claim entitlement to any advantage available to improve their professional qualifications and social advancement, such as a maintenance grant in an educational institution not covered by Article 7(3).[121] On the other hand, the Court imposed other limits on the ability of workers to invoke Article 7(2) in this way, by requiring that although they did not have to be in the employment relationship just before the course of study nor to remain in employment during the course of study, there must be some continuity or link between the previous work and the purpose of the studies in question.[122] The one exception allowed by the Court was where a worker involuntarily became unemployed and was 'obliged by conditions on the job market to undertake occupational retraining in another field of activity'.[123]

The reason for the limitations imposed by the Court on Article 7(2) and (3) is probably that the status of worker entitles EC nationals and their families

[120] Case 39/86, *Lair* [1988] ECR 3161, [1989] 3 CMLR 545.

[121] See Case 235/87, *Matteucci* v. *Communauté Français de Belgique* [1988] ECR 5589, [1989] 1 CMLR 357 in which the Court held that Art. 7(2) extended to cover grants which would enable an EC worker to pursue studies abroad, if such grants were made available to nationals.

[122] [1988] ECR 3161, para. 37.

[123] *Ibid.*

to a very substantial range of social and other benefits, so that it is important to the Member States that the people claiming such benefits are genuine workers. If they give up work to pursue education or training, they will no longer be economically active, and the states evidently fear that this could become a way for people to gain generous educational benefits after a short and purely instrumental period of employment. For that reason, although it has ruled that a fixed mimimum period of employment cannot be required by the Member States,[124] the Court read the term 'vocational schools' in Article 7(3) very narrowly, and has required that any educational course pursued by virtue of Article 7(2) must be specifically related to the worker's previous employment.

It is also clear from the ruling in *Brown*, discussed earlier, that not only must there be a link between the previous employment and the subsequent studies, but the employment must not be 'ancillary' to the main purpose of pursuing a course of study.[125]

(c) Students

The third category of persons who could claim educational rights under Community law was developed by the Court, not in the context of workers and Regulation 1612/68, but by virtue of what were formerly Article 7 and Article 128 of the EEC Treaty (now, confusingly, Article 6 and Article 127 of the EC Treaty). Article 7 contained the general prohibition on discrimination on grounds of nationality 'within the scope of application' of the Treaty. Article 128 provided that the Council should 'lay down general principles for implementing a common vocational training policy'.

In the case of *Forcheri*, the Court held that the Italian spouse of an Italian worker who was employed in Belgium was entitled, by virtue of these two provisions, to be admitted to the host state's educational courses related to vocational training, without having to pay an enrolment fee which was not charged to nationals.[126]

This ruling was developed subsequently in the case of *Gravier*, in which a French student wishing to study strip-cartoon art in Belgium challenged the imposition on her of an enrolment fee which Belgian nationals did not have to pay. Unlike the applicant in *Forcheri*, Gravier had no family members in Belgium and so had no right of residence there, apart from her claim as a student to such a right:

[124] See also Case 157/84, *Frascogna* v. *Caisse des Dépôts et Consignations* [1985] ECR 1739 on the requirement of a fixed period of residence, and Cases C–3/90, n. 37 above, and C–357/89, n. 36 above.

[125] Case 197/86, n. 42 above.

[126] Case 152/82, *Forcheri* v. *Belgium* [1983] ECR 2323, [1984] 1 CMLR 334.

Case 293/83, Gravier v. City of Liège [1985] ECR 593, [1985] 3 CMLR 1

Françoise Gravier was an art student of French nationality who was charged an enrolment fee (*minerval*) for a course in strip-cartoon art in Liège in Belgium, which Belgian nationals were not required to pay. She brought judicial proceedings claiming exemption from the *minerval*, and the question whether Article 7 of the Treaty prohibited Member States from treating their own nationals more favourably in the area of education was raised before the Court.

THE ECJ

15. Such unequal treatment based on nationality must be regarded as discrimination prohibited by Article 7 of the Treaty if it falls within the scope of the Treaty.

. . .

19. The first remark which must be made in that regard is that although educational organization and policy are not as such included in the spheres which the Treaty has entrusted to the Community institutions, access to and participation in courses of instruction and apprenticeship, in particular vocational training, are not unconnected with Community law.

. . .

21. With regard more particularly to vocational training, Article 128 of the Treaty provides that the Council is to lay down general principles for implementing a common vocational training policy capable of contributing to the harmonious development both of the national economies and of the common market. The first principle established in Council Decision 63/266 of 2 April 1963 laying down those general principles states that 'the general principles must enable every person to receive adequate training, with due regard for freedom of choice of occupation, place of training and place of work.'

. . .

23. The common vocational training policy referred to in Article 128 of the Treaty is thus gradually being established. It constitutes, moreover, an indispensable element of the activities of the Community, whose objectives include *inter alia* the free movement of persons, the mobility of labour, and the improvement of the living standards of workers.

24. Access to vocational training is in particular likely to promote free movement of persons throughout the Community, by enabling them to obtain a qualification in the Member State where they intend to work and by enabling them to complete their training and develop their particular talents in the Member State whose vocational training programmes include the special subject desired.

25. It follows from all the foregoing that the conditions of access to vocational training fall within the scope of the Treaty.

Accordingly, the Court, confirming that vocational training fell within the scope of the Treaty,[127] held that the imposition of a *minerval* only on students

[127] See also para. 10 of the ruling in the *Erasmus* case: Case 242/87, *Commission* v. *Council* [1989] ECR 1425, [1991] 1 CMLR 478 where the Court held that the task of implementing the principles of the common vocational training policy was for the Member States and the Community working in co-operation.

who were nationals of other Member States, as a condition of access to such training, was contrary to Article 7 of the Treaty.[128] Given the financial burden which could be imposed on the Member States if they were required to treat all students of EC nationality on an equal footing with national students in conditions of access to vocational training, the *Gravier* ruling clearly had far-reaching potential. There were, however, two limits which the Court could place upon it: first, on what could constitute a course of 'vocational training' and secondly on what the 'conditions of access' were.

As regards the first, the Court placed very few limits on the concept of vocational training, and interpreted it in a far more expansive way than it had the 'vocational schools' for workers in Article 7(3) of Regulation 1612/68.[129] In *Gravier*, the Court ruled that any form of education which prepared for or provided skills for a profession, trade or employment would consitute vocational training, even if the programme included 'an element of general education'.[130] Subsequently, in *Blaizot*, the Court held that university education could constitute vocational training, unless the course was one intended for people to improve their general knowledge rather than to prepare themselves for an occupation:[131]

> With regard to the issue whether university studies prepare for a qualification for a particular profession, trade or employment, it must be emphasized that that is the case not only where the final academic examination directly provides the required qualification for a particular profession, trade or employment but also in so far as the studies in question provide specific training and skills, that is to say where a student needs the knowledge so acquired for the pursuit of a profession, trade or employment, even if no legislative or administrative provisions make the acquisition of that knowledge a prerequisite for that purpose.[132]

The Court decided to limit the retroactivity of its ruling in *Blaizot*, taking account of Belgium's fear that it would 'throw the financing of university education into chaos'. The Court agreed to do so because the Community's vocational policy had been developing, and it had been reasonable for the Belgian Government, on the basis of earlier communications with the Commission, to

[128] For subsequent litigation over continuing forms of discrimination in the Belgian higher education system, see Case 42/87, *Commission* v. *Belgium* [1988] ECR 5445, [1989] 1 CMLR 457 and Case C–47/93 *Commission* v. *Belgium* [1994] ECR I–1593.

[129] See Case 39/86, *Lair* n. 120 above.

[130] Case 293/83, *Gravier* v. *City of Liège* [1985] ECR 593, [1985] 3 CMLR 1, para. 30. On this point, see Case 263/86, *Belgium* v. *Humbel* [1988] ECR 5365, [1989] 1 CMLR 393. See also Case 242/87, *Commission* v. *Council* [1989] ECR 1425, [1991] 1 CMLR 478 in which the Court found that the Council had not exceeded its competence in enacting Dec. 87/327 adopting the EC action scheme for the mobility of university students (Erasmus).

[131] Case 24/86, *Blaizot* v. *University of Liège* [1988] ECR 379, [1989] 1 CMLR 57, para. 20. The ECJ drew for support on Art. 10 of the Council of Europe's European Social Charter, which treats university education as a form of vocational training.

[132] *Ibid.*, para. 19.

assume that the *minerval* in respect of university education was not contrary to Community law.[133]

The Court's concern about the effect of its development of the scope of vocational education under Article 128 on the financing of the Member States' educational systems seems to have led it to take a more cautious stance with regard to the second criterion mentioned above, the 'conditions of access' to vocational training.[134] In *Lair*, the Court was asked whether a maintenance and training grant provided by the state to pursue university study fell within the scope of the Treaty.[135] The Court ruled that only grants which were intended to cover charges relating specifically to access to vocational training, such as registration and tuition fees, were covered by the prohibition on discrimination:

> Subject to that reservation, it must be stated that at the present stage of development of Community law assistance given to students for maintenance and for training falls in principle outside the scope of the EEC Treaty for the purposes of Article 7. It is, on the one hand, a matter of educational policy, which is not as such included in the spheres entrusted to the Community institutions (see *Gravier*) and, on the other, a matter of social policy, which falls within the competence of the Member States in so far as it is not covered by specific provisions of the EEC Treaty.[136]

In *Raulin*, the Court held that the principle of non-discrimination deriving from Articles 7 and 128, meant that an EC national who had been admitted to a vocational training course in another Member State must have a right of residence in that state for the duration of the course.[137] Since it derived from the Treaty, that right was independent of the possession of a residence permit, but the Court held that the Member State could legitimately impose conditions on it 'such as the covering of maintenance costs and health insurance'.[138] There is a form of co-operative dialogue taking place between the legislative and judicial organs of the Community which is interesting to observe in this context. It is significant that the right of residence recognized by the Court corresponds exactly with the right of residence for students to be found in Directive 90/366, which was adopted by the Council in 1990, but which had not come into effect when the facts giving rise to the Raulin case first arose.[139]

[133] Contrast the refusal to limit the retroactivity of its ruling in Case 309/85, *Barra* [1988] ECR 355, [1988] 2 CMLR 409.

[134] Note that in Case C–109/92, *Wirth* v. *Landeshauptstadt Hannover* [1993] ECR I–6447, the ECJ ruled that private educational institutes, which operated to make a profit, would fall within Art. 59 EC on the freedom to provide commercial services.

[135] Case 39/86, n. 120 above.

[136] *Ibid.*, para. 15. See also Case 197/86, n. 42 above.

[137] Case C–357/89, n. 36 above.

[138] *Ibid.*, para. 39.

[139] Dir. 90/366 was annulled by the ECJ on procedural grounds in Case C–295/90, *European Parliament* v. *Council* [1992] ECR I–4193, [1992] 3 CMLR 281, but replaced in 1993 by a virtually identical measure, Dir. 93/96, [1993] OJ L317/59. For another example of this 'dialogue' between the ECJ, the legislative powers, and the Member States, see the so-called Barber Protocol and Case C–109/91, *Ten Oever* v. *Stichting Bedrijfspensioenfonds voor het Glazenwassers- en Schoonmaakbedrijf* [1993] ECR I–4879 below at 825–7.

In defining the scope of the Treaty right of residence, the Court was clearly taking account of the conditions which had been agreed by the Member States in the Directive, which in turn reflect the content of the Court's earlier rulings in cases such as *Lair*.

How, then, has the addition by the TEU of Article 126 of the EC Treaty, and its amendment of Article 128 (now appearing as Article 127), affected this area of education within Community law? It has been pointed out in the context of education that Article C of the TEU makes it clear that the *acquis communautaire* is to be respected.[140] To a large extent this means that the existing law on vocational education is to be built on, and added to, rather than replaced. One result which would seem to flow from the combination of Article 6 and Article 126 is that a claim for equal conditions of access to a host Member State's general educational courses could now be made by an EC national, without needing to show any vocational element in the course. In other words, the exclusion in *Blaizot* of courses which are to improve 'general knowledge' only will no longer exist. It has also been suggested that the Community now has the power under Article 6 to pass legislation governing the wider conditions under which education for Community nationals is to be provided, included formerly excluded areas such as maintenance grants and financing.[141]

The new provisions are also carefully worded in such a way as to recognize the primary responsibility of the Member States for their own educational systems, and to indicate that the Community's role is to be supplementary and co-operative. Furthermore, Article 126, in similar terms to the provisions of the revised Article 127 on vocational training and the new Article 128 on culture, expressly provides that no attempt is to be made to harmonize or to jeopardize the diversity of the Member States in these areas. Article 126 provides that the Council is to adopt 'incentive measures' under the so-called co-decision procedure of Article 189B, and it lists various projects at which Community action should be aimed, including the development of the European dimension in education, promoting co-operation between educational establishments, exchanges of information between Member States, and encouraging the mobility of students and teachers. Article 127, on the other hand, provides that the Council shall adopt 'measures' under the co-operation procedure of Article 189C (replacing the previous procedure under what used to be Article 128, whereby the Council could adopt measues by simple majority without consulting the European Parliament) to further a range of listed objectives in the area of vocational training, retraining, and reintegration. Although the boundary between vocational and other education is a difficult one to draw, it would appear to be important on account of the two different legislative procedures provided in Article 126 and 127 respectively. Finally, co-operation with third countries and with international organizations is to be

140 K. Lenaerts, 'Education in European Community Law after "Maastricht"' (1994) 31 CMLRev. 7.

141 *Ibid.* 15–16.

fostered both in the sphere of education under Article 126 and of vocational training under Article 127.

Koen Lenaerts, a judge of the CFI, has summarized the current position on education in Community law as follows:

K. Lenaerts, Education in European Community Law after 'Maastricht'[142]

The new Articles 126 and 127 consolidate the acquis communautaire with regard to educational and vocational-training policy by introducing a legally certain, constitutional basis for that policy and democratizing the relevant decision-making procedures. In addition, education has been taken out of its one-sided, economically-oriented perpective. The Community may henceforward contribute to 'the development of quality education' irrespective of the vocational aim of the education . . .

Both provisions embody an expression of the principle of subsidiarity . . . The confirmation of the responsibility of the Member States (or their constituent entities) for the content of teaching, the organization of the education system (or the content and organization of vocational training) and the safeguarding of their cultural and linguistic identity boils down to the introduction of an irrebuttable presumption that they are better placed to deal with these policy matters. Community action is confined to aspects of educational and vocational-training policy which are manifestly cross-border and for which it would be difficult for each Member State to act efficiently on an individual basis.

10. CITIZENSHIP

One of the major symbolic changes made by the TEU to the EEC Treaty was to rename it the European Community Treaty, omitting the central word 'economic'. Further, in addition to the conferral on the Community of new, wider areas of social and political competence such as culture and education, Part Two of the EC Treaty, consisting of Articles 8 to 8e, is entitled 'Citizenship of the Union'.[143] This was by no means a new and sudden addition, since the idea of Community citizenship, and the rhetoric of a 'People's Europe', have been in circulation for a long time.[144]

Article 8 provides:

1. Citizenship of the Union is hereby established.

142 *Ibid.* 40–41.

143 See C. Closa, 'The concept of Citizenship in the Treaty on European Union' (1992) 29 CMLRev. 1137, S. O'Leary, 'Nationality Law and Community Citizenship: A Tale of Two Uneasy Bedfellows' (1992) 12 YBEL 353. See also the Commission Report on Citizenship of the Union, COM(93)702.

144 See e.g. 'Towards a Citizens' Europe' Bull. EC, Supp. 7–1975, 11, and the report on 'A People's Europe' following the Fontainebleu summit of the European Council, COM(84)446 Final. For a discussion of the general background to this area, see O'Keeffe, 'Union Citizenship' in D. O'Keeffe and P. Twomey (eds.), *Legal Issues of the Maastricht Treaty* (Chancery, 1994.) 87.

> Every person holding the nationality of a Member State shall be a citizen of the Union.
>
> 2. Citizens of the Union shall enjoy the rights conferred by this Treaty and shall be subject to the duties imposed thereby.

Article 8a provides:

> 1. Every citizen of the Union shall have the right to move and reside freely within the territory of the Member States, subject to the limitations and conditions laid down in this Treaty and by the measures adopted to give it effect.
>
> 2. The Council may adopt provisions with a view to facilitating the exercise of the rights referred to in paragraph 1; save as otherwise provided in this Treaty, the Council shall act unanimously on a proposal from the Commission and after obtaining the assent of the European Parliament.

At first sight, this seems quite a dramatic provision, which might suggest that since the community is no longer purely an economic Community, the status of 'worker' under Article 48 is no longer of such importance. If the right to move freely and to reside in any Member State is no longer tied to economic status but to a notion of Union citizenship, any EC national, employed or not, could move freely throughout the Community and reside in any Member State. However, closer analysis of Article 8 shows that this is unlikely to be so. Although a range of 'political' rights is conferred by Articles 8b to 8e, these are limited, and of less significance than the right to move freely and to reside in other Member States. Further, the crucial restriction on the right to move and to reside in Article 8 is that it is subject to such limits and conditions as are laid down in the Treaty or in secondary legislation.[145]

In fact, in 1990, two years before the TEU was signed, the Council had already adopted three Directives which guaranteed rights of residence to categories of persons other than workers.[146] These were Directive 90/366, governing students exercising the right to vocational training, Directive 90/365, governing employed and self-employed people who had ceased to work but without necessarily having moved to another Member State, and Directive 90/364 as a catch-all governing all those persons who do not already enjoy a right of residence under Community law.

The Directives require Member States to grant the right of residence, evidenced by a residence permit, to those persons and to certain of their family members (a more restricted category than under Regulation 1612/68), provided that they have adequate resources so as not to become a burden on the social assistance schemes of the Member States and are all covered by

[145] A ref. is currently pending before the ECJ in Case C–229/94, n. 17 above, on whether Art. 8(a)(1) confers rights of free movement additional to those which existed under the EEC Treaty prior to the TEU amendments.

[146] The original proposals for dirs. of this kind were made by the Commission as early as 1980. See COM(80)358.

sickness insurance. The Directives allow the spouse and dependent children of those who come within their scope to take up employment, if they are non-Community nationals, and the rights set out in these measures are subject to the same derogations on grounds of public policy, security, and health as are those under Article 48. It is clear that the concerns of the Member States were taken into account in adopting these Directives, and although the right of residence may no longer be dependent on the exercise of an economic activity, it is certainly dependent on the enjoyment of a degree of wealth or financial self-sufficiency. Only those non-workers who can afford to support themselves and their families will derive any benefit from the Directives, and even the benefits which could be derived are very limited.

Considering the provisions of Article 8 of the Treaty in the context of these Directives, it seems likely that the 'limits and conditions' to which the right of residence of citizens may be subject will include the financial and other conditions set by the Directives. Thus it seems that the right of residence which Article 8 guarantees to all 'citizens of the Union' goes no further than did these Directives, unless the Council should choose in the future to provide for a more generous right of residence in accordance with its powers under Article 8a(2).

The rights and the status conferred by the section of the Treaty on Union citizenship are in addition to, and do not replace or alter, the rights enjoyed by Member State nationals by virtue of their own nationality and citizenship. The question of who is a Member State national remains entirely for each Member State to decide. The remainder of the section confers a number of rights, which, although limited in their range, are of some practical and symbolic importance. Article 8b, which provoked controversy on account of its incompatibility with constitutional provisions in some Member States and which thus allows for the possibility of derogations, provides that citizens of the Union shall have the right in a Member State other than that of their nationality to vote and to stand as a candidate both in municipal and in European Parliament elections.[147] Article 8c provides that they have the right, in a third country where their own Member State is not represented, to the protection of the diplomatic authorities of any Member State. Article 8d provides a Treaty basis for an existing practice, by declaring that citizens shall have the right to petition the European Parliament, and it also states that they may apply to the Ombudsman, an office newly established under Article 138e of the Treaty.[148] Finally, Article 8e requires the Commission to report every three years on the application of these provisions on citizenship, and, in what could become an important provision, the Council is empowered 'to adopt provisions to strengthen or to add to the rights laid down' in this part of the Treaty. However, the Council must act unanimously and Article 8e envisages

[147] See Council Dir. 93/109 on exercising the right to vote in European Parliament elections: [1993] OJ L329/34. See also the res. of the European Parliament on the implementation of this Dir.: [1994] OJ C44/159. On the right to vote and stand in municipal elections see [1994] OJ C 105/8.

[148] See Ch. 2 64–5.

that such action may require constitutional amendment at the nationa level.[149]

It was noted at the beginning of this Chapter that the original provisions o the EEC Treaty on workers may have been meant to extend to workers of an nationality, who were living and working within the Community, but that th Court subsequently adopted the narrower reading in Regulation 1612/68 tha only Community nationals were covered. Unfortunately, the opportunity t remedy the exclusion of this large category of lawful Community residents wa not taken in the TEU, and, with the exception of the right to petition th Parliament and the right to complain to the Ombudsman under Article 138 and 138e, the rights of citizenship created do not extend to non-Communit nationals who are resident within the Community.[150] The exclusion of non Community nationals from the rights and the protection of Community law both before and after the TEU, has attracted strong criticism from many quar ters.[151]

H. D'Oliveira, Expanding External and Shrinking Internal Borders: Europe's Defence Mechanisms in the Areas of Free Movement, Immigration and Asylum[152]

There is one category of non-nationals of Member States which derives freedom of movement from EC legislation: the groups of family members as defined in several Directives. The large groups of non-Member State nationals, however, who have established themselves in the territories of the Member States as workers or as a result of family reunification or formation have systematically been excluded from the Community framework. Although they form part and parcel of the population of the countries of the EC, many have been born there, received their education in these countries etc., their position is grossly neglected both by the EC and in intergovernmental co-operation.

In view of their inferior status and the disadvantage suffered by such persons under Community law, it has been questioned whether the human, as opposed to the economic, side of the free movement of persons can really be said to be the most important.

J. Weiler, The Transformation of Europe[153]

The Treaty provisions prohibiting discrimination on grounds of nationality, allowing the free movement of workers and their families, and generally supporting a

[149] Denmark entered various reservations about the concept of Union citizenship in a 'Unilateral Declaration' at the 1992 Edinburgh summit, after the initial rejection by referendum in that Member State of the TEU.

[150] Contrast the non-binding 1989 Community Charter of Fundamental Social Rights for workers, signed by 11 of the then Member States, excluding the UK, some of whose provisions also cover workers who are non-EC nationals: COM(89)471.

[151] See O'Keeffe, n. 76 above, 285–7.

[152] D. O'Keeffe and P. Twomey (eds.), n. 144 above, 261, 267.

[153] (1991) 100 Yale L.J. 2403, 2480. For another pre-TEU criticism of the treatment of non-

rich network of transnational social transactions may be viewed not simply as creating the optimal conditions for the free movement of factors of production in the common market. They also serve to remove nationality and state affiliation of the individual, so divisive in the past, as the principal referent for transnational human intercourse . . .

. . . It would be more than ironic if a polity with its political process set up to counter the excesses of statism ended up coming round full circle and transforming itself into a (super) state. It would be equally ironic that an ethos that rejected the nationalism of the Member States gave birth to a new European nation and European nationalism . . .

. . . We have made little progress if the *Us* becomes European (instead of German or French or British) and the *Them* becomes those outside the Community or those inside who do not enjoy the privileges of citizenship.

These comments bring to mind the early promises noted at the beginning of this Chapter, that the Community was not to be an 'inward-looking rich man's club', and that the human, rather than simply the economic, aspects of freedom of movement were of central importance. Thus far, the provisions of the Treaty on citizenship and related provisions on freedom of movement for persons have not very effectively substantiated these claims.

11. FURTHER READING

(a) Books

BURROWS, F., *Free Movement in European Community Law* (Clarendon Press, 1987)

MEEHAN, E., *Citizenship and the European Community* (Sage, 1993)

SCHERMERS, H. *et. al.* (eds.), *Free Movement of Persons in Europe* (Martinus Nijhoff, 1991)

(b) Articles

CLOSA, C., 'The concept of Citizenship in the Treaty on European Union' (1992) 29 CMLRev. 1137

D'OLIVEIRA, H., 'Expanding External and Shrinking Internal Borders: Europe's Defence Mechanisms in the Areas of Free Movement, Immigration and Asylum' in O'Keeffe and Twomey (eds.), *Legal Issues of the Maastricht Treaty* (1994) 261

LENAERTS, K., 'Education in European Community Law after "Maastricht" ' (1994) 31 CMLRev. 7

MANCINI, G. F., 'The Free Movement of Workers in the Case-Law of the European Court of Justice' in D. Curtin and D. O'Keeffe (eds.), *Constitutional Adjudication in European Community and National Law* (1992), 67

Community nationals, see 'Symposium on the Status of Non-Community Nationals in Community Law' (1992) EJIL 36–91.

O'Keeffe, D., 'Judicial Interpretation of the Public Service Exception to the Free Movement of Workers' in D. Curtin and D. O'Keeffe (eds.), *Constitutional Adjudication in European Community Law and National Law* 89

—— 'Trends in the Free Movement of Persons' in J. O'Reilly (ed.), *Human Rights and Constitutional Law* (1992), 262

—— 'Union Citizenship' in D. O'Keeffe and P. Twomey (eds.), *Legal Issues of the Maastricht Treaty* (1994), 87

Watson, P., 'Free Movement of Workers: A one-way ticket?' (1993) 22 ILJ 68

16

Freedom of Establishment and to Provide Services

1. INTRODUCTION

Article 48, we have seen, provides for the free movement of employed persons throughout the Community, by requiring Member States to ensure equal treatment between workers from other Member States and their own workers. The other two chapters of the Treaty which are central to the free movement of persons are the chapter on establishment which encompasses Articles 52 to 58, and, to a lesser extent, the chapter on services which encompasses Articles 59 to 66. These chapters essentially cover freedom of movement for the self-employed and for companies, and, like Article 48, they embody the principle of non-discrimination on grounds of nationality. Freedom of establishment, roughly speaking, requires the removal of restrictions on the right of individuals and companies to maintain a permanent or settled place of business in a Member State. Establishment has been defined as 'the actual pursuit of an economic activity through a fixed establishment in another Member State for an indefinite period'.[1] The free movement of services, on the other hand, generally requires the removal of restrictions on the provision of services between Member States, where either the provider is supplying services in a state in which that person does not maintain an establishment, or the recipient is travelling to receive services in a Member State other than that in which the recipient is established. It is also possible for the service itself to 'move' without the provider or the recipient moving, for example where the provision of the service takes place by telecommunication.

It will be seen that, although the principle of non-discrimination set out in Article 6—formerly Article 7—of the Treaty is a very important part of these two chapters[2]—in that, as a general rule, the non-national who is established in a Member State must be treated in the same way as a national, and the non-established provider or recipient of services must be treated in the same way as a provider or recipient who is established in the Member State—the Court of Justice has appeared to go beyond the notion of discrimination and to state that even non-discriminatory restrictions might be prohibited by the Treaty

[1] Case C–221/89 *R.* v. *Secretary of State for Transport, ex p. Factortame* [1991] ECR I–3905, [1991] 3 CMLR 589, para. 20.

[2] See Case 2/74, *Reyners* v. *Belgium* [1974] ECR 631, 660, [1974] 2 CMLR 305, paras. 15–16.

provisions. However, as will be seen below, the concept of 'discriminatory measures' is not a very sharply defined one, so that (as in the context of free movement of goods) the distinction between discriminatory and non-discriminatory measures is not always clear.

(a) The Three Chapters

The similarities between the various chapters on the free movement of persons and services have often been stressed. Advocate General Mayras in *Van Binsbergen* pointed out that the principle of equality of treatment and non-discrimination on grounds of nationality in what was then Article 7 lay behind Articles 48, 52, and 59 to 60 alike.[3] On the other hand, there are differences too, and these can be seen in contrasting the common features shared by two of the three chapters with the third. Articles 48 and 52, for example, are often compared from the point of view of the requirement of equal treatment of persons who are *settled* in a Member State other than that of their nationality, either in an employed or a self-employed capacity,[4] whereas the similarities between Articles 52 and 59 are evident when considering at what stage a self-employed person providing regular services into or within a Member State may be considered to be sufficiently connected with that state to be established, rather than merely providing services there.[5] Equally Articles 59 and 48 are linked by virtue of the fact that they both concern economic activities engaged in by Community nationals throughout the Community, the only difference being the employed or self-employed status of the person. In *Walrave and Koch*, the Court stated that these two provisions were to be similarly construed:

> The activities referred to in Article 59 are not to be distinguished by their nature from those in Article 48, but only by the fact that they are performed outside the ties of the contract of employment.[6]

On the other hand, Article 59 has also been contrasted with Articles 48 and 52 as being less concerned with the equal treatment of foreigners and nationals, and more concerned with the mobility of the services themselves and with setting up a single market,[7] by analogy with the Treaty provisions on free movement of goods and the abolition of quantitative restrictions under Article

[3] Case 33/74, *Van Binsbergen* v. *Bestuur van de Bedrijfsvereniging voor de Metaalnijverheid* [1974] ECR 1299, [1975] 1 CMLR 298.

[4] See Mayras A.G. in Case 2/74, n. 2 above.

[5] See Cases 205/84, *Commission* v. *Germany* [1986] ECR 3755, [1987] 2 CMLR 69, para. 22, and 33/74, n. 3 above, para. 13. See also the opinion of Jacobs A.G. in Case C–76/90, *Säger* v. *Dennemeyer & Co Ltd* [1991] ECR I–4221, [1993] 3 CMLR 639.

[6] Case 36/74, *Walrave and Koch* v. *Association Union Cycliste Internationale* [1974] ECR 1405, [1975] 1 CMLR 320, para. 23.

[7] See Warner A.G. in Case 52/79, *Procureur du Roi* v. *Debauve* [1980] ECR 833, 872, [1981] 2 CMLR 362.

30.[8] The Court has often stated that not all of the regulatory rules applicable to persons established within a Member State should be applied to persons who are merely providing services there on a temporary basis.

This theme of eliminating discrimination versus ensuring mobility, of equal treatment versus the creation of a single market, will be seen throughout the discussion in this chapter of the provisions on establishment and services. It is interesting and important for several reasons. First, because the Court has ruled that only the narrow grounds of exception in Articles 56 and 66 of the Treaty—the derogations on grounds of public policy, security, or health—can be relied upon to justify discriminatory restrictions,[9] whereas a much wider range of public-interest justifications can be relied on where the restriction is non-discriminatory. Secondly, it is important because to extend the scope of the Treaty provisions to genuinely non-discriminatory restrictions can often be seen to reach further into sensitive areas of national policy, in circumstances which might at first appear to have little to do with the abolition of barriers to the nationals and companies of other Member States performing economic activities. This will become evident from an examination of cases concerning issues such as abortion, lotteries, and the regulation of broadcasting.

The chapter will begin with a consideration of the law relating to freedom of establishment, in the context of both natural persons and of legal or artificial persons, and an examination of the law on the free movement of services will follow. The question of mutual recognition of qualifications is important to both areas, as is clear from Articles 57 and 66 of the Treaties, and indeed also to the free movement of workers.[10] However, litigation and problems relating to the non-recognition of qualifications occur more frequently in the context of the right of establishment, generally when Community nationals wish to join a professional body in the State in which they wish to base their practice. For this reason the legislation on harmonization and mutual recognition of qualifications will be dealt with in the section on freedom of establishment. The derogations from the free movement of persons on grounds of public policy, security, and health under Articles 48, 56, and 66 will be discussed together in Chapter 17, since Directive 64/221, which regulates the

[8] See Jacobs A.G. in Case C–76/90, n. 5 above, at 4234–5, and Gulmann A.G. in Case C–275/92, *H.M. Customs and Excise* v. *Schindler* [1994] ECR 1039, 1059. The close relationship between the free movement of goods and of services can be seen in Case 155/73 *Sacchi* [1974] ECR 409, [1974] 2 CMLR 177 in which the ECJ ruled that the broadcasting of TV signals fell within the Treaty rules relating to services, whereas materials such as video or sound tapes are covered by the provisions on free movement of goods.

[9] See Case 352/85, *Bond van Adverteerders* v. *Netherlands* [1988] ECR 2085, [1989] 3 CMLR 113, paras. 32–3.

[10] See the Opinion of Van Gerven A.G. in Case 340/89, *Vlassopoulou* v. *Ministerium für Justiz, Bundes- und Europaangelegenheiten Baden-Württemberg* [1991] ECR 2357, [1993] 3 CMLR221. See also Art. 2 of Dir. 92/51, [1992] OJ L209/29, making many of the earlier transitional recognition Dirs., which had been applicable only to the self-employed, applicable also to the pursuit of those same activities as an employed person.

exercise of the three derogations, applies both to employed and to self-employed persons.

(b) The Secondary Legislation

Directive 73/148 was passed, under the terms of Articles 54 and 63 of the Treaty, to provide for the abolition of restrictions on movement and residence within the Community for nationals of Member States with regard to establishment and the provision of services.[11] This measure is similar to Directive 68/360 in the context of workers, regulating the terms and conditions of entry of other Member State nationals and their families. Article 1 covers those wishing to establish themselves or to provide or receive services, and their families, which include the same family members as those listed in Regulation 1612/68 on workers. The Directive requires Member States to guarantee the right to enter and to leave a Member State for those purposes, without any visa requirements other than for non-EC nationals.[12] A right of permanent residence evidenced by a permit is to be granted to those who establish themselves in a self-employed activity, and a right of temporary residence for those providing or receiving services which is of equal duration with the length of the services.[13] The right of temporary residence is to be formalized by the issue of a 'right of abode' where the period during which services are provided or received exceeds three months.[14] All that is needed to apply for a residence permit or right of abode is an identity card or passport and proof of being one of the persons covered by the Directive.[15]

Directive 75/34 provides for the right of nationals of a Member State to remain in the territory of another Member State after having pursued an activity there in a self-employed capacity, and to be entitled to equality of treatment with nationals as under Directive 73/148.[16] The conditions which must be satisfied by the person in order to qualify for this right are very similar to those which apply to employed persons under Directive 1251/70, and like that Directive they apply also to the family members who are listed therein.[17]

(c) Articles 55 and 66: The Official-Authority Exception

Article 55 of the Treaty, which is extended by Article 66 to cover the chapter on services, states that the provisions of the chapter on freedom of establishment shall not apply 'so far as any given Member State is concerned, to activities which in that State are connected, even occasionally, with the exercise of official authority'. This provision has a similar role to that of the public-service derogation in Article 48(4), but this time in the context of the self-employed.

[11] Dir. 73/148, [1973] OJ L172/14. [12] *Ibid.*, Arts. 2–3. [13] *Ibid.*, Art. 4(2).
[14] *Ibid.* [15] *Ibid.*, Art. 6.
[16] [1975] OJ L14/10. Dir. 75/35: [1975] OJ L14/14 makes the provisions of Dir. 64/221 applicable also to these persons. See further Ch. 17 on Dir. 64/221.
[17] See Ch. 15, n. 20 and text.

Advocate General Mayras gave a useful definition of official authority, which brings to mind some of the descriptions we have seen of what is characteristic of public-service employment under Article 48(4):

> Official authority is that which arises from the sovereignty and majesty of the State; for him who exercises it, it implies the power of enjoying the prerogatives outside the general law, privileges of official power and powers of coercion over citizens.[18]

The wording of Article 55 refers to those 'activities' which are connected with the use of official power, rather than to professions or vocations within which official authority might, under certain circumstances, be exercised. Questions over the interpretation of the provision first arose in the *Reyners* case, in which the Conseil d'Etat asked the Court whether, within the legal profession of *avocat*, only those activities which were connected with the exercise of official authority were excepted from the Treaty rules, or whether the whole of the profession was excepted by reason of the fact that it comprised activities connected with the exercise of such authority. According to the Luxembourg Government, the whole profession should be excepted because it was 'connected organically' with the public service of the administration of justice, in that it involved a set of strict conditions for admission and discipline, and participation by the *avocat* in the course of judicial procedures was largely obligatory:

Case 2/74, Reyners v. Belgium
[1974] ECR 631, [1974] 2 CMLR 305

The facts are set out in Chapter 4.[19]

THE ECJ

43. Having regard to the fundamental character of freedom of establishment and the rule on equal treatment with nationals in the system of the Treaty, the exceptions allowed by the first paragraph of Article 55 cannot be given a scope which would exceed the objective for which this exemption clause was inserted.

44. The first paragraph of Article 55 must enable Member States to exclude non-nationals from taking up functions involving the exercise of official authority which are connected with one of the activities of self-employed persons provided for in Article 52.

45. This need is fully satisfied when the exclusion of nationals is limited to those activities which, taken on their own, constitute a direct and specific connection with the exercise of official authority.

46. An extension of the exception allowed by Article 55 to a whole profession would be possible only in cases where such activities were linked with that profession in such a way that freedom of establishment would result in imposing on

[18] Case 2/74, n. 2 above, at 664 (ECR). [19] See 159.

the Member State concerned the obligation to allow the exercise, even occasionally, by non-nationals of functions appertaining to official authority.

47. This extension is on the other hand not possible when, within the framework of an independent profession, the activities connected with the exercise of official authority are separable from the professional activity in question taken as a whole.

. . .

51. Professional activities involving contacts, even regular and organic, with the courts, including even compulsory cooperation in their functioning, do not constitute, as such, connection with the exercise of official authority.

52. The most typical activities of the profession of avocat, in particular, such as consultation and legal assistance and also representation and the defence of parties in court, even when the intervention or assistance of the avocat is compulsory or is a legal monopoly, cannot be considered as connected with the exercise of official authority.

53. The exercise of these activities leaves the discretion of judicial authority and the free exercise of judicial power intact.

The reasoning of the Court is very similar to that used in the context of the public-service derogation in Article 48(4), in the sense that the exception must have a single Community definition and that it cannot be given a scope which would exceed its purpose. If specific activities which involve exercising official authority are severable from the rest of a profession, then Article 55 cannot apply to the profession as a whole. And in the legal context, even if lawyers participate in various ways in the administration of justice, so long as their activities do not interfere with judicial discretion, they do not involve the necessary 'direct and specific connection' with the exercise of official power or authority.

In proceedings brought by the Commission against Greece, for failure to implement Directive 82/470 on freedom of establishment and freedom to provide services in the context of certain transport and travel agency activities, the Greek Government sought to argue that the activity of traffic-accident expert was covered by Article 55.[20] The Court rejected the argument, pointing out that the reports of such experts did not bind the courts, and, repeating its ruling in *Reyners*, that they left intact the exercise of judicial power and discretion. Similarly in the case of *Thijssen*, the Court ruled that the post of commissioner of insurance companies and undertakings was not excluded from the provisions of the chapter on establishment or services by Article 55.[21] Although the post involved monitoring companies and reporting on possible infringements of the penal code, the power to prevent insurance companies from implementing certain decisions was not a definitive power, and did not

[20] Case C–306/89, *Commission* v. *Greece* [1991] ECR I–5863, [1994] 1 CMLR 803. See also Case C–272/91, *Commission* v. *Italy* [1994] ECR I–1409 on operating a computerization system for a national lottery.

[21] Case C–42/92, *Thijssen* v. *Controledienst voor de Verzekeringen* [1993] ECR I–4047.

affect the final power of approval or refusal of the *Office de Contrôle des Assurances*.

2. THE RIGHT OF ESTABLISHMENT

Article 52 of the Treaty provides:

> Within the framework of the provisions set out below, restrictions on the freedom of establishment of nationals of a Member State in the territory of another Member State shall be abolished by progressive stages in the course of the transitional period. Such progressive abolition shall also apply to restrictions on the setting up of agencies, branches, or subsidiaries by nationals of any Member State established in the territory of any Member State.
>
> Freedom of establishment shall include the right to take up and pursue activities as self-employed persons and to set up and manage undertakings, in particular companies or firms within the meaning of the second paragraph of Article 58, under the conditions laid down for its own nationals by the law of the country where such establishment is effected, subject to the provisions of the chapter relating to capital.

The first paragraph of the Article is negatively worded, requiring the gradual abolition of restrictions on freedom of establishment, whether that is a primary or a secondary establishment, and the second is positively worded, indicating that freedom of establishment entails the right for self-employed persons to pursue their activities on an equal footing with the nationals of the Member State in which they are established. The reference to capital reflects the fact that there is a separate chapter on the free movement of capital, which was subject to different rules and to a more gradual liberalization.[22]

It is clear from the wording of Article 52 that there are two possible limitations on its scope. First, in paragraph one, reference is made to the position of nationals in a Member State *other than that of their nationality*, which would imply that Article 52 cannot be invoked by nationals in their own Member State against restrictions on their freedom to establish themselves. And, secondly, paragraph two refers to the right of establishment in a Member State 'under the conditions laid down for its own nationals'. In other words, the Article prohibits discrimination, but so long as the person exercising the right of establishment is treated in the same way as a national of that Member State, there can be no ground for complaint under Article 52. However, it will be seen in the discussion below that, although this may initially have been the meaning given to the provision, its interpretation has

[22] See Case 203/80, *Casati* [1981] ECR 2595, [1982] 1 CMLR 365. Arts. 67–73 EEC were replaced, following the amendments made by the TEU, by Arts. 73b-g. See J. Usher, *The Law of Money and Financial Services in the European Community* (Oxford, 1992), Ch. 2.

broadened since then, and the scope of Article 52 is wider than its language might suggest.

Article 53 is a standstill provision, prohibiting any new restrictions, and Article 54 requires the Council to draw up a general programme for the abolition of restrictions on establishment, and to issue directives to attain freedom for particular activities. Article 57 also requires the Council to issue directives for the mutual recognition of diplomas and other qualifications, and Article 58 places companies in the same position as natural persons for the purpose of the application of this chapter of the Treaty. These provisions will be discussed in more detail below.

First, the General Programme, which was adopted pursuant to Article 54 in 1961, makes it clear that discriminatory restrictions are the target of the Treaty provisions on establishment.[23] It requires the elimination of restrictive laws and administrative practices which treat nationals of other Member States differently from nationals of the state concerned, and it lists a range of examples of the sorts of restrictions which must be abolished. These include the attachment of conditions such as licences, periods of residence, tax burdens, and various other measures which make more difficult the exercise of activities by the self-employed or by companies. The Programme also requires the elimination of restrictions on the powers which usually attach to the exercise of such activities, listing as examples the power to enter contracts, to acquire property, to have access to credit, and to receive State aids.

It is made clear that not only directly but also indirectly discriminatory restrictions on the exercise of activities by the self-employed are to be abolished, which 'although applicable irrespective of nationality, their effect is exclusively or principally, to hinder the taking up or pursuit of such activity by foreign nationals'. The Programme also allowed for the application of a transitional system, pending the mutual recognition of diplomas and qualifications, and there was a considerable amount of legislative activity in this field.

(a) The Effect of Article 52

In *Reyners*, one of the earliest cases concerning freedom of establishment, the Court, as has been seen earlier in Chapter 4, ruled that Article 52 of the Treaty was directly effective.[24] The ruling was made, despite the failure on the part of the Council to adopt all of the necessary implementing legislation envisaged under Article 54(2), and despite the fact that the stringent conditions for direct effect which had been set out in the *Van Gend* decision did not appear to have been met.[25] Before examining the Court's ruling, it is worth inquiring why the

[23] See the General Programme for the Abolition of Restrictions on the Freedom of Establishment of 18 Dec. 1961 ([1962] OJ 36/62), OJ Spec. Edn., Second Ser., IX.

[24] Case 2/74, n. 2 above. In Case 6/64, *Flaminio Costa* v. *ENEL* [1964] ECR 585, [1964] CMLR 425, the ECJ had ruled that Art. 53, the standstill provision, was directly effective.

[25] See Ch. 4, 156–65.

necessary legislation had in 1974 not yet been adopted. Apart from the slow progress of legislative procedures in Council in the aftermath of the Luxembourg Accords, the process of opening the professions, and in particular the legal profession, to non-nationals met with very considerable opposition in the Member States. This much can be seen from the comments of Advocate General Mayras in the case:

> This problem . . . is one of those which have, since the coming into force of the Treaty, given rise to the most lively controversies and the most marked divergences between the Bars and between the national Governments, to the point where action by the Community organs has been paralysed and no positive measure has until now been able to be taken to free the activities of the *avocat* at a Community level.[26]

It will be remembered that Reyners was a Dutch national who had obtained his legal education in Belgium, and who was refused admission to the Belgian Bar solely on the ground that he lacked Belgian nationality. The Court ruled that, despite the requirement in the Treaty that directives be adopted, Article 52 laid down a precise result which was to be achieved by the end of the transitional period, namely the requirement of non-discrimination on grounds of nationality. This was a result 'the fulfilment of which had to be made easier by, but not made dependent on, the implementation of a programme of progressive measures'.[27] Since no directive was required in Reyners' situation to remove the clearly discriminatory restriction which confronted him, he could invoke Article 52 directly. The Court did acknowledge, however, that the directives had 'not lost all interest since they preserve an important scope in the field of measures intended to make easier the effective exercise of the right of freedom of establishment'.[28]

In what circumstances, then, would the existence of directives be necessary before Article 52 could be invoked and relied upon by a Community national seeking to exercise the right of establishment in another Member State? In what circumstances would Article 52 lack direct effect? One example of an area which was clearly regarded in the Treaty provisions and in the General Programme as being in need of legislative co-ordination was that concerning the divergences between the educational, vocational, and other qualifications existing in the different Member States. If a doctor, qualified to practise medicine in Italy, were to seek to set up practice in the United Kingdom, could she rely on Article 52 of the Treaty to require the United Kingdom authorities to permit her to practise even though the systems of medical training in the two countries were very different? Clearly Community legislative intervention was needed to attempt some kind of co-ordination of the varying requirements of different states for the same professional qualification.

[26] [1974] ECR 631, 658. [27] *Ibid.*, para. 26. [28] *Ibid.*, para. 31.

However, even before such legislation was passed under Article 57, several cases came before the Court in which it was argued that, even in the absence of directives, and even where the restriction was not clearly based on the criterion of nationality, Article 52 could be relied on by an EC national seeking to practise a profession in another Member State. In *Thieffry*, a Belgian national, who obtained a doctorate in law in Belgium and practised as an advocate for some years in Brussels, subsequently obtained French university recognition of his qualifications as equivalent to a degree in French law, and obtained a certificate of aptitude for the profession of *avocat*.[29] However, he was refused admission to the training stage as an advocate at the Paris Bar, on the ground that he lacked a degree in French law. Although the Court agreed that freedom of establishment could be subject to the observance of professional rules justified by the general good, it ruled that national authorities, including the responsible professional bodies, had a duty to ensure that their practices were in accordance with Treaty objectives:

> Consequently, if the freedom of establishment provided for by Article 52 can be ensured in a Member State either under the provisions of the laws and regulations in force, or by virtue of the practices of the public service or of professional bodies, a person subject to Community law cannot be denied the practical benefit of that freedom solely by virtue of the fact that, for a particular profession, the directives provided for by Article 57 of the Treaty have not yet been adopted.[30]

Accordingly, if Thieffry had already obtained what was recognized (both professionally and academically) to be an equivalent qualification, and had satisfied the necessary practical training requirements, the state authorities would not be justified in refusing him admission to the Bar solely on the ground that he did not possess a French qualification.[31] The absence of Community directives regulating or co-ordinating particular professional qualifications was no obstacle to the direct effectiveness of Article 52, and the obligation it imposed on Member States to ensure, where they could under national law, the free exercise of the right of establishment.

The Court developed its argument in *Thieffry* further in subsequent decisions, ruling that Article 52 precluded the competent national authorities from simply refusing, without further explanation, to allow nationals of another Member State to practise their trade or profession on the ground that their qualification was not equivalent to the corresponding national qualification. We can see in the following case that the Treaty provisions, both on free movement of workers and on freedom of establishment, have the effect of imposing specific, positive obligations on national authorities and professional

[29] Case 71/76, *Thieffry* v. *Conseil de l'Ordre des Avocats à la Cour de Paris* [1977] ECR 765, [1977] 2 CMLR 373.

[30] *Ibid.*, para. 17.

[31] See also Case 11/77, *Patrick* v. *Ministre des Affairs Culturelles* [1977] ECR 1199, [1977] 2 CMLR 523.

bodies to take steps to secure freedom of establishment even in the absence of Community or national legislation providing for equivalence or recognition of qualifications:

Case 222/86, UNECTEF v. Heylens
[1987] ECR 4097, [1989] 1 CMLR 901

Heylens was a Belgian national who held a Belgian football trainer's diploma, and was taken on as trainer of a Lille football team in France. His application for recognition of the equivalence of his diploma to the corresponding French diploma was refused by the Ministry of Sport, without giving him reasons for the decision. When he continued to practise as a trainer, he was prosecuted by UNECTEF, the French football trainers' union. The French court referred to the ECJ the question of the compatibility with Community law of the French system for deciding on the equivalence of diplomas.

THE ECJ

10. In the absence of harmonization of the conditions of access to a particular occupation, the Member States are entitled to lay down the knowledge and qualifications needed in order to pursue it and to require the production of a diploma certifying that the holder has the relevant knowledge and qualifications.

. . .

13. Since it has to reconcile the requirement as to the qualifications necessary in order to pursue a particular occupation with the requirements of the free movement of workers, the procedure for the recognition of equivalence must enable the national authorities to assure themselves, on an objective basis, that the foreign diploma certifies that its holder has knowledge and qualifications which are, if not identical, at least equivalent to those certified by the national diploma. That assessment of the equivalence of the foreign diploma must be effected exclusively in the light of the level of knowledge and qualifications which its holder can be assumed to possess in the light of that diploma, having regard to the nature and duration of the studies and practical training which the diploma certifies that he has carried out.

The Court concluded that, where employment was dependent on possession of a diploma, the Treaty required that it be possible for a national of a Member State to obtain judicial review of a decision of the authorities of another Member State, refusing to recognize the equivalence of a diploma, and for that national to ascertain the reasons for the decision.[32] This line of reasoning was continued in the case of *Vlassopoulou*, where, in the absence of national recognition or of Community legislation on the co-ordination or the mutual recognition of legal qualifications, the Court held that Article 52 imposed an obligation on Member State authorities to examine closely and compare the qualifications of a Community national wishing to practise in that state, and to take into account any further knowledge subsequently acquired in the host state:

32 See Ch. 5 at 208 for a discussion of the importance of this case in the context of remedies.

Case 340/89, Vlassopoulou v. Ministerium für Justiz, Bundes- und Europaangelegenheiten Baden-Württemberg [1991] ECR 2357, [1993] 2 CMLR 22

The applicant was a Greek national who had obtained a law degree in Athens and had been admitted to the Athens Bar. Much of her professional practice over several years was in the field of German law and was focused in Mannheim, Germany. Her application for admission to the Bar and authorization to practise at the Mannheim courts was rejected on the ground that she lacked the necessary qualifications, which included the passing of the First and Second German State Examinations. The Court was asked by the German Federal Supreme Court whether it was permissible to refuse access for this reason.

THE ECJ

15. It must be stated in this regard that, even if applied without any discrimination on the basis of nationality, national requirements concerning qualifications may have the effect of hindering nationals of the other Member States in the exercise of their right of establishment guaranteed to them by Article 52 of the EEC Treaty. That could be the case if the national rules in question took no account of the knowledge and qualifications already acquired by the person concerned in another Member State.

16. Consequently, a Member State which receives a request to admit a person to a profession to which access, under national law, depends upon the possession of a diploma or a professional qualification must take into consideration the diplomas, certificates and other evidence of qualifications which the person concerned has acquired in order to exercise the same profession in another Member State by making a comparison between the specialized knowledge and abilities certified by those diplomas and the knowledge and qualifications required by the national rules.

Thus the national authorities are required to consider any education and training received by the person which is indicated by the certificate or diploma held by that person, and to contrast the knowledge and skills acquired with those which are required by the domestic qualification.[33] If they are found to be equivalent, the Member State *must* recognize the qualification, and if they are not so found, the state is obliged to go on to assess whether any knowledge or practical training the person may have acquired in the host Member State, through study or experience, is sufficient to make up for what was lacking in that person's qualification.

It is clear that the applicability and effect of Article 52 has developed considerably since the case of *Reyners*, in which the Court held that in the absence of legislation by the Council, at least the non-discrimination 'core' of the Article was directly effective, so that straightforward discrimination on grounds of nationality was a breach of that provision. Now, even where there is no legislation to co-ordinate or to recognize qualifications acquired within the Community, and Member States may have very diverse educational and

[33] See also Case C–104/91, *Borrell* [1992] ECR I–3001.

training systems, there will be a breach of Article 52 if the national authorities do not conduct a thorough examination of the basis for the qualification held by the Community national in question. And, further, there will be a breach of Article 52 if they do not go on to inform the person concerned why the qualification held is not sufficient, respecting that person's rights in the process.

It is striking that the ruling of the Court in *Vlassopoulou* is so similar in its approach to the provisions of Council Directive 89/48 on the mutual recognition of higher-education diplomas.[34] This Directive was not applicable to Vlassopoulou's situation, since the time limit for its implementation had not then expired. Advocate General Van Gerven discussed the new legislation, and said that the difference between its provisions and the effect of the Treaty alone was that, unlike the Directive, Article 52 did not of itself give EC nationals the right to establish themselves in any Member State, subject only to the possible requirement of completion of an adaptation period. Rather, Article 52 simply required the Member State to take into account qualifications and training already received, and only if it were found that these were *equivalent* to the Member State's requirements could an EC national place reliance on them. Article 52 could not of itself be relied upon to impose an obligation on the state to provide facilities for such a person to complete an adaptation period which would bring his or her qualification and training up to the level required for that Member State.

Even given this difference, however, the interpretation of the effect of Article 52 in cases such as *Heylens* and *Vlassopoulou*, from the point of view of the obligation to compare qualifications carefully, to recognize equivalence, and to provide adequate reasons for a refusal of recognition, brings it very close indeed to the position under the new legislative measures, and reflects the dialogue between the Community's legislative and judicial organs which has been noted before.[35] The effect of Article 52 is that a Member State can no longer simply refuse someone entry to a profession or to practise a trade solely on the ground that he or she lacks the domestic qualification. And this is true even where the position in national law is more complex than in *Thieffry* and *Patrick*, in that there is as yet no domestic recognition of the foreign qualification.

(b) Harmonization and Mutual Recognition of Qualifications

The comments of Advocate General Mayras in *Reyners*, cited above, indicated some of the difficulties encountered in the attempt to implement Community legislation on the mutual recognition of formal qualifications. Yet this was clearly a vital task in the creation of a Community which would be genuinely open to those wishing to exercise a trade, profession, or other self-employed activity in any Member State other than that in which the qualification was obtained.

[34] [1989] OJ L19/16. [35] See Ch. 15, nn. 138–9 and text.

Initially, the legislative institutions pursued a 'harmonisation' or 'co-ordination' approach, which sought to take specific sectors of economic or professional life, and to obtain agreement from all the Member States on the minimum standard of the training and education needed for a qualification in that field. Generally, for each sector, two directives would be passed, one specifying the general level of the education and training necessary to pursue that activity or profession, and the second listing the qualifications and diplomas awarded in the various Member States which satisfied those conditions for recognition. These directives mainly covered activities in the medical and health-related sphere—general practitioners, nurses, pharmacists, veterinary surgeons—and also architects. There were other directives on various activities such as small craft, food and beverage, wholesale, intermediary, retail, and coal-trade industries, and a directive on lawyers' services in 1977. A directive on the right of establishment for lawyers, although much discussed and debated, has never been adopted.

Clearly, to gain agreement on the content of such directives, and to get them through the Community legislative process, was an arduous task. In 1974, the Council adopted a resolution, a non-binding act, on the mutual recognition of formal qualifications, expressing the wish that future work on mutual recognition be based on 'flexible and qualitative criteria', and that directives 'should resort as little as possible to the prescription of detailed training requirements'.[36] However, following the 1984 summit of the European Council at Fontainebleu, an approach which moved away from co-ordinating or harmonizing the requirements for qualification was adopted. Directive 89/48 was eventually adopted five years later, providing for 'a general system for the recognition of higher-education diplomas awarded on completion of professional education and training of at least three years' duration'.[37] The aim and content of this Directive were officially summarized in the Bulletin of the Community, shortly before the final adoption of the legislation:

> The Directive differs from previous 'sectoral' directives in several respects.
>
> First, it is general in nature, in that the new system is intended to apply to all regulated professions for which university-level training of at least three years is required and which are not covered by a specific directive.
>
> Second, recognition is to be based on the principle of mutual trust, without prior coordination of the preparatory educational and training courses for the various professions in question. As a basic principle, a host Member State may not refuse entry to a regulated profession to a national of a Member State who holds the qualifications necessary for exercise of that profession in another Member State.
>
> Third, recognition is granted to the 'end product' i.e. to fully qualified professionals who have already received any professional training required in addition to their university diplomas . . .
>
> Fourth, where there are major differences in education and training, or in the

[36] [1974] OJ C98/1. [37] [1989] OJ L19/16.

structure of a profession, the draft Directive provides for compensation mechanisms, i.e. either an adaptation period or an aptitude test.[38]

Thus in a single legislative measure a general system of recognition was established, avoiding the need for the time-consuming and contentious process of securing agreement on the minimum standard required for every specific trade or profession. However, there are obviously disadvantages to this approach, in that, unlike the harmonization approach of the earlier directives, it does not provide an automatic guarantee to those who hold specified qualifications that they will be accepted by any Member State of the Community. Compliance with the criteria set out in Directive 89/48 guarantees only a starting point for the person wishing to practise a trade or profession, and the diploma or other qualification held by that person will be subject to scrutiny and control by the authorities of the host Member State. The Member States remain free, where either the content of the education or training received is inadequate or the structure of the profession it represents is different, to impose the additional requirements of an aptitude test or an adaptation period.

The basic thrust of the Directive is that, if a Community national wishes to pursue a regulated profession in any Member State, the competent authorities in the Member State may not refuse permission on the ground of inadequate qualifications if the person satisfies certain conditions. In brief, the conditions to be satisfied are that the person has pursued the equivalent of a three-year higher-education course in the Community, and has completed the necessary professional training in order to be qualified to take up the regulated profession in question.[39] Satisfaction of these conditions does not mean that the person must be permitted to pursue that profession: what it means is that the competent authorities in the host Member State may not refuse permission solely on the ground of inadequate qualifications. If the qualifications are considered adequate, then permission to practise should be given. However, if the duration of the person's training and education is at least one year less than that required in the host State, Article 4(a) of the Directive allows the Member State to require certain evidence of professional experience. If, on the other hand, the matters covered by the person's education and training differ substantially from those covered by the host state qualification, or if the host state profession comprises specific regulated activities which are not within the profession regulated in the Member State where the qualification was obtained, Article 4(b) allows the Member State to require the completion of an adaptation period or that an aptitude test be taken. The applicant is to have the

[38] Bull. EC 6–1988, 11.

[39] According to J. Pertek in 'Free Movement of Professionals and Recognition of Higher Education Diplomas' (1992) 12 YBEL 293, a profession is regulated within the meaning of the Dir. 'if it is usually pursued under a professional denomination, the use of which is reserved to the holders of a diploma by rules laid down by a public authority, this monopoly is protected by the existence of penal sanctions'.

choice between test or adaptation period, except in instances specified by the Directive, such as in the case of professions requiring precise knowledge of national law, in which case the Member State may stipulate which of the two is required.

Following on from Directive 89/48, the Council adopted Directive 92/51 which is supplementary to and follows the same approach as the system for recognition established by the earlier Directive. The 1992 Directive covers education and training other than the three-year higher-education requirement of Directive 89/48. It covers *diplomas* which are awarded after a post-secondary course (other than higher-education courses covered by Directive 89/48) of at least one year in length, and which qualify the holder to take up a regulated profession. It also covers *certificates* which are awarded after educational or training courses other than these post-secondary courses of one year's duration, or after a probationary or professional practice period, or after vocational training, which qualify the holder to take up a regulated profession.

Although there are clearly many advantages to the system which has been established by these two measures, the move towards recognition which allows Member States to control and to supervise the process of recognition at each step, rather than the provision for automatic recognition in the earlier sectoral Directives also has its drawbacks. Some of these problems, stemming from the responses of the Member States, are highlighted in the following discussion:

J. Pertek, Free Movement of Professionals and Recognition of Higher Education Diplomas[40]

First, there is a reluctance to acknowledge that an activity is regulated within the meaning of the Directive, i.e. that there are obstacles to free movement, the origin of which is to be found in public regulations . . .

Secondly, there is the problem of putting the general system's basic principle, i.e. mutual trust, into full effect. The tendency in most of the Member States is to reverse the principle and the exception. This means, on the one hand, that countervailing and controlling measures are generally considered justified. This implies, on the other hand, that these measures are extremely strict.

Thirdly, there is a clear preference in the Member States to use an aptitude test as the corrective measure required of the applicants. This results in a wide interpretation of the derogation from the rule allowing the applicant to choose between an adaptation period and a test; it is doubtful whether some professions, such as the profession of '*commissaire-priseur*' in France, may truly be considered as a legal profession within the definition of the Directive. In this case, when the right to choose is clearly reserved for the State, the migrant is usually required to take an aptitude test and this test may be very strict . . .

Finally, there is the problem of guaranteeing in concrete terms the rights of the people who could benefit from the system. In other words, one can see a tendency to adhere to equal treatment. As emphasized by the Court of Justice, the legit-

[40] 'Free Movement of Professionals and Recognition of Higher Education Diplomas' (1992) 12 YBEL 320–1.

imate requirement concerning the possession of diplomas is a barrier to the effective exercise of the freedom guaranteed by the Treaty, and the Directives on the recognition of diplomas aim precisely at facilitating this effective exercise. One could then expect national measures to secure recognition by setting up clear rules rather than merely indicating what the competent authority will examine or decide.

Another danger is linked to the choice of the competent authority. If the designated competent authority is the body which represents the profession, the fear may exist of a tendency towards protectionism or even hostility against migrants arriving to compete with the members of the profession.

Despite the shortcomings of the new approach, however, it would now appear, since the adoption of these two major directives on the mutual recognition of qualifications, alongside the earlier series of 'sectoral' harmonizing directives, that almost anyone who has obtained any kind of professional qualification will be able to rely on these measures to prevent a Member State from simply refusing to permit that person to practise on grounds of inadequate qualifications. One conclusion which might be drawn from this is that the rulings in *Heylens* and *Vlassopoulou* on the direct effect of Article 52 in the context of mutual recognition have lost their relevance. However, it is possible that there may yet be cases in which the education or training received does not fall within the directives, or is said by a Member State not to satisfy all of the conditions in the directives, for example in the case of persons who have not completed a formal course of secondary education but who nevertheless have gone on to complete a vocational course or other professional training. In such cases, the basic principle underlying *Vlassopoulou* and *Heylens*, stemming directly from the Court's interpretation of Article 52 of the Treaty, will be important to protect the person who seeks to exercise the right to practise in a self-employed capacity. The requirement to give proper reasons for the non-recognition of a qualification, as well as the requirement of access to a judicial remedy to contest a refusal of recognition or a requirement to undertake an aptitude test or adaptation period will remain valuable.[41]

As with most of the Treaty provisions on free movement of persons, neither the sectoral directives nor the general mutual-recognition directives cover non-Community nationals. Nor do they apply to qualifications obtained outside the Community, although under Directives 89/48 and 92/51 a diploma awarded within the Community may, in certain circumstances, take into account education or training received outside the Community. However, at the same time as the adoption of Directive 89/48, the Council passed a recommendation encouraging the Member States to recognize diplomas and other evidence of formal qualifications obtained in non-member countries by Community nationals.[42]

[41] For those whose qualifications are covered by the Dirs., these requirements of reasoning and access to a judicial remedy are set out in Art. 8 of Dir. 89/48 and Art. 12 of Dir. 92/51.

[42] Council Rec. 89/49: [1989] OJ L19/24.

In two recent decisions, the Court had to rule on the rights of EC nationals who had obtained qualifications outside the Community, and who now sought to exercise their right of establishment under Article 52 of the Treaty. The first set of proceedings involved one of the sectoral directives which dealt with the profession of dentistry, whereas the other involved Directive 89/48 and the general system for mutual recognition.

In the case of *Tawil-Albertini*, a French national obtained in Lebanon a dental qualification, which was subsequently recognized by the Belgian authorities as equivalent to the corresponding Belgian qualification, and which authorized him to practise in Belgium.[43] He was also authorized to practise in two other Member States, but his application to the French authorities for permission to practise in France was refused. The qualifications listed in Council Directive 78/686 on mutual recognition of dental qualifications did not include any qualification obtained outside the Member States, but since his qualification had been recognized as equivalent to the Belgian diploma, he argued that it was also covered by the Directive. The Court held that the mutual recognition of qualifications in dentistry awarded by the Member States was based on the guarantees of specific minimum criteria set out in the co-ordination Directive. In the case of non-Member States, co-ordination of training could only be brought about by agreements between the states in question, so that although any Member State could recognize the equivalence of a non-member country's qualifications, this would not bring those qualifications within the scope of the Community directive on dentistry and could not bind other Member States which did not recognize those qualifications. This ruling is presumably also applicable not just to the dentistry directive but also to any of the sectoral or mutual-recognition directives.

In *Haim*, although the applicant did not hold one of the qualifications listed in Council Directive 78/686 on mutual recognition of dental qualifications, he was authorized to practise as a dentist in Germany.[44] When he applied to work on a social-security scheme in Germany, however, he was informed that he would have to complete a further two-year preparatory training period. He argued that his experience working for eight years as a dentist of a social-security scheme in Belgium should be taken into account, and the Court, citing *Vlassopoulou*, ruled in his favour:

> The competent national authority, in order to verify whether the training period requirement prescribed by the national rules is met, must take into account the professional experience of the plaintiff in the main proceedings, including that which he has acquired during his appointment as a dental practitioner of a social security scheme in another Member State.[45]

[43] Case C–154/93, *Tawil-Albertini* v. *Ministre des Affairs Sociales* [1994] ECR I–451.

[44] Case C–319/92, *Haim* v. *Kassenzahnärtzliche Vereinigung Nordrhein* [1994] ECR I–425, [1994] 2 CMLR 169.

[45] *Ibid.*, para. 28.

Thus, although non-member country qualifications are excluded from the coverage of the directives, if a Member State chooses to recognize such a qualification, it must also take into account, in determining whether a national training period condition has been fulfilled, any practical training or professional experience obtained in another Member State.

Both Haim and Tawil-Albertini were Community nationals who had obtained non-member country qualifications. However, as was seen in the law relating to the free movement of workers, nationals of non-member countries who are established in the Community have no rights of recognition or permission to practise under Community law. Non-member country nationals who have undergone the self-same education and training as Community nationals within a Member State and who have thus obtained Community qualifications which are listed within the directives, remain without any independent Community rights to recognition or establishment.

(c) The Scope of Article 52

(i) Does Article 52 Cover only Discriminatory Restrictions? It has been noted above that the wording of Article 52 suggests that what is required is the equal treatment of nationals and non-nationals. Since it guarantees the right for nationals of a Member State to establish themselves in another Member State 'under the conditions laid down for its own nationals', it would appear that EC nationals have no ground for complaint under Article 52 if the same provisions are applied to them as to nationals of the host Member State. This interpretation is supported by the emphasis on non-discrimination in the General Programme, as set out above, and it is consistent with some of the statements of the Court in its case law on Article 52. In *Commission* v. *Belgium*,[46] which is discussed further below, restrictions were placed on the provision of clinical biology services by laboratories. Although the effect of these restrictions appeared to be to require those engaged in clinical laboratory testing to maintain their primary establishment in Belgium, they did not refer to the nationality of the person or to the seat of the company providing the services. However, in answer to the argument that the restrictions were in breach of Article 52 by hindering secondary establishment, the Court stated:

> It is clear from [Article 52] and its context that, provided that such equality of treatment is respected, each Member State is, in the absence of Community rules in this area, free to lay down rules for its own territory governing the activities of laboratories providing clinical biology services.
>
> Secondly . . . Article 52 is intended to ensure that all nationals of Member States who establish themselves in another Member State, even if that establishment is only secondary, for the purpose of pursuing activities there as a self-employed person receive the same treatment as nationals of that State and it prohibits, as a

[46] Case 221/85, *Commission* v. *Belgium* [1987] ECR 719, [1988] 1 CMLR 620.

restriction on freedom of establishment, any discrimination on grounds of nationality.[47]

Advocate General Lenz in the case put the point even more strongly than the Court:

> There appears to be no basis for arguing that national rules on the exercise of a profession which are applied without distinction to a State's own nationals and those of another Member State could be tested by reference to the principle of proportionality even if the scope of the freedom of establishment governed by Community law is not affected . . . Provided that the measure in question is applied indiscriminately to the nationals of all Member States, it is not necessary to consider whether it is appropriate or proportionate from the point of view of Belgian law.[48]

There are other rulings which lend support to the reading of Article 52 which restricts its scope to discriminatory rules, providing for unequal treatment. In the case of *Fearon*, the legislation allegedly in breach of Article 52 provided that, in order for a company to benefit from an exemption from the compulsory purchase of its land, its members and shareholders would have to reside on the land.[49] This residence requirement was imposed in pursuance of a national policy on rural agricultural holdings, in an attempt to prevent speculation in such land. In its answer to the question whether the legislation was compatible with Article 52, although the Court's reasoning is not entirely clear, it is evident that its perception that the rule did not distinguish between nationals and non-nationals was important:

> That question must be answered in the affirmative if the obligation to reside on or near land is imposed by a Member State, within the framework of legislation concerning the ownership of rural land which is intended to achieve the objectives set out above, both on its own nationals and on those of the other Member States and is applied to them equally. A residence requirement so delimited does not in fact amount to discrimination which might be found to offend against Article 52 of the Treaty.[50]

However, in many other cases, the Court has appeared to move away from the emphasis on unequal treatment, and to state that even 'equally applicable' restrictions may be contrary to Article 52. In *Klopp*, a German lawyer was refused admission to the Paris Bar on the sole ground that he already main-

[47] Case 221/85, *Commission* v. *Belgium* [1987] ECR 719, [1988] 1 CMLR 620, paras. 9–10.
[48] [1987] ECR 719, 732.
[49] Case 182/83, *Robert Fearon and Co* v. *Irish Land Commission* [1984] ECR 3677, [1985] 2 CMLR 228.
[50] *Ibid.*, para. 10.

tained an office as a lawyer in another Member State.[51] The statutes of the Paris Bar, which applied equally to nationals and non-nationals, provided that a lawyer could have only one office, which must be within the district of the court at which that lawyer was admitted. It might be thought, on the basis of the reasoning in the *Belgium* case, that the Court would find no breach of Article 52, since nationals and non-nationals alike who wished to practise at the Paris Bar were to be restricted to a single place of practice. Yet the Court held that, although it was for the states to regulate the exercise of professions in their own territory, they could not require a lawyer who wished to practise there to have only one establishment throughout the Community, since Article 52 specifically included the freedom to set up more than one place of work in the Community. There were less restrictive ways, given modern methods of transport and telecommunications, of ensuring that lawyers should practise so as to maintain sufficient contact with their clients and the judicial authorities, and to obey the rules of the profession. Yet *Klopp* is not of itself authority for a general proposition that even non-discriminatory rules which restrict freedom of establishment may breach Article 52: a narrower reading is that a non-discriminatory rule which has the effect of preventing the exercise of a secondary establishment in another Member State is contrary to the Treaty, since Article 52 clearly guarantees the right to maintain a second place of establishment.[52]

Similar issues arose in the cases of *Wolf*[53] and *Stanton*,[54] in which the Court ruled that 'indistinctly applicable' rules on social-security exemptions for the self-employed were impermissible, because they were an excessive impediment to the pursuit of occupational activities in more than one Member State. The Court stated clearly that the legislation did not contain any direct or indirect discrimination on grounds of nationality.[55] However, because the legislation 'might place Community citizens at a disadvantage when they wish to extend their activities beyond the territory of a single Member State',[56] and it was not justified by any additional social security protection given to those citizens, it was incompatible with Article 52.

However, the proposition that even non-discriminatory rules which do not render impossible or difficult the exercise of the right of secondary establishment guaranteed by Article 52 might be contrary to Article 52 is supported by other case law. In *Gullung* the Court held that even a rule applicable without distinction to nationals and non-nationals (such as that all practising lawyers must be registered at the Bar in that Member State, where registration was

[51] Case 107/83, *Ordre des Avocats* v. *Klopp* [1984] ECR 2971, [1985] 1 CMLR 99.

[52] See also Cases 96/85, *Commission* v. *France* [1986] ECR 1475, [1986] 3 CMLR 57, and C–351/90, *Commission* v. *Luxembourg* [1992] ECR I–3945, [1992] 3 CMLR 124, in which similar single-practice rules for doctors, dentists, and vets were contrary to Art. 52, since they went beyond what was necessary to ensure continuity of patient care. The Luxembourg rule was, in any case, directly discriminatory in part. See also Case C–106/91, *Ramrath* v. *Ministre de la Justice* [1992] ECR I–3351.

[53] Cases 154–155/87, *RSVZ* v. *Wolf* [1988] ECR 3897.

[54] Case 143/87 *Stanton* v. *INASTI* [1988] ECR 3877, [1989] 3 CMLR 761.

[55] *Ibid.*, para. 9.

[56] *Ibid.*, para. 13.

open to nationals of all Member States without discrimination) might breach Community law on freedom of establishment, unless it was objectively justified.[57]

There are several explanations for the Court's apparent extension of Article 52 to cover national rules which apply equally to nationals and to non-nationals alike. One is to focus not on the wording of the second part of Article 52, which refers to equal treatment, but on the first part, which simply requires restrictions on freedom of establishment to be abolished, without stating whether the restrictions referred to are only those which are applied exclusively to nationals of other Member States. The reason the Treaty might prohibit such restrictions, even when they do not make distinctions based on nationality, is that many apparently equally applicable rules in fact bear more heavily on non-nationals than on nationals. This was seen above in the context of recognition of qualifications. But this might lead us to the conclusion that in fact we are simply saying that equally applicable rules can be discriminatory in their effect (indirectly discriminatory) so that we are back to the initial proposition that Article 52 only applies to restrictions which are discriminatory, although this includes indirectly as well as directly discriminatory restrictions. Looking back at the cases in which the Court has apparently extended the scope of Article 52 to cover non-discriminatory restrictions, it may be found that many of the restrictions which appeared to provide for equal treatment could in fact be categorized as indirectly discriminatory, in that they would bear more heavily on non-nationals than on nationals.[58]

In cases such as *Belgium* and *Fearon*, above, although the Court appeared to give judgment on the basis that the legislation was compatible with Article 52 because there was no discrimination, there was in fact, looking more closely at the cases, an unequal burden imposed on non-nationals or on companies with their primary establishment elsewhere. In the *Belgium* case, the legislation clearly had a more restrictive impact on clinical laboratories whose primary establishment was in a Member State other than Belgium. And in *Fearon*, the residence requirement was more likely to restrict non-national shareholders who wished to participate in the formation of an Irish company. Yet this is not to say that the conclusions of the Court were wrong, since in both cases the unequal burden was probably justified by public policy interests. In the *Belgium* case, it was stated that the Government wished to prevent excessive recourse to clinical biology services,[59] presumably on grounds of protection of public health, and in *Fearon*, the policy embodied in the Land Acts was a national agricultural policy which was consistent with broader Community aims.

[57] Case 292/86, *Gullung* v. *Conseil de l'Ordre des Avocats* [1988] ECR 111, [1988] 2 CMLR 57. See also Case 271/82, *Auer* v. *Ministère Public* [1983] ECR 2727, [1985] 1 CMLR 123, para. 18 in which a registration requirement was said to be justified if it sought to ensure 'the observance of moral and ethical principles and the disciplinary control of the activity'.

[58] See G. Marenco, 'The Notion of a Restriction on the Freedom of Establishment and the Provisions of Services in the Case Law of the ECJ' (1991) 11 YBEL 111.

[59] Case 221/85, *Commission* v. *Belgium* [1987] ECR 719, [1988] 1 CMLR 620, para. 8.

Further, the single-practice restrictions in cases like *Klopp*, although they appeared equally applicable since they could adversely affect nationals as well as non-nationals, were likely in practice to be indirectly discriminatory. This is because most of those who would wish to set up a secondary place of establishment in a host Member State would be nationals of other Member States who are likely to have their primary place of establishment in their Member State of origin. Thus, a single-practice rule can be seen as an indirectly discriminatory rule which is not justified by any overriding public policy interest that could not be satisfied by less restrictive means. Equally, in cases like *Stanton* and *Wolf*, the legislation clearly disadvantaged those whose principal occupation or professional activities were in a Member State other than Belgium. Again, in the majority of cases these are more likely to be non-nationals than nationals, and there was no adequate justification for the unequal burden. Finally in *Gullung*, the requirement of registration with a professional body would impose a second or additional requirement on those who were already established in another Member State, who again were more likely to be non-nationals.

Thus it could be said that Article 52 prohibits restrictions which are directly or indirectly discriminatory on grounds of nationality (or, in the case of a company, place of registration or primary establishment), unless they are objectively justified by a sufficiently pressing public interest. However, in the case of *Bond* concerning freedom to provide services, a distinction was drawn by the Court between rules which are apparently intended to discriminate and those which are genuinely equally applicable but which happen to impose an unequal burden on non-nationals.[60] In the case of what could be called 'deliberately discriminatory restrictions'—be they overt or covert, the Member State may rely for justification only on the express derogations on grounds of public policy, security, and health in Article 56 of the Treaty.[61] These, it will be seen in the next chapter, have been carefully circumscribed both by the Court and in secondary legislation.[62] On the other hand, when the unequal treatment stems from a genuinely equally applicable rule which was not a hidden or covert discrimination, there is a wider and open-ended range of public-interest grounds which may be relied upon to justify the restrictive measure. Although the Court has ruled to this effect in relation to Article 59 rather than Article 52, it would seem that its reasoning on the freedom to provide services in *Bond*—which follows the pattern of its reasoning on justifying discriminatory restrictions on the free movement of goods[63]—should also apply by analogy to freedom of establishment. On the other hand, the Court in the case of *Bachmann* appeared to take a different view in the context of free movement of workers under Article 48, and to hold that discriminatory restrictions could be justified without recourse to the specific public policy,

[60] Case 352/85, n. 9 above.

[61] *Ibid.*, paras. 32–3.

[62] See e.g. Case C–211/91, *Commission* v. *Belgium* [1992] I–6757 on restricting access to cable TV networks.

[63] See Ch. 14.

security, or health exceptions.[64] However, it may be that the Court in *Bachmann* might not have considered the tax restriction to be deliberately discriminatory, but instead to be a genuinely equally applicable measure which indirectly burdened non-national workers.[65] This might explain why the measure could be justified on grounds other than those set out in Article 48. On this assumption, deliberately discriminatory restrictions on freedom of establishment under Article 48 or under Article 52 could only be justified by reference to the express exceptions in Article 48(3) or Article 56 of the Treaty.

In most of the case law on Article 52 examined above, the restrictions in question were in some way directly or indirectly discriminatory. However, that is not to say that genuinely non-discriminatory restrictions (i.e. those which cannot really be said to impose more of a burden on non-nationals than on nationals) do not fall within the scope of the Article. Recently in the case of *Kraus*, which will be discussed below in the context of 'reverse discrimination', the Court ruled that a provision of law in a Member State which required special permission for the use of a foreign academic title could be contrary to Article 52, on the ground that any national rule which restricts the exercise of freedom of establishment of nationals or non-nationals would be contrary to that Article unless adequately justified.[66] It may, of course, be argued that the restriction in *Kraus* was in fact indirectly discriminatory, since a greater number of non-nationals than nationals will hold foreign academic degrees, but the Court's judgment seems to imply that, even if just as many or more German nationals than non-nationals established in Germany were obtaining LL.M. degrees in other Member States, the restriction would still fall within the scope of Article 52 despite its non-discriminatory nature. The fact that the complainant in the case was a German national adds force to this suggestion.

Even if it is true—as it is in the free movement of goods and of services—that the vast majority of cases which come before the Court involve restrictions which fall more heavily on non-nationals or non-nationally-based companies than on nationals or nationally established companies, the Court has nonetheless stressed in its decisions that non-discriminatory restrictions will also fall within the scope of the establishment provisions. This would seem to indicate that, if a truly non-discriminatory provision were in question, the Court would require it to demonstrate an objective justification and to comply with the principles of necessity and proportionality before it could be said to be compatible with Article 52. This issue will be examined in relation to Article 59 and the free movement of services, below.

[64] Case C–204/90, *Bachmann* v. *Belgium* [1992] ECR I–249, [1993] 1 CMLR 785. See Ch. 15, 658–9.

[65] This same uncertainty over whether a measure is discriminatory or not can be seen across a range of different substantive areas of law. For case C–132/92, *Roberts* v. *Birds Eye Walls Ltd* [1993] ECR I–5579, [1993] 3 CMLR 622 on sex discrimination, see Ch. 18, 833–4, and see case C–2/90, *Commission* v. *Belgium* [1992] ECR I–4431 on free movement of goods, Ch. 14, 599, n. 26.

[66] Case C–19/92, *Kraus* v. *Land Baden-Württemberg* [1993] ECR I–1663.

(ii) The 'Reverse Discrimination' Question: Can Nationals Rely on Article 52 in their Own Member State? The second potential limitation on the scope of Article 52, mentioned above, derives from the fact that its wording refers to the situation of nationals wishing to establish themselves in a state other than that of their nationality. This implies that nationals setting up a practice or a business in the Member State of their own nationality cannot complain under Article 52 of any domestic regulation of those activities. A Member State is clearly obliged, under Article 52 and Directive 73/148, not to restrict its own nationals who wish to *leave* the territory in order to set up an establishment in another Member State.[67] But where the situation concerns nationals established in the Member State of their nationality who seek to rely on Article 52 to challenge a restriction there, the case law of the Court has been more complex, and has undergone change over the years.

One obvious way in which nationals wishing to establish in their own Member State may be disadvantaged in a similar way to nationals of other Member States is if the qualifications they have obtained in another Member State are not recognized. In the case of *Knoors*, the Court appeared to take a generous view, which would allow nationals to plead Article 52 in the Member State of their own nationality:[68]

Case 115/78, Knoors v. Secretary of State for Economic Affairs [1979] ECR 399, [1979] 2 CMLR 357

The applicant was a Dutch national who had practised as a plumber in Belgium. He was refused permission to practise as a plumber in The Netherlands, despite the fact that the Council had passed Directive 64/427 governing certain trade skills, which covered the training and experience he had acquired. The Dutch authorities argued that he could not rely on the provisions of the Directive since he was a national seeking to establish himself in his own Member State, and they argued further that the danger in nationals seeking to rely in their own Member States on qualifications obtained elsewhere was that they might evade the application of their national provisions relating to qualification for a trade.

THE ECJ

15. The General Programme for the abolition of restrictions on freedom to provide services, in the first indent of Title I, defines as beneficiaries the nationals of Member States who are established within the Community without making any distinction as to the nationality or residence of the persons concerned.

16. The same idea is expressed by Title I of the General Programme for the abolition of restrictions on freedom of establishment, which designates as beneficiaries, in the first and third indents, the 'nationals of the Member States' without any distinction as regards nationality or residence.

17. It may therefore be stated that Directive No 64/427 is based on a broad definition of the 'beneficiaries' of its provisions, in the sense that the nationals of all

[67] See Art. 2 of the Directive.

[68] See also Case 246/80, *Broekmeulen* v. *Huisarts Registratie Commissie* [1981] ECR 2311, [1982] 1 CMLR 91.

Member States must be able to avail themselves of the liberalizing measures which it lays down, provided that they come objectively within one of the situations provided for by the Directive, and no differentiation of treatment on the basis of their residence or nationality is permitted.

. . .

19. This interpretation is justified by the requirements flowing from freedom of movement for persons, freedom of establishment and freedom to provide services, which are guaranteed by Articles 3(c), 48, 52 and 59 of the Treaty.

20. In fact these liberties, which are fundamental in the Community system, could not be fully realized if the Member States were in a position to refuse to grant the benefit of the provisions of Community law to those of their nationals who have taken advantage of the facilities existing in the matter of freedom of movement and establishment and who have acquired, by virtue of such facilities, the trade qualifications referred to by the Directive in a Member State other than that whose nationality they possess.

. . .

24. Although it is true that the provisions of the Treaty relating to establishment and the provision of services cannot be applied to situations which are purely internal to a Member State, the position nevertheless remains that the reference in Article 52 to 'nationals of a Member State' who wish to establish themselves 'in the territory of another Member State' cannot be interpreted in such a way as to exclude from the benefit of Community law a given Member State's own nationals when the latter, owing to the fact that they have lawfully resided on the territory of another Member State and have there acquired a trade qualification which is recognized by the provisions of Community law, are, with regard to their State of origin, in a situation which may be assimilated to that of any other persons enjoying the rights and liberties guaranteed by the Treaty.

However, despite this apparently flexible approach, it became clear from subsequent rulings that the existence of a directive recognizing the 'foreign' qualification of the Member State national was crucial, and that Article 52 of itself would not avail nationals established in the Member State of their nationality. This was made apparent by the ruling in *Auer*,[69] in which a naturalized French citizen had obtained a veterinary qualification in Italy but was not permitted to practise in France, apparently because, in the absence of a Community directive on the subject, the Italian qualification was not equivalent to that required in France. Unusually the Court, following Advocate General Warner, chose to interpret Article 52 in a literal and rather restrictive manner. The Court referred to the express wording of Article 52 and ruled on this basis that 'Article 52 concerns only—and can concern only—in each Member State the nationals of other Member States, those of the host Member State coming already, by definition, under the rules in question'.[70]

The Court did agree that the mere application of the rule of national treatment would not ensure complete freedom of establishment 'as such application retains all obstacles other than those resulting from the non-possession of

[69] Case 136/78, *Ministère Public* v. *Auer* [1979] ECR 437, [1979] 2 CMLR 373.

the nationality of the host State, and in particular, those resulting from the disparity of the conditions laid down by the different national laws for the acquisition of an appropriate professional qualification'.[71] But, in the view of the Court, what was needed to ensure complete freedom of establishment was the adoption by the Council of directives on mutual recognition of diplomas and qualifications. When directives of this kind are passed, they generally do not distinguish between nationals of the Member State in question and nationals of other Member States so that they can be invoked either by nationals in their own Member State or by non-nationals. This was true of the Directive in *Knoors*, above, and has also been true of the harmonization and the mutual-recognition directives since that time.

Indeed, after the facts which gave rise to Auer's first prosecution, the Council adopted Directives 78/1026 and 78/1027 governing veterinary qualifications and practice, which covered the Italian qualification Auer had obtained.[72] When, after a subsequent prosecution, the case came again before the Court, it agreed that he could rely directly on the Directives, despite the fact that France had not implemented them.[73] In other words, he was no longer, as a national in his own Member State, relying solely on the provisions of Article 52 in a way which might 'evade' national requirements of qualification.

In the case of *Bouchoucha*, the Court gave a ruling similar to that in the first *Auer* case.[74] Bouchoucha was a French national who had obtained a diploma in osteopathy in the United Kingdom. He was subsequently prosecuted in France for practising as an osteopath, without being qualified as a doctor, which was required under French law for the practice of osteopathy. Council Directives 75/362 and 75/363 concerned the harmonization and mutual recognition of medical qualifications, but did not define the activities of a 'doctor', and there were no Community measures specifically relating to osteopathy. The Court ruled that:

> in the absence of Community legislation on the professional practice of osteopathy each Member State is free to regulate the exercise of that activity within its territory, without discriminating between its own nationals and those of the other Member States.[75]

The Court evidently felt that this was one of the examples of an attempted 'abuse' situation, in which a Member State had a legitimate interest in preventing its own nationals from evading the provisions of national legislation by attempting to rely on a lower qualification obtained in another Member State. Interestingly, its approach was quite different from that seen in *Heylens* and *Vlassopoulou*, above, where nationals of other Member States were

[70] *Ibid.*, para. 20. [71] *Ibid.*, para. 21. [72] [1978] OJ L362/1.
[73] Case 271/82, n. 57 above.
[74] Case C–61/89, *Bouchoucha* [1990] ECR I–3551, [1992] 1 CMLR 1033.
[75] *Ibid.*, para. 12.

seeking to rely in a host Member State on their national qualifications, despite the fact that there was no Community directive governing those qualifications and therefore no mutual recognition. In *Heylens* and *Vlassopoulou*, the host Member State was required at least to examine the nature and content of the qualification offered by the practitioner, and to give reasons for its lack of equivalence with the corresponding domestic qualification, if indeed that was the result of the examination. In *Bouchoucha*, on the other hand, where the national was attempting to rely on Article 52 in his own Member State, the Court simply held that, in the absence of Community recognition or of any directive in the area, Member States were free to regulate a profession in a non-discriminatory manner, without necessarily having to examine degrees of knowledge and training attested to by the qualification offered by the national.[76]

The situation in *Bouchoucha* is less likely to arise again now, since a national who has obtained a qualification in another Member State and has returned to practise in her Member State of origin will probably be covered by the provisions of either Directive 89/48 or Directive 92/51, which include most trade or professional qualifications and which are not restricted to nationals establishing themselves in a Member State other than that of their nationality. However, as was suggested above, it is possible to envisage a situation in which a qualification is not covered by a harmonization directive, or by either of the two mutual-recognition directives, for example where the necessary secondary course which is a prerequisite under the recognition directives has not been completed. In the case of non-nationals in a host Member State, the interpretation of Article 52 in *Heylens* and *Vlassopoulou* provides a partial answer, but *Bouchoucha* might indicate that nationals established in their own Member State are left without redress under Community law since they are not covered by Article 52 alone.

To judge by the recent ruling in *Kraus*, however, it may be that there is, in fact, redress available under Community law, because the Court ruled in that case that a national in the Member State of his nationality—a German national who had obtained a one-year postgraduate LL.M. degree in Edinburgh and had returned to Germany—could rely on Article 52 when there was no mutual recognition directive in force to govern his qualification.[77] The facts of the case arose before the coming into force of Directive 92/51, which gives recognition to educational courses of less than three years, and there was no Community measure of any kind in respect of his degree. The case did not actually concern a refusal to recognize the knowledge or qualification attested to by the degree, or a refusal to permit the practice of a profession, but simply a refusal of permission to use the title of such a foreign degree without having to obtain (at substantial cost) prior permission.[78] The

[76] See also Cases C–330–331/90, *Ministero Fiscal* v. *Lopez Brea* [1992] ECR I–323.

[77] Case C–19/92, n. 66 above.

[78] See Art. 7 of Dir. 89/48 and Art. 11 of Dir. 92/51 on the right to use the lawful academic title from the Member State where the qualification was received.

Court ruled that freedom of movement for workers and the right of establishment under Articles 48 and 52 constituted fundamental liberties, which could not be fully implemented if Member States could refuse to allow their own nationals, who had availed themselves of those freedoms and had as a result acquired qualifications in another Member State, to benefit from them. However, the Court ultimately ruled that, in the absence of harmonization or recognition, the Member State could regulate the conditions relating to the use of the degree title, so long as it was not done in an excessive or disproportionate manner. The main interest in the case from the point of view of the application of Article 52 to nationals established in their own Member State, however, is that such nationals may rely on Article 52 even in the absence of any Community legislation providing for recognition. To this extent, *Kraus* represents a change in position from that indicated in the first *Auer* case. Further, the requirement that the Member State's regulation of the use of degree titles must not be excessive or disproportionate is certainly more than the Court required in *Bouchoucha*, where it simply ruled that, in the absence of Community legislation, the Member State was free to regulate the exercise of a profession in a non-discriminatory manner.

That is not to say, however, that nationals will always be free to rely on Article 52 to challenge a restriction on their freedom to establish themselves in their own Member State. It is only where there is a 'Community element' present, such as the fact of having pursued an educational course and obtained a qualification in another Member State, that Article 52 can come into play. Otherwise, the situation may be held to be a 'wholly internal' one, as was seen in the case law on free movement of workers.[79] An example of a wholly internal situation, in which the qualifications of nationals who were established in their own Member State had also been obtained in that state, can be found in the case of *Niño*.[80] Criminal proceedings were brought in Italy against four Italian nationals who had, without having the required authorization to practice as medical doctors, provided pranotherapy and biotherapy treatment. They argued that they should not be refused the freedom to practise their profession solely on the ground that a directive relating to the practice of such therapy had not yet been adopted under Article 57. The Court held that the situation was in a purely national setting, and that the Community provisions on freedom of establishment were not applicable.[81] Even if a national is resident in a Member State other than that of his nationality, if he maintains his place of establishment and professional practice in his own Member State, the Court has ruled that he cannot rely on Article 52 to challenge tax provisions of his own state which favour those who are resident within the Member State over non-residents.[82] As a national who is established in his own Member State and paying tax there, and who is not being restricted from

[79] e.g. Case 175/78, *R.* v. *Saunders* [1979] ECR 1129, [1979] 2 CMLR 216.

[80] Cases 54 and 91/88 and 14/89, *Niño and others* [1990] ECR 3537, [1992] 1 CMLR 83.

[81] See also Case 204/87, *Bekaert* [1988] ECR 2029, [1988] 2 CMLR 655.

[82] Case C–112/91, *Werner* v. *Finanzamt Aachen-Innenstadt* [1993] ECR I–429.

setting up a place of establishment in another Member State, he may not invoke Article 52 of the Treaty. Rather than treating the case as one in which there was a certain restriction on his freedom to establish owing to the tax 'encouragement' to reside in the Member State of establishment, but that the restriction was justified for legitimate tax reasons, the Court simply held Article 52 to be inapplicable.

(iii) Are Restrictions on Social Benefits Contrary to Article 52? It has been seen that, apart from restrictions which discriminate directly on grounds of nationality, many less direct measures may constitute restrictions on freedom of establishment within the meaning of Article 52. The non-recognition of professional qualifications and the single-practice rule are two examples which have been discussed, and the General Programme also referred to various others, such as the right to buy property and to obtain credit, which were linked to the exercise of the activity in question.

However, there is no equivalent in the law on freedom of establishment to Regulation 1612/68 on the rights of workers and their families in the context of Article 48, and in particular no provision like Article 7(2) of that measure which guarantees the same social and tax advantages to non-national workers as are available to nationals. There is no mention of a right to housing, nor of educational rights for the children of non-nationals who are established in a self-employed capacity. However, although the self-employed have not been accorded the same level of protection by secondary Community legislation as workers, the Court has read Article 52 in such a way as to prohibit national measures which confer certain social advantages on nationals or on companies maintaining their primary establishment in that Member State, to the exclusion of non-nationals or companies maintaining a secondary establishment there. It will be remembered that, under Article 48 of the Treaty and Article 7(2) of Regulation 1612/68, the Court had held that the advantages in question did not have to be those linked with employment, so that virtually any difference in treatment of a worker or a worker's family would be a possible breach of Article 48. In the context of Article 52, on the other hand, the Court has held that the prohibition on discrimination is concerned with 'the rules relating to the various general facilities which are of assistance in the pursuit of [occupational] activities'.[83]

In *Steinhauser*,[84] a restriction on renting premises for business purposes, and in *Stanton*,[85] the refusal of certain social security exemptions, were held to constitute restrictions on the right of establishment within Article 52. Similarly it will be seen below that the denial of certain tax advantages to companies whose primary establishment or registered office is not in the state may

[83] Case 63/86, *Commission* v. *Italy* [1988] ECR 29, [1989] 2 CMLR 601.

[84] Case 197/84, *Steinhauser* v. *City of Biarritz* [1985] ECR 1819, [1986] 1 CMLR 53.

[85] Case 143/87 n. 54 above, discussed above. See also Case 79/85, *Segers* [1986] ECR 2375, [1987] 2 CMLR 247 on the right of employees of a company to be affiliated to a social security scheme.

infringe Article 52.[86] Such measures, although they may not directly regulate or curb the right of establishment, nevertheless constitute disadvantages for those exercising rights under Article 52. However, it can be seen that, unlike the restrictions on social advantages for workers which are prohibited by Article 48,[87] the link between the enjoyment of the social benefit and the ability to carry on the self-employed activity is important in the context of Article 52 and, indeed, as will be seen below, of Article 59. In the following case, it was held that a nationality requirement for access to reduced-rate mortgage loans and to social housing was contrary to Article 52, despite Italy's argument that, in the absence of legislation like Article 9 of Regulation 1612/68 on workers, housing did not have to be provided on the same terms as for nationals:

Case 63/86, Commission v. Italy
[1988] ECR 29, [1989] 2 CMLR 601

THE ECJ

16. If complete equality of competition is to be assured, the national of a Member State who wishes to pursue an activity as a self-employed person in another Member State must therefore be able to obtain housing in conditions equivalent to those enjoyed by those of his competitors who are nationals of the latter State. Accordingly any restriction placed not only on the right of access to housing but also on the various facilities granted to those nationals in order to alleviate the financial burden must be regarded as an obstacle to the pursuit of the occupation itself.

17. That being so, housing legislation, even where it concerns social housing, must be regarded as part of the legislation that is subject to the principle of national treatment which results from the provisions of the Treaty concerning activities as self-employed persons.

(d) Establishment of Companies

Article 58 of the Treaty provides:

Companies or firms formed in accordance with the law of a Member State and having their registered office, central administration or principal place of business within the Community shall, for the purposes of this Chapter, be treated in the same way as natural persons who are nationals of Member States.

'Companies or firms' means companies or firms constituted under civil or commercial law, including co-operative societies, and other legal persons governed by public or private law, save for those which are non-profit making.

[86] Case 270/83, *Commission* v. *France* [1986] ECR 273, [1987] 1 CMLR 401.

[87] See e.g. Cases 207/78, *Ministère Public* v. *Even and ONPTS* [1979] ECR 2019, [1980] 2 CMLR 71 and 65/81, *Reina* v. *Landeskreditbank Baden-Württemberg* [1982] ECR 33, [1982] 1 CMLR 744.

Despite the fact that Article 58 requires companies to be treated in the same way as nationals for the purposes of the Treaty provisions on freedom of establishment, this is not strictly possible, since there are many differences between natural and legal persons. It may be easier, for example, to recognize what is a primary as opposed to a secondary establishment in the case of the registered office of a company and one of its subsidiaries or its branches, than it is in the case of a professional who has two places of practice in two different Member States. Further, despite the many directives on company law which have been adopted, considerable differences between the Member States remain in the way they regulate companies and their activities.

The definition of a company in Article 58 is broad and open-ended, referring to 'legal persons governed by private or public law', but it excludes non-profit-making companies. This exclusion is consistent with the exclusion from the scope of Article 48 of workers who are not remunerated, and services which are not provided for remuneration from the scope of Article 59, and it reflects what is still, despite the changes made in other areas by the TEU, the essentially commercial focus of the free movement provisions.[88]

It is clear that, so long as a company is formed in accordance with the law of a Member State and has its registered office there and its principal place of business *somewhere* in the Community, it will be established in the first Member State within the meaning of Articles 52 and 58. The Court made it clear in the case of *Segers* that this would hold true even if the company conducted no business of any kind in that Member State, but instead conducted its business through one of the various forms of secondary establishment—such as a subsidiary, branch, or agency—in another Member State.[89] In the *Insurance Services* case, the Court held that even an office managed for a company by an independent person on a permanent basis would amount to establishment in that Member State.[90] This latter form of establishment would amount to a secondary establishment, since the registered office or seat of the company, and its principal place of business, would presumably be elsewhere in the Community. A company only has a right of secondary establishment if it already has its principal place of business, or central or registered office within the Community.

Many of the cases which have come before the Court concerned restrictions or disadvantages imposed by Member States on companies whose registered offices were in a different Member State. In *Commission* v. *France*, the Court drew an analogy between the location of the registered office of a company and the place of residence of a natural person.[91] It ruled in the proceedings against France that discrimination in tax laws against branches or agencies in a Member State, by on the one hand taxing them on the same basis as

[88] The fact that a company is non-profit-making does not, however, mean that it is not engaged in economic activity. For an illustration of this point in a different context see Case C–382/92, *Commission* v. *UK* [1994] ECR I–2435, para. 45.

[89] Case 79/85, n. 85 above, para. 16.

[90] Case 205/84, n. 5 above, para. 21.

[91] Case 270/83, n. 5 above, para. 18.

companies whose registered office is in that state yet on the other hand not giving them the same tax advantages as such companies, was an infringement of Article 52. Neither the lack of harmonization of the tax laws of the different Member States (e.g. the possibility that the tax position of the company was more favourable in the Member State in which it was registered) nor the risk of tax avoidance by companies could justify the restriction. According to the Court, Article 52 'expressly leaves traders free to choose the appropriate legal form in which to pursue their activities in another Member State and that freedom of choice must not be limited by discriminatory tax provisions'.[92] However, the Court did not rule out the possibility that a distinction based on the location of the registered office of a company or the place of residence of a natural person could, under certain conditions, be justified in an area such as tax law.[93]

In *Segers*, the Court ruled that, where a company had exercised its right of establishment under the Treaty, Articles 52 and 58 prohibited the Member States from excluding the company's director from a national sickness insurance benefit scheme solely on the ground that the company was formed in accordance with the law of another Member State where it also had its registered office but did not carry on any business.[94] Again, in this case, the discrimination or disadvantage was on the ground that the registered office of the company was not within the Member State in question.[95] And although the discrimination was practised against the manager, rather than against the company, the Court ruled that 'discrimination against employees in connection with social security protection indirectly restricts the freedom of companies of another Member State to establish themselves through an agency, branch or subsidiary'.[96] Nor was the discrimination justified under Article 56 on the ground of the need to combat fraud, because the Court held that the refusal of sickness benefit was not an appropriate means of preventing fraud.

In other cases, the alleged discrimination against a company which had its registered office or primary place of establishment in another Member State was not as in the cases of *France* and *Segers*, but rather indirect or covert. In the *Clinical Biology Services* case discussed above, the Commission claimed

[92] *Ibid.*, para. 22. See also Case C–330/91, *R.* v. *Inland Revenue Commissioners, ex p. Commerzbank AG* [1993] ECR I–4017, [1993] 3 CMLR 457 in which the ECJ held that tax disadvantages imposed on a company not on the basis of its seat, but on the basis of its fiscal residence were indirectly discriminatory, since in practice most companies are fiscally resident in the state in which they have their seat. See also Case C–1/93, *Halliburton Services BV* v. *Staatssecretaris van Financiën* [1994] ECR I–1137, [1994] 3 CMLR 377.

[93] [1986] ECR 273, para. 19. For an example of tax treatment which differentiated on the basis of the place of residence of a natural person, yet which was compatible with Art. 52, see case C–112/91, n. 82 above, and text.

[94] Case 79/85, n. 85 above, para. 19.

[95] In Case 93/89, *Commission* v. *Ireland* [1991] ECR I–4569, [1991] 3 CMLR 697, there was a breach of Art. 52 where the state required nationals of other Member States who owned a vessel registered in Ireland to set up and establish a company in Ireland. However, this is really a restriction on individuals, rather than a restriction on a company which is established in another Member State.

[96] [1986] ECR 2375, para. 15.

that Belgian social-security legislation, which effectively required all members, partners, or directors of companies which operated a laboratory providing clinical biology services to be persons who were authorized to carry out medical analyses, was incompatible with Article 52 and 58.[97] The Commission argued that the effect of this legislation was that it was impossible for companies established in any other Member State to set up secondary establishments, such as a branch or a subsidiary company, in Belgium. The legislation was very unlikely to affect laboratories whose primary establishment was in Belgium, since the company's medically qualified personnel would in all probability be based there. Surprisingly, the Court found that there was neither direct nor indirect discrimination,[98] but the ruling might also be explained on the basis that the restrictive effect on companies whose primary establishment was not in Belgium was in any case justified in the interests of protecting public health, in that it prevented excessive recourse to clinical biology testing.[99]

However, in a subsequent case, the Court looked more closely at a restriction which on its face was not discriminatory, since it 'applied without distinction' to companies registered in the Member State and those registered elsewhere.[100] The Commission argued to the Court that it was indirectly discriminatory and not justified under Article 56:

Case 3/88, Commission v. Italy
[1989] ECR 4035, [1991] 2 CMLR 115

The Commission brought proceedings under Article 169 against Italy on the basis that Italian legislation, providing that only companies in which the state owned a majority of the shares could obtain state contracts for developing data-processing systems for public authorities, was contrary to Articles 52 and 59 of the Treaty. The Italian Government argued that the laws made no distinction on the basis of the nationality of companies which could conclude the contracts, and that the Italian State owned shares not only in Italian companies but also in companies of other Member States.

THE ECJ

9. Although the laws and decree-laws in issue apply without distinction to all companies, whether of Italian or foreign nationality, they essentially favour Italian companies. As the Commission has pointed out, without being contradicted by the Italian Government, there are at present no data-processing companies from other Member States all or the majority of whose shares are in Italian public ownership.

10. In justification of the public ownership requirement, the Italian Government claims that it is necessary for the public authorities to control the performance of the contracts in order to adapt the work to meet developments which were unforeseen at the time when the contracts were signed. It also claims that for certain types of activity which the companies have to carry out, particularly in strategic

[97] Case 221/85, n. 46 above. [98] *Ibid.*, para. 11. [99] *Ibid.*, para. 8.
[100] See also Case C–272/91, n. 20 above.

sectors, which involve, as in the present case, confidential data, the State must be able to employ an undertaking in which it can have complete confidence.

11. In that regard it must be stated that the Italian Government had sufficient legal powers at its disposal to be able to adapt the performance of contracts to meet future and unforeseeable circumstances and to ensure compliance with the general interest, and that in order to protect the confidential nature of the data in question the Government could have adopted measures less restrictive of freedom of establishment and freedom to provide services than those in issue, in particular by imposing a duty of secrecy on the staff of the companies concerned, breach of which might give rise to criminal proceedings. There is nothing in the documents before the court to suggest that the staff of companies none of whose share capital is in Italian public ownership could not comply just as effectively with such a duty.

The Court also rejected the invocation of the public-policy exception under Article 56, given the nature of the data in question. It took the view that any possible threat to public policy, if companies from other Member States were awarded the contracts, could be averted by the imposition of a duty of secrecy to preserve the confidential nature of data, without needing to restrict freedom of establishment.

Thus indirect discrimination against a company which is not registered in the Member State in question is also prohibited by Articles 52 and 58. However, can a company whose registered office is in fact in a particular Member State invoke those provisions to challenge national legislation which allegedly restricts its freedom of establishment? In the case of *Fearon*, the Court appeared to reject this suggestion.[101] Robert Fearon & Co. was registered under Irish law as an Irish company, but wished to challenge a provision of the Land Acts under which it was denied the benefit of an exception to the powers of compulsory acquisition of land. The exception was only available to companies all of whose members and shareholders resided on or within three miles of the land. Fearon & Co. could not benefit from the exception since several of its members lived in England, and it argued that the legislation was in breach of Article 58 of the Treaty. The Court, however, viewed the situation as an internal one, rather as it had in the *Niño* case concerning natural persons,[102] and ruled that Article 58 was not applicable to the situation:

As the Commission rightly points out, Article 58 of the Treaty, to which the national court's question refers, does not govern the solution of the matter in litigation in the main proceedings. The effect of that article is to assimilate, for the purposes of giving effect to the chapter relating to the right of establishment, companies or firms formed in accordance with the law of a Member State and having their registered office, central administration or principal place of business within the Community, to natural persons who are nationals of one of the Member

[101] Case 182/83, n. 49 above.

[102] Cases 54 and 91/88 and 14/89, n. 80 above and text.

> States. In this case, Fearon & Company Limited is an Irish company for the purposes of Article 58 of the EEC Treaty, it cannot claim in Ireland the benefit of the right of establishment granted to companies formed under the laws of other Member States.[103]

As was seen from the discussion above, however, the Court went on to consider the applicability of Article 52 to the situation of the shareholders as natural persons, rather than to the situation of the company. Ultimately the Court concluded that, although the individual shareholders' right to participate in a company was restricted by the residence requirement, that restriction did not infringe Article 52 since it was applied to nationals and non-nationals alike in pursuance of a legitimate national policy.[104]

The *Fearon* ruling does not, however, mean that a company registered in a Member State can never invoke the provisions on freedom of establishment to challenge a national rule. Just as in the case of natural persons established in their own Member State who may invoke Article 52 if there is a 'Community element' in the case, a registered company can invoke the Treaty provisions to challenge a national rule which, for example, restricts its ability to set up a second establishment in another Member State. If a national rule sought to prevent a company which was registered in its territory from establishing a branch or an agency in another Member State, Articles 52 and 58 could be invoked by the company. Although companies are not covered by Directive 73/148, Article 2 of which guarantees to natural persons the right to leave their Member State, they have been held to have similar rights under the provisions of the Treaty itself.

This much is made clear in the *Daily Mail* case.[105] However, that case also indicates that there are limits to the freedom accorded at this stage, under the Treaty, to companies registered in one Member State to move to another Member State. In particular, the Treaty provisions on freedom of establishment do not give companies the right, without any restriction or impediment from the Member State in which they are registered, to move their registered office or their central management and control to another Member State, whilst retaining an establishment in the first Member State. That is not to say that a company does not have the right under Community law to move its registered office or its central place of administration, for example, to a state in which the tax position would be more favourable, but simply that it may in doing so be subject to the conditions and restrictions laid down by the Member State from which it wishes to move. The reason for this is that the laws of the Member States on what constitutes the place of incorporation or

[103] [1984] ECR 3677, para. 8.

[104] Contrast case C–221/89 n. 1 above, where the nationality and residence requirements for the shareholders and directors of a company who wished to own and register a ship in a Member State did unjustifiably infringe Art. 52.

[105] Case 81/87, *R.* v. *HM Treasury and Commissioners of Inland Revenue, ex p. Daily Mail and General Trust PLC* [1988] ECR 5483, [1988] 3 CMLR 713.

the real head office of the company are not harmonized, and have not been the subject of Community directives, so that different Member States may legitimately have different views and different ways of regulating how a transfer of head office may be effected:[106]

Case 81/87, R. v. H.M. Treasury and Commissioners of Inland Revenue, ex parte Daily Mail and General Trust PLC [1988] ECR 5483, [1988] 3 CMLR 713

Under United Kingdom law, companies resident outside the United Kingdom were liable to tax only on income arising in the United Kingdom (there was no advance corporation tax or tax on capital gains), residence being defined as having central management and control of trade business exercised in the United Kingdom. Daily Mail, which was a company resident in the United Kingdom, wished to transfer its residence to The Netherlands and to set up a subsidiary or branch in the United Kingdom instead. Permission to make such a transfer was required by statute to be sought from the Treasury, which could require Daily Mail first to liquidate some of its assets. The company challenged the requirement of permission before the High Court, arguing that, since the transfer of central management and control to The Netherlands constituted a transfer of establishment, the requirement of consent from the Treasury was a restriction on its freedom of establishment, contrary to Article 52 and 58 of the Treaty.

THE ECJ

16. Even though those provisions are directed mainly to ensuring that foreign nationals and companies are treated in the same way as nationals of that State, they also prohibit the Member State of origin from hindering the establishment in another Member State of one of its nationals or of a company incorporated under its legislation which comes within the definition contained in Article 58 . . . In regard to natural persons, the right to leave their territory for that purpose is expressly provided for in Directive 73/148 . . .

17. In the case of a company, the right of establishment is generally exercised by the setting-up of agencies, branches or subsidiaries, as is expressly provided for in the second sentence of the first paragraph of Article 52 . . . A company may also exercise its right of establishment by taking part in the incorporation of a company in another Member State, and in that regard Article 221 of the Treaty ensures that it will receive the same treatment as nationals of that Member State as regards participation in the capital of the new company.

18. The provision of United Kingdom law at issue in the main proceedings imposes no restriction on transactions such as those described above. Nor does it stand in the way of a partial or total transfer of the activities of a company incorporated in the United Kingdom to a company newly incorporated in another Member State, if necessary after winding-up and, consequently, the settlement of the tax position of the United Kingdom company. It requires Treasury consent only where such a company seeks to transfer its central management and control

[106] Art. 220 EC recognizes the need for the adoption of agreements for the mutual recognition of companies and the retention of legal personality in the event of transfer of their seat from one country to another, but the Convention on the Mutual Recognition of Companies, which was adopted pursuant to this Art. in 1968, has not come into force.

out of the United Kingdom while maintaining its status as a United Kingdom company.

19. In that regard it should be borne in mind that, unlike natural persons, companies are creatures of the law and, in the present state of Community law, creatures of national law. They exist only by virtue of the varying national legislation which determines their incorporation and functioning.

20. As the Commission has emphasized, the legislation of the Member States varies widely in regard to both the factor providing a connection to the national territory required for the incorporation of a company and the question whether a company incorporated under the legislation of a Member State may subsequently modify that connecting factor. Certain states require that not merely the registered office but also the real head office, that is to say the central administration of the company, should be situated on their territory, and the removal of the central administration from that territory thus presupposes the winding-up of the company, with all the consequences that winding-up entails in company law and tax law. The legislation of other States permits companies to transfer their central administration to a foreign country but certain of them, such as the United Kingdom, make that right subject to certain restrictions, and the legal consequences of a transfer, particularly in regard to taxation, vary from one Member State to another.

. . .

23. It must therefore be held that the Treaty regards the differences in national legislation concerning the required connecting factor and the question whether—and if so how—the registered office or real head office of a company incorporated under national law may be transferred from one Member State to another as problems which are not resolved by the rules concerning the right of establishment but must be dealt with by future legislation or conventions.

24. Under those circumstances, Articles 52 and 58 of the Treaty cannot be interpreted as conferring on companies incorporated under the law of a Member State a right to transfer their central management and control and their central administration to another Member State while retaining their status as companies incorporated under the legislation of another Member State.

3. FREE MOVEMENT OF SERVICES

If the right of establishment entails the pursuit of an economic activity from a fixed base in a Member State for an indefinite period, the freedom to provide services by contrast entails the carrying out of an economic activity for a temporary period in a Member State in which either the provider or the recipient of the service is not established. Indeed, if a person or an undertaking maintains a permanent base in a Member State, even if only an office, it cannot avail itself of the right to provide services in that state but will be governed by the provisions on freedom of establishment.[107] Further, the Court

[107] Case 205/84, n. 5 above, para. 21. Note, however, that the earlier decision in Case 39/75, *Coenen* v. *Sociaal-Economische Raad* [1975] ECR 1547, [1976] 1 CMLR 30 is somewhat contradictory on this point.

has stated that, if someone directs most or all of his or her services at the territory of a particular Member State but keeps his or her place of establishment outside that State in order to evade its professional rules, that person may be treated as being established within the Member State, and thus covered not by Article 59 but by Article 52.[108] This would mean that all of the professional rules which that person was attempting to evade, by keeping a place of establishment in a different Member State, could be applied to them as though they were established in the regulating state.

Article 59 provides:

> Within the framework of the provisions set out below, restrictions on freedom to provide services within the Community shall be progressively abolished during the transitional period in respect of nationals of Member States who are established in a State of the Community other than that of the person for whom the services are intended.
>
> The Council may, acting by a qualified majority on a proposal from the Commission, extend the provisions of this Chapter to nationals of a third country who provide services and who are established within the Community.

In order to avail him or herself of the right to provide services. Article 59 indicates that the person in question, natural or legal, must already have a place of establishment in the Community. This point is emphasized in the General Programme on freedom to provide services, which stipulates that the right to provide services shall be available only to nationals who are established in the Community, or to companies formed under the laws of a Member State and having their seat, centre of administration, or main establishment within the Community.[109] If only the seat of a company is situated within the Community, the General Programme requires that its activity should have a real and continuous link with the economy of a Member State, other than a link of nationality. Without that economic foothold within the Community, there is no right under Community law for a Community national or a company established outside the Community to provide temporary services within the Community. What he or she must first do is to set up an establishment in one of the Member States, and then, from that established base, he or she may provide temporary services in other Member States.

Article 60 provides:

> Services shall be considered to be 'services' within the meaning of this Treaty where they are normally provided for remuneration, in so far as they are not

[108] Case 33/74, Van Binsbergen n. 3 above, para. 13. See also Case 205/84, n. 5 above, para. 22. For an example of a justified state restriction to prevent an abuse where a provider of services was established outside The Netherlands in order to evade broadcasting regulations, yet was directing its services at The Netherlands, see Cases C–148/91, *Vereniging Veronica Omroep Organisatie* v. *Commissariaat voor de Media* [1993] ECR I–487 and C–23/93, *TV10 SA* v. *Commissariaat voor de Media*, 5 Oct. 1994.

[109] See the 1961 General Programme, n. 23 above.

governed by the provisions relating to freedom of movement for goods, capital and persons.

'Services' shall in particular include

(a) activities of an industrial character;
(b) activities of a commercial character;
(c) activities of craftsmen;
(d) activities of the professions.

Without prejudice to the provisions of the Chapter relating to the right of establishment, the person providing a service may, in order to do so, temporarily pursue his activity in the State where the service is to be provided, under the same conditions as are imposed by that State on its own nationals.

Article 60 first makes it clear that services must be paid for if they are to fall within this part of the Treaty. Secondly, it appears to indicate that what the freedom to provide services requires is equal treatment or non-discrimination on grounds of nationality, and this is partly supported by Article 65, which provides that 'as long as restrictions on freedom to provide services have not been abolished, each Member State shall apply such restrictions without distinction on grounds of nationality or residence'. Thirdly, Article 60 refers only to the provider moving to the Member State in which the service is provided, and does not expressly cover the situation of a person travelling to another Member State in order to receive services there.[110]

Article 60 makes it clear that the provisions on free movement of services will only apply in so far as a particular restriction is not covered by the provisions on free movement of goods, persons, or capital. Article 61 also excludes transport services from the chapter on services since transport is dealt with elsewhere in the Treaty,[111] and provides that banking and insurance services connected with capital movements are to be dealt with in line with the Treaty provisions on movement of capital.[112] The 'official authority' exception and the public policy, security, and health derogations provided for in Articles 55 and 56 in the context of establishment are made applicable to the free movement of services by Article 66. These derogations, as in the case of workers and establishment, are regulated by the provisions of Directive 64/221.[113]

Like Article 54 in the chapter on establishment, Article 63 provides for a General Programme to be drawn up, and for directives to be issued by the Council so as to liberalize specific services. The General Programme was drawn up and adopted at the same time as that on establishment, and its provisions are very similar, setting out two lists of the sorts of restrictions which are to be abolished: those which impose restrictions and conditions on the actual provision of the service, and those which limit the powers normally enjoyed by a self-employed person engaged in such activity. As in the case of

[110] See below, 757–8.
[111] See Arts. 74–84 EC.
[112] See now Arts. 73(a)–(h), and, prior to the TEU, Arts. 67–73 on capital and payments.
[113] See Ch. 17.

the General Programme on establishment, the emphasis in the programme on the provision of services is on the abolition of discrimination.

(a) The effect of Article 59

In many ways, then, the chapter on the provision of services appears very similar to that on establishment, except that the activity in question is pursued on a temporary rather than a permanent basis in a Member State. Shortly after the *Reyners* case first established that Article 52 was directly effective, the *Van Binsbergen* case in which the direct effect of Article 59 was in issue came before the Court.[114] The United Kingdom and Irish Governments intervened to argue, despite the conclusion in *Reyners* on Article 52, that the area of provision of services was subject to even greater problems of control and discipline than that of establishment. They argued for this reason that Articles 59 and 60 should not be held to have direct effect, and the only satisfactory method of resolving the problems was by the passing of directives as provided for under Articles 63(2) and 57(1):

Case 33/74, Van Binsbergen v. Bestuur van de Bedrijfsvereniging voor de Metaalnijverheid
[1974] ECR 1299, [1975] 1 CMLR 289

A Dutch national acting as legal adviser to Van Binsbergen, in respect of proceedings before a Dutch social security court, transferred his place of residence from The Netherlands to Belgium during the course of the proceedings. He was told that he could no longer represent his client since, under Dutch law, only persons established in The Netherlands could act as legal advisers. He invoked Article 59, and a reference was made to the Court to determine whether Article 59 had direct effect, and whether the Dutch rule was compatible with the prohibition in Articles 59 and 60 on restrictions on the freedom to provide services.

THE ECJ

20. With a view to the progressive abolition during the transitional period of the restrictions referred to in Article 59, Article 63 has provided for the drawing up of a 'general programme'—laid down by Council Decision of 18 December 1961—to be implemented by a series of directives.

21. Within the scheme of the chapter relating to the provision of services, these directives are intended to accomplish different functions, the first being to abolish, during the transitional period, restrictions on freedom to provide services, the second being to introduce into the law of Member States a set of provisions intended to facilitate the effective exercise of this freedom, in particular by the mutual recognition of qualifications and the coordination of laws with regard to the pursuit of activities as self-employed persons.

22. These directives also have the task of resolving the specific problems resulting from the fact that where the person providing the service is not established, on a habitual basis, in the State where the service is performed he may not be fully subject to the professional rules of conduct in force in that State.

[114] Case 33/74, n. 3 above.

> . . .
>
> 24. The provisions of Article 59, the application of which was to be prepared by directives issued during the transitional period, therefore became unconditional on the expiry of that period.
>
> 25. The provisions of that article abolish all discrimination against the person providing the service by reason of his nationality or the fact that he is established in a Member State other than that in which the service is to be provided.
>
> 26. Therefore, at least as regards the specific requirement of nationality or of residence, Articles 59 and 60 impose a well-defined obligation, the fulfilment of which by the Member States cannot be delayed or jeopardized by the absence of provisions which were to be adopted in pursuance of powers conferred under Articles 63 and 66.

What the Court did in this case was to examine the reason for the provisions of the Treaty on the adoption of directives, which it identified as being twofold: first, a negative function in abolishing restrictions and, secondly, a positive function in facilitating the freedom to provide services. An example of the latter would be the adoption of directives to harmonize or provide for mutual recognition of qualifications. In so far as the first was concerned, where the restriction was a straightforward one on the ground of nationality, or on the ground of the place of establishment, the Court considered that no directive could be necessary before a national whose freedom to provide services had been restricted could rely on the provisions of Article 59 itself. By the end of the transitional period, it had become effective. The residence requirement in this case was a particularly straightforward infringement of that provision:

> 11. In particular, a requirement that the person providing the service must be habitually resident within the territory of the State where the service is to be provided may, according to the circumstances, have the result of depriving Article 59 of all useful effect, in view of the fact that the precise object of that Article is to abolish restrictions on freedom to provide services imposed on persons who are not established in the State where the service is to be provided.

It will be noted that the lawyer in this case was a national who sought to rely, in the Member State of his own nationality, on the provisions of Article 59. Unlike in the case of establishment, this is not problematic since Article 59, by contrast with Article 52, does not expressly restrict its coverage to the situation of a national in a Member State other than that of her nationality. Instead, the relevant factor for the application of Article 59 is that the provider must be established in a Member State other than that of the person for whom the service is to be provided, which was true of the lawyer and his client in the *Van Binsbergen* case.

(b) The Scope of Article 59

(i) The Need for an Inter-State Element As in the context of workers and establishment, however, the provisions of the Treaty on freedom to provide services will not be relevant in what is considered to be a 'wholly internal situation'. The Court made this clear in the case of *Debauve*, in which criminal proceedings were brought against Belgian cable television companies for infringing a prohibition on the transmission of broadcasts of commercial advertisements in Belgium.[115] In its discussion of the scope of application of Article 59, the Court held that 'the provisions of the Treaty on freedom to provide services cannot be applied to activities whose relevant elements are confined within a single Member State'.[116]

In the case of *Koestler*, a bank in France carried out certain stock-exchange orders and account transactions for a customer established in France.[117] From these facts alone, given that both the provider and the recipient of services were established in the same Member State, it might be thought that there could be no inter-state provision of services such as would attract the application of the Treaty provisions. However, because the customer moved, before the contractual relationship with the bank was terminated, to establish himself in Germany, the Court ruled that there was a provision of services within the meaning of Article 60.

In the cases of *Coditel*[118] and *Bond*,[119] which, like *Debauve*, concerned the provision of broadcasting services, the Court was specifically asked whether there could be a provision of services within the meaning of the Treaty where the providers and recipients were firmly established in the same Member State. It will be remembered that Article 59 refers to a provider who is established 'in a State of the Community other than that of the person for whom the services are intended'. This requirement did not appear to be fulfilled on the facts as presented by the national courts in these two cases, but there was a certain inter-state element, in that the substance of the services, the cable television broadcasts, originated in another Member State.

In *Coditel*, a Belgian distribution company brought an action against a Belgian cable television company for damage caused through breach of its exclusive distribution rights for a certain film in Belgium. The film was transmitted in Germany but had been picked up in Belgium by subscribers to the cable company, and the cable company relied in its defence on Articles 59 to 60 of the Treaty. Since both recipients and providers of the broadcasting service appeared to be established in the same Member State, the Court was asked whether the Treaty provisions were applicable to the situation. The Court chose to answer first the second question which had been referred,

[115] Case 52/79, n. 7 above. [116] *Ibid.*, para. 9.

[117] Case 15/78, *Société Générale Alsacienne de Banque SA* v. *Koestler* [1978] ECR 1971, [1979] 1 CMLR 89.

[118] Case 62/79, *Compagnie Générale pour la Diffusion de la Télévision, Coditel* v. *SA Ciné Vog Films* [1980] ECR 881, [1981] 2 CMLR 362.

[119] Case 352/85, n. 9 above.

namely whether Articles 59 and 60 permitted the holder of an exclusive performing right to prevent the transmission of a film when it has been picked up from a lawful broadcast in another Member State. Having ruled that a restriction of this kind, which arose out of national legislation for the protection of industrial property rights and which was not intended as a market-dividing barrier, was not contrary to Article 59, the Court decided not to address the first question at all.[120]

Another opportunity to address the question arose in the case of *Bond*, but although Advocate General Mancini gave his opinion on the matter, the Court again avoided the question:

Case 352/85, Bond van Adverteerders v. Netherlands
[1988] ECR 2085, [1989] 3 CMLR 113

An association of Dutch advertisers and several advertising groups brought an application in the Hague District Court for the suspension of certain restrictive broadcasting regulations which were applied to them. The rules were designed to prohibit the distribution by cable of radio and television programmes transmitted from other Member States, which contained advertising intended especially for the public in the Netherlands, or which contained subtitles in Dutch. One of the questions the Court of Justice was asked was whether there was a provision of services within Article 59, when cable operators established in a Member State, whose customers or subscribers were also within that Member State, received programmes supplied from abroad via cable.

THE ECJ

14. It must be held that the transmission of programmes at issue involves at least two separate services. The first is provided by the cable network operators established in one Member State to the broadcasters established in other Member States and consists of relaying to network subscribers the television programmes sent to them by the broadcasters. The second is provided by the broadcasters established in certain Member States to advertisers established in particular in the Member State where the programmes are received, by broadcasting advertisements which the advertisers have prepared especially for the public in the Member State where the programmes are received.

15. Each of those services are transfrontier services for the purposes of Article 59 of the Treaty. In each case the suppliers of the service are established in a Member State other than that of certain of the persons for whom it is intended.

16. The two services in question are also provided for remuneration within the meaning of Article 60 of the Treaty. Firstly, the cable network operators are paid, in the form of fees which they charge their subscribers, for the service which they provide for the broadcasters. It is irrelevant that the broadcasters generally do not themselves pay the cable network operators for relaying their programmes. Article 60 does not require the service to be paid for by those for whom it is performed. Secondly, the broadcasters are paid by the advertisers for the service which they perform for them in scheduling their advertisements.

[120] [1980] ECR 831, paras. 10 and 15.

ADVOCATE GENERAL MANCINI

It appears to me that in . . . *Luisi and Carbone* . . . the Court recognized that, in order for Article 59 *et seq.* to apply, the provision of services need not necessarily cross a frontier and may well be carried out in all its elements within the frontiers of a single Member State. In my opinion in that case I argued with particular regard to tourism, medical treatment and education that the provisions on freedom of movement are addressed not only to providers of services but also to users . . . . Compared with the activities I have just mentioned, television is different only in so far as neither the provider nor the user is compelled to move. It is different in that regard only because, owing to its indivisible nature and its ability to be enjoyed at increasing distances from the State in which the programmes are broadcast, it is a provision of services which is neither domestic nor trans-frontier but—and this is the definitive outcome of research—a provision of services which is without frontiers.[121]

Advocate General Mancini's argument is an innovative one, focusing not on the provider and the recipient, nor on the requirement in Article 59 that each should be established in a different Member State, but instead on the nature of the services themselves as being capable of transcending frontiers. The Court, however, chose not to adopt this approach in the case, and it relied instead on a traditional analysis by identifying two separate examples of a provider and a recipient established in different Member States.

(ii) The Freedom to Receive Services Article 59 expressly refers to the freedom to *provide* services, and Article 60 to the rights of the *provider* of services, but makes no mention of the recipient of the services. However, Article 1 of Directive 64/221, which regulates the public-policy, security, and health derogations provided for in Articles 56 and 66 of the Treaty, protects the position of a recipient of services who resides in or travels to another Member State for that purpose.[122] Article 1(b) of Directive 73/148 also requires the abolition of restrictions on the movement and residence of 'nationals wishing to go to another Member State as recipients of services'. It was not until its ruling in *Luisi and Carbone* that the Court confirmed that the Treaty Articles themselves extended to cover the situation of recipients as well as providers of services:

Case 286/82 and 26/83, Luisi and Carbone v. Ministero del Tesoro [1984] ECR 377, [1985] 3 CMLR 52.

Luisi and Carbone were two Italian residents who were fined for exceeding the maximum permitted amount of foreign currency which could be exported from Italy for use abroad. They argued that, as they had exported the currency in order to pay for services as tourists and for medical treatment in another Member State, the currency restrictions were contrary to Community law. The Court was asked

121 [1988] ECR 2085, 2114. 122 See Ch. 17.

whether the circumstances fell within Articles 67 and 68 of the Treaty on movements of capital, which were not then subject to compulsory liberalization, or whether they were covered by the rules on the liberalization of payments connected with the provision of services under Article 106(1) and Articles 59 and 60 of the Treaty.

THE ECJ

10. By virtue of Article 59 of the Treaty, restrictions on freedom to provide such services are to be abolished in respect of nationals of Member States who are established in a Member State other than that of the person for whom the service is intended. In order to enable services to be provided, the person providing the services may go to the Member State where the person for whom it is provided is established or else the latter may go to the State in which the person providing the service is established. Whilst the former case is expressly mentioned in the third paragraph of Article 60, which permits the person providing the service to pursue his activity temporarily in the Member State where the service is provided, the latter case is the necessary corollary thereof, which fulfils the objective of liberalizing all gainful activity not covered by the free movement of goods, persons and capital.

. . .

14. Among the restrictions on the freedom to provide services which must be abolished, the General Programme mentions, in section C of Title III, impediments to payments for services, particularly where, according to section D of Title III and in conformity with Article 106(2), the provision of such services is limited only by restrictions in respect of the payments therefor . . . Those provisions were implemented by Council Directive 63/340/EEC of 31 May 1963 on the abolition of all prohibitions on or obstacles to payments for services where the only restrictions on exchange of services are those governing such payments . . .

15. However, both the General Programme and the aforesaid directive reserve the right for Member States to verify the nature and genuineness of transfers of funds and of payments and to take all necessary measures in order to prevent contravention of their laws and regulations, 'in particular as regards the issue of foreign currency to tourists'.

16. It follows that the freedom to provide services includes the freedom, for the recipients of services, to go to another Member State in order to receive a service there, without being obstructed by restrictions, even in relation to payments and that tourists, persons receiving medical treatment and persons travelling for the purposes of education or business are to be regarded as recipients of services.

This ruling was confirmed in several later judgments, most notably in *Cowan*, in which the Court held that the refusal to compensate a British tourist who had been attacked while in Paris was a restriction within the meaning of Article 59, without specifying exactly what service he had received.[123]

[123] Case 186/87 *Cowan* v. *Le Trésor Public* [1989] ECR 195, [1990] 2 CMLR 613. For an inroad into this extension of the freedom to receive services, see Prot. 1 attached to the EC Treaty by the TEU, preserving Denmark's right to exclude non-nationals from acquiring second homes in Denmark.

iii) The Economic Nature of the Services: Remuneration Whether a provision of services falls within Articles 59 to 60 of the Treaty depends not just on the inter-state element, but also, as Article 60 makes clear, on the services being economic in nature, in that they are provided for remuneration. The Court has ruled that remunerated services do not lose their economic nature either because of an 'element of chance' inherent in the return, or because of the recreational or sporting nature of the services.[124] In *Bond*, above, the Court ruled that the remuneration did not have to come from the recipient of the services, so long as there was remuneration from some party.[125]

But what if the remuneration for the service is provided by the state? This issue arose in the case of *Gravier*, in which the Court was asked whether students receiving vocational training in a Member State other than that of their nationality were recipients of services within the meaning of Article 59.[126] The Court did not address the question in its ruling, but Advocate General Slynn considered that educational services were not remunerated within the meaning of Article 60 if the remuneration came from the state through public taxes. The Court subsequently, in a case concerning a course taught under the national educational system, took a similar view:

Case 263/86, Belgium v. Humbel
[1988] ECR 5365, [1989] 1 CMLR 393.

THE ECJ

17. The essential characteristic of remuneration thus lies in the fact that it constitutes consideration for the service in question, and is normally agreed upon between the provider and the recipient of the service.

18. That characteristic is, however, absent in the case of courses provided under the national education system. First of all, the State, in establishing and maintaining such a system, is not seeking to engage in gainful activity but is fulfilling its duties towards its own population in the social, cultural and educational fields. Secondly, the system in question is, as a general rule, funded from the public purse and not by pupils or their parents.

19. The nature of the activity is not affected by the fact that pupils or their parents must sometimes pay teaching or enrolment fees in order to make a certain contribution to the operating expenses of the system.

Following the logic of this decision, the Court ruled in the case of *Wirth* that, although most institutions of higher education were financed from public funds, those which sought to make a profit and which were financed mainly

124 Case C–275/92, Schindler, n. 8 above, paras. 33–4. See the similar rulings on the concept of an economic activity under Art. 48 in Cases 36/74, Walrave, n. 6 above, and 13/76, *Donà* v. *Mantero* [1976] ECR 1333, [1976] 2 CMLR 578.

125 Case 352/85, n. 9 above.

126 Case 293/83, *Gravier* v. *City of Liège* [1985] ECR 593, 603, [1985] 3 CMLR 1.

out of private funds, for example by students or their parents, could constitute providers of services within Articles 59 and 60.[127]

The reasoning on which these cases are based, which distinguishes service remunerated by the state, such as educational courses, from privately remunerated services, may prove to be problematic. The distinction is based on the assumption that the latter are provided as an economic service for profit, while the former are not provided with a profit motive but as part of the state's social and educational policy. Certainly if the state provides some services such as educational services, totally without charge, it would seem that these could never be seen as being provided on an economic basis with a view to a profit. However, if a service is subsidized by the state rather than provided free, it is possible that it would be considered economic in nature, since the service would also be partly remunerated—and not just by making a contribution, as the Court suggested in paragraph 19 of the judgment in *Humbel*—by the person who pays the subsidized cost of it. Further, although fee-paying schools may be profit-making, the educational motive for providing such services may be as important or more important than the commercial motive. The line between wholly state-funded services and partly state-funded services, or between services which are economic in nature and those which are provided within the context of educational and cultural policy is not a clear one.

The question of remuneration arose less directly in the case of *Grogan*.[128] While the Court held that the provision of a medical service such as abortion for remuneration fell within the scope of Articles 59 and 60,[129] a restriction on the voluntary distribution by student bodies of information about that service in another Member State did not. This was because, on the facts of the case, the student distributors received no payment or other remuneration from the providers of the actual service in the other Member State. In the absence of such an economic link between the restriction on information and the freedom to provide the service, the connection between them was 'too tenuous' to attract the application of Articles 59 and 60.

(iv) Can Illegal Activities Constitute Services within Articles 59–60? Several cases have raised the question of 'illegal' or 'immoral' services, in other words activities which are lawful in certain states but not in others. Clearly if someone established in a Member State in which a particular activity is lawful wishes to provide services in another Member State in which it is not lawful, the second state may have very good reasons for prohibiting or restricting the provision of that service. A first question which the Court has had to address in this context is whether such activities, on whose legality the Member States

[127] Case C–109/92, *Wirth* v. *Landeshauptstadt Hannover* [1993] ECR I–6447.

[128] Case C–159/90, *SPUC* v. *Grogan* [1991] ECR I–4685, [1991] 3 CMLR 849.

[129] On the implications of the possibility that such information could concern publicly rather than privately funded abortions, see S. O'Leary, 'The Court of Justice as a Reluctant Constitutional Adjudicator' (1992) 17 ELRev. 138.

cannot agree, can constitute 'services' in Community law, so as to bring them within the scope of Articles 59 and 60.

In *Koestler*, the Court ruled that Germany's refusal to allow a French bank which had provided services for a German national, including a stock-exchange transaction which was treated as an illegal wagering contract in Germany but not in France, to recover from that client was not contrary to Article 59 if the same refusal would apply to banks established in Germany.[130] However, the fact that the services were considered to be illegal in Germany did not lead the Court to say that Article 59 did not apply to the situation. Instead, it was held that the conclusion of the wagering contract could constitute a service, but the regulating Member State would be justified in refusing to allow the bank to sue for recovery because of the illegality of the contract in that state.

In *Grogan*, the Court was asked to rule on whether the provision of abortion was a service within the meaning of the Treaty, in order to determine whether the restriction in one Member State on information about the provision of abortion in another state was contrary to Article 59.[131] In response to the argument of one of the parties that abortion could not be categorized as a service on the ground that it was immoral, the Court ruled that it was not for it 'to substitute its assessment for that of the legislature in those Member States where the activities are practiced legally'.[132] However, the fact that abortion constitutes a service within the meaning of the Treaty does not mean that a Member State in which that activity is illegal may not prohibit or restrict the provision of such services in its territory from providers who are established in another Member State, as was made clear in the case of *Koestler*. What is less clear is whether a Member State could, compatibly with the Treaty, refuse to allow its own nationals to travel to another Member State to receive services which are lawfully provided there, but which are illegal in the first Member State. Advocate General Van Gerven in *Grogan* seemed to take the view that this would constitute a disproportionate restriction on the freedom to travel to receive services, but the Court did not rule on the matter.

The recent ruling in *Schindler* confirms the Court's approach in *Grogan* and *Koestler* to services which are not legally performed in all Member States:

Case C–275/92, Customs and Excise v. Schindler
[1994] ECR 1039

The defendants were agents of SKL, a public body responsible for organizing class lotteries on behalf of certain Länder (territories) in Germany, whose job involved promoting and selling tickets for SKL lotteries. The postal authorities in the United Kingdom intercepted a number of envelopes sent from The Netherlands, which contained invitations and application forms to participate in a lottery.

[130] Case 15/78, n. 117 above. [131] Case C–159/90, n. 128 above.
[132] *Ibid.*, para. 20.

When the Schindlers were charged with an offence against United Kingdom legislation governing lotteries, they argued that the legislation was incompatible with the Treaty, and a reference was made to the Court. Five of the eight Member State governments which intervened in the case argued that lotteries were not an 'economic activity' within the meaning of the Treaty, since they were traditionally prohibited or operated by public authorities in the public interest.

THE ECJ

27. The services at issue are those provided by the operator of the lottery to enable purchasers of tickets to participate in a game of chance with the hope of winning, by arranging for that purpose for the stakes to be collected, the draws to be organized and the prizes or winnings to be ascertained and paid out.

28. Those services are normally provided for remuneration constituted by the price of the lottery ticket.

. . .

31. Admittedly, as some Member States point out, lotteries are subject to particularly strict regulation and close control by the public authorities in the various Member States of the Community. However, they are not totally prohibited in those States. On the contrary, they are commonplace. In particular, although in principle lotteries are prohibited in the United Kingdom, small-scale lotteries for charitable and similar purposes are permitted, and, since the enactment of the appropriate law in 1993, so is the national lottery.

32. In these circumstances, lotteries cannot be regarded as activities whose harmful nature causes them to be prohibited in all the Member States and whose position under Community law may be likened to that of activities involving illegal products (see, in relation to drugs, the judgment in Case 294/82, *Einberger* v. *Hauptzollamt Freiburg* [1984] ECR 1177) even though, as the Belgian and Luxembourg Governments point out, the law of certain Member States treats gaming contracts as void. Even if the morality of lotteries is at least questionable, it is not for the Court to substitute its assessment for that of the legislatures of the Member States where the activity is practised legally.

It would seem, then, that provided it is lawful in some Member States (*quaere* whether one Member State would be sufficient), a remunerated activity will constitute a service within the meaning of Article 59 of the Treaty, although other Member States will remain free to regulate and restrict it, so long as they do so without arbitrary discrimination on grounds of nationality or place of establishment.

(v) Are Restrictions on Social Benefits Contrary to Article 59? We have seen in the context of freedom of establishment that, despite the absence of secondary legislation such as Regulation 1612/68 for workers, restrictions on certain social advantages and benefits which are linked to the exercise of the self-employed activity may fall within prohibition in the Treaty. The same is also true of the free movement of services, as the Court has made clear in the Italian housing case, which was discussed above in the context of establish-

ment.[133] The Court ruled that a nationality requirement for access to reduced-rate mortgage loans and to social housing was contrary to Article 52 on freedom of establishment, but the Italian Government argued that access to publicly built housing could not possibly be relevant to the exercise of the right to provide services, since that was precisely the right to do so without having to have a house or place of residence in that state. The Court did not agree:

Case 63/86, Commission v. Italy
[1988] ECR 29, [1989] 2 CMLR 601.

THE ECJ

18. It is true, as the Italian Government has contended, that in practice not all instances of establishment give rise to the same need to find permanent housing and that as a rule that need is not felt in the case of the provision of services. It is also true that in most cases the provider of services will not satisfy the conditions, of a non-discriminatory nature, bound up with the objectives of the legislation on social housing.

19. However, it cannot be held to be *a priori* out of the question that a person, whilst retaining his principal place of establishment in one Member State, may be led to pursue his occupational activities in another Member State for such an extended period that he needs to have permanent housing there and that he may satisfy the conditions of a non-discriminatory nature for access to social housing. It follows that no distinction can be drawn between different forms of establishment and that providers of services cannot be excluded from the benefit of the fundamental principle of national treatment.

Thus, although the Court recognized that it was unlikely that providers of temporary services would satisfy the criteria necessary for eligibility for social housing, it ruled that if they did satisfy such criteria (which were presumably means-based, and dependent on the length of time to be spent in the state) they must be given the benefit of such equal treatment. As in the case of establishment, however, it seems that the benefit in question must be in some way connected with facilitating the pursuit or exercise of the occupation, so that the denial of the benefit actually constitutes an obstacle to its exercise.

In the case of *Cowan*, a British tourist in France was refused state compensation for victims of violent crime, which was available to nationals and to residents.[134] The Court cited the general prohibition on discrimination 'within the scope of application of this Treaty' in Article 6 (formerly Article 7) thereof,[135] and referred to its ruling in *Luisi and Carbone*, to the effect that tourists were covered by Article 59 as recipients of services:

[133] Case 63/86, *Commission* v. *Italy* [1988] ECR 29, [1989] 2 CMLR 601.

[134] Case 186/87, n. 123 above.

[135] For a case in which the ECJ ruled that Art. 7, as it then was, could found a claim for discrimination in treatment, without needing to link it to another specific Treaty provision, see Cases C–92/92 and C–326/92, *Phil Collins* v. *Imtrat Handeslgesellschaft* [1993] ECR I–5145, [1993] 3

> When Community law guarantees a natural person the freedom to go to another Member State, the protection of that person from harm in the Member State in question, on the same basis as that of nationals and persons residing there, is a corollary of that freedom of movement. It follows that the prohibition of discrimination is applicable to recipients of services within the meaning of the Treaty as regards protection against the risk of assault and the right to obtain financial compensation provided for by national law when that risk materialises. The fact that the compensation at issue is financed by the Public Treasury cannot alter the rules regarding the protection of the rights guaranteed by the Treaty.[136]

More recently, in proceedings against Spain, the Court ruled that a system under which Spanish nationals and residents were entitled to free admission into national museums, while other Member State nationals over 21 had to pay an entrance fee, was contrary to Articles 7 and 59 of the Treaty.[137] At first sight, cases like this and like *Cowan* seem to be at odds with *Humbel*, in which the Court ruled that Article 59 did not cover the receipt of state-funded services within the educational, social, and cultural field. Since the state would pay the compensation in *Cowan*, and would presumably fund the museum in the Spanish case, why does a refusal of such benefits constitute a restriction on the freedom to receive services within Articles 59 and 60? The answer would seem to be that the compensation in *Cowan* and the entrance fee in the Spanish case are not in themselves the 'service' being received, and if they were, since they were remunerated by the state, they would not fall within the scope of Article 59. But the services being received in these cases, although they are not specifically identified by the Court, are other services for which, as tourists, the recipients provide remuneration. Presumably the services of hotels, restaurants and other such establishments are the services received by tourists which bring them within the scope of the Treaty. If, whilst in the course of a temporary stay in a Member State in order to receive remunerated services of this nature, such tourists are denied equal treatment with nationals in matters such as compensation for assault and entry fees to museums, they may be able to invoke Article 59 of the Treaty. The denial of such benefits can be seen to be at least loosely linked with the enjoyment of services as a tourist, although in the case of *Cowan* in particular, the link may seem rather tenuous. However, to take a more extreme example, it seems unlikely that if, during the course of a two-month holiday as a tourist in another Member State, a Community national invoked Article 59 to challenge the refusal of admission on equal terms to a three-week educational course which was free for nationals, the Court would find any breach of that provision.

CMLR 773. However, Art. 7 will not apply where another specific Treaty provision such as Art. 52 applies: see Case C–1/93, *Halliburton*, n. 92 above.

[136] [1989] ECR 195, para. 17.

[137] Case C–45/93, *Commission* v. *Spain* [1994] ECR I–911.

(c) Justifying Restrictions on the Free Movement of Services

As in the case of workers and establishment, once a restriction on the freedom to provide services is found to exist, it is open to the Member States to try to justify it on grounds of public policy, security, or health. Article 66 makes those three grounds of exception set out in Article 56 applicable also in the sphere of services. The nature of these exceptions and the secondary legislation relating to them are discussed in more detail in Chapter 17. However, alongside these express exceptions, the Court has also developed a justificatory test similar to the *Cassis de Dijon* 'rule of reason' in the free movement of goods context.[138] The structure of the test is the same in the present context, in that once a non-discriminatory restriction on the free movement of services has been found to exist, that restriction will contravene Article 59 unless it can be shown to be objectively justified in pursuance of a public interest. The origins of this approach in the services context can be seen in the case of *Van Binsbergen*.[139]

It was seen above that in that case the Member States had argued to the Court that there were greater dangers in the area of freedom to provide services than in the area of establishment, since the evasion of national regulation and control would be easier where the providers of services were not resident, or only temporarily rather than permanently present, within the state where the service was provided. These concerns were acknowledged by Advocate General Mayras.

> A fundamental aspect of the difference between, on the one hand, mere occasional provision of services, even temporary activities and, on the other hand, establishment, is that the person providing services falls outside the competence and control of the national authorities of the country where the services are provided.[140]

The Court addressed this issue by indicating that, although a residence requirement would probably be excessive in this case, not every such restriction would be incompatible with Article 59:[141]

> 12. However, taking into account the particular nature of the services to be provided, specific requirements imposed on the person providing the service cannot be considered incompatible with the Treaty where they have as their purpose the application of professional rules justified by the general good—in particular rules relating to the organization, qualifications, professional ethics, supervision and liability—which are binding upon any person established in the State in which the

[138] See Ch. 14. [139] Case 33/74, n. 3 above. [140] [1974] ECR 1299, 1317.

[141] See also Case 39/75, *Coenen*, n. 107 above, para. 9, in which the ECJ ruled that a residence requirement could be justified only where no other less restrictive rule would suffice.

service is provided, where the person providing the service would escape from the ambit of those rules being established in another Member State.

. . .

14. In accordance with those principles, the requirement that persons whose functions are to assist the administration of justice must be permanently established for professional purposes within the jurisdiction of certain courts or tribunals cannot be considered incompatible with the provisions of Article 59 and 60, where such requirement is objectively justified by the need to ensure observance of professional rules of conduct connected, in particular, with the administration of justice and with respect for professional ethics.

It can be seen that several conditions are laid down by the Court in these passages which must be satisfied if a restriction on the freedom to provide services is to be compatible with Article 59. In the *first* place, the restriction must be adopted in pursuance of a legitimate public interest which is not incompatible with Community aims, such as the enforcement of professional rules which are intended to ensure the observance of ethical conduct, proper qualification requirements, and other matters relating to supervision and liability. In the *second* place, they must be rules which are equally applicable to persons established within the state, and which would be evaded if the person providing services was established outside the state.

Thirdly, the Court made clear that the restriction imposed on the provider of services would have to be 'objectively justified' by the need to observe the legitimate professional rules in question. This objective justification involves the application of a proportionality test, looking first to see whether there is a genuine need for the rule, whether it is appropriate in achieving its aim, and whether the interest pursued by the rule could not be satisfied by other, less restrictive means. In *Van Binsbergen* itself, the Court ruled that the public interest in the proper administration of justice could be ensured by requiring an address for service to be maintained within the state, rather than a residence there.

In the subsequent case of *Webb*, the Court elaborated further on the requirement of 'objective justification' of restrictive rules:[142]

Case 279/80, Criminal proceedings against Webb [1981] ECR 3305, [1982] 11 CMLR 719

Webb was the manager of a company established in the United Kingdom, and licensed there to provide manpower. The company was paid for recruiting technical staff and making them available, on a temporary basis, for businesses located in The Netherlands. No contract of employment would exist between the staff and the businesses. Webb was prosecuted for having supplied workers in this way, without possessing a licence issued by the Dutch authorities. On a reference to the

142 See also Cases 110–111/78, *Ministère Public* v. *Van Wesemael* [1979] ECR 35, [1979] 3 CMLR 87.

Court of Justice, the compatibility of the licence requirement with Article 59 was considered.

> THE ECJ
>
> 17. In cases 110 and 11/78 *Van Wesemael* [1979] ECR 35, the Court held that, regard being had to the particular nature of certain services, specific requirements imposed on the provider of the services cannot be considered incompatible with the Treaty where they have as their purpose the application of rules governing such activities. However, the freedom to provide services is one of the fundamental principles of the Treaty and may be restricted only by provisions which are justified by the general good and which are imposed on all persons or undertakings operating in the said State in so far as that interest is not safeguarded by the provisions to which the provider of the service is subject in the Member State of his establishment.

One of the factors to consider in deciding whether a restriction on the provision of services is objectively justified, then, is whether the provider is subject to similar regulations or restrictions in the Member State in which that person is established. If so, then the imposition of a such a requirement duplicates a condition already satisfied, and accordingly, since it is not necessary, it will not be justified. It can also be seen that what might appear to be equal treatment, in the application of the same rules to providers of services established in the host state and those established in other Member States, may be unequal in its application since it forces those established elsewhere to satisfy the same licence requirement or conditions twice. Despite this unequal impact, however, the rules were not perceived by the Court to be deliberately discriminatory, which meant that they could be justified without having to invoke the grounds in Article 56 of the Treaty.[143]

Applying its objective justification test to the licence requirement in *Webb*, the Court held that the provision of manpower was sensitive from an occupational and a social point of view, so that the aims of preserving the interests of the workforce and of ensuring good relations on the labour market were part of a legitimate state policy.[144] Having identified a legitimate aim, the Court considered whether the licence requirement used to pursue that aim were proportionate:

> 20. Such a measure would be excessive in relation to the aim pursued, however, if the requirements to which the issue of a licence is subject coincided with the proofs and guarantees required in the State of establishment. In order to maintain

[143] Case 352/85, n. 9 above. See n. 60 above and text.

[144] Contrast Case C–113/89, *Rush Portuguesa* v. *Office National d'Immigration* [1990] ECR I–1417, [1991] 2 CMLR 818, in which the ECJ ruled that the requirement of work permits for members of staff who were non-member country nationals, of a company providing temporary services in a Member State other than that in which it was established, was incompatible with Art. 59. See also Case C–43/93, *Raymond Vander Elst* v. *Office des Migrations Internationales*, [1994] ECR I–3803. In both cases, however, it was permissible for the host Member State to apply its own labour legislation to these workers.

> the principle of freedom to provide services the first requirement is that in considering applications for licences and in granting them the Member State in which the service is to be provided may not make any distinction based on the nationality of the provider of the services or the place of his establishment; the second requirement is that it must take into account the evidence and guarantees already furnished by the provider of the services for the pursuit of his activities in the Member State of his establishment.

The three conditions of the justificatory test set out in *Van Binsbergen* can be seen clearly here: the restriction must pursue a justified aim, it must be equally applicable to nationals, non-nationals, and those established within and outside the Member State alike, and it must not be more restrictive or burdensome than is necessary. Another way of putting the third condition is that there must be no less restrictive means of achieving the same aim. In particular, a restriction such as a licensing requirement will be unduly burdensome if it duplicates requirements already satisfied in the Member State in which the provider is established. It is possible that a fourth condition of the test is the requirement that the restrictive measure should respect fundamental rights. Certainly when one of the exceptions in Article 56 is invoked in order to justify a restriction on freedom of establishment or freedom to provide services, the Court has ruled that the restriction must also be compatible with the fundamental rights which are protected as part of Community law.[145] Whether or not this requirement will also extend to the justification of indistinctly applicable restrictions on public-interest grounds other than under the express exceptions of Article 56, remains to be seen.[146]

The Court frequently indicates which requirements or restrictions might be disproportionate or unnecessary,[147] although when the issue arises in Article 177 proceedings, the actual application of the proportionality test to the national restriction is often left to the national court, which has all of the relevant facts before it, to determine.[148]

On the other hand, in Article 169 infringement proceedings, when the Court is asked to rule specifically on the compatibility of Member State legislation with Article 59, it will apply the proportionality test directly to the restriction

[145] Case C–260/89, *Elliniki Radiophonia Tileorassi AE* v. *Dimotiki Etairia Pliroforissis and Sotirios Kouvelas* [1991] ECR 2925, [1994] 4 CMLR 540, para. 42.

[146] Van Gerven A.G. in Case C–159/90, n. 128 above, argued that it should. See G. de Búrca, 'Fundamental Human Rights and the Reach of EC law' [1993] O.J.L.S. 283 and the discussion in Ch. 7, 319–21.

[147] See e.g. Case 16/78, *Choquet* [1978] ECR 2293, [1979] 1 CMLR 535, where the ECJ ruled that although the requirement of a domestic driving licence for a Member State national established in another Member State, who already holds a licence in the Member State of origin, was not of itself incompatible with Art. 59, it would fall foul of that provision if it imposed disproportionate conditions, such as the insistence on a driving test which duplicated a test taken in another state, or linguistic difficulties in checking procedures, or exorbitant charges for formalities. See also Case C–76/90, *Säger*, n. 5 above on the provision of patent-renewal services.

[148] See the Opinion of Slynn A.G. in Case 279/80, *Webb* [1981] ECR 3305, 3334, [1982] 1 CMLR 719.

n question.[149] This can be seen in the insurance-services cases, in which an authorization and a residence requirement were imposed on companies established in other Member States which were providing certain kinds of insurance services in Germany:[150]

Case 205/84, Commission v. Germany
[1986] ECR 3755, [1987] 2 CMLR 69

Under provisions of German law, where insurance undertakings in the Community wished to provide certain kinds of direct insurance services in Germany through agents or intermediaries, such undertakings were required to be established and authorised in Germany. Secondly, in its legislation implementing Council Directive 78/473, where co-insurance services were concerned, Germany provided that the leading insurer, in the case of risks situated in Germany, must also be established in Germany and must be authorized as sole insurer of those risks. The Commission argued that these provisions breached Articles 59 and 60 of the Treaty.

THE ECJ

28. It must be stated that the requirements in question in these proceedings, namely that an insurer who is established in another Member State, authorized by the supervisory authority of that State and subject to the supervision of that authority, must have a permanent establishment within the territory of the State in which the service is provided and that he must obtain a separate authorization from the supervisory authority of that State, constitute restrictions on the freedom to provide services in as much as they increase the cost of such services in the State in which they are provided, in particular where the insurer conducts business in that State only occasionally.

29. It follows that those requirements may be regarded as compatible with Articles 59 and 60 of the EEC Treaty only if it is established that in the field of activity concerned there are imperative reasons relating to the public interest which justify restrictions on the freedom to provide services, that the public interest is not already protected by the rules of the State of establishment and that the same result cannot be obtained by less restrictive rules.

The Court accepted that the insurance sector was a sensitive area, that the protection of the policy-holder and the insured person was an important objective, and that the existing co-ordination directives on insurance had not dealt with all important matters concerning the reserves and assets of insurance companies. This meant that the first part of the test for justification was satisfied: there was a legitimate public interest at stake. Since the residence and authorization requirements were non-discriminatory, or 'equally applicable',

[149] See e.g. the Lawyers' Services case, Case 427/85, *Commission* v. *Germany* [1988] ECR 1123, [1989] 2 CMLR 677, para. 26.

[150] See also Case 206/84, *Commission* v. *Ireland* [1986] ECR 3817, [1987] 2 CMLR 150 and cases 220/83, *Commission* v. *France* [1986] ECR 3663, [1987] 2 CMLR 113 and 252/83, *Commission* v. *Denmark* [1986] ECR 3713, [1987] 2 CMLR 169 on life insurance.

the Court went on to the third stage of the proportionality test: did they go beyond what was necessary? The Court ruled that the authorization requirement was justified so long as its conditions did not duplicate those already satisfied in the Member State of establishment. However, the establishment condition did not fare so well. The Court repeated its statement in *Van Binsbergen* that a residence requirement could entirely undermine the aim of Article 59 and that it would have to be shown to be 'indispensable for attaining the objective pursued'.[151] In this case the Court was not convinced that there were no less restrictive means open to the responsible national authorities:

> It must also be shown that those authorities cannot, even under an authorization procedure, carry out their supervisory tasks effectively unless the undertaking has in the aforesaid State a permanent establishment at which all the necessary documents are kept. That has not been shown to be the case.[152]

In the subsequent 'tourist guide' cases, the Court found licence requirements to be disproportionate although they did not necessarily duplicate conditions already satisfied.[153] To take one of the cases as a representative example, Italian law made the provision of services by tourist guides accompanying groups of tourists from another Member State subject to possession of a licence which would be issued after a specific qualifying examination:

> The general interest in consumer protection and in the conservation of the national historical and artistic heritage can constitute an overriding reason justifying a restriction on the freedom to provide services. However, the requirement in question contained in the Italian legislation goes beyond what is necessary to ensure the safeguarding of that interest inasmuch as it makes the activities of a tourist guide accompanying groups of tourists from another Member State subject to possession of a licence.[154]

Given the nature of a tour guide's activities, the Court concluded that the licence requirement could reduce the number of guides qualified to travel with a group, and so could lead a tour operator to have recourse to local guides established in the Member State in which the service is to be performed. This might not be to the benefit of the tourists since they could be deprived of 'a guide who is familiar with their language, their interests and their specific expectations'.[155] In other words, since the restriction could have adverse effects for tourists, it could not really be said to pursue effectively the public interest in consumer protection. The Court also felt that the competition

[151] [1986] ECR 3755, para. 52.

[152] *Ibid.*, paras. 54–5.

[153] See Cases C–180/89, *Commission* v. *Italy* [1991] ECR I–709; C–154/89, *Commission* v. *France* [1991] ECR I–659; C–198/89, *Commission* v. *Greece* [1991] ECR I–727; and C–375/92, *Commission* v. *Spain* [1994] ECR I–923.

[154] Case C–180/89, *Commission* v. *Italy* [1991] ECR I–709.

[155] *Ibid.*, para. 22.

which tour operators faced made it likely that, in the need to maintain their reputation, they would be selective in employing tour guides and in this way would exercise control over the quality of their services. In other words, the danger of under-qualified guides distorting Italian history and culture could be avoided without imposing a restrictive licence requirement.

In a further series of cases which concerned broadcasting restrictions, the Court held that, although the promotion of cultural policy through ensuring a balance of programmes and restricting the content and frequency of advertisements was a legitimate aim, it could not be pursued in a discriminatory or a protectionist manner.[156]

(d) Are Non-Discriminatory Restrictions covered by Article 59?

The cases examined in the last section also raise the question, which was discussed above in relation to establishment, whether truly non-discriminatory restrictions come within the scope of Article 59, and thus need to be subjected to the 'objective justification' test. Several factors appear to lend support to the proposition that non-discriminatory restrictions are within the scope of that Article. In the first place, one of the three conditions we have seen in the test for objective justification is that the restriction must be indistinctly applicable. In the second place, the Court has ruled that Article 59 does not permit Member States to apply all of the rules which are applicable to persons established within the Member State to those who are supplying services on a temporary basis there: 'were it to do so the provisions securing freedom to provide services would be deprived of all practical effect'.[157] However, although it might appear from these statements that even non-discriminatory restrictions will be caught by Article 59, it is often the case, as was seen above in the discussion of establishment, that the equal application of such rules to both categories of person will impose a heavier burden on the non-national or the person who is established in another Member State than on the national or the person domestically established. Thus a licensing requirement which, as in *Webb*, is applied even-handedly to nationals and non-nationals alike, will clearly affect non-nationals in a different way if they have already had to satisfy the conditions for a licence in the Member State of their nationality or of establishment. On examination, it can be seen that most of the services cases mentioned above fall into this category. The restrictions or regulations in question are not intended to be discriminatory—since if they were, only Article 56 could be invoked to justify them—but they inadvertently burden non-nationals and non-established persons more heavily than nationals or established persons.

[156] See Cases 352/85, n. 9 above; C–288/89, *Stichting Collectieve Antennevoorsiening Gouda* v. *Commissariaat voor de Media* [1991] ECR I–4007; and C–353/89, *Commission* v. *Netherlands* [1991] ECR I–4069.

[157] Case C–180/89, n. 153 above, para. 15. See also Cases 279/80, n. 148 above, para. 16; and C–76/90, n. 147 above.

An example of a rule which arguably burdened established providers of services to the same extent as non-established providers, yet which was found to be incompatible with Article 59 can be seen in the case involving the Directive on lawyers' services:[158]

Case 427/85, Commission v. Germany [1988] ECR 1123, [1989] 2 CMLR 677

The Commission brought proceedings against Germany, alleging that its implementation of Directive 77/249 on the effective exercise by lawyers of freedom to provide services was inadequate and in breach of the Treaty. The main argument centred on provisions of the German legislation which implemented the concept of 'work in conjunction' allowed by the Directive, requiring lawyers who were not established in Germany to provide various legal services in conjunction with local lawyers and under specific conditions. One of these provisions contained a rule of territorial exclusivity, which provided that, in order to practise before certain of the higher German courts, a lawyer must first be admitted to practise before that judicial authority. The Commission argued that this rule should not be applied to lawyers established in other Member States who were providing services in Germany.

THE ECJ

38. It appears that this difference of views is concerned essentially with the question whether the Federal Republic of Germany is entitled to impose upon lawyers providing services the same conditions as it applies to German lawyers not admitted to practise before the court in question. The provisions of the Directive do not provide an answer to that question; it must be considered in the light of the principles governing the freedom to provide services deriving from Articles 59 and 60 of the Treaty.

. . .

41. The rule of territorial exclusivity contained in paragraph 52(2) of the Bundesrechtsanwaltsordnung is precisely part of national legislation normally relating to a permanent activity of lawyers established in the territory of the Member State concerned, all such lawyers having the right to gain admission to practise before one, and sometimes two, German judicial authorities, and to pursue before them all the activities necessary for representation of clients or the defence of their interests. On the other hand, a lawyer providing services who is established in another Member State is not in a position to be admitted to practise before a German court.

42. In those circumstances, it must be stated that the rule of territorial exclusivity cannot be applied to the activities of a temporary nature pursued by lawyers established in other Member States, since the conditions of law and fact which apply to those lawyers are not in that respect comparable to those applicable to lawyers established on German territory.

[158] Dir. 77/249: [1977] OJ L78/17. See also Case 292/86, n. 57 above, for discussion of the requirements of the Dir. relating to professional ethics; and more recently case C–294/89, *Commission* v. *France* [1991] ECR I–3591, [1993] 3 CMLR 569.

Unlike the cases of *Webb*,[159] *Van Wesemael*,[160] and *Choquet*,[161] the rule in this case cannot necessarily be said to burden a lawyer established in another Member State more heavily than a lawyer established in Germany, since it does not, for example, duplicate the conditions of a licence requirement already satisfied in the state of establishment. On the other hand, the Court based its reasoning on the fact that a lawyer established in another state was in a different and less advantaged position because that person would not have the advantages of a place of establishment in Germany, yet would be required to go through the procedures for admission to practise there. However, as Advocate General da Cruz Vilaça pointed out, this did not disadvantage the lawyer established in another Member State any more than it would disadvantage German lawyers established and admitted to practise before the judicial authorities in different Länder (territories), from the Land in which the legal service was to be provided. To accept the Commission's argument and to make the territoriality rule inapplicable to non-German-based lawyers would, he felt, give them considerable advantages over lawyers established in Germany. If the Advocate General's analysis of the impact of the rule is accepted, this case provides support for the view that even genuinely non-discriminatory restrictions on the freedom to provide services will breach Article 59 unless objectively justified.

In the case of *Säger* v. *Dennemeyer*, Advocate General Jacobs considered the debate over the scope of Article 59, and in particular the question whether truly non-discriminatory restrictions were covered by that provision, so that they would have to be objectively justified.[162] The case concerned the provision of patent-renewal services in Germany by a company established in England, when under German legislation activities relating to the maintenance of industrial property rights were apparently reserved to patent agents. The United Kingdom had intervened in the case to argue to the Court that Article 59 did not apply to non-discriminatory measures of this kind. Reference was made to the decision in *Koestler*,[163] on which several Member States had relied in support of the proposition that, in the absence of discrimination or unequal application, a restriction would not breach Article 59.[164] Advocate General Jacobs noted that in most of the cases already decided under Article 59 there had been some element of overt or covert discrimination, in other words, that despite the apparently indistinctly applicable rules, some kind of unequal burden had been imposed. However, he went on to consider whether genuinely non-discriminatory restrictions should fall within the scope of Articles 59 to 60:

> It does not seem unreasonable that a person establishing himself in a Member State should as a general rule be required to comply with the law of that State in

[159] Case 279/80, n. 148 above.

[160] Cases 110–111/78, n. 142 above.

[161] Case 16/78, n. 147 above.

[162] Case C–76/90, n. 147 above.

[163] Case 15/78, n. 117 above. See n. 130 above and text. See also the discussion in the Opinion of Gulman A.G. in Case C–275/92, n. 8 above.

[164] Another decision which has been cited in support of this proposition is Case 52/79, n. 7 above, in particular para. 16.

all respects. In contrast, it is less easy to see why a person who is established in one Member State and who provides services in other Member States should be required to comply with all the detailed regulations in force in each of those States. To accept such a proposition would be to render the notion of a single market unattainable in the field of services.

For this reason, it may be thought that services should rather be treated by analogy with goods, and that non-discriminatory restrictions on the free movement of services should be approached in the same way as non-discriminatory restrictions on the free movement of goods under the '*Cassis de Dijon*' line of case-law. That analogy seems particularly appropriate where, as in the present case, the nature of the service is such as not to involve the provider of the service in moving physically between Member States but where instead it is transmitted by post or telecommunications . . .

The truth is that the provision of services covers a vast spectrum of different types of activity. At one extreme, it may be necessary for the provider of the service to spend a substantial period of time in the Member State where the service is provided: for example, an architect supervising the execution of a large building project . . .

At the other extreme, the person providing the service might transmit it in the form of a product: for example, he might provide an educational service by posting a series of books and video-cassettes: here there is an obvious analogy with the free movement of goods, and the case might even be considered to fall under Article 30, rather than under Article 59.

. . . I do not think that it can be right to state as a general rule that a measure lies wholly outside the scope of Article 59 simply because it does not in any way discriminate between domestic undertakings and those established in other Member States. Nor is such a view supported by the terms of Article 59: its expressed scope is much broader. If such a view were accepted, it would mean that restrictions on the freedom to provide services would have to be tolerated, even if they lacked any objective justification, on condition that they did not lead to discrimination against foreign undertakings. There might be a variety of restrictions in different Member States, none of them intrinsically justified, which collectively might wholly frustrate the aims of Article 59 and render impossible the attainment of a single market in services. The principle should, I think, be that if an undertaking complies with the legislation of the Member State in which it is established it may provide services in another Member State, even though the provision of such services would not normally be lawful under the laws of the second Member State. Restrictions imposed by those laws can only be applied against the foreign undertaking if they are justified by some requirement that is compatible with the aims of the Community.[165]

Advocate General Jacobs in this passage recommends an approach to Article 59 which does not look to see whether a restriction unequally burdens a non-national or a provider of services who is established in another Member State, but which simply asks the sort of question which is asked in the free movement of goods context: is this measure a restriction on the free movement of

[165] [1991] ECR I–4221, 4234–5.

inter-state services? If it is, he would apply the proportionality test to see whether the restriction is objectively justified. Jacobs emphasizes the link between the provision of services and the movement of goods in a case such as *Säger*, where the presence of the provider of services in the Member State's territory is not even necessary, and where such services are likely to be provided at the same time in many different Member States which maintain different levels of regulation and control. In such circumstances, he considers that if the provider is already regulated in the Member State in which that person is established, any further restrictions by the Member State in which the services are provided must be shown to be objectively justified if they are to be compatible with Article 59.

It is evident that such an approach by the Court would be an intrusive one, since any national law which regulates the domestic market—and these can often be measures which are not specifically intended to be market-regulating, but rather legislation which pursues other important national policies—will be subjected to rigorous scrutiny by the Court for justification.[166] It is not clear whether the Court will take such an approach, since in most cases there has been an unequal burden or a discriminatory effect of some kind, or a desire to protect some part of the domestic market from foreign competition.[167] Another possible argument against such an approach is that, in the free movement of goods context, the Court has narrowed its approach to the scope of Article 30, so that not every non-discriminatory measure which indirectly affects inter-state trade is to be subjected to the proportionality test, and there are indications that it may apply this approach also in the context of services.[168]

On the other hand, there have been cases in which restrictions which appear to be genuinely non-discriminatory—such as the territoriality rule in the *Lawyers' Services* case—have been held to fall within the scope of Article 59, and the recent ruling on lottery restrictions in *Schindler* supports the view that the Court is taking this approach.[169] The effect of this ruling is that, although such regulation could be justified on grounds of the dangers of fraud and of

[166] Consider, e.g., the restriction on information about abortion in case C–159/90, n. 128 above, which the A.G. but not the ECJ subjected to the test for justification.

[167] See G. Marenco, 'The Notion of a Restriction on the Freedom of Establishment and the Provisions of Services in the Case Law of the Court' (1991) 11 YBEL 111. And see Case C–379/92, *Peralta*, [1994] ECR I–3453, para. 51, where, in the absence of any direct or indirect discrimination or any advantage for domestic interests, Art. 59 was held not to apply to a prohibition on discharging harmful chemicals at sea.

[168] See Case C–267–268/91, *Keck and Mithouard* [1993] ECR I–6097 and the discussion in Ch. 14, and see Case C–379/92, *Peralta*, n. 167 above. See also, however, the opinion of Jacobs A.G. in Case C–412/93, *Leclerc-Siplec* v. *TF1 Publicité*, 24 Nov. 1994, who argues that a requirement of discrimination is inconsistent in principle with the aim of the Treaty to establish a single market.

[169] Case C–275/92, n. 8 above, para. 43. See also the view of J. Art, 'Legislative Lacunae, The Court of Justice and Freedom to Provide Services' in *Constitutional Adjudication in European Community Law and National Law*, ed. Curtin and O'Keeffe (Butterworths Ireland, 1992) 121, on Case C–288/89, *Gouda*, n. 156 above. Contrast the view of G. Marenco on this case, n. 167 above, 142–147.

damaging individual and social consequences, a decision to restrict or prohibit the activities of lotteries—which are clearly non-discriminatory restrictions—would otherwise be caught by Article 59. Whether the Court will continue this broad reading of Article 59 in later cases, or whether it will modify its approach along the lines of the developments in the free movement of goods case law, remains to be seen.

4. FURTHER READING

(a) Books

BURROWS, F., *Freedom of Movement in European Community Law* (Clarendon Press, 1987), Chs. 5 and 6

KAPTEYN, P. J. G., and VERLOREN VAN THEMAAT, P., *Introduction to the Law of the European Communities*, ed. L. Gormley (Kluwer, 1989) Ch. VII, 5

(b) Articles

ART, J., 'Legislative Lacunae, The Court of Justice and Freedom to Provide Services' in *Constitutional Adjudication in European Community Law and National Law*, eds. D. Curtin and D. O'Keeffe (Butterworths Ireland, 1992), 121

EDWARD, D., 'Establishment and Services: An Analysis of the Insurance Cases' (1987) 12 ELRev. 231

LONBAY, J., 'Picking Over the Bones: Rights of Establishment Reviewed' (1991) 16 ELRev. 507

MARENCO, G., 'The Notion of a Restriction on the Freedom of Establishment and the Provisions of Services in the Case Law of the Court' (1991) 11 YBEL 111

O'LEARY, S., 'The Court of Justice as a Reluctant Constitutional Adjudicator: An Examination of the Abortion Case' (1992) 16 ELRev. 138

PERTEK, J., 'Free Movement of Professionals and Recognition of Higher Education Diplomas' (1992) 12 YBEL 293

17

The Public Policy, Security, and Health Derogations: Directive 64/221

1. INTRODUCTION

We have seen that in the chapters on free movement of workers, freedom of establishment, and free movement of services alike, the Treaty provided for similar grounds of derogation from the requirements of these chapters. Article 48(3) sets out the rights attaching to freedom of movement for workers, but states that these are 'subject to limitations justified on grounds of public policy, public security or public health'. Article 56(1), in the chapter on establishment, states that 'the provisions of this chapter and measures taken in pursuance thereof shall not prejudice the applicability of provisions laid down by law, regulation or administrative action providing for special treatment for foreign nationals on grounds of public policy, public security or public health'. Article 66 makes the provisions of Article 56 applicable also to the free movement of services.

As might be expected, just as the Court of Justice has interpreted the freedoms in the three chapters expansively, and the public service and official-authority exceptions of Articles 48(4) and 55 restrictively, the public policy, security, and health derogations have been carefully circumscribed and given a narrow scope. Unlike the public service and official authority exceptions, however, the scope of these derogations is not determined solely by the Court, but has been further defined in secondary legislation. Directive 64/221 was adopted pursuant to Article 56(2) of the Treaty, which provides for the issuing of directives to co-ordinate these public policy, security, and health measures.[1] Despite the fact that its preamble mentions only Article 56 and not Article 48, the Directive applies to the employed as well as to the self-employed, and to recipients of services. It applies only to natural persons, however, so that the application of the derogations to companies under the establishment and services chapters is governed only by Article 56 and by the general principles of Community law.[2] These include the principles of non-

[1] [1963–4] OJ Spec. Ed. 117.

[2] For examples of the application of Arts. 56 and 66 to companies, see Cases 3/88, *Commission* v. *Italy* [1989] ECR 4035, [1991] 2 CMLR 115, and 352/85, *Bond van Adverteerders* v. *Netherlands* [1988] ECR 2085, [1989] 3 CMLR 113, discussed in Ch. 16. Although Art. 56 appears to permit only 'special treatment for foreign nationals', it is likely, since the Court has held that Arts. 52 and 59 protect also nationals in their own Member State and companies which have their primary

discrimination and of proportionality, which are also a part of the test for justifying certain restrictions on establishment and the provision of services which the Court has developed alongside Article 56.[3] A further important limit recently articulated by the Court is the requirement that Member States should respect the fundamental rights of the person when invoking one of the derogations.[4]

It has been seen that the public service and official authority exceptions relate to the nature of the work or activity to be undertaken, and that they allow for the exclusion of all non-nationals or foreign companies from certain kinds of work involving the exercise of public power or official authority. The public policy, security, and health derogations, by contrast, are concerned not so much with a certain kind of work or activity as with the specific characteristics of particular persons. A final distinction between the two categories of exception or derogation is that, whereas the scope and content of the public service and official authority derogations have firmly been delimited by the Court, there is no single uniform interpretation of the public policy exception and Member States retain a degree of discretion in defining its content.

In particular, the nature of the activities and conduct which may be considered to be contrary to public policy or public security remain, to a certain extent, within the discretion of the Member States. However, the limits to the exercise and scope of the exceptions are set by the general principles of law such as the principles of non-discrimination, proportionality, protection for fundamental rights, as well as by the various safeguards set out in Directive 64/221.

The Directive sets out to co-ordinate all measures relating to entry and deportation from their territory and issue or renewal of residence permits which Member States can adopt on grounds of public policy, security, and health, in relation to the employed, the self-employed, recipients of services, and the families of each. The first limit imposed in Article 2(1) is that none of the grounds shall be invoked 'to service economic ends'. In other words, a Member State cannot plead a ground such as high unemployment to justify deporting or refusing entry to another EC national who wishes to take up employment or an activity as a self-employed person in the state. Article 3 places other limits on the use of the public policy and security exceptions, and will be examined further in the cases below.

Article 4 concerns the public health exception and refers to the illnesses listed in the Annex, stating that diseases or disabilities occurring after the issue of a first residence permit shall not justify refusal to renew the permit or

establishment there, that the derogations may be invoked to permit special treatment for such companies and nationals in their own Member State.

[3] See Ch. 16, pt. 3(c).

[4] See Case C–260/89, *Elliniki Radiophonia TileorassiAE* v. *Dimotiki Etaria Pliroforissis* [1991] ECR I–2925, [1994] 4 CMLR 540, and the earlier Case 36/75, *Rutili* v. *Minister for the Interior* [1975] ECR 1219, [1976] 1 CMLR 140. See S. Hall, 'The ECHR and public policy exceptions to the free movement of workers under the EEC Treaty' (1991) 16 ELRev. 466, and see Ch. 7 for a fuller discussion.

expulsion. The diseases listed in the Annex are under two main headings. The first concerns diseases which may endanger public health, and covers those which are subject to quarantine listed by the World Health Organization: active tuberculosis, syphilis, and contagious or infectious diseases which are the subject of measures for the protection of nationals. The second concerns diseases and disabilities threatening public policy or security and it includes drug-addiction and profound mental disturbance. Article 4 is a standstill clause, and Articles 5 to 9 set out a range of procedural protections for the person in relation to the way in which decisions concerning entry, residence permits, and expulsion must take place, and may be challenged. These provisions have given rise to a considerable amount of litigation, too, as will be seen in cases discussed below. It is notable that most of the cases concern the public policy exception, which is a less clearly defined and more amorphous concept than that of public security or public health. Genuine threats to public security from the personal conduct of one person appear to have been infrequent,[5] and the careful delimitation of the public-health exception leaves little scope for manœuvre beyond those limits by the Member States.

2. THE DISCRETION OF THE MEMBER STATES

(a) What Conduct Can Justify the Invocation of the Derogations?

One of the early and well-known cases in which the Court was called upon to interpret the public policy exception, and the provisions of Directive 64/221, gives an indication of the degree of discretion which Member States retain in this context. The exception was invoked by the United Kingdom in an attempt to justify the refusal of permission to enter the state to a Dutch woman who had come to work for the Church of Scientology, a quasi-religious organization which was considered by the state to be anti-social and harmful:

Case 41/74, Van Duyn v. Home Office
[1974] E.C.R 1337, [1975] 1 CMLR 1.

The facts are set out in Chapter 4.[6]

THE ECJ

10. It emerges from the order making the reference that the only provision of the Directive which is relevant is that contained in Article 3(1) which provides that 'measures taken on grounds of public policy or public security shall be based exclusively on the personal conduct of the individual concerned'.

. . .

[5] Note that Art. 223 EC provides for a further exception to the rules of the Treaty (and not just to the free movement rules) where a Member State considers that the essential interests of its security are at stake.

[6] At 176.

17. It is necessary, first, to consider whether association with a body or an organization can in itself constitute personal conduct within the meaning of Article 3 of Directive No 64/221. Although a person's past association cannot, in general, justify a decision refusing him the right to move freely within the Community, it is nevertheless the case that present association, which reflects participation in the activities of the body or of the organization as well as identification with its aims or designs, may be considered a voluntary act of the person concerned and, consequently, as part of his personal conduct within the meaning of the provision cited.

18. This third question further raises the problem of what importance must be attributed to the fact that the activities of the organization in question, which are considered by the Member State as contrary to the public good are not however prohibited by national law. It should be emphasized that the concept of public policy in the context of the Community and where, in particular, it is used as a justification for derogating from the fundamental principle of freedom of movement for workers, must be interpreted strictly, so that its scope cannot be determined unilaterally by each Member State without being subject to control by the institutions of the Community. Nevertheless, the particular circumstances justifying recourse to the concept of public policy may vary from one country to another and from one period to another, and it is therefore necessary in this matter to allow the competent national authorities an area of discretion within the limits imposed by the Treaty.

19. It follows from the above that where the competent authorities of a Member State have clearly defined their standpoint as regards the activities of a particular organization and where, considering it to be socially harmful, they have taken administrative measures to counteract these activities, the Member State cannot be required, before it can rely on the concept of public policy, to make such activities unlawful, if recourse to such a measure is not thought appropriate in the circumstances.

20. The question raises finally the problem of whether a Member State is entitled, on grounds of public policy, to prevent a national of another Member State from taking gainful employment within its territory with a body or organization, it being the case that no similar restriction is placed upon its own nationals.

21. In this connection, the Treaty, while enshrining the principle of freedom of movement for workers without any discrimination on grounds of nationality, admits, in Article 48(3), limitations justified on grounds of public policy, public security or public health to the rights deriving from this principle. Under the terms of the provision cited above, the right to accept offers of employment actually made, the right to move freely within the territory of Member States for this purpose, and the right to stay in a Member State for the purpose of employment are, among others all subject to such limitations. Consequently, the effect of such limitations, when they apply, is that leave to enter the territory of a Member State and the right to reside there may be refused to a national of another Member State.

22. Furthermore it is a principle of international law, which the EEC Treaty cannot be assumed to disregard in the relations between Member States, that a State is precluded from refusing its own nationals the right of entry or residence.

The contrast with the public service exception, given the lack of uniformity between Member States' application of the public policy concept is evident in paragraph 18, where the Court accepts that the states will retain a certain discretion since 'the particular circumstances justifying recourse to the concept of public policy may vary from one country to another and from one period to another'. Thus the practice of Scientology could legitimately be considered to be against public policy in one Member State, even if all of the other Member States tolerated or approved of it. Advocate General Mayras commented on this in the context of the related public security concept:

> I did not think, contrary to the opinion of the Commission, that it is possible to deduce a Community concept of public security. That concept remains, at least for the present, national, and this conforms with reality inasmuch as the requirements of public security vary, in time and in space, from one State to another.[7]

The Court in its judgment also made clear that, although membership alone will not constitute personal conduct as required by Article 3 of the Directive, active participation and identification with the aims of an organization may do so.

(b) *What Steps may Member States take Against Non-Nationals?*

A second important point made in the *Van Duyn* ruling is that, so long as it adopts some administrative measures to counteract its activities, a state is not required to criminalize or to ban a particular organization, before it can rely on the public policy exception. Given that the United Kingdom could not deport its own nationals for working for the Church despite its public policy against them, the Court seemed prepared to accept that the deportation of a non-national for the same activity was an acceptable use of the public policy derogation. However, the point made in paragraph 19 of the judgment, that some administrative measures must be taken by the state against the activities in question, if it is to rely on Article 48(3), is not elaborated further, so that it is not clear what a Member State must do in relation to a particular organization or a particular activity before it can rely on the public policy concept against non-nationals. The background to the *Van Duyn* case in the United Kingdom was that there had been a statement made by the Minister of Health during a debate in Parliament in 1968, expressing strong official disapproval of the activities of the Church of Scientology, but stating that there was no power to prohibit the practice of scientology. This was noted by Advocate General Mayras as 'one of the consequences of a liberal government', but which should not prevent the United Kingdom from refusing entry to non-nationals who intended to work for the organization.

The *Van Duyn* case has attracted considerable critical comment, in relation

[7] [1974] ECR 1337, 1357.

to the Court's acceptance of the disparity of treatment between nationals and non-nationals.[8] If the activity really was contrary to public policy to such an extent that non-nationals could be refused entry or be deported, surely some other measures had to be taken against nationals engaging in that activity than simply a statement to Parliament condemning the organization? It is true, as the Court said, that despite the principle of non-discrimination in Articles 7 (now 6) and 48(2) and underlying Articles 52 and 60 of the Treaty, there is an inevitable discrimination between nationals and non-nationals, in that the latter can be deported and the former cannot. However, the element of discrimination could be lessened, by providing for more restrictive measures against the practice of the activity on the part of nationals. If it were thought undesirable to take any such restrictive measures in a liberal state, why would it be desirable to deport non-nationals for the same conduct?

This issue arose in the *Adoui* case, where the Court addressed the question whether deportation in such circumstances could amount to unnecessary or arbitrary discrimination on grounds of nationality:

Case 115 and 116/81, Adoui and Cornuaille v. Belgian State [1982] ECR 1665, [1982] 3 CMLR 631.

Adoui and Cornuaille were both French nationals working in Belgium. Adoui's application to the City of Liège for a residence permit was refused for reasons of public policy, the reason given being that she worked in a bar that was 'suspect from the point of view of morals'. An order to leave the country was subsequently made against her. Cornuaille had similarly been contacted by the police, and a recommendation had been made by the Consultative Committee for Aliens that she be deported. Both separately challenged these decisions before the Belgian courts, and references were made to the Court, asking whether a Member State could, under Article 48(3), deport a national of another Member State because of activities which, when carried out by the host state's own nationals, did not give rise to any repressive measures.

THE ECJ

6. Those questions are motivated by the fact that prostitution as such is not prohibited by Belgian legislation, although the Law does prohibit certain incidental activities, which are particularly harmful from the social point of view, such as the exploitation of prostitution by third parties and various forms of incitement to debauchery.

7. The reservations contained in Articles 48 and 56 of the EEC Treaty permit Member States to adopt, with respect to the nationals of other Member States and on the grounds specified in those provisions, in particular grounds justified by the requirements of public policy, measures which they cannot apply to their own nationals, inasmuch as they have no authority to expel the latter from the national

[8] See e.g. G. Slynn, *Introducing a European Legal Order* (Stevens & Son, 1992) 108; F. Mancini, 'The Free Movement of Workers in the Case Law of the European Court of Justice' in *Constitutional Adjudication in European Community and National Law*, ed. D. Curtin and D. O' Keeffe (Butterworths Ireland, 1992), 75; A. Arnull, *The General Principles of Law and the Individual* (Leicester University Press, 1990), 93–6.

territory or to deny them access thereto. Although that difference of treatment, which bears upon the nature of the measures available, must therefore be allowed, it must nevertheless be stressed that, in a Member State, the authority empowered to adopt such measures must not base the exercise of its powers on assessments of certain conduct which would have the effect of applying an arbitrary distinction to the detriment of nationals of other Member States.

8. . . . Although Community law does not impose upon the Member States a uniform scale of values as regards the assessment of conduct which may be considered as contrary to public policy, it should nevertheless be stated that conduct may not be considered as being of a sufficiently serious nature to justify restrictions on the admission to or residence within the territory of a Member State of a national of another Member State in a case where the former Member State does not adopt, with respect to the same conduct on the part of its own nationals repressive measures or other genuine and effective measures intended to combat such conduct.

The Court's emphasis here is on the need to take 'genuine and effective' repressive measures against the activities of nationals, if it is to use that same conduct as a reason for deporting or refusing entry to non-nationals. While that does seem to represent a tighter reading of the public policy exception than in *Van Duyn*, the Court gave no examples of the kind of repressive measures which a state might take. If the Court adheres to that part of its ruling in *Van Duyn* which suggested that it was not necessary to make unlawful or to ban the Church of Scientology before it could be considered contrary to public policy, then what sorts of steps must a Member State take against nationals if it is to be permitted to exclude or deport non-nationals? If it is not necessary to ban the Church of Scientology or to prosecute its active members, what other repressive measures against nationals could be taken which would be sufficiently repressive? Perhaps the official disapproval and the parliamentary debate in the United Kingdom were in fact sufficient, so that (contrary to the views of several commentators) the *Van Duyn* case would be decided in the same way even after *Adoui*. Certainly the applicants in *Adoui*, seeking to distinguish *Van Duyn* from their case, argued that in fact the United Kingdom Government had taken sufficiently restrictive measures and had demonstrated an unequivocal attitude towards the Church of Scientology.

The obligation to minimize, as far as possible, the discrimination in treatment of nationals and non-nationals in the exercise of the exceptions is also emphasized in the Court's ruling in *Rutili*:

Case 36/75 Rutili v Minister for the Interior
[1975] ECR 1219, [1976] 1 CMLR 140.

The applicant was an Italian national, married to a French woman, who had been resident in France since his birth and was now working there as a trade union official. He held a privileged resident's permit until 1968 when various deportation and restriction orders were made against him. Eventually the Minister for the

Interior prohibited him from residing in certain French territories (*départements*), and when he applied in 1970 for a residence permit for a national of an EEC Member State, his permit included a prohibition on residence in these territories. He challenged the limitation to the territorial validity of his permit before the French courts, and a reference was made to the Court for an interpretation of Article 48 and Directive 64/221.

THE ECJ

28. Accordingly, restrictions cannot be imposed on the right of a national of any Member State to enter the territory of another Member State, to stay there and to move within it unless his presence or conduct constitutes a genuine and sufficiently serious threat to public policy.

29. In this connexion Article 3 of Directive No 64/221 imposes on Member States the duty to base their decision on the individual circumstances of any person under the protection of Community law and not on general considerations.

30. Moreover, Article 2 of the same directive provides that grounds of public policy shall not be put to improper use by being invoked to service economic ends.

31. Nor, under Article 8 of Regulation No 1612/68, which ensures equality of treatment as regards membership of trade unions and the exercise of rights attaching thereto, may the reservation relating to public policy be invoked on grounds arising from the exercise of those rights.

The Court ruled that the term 'measures' in Directive 64/221 should have a broad construction, covering not only national legislative measures but also individual decisions taken, and that they should therefore be subject to judicial control as required by the Directive:

46. Right of entry into the territory of Member States and the right to stay there and to move freely within it is defined in the Treaty by reference to the whole territory of those States and not by reference to its internal subdivisions.

47. The reservation contained in Article 48(3) concerning the protection of public policy has the same scope as the rights the exercise of which may, under that paragraph, be subject to limitations.

48. It follows that prohibitions on residence under the reservation inserted to this effect in Article 48(3) may be imposed only in respect of the whole of the national territory.

49. On the other hand, in the case of partial prohibitions on residence, limited to certain areas of the territory, persons covered by Community law must, under Article 7 of the Treaty and within the field of application of that provision, be treated on a footing of equality with the nationals of the Member State concerned.

On an initial reading of *Rutili*, it might seem odd that while Article 48(3) (and, presumably, Article 56 by analogy), and Directive 64/221 allow a Member State to take quite a drastic step—namely deportation—in relation to someone who is considered to be a threat to public policy, they do not allow a more restrained measure, such as a limited restriction order barring entry only to some parts of the territory. But the reasoning behind this conclusion is as follows: if the person in question is a very serious threat indeed to public policy, then the state should be able to justify a deportation order as required under Directive 64/221. But if the conduct in question is not so serious as to warrant expulsion, then any lesser restriction such as a partial territorial exclusion order can only be imposed on a non-national to the same extent to which it would be imposed on a national engaged in the same conduct.

(c) The 'Personal Conduct' Requirement

The only guidance given by Directive 64/221 on what might constitute 'personal conduct' serious enough to give grounds for invoking the public policy or security exception is negative, in that Article 3(2) provides that previous criminal convictions in themselves are not sufficient. A series of cases involving criminal convictions has fleshed out this provision:

Case 67/74, Bonsignore v. Oberstadtdirektor der Stadt Köln [1975] ECR 297, [1975] 1 CMLR 472.

Bonsignore was an Italian national who came to Germany to work as a chemical worker. Three years later, he fatally injured his younger brother while handling a pistol for which he had no firearms permit. Although he was convicted of causing death by negligence, no punishment was imposed upon him by the court. However, a deportation order was subsequently made against him, and on his appeal, a reference was made to the Court. The principal question was whether Community law permitted a Member State national to be deported for reasons of a general preventive nature, or whether the preventive reasons had to be specific to the individual. The German authority responsible for the deportation argued to the Court that reprehensible conduct such as unlawful possession of firearms by aliens was regarded as of particular danger to the peaceful, secure coexistence of Germans and foreigners.

THE ECJ

5. According to Article 3(1) and (2) of Directive No 64/221, 'measures taken on grounds of public policy shall be based exclusively on the personal conduct of the individual concerned' and 'previous criminal convictions shall not in themselves constitute grounds for the taking of such measures'.

. . .

6. With this in view, Article 3 of the directive provides that measures adopted on grounds of public policy and for the maintenance of public security against the nationals of Member States of the Community cannot be justified on grounds extraneous to the individual case, as is shown in particular by the requirement set out in paragraph (1) that 'only' the 'personal conduct' of those affected by the measures is to be regarded as determinative.

As departures from the rules concerning the free movement of persons constitute exceptions which must be strictly construed, the concept of 'personal conduct' expresses the requirement that a deportation order may only be made for breaches of the peace and public security which might be committed by the individual affected.

Accordingly, the Court ruled that deportation of a 'general preventive nature' was prohibited by Article 3 of the Directive. The combination of the 'personal conduct' requirement and the condition that criminal convictions in themselves were insufficient as a ground led the Court to conclude that more would be required if Bonsignore, on whom the German sentencing court had obviously taken pity in view of the tragic killing of his brother, was to be deported. Advocate General Mayras went somewhat further in his criticism of such preventive use of the power to deport:

> I am, for my part, rather sceptical as to the real deterrent effect of a deportation which is ordered 'to make an example' of the individual concerned . . . ,
>
> In point of fact, one cannot avoid the impression that the deportation of a foreign worker, even a national of the Common Market, satisfies the feeling of hostility, sometimes verging on xenophobia, which the commission of an offence by an alien generally causes or revives in the indigenous population.[9]

However, the fact that past criminal convictions cannot in themselves justify the adoption of measures on grounds of public policy or security does not mean that criminal convictions can never be relevant to the reasons a Member State has for invoking one of the exceptions. In *Bouchereau*, the Court explained the circumstances in which a past conviction might in fact be relevant:

Case 30/77, R v. Bouchereau [1977] ECR 1999, [1977] 2 CMLR 800

Bouchereau was a French national working in England, who was twice convicted there of unlawful possession of drugs. After the second conviction, the court wished to recommend to the Secretary of State that he be deported. A reference was made to the Court, asking whether such a judicial recommendation would be a 'measure' within Directive 64/221, and asking in what way a criminal conviction might be taken into account in deciding to recommend deportation. The Court ruled that the concept of a 'measure' included a judicial recommendation, which was an important step in the process.

THE ECJ

26. According to the terms of the order referring the case to the Court, that question seeks to discover whether, as the defendant maintained before the national court, 'previous criminal convictions are solely relevant in so far as they manifest a present or future intention to act in a manner contrary to public

[9] [1975] ECR 297, 315.

policy or public security' or, on the other hand, whether, as Counsel for the prosecution sought to argue, although 'the court cannot make a recommendation for deportation on grounds of public policy based on the fact alone of a criminal conviction' it 'is entitled to take into account the past conduct of the defendant which resulted in the criminal conviction'.

27. The terms of Article 3(2) of the directive, which states that 'previous criminal convictions shall not in themselves constitute grounds for the taking of such measures' must be understood as requiring the national authorities to carry out a specific appraisal from the point of view of the interests inherent in protecting the requirements of public policy, which does not necessarily coincide with the appraisals which formed the basis of the criminal conviction.

28. The existence of a previous criminal conviction can, therefore, only be taken into account in so far as the circumstances which gave rise to that conviction are evidence of personal conduct constituting a present threat to the requirements of public policy.

29. Although in general, a finding that such a threat exists implies the existence in the individual concerned of a propensity to act in the same way in the future, it is possible that past conduct alone may constitute such a threat to the requirements of public policy.

. . .

35. In so far as it may justify certain restrictions on the free movement of persons subject to Community law, recourse by a national authority to the concept of public policy presupposes, in any event, the existence, in addition to the perturbation of the social order which any infringement of the law involves, of a genuine and sufficiently serious threat to the requirements of public policy affecting one of the fundamental interests of society.

The judgment states that the relevance of a criminal conviction is in whether it reveals that person to be a *present* and not just a past danger to the requirements of public policy. A present danger does not necessarily mean that the person is likely to commit such offences in the future, and indeed the Court expressly rules that past conduct alone might well be enough to indicate a present danger, although it does not go much further in explaining how someone who would not commit future offences might nevertheless be a present danger. The *Bouchereau* judgment also elaborates a little further on the 'genuine and sufficiently serious threat to public policy', which was referred to earlier in *Rutili*. It must be something more than the disruption which any breach of the law causes, and the public policy which it threatens must affect one of society's 'fundamental interests'. This sends a clear message to the Member States that the exception is not to be lightly invoked, and that very substantial grounds must be shown before conduct, whether or not of a criminal nature, will be accepted as a threat to public policy within the meaning of Article 48(3). However, the Court's failure to suggest how past criminal conduct in itself, without any likelihood of reoffending, may constitute such a serious threat, to some extent subverts the provision in Article 3 of the Directive that previous convictions in themselves cannot constitute grounds for invoking one of the exceptions.

The issue of past criminal convictions arose again in the case of *Santillo*.[10] After Santillo had served a prison sentence for violent sexual offences, a decision to deport him was based on a recommendation made several years earlier by the sentencing court. The Court ruled that it was 'indeed essential that the social danger resulting from a foreigner's presence should be assessed at the very time when the decision ordering expulsion is made against him as the factors to be taken into account, particularly those concerning his conduct, are likely to change in the course of time'.[11] In a recent case in the United Kingdom, the court ruled that the past conduct of a consultant psychiatrist, who had been convicted of conspiracy to import heroin, was sufficient, despite the absence of any propensity to reoffend, to justify deportation on grounds of public policy.[12] According to the court he had committed 'a very serious and horrifying offence in a field where there is grave danger' and one which was especially 'repugnant to the public, when committed by a doctor'.[13] The fact that the requirements of public policy would not, in the court's view, have adequately been served by the imposition of a prison sentence and the striking off of the defendant as a practising psychiatrist suggests that there may be some substance in Advocate General Mayras' comments about the particular hostility aroused by the commission of an offence by an 'alien'.[14]

(d) The Procedural Protections under Directive 64/221

It has been said that the aim of Directive 64/221 was 'substantially to reduce the discretionary power of the States . . . by requiring that the individual position of such workers should be given a thorough examination which is subject to review by the courts'.[15] Whereas the provisions in the first half of the Directive set certain limits to what can constitute a public policy, security, or health ground, the provisions in the latter part of the Directive set out a framework of procedural rights which the Member State must provide for a worker against whom one of the grounds is being invoked.

Article 5 provides that a decision to grant or refuse a first residence permit should be made as soon as possible and not later than six months from the date of application, allowing for temporary residence pending the decision. The host country, in essential cases, may ask the Member State of origin for information regarding any previous police record.

Article 6 provides that the person is to be informed of the grounds of public policy, security, or health on which the decision is taken, unless this is

[10] Case 131/79, *R.* v. *Secretary of State for Home Affairs, ex p. Mario Santillo* [1980] ECR 1585, [1980] 2 CMLR 308.

[11] *Ibid.*, para. 18.

[12] *R,* v. *Home Secretary, ex parte Marchon* [1993] 2 CMLR 132.

[13] *Ibid.* 137.

[14] See n. 9 above.

[15] Mayras A.G. in Case 67/74, *Bonsignore* v. *Oberstadtdirektor der Stadt Köln* [1975] ECR 297, 316, [1975] 1 CMLR 472.

contrary to the interests of state security.[16] It was held in *Adoui*,[17] that the reasons given for expulsion must be sufficiently detailed to enable the person to protect her or his interests. Under Article 7, official notification to the person concerned of any decision of refusal or expulsion is required. A period of time to leave must be given in the notice, and except in cases of urgency it must be at least fifteen days where the person has not yet been granted a residence permit, and at least a month in all other cases.

Articles 8 and 9 provide for the legal remedies against a decision of refusal of issue or renewal of a permit or an expulsion. These are set out in more detail in the cases and discussion which follow.

In *Royer*, the Court was asked whether a decision ordering expulsion or a refusal to issue a residence permit could give rise to immediate measures of execution or whether that decision could only take effect after remedies before the national courts were exhausted.[18] The Court had an opportunity to rule on the relationship between Article 8, which requires the same remedies to be available, in the event of an expulsion order, as are available to nationals against acts of the administration, and Article 9, which guarantees that in the absence of an effective appeal against the administrative decision the worker must at least be able to exercise rights of defence before an independent 'competent authority':

Case 48/75, Royer [1976] ECR 497, [1976] 2 CMLR 619

The facts are set out in Chapter 15.[19]

THE ECJ

56. However, this guarantee would become illusory if the Member States could, by the immediate execution of a decision ordering expulsion, deprive the person concerned of the opportunity of effectively making use of the remedies which he is guaranteed by Directive No 64/221.

57. In the case of the legal remedies referred to in Article 8 of Directive No 64/221, the party concerned must at least have the opportunity of lodging an appeal and thus obtaining a stay of execution before the expulsion order is carried out.

58. This conclusion also follows from the link established by the directive between Articles 8 and 9 thereof in view of the fact that the procedure set out in the latter provision is obligatory *inter alia* where the legal remedies referred to in Article 8 'cannot have suspensory effect'.

59. Under Article 9 the procedure of an appeal to a competent authority must precede the decision ordering expulsion except in cases of urgency.

[16] In C–229/94, *R.* v. *Secretary of State for the Home Department, ex p. Adams*, one of the questions referred on 29 July 1994 by the Div. Ct. to the ECJ concerned what the principle of proportionality required in a case involving a restriction on freedom of movement, not under Art. 48 but under the new Art. 8a(1), where the state's interest in national security and the applicant's freedom of expression were both in issue.

[17] Case 115 and 116/81, *Adoui and Cornuaille* v. *Belgian State* [1982] ECR 1665, [1982] 3 CMLR 631.

[18] Case 48/75, *Royer* [1976] ECR 497, [1976] 2 CMLR 619.

[19] At 682.

60. Consequently, where a legal remedy referred to in Article 8 is available the decision ordering expulsion may not be executed before the party concerned is able to avail himself of the remedy.

61. Where no such remedy is available, or where it is available but cannot have suspensory effect, the decision cannot be taken—save in cases of urgency which have been properly justified—until the party concerned has had the opportunity of appealing to the authority designated in Article 9 of Directive 64/221 and until this authority has reached a decision.

Subsequently, in the case of *Pecastaing*, the Court ruled that Articles 8 and 9 did not require Member States to allow the non-national to remain in the country for the duration of appeal or review procedures, so long as it was nevertheless possible to obtain a fair hearing and to have an adequate defence presented.[20] As for cases of urgency, in which neither suspension of the decision to deport nor recourse, before expulsion, to the opinion of a competent authority is required, the Court ruled that the determination of the existence of urgency was not a judicial matter but one for the administrative authority to make.[21]

Further elaboration on the concept of an 'opinion of a competent authority' in Article 9 of the Directive is to be found in the case of *Santillo*.[22] Noting that Member States were left 'a margin of discretion in regard to the nature of the authority', the Court held that a recommendation for deportation made by a criminal court at the time of conviction could satisfy this requirement, provided that:

> all the factors to be taken into consideration by the administration are put before the competent authority, if the opinion of the competent authority is sufficiently proximate in time to the decision ordering expulsion to ensure that there are no new factors to be taken into consideration, and if both the administration and the person concerned are in a position to take cognizance of the reasons which led the 'competent authority' to give its opinion—save where grounds touching the security of the State referred to in Article 6 of the directive make this undesirable.[23]

The requirement to consider any new grounds put forward by the appellant also applies in the context of someone who has been properly expelled, but

[20] Case 98/79, *Pecastaing* v. *Belgium* [1980] ECR 691, [1980] 3 CMLR 685.

[21] For criticism of this judgment, in particular regarding the determination of 'urgency' see D. O'Keeffe, 'Practical Difficulties in the Application of Art. 48 of the EEC Treaty' (1982) 19 C.M.L.Rev. 35, 36–9.

[22] Case 131/79, n. 10 above. See also Cases 115 and 116/81, *Adoui* n. 17 above, where the ECJ stressed the need for the absolute independence of the authority. In *R.* v. *Secretary of State for the Home Department, ex p. Gallagher* [1994] 3 CMLR 295, a reference under Art. 177 was made by the English CA to see whether the requirement of a fully independent 'competent authority' was satisfied by the opinion of a civil servant appointed by the Home Secretary.

[23] [1980] ECR 1585, para. 14.

who after a time seeks permission to re-enter. It was held in *Adoui* that a national, after expulsion, may re-apply for a residence permit and, if a reasonable period has elapsed, the authorities must consider the arguments put forward by that person purporting to show that there has been a material change in circumstances.[24]

3. FURTHER READING

HALL, S., 'The ECHR and public policy exceptions to the free movement of workers under the EEC Treaty' (1991) 16 ELRev. 466

O'KEEFFE, D., 'Practical Difficulties in the Application of Article 48 of the EEC Treaty' (1982) 19 CMLRev. 35

[24] Cases 115 and 116/81, n. 17 above.

18

Equal Treatment of Women and Men

1. INTRODUCTION

The main Treaty provisions on what can broadly be called social policy are now contained in Articles 117 to 125 of the EC Treaty. These are followed, after the amendments of the TEU, by Articles relating to education, culture, and public health, as well as a later chapter dealing with economic and social cohesion. It is the Treaty chapter specifically entitled 'social policy', however, which contains the most important provisions forming the basis for Community legislative action in this sphere. Articles 117 to 118b declare the Member States' agreement on the need to improve the working conditions and living standard of workers as well as to co-operate on various other aspects of social and vocational policy, and Article 118a in particular contains specific legislative powers in the area of health and safety of workers, which were added by the Single European Act in 1986. Further, the Protocol and the Agreement on Social Policy annexed by the TEU to the EC Treaty provide an additional basis for action in the field of labour policy—including equality between men and women with regard to the labour market—on the part of fourteen of the fifteen Member States, the United Kingdom having chosen to exclude itself from the application of that Agreement.[1] Articles 123 to 125 concern the European Social Fund, which was established to provide financial assistance for some of the social-policy objectives of the Community, such as to support vocational training and to promote employment, in particular amongst disadvantaged groups such as the long-term unemployed, migrant workers, or women returning to work.

The Treaty provision on which this Chapter is primarily focused is Article 119, which establishes the principle of equal pay for equal work. However, Community law is concerned not only with equal pay between men and women but also with their equal treatment in a broader sense. This Chapter will examine the scope and the limits of the equal treatment principle in Community law, its development through the primary and secondary legislation and through the decision-making of the Court of Justice. It is a very interesting area of law for many reasons, not least because of the practical, social,

[1] See generally P. Watson 'Social Policy after Maastricht' (1993) 30 CMLRev. 481; E. Whiteford, 'Social Policy after Maastricht' (1993) 18 ELRev. 202; E. Szyszczak, 'Social Policy: A Happy Ending or a Reworking of the Fairy Tale' in *Legal Issues of the Maastricht Treaty*, ed. O'Keeffe and Twomey, (Chancery, 1994), 313.

and cultural importance of developments in this field. In the first place, it is a body of law which reveals the persistent tension, evident in many other areas of Community law, between the economic and the social objectives of the Community.[2] Secondly, it highlights questions about the division of competence between the Community and the Member States in the sphere of social policy.[3] Thirdly, it provides a very good illustration of the interaction and dialogue—which is certainly not always of a harmonious kind—between the Community's political and judicial branches in the law-making process.[4] Despite various legislative extensions and developments beyond the area of pay, the equal treatment principle is limited in scope, and is confined, in keeping with the essentially economic focus of the Community, to employment-related sex discrimination.

It is undoubtedly a very complex branch of law, in part because of the unclear boundaries between various kinds of sex discrimination which are governed by distinct legal regimes. Community law in this area is divided principally into three parts: equal pay, equal treatment, and social security. Although the basic principle of non-discrimination on grounds of sex is common to all three, each is governed by different legal provisions, so that the distinction drawn between them is significant. In brief, equal pay is governed by Article 119 and Directive 75/117, equal treatment by Directives 76/207 and 86/613 (and, it could be said, by Directive 92/85 on pregnancy, although whether protection in the event of pregnancy constitutes 'special' treatment or equal treatment is a matter for debate), and social security by Directives 79/7 and 86/378. However, the division between the three categories has become blurred in various ways. In the first place, the distinction between pay and occupational social security has been eroded by the Court of Justice's reading of Article 119, thus undermining much of Directive 86/378. Further, the distinction between matters which fall under the Equal Treatment Directive and those which fall under the Social Security Directive has not always been clearly drawn. And finally, the distinction between what constitutes social security, which falls within Community sex discrimination law, and other forms of social assistance, which remain as yet a matter for the Member States, has also been problematic. There has also been a considerable amount of 'soft law' in the area of equal treatment, with the adoption of memoranda, resolutions, and recommendations on matters such as sexual harassment and child care.[5] Further, the Commission has adopted action programmes to

[2] In an early decision, Case 28/66, *Netherlands* v. *Commission* [1968] ECR 1, 12, the ECJ ruled that the social aims of the ECSC Treaty set out in Art. 2 were not necessarily to be of secondary importance to the aims of establishing a common market.

[3] The hostility of the UK to the adoption of the Pregnancy Dir. under the health and safety provisions of the Treaty is evidence of this, as is the more recent controversy over the legal basis for a proposed Parental Leave Dir., which is, as a result, to be based on the Agreement on Social Policy.

[4] See, in particular below, 818–35, the developments in the law relating to sex discrimination in occupational pensions.

[5] On sexual harassment see Commission Rec. 92/131 and Code, [1992] OJ L49/1, and on child care see Council Rec. 92/241: [1992] OJ L123/16. In June 1994 the Commission adopted a

promote equality in the workplace, most recently in its Third Action Programme for 1991–5, and a fourth programme is due to be adopted in 1995.[6]

Briefly, the differences in the Community's current legal treatment of these various categories of sex discrimination are as follows: first, of the three, matters of equal pay are subject to the more stringent legal regulation, since there are no express exceptions, and since Article 119 is both vertically and horizontally directly effective; secondly, matters of equal treatment in employment are subject to less strict regulation in that there are several exceptions within Directive 76/270, the Directive is only vertically effective and its efficacy has therefore been subject to the varying methods of enforcement of directives; finally, the prohibition on sex discrimination in social security relates to protection against certain specified risks only, is subject to various exceptions, and is contained in Directives which are again of vertical direct effect only.

These three specific areas of sex-discrimination law apart, the Court has stated that the general principle of equal treatment between men and women is a fundamental one in the Community legal order. In *Sabbatini*[7] and *Airola*,[8] the Court held that the *Community* was bound by the principle of non-discrimination on grounds of sex in the treatment of its staff. Subsequently the Court ruled that the elimination of sex discrimination was one of the fundamental personal human rights which had to be protected within Community law.[9] However, this status for the principle did not ensure that it would be directly applicable against Member States, so as to prohibit laws permitting unequal treatment of men and women, since the Community had not yet assumed competence in the area of equal treatment at work and could only, at that stage, prohibit the states from maintaining unequal pay between men and women.[10]

As a general comment before examining the relevant provisions and cases in detail, the concept of equality and of non-discrimination which underlies this area of Community law has been criticized as a strictly formal concept which takes little account of the differences in the social and material circumstances of men and women. By insisting on identical treatment for men and women who are similarly situated, it has been argued that Community law ignores the disadvantages faced by women as opposed to men, and the different patterns of their working and family lives.[11]

Memorandum on Equal Pay for Work of Equal Value: for comment see T. Gill, 'Equal Pay' (1994) 23 ILJ 359.

[6] See the Commission White Paper on European Social Policy: COM(94)333.

[7] Case 20/71, *Sabbatini* [1972] ECR 345, [1972] CMLR 945.

[8] Case 21/74, *Airola* [1972] ECR 221. See also Cases 75, 117/82, *Razzouk and Beydoun* v. *Commission* [1984] ECR 1509, paras. 16–17.

[9] Case 149/77, *Defrenne* v. *Sabena* [1978] ECR 1365, [1978] 3 CMLR 312, paras. 26–7 (the third *Defrenne* case). See C. Docksey, 'The Principle of Equality between Women and Men as a Fundamental Right under Community Law' (1991) 20 ILJ 258.

[10] Case 149/77, n. 9 above, para. 30.

[11] See S. Fredman, 'European Community Discrimination Law: A Critique' (1992) 21 ILJ 119; G. More, ' "Equal Treatment" of the Sexes: What Does "Equal" Mean?' (1993) 1 *Feminist Legal Studies* 45.

2. EQUAL PAY

Whatever may have been the status of the principle of equal treatment between the sexes more generally, it was certainly clear from the Treaty that the principle of equal pay was firmly within the scope of Community competence, and was applicable to the Member States.

Article 119 provides:

> Each Member State shall during the first stage ensure and subsequently maintain the application of the principle that men and women should receive equal pay for equal work.
>
> For the purpose of this Article, 'pay' means the ordinary basic or minimum wage or salary and any other consideration, whether in cash or in kind, which the worker receives, directly or indirectly, in respect of his employment from his employer.
>
> Equal pay without discrimination based on sex means:
>
> (a) that pay for the same work at piece rates shall be calculated on the basis of the same unit of measurement;
>
> (b) that pay for work at time rates shall be the same for the same job.

The presence of Article 119 in the original EEC Treaty prompts the question: what was the impetus for a principle of equal pay between the sexes in the setting up of this distinctly economic community, given that there is no mention of sex discrimination or of equal treatment in the Treaty, other than in this context of pay? According to various writers, the historical explanation for Article 119 is the French concern that France would be at a competitive disadvantage through observing the principle of equal pay for equal work more thoroughly than it was observed in other Member States.[12] In other words, concern over the oppression of women in the labour market or more generally in economic life is unlikely to have been the primary factor motivating the drafters of Article 119. However, that historical explanation apart, it can now be said that Article 119 and the other provisions of Community sex-discrimination law are viewed and interpreted not primarily as an instrument of economic policy, but also as an important part of Community social policy. The original aims listed in the Preamble and in Article 2 of the Treaty and the activities envisaged in Article 3 included the raising of the standard of living and the improvement of employment opportunities for workers, objectives which clearly have a social aspect and which form part of the context within which Article 119 should be read.

Thus the theme, which was emphasized in the chapter on free movement of workers, that many of the Treaty's provisions have mixed objectives can be

[12] See P. J. G. Kapteyn and P. Verloren van Themaat, *Introduction to the Law of the European Communities* (2nd edn., L. Gormley, Kluwer, 1989), 632.

very clearly seen in the area of equal pay and equal treatment. On the one hand, just as the free movement of workers was intended to liberalize the market and to further the economic aims of creating a single trading entity in Europe, the equal treatment provisions were intended to 'level the playing field', to ensure that employers in no one Member State would have the competitive advantage over those in another Member State that women were cheaper than men to employ. On the other hand, just as the provisions on free movement of workers are interpreted by the Court as being intended to enhance the standard of living of individual workers and to confer rights directly on them and on their families, so the Court has also ruled that Article 119 has a social and not just an economic aim. This much can be seen from the first *Defrenne* case, in which the Belgian Government argued that Article 119 had only an economic objective, namely 'to avoid discrepancies in cost prices due to the employment of female labour less well paid for the same work than male labour'.[13] The Court rejected this view in the second *Defrenne* case:

Case 43/75, Defrenne v. Sabena
[1976] ECR 455, [1976] 2 CMLR 98

The facts are set out in chapter 4.[14]

THE ECJ

8. Article 119 pursues a double aim.

9. First, in the light of the different stages of the development of social legislation in the various Member States, the aim of Article 119 is to avoid a situation in which undertakings established in States which have actually implemented the principle of equal pay suffer a competitive disadvantage in intra-Community competition as compared with undertakings established in States which have not yet eliminated discrimination against women workers as regards pay.

10. Secondly, this provision forms part of the social objectives of the Community, which is not merely an economic union, but is at the same time intended, by common action, to ensure social progress and seek the constant improvement of the living and working conditions of their peoples, as is emphasized by the Preamble to the Treaty.

. . .

12. This double aim, which is at once economic and social, shows that the principle of equal pay forms part of the foundations of the Community.

We saw in Chapter 4, however, that various of the Member States had avoided the implementation of the equal pay principle for some years, eventually arguing unsuccessfully to the Court in the case above that Article 119 lacked direct effect. However, the Court ruled that Article 119 had been directly effective since the end of the first stage of the transitional period, and

[13] See Case 80/70, *Defrenne* v. *Belgium* [1971] ECR 445, [1974] 1 CMLR 494.

[14] At 162.

that its direct effectiveness could not be affected by any implementing provision either of the states or of the Community. Nevertheless, the Court was swayed by the arguments of the Member States on the seriousness for them of the financial consequences of such a ruling, and it agreed that on account of the likely incorrect understanding of the Member States of the effects of Article 119, due in part to the fact that the Commission had not brought earlier infringement proceedings against them, its ruling should only have effect prospectively. This meant that only those who had already brought legal proceedings or made a claim could rely on Article 119 in respect of pay claims for periods prior to the date of judgment. Prospective overruling of this kind by the Court has been rare, and although it generally cites the principle of legal certainty in support of its decision to limit the past effects of its ruling, the cases tend to be those in which there are considerable financial implications for the Member States or their industries.[15]

(a) Directive 75/117

In its discussion of cases which might require further legislation before Article 119 could be applied, the Court in *Defrenne (No 2)* made reference to Directive 75/117 which had recently been adopted to extend the 'narrow criterion of equal work' to cover work of equal value.[16] The Directive was based on Article 100 of the Treaty, which is the provision designed to deal with the approximation of the laws of the Member States.[17] The twin aims—economic and social—of the equal pay principle can be seen reflected in the preamble to the measure, which mentions equal pay as 'an integral part of . . . the functioning of the common market' and refers to the recognition by the Council in its resolution on a social action programme 'that priority should be given to action taken on behalf of women as regards . . . working conditions, including pay'.

The basic thrust of the Directive is to require the elimination of sex discrimination in pay in cases involving the same work or work to which equal value is attached, and to require job classification schemes to be similarly free from discrimination.[18] Member States are to abolish any such discrimination in legislative or administrative provisions[19] and to ensure that any breaches of the equal pay principle in collective agreements or contracts are rendered void or amended.[20] In addition to these 'negative' obligations, the Directive also

15 See also p. 820–5 below, Case 262/88, *Barber* v. *Guardian Royal Exchange* [1990] ECR 1889, [1990] 2 CMLR 513, and see above p. 704–5 Case 24/86, *Blaizot* v. *University of Liège* [1988] ECR 379, [1989] 1 CMLR 57. Contrast Case C–200/90, *Dansk Denkavit and Poulsen* v. *Skatteministeriet* [1992] ECR I–2217.

16 [1976] ECR 455, para. 20.

17 Dir. 75/117 of 10 Feb. 1975: [1975] OJ L45/19.

18 Art. 1. See Case 237/85, *Rummler* [1986] ECR 2101, [1987] 3 CMLR 127 where the Court ruled that the use of criteria such as muscle-demand for the purpose of determining rates of pay was permitted by Dir. 75/117. For criticism of the Court's acceptance of such criteria as 'objective', whilst simultaneously ruling that criteria based on values appropriate only to female workers would be discriminatory see S. Fredman, n. 11 above, 123.

19 Art. 3.

20 Art. 4.

imposes a positive obligation on the states to take effective measures to ensure that the equal pay principle is observed.[21] Other provisions of the Directive which are similar to those to be found in the Equal Treatment and Social Security Directives are the requirement that employees should be able to pursue their claims by judicial process,[22] that complainants should be protected against dismissal,[23] and that employees should be properly informed of their rights.[24]

According to Advocate General Trabucchi in *Defrenne (No 2)*, Directive 75/117 did not and could not restrict the original scope of Article 119.[25] Indeed it can be said of all Community secondary legislation that, although it can supplement or give effect to primary Treaty provisions, it cannot restrict or reduce them. Further, the fact that the Directive was intended to apply the equal-pay principle not just to 'similar work' but also to 'work of equal value' does not mean that Article 119 does not of itself cover the latter. As in the case of the relationship between Article 48 and Regulation 1612/68, discussed in Chapter 15, Directive 75/117 fleshes out the provisions of Article 119, but the rights are said by the Court to stem directly from the Treaty. Thus the direct effect of Article 119 can be invoked against a private employer in a case concerning work of equal value, avoiding arguments about the horizontal direct effect of the Directive.

The principle of equal pay is not difficult to apply when two employees are being paid different rates for the same work, but it becomes more difficult when the work performed by each is quite different, but is alleged to be of equal value. Directive 75/117 was intended to address this problem, to facilitate the enforcement of the aims of Article 119, and to place an onus on the Member States to ensure its proper application and its effectiveness. However, the Commission was not satisfied with the steps taken by all of the Member States to implement the Directive.

Case 61/81, Commission v. United Kingdom [1982] ECR 2601, [1982] 3 CMLR 284

The Commission brought infringement proceedings against the United Kingdom on the basis of its alleged failure to ensure the proper implementation of Directive 75/117 on equal pay. In particular, the Commission complained of the failure of the United Kingdom to ensure a job-classification system which would assist in determining whether work is 'of equal value' with other work. The United Kingdom 1970 Equal Pay Act did not permit the introduction of such a classification system without the employer's consent, and the Act did not provide for any other way of determining pay for work to which equal value was attributed.

THE ECJ

6. The United Kingdom attempts to justify that state of affairs by pointing out that Article 1 of the Directive says nothing about the right of an employee to insist

[21] Art. 6. [22] Art. 2. [23] Art. 5. [24] Art. 7.

[25] See also, p. 829 below, the discussion in Case 110/91, *Moroni* v. *Collo GmbH* [1993] ECR I–6591 of the interaction between Dir. 86/378 and Art. 119.

on having pay determined by a job classification system. On that basis it concludes that the worker may not insist on a comparative evaluation of different work by the job classification method, the introduction of which is at the employer's discretion.

7. The United Kingdom's interpretation amounts to a denial of the very existence of a right to equal pay for work of equal value where no classification has been made. Such a position is not consonant with the general scheme and provisions of Directive 75/117. The recitals in the preamble to that Directive indicate that its essential purpose is to implement the principle that men and women should receive equal pay contained in Article 119 of the Treaty and that it is primarily the responsibility of the Member States to ensure the application of this principle by means of appropriate laws, regulations, and administrative provisions in such a way that all employees in the Community can be protected in these matters.

8. To achieve that end the principle is defined in the first paragraph of Article 119 so as to include under the term 'the same work' the case of 'work to which equal value is attributed', and the second paragraph emphasizes merely that where a job classification system is used for determining pay it is necessary to ensure that it is based on the same criteria for both men and women and so drawn up to exclude any discrimination on grounds of sex.

9. It follows that where there is disagreement as to the application of that concept a worker must be entitled to claim before an appropriate authority that this work has the same value as other work and, if that is found to be the case, to have his rights under the Treaty and the Directive acknowledged by a binding decision. Any method which excludes that option prevents the aims of the Directive from being achieved.

Clearly, then, it is not sufficient for a Member State to leave it to employers to determine what amounts to work of equal value, since this would effectively leave an employee without redress in the event of a disagreement over the value of particular work. The obligation on the Member State to ensure that the aims of Article 119 and the Directive are achieved requires, if not a specific job classification system, at least the provision of an authority before which an employee can make a claim, if necessary in the context of adversarial proceedings.

The difficulties facing employees who wish to make an equal-pay claim were illustrated in the next case, in which the Court ruled that employers were not entitled to maintain pay practices which were opaque and which did not readily enable the criteria on which they were based to be determined:

Case 109/88, Handels og Kontorfunktionærernes Forbund i Danmark v. Dansk Arbejdsgiverforening, acting on behalf of Danfoss [1989] ECR 3199, [1991] 1 CMLR 8

The Union of Commercial and Clerical Employees in Denmark had brought Danfoss, an employer, before the Industrial Arbitration Board. The case was brought for the benefit of two female employees, and was based on the principle of equal pay. Danfoss paid the same basic wage to employees in the same wage group, but it also awarded individual pay supplements which were calculated on the basis of mobility, training, and seniority. Each of the two female employees worked within a different wage group, and within these two wage groups it was shown that a man's average wage was higher than that of a woman. The Board referred several questions to the Court.

THE ECJ

10. It is apparent from the documents before the Court that the issue between the parties to the main proceedings has its origin in the fact that the system of individual supplements applied to basic pay is implemented in such a way that a woman is unable to identify the reasons for a difference between her pay and that of a man doing the same work. Employees do not know what criteria in the matter of supplements are applied to them and how they are applied. They know only the amount of their supplemented pay without being able to determine the effect of the individual criteria. Those who are in a particular wage group are thus unable to compare the various components of their pay with those of the pay of their colleagues who are in the same wage group.

11. In those circumstances the questions put by the national court must be understood as asking whether the Equal Pay Directive must be interpreted as meaning that where an undertaking applies a system of pay which is totally lacking in transparency, it is for the employer to prove that his practice in the matter of wages is not discriminatory, if a female worker establishes, in relation to a relatively large number of employees, that the average pay for women is less than for men.

12. In that respect, it must first be borne in mind that in its judgment of 20 June 1988 in Case 318/86 *Commission* v. *France* [1988] ECR 3559, paragraph 27, the Court condemned a system of recruitment, characterized by a lack of transparency, as being contrary to the principle of equal access to employment on the ground that the lack of transparency prevented any form of supervision by the national courts.

13. It should next be pointed out that in a situation where a system of individual pay supplements which is completely lacking in transparency is at issue, female employees can establish differences only in so far as average pay is concerned. They would be deprived of any effective means of enforcing the principle of equal pay before the national courts if the effect of adducing such evidence was not to impose upon the employer the burden of proving that his practice in the matter of wages is not in fact discriminatory.

14. Finally, it should be noted that under Article 6 of the Equal Pay Directive Member States must, in accordance with their national circumstances and legal systems, take the measures necessary to ensure that the principle of equal pay is applied and that effective means are available to ensure that it is observed. The concern for effectiveness which thus underlies the Directive means that it must be interpreted as implying adjustments to national rules on the burden of proof in special cases where such adjustments are necessary for the effective implementation of the principle of equality.

13. To show that his practice in the matter of wages does not systematically work to the disadvantage of female employees the employer will have to indicate how he has applied the criteria concerning supplements and will thus be forced to make his system of pay transparent.

In *Commission* v. *United Kingdom* above, the concern for the effectiveness of the equal pay principle, which underlies Directive 75/117, meant that the Member States had to take steps to ensure an adequate method for employees to determine whether their work was of equal value with that of another. In *Danfoss*, however, the Court decided that the principle of effectiveness could require the employer, by way of a reversal of the normal onus of proof, to show that a non-transparent pay policy did not discriminate on grounds of sex. The difficulty of determining on what basis supplements were paid had meant that the complainant employees could only show that the average pay across a group of women was lower than the average pay of men. If the normal burden of proof were to apply, it would be difficult or indeed impossible for an affected employee to show that pay discrimination had, in fact, occurred. What is particularly interesting about the *Danfoss* case is that the Commission in 1988 had proposed a directive on reversing the burden of proof in sex-discrimination cases, but this had been blocked in the Council.[26] But the Court, overriding the Member State objections reflected in the non-adoption of this proposal, nevertheless achieved a similar result in the field of pay, in its ruling in *Danfoss*.[27] This particular dynamic, where the Court can be seen to assert its authority over the states and over the Community legislative process in the field of sex discrimination, will be seen again below in the context of the Court's rulings on occupational pensions.

(b) Indirect Discrimination in Pay and Objective Justification

We saw in Chapter 4 that the Court in *Defrenne (No 2)* drew a distinction between discrimination which could be identified 'solely with the aid of the criteria based on equal work and equal pay referred to by the article' and indirect and disguised discrimination 'which can only be identified by reference to more explicit implementing provisions of a Community or national character'.[28] According to the Court, while Article 119 could have direct effect in the former type of case, it could not in the latter. Further legislation would be required in the second case before certain kinds of indirect discrimination could be identified and targeted. However, in a case in which pay provisions in legislation or in a collective-bargaining agreement could be seen 'on a purely legal analysis' to be discriminatory on grounds of sex, Article 119 would have direct effect, since a court is 'in a position to establish all the facts which enable it to decide whether a woman is receiving lower pay than a male worker performing the same tasks'.[29]

26 [1988] OJ C176/5. For comment on this aspect of *Danfoss*, see J. Shaw, 'The Burden of Proof and the Legality of Supplementary Payments in Equal Pay Cases' (1990) 15 ELRev. 260, 263–4. In its 1994 White Paper on Social Policy, COM(94)333, the Commission indicated that it would attempt again to gain agreement on the adoption of the proposed dir., but would withdraw it if agreement had not been reached by the end of 1994.

27 For criticism of the draft dir., see E. Ellis, *European Community Sex Equality Law* (Clarendon Press, 1992), 156–8.

28 N. 16 above, para. 18. See Ch. 4, 162–3.

29 *Ibid.*, para. 23.

Indirect discrimination is a concept which has been discussed in Chapters 14, 15, and 16 in the context of discriminatory restrictions on freedom of movement in the Community. In the context of equal treatment of women and men, the concept of indirect discrimination is one which is familiar in other jurisdictions—in particular in the United States—as a means of confronting and redressing systemic discrimination. Thus, where a rule or a practice, although not framed in terms which apply only to one sex, has the effect of disadvantaging a considerably higher percentage of one sex, that rule or practice will be indirectly discriminatory.

The Court's analysis in *Defrenne (No 2)* of what it called 'indirect and disguised' discrimination was subsequently confirmed by its ruling in *Macarthys Ltd* v. *Smith*.[30] In this case the Court said that, for the purpose of determining discrimination in pay between men and women, comparisons were to be confined to parallels drawn between work actually done by employees of different sex within the same establishment or service,[31] although the employment need not be contemporaneous.[32] Comparisons with a hypothetical male worker would take the situation outside the direct effect of Article 119, since the identification of discrimination in that case implied 'comparative studies of entire branches of industry and therefore requires, as a prerequisite, the elaboration by the Community and national legislative bodies of criteria of assessment'.[33] However, even if a comparator doing the same work or work of equal value within the same establishment cannot be found, no legislation is needed and Article 119 will be directly effective if a woman is paid less than a man who is doing work of *lower* value within the same establishment.[34] This apparently self-evident conclusion had not recommended itself to the national court in the case.[35] However, the case is not authority for the proposition that Article 119 of itself requires proportionate pay, so that, although a woman in such circumstances is entitled to at least the same pay as a man doing work of lower value, she cannot necessarily rely directly on Article 119 for payment of a higher wage which would reflect the value of her work.

It was pointed out in a subsequent case by Advocate General Warner that the language used by the Court in *Defrenne (No 2)*, to indicate when Article 119 would not have direct effect, was puzzling, since it implied that the Article could not have direct effect where discrimination was 'indirect' or 'disguised'.[36] However, the case law since then establishes that the existence of

[30] Case 129/79, *Macarthys Ltd* v. *Smith* [1980] ECR 1275, [1980] 2 CMLR 205, paras. 14–15.

[31] On whether Art. 119 extends to comparisons with workers in other establishments, see E. Ellis, n. 27 above, 62–3.

[32] See also Case C–200/91, *Coloroll Pension Trustees Ltd* v. *James Richard Russell*, [1994] ECR I–4389, paras. 103–4.

[33] It is not clear after this judgment whether a woman complaining of unequal pay can point to a male comparator in a different establishment.

[34] Case 157/86, *Murphy* v. *Bord Telecom Eireann* [1988] ECR 673, [1988] 1 CMLR 879.

[35] *Murphy* v. *Bord Telecom Eireann* [1986] ILRM 483.

[36] See the comments of Warner A.G. in Case 69/80 *Worringham and Humphreys* v. *Lloyd's Bank Ltd.* [1981] ECR 767, 803, [1981] 2 CMLR 1, arguing that it was not accurate to say that Art. 119 could not have direct effect in the case of covert or indirect discrimination.

ndirect discrimination does not preclude the direct effect of Article 119, and that such discrimination can be identified on what the Court called a 'purely legal analysis' without the need for further implementing legislation. This was first established in the *Jenkins* case:

Case 96/80, Jenkins v. Kingsgate (Clothing Productions) Ltd [1981] ECR 911, [1981] 2 CMLR 24

The complainant was a part-time female employee of Kingsgate, who considered that the fact that she was paid a lower hourly rate than her full-time male colleagues performing the same work was a breach of the equal-pay principle. She brought an action before the Industrial Tribunal claiming a breach of the United Kingdom Equal Pay Act 1970, which provided for equal pay whenever a woman was employed on 'like work' with a man in the same employment. Her employer acknowledged that the work was 'like work' but argued that the different pay rates were, in accordance with section 1(3) of the Act, due to a material difference other than the difference of sex.

THE ECJ

9. It appears from the first three questions and the reasons stated in the order making the reference that the national court is principally concerned to know whether a difference in the level of pay for work carried out part-time and the same work carried out full-time may amount to discrimination of a kind prohibited by Article 119 of the Treaty when the category of part-time workers is exclusively or predominantly comprised of women.

10. The answer to the questions thus understood is that the purpose of Article 119 is to ensure the application of the principle of equal pay for men and women for the same work. The differences in pay prohibited by that provision are therefore exclusively those based on the difference of the sex of the workers. Consequently, the fact that part-time work is paid at an hourly rate lower than pay for full-time work does not amount per se to discrimination prohibited by Article 119 provided that the hourly rates are applied to workers belonging to either category without distinction based on sex.

11. If there is no such distinction, therefore, the fact that work paid at time rates is remunerated at an hourly rate which varies according to the number of hours worked per week does not offend against the principle of equal pay laid down in Article 119 of the Treaty, in so far as the difference in pay between part-time work and full-time work is attributable to factors which are objectively justified and are in no way related to any discrimination based on sex.

12. Such may be the case, in particular, when by giving hourly rates of pay which are lower for part-time work than those for full-time work the employer is endeavouring, on economic grounds which may be objectively justified, to encourage full-time work irrespective of the sex of the worker.

13. By contrast, if it is established that a considerably smaller percentage of women than of men perform the minimum number of weekly working hours required in order to be able to claim the full-time hourly rate of pay, the inequality in pay will be contrary to Article 119 of the Treaty where, regard being had to the difficulties encountered by women in arranging to work that minimum

number of hours per week, the pay policy of the undertaking in question cannot be explained by factors other than discrimination based on sex.

14. Where the hourly rate of pay differs according to whether the work is part-time or full-time it is for the national courts to decide in each individual case whether, regard being had to the facts of the case, its history and the employer's intention, a pay policy such as that which is at issue in the main proceedings although represented as a difference based on weekly working hours is or is not in reality discrimination based on the sex of the worker.

The reasoning in this judgment is somewhat muddled. Although the Court stated in paragraph 10 that the only differences in pay prohibited by Article 119 are those based on sex, it would appear from the rest of the judgment that this does not mean that only pay differences which are deliberately or directly discriminatory on grounds of sex will breach that provision. On the contrary the Court emphasizes in the following paragraph that, even where there is no sex-based distinction, the difference in hourly pay between part-time and full-time workers will be compatible with Article 119 only 'insofar as they are objectively justified'. In paragraph 12 the Court gives an example of what it appears to consider a legitimate policy which an employer might be pursuing by maintaining different pay rates for part- and full-time work, namely to encourage a greater number of full-time workers.[37] However, although this might seem to conclude the issue against female workers—who, Advocate General Warner noted in his opinion, constitute 90 per cent of part-time workers in the Community—the Court makes it clear that the issue is one for the national court to weigh. If the employer claims that the differential pay policy is justified in the interests of recruiting full-time workers, yet it is clear that a much smaller proportion of women than of men can, on account of family responsibilities, manage to work full-time, paragraph 13 seems to indicate that the onus remains on the employer to show that the pay policy is genuinely justified on grounds other than sex. Whether the 'recruitment of full-time workers' would of itself constitute adequate justification remains to be decided by the national court, taking into account not just the employer's intention but all of the facts of the case and its history.The broadening of the formal criterion of direct sex-based discrimination in *Jenkins*, to include the less obvious but equally or even more pervasive forms of pay discrimination affecting women, was an important development. However, the development alongside it of an equally broad and relatively undefined concept of objective justification reduces its significance and impact.

Exactly what can constitute objective justification remains unclear, in part because the Court generally, as in *Jenkins*, leaves the matter to be decided by the national court. Not only does this introduce the problem of differences amongst the tribunals of the various Member States on whether a certain

[37] See more recently the decision of the ECJ in the context of equal treatment, rather than pay, where it ruled that the interests of the enterprise might justify discrimination against part-time workers: Case C–189/91, *Kirshammer-Hack* v. *Sidal* [1993] ECR I–6185.

ndirectly discriminatory pay policy is justified, but it is not clear what factors nay or may not constitute an objective justification. The Court has gradually begun to give guidance on the latter question, and has done so increasingly in more recent case law, declaring some grounds of justification to be too general, and indicating that others may be sufficient. However, the problems of nconsistency and lack of certainty arising from the fact that the issue is ultimately to be decided by national courts still remain, thus contributing to the volume of expensive and possibly duplicated litigation in different Member States.

In the case of *Bilka*, the Court expanded further on the meaning of 'objective justification' and formulated a test similar to the three-part proportionality test which it developed when examining state justifications for restrictions on the free movement of goods and services:[38]

Case 170/84, Bilka-Kaufhaus GmbH v. Karin Weber von Hartz [1986] ECR 1607, [1986] 2 CMLR 701.

Bilka was a department store which had established a supplementary occupational pension scheme for its employees, as part of their contracts of employment. Part-time employees could obtain pensions under the scheme only if they had worked full-time for at least 15 years over a total period of 20 years. Since Karin Weber did not fulfil these conditions, Bilka refused to pay her a pension under the scheme. She claimed before the German courts that the scheme infringed Article 119 of the Treaty, arguing that female workers were more likely than their male colleagues to take part-time work so as to be able to care for their families and children. On a reference under Article 177, the Court referred to its ruling in *Jenkins* v. *Kingsgate* and adopted the same reasoning in this context.

THE ECJ

29. If, therefore, it should be found that a much lower proportion of women than men work full time, the exclusion of part-time workers from the occupational pension scheme would be contrary to Article 119 of the Treaty where, taking into account the difficulties encountered by women workers in working full-time, that measure could not be explained by factors which exclude any discrimination on grounds of sex.

30. However, if the undertaking is able to show that its pay practice may be explained by objectively justified factors unrelated to any discrimination on grounds of sex there is no breach of Article 119.

. . .

33. In its observations Bilka argues that the exclusion of part-time workers from the occupational pension scheme is intended solely to discourage part-time work, since in general part-time workers refuse to work in the late afternoon and on Saturdays. In order to ensure the presence of an adequate workforce during those periods it was therefore necessary to make full-time work more attractive than part-time work, by making the occupational pension scheme open only to

[38] See 818–19 below for further discussion of *Bilka* in the context of what constitutes pay under Art. 119.

full-time workers. Bilka concludes that on the basis of the judgment of 31 March 1981 it cannot be accused of having infringed Article 119.

. . .

36. It is for the national court, which has sole jurisdiction to make findings of fact, to determine whether and to what extent the grounds put forward by an employer to explain the adoption of a pay practice which applies independently of a worker's sex but in fact affects far more women than men may be regarded as objectively justified economic grounds. If the national court finds that the measures chosen by the employer correspond to a real need on the part of the undertaking, are appropriate with a view to achieving the objectives pursued and are necessary to that end, the fact that the measures affect a far greater number of women than men is not sufficient to show that they constitute an infringement of Article 119.

37. The answer to question 2(a) must therefore be that under Article 119 a department store company may justify the adoption of a pay policy excluding part-time workers, irrespective of their sex, from its occupational pension scheme on the ground that it seeks to employ as few part-time workers as possible, where it is found that the means chosen for achieving that objective correspond to a real need on the part of the undertaking, are appropriate with a view to achieving the objective in question and are necessary to that end.

The proportionality requirement can be seen here in paragraph 36. An indirectly discriminatory measure of this kind may be justified, on the Court's reasoning, if, first, the measure answers a 'real need' of the employer; secondly, the measures are 'appropriate' to achieve the objectives they pursue; and, finally, the measures are 'necessary' to achieve those objectives. Phrased in slightly different language, this test corresponds broadly to the 'rule of reason' test for proportionality in the free movement of goods and services context. Again, however, it can be seen that the Court does not say whether it considers the discrimination against part-time workers in this case to be justified, and although it appears to accept that the encouragement of full-time workers is an acceptable policy, it does not state whether the pursuit of this policy justifies the disadvantage in pay to women. Ultimately, the proportionality test is left for the national courts to apply.

Some years after *Bilka*, the Court was faced with a similar case involving the exclusion of part-time workers from sick-pay provision. The issue of indirect sex discrimination was the same, given that the affected group constituted part-time workers, but on this occasion the provisions in question were contained in national legislation, rather than in the act of an employer:

Case 171/88, Rinner-Kühn v. FWW Spezial-Gebäudereinigung GmbH [1989] ECR 2743, [1993] 2 CMLR 932

The complainant worked for an office-cleaning company normally for ten hours a week. She brought proceedings against her employer on the ground that she was refused wages while absent from work owing to illness. German legislation required employers to provide up to six weeks of sick pay, but excluded from its scope those employees who normally worked no more than ten hours a week. The national court asked the Court whether such legislation was compatible with Article 119 and Directive 75/117, even though the proportion of women adversely affected by the exclusion was considerably greater than that of men.

THE ECJ

12. In such a situation, it must be concluded that a provision such as that in question results in discrimination against female workers in relation to male workers and must, in principle, be regarded as contrary to the aim of Article 119 of the Treaty. The position would be different only if the distinction between the two categories of employee were justified by objective factors unrelated to any discrimination on grounds of sex . . .

13. In the course of the procedure, the German Government stated, in response to a question put by the Court, that workers whose period of work amounted to less than 10 hours a week or 45 hours a month were not as integrated in, or as dependent on, the undertaking employing them as other workers.

14. It should, however, be stated that those considerations, in so far as they are only generalizations about certain categories of workers, do not enable criteria which are both objective and unrelated to any discrimination on grounds of sex to be identified. However, if the Member State can show that the means chosen meet a necessary aim of social policy and that they are suitable and requisite for attaining that aim, the mere fact that the provision affects a much greater number of female workers than male workers cannot be regarded as constituting an infringement of Article 119.

It is significant that the Court applied the same 'indirect-discrimination' and 'objective-justification' analysis to the legislative provisions in this case as it did to the employer agreements in *Jenkins* and in *Bilka*. Advocate General Darmon had argued against the establishment of a presumption of indirect discrimination requiring justification, whenever a national legislative provision was seen to have an adverse impact on a far greater number of women than men. In his view, employer agreements such as that in *Bilka* were 'rules of law of modest status' whereas legislative provisions which might have taken into account many 'social, economic, and political' circumstances other than the adverse effects on women were of a different order and should not have to be justified simply on the ground of their adverse effects on women.[39] From the fact that the proposed Commission directive on reversing the burden of proof in sex-discrimination cases has never been adopted, he deduced that there was no rule requiring reversal where discriminatory effects only could be shown.[40] The Court, however, applied the same analysis as it had done in *Bilka*. Thus the onus is on the employee—save in a case like *Danfoss*, above, where the employer's system is insufficiently transparent—to show in the first instance

[39] See below, however, that in the context of *social security* legislation, the Court in fact applies the proportionality test loosely, leaving a considerable 'margin of discretion' to the states, which makes indirectly discriminatory practices very easy to justify.

[40] For the Commission proposal, see [1988] OJ C176/5.

that those receiving lower payments are predominantly or disproportionatel[y] women. The onus then shifts to the employer to justify such indirect discrim[in]ation, without the employee having to impute a discriminatory intent or t[o] prove that the pay policy is in some way based on sex.[41]

The proportionality test was phrased slightly differently in *Rinner-Kühn* where discrimination by the state rather than by the employer was in issue. The 'real need of the employer' mentioned in *Bilka* was replaced in *Rinner-Kühn* by a 'necessary aim' of social policy, and rather than requiring the mean[s] chosen to achieve that aim to be 'appropriate and necessary', the Court i[n] *Rinner-Kühn* said it must be 'suitable and requisite'. The thrust of the test however, remains essentially the same, its aim being to require the responsibl[e] authority to demonstrate that any discrimination which does occur is effectiv[e] in achieving a legitimate purpose and goes no further than is necessary t[o] achieve that purpose. The Court also gave a little more guidance on what ma[y] or may not constitute objective justification, in stating that generalized con[]siderations about the tendency of full-time as opposed to part-time workers t[o] integrate more in the working establishment could not constitute goo[d] grounds for indirect discrimination, but indicating that 'social policy' aim[s] might do so.[42]

Similarly in the case of *Danfoss*, discussed above, the Court gave some indi[]cation of the kind of justification for indirect discrimination which might b[e] acceptable.[43] Having decided that the onus was on the employer, whose cri[]teria for supplementary pay were not transparent, to explain the system of pa[y] clearly, the Court considered whether these criteria, which included factor[s] such as mobility, training, and length of service of employees, might be indi[]rectly discriminatory. 'Mobility'—a term used, somewhat oddly, apparently t[o] describe characteristics such as enthusiasm and initiative—was, in the Court'[s] view, a neutral criterion which should not disadvantage women unless th[e] employer misapplied it. However, if mobility meant adaptability to hours an[d] places of work, then the Court considered that it could disadvantage wome[n] because of family and household duties for which they so often bear respons[]ibility. The criteria of training and length of service, too, although 'neutral', could disadvantage women. However, the Court took the view that they could be objectively justified if the employer could show, for example, that it was o[f] importance for the performance of specific tasks that the employee could be adaptable and mobile, or had valuable experience due to the length of service.

[41] See J. Shaw, 'Sick Pay for Cleaners', (1989) 14 ELRev. 428, for criticism of the A.G.'s argument and the difficulties it would pose for employees.

[42] In the UK, the HL in *Equal Opportunities Commission* v. *Secretary of State for Employment* [1994] 1 WLR 409 concluded that, although the aim of increasing the availability of part-time work was a proper social policy aim, discrimination against part-time workers in pay or in the requirement of qualifying periods for statutory protection was neither a suitable nor a requisite means of achieving that aim. Contrast the decision of the ECJ in Case C–189/91, n. 37 above.

[43] Case 109/88, *Handels- og Kontorfunktionærernes Forbund i Danmark* v. *Dansk Arbejdsgiverforening, acting on behalf of Danfoss* [1989] ECR 3199, [1991] 1 CMLR 8.

However, despite these guidelines, the question of objective justification again was left to the national court to decide.

An instance of indirect discrimination stemming, not from legislative provisions nor from an occupational scheme established by an employer, but from a provision in a collective-bargaining agreement, arose in the case of *Kowalska*. In *Defrenne (No 2)*, the Court had ruled that Article 119 would apply not just to legislative provisions but also to discriminatory provisions contained in collective-bargaining agreements, but the concept of indirect discrimination prohibited by Article 119 had not been developed at that stage:

Case 33/89, Kowalska v. Freie und Hansestadt Hamburg [1990] ECR 2591

The plaintiff was an employee of Hamburg City, who challenged the refusal to award her a severance grant on her retirement. Under the terms of the Civil Service Employees' Collective Agreement, only full-time employees were entitled to such a severance grant. It was accepted that the part-time work-force contained a much larger number of women than of men. The Court, on a reference from the German Labour Court, considered whether a term such as that relating to the severance grant would be contrary to Article 119.

THE ECJ

12. The prohibition of discrimination between male and female workers contained in [Article 119], being mandatory, not only applies to the action of public authorities but extends also to all agreements which are intended to regulate paid labour collectively, as well as to contracts between individuals . . .

13. It is apparent from the documents before the Court that the collective agreement at issue allows the severance grant to be paid only to full-time workers on termination of the employment relationship. A collective agreement like the one at issue, which allows employers to maintain a difference in total pay as between two categories of workers—those who work a specified minimum number of hours each week and those who, whilst performing the same tasks, do not work that minimum number of hours—leads to discrimination against female workers as compared with male workers in cases where a considerably lower percentage of men than of women work part time. Such an agreement must, in principle, be regarded as infringing Article 119 of the Treaty.

As in its previous case law, the Court held that the *prima facie* infringement might be objectively justified, but again left the answer to be decided by the national court.[44]

Nimz, too, decided shortly after *Kowalska*, involved a challenge to a term in a collective agreement, this time a system of salary classification based on rules relating to length of service. Only half of the period of service of specified part-time workers was taken into account in calculating their salary grade,

[44] In cases C-3/99, C-409 & C-425/92, C-34, C-50 & C-78/93, *Stadt Lengerich* v. *Helmig*, judgment of 15 December 1994, the Court ruled that there was no indirect discrimination where collective agreements restricted payment of overtime supplements to cases where the normal working hours fixed for full-time workers were exceeded.

which amounted to indirect discrimination against women. This time the Court, rather than simply referring to the justification offered by the employer, indicated its disapproval of certain grounds:

Case 184/89, Nimz v. Freie und Hansestadt Hamburg [1991] ECR 297, [1992] 3 CMLR 699

THE ECJ

13. In this regard, the City of Hamburg claimed during the procedure that full-time employees or those who work for three-quarters of normal working time acquire more quickly than others the abilities and skills relating to their particular job. The German Government also relied on their more extensive experience.

14. It should however, be stated that such considerations, in so far as they are no more than generalizations about certain categories of workers, do not make it possible to identify criteria which are both objective and unrelated to any discrimination on grounds of sex . . . Although experience goes hand in hand with length of service, and experience enables the worker in principle to improve performance of the tasks allotted to him, the objectivity of such a criterion depends on all the circumstances in a particular case, and in particular on the relationship between the nature of the work performed and the experience gained from the performance of that work upon completion of a certain number of working hours. However, it is a matter for the national court, which alone is competent to evaluate the facts, to determine in the light of all the circumstances whether and to what extent a provision in a collective agreement such as that here at issue is based on objectively justified factors unrelated to any discrimination on grounds of sex.

This ruling underscores the point made in *Rinner-Kühn*, that general assumptions or assertions about the attributes of part-time workers are unlikely to constitute adequate grounds for justifying a measure which has a disproportionately adverse impact on one sex. Even the argument relating to the greater experience of full-time workers was not in itself sufficient as a justification, since the Court considered that it depended very much on the nature of the work performed and on whether such experience could really only be gained through completing a minimum number of hours per week. However, it is clear that a criterion of seniority is likely to disadvantage women disproportionately, given the frequent interruption of their career patterns on account of family responsibilities.

It must be noted that although, in the absence of firm guidance from the Court, the disparities amongst the Member States which are likely to arise from the conclusions of different national courts on whether particular discriminatory practices can be objectively justified or not is very problematic, it is evident that the Article 177 reference procedure does not always provide the best forum for an analysis of the justification put forward by an employer or a state, unless the factual information provided to the Court is very thorough.

The application of the equal pay principle to less obvious and more systemic forms of pay discrimination can be seen in the recent case of *Enderby*:

Case 127/92, Enderby v. Frenchay Health Authority and the Secretary of State for Health [1993] ECR 5535, [1994] 1 CMLR 8

Enderby, who was employed as a speech therapist by the defendant authority, brought proceedings before the Industrial Tribunal claiming that she had been discriminated against on grounds of sex. She argued that members of her profession, which was overwhelmingly a female profession, were paid appreciably less well than members of comparable professions whose jobs were of equal value to hers. She cited in particular the higher pay received by clinical psychologists and pharmacists, since these were professions in which, at an equivalent professional level, there were more men than women. The Court of Appeal requested from the Court an interpretation of Article 119 in the context of the case.

THE ECJ

7. In its first question, the Court of Appeal wishes to know whether the principle of equal pay for men and women requires the employer to prove, by providing objective justification, that a difference in pay between two jobs assumed to be of equal value, of which one is carried out almost exclusively by women and the other predominantly by men, does not constitute sex discrimination.

. . .

13. It is normally for the person alleging facts in support of a claim to adduce proof of such facts. Thus, in principle, the burden of proving the existence of sex discrimination as to pay lies with the worker who, believing himself to be the victim of such discrimination, brings legal proceedings against his employer with a view to removing the discrimination.

14. However, it is clear from the case law of the Court that the onus may shift when that is necessary to avoid depriving workers who appear to be the victims of discrimination of any effective means of enforcing the principle of equal pay . . . (judgments in case 170/84 *Bilka-Kaufhaus* [1986] ECR 1607, at paragraph 31, Case C–33/89 *Kowalska* [1990] ECR I–2591 at paragraph 16, and C–184/89 *Nimz* [1991] ECR I-297 at paragraph 15) . . . (judgment in Case 109/88 *Danfoss* [1989] ECR 3199 at paragraph 16).

15. In this case, as both the FHA and the United Kingdom observe, the circumstances are not exactly the same as in the cases just mentioned. First, it is not a question of *de facto* discrimination arising from a particular sort of arrangement such as may apply, for example, in the case of part-time workers. Secondly, there can be no complaint that the employer has applied a system of pay wholly lacking in transparency since the rates of pay of NHS speech therapists and pharmacists are decided by regular collective bargaining processes in which there is no evidence of discrimination as regards either of those two professions.

16. However, if the pay of speech therapists is significantly lower than that of pharmacists and if the former are almost exclusively women while the latter are predominantly men, there is a *prima facie* case of sex discrimination, at least where the two jobs in question are of equal value and the statistics describing that situation are valid.

17. It is for the national court to assess whether it may take into account those statistics, that is to say, whether they cover enough individuals, whether they illustrate purely fortuitous or short-term phenomena, and whether, in general, they appear to be significant.

18. Where there is a prima facie case of discrimination, it is for the employer to show that there are objective reasons for the difference in pay. Workers would be unable to enforce the principle of equal pay before national courts if evidence of a *prima facie* case of discrimination did not shift to the employer the onus of showing that the pay differential is not in fact discriminatory.

Although the reference had been made from the national court on the assumption that the two jobs were of equal value, *Enderby* illustrates the problem of establishing whether work which is performed predominantly by women is undervalued in comparison to work which is performed predominantly by men.[45] In the case of part-time and full-time workers, it is clear that the actual tasks being done are the same, whereas in the case of two quite distinct types of work, and in the absence of a job-classification scheme, it is considerably more difficult to establish this. A second difficulty is in showing that the justification offered for the pay differential between two different but equally valuable sorts of work is not adequate, given the adverse impact of that pay differential on one sex.[46] The onus is on the employer to show justification, but it will often be difficult for the employee to try to counter the justifications offered, when broad economic grounds are pleaded. This can be seen in *Enderby* where one of the justifications offered—that the process of reaching the terms of pay, through non-discriminatory collective-bargaining processes, was fair in each case—was rejected by the Court, whereas the other—that the needs of the market, given the shortfall of applicants in one of the two types of work, led to different salary levels—clearly carried greater weight and could be very difficult for an employee to counter. Consistently with its increasing willingness to indicate whether certain grounds can constitute objective justification, the Court ruled that the separate bargaining processes could not of themselves justify the discrimination, since otherwise the employer could 'easily circumvent the principle of equal pay by using separate bargaining processes'.[47] By way of contrast the Court ruled that the needs of the market might constitute adequate justification, depending on whether the proportion of the increase in pay was in fact attributable to the need to attract suitable candidates to the less popular job. The case shows

[45] The fact that speech therapists in general are paid less than psychologists would not be a concern of Community law unless the lower-paid group was disproportionately composed of women, or indeed of men. The Commission in *Enderby* argued to the Court that the requirement of showing a substantially greater adverse impact on one sex avoided 'the danger of converting the rule against sex discrimination into a general obligation of equal pay independent of such discrimination'.

[46] It has been argued, with regard to the question whether there was indirect discrimination in the first place, that more should be done than just to show that statistically there are more women than men in a particular job, but also that it must be shown that there was some link with sex, such as that the nature of the work which enabled people to work part-time made it much more attractive to women, whereas the low pay made it much less attractive to men. See F. Herbert, 'Social Security and Indirect Discrimination' in *Equality of Treatment between Women and Men in Social Security*, ed. C.McCrudden (Butterworths, 1994). However, the Court in para. 16 of *Enderby* did not require any such link.

[47] [1993] ECR I–5535, para. 22.

some of the weakness of the concept of indirect sex discrimination, and indeed of law, in addressing inequality within the labour market. The fact that women traditionally tend to pursue certain careers and professions which allow for flexibility, even if they offer less competitive salary rates than in other professions which attract a greater number of men, means that women's pay is likely remain at lower levels than other work which is objectively equal in value.

Like the cases of *Nimz*[48] and *Kowalska*,[49] *Enderby* also shows that there may be a conflict between the principle of non-discrimination on grounds of sex and the collective-bargaining process, which was described by the Health Authority in its defence as 'a process of industrial democracy in which those affected by the terms and conditions of employment can participate', sometimes after many years of negotiation and exhaustive studies. The Court, however, made clear in this group of cases that the prohibition on sex discrimination, direct or indirect, must take priority over the autonomy of the industrial-bargaining process.

The concept of indirect discrimination has clearly had some effect in helping to promote the reality of equal pay for women in employment, by moving away from a formal analysis of whether the same rules are applied to women as those which are applied to men, regardless of the disadvantageous impact which those rules prove to have for women as a group. However, despite these advantages, the shortcomings of the approach, in particular of the Court's use of the 'objective justification' test, have also been noted.[50] The relative ease with which the commercial objectives of the undertaking or employer—such as the need to alleviate constraints on 'small or medium-sized enterprises'—can defeat the claim of indirect discrimination undermines its usefulness in remedying the considerable disadvantages suffered by women in the labour market.[51]

S. Fredman, European Community Discrimination Law: A Critique[52]

Indirect discrimination goes some way towards acknowledging the problematic male norm. Recognizing that certain practices obstruct the free entry of women into the labour force, indirect discrimination addresses situations in which employment practices or conditions, although treating both sexes alike in a formal sense, have the effect of excluding more women than men. In this way, the principle of equality of treatment is extended to incorporate, prima facie,

[48] Case C–184/89, *Nimz* v. *Freie und Hansestadt Hamburg* [1991] ECR I–297, [1992] 3 CMLR 699.

[49] Case C–33/89, *Kowalska* [1990] ECR I–2591.

[50] G. More, n. 11 above, 70; E. Szyszczak, 'L'Espace Social Européenne: Reality, Dreams or Nightmares?' [1990] German Yearbook of International Law 284, 296.

[51] See Case C–189/91, n. 37 above. See T. Hervey, 'Small Business Exclusion in German Dismissal Law' [1994] ILJ 267. Note that the Commission's two proposals for dirs. providing protections for part-time workers have never been adopted. See [1990] OJ C254/4 and C254/6. See also Case C-297/93 *Grau-Hupka*, 13 Dec. 1994, where the ECJ found no indirect discrimination despite the pay disadvantage of women who worked part-time while in receipt of a reduced pension.

[52] N. 11 above, 125.

divergences from a strictly male norm. However, there are two major limitations on the reach of indirect discrimination. Firstly, disproportionate impact does no more than establish a prima facie case of indirect discrimination. The employer is still permitted to defend indirectly discriminatory practices by arguing that they are justified for reasons which are not due to the sex of the worker. In effect then, the anti-discrimination principle is not a 'fundamental right', as it is frequently proclaimed to be, but merely a presumption which can be trumped by other considerations. Secondly, in its practical application, indirect discrimination does not make sufficiently radical inroads into the male norm. Although it has some redistributive effect, it does not demand a resolution of the underlying structural problems which disadvantage women in the workplace.

(c) The Breadth of Article 119: What Can Constitute 'Pay'?

This relatively simple question has not given rise to simple answers, despite the guidance given in Article 119 itself as to the meaning of the term 'pay'. The Court has given the term an increasingly wide scope, which, although it may advance the cause of at least formal financial equality between men and women in employment matters, has also given rise to uncertainty and confusion on account of the apparent overlap between pay and social security. The Court's widening of the concept of pay may indicate a desire to assert its hegemony in the context of Article 119, in particular since its rulings have undermined Community legislative measures—and thus the bargains struck by the Member States in the Council when adopting those measures—in this area. We will see, however, that the Court has not always asserted itself against the wishes of the Member States, but has at other times responded to the political context by retreating from some of its more expansive rulings.

In the first *Defrenne* case, which was brought against the Belgian State rather than against the employer, Sabena, the Court had an early opportunity to rule on what has since become a very tangled relationship between pay and pensions:

Case 80/70, Defrenne v. Belgium
[1971] ECR 445, [1994] 1 CMLR 494

The Court was asked to rule on whether a Belgian law concerning retirement pensions, which excluded air hostesses from its scope, fell within the ambit of Article 119. The retirement pension was granted under the terms of social security financed by contributions from workers, employers, and by State subsidy. Defrenne argued that there was a direct and necessary link between the retirement pension and salary, since certain conditions of the employment directly influenced the amount of the pension. She further argued that the state was not involved in financing the pension scheme. The Commission, by contrast, argued that social security benefits in general and pensions in particular must be excluded from the scope of Article 119.

THE ECJ

5. According to the first paragraph of Article 119 of the EEC Treaty Member States are required to ensure the application of the principle of equal pay for equal work.

6. The provision in the second paragraph of the article extends the concept of pay to any other consideration, whether in cash or in kind, whether immediate or future, provided that the worker receives it, albeit indirectly, in respect of his employment from his employer.

7. Although consideration in the nature of social security benefits is not therefore in principle alien to the concept of pay, there cannot be brought within this concept, as defined in Article 119, social security schemes or benefits, in particular retirement pensions, directly governed by legislation without any element of agreement within the undertaking or the occupational branch concerned, which are obligatorily applicable to general categories of workers.

8. These schemes assure for the workers the benefit of a legal scheme, the financing of which workers, employers and possibly the public authorities contribute in a measure determined less by the employment relationship between the employer and the worker than by considerations of social policy.

9. Accordingly, the part due from the employers in the financing of such schemes does not constitute a direct or indirect payment to the worker.

10. Moreover the worker will normally receive the benefits legally prescribed not by reason of the employer's contribution but solely because the worker fulfils the legal conditions for the grant of benefits.

11. These are likewise characteristics of special schemes which, within the framework of the general system of social security established by legislation, relate in particular to certain categories of workers.

Although the Court stressed that 'consideration in the nature of social security benefits' was not in itself excluded from the concept of pay, the factors which went to exclude the employer's contributions to the retirement pension in this case from the scope of Article 119 were threefold: first, the pension scheme was directly governed by legislation; secondly, there was no agreement on the scheme within the particular company or occupational branch concerned; and thirdly, the retirement scheme was *obligatorily* applicable to *general* categories of workers. The determining role of the state and the lack of involvement of the particular employer are clearly crucial, and the Court summed up the defining features which excluded the pension from Article 119 by stating that the pension scheme was set up essentially as a matter of social policy and not as a part of the employment relationship in question. The Court's definition of the difference between pay and social security is important, since equal treatment in social security is not covered by Article 119, but primarily by Directive 79/7, whereas we shall see that occupational social security is covered in part by Article 119 and in part by Directive 86/378. The significance of the different legal provisions is in the fact that the Directives contain many exceptions, and are of vertical direct effect only, whereas Article 119 is without exceptions and is both horizontally and vertically directly effective.

The wide interpretation of the concept of pay in Article 119 can be seen in the case law. In *Garland* v. *British Rail Engineering*,[53] the Court ruled that the fact that female employees could on retirement no longer enjoy travel facilities for their spouses and dependent children, whilst male employees continued to do so, constituted discrimination contrary to the Treaty. Since they were benefits conferred in respect of employment, even if after retirement and irrespective of any specific contractual obligation, they were held to be pay within the meaning of Article 119. Similarly in *Kowalska*, the Court ruled that a severance grant was covered by Article 119 since it was compensation to which a worker was entitled by reason of her employment, even though it was not paid in the course of employment but rather on termination of the employment relationship, so as to help the worker to adjust.[54] In *Nimz*, the complainant was not challenging pay rates in themselves, but rather the rules governing the system of salary-classification into grades, and the Court confirmed that such rules fell within the concept of pay in Article 119, since they directly governed changes in employees' salaries.[55]

In *Worringham*, an action was brought by two female employees of Lloyds Bank who claimed that the bank was in breach of its obligations by paying its male staff under 25 years a higher gross salary than its female staff of the same age engaged in the same work.[56] Contributions to a retirement scheme were compulsory for men under 25 but not for women under 25, and in order to cover their contribution, the bank added a sum equal to that amount to the gross salary for men. Since the calculation of various other benefits was linked to gross salary, the Court ruled that there was a breach of the equal-pay principle:

> Although, where women are not required to pay contributions, the salary of men after deduction of the contributions is comparable to that of women who do not pay contributions, the inequality between the gross salaries of men and women is nevertheless a source of discrimination contrary to Article 119 of the Treaty since because of that inequality men receive benefits from which women engaged in the same work or work of equal value are excluded, or receive on that account greater benefits or social advantages than those to which women are entitled.[57]

In *Rinner-Kühn*, the Court ruled that statutory sick pay, that is, wages which an employer is required by law to continue to pay an employee in the event of illness, fell within the meaning of pay in Article 119.[58] However, it is

[53] Case 12/81, *Garland* v. *British Rail Engineering Ltd* [1982] ECR 359, [1982] 1 CMLR 696.

[54] Case C–33/89, n. 49 above, para. 10.

[55] Case C–184/89, n. 48 above.

[56] Case 69/80, n. 36 above. See also Case 23/83, *Liefting* v. *Directie van het Academisch Ziekenhuis bij de Universiteit van Amsterdam* [1984] ECR 5225.

[57] Case 69/80, n. 36 above, para. 25.

[58] Case 171/88, *Rinner-Kühn* v. *FWW Spezial-Gebäudereinigung GmbH* [1989] ECR 2743, [1993] 2 CMLR 932, para. 7.

clearly difficult to distinguish this kind of pay from a social-security benefit.[59] Although these wages were to be paid by the employer, in the case of employees who worked a certain number of hours for a particular period of time, 80 per cent of such payment was thereafter to be reimbursed by the state. Given this fact, the wages would seem to be paid more as a matter of 'social policy' as suggested in *Defrenne (No 1)*, than as pay as part of the contract of employment within Article 119.[60] Clearly it is in an employee's interests that such sick pay is classified as pay rather than social security, given that Article 119, unlike Directive 79/7, is directly effective both against the state and against private employers. However, the lack of clarity about precisely what it is that determines whether a benefit constitutes social security or pay is not helpful either to employers, employees, or to the Member States in the long run, and it gives rise to lengthy and costly litigation.

In the case of *Barber*, Advocate General Van Gerven attempted to explain why payments which were required under statute, such as the statutory minimum redundancy payment, did not necessarily constitute social security benefits, but could constitute pay:[61]

> The fact that the employer's duty to pay compensation is dictated by social security considerations is not, in my view, sufficient to prevent a minimum payment from falling within the scope of Article 119. The same situation arises with regard to statutory provisions on the minimum wage. It would seem to be self-evident that the salary paid by an employer falls in its entirety within Article 119 even though it is wholly or partly subject to statutory provisions on the minimum wage.
>
> As stated earlier, the crux of the matter is the existence of an unseverable causal connection between the employment and the benefit.

The Court evidently agreed with this analysis, and ruled that severance benefits, including statutory redundancy payments, would constitute pay within the meaning of Article 119:

> 13. As regards, in particular, the compensation granted to a worker in connection with his redundancy, it must be stated that such compensation constitutes a form of pay to which the worker is entitled in respect of his employment, which is paid to him upon termination of the employment relationship, which makes it possible to facilitate his adjustment to the new circumstances resulting from the loss of his employment and which provides him with a source of income during the period in which he is seeking employment.
>
> 14. It follows that compensation granted to a worker in connection with his

[59] See also Case C–360/90, *Arbeiterwohlfahrt der Stadt Berlin* v. *Bötel* [1992] ECR I–3589, [1992] 3 CMLR 446, in which statutorily required compensation payments to workers attending training courses were held to constitute pay.

[60] Darmon A.G. did not take this view and emphasized the fact that the sick pay was directly related to the wages paid and to the hours and service of the employee. See J. Shaw, n. 41 above.

[61] Case C–262/88, n. 15 above.

redundancy falls in principle within the concept of pay for the purposes of Article 119 of the Treaty.

15. At the hearing, the United Kingdom argued that the statutory redundancy payment fell outside the scope of Article 119 because it constituted a social security benefit and not a form of pay.

16. In that regard it must be pointed out that a redundancy payment made by the employer, such as that which is at issue, cannot cease to constitute a form of pay on the sole ground that, rather than deriving from the contract of employment, it is a statutory or ex gratia payment.

17. In the case of statutory redundancy payments it must be borne in mind that, as the Court held in its judgment of 8 April 1976 in Case 43/75 *Defrenne* v. *Sabena* [1976] ECR 455 paragraph 40, Article 119 of the Treaty also applies to discrimination arising directly from legislative provisions. This means that benefits provided for by law may come within the concept of pay for the purposes of that provision.

18. Although it is true that many advantages granted by an employer also reflect considerations of social policy, the fact that a benefit is in the nature of pay cannot be called in question where the worker is entitled to receive the benefit in question from his employer by reason of the existence of the employment relationship.

The most significant developments in the area of uncertainty between pay and social security, however, came in the rulings relating to occupational pensions in the cases of *Barber* and *Bilka-Kaufhaus*,[62] along with the flood of litigation which followed on from the *Barber* ruling.[63]

The Court first addressed the issue of occupational pension schemes directly in *Bilka-Kaufhaus*. At the time judgment was given, a proposal for what subsequently became Directive 86/378 on occupational social security, to supplement Directive 79/7 on statutory social security, was being considered by the Council of Ministers. The terms of the 1986 Directive show that the institutions considered occupational pensions to be a matter of social security and not of pay, so that they were dealt with in a manner similar to matters covered by Directive 79/7, rather than under Article 119. However, the Court in *Bilka* took a different view, in the context of a supplementary occupational pension scheme entirely financed by the employer:

Case 170/84 Bilka-Kaufhaus GmbH v. Karin Weber von Hartz [1986] ECR 1607, [1986] 2 CMLR 701.

The facts are set out at p. 805 above.

THE ECJ

20. It should be noted that according to the documents before the Court the occupational pension scheme at issue in the main proceedings, although adopted

[62] Case 170/84, *Bilka-Kaufhaus GmbH* v. *Karin Weber von Hartz* [1986] ECR 1607, [1986] 2 CMLR 701.

[63] See further below, pp. 825–35.

in accordance with the provisions laid down by German legislation for such schemes, is based on an agreement between Bilka and the staff committee representing its employees and has the effect of supplementing the social benefits paid under national legislation of general application with benefits financed entirely by the employer.

21. The contractual rather than the statutory nature of the scheme in question is confirmed by the fact that, as has been pointed out above, the scheme and the rules governing it are regarded as an integral part of the contracts of employment between Bilka and its employers.

22. It must therefore be concluded that the scheme does not constitute a social security scheme governed directly by statute and thus does not fall outside the scope of Article 119. Benefits paid to employees under the scheme therefore constitute consideration received by the worker from the employer in respect of his employment, as referred to in the second paragraph of Article 119.

By contrast with the statutory pension scheme in *Defrenne (No 1)*, the Court in this case highlighted three factors: (1) the contractual nature of the pension scheme, (2) the fact that it was not directly governed by statute but by the agreement between employer and employee, and (3) that it was not financed in part by the public authorities but entirely by the employer. The fact that the employer chose to arrange the scheme in a way which corresponded to the statutory social-security scheme was held to be irrelevant, and the benefits paid to employees under the occupational scheme thus constituted pay under Article 119.

Although this decision should have sent a warning to the institutions which were in the process of adopting Directive 86/378 and treating occupational pensions as social security, not subject to Article 119, the Directive was nevertheless adopted in 1986. This difference of view between the Member States in the Council, on the one hand, and the Court, on the other, was starkly highlighted in the *Barber* case set out below, where the Court once again asserted its authority over the legislative institutions by reading Article 119 in such a way as to render much of Directive 86/378 redundant.[64]

In the subsequent case of *Newstead*, the Court had to consider whether compulsory *contributions of employees* to a contracted-out occupational pension scheme constituted pay within Article 119.[65] Bilka had ruled that *payments to employees* from a supplementary occupational pension scheme constituted pay. It was held in *Newstead*, however, following on from *Worringham*,[66] that, so long as gross salary was unaffected, compulsory deductions in net pay from all male employees to contribute to an occupational scheme providing for widows' pensions did not fall within Article 119. One of the reasons given by the Court was that, since the scheme was in part a substitute for the statutory pension scheme, it was to be treated like a

64 For another example of this Court/Member State dynamic, see the comment on *Danfoss*, nn. 26 and 27 above and text.

65 Case 192/85, *Newstead* v. *Department of Transport* [1987] ECR 4735, [1988] 1 CMLR 219.

66 Case 69/80, n. 36 above. See above, 816.

contribution to a statutory social-security scheme falling outside the scope of Article 119. Thus, whereas the payments to employees from a non-contracted-out occupational scheme in *Bilka* were 'pay' even though the scheme was adapted to correspond with the statutory social-security scheme, *Newstead* ruled that deductions from employees' pay to fund a contracted-out occupational pension scheme were not pay, but were in the nature of contributions to social-security benefits and thus not within Article 119. It will become clear after considering the case of *Barber* and subsequent decisions below, that the authority of *Newstead* is now very weak, if indeed it has not been overridden.[67] It has been suggested that *Newstead* may remain as authority for the narrow proposition that employee contributions to a widow's pension fund are a matter of social security, rather than pay,[68] but in the light of the case law since *Barber*, this is now unlikely.[69]

Despite the judgment in *Bilka*, then, and perhaps on account of the opposing trend of the judgment in *Newstead*, the ruling in the case of *Barber*, in which the issue of 'contracted-out' occupational pension schemes was directly addressed, came as a shock. Many had assumed, in spite of the *Bilka* ruling, that, if an occupational pension scheme was contracted out, in other words where it was set up by an employer in direct substitution for and in fulfilment of the obligations of the statutory scheme, payments of benefits to employees (and also, according to *Newstead*, deductions from the net pay of employees) would, by analogy with that statutory scheme, be treated as social security rather than as pay:

Case C–262/88, Barber v. Guardian Royal Exchange Assurance Group [1990] ECR I–1889, [1990] 2 CMLR 513

Barber was an employee of Guardian and was made redundant at the age of 52. He belonged to an occupational pension scheme set up and wholly financed by Guardian, which was regarded by the United Kingdom Occupational Pensions Board as a 'contracted-out' scheme under Social Security legislation, and thus as a substitute for the earnings-related part of the state pension scheme. This meant that members of the contracted-out scheme would contractually waive that part of the state pension scheme. Barber claimed that the terms of redundancy relating to his entitlement to an early retirement pension were in breach of Article 119. Under those terms, a woman would be entitled to an immediate pension on reaching the age of 50, whereas for a man the relevant age was 55. The Court was asked whether redundancy-related benefits, including a private occupational pension, fell within the terms of Article 119 or Directive 75/117.

[67] See below, 829.

[68] D. Curtin, 'Scalping the Community Legislator: Occupational Pensions and "Barber"' (1990) CMLRev. 475, 480–1.

[69] The payments in *Newstead* would have to be distinguished from the payments made in Case C–152/91, *Neath* v. *Hugh Steeper Ltd* [1993] ECR I–6935, para. 31, which were held, following *Barber*, to constitute pay. See 829–31 below.

THE ECJ

22. It must be pointed out in that regard that, in its judgment of 25 May 1971 in Case 80/70 *Defrenne* v. *Belgium* [1971] ECR 445, paragraphs 7 and 8, the Court stated that consideration in the nature of social security benefits is not in principle alien to the concept of pay. However, the Court pointed out that this concept, as defined in Article 119, cannot encompass social security schemes or benefits, in particular retirement pensions, directly governed by legislation without any element of agreement within the undertaking or the occupational branch concerned, which are compulsorily applicable to general categories of workers.

23. The Court noted that those schemes afford the workers the benefit of a statutory scheme, to the financing of which workers, employers and possibly the public authorities contribute in a measure determined less by the employment relationship than by considerations of social policy.

24. In order to answer the second question, therefore, it is necessary to ascertain whether those considerations also apply to contracted-out private occupational schemes such as that referred to in this case.

25. In that regard it must be pointed out first of all that the schemes in question are the result either of an agreement between workers and employers or of a unilateral decision taken by the employer. They are wholly financed by the employer or by both the employer and the workers without any contribution being made by the public authorities in any circumstances. Accordingly, such schemes form part of the consideration offered to workers by the employer.

26. Secondly, such schemes are not compulsorily applicable to general categories of workers. On the contrary, they apply only to workers employed by certain undertakings, with the result that affiliation to those schemes derives of necessity from the employment relationship with a given employer. Furthermore, even if the schemes in question are established in conformity with national legislation and consequently satisfy the conditions laid down by it for recognition as contracted-out schemes, they are governed by their own rules.

27. Thirdly, it must be pointed out that, even if the contributions paid to those schemes and the benefits which they provide are in part a substitute for those of the general statutory scheme, that fact cannot preclude the application of Article 119. It is apparent from the documents before the Court that occupational schemes such as that referred to in this case may grant to their members benefits greater than those which would be paid by the statutory scheme, with the result that their economic function is similar to that of the supplementary schemes which exist in certain Member States, where affiliation and contribution to the statutory scheme is compulsory and no derogation is allowed. In its judgment of 13 May 1986 in Case 170/84 *Bilka-Kaufhaus* v. *Weber von Hartz* [1986] ECR 1607, the Court held that the benefits awarded under a supplementary pension scheme fell within the concept of pay, within the meaning of Article 119.

28. It must therefore be concluded that, unlike the benefits awarded by national statutory social security schemes, a pension paid under a contracted-out scheme constitutes consideration paid by the employer to the worker in respect of his employment and consequently falls within the scope of Article 119 of the Treaty.

29. That interpretation of Article 119 is not affected by the fact that the private occupational scheme in question has been set up in the form of a trust and is administered by trustees who are technically independent of the employer, since Article 119 also applies to consideration received indirectly from the employer.

The distinction between social security and pay, which is one of the central issues of the *Barber* litigation, was very important in relation to pensions, because of the exceptions to the equal-treatment principle which were allowed under Social Security Directive 79/7 in relation to pensionable age and related benefits.[70] No such exception exists under Article 119, and companies which had operated contracted-out occupational pension schemes had proceeded on the assumption that they could maintain discriminatory pensionable ages as between men and women. In *Barber*, however, despite the strong submissions of various Member States, the Court made it clear that this assumption had not been well-founded.

The question was, in essence, whether contracted-out occupational pension schemes were governed by the principle set out in *Defrenne (No 1)*,[71] in which case they were social security, or that in *Bilka*, in which case they were pay. The Court adopted a similar analysis to that in *Bilka*, focusing on three features of the contracted-out scheme: first, it was agreed and entirely financed by the employer, not imposed directly by statute;[72] secondly, unlike most social security benefits the scheme was not compulsorily applicable to general categories of employees and although in conformity with national legislation, was governed by its own rules; and finally, although it was intended in substitution for the statutory scheme, its provisions could also go further and provide additional benefits, thereby making it indistinguishable from supplementary schemes such as those in *Bilka*. The fact that the fund was administered by trustees did not prevent the benefits paid from constituting pay, and this point was underlined in the subsequent ruling in *Coloroll* where the Court held that Article 119 could be relied upon directly as against the trustees, who were bound in their duties by the equal treatment principle.[73]

Having thus ruled that private 'contracted-out' occupational pension schemes could fall within the scope of Article 119, the Court went on to consider, first, whether different pension entitlements on redundancy for men and women, such as those in issue in the case, were contrary to Article 119, and, secondly, whether equal pay had to be ensured with respect to each element of pay or only on the basis of an overall assessment of the consideration paid to workers:

> 32. In the case of the first of those two questions thus formulated, it is sufficient to point out that Article 119 prohibits any discrimination with regard to pay as between men and women, whatever the system which gives rise to such inequality. Accordingly, it is contrary to Article 119 to impose an age condition which differs according to sex in respect of pensions paid under a contracted-out scheme,

[70] See further p. 870 below, Pt. 4(a)(iv).

[71] Case 80/70, n. 13 above.

[72] The ECJ made it clear subsequently in Case C–200/91, *Coloroll* n. 32 above, para. 88, that all benefits payable to an employee under an occupational pension scheme, whether the scheme was contributory or non-contributory—i.e. whether or not the employee also made contributions—consituted pay within Art. 119.

[73] Case C–200/91, *ibid.*, para. 24.

even if the difference between the pensionable age for men and that for women is based on the one provided for by the national statutory scheme.

. . .

34. With regard to the means of verifying compliance with the principle of equal pay, it must be stated that if the national courts were under an obligation to make an assessment and a comparison of all the various types of consideration granted, according to the circumstances, to men and women, judicial review would be difficult and the effectiveness of Article 119 would be diminished as a result. It follows that genuine transparency, permitting an effective review, is assured only if the principle of equal pay applies to each of the elements of remuneration granted to men or women.

This conclusion was one which had serious repercussions throughout the Community, and which fundamentally changed the way employers and others in the Member States would henceforth have to organize their pension schemes. Some of the radical effects of the ruling are discussed in the following commentary:

D. Curtin, Scalping the Community Legislator: Occupational Pensions and Barber[74]

One of the major points to emerge from the Court's decision in *Barber* is that the limitation originally imposed by the Court as to the scope of the direct effect of Article 119 is, to all intents and purposes, redundant. It has been consistently argued over the years that highly complex problems such as the different life expectancies of men and women, different retirement ages, putative pensionable service during maternity leave etc. all militated against direct effect being ascribed to Article 119 in the pensions sphere in the absence of implementing legislation. The view was that since pension benefits were not tangible and calculable in money terms, detailed criteria determining how equality had to be achieved would have to be established through appropriate measures at either Community level or national level. However the Court's judgment in *Barber* adopts the approach that once the question of deciding that occupational benefits fall within the scope of 'pay' in Article 119 has been answered, the national court will *ipso facto* be in a position to decide whether the litigant receives less pay than a member of the opposite sex engaged in the same work. What is radical about this approach is that it confirms that equal treatment in the pension context does not require that the total amount of a particular benefit be mathematically equal since neither the costs nor the value of total pension benefits received will ever be known in advance. What seems to be required is rather that the rate at which the benefit is enjoyed be equal.

The radical nature of the *Barber* judgment, unsurprisingly, met with criticism from Member States and from employers alike, as the argument of a defendant employer in one of the subsequent cases arising out of *Barber* shows:

[74] N. 68 above, 484.

> The *Barber* judgment . . . did not take sufficient account of the requirements of social policy which underlie occupational pension schemes such as that involved in this case . . . The test of equality which the Court of Justice applies to the factual justification for differential provisions in occupational pension schemes is stricter than that which it applies to statutory pension schemes.
>
> Community legislation had itself taken account of this unavoidable link between statutory and occupational pensions by providing for the gradual and parallel application of the principle of equal treatment (see Directive 86/378/EEC). However, it is very disturbing, from the point of view of social policy and the protection of legitimate expectations, when a decision of the Court of Justice bypasses the provisions of a directive by means of an interpretation of Article 119.[75]

Despite such criticisms, it was certainly clear that occupational pensions would henceforth have to be organized differently to comply with the *Barber* ruling. What was also of considerable concern to those affected, however, was the prospect of claims being made by all those who had, in the past, been adversely affected by the discriminatory conditions of pension schemes. No doubt in reaction to some of these concerns, the Court decided, as it had done in the first *Defrenne* case, to limit the retroactivity of its ruling. This decision was made partly in response to submissions made by the United Kingdom concerning the serious financial consequences the ruling would have, given the number of workers affiliated to contracted-out schemes which had derogated from the principle of equality between men and women by providing for different pensionable ages.[76] The Court agreed that the Member States and the other parties concerned had been entitled, in light of the authorization in the two Social Security Directives to defer implementation of the equal-treatment principle in relation to pensionable ages, to consider that Article 119 did not apply to pensions paid under contracted-out schemes:

> 44. In those circumstances, overriding considerations of legal certainty preclude legal situations which have exhausted all their effects in the past from being called in question where that might upset retroactively the financial balance of many contracted-out pension schemes. It is appropriate, however, to provide for an exception in favour of individuals who have taken action in good time in order to safeguard their rights. Finally, it must be pointed out that no restriction on the effects of the aforesaid interpretation can be permitted as regards the acquisition of entitlement to a pension as from the date of this judgment.
>
> 45. It must therefore be held that the direct effect of Article 119 of the Treaty may not be relied upon in order to claim entitlement to a pension with effect from a date prior to that of this judgment, except in the case of workers or those claiming under them who have before that date initiated legal proceedings or raised an equivalent claim under the applicable national law.

[75] See Case C–110/91 *Moroni*, n. 25 above.

[76] In particular, the UK argued that, unless the retroactive effect of the judgment was limited, the increase in cost would run to between £33 and 45 billion, with disastrous effects for the UK economy as a whole.

Despite the fact that they were intended to ensure a degree of legal certainty by restricting the retroactive effect of the decision, these paragraphs in fact gave rise to a great deal of uncertainty about the precise limits which had been placed upon the ruling. Several questions remained to be answered, and these came before the Court in the course of litigation which arose in different Member States. There had been considerable debate over the many possible meanings of paragraphs 44 and 45 of the judgment, in particular on whether Article 119 could be relied on in relation to periods of service completed before the date of the judgment when no pension payments in respect of those periods had yet been received, or whether it could only be relied on in relation to periods of service completed after the date of the judgment. Clearly the latter interpretation was the one which would have the least serious financial consequences for employers.

Before those cases were heard, however, the concern aroused by *Barber* in the Member States had prompted the annexation of an additional Protocol to the EC Treaty by the TEU, which was being negotiated at the time, purporting to limit the retroactive effect of the judgment in the way stated above. In other words, the Protocol stipulated that, with the exception of those who had already instituted a legal claim, only pay attributable to periods of service completed after 17 May 1990—the date of the *Barber* judgment—would constitute pay within Article 119.

It is interesting to see how, in the litigation which subsequently arose and which is discussed below, the Court's explanation of paragraphs 44 to 45 of the ruling in *Barber* managed, without mentioning the Protocol, to correspond with its terms. An awkward conflict of Community laws was prevented: the interpretation of the Court of the effect in a particular case of Article 119, and a Protocol purporting to limit Article 119 in this context, which, being attached to the EC Treaty, is of Treaty status.[77] The Protocol would override any conflicting judgment of the Court on the scope of Article 119, as soon as the TEU came into effect. Undoubtedly the Protocol was intended by the Member States to ensure that their desired interpretation of the scope of Article 119 would prevail, in the event that the Court chose a different and wider interpretation of the reach of the *Barber* ruling on Article 119.[78] Despite the brave attempt of Advocate General Van Gerven in a subsequent opinion to show that the Protocol was not intended to amend Article 119 or to call into question the Court's case law, it is clear that this is exactly what it would have done when the TEU came into effect, had the Court in one of the post-*Barber* cases given the scope of Article 119, as interpreted in *Barber*, a wider reading.[79]

[77] See Art. 239 EC.

[78] See D. Curtin, 'The Constitutional Structure of the Union: A Europe of Bits and Pieces' (1992) 29 CMLRev. 17, 51.

[79] See para. 23 of his one opinion in Cases C–109/91, *Ten Oever* v. *Stichting Bedrijfspensioenfonds voor het Glazenwassersen Schoonmaakerbedrijf*. [1993] ECR I–4879, C–110/91, n. 25 above, C–152/91, n. 69 above, and C–200/91 n. 32 above, as well as his comments in *Equality of Treatment between Women and Men in Social Security*, n. 46 above. See more generally T. Hervey

However, although it adopted a similar approach to the retroactivity of *Barber* as that in the Protocol, the Court also chose in further case law to reassert its independence by limiting the potential reach of that Protocol, ruling in *Fisscher* and *Vroege* that it had to be read 'in conjunction with the *Barber* judgment and cannot have a scope wider than the limitation of its effects in time'.[80] This meant that the Protocol related only to benefits and not to the right to join or belong to an occupational pension scheme. Thus discriminatory conditions of membership of an occupational scheme, such as a full-time requirement, or the exclusion of married women, were governed by *Bilka* rather than by the Protocol. The Court found that the reasons for limiting the retroactivity of the *Barber* ruling—i.e. the fact that the discrimination in pension schemes could reasonably have been considered to be permissible under Directive 86/378—did not apply to the issues in *Bilka*, which was decided before the Directive had been adopted. Thus, subject to the application of national time limits for bringing an action,[81] Article 119 could be relied on to challenge a discriminatory exclusion from a pension scheme as from the date of the *Defrenne (No 2)* judgment, on which Article 119 was held to be directly effective. On first consideration, the effects of these judgments might seem even more radical than those of *Barber* would have been without the temporal limitation on the ruling, since the employees claiming entitlement to pension benefits for past work would have made no financial contributions at all to the scheme on account of their exclusion. However, the Court also ruled that the right retroactively to join a pension scheme did not mean that such workers could avoid paying the value of the past contributions.[82] It is unlikely that many part-time working women or married women who were excluded from a pension scheme would now be able to afford the cumulative cost of those contributions.

It can be seen that the simple question posed at the beginning of this section, namely what constitutes pay within Article 119 for the purposes of the equal pay principle, yields anything but a simple answer. The series of questions which arose out of the *Barber* ruling indicate the complexity and confusion surrounding the whole area. In *Ten Oever*, the Court clarified the meaning of paragraphs 44 to 45 concerning the limits on the retroactive effect of that ruling, and followed the approach which had been adopted in the Protocol to the TEU:

'Legal Issues concerning the Barber Protocol' in *Legal Issues of the Maastricht Treaty*, n. 1 above, 329.

[80] Cases C–128/93 *Fisscher* v. *Voorhuis Hengelo BV and Stichting Bedrijfspensioenfonds voor de Detailhandel* [1994] ECR I–4583, and C–57/93, *Vroege* v. *NCIV Institut voor Volkshuisvesting BV and Stichting Pensioenfonds NCIV* [1994] ECR I–4541. See also Case C–7/93, *Bestuur van het Algemeen Burgerlijk Pensioenfonds* v. *Beune* [1994] ECR I–4471.

[81] As in the Court's general case law on remedies, the rules relating to national time limits must be no less favourable than for similar actions of a domestic nature and must not render impossible the exercise of the right: see *Fisscher*, n. 80 above, para. 39.

[82] Case C–128/93 n. 80 above, para. 37.

Case C-109/91, Ten Oever v. Stichting Bedrijfspensioenfonds voor het Glazenwassers- en Schoonmaakbedrijf [1993] ECR I–4879

THE ECJ

15. In essence, the second question asks the Court to state the precise scope of the limitation of the effects in time of the *Barber* judgment.

16. The precise context in which that limitation was imposed was that of benefits (in particular, pensions) provided for by private occupational schemes which were treated as pay within the meaning of Article 119 of the Treaty.

17. The Court's ruling took account of the fact that it is a characteristic of this form of pay that there is a time-lag between the accrual of entitlement to the pension, which occurs gradually throughout the employee's working life, and its actual payment, which is deferred until a particular age.

18. The Court also took into consideration the way in which occupational pension funds are financed and thus of the accounting links existing in each individual case between the periodic contributions and the future amounts to be paid.

19. Given the reasons explained in paragraph 44 of the *Barber* judgment for limiting its effects in time, it must be made clear that equality of treatment in the matter of occupational pensions may be claimed only in relation to benefits payable in respect of periods of employment subsequent to 17 May 1990, the date of the *Barber* judgment, subject to the exception in favour of workers or those claiming under them who have, before that date, initiated legal proceedings or raised an equivalent claim under the applicable national law.

The other matter decided by the Court in *Ten Oever* was that Article 119 covered not just pension benefits payable to an employee, but also to the employee's survivor—in this case a widow's pension—since the crucial factor was that the pension was paid by reason of the employment relationship between the employee and employer. Following on from this in the case of *Coloroll*, the Court ruled that Article 119 could be relied upon against the employer or the trustees of the pension scheme, not just by an employee under the scheme, but also by the employee's dependants.[83]

The limit placed on the retroactive effects of the *Barber* ruling was not, however, sufficient to answer the concerns of those affected by the decision, and in its argument to the Court in *Ten Oever*, the German Government took the opportunity to voice its sharp criticism of the Court's extension of Article 119 in the grey area between social security and pay:

> Benefits paid to survivors under a collective company pension scheme cannot be regarded as 'pay' within the meaning of Article 119 and therefore as (indirect) consideration for the work performed by the worker since the pension aspect, and thus the 'social security' aspect, is predominant in those benefits. A survivor's pension benefit is not so closely linked to the deceased person's service but, on the contrary, reflects the social policy aspect of compensating for a deficit which

[83] Case C–200/91 n. 32 above, paras. 17–19.

women have in the matter of pensions owing to the traditional allocation of roles. If it is considered that such an allocation is no longer justified in these modern times, the possibility of also providing for widowers' pensions should be regulated by legislation and not by the courts.[84]

In the case of *Moroni* the Court was asked whether the ruling in *Barber* applied in the same way to supplementary pension schemes as it did to contracted-out schemes.[85] It might be thought that this had been decided in *Bilka*, but the issue in *Bilka* was the compatibility with Article 119 of the total exclusion from a supplementary pension scheme of part-time workers, whereas the issue in *Moroni* was whether discriminatory pensionable ages in such a scheme were contrary to Article 119. The Court cited the same reasoning used in *Bilka*, and held that sums paid out under a supplementary occupational pension scheme did constitute pay, and that the discriminatory effects of setting different retirement ages were just as much a feature of supplementary occupational pension schemes as they were of contracted-out schemes such as that in *Barber*.[86] The argument made by the German Government that there was a strong link between the statutory social-insurance scheme and the supplementary occupational pension scheme, and that the latter was a form of social welfare rather than pay, did not sway the Court.[87]

In a long and rather confusing judgment in the case of *Beune*, concerning civil service pensions, the Court reviewed the criteria it had developed in its case law from *Defrenne (No 1)* to *Ten Oever* for determining whether a pension scheme constituted pay under Article 119 or social security under Directive 79/7.[88] Ultimately, having considered the criteria of agreement between employer and employee rather than statutory origin, absence of public funding of a scheme, the provision of benefits supplementary to state social security benefits, the Court concluded that the 'decisive' though not the 'exclusive' criterion (which seems to mean 'necessary' but not 'sufficient') was that set out in Article 119 itself: i.e. that the pension is paid to the worker by reason of the employment relationship between the worker and the former employer.[89] Consequently, even if the civil-service pension scheme was affected by 'considerations of social policy, of State organisation, or of ethics or even budgetary preoccupations'—i.e. factors which would normally point to its classification as a state social-security scheme rather than pay—the Court concluded that these could not prevail if three other factors were also present: if the pension paid by a public employer (1) concerned only a particular category of workers rather than general categories, (2) was directly related

[84] [1993] ECR I–4879.
[85] Case C–110/91, n. 25 above.
[86] *Ibid.*, para. 16.
[87] See also Case C–173/91 *Commission* v. *Belgium* [1993] ECR I–673, [1993] 2 CMLR 165, in which redundancy supplements were held to consitute pay within Art. 119, despite the argument of the Belgian Government that, being like early state retirement pensions, they constituted a form of social security falling within the exception in Art. 7(1)(a) of Dir. 79/7.
[88] Case C–7/93, n. 80 above.
[89] *Ibid.*, paras. 43–4.

to the period of service, and (3) was calculated, in its amount, by reference to the civil servant's last salary, then it was comparable to a pension paid by a private employer and would constitute pay.[90]

The relationship between Directive 86/378 and Article 119 was also raised in both *Beune* and *Moroni*, and the Court ruled quite simply that, whenever the legal criteria of pay and equal work could be identified, an employee could rely directly on Article 119. Thus Article 8 of the Directive, which purported to allow the postponement until 1993 of the establishment of equal pensionable ages in occupational schemes, has effectively been overridden in this context, since the Court held that it could not prevent an affected employee from relying directly on Article 119 of the Treaty.[91] Subsequently, in the *Coloroll* case, the Court ruled that the limitation on the retroactive effect of the *Barber* ruling applied to discriminatory age conditions in non-contracted-out and contracted-out occupational schemes alike.[92]

Among the various other issues raised in the cases of *Neath* and *Coloroll* was the question whether payments by an employer to a contracted-out occupational pension scheme (rather than payments to an employee, as in *Barber*) were covered by Article 119.[93] This question arose because actuarial calculations of the different life expectancies of men and women were used in determining the sums payable by an employer into the scheme. In both cases, a 'defined-benefit' pension scheme was in issue, under which employees would receive a pension, the criteria for which were fixed in advance, e.g. by reference to a fraction of their final year's salary for each year of service. It was held that contributions of *employees* to the scheme must consist of an identical amount for men and women, since, according to *Worringham*,[94] employee contributions were pay within Article 119. However, in such defined-benefit schemes, *employers'* contributions varied over time and were adjusted to take account of the pensions which would have to be paid. As a consequence of using the sex-based actuarial factors in calculating such employers' contributions, the amount which a male employee would receive on redundancy either in the form of a capital sum, transfer benefits, or a deferred pension would be less than that which a woman would receive. The Commission argued that such sums constituted pay, and that the differences in pay between men and women could not be justified by reference to the statistical data based on the average life expectancy of the two sexes, since the right to equal pay was given to employees individually, rather than as members of a class. Advocate General Van Gerven agreed and took the view that, in so far as it gave rise to different employee contributions or to different employee benefits (such as

[90] *Ibid.*, para. 45.

[91] *Ibid.*, paras. 64–5, and Case C–110/91, n. 25 above, paras. 25–6.

[92] Case C–200/91, n. 32 above, para. 71. It had been argued that it was clear, since the ruling in *Bilka* in 1986, that supplementary occupational pension schemes were covered by Art. 119, but neither the A.G. nor the Court accepted this. In the case of a pension benefit payable not according to length of service, but e.g. on the happening of an event such as the death of the employee, the Court held that the limit on the retroactive effect of the *Barber* ruling applied if the event took place before 17 May 1990. Contrast *Fisscher*, *Vroege*, and *Beune*, n. 80 above.

[93] Case C–152/91, n. 69 above.

[94] Case 69/80, n. 36 above.

lump sums or transfer value), the use of sex-based actuarial factors to ascertain the funding needed for a pension scheme was contrary to Article 119.[95] The Court, however, did not follow this view. In a defined-benefit scheme, the Court held that the pension which was promised according to fixed criteria constituted pay, since it represented the employer's 'commitment' to the employee. However, the Court considered that employer contributions were paid in order to ensure the adequacy of the funds to cover the cost of the promised pension, and although the pension constituted 'pay' within Article 119, neither the contributions of the employer nor the value of those contributions as represented by a lump sum or transfer benefits would fall within Article 119.[96]

Thus, having in a series of cases broadened out the concept of pay, eroding the distinction between pay and occupational social security, and creating a distinction between the latter and state social security, the Court drew back in *Neath* and *Coloroll.* Despite the force of the Advocate General's submission that, once a capital sum or transfer value was paid on behalf of an employee, it should be seen as pay within Article 119, the Court ruled that employers' contributions to defined-benefit occupational pension schemes did not fall within Article 119. The contrary argument of the Commission reflected the proposal it had originally put forward for what became Directive 86/378, excluding the possibility of relying on different actuarial factors for men and women based on life-expectancy.[97] The Council had rejected this proposal in adopting that Directive, and the Court in *Neath* took a similar view to the Council, thus leaving some scope of application for the Directive which it had so fundamentally undermined in the *Barber* ruling. It is not clear from the rulings in *Neath* and *Coloroll,* however, whether Article 119 applies to contributions paid by an employer into what is called a 'money-purchase' scheme, as opposed to a 'defined-benefit' scheme. In contrast with the latter scheme, in which the criteria for the pension to be paid are fixed in advance even though the employer's contributions to the funding of the scheme will vary, the pension is paid in a money-purchase scheme by reference to the amount of the contributions which the employer has made to the scheme. It is not clear whether the Court will eventually rule that these, like the employer's contributions to a defined-benefit scheme, fall outside Article 119, or whether, given the direct link between the amount the employee will receive by way of pension and the contributions made by the employer, the Court will find the contributions to fall within the scope of Article 119. If it took the latter view, this would mean that sex-based actuarial factors could be used in calculating an employer's contributions in a defined-benefit scheme, but not in a money-

[95] The A.G. was impressed by the fact that many differences in risk factors other than life expectancy were ignored in calculating the financing of the pension scheme e.g. risks associated with certain occupations, health risks, or smoking. He also noted that no state pension scheme, as opposed to private occupational schemes, found it necessary to use such sex-based actuarial calculation factors.

[96] *Neath*, n. 69 above, paras. 31–2 and *Coloroll*, n. 32 above, paras. 80–1.

[97] See [1983] OJ C134/7.

purchase scheme, which would muddy the waters of pension-scheme financing even further! However, although this question was not resolved in *Coloroll*, the Court did rule that certain pension benefits purchased by voluntary *employee* contributions, if they were managed in a fund separately from the normal occupational pension scheme, would not fall within Article 119 and thus would not constitute pay.[98] Thus *Neath* and *Coloroll* represent certain inroads into the broad principle established by *Barber*, that occupational pensions constitute pay within Article 119. Employer contributions to a defined-benefit pension scheme, as well as benefits paid to employees as a result of separately managed additional voluntary contributions, would fall outside Article 119.

One of the main questions remaining to be answered concerned what measures could be taken in order to comply with the *Barber* ruling. In *Coloroll*, the Court ruled that, between the date of the latter ruling and the date of entry into force of measures designed to eliminate discrimination contrary to Article 119, 'correct implementation of the principle of equal pay requires that the disadvantaged employees should be granted the same advantages as those previous enjoyed by other employees'. In other words, until amending measures were adopted, pension schemes could only 'level up', by giving men the same advantages as women enjoyed. This principle was first enunciated in *Defrenne (No 2)*,[99] in which the Court held that compliance with the equal pay principle could not be achieved other than by raising the lowest salaries, since Article 119 appeared in the context of the harmonization of working conditions while maintaining an improvement in those conditions. However, the Court in *Coloroll* took a more limited approach than that perhaps implied in *Defrenne*, and applied the 'levelling-up' or improvement in conditions of pay only to the transitional stage between the date of the *Barber* ruling and the date on which measures were adopted to comply with it.[100] The Court ruled further that, during this transitional stage, it was not open to the pension scheme or the employer to plead that a levelling-down approach was objectively justified by reason of the financial difficulties for the pension scheme, since 'the space of time involved is relatively short and attributable in any event to the conduct of the scheme administrators themselves'.[101] However, once equalizing measures were adopted, 'Article 119 does not then preclude measures to achieve equal treatment by reducing the advantages of the persons previously favoured'.[102] On the other hand, with regard to the period before the date of the *Barber* ruling, during which the pensionable age for women under these occupational schemes was lower than that for men, the Court made clear that, since it had ruled that discrimination was permissible prior to that date, Community law provided no justification for equalizing the

[98] Case C–200/91, n. 32 above, paras. 90–3.

[99] Case 43/75, *Defrenne* v. *Sabena* [1976] ECR 1365, [1978] 2 CMLR 98, para. 15.

[100] See this approach also in the cases of indirect discrimination in pay and social security, below at 878–80.

[101] Case C–408/92 *Smith* v. *Advel Systems Ltd* [1994] ECR I–4435, para. 30.

[102] *Coloroll*, n. 32 above, para. 33.

positions of men and women during that earlier period by retroactively reducing the advantages enjoyed by women. In other words, Community law had nothing to say about the age discrimination between men and women in occupational pension schemes prior to 17 May 1990, and if a Member State sought to equalize the positions of men and women by retroactive reduction of women's advantages, the justifiability of this would be a matter for national law. The Court reiterated this point in *Smith* v. *Advel*, decided on the same day as *Coloroll*, but it ruled further that, once an employer took steps for the future to comply with Article 119, the achievement of equality could not be made progressive:

> The step of raising the retirement age for women to that for men, which an employer decides to take in order to remove discrimination in relation to occupational pensions as regards benefits payable in respect of future periods of service, cannot be accompanied by measures, even if only transitional, designed to limit the adverse consequences which such a step may have for women.[103]

It is noticeable that the Court uses the language of 'advantage' in the occupational pensions case law to describe the position of women, since the retirement age for women was generally, being linked to that of state pension schemes, lower than that for men. However, it has been pointed out that the language of 'advantage' or 'favoured group' is hardly appropriate to apply to women in the context of pensions, given the nature and pattern of the working life which most working women, in contrast to most working men, are forced to pursue:

> It would be misleading to consider this matter of 'more' or 'less' favoured groups at a theoretical level. Unquestionably, the less favoured group is in reality composed of women, who have worked and contributed to the scheme but receive very low pensions because of the level of pay which they earned during their working life, itself frequently shorter than the men's.[104]

It is perhaps this perception of male workers as the disadvantaged group that led the Court recently to permit what could be seen as direct discrimination in pay by an employer, so as to compensate for the relative disadvantage of men as opposed to women in the context of pensionable ages. Although the case was decided by the Court on the basis that there was no real discrimination, it appears in fact more like a case where discrimination in pay was permitted to make up for what was perceived to be an existing inequality.

[103] Case C–408/92, n. 101 above, para. 27. See also Case C–28/93 *Van den Akker* v. *Stichting Shell Pensioenfonds* [1994] ECR I–4527, as regards the impermissibility of any advantages for women once a uniform retirement age for men and women is introduced.

[104] D. de Vos, 'Pensionable Age and Equal Treatment from Charybdis to Scylla' (1994) 23 ILJ 175, 179.

Case C-132/92, Roberts v. Birds Eye Walls Ltd [1993] ECR I–5579, [1993] 3 CMLR 822

Mrs Roberts, who was forced to retire on grounds of ill-health before reaching the statutory retirement age, challenged the amount of the bridging pension paid to her under the occupational pension scheme to which she had been affiliated. The bridging pension was an *ex gratia* payment—entirely financed by the employer—to employees who were forced to retire on grounds of ill health before reaching the statutory retirement age. The purpose of the bridging pension was said to be both to place employees in the financial position they would have been in had they not been forced to retire early, and to place the overall financial treatment of men and women in identical situations on an equal footing. For male and female employees retiring before the age of 60, when neither had reached state pensionable age, the bridging pension included an amount corresponding to the proportion of the state pension attributable to periods of service. After 60, however, the amount of the bridging pension paid to a woman was reduced on the ground that she was in receipt of a state pension, whereas the bridging pension paid to a man was not reduced until the age of 65, when he would receive a state pension.

THE ECJ

17. It should be noted that the principle of equal treatment laid down by Article 119 of the Treaty, like the general principle of non-discrimination which it embodies in a specific form, presupposes that the men and women to whom it applies are in identical situations.

18. However, that would not appear to be so where the deferred payment which an employer makes to those of his employees who are compelled to take early retirement on grounds of ill-health is regarded as a supplement to the financial resources of the man or woman concerned.

19. It follows clearly from the mechanism for calculating the bridging pension that the assessment of the amount thereof is not frozen at a particular moment but necessarily varies on account of changes occurring in the financial position of the man or woman concerned with the passage of time.

20. Accordingly, although until the age of 60 the financial position of a woman taking early retirement on grounds of ill-health is comparable to that of a man in the same situation, neither of them as yet entitled to payment of the State pension, that is no longer the case between the ages of 60 and 65 since that is when women, unlike men, start drawing that pension. That difference as regards the objective premise, which necessarily entails that the amount of the bridging pension is not the same for men and women, cannot be considered discriminatory.

21. What is more, given the purpose of the bridging pension, to maintain the amount for women at the same level as that which obtained before they received the State pension would give rise to unequal treatment to the detriment of men who do not receive the State pension until the age of 65.

Birds Eye Walls is quite a surprising judgment, since, although men and women under a private occupational scheme clearly received different bridging pensions after the age of 60, the Court held that this was not discriminatory within Article 119. Instead, the Court focused on the fact that men and women over 60 were differently situated, since women were generally in receipt of a state pension by that age. However, this is a departure from the reasoning of the Court in earlier cases such as *Worringham*, where the difference in the actual gross sum paid by an employer to men as opposed to women was held to be discriminatory, regardless of the fact that men were paid the extra sum in order to compensate for a deduction from their earnings to which women were not subject—in other words, regardless of the fact that men and women were not 'similarly situated' in that case either.[105] Further, the ruling seems to go against the trend of the Court's judgments in its earlier cases such as *Roberts*, in which it was not permissible for employers to link the granting of pensions on voluntary redundancy to the state social-security scheme where the state scheme still maintained discriminatory retirement ages for men and women.[106] Equality of age limits for the grant of a pension on voluntary redundancy, ignoring the different state pensionable ages, was required by the Court in *Roberts*. By way of contrast, although the employer in *Birds Eye Walls* was not seeking to replicate the discrimination in the state system in its bridging pension scheme, it was introducing discrimination between men and women in its scheme in order to counterbalance the effects of the state system, rather than paying equal bridging pensions and ignoring the continuing discrimination in the state system. The approach of the Court in *Birds Eye Walls*, in not requiring equal pay where men and women are not 'identically situated', has been criticized for its sudden departure from past principles, but the fact that it was decided by only a three-judge chamber might indicate that it does not necessarily reflect the thinking of or carry the weight of a decision of the whole court.

B. Fitzpatrick, Equality in Occupational Pension Schemes[107]

How remarkable it is that, the Court having propounded equality irrespective of sex as a fundamental right in Community law for nearly 20 years, a three man chamber of the Court should now discover 'equality of outcomes'—but not for women who, generally speaking, receive much lower benefits in occupational pension schemes, but rather for men upon whose stereotyped working lives the discriminatory structure of pension schemes is based?

. . .

Although *Birds Eye Walls* was decided upon the concept of equality, these conclusions call into question aspects of the Court's case law upon the concept of pay within Article 119. In *Barber*, the Court concluded . . . that each component part of the payment package had to be judged autonomously on grounds of equality. It was not permissible to set off parts of the remuneration package against each other. Here we are suddenly told that, because of a payment's purpose, it can be set off against, not merely another part of the employer's remuneration package, but rather a *State* benefit. And yet, the focus of the Court's judgment in *Barber*

[105] Case 69/80, n. 36 above.

[106] Case 151/84, *Roberts* v. *Tate & Lyle Industries* [1986] ECR 703, [1986] 1 CMLR 714.

[107] (1994) 23 1 LJ 155, 163.

. . . has been to break the links between pay and welfare which bedevilled cases such as *Burton* and *Newstead.*

The decisions in this whole area of pay and pensions, in particular surrounding the shifting borderline between pay and social security, raise pertinent questions about the respective roles of the political institutions and the Court in matters of equality and social policy. On the one hand, social security is an area which has been seen in Community law as a complex matter requiring gradual legislative progress rather than immediate change. With the involvement of all representatives of the Member States through the legislative institutions, compromises such as those in Directive 79/7 and 86/378 were drawn up to enable national authorities more gradually to adapt the financial structures and systems of benefits which had developed over many years on the basis of social policies which provided for different pensionable and retirement ages of men and women. On the other hand, Article 119 embodies a straightforward principle of equal pay for equal work, which appeared to involve none of the complexities of adapting a pension scheme, and which was to be 'policed' by the Court through the cases which came before it. The Court has taken an active stance in promoting its conception of the equal pay principle as a 'fundamental principle' of the Community legal order. However, the Court's interpretation of pay has clashed with the legislative policy of the Community institutions in the occupational pensions context, and the ringing criticisms of the Court in arguments such as those of the parties in *Moroni* and *Ten Oever* provide evidence of this tension.

3. EQUAL TREATMENT

(a) Equal Treatment as a General Principle

The terms of Article 119 quite clearly establish the principle of equal pay for equal work, but they do not expressly refer to the equal treatment of men and women other than in terms of pay. This is quite consistent with the historical explanation for Article 119, suggested above, which was to ensure equal conditions of competition for businesses operating in the different Member States, by ensuring that no advantage could be obtained by states which permitted female labour to be secured at lower cost than male labour. However, the other aim of Article 119, i.e. the social rather than the economic objective, would evidently be better achieved in the context of a general commitment to equality between women and men, at least in the context of the workplace. In the third *Defrenne* case, it was argued to the Court that the principle of equal treatment of men and women was in fact a fundamental principle of Community law:

Case 149/77, Defrenne v. Sabena (No 3)
[1978] ECR 1365, [1978] 3 CMLR 312

Following the preliminary ruling of the Court in *Defrenne (No 2)* for violation of the principle of equal pay, the plaintiff appealed against the dismissal by the national court of certain heads of her claim. She argued that compulsory termination of her employment contract at age 40, when no such condition attached to male stewards engaged in the same work, was contrary to Article 119. The Conseil d'Etat referred several questions to the Court, this time to discover whether Article 119 or the general principles of Community law required the elimination of sex discrimination in working conditions other than remuneration.

THE ECJ

15. The field of application of Article 119 must be determined within the context of the system of the social provisions of the Treaty, which are set out in the chapter formed by Article 117 *et seq.*

16. The general features of the conditions of employment and working conditions are considered in Articles 117 and 118 from the point of view of the harmonization of the social systems of the Member States and of the approximation of their laws in that field.

17. There is no doubt that the elimination of discrimination based on the sex of workers forms part of the programme for social and legislative policy which was clarified in certain respects by the Council Resolution of 21 January 1974 (OJ C13/.1).

. . .

19. In contrast to the provisions of Articles 117 and 118, which are essentially in the nature of a programme, Article 119, which is limited to the question of pay discrimination between men and women workers, constitutes a special rule, whose application is linked to precise factors.

20. In those circumstances it is impossible to extend the scope of that article to elements of the employment relationship other than those expressly referred to.

21. In particular, the fact that the fixing of certain conditions of employment—such as a special age-limit—may have pecuniary consequences is not sufficient to bring such conditions within the field of application of Article 119, which is based on the close connection which exists between the nature of the services provided and the amount of remuneration.

. . .

23. It is, therefore, impossible to widen the terms of Article 119 to the point, first, of jeopardizing the direct applicability which that provision must be acknowledged to have in its own sphere and, secondly, of intervening in an area reserved by Articles 117 and 118 to the discretion of the authorities referred to therein.

Significantly the Court did not stop at this, but went on to say that the elimination of sex discrimination was a fundamental personal human right, and thus part of the general principles of Community law the observance of which the Court must ensure. In its previous rulings in *Sabbatini* [108] and *Airola*,[109]

[108] Case 20/71, n. 7 above. [109] Case 21/74, n. 8 above.

t had recognized that the Community had to ensure equality of working conditions as between men and women in respect of its own staff. However, this was to be contrasted with the positions of the Member States, at the stage of development of Community law at that time:

> 30. On the other hand, as regards the relationships of employer and employee which are subject to national law, the Community had not, at the time of the events now before the Belgian courts, assumed any responsibility for supervising and guaranteeing the observance of the principle of equality between men and women in working conditions other than remuneration.

Since the time of the events giving rise to the case, Directive 76/207 on equal treatment in conditions of employment, based on Article 235 of the Treaty, had been adopted.[110] Advocate General Capotorti in *Defrenne (No. 3)* pointed out that the Directive's preamble linked it to Article 117 and to the Council's 1976 Resolution on a social action programme. Had that Article been directly effective, he commented, the Equal Treatment Directive would not have been necessary.[111] The somewhat uncertain legal basis of the Directives on sex discrimination highlights the weakness of the social-policy provisions of the Treaty. Directive 75/117 on equal pay, we have seen, was based on Article 100 of the Treaty, Directives 76/207 on equal treatment and 79/7 on state social security are primarily based on Article 235, and Directives 86/378 on occupational social security and 86/613 on equal treatment for the self-employed are based on Articles 100 and 235 jointly.[112]

(b) Directive 76/207

The aim of the Directive is to secure equal treatment between men and women in three broad, employment-related areas, namely access to employment and promotion, vocational training, and working conditions. Matters of social security are not within its scope by virtue of Article 1(2), which provides that the Council is to adopt future legislation on equal treatment in social security.[113] The equal-treatment principle is defined in Article 2 to mean any discrimination 'on grounds of sex either directly or indirectly by reference in particular to marital or family status'. Many of its provisions are similar to Directive 75/117 on equal pay, in that the Member States are required to abolish all legislative and administrative provisions in those three areas which discriminate on grounds of sex, and to ensure that any provisions of measures such as collective agreements and individual employment contracts are similarly abolished.[114] The provisions on access to a legal remedy, protecting

110 [1976] OJ L39/40.

111 N. 9 above, 1387.

112 Dir. 92/85 on pregnancy, however, is expressly based on one of the post-SEA social policy provisions of the Treaty, Art. 118a. See further p. 857 below.

113 This was subsequently done with the adoption of Dir. 79/7: [1979] OJ L6/24.

114 Dir. 76/207, Arts. 3, 4, and 5.

complainants and ensuring that those affected know of their rights are also similar to those in the Equal Pay Directive.[115]

The Directive is distinctive, however, in that, unlike the equal-pay provisions, it permits several exceptions to the equal-treatment principle. Article 2 sets out three matters which Member States may exclude from the principle. The first, in Article 2(2), relates to occupational activities, including training in respect of which 'by reason of their nature or the context in which they are carried out' the sex of the worker constitutes a determining factor. An example of this might be an occupation such as acting, which may legitimately require a person of specified sex to perform a role.

The scope of Article 2(2) was considered in the *Male Midwives* case in the United Kingdom.[116] The Court found that legislation which limited access for men to the profession of midwife was in conformity with the exception in Article 2(2), in view of the fact that 'personal sensitivities' could play an important role in the relationship between midwife and patient. The arguments of the Commission and the Advocate General that this could be adequately catered for by giving the patient the choice whether to have a male or female midwife were not addressed by the Court, which ruled that the United Kingdom had 'not exceeded the limits of the power granted to the Member States by Articles 9(2) and 2(2) of the Directive'.[117]

The provision was also considered in *Johnston* v. *Chief Constable of the RUC*, in which the RUC sought to justify its decision not to employ women as full-time members of the RUC Reserve on the basis of Article 2(2).[118] It was argued that if women were permitted to carry and use firearms, they would be at greater risk of becoming targets for assassination. The Commission, however, argued that the occupational activity of an armed police officer could not be considered an activity for which the sex of the officer was a determining factor, and that if an exception was to be made in relation to specific duties, the principle of proportionality would have to be observed. The Court accepted the argument of the United Kingdom that the carrying of firearms by policewomen might create additional risks of assassination, without requiring any evidence to support the implication that women could not be trained to use firearms just as safely and effectively as men.[119] Hence the Court accepted that the sex of police officers could constitute a 'determining factor' for carrying out certain policing activities.[120] However, it left the actual decision on the facts of the case for the national court, taking

[115] Dir. 76/207, Arts. 6, 7, and 8 respectively.

[116] Case 165/82, *Commission* v. *UK* [1983] ECR 3431, [1984] 1 CMLR 44.

[117] *Ibid.*, para. 20.

[118] Case 222/84, *Johnston* v. *Chief Constable of the Royal Ulster Constabulary* [1986] ECR 1651, [1986] 3 CMLR 240.

[119] See S. Fredman, n. 11 above, 128; G. More, n. 11 above, 52–3.

[120] See also Case 318/86, *Commission* v. *France* [1988] ECR 3559, [1989] 3 CMLR 663, para. 27, where the Court accepted that certain police duties could involve sex-specific duties, but nevertheless condemned France's separate recruitment systems for men and women, since they lacked transparency and made it impossible for the Community to supervise the use of Art. 2(2) of the Dir.

into account the principle of proportionality. This meant, for example, that the national court had to decide 'whether the refusal to renew Mrs Johnston's contract could not have been avoided by allocating to women duties which, without jeopardizing the aims pursued, can be performed without firearms'.[121]

The second area which may be excluded from the principle of equal treatment is set out in Article 2(3) and relates to provisions adopted by the Member States 'concerning the protection of women, particularly as regards pregnancy and maternity'. In so far as matters such as maternity leave are concerned, the 1992 Pregnancy Directive now goes further than simply allowing Member States to maintain protective provisions and imposes a requirement on them to provide a minimum of employment protection for women who are pregnant, breast-feeding, or who have recently given birth.[122] However, the new Directive specifically states that it does not provide any ground for Member States to reduce the existing levels of protection they provide, if these are higher than the requirements of the Directive.

The third area of 'exception' to the principle of formal equality is in Article 2(4) of the Directive. This relates to what might be called measures of positive discrimination, in other words measures designed to redress existing inequalities between men and women, and to 'promote equal opportunity for men and women' in the three areas covered by the Directive.[123] This provision has been narrowly read by the Court, so that a provision of French law which permitted collective agreements to provide special rights for women—including shorter working hours for older women, the obtaining of leave when a child was ill, the granting of extra days of leave in respect of children—was held not to be justified by Article 2(4).[124] France had not adequately shown that 'the generalized preservation of special rights for women' would reduce actual instances of inequality in social life.[125] Although the assumption of the Court and the Advocate General in this case seemed to be that there was no inequality facing women which required these advantages, the Commission had made a different argument against the French laws, namely that 'the evolution of society is such that in many cases working men, if they are fathers, must share the tasks previously performed by the wife as regards the care and organisation of the family'.[126] A similar argument about the roles of men and women, to the effect that such rights or advantages should not depend on sex, was made by Advocate General Jacobs in a case concerning 'positive discrimination' in national social-security benefits in favour of women, where the Court found a breach of the equal-treatment principle of Directive 79/7.[127] It has been pointed out, however, that there are difficulties with arguments which claim that measures which positively discriminate reinforce traditional

[121] [1986] ECR 1651, para. 39.

[122] Dir. 92/85, [1992] OJ L348/1.

[123] There is another exception of sorts in Art. 4(c) of the Dir. which provides that equal treatment in access to vocational training is to be ensured 'without prejudice to the freedom granted in certain Member States to certain private training establishments'.

[124] Case 312/86, *Commission* v. *France* [1988] ECR 6315, [1989] 1 CMLR 408.

[125] *Ibid.*, para. 15.

[126] *Ibid.* 6322.

[127] Case 373/89, *Integrity* v. *Rouvroy* [1990] ECR 4243, para. 14 of his Opinion.

assumptions, such as that the female is always the primary carer, or that the male is always the main breadwinner.

S. Fredman, European Community Discrimination Law: A Critique[128]

Such an argument correctly highlights the need for close examination of measures purporting to benefit women. Any measure giving advantages to a group defined according to gender runs the risk of over- or under-inclusiveness and may well perpetuate damaging stereotypes. However, this in itself does not imply that anti-discrimination legislation should aspire to neutrality and thereby ignore disadvantage. The risks referred to need to be balanced against the possible gains of such criteria in reducing gender disadvantage. It may well be that social security is too costly and administratively too complex to test each person on an individual basis. In that case, it may be more advantageous overall to define a group according to gender than not to offer the benefit at all. On the other hand, the perpetuation of a stereotype may be more damaging than the overall benefit. Thus, discriminatory criteria should not be rejected out of hand, but instead scrutinized closely to discover whether they perpetuate disadvantage, or go some way towards alleviating it.

With respect to measures which contravene the equal-treatment principle in access to employment or conditions of work, however, Member States are required to ensure the revision of such provisions 'when the concern for protection which originally inspired them is no longer well founded'.[129]

Positive action in favour of women is also now provided for, not within the Equal Treatment Directive, but under the Agreement on Social Policy annexed to the TEU, which was signed by all of the Member States except the United Kingdom. After setting out the equal-pay principle of Article 119 of the EC Treaty, Article 6(3) of the Agreement provides:

> This Article shall not prevent any Member State from maintaining or adopting measures providing for specific advantages in order to make it easier for women to pursue a vocational activity or to prevent or compensate for disadvantages in their professional careers.

It is not yet clear what effect this provision might be given, but while Advocate General Van Gerven has suggested that it cannot be used to deviate from past case law which e.g. prohibits advantageous pension payments for women to make up for their past disadvantage,[130] another commentator has suggested that the Court has, in a sense, already approved such measures of positive discrimination in pay in favour of men in *Bird Eye Walls*.[131]

[128] N. 11 above, 129.

[129] Arts. 3(2)(c) and 5(2)(c).

[130] W. Van Gerven in *Equality of Treatment between Women and Men in Social Security*, n. 46 above.

[131] B. Fitzpatrick, 'Equality in Occupational Pension Schemes' (1994) 23 ILJ 155, 162 n. 107 above.

Further, it has been suggested that any measures adopted under the Agreement on Social Policy do not constitute Community law, but rather inter-governmental agreements between the Member States which signed it.[132]

The Court has also addressed the question whether there are exceptions to the principle of equal treatment other than those expressly set out in Directive 76/207. In *Johnston*, it rejected the argument that the Directive was subject to a general public-safety proviso which was applicable across the whole of the Treaty, similar to the specific derogations expressly provided in the context of free movement of persons, services, goods, and in serious military situations.[133] However, in the cases of *Levy*[134] and *Minne*,[135] the Court acknowledged that the Member States were entitled to maintain a provision which was in breach of the Equal Treatment Directive, if the adoption of that provision had been necessary to ensure performance by the Member State, under Article 234 of the Treaty, of obligations arising from agreements concluded with non-member countries before the entry into force of the EC Treaty. In those cases, the agreement in question was Convention No 89 of the International Labour Organization, which concerned night-work of women employed in industry, and which was apparently incompatible with Article 5 of the Equal Treatment Directive. However, the Court imposed certain limits on the scope of the Article 234 exception by requiring the national court to ascertain two things: first, the extent to which the obligations under that Convention actually constituted an obstacle to the application of the Directive, and secondly the extent to which the national provisions which breached the Equal Treatment Directive were designed to implement the Convention.[136]

(c) The Distinction between Conditions of Work, Pay, and Social Security

We have seen above how the distinction between pay and social security has given rise to a great deal of confusion, on account of the different provisions of law regulating each. Similarly, the distinction between equal pay and equal treatment in conditions of work, as well as between the latter and equal treatment in social security has not always been entirely clear.

The distinction between pay and conditions of work arose in the case of

132 D. Curtin, 'The Constitutional Structure of the Union: A Europe of Bits and Pieces' (1992) 29 CMLRev. 17, 56–7. The author suggests also that Art. 6(3) should not affect the interpretation of Art. 119. See also the arguments of E. Whiteford, 'Social Policy after Maastricht' (1993) 18 ELRev. 202.

133 Case 222/84, n. 118 above. The specific derogations mentioned by the Court were those in Arts. 36, 48, 56, 223, and 224 EC.

134 Case C–158/91, *Ministère Public and Direction du Travail et de l'Emploi* v. *Levy* [1993] ECR I–4287. Contrast the earlier Case C–345/89, *Ministère Public* v. *Stoeckel* [1991] ECR I–4047.

135 Case C–13/93, *Office Nationale de l'Emploi* v. *Minne* [1994] ECR I–371.

136 The issue of this ILO Convention was addressed in a Commission Communication in 1987 (COM(87)105), in which it had indicated that a ban on night work for women was incompatible with the Equal Treatment Dir. Thus the Member States were required to denounce Convention no. 89 in 1992, when the opportunity to do so in accordance with the terms of ILO Conventions arose. See N. Wuiame, 'Night Work for Women—*Stoeckel* Revisited' (1994) 23 ILJ 95.

Bilka, in which the Court ruled that the exclusion of part-time workers from a supplementary occupational pension scheme constituted indirect discrimination in pay.[137] The Court had also been asked, in the same case, whether Article 119 imposed an obligation on employers to organize their occupational pension schemes in a way which took into account the fact that women's family responsibilities prevented them from fulfilling the pension requirements. The argument was based on Article 119, presumably because Directive 76/207 does not appear to impose any positive obligations which would be 'horizontally effective' against employers, to ensure that they take steps to promote equal opportunities. The Court, however, denied that Article 119 could have any such effect:

> 41. It must be pointed out that . . . the scope of Article 119 is restricted to the question of pay discrimination between men and women workers. Problems related to other conditions of work and employment, on the other hand, are covered generally by other provisions of Community law, in particular Articles 117 and 118 of the Treaty, with a view to the harmonization of the social security systems of Member States and the approximation of their legislation in that area.
>
> 42. The imposition of an obligation such as that envisaged by the national court in its question goes beyond the scope of Article 119 and has no other basis in Community law as it now stands.[138]

This issue illustrates some of the limits of a legal approach based on discrimination in ensuring equal conditions for men and women, given the differences in the existing social and material circumstances of women and men. According to the opinion of the Advocate General in *Bilka*, although employers were required not to exploit 'the socio-cultural constraints faced by working women', neither were they under any additional obligations which would restrict their normal freedom to determine staff policy.[139]

The complex relationship between equal treatment in working conditions, equality in social security, and equal pay can be seen in a series of cases beginning with that of *Burton*.[140] Burton was an employee of the British Railways Board whose application for voluntary redundancy was rejected on the ground that he was two years below the minimum age of 60 which had been set for male employees. Since the minimum age for women was 55, he complained to an Industrial Tribunal of sex discrimination. The Court was asked whether the different age conditions in access to voluntary redundancy was contrary to Directive 76/207, and it ruled that they were not. In the Court's view, the reason for the different age conditions was not to discriminate on grounds of sex, but because the terms of the redundancy scheme had been tied by the employer to the national statutory retirement scheme. And the national scheme, which maintained different pensionable ages for men and women, was

[137] Case 170/84, n. 62 above. [138] *Ibid.* [139] [1986] ECR 1607, 1618.
[140] Case 19/81, *Burton* v. *British Railways Board* [1982] ECR 555, [1982] 2 CMLR 136.

covered by the exception in Social Security Directive 79/7. In other words, the voluntary redundancy scheme, although it was clearly not statutory social security within Directive 79/7 and was in principle, according to the Court, 'dismissal' within Directive 76/207, could be arranged so as to correspond with the statutory scheme including the different pensionable ages, without being found in breach of the equal treatment Directive.

In the subsequent case of *Roberts*, the complainant was a member of an occupational pension scheme which provided for the compulsory retirement with a pension at age 65 for men and 60 for women.[141] At the time, since it was before the judgment in *Bilka*,[142] the pension scheme would not have been considered to be pay within Article 119. Under its compulsory redundancy terms, the company provided that both men and women could receive an immediate early pension at age 55. Since Roberts was 53 when she was made redundant, she did not receive a pension. She argued that the scheme was in breach of the equal-treatment principle, since men could receive an early pension ten years before their normal retirement age, whereas women could only receive one five years before. This time, the Court decided the case on the basis of the Equal Treatment Directive, and appeared to narrow the scope of the exception in the Social Security Directive. The complaint was not about the terms on which an early pension was granted, in the Court's view, but about the terms of dismissal:

Case 151/84, Roberts v. Tate & Lyle Industries
[1986] ECR 703, [1986] 1 CMLR 714

THE ECJ

32. In the judgment in the *Burton* case the Court has already stated that the term 'dismissal' contained in that provision must be given a wide meaning. Consequently, an age limit for the compulsory redundancy of workers as part of a mass redundancy falls within the term 'dismissal' construed in that manner, even if the redundancy involves the grant of an early retirement pension.

33. Even though the retirement scheme at issue does not *prima facie* discriminate between men and women with regard to the conditions for dismissal, it is still necessary to consider whether the fixing of the same age for the grant of an early pension nevertheless constitutes discrimination on grounds of sex in view of the fact that under the United Kingdom statutory social security scheme the pensionable age for men and women is different. Under United Kingdom legislation the minimum qualifying age for a State retirement pension is 60 for women and 65 for men.

34. As the Court emphasized in its judgment in the *Burton* case, Article 7 of Directive No 79/7 expressly provides that the Directive does not prejudice the right of Member States to exclude from its scope the determination of pensionable age for the purposes of granting old-age and retirement pensions and the possible

141 Case 151/84, n. 106 above. See also Case 262/84, *Beets-Proper* v. *Van Lanschot Bankiers* [1986] ECR 773, [1987] 2 CMLR 616.

142 Case 170/84, n. 62 above.

consequences thereof for other benefits falling within the statutory social security schemes. The Court thus acknowledged that benefits linked to a national scheme which lays down a different minimum pensionable age for men and women may lie outside the ambit of the aforementioned obligation.

35. However, in view of the fundamental importance of the principle of equality of treatment, which the Court has reaffirmed on numerous occasions, Article 1(2) of Directive No 76/207, which excludes social security matters from the scope of that directive, must be interpreted strictly. Consequently, whereas the exception to the prohibition of discrimination on grounds of sex provided for in Article 7 (1) (a) of Directive No 79/7 concerns the consequences which pensionable age has for social security benefits, this case is concerned with dismissal within the meaning of Article 5 of Directive No 76/207. In those circumstances the grant of a pension to persons of the same age who are made redundant amounts merely to a collective measure adopted irrespective of the sex of those persons in order to guarantee them all the same rights.

The implication in paragraph 35 of the judgment is that if Roberts' employer had done as the employer in *Burton* had done, and had tied the age for receipt of an immediate pension on compulsory redundancy to the statutory social-security scheme, it would not have been able to gain the benefit of the exception in Directive 79/7 for pensionable ages in statutory social-security schemes. Because the redundancy was classified by the Court as dismissal, the receipt of a pension on redundancy was a condition of dismissal within the scope of Directive 76/207. The fact that the age conditions for men and women were identical meant that there was no breach of the equal treatment principle in that Directive, whereas if they had been linked with statutory pensionable ages there would have been a breach. In *Burton*, on the other hand, the Court allowed the linking of age conditions for *voluntary* redundancy to the statutory social-security scheme with its different pensionable ages, to benefit by association with the exception in Directive 79/7, and to avoid being in breach of the Equal Treatment Directive. According to the Court in *Roberts*, however, the exception in Article 7(1)(a) of Directive 79/7 concerned 'the consequences which pensionable age has for social security benefits' and the grant of a pension on compulsory redundancy was not a social security benefit within Directive 79/7 but a condition governing dismissal within Directive 76/207.

It is interesting that the Court gave a narrow reading in this case to the exception in Directive 79/7. Article 7(1)(a) in fact allows Member States to exclude from the scope of the equal-treatment principle 'the determination of pensionable age for the purposes of granting old-age and retirement pensions and the possible consequences thereof for other benefits'. It might therefore have been arguable that the pension on redundancy was a benefit, albeit not a statutory but an occupational benefit, which could legitimately be affected by different statutory pensionable ages for men and women. But the Court stated in paragraph 35 that the benefits which were covered by the exception in the Directive were 'social-security benefits', and once it had categorized the early pension as a condition governing dismissal, this did not fall within the exception but instead within the Equal Treatment Directive. The precise scope of Article 7(1)(a) will be examined further in the discussion of Directive 79/7 and equal treatment in social security, below.

The narrowing of the scope of the exception in Directive 79/7 continued in the case of *Marshall*.[143] In this case, the Court was dealing, not with voluntary or compulsory redundancy, but with a compulsory *retirement* provision which mirrored the different statutory pensionable ages for men and women. Marshall was required to retire some time after reaching the age of 60, which was the statutory pensionable age and the compulsory retirement age which the company had set for women. Taking the same approach and repeating much of its ruling in *Roberts*, the Court dealt with the compulsory retirement as dismissal falling within the scope of the Equal Treatment Directive, rather than as a consequence of the different statutory pensionable ages falling within the scope of the exception in Article 7(1)(a) of the Social Security Directive.

The further complication which arises from these cases concerns the relationship between social security and pay, which was examined above. It became clear after the later rulings in *Bilka*, *Barber*, and *Moroni*, that payments made on redundancy and under occupational social-security schemes constituted pay within Article 119, and that the discriminatory effects of setting different pensionable ages were in breach of the principle of equal pay. Only state social-security schemes could benefit from the exception in Article 7(1)(a) of Directive 79/7. Thus the approach in *Burton*, where the Court treated the age condition for voluntary redundancy as falling alongside the statutory pensionable ages with which it was linked, thus as a condition of work which could, despite Directive 76/207, benefit from the exception in Directive 79/7, would no longer be possible. Despite the later attempts of Advocate General Van Gerven to distinguish the case,[144] *Burton*, as another commentator put it, appears to have been overruled '*sotto voce*' so that discriminatory age conditions for access to voluntary redundancy benefits would now breach the equal-pay principle of Article 119, rather than constituting dismissal within Directive 76/207 or being covered by the exception in Directive 79/7.[145]

The distinction between discrimination in conditions of work under Directive 76/207 and discrimination in social security under Directive 79/7 arose also in the case of *Jackson and Cresswell*, where the Court held that a scheme of benefits would not be excluded from the scope of Directive 76/207

143 Case 152/84, *Marshall* v. *Southampton and South-West Hampshire Area Health Authority (Teaching)* [1986] ECR 723, [1986] 1 CMLR 688. See Ch. 4 181–3 for a discussion of the aspects of the case dealing with the direct effect of dirs.

144 See his Opinion in *Barber*, n. 15, above, suggesting that the age condition for voluntary redundancy in *Burton* might be seen as a condition of 'access to pay' falling outside Art. 119, whereas *Bilka* could be distinguished since it concerned the amount of pay within Art. 119, and *Barber* could be distinguished since it concerned compulsory redundancy. The Court in *Barber* did not attempt to draw any such distinction.

145 D. Curtin, n. 68 above.

solely because it was formally part of a national social-security system.[146] However, the subject matter of any scheme falling within Directive 76/207 must concern access to employment, access to promotions, vocational training, or conditions of work. As a result, an income-support scheme, the purpose of which was to supplement the income of those with inadequate means of subsistence, could not be brought within the scope of the Directive solely because the method for calculating eligibility could affect a single mother's ability to take up vocational training or employment.[147]

(d) Equal Treatment and Pregnancy

We have seen that Article 2(3) of Directive 76/207 provides that the Directive is to be without prejudice to provisions concerning the protection of women, particularly as regards pregnancy and maternity. This is designed to prevent any challenge on grounds of equal treatment in EC law to national employment provisions granting leave or other special conditions to women who are pregnant or have given birth, rather than to impose any obligation to adopt such provisions.

In the case of *Hofmann*, however, a challenge was brought on the basis of the Equal Treatment Directive against provisions of German law relating to maternity leave. The argument was not that all men should have the same entitlement to leave as women before and after childbirth, but that the Directive only permitted derogation from the equal treatment principle in so far as this was done in order to protect women before and after childbirth, and if the provision of leave went beyond that function, e.g. in order to care for the child in the longer term, then it should be open on an equal basis to men and to women who would wish to do this:

Case 184/83, Hofmann v. Barmer Ersatzkasse
[1984] ECR 3047, [1986] 1 CMLR 242

Hofmann obtained unpaid leave from his employer in order to care for his newborn child, to enable the child's mother to avoid a detrimental interruption to a career she had just begun. The period of time he requested was that between the expiry of the statutory eight weeks following childbirth available to the mother, during which German legislation provided that women may not work, and the date the child reached six months of age. The law provided that mothers were entitled to maternity leave from the end of the mandatory eight week 'protective period' until the child was six months old. Since the mother in this case had not taken maternity leave after the eight-week period, and since Hofmann had cared for the child from that time on, he applied for payment during the period of maternity leave provided by law. His application was rejected on the ground that the law had deliberately allowed only mothers to claim maternity leave. The

[146] Cases C–63–64/91, *Jackson* v. *Chief Adjudication Officer* [1992] ECR I–4737, [1992] 3 CMLR. 389, para. 27.
[147] *Ibid.*, paras. 29–30.

plaintiff argued that the legislation was incompatible with Directive 76/207, and the Court began by examining the provisions and preamble to the Directive.

THE ECJ

24. It is apparent from the above analysis that the Directive is not designed to settle questions concerned with the organization of the family, or to alter the division of responsibility between parents.

25. It should further be added, with particular reference to paragraph (3), that, by reserving to member States the right to retain, or introduce provisions which are intended to protect women in connection with 'pregnancy and maternity', the directive recognizes the legitimacy, in terms of the principle of equal treatment, of protecting a woman's needs in two respects. First, it is legitimate to ensure the protection of a woman's biological condition during pregnancy and thereafter until such time as her physiological and mental functions have returned to normal after childbirth; secondly, it is legitimate to protect the special relationship between a woman and her child over the period which follows pregnancy and childbirth, by preventing that relationship from being disturbed by the multiple burdens which would result from the simultaneous pursuit of employment.

26. In principle, therefore, a measure such as maternity leave granted to a woman on expiry of the statutory protective period falls within the scope of Article 2(3) of Directive 76/207, inasmuch as it seeks to protect a woman in connection with the effects of pregnancy and motherhood. That being so, such leave may legitimately be reserved to the mother to the exclusion of any other person, in view of the fact that it is only the mother who may find herself subject to undesirable pressures to return to work prematurely.

27. Furthermore, it should be pointed out that the Directive leaves Member States with a discretion as to the social measures which they adopt in order to guarantee, within the framework laid down by the Directive, the protection of women in connection with pregnancy and maternity and to offset the disadvantages which women, by comparison with men, suffer with regard to the retention of employment. Such measures are, as the Government of the United Kingdom has rightly observed, closely linked to the general system of social protection in the various Member States. It must therefore be concluded that the Member States enjoy a reasonable margin of discretion as regards both the nature of the protective measures and the detailed arrangements for their implementation.

By conferring a 'margin of discretion' on the Member States with regard to the exception in Article 2(3) of the Directive, the Court could dismiss the arguments of the plaintiff and of the Commission that, if the father were given the option not only of taking care of the child but also of attending to the upkeep of the household, by the provision of a period of non-discriminatory parental leave, that would be an equally effective means of relieving the mother of the burdens which might impair her health. Normally, exceptions to fundamental rules are strictly construed by the Court, as with Article 7(1)(b) of Directive 79/7 in *Roberts* and *Marshall* above, but in the context of the derogation for pregnancy and maternity protection, the Court chose to apply a looser test than its usual examination of whether a derogating measure was strictly 'necessary' to achieve its aim. It is arguable that, despite the statement in paragraph 24 to the effect that the Directive was not meant to settle questions of 'the organization of the family' or 'the division of responsibility between parents', that in fact by choosing a broad interpretation of the exception in Article 2(3), the Court was supporting the continuation by the Member States of the traditional division of responsibility which entrenches the role of the mother as primary carer, and which, by protecting 'the special relationship between a woman and her child', deprives the father of the opportunity to develop such a relationship in the period after birth, by refusing to give the parents a choice as to who shall take leave.[148] Both the Court and the Advocate General appeared to assume that, even after the eight-week protective period, a mother was in an objectively different position from a father, in that she would bear other burdens and responsibilities, so that she should be relieved from also having to return to work. Of course if the extended period of leave were open to the father or the mother, the father, if the parents so wished, could take on those multiple burdens of household and caring duties, and he in turn could be relieved from having to return to work. On the other hand, it must be admitted that if the Court had read the exception more restrictively, thus preventing Member States from providing protection for women only other than while this was necessary to protect women's biological condition during and after pregnancy and childbirth, the Member States would have been free to 'level down' as well as to 'level up'. In other words they could, compatibly with the Directive, abolish discrimination between men and women by abolishing more extended maternity leave for women, rather than by providing a more extended parental leave for men and women alike.

An even clearer example of the reinforcement, through the interpretation of Article 2(3), of the view that only the mother does or should develop a special relationship with a child after birth is in the case of *Commission* v. *Italy*, which concerned national laws giving compulsory maternity leave to the mother of an adopted child under 6 years of age, but not to the father.[149] The explanation which the Court accepted related to Italy's 'legitimate concern to assimilate as far as possible the conditions of entry of the child into the adoptive family to those of the arrival of a newborn child in the family during the very delicate initial period'.[150] It is difficult to see why the initial three-month period is not an equally delicate period for an adoptive father as it is for an adoptive mother, and when the child is more than several months old, it is clearly impossible in any case to assimilate the conditions of its arrival to those of a newborn child.

Legislation actually requiring Member States to provide a period of maternity leave for women would have to await the 1992 Pregnancy Directive, and legislation providing for parental leave longer still. Although the Commission had already, by the time of the *Hofmann* decision, presented a proposal for a

[148] See S. Fredman, n. 11 above, 127 and N. Burrows, 'Maternity Rights in Europe—An Embryonic Legal Regime' (1991) 11 YBEL 273, 285.
[149] Case 163/82, *Commission* v. *Italy* [1983] ECR 3273, [1984] 3 CMLR 169.
[150] *Ibid.*, para. 16.

parental leave directive to the Council,[151] this was never adopted. Despite the Commission's attempt to secure its adoption again in 1994,[152] the proposal was blocked by the United Kingdom, which means that, if such legislation is to be adopted, it will have to be brought forward under the Agreement on Social Policy without the United Kingdom's participation.

The exception in Article 2(3) clearly covers provisions for the protection of women in the case of pregnancy or maternity, but it was not clear whether it could also cover other protective measures. This arose in *Johnston*, in which the Court ruled that it was clear from the express reference to pregnancy and maternity in Article 2(3) that the Directive was intended to protect a woman's biological condition and the special relationship which exists between a woman and her child, and could not be used to justify a policy of not recruiting women to the RUC Reserve simply because 'public opinion demands that women be given greater protection than men against risks which affect men and women in the same way'.[153] This limit on the scope of Article 2(3) was emphasised again in the case of *Stoeckel*, in which the Court ruled that Article 5 of the Directive, which requires equal treatment of men and women in conditions of work, precluded Member States from prohibiting night-work for women where it was not prohibited for men.[154] The *Stoeckel* ruling was confirmed and extended in the later case of *Minne*, where the Court held that, even if legislation prohibited night-work for men and women alike, it was nevertheless contrary to Article 5 for such legislation to provide different derogations from the prohibition for men and for women.[155] Only in the context of pregnancy and maternity would a ban on night-work for women be acceptable.[156]

In the proceedings brought by the Commission against France for inadequate implementation of Directive 76/207, the Court ruled that legislation allowing for the provision of 'special rights' for women not connected with pregnancy or maternity could not come within the scope of Article 2(3) of the Directive.[157] Some of the special rights, such as sick days in the case of children's illness, days off at the beginning of the school year, and the shortening of working hours for women over 59 related to the protection of women in their capacity as parents or as older workers, which were categories to which both men and women could equally belong.

Although the exceptions in Directive 76/207 *permitted* Member States to maintain protective provisions which discriminated in favour of women in relation to pregnancy and maternity, it was not clear for some years whether

[151] See [1983] OJ C333/6 as amended, [1984] OJ C316/7. See also the Council Rec. on Child Care: [1992] OJ L123/16.

[152] See the Commission White Paper on European Social Policy, COM(94)333, pt. V.

[153] [1986] ECR 1651, para. 44.

[154] Case C–345/89, *Criminal Proceedings against Stoeckel* [1991] ECR I–4047, [1993] 3 CMLR 637.

[155] Case C–13/93, n. 135 above.

[156] See Case C–421/92, *Habermann-Beltermann* v. *Arbeiterwohlfahrt, Bezirksverband* [1994] ECR I–1657, [1994] 2 CMLR 681, below.

[157] Case 312/86, n. 124 above and text.

it also *prohibited* measures which discriminated against women on grounds of pregnancy. In other words, was a dismissal on grounds of pregnancy a breach of the equal-treatment principle, or was it impossible to compare the position of a pregnant woman with a man in order to determine whether they had been unequally treated? This question was addressed by the Court in the case of *Dekker*:

Case C–177/88, Dekker v. Stichting Vormingscentrum voor Jong Volwassenen [1990] ECR I–3941

Dekker applied for the post of instructor at the defendant's training centre (VJV) for young adults, and informed the applications' committee that she was three months pregnant. Although she was put forward by the Committee as the most suitable candidate for the job, VJV informed her that she would not be appointed. The reason given was that VJV's insurer would not reimburse the benefits VJV would be obliged to pay her during her maternity leave, which meant that it would be financially unable to employ a replacement during her absence and would be short-staffed. The Dutch Supreme Court asked the Court to determine whether the employer was in breach of the Equal Treatment Directive.

THE ECJ

10. Consideration must be given to the question whether a refusal of employment in the circumstances to which the national court has referred may be regarded as direct discrimination on grounds of sex for the purposes of the Directive. The answer depends on whether the fundamental reason for the refusal of employment is one which applies without distinction to workers of either sex or, conversely, whether it applies exclusively to one sex.

11. The reason given by the employer for refusing to appoint Mrs Dekker is basically that it could not have obtained reimbursement from the Risicofonds of the daily benefits which it would have had to pay her for the duration of her absence due to pregnancy, and yet at the same time it would have been obliged to employ a replacement. That situation arises because, on the one hand, the national scheme in question assimilates pregnancy to sickness and, on the other, the Ziekengeldreglement contains no provision excluding pregnancy from the cases in which the Risicofonds is entitled to refuse reimbursement of the daily benefits.

12. In that regard it should be noted that only women can be refused employment on grounds of pregnancy and such a refusal therefore constitutes direct discrimination on grounds of sex. A refusal of employment on account of the financial consequences of absence due to pregnancy must be regarded as based, essentially, on the fact of pregnancy. Such discrimination cannot be justified on grounds relating to the financial loss which an employer who employed a pregnant woman would suffer for the duration of her maternity leave.

. . .

17. It should be stressed that the reply to the question whether the refusal to employ a woman constitutes direct or indirect discrimination depends on the reason for that refusal. If that reason is to be found in the fact that the person concerned is pregnant, then the decision is directly linked to the sex of the candidate.

In those circumstances the absence of male candidates cannot affect the answer to the first question.

The reason given by the Court in *Dekker* for why such refusal of employment on grounds of pregnancy is direct sex discrimination is that pregnancy is a condition which applies to women only. Would this mean that, if certain physical or medical conditions applied only to men, such refusal or dismissal on grounds of absence due to such a condition would be considered sex discrimination in breach of Directive 76/207? In the case of *Hertz*, below, the Court ruled that dismissal on grounds of sickness to which one sex only is susceptible would not constitute discrimination on grounds of sex, since both sexes were equally exposed to illness.[158] Yet the reason given by the Court for dismissal on grounds of pregnancy constitutes sex discrimination seems formal and inadequate, since its only basis is that, since pregnancy is a condition affecting only women, such dismissal must constitute sex discrimination. Surely the reason pregnancy-related dismissal is seen as impermissible discrimination is not just that it is a condition 'which applies to women only', but that it is a unique condition which is also of social value. Protection against pregnancy-based dismissal should exist because the role women play in reproduction and childbirth is an important one in which employers, men, and society as a whole have an interest.[159] Indeed, this was acknowledged by Advocate General Tesauro, who stated in the context of Directive 76/207 that 'it would be paradoxical if recognition of the social function of maternity, and consequent protection of pregnant women, should come about through their exclusion from the labour market'.[160] In his view, Article 2(3) and the provisions for protection of women in the event of pregnancy could not properly be considered as a derogation from the equal treatment principle, since 'they seek rather to ensure that principle operates in substance, by permitting such 'inequalities' as are necessary in order to achieve equality'.[161]

What the ruling in *Dekker* established was that the refusal to employ a worker for financial reasons consequent upon her pregnancy constitutes sex discrimination, but it remained unclear how far the principle would be applied. If the refusal were on grounds of other pregnancy-related factors, such as illness arising from pregnancy, or because of a legislative prohibition on women performing certain work during pregnancy, or because of unavailability for essential work while absent during pregnancy, would it still constitute sex discrimination contrary to Directive 76/207? These questions were

158 Case C–179/88 *Handels- og Kontorfuntionærernes Forbund i Danmark* v. *Dansk Arbejdsgiverforening* [1990] ECR I–3979.

159 See generally S. Fredman, 'A Difference with Distinction: Pregnancy and Parenthood Reassessed' (1994) 110 LQR 106.

160 See his opinion in Case C–421/92, *Habermann-Beltermann* n. 156 above, 1664 (ECR).

161 *Ibid.* See S. Fredman, n. 159 above, for an argument that employment protection in the event of pregnancy should not be seen as a means of ensuring 'equality' for women, but as a means of acknowledging the value of childbirth and parenting.

addressed by the Court in the following three cases of *Hertz*, *Habermann-Beltermann*, and *Webb*.

In *Hertz*, the matter of dismissal on account of absence owing to sickness originating in pregnancy was in issue. The employees' union argued that protection against dismissal owing to illness caused by pregnancy was unlimited in time, but the Court did not accept this interpretation of the Equal Treatment Directive:

Case C–179/88, Handels- og Kontorfunktionærernes Forbund i Danmark v. Dansk Arbejdsgiverforening [1990] ECR I–3979

Hertz was employed as a part-time saleswoman for Aldi Marked, and gave birth a year later to a child. The period of pregnancy was complicated and she was on sick leave with the consent of her employer for most of it. Six months after resuming employment on the expiry of her twenty-four week maternity leave, she became ill again and was on sick leave for 100 working days between June 1984 and June 1985. In June 1985 she was given notice of dismissal, on the ground of her absences. Both parties agreed that the absences between 1984 and 1985 were to due to complications which arose from her pregnancy the previous year, but her employer stated that it was normal practice to dismiss employees who were so often ill. The Court was asked whether this was in breach of the Equal Treatment Directive.

THE ECJ

13. It follows from [Articles 1(1), 2(1), 2(3) and 5(1)] of the Directive quoted above that the dismissal of a female worker on account of pregnancy constitutes direct discrimination on grounds of sex, as is a refusal to appoint a pregnant woman (see judgment in case C–177/88 *Dekker* v. *VJM-Centrum* [1990] ECR I–3941).

14. On the other hand, the dismissal of a female worker on account of repeated periods of sick leave which are not attributable to pregnancy or confinement does not constitute direct discrimination on grounds of sex, inasmuch as such periods of sick leave would lead to the dismissal of a male worker in the same circumstances.

15. The Directive does not envisage the case of an illness attributable to pregnancy or confinement. It does, however, admit of national provisions guaranteeing women specific rights on account of pregnancy and maternity, such as maternity leave. During the maternity leave accorded to her pursuant to national law, a woman is accordingly protected against dismissal due to absence. It is for every Member State to fix periods of maternity leave in such a way as to enable female workers to absent themselves during the period in which the disorders inherent in pregnancy and confinement occur.

16. In the case of an illness manifesting itself after the maternity leave, there is no reason to distinguish an illness attributable to pregnancy or confinement from any other illness. Such a pathological condition is therefore covered by the general rules applicable in the event of illness.

17. Male and female workers are equally exposed to illness. Although certain

disorders are, it is true, specific to one or other sex, the only question is whether a woman is dismissed on account of absence due to illness in the same circumstances as a man; if that is the case, then there is no direct discrimination on grounds of sex.

How far the protection against dismissal on grounds of pregnancy should go in this context is a difficult question, and Advocate General Darmon in the case admitted that he was 'tempted to propose a solution whereby medical conditions which were directly, definitely and preponderantly due to pregnancy or confinement would enjoy a sort of "immunity" in the sense that the principle of equality of treatment would restrain the employer from dismissing his employee for a reasonable period after the event in question'.[162] He decided ultimately against this, stating that such a solution was a matter for legislation. He chose the compromise which the Court also adopted, which makes the extent of protection against dismissal for pregnant women dependent on whatever maternity leave is granted by national legislation. This means that Directive 76/207 would not apply uniformly in the different Member States, but would vary according to the length of maternity leave provided in each. Again, however, this will now be affected by the provisions on maternity leave in Directive 92/85, which came into effect in October 1994 and which require Member States to provide a minimum period of fourteen weeks' leave.

The approach adopted by the Court in *Hertz* has been criticized as an example of the limitations of a model of equality which requires women to be compared with men, for the purposes of treating them in the same way, except in certain 'exceptional' cases such as pregnancy, which are permitted by Directive 76/207, when they are entitled to 'special' treatment which recognizes their difference from men. It is argued instead in the following extract that what is needed is a recognition of the specific social disadvantages faced by women in order to ensure that they enjoy substantive equality:

G. More, Reflections on Pregnancy Discrimination under European Community Law[163]

It is apparent that the Equal Treatment Directive is constructed wholly within the 'sameness–difference' paradigm of equality. Gender neutrality—identical treatment—is the norm, but in certain areas where gender difference has proved problematic, such as maternity and occupational requirements, a special exception to the norm is permitted. The Equal Treatment Directive incorporates, therefore, both identical treatment and special standards, with man as the undeniable measure for both . . .

The decision in *Hertz* means that women are only guaranteed protection from dismissal relating to their pregnancy during the period of national statutory

[162] See para. 43 of his Opinion.
[163] [1992] *Journal of Social Welfare and Family Law* 48, 53–4.

maternity leave. This leaves 'abnormal' pregnancies, such as Ms Hertz's, without protection—a decision justified in the Advocate General's opinion on the basis that the possible 'financial difficulties' faced by the employer, and the risks to the 'efficient operation of the company' should override the interests of the exceptional case . . .

. . . Were the issue of pregnancy to be approached in an alternative way, however, and discrimination in law used as a way to remedy the disadvantages faced by pregnant women in the labour market, then the question of 'special rights' and of the point at which they are limited, would not arise (meaning, therefore, that 'abnormal pregnancies' could also be guaranteed protection). Yet, as long as legal protection from dismissal on grounds of pregnancy is conceptualised as preferential treatment for women, then women's disadvantaged status is obscured.

In *Habermann-Beltermann*, the Court was asked whether it was compatible with Directive 76/207 for an employee, who had chosen to work nights only, to be dismissed on becoming pregnant, because of national legislation which prohibited the assignment of night work to women who were pregnant or breast-feeding. A related question was whether it was compatible with the Directive for her contract of employment to be declared void for mistake—since her employer did not know that she was pregnant when she was hired—given that the legislation provided that any term in an employment contract breaching the prohibition on night work would be void:

Case C–421/92, Habermann-Beltermann v. Arbeiterwohlfahrt, Bezirksverband [1994] ECR I–1657, [1994] 2 CMLR 681

THE ECJ

15. It is clear that the termination of an employment contract on account of the employee's pregnancy, whether by annulment or avoidance, concerns women alone and constitutes, therefore, direct discrimination on grounds of sex . . .

16. However, the unequal treatment in a case such as this, unlike the *Dekker* case referred to by the national court, is not based directly on the woman's pregnancy but is the result of the statutory prohibition on night-time work during pregnancy.

17. The basis for that prohibition, laid down by section 8(1) of the Mutterschutzgesetz, is Article 2(3) of the directive, according to which the directive is without prejudice to the provisions concerning the protection of women, particularly as regards pregnancy and maternity.

18. The question, therefore, is whether the Directive precludes compliance with the prohibition on night-time work by pregnant women, which is unquestionably compatible with Article 2(3), from rendering an employment contract invalid or allowing it to be avoided on the ground that the prohibition prevents the employee from doing the night-time work for which she was engaged.

. . .

23. In this case, the questions submitted for a ruling relate to a contract without a fixed term and the prohibition on night-time work by pregnant women

therefore takes effect only for a limited period in relation to the total length of the contract.

24. In the circumstances, to acknowledge that the contract may be held to be invalid or be avoided because of the temporary inability of the pregnant employee to perform the night-time work for which she was engaged would be contrary to the objective of protecting such persons pursued by Article 2(3) of the Directive, and would deprive the Directive of its effectiveness.

25. Accordingly, the termination of a contract without a fixed term on account of the woman's pregnancy, whether by annulment or avoidance, cannot be justified on the ground that a statutory prohibition, imposed because of pregnancy, temporarily prevents the employee from performing night-time work.

Thus, in contrast to *Levy* and *Minne*, where pregnancy was not in issue,[164] a prohibition on night-work by pregnant women is, by virtue of Article 2(3), perfectly compatible with the Equal Treatment Directive. However, to terminate a woman's contract of employment on account of such a prohibition is in breach of the Directive, since it would undermine the basic aim of Article 2(3) and of the Directive as a whole, which is intended not just to protect women's physical condition but also to protect them against disadvantage in employment on account of the pregnancy.

It will be noted that the Court specifically limited its ruling to the case of a woman working without a fixed term contract. This seems to imply that, if the contract was for a fixed term during which she was unable to fulfil the terms of employment on account of pregnancy, dismissal might not be contrary to the Equal Treatment Directive. This issue was of importance also in the case of *Webb*, which concerned a woman who was dismissed when she discovered, shortly after being employed as replacement for another employee who would soon be absent on maternity leave, that she herself was pregnant. In addressing the question whether dismissal in these circumstances was in breach of the Equal Treatment Directive, the Court made extensive reference to the recently adopted Pregnancy Directive which was soon to come into effect.

Case C–32/93, Webb v. EMO Air Cargo (United Kingdom) Ltd [1994] ECR I–3567, [1994] 2 CMLR 729

THE ECJ

21. In view of the harmful effects which the risk of dismissal may have on the physical and mental state of women who are pregnant, have recently given birth or are breastfeeding, including the particularly serious risk that pregnant women may be prompted voluntarily to terminate their pregnancy, the Community legislature subsequently provided, pursuant to Article 10 of Council Directive 92/85 on the introduction of measures to encourage improvements in the safety and health at work of pregnant workers and workers who have recently given birth or are breastfeeding, by prohibiting dismissal during the period from the beginning of their pregnancy to the end of their maternity leave.

[164] See nn. 134 and 135 above.

22. Furthermore, Article 10 of Directive 92/85 provides that there is to be no exception to, or derogation from, the prohibition on the dismissal of pregnant women during that period, save in exceptional cases not connected with their condition.

23. The question submitted by the House of Lords, which concerns Directive 76/207, must take account of that general context.

24. First, in response to the House of Lords inquiry, there can be no question of comparing the situation of a woman who finds herself incapable, by reason of pregnancy discovered very shortly after the conclusion of the employment contract, of performing the task for which she was recruited with that of a man similarly incapable for medical or other reasons.

25. As Mrs Webb rightly argues, pregnancy is not in any way comparable with a pathological condition, and even less so with unavailability for work on non-medical grounds, both of which are situations that may justify the dismissal of a woman without discriminating on grounds of sex. Moreover, in *Hertz*, cited above, the Court drew a clear distinction between pregnancy and illness, even where the illness is attributable to pregnancy but manifests itself after the period of maternity leave. As the Court pointed out, in paragraph 16, there is no reason to distinguish such an illness from any other illness.

26. Furthermore, contrary to the submission of the United Kingdom, dismissal of a woman recruited for an indefinite period cannot be justified on grounds relating to her inability to fulfil a fundamental condition of her employment contract. The availability of an employee is necessarily, for the employer, a precondition for the proper performance of the employment contract. However, the protection afforded by Community law to a woman during pregnancy and after childbirth cannot be dependent on whether her presence at work during maternity is essential to the proper functioning of the undertaking in which she is employed. Any contrary interpretation would render ineffective the provisions of the Directive.

27. In circumstances such as those of Mrs Webb, termination of a contract for an indefinite period on grounds of the woman's pregnancy cannot be justified by the fact that she is prevented, on a purely temporary basis, from performing the work for which she has been engaged: see *Habermann-Beltermann*.

The case of women employed on fixed-term contracts, of whatever length, who are dismissed owing to pregnancy was expressly left undecided by the Court. In Advocate General Tesauro's view, the reason Webb should not be dismissed, despite the fact that she was unable to work during the period of another employee's maternity leave for which she was specifically recruited, was that 'her inability to carry out the task for which she was engaged affects only a limited period in relation to the total length of the contract'.[165] It is possible then that, even on the view of the Advocate General and the Court, women on fixed-term contracts should also be protected against dismissal if they can still fulfil a reasonable proportion of their contract. Certainly the same social and moral considerations in relation to the protection of pregnant women in employment still apply when the contract is not indefinite, since, if

[165] [1994] ECR I–3567, 3573–4.

anything, such women are in an even more vulnerable and disadvantaged position. It is certainly open to question whether the economic arguments against protection should prevail, since the issue is not even whether such an employee would be entitled to paid leave, but simply whether she should be protected against dismissal. The economic argument would relate primarily to the cost of recruiting and training another employee, but the question is whether this interest should take precedence over the protection of pregnant women in the workforce.

In both *Habermann-Beltermann* and *Webb*, it is noteworthy that the interpretation given by the Court of Directive 76/207 corresponds with the provisions of the Pregnancy Directive—by providing essentially that dismissal for any pregnancy-related reason *during the period of maternity leave* is impermissible.[166]

(e) The Pregnancy Directive

In a move away from the treatment of pregnancy as an issue of 'equal treatment between men and women', Directive 92/85 is expressly based on Article 118a of the Treaty on the health and safety at work of workers, under which legislation could be adopted by a qualified majority vote of the Council.[167] The preamble to the Directive also refers to the 1989 Charter of Fundamental Social Rights for Workers, which was signed in 1989 by eleven of the then twelve Member States, excluding the United Kingdom, and which has provided the impetus for various legislative initiatives in the field of social policy.[168] The chosen legal base, unsurprisingly, met with objection from the United Kingdom which wished to confine 'health and safety' to narrower issues such as fencing of machinery and dangerous substances at work.[169] However, the Directive was adopted after considerable negotiation and compromise, which included, again at the insistence of the United Kingdom, the setting of the minimum level of pay for workers on maternity leave at the level of sick pay, despite the arguments against drawing any parallels between sickness and pregnancy.

The Directive introduces a requirement of minimum protection by the Member States for three categories of female workers: pregnant workers, workers who have recently given birth, and workers who are breast-feeding. It is expressly stated that the Directive cannot be used to justify any reduction in higher levels of protection already provided in Member States, since they

166 See, however, J. Jacqmain 'Pregnancy as Grounds for Dismissal' (1994) 23 ILJ 355, 358, suggesting that there may be a conflict between Dir. 76/207 and Dir. 92/85 in a situation where a pregnant woman applies for a job for which she is fully qualified, but which necessarily entails exposure to risks which are listed in the latter Dir., when no alternative work is available.

167 [1992] OJ L348/1. For a critical analysis of the Dir. and of the various possible explanations for its adoption see V. Cromack, 'The EC Pregnancy Dir.: Principle or Pragmatism?' [1993] JSWFL 261.

168 COM(89)471.

169 For a discussion of some of the background to the Dir., see N. Burrows, n. 148 above.

have committed themselves under the Treaty 'to encouraging improvement while maintaining the improvements made'. Thus it is clear that this is not a fully harmonizing Directive, and it does not attempt to require uniform rights of maternity leave for women in all of the Member States.

The Directive provides for guidelines to be drawn up by the Commission on substances and processes which are considered hazardous or stressful to those three categories of workers. It requires employers to assess the extent to which such women are exposed to specified risks and, under Article 5, to take appropriate action further to these assessments, such as adjusting their working hours or working conditions, moving them to another job, or granting them leave. Article 7 provides that they cannot be obliged to perform night work for a period to be set by national law, and the option of day work or, in the alternative, extended maternity leave must be possible. Article 6 provides that pregnant or breast-feeding workers cannot be required to carry out duties involving the risk of exposure to specified substances, and Article 9 stipulates that pregnant workers must be entitled, where necessary, to time off work without loss of pay to attend ante-natal examinations.

The core provision on maternity leave is contained in Article 8, which specifies that the three categories of workers are to be given a minimum of fourteen continuous weeks' maternity leave before and/or after confinement, including at least two weeks of compulsory maternity leave. This is bolstered by Article 10, which requires Member States to prohibit the dismissal of such workers during the period of maternity leave, other than in exceptional cases unconnected with pregnancy. The requirement of access to a judicial remedy which was seen in the Equal Pay and Equal Treatment Directives is to be found in Article 12 of the Pregnancy Directive. Under Article 11, the right to maintenance of payment and other employment rights must be protected in the case of those workers who are on leave in the circumstances provided in Articles 5, 6, and 7. Significantly, the same is not required in the case of workers who are on maternity leave as provided in Article 8. Instead, Article 11 specifies that they must be entitled to an 'adequate allowance' of not less than the amount of statutory sick pay. Further, eligibility for this allowance can be subjected by national legislation to conditions, other than a condition which requires previous employment of more than twelve months prior to confinement. From this it might be concluded that, if a Member State chose to do so, it could exclude fixed-term or part-time workers from eligibility for an allowance while on maternity leave.[170] However, such workers now appear to be protected, under Article 10, from dismissal during the new fourteen-week leave period to which all women who are giving birth are entitled. Thus the case of dismissal of a pregnant employee on a fixed-term contract, which the Court in *Habermann-Beltermann* and the Advocate General in *Webb* implied

[170] A reference is currently pending before the Court on whether Art. 119, Dir. 75/117, or Dir. 76/207 require a woman to be paid full pay while on maternity leave. The facts of the case would have arisen before the coming into force of Dir. 92/85: case C–342/93, *Gillespie* v. *Department of Health*, [1993] OJ C215/15.

would not breach the Equal Treatment Directive, would now breach Article 10 of the Pregnancy Directive. It has been pointed out, however, that the Directive does not cover the *Dekker* situation, i.e. that of refusal to employ a woman on grounds of pregnancy, and for this situation it will still be necessary to rely on the concept of discrimination under the Equal Treatment Directive with the problem of hypothetical male comparator to which that approach gives rise.[171]

(f) Directive 86/613

Since Directive 76/207 deals with equal treatment in relation to employed persons, Directive 86/613 was adopted under Articles 100 and 235 of the Treaty in order to apply the principle of equal treatment also to the self-employed.[172] Article 2 sets out the personal scope of the Directive, providing that it applies to the self-employed 'including farmers and members of the liberal professions' as well as their spouses who are not employees or partners, but who participate in the same activities. Article 3 sets out the principle of equal treatment in a similar way to that in the other Equal Treatment and Social Security Directives. Articles 4 to 8 then set out the 'material scope' of the scheme, which requires Member States to take action to eliminate sex discrimination in a range of matters, such as establishing a business or activity, forming a company, and providing for social-security schemes for spouses of the self-employed. Member States are also to 'examine under what conditions' the recognition of the work of spouses may be encouraged, and under what conditions female self-employed workers or wives of such workers may be protected in the event of pregnancy or motherhood—specifically, the Directive mentions access to temporary replacements or national social services and entitlement to cash benefits under public social-security or social-protection schemes.

(g) Sexual Harassment

In 1991, having commissioned a report on the Dignity of Women at Work, the Commission adopted a Recommendation on the protection of the dignity of employees at work, setting out guidelines on what may or may not constitute sexual harassment in the work-place and calling on Member States to encourage employees to implement its Code of Practice.[173] The recommendation was annexed to the Code of Practice on measures to combat sexual harassment. While recommendations in themselves are a form of non-binding or soft law, they are not without legal effect in national law since they may be used in the interpretation of relevant national law.[174] Further, the recommendation may

[171] V.Cromack, n. 167 above.

[172] See [1986] OJ L359/56 and COM(94) 163.

[173] Rec. 92/131: [1992] OJ L49/1. See also the Council Res. on the protection of the dignity of men and women at work: [1990] OJ C157/3.

[174] Case C–322/88, *Grimaldi* v. *Fonds des Maladies Professionelles* [1989] ECR 4407, [1991] 2 CMLR 265.

prompt changes in employment practices by virtue of the very fact that it has been adopted at Community level.[175]

According to the author of the report which had been commissioned, the Commission accepted that sexual harassment is, in principle, contrary to Equal Treatment Directive 76/207, and thus also contrary to any national provisions implementing the Directive.[176] If the Recommendation has not, within the three years for which it provides, been made effective, it has been suggested that 'the pressure for a Community Directive . . . is likely to be intense'.[177]

4. SOCIAL SECURITY

The two main legislative provisions in the field of social security are Directive 79/7 on statutory social security,[178] and Directive 86/378 on occupational social security.[179] However, as we have seen, the expanding interpretation of Article 119 has undermined much of the latter Directive, greatly reducing its scope. Little remained of the original, and the Commission has recently introduced a proposal to amend it in the light of the Court's rulings.[180]

(a) Directive 79/7

Directive 79/7, which was anticipated by Article 1(2) of Directive 76/207, was adopted on the basis of Article 235, and its purpose is said to be the progressive implementation of the principle of equal treatment for men and women in the field of social security.[181] The term "progressive" is significant here, since, unlike Directive 75/117 on equal pay, Directive 79/7 provided various exceptions to the equal-treatment principle, and allowed Member States a considerably longer period of time to adapt their laws to its requirements than was allowed to them under the Equal Treatment Directive.

Article 2 establishes the personal scope of the Directive, setting out two broad categories of person to which it applies. First, it covers the 'working population', which is subdivided into three categories: (i) those who are employed or self-employed, (ii) those under (i) whose work is interrupted by illness, accident, or involuntary unemployment, and (iii) those who are seeking employment. Secondly, it covers retired or invalided employees and

[175] On the impact of the Rec. and Code, see J. Dine and B. Watt, 'Sexual Harassment: Hardening the Soft Law' (1994) 19 ELRev. 104, and T. Lester 'Some Reflections on the European Community's Code of Conduct on Sexual Harassment' [1994] JSWFL 354.

[176] See M. Rubenstein, (1992) 21 ILJ 70. See also the argument of E. Ellis to this effect in *European Community Sex Equality Law* (Clarendon Press, 1991), 148–52.

[177] *Ibid.* 74. See also European Parliament Res. A3–0043/94 urging the Member States to require employers to appoint a sexual harassment counsellor and to adopt other preventive measures: [1994] OJ C61/246.

[178] [1979] OJ L6/24.

[179] [1986] OJ L225/40, as amended in [1986] OJ L283/27.

[180] See 819–35.

self-employed persons. Thus, in keeping with the Equal Pay and Equal Treatment Directives, Directive 79/7 covers only *employment-related* social security.

Article 3, which sets out the material scope of the Directive, then indicates that it does not cover all forms of employment-related social security. Rather, it covers those statutory schemes which provide protection against five specified risks, as well as social assistance which is intended to supplement or replace those statutory schemes. The five categories of risk are sickness, invalidity, old age, accidents at work and occupational diseases, and finally unemployment. Article 3(2) specifies that the Directive will not apply to provisions concerning survivors' benefits or family benefits, except family benefits due in respect of one of the five listed risks. Article 3(3) indicates that occupational social security is not covered, and provides for the adoption of later legislation in that sphere—Directive 86/378 being the later example of such legislation.[182]

The basic principle of equal treatment is set out in Article 4(1), providing that there is to be no discrimination on ground of sex, either directly or indirectly, by reference in particular to marital or family status. Examples of the prohibited forms of discrimination are listed: no discrimination in the scope of schemes or conditions of access, nor in the obligation to contribute and the calculation of contributions, nor in the calculation of benefits, the conditions governing their duration, and the retention of entitlement to such benefits. Provisions concerning the protection of women on grounds of maternity are again specifically exempted.[183] The Member States are required, as in the other equality Directives, to take the necessary measures to ensure any provisions in breach of the equal-treatment principle are abolished, and they are required to provide an adequate remedy for those who feel aggrieved.[184]

The permissible exceptions to the scope of the Directive are set out in Article 7(1). Five specific matters are listed which the Member States may choose to exclude from the application of the Directive. The first, which was mentioned above in relation to the cases of *Marshall* and *Roberts* on the Equal Treatment Directive, relates to the 'determination of pensionable age for the purposes of granting old-age and retirement pensions and the possible consequences thereof for other benefits'.[185] This has been the subject of much litigation. The second exception concerns advantages in respect of old-age pension schemes for persons who have brought up children and the acquisition of benefit entitlements following periods of interruption of employment due to the bringing up of children. The third concerns the granting of old-age

[181] Dir. 79/7, Art. 1. Dirs. and other measures on social security can now be adopted unanimously by the Member States using the machinery of the Council, but without the participation of the UK, under the provisions of the Agreement on Social Policy.

[182] A third draft Dir. on Social Security was proposed by the Commission in 1987 to remove the exceptions provided for in Dirs. 79/7 and 86/378, but it was never adopted. See [1987] OJ C309/10 and more generally see K. Banks, 'The Current Status of the Social Security Dirs.' in *Equality of Treatment Between Women and Men in Social Security*, n. 46 above.

[183] Art. 4(2).

[184] Arts. 5 and 6.

[185] Art. 7(1)(a).

or invalidity benefit entitlements 'by virtue of the derived entitlements of a wife', the fourth the granting of increases in long-term invalidity, old-age, accidents-at-work, and occupational-disease benefits for a dependent wife, and the fifth the consequences of the exercise of a right of option not to acquire rights or incur obligations under a statutory scheme.[186] However, these areas of permissible exception are not to be static, since Article 7(2) requires Member States to examine periodically any areas they have excluded, to see whether the justification for exclusion has altered in the light of social developments. Further, Member States must communicate to the Commission the provisions adopted pursuant to Article 7(2) and to inform it of their reasons for maintaining existing provisions under Article 7(1), as well as the possibilities for future review of such derogations. The period for implementation of the Directive was six years, which meant that it was required to be fully in force in the Member States at the end of 1984.

(i) Direct Effect of Directive 79/7 The direct effect of the equal-treatment principle in Article 4(1) of the Directive was confirmed in the *FNV* case, in which the Court was asked whether it could be relied upon after the deadline for implementation, either if the Member States failed to implement it or if they implemented it only partially. The Court ruled that, despite the fact that Article 5 envisaged that Member States would take steps to abolish discrimination, this did not prevent the clear and precise principle in Article 4(1) from having direct effect in the absence of implementation:

Case 71/85, Netherlands v. Federatie Nederlandse Vakbeweging [1986] ECR 3855, [1987] 3 CMLR 767

FNV, the defendant trade-union federation, brought an action against The Netherlands challenging the state's refusal to cease to apply the Law on Unemployment Benefit after 23 December 1984, the date by which Member States had to have implemented the provisions of Directive 79/7. The law in question contained a 'breadwinner' rule which excluded certain categories of married female workers from the right to unemployment benefit. Although the Dutch Government subsequently abolished this rule, it was provided that those whose unemployment had begun before 23 December 1984 would still be affected by the rule.

THE ECJ

18. It must be pointed out that, standing by itself, and in the light of the objective and contents of Directive 79/7/EEC, Article 4(1) precludes, generally and unequivocally, all discrimination on grounds of sex. The provision is therefore sufficiently precise to be relied upon in legal proceedings by an individual and applied by the courts. However, it remains to be considered whether the prohibition of discrimination which it contains may be regarded as unconditional, having regard to the exceptions provided for in Article 7 and to the fact that according to the

186 Art. 7(1)(b)–(e).

wording of Article 5, Member States are to take certain measures in order to ensure that the principle of equal treatment is applied in national legislation.

The Court ruled that Article 7 was not relevant since it simply excluded certain clearly defined areas from the equal-treatment principle of Article 4. Nor could Article 5, which obliges Member States to adopt the measures necessary to abolish infringements of the equal-treatment principle, be seen as imposing conditions on the clear prohibition on discrimination.

> 21. Consequently, Article 4(1) of the Directive does not confer on Member States the power to make conditional or to limit the application of the principle of equal treatment within its field of application and it is sufficiently precise and unconditional to allow individuals, in the absence of implementing measures adopted within the prescribed period, to rely upon it before the national courts as from 2 December 1984 in order to preclude the application of any national provision inconsistent with that article.
>
> . . .
>
> 25. . . . a Member State may not invoke its discretion with regard to the choice of methods for implementing the principle of equal treatment in the field of social security laid down in Directive 79/7/EEC in order to deny all effect to Article 4(1) thereof, which may be invoked in legal proceedings even though the said Directive has not been implemented in its entirety.

Subsequently, in *Borrie Clark*, the Court ruled that it was contrary to Article 4(1) of the Directive for a Member State, by means of legislation passed after the coming into effect of the Directive, to extend the discriminatory effects of an old benefit to the criteria for eligibility for a new benefit.[187] The case concerned an application for a severe-disablement allowance, which had been brought in to replace the earlier invalidity allowance. The invalidity allowance had discriminated against married women by requiring them not only to be incapable of continuing to work, but also 'incapable of performing normal household duties'. When the new severe-disablement allowance was introduced, it was provided that those who had qualified for the previous invalidity pension would be entitled to the new allowance, thus continuing the discriminatory criteria for eligibility. This was not permissible, and Article 4(1) could be directly relied on by the affected applicant.[188]

(ii) Personal scope The personal scope of the Directive was given a broad reading by the Court in *Drake*, in which a woman who had given up work in order to care for her disabled mother was refused an invalid care allowance under national legislation on the ground that such an allowance was not

[187] Case 384/85, *Borrie Clark* v. *Chief Adjudication Officer* [1987] ECR 2865, [1987] 3 CMLR 277.

[188] See also Case 80/87, *Dik* v. *College van Burgemeester en Wethouders* [1988] ECR 1601, [1989] 2 CMLR 963.

payable to a married woman who was living with her husband. No such restriction was imposed by the legislation on a married man who was living with his wife, but when the applicant challenged the compatibility of the legislation with Directive 79/7, the Adjudication Officer took the view that she did not fall within the personal scope of the Directive:

Case 150/85, Drake v. Chief Adjudication Officer [1986] ECR 1995, [1986] 3 CMLR 43

THE ECJ

21. According to Article 3(1), Directive 79/7 applies to statutory schemes which provide protection against, inter alia, the risk of invalidity . . . and social assistance in so far as it is intended to supplement or replace the invalidity scheme . . . In order to fall within the scope of the Directive, therefore, a benefit must constitute the whole or part of a statutory scheme providing protection against one of the specified risks or a form of social assistance having the same objective.

22. Under Article 2, the term 'working population', which determines the scope of the directive, is defined broadly . . . That provision is based on the idea that a person whose work has been interrupted by one of the risks referred to in Article 3 belongs to the working population. That is the case of Mrs. Drake, who has given up work solely because of one of the risks listed in Article 3, namely the invalidity of her mother. She must therefore be regarded as a member of the working population for the purposes of the Directive.

23. Furthermore, it is possible for the Member States to provide protection against the consequences of the risk of invalidity in various ways. For example, a Member State may, as the United Kingdom has done, provide for two separate allowances, one payable to the disabled person himself and the other payable to a person who provides care, while another Member State may arrive at the same result by paying an allowance to the disabled person at a rate equivalent to the sum of those two benefits. In order, therefore, to ensure that the progressive implementation of the principle of equal treatment referred to in Article 1 of Directive 79/7 and defined in Article 4 is carried out in a harmonious manner throughout the Community, Article 3(1) must be interpreted as including any benefit which in a broad sense forms part of one of the statutory schemes referred to or a social assistance provision intended to supplement or replace such a scheme.

24. Moreover the payment of the benefit to a person who provides care still depends on the existence of a situation of invalidity inasmuch as such a situation is a condition *sine qua non* for its payment, as the Adjudication Officer admitted during the oral procedure. It must also be emphasized that there is a clear economic link between the benefit and the disabled person, since the disabled person derives an advantage from the fact that an allowance is paid to the person caring for him.

25. It follows that the fact that a benefit which forms part of a statutory invalidity scheme is paid to a third party and not directly to the disabled person does not place it outside the scope of Directive 79/7. Otherwise, as the Commission emphasized in its observations, it would be possible, by making formal changes to existing benefits covered by the directive, to remove them from its scope.

Thus, although Mrs Drake had not given up work because she had become an invalid, the fact that she had given up work in order to care for someone else who had was sufficient to bring her within the scope of the Directive. The care allowance was treated by the Court in the same way as the mother's severe-disablement allowance, being simply the legislature's way of dividing up the payment of social-security benefits consequent on invalidity.

The Social Security Directive is strictly employment-related, in that it does not cover someone who has never worked. This was established in the case of *Achterberg-te Riele*, in which the Court also ruled that persons who give up work for a reason other than one of the five listed in the Directive—e.g. to look after children—fall outside of its scope.[189] Benefits such as old-age pensions and invalidity allowances, which are referred to in Article 3, will only fall within the scope of the Directive when they are claimed by someone who is within one of the categories of person in Article 2:

> This interpretation is in conformity with the objectives of Community law and the wording of the other provisions in the same field as Directive 79/7. Article 119 . . . Directive 75/117 . . . and Directive 76/207 . . . implement equal treatment between men and women not generally but only in their capacity as workers.[190]

These conditions were tightened further in the case of *Johnson* where the Court ruled that in order to be covered by the Directive, not only must one of the risks listed in the Directive have materialized, but the person in question must have either given up employment, or been obliged to give up seeking employment *at the time of materialization of the risk*.[191] Johnson had given up work for some years in order to care for her child and in the meantime had developed a serious back condition which rendered her unable to return to work. She was refused an invalidity pension or severe-disablement allowance because she was cohabiting with her partner, and since this restriction did not apply to men and thus was discriminatory, she argued that it was in breach of Directive 79/7. Despite the Commission's argument that, since those who give up work to look after children are largely women, and that they would be at a considerable disadvantage if they were excluded from the Social Security Directive on account of an illness or disability *subsequently* arising, the Court ruled that they would not be within the personal scope of the Directive, and shifted the responsibility for removing the disadvantage faced by women on to the Community legislature:[191a]

189 Cases 48, 106, and 107/88, *Achterberg-te Riele* v. *Sociale Versekeringsbank, Amsterdam* [1989] ECR 1963, [1990] 3 CMLR 323.

190 *Ibid.*, para. 12.

191 Case C–31/90, *Johnson* v. *Chief Adjudication Officer* [1991] ECR I–3723, [1991] 3 CMLR 917, paras. 18–23.

191a See also Case C–297/93 *Grau-Hupka* v. *Stadtgemeinde Bremen*, 13 Dec. 1994, even where such disadvantage affects women's pay.

Case C–31/90 Johnson v. Chief Adjudication Officer [1991] ECR I–3723, [1991] 3 CMLR 917

THE ECJ

25. It must be observed, however, that according to the first recital of the preamble to Directive 79/7/EEC and Article 1 thereof, the Directive has in view only the progressive implementation of the principle of equal treatment for men and women in matters of social security. As far as the social protection of mothers remaining at home is concerned, it follows from Article 7(1)(b) . . . that the acquisition of entitlement to benefits following periods of interruption of employment due to the upbringing of children is still a matter for the Member States to regulate.

26. In those circumstances, it is for the Community legislature to take such measures as it considers appropriate to remove the discrimination which still exists in this regard in some bodies of national legislation.

This represents a tighter reading of the personal scope of the Directive, since it excludes someone who wishes to seek employment but cannot do so on account of a disability or illness he or she has suffered, and it firmly underlines the employment-related focus of the Social Security Directive. Where the person seeking a benefit does satisfy the conditions of the Directive, however, the Court has ruled that the right to rely on the Directive is not confined to that person. In *Verholen*, one of the applicants before the Dutch court was the husband of a woman who was claiming sex discrimination in the conditions for determining affiliation of an old-age pension scheme.[192] The national court, of its own motion, raised the question of the applicability of Directive 79/7 and among the questions referred to the Court was that whether someone other than the person entitled to the benefit could rely on the measure:

> It should be pointed out straight away that the right to rely on the provisions of Directive 79/7 is not confined to individuals coming within the scope *ratione personae* of the Directive, in so far as the possibility cannot be ruled out that other persons may have a direct interest in ensuring that the principle of non-discrimination is respected as regards persons who are protected.[193]

Accordingly, because the claimant's husband had suffered the effects of the discriminatory national legislation concerning his spouse, in that his pension would also be reduced, he could invoke the provisions of the Directive so long as his spouse came within its personal scope, even though he himself did not.[194]

[192] Cases C–87–89/90, *Verholen and Others* v. *Sociale Versekeringsbank* [1991] ECR I–3757, [1994] 1 C.M.L.R 157.

[193] *Ibid.*, para. 22.

[194] See also Case C–200/91, n. 32 above, para. 19.

iii) Material Scope With regard to the material scope of the Directive, lthough the Court began by giving Article 3 quite a broad reading, there has een a move away from this approach in more recent cases, in which social-ecurity benefits have been excluded from the scope of the Directive although hey appear to be linked to the risks which are set out in Article 3. In *Drake* t has been seen that the Court held that an invalid care allowance could be a enefit falling within the scope of the Directive because it was indirectly of enefit to the disabled person who would receive the care. However, it can be een from the following cases that the link between one of the risks listed—uch as invalidity—and the benefit paid must be quite strong before the bene-it will be deemed to fall within the scope of the Directive:

Case 243/90, R. v. Secretary of State for Social Security, ex parte Smithson [1992] ECR I–467, [1992] 1 CMLR 1061

In determining eligibility for housing benefit, United Kingdom law provided that a person's income must fall below a certain notional level. The criteria to be used in determining that notional level included matters such as receipt of invalidity benefit and of a 'higher pensioner premium', i.e. criteria related to protection against risks covered by Directive 79/7. Mrs Smithson contested the determination of her income for the purposes of determining eligibility for housing benefit, and argued that, since the rules governing eligibility for invalidity benefit were clearly discriminatory as between men and women, the criteria for calculation of housing benefit were also discriminatory and in breach of Directive 79/7.

THE ECJ

13. In [*Drake*], the Court held that a benefit constituted part of the statutory scheme providing protection against the risk of invalidity despite the fact that it was paid partly to the beneficiary himself and partly to the person providing care; it was emphasised in this regard that the payment of the benefit to a person who provided care still depended on the existence of invalidity inasmuch as the latter was an essential condition for such payment, and pointed out the clear economic link between the benefit and the disabled person, who derived an advantage from the fact that an allowance was paid to the person caring for him.

14. It is therefore clear that although the mode of payment is not decisive as regards the identification of a benefit as one which falls within the scope of Directive 79/7, in order to be so identified the benefit must be directly and effectively linked to the protection provided against one of the risks specified in Article 3(1) of the Directive.

15. However, Article 3(1)(a) of Directive 79/7 does not refer to statutory schemes which are intended to guarantee any person whose real income is lower than a notional scheme calculated on the basis of certain criteria a special allowance enabling that person to meet housing costs.

16. The age and invalidity of the beneficiary are only two of the criteria applied in order to determine the extent of the beneficiary's financial need for such an allowance. The fact that those criteria are decisive as regards eligibility for the

higher pensioner premium is not sufficient to bring that benefit within the scope of Directive 79/7.

17. The premium is an inseparable part of the whole benefit which is intended to compensate for the fact that the beneficiary's income is insufficient to meet housing costs, and cannot be characterised as an autonomous scheme intended to provide protection against one of the risks listed in Article 3(1) of Directive 79/7.

The Court in this case took a narrower approach to the material scope of Directive 79/7 than it had done earlier in *Drake*. In *Drake*, the allowance was not to protect the recipient against invalidity, but to make up for the loss of income on the part of the recipient who has given up work to care for an invalid. Thus the benefit is linked to invalidity, but indirectly, since the invalid is not a direct recipient of the financial benefit. The reference to methods of funding in paragraph 14 may indicate that the mere fact that the benefit is non-contributory does not mean that it falls outside the scope of the Directive. However, in *Smithson*, the Court nevertheless took the view that housing benefit was not within the scope of the Directive even though the criteria for calculating the benefit included two of the risks covered in the Directive—age and invalidity. The link between these criteria for calculating the benefit and the aim of the benefit—i.e. to provide for those whose income was inadequate to cover housing costs—was held to be insufficiently strong to conclude that the housing benefit was intended to protect against the risks of old age or invalidity. It is arguable that if this approach had been taken in *Drake*, looking strictly at the intended aim of the benefit, the conclusion might have been that the aim of the invalid care allowance was to provide a source of income to someone who had given up work to care for another. The link between the protection against the risk of invalidity and the care allowance was indirect, just as the link between the protection against the risk of old age or invalidity and the housing benefit was indirect. The conclusion of the Court in *Smithson* seems to be that the housing benefit was really a form of social assistance and was not intended to supplement or replace one of the listed social security benefits, and it represents a more restrictive approach to determining the scope of the equal treatment principle in Community social security under Community law.

This tightening up of the scope of the Directive continued in *Jackson and Cresswell*, where the question was whether supplementary allowance or income support could be said, in certain circumstances, to fall within the scope of the Directive as a form of protection against the risk of unemployment. The applicants argued that the reduction in their benefits was in breach of Directive 79/7, since it was a consequence of their not being able to deduct child-minding expenses when calculating their income in order to determine the amount of benefit they should receive. The prohibition on deduction of child-minding expenses was argued to be indirectly discriminatory against women. However, despite the argument of Advocate General Van Gerven that the link between protection against unemployment and the benefits in issue in his case was much closer than the link between protection against invalidity and old age and the benefits in issue in *Smithson*, the Court ruled that the benefits were not 'directly and effectively' linked to protection against the risk of unemployment.

Cases C–63–64/91, Jackson v. Chief Adjudication Officer [1992] ECR I–4737, [1992] 3 CMLR 389

THE ECJ

17. . . . Article 3(1)(a) of Directive 79/7 does not refer to a statutory scheme which, on certain conditions, provides persons with means below a legally defined limit with a special benefit designed to enable them to meet their needs.

18. That finding is not affected by the circumstance that the recipient of the benefit is in fact in one of the situations covered by Article 3(1) of the Directive.

19. Indeed in *Smithson*, cited above, the Court held with regard to a housing benefit that the fact that some of the risks listed in Article 3(1) of Directive 79/7 were taken into account in order to grant a higher benefit was not sufficient to bring that benefit within the scope of the Directive.

20. Consequently, exclusion from the scope of Directive 79/7 is justified *a fortiori* where, as in the case at issue in the main proceedings, the law sets the amount of the theoretical needs of the persons concerned, used to determine the benefit in question, independently of any consideration relating to the existence of any of the risks listed in Article 3(1) of the Directive.

21. Moreover, in certain situations, in particular those of the appellants in the main proceedings, the national schemes at issue exempt claimants from the obligation to be available for work. That shows that the benefits in question cannot be regarded as being directly and effectively linked to protection against the risk of unemployment.

Thus, whereas the Advocate General argued for an approach to the material scope of Directive 79/7 which did not focus exclusively on the intention or aim of the statutory scheme but also on its overall effect in providing protection against one of the risks in the Directive, the Court concentrated on the need which the scheme was 'designed' to meet. The problem with an approach which is largely intention-oriented, however, is that it may enable the Member States to structure their social-security and assistance schemes so as to avoid the application of the equal-treatment principle to many benefits which do, in fact, provide protection against one or more of the risks set out in the Directive.[195]

In *Steenhorst-Neerings*, the question arose whether a provision governing the cumulability of benefits, one of which was covered by the Directive and the other of which was not, would fall within its scope.[196] The Court ruled in

[195] See J. Sohrab, 'Women and Social Security Law: The Limits of EEC Equality Law' [1994] JSWFL 5.

[196] Case C–338/91, *Steenhorst-Neerings* v. *Bestuur van de Bedrijfsvereniging voor Detailhandel, Ambachten en Huisvrouwen* [1993] ECR I–4975.

that case that although survivor's benefits were in themselves outside the scope of the Directive, if invalidity benefits were to be withdrawn when a woman receiving them became entitled to a widow's pension, this would breach Article 4(1) of the Directive, since invalidity benefits fell clearly within its scope.

(iv) The Exceptions in Article 7 We have seen that the Council in adopting Directive 79/7 did not attempt to require the states to bring about immediate equality between women and men in social security, but rather permitted the gradual introduction of equal treatment in certain areas which would require considerable financial restructuring of existing state schemes. The exact scope of these exceptions, however, is not clear from the provisions of the Directive and has given rise to a considerable amount of litigation. The most frequently litigated point is that which has briefly been considered above in relation to conditions of dismissal under the Equal Treatment Directive, and that is the derogation concerning the determination of pensionable age.

Case C–9/91, R. v. Secretary of State for Social Security ex parte Equal Opportunities Commission [1992] ECR I–4927, [1992] 3 CMLR 233

The pensionable age in the United Kingdom was 65 for men and 60 for women. The Equal Opportunities Commission (EOC) sought judicial review of the contributory state pension scheme, claiming that it discriminated against men on grounds of sex, by requiring men to pay contributions for 44 years and women for 39 years in order to qualify for a full basic pension. Further, men working between the ages of 60 and 64 paid pension contributions whereas women working between those ages did not. The United Kingdom Government argued that the differences in treatment could be justified under the derogation in Article 7(1)(a) of Directive 79/7.

THE ECJ

13. Since the text of the derogation refers to 'the determination of pensionable age for the purpose of granting old-age and retirement pensions', it is clear that it concerns the moment from which pensions become payable. The text does not, however, refer expressly to discrimination in respect of the extent of the obligation to contribute for the purposes of the pension or the amount thereof. Such forms of discrimination therefore fall within the scope of the derogation only if they are found to be necessary in order to achieve the objectives which the Directive is intended to pursue by allowing Member States to retain a different pensionable age for men and women.

. . .

15. Although the preamble to the Directive does not state the reasons for the derogations which it lays down, it can be deduced from the nature of the exceptions contained in Article 7(1) of the Directive that the Community legislature intended to allow Member States to maintain temporarily the advantages accorded to women with respect to retirement in order to enable them progres-

sively to adapt their pension systems in this respect without disrupting the complex financial equilibrium of those systems, the importance of which could not be ignored. Those advantages include the possibility for female workers of qualifying for a pension earlier than male workers, as envisaged by Article 7(1)(a) of the directive.

16. In a system such as the one concerned in the main proceedings, whose financial equilibrium is based on men contributing for a longer period than women, a different pensionable age for men and women cannot be maintained without altering the existing financial equilibrium, unless such inequality with respect to the length of contribution periods is also maintained.

Any more limited interpretation of the derogation, the Court ruled, would render it entirely ineffective, since the financial upheaval which the exception was intended to allow the states to avoid by readjusting the financing of pension schemes over a period of years would have to be faced by them before the deadline for implementation of the Directive. Thus the maintenance of different pensionable ages was not the only form of discrimination permitted by Article 7(1)(a), but 'also forms of discrimination such as those described by the national court which are necessarily linked to [the difference in statutory pensionable ages]'.

The derogation in Article 7(1)(a) extends not just to the setting of different pensionable ages, but also, as has been seen in the cases of *Burton* and *Roberts*,[197] above, to 'the possible consequences thereof for other benefits'. The case of *Thomas* raised the question whether the scope of the derogation was exceeded, where the cessation of entitlement to invalid-care and severe-disablement allowances was linked to the attainment of statutory retirement age, which was 65 for men and 60 for women.[198] Having considered its reasoning in the *EOC* case in relation to discrimination in contribution periods, the Court ruled that the same sort of link between the discrimination and the difference in pensionable ages was necessary when the complaint concerned discrimination as regards 'other benefits'. The requisite link was held not to exist in the case of disablement and invalid-care allowances, since:

the grant of benefits under non-contributory schemes, such as severe disablement allowance and invalid care allowance, to persons in respect of whom risks have materialised, regardless of the entitlement of such persons to an old-age pension by virtue of contribution periods completed by them, has no direct influence on the financial equilibrium of the contributory pension schemes.[199]

[197] Cases 19/81, n. 140 above, and 151/84, n. 106 above. See also Cases 262/84, n. 141 above and 152/84, n. 143 above.

[198] Case C–328/91, *Secretary of State for Social Security* v. *Thomas* [1993] ECR I–1247, [1993] 3 CMLR 880.

[199] *Ibid.*, para. 14.

It has been noted above that, although Article 7(1) sets out derogations to the scope of application of the Directive, Article 7(2) encourages Member States to carry out periodical examinations of any areas excluded under Article 7(1) to see whether such exclusions are still justified in the light of social changes, and to inform the Commission of the reasons for continuing to exclude as well as the future prospects for review. Once the Member State has acted to abolish discrimination from a previously exempt area, however it cannot rely on the derogation to continue discriminatory practices in that area. In *Van Cant*, the applicant was challenging the provisions of Belgian legislation which in 1990 had abolished discriminatory pensionable ages and had fixed entitlement to a retirement pension for both men and women at age 60.[200] However, the method for calculating the amount of the pension, which had been based on the forty most favourable years for women and forty-five for men, remained unchanged so that it now favoured women. The Court ruled that, once discriminatory retirement ages had been abolished, Article 7(1)(a) could no longer be relied on to justify maintaining a difference in calculating the retirement pension which was linked to that difference in retirement ages.

In *Bramhill*, however, a more progressive abolition of discrimination which was the subject of an exception in Article 7(1)(d) was held to be compatible with the Directive.[201] The case involved the scope of the derogation concerning increases in benefits for a 'dependent wife' in that provision. The applicant was refused an increase, in respect of her dependent husband, on the pension she had received when she retired at 60, on the ground that she did not satisfy the conditions in the social-security legislation. The conditions, which required her to have been in receipt of certain benefits for adult dependents prior to retirement, were clearly discriminatory since they did not apply to a married man in similar circumstances, but the United Kingdom argued that the provision was covered by the derogation in Article 7(1)(d). According to Mrs Bramhill, the derogation applied to increases in benefit for a dependent *wife* only, and did not apply to an increase in pension like that in the present case, which had been made available by legislation in 1984 in respect of dependent husbands and wives alike. She argued that, since the benefit was made available for both, whereas before the amending legislation in 1984 it had been available for dependent wives only, it fell outside the scope of the exception and the discriminatory conditions were thus in breach of Article 4(1):

> To interpret the Directive in the way contended for by Mrs Bramhill, which would mean that in the case of benefits which a Member State has excluded from the scope of the Directive pursuant to Article 7(1)(d) it could no longer rely on the derogation provided for by that provision if it adopted a measure which, like that in question in the main proceedings, has the effect of reducing the extent of unequal treatment based on sex, would therefore be incompatible with the

[200] Case C–154/92, *Van Cant* v. *Rijksdienst voor Pensionen* [1993] ECR I–3811.
[201] Case C–420/92, *Bramhill* v. *Chief Adjudication Officer* [1994] ECR I–3191.

purpose of the Directive and would be likely to jeopardize the implementation of the aforesaid principle of equal treatment.[202]

The difference between *Van Cant* and *Bramhill* would seem to be that, once a Member State abolishes a discriminatory provision in an area which has previously been excepted under Article 7(1), it cannot retain other associated forms of discrimination which existed only because of the now-abolished provision. However, where the state chooses not to abolish the original discrimination, but to alleviate it progressively by means of gradually improving the position of the disadvantaged sex, this cannot be said to be outside the scope of the derogation.

Article 7(1)(c) permits the exclusion from the Directive of the granting of old-age benefits by virtue of the derived entitlements of a wife. This provision was interpreted in the case of *Van Munster*, in which it was held that the principle of equal treatment in Directive 79/7 permitted a Member State to refuse a retired worker the higher rate of pension which its legislation provided for persons with dependent spouses, where that worker's spouse was entitled in her own right to a retirement pension in another Member State.[203]

(v) Indirect Discrimination in Social Security We have seen above that in the context of pay, Article 119 has been interpreted so as to prohibit both direct and indirect discrimination on grounds of sex. In the social-security context, this is not left to interpretation but is expressly stated in Article 4(1) of Directive 79/7. The following case indicates that the Court has developed the concept of indirect discrimination and objective justification in a very similar way to that seen above in the context of pay:

Case 30/85, Teuling v. Bedrijfsvereniging voor de Chemische Industrie [1987] ECR 2497, [1988] 3 CMLR 789

Under Dutch law, all employed persons suffering from an incapacity for work, regardless of sex or civil status, were entitled to a net minimum benefit equal to 70 per cent of the statutory minimum wage. That minimum could be increased under certain conditions by means of supplements to 100 per cent, but in practice this was only for beneficiaries having family responsibilities, such as a dependent spouse or children. Mrs. Teuling claimed that this system of entitlement to benefits was indirectly discriminatory against women and thus incompatible with Article 4(1) of Directive 79/7.

202 *Ibid.*, para. 21.

203 Case C–165/91, *Van Munster* v. *Rijksdienst voor Pensionen*, [1994] ECR I–4661. However, the Court did require, where the differences in social security systems between two Member States were such that a worker was disadvantaged by having moved to work in a different Member State, that the national authorities should, in so far as possible, interpret their own social-security provisions in such a way as to avoid constituting a deterrent to the free movement of the worker under Art. 48 and 51.

THE ECJ

13. In that regard, it should be pointed out that a system of benefits in which, as in this case, supplements are provided for which are not directly based on the sex of the beneficiaries but take account of their marital status or family situation, and in respect of which it emerges that a considerably smaller proportion of women than of men are entitled to such supplements, is contrary to Article 4(1) of the Directive if that system of benefits cannot be justified by reasons which exclude discrimination on grounds of sex.

14. It appears from the documents before the Court that according to statistics provided to the Commission by the Netherlands Government a significantly greater number of married men than married women receive a supplement linked to family responsibilities. According to the plaintiff and the Commission, that results from the fact that in the Netherlands there are at present considerably more married men than married women who carry on occupational activities, and therefore considerably fewer women who have a dependent spouse.

15. In such circumstances a supplement linked to family responsibilities is contrary to Article 4(1) of the Directive if the grant thereof cannot be justified by reasons which exclude discrimination on grounds of sex.

16. In that regard, the supplements at issue must be considered. According to the Netherlands Government, the General Law does not link benefits to the salary previously earned by the beneficiaries but seeks to provide a minimum subsistence income to persons with no income from work. It must be observed that such a guarantee granted by Member States to persons who would otherwise be destitute is an integral part of the social policy of the Member States.

17. Consequently, if supplements to a minimum social security benefit are intended, where beneficiaries have no income from work, to prevent the benefit from falling below the minimum subsistence level for persons who, by virtue of the fact that they have a dependent spouse or children, bear heavier burdens than single persons, such supplements may be justified under the Directive.

18. If a national court, which has sole jurisdiction to assess the facts and interpret the national legislation, finds that supplements such as those in this case correspond to the greater burdens which beneficiaries having a dependent spouse or children must bear in comparison with persons living alone, serve to ensure an adequate minimum subsistence income for those beneficiaries and are necessary for that purpose, the fact that the supplements are paid to a significantly higher number of married men than of married women is not sufficient to support the conclusion that the grant of such supplements is contrary to the Directive.

Clearly here, although it was left ultimately to the national court to say whether the supplements corresponded to the additional burden borne by those with dependent families, the Court felt that the indirect discrimination could be justified on the grounds of social policy which were put forward.[204]

[204] See also Case 102/88, *Ruzius-Wilbrink* v. *Bestuur van de Bedrijfs vereniging voor Overheidsdiensten* [1989] ECR 4311, [1991] 2 CMLR 202 where there was indirect discrimination against part-time workers in eligibility for invalidity benefits. The Court did not accept, as a justification, the claim that it would be unjust to grant such workers benefits which would exceed the income they had previously received.

Some years later, in proceedings against Belgium, the Court appeared to widen the discretion left to the Member States in justifying indirect discrimination in unemployment allowances, this time in favour of those with dependent family members, who were predominantly men.[205] Belgium argued that the discrimination reflected a necessary aim of social policy, since it recognized the greater burdens of unemployment for households with only one income. The Commission in response argued that the scheme of benefits would not be compatible with the equal-treatment principle unless its aim was to provide minimum means of subsistence, rather than to award replacement income for a lost salary. The Commission's argument appeared to have support in paragraph 16 of the Court's judgment in *Teuling*, above, but both the Advocate General and the Court disagreed with the Commission in this case. They took the view that the relevant criterion was whether the supplements corresponded to the greater burdens resulting from a spouse or children not in receipt of income, and that the principle of taking previous income into account was not in breach of the equal-treatment principle. The Court ruled that the aims of the Belgian scheme 'form part of a social policy which in the current state of Community law is a matter for the Member States which enjoy a reasonable margin of discretion as regards both the nature of the protective measures and the detailed arrangements for their implementation'.[206]

In the case of *De Weerd*, however, the Court held that although an indirectly discriminatory national measure, such as a previous income requirement for eligibility for incapacity benefits, could be justified on social policy grounds, a Member State's budgetary policy could not of itself constitute adequate justification for such discrimination:

Case C–343/92, De Weerd v. Bestuur van de Bedrijfsvereniging voor de Gezondheid, Geestelijke en Maatschappelijke Belangen [1994] ECR I–571, [1994] 2 CMLR 325

THE ECJ

35. Nevertheless, although budgetary considerations may influence a Member State's choice of social policy and affect the nature or scope of the social protection measures it wishes to adopt, they cannot themselves constitute the aim pursued by that policy and cannot, therefore, justify discrimination against one of the sexes.

36. Moreover, to concede that budgetary considerations may justify a difference in treatment as between men and women which would otherwise constitute indirect discrimination on grounds of sex, which is prohibited by Article 4(1) of Directive 79/7, would be to accept that the application and scope of as fundamental a rule of Community law as that of equal treatment between men and women might vary in time and place according to the state of the public finances of the Member States.

205 Case C–229/89, *Commission* v. *Belgium* [1991] ECR I–2205, [1993] 2 CMLR 403.

206 *Ibid.*, para. 22. See also Case C–221/91, *Molenbroek* v. *Bestuur van de Soziale Verzekeringsbank* [1992] ECR I–5943 where the state was accorded a similar margin of discretion in justifying indirect discrimination in the award of supplementary pensions for dependent spouses.

The same criticisms of indirect discrimination and objective justification are applicable in the context of social security as those which have been noted in the equal-pay and equal-treatment context. Indeed, in the social-security field the Court seems to allow an even wider discretion to Member States as regards their reasons for such discrimination.[207] Further, Directive 79/7 and the whole area of equal treatment in Community social-security law has been the subject of a more wide-ranging critique on account of its narrow focus and, once again, its use of a male norm and pattern of working life against which to measure standards of treatment.

J. Sohrab, Women and Social Security Law: The limits of EEC Equality Law[208]

EEC equality law has had an important impact on national social security systems. Many forms of direct discrimination have been eliminated. However, two outstanding problems with the Directive remain. The first is what kind of equality can the Directive promote and is this enough to produce equality of outcomes between men and women? We have seen that the Directive applies only to workers claiming broadly employment-related, rather than social assistance, benefits. In so doing the Directive, it is argued, perpetuates a market/family dichotomy, which hinders progress towards equality of outcomes. Women are not situated similarly to men in relation to employment and to caring responsibilities. Women's situation in one of these spheres cannot be seen in isolation from their situation in the other.

This leads us to the second problem, how strong is the concept of indirect discrimination? Once rules have been formally equalised the crucial part of Article 4(1) of the Directive becomes the prohibition of indirect discrimination. We have seen, however, that in implementing the Directive Member States may easily create indirect discrimination. Since men and women are not similarly situated, in many instances formally equal benefit rules can only help those women gain access to benefits who most closely conform to underlying structures of benefit entitlement . . . It is clear then that where the underlying structures do not fit closely with women's employment and life patterns, equality of outcomes will remain elusive. A strong concept of indirect discrimination could be used to challenge both levelling down and benefit rules which do not allow women in practice to gain benefits in their own right. In cases that do not directly concern workers, however, the Court seems reluctant to engage in such a radical enterprise. The real challenge to equality law in the future is to promote a social security system in which women are no longer penalised, in terms of a lack of financial independence, for not conforming to the 'typical (male) employment pattern.' This should also mean encouraging men to participate to a greater extent in caring.

[207] See F. Herbert, 'Social Security and Indirect Discrimination' in *Equality of Treatment between Women and Men in Social Security*, n. 46 above.

[208] [1994] JSWFL 5, 16.

(b) Directive 86/378

Directive 86/378, which was based on Articles 100 and 235 of the Treaty and had been anticipated in Article 4(3) of Directive 79/7, was intended—before the judgment in *Barber* had been given—to extend the principle of equal treatment from state social-security schemes, which were covered in Directive 79/7, to those in private or occupational social-security schemes. These are defined in Article 2 as schemes, whose membership is optional or compulsory, which are intended to provide workers or self-employed persons in an economic sector or undertaking with benefits intended to supplement or replace those provided by statutory social-security schemes. Certain schemes are excluded by Article 2, such as individual contracts, insurance contracts to which the employer is not a party, and individual options for additional benefits. Article 3 sets out the personal scope of the Directive, covering the working population in terms very similar to those of Article 2 of Directive 79/7, except that, in addition to covering those whose work is interrupted by illness, accident, or involuntary unemployment, it also covers interruption by maternity. Article 4 sets out the material scope of the Directive, and again the risks covered are almost exactly the same—sickness, invalidity, old-age including early retirement, industrial accidents and occupational diseases, and unemployment. Article 4(b) also provides that any other social benefits provided for in an occupational scheme, such as family or survivor's benefits, will fall within the scope of the Directive in so far as they constitute consideration for the worker by reason of the worker's employment. Article 5 sets out the principle of equal treatment in terms virtually identical to those of Article 4 of Directive 79/7, and Article 6 sets out ten examples of provisions which contravene the principle of equal treatment by discriminating on the basis of sex, or marital or family status.

Articles 7 and 8 impose specific obligations on Member States to take the necessary steps to ensure that provisions of schemes which contravene the equal-treatment principles will be annulled or amended, at the latest by January 1993. Thus a seven-year period for achieving equality in occupational pensions was envisaged. However, Article 9, in a manner similar to Article 7 of Directive 79/7, then provides for three derogations, matters in relation to which Member States may defer the application of the principle of equal treatment. The first derogation is the same as that in Article 7(1)(a) of Directive 79/7, i.e. the determination of pensionable age, etc., except that it is to apply only until the date on which equality is achieved in statutory schemes or until equality is required by a directive. The second derogation relates to survivors' pensions, again until equality is achieved in statutory schemes or until a directive requires it. The final derogation concerns the application of different actuarial factors for men and women with regard to setting worker contributions, or with regard to setting employer contributions in 'contribution-defined' schemes (i.e. money-purchase schemes, as explained above). This derogation was to apply for a thirteen-year period from the date of notification of the Directive.

However, we have seen above that as the Court in *Barber*, and in the series of cases which followed it, has expanded the definition of pay in Article 119 to include benefits paid under an occupational pension scheme, much of this Directive has become redundant or has been overridden. With the exception of occupational schemes covering the self-employed (who do not come within the scope of Article 119), employer contributions to defined-benefit schemes (held in *Neath* and *Coloroll* to be outside Article 119), and benefits paid to workers as a result of additional voluntary contributions (held in *Coloroll* to be outside Article 119), the Directive lost most of its relevance, and the Commission has introduced a legislative proposal to amend it in light of these changes.

5. REMEDIES

The issue of remedies has been discussed more generally in chapter 5 dealing specifically with that issue, but it is worth noting in the context of this Chapter how many of the cases on remedies have arisen in the sphere of sex discrimination.[209] If Member States have delayed properly implementing Article 119 or the directives in this area (often because of the costs they may involve for the state), then, even though the affected parties may rely on the direct effect of those directives against the state, it is often unclear, in the absence of national remedial legislation in that sphere, how the breach of their rights will be remedied.

In the second *Defrenne* case, the Court appeared to reject the possibility of 'levelling down' salaries in order to comply with the equal-pay principle:

> In particular, since Article 119 appears in the context of the harmonisation of working conditions while the improvement is being maintained, the objection that the terms of this article may be observed in other ways than by raising the lowest salaries may be set aside.[210]

Subsequently, in the context of social security rather than pay in the *FNV* case, the Court, having ruled that Article 4(1) of Directive 79/7 was directly effective from the date on which it should have been implemented, went on to state what the proper 'point of reference' was, pending such proper implementation:

> It follows that until such time as the national government adopts the necessary implementing measures women are entitled to be treated in the same manner, and

[209] See C. McCrudden, 'The Effectiveness of European Equality Law: National Mechanisms for Enforcing Gender Equality Law in the Light of European Requirements' (1993) 13 OJLS 320.

[210] Case 43/75, n. 99 above, para. 15.

to have the same rules applied to them, as men who are in the same situation, since, where the directive has not been implemented, those rules remain the only valid point of reference.[211]

This formula has since been repeated in many other cases in the context of adopting the appropriate transitional measures where there has been discrimination on grounds of sex. We have seen in the case of *Cotter* in Chapter 5 that, where Irish social welfare legislation had discriminated against married women in breach of Directive 79/7, the Court would not allow the state to plead the principle of unjust enrichment in order to deny the applicants a remedy against its own past unlawful conduct.[212] Following the approach in *FNV*, in the absence of implementing measures, the women were entitled to have the same rules applied to them as applied to men who were in the same situation, on the basis that those rules remained 'the only valid point of reference'.[213] Thus there was no question of having first to await the adoption of remedial legislation. The transitional 'levelling-up' requirement meant that, until the legislature decided how to implement the Directive and to remedy the discrimination, the disadvantaged group would be entitled to the same benefits as the advantaged group.

Although *Cotter* concerned direct discrimination in breach of Article 4(1) of Directive 79/7, the same approach was adopted in the case of *Ruzius*,[214] in the context of indirect discrimination in social-security legislation, and in *Nimz* [215] and *Kowalska*,[216] in the context of indirect discrimination in pay under Article 119.[217] Whereas *Cotter* and *Ruzius* involved legislative measures, however, both *Nimz* and *Kowalska* concerned provisions of collective bargaining agreements which were allegedly discriminatory. The significance of the fact that the discriminatory term was contained in a collective-bargaining agreement was that, unlike a legislative provision or a contract drafted by the employer, it was open to the defendant in *Kowalska* to argue that the terms of the agreement should not be struck down and replaced, on account of their incompatibility with Article 119, since this would infringe the 'freedom of contract' of the negotiating parties. The Court, however, relied on the reasoning in *Ruzius*, and ruled that, on a finding of unjustified indirect discrimination by a national court, the favourable terms of the agreement should be extended to the previously disadvantaged party:

211 Case 71/85, *Netherlands* v. *Federatie Nederlandse Vakbeweging* [1986] ECR 3855, [1987] 3 CMLR 767, para. 22.

212 Case C–377/89, *Cotter and McDermott* v. *Minister for Social Welfare and Attorney General* [1991] ECR I–1155, [1991] 3 CMLR 507.

213 *Ibid.*, para. 18.

214 Case 102/88, *Ruzius Wilbrink* v. *Bestuur van de Bedrijsvereniging voor Overheidsdiensten* [1989] ECR 4311, [1991] 2 CMLR 202, para. 20.

215 Case C–184/89, n. 48 above.

216 Case C–33/89, n. 49 above.

217 See also Case C–7/93, *Beune* n. 80 above, para. 53 and, in the social security context case C–154/92, *Van Cant* n. 200 above.

It must therefore be stated in reply to the second question that, where there is indirect discrimination in a clause in a collective wage agreement, the class of persons placed at a disadvantage by reason of that discrimination must be treated in the same way and made subject to the same scheme, proportionately to the number of hours worked, as other workers, such scheme remaining, for want of correct transposition of Article 119 of the EEC Treaty into national law, the only valid point of reference.[218]

In *Nimz*, too, despite the arguments made about the autonomy in bargaining enjoyed by the parties to the agreement, the Court referred to its well-established case law on the duty of national courts to give full and immediate effect to Community law:

20. It is equally necessary to apply such considerations to the case where the provision at variance with Community law is derived from a collective labour agreement. It would be incompatible with the very nature of Community law if the Court having jurisdiction to apply that law were to be precluded at the time of such application from being able to take all necessary steps to set aside the provisions of a collective agreement which might constitute an obstacle to the full effectiveness of Community rules.

21. The answer to the second question must therefore be that, where there is indirect discrimination in a provision of a collective agreement, the national court is required to set aside that provision, without requesting or awaiting its prior removal by collective bargaining or any other procedure, and to apply to members of the group disadvantaged by that discrimination the same arrangements as are applied to other employees, arrangements which, failing the correct application of Article 119 of the EEC Treaty in national law, remain the only valid system of reference.[219]

Advocate General Darmon explained that this would not affect autonomy of bargaining, any more than the equal treatment rules affect the Member States' legislative powers, since bargaining power simply must be exercised having regard to the need to observe the requirements of equal treatment.[220] However, once the legislature or the employer responsible for the discrimination takes measures to abolish the discriminatory provisions, there is no 'levelling-up' requirement. Although this was not made clear in the original *Defrenne (No 2)* ruling, the Court has ruled subsequently that when action is taken to eliminate sex discrimination, the benefits may be abolished altogether rather than being provided for both sexes. This can be seen most recently in the case of *Coloroll*, concerning the equalization of pensionable ages in a private occupational-pension scheme. After ruling that, in the absence of measures adopted to bring about equal treatment, the only proper way of complying with Article 119 was to grant to the person previously disadvantaged

[218] N. 49 above, para. 20. [219] C–184/89, n. 48 above. [220] *Ibid.*, 312.

the same advantages as the persons in the favoured class, the Court continued:

> The situation is different as regards periods of service completed after the entry into force of rules to eliminate discrimination, since Article 119 does not then preclude measures to achieve equal treatment by reducing the advantages of the persons previously favoured. Article 119 merely requires that men and women should receive the same pay for the same work without imposing any specific level of pay.[221]

In *Emmott*,[222] *Cotter*,[223] and *Marshall (No 2)*,[224] the Court stressed the importance of ensuring the effectiveness of Community sex-discrimination law, by requiring the provision of adequate national remedies. In all three cases, as is discussed in more detail in Chapter 5, the Court ruled that particular national rules—both procedural and substantive—must be set aside where they have the effect of depriving an aggrieved person of an effective remedy. In *Cotter*, the national rule in question was a principle of unjust enrichment which would have barred the plaintiff's remedy, in *Marshall* it was a ceiling on damages in a statute and a prohibition on the award of interest by certain tribunals, and in *Emmott*, it was a time limit within which proceedings had to be brought. Further, in *Marshall (No 2)*, the Court ruled that the fixing of a ceiling on damages could not constitute proper implementation of the remedial provision (Article 6) of the Equal Treatment Directive, since such a ceiling could limit the amount of compensation to a sum which was not at all adequate to compensate for damage incurred as a result of sex discrimination.[225]

The requirement to do all that is necessary to give effect to Community law, once it has been established that there is discrimination, applies not just to the national courts, in accordance with cases such as *Von Colson*,[226] but also to those authorities who are responsible for the scheme in question. In *Coloroll*, the Court was asked whether, where rules of a pension scheme were incompatible with the principle of equal pay, the Trustees would be obliged to disregard those rules in administering the scheme, or whether they must amend the rules so as to comply with the equal-pay principle.[227] The Court responded as follows:

221 Case C–200/91, *Coloroll* n. 32 above, para. 33.

222 Case C–208/90, *Emmott* v. *Minister for Social Welfare* [1991] ECR I–4269, [1991] 3 CMLR 894.

223 Case C–377/89, n. 212 above.

224 Case C–271/91, *Marshall* v. *Southampton and South West Area Health Authority (Teaching) (No 2)* [1993] ECR I–4367, [1993] 3 CMLR 293.

225 *Ibid.*

226 Case 14/83, *Von Colson and Kamann* v. *Land Nordrhein-Westfalen* [1984] ECR 1891, [1986] 2 CMLR 430. See the discussion in Ch. 5.

227 Case C–200/91, n. 32 above.

In so far as the relevant rules of national law prohibit them from acting beyond the scope of their powers or in disregard of the provisions of the trust deed, employers and trustees are bound, in order to ensure compliance with the principle of equal treatment, to use all the means available under domestic law, such as recourse to the national courts, especially where, as seems to be the case in this instance, involvement of the national courts is necessary to amend the provisions of the pension scheme or the trust deed.[228]

The effect of *Emmott*, which stated that, until a directive had been properly implemented, a Member State could not invoke a national time limit for implementing proceedings, was, however, limited by the subsequent ruling in *Steenhorst-Neerings*.[229] In the latter case, it had been established that a provision of Dutch social security law was discriminatory on grounds of sex, but it was provided by legislation that invalidity benefits would not be payable retroactively for more than one year before the date on which they were claimed. This was not, therefore, a time limit for bringing proceedings, but a temporal limitation on the extent to which compensation for past discrimination could be recovered. Arguably, on the same basis as the rule prohibiting the award of interest on damages in *Marshall (No 2)*, this limit on the amount which could be awarded to a victim of discrimination would undermine the effectiveness of the compensation remedy. However, the Court dismissed the Commission's argument that on the basis of *Emmott* such a limitation could not operate until the Directive was properly implemented. Placing surprising emphasis on the administrative convenience and financial concerns of the Member States—which, arguably, were equally present in *Emmott*—the Court found that the limiting provision was justified. It noted that the effect of the domestic rule in *Emmott* had been to prevent a claim being brought at all:

23. On the other hand, the aim of the rule restricting the retroactive effect of claims for benefits for incapacity for work is quite different from that of a rule imposing mandatory time-limits for bringing proceedings. As the Government of the Netherlands and the defendant in the main proceedings explained in their written observations, the first type of rule, of which examples can be found in other social security laws in the Netherlands, serves to ensure sound administration, most importantly so that it may be ascertained whether the claimant satisfied the conditions for eligibility and so that the degree of incapacity, which may well vary over time, may be fixed. It also reflects the need to preserve financial balance in a scheme in which claims submitted by insured persons in the course of a year must in principle be covered by the contributions collected during that same year.[230]

[228] Case C–200/91, n. 32 above, para. 28. Although the adequacy of a remedy would clearly be affected if there were insufficient funds to compensate the affected employees, the Court in *Coloroll*, rather than prescribing Community rules to be applied, ruled that problems of this kind were to be resolved on the basis of national law in the light of the principle of equal pay.

[229] Case C–338/91, n. 196 above. See Ch. 5, 221–3.

[230] *Ibid.*

After this decision, a similar case came before the Court in *Johnson (No 2)*, in which the ruling in *Steenhorst-Neerings* was confirmed and indeed extended.[231] The United Kingdom legislative provision in issue in *Johnson* limited to one year only the retroactive effect of a claim for benefits for incapacity for work. The applicant sought, however, to distinguish the provision from that in *Steenhorst-Neerings*, since the two concerns which the Court had cited in favour of the restrictive national procedural rule in the earlier case—administrative convenience and the need for financial balance—did not apply to the benefit she sought. Administrative convenience would not be affected since the onus of proof was on applicants to show that they had suffered incapacity in a particular year, and financial balance would be unaffected since the benefit was non-contributory. The Court, however, rejected her arguments and based its ruling firmly on the 'national procedural autonomy' conditions in its older case law, ignoring the possible inadequacy or ineffectiveness of the remedy for past discrimination.[232] It ruled instead that the restrictive United Kingdom provision was identical to that in *Steenhorst-Neerings*, did not discriminate between Community-based actions and domestic actions, and did not render the exercise of the right impossible.

6. CONCLUSION

One issue which has been highlighted throughout this chapter, in all of the different areas of Community sex-discrimination law, is the fact that the law has had only limited success in eliminating the disadvantage faced by women in the labour market. This is explicable in part on the basis that Community law adopts a very formal notion of equality, based on the pattern of a normal male working life, and that, in restricting its focus to the work-place, it does not take into account the realities of family life and social circumstances which affect women's participation in the labour market. However, it is also true that it is not just Community law, but law in general, which may be inadequate for the purposes of genuinely ensuring equality for women and men at work. The following extracts identify the limits of law, and, in the second case, suggest that other kinds of action are necessary if the underlying disadvantages are to be addressed and remedied:

N. Burrows and S. Prechal, Gender Discrimination Law of the European Community[233]

Disguised discrimination relates to the underlying causes of discrimination, for example in the way that job segregation relates to the overall problem of inequality of incomes. Very often legislation is not aimed at this type of discrimination;

[231] Case C–410/92, 6 Dec. 1994.

[232] See Ch. 5 for further discussion of these conditions.

[233] (Dartmouth, 1990), 10.

indeed, it is questionable whether or not the law would be capable of eliminating it. Therefore, one of the major questions faced by the Court is to determine the limits of Community law in matters relating to discrimination . . . this is a particularly difficult question in the area of sex-based discrimination.

S. Fredman, European Community Discrimination Law: A Critique[234]

Both specific rights and the broad anti-discrimination principle have a role to play. But the law is necessarily limited in this context. Legal strategies must be accompanied by a much more radical focus on structural disadvantage and the causes thereof. The primary requirement is a restructuring of the work environment to take account of family needs, and this demands not only effective legal concepts but also more widespread political and social mobilisation and the appropriate resource allocation. Some steps in this direction have been taken at EC level. There is a well organized women's lobby within the Community, and EC Action programmes have established initiatives for women's training and enterprise creation, as well as promising measures such as the financing of child-care facilities in rural areas. The law alone cannot bear the burden of radical institutional change: it needs to be accompanied by a more sustained development of alternative initiatives such as these.

7. FURTHER READING

(a) Books

ELLIS, E., *European Community Sex Equality Law* (Clarendon Press, 1992)

MCCRUDDEN, C. (ed.), *Women, Employment and European Equality Law* (Eclipse, 1987)

—— (ed.), *Equality of Treatment between Women and Men in Social Security* (Butterworths, 1994)

NIELSEN, R., and SZYSZCSAK, E., *The Social Dimension of the European Community* (2nd edn., Handelshjskolens Forlag, Copenhagen, 1993)

PRECHAL, S., and BURROWS, N., *Gender Discrimination Law of the European Community* (Dartmouth, 1990)

(b) Articles

BURROWS, N., 'Maternity Rights in Europe—An Embryonic Legal Regime' (1991) 11 YBEL 273

CROMACK, V., 'The EC Pregnancy Directive: Principle or Pragmatism?' [1993] JSWFL 261

CURTIN, C., 'Scalping the Community Legislator: Occupational Pensions and "*Barber*"' (1990) 27 CMLRev. 475

DOCKSEY, C., 'The Principle of Equality between Women and Men as a Fundamental Right under Community Law' (1991) 20 ILJ 58

[234] N. 11 above, 134.

FREDMAN, S., 'European Community Discrimination Law: A Critique' (1992) 21 ILJ 119

MCCRUDDEN, C., 'The Effectiveness of European Equality Law: National Mechanisms for Enforcing Gender Equality Law in the Light of European Requirements' (1993) 13 OJLS 320

MORE, G., '"Equal Treatment" of the Sexes: What Does "Equal" Mean?' (1993) 1 *Feminist Legal Studies* 45

SOHRAB, J., 'Women and Social Security Law: The Limits of EEC Equality Law' [1994] JSWFL 5

SZYSZCZAK, E., 'L'Espace Social Européenne: Reality, Dreams or Nightmares?' [1990] *German Yearbook of International Law* 284

WHITEFORD, E., 'Social Policy after Maastricht' (1993) 18 ELRev. 202

19

Competition Law: Article 85

1. INTRODUCTION

Competition law has always played an important part in Community law. The precise role served by this aspect of Community law is, however, contestable. A number of differing objectives may lay at the heart of competition policy, not all of which are mutually compatible.

One such objective is to *enhance efficiency*, in the sense of maximizing consumer welfare and achieving the optimal allocation of resources. Traditional economic theory indicates that goods and services will be produced in the most efficient manner in circumstances of perfect competition, or more realistically, in circumstances of workable competition.[1] There is, as will be seen below, considerable disagreement between economists on a large number of matters relating to competition policy. Notwithstanding this diversity of opinion, there is also considerable uniformity of view on the fact that certain types of agreement or behaviour can have a distorting and deleterious impact on the market. Thus, for example, an agreement between the major producers of cement to fix the prices at which they will sell their goods will be likely to result in higher prices for cement, and also in the production of less cement, than would otherwise be produced in conditions of ordinary competition. Throughout the course of this Chapter we will be examining the nature of the anti-competitive effects of certain types of agreements, and the way in which they can distort the market. We will also be examining the areas in which there is more disagreement between economists concerning the effects of certain types of agreements, and hence less certainty concerning the nature of the competition rules which should apply in these instances.

Efficiency is not the only goal which competition policy may strive to attain. A second objective may be to *protect consumers and smaller firms* from large aggregations of economic power, whether in the form of the monopolistic dominance of a single firm or of agreements whereby rival firms co-ordinate their activity so as to act as one unit. Advocates of this approach may support it for varying reasons. Some may be concerned at the threat which such aggregations of economic power have for political liberty, the democratic

[1] For discussion of the basic economic concepts see F. Scherer and D. Ross, *Industrial Market Structure and Economic Performance* (3rd edn., Houghton Mifflin, 1990); R. Lipsey, *An Introduction to Positive Economics* (7th edn., Weidenfeld & Nicolson, 1989); O. Williamson, *Antitrust Economics* (Blackwell, 1987).

process, and the like. Others may favour it because it gives greater opportunities for small and medium-sized firms to enter the market without being 'devoured' by their stronger rivals.

A third objective of EC competition law is to help in the *creation of a single European market*, and to prevent this aspiration from being frustrated by the activities of private undertakings. The relationship between this aspect of substantive Community law and other parts of substantive law was touched on in the earlier discussion which presented an overview of the economic aims of the Community.[2] It warrants brief repetition here. Certain aspects of Community law are concerned with the creation of a single European market, and therefore prohibit devices such as tariffs, quotas, and the like which can impede the attainment of this goal. The effectiveness of such Community norms would, however, be radically undermined if private undertakings could themselves partition the Community market along national lines. A brief example will make this clear. Let us imagine that our cement producers wish not only to fix prices as between themselves, but also wish to limit competition by dividing the Community market. They may desire to do this in order to live a quiet life, rather than undergo the rigours of a more aggressive competitive strategy in which the outcome may be uncertain. Our cement producers decide, therefore, that the best strategy for this live-and-let-live ideal is to allow each of the firms exclusive control of their respective national markets. The German cement producer will not sell directly into France or Italy or the United Kingdom, and the other producers accept reciprocal obligations. Each of the producers also pledges to try and prevent cross-border sales by third parties to whom they have sold their goods. The effect of all this is to partition the Community market along national lines and to impede the attainment of a single Community market. Not surprisingly, the Community competition authorities have shown themselves to be particularly antagonistic to such agreements. The goal of the creation of a single market is furthered not only by preventing firms from creating trade barriers between Member States. It is also enhanced by encouraging the economic players to operate on a Community-wide scale; to consider the entirety of the EC as their domestic market.

The preceding objectives may lead to the same results in a particular case. This harmony is not, however, always to be found. As will be seen below, there are a number of areas in which the policy objectives can produce differing prescriptions, necessitating a choice between them. As will also be seen, this choice is not always made explicitly, but has to be inferred from the reasoning used by the Commission and the Court.

An additional variable serves to complicate matters further. Even when the objectives do suggest the same conclusion in a particular instance, these policy objectives may themselves be in conflict with other aims of the Community. There may, for example, be policies aimed at benefiting particular regions of the Community which are disadvantaged, and the fulfilment of

[2] See, above 548–50.

such goals may, on occasion, require a trade-off between the objectives of competition policy and those of regional policy. The existence of these tensions will be made evident in the ensuing discussion.

Article 85 of the Treaty is the principal weapon to control anti-competitive behaviour by cartels:

> 1. The following shall be prohibited as incompatible with the common market; all agreements between undertakings, decisions by associations of undertakings and concerted practices which may affect trade between Member States and which have as their object or effect the prevention, restriction or distortion of competition within the common market, and in particular those which:
>
> (a) directly or indirectly fix purchase or selling prices or any other trading conditions;
> (b) limit or control production, markets, technical development, or investment;
> (c) share markets or sources of supply;
> (d) apply dissimilar conditions to equivalent transactions with other trading parties, thereby placing them at a competitive disadvantage;
> (e) make the conclusion of contracts subject to acceptance by the other parties of supplementary obligations which, by their nature or according to commercial usage, have no connection with the subject of such contracts;
>
> 2. Any agreements or decisions prohibited pursuant to this Article shall be automatically void.
>
> 3. The provisions of paragraph 1 may, however, be declared inapplicable in the case of:
>
> —any agreement or category of agreements between undertakings;
> —any decision or category of decisions by associations of undertakings;
> —any concerted practice or category of concerted practices;
>
> which contributes to improving the production or distribution of goods or to promoting technical or economic progress, while allowing consumers a fair share of the resulting benefit, and which does not:
>
> (a) impose on the undertakings concerned restrictions which are not indispensable to the attainment of these objectives;
> (b) afford such undertakings the possibility of eliminating competition in respect of a substantial part of the products in question.

2. UNDERTAKINGS

Article 85(1) catches agreements etc. which are made by undertakings, but the Treaty does not provide a definition of this term. The competition authorities have, not surprisingly, taken a broad view of it. In *Polypropylene*, the Commission held that the term 'undertaking' was not confined to those entities which possessed legal personality, but covered any entity which was engaged in commercial activity.[3] This has been held to include: corporations, partnerships, individuals, trade associations, state-owned corporations, and co-operatives.[4] While state-owned corporations can qualify as undertakings for the purpose of Article 85 when they operate in a commercial context, this may not be so when they are exercising their public-law powers.[5]

In certain circumstances firms which are legally distinct may, however, be treated as a single unit because of the close economic link between them. This may be the case with agreements made between parent and subsidiary, where the Court or Commission decide that they are, in reality, to be regarded as one economic unit, so that any agreement which has been made is best regarded as an internal allocation of function or role within that economic unit, as opposed to a relationship which comes within Article 85(1).[6]

Changing the legal form of an undertaking will not, however, allow the new legal entity to escape liability for acts done by its predecessor, if there is a functional and economic continuity between the original undertaking and that into which it has merged.[7]

3. AGREEMENTS, DECISIONS AND CONCERTED PRACTICES

Article 85 states that there must be an agreement, decision or concerted practice in order for the behaviour to be caught by the competition rules. The rationale for this range of terms is easy to explain. Businessmen who enter agreements of the kind indicated above are likely to know that they are making an agreement which is illegal. They are unlikely to spell out the agreement explicitly, and will normally do so in a covert fashion. If the rules on competition law only operated when an explicit, formal agreement was made then they would be of little practical use. All legal systems which regulate anti-competitive activity therefore have provisions which are designed to catch less formal species of agreements.[8] The *Quinine Cartel* case provides a good example of this aspect of competition law:

[3] [1986] OJ L230/1, [1988] 4 CMLR 347, 402. This issue was not dealt with on appeal: Case T–7/89, *SA Hercules Chemicals NV* v. *Commission* [1991] ECR II–1711, [1992] 4 CMLR 84.

[4] R. Whish, *Competition Law* (3rd edn., Butterworths, 1993), 187–90.

[5] *Ibid.* 189.

[6] See e.g. Case 22/71, *Béguelin Import* v. *GL Import-Export* [1971] ECR 949, [1972] CMLR 81; *Racal Group Services* [1989] OJ L43/27, [1990] 4 CMLR 627; *NV IGMO* v. *Ijsselcentrale* [1991] OJ L28/32, [1992] 5 CMLR 154.

[7] Cases 29 and 30/83, *Compagnie Royale Asturienne des Mines SA and Rheinzik GmbH* v. *Commission* [1984] ECR 1679, [1985] 1 CMLR 688; *Welded Steel Mesh* [1989] OJ L260/1, [1991] 4 CMLR 13.

[8] See, *e.g*, in the UK, Restrictive Trade Practices Act 1976, ss. 6, 43; and in the USA, Sherman Act 1890, s. 1.

Cases 41, 44 and 45/69, ACF Chemiefarma NV v. Commission [1970] ECR 661

A number of firms agreed to fix prices and divide the market in quinine. They made an agreement to this effect which affected trade with non-Member States (the export agreement). They also made a gentlemen's agreement which extended this to sales within the common market.

THE ECJ

106. The applicant complains that the Commission considered that the export agreement relating to trade with third countries and the gentlemen's agreement governing the conduct of its members in the Common Market constituted an indivisible entity as far as Article 85 was concerned.

107. The applicant states that the gentlemen's agreement, unlike the export agreement, did not constitute an agreement within the meaning of Article 85(1) and in any event it definitively ceased to exist from the end of October 1962.

108. The conduct of the parties to the export agreement does not in the applicant's view indicate that they continued the restrictions on competition which were originally provided for in the gentlemen's agreement.

109. The opposite conclusions reached by the contested decision are therefore alleged to be vitiated because they are based on incorrect findings.

110. The gentlemen's agreement, which the applicant admits existed until the end of October 1962, had as its object the restriction of competition within the Common Market.

111. The parties to the export agreement mutually declared themselves willing to abide by the gentlemen's agreement and concede that they did so until the end of October 1962.

112. This document thus amounted to the faithful expression of the joint intention of the parties to the agreement with regard to their conduct in the Common Market.

113. Furthermore it contained a provision to the effect that infringement of the gentlemen's agreement would *ipso facto* constitute an infringement of the export agreement.

114. In those circumstances account must be taken of this connexion in assessing the effects of the gentlemen's agreement with regard to the categories of acts prohibited by Article 85(1).

115. The defendant bases its view that the gentlemen's agreement was continued until February 1965 on documents and declarations emanating from the parties to the agreement the tenor of which is indistinct and indeed contradictory so that it is impossible to conclude whether those undertakings intended to terminate the gentlemen's agreement at their meeting on 29 October 1962.

116. The conduct of the undertakings in the Common Market after 29 October 1962 must therefore be considered in relation to the following four points: sharing out of domestic markets, fixing of common prices, determination of sales quotas and prohibition against manufacturing synthetic quinidine.

117. The gentlemen's agreement guaranteed protection of each domestic market for the producers in the various Member States.

118. After October 1962 when significant supplies were delivered on one of those markets by producers who were not nationals, as for example in the case of

sales of quinine and quinidine in France, there was a substantial alignment of prices conforming to French domestic prices which were higher than the export prices to third countries.

119. It does not appear that there were alterations in the insignificant volume of trade between the other Member States referred to by the clause relating to domestic protection in spite of considerable differences in the prices prevailing in each of those States.

120. The divergences between the domestic legislation of those States cannot by itself explain those differences in price or the substantial absence of trade.

121. Obstacles which might arise in the trade in quinine and quinidine from differences between national legislation governing pharmaceutical products under trade-mark cannot relevantly be invoked to explain those facts.

122. The correspondence exchanged in October and November 1963 between the parties to the export agreement with regard to the protection of domestic markets merely confirmed the intention of those undertakings to allow this state of affairs to remain unchanged.

123. This intention was subsequently confirmed by Nedchem during the meeting of the undertakings concerned in Brussels on 14 March 1964.

124. From those circumstances it is clear that with regard to the restriction on competition arising from the protection of the producers' domestic markets the producers continued after the meeting on 29 October 1962 to abide by the gentlemen's agreement of 1960 and confirmed their common intention to do so.

The *Quinine Cartel* case serves as a good example of the approach of the Court. Informal agreements can be caught under Article 85, and the mere fact that the parties claim to have terminated them will not be taken to be conclusive. The Court will examine the facts with care, in order to determine whether it is economically plausible to imagine that the pricing behaviour of the parties could have been achieved in the absence of some form of collusion.

The Commission, which makes the initial determination of an infringement of Article 85, has continued to take an expansive view of the meaning of 'agreement'. Thus, in *Polypropylene*,[9] the Commission held that there was a single agreement covering firms in the petrochemical industry which had continued over many years. It was willing to hold that there was such an overall agreement even though the agreement was oral, even though there were no sanctions for breach, and even though it was not legally binding. Moreover, the finding of a single overall agreement facilitated a finding of guilt against the fifteen firms involved, notwithstanding the fact that not all the firms had taken part in all aspects of the cartel. An agreement existed if the parties reached a consensus on a plan which limited, or was likely to limit, their commercial freedom by determining the lines of their mutual action or abstention from action in the market. The CFI upheld the Commission in this respect,[10]

[9] [1986] OJ L230/1, [1988] 4 CMLR 347. See also *PVC* [1989] OJ L74/1, [1990] 4 CMLR 345, reversed on other grounds in Case C–137/92P *Commission* v. *BASF AG*, 15 June 1994; *LdPE* [1989] OJ L74/21, [1990] 4 CMLR 382; *Italian Flat Glass* [1989] OJ L33/44, [1990] 4 CMLR 535.

[10] Case T–7/89, n. 3 above, paras. 262–4.

holding that the firms' pattern of conduct was in pursuit of a single economic aim, namely the distortion of the market in question. It would therefore be artificial to split up this continuous conduct into a number of separate infringements. In a further series of cases concerning the polypropylene saga, the CFI has, moreover, held that for there to be an agreement within Article 85 it is sufficient that the undertakings in question should have expressed their joint intention to conduct themselves on the market in a specific way. Such is the case where there were common intentions between undertakings to achieve price and sales-volume targets.[11]

This expansive interpretation of the term 'agreement' should be borne in mind when considering the construction of the term 'concerted practice', particularly given that the Commission has consistently held that collusion may present elements of both forms of co-operation.

Even if the competition authorities are unable to prove the existence of an agreement in the above sense, the undertakings will still be caught by Article 85 if it is decided that there is a concerted practice. The precise meaning of this phrase will be considered below, in the light of the decision in the *Dyestuffs* case. A better understanding of that decision will, however, be gained by reflecting on the problems which terms such as 'concerted practice' present for competition authorities. Two principal factors have to be taken into account in deciding on the construction to be given to a term such as 'concerted practice'.

On the one hand, there is the fact, touched upon already, that firms can be very devious. They may well have colluded, but they may have been astute enough to destroy all paper evidence of that collusion; or they may never have committed anything to paper at all, relying instead on understandings and verbal exchanges. The collusion may be real nonetheless, and the construction of a term such as concerted practice must be flexible enough to capture this 'fact' of business life.

On the other hand, if the term is interpreted too broadly it may label certain behaviour as collusion, even though the identity of pricing policy between the parties is not in fact the result of collusion at all, but rather a rational, natural response of firms in that type of market. This idea requires a brief explanation. In normal competitive markets, firms will compete and it is unlikely that they will price at the same level without some species of collusion, because of differences in cost structures and the like. Some economists have, however, maintained that matters are different in markets which are oligopolistic. These markets have the following characteristics: there are relatively few sellers; there are high barriers to entry, in the sense that it is difficult for new firms to enter the market; there is relatively little in the way of product-differentiation; and prices tend to be transparent, in that price changes are easily detectable by competitors. In these markets it has been argued that firms will naturally end up pricing at the same level, not because of any collusion

[11] Case T–9/89, *Huls AG* v. *Commission* [1992] ECR II–499; Case T–11/89, *Shell International Chemical Company Ltd* v. *Commission* [1992] ECR II–757.

as such, but rather because each of the firms independently recognizes their mutual interdependence. If any one of the firms attempts to increase its market share at the expense of one of the other firms, by cutting prices, this will simply lead to a response from the others, with the result that there is a downward spiral of prices but no actual increase in market share for any of the firms involved. No unilateral price increase could be made by any one of the firms, because its customers would switch their trade to one of the other companies in the oligopolistic market. Moreover, the uniformity of prices which is said to be expected in an oligopoly will, on this theory, arise even if the respective firms have differing cost structures, because the nature of the demand curve facing the industry assumes a peculiar 'kinked' form.[12] The relevance of this theory for the purposes of Article 85 is readily apparent. *If* the uniformity of price which exists in a particular market really is the result of rational, natural action by the parties in an oligopoly, and there is no actual collusion as such, then it is neither rational nor fair to penalize such parties through fines and the like for colluding. In the parlance of industrial economics, the problem is no longer *behavioural*, in the sense that the parties are engaging in behaviour different from that which would exist in normal circumstances in that type of market; the problem is rather *structural*, in the sense that a market with this type of structure will naturally generate this type of response by the firms involved therein. On this view, if there is concern about the effects of oligopoly, then a structural solution should be sought to a structural problem.

The theory considered above has, however, been criticized. The following extract contains a succinct summary of this criticism:

R. Whish, Competition Law[13]

The theory of interdependence has attracted criticism. Four particular problems with it have been pointed out. The first is that the theory overstates the interdependence of oligopolists. Even in a symmetrical three-firm oligopoly one firm might be able to steal a march on its rivals by cutting its price if, for example, there would be a delay before the others discovered what it had done: in the meantime the price- cutter may make sufficient profit to offset the cost of any subsequent price-war . . .

A second problem is that the theory of oligopoly presents too simplistic a picture of industrial market structures. In a symmetrical oligopoly where producers produce identical goods at the same costs interdependence may be strong, but in reality market conditions are more complex. The oligopolists themselves will almost inevitably have different cost levels; they may be producing differentiated goods and will usually command at least some consumer loyalty; and their market shares will not be equal . . . Many other factors affect the competitive environment in which oligopolists function. The concentration of the market on the

[12] See, F. Scherer, n. 1 above, Ch. 5; Sweezy, 'Demand under Conditions of Oligopoly' (1937) 47 JPol. Econ. 568; G. Stigler, 'The Kinked Oligopoly Demand Curve' (1947) 55 JPol. Econ. 431.

[13] N. 4 above, 469–70.

buying side is important: the more concentrated it is, the less the oligopolists might compete with one another since it will be relatively easy to detect attempts to attract the custom of particular customers. The transparency of price information is significant: the easier it is to conceal the price of goods from competitors, the less will be the interdependence or mutual awareness of the oligopolists . . .

A third problem with the theory of interdependence is that it fails to explain why in some oligopolistic markets competition is intense. Firms quite clearly do compete with one another in some oligopolies. Such competition may take various forms. Open price competition may be limited, although price wars do break out periodically in some oligopolistic markets . . . Where open price competition is restricted, this does not mean that secret price cutting does not occur . . . Non-price competition may be particularly strong in oligopolistic markets. This may manifest itself in various ways: offering better quality products and after sales service; striving for a lead in technical innovation and research and development . . . ; and by making large investments in advertising to improve brand image . . .

A fourth objection to the theory of oligopolistic interdependence is that it does not explain satisfactorily its central proposition, which is that oligopolists can earn supra-competitive profits without actually colluding. The interdependence theory says that they cannot increase price unilaterally because they will lose custom to their rivals, and yet to earn supra-competitive profits, prices must have been increased from time to time: how could this have been achieved without collusion? A possible answer to this is that a pattern of price leadership develops whereby one firm raises its price and this acts as a signal for the others to follow suit. Prices therefore remain parallel without conspiracy amongst the oligopolists, although this is not particularly convincing . . .

Having considered the economic problems which exist in this area it is now time to consider the interpretation given by the ECJ to the term 'concerted practice'. The leading decision is the *Dyestuffs* case:

Case 48/69, ICI v. Commission [1972] ECR 619, [1972] CMLR 557

The Court considered allegations that there had been concerted practices in the dyestuffs industry. As will be apparent from the extract which follows, the firms attempted to argue that any identity of price was the result of the oligopolistic nature of the market. The extract begins with the Court providing a definition of concerted practice.

THE ECJ

64. Article 85 draws a distinction between the concept of 'concerted practices' and that of 'agreements between undertakings' or of 'decisions by associations of undertakings'; the object is to bring within the prohibition of that Article a form of coordination between undertakings which, without having reached the stage where an agreement properly so-called has been concluded, knowingly substitutes practical cooperation between them for the risks of competition.

65. By its very nature, then, a concerted practice does not have all the elements

of a contract but may *inter alia* arise out of coordination which becomes apparent from the behaviour of the participants.

66. Although parallel behaviour may not by itself be identified with a concerted practice, it may however amount to strong evidence of such practice if it leads to conditions of competition which do not correspond to the normal conditions of the market, having regard to the nature of the products, the size and number of the undertakings and the volume of the said market.

67. This is especially the case if the parallel conduct is such as to enable those concerned to attempt to stabilize prices at a level different from that to which competition would have led, and to consolidate established positions to the detriment of effective freedom of movement of the products in the Common Market and of the freedom of consumers to choose their suppliers.

68. Therefore the question whether there was concerted action in this case can only be correctly determined if the evidence upon which the contested decision is based is considered, not in isolation, but as a whole, account being taken of the specific features of the market in the products in question.

[*The Court found that 80 per cent of the dyestuffs market was supplied by ten producers; that these firms possessed differing cost structures; that there were a large number of dyes produced by each firm; that while standard dyes could be replaced by other products relatively easily, this was not the case with specialist dyes; that the market for specialist dyes tended to be oligopolistic; that the Community market in dyestuffs consisted of five separate national markets which had different price levels; and that this division along national lines was in part due to the need to supply local assistance to users of the product, and also to ensure immediate delivery of quantities which were often small. The Court then considered price increases which occurred in 1964, 1965, and 1967. It found that the increases were factually connected, and then continued as follows:*]

88. In 1964 all the undertakings in question announced their increases and immediately put them into effect, the initiative coming from Ciba-Italy which, on 7 January 1964, following instructions from Ciba-Switzerland, announced and immediately introduced an increase of 15%. This initiative was followed by the other producers on the Italian market within two or three days.

89. On 9 January ICI Holland took the initiative in introducing the same increase in the Netherlands, whilst on the same day Bayer took the same initiative on the Belgo-Luxembourg market.

. . .

91. As regards the increase of 1965 certain undertakings announced in advance price increases amounting, for the German market, to an increase of 15% for products whose prices had already been similarly increased on the other markets, and to 10% for products whose prices had not yet been increased. These announcements were spread over the period between 14 October and 28 December 1964.

92. The first announcement was made by BASF, on 14 October 1964, followed by an announcement by Bayer on 30 October and by Casella on 5 November.

93. These increases were simultaneously applied on 1 January 1965 on all the markets except for the French market because of the price freeze in that State, and the Italian market where, as a result of the refusal by the principal Italian producer, ACNA, to increase its prices on the said market, the other producers also decided not to increase theirs.

. . .

95. Otherwise the increase was general, was simultaneously introduced by all the producers mentioned in the contested decision, and was applied without any differences concerning the range of products.

[*The Court then considered a similar pattern in relation to the 1967 price increases. It continued as follows:*]

99. Viewed as a whole, the three consecutive increases reveal progressive cooperation between the undertakings concerned.

100. In fact, after the experience of 1964, when the announcement of the increases and their application coincided, although with minor differences as regards the range of products affected, the increases of 1965 and 1967 indicate a different mode of operation. Here, the undertakings taking the initiative, BASF and Geigy respectively, announced their intentions of making an increase some time in advance, which allowed the undertakings to observe each other's reactions on the different markets, and to adapt themselves accordingly.

101. By means of these advance announcements the various undertakings eliminated all uncertainty between them as to their future conduct and, in doing so, also eliminated a large part of the risk usually inherent in any independent change of conduct on one or several markets.

102. This was all the more the case since these announcements, which led to the fixing of general and equal increases in prices for the markets in dyestuffs, rendered the market transparent as regard the percentage rates of increase.

103. Therefore, by the way in which they acted, the undertakings in question temporarily eliminated with respect to prices some of the preconditions for competition on the market which stood in the way of the achievement of parallel uniformity of conduct.

104. The fact that this conduct was not spontaneous is corroborated by an examination of other aspects of the market.

105. In fact, from the number of producers concerned it is not possible to say that the European market in dyestuffs is, in the strict sense, an oligopoly in which price competition could no longer play a substantial role.

106. These producers are sufficiently powerful and numerous to create a considerable risk that in times of rising prices some of them might not follow the general movement but might instead try to increase their share of the market by behaving in an individual way.

107. Furthermore, the dividing-up of the Common Market into five national markets with different price levels and structures makes it improbable that a spontaneous and equal price increase would occur on all the national markets.

. . .

109. Therefore, although parallel conduct in respect of prices may well have been an attractive and risk-free objective for the undertakings concerned, it is hardly conceivable that the same action could be taken spontaneously at the same time, on the same national markets and for the same range of products.

. . .

111. As regards the increases of 1965 and 1967 concertation took place openly, since all the announcements of the intention to increase prices with effect from a certain date and for a certain range of products made it possible for producers to decide on their conduct regarding the special cases of France and Italy.

112. In proceeding in this way, the undertakings mutually eliminated in

advance any uncertainties concerning their reciprocal behaviour on the different markets and thereby also eliminated a large part of the risk inherent in any independent change of conduct on those markets.

113. The general and uniform increase on those different markets can only be explained by a common intention on the part of those undertakings, first, to adjust the level of prices and the situation resulting from competition in the form of discounts, and secondly, to avoid the risk, which is inherent in any price increase, of changing the conditions of competition.

The approach of the Court emerges clearly in the above extract,[14] and in other judgments on this topic.

On the one hand, the formal burden of proving an infringement of Article 85 will rest with the Commission, and the mere existence of parallel conduct will not, in itself, be sufficient to prove the existence of a concerted practice. Thus, if the parties can show that, although there is parallel behaviour, there are explanations for what has taken place other than the existence of concertation, then they may be exonerated.[15] It is equally the case that the Court will investigate whether there really is 'room' for the competition rules to operate in a particular context. Thus, in relation to one of the allegations of a concerted practice in the *Sugar Cartel* case, the Court found that the degree of state regulation of the Italian sugar market left no appreciable room in which Article 85 could operate.[16]

On the other hand, the Court will not lightly accede to arguments that uniformity of price has been produced as the result of oligopolistic market structure. It will examine the factual evidence relating to the nature of the market, and the way in which the firms behaved therein. If the facts do not indicate that the market structure will naturally lead to price uniformity, *and* if there are other factors which are indicative of collusion, then the onus may effectively shift to the firms to suggest how the identity of price came about without some element of concertation. It is, moreover, clear that there can be a concerted practice even though there is no actual 'plan' operative between the parties. In the *Sugar Cartel* case one of the defences raised by parties accused of operating a concerted practice to protect the Dutch market was that the concept of a concerted practice must involve the existence of a plan. This contention was rejected by the Court. No actual plan was required for a concerted practice to exist. The key idea was that each undertaking should operate independently on the market:[17]

Although it is correct to say that this requirement of independence does not deprive economic operators of the right to adapt themselves intelligently to the

[14] See also Case 172/80, *Gerhard Züchner* v. *Bayerische Vereinsbank AG* [1981] ECR 2021, [1982] 1 CMLR 313.

[15] Cases 29 and 30/83, n. 7 above.

[16] Cases 40–8, 50, 54–6, 111, 113 and 114/73, *Cooperatieve verenigning 'Suiker Unie' UA* v. *Commission* [1975] ECR 1663, 1916–24, [1976] 1 CMLR 295.

[17] *Ibid.* 1942.

> existing and anticipated conduct of their competitors, it does however strictly preclude any direct or indirect contact between such operators, the object or effect whereof is either to influence the conduct on the market of an actual or potential competitor or to disclose to such a competitor the course of conduct which they themselves have decided to adopt or contemplate adopting on the market.

That there can be differences of opinion as to which side of the line a case falls on is aptly demonstrated by *Wood Pulp*.[18] The Commission considered allegations of concerted practices by a large number of producers of wood pulp. In reaching the conclusion that there was a concerted practice, the Commission was strongly influenced by the nature of the market. It felt that this was not oligopolistic in nature, since there were a large number of firms operating on the market. The fact that they charged similar prices, and made uniform alterations to them simultaneously, was itself *prima facie* evidence that they were acting in concert. A significant part of the Commission's findings was annulled by the ECJ.[19] It held that parallel conduct cannot be regarded as proof of concertation unless concertation constitutes the only plausible explanation for the conduct. Article 85 did not deprive firms of the ability to adapt their behaviour intelligently to that of their competitors.[20] It held, moreover, that the parallelism of the prices and the price trends could satisfactorily be explained by the oligopolistic tendencies of the market and the specific circumstances prevailing during the relevant period.[21]

It may be no coincidence that the *juge rapporteur* in *Wood Pulp* was Joliet who had, a number of years earlier, expressed misgivings about the possible impact of the *Dyestuffs* case.[22] What the *Wood Pulp* case signifies is that the ECJ will not be readily convinced that parallel behaviour, in and of itself, is sufficient to establish a concerted practice. It will only be evidence of a concerted practice if there is no other plausible explanation for the parellelism. In the long term the Court's decision may be of most significance in its insistence that rigorous economic analysis may be required in order to determine whether there is another plausible explanation for the parties' conduct. It was just such expert evidence which destroyed the Commission's case before the Court. In the absence of some form of overt communication between the parties, the Commission will have to be ready to defend its assumptions against experts who can suggest some innocent explanation for the challenged behaviour.[23]

The *Polypropylene* cases provide a good contrast to *Wood Pulp*. In a series of decisions the CFI cited the definition of concerted practice given in the

[18] [1985] OJ L85/1, [1985] 3 CMLR 474.

[19] Cases 89, 104, 114, 116–17, 125–29/85, *A. Ahlström Oy* v. *Commission* [1993] ECR I–1307, [1993] 4 CMLR 407.

[20] *Ibid.*, para. 71.

[21] *Ibid.*, paras. 126–7.

[22] R. Joliet, 'La Notion de Pratique Concertée et l'Arrêt dans une Perspective Comparative' [1974] CDE 251.

[23] G. Van Gerven and E. N. Varona, 'The *Wood Pulp* Case and the Future of Concerted Practices' (1994) 31 CMLRev. 575.

Sugar Cartel case and then proceeded to hold that participation in meetings concerning the fixing of price and sales-volume targets during which information is exchanged between competitors about the prices which they intend to charge, their profitiability thresholds, the sales volumes they judge to be necessary, or their sales figures constituted a concerted practice, since the participant undertakings could not fail to take account of the information thus disclosed in determining their conduct on the market.[24]

4. THE OBJECT OR EFFECT OF PREVENTING, RESTRICTING, OR DISTORTING COMPETITION

Article 85(1) of the Treaty requires that the agreement, decision, or concerted practice has the object or effect of preventing, restricting, or distorting competition in the Common Market. The interpretation of this phrase has generated a significant body of literature, as commentators have proffered rival views on what the Court is, and what it should be, doing under Article 85(1). Let us begin by understanding the nature of the problem.

(a) *The Nature of the Problem*

Article 85(1) captures *all* agreements which have as their object or effect the prevention etc. of competition. This immediately presents us with two related problems.

One is that all contracts concerning trade impose restraints in some manner, 'to bind, to restrain is of their very essence'.[25] Now one could in theory stipulate that every contract was caught by the rules on competition law, but this would be both absurd and impractical. An endemic problem for legal systems which possess a competition policy is to find the best way of resolving this conundrum.

The second problem is that an agreement may have features which both enhance competition and restrict it. This can be explained briefly. Imagine that a supplier wishes to break into a new market, and decides to use Brown as its distributor for a particular area. Brown may only be willing to risk marketing the new product if he is given certain incentives and protection. This may take the form of a commitment from the supplier that it will not supply any other firm in the same area. Now in this instance there is undoubtedly some restriction of competition, in the sense that the supplier has undertaken not to sell to any firm other than Brown in the designated area. However, it is also the case that the whole agreement may enhance competition, since there is now a new product being marketed in the relevant area which was not there before, and which could *only* be marketed under these conditions.

[24] See *e.g.* Case T–11/89, n. 11 above.
[25] *Chicago Board of Trade* v. *US* 246 US 231 (1918).

The appropriate form of response to these related problems is, as stated above, a contentious issue. A central aspect of this debate has been the extent to which the EC should follow the approach in the United States, and utilize a distinction between a rule of reason and *per se* rules, as a method of tackling the problems mentioned above. A brief glance at the United States experience is, therefore, necessary in order to understand the diversity of opinion in the EC.

(b) The Experience in the United States

The dilemmas identified above are patently evident in the language of section 1 of the Sherman Act, which states that every contract, combination, or conspiracy in restraint of trade is illegal. These dilemmas were apparent to the courts which made the early pronouncements on the ambit of the Sherman Act. Did section 1 really render illegal every restraint of trade, did this embrace ordinary contracts, and was it possible to make trade-offs between the pro- and anti-competitive effects of an agreement? A range of answers was forthcoming to these questions.

One response was to use the language of ancillary restraints. If the restraint was deemed to be merely ancillary to the main purpose of a lawful contract, as in the case of a covenant on sale which imposed reasonable limits on the freedom of action of the covenantee, then it would be lawful; if the restraint was solely to limit competition then it would be illegal.[26]

Another response was to sow the seeds of the rule of reason. In *Standard Oil* v. *US* White CJ stated that a standard of reason had to be applied in order to determine whether a restraint was within the Sherman Act, and that only undue or unreasonable restraints should be condemned.[27] The precise meaning of this emergent idea was contested, and this is still the case to some extent even today.[28] The analysis mandated by the concept does, however, appear to demand a broad inquiry as to whether the restrictions in the agreement increase or decrease competition in the market as a whole. The pro- and anti-competitive effects of the agreement are weighed in order to determine whether the agreement is one which suppresses or promotes competition.[29] Controversy continues to exist in relation to two related matters.

On the one hand, there is, as will be seen below,[30] continuing disagreement on what the effects of particular types of agreement actually are, and therefore whether they should be prohibited or not.

On the other hand, there is disagreement on the range of considerations which should be taken into account within this analysis. For some this should be restricted to factors of a strictly economic nature; others wish to be more

[26] *US* v. *Addystone Pipe and Steel Co* 175 US 211 (1889).

[27] 221 US 1 (1911).

[28] R. Bork, 'The Rule of Reason and the Per Se Concept: Price Fixing and Market Division' (1965) 74 Yale LJ 775.

[29] *National Society of Professional Engineers* v. *US* 435 US 679, 691–2 (1978).

[30] See below, 919–23.

wide-ranging in their inquiry, or are willing to ascribe economic value to factors of a more social nature.[31]

Properly understood, *per se* rules develop from a rule-of-reason analysis. The relationship is as follows. The type of market inquiry demanded by the rule of reason may be time-consuming and costly. With the passage of time the courts came to identify certain types of agreement which were conclusively presumed to be 'without redeeming virtue' and which had a 'pernicious effect on competition'. The courts condemned these without the need for any elaborate inquiry as to whether they had an impact on the market. Not surprisingly the types of case held to fall within this category were those which were most obviously anti-competitive, such as horizontal price-fixing[32] and market division.[33] In these instances the proof of the existence of the agreement was sufficient to condemn it, obviating the need for more detailed market investigation.[34]

(c) The Academic Debate in the EC

An interesting debate now exists on how far we should resolve the problems outlined above by adopting the idea of a rule of reason within Community law. A number of factors should be noted in order to understand the materials which follow.

The first is that one of the obvious differences between the system in the United States and that in the EC is that the latter has a mechanism, in the form of Article 85(3), whereby agreements which are held to restrict competition can be exempted following an economic analysis. No such provision exists in the United States, and this renders the need for some species of rule-of-reason analysis the more necessary in that country. Notwithstanding this difference the authors in the first extract begin their argument by pointing out that the regime under Community law, whereby an agreement is caught by Article 85(1) and then exempted under Article 85(3), works less than perfectly, in part because of the work-load which this imposes on the Commission.

The second point to note is that national courts are able to apply Article 85(1), but they cannot pass judgment on Article 85(3). A formalistic interpretation of Article 85(1), which serves to capture a very wide range of agreements and which reserves almost all the economic analysis for Article 85(3), does not, therefore, leave much room for the national courts to play a significant part in the administration of the competition rules. Whether it would be

[31] Compare R. Bork, *The Antitrust Paradox: A Policy at War with Itself* (Basic Books, 1978), with E. Fox, 'The Modernization of Antitrust: A New Equilibrium' (1981) 66 Cornell LRev. 1140 and 'The Politics of Law and Economics' (1986) 61 NYUL.Rev. 554.

[32] *US* v. *Trenton Potteries Co* 273 US 392 (1927).

[33] *US* v. *Topco Associates* 405 US 596 (1972).

[34] Because classification as a price-fixing agreement can have these serious consequences the courts will, on occasion, strive to avoid characterizing a case in this way, if they believe that it has redeeming features, notwithstanding an element of price control: *National Collegiate Athletic Assn.* v. *Board of Regents of the University of Oklahoma* 468 US 85 (1984).

desirable for them to be able to play a larger role is one of the debating points in the following discussion:

I. Forrester and C. Norall, The Laïcization of Community Law: Self-Help and the Rule of Reason: How Competition is and Could be Applied[35]

At least from a theoretical point of view, so long as exemption is legally necessary but unavailable in many if not most cases, the consequences appear to be rather serious. An agreement caught by paragraph 1 of Article 85 is void and unenforceable under paragraph (2) if it has not been exempted under paragraph (3). A system which purports to make so much depend on the issuance of exemptions which it is unable as a practical matter to deliver is open to rather harsh criticism. Far from creating legal certainty, it is a source of uncertainty.

[*The same theme is explored at a later stage in the passage:*]

The system theoretically requires resort to the notification procedure to ensure the legality of conduct, but very few notifications are, so far as the outside world can see, acted upon; the resources of the Commission in the enforcement field are limited, and the circumscribed powers at its disposal do not lend themselves to the efficient and accurate discovery of the truth; the large potential resource which is the national court systems in the Member States is not used to any significant extent; non-compliance is too common; and the system by its terms purports not to permit businessmen and their legal advisers to reach their own conclusions regarding the legitimacy of matters caught by Article 85(1).

[*The authors proffer a number of suggestions for improvement to the system:*]

It is submitted that the time is ripe for a number of changes. The characteristics of a mature, coherent and properly functioning system of competition law are that it permeates the consciousness of the economic and legal system, and is applied almost routinely by businessmen, lawyers and judges on their own responsibility. In such a system, the role of law enforcement officials like the Commission should be not to exercise a theoretically all-embracing but practically unworkable surveillance over an immense number of individual transactions and agreements, but rather to observe the scene as a whole, to formulate policy, and for the rest to concentrate necessarily limited resources on carefully selected targets where intervention is necessary and effective. National courts should be genuinely available for the resolution of competition law problems, whether raised by complainants or by others.

Among the steps which should be taken is a relaxing of the interpretation of paragraph (1) of Article 85 so as to broaden the number of cases where economic behaviour can be said to comply with Article 85 without having to resort to the criteria or procedures of paragraph (3) . . .

[*This same theme is developed at a later stage:*]

The intensity of the debate over whether Europe has or should have a rule of reason is not principally about the meaning of the language of Article 85(1). It fundamentally concerns who shall interpret and apply the competition rules. By arguing against a rule of reason, the Commission is seeking to maximize the number of cases about which it receives detailed information through the notification

[35] (1984) 21 CMLRev. 11, 16, 17–18, 32, 37, 38.

process. However, the Commission is physically unable to deal with its present caseload . . .

The core of our argument is that it would be desirable if the EEC competition rules could evolve away from the twin principles of the substantive primacy of Article 85(3) and the procedural insistence on the necessity of obtaining exemption from the Commission.

. . .

The Commission should view more favourably a competition analysis based on Article 85(1) rather than under Article 85(3). It would inject flexibility and realism, and would not involve any relinquishing of power.

The following extract provides further arguments in favour of the adoption of a rule of reason analysis within the Community:

V. Korah, The Rise and Fall of Provisional Validity—The Need for a Rule of Reason in EEC Antitrust[36]

The provision in Article 85(2) that agreements that infringe Article 85 should be void, at least to the extent of the infringement, has created considerable difficulties. The theories of competition and welfare developed by the classical economists and most of their successors are based on the assumption of private property and contractual rights. It will pay businessmen to make contracts and investments in reliance on them only to the extent that they expect them to be performed or enforceable. Where the contractual collaboration is undesirable, the sanction of nullity may be of some use and can do little harm. But apart from the area to which a *per se* rule applies in the United States, restraints that are ancillary to pro-competitive collaboration should generally be enforceable.

The Community Court and Commission have not developed the same theory of *per se* offences so brilliantly developed in the early cases under the Sherman Act. Naked restraints on pricing, market sharing, and some kinds of collective boycott . . . are likely to be condemned with fairly short reasoning if they are found capable of restricting trade between Member States, but more market analysis is required in the case of ancillary restraints. In *Consten & Grundig*, the Court seems to have developed a *per se* rule against absolute territorial protection conferred by export bans . . ., and this has been consistently applied by the Commission, despite mounting criticism. For all other restraints, however, the Court seems to be applying a rule of reason, requiring an analysis of the actual or intended effects in the light of market conditions.

The Commission, however, habitually analyzes agreements under Article 85(1) in the formalistic way developed by the German case law . . ., and condemns any restriction on the conduct of the parties, or third parties, provided the restriction has, or may be expected to have, appreciable effects on the market. Only under Article 85(3) does the Commission usually try to balance any pro- and anti-competitive effects.

If national courts adopt the Commission's practice, it is feared that many desirable contracts which restrict only competition that could not take place without

[36] (1981) 3 Nw.JInt.Law and Bus. 320, 354–5.

such an agreement, or which restrict competition less than they increase it, may not be made. The Commission grants few exemptions . . . Important agreements are unlikely to be exempted unless certain clauses are altered. These alterations may help one party more than the other, and the whole contract may have to be renegotiated after the parties have been implementing it, when their relative bargaining power may have been altered as a result of the collaboration. This is a considerable disincentive to notification.

. . .

There is fear that European firms that may have to compete in world markets may fall behind technologically or have to merge completely, so as to reduce the risk of collaboration. Market analyses are difficult, especially for lawyers and bureaucrats. But if such analyses are not made, agreements that may have overall desirable consequences should not be controlled. This means that national courts will have to be strong in resisting claims that agreements are anti-competitive just because some competitor is harmed.

Calls for the recognition of a rule of reason within Article 85(1) have come from a number of other sources.[37] In order for there to be a debate there must, of course, be an opposing view. The work of Whish and Sufrin represents the most complete statement of this contrasting position. There are a number of aspects to their argument. One is that the case law of the Court does not, properly understood, signify acceptance of a rule of reason in EC law; or that, at the least, differing labels express the essence of what the ECJ is doing better than the simple adoption of labels from the United States. This aspect of the matter will be considered below, after the case law has been evaluated.[38] A second aspect of their thesis is that there are very real differences between the antitrust laws of the United States and the EC, which render any transfer of terminology of limited utility:[39]

R. Whish and B. Sufrin, Article 85 and the Rule of Reason[40]

The call for the adoption of a US-style rule of reason should be resisted and, indeed, there is much to be said for dropping this term (and the terms 'ancillary restraint' and 'per se illegality') from EEC antitrust law altogether, on the basis that they do more to confuse than to clarify. EEC competition law requires its own vocabulary, carefully honed to express its own particular tensions.

One ground for jettisoning the term 'rule of reason' from the vocabulary of EEC competition law is that it is now used in other areas of the law, for example, in the provisions on free movement of goods . . .

A different reason for abandoning this terminology in EEC competition law is that it invites misleading comparison with antitrust law analysis in the United States. We have suggested above that the context of US antitrust law is so

[37] See e.g. R. Joliet, *The Rule of Reason in Antitrust Law: American, German and Common Market Laws in Comparative Perspective* (Hague, 1967); M. Schecter, 'The Rule of Reason in European Competition Law' [1982] 2 LIEI 1; V. Korah, 'EEC Competition Policy—Legal Form or Economic Efficiency' (1986) 39 CLP 85.

[38] See, below, 905–13.

[39] (1987) 7 YBEL 12–20.

[40] *Ibid.* 36–7.

dissimilar from that of the EEC that comparative analysis should be undertaken with great caution.

Quite apart from the issue of terminology, the writers have other doubts about the wisdom of analysing Article 85(1) in a way that relies on an approach similar to that of the Sherman Act. It would not help the cause of certainty.

. . .

The matter of certainty is, of course, important. It is in no one's interest to retard beneficial collaboration between firms striving to compete in a competitive international market. However, the best answer to this problem is for the Commission to continue to improve its procedures, to publish block exemptions where this is possible, and to develop such notions as objective necessity and potential competition. We also expect its sophistication in dealing with economics to continue to improve, but do not consider that this goes hand in hand with rule-of-reason analysis. This would stifle the proper application of Article 85 which, precisely because of its more ample wording, does not bear the same intellectual burden that the words 'restraint of trade' do in the Sherman Act. We doubt, too, that it would be helpful to draw the national courts further into the application of Article 85 by asking them to undertake extensive economic analysis under Article 85(1). We are happy for them to enforce the competition rules against blatant cartels and abuses of a dominant position. We do not consider them to be appropriate fora for deciding upon complex economic issues.

(d) The Case Law in the EC

The academic debate considered above provides a fitting framework within which to evaluate the case law of the ECJ. In reading the materials which follow two matters should be borne in mind: how far is the Court balancing the pro- and anti-competitive effects of an agreement to determine whether it is caught within Article 85(1), and how far is the terminology of the rule of reason an apt way of describing this approach?

Case 56/65, Société Technique Minière v. Maschinenbau Ulm GmbH [1966] ECR 235, [1966] CMLR 357

The case concerned an exclusive supply contract, whereby STM had the exclusive right to sell in France certain grading equipment produced by Maschinenbau Ulm (MBU), a German undertaking. The contract did not, however, insulate the French territory: STM could sell the goods outside France, and parallel imports could be obtained from other countries. A contract dispute between STM and MBU led the former to argue that this contract was invalid under Article 85.

THE ECJ

Finally, for the agreement at issue to be caught by the prohibition contained in Article 85(1) it must have as its 'object or effect the prevention, restriction or distortion of competition within the Common Market'.

The fact that these are not cumulative but alternative requirements, indicated by the conjunction 'or', leads first to the need to consider the precise purpose of the agreement, in the economic context in which it is to be applied. This interference with competition referred to in Article 85(1) must result from all or some of the clauses of the agreement itself. Where, however, an analysis of the said clauses does not reveal the effect on competition to be sufficiently deleterious, the consequences of the agreement should then be considered and for it to be caught by the prohibition it is then necessary to find that those factors are present which show that competition has in fact been prevented or restricted or distorted to an appreciable extent.

The competition in question must be understood within the actual context in which it would occur in the absence of the agreement in dispute. In particular it may be doubted whether there is an interference with competition if the said agreement seems really necessary for the penetration of a new area by an undertaking. Therefore, in order to decide whether an agreement containing a clause 'granting an exclusive right of sale' is to be considered as prohibited by reason of its object or its effect, it is appropriate to take into account in particular the nature and quantity, limited or otherwise, of the products covered by the agreement, the position and importance of the grantor and the concessionaire on the market for the products concerned, the isolated nature of the disputed agreement or, alternatively, its position in a series of agreements, the severity of the clauses intended to protect the exclusive dealership or, alternatively, the opportunities allowed for other commercial competitors in the same products by way of parallel re-exportation and importation.

Cases 56 and 58/64, Etablissements Consten SARL and Grundig-Verkaufs-GmbH v. Commission [1966] ECR 299, [1966] CMLR 418

Grundig granted to Consten a sole distributorship for its electronic products in France. Consten had an obligation to take a minimum amount of the product; it had to provide publicity and after sales service; and it undertook not to sell the products of competing manufacturers. Moreover, the French territory was in effect insulated, in the sense that there was absolute territorial protection: Consten undertook not to sell the goods outside the contract territory; a similar prohibition existed on other Grundig distributors in other countries; and Grundig assigned to Consten its trade-mark, GINT, which Consten could use against any unauthorized sales in France. In 1961 a company called UNEF bought Grundig goods from sellers in Germany and sold them in France more cheaply than Consten. The latter brought an action for infringement of its trade-mark, and UNEF contended that the whole agreement between Grundig and Consten violated Article 85.

THE ECJ

The applicants and the German Government maintain that since the Commission restricted its examination solely to Grundig products the decision was based upon a false concept of competition . . . contained in Article 85(1), since this concept applies particularly to competition between similar products of different makes; the Commission, before declaring Article 85(1) to be applicable, should, by basing itself upon the 'rule of reason', have considered the economic effects of the disputed contract upon competition between the different makes. There is a presumption that vertical sole distributorship agreements are not harmful to competition and in the present case there is nothing to invalidate that presumption. On the contrary, the contract in question has increased the competition between similar products of different makes.

The principle of freedom of competition concerns the various stages and manifestations of competition. Although competition between producers is generally more noticeable than that between distributors of products of the same make, it does not thereby follow that an agreement tending to restrict the latter kind of competition should escape the prohibition of Article 85(1) merely because it might increase the former.

Besides, for the purpose of applying Article 85(1), there is no need to take account of the concrete effects of an agreement once it appears that it has as its object the prevention, restriction or distortion of competition.

Therefore, the absence in the contested decision of any analysis of the effects of the agreement on competition between similar products of different makes does not, of itself, constitute a defect in the decision.

[*The Court considered the system of absolute territorial protection established by the agreement between Consten and Grundig. It then continued as follows:*]

The situation as ascertained above results in the isolation of the French market and makes it possible to charge for the products in question prices which are sheltered from all effective competition. In addition, the more producers succeed in their efforts to render their own makes of product individually distinct in the eyes of the consumer, the more the effectiveness of competition between producers tends to diminish. Because of the considerable impact of distribution costs on the aggregate cost price, it seems important that competition between dealers should also be stimulated. The efforts of the dealer are stimulated by competition between distributors of products of the same make. Since the agreement thus aims at isolating the French market for Grundig products and maintaining artificially, for products of a very-well known brand, separate national markets within the Community, it is therefore such as to distort competition in the Common Market.

It was therefore proper for the contested decision to hold that the agreement constitutes an infringement of Article 85(1). No further considerations, whether of economic data . . . or of the correctness of the criteria upon which the Commission relied in its comparisons between the situations of the French and German markets, and no possible favourable effects of the agreement in other respects, can in any way lead, in the face of the above-mentioned restrictions, to a different solution under Article 85(1).

The general issues concerning vertical restraints will be considered more fully below.[41] For the moment we should concentrate on the meaning ascribed by the Court to the terms 'object' or 'effect' within Article 85.

It is clear from the judgment in the *STM* case that the Court, even at this early date, accepted that the words of Article 85 were to be read disjunctively, in the sense that if the object or purpose of the agreement was anti-competitive then it could be condemned without pressing further. On this hypothesis agreements which are particularly heinous and indefensible, such as horizontal price-fixing, market-division, collective boycotts, and the like would be

[41] See below, 919–36.

condemned without any further analysis of the market circumstances.[42] If one were using the language of the United States' courts, such agreements would be *per se* illegal.

Where the anti-competitive quality of an agreement is not evident from its objective then one must press further and consider its effects,[43] as has been emphasized once again by the ECJ in the *Delimitis* case.[44] The contrast between the *STM* case and the decision in *Consten and Grundig* is instructive in this respect. It is clear that the *STM* case does countenance some species of economic analysis within Article 85(1). It is clear also that the ECJ took into account the fact that the exclusive-supply contract may have been a necessary step in allowing MBU to penetrate the French market; *and* that this was something to be encouraged. The response of the Court in *Consten and Grundig* to the argument concerning the rule of reason must be seen in the light of the facts of that case. The parties sought to use that doctrine as a basis for legitimating a scheme which gave absolute territorial protection to the French distributor. Now it may well be the case that if one were engaging in a pure economic analysis, which involved trade-offs between the pro- and anti-competitive effects of an agreement, then even absolute territorial protection might be warranted: the protection might be necessary to enable the manufacturer to penetrate a new market, and any reduction in intra-brand competition would be more than offset by an increase in inter-brand competition.[45] However, as indicated at the beginning of this Chapter, the Community rules on competition have been strongly influenced by the desire to create a single market. Agreements which contain provisions which have the effect of partitioning the market along national lines are, therefore, likely to be treated harshly by the ECJ. The *Consten and Grundig* case should not be perceived as rejecting economic analysis within Article 85(1), but rather as indicating that such analysis cannot serve to validate absolute territorial protection.

Economic analysis is apparent in a number of other ECJ decisions. In *Coditel*[46] the Court held that the grant of an exclusive copyright licence to exhibit a film in a Member State would not, in itself, infringe Article 85(1), even though the effect of this was to prevent transmission of that film by cable from a neighbouring Member State. It was for the national courts to determine whether the restrictions thereby created were artificial and unnecessary in terms of the needs of the cinematographic industry. The *Nungesser* case furnishes a further example of this approach:

[42] See also Case 45/85, *Verband der Sachversicherer eV* v. *Commission* [1987] ECR 405, [1988] 4 CMLR 264, para. 39.

[43] Case 23/67, *Brasserie de Haecht SA* v. *Wilkin* [1967] ECR 407, [1968] CMLR 26; Case 5/69, *Völk* v. *Vervaecke* [1969] ECR 295, [1969] CMLR 273; *Mars GmbH* [1993] OJ L183/1, [1994] 4 CMLR 51, para. 127.

[44] Case C–234/89, *Delimitis* v. *Henninger Bräu AG* [1991] ECR I–935, [1992] 5 CMLR 210.

[45] Intra-brand competition is competition between distributors of the same product; inter-brand competition is competition between those who distribute goods of the same kind, e.g. different brands of stereo equipment.

[46] Case 262/81, *Coditel SA* v. *Ciné-Vog Films SA* [1982] ECR 3381, [1983] 1 CMLR 49.

Case 258/78, L. C. Nungesser KG and Kurt Eisele v. Commission [1982] ECR 2015, [1983] 1 CMLR 278

The case was concerned with a contract made between INRA, a French research institute specializing in the development of plant seeds, and Eisele, a German supplier of seeds. The contract gave Eisele, and through him Nungesser, absolute territorial protection: INRA would not sell the seed to any other undertaking in Germany, and would prevent third parties from doing so; Eisele could use the plant breeder's rights assigned to him by INRA to prevent third parties selling into Germany. The Commission found that the agreement was in violation of Article 85(1). The applicant argued, *inter alia*, that the exclusive licence was necessary to enable INRA to enter a new market, and compete with comparable products therein, since no trader would risk launching a new product unless he were given protection from competition from the licensor and from other licensees. The Court distinguished between an open exclusive licence, whereby the owner merely undertakes not to compete himself, nor to grant licences to others in the same territory; and an exclusive licence with absolute territorial protection, under which all competition from third parties is eliminated.

THE ECJ

54. That point having been clarified, it is necessary to examine whether, in the present case, the exclusive nature of the licence, in so far as it is an open licence, has the effect of preventing or distorting competition within the meaning of Article 85(1) of the Treaty.

. . .

56. The exclusive licence which forms the subject-matter of the contested decision concerns the cultivation and marketing of hybrid maize seeds which were developed by INRA after years of research and experimentation and were unknown to German farmers at the time when the cooperation between INRA and the applicants was taking shape. For that reason the concern shown by the interveners as regards the protection of new technology is justified.

57. In fact, in the case of a licence of breeders' rights over hybrid maize seeds newly developed in one Member State, an undertaking in another Member State which was not certain that it would not encounter competition from other licensees for the territory granted to it, or from the owner of the right himself, might be deterred from accepting the risk of cultivating and marketing that product; such a result would be damaging to the dissemination of a new technology and would prejudice competition in the Community between the new product and similar existing products.

58. Having regard to the specific nature of the products in question, the Court concludes that, in a case such as the present, the grant of an open exclusive licence, that is to say a licence which does not affect the position of third parties such as parallel importers and licensees for other territories, is not in itself incompatible with Article 85(1) of the Treaty.

[*In relation to those aspects of the agreement which conferred absolute territorial protection, the Court, however, continued to follow* Consten and Grundig, *and to hold that these were illegal*].

Case 161/84, Pronuptia de Paris GmbH v. Pronuptia de Paris Irmgard Schillgallis [1986] ECR 353, [1986] 1 CMLR 414

The case was concerned with franchising arrangements for wedding apparel. Under the franchise, the franchisor undertook the following principal obligations: it granted the franchisee the exclusive right to use the Pronuptia mark for a certain area; it agreed not to open another shop in that area, or aid any third party to do so; and it assisted the franchisee in setting up the store, providing know-how etc. In return the franchisee, who remained the owner of the business, agreed to the following: to use the Pronuptia name; to pay the franchisor a royalty on turnover; to purchase 80 per cent of its requirements for wedding dresses from the franchisor; to take account of the recommended resale prices proposed by the franchisor; and not to compete with any Pronuptia business. The Court noted the diversity in types of franchise agreement: there were service, production, and distribution franchise agreements. The judgment is directed at distribution franchises.

THE ECJ

15. In a distribution system such as this, an enterprise which has established itself as a distributor in a market and which has thus been able to perfect a range of commercial methods gives independent businessmen the chance, at a price, of establishing themselves in other markets by using its mark and the commercial methods which created the franchisor's success . . . At the same time this system gives businessmen who lack the necessary experience access to methods which they could otherwise only acquire after prolonged effort and research and allows them also to profit from the reputation of the mark . . . Such a system, which permits the franchisor to take advantage of his success, is not by itself restrictive of competition. For it to function two conditions must be satisfied.

16. First, the franchisor must be able to communicate his know-how to the franchisees and provide them with the necessary assistance in putting his methods into effect, without running the risk that this know-how will aid his competitors, even indirectly. It thus follows that those clauses which are essential to prevent this risk do not constitute restrictions on competition in the sense of Article 85(1). These include the prohibition on the franchisee opening, for the duration of the franchise or for a reasonable period after its termination, a shop with an identical or similar purpose in an area where he could be in competition with one of the members of the network. The same applies to the obligation on the franchisee not to sell his shop without the prior approval of the franchisor: this clause serves to ensure that the benefit of the know-how and assistance provided does not go directly to a competitor.

17. Secondly, the franchisor must be able to take appropriate measures to preserve the identity and reputation of the network which is symbolised by the mark. It thus follows that those clauses which provide a basis for such control as is indispensable for this purpose also do not constitute restrictions on competition in the sense of Article 85(1).

18. This covers then the obligation on the franchisee to apply the commercial methods developed by the franchisor and to utilise the know-how provided.

19. This is also the case with the franchisee's obligation only to sell the merchandise covered by the agreement in premises set up and decorated according to

> the franchisor's specifications, which have as their purpose to guarantee a uniform image corresponding to specified requirements.
>
> . . .
>
> 21. Thanks to the control exercised by the franchisor over the selection of goods offered by the franchisee, the public can find at each franchisee's shop merchandise of the same quality . . . A clause prescribing that the franchisee can only sell products provided by the franchisor or by suppliers selected by him must, in these circumstances, be considered necessary for the protection of the reputation of the network. It must not, however, operate to prevent the franchisee from obtaining the products from other franchisees.

Other cases exemplify the same type of approach by the Court. Thus, in *Remia*[47] it was held that non-competition clauses included in the sale of an undertaking would not come within Article 85(1). Such clauses were necessary to give effect to the sale, since otherwise the vendor, with his specialist knowledge of the transferred undertaking, could simply win back the custom from the purchaser of that undertaking. Clauses of this type could, therefore, enhance competition by leading to an increase in the number of undertakings on the relevant market.

This species of analysis will, however, only exclude certain clauses from the operation of Article 85(1). Thus, in the *Remia* case the Court held that the non-competition clause must be limited in time and scope,[48] while in *Pronuptia*,[49] the Court decided that certain clauses were not necessary for the integrity of the franchise agreement and were restrictive of competition within Article 85(1). This was particularly the case for those clauses which partitioned the market between franchisor and franchisee, or between franchisees themselves. Thus, the obligation on the franchisor not to allow other franchisees to open shops outside their allotted territory was held to fall foul of the *Consten and Grundig* principle. The fact that such a clause might be necessary for any franchisee to make the initial investment was recognized by the Court, but was considered to be of relevance only within Article 85(3).

(e) Economic Analysis within Article 85(1): An Evaluation

The preceding discussion has considered the views of academics on the appropriate method of interpreting Article 85(1), and has also reviewed the case law of the Court in this area. What conclusions should be drawn in the light of this material on whether we do, or should possess, a rule of reason in the EC?

First, it is reasonably clear that the ECJ does condemn certain types of agreement on the basis of their object or purpose, without any extensive market analysis, and in this sense it effectively proscribes these agreements as *per se* illegal. It is also clear that the Court is engaging in some form of economic

[47] Case 42/84, *Remia BV and Verenigde Bedrijven Nutricia NV* v. *Commission* [1985] ECR 2545, [1987] 1 CMLR 1.

[48] *Ibid.*

[49] Case 161/84, [1986] ECR 353, 382–5, [1986] 1 CMLR 414, 445.

analysis within Article 85(1), although the Commission has not always been so enthusiastic in this regard.[50] While the Court has not employed the language of the rule of reason, there is evidence of a balancing of the pro- and anti-competitive effects of an agreement, subject to the caveats made above.

Secondly, whether one believes that the label 'rule of reason' is the most helpful explanatory tag to describe what the Court has been doing, or whether one believes that different labels are more instructive, is then a matter for further debate. Some commentators, as is apparent from the above extracts, would be content with importing the United States terminology. Others prefer labels which do not come with any particular foreign connotation. Thus, Whish argues that there are more finely tuned ways of regarding the ECJ's jurisprudence in this area. He contends that cases such as *Remia* and *Pronuptia* are explicable because the restrictions therein were *objectively necessary* for the success of the agreements in which they were contained; any such agreement would have to contain such provisions in order for it to achieve its ends. The argument is that these should be distinguished from other decisions, such as *STM* and *Nungesser*. In these latter cases it is argued that the issue was whether the *commercial risk* undertaken by the distributor or licensee warranted some degree of exclusivity and protection, a matter which requires a degree of market analysis not dissimilar to the rule of reason in the United States.[51]

This distinction should not serve to mask the underlying similarity between the two groups of cases. In both groups the issue at base is whether the agreement as a whole will have pro- or anti-competitive effects. Any distinction resides in the fact that in the former class of case it can be contended that certain restrictions will always be necessary for that type of agreement, whereas in the latter group a market analysis will be required to determine the degree of exclusivity which is needed. Even this line may prove to be shaky, since the precise content of restrictions which are deemed to be objectively necessary for that type of agreement may only be capable of being made in the light of a more complete market analysis.[52]

Thirdly, it is clear that the object behind the categorization mentioned immediately above is to demarcate the Court's role within Article 85(1). Thus, Whish is clear in his view that economic analysis outside cases of objective necessity is not particularly helpful: it produces delay, uncertainty, and places too great a demand on the national courts.[53] Whether this is so is contestable, and, as seen from the extracts considered above, is a matter which continues to divide commentators in this area.

A final, albeit somewhat paradoxical, point is worthy of note. In so far as some commentators do prefer the language of objective necessity to using terms such as the 'rule of reason' in the context of Article 85, this fits some-

[50] See e.g. the extract from Korah, above 903–4.

[51] R. Whish, n. 4 above, 210–11.

[52] This would apply, e.g., to the length and duration of permissible non-competition clauses made pursuant to the sale of an undertaking.

[53] N. 51 above.

what uneasily with the use of the phrase the rule of reason in other areas of Community law, most notably within Article 30. The rule of reason is employed within Article 30 as a mechanism for describing those restrictions on the free movement of goods which *are* objectively necessary to safeguard public health, consumer protection, and the like.[54]

5. THE EFFECT ON TRADE BETWEEN MEMBER STATES

In order for Article 85(1) to apply, the agreement etc. must have an effect on trade between Member States. This hurdle is of significance since if it is not satisfied the matter will remain within the jurisdiction of the relevant Member State. The hurdle has not, however, proven difficult for the Court to surmount. It has adopted a broad test and applied it in a similar fashion. In the *STM* case the ECJ held that the test was whether it was possible to 'foresee with a sufficient degree of probability on the basis of a set of objective factors of law or of fact that the agreement in question may have an influence, direct or indirect, actual or potential, on the pattern of trade between Member States'.[55] The latitude of the test is apparent from its principal parts.[56] The ability to focus on potential or indirect effects on trade means that it will be very rare for the Community to lack jurisdiction. Moreover, the mere fact that all the parties to the agreement are from one Member State will not preclude the application of Article 85(1): such an agreement will be held to have increased the compartmentalization of the Community along national lines, and rendered it more difficult for firms from other states to penetrate that national market.[57] Nor will the Court's jurisdiction be barred merely because the agreement relates to trade outside the EEC if it might have an impact on trade within the Community.[58]

[54] See above, Ch. 14.

[55] Case 56/65, [1966] ECR 235, 249. Moreover, provided that the agreement has this effect, it is not necessary for each of the restrictions to do so: Case 193/83, *Windsurfing International Inc.* v. *Commission* [1986] ECR 611, [1986] 3 CMLR 489.

[56] See Whish, n. 4 above, 215–23. See also *Welded Steel Mesh* [1989] OJ L260/1, [1991] 4 CMLR 13.

[57] Case 8/72, *Vereeniging van Cementhandelaren* v. *Commission* [1972] ECR 977, [1973] CMLR 7; Case 246/86, *Société Coopérative des Asphalteurs Belges (BELASCO)* v. *Commission* [1989] ECR 2117 [1991] 4 CMLR 96; Case T–66/89, *Publishers Association* v. *Commission (No 2)* [1992] ECRII–1995 [1992] 5 CMLR 120.

[58] See e.g. *Franco-Japanese Ballbearings Agreement* [1974] OJ L343/19, [1975] 1 CMLR D8; *French and Taiwanese Mushroom Packers* [1975] OJ L29/26, [1975] 1 CMLR D83.

6. THE *DE MINIMIS* DOCTRINE

An agreement will not be caught by Article 85(1) if it does not have an appreciable impact on competition or on inter-state trade.[59] This principle has been imbued with greater specificity by the Commission notice which delineates the boundaries of agreements deemed to be of minor importance.[60] Agreements which are covered by the notice do not have to be notified, thereby easing the workload of the Commission (paragraph 4 of the notice). Equally important is the assurance that the Commission will not, as a general rule, open proceedings against firms covered by the notice; nor will it impose fines on such firms who have failed to notify an agreement due to an error in calculating their market share, and who therefore believed that they were covered by the notice, unless the firms were negligent (paragraph 5).

The principal definition is provided by paragraph 7. Agreements concerning goods or services will not fall within Article 85(1) if:

> —the goods or services which are the subject of the agreement . . . together with the participating undertakings' other goods or services which are considered by users to be equivalent in view of their characteristics, price and intended use, do not represent more than 5% of the total market for such goods or services . . . in the area of the common market affected by the agreement and
> —the aggregate annual turnover of the participating undertakings does not exceed 200 million ECU.[61]

7. EXEMPTION UNDER ARTICLE 85(3)

Even if an agreement is held to be within Article 85(1) it can gain exemption under Article 85(3). In order to do so the agreement must satisfy four conditions: it must improve the production or distribution of goods or promote technical or economic progress; consumers must receive a fair share of the resulting benefit; it must contain only restrictions which are indispensable to the attainment of the agreement's objectives; and it cannot lead to the elimination of competition in respect of a substantial part of the products in question. Exemption can be granted on an individual basis, or there can be block exemptions which exempt categories of agreement, provided that they only contain certain terms. These two methods of gaining exemption will be examined in turn.

[59] Case 5/69, n. 43 above.

[60] Notice on Agreements of Minor Importance [1986] OJ C231/2. For the extent to which the Court may nonetheless apply the competition rules, see Whish, n. 4 above, 223–7.

[61] Subsequent paragraphs provide definitions or guidance on matters such as the meaning of 'undertaking', and the way in which the geographic and product market will be calculated.

(a) Individual Exemption

The Commission has the sole power to grant exemptions under Article 85(3), subject to review by the Court. It is readily apparent that the precise factors which will lead the Commission to exempt an agreement will differ from case to case. The type of reasoning employed can, however, be exemplified by considering two cases, one involving a decision by the Commission, the other a review judgment of the Court:

Re Bayer and Gist-Brocades NV
[1976] OJ L30/13, [1976] 1 CMLR D98

Bayer and Gist-Brocades (GB) made a specialization agreement whereby the former made 6-APA, an intermediate penicillin product, and GB made raw penicillin. Prior to the agreement both firms had made both products. The specialization agreement was supported by reciprocal supply contracts, under which each firm agreed to supply the requirements of the other: Bayer would supply 6-APA to GB, and GB would supply raw penicillin to Bayer. There were a number of other clauses to the agreement, which are adverted to by the Commission in its decision. The agreement was found to be in breach of Article 85(1), and the Commission then turned its attention to Article 85(3).

THE COMMISSION

57. 1. For the agreements to contribute to the improvement of production or distribution, or to promote technical and economic progress, they must objectively constitute an improvement on the situation that would otherwise exist. The fundamental principle in this respect, established at the time the Common Market was formed, lays down that fair and undistorted competition is the best guarantee of regular supply on the best terms. Thus the question of contribution to economic progress within the meaning of Article 85(3) can only arise in those exceptional cases where the free play of competition is unable to produce the best result economically speaking.

. . .

59. Account must . . . be taken of the limitations on Bayer's ability to expand its raw penicillin plants to cover rising supply requirements. The quality and yield of Bayer's raw penicillin strain were very low, and an increase in yield could not be expected. In order to improve production of raw penicillin, Bayer had to obtain the aid of a firm experienced in fermentation techniques . . . At the same time this arrangement with Gist made it possible for Bayer to change from raw penicillin to the manufacture of 6-APA in larger quantities and under modernised conditions. The agreements therefore contribute to the improvement of production.

60. 2. As a result of the agreements both firms have been able to expand their production to an extent which should allow the consumer to enjoy the resulting benefit. These benefits will stem from the improved production which the combined technical knowledge of the firms makes possible . . . The greater number of end-products available on the market and the general trend to lower prices show that the consumer is receiving a fair share of the benefits of the agreement.

However, in order that the Commission may follow developments on the market, certain obligations should be imposed upon the parties.

61. 3. All of the clauses to the agreement as amended are indispensable to the attainment of the stated objectives.

62. (a) The decision by each firm that for the duration of the agreement it will not manufacture the specialised product on which the other will concentrate is essential, as are the long-term mutual supply contracts . . .

. . .

65. (c) The no-challenge clause in the licensing agreement has . . . been removed as an unnecessary restriction. If Gist-Brocades and Bayer, two of the world's largest 6-APA manufacturers, had continued to agree not to contest the validity of each other's patents, the result might have been that third parties would have been prevented from exploiting freely for the benefit of the consumer processes which did not in fact merit the protection of a patent.

. . .

68. 4. The agreements do not afford the undertakings concerned the possibility of eliminating competition in respect of a substantial part of the products in question.

[*The Commission reached this conclusion after taking into account the market shares possessed by the two companies in respect both of raw penicillin and 6-APA.*]

The reasoning of the Court in the *Nungesser* case reinforces the importance of breaking down national barriers and creating a single market. The conditions of Article 85(3) will not be satisfied if the agreement contains terms which partition the Community market:

Case 258/78, L. C. Nungesser KG and Kurt Eisele v. Commission [1982] ECR 2015, [1983] 1 CMLR 278

The facts of the case have been set out above. It will be remembered that the Court held that the clauses in the agreement which gave absolute territorial protection were caught by Article 85(1). The Commission had also refused an exemption under Article 85(3) for certain aspects of the agreement because of this territorial protection. The applicants argued that the Court should overturn this part of the Commission's decision.

THE ECJ

73. . . . The decision states that Mr Eisele enjoyed absolute territorial protection in respect of the distribution in Germany of the seeds for which he had exclusive rights, and that by its absolute nature the sole and direct consequence of such protection was to prevent all imports through other channels of the original products, namely INRA seeds originating in France, despite a persistent demand for such seeds in Germany, which in itself is not capable of contributing to an improvement in the production or distribution of goods within the meaning of Article 85(3) . . .

74. The Caisse de Gestion des Licences Végétales disputed that reasoning. In its view, the territorial protection enjoyed by the licensee in the present case was

rather a relative protection on account of the presence on the market of numerous varieties of maize seed which could be substituted for INRA varieties and which could thus enter into direct competition with those varieties.

75. However, the Commission rightly stated in reply that that view put forward by the Caisse . . . concerns the problem of the demarcation of the market; that is a problem which arises when the Commission has to examine whether an agreement affords 'the possibility of eliminating competition in respect of a substantial part of the products in question' . . . but which is not relevant to the question whether an agreement is capable of improving the production or distribution of goods.

76. It must be remembered that under the terms of Article 85(3) . . . an exemption from the prohibition contained in Article 85(1) may be granted in the case of an agreement between undertakings which contributes to improving the production or distribution of goods or to promoting technical progress, and which does not impose on the undertakings concerned restrictions which are not indispensable to the attainment of those objectives.

77. As it is a question of seeds intended to be used by a large number of farmers for the production of maize, which is an important product for human and animal foodstuffs, absolute territorial protection manifestly goes beyond what is indispensable for the improvement of production or distribution or the promotion of technical progress, as is demonstrated . . . by the prohibition agreed to by both parties to the agreement, of any parallel imports of INRA maize seeds into Germany even if those seeds were bred by INRA itself and marketed in France.

78. It follows that the absolute territorial protection conferred on the licensee . . . constituted a sufficient reason for refusing to grant an exemption under Article 85(3) . . . It is therefore no longer necessary to examine the other grounds set out in the decision for refusing to grant such an exemption.

The following extract serves to give an overall impression of the Commission's approach under Article 85(3):

R. Whish, Competition Law[62]

In practice the Commission has considerable discretion when dealing with agreements under Article 85(3). The provisions themselves are drafted liberally and the Commission has not found it difficult to apply them in a way which promotes those types of agreement which it considers desirable. It would not uphold price fixing, market sharing, discrimination against Community nationals or the conferment of absolute territorial protection on distributors or licensees except in the most exceptional cases. However, it has encouraged distribution agreements, research and development, specialisation in production, licensing of intellectual property and know-how, rationalisation of trade fairs and even crisis cartels. It should also be borne in mind that the various block exemptions are based upon the principles incorporated in Article 85(3). In granting individual exemptions, the Commission has been particularly keen to assist 'small and medium-sized undertakings'. The block exemptions also tend to favour such firms. However, . . . agreements between large firms may be permitted, and it seems to be the case that

[62] *Competition Law*, n. 4 above, 235–6.

in recent years more agreements between major undertakings have been permitted than before, particularly where they were themselves subject to competition from large firms established outside the EEC . . .

. . .

There are however problems with the application of Article 85(3). The delays experienced in obtaining an exemption are unfortunate because of the uncertainty and inconvenience which result. It is thought that many firms do not bother to notify their agreements to the Commission, preferring to take the risk that beneficial projects in which they take part will not be discovered or will not be severely punished if they are.

(b) Block Exemption

Article 85(3) allows the Commission to declare the provisions of Article 85(1) inapplicable to a category of agreements. This is the foundation for the series of block exemptions which the Commission has promulgated, acting under delegated authority from the Council.[63] The object of such exemptions is to exclude a generic type of agreement from the ambit of Article 85(1), thereby obviating the need for separate and time-consuming individual exemptions. In some ways the technique of block exemption is conceptually similar to the evolution of *per se* rules, although the result produced is to exclude rather than condemn the agreement: experience with individual agreements leads to the conclusion that certain types of such agreement, which contain particular terms, warrant exemption. A block exemption encapsulates this conclusion. It serves also to give more definite guidance to firms and their legal advisers. Standardized contracts can be devised which will comply with the requirements of the relevant block exemption. Although the contents of the block exemptions differ, they possess certain structural features in common.

First, agreements which come within the terms of a block exemption do not need to be notified to the Commission, and this will be specified in the opening recital of the exemption.[64] Secondly, the regulation containing the block exemption will state, in the recitals, the reasons it has been seen fit to produce a block exemption covering this area; the advantages secured by the agreements which are to be exempted will be explained. Thirdly, the substance of the exemption will then specify: certain 'white' clauses which, although falling within Article 85(1), are to be exempted; certain 'black' clauses which will prevent the grant of an exemption; and certain 'grey' clauses, which may or may not fall within Article 85(1), but which are in any event permitted by the

[63] See above, 128–31.

[64] Some of the block exemptions contain what is known as an opposition procedure, whereby certain agreements which do not satisfy all the conditions for inclusion in the exemption can benefit from an accelerated exemption procedure, provided that they do notify the Commission of their agreement, and provided that the Commission takes no action within a certain period of time: see e.g. Reg. 417/85, Art. 4. For difficulties with this procedure see J. Venit, 'The Commission's Opposition Procedure—Between the Scylla of Ultra Vires and the Charybdis of Perfume: Legal Consequences and Tactical Considerations' (1985) 22 CMLRev. 167.

exemption. The block exemptions will normally also contain provisions which limit the size of the firms which can take advantage of them.

Such exemptions have been made for a number of areas, including: specialization agreements;[65] research and development;[66] exclusive distribution;[67] exclusive purchasing;[68] patent licensing;[69] franchising;[70] and know-how licensing.[71] The structure and operation of block exemptions will be examined more closely in the context of vertical restraints, which will be considered below.

8. VERTICAL RESTRAINTS

Space precludes a detailed analysis of all the varying types of restraint which competition authorities have to deal with. However, it is also the case that consideration of the general principles which operate within EC competition law only take one so far. The remainder of this Chapter will, therefore, be devoted to an examination of one important area of competition policy, that of vertical restraints. These are agreements which are made between parties at differing levels of the production process, a typical example being a distribution agreement between a manufacturer of a product and a retailer. There are a number of reasons for focusing on this species of agreement: one is that there is greater controversy in this area than in many others about the extent to which these agreements are economically harmful, and hence disagreement about the 'correct' approach for competition policy; a second reason for the focus on vertical restraints is that they are of considerable practical importance in the way that business is organized; a third rationale is that the law's response to vertical restraints exemplifies the application of many of the general principles considered earlier in this Chapter. Let us begin, therefore, with an examination of the opposing arguments concerning the extent to which vertical restraints are harmful or not.

(a) The Economic Debate

There is considerable diversity of opinion whether vertical restraints are economically harmful or not. Broadly speaking there are two schools of thought: there are those who believe that this species of restraint is not harmful at all, or only where there is some real degree of market power at the production level; others adopt a more wary attitude, and believe that vertical restraints may produce a variety of anti-competitive effects, and that therefore it is correct for competition policy to subject them to some scrutiny.

[65] Reg. 417/85, [1985] OJ L53/1, as amended by Reg. 151/93, [1993] OJ L21/8.
[66] Reg. 418/85, [1985] OJ L53/5, as amended by Reg. 151/93, [1993] OJ L21/8.
[67] Reg. 1983/83, [1983] OJ L173/1.
[68] Reg. 1984/83, [1983] OJ L173/5.
[69] Reg. 2349/84, [1984] OJ L219/15, as amended by Reg. 151/93, [1993] OJ L21/8.
[70] Reg. 4087/88, [1988] OJ L359/46.
[71] Reg. 559/89, [1989] OJ L61/1, as amended by Reg. 151/93, [1993] OJ L21/8.

The essence of the former view can be presented as follows. A manufacturer of a product will have to decide how to market that product. A number of options are open to the firm: it might decide to establish its own retail outlets; it might decide to establish a joint venture with a company which has expertise in the retailing area; it might determine that retailing is best done by different firms, and simply sell its products through any outlet which is willing to stock them; a further option would be to sell through certain specialized shops, on the basis that the product requires sales expertise in that area; or it might conclude that the optimum marketing technique is to sell through certain retail outlets, each of which would be given exclusive rights to distribute the product in that geographical area, either because retailers would only take the goods on these terms, or because this will maximize total sales. This list of distributive techniques is by no means exhaustive, but merely indicative of the range of options open to the manufacturer. The argument of those who do not see vertical restraints as harmful has two parts.

One is that the manufacturer will choose whichever of the above options is felt to be the most efficient way of marketing the product. It will, for example, only use independent retailers on the assumption that this is a more efficient marketing technique than establishing its own outlets. And it will only give such outlets exclusivity on the assumption that this will lead to greater sales than if exclusivity had not been given. Now, it may be wrong in its assumptions, but if this is so then the market will 'punish' it, through reduced sales or by the ultimate sanction of bankruptcy. In any event, it is not the function of competition authorities to play at management consultancy and to try and devise a better marketing strategy for the manufacturer, partly because that is not their function and partly because they are in a less good position than the manufacturer itself to make this choice. It is, moreover, a central facet of the argument in favour of the legality of vertical restraints that a manufacturer which imposes such restraints will not be restricting output to any greater degree than it would otherwise be doing, and will not be taking any greater monopoly profit, if such is available in the circumstances, through the presence of a vertical restraint than it would otherwise be able to extract from that market.

The second part of the argument develops from the preceding foundations, and has two parts.

On the one hand, given that the manufacturer will be devising the marketing strategy which is conceived to be the most efficient, then any restraints which are imposed are either outweighed by the pro-competitive effects of the agreement and/or are necessary to persuade the distributor to undertake the marketing of the goods at all. An example will serve to clarify this idea. Imagine that a producer wishes to enter a new geographical market. It does not have retailing expertise, and therefore wishes to use an independent retailer. If the product is to be noticed within this new market it may require expenditure on advertising, and also a commitment to provide both pre- and post-sales service. A retailer may well not be willing to undertake this expense unless it is accorded some exclusivity in the sales process. If this is not forthcoming the retailer will encounter what is known as the free-rider problem: that retailer will expend money on advertising, pre-sales service, and the like, only to witness the sales being taken by a rival retailer who has not had to expend money in this manner. Now it is, of course, the case that the grant of such exclusivity will necessarily restrict intra-brand competition between retailers of the same product. However, it is felt that in most markets this species of competition is relatively unimportant in that prices will be controlled by the existence of inter-brand competition: a retailer of Sony stereos who has exclusivity in a certain area will not be able to raise prices significantly since there will be competition from other stereo brands.

On the other hand, those who contend that vertical restraints should be lawful do not accept that these restraints produce certain anti-competitive effects. The nature of these effects will be considered in more detail below.

One of the prominent exponents of the view outlined above is Bork, and the following extract provides a summary of the argument:

R. Bork, The Antitrust Paradox, A Policy at War with Itself[72]

We have seen that vertical price fixing (resale price maintenance), vertical market division (closed dealer territories), and, indeed, all vertical restraints are beneficial to consumers and should for that reason be completely lawful. Basic economic theory tells us that the manufacturer who imposes such restraints cannot intend to restrict and must (except in the rare case of price discrimination, which the law should regard as neutral) intend to create efficiency. The most common efficiency is the inducement or purchase by the manufacturer of extra reseller sales, service or promotional effort.

The proposal to legalize all truly vertical restraints is so much at variance with conventional thought on the topic that it will doubtless strike many readers as troublesome, if not bizarre. But I have never seen any economic analysis that shows how manufacturer-imposed resale price maintenance, closed dealer territories, customer allocation clauses, or the like can have the net effect of restricting output. We have too quickly assumed something that appears untrue.

Perhaps the ambiguity of the word 'restraint' accounts for some of our confusion on this topic. When the Supreme Court speaks of a restraint it often, or even usually, refers to the manufacturer's control of certain activities of his resellers or to the elimination by the manufacturer of some forms of rivalry among his resellers. There is, of course, nothing sinister or unusual about using 'restraint' in that sense. It is merely a form of vertical integration by contract, a less complete integration than that which would obtain if the manufacturer owned his outlets and directed their activities. It is merely one instance of the coordination of economic activities which is ubiquitous in the economic world and upon which our

[72] (1978), 297–8. See also R. Bork, 'The Rule of Reason and the *Per Se* Concept in Price Fixing and Market Division II' (1966) 75 Yale LJ 373 . For the debate on this issue see, J. R. Gould and B. S. Yamey, 'Professor Bork on Vertical Price Fixing' (1967) 76 Yale LJ 722; R. Bork, 'A Reply to Professors Gould and Yamey' (1967) 76 Yale LJ 731; J. R. Gould and B. S. Yamey, 'Professor Bork on Vertical Price Fixing: A Rejoinder' (1968) 77 Yale LJ 936.

> wealth depends. The important point is that such vertical control never creates 'restraint' in that other common meaning, restriction of output. Perhaps, if we are more careful about the ambiguity of the word and make it clear in which sense we use it, our reasoning about antitrust problems, including the problem of vertical restraints, will improve.[73]

Those commentators who adopt a more wary approach to vertical agreements do so for a variety of reasons. They perceive a number of possible dangers to the competitive process flowing from such agreements. Four may be briefly considered here.

The first is market foreclosure. If a producer has made exclusive contracts with certain outlets to sell only its brand of a particular product, then it may be difficult for other producers to secure outlets for their own sales. This is especially the case in those instances where either the best outlets have already been taken or the number of outlets for distributing a particular product is limited by the nature of that product or by external factors such as planning laws.

A second concern is that consumers will be harmed, in particular by certain types of vertical restraint. Resale-price maintenance is one of the most commonly cited instances of this, although the existence of such harm has been vigorously contested.[74] Consumer harm is said to be apparent in other ways. Thus, it is argued that systems of selective or exclusive distribution force a 'package' on consumers which includes the basic price of the product, plus advertising costs, after-sales service, and the like, even though some consumers would prefer to take the raw product itself and worry about maintenance etc. themselves.

A third disadvantage which is said to attend vertical agreements is that they can serve as a mask for cartels between producers or distributors. A producer may grant an exclusive distribution right to a distributor in circumstances in which the latter has agreed with other distributors of competing products to divide the market horizontally: the consequence will be that inter- as well as intra-brand competition is reduced. Once again the cogency of this objection has been strongly contested, both in empirical terms (does this really happen, and is it really exacerbated by the existence of the vertical agreement?), and in terms of the appropriate policy response (if it does occur then attack the real problem itself, the horizontal agreement, not the vertical one)[75].

A final source of concern with vertical agreements is peculiar to the EC, and has been touched upon a number of times in the above discussion. Community competition law is not concerned solely with efficiency. The creation of a single European market is also of prime importance. Agreements which either explicitly or implicitly divide the market along national or regional lines will, therefore, be treated particularly severely by the competition authorities, as

[73] See also F. Easterbrook, 'Vertical Arrangements and the Rule of Reason' (1984) 53 Antitrust LJ 135; B. Bock, 'An Economist Appraises Vertical Restraints' (1985) 30 Antitrust B. 117.

[74] See above, n. 72.

[75] See, R. Bork, n. 31 above, Ch. 14.

exemplified by the Court's continuing opposition to agreements which attempt to provide absolute territorial protection.

In the following extract Comanor expresses the concerns of this second, more cautious, school of thought. He reviews some of the arguments utilized by those such as Bork, but does not believe that vertical agreements should always be regarded as legal:

W. Comanor, Vertical Price-Fixing, Vertical Market Restrictions, and the New Antitrust Policy[76]

When vertical restraints are used to promote the provision of distribution services, the critical issue for antitrust purposes remains whether consumers are better served by lower prices and fewer services or by higher prices and more services. In its *Spray-Rite* brief, the Department of Justice suggested that pure vertical restraints always lead to increased consumer welfare. This position is unfounded, and a more hostile treatment of vertical restraints is appropriate.

Because vertical restraints can either enhance or diminish consumer welfare, depending upon the situation, it is tempting to apply the rule of reason on a case-by-case basis . . . Yet it is no easy task to determine whether particular restraints increase or decrease efficiency: the answer depends in each case largely on the relative preferences of different groups of consumers. In the interests of judicial economy, therefore, it may be more expeditious to set general policy standards, even though they will sometimes lead to improper results.

Vertical restraints that concern established products are more likely to reduce consumer welfare. Large numbers of consumers are already familiar with such products and are therefore unlikely to place much value on acquiring further information about them. In this context, stringent antitrust standards should be applied to vertical price and non-price restraints alike. This approach could take the form either of a direct *per se* prohibition, or of a modified rule of reason analysis under which the defendant would be required to demonstrate that the restraints have benefited consumers generally. By contrast, in the case of new products or products of new entrants into the market, vertical restraints are less likely to lessen consumer welfare, because their novelty should create greater demand for information. In these circumstances, the restraints should be permissible, or at the least should be treated more leniently in any modified rule of reason analysis.

In the discussion which follows the approach of the EC to certain types of vertical restraint will be considered, with reference to the economic literature where this is appropriate. There are, as the preceding analysis indicated, varying ways in which a producer may choose to market his product. We will begin with one of the most common, the exclusive-distribution agreement.

(b) Exclusive Distribution

The essential idea behind an exclusive-distribution agreement (EDA) is that the producer agrees to supply only to a particular distributor within a

[76] (1985) 98 Harv. LRev. 983, 1001–2.

particular territory. This central idea may be buttressed by attempts to prevent third parties from selling into the contract territory of the designated distributor, either by imposing contract terms to that effect in agreements which the producer has with other distributors and/or by assigning to the designated distributor trade mark rights which will enable the latter to stop such infringements. As we have seen in the previous discussion, this type of agreement may be necessary to persuade a distributor to market a new product or to market an existing product in a new area; or to do so with the degree of financial commitment desired by the producer. An EDA may also be beneficial to the producer by facilitating the efficient distribution of his goods, in the sense that he will not have to incur transport costs etc. to multiple sites.

The central issue is whether an EDA will be caught be Article 85(1), and whether it will be exempted under Article 85(3), either individually or pursuant to a block exemption.

The applicability of Article 85(1) to an EDA has been touched on in the earlier discussion of the general principles which underlie that Article. It is clear that such agreements can be caught by Article 85(1), and that, in the view of the Court, the vertical restraint must be considered in its factual, legal, and economic context in order to consider whether it is in fact within that Article (*STM* and *Brasserie de Haecht*).[77] It is also reasonably clear that the Commission has, however, often adopted a formalistic attitude, eschewing the more general contextual approach advocated by the Court.[78]

R. Whish, Competition Law[79]

The Commission seems to regard any exclusive distribution agreement as infringing Article 85(1), even where it does not confer absolute territorial protection upon the distributor in question . . . Exclusivity as to customers as well as territories will be held to infringe Article 85(1).

Some other terms commonly found in exclusive distribution agreements will generally be held not to infringe Article 85(1). For example positive obligations imposed upon a distributor to advertise goods, to package them in the way the producer requires, to sell them under its trade mark, to stock spare parts and to stock the complete range of a producer's goods tend to be regarded as normal terms of such agreements and to fall outside Article 85 altogether. Generally speaking other contractual provisions providing for minimum sales, advance payments and pass-over payments would not be caught, although it is important to emphasise that the Commission will always look carefully to see whether in practice any particular term in an agreement has anti-competitive effects. The Commission will normally hold that restrictions imposed upon a distributor as to its own right to resell the products as it wishes infringes Article 85(1) . . . Without considering such terms in their economic context, the Commission has tended to object to such provisions because they remove the distributor's freedom and lead to a greater rigidity at the various levels of distribution. To this however there is

[77] See above, 905–6. [78] Whish, n. 4 above, 580–1; Korah, n. 36 above.

[79] N. 4 above, 564–5.

an important exception since both the Commission and the Court have indicated that in certain circumstances the restrictive provisions of selective distribution networks might fall outside Article 85(1) altogether.

Notwithstanding the divergence of approach between Court and Commission, it is apparent from their combined jurisprudence that certain types of restrictions within an EDA are especially likely to fall within the ambit of Article 85(1). Thus, export bans which prohibit a distributor from exporting the product outside a designated area will be judged particularly severely, as will any other attempt to establish absolute territorial protection for a distributor.[80] Indirect attempts to attain the same end will also be condemned, as in the case of customer guarantees which are only available if the product is bought from the distributor in that state.[81] The *Konica* case provides another example of this principle in operation:

Commission v. Konica UK Limited and Konica Europe GmbH
[1988] OJ L78/34, [1988] 4 CMLR 848

The case was concerned with a scheme one object of which was to prevent film which had been parallel imported into Germany from the United Kingdom from being sold there. Prices for Konica film were higher in Germany than in the United Kingdom, hence the incentive to import into Germany from the United Kingdom. In order to protect its German distributors from these sales of Konica film at cheaper prices, Konica bought up the cheap film itself. It attempted to justify this by contending that its marketing strategy in Germany was to sell its film only through specialist outlets, and that this strategy was being undermined by the parallel import of cheaper film from the United Kingdom being sold through non-specialist shops.

THE COMMISSION

41. The export ban imposed on a number of dealers by Konica UK had the object and effect of restricting competition within the Common Market. Its aim was to restrain dealers in the United Kingdom . . . from selling to customers in other Member States, so that these would not compete with dealers under contract to Konica Europe. Such a ban leads to artificial divisions in the Common Market and impedes the establishment of a single market between the Member States, which is a basic objective of the EEC Treaty.

42. The buying-up undertaking given by Konica Europe to prevent the resale of parallel imported Konica film in the Federal Republic of Germany had the same aim, namely to protect the dealers supplied by Konica Europe against competition from parallel imported Konica film so that their margins were not eroded.

43. The intention of Konica UK and Konica Europe to restrict competition

[80] Case 19/77, *Miller International Schallplatten GmbH* v. *Commission* [1978] ECR 131, [1978] 2 CMLR 334; Case C–279/87, *Tipp-Ex GmbH & Co KG* v. *Commission* [1990] ECR I–261; Case T–43/92, *Dunlop Slazenger International Ltd* v. *Commission*, 7 July 1994.

[81] Case 31/85, *ETA Fabriques d'Ebauches* v. *DK Investments SA* [1985] ECR 3933, [1986] 2 CMLR 674.

within the Common Market is clear from their joint efforts to identify the dealers who were 'grey' exporting or importing Konica film.

. . .

45. As far as Konica Europe's buying-up undertaking is concerned, this largely eliminated intra-brand competition and its impact on the prices of Konica film in the Federal Republic of Germany which would have benefited the German consumer. The buying-up commitment was also inextricably linked to the action taken by Konica UK; it was part of a deliberate policy in the Konica group to isolate national markets from one another.

If an EDA is caught by the provisions of Article 85(1) the parties may either seek individual exemption or try and bring themselves within the terms of the relevant block exemption. The principles which govern the former have been examined above,[82] and therefore attention will be focused on the principles of the block exemption.[83] Article 1 of Regulation 1983/83 provides that:

> Pursuant to Article 85(3) of the Treaty and subject to the provisions of this Regulation, it is hereby declared that Article 85(1) of the Treaty shall not apply to agreements to which only two undertakings are party and whereby one party agrees with the other to supply certain goods for resale within the whole or a defined area of the common market only to that other.

It is clear from this Article that the distributor may be granted exclusivity within the designated area, and the effect of Article 2(1) is to allow the supplier of the goods to undertake an obligation not himself to sell within that area. Absolute territorial protection is not, however, possible, and the supplier of the goods could not undertake not to supply those outside the contract territory, even though they might well then sell into that area. To qualify under Article 1 the EDA must be bilateral,[84] and the goods must be supplied for resale.[85] It is equally important that the agreement should come within the spirit of the Regulation: attempts to use it to gain exemption for agreements which are not, in reality, distribution agreements at all will not be successful. Thus in *Siemens/Fanuc* the Commission refused to apply a block exemption to what was, in effect, a horizontal market-sharing agreement between rival companies.[86]

Article 2 then specifies certain other restrictions which will be allowed:

[82] See above, 915–17.

[83] V. Korah, *Exclusive Dealing Agreements in the EEC: Reg. 67/67 Replaced* (ESC Publishing, 1984).

[84] This, however, can be satisfied if there are more than two actual firms involved. One side of the EDA may be comprised of more than one firm provided that they are economically one unit.

[85] There can clearly be uncertainty over the interpretation of this phrase: see Commission, *Notes of Guidance* [1984] OJ C101/2, paras. 15–16.

[86] [1985] OJ L376/29, [1988] 4 CMLR 945.

1. Apart from the obligation referred to in Article 1 no restriction shall be imposed on the supplier other than the obligation not to supply the contract goods to users in the contract territory.

2. No restriction on competition shall be imposed on the exclusive distributor other than:

(a) the obligation not to manufacture or distribute goods which compete with the contract goods;
(b) the obligation to obtain the contract goods for resale only from the other party;
(c) the obligation to refrain, outside the contract territory and in relation to the contract goods, from seeking customers, from establishing any branch and from maintaining any distribution depot.

3. Article 1 shall apply notwithstanding that the exclusive distributor undertakes all or any of the following obligations:

(a) to purchase complete ranges of goods or minimum quantities;
(b) to sell the contract goods under trademarks, or packed and presented as specified by the other party;
(c) to take measures for promotion of sales, in particular:
—to advertise,
—to maintain a sales network or stock of goods,
—to provide customer and guarantee services,
—to employ staff having specialised or technical training.

The restrictions permitted under Article 2 relate to intra- and inter-brand competition. The former is covered, in varying ways, by Article 2(1), 2(2)(b), and 2(2)(c). Thus, Article 2(1) permits the distributor to be protected against intra-brand competition from the supplier himself; Article 2(2)(b) sanctions clauses which oblige the distributor to obtain the contract goods only from the supplier;[87] and Article 2(2)(c) permits restrictions on the distributor from seeking customers outside the contract territory, and hence from invading the territory of a different distributor. This latter provision does not, however, sanction absolute territorial protection, since it does not enable the supplier to prevent sales outside the area, but only to prevent the distributor from actively seeking such sales or establishing a depot. Article 2(2)(a), by way of contrast, deals with inter-brand competition, and allows the supplier to stipulate that the distributor should not sell competing goods, the rationale being that this would diminish the degree of commitment to selling the goods covered by the EDA.

All block exemptions contain a 'black' list, and the existence of the matters mentioned will prevent the block exemption from applying. These are specified in Article 3 and are four in number.

Article 3(a) precludes reciprocal EDAs between manufacturers of identical or equivalent goods. The objective is to prevent the block exemption from

[87] Exclusive purchasing is, therefore, permitted under the block exemption concerned with distribution.

being used in situations such as *Siemens/Fanuc*, in which rival manufacturers grant each other an EDA, but where in reality there is a horizontal market-sharing agreement. Article 3(b) extends this idea and prohibits a non-reciprocal EDA between manufacturers of identical or equivalent goods, unless one of the firms is relatively small, with a turnover of no more than 100 million ECU. The rationale is that to distribute one's goods through a rival company in another area is unlikely to be good for competition, may well be a mask for market sharing, and is probably unnecessary, in the sense that other distribution possibilities could be arranged. The size qualification serves to recognize that there may be instances where a small concern could legitimately seek to market its product in this manner.

Article 3(c) and (d) have a different purpose. Both are concerned, in differing ways, with the preservation of intra-brand competition. The former precludes the application of Article 1 of the Regulation where users of the contract goods in the territory can obtain them only from the designated distributor and have no alternative source of supply outside the area. This provision serves as a longstop, and is indicative of the Community's desire that intra-brand competition should not be eroded entirely.

Article 3(d) approaches the matter from a different perspective, by 'policing' possible interference with parallel imports. It demonstrates the Community's opposition to absolute territorial protection, and its commitment to a single market. The Article stipulates that the Regulation will not apply where one or both of the parties to the EDA make it difficult for users etc. to obtain the contract goods from other dealers. Thus, the use, for example, of intellectual property rights to prevent parallel imports would be caught by this provision.

In addition to the 'black' list in Article 3, the Commission may withdraw the benefit of the exemption if the agreement has effects which are incompatible with Article 85(3). These include the absence of effective inter-brand competition (Article 6(a)); that access to distribution outlets by different suppliers within the contract territory has been made difficult (Article 6(b)); or that the distributor has refused to supply the contract goods, which are not obtainable elsewhere in the territory on suitable terms, without objective cause, or sells the goods at excessive prices (Article 6(d)).

(c) Selective Distribution

The approach of the Court and the Commission to selective-distribution agreements (SDA) stands in marked contrast to that adopted towards EDAs. A selective-distribution system is one in which the supplier chooses to distribute the goods only through certain outlets, normally those which fulfil certain criteria concerning expertise. As will be seen, the Court has held that such agreements do not necessarily fall within Article 85(1). *Metro* is the seminal case:

Case 26/76, Metro-SB-Großmarkte GmbH & Co KG v. Commission and SABA [1977] ECR 1875, [1978] 2 CMLR 1

Metro was a wholesaler of goods in Germany. It operated a system of self-service wholesaling and a cash-and-carry service, which enabled it to undercut the prices charged by other wholesalers. Metro applied to SABA to be allowed to stock the electronic equipment produced by the latter, but SABA refused to supply it, claiming that it did not fulfil the conditions that SABA required before supplying its goods. Metro complained to the Commission that SABA's policy was in breach of Article 85(1), but the Commission found in favour of SABA after the latter had amended its terms of trade in certain respects. Metro then sought to have this decision of the Commission annulled.

THE ECJ

20. . . . In the sector covering the production of high quality and technically advanced consumer durables, where a relatively small number of large and medium-scale producers offer a varied range of items which, or so consumers may consider, are readily interchangeable, the structure of the market does not preclude the existence of a variety of channels of distribution adapted to the peculiar characteristics of the various producers and to the requirements of the various categories of consumers. On this view the Commission was justified in recognising that selective distribution systems constituted, together with others, an aspect of competition which accords with Article 85(1), provided that the resellers are chosen on the basis of objective criteria of a qualitative nature relating to the technical qualifications of the reseller and his staff and the suitability of his trading premises and that such conditions are laid down uniformly for all potential resellers and are not applied in a discriminatory fashion.

21. It is true that in such systems of distribution price competition is not generally emphasised either as an exclusive or indeed as a principal factor . . . However, although price competition is so important that it can never be eliminated, it does not constitute the only effective form of competition or that to which absolute priority must in all circumstances be accorded . . . For specialist wholesalers and retailers the desire to maintain a certain price level, which corresponds to the desire to preserve, in the interests of consumers, the possibility of the continued existence of this channel of distribution in conjunction with new methods of distribution based on a different type of competition policy, forms one of the objectives which may be pursued without necessarily falling under the prohibition of Article 85(1), and if it does fall thereunder, either wholly or in part, coming within the framework of Article 85(3) . . .

The significance of the *Metro* decision resides in the fact that, when the conditions elaborated therein are fulfilled, the SDA is held not to be within Article 85(1) at all. The principle enunciated in that case has oft been cited since then.[88] There are, however, a number of limits to the application of that principle.

[88] See e.g. Case 210/81, *Demo-Studio Schmidt* v. *Commission* [1983] ECR 3045, [1984] 1 CMLR 63; Case 107/82, *AEG-Telefunken AG* v. *Commission* [1983] ECR 3151, [1984] 2 CMLR 325; Case C–376/92, *Metro SB-Großmärkte GmbH & Co KG* v. *Cartier SA* [1994] ECR I–15.

First and foremost, the product has to be of the kind in relation to which the Court and the Commission believe that it is justifiable to limit price competition and to operate the regime of selective distribution with an element of non-price competition. Products which have qualified in this respect tend to be those which require specialist sales staff who have expertise in that area,[89] or goods where brand image is of particular importance.[90] Plumbing fittings are, by way of contrast, not deemed to be a technically advanced product which necessitates a selective-distribution system.[91]

A second, and equally important, facet of the *Metro* principle is that it only operates to legitimate outlets which are chosen on the basis of qualitative criteria. Whether it is sensible, as a matter of competition policy, to distinguish between qualitative and quantitative constraints will be examined below. What is clear is that it can be extremely difficult to determine whether a particular requirement for a distributor to be acceptable to a supplier should really be classified as qualitative or not.[92] Subject to this uncertainty, the *Metro* principle does not allow a supplier to impose quantitative limits on those who can distribute the product, or to discriminate as between distributors.[93]

The logic of the distinction drawn between qualitative and quantitative criteria for restrictions on distribution is questionable, to say the least. As the previous discussion of the economics underlying vertical restraints indicated, producers will tend to choose that method of distributing their goods which they believe will best maximize their sales in the medium term. Whether they believe that this is best achieved by qualitative or quantitative criteria, or a mixture of both, will vary depending upon the nature of the product etc. The pro- and anti-competitive effects of such distribution strategies will not, however, differ radically depending on which of these criteria is chosen. The following extract from Chard brings this out clearly. The author reviews the Commission's analysis of the terms of SDAs, and is critical of its evaluation on whether those terms have pro- or anti-competitive effects.

J. S. Chard, The Economics of the Application of Article 85 to Selective Distribution Systems[94]

It should be clear from this discussion of the economic effects of qualitative and quantitative selection criteria that the Commission's attempts to distinguish between the criteria is essentially arbitrary and confusing. To be meaningful,

[89] Such as electronic equipment: *AEG*; audiovisual equipment: *Demo-Studio Schmidt*; computers: *IBM Personal Computers* [1984] OJ L118/24, [1984] 2 CMLR 342.

[90] Such as ceramic tableware: *Villeroy & Boch* [1985] OJ L376/15, [1988] 4 CMLR 461; jewellery: *Murat* [1983] OJ L348/20, [1984] 1 CMLR 219.

[91] *Grohe* [1985] OJ L19/17, [1988] 4 CMLR 612.

[92] Whish, n. 4 above, 590–1.

[93] See Case 107/82, n. 88 above; Cases 25 and 26/84, *Ford* v. *Commission* [1985] ECR 2725, [1985] 3 CMLR 528; *Bayo-N-Ox* [1990] OJ L21/71, [1990] 4 CMLR 930; *Yves Saint Laurent* [1990] OJ C320/11, [1991] 4 CMLR 163.

[94] (1982) 7 ELRev. 83, 97, 100–1. See also C. Vajda, 'Selective Distribution in the European Community' (1979) 13 JWTL 409.

qualitative criteria must have a quantitative effect . . . while quantitative criteria may have qualitative implications. With regard to the latter aspect for example, in *Omega*, the Commission recognised that the number of concessionaires needed to be limited otherwise no concessionaire could attain a sufficient turnover to be able to undertake service and guarantee commitments. Thus, qualitative and quantitative criteria should be subject to the same analytical procedure.

[*The author suggests that a proper economic analysis along the following lines is required:*]

First, the Commission should examine whether there is direct evidence of collusion between manufacturers and/or distributors of different brands or whether the restriction embraces so large a fraction of the market . . . as to make cartelisation a plausible motivation for the restriction. If it finds the answer is no . . . there should be a presumption that the restriction has pro-competitive effects. The parties to the agreements in question can be expected to indicate the alleged pro-competitive effects and the Commission should not query these too closely. It should not be tempted to second-guess business judgments as to what arrangements would or would not provide adequate means for achieving the pro-competitive effects and attach conditions to the granting of negative clearance or exemption under Article 85(3), as its record in this respect does not inspire confidence. Secondly, if there is some evidence of restrictions in competition between manufacturers and/or distributors, but the evidence is not conclusive, . . . the Commission should carefully examine whether pro-competitive effects are being achieved, . . . the burden of justification being shifted firmly onto the defendant . . .

What evidence there is seems to cast doubt on the likely importance of anti-competitive effects while pro-competitive effects seem likely to be more common. A more rigorous investigation by the Commission of the competitive effects of selective distribution systems along the lines suggested could, therefore, lead to more distribution arrangements with restrictions on cross supplies, quantitative selection criteria, and restrictions of like effect, resulting in the protection of distributors from competition by other distributors of the same manufacturer's brand, being allowed under EEC rules of competition. If anti-competitive effects are usually absent, then the greater freedom of manufacturers to choose the distribution arrangements which suit them best will tend to result in the most efficient forms of arrangements being used.

The link between the analysis advanced by Chard and the economic thesis advocated by Bork is evident in the preceding extract. It should, however, be noted that the greater leniency shown by the competition authorities to SDAs as opposed to EDAs may be partially explained by the importance which the Community attaches to the attainment of a single European market. EDAs are more likely to divide the Community along national lines than are SDAs and, as seen above, the EC is particularly antagonistic towards such forms of market division. In any event, the extent to which Community law is willing to exclude SDAs from the ambit of Article 85(1) now has to be seen in the light of *Metro (No 2)*:

Case 75/84, Metro-SB-Großmarkte GmbH & Co KG v. Commission (No.2)
[1986] ECR 3021, [1987] 1 CMLR 118

The Commission had renewed an exemption for SABA's selective-distribution system. Metro, the original objector, sought to contest the renewal of the SDA. In the original decision the Court had intimated that its view (that SDAs were compatible with Article 85(1)), might be different if, in a particular area, the existence of a large number of SDAs similar to that operated by SABA eliminated firms such as Metro from this part of the market. In this second case, Metro argued that this had now occurred, and that therefore the exemption for the SABA SDA should not be renewed.

THE ECJ

40. It must be borne in mind that, although the Court has held in previous decisions that 'simple' selective distribution systems are capable of constituting an aspect of competition compatible with Article 85(1), there may nevertheless be a restriction or elimination of competition where the existence of a certain number of such systems does not leave any room for other forms of distribution based on a different type of competition policy or results in a rigidity in price structure which is not counterbalanced by other aspects of competition between other products of the same brand and by the existence of effective competition between different brands.

41. Consequently, the existence of a large number of selective distribution systems for a particular product does not in itself permit the conclusion that competition is restricted or distorted. Nor is the existence of such systems decisive as regards the granting or refusal of exemption under Article 85(3), since the only factor to be taken into consideration in that regard is the effect which such systems actually have on the competitive situation. Therefore the coverage ratio of selective distribution systems for colour television sets, to which Metro refers, cannot in itself be regarded as a factor preventing an exemption from being granted.

42. It follows that an increase in the number of 'simple' selective distribution systems after an exemption has been granted must be taken into consideration, when application for renewal of that exemption is being considered, only in the special situation in which the relevant market was already so rigid and structured that the element of competition inherent in 'simple' systems is not sufficient to maintain workable competition. Metro has not been able to show that a special situation of that kind exists in the present case.

43. As regards the effect on the market of the existence of selective distribution systems other than 'simple' systems, the Commission in renewing the exemption based itself on the relatively small market share covered by the SABA system and on the fact that that system is distinguished from 'simple' systems only by the existence of obligations pertaining to the promotion of sales. By so doing, it did not misdirect itself in exercising its discretion to assess, within the framework of Article 85(3), the economic context in which the SABA system is situated.

The judgment in *Metro (No 2)* clearly builds upon the cautionary remarks uttered in the earlier *Metro* case. The situations in which a market analysis will be required in order to determine whether an SDA is within Article 85(1) are, however, bound to render it more difficult to predict whether a particular SDA will be caught by that Article. Moreover, as Whish has remarked, it would seem that either the creation of one further SDA takes it, but not those already existing, outside Article 85(1), which would be unfair to the 'new' SDA; or the creation of the most recent SDA has the effect of retrospectively bringing the previous SDAs within the ambit of Article 85(1), which would be odd, to say the least.[95]

(d) Franchising

The essence of a franchise agreement differs from that of the other methods of distribution considered thus far.[96] The franchisor will allow the franchisee to use certain intellectual-property rights which belong to the former, such as trade names, logos, and the like. The premises on which the goods are sold are owned by the franchisee, who pays a royalty to the franchisor for the use of the trade name etc. Franchises, therefore, benefit both parties: the franchisor receives a payment for the use of its intellectual-property rights; the franchisee is enabled to start an independent business, but with the assurance that the product and sales methods have been tried and tested elsewhere.

It is of the essence of a franchise that the franchisor will require the franchisee to comply with certain standards and methods of sale for the product in question; failure to meet such standards by any particular franchisee can harm both the franchisor and other franchisees by damaging the reputation of the product and trade name. It is also central to the franchising system that the franchisor be enabled to impose terms which serve to protect the intellectual-property rights which have been assigned to the franchisee. In the seminal *Pronuptia* case the Court held that terms which related to both of the above issues were not caught by Article 85(1) at all, but that other restrictions in the agreement, such as those which could divide the market territorially, would have to seek exemption under Article 85(3).[97] Thus, in *Yves Rocher* the Commission held that a franchise agreement under which the franchisor appointed only one franchisee for a particular area, agreed not to compete with the latter in that area, and forbade franchisees from opening more than one shop resulted in a degree of market-sharing which brought the agreement within Article 85(1).[98] The Commission has produced other decisions which have built upon the judgment of the Court in *Pronuptia*.[99]

There is now a block exemption to cover certain types of franchise agreements. Regulation 4087/88[100] provides a block exemption for distribution and

[95] Whish, n. 4 above, 594.

[96] See generally, V. Korah, *Franchising and the EEC Competition Rules* (ESC Publishing, 1989).

[97] Case 161/84, n. 49 above. The case is set out in the text, above, 910–11. See J. Venit, '*Pronuptia*: Ancillary Restraints or Unholy Alliances' (1986) 11 ELRev. 213.

[98] [1987] OJ L8/49, [1988] 4 CMLR 592, 607.

[99] See e.g. *Computerland* [1987] OJ L222/12, [1989] 4 CMLR 259; *ServiceMaster Ltd* [1988] OJ L332/38, [1989] 4 CMLR 581.

[100] [1988] OJ L359/46.

service franchises; it does not cover those instances where the franchisee produces the goods. The recital to the Regulation recognizes the benefits that franchise agreements can produce. They facilitate the establishment of a uniform distribution network by the franchisor without the need for major investment in the establishment of retail outlets; and they render it easier for firms to enter the retailing market with the aid of the franchisor's expertise, and thereby to increase inter-brand competition.

Article 1(1) establishes the basic exemption for distribution and service franchises, and master franchises are exempted by Article 1(2). The concept of a franchise is addressed in Article 1(3): it connotes a package of industrial or intellectual-property rights relating to trade marks, trade names, shop signs, utility models, designs, copyright, know-how, or patents, to be exploited for the resale of goods or the provision of services.

Article 2 then proceeds to exempt certain clauses which appear in franchise agreements. The franchisor is permitted to undertake not to allow others to exploit the franchise on the franchisee's territory, not to exploit the franchise there itself, and not to supply its goods to third parties. The franchisee is allowed to undertake to exploit the franchise only from the contract premises, not actively to seek customers outside the contract territory, and not to manufacture, sell, or use in the course of the provision of services goods which compete with the franchisor's goods which are the subject matter of the franchise.

Article 3(1) then proceeds to list a number of obligations which are permitted, on the condition that they are necessary either to protect the franchisor's intellectual-property rights or to preserve the reputation of the franchise system. These are imposed on the franchisee and include, *inter alia*, obligations to sell or use goods which meet minimum quality specifications laid down by the franchisor, manufactured by the franchisor or by parties designated by it, where it is impractical, due to the nature of the goods, to apply objective quality criteria; not to engage in business which competes with the franchisor; to offer minimum ranges of goods, keep minimum stocks, and achieve minimum turnover; and to pay the franchisor certain sums for advertising, and itself to undertake advertising subject to approval by the franchisor. Article 3(2) then lists further obligations which may be imposed on the franchisee. These include obligations: to attend training courses, to comply with standards of presentation established by the franchisor, and not to assign the rights under the franchise agreement.

While Articles 2 and 3 stipulate the restrictions which may be imposed, Article 4 establishes certain conditions which must be met if the block exemption is to be used. These include, *inter alia*, that the franchisee must be free to obtain the franchise goods from other franchisees, and that any guarantee for the goods should apply irrespective of which member of the franchise network it was purchased from.

As is normal with block exemptions there is a black list, and this is to be found in Article 5. The Regulation will not apply in certain circumstances, which include: franchise agreements made between rival firms; where the franchisee is precluded from obtaining goods of equivalent quality to those offered by the franchisor, and this is not warranted as a means to protect the franchisor's know-how or reputation; where the franchisee is obliged, without objective justification, to sell goods made by the franchisor or someone designated by him; where the franchisor seeks to fix resale prices; or the franchisor attempts to prevent the franchisee from challenging any intellectual-property rights.

(e) *Exclusive Purchasing*

Exclusive-purchasing agreements (EPAs) are those in which one party agrees to buy all it needs of a particular product from a particular supplier. Common examples include petrol stations which stock only one brand of petrol, and public houses which carry only one general brand of beer.

Whether EPAs are within the ambit of Article 85(1) requires a market analysis: if the agreement, considered in its legal, factual, and economic context, could have the effect of restricting, preventing, or distorting competition then it will be within the ambit of Article 85(1).[101] In deciding whether this is so, the competition authorities will take account of clauses which, although not constituting an obligation as such on the reseller to purchase all its requirements of a particular product from a particular supplier, nonetheless constitute inducements to do so. Offering discounts to the reseller is one obvious form which such indirect inducements can take.

The parties to an EPA can seek exemption either on an individual basis or pursuant to the block exemption which covers this area. The preamble to Regulation 1984/83 expresses the Community's view of such agreements. It recognizes that they can be beneficial by enabling the supplier to plan production and to render distribution more efficient; such agreements also enable the purchaser to ensure a supply of the goods in question, and operate as an inducement to the purchaser of the goods to promote their sales.[102] The Community is also concerned that EPAs can serve to foreclose a section of the market, by making it more difficult for other sellers to find an outlet for their goods. The block exemption excludes certain EPAs from Article 85(1), the majority of these being for the short and medium-term duration. There are special provisions dealing with beer and petrol, principally because in these industries it is common for the supplier of the product to invest heavily in the premises from which the goods are resold.[103] The structure of the Regulation follows closely that which was examined in the context of exclusive distribution.

Article 1 of Regulation 1984/83 provides that Article 85(1) does not apply to bilateral EPAs, under which the reseller agrees with the supplier that it will

[101] Case 23/67, n. 43 above; Case C–234/89, n. 44 above; Case C–393/92, *Municipality of Almelo* v. *NV Energiebedriff Ijsselmij*, 27 Apr. 1994.

[102] [1983] OJ L173/5, paras. 5–6.

[103] *Ibid.*, paras. 13–15.

only purchase certain goods for resale from the supplier or from a connecte undertaking, or from another undertaking which the supplier has entruste with the sale of the goods.

Article 2 of the Regulation then proceeds to specify certain other restric tions which are allowed. Thus, Article 2(1) enables the supplier itself to agre not to distribute the contract goods in the reseller's area and at the reseller' level of distribution;[104] and Article 2(2) sanctions restrictions which preclud the reseller from manufacturing or distributing goods which compete with th contract goods. Article 2(3) then permits a range of obligations being under taken by the reseller, which include the obligation to purchase a complet range of goods, to purchase minimum quantities, and to undertake a variet of sales promotion, such as advertising, customer services, and the like.

Article 3 of the Regulation contains the black list. Article 3(a) and (b) ar the equivalent of Article 3(a) and (b) of Regulation 1983/83, and prevent th exemption from being used between rival manufacturers. Article 3(c) is, how ever, distinctive. It provides that the block exemption will not apply where th exclusive-purchasing obligation is agreed to for more than one type of prod uct, where these are not connected to each other by nature or commercia usage. The objective of this provision is to prevent the reseller from being sub jected to tie-ins and full-line forcing by the supplier. This occurs where th supplier attempts to make the availability of one product dependent on th buyer taking another product or a whole group of products which are no within the same range. Article 3(d) stipulates that the EPA cannot be for ar indefinite duration, or for more than five years. This reflects the Community's concern with foreclosure of outlets to other suppliers.[105] Apart from the special rules which relate to beer and petrol, the remainder of the Regulation follows the pattern of that discussed in the context of exclusive distribution.

9. FURTHER READING[106]

Areeda, P., *Antitrust Law: An Analysis of Antitrust Principles and their Application* (Little Brown, 1989)

Bellamy, C., and Child, G., *Common Market Law of Competition* (4th edn., Sweet & Maxwell, 1994)

Bork, R. H., *The Antitrust Paradox: A Policy at War with Itself* (Basic Books, 1978)

Demsetz, H., *Efficiency, Competition and Policy* (Oxford University Press, 1989)

Frazer, T., *Monopoly, Competition and the Law* (2nd edn, Harvester, 1992);

Goyder, D., *EEC Competition Law* (2nd edn., Clarendon Press, 1992)

[104] If the supplier agreed not to supply to any other reseller then this would amount to an exclusive-distribution agreement, and would have to be dealt with under Reg. 1983/83.

[105] Special rules operate for beer and petrol.

[106] There is a truly voluminous literature on this topic. For this reason the references will be confined to books.

GREEN, N., *Commercial Agreements and Competition Law: Practice and Procedure in UK and EEC* (2nd edn., Graham & Trotman, 1992)

JOLIET, R., *The Rule of Reason in Antitrust Law—American, German and Common Market Laws in Comparative Perspective* (Hague, 1967)

JONES, C., VAN DER WOUDE, M., and LEWIS, X., *EEC Competition Law Handbook* (Sweet & Maxwell, 1992)

KORAH, V., *Know-how Licensing Agreements and the EEC Competition Rules: Regulation 556/89* (ESC Publishing, 1989)

—— *An Introductory Guide to EEC Competiton Law and Practice* (5th edn., ESC Publishing, 1994)

—— and ROTHNIE, W., *Exclusive Distribution and the EEC Competition Rules: Regulations 1983/83 and 1984/83* (2nd edn., Sweet & Maxwell, 1992)

POSNER, R., *Antitrust Law* (Chicago, 1978)

SCHERER F., and ROSS, D., *Industrial Market Structure and Economic Performance* (3rd edn., Houghton Mifflin, 1991)

SULLIVAN, L., *Antitrust* (West, 1977)

WHISH, R., *Competition Law* (3rd edn., Butterworths, 1993)

20

Competiton Law: Article 86

1. INTRODUCTION

In the previous chapter we considered the applicability of Article 85 to horizontal and vertical restraints on competition. In this Chapter we focus attention upon the other principal provision of the Treaty which is concerned with competition policy: Article 86. It reads as follows:

> Any abuse by one or more undertakings of a dominant position within the common market or in a substantial part of it shall be prohibited as incompatible with the common market in so far as it may affect trade between Member States. Such abuse may, in particular, consist in:
>
> (a) directly or indirectly imposing unfair purchase or selling prices or unfair trading conditions
>
> (b) limiting production, markets or technical development to the prejudice of consumers
>
> (c) applying dissimilar conditions to equivalent transactions with other trading parties, thereby placing them at a competitive disadvantage
>
> (d) making the conclusion of contracts subject to acceptance by the other parties of supplementary obligations which, by their nature or according to commercial usage, have no connection with the subject of such contracts.

A number of features of this Article should be noted at the outset.

First, the essence of Article 86 is the control of market power. The paradigm instance for the application of the Article is the single, dominant firm which abuses its market power in one of the ways exemplified above, by, for example charging unfair selling prices. Two things are, however, immediately apparent from the wording of this Article. On the one hand, the text of Article 86 makes it clear that one or more undertakings may be held to have abused a dominant position; the problems which are generated by this language will be examined in due course.[1] On the other hand, it is also readily apparent that the instances of abusive behaviour are themselves only examples. They do not exhaust the definition of abusive conduct.

A second feature to note about Article 86 is that its constituent elements,

[1] See below, 972–5.

such as the existence of a dominant position, demand an economic analysis in order to determine whether they are met in any particular circumstances. Moreover, as will be seen below, the application of the basic economic ideas to the facts of particular cases can itself be controversial.

A third aspect of the Article is less obvious. Article 86 does not prohibit market power or monopoly *per se*. It proscribes the *abuse* of market power. This point warrants brief explanation here, and it is one to which we will return throughout the course of the ensuing analysis. Firms are encouraged to compete, to engage in a market 'race', with the objective, *inter alia*, of ensuring that the most efficient players will emerge successful at the end of the contest. This contest never actually ends, since even those who are winners at any one point in time will have to face the potential of competition from new market entrants. In any event, it would be odd although not logically impossible, to state that those who do emerge as the winners from the race at any one point in time should, *from that fact alone*, face the possibility of legal penalty or proscription. This would have the effect of penalizing the winner, who may have attained a species of market power by dint of being more efficient than the rest of the field. It is for this reason that most systems of competition policy stop short of proscribing market power *per se*. The thrust of this policy is directed at the *behaviour* of the firm with market power, rather than the *existence* of the power in and of itself. This is reflected within Article 86 by the fact that the Treaty speaks of *abuse* of a dominant position being prohibited, as opposed to dominance *per se*.

There is, however, a conundrum the essence of which can be stated as follows. While one can comprehend the distinction stated above, it is more difficult to maintain this in practice than might initially be thought. An example will serve to demonstrate this. Article 86(a) prohibits unfair selling prices by those with a dominant position. This would appear to be a classic form of abusive market behaviour: the firm with market power charges significantly too much. This seems straightforward. It may well be in some instances. The problem is, none the less, not so easily avoided. This is because the behaviour of a rational monopolist will be to market the goods at a price which is higher than that which exists under ordinary competitive conditions. It is part of standard economic doctrine that a monopolist will behave in this manner, and that it will do so because that is the way in which it will maximize its profits. There is then a choice for the competition authorities. They may categorize such behaviour as being in breach of Article 86(a) by denominating the selling price as unfair. This is clearly an option, but the effect of pursuing this line would be, in effect, to prohibit monopoly *per se*. It would be to categorize the standard, economically rational, pricing behaviour of the monopolist as illegal. The alternative would be to interpret the phrase 'unfair selling price' differently, and only to proscribe pricing behaviour which is in some way excessively high, or indeed low, even by the standard of the monopolist or one possessed of market power. Precisely why a firm possessed of this degree of market power would actually wish to price in this manner is another matter.

Now it might be argued in the light of the above that we should indeed prohibit market power *per se*, given that those possessed of such power are likely to price at a level higher than that which appertains in ordinary competitive markets, and given also that they are likely to limit production to a greater extent than that which would operate in ordinary market conditions. While this would, in principle, be possible, the problems with such a strategy must be fully appreciated. Two such problems can be briefly outlined here.

One is that such an approach would entail a very different type of control over market power than that which is commonly exercised by competition authorities. If the ordinary, rational pricing and output policies of the monopolist are to be treated in this manner, then this would necessitate some species of continuing regulatory control over the policies of firms in this position. Regulatory structures of this kind can be established, and do indeed exist for certain industries in the United Kingdom, most notably those operating in the post-privatization spheres such as gas, telecommunications, and electricity. This type of control is, however, different from that exercised by competition authorities.

The other problem with the proscription of market power *per se* is that it might well be undesirable because the firm possessed of such power might have attained this position through superior efficiency and lower costs. One would, therefore, be penalizing the winner of the competitive race even though the victory was achieved through legitimate means.

Difficulties of the kind outlined above will be returned to in the course of the following analysis. This Chapter will be structured as follows. There will be a *general* discussion of the elements which make up Article 86, such as the concepts of dominance and abuse. Within this discussion there will be an investigation of some of the more *particular* abusive modes of behaviour, such as price discrimination and predation, and the problems which attend these concepts.

2. DOMINANT POSITION: THE PRODUCT MARKET

Article 86 requires that the undertaking[2] or undertakings be in a dominant position before the prohibitions on abusive behaviour are applicable. The Article does not provide any formalistic definition[3] of what is to constitute dominance, and therefore the application of this term necessitates an economic analysis. An undertaking cannot be dominant in the abstract.

[2] The definition of an undertaking is the same as in the context of Art. 85, on which see above, 888–9. For a recent example of a body which was not deemed to be an undertaking for the purposes of Art. 86, see Case C–364/92, *SAT Fluggesellschaft mbH* v. *Eurocontrol*, 19 Jan. 1994. The problems of applying Art. 86 to joint dominance are dealt with below, 972–5.

[3] For an example of a formalistic definition see Fair Trading Act 1973, ss. 6–8.

Dominance can only be assessed in relation to three essential variables: the product market, the geographical market, and the temporal factor. The first of these factors will be examined in this section, the second and third in the sections which follow.

Any firm will only have market power in the context of the supply of particular goods or services. The determination of the relevant product market is, therefore, crucial. Other things being equal, the narrower the definition of the product market the easier it is to conclude that an undertaking has the requisite dominance for the purposes of Article 86. It is not, then, surprising to find that many cases under Article 86 have been fought out on this terrain, with the firm contesting that the Commission has adopted a narrow and inaccurate definition of the relevant product.

How should one decide on the scope of the product market? The general approach of the Commission and the Court has been to focus upon *interchangeability*: the extent to which the goods or services under scrutiny are interchangeable with other products.[4] This pushes the question one stage further back. How does one measure interchangeability? This question can be answered, in principle, by looking at both the demand and supply sides of the market.

From the *demand side* the idea of interchangeability requires some investigation of cross-elasticities of the product in question. The basic idea here is simple. Cross-elasticity is high where an increase in the price of one product, for example beef, will lead buyers to switch in significant numbers to lamb or pork. The existence of high cross-elasticity indicates that the products are in reality part of the same market. It may, however, be difficult to obtain reliable data on the relative cross-elasticities of differing products. In these circumstances the Commission and the Court may well look to related factors in order to determine whether the products really are interchangeable. These factors will include the prices of the two products, and their physical characteristics. For example, wines may vary significantly in price and quality. An increase in the price of a top-quality wine may not lead buyers to switch to 'plonk', although it may lead them to buy more of another high-grade wine which has not increased in price to such a degree. The relevance of the physical characteristics of the product is exemplified by the *United Brands* case, in which the Court took into account the taste, seedlessness, and softness of bananas in order to determine whether they constituted a separate market from other fruits.[5]

The degree of interchangeability between products may also be affected by factors on the *supply side*. Even if firms are producing differing products it may be relatively simple for one such firm to adapt its machinery to make the goods produced by a rival. In these circumstances the two products may be

[4] See e.g. Case 27/76, *United Brands Company and United Brands Continentaal BV* v. *Commission* [1978] ECR 207, [1978] 1 CMLR 429.

[5] *Ibid.*

thought to be part of the same market.[6] As will be seen below, adaptability of production lines was a factor taken into account in the *Michelin* case.

The following cases provide a sense of how the Court goes about defining the relevant product market, and the problems that this can entail:

Case 27/76, United Brands Company and United Brands Continentaal BV v. Commission [1978] ECR 207, [1978] 1 CMLR 429

United Brands produced bananas, and was accused of a variety of abusive practices which were said to infringe Article 86. These practices will be examined below. An initial issue concerned the definition of the relevant product market. UB argued that bananas were part of a larger market in fresh fruit, and produced studies designed to show that cross-elasticity between bananas and other fruits was high. The Commission contended that cross-elasticity was in fact low, and that bananas were a distinct market in part because they constituted an important part of the diet of certain sections of consumers, and in part because they had specific qualities which made other fruits unacceptable as substitutes.

THE ECJ

22. For the banana to be regarded as forming a market which is sufficiently differentiated from other fruits it must be possible for it to be singled out by such special features distinguishing it from other fruits that it is only to a limited extent interchangeable with them and is only exposed to their competition in a way that is hardly perceptible.

23. The ripening of bananas takes place the whole year round without any season having to be taken into account.

. . .

27. Since the banana is a fruit which is always available in sufficient quantities the question whether it can be replaced by other fruits must be determined over the whole of the year for the purpose of ascertaining the degree of competition between it and other fresh fruit.

28. The studies of the banana market on the Court's file show that on the latter market there is no significant long term cross-elasticity any more than . . . there is any seasonal substitutability in general between the banana and all the seasonal fruits, as this only exists between the banana and two fruits (peaches and table grapes) in one of the countries (West Germany) of the relevant geographical market.

29. As far as concerns the two fruits available throughout the year (oranges and apples) the first are not interchangeable and in the case of the second there is only a relative degree of substitutability.

30. This small degree of substitutability is accounted for by the specific features of the banana and all the factors which influence consumer choice.

31. The banana has certain characteristics, appearance, taste, softness, seedlessness, easy handling, a constant level of production which enable it to satisfy

[6] This was a factor said to be of relevance in Case 6/72, *Europemballage Corporation and Continental Can Co Inc* v. *Commission* [1973] ECR 215, [1973] CMLR 199.

the constant needs of an important section of the population consisting of the very young, the old and the sick.

32. As far as prices are concerned two FAO studies show that the banana is only affected by the prices—falling prices—of other fruits (and only of peaches and table grapes) during the summer months and mainly in July and then by an amount not exceeding 20 per cent.

. . .

34. It follows from all these considerations that a very large number of consumers having a constant need for bananas are not noticeably or even appreciably enticed away from the consumption of this product by the arrival of fresh fruit on the market and that even the seasonal peak periods only affect it for a limited period of time from the point of view of substitutability.

35. Consequently the banana market is a market which is sufficiently distinct from the other fresh fruit market.

Case 322/81, Nederlandsche Banden-Industrie Michelin NV v. Commission [1983] ECR 3461, [1985] 1 CMLR 282

The Commission brought an action under Article 86 against Michelin based on the practice of awarding discounts on tyre sales which were not related to objective differences in costs. The allegation was, therefore, that the discounts were granted so as to tie purchasers to Michelin. Michelin was held to have a dominant position in the market for new replacement tyres for lorries, buses and similar vehicles. Michelin argued that this definition of the product market was arbitrary and artificial, and that regard should also be had to tyres for cars and vans, and to retreads.

THE ECJ

37. As the Court has repeatedly emphasised . . . for the purposes of investigating the possibly dominant position of an undertaking on a given market, the possibilities of competition must be judged in the context of the market comprising the totality of the products which, with respect to their characteristics, are particularly suitable for satisfying constant needs and are only to a limited extent interchangeable with other products. However, it must be noted that the determination of the relevant market is useful in assessing whether the undertaking concerned is in a position to prevent effective competition from being maintained and behave to an appreciable extent independently of its competitors and customers and consumers. For this purpose, therefore, an examination limited to the objective characteristics only of the relevant products cannot be sufficient: the competitive conditions and the structure of supply and demand must also be taken into consideration.

38. Moreover, it was for that reason that the Commission and Michelin NV agreed that new, original-equipment tyres should not be taken into consideration in the assessment of market shares. Owing to the particular structure of demand for such tyres characterised by direct orders from car manufacturers, competition in this sphere is in fact governed by completely different factors and rules.

39. As far as replacement tyres are concerned, the first point which must be made is that at the user level there is no interchangeability between car and van

tyres on the one hand and heavy-vehicle tyres on the other. Car and van tyres therefore have no influence at all on competition on the market in heavy-vehicle tyres.

40. Furthermore, the structure of demand for each of these groups of products is different. Most buyers of heavy-vehicle tyres are trade users . . . for whom . . . the purchase of replacement tyres represents an item of considerable expenditure . . . On the other hand, for the average buyer of car or van tyres the purchase of tyres is an occasional event . . .

41. The final point which must be made is that there is no elasticity of supply between tyres for heavy vehicles and car tyres owing to significant differences in production techniques and in the plant and tools needed for their manufacture. The fact that time and considerable investment are required in order to modify production plant for the manufacture of light-vehicle tyres instead of heavy-vehicle tyres or *vice versa* means that there is no discernible relationship between the two categories of tyre enabling production to be adapted to demand on the market.

. . .

45. In establishing that Michelin NV has a dominant position the Commission was therefore right to assess its market share with reference to replacement tyres for lorries, buses and similar vehicles and to exclude consideration of car and van tyres.

The nature of the particular product market may indeed be particularly narrow as the next case illustrates:[7]

Case 22/78, Hugin Kassaregister AB and Hugin Cash Registers Limited v. Commission [1979] ECR 1869, [1979] 3 CMLR 345

Hugin was held by the Commission to be in breach of Article 86 by refusing to supply spare parts for its cash registers to Liptons, which competed with Hugin in servicing Hugin's machines. The Commission defined the relevant market as being spare parts for Hugin machines which were needed by independent repairers. Hugin argued that the proper product market was cash registers in general, which was very competitive. The Court found that users of cash registers would require the services of a specialist to service the machines. It continued as follows.

THE ECJ

7. . . . there exists a separate market for Hugin spare parts at another level, namely that of independent undertakings which specialize in the maintenance and repair of cash registers, in the reconditioning of used machines and in the sale of used machines and the renting out of machines. The role of those undertakings on the market is that of businesses which require spare parts for their various activities. They need such parts in order to provide services for cash register users in the form of maintenance and repairs and for the reconditioning of used machines

[7] See also Case 26/75, *General Motors Continental NV* v. *Commission* [1975] ECR 1367, [1976] 1 CMLR 95.

and for re-sale and renting out. Finally, they require spare parts for the maintenance and repair of new or used machines belonging to them which are rented out to their clients. It is, moreover, established that there is a specific demand for Hugin spare parts, since those parts are not interchangeable with spare parts for cash registers of other makes.

8. Consequently the market thus constituted by Hugin spare parts required by independent undertakings must be regarded as the relevant market for the purposes of the application of Article 86 to the facts of the case . . .

9. It is necessary to examine next whether Hugin occupies a dominant position on that market. In this respect Hugin admits that it has a monopoly in new spare parts. For commercial reasons any competing production of spare parts which could be used in Hugin cash registers is not conceivable in practice. Hugin argues nevertheless that another source of supply does exist, namely the purchase and dismantling of used machines. The value of that source is disputed by the parties. Although the file appears to show that the practice of dismantling used machines is current in the cash register sector it cannot be regarded as constituting a sufficient alternative source of supply . . .

10. On the market for its own spare parts, therefore, Hugin is in a position which enables it to determine its conduct without taking account of competing sources of supply. There is therefore nothing to invalidate the conclusion that it occupies, on that market, a dominant position within the meaning of Article 86.

That the definition of the appropriate product market can be contentious is demonstrated by the following comment on the *Hugin* case:

E. Fox, Monopolization and Dominance in the US and the EC: Efficiency, Opportunity and Fairness[8]

In *Hugin Liptons*, the Court of Justice defined the market as spare parts for Hugin machines in view of the demand by independent servicers and renting agents. In doing so it ignored facts that US courts would deem material; namely that the independents could get spare parts for the other cash registers from their producers and that Liptons could be expected to shift its business to the servicing and renting of more cash registers produced by other firms. A healthy market of independents who serviced and rented cash registers (made by other producers) would have remained.

When one asks whether Hugin's termination of Liptons was an effort to monopolize, the misfit of the monopoly framework becomes plain. Hugin was not a dominant cash register firm. It surely could not get a monopoly by charging a supracompetitive price for spare parts, and it would undercut its competitive attractiveness as a supplier of new machines if it developed a reputation for overcharging for repairs. Only two hypotheses seem plausible. Either Hugin was charging a low price for service and was providing rapid reliable service itself or through its authorized distributors, so as to wage more effective competition against its highly aggressive competitors, or Hugin wanted to keep the servicing business for itself and its authorized distributors and they were providing at least as good a price/service package as Liptons.

[8] (1986) 61 Notre Dame LRev. 981, 1003–4.

One further brief example may be given which illustrates the problems which can arise concerning the determination of the relevant product market. In *Commercial Solvents*[9] the applicant companies were said to violate Article 86 by refusing to supply another company, Zoja, with a raw material which the latter then used to make ethambutol, an anti-tuberculosis drug. The applicant companies argued that ethambutol was not itself a product market, but only part of the wider market for anti-tuberculosis drugs; and that therefore it was not possible to establish the existence of a separate market in the raw material used for the making of ethambutol. The Court disagreed and held that it was, in fact possible to distinguish a market in the raw material for the manufacture of a product from the market on which the finished product was itself sold. This was so even if the market for the derivative did not constitute a self-contained market.

3. DOMINANT POSITION: THE GEOGRAPHIC MARKET AND THE TEMPORAL FACTOR

In order to determine whether an undertaking has the requisite dominance for the purposes of Article 86 it is necessary to make some judgement as to the relevant geographic market in which it operates. Some types of goods or services can be supplied without differentiation over a wide area; others may be supplied within a narrower area, because of technical or practical reasons which render wider distribution problematic. Transport costs are a factor of obvious importance in this regard. The *United Brands* case provides insights into this aspect of the Court's thinking:

Case 27/76, United Brands Company and United Brands Continentaal BV v. Commission [1978] ECR 207, [1978] 1 CMLR 429

The facts have been set out above. One of the grounds on which UB challenged the findings of the Commission was that the latter had misconstrued the nature of the geographic market. The Commission had excluded France, Italy, and the United Kingdom from the applicable market, because of particular trading conditions which existed there. The applicants accepted this, but contended that trading conditions were also different in each of the other countries which had been treated by the Commission as the relevant geographic market.

THE ECJ

44. The conditions for the application of Article 86 to an undertaking in a dominant position presuppose the clear delimitation of the substantial part of the

[9] Cases 6 and 7/73, *Istituto Chemioterapico Italiano SpA and Commercial Solvents* v. *Commission* [1974] ECR 223, [1974] 1 CMLR 309. Product-market definition has played a part in other cases such as *Continental Can*, n. 6 above, and Case 85/76, *Hoffmann-La Roche and Co AG* v. *Commission* [1979] ECR 461, [1979] 3 CMLR 211.

Common Market in which it may be able to engage in abuses which hinder effective competition and this is an area where the objective conditions of competition applying to the product in question must be the same for all traders.

45. The Community has not established a common organisation of the agricultural market in bananas.

46. Consequently import arrangements vary considerably from one Member State to another and reflect a specific commercial policy to the States concerned. [*The Court then examined the special arrangements for bananas in France, Italy and the United Kingdom. These arrangements differed in detail, but in general entailed preferential treatment for bananas coming from overseas territories of the three countries, or from the Commonwealth. It continued as follows:*]

51. The effect of the national organisation of these three markets is that the applicant's bananas do not compete on equal terms with the other bananas sold in these States which benefit from a preferential system and the Commission was right to exclude these three national markets from the geographic market under consideration.

52. On the other hand the six other States are markets which are completely free, although the applicable tariff provisions and transport costs are of necessity different but not discriminatory, and in which the conditions of competition are the same for all.

53. From the standpoint of being able to engage in free competition these six States form an area which is sufficiently homogeneous to be considered in its entirety.

In some instances the scope of the geographical market will be relatively straightforward. This was the case in *British Telecommunications*,[10] where the issue was whether BT had abused its dominant position with regard to message-forwarding agencies in the United Kingdom: the geographical market was the United Kingdom, within which BT, at the time, had a monopoly in the provision of telecommunication services. In other instances the scope of the geographical market may be influenced by factors such as transport costs. Thus, in *Napier Brown–British Sugar* the Commission held that in determining whether a United Kingdom company holds a dominant position in the production and sale of sugar the relevant market was Great Britain, since imports were very limited and acted as a complement to British sugar, rather than an alternative.[11]

In the absence of such special factors, then, the relevant geographic market has been held in *Hilti* to be the entire EC.[12]

As stated above, markets may also have a temporal quality or element to them. Thus, a firm may possess market power at a particular time of year, during which competition from other products is low because these other products are only available seasonally. It is equally important to note that the

[10] [1982] OJ L360/36, [1983] 1 CMLR 457. On appeal see Case 41/83, *Italy* v. *Commission* [1985] ECR 873, [1985] 2 CMLR 368.

[11] [1988] OJ L284/41, [1990] 4 CMLR 196.

[12] [1988] OJ L65/19, [1989] 4 CMLR 677, upheld on appeal: Case C–53/92P *Hilti AG* v. *Commission* 2 Mar. 1994.

very definition of the product market will have a temporal dimension to it, in the sense that technological progress and changes in consumer habits will shift boundaries between markets.[13]

4. DOMINANT POSITION: MARKET POWER

Once the Court has defined the relevant product, geographical, and temporal elements of the market, it has then to decide whether the undertaking is dominant within that sphere. Some measurement of the market power possessed by the undertaking is, therefore, necessary. The legal test employed by the Court emerges in the following passage from the *United Brands* case:[14]

> The dominant position referred to in this Article relates to a position of economic strength enjoyed by an undertaking which enables it to prevent effective competition being maintained on the relevant market by giving it the power to behave to an appreciable extent independently of its competitors, customers and ultimately of its consumers.

This test was quoted with approval in *Hoffmann-La Roche*, and the Court then added the following rider:[15]

> Such a position does not preclude some competition, which it does where there is a monopoly or a quasi-monopoly, but enables the undertaking which profits by it, if not to determine, at least to have an appreciable influence on the conditions under which that competition will develop, and in any case to act largely in disregard of it so long as such conduct does not operate to its detriment. A dominant position must also be distinguished from parallel courses of conduct which are peculiar to oligopolies in that in an oligopoly the courses of conduct interact, while in the case of an undertaking occupying the dominant position the conduct of the undertaking which derives profits from that position is to a great extent determined unilaterally. The existence of a dominant position may derive from several factors which, taken separately, are not necessarily determinative but among these factors a highly important one is the existence of very large market shares.

It is apparent from the Court's case law that an undertaking which has a statutory monopoly may be dominant for the purposes of Article 86. The grant of the statutory monopoly confers no immunity from EC competition law, subject to the application of Article 90(2).[16]

[13] *Elopak Italia Srl* v. *Tetra Pak (No 2)* [1992] OJ L72/1, [1992] 4 CMLR 551.
[14] Case 27/76, [1978] ECR 207, [1978] 1 CMLR 429, 487–8.
[15] Case 85/76, n. 9 above, para. 39.
[16] Case 41/83, n. 10 above. See further Ch. 24.

In the more common situation in which there is no statutory monopoly, the Court will consider two types of evidence to determine whether the firm has market power: the market share possessed by the undertaking and the extent to which there are other factors which serve to reinforce its dominance. These will be considered in turn.

The actual size of the *market share* possessed by the undertaking will clearly be central to the determination of whether it has market power in the sense set out above. Precisely what market share will serve to render the undertaking liable to Article 86 proceedings is impossible to state with absolute accuracy. Certain guidelines can, none the less, be articulated. Few firms, other than those which do possess a statutory monopoly, will actually have 100 per cent of the market. Nor is a market share of this size necessary in order for Article 86 to 'bite'. Indeed, undertakings with significantly less of a market share than is commonly understood by the layman's sense of monopoly may be deemed to have a sufficient share of the market for the purposes of Article 86. Thus, in *United Brands* UBC's 40 to 45 per cent of the market was held to be sufficient, although the Court also considered other factors which were indicative of its dominance.[17] On the other hand, in *Hoffmann-La Roche* the Court overturned a Commission finding that the firm was dominant in the market for B3 vitamins, in which it had only 43 per cent, principally because it was not satisfied that there were other factors sustaining the conclusion that the undertaking had dominance in this market.[18] In the *Hoffmann-La Roche* case the Court did, however, also make it clear that, save in exceptional circumstances, the existence of a very large market share, which was held for some time, would in itself be indicative of dominance: it would secure for the undertaking concerned the freedom of action which was the hallmark of a dominant position.[19] And more recently in the *Akzo* case[20] the ECJ has held that a market share of 50 per cent could be said to be very large, and hence indicative of a dominant position.

The question which *other factors serve to indicate dominance* is problematic for the following reasons.

On the one hand, it is clear that, as a matter of principle, the Court should pay attention to factors other than market share in determining dominance, since, even if a firm does possess a relatively large market share this may be fragile because of the possibilities of new entrants on to the market. An essential aspect of the analysis must, therefore, be how far there are *barriers to entry* which render it difficult for other firms to penetrate this market.

On the other hand, considerable controversy surrounds the more particular meaning to be ascribed to the concept of barriers to entry. *For some* it is a broad idea which embraces almost anything which makes it particularly

[17] Case 27/76, n. 14 above.

[18] Case 85/76, n. 9 above.

[19] *Ibid.*, para. 41. Case T–30/89, *Hilti AG* v. *Commission* [1991] ECR II–1439, [1992] 4 CMLR 16, para. 92: a market share of 70% was, in itself, indicative of market dominance.

[20] Case C–62/86, *Akzo Chemie BV* v. *Commission* [1991] ECR I–3359, [1993] 5 CMLR 215, para. 60.

difficult for a new firm to enter the market. This construction of the term places more firms at risk of being defined as dominant for the purposes of Article 86. *For others* the term has, or should have, a much narrower construction. Those who are in this camp are particularly concerned at the possibility that matters will be characterized as barriers to entry when they are merely indicative of the superior efficiency of the incumbent firm. We see here one manifestation of the dilemma articulated in the introduction to the discussion: the difficulty of drawing the boundary between legitimate competitive activity and winning by means which are in some way deemed to be unfair or illegitimate. The following extract from Bork exemplifies this aspect of the argument:

R. Bork, The Antitrust Paradox, A Policy at War with Itself[21]

The concept of barriers to entry is crucial to antitrust debate. Those who advocate extensive and increasing legal intervention in market processes cite the existence of entry barriers as a reason to believe that unassisted market forces very often fail to produce adequate results . . . The ubiquity and potency of the concept are undeniable.

Yet it is demonstrable that barriers of the sort these commentators and jurists believe they see do not exist. They are the ghosts that inhabit antitrust theory. Until the concept of barriers to entry is thoroughly revised, it will remain impossible to make antitrust law more rational or, indeed, to restrain the growth of its powerful irrational elements.

We may begin by asking what a 'barrier to entry' is. There appears to be no precise definition, and in current usage a 'barrier' often seems to be anything that makes the entry of new firms into an industry more difficult. It is at once apparent that an ambiguity lurks in the concept, and it is this ambiguity that causes the trouble. When existing firms are efficient and possess valuable plant, equipment, knowledge, skill, and reputation, potential entrants will find it correspondingly more difficult to enter the industry, since they must acquire those things . . . But these difficulties are natural; they inhere in the nature of the tasks to be performed. There can be no objection to barriers of this sort. Their existence means only that when market power is achieved by means other than efficiency, entry will not dissipate the objectionable power instantaneously, and law may therefore have a role to play. If entry were instantaneous, market forces would break up cartels before a typist in the Antitrust Division could rap out a form complaint . . .

The question for antitrust is whether there exist artificial entry barriers. These must be barriers that are not forms of superior efficiency and which yet prevent the forces of the market—entry or the growth of smaller firms already within the industry—from operating to erode market positions not based on efficiency. Care must be taken to distinguish between forms of efficiency and artificial barriers. Otherwise the law will find itself—indeed, it has found itself—attacking efficiency in the name of market freedom. Joe Bain, whose work has done much to popularize the concept, lists among entry barriers such things as economies of scale,

[21] (Basic Books, 1978), 310–11.

capital requirements, and product differentiation.[22] There may be disagreement about two of these barriers, but it is clear that at least one of them, economies of scale, is a form of efficiency. Uncritical adapters of Bain's work have not sufficiently inquired whether the others may not also be efficiencies.

Before examining some claimed entry barriers to determine whether they are efficiencies or artificial clogs upon competition, it should be noted that . . . an artificial barrier is, of course, an exclusionary practice . . . Every barrier will be either a form of efficiency deliberately created or an instance of deliberate predation. There is no 'intermediate case' of non-efficient and unintended exclusion. Failure to bear that in mind leads to serious policy mistakes.

The Court's actual approach can be gleaned by considering its case law. The *Hoffmann-La Roche*[23] case furnishes a good example of the Court's reasoning. The case was concerned with alleged abusive behaviour by the undertaking in relation to vitamins. Having defined the relevant markets which were in issue, the Court then proceeded to consider whether HLR had dominance in these areas. The market share which it possessed was taken into account, and the ECJ then evaluated the relevance of other factors which might be indicative of market power. The Commission had listed a number of such factors, some of which were rejected by the Court, others of which it accepted. The ECJ rejected, for example, the fact that HLR had retained its market share, since this might have resulted from effective competitive behaviour as from a position which ensured that HLR could behave independently of competitors.[24] The Court also rejected the fact that HLR produced a wider range of vitamins than other undertakings, since the Commission itself had found that each group of the vitamins constituted a separate market.[25] The following factors were, however, deemed to be of relevance:[26]

On the other hand the relationship between the market shares of the undertaking concerned and of its competitors, especially those of the next largest, the technological lead of an undertaking over its competitors, the existence of a highly developed sales network and the absence of potential competition are relevant factors, the first because it enables the competitive strength of the undertaking in question to be assessed, the second and third because they represent in themselves technical and commercial advantages and the fourth because it is the consequence of the existence of obstacles preventing new competitors from having access to the market.

The ECJ has persisted in taking a relatively wide view of barriers to entry, which places more firms in danger of Article 86 proceedings. The following

[22] The reference is to J. Bain, *Barriers to New Competition* (Harvard University Press, 1956), Ch. 1.

[23] Case 85/76, n. 9 above.

[24] *Ibid.*, para. 44. The ECJ did, however, state that if there is a dominant position then its retention may be indicative that abusive behaviour within Art. 86 has been used to maintain this dominance.

[25] *Ibid.*, paras. 45–6.

[26] *Ibid.*, para. 48.

factors have been deemed to be indicative of dominance and market power. It is questionable whether a number of these factors ought to be regarded as barriers to entry in the light of the argument advanced by Bork.

Thus, *economies of scale* have been considered to be relevant in assessing the market power of a particular firm,[27] as has the capital strength of the undertaking and its access to capital markets.[28] However, as seen above, the former is almost certainly indicative of efficiency. As for the latter, many commentators would contend that access to capital is not a barrier to entry, either because the capital markets are efficient, in the sense of accurately reflecting the cost of capital to a particular firm, or because any inefficiency in this regard is best dealt with through the reform of capital markets themselves.

It is equally questionable whether the existence of *vertical integration* should be regarded as a factor indicating dominance.[29] The motivation for a firm to become vertically integrated was considered in the previous chapter,[30] and it was seen that the rational firm would normally only choose to integrate vertically if that was the most efficient method of marketing its product.[31]

It is also doubtful whether *superior technology* should be perceived as a barrier to entry, even though the Court has consistently regarded it in this manner.[32] Any new firm wishing to enter the market should expect to have to expend money on developing technology and know-how, and these costs will not necessarily be any greater than for the incumbent firm. Moreover, the protection afforded to firms by industrial and intellectual-property rights is given precisely as a reward for, and incentive to, inventiveness. Given that this is so, it might be thought to be odd that the presence of superior technology should render a firm more likely to be caught under Article 86.

It might be argued, by way of response, that it is perfectly legitimate for the Court to take account of the preceding factors, since it is only seeking to determine whether the firm has some dominance, not whether it has actually abused that dominance and hence laid itself open to penalties. However, a finding of dominance will lay the firm open to investigation with attendant costs for the company, and these costs may be very significant.

Other factors which the Court has taken into account as indicative of dominance include *legal provisions* within Member States which render it more difficult for new firms to break into the market. This is exemplified by the *Hugin* case, where the Court was influenced in finding dominance in the making of spare parts by the fact that other firms would be wary of doing so lest they be in breach of the Design Copyright Act 1968.[33] Other forms of intellectual or industrial-property rights will also be of relevance in this respect.[34]

[27] Case 27/76, n. 14 above. [28] *Ibid.* [29] *Ibid.* See also Case 85/76, n. 9 above.

[30] See above, 919–21.

[31] It is, moreover, doubtful whether the existence of vertical integration enables the firm with some dominance to achieve any greater monopoly profit than it would do without the vertical integration.

[32] See e.g. *United Brands*, n. 14 above; *Hoffmann-La Roche*, n. 9 above; *Michelin*, n. 35 below.

[33] Case 22/78, [1979] ECR 1869, [1979] 3 CMLR 345.

[34] Case T–30/89, n. 19 above, para. 93: patent and copyright protection were of relevance in securing dominance.

It is also clear that the Court can and will take into account, in determining dominance, the *conduct of the firm* which is alleged to be the actual abusive behaviour, notwithstanding the apparent circularity that this entails. Thus, in the *Michelin* case the Court took account of Michelin's price discrimination, as an indication of its dominance, even though it noted the circularity thereby involved.[35]

It is difficult to regard the Court's decisions in this area as entirely satisfactory. The problem of drawing the line between healthy and legitimate competition and winning by illegitimate means is ever-present. This problem was highlighted at the beginning of the discussion, and picked up again in the quotation from Bork set out above. It is echoed once again by Whish who, commenting on the Court's case law, states:[36]

> The position is delicate because conduct which might in reality be competitive may be condemned as abusive under Article 86 if carried on by a firm wrongly held to be dominant. If this happens, Article 86 could have the paradoxical effect of discouraging firms, fearful of being held to be dominant, from competing on the merits.

5. ABUSE: GENERAL PRINCIPLES

(a) General Problems of Interpretation

An undertaking will only be condemned under Article 86 if it has *abused* its dominant position: dominance *per se* is, as stated at the beginning, no offence. The construction which is accorded to the concept of abuse is, however, particularly important, given that Article 86 has no analogue to Article 85(3). There is, in other words, no form of exemption as such if an undertaking is held to have abused its power.

There are two related, but distinct, problems in deciding what meaning is to be ascribed to this important term.

The first is to decide *who* the Article is intended to protect: is this consumers, competitors, or both? If the answer is 'both', then might there not be certain instances in which the interests of consumers and competitors clash? Behaviour by a dominant undertaking which in some way injures a competitor will not necessarily be injurious to consumers.

The second problematic issue relates to the *kinds* of behaviour which will actually count as abusive. It should be remembered that such behaviour must be distinguished from the pursuit of a normal competitive strategy. It should also be remembered that the assumption is that dominance *per se* is not forbidden. It would, therefore, be odd to conclude that the ordinary, rational pricing and output decisions of the dominant firm were themselves to be

[35] Case 322/81, [1983] ECR 3461, [1985] 1 CMLR 282.

[36] Whish, *Competition Law* (3rd edn., Butterworths, 1993), 268.

classified as abusive. To do so would, in reality, mean that Community law was in fact proscribing those with dominant market power *per se*. Having said this, it is also clear that Article 86 does explicitly prohibit unfair pricing and limits on productive capacity, and that some meaning must, therefore, be ascribed to these terms.

One response to this second problem would be to confine the concept of abuse to practices, such as price discrimination, predation, tying, and the like, which look 'bad' or 'abnormal', even for the firm with dominance. The problem is not so easily resolved since, as will be seen, there is considerable disagreement among economists, both as to whether these activities are in fact harmful, and as to how they are to be measured. The application of Article 86 can, therefore, be particularly controversial, and these problems will be adverted to in the course of the following analysis.

(b) Exploitation and Anti-Competitive Practices

It is common to subdivide the situations to which Article 86 can apply into at least two types: exploitation and anti-competitiveness.[37] The former signifies behaviour which is harmful to consumers. The latter, generally, connotes conduct which is deleterious to competitors, actual or potential. This division should not, however, be treated too rigidly, and in any event the same conduct by the dominant firm may be both exploitative and anti-competitive.

Although it is now clear that Article 86 covers both exploitation and anti-competitive behaviour, this was not so apparent at the inception of the Treaty. Indeed some commentators, such as Joliet, argued strenuously that the Article should be restricted to clear forms of exploitative behaviour which were harmful to consumers in particular, and that there should be some real link between the harm and the market power possessed by the dominant undertaking.[38] In reaching this conclusion Joliet was influenced in part by the wording of Article 86 itself, and in part by the need to avoid what he perceived as a danger in the United States' case law, where the courts had, on occasion, come close to outlawing market power *per se*. This construction of Article 86 was rendered untenable by the ECJ's decision in *Continental Can*, which will be considered in the next section.

6. ABUSE: PARTICULAR EXAMPLES

(a) Abuse and Mergers

Community law relating to mergers will be considered in detail in the next chapter. As will become apparent from that discussion the Community has

[37] See, e.g., Whish, *ibid.*, 271–2; J. Temple Lang, 'Monopolisation and the Definition of Abuse of a Dominant Position under Art. 86 EEC Treaty' (1979) 16 CMLRev. 345.

[38] R. Joliet, *Monopolization and Abuse of a Dominant Position* (Hague, 1970).

waited a long time for a specific regulation concerning mergers. The ECJ made it clear in the *Continental Can* case that some mergers at least would be caught by Article 86 itself. The case is also of more general importance for the interpretation of the meaning of abuse within Article 86:

Case 6/72, Europemballage Corporation and Continental Can Co Inc v. Commission [1973] ECR 215, [1973] CMLR 199

Continental Can (CC) was a United States manufacturer of metal packaging which had a presence in Europe through a German firm (SLW), which it acquired in 1969. In 1970 it sought to purchase, through its subsidiary Europemballage, a controlling interest in a Dutch company, TDV. The Commission found that CC had a dominant position in Europe for certain types of packaging through SLW, and that there had been an abuse of that position by the purchase of TDV. CC argued before the Court that there had been no abuse.

THE ECJ

20. . . . The question is whether the word 'abuse' in Article 86 refers only to practices of undertakings which may directly affect the market and are detrimental to production or sales, to purchasers or consumers, or whether this word refers also to changes in the structure of an undertaking, which lead to competition being seriously disturbed in a substantial part of the Common Market.

21. The distinction between measures which concern the structure of the undertaking and practices which affect the market cannot be decisive, for any structural measure may influence market conditions, if it increases the size and the economic power of the undertaking.

22. In order to answer this question one has to go back to the spirit, general scheme and wording of Article 86, as well as to the system and objectives of the Treaty . . .

23. Article 86 is part of the chapter devoted to the common rules on the Community's policy in the field of competition. This policy is based on Article 3(f) of the Treaty according to which the Community's activity shall include the institution of a system ensuring that competition in the Common Market is not distorted . . .

24. But if Article 3(f) provides for the institution of a system ensuring that competition in the Common Market is not distorted, then it requires *a fortiori* that competition must not be eliminated. This requirement is so essential that without it numerous provisions of the Treaty would be pointless. Moreover, it corresponds to the precept of Article 2 of the Treaty according to which one of the tasks of the Community is 'to promote throughout the Community a harmonious development of economic activities'. Thus the restraints on competition, which the Treaty allows under certain conditions because of the need to harmonise the various objectives of the Treaty, are limited by the requirements of Articles 2 and 3. Going beyond this limit involves the risk that the weakening of competition would conflict with the aims of the Common Market.

25. . . . Articles 85 and 86 seek to achieve the same aim on different levels, *viz.* the maintenance of effective competition within the Common Market. The restraint on competition, which is prohibited if it is the result of behaviour falling

under Article 85, cannot become permissible by the fact that such behaviour succeeds under the influence of a dominant undertaking and results in the merger of the undertakings concerned. In the absence of explicit provisions one cannot assume that the Treaty, which prohibits in Article 85 certain decisions of ordinary associations of undertakings restricting competition without eliminating it, permits in Article 86 that undertakings, after merging into an organic unity, should reach such a dominant position that any serious competition is practically rendered impossible. Such a diverse legal treatment would make a breach in the entire competition law which could jeopardise the proper functioning of the Common Market. If, in order to avoid the prohibitions in Article 85, it sufficed to establish such close connections between the undertakings that they escaped the prohibition of Article 85 without coming within the scope of Article 86, then, in contradiction to the basic principles of the Common Market, the partitioning of a substantial part of the Common Market would be allowed . . .

26. It is in the light of these considerations that the condition imposed by Article 86 is to be interpreted whereby in order to come within the prohibition a dominant position must have been abused. The provision states a certain number of abusive practices which it prohibits. The list merely gives examples, not an exhaustive enumeration of the sort of abuses of a dominant position prohibited by the Treaty. As may further be seen from subparagraphs (c) and (d) of Article 86(2), the provision is not only aimed at practices which may cause damage to the consumer directly, but also at those which are detrimental to them through their impact on an effective competition structure, such as is mentioned in Article 3(f) of the Treaty. Abuse may therefore occur if an undertaking in a dominant position strengthens such position in such a way that the degree of dominance reached substantially fetters competition, i.e. that only undertakings remain in the market whose behaviour depends on the dominant one.

27. Such being the meaning and scope of Article 86 of the EEC Treaty, the question of the link of causality raised by the applicants which in their opinion has to exist between the dominant position and its abuse, is of no consequence, for the strengthening of the position of an undertaking may be an abuse and prohibited under Article 86 of the Treaty, regardless of the means and the procedure by which it is achieved, if it has the effects mentioned above.

The decision in *Continental Can* is of seminal importance for the construction of Article 86, both in terms of the reasoning employed and the result.

The *reasoning* of the ECJ provides a clear example of the teleological approach which has been encountered in other areas of Community law. Reference is made to, and reliance is placed on, the general principles in the Treaty, as a guide to the appropriate construction of the more particular Articles. The competition provisions are read as a whole, and the interpretation accorded to Article 86 is strongly influenced by the desire to avoid any 'gap' in the coverage of this part of the Treaty.

The *result* of the case signals the intent of the ECJ that Article 86 should be held to cover situations where the competitive market structure was placed in jeopardy. Article 86 certainly included classic forms of *behavioural* abuse, which operated directly to the detriment of consumers. It was now clear that it would also embrace *structural* abuse, in the sense of action which would weaken the competitive market structure. It was *Continental Can* which made it apparent that Article 86 would be held to cover anti-competitiveness, where the primary and direct injury was to competitors. This construction of the Article was reinforced by the Court's negation of the need for any real causal link between the dominance and the impugned action. On the facts of the case there did not need to be any proof that it was CC's 'economic muscle' which had forced the merger on a reluctant undertaking. The fact that the merger did in fact result in damage to the competitive market structure sufficed.[39]

The decision in *Continental Can* received a mixed reception when it first appeared, with certain commentators being critical of the reasoning employed as well as the result. The Court has, however, persisted in its approach[40] as the cases in the following sections will demonstrate.

(b) Abuse and Refusal to Supply

The obligation on a firm which occupies a dominant position to supply to other firms which wish to purchase its products is exemplified by the decision in the *Commercial Solvents* case:

Cases 6 and 7/73, Istituto Chemioterapico Italiano SpA and Commercial Solvents v. Commission
[1974] ECR 223, [1974] 1 CMLR 309

Commercial Solvents Corporation (CSC) made raw materials, nitropropane and aminobutanol, which were then used to make ethambutol, a drug for tuberculosis. CSC acquired 51 per cent of an Italian company, Istituto, which bought the raw material from CSC and sold it to another Italian company, Zoja, the latter then using it to manufacture ethambutol-based products. Istituto sought to acquire Zoja, but the negotiations were unsuccessful. Istituto then increased its price to Zoja, and Zoja found an alternative source of supply from other customers of CSC. This alternative source of supply then dried up, principally because CSC instructed those to whom it sold the raw material not to sell it on to firms such as Zoja. CSC then stated that it was no longer going to sell the raw material, but that it would instead integrate vertically down-market, in the sense that it would use the raw material for its own production of the finished product. When Zoja sought to re-order the raw material from CSC the latter refused to supply.

THE ECJ

25. However, an undertaking being in a dominant position as regards the production of raw material and therefore able to control the supply to manufacturers

[39] See generally, P. Vogelenzang, 'Abuse of a Dominant Position in Art. 86: The Problem of Causality and Some Applications' (1976) 13 CMLRev. 61.

[40] In Case C–393/92, *Municipality of Almelo* v. *NV Energiebedrijf Ijsselmij* 27 Apr. 1994, the ECJ held that an exclusive-purchasing obligation constituted an abuse for the purposes of Art. 86, and that this was so without any need to find that the purchasing obligation had been forced on the firms by the dominant undertaking.

of derivatives, cannot, just because it decides to start manufacturing these derivatives (in competition with its former customers) act in such a way as to eliminate their competition which, in the case in question, would amount to eliminating one of the principal manufacturers of ethambutol in the Common Market. Since such conduct is contrary to the objectives expressed in Article 3(f) of the Treaty and set out in greater detail in Article 85 and 86, it follows that an undertaking which has a dominant position in the market in raw materials and which, with the object of reserving such raw material for manufacturing its own derivatives, refuses to supply a customer, which is itself a manufacturer of these derivatives, and therefore risks eliminating all competition on the part of this customer, is abusing its dominant position within the meaning of Article 86. In this context it does not matter that the undertaking ceased to supply in the spring of 1970 because of the cancellation of the purchases by Zoja, because it appears from the applicants' own statement that, when the supplies provided for in the contract had been completed, the sale of aminobutanol would have stopped in any case.

Now this may appear to be a classic case of abusive behaviour: CSC, the dominant firm, teaches Zoja a lesson by making it clear that if the latter seeks an alternative source of supply which later dries up, then Zoja cannot necessarily expect CSC to resume supplies. The case could well have been decided in this way, and this would probably have been justified on the facts. However the reasoning of the Court is phrased in broader terms. It specifically addresses the situation where the refusal to supply is based on a desire by the dominant firm to integrate vertically down into the finished-product market: such a refusal is still deemed an abuse for the purpose of Article 86. Why then is this more controversial?

The reason is similar to that which we encountered when discussing vertical restraints in the context of Article 85.[41] A rational firm will only seek to enter a new phase of the market downstream if it believes that it can produce the finished product more efficiently than the incumbent firms. If it is correct in this calculation then the consumer will benefit by the product being cheaper. If it is wrong then it will suffer accordingly. It may well be true that the effect of this is that existing firms making the finished product will no longer be able to do so, if the dominant firm does not have enough of the raw material for its own needs and those of its rivals.[42]

This type of case then exemplifies the tension mentioned at the beginning of this Chapter as to whether Article 86 is intended to protect consumers or competitors/the competitive market structure. There may, in other words, be situations in which actions by a dominant firm may benefit consumers but be harmful to its competitors. *Commercial Solvents* signals the intent of the Court that, if forced to choose between these, it will opt to protect the latter.

It may be possible to 'square this circle' by arguing that in the medium or long term the consumer will in fact be better off if there are more competitors

[41] See above, 919–21.

[42] On the facts of the case the ECJ was not convinced that CSC could not meet its own needs and those of Zoja: [1974] ECR 223, para. 28.

at the finished-product-market level; and that if the dominant firm really is more efficient than a firm such as Zoja then the latter will not, in any event, survive. This reconciliation is, however, not perfect: the finished-product market may, for example, be of a nature that it can only support one firm.

Notwithstanding the difficulties with the reasoning in *Commercial Solvents* the Commission and the Court have built upon the case, and have condemned refusals to supply existing customers unless there is some objective justification.[43] It has not been easy for dominant firms to satisfy the Court that such justification exists.[44] This is apparent from the decision in *United Brands*:

Case 27/76, United Brands Company and United Brands Continentaal BV v. Commission
[1978] ECR 207, [1978] 1 CMLR 429

One of the allegations of abusive behaviour by UB was that it had refused to supply to Olesen who was a distributor in Denmark. UB argued that it had refused to continue supplying Olesen because the latter, having failed to secure preferential treatment from UB for the Danish market, then started to sell a competitor's product and to neglect the sale of UB's produce.

THE ECJ

182. . . . it is advisable to assert positively from the outset that an undertaking in a dominant position for the purpose of marketing a product—which cashes in on the reputation of a brand name known to and valued by the consumers—cannot stop supplying a long standing customer who abides by regular commercial practice, if the orders placed by that customer are in no way out of the ordinary.

183. Such conduct is inconsistent with the objectives laid down in Article 3(f) of the Treaty, which are set out in greater detail in Article 86, especially in paragraphs (b) and (c), since the refusal to sell would limit markets to the prejudice of consumers and would amount to discrimination which might in the end eliminate a trading party from the relevant market.

[*The Court then reviewed the reasons given by UB for discontinuing supplies to Olesen. It continued as follows:*]

189. Although it is true, as the applicant points out, that the fact that an undertaking is in a dominant position cannot disentitle it from protecting its own commercial interests if they are attacked, and that such an undertaking must be conceded the right to take such reasonable steps as it deems appropriate to

[43] One case where the Court overturned the decision of the Commission was in *BP* which arose out of the OPEC oil crisis in 1973: Case 77/77, *Benzine en Petroleum Handelsmaatschappij BV, British Petroleum Raffinaerij Nederland NV and British Petroleum Maatschappij Nederland BV* v. *Commission* [1978] ECR 1513, [1978] 3 CMLR 1744. The complainant company argued that BP had abused its dominant position by reducing supplies to it during the oil shortage to a greater extent than it had done in relation to other customers. The Commission found in favour of the complainant. This decision was overturned by the ECJ on the ground that the complainant was not a regular customer of BP, but the Court also affirmed that it would be an abuse, even during a time of short supply due to external factors, for a dominant firm to reduce supplies to firms which were in a comparable situation in a way which placed them at a comparative disadvantage.

[44] Case T–65/89, *BPB Industries plc and British Gypsum Ltd* v. *Commission* [1993] ECR II–389, [1993] 5 CMLR 32.

protect its said interests, such behaviour cannot be countenanced if its actual purpose is to strengthen this dominant position and abuse it.

190. Even if the possibility of counter-attack is acceptable that attack must still be proportionate to the threat taking into account the economic strength of the undertakings confronting each other.

191. The sanction consisting of refusal to supply by an undertaking in a dominant position was in excess of what might, if such a situation were to arise, reasonably be contemplated as a sanction for conduct similar to that for which UBC blamed Olesen.

192. In fact UBC could not be unaware of that fact that by acting in this way it would discourage other ripener/distributors from supporting the advertising of other brand names and that the deterrent effect of the sanction imposed upon one of them would make its position of strength on the relevant market that much more effective.

193. Such a course of conduct amounts therefore to a serious interference with the independence of small and medium sized firms in their commercial relations with the undertaking in a dominant position and this independence implies the right to give preference to a competitors' goods.

It is unclear from the case precisely what type of reaction by UB would have been considered to be proportionate and lawful in the light of Olesen's behaviour. Given that refusal to supply was held to be unlawful, what could UB have done in the circumstances?

It is also unclear whether the rules on refusal to supply will apply to new customers as opposed to existing customers. The case law has certainly come close to condemning such refusals. Thus in *Boosey & Hawkes*[45] the Commission found against B & H which had refused to supply brass-band instruments to a customer which had begun manufacturing in competition with it. The fact that a customer of a dominant producer had become associated with a competitor of that manufacturer would not normally entitle the dominant producer to withdraw all supplies immediately or take reprisals against that customer. This was not, said the Commission, a proportionate response. In the *GVL* case[46] the ECJ held that it was an abuse of Article 86 for a national copyright-collecting society to refuse to admit to its membership nationals of other Member States. The fact that the discrimination was based on nationality may, however, explain the Court's approach in this case. In the *BPB* case[47] the CFI held that, in deciding how to allocate supplies in times of shortage, a firm must use an objective criterion; and that favouring loyal customers, even marginally, over others did not meet this test.

What is clear is that Article 86 can apply to a refusal to supply a product which is required by another party to produce a different product, and that this is so even if the second product is in competition with the first and even

[45] [1987] OJ L286/36, [1988] 4 CMLR 67.

[46] Case 7/82, *GVL* v. *Commission* [1983] ECR 483, [1983] 3 CMLR 645.

[47] Case T–65/89, n. 44 above.

if the producer of the first product enjoys an intellectual property right. This is exemplified by the *RTE* case:

Case T-69/89, Radio Telefis Eireann v. Commission [1991] ECR II–485, [1991] 4 CMLR 586[48]

RTE was a statutory authority providing broadcasting services, and it reserved the exclusive right to publish a weekly schedule of TV programmes for its channels in Ireland. An Irish company, Magill, sought to publish a weekly guide which would have information on all the available channels. RTE wished to prevent this, claiming that it infringed its copyright in the weekly schedule for its channels. The Commission found this to be an abuse of Article 86 and RTE challenged this before the CFI. The CFI accepted that the specific subject matter[49] of a copyright would enjoy protection under Community law, and in that sense the exclusive right to reproduce the protected work would not be an abuse for the purposes of Article 86. However, the copyright owner would not be protected if the manner of the exercise of the right was contrary to Article 86. It then continued as follows.

THE CFI

73. In the present case, it must be noted that the applicant, by reserving the exclusive right to publish its weekly television programme listings, was preventing the emergence on the market of a new product, namely a general television magazine likely to compete with its own magazine, the RTE Guide. The applicant was thus using its copyright in the programme listings which it produced in order to secure a monopoly in the derivative market of weekly television guides . . .

Conduct of that type—characterised by preventing the production and marketing of a new product, for which there is potential consumer demand, on the ancillary market of television magazines and thereby excluding all competition from that market solely in order to secure the applicant's monopoly—clearly goes beyond what is necessary to fulfil the essential function of the copyright as permitted in Community law.

Cases such as *RTE* come close to endorsing what has been termed an 'essential facilities doctrine'. This is the 'idea that the owner of a facility which is not replicable by the ordinary process of innovation and investment, and without access to which competition on a market is impossible or seriously impeded, has to share it with a rival'.[50] This idea is apparent in other cases. Thus in *London European Airways/Sabena*[51] the Commission held that an airline's refusal to allow access to its computer reservation system without a tie-in constituted an abuse for the purposes of Article 86. More recently in the *Sealink* case[52] the Commission pursued the same theme. Sealink was the

[48] See also Case T–70/89, *British Broadcasting Corporation and British Broadcasting Corporation Enterprises Ltd* v. *Commission* [1991] ECR II–535, [1991] 4 CMLR 649; Case 238/87, *Volvo AB* v. *Erik Veng (UK) Ltd* [1988] ECR 6211, [1988] 4 CMLR 122.

[49] See below, Ch. 23, for a discussion of this issue.

[50] Whish, n. 36 above, 618.

[51] [1988] OJ L317/47, [1989] 4 CMLR 662.

[52] [1992] 5 CMLR 255.

owner of the port of Holyhead. It also operated a ferry service to Ireland. It was claimed by a rival ferry company that Sealink had organized the sailing schedules from the port in a way which was most inconvenient for the rival company. The Commission held that it was an abuse of Article 86 for the owner of an essential facility to use its power in one market to strengthen its position on another related market, and that this would occur if it granted its competitors access to the related market on terms which were less favourable than those for its own services without any objective justification.[53] There are, however, dangers in the essential facilities doctrine. As Whish states:[54]

> Such an idea has to be treated with the utmost caution because of the dangers inherent in it—what incentive is there to innovate and invest if antitrust law deprives one of the fruits of the effort and expense by forcing one to share? For this reason it is argued that the application of the essential facilities doctrine needs to be seen as a very rare exception to the normal principle that one has a right to keep one's creations to oneself.

(c) Abuse and Price Discrimination

Article 86(c) explicitly prohibits the application of dissimilar trading conditions to equivalent transactions and, as will be seen below, the Court has condemned various forms of price discrimination on a number of occasions. Before examining the Court's case law it is important to understand the rudiments of the economic ideas which underlie this area, since a failure to do so can lead to error and confusion.

The term 'price discrimination' is, in some ways, an unfortunate and tendentious one: the very language suggests that differences in the price at which goods are offered are themselves 'bad'. The matter is not so simple for two connected reasons.

On the one hand, price discrimination only exists where goods are sold or purchased at prices which are not related to differences in costs. Thus, price discrimination can cover the situation in which the same product is sold at different, non-cost-related prices; *and* it can also cover the situation where the goods are sold at the same price, even though there are real cost differences entailed.

On the other hand, it is by no means always self-evident that price discrimination is in fact 'bad' in economic terms; or the cure may turn out to be worse than the disease. This requires a little by way of explanation.

Discrimination can occur in a variety of ways. It may be *geographical*, whereby the undertaking prices at different levels for different local markets, and then seeks to insulate one from the other in order to prevent arbitrage (reselling) between them. It may assume the form of *discounts* or *rebates* which are not related to any differences in costs, but have the objective of tying

[53] [1992] 5 CMLR 255, para. 41. [54] N. 36 above, 618.

customers closer to that producer, with the correlative effect of rendering it more difficult for others to penetrate that market. It might also, in theory at least, appear as *predatory pricing*, whereby the dominant firm seeks to protect its dominance by dropping its prices below a certain level in order to deter a would-be entrant to the market, the idea being that it will then raise them again to reap monopoly profits when it has 'seen the other firm off'.

It is common also to distinguish price discrimination according to the nature of the injured party. *Primary-line injury* refers to harm suffered by a competitor at the same level of the market as the dominant firm. Loyalty rebates and the like provide the classic kind of price discrimination which produces primary-line injury, by making it more difficult for a competitor to break into the market. *Secondary-line injury*, by way of contrast, is concerned with harm to the purchaser of the product. This is exemplified by uniform delivered pricing, whereby goods are sold at the same price irrespective of the fact that, for example, one customer is closer to the factory than the other, and therefore transport costs are different in the two instances.

Having identified the principal species of price discrimination, why then is there any debate about whether it is 'bad', or whether the cure is not worse than the disease? Surely non-cost-related price differences are always to be deplored and outlawed. There are three reasons why this is not so self-evident.

The first reason concerns *measurement* or *assessment*. All species of price discrimination are dependent upon an assessment of the relative costs of production in different instances, and this may not be an easy thing to do. This is particularly problematic in relation to certain kinds of discrimination, such as predatory pricing. If a new firm enters the market then one would expect the existing dominant firm to respond in some manner, for this is the essence of competition. When does this response cross the line between a 'proper' competitive strategy and 'improper' predation? The problem is especially acute in relation to predation, since commentators disagree on whether a court has correctly measured predation in any one case; on what the test for predation should actually be, i.e. on the pricing levels which constitute predation;[55] and upon the empirical likelihood that predation would, in any event, be a rational course of conduct for a dominant firm.[56]

It is this problem which has led some to argue that legal intervention can be ineffective or worse than the disease.[57] Either the court might choose the criterion which a particular commentator believes to be correct, but misapply it to the facts of the instant case; or it might select the criterion which the

[55] See e.g. P. Areeda and D. Turner, 'Predatory Pricing and Related Practices under Section 2 of the Sherman Act: A Comment' (1975) 88 Harv. LRev. 697; F. M. Scherer, 'Predatory Pricing and the Sherman Act: A Comment' (1976) 89 Harv. LRev. 869; O. Williamson, 'Predatory Pricing: A Strategic and Welfare Analysis' (1977) 87 Yale LJ 284; J. Brodley and G. Hay, 'Predatory Pricing: Competing Economic Theories and the Evolution of Legal Standards' (1981) 66 Corn. LRev. 738.

[56] Thus commentators, such as R. Bork, n. 21 above, 144–59, are sceptical whether a dominant firm really could suffer losses in the short term, drive the new entrant out of the market, and then reap monopoly profits.

[57] *Ibid.*

commentator believes to be wrong; or the very existence of the legal rule may have an adverse, dampening effect on competition. The last of these arguments merits brief further comment. The existence of a legal proscription against, for example, predatory pricing can be a weapon in the hands of a firm which is breaking into the market. Let us imagine that the dominant firm responds to this intervention by cutting prices in a manner which it believes is a legitimate competitive response. Let us also imagine that this is, in fact objectively so, and that it is not predation. Notwithstanding this 'objective fact' it is still open to the new entrant to threaten the dominant firm with a legal action, alleging predation. Given the cost of legal proceedings, and given the uncertainties concerning the test which will be applied etc., the dominant firm might still decide to 'go easy' in its competitive response in order to reduce the risk of litigation.[58] In this sense the legal rules could well do more harm than good.

The second reason price discrimination is not self-evidently bad relates to *allocative efficiency*. In terms of general economic theory monopoly is perceived to be bad because the monopolist will restrict output to a greater extent than that which would prevail under more normal competitive conditions, with the consequence that there will be a misallocation of resources within society.[59] The key question is, therefore, whether this misallocation will be greater under a regime which requires the charging of a single price to all customers or under one which permits price discrimination? This depends upon whether the price discrimination would have the effect of further restricting output or whether it might not actually lead to an increase in output. The following extract takes up this theme:

W. Bishop, Price Discrimination under Article 86: Political Economy in the European Court[60]

If a monopolist were able to charge each customer exactly that customer's maximum price, then the monopolist would realise very large profits, but output would be identical to that under perfect competition with not a single sale being sacrificed because of higher price. This is called perfectly discriminating monopoly and is very rare, perhaps non-existent.

Much more important is imperfect price discrimination—different prices in a number of different markets or for different classes of customers. British Rail for example discriminates by offering special discounts to students for no reason other than that most of them would not travel by train otherwise, and a little more revenue is better than none at all when it costs virtually nothing to carry an extra passenger outside peak hours.

In *United Brands* the court condemned imperfect price discrimination when practised on a regional basis so as to divide the common market into a number

[58] This may be particularly the case in legal systems which award the successful litigant treble damages, as is the case in the US.

[59] See any basic work on economics, e.g., G. Stigler, *The Theory of Price* (3rd edn., Macmillan 1966).

[60] (1981) 44 MLR 282, 287–8. See also Bork, n. 21 above, 394–8.

of sub-markets with different, discriminatory prices. However it is not at all clear that imperfect price discrimination generally reduces output below the level that would prevail under simple monopoly. Whether output under imperfectly discriminating monopoly is nearer the perfectly competitive or further from it will depend upon the facts of each case. Unfortunately in any real case the facts are extremely difficult to ferret out—in practice usually impossible to ascertain at all.

Moreover, as several economists have demonstrated, it is conceivable that price discrimination in practice may reduce economic efficiency, *i.e.* increase the misallocation of money and resources, even if it increases output as compared with output in the absence of discrimination. Probably the best we can do is to adopt one general rule on price discrimination. Many economists guess that price discrimination is probably on balance efficient, assuming that there will be monopoly anyway. Certainly there is no reason to believe that a rule prohibiting it will promote more efficient allocation of resources. Furthermore it is clear that enforcing the prohibition will lead both enforcers and defendants to incur costs that consume real social resources.

The third reason rules against price discrimination may be undesirable, or the cure may be worse than the disease, relates to *fairness*. Now this may seem to be intuitively odd, for many might regard price discrimination as unfair. After all why should some pay more for the same product than others? Economists often express agnosticism on this issue, on the basis that it is not for them to express any prescriptive opinion on the *income* and *distributive* effects of certain policies. Some do, however, point out that the argument that price discrimination is unfair is a good deal less self-evident than might normally be thought. Bishop provides a succinct formulation of the counter-argument:

W. Bishop, Price Discrimination under Article 86: Political Economy in the European Court[61]

The rule in *United Brands* requires any monopolist who hitherto has discriminated in price between national submarkets to discontinue this practice. Henceforth such a monopolist must charge the same price (with due allowance for cost differences). Generally speaking discriminating monopolists will find it profitable to charge higher prices in higher income countries . . . than in lower income countries . . . Suppose these firms are now required to charge only one price. Almost certainly the profit maximising price will lie somewhere between the highest and lowest discriminatory prices that such a firm could charge . . . consider the effect on income distribution as between high and low income countries. German consumers of (say) bananas get them at a lower price than before. Also some German consumers who did not buy bananas before do buy them now. All these German consumers are better off. Some British consumers who bought before now drop out of the market because the price is too high. Remaining British consumers pay more. All these British consumers are worse off. So, though efficiency effects in

[61] Bishop, n. 60 above, 288–9, italics in the original.

this example are ambiguous, distributional effects are quite clear: income is redistributed away from Britain and toward Germany. The general effect of *United Brands* is clear—*it redistributes income away from consumers in the poorer regions of Europe and toward consumers in the richer regions.*

Now, an objection to the preceding analysis might be cast in the following form. It might be argued that this analysis ignores the importance of the creation of a *single market*, a factor which, as has been seen in other contexts, is of considerable importance within Community law. It is this which serves both to explain and justify the Court's opposition to forms of market behaviour which entail divisions along national lines. While the hostility of the Community authorities to barriers along national lines is undoubtedly an important factor, it should not be viewed as a self-evident justification for any and every aspect of the ECJ's jurisprudence, quite simply because the argument might not 'really work' in certain instances. We can lose sight of substance by concentrating upon form or labels. The rationale for a single market in economic terms was to create greater efficiency:[62]

> To that end striking down arrangements in which arbitrary national barriers are preserved is a goal of the Community institutions. But that is very different from charging different prices in geographically separated markets, simply because the markets happen to be different countries. It is also very different when the effect of prohibiting the practice is possibly to induce greater misallocation of resources and certainly to redistribute wealth from the poor to the rich. The common European market was set up *as a means to the opposite ends*, so a general appeal to that means cannot justify the decision.

Some of the seminal decisions of the ECJ concerning price discrimination can now be considered:

Case 27/76, United Brands Company and United Brands Continentaal BV v. Commission [1978] ECR 207, [1978] 1 CMLR 429

The general facts of the case were set out above. UB was accused of abusive behaviour for a number of different reasons. The present discussion will focus on price discrimination. UB shipped bananas from Central America to Europe. Some of these bananas bore the brand name 'Chiquita', and these tended to fetch a higher price. UB sold the goods to ripeners, who sold them to wholesalers, who in turn sold to retailers. The bananas were landed at two ports, but there were no real differences in unloading costs. The Commission alleged that UB sold the bananas at different prices in different Member States, and that it did so without objective justification. The essence of UB's response was to contend that the price

[62] Bishop, n. 60 above, 288–9, italics in the original.

differentials reflected market forces, *viz.* the average anticipated market price in each state; that the Community had not established a single banana market; and that, therefore, it was not possible to avoid differences in the individual supply/demand situations in the different countries.

THE ECJ

227. Although the responsibility for establishing the single banana market does not lie with the applicant, it can only endeavour to take 'what the market can bear' provided that it complies with the rules for the regulation and coordination of the market laid down by the Treaty.

228. Once it can be grasped that differences in transport costs, taxation, customs duties, the wages of the labour force, the conditions of marketing, the differences in the parity of the currencies, the density of competition may eventually culminate in different retail selling price levels according to the Member States, then it follows that those differences are factors which UBC only has to take into account to a limited extent since it sells a product which is always the same and at the same place to ripener/distributors who—alone—bear the risks of the consumers' market.

229. The interplay of supply and demand should, owing to its nature, only be applied to each stage where it is really manifest.

230. The mechanisms of the market are adversely affected if the price is calculated by leaving out one stage of the market and taking into account the law of supply and demand as between the vendor and the ultimate consumer and not as between the vendor (UBC) and the purchaser (the ripener/distributor).

231. Thus, by reason of its dominant position UBC . . . was in fact able to impose its selling price on the intermediate purchaser . . .

232. These discriminatory prices, which varied according to the circumstances of the Member States, were just so many obstacles to the free movement of goods and were intensified by the clause forbidding the resale of bananas while still green and by reducing the deliveries of the quantities ordered.

233. A rigid partitioning of national markets was thus created at price levels which were artificially different, placing certain distributor/ripeners at a competitive disadvantage, since compared with what it should have been competition had thereby been distorted.

There is much which is confusing in this extract, which does not represent the Court's most lucid reasoning. This is apparent both from what the Court does and does not say.

In terms of the former, the reasoning which is employed is punctuated by the use of concepts which are mistakenly applied. It is, for example, central to the ECJ's judgment that UB would only have to take account of the many factors which differentiated the various retail markets to a limited extent; and that the risks would instead be borne by the distributors/ripeners.[63] This is highly questionable. It is readily apparent that a manufacturer may well bear the risk of differing demand conditions at the retail level; that, on the facts of the case, UB almost certainly did bear these risks; and that had it wished to

[63] Para. 228.

shift these risks to the distributors, then it would have been necessary for it to have given financial inducements to the latter.[64] The Court's references to the markets in which supply and demand is really manifest are equally problematic.[65]

In terms of what the Court does not say, the judgment omits any consideration of the general issue whether price discrimination can be beneficial.

One of the other major decisions which turned upon price discrimination was the *Hoffmann-La Roche* case:

Case 85/76, Hoffmann-La Roche & Co AG v. Commission [1979] ECR 461, [1979] 3 CMLR 211

The case turned on certain abusive practices which were engaged in by HLR in the markets for vitamins. One aspect of this behaviour was concerned with HLR's practice of giving rebates.

THE ECJ

89. An undertaking which is in a dominant position on a market and ties purchasers—even if it does so at their request—by an obligation or promise on their part to obtain all or most of their requirements exclusively from the said undertaking abuses its dominant position within the meaning of Article 86 of the Treaty, whether the obligation in question is stipulated without further qualification or whether it is undertaken in consideration of the grant of the rebate. The same applies if the said undertaking, without tying the purchasers by a formal obligation, applies, either under the terms of agreements concluded with these purchasers or unilaterally, a system of fidelity rebates, that is to say discounts conditional on the customer's obtaining all or most of its requirements—whether the quantity of its purchases be large or small—from the undertaking in the dominant position.

90. Obligations of this kind . . . are incompatible with the objective of undistorted competition within the Common Market, because . . . they are not based on an economic transaction which justifies this burden or benefit but are designed to deprive the purchaser of or restrict his possible choices of sources of supply and to deny other producers access to the market. The fidelity rebate, unlike quantity rebates exclusively linked with the volume of purchases from the producer concerned, is designed through the grant of a financial advantage to prevent customers from obtaining their supplies from competing producers. Furthermore, the effect of fidelity rebates is to apply dissimilar conditions to equivalent transactions with other trading parties in that two purchasers pay a different price for the same quantity of the same product depending on whether they obtain their supplies exclusively from the undertaking in a dominant position or have several sources of supply. Finally, these practices by an undertaking in a dominant position and especially on an expanding market tend to consolidate this position by means of

[64] The mere fact that a manufacturer possesses some degree of market power does not somehow mean that it is immune to the conditions in particular retail markets, particularly where the *degree* of that power will be directly related to conditions in differing retail markets: see, Bishop, n. 60 above, 285–6.

[65] *Ibid.* 284–5. For a more recent instance of discrimination on geographical lines see *Elopak Italia Srl* v. *Tetra Pak (No 2)*, n. 13 above, para. 154.

a form of competition which is not based on the transaction effected and is therefore distorted.

91. For the purpose of rejecting the finding that there has been an abuse of a dominant position the interpretation suggested by the applicant that an abuse implies that the use of the economic power bestowed by the dominant position is the means whereby the abuse has been brought about cannot be accepted. The concept of abuse is an objective concept relating to the behaviour of an undertaking in a dominant position which is such as to influence the structure of the market where, as a result of the very presence of the undertaking in question, the degree of competition is weakened and which, through recourse to methods different from those which condition normal competition in products or services on the basis of the transactions of commercial operators, has the effect of hindering the maintenance of the degree of competition still existing in the market or the growth of that competition.

The ECJ's antipathy to price discrimination in the form of loyalty rebates emerges clearly in the above extract. The Court, moreover, made it clear that the existence of the 'English clause', whereby a purchaser could buy elsewhere if the goods could be obtained on more favourable terms, did not serve to exonerate HLR, for a number of reasons, *inter alia*, that such a clause could give valuable information to HLR on a competitor's prices.[66] The ECJ also reiterated the point which had been made in the *Continental Can* case: there was no need under Article 86 to prove that the abuse had been brought about by means of the firm's market power. The concept of abuse was 'objective', and could apply to any behaviour which influenced the *structure* of the market and weakened competition.[67]

Later cases demonstrate the continued hostility of the competition authorities to rebate or discount schemes of this kind. Such behaviour was condemned in the tyre market in *Michelin,*[68] and in the market for cartons in *Tetra Pak (No 2)*.[69] It was also condemned in *Eurofix-Bauco* v. *Hilti*. Hilti made fasteners and nail guns for the building industry, and it produced the nails etc. which could be used with the guns. Other firms could make these latter products, but Hilti used a variety of practices (such as tying and discriminatory pricing) which had the objective of preventing customers from buying their nails from other firms.[70]

(d) Abuse and Predatory Pricing

Predatory pricing has already been touched on when discussing price discrimination. It is now time to focus more specifically on this type of abusive behaviour. *Akzo* is the leading case on the point:

66 Case 85/76, n. 9 above, para. 107.

67 *Ibid.*, para. 91.

68 Case 322/81, n. 35 above.

69 *Elopak (No 2)*, n. 13 above, paras. 154, 160–1.

70 [1988] OJ L65/19, [1989] 4 CMLR 677. On appeal, Case T–30/89, n. 19 above.

Case C–62/86, Akzo Chemie BV v. Commission [1991] ECR I–3359, [1993] 5 CMLR 215

Akzo, which was based in Holland, and ECS, a smaller United Kingdom firm, both made organic peroxides. Benzoyl peroxide could be used in both the flour and the plastics markets. ECS was initially engaged in the flour market, but then moved into the plastics market in 1979 and solicited some of Akzo's customers. Akzo had a meeting with ECS at which it threatened that it would take aggressive action on the flour market unless ECS withdrew from the plastics market. ECS ignored the threats, which Akzo then put into operation. Akzo targeted certain of ECS's customers in the flour market, and offered them prices which were below previous rates and below average total cost. Akzo subsidized these low prices by money drawn from the plastics sector. ECS's business fell significantly as a result of this action. The Court quoted the test of abuse from *Hoffmann-La Roche*, which was set out above,[71] and then reasoned as follows.

THE ECJ

70. It follows that Article 86 prohibits a dominant undertaking from eliminating a competitor and thereby strengthening its position by using methods other than those which come within the scope of competition on the basis of quality. From that point of view, however, not all competition by means of price can be regarded as legitimate.

71. Prices below average variable costs (that is to say, those which vary depending on the quantities produced) by means of which a dominant undertaking seeks to eliminate a competitor must be regarded as abusive. A dominant undertaking has no interest in applying such prices except that of eliminating competitors so as to enable it subsequently to raise its prices by taking advantage of its monopolistic position, since each sale generates a loss, namely the total amount of the fixed costs (that is to say, those which remain constant regardless of the quantities produced) and, at least, part of the variable costs relating to the unit produced.

72. Moreover, prices below average total costs, that is to say, fixed costs plus variable costs, but above average variable costs, must be regarded as abusive if they are determined as part of a plan for eliminating a competitor. Such prices can drive from the market undertakings which are perhaps as efficient as the dominant undertaking but which, because of their smaller financial resources, are incapable of withstanding the competition waged against them.

The ECJ found on the facts of the case that Akzo had been in breach of the principles set out above: it had at various times offered customers of ECS prices which were lower than Akzo's own average total or variable costs, and it had done so as part of a deliberate strategy to remove ECS from the plastics market. The behaviour of Akzo was particularly blatant in the circumstances of the case, and also, it must be said, rather ill-advised in business terms. If a firm is intending to drive another out of a sector of the market, then the last thing that a manager of the dominant firm should be doing is

[71] See above, 948.

committing to paper this aggressive strategy, given that the Commission might gain access to such information. Yet this is exactly what a manager of Akzo did in this case.[72] The unequivocally wrongful intent of Akzo should not, however, lead us to underestimate the difficulties which a rule against predatory pricing presents for a system of competition policy. A number of these difficulties were touched on in the discussion of price discrimination, but they should be borne in mind in this specific context.

First, there is the continuing disagreement about what is the proper definition of predation in economic terms.[73]

Secondly, there is the fact that the existence of this ground of challenge may do more harm than good. It may be a potent weapon in the hands of a firm which can use it as a weapon against the incumbent dominant firm. The line between vigorous price competition and illegal predation may be a fine one. A dominant firm may feel that it should not pursue price competition as vigorously as it might otherwise have done, lest this should leave it open to allegations of predatory abuse. Even if these allegations are in the end regarded as unfounded the cost of defending an action may be high and may be a potent disincentive to risking legal proceedings. This is all the more so given that, on the test propounded in *Akzo*, intention becomes of crucial importance where prices are below average total costs but above average variable costs. It may be extremely difficult, in such circumstances, to distinguish between an intent to compete energetically in the market from an intent to eliminate a competitor.

Finally, there are those who continue to doubt whether a rational firm would engage in predation. The potential gains from successful predation appear to be straightforward: the dominant firm lowers its prices, takes a loss in the short term, drives out the smaller firm, and then reaps high monopoly profits in the relevant market. The economic reality is much less certain. In order for predation to be a successful and rational strategy the future flow of profits has to exceed the present losses incurred as a result of the drop in price. This is not theoretically impossible, but it is more difficult to achieve than might initially be thought. Predation is, in this sense, a war of attrition, with the outcome to be determined by the combatants' relative losses and reserves: the 'war will be a *blitzkrieg* only if the predator has greatly disproportionate reserves or is able to inflict very disproportionate losses'.[74] Significant obstacles stand in the way of a successful campaign: the losses during the battle will be higher for the predator than the victim; any anticipated monopoly profits must be discounted at current interest rates; and the predator will have to gauge the likelihood of another competitor entering the market, should it seek to reap excessive monopoly profits having disposed of the original combatant.[75] The prospect that future entrants would be deterred from entry by witnessing the plight of the victim is often accorded undue weight. The greater the monopoly profits now being reaped by the predator, the greater the

[72] [1993] 5 CMLR 215, 223–4. [73] See above, n. 55. [74] Bork, n. 21 above, 147.
[75] *Ibid.* 149–55.

incentive for new entrants. For the predator to seek to engage in another battle to drive out this new entrant would lead it to incur ever more losses in the hope of obtaining the desired monopoly returns once it has the field to itself.

So what then of Akzo on the facts of the above case? Was it behaving rationally in the circumstances? This depends upon the criterion set out above: would its present losses be outweighed by future gains? The answer to this is unclear, but it is not self-evident that the future gains would have compensated for the money lost in the battle. It must, however, be said that while Akzo was inept by consigning its strategy to paper, it was, in one respect, more astute. The losses to the predator from the campaign will be lower if it can price discriminate, by charging higher prices to its traditional customers, while poaching ECS's customers by billing them at a lower price. It appears from the facts of the case that Akzo did in fact do this, though how long this strategy could have been maintained is more debatable.

Notwithstanding the difficulties associated with the detection of predatory pricing the competition authorities continue to base a breach of Article 86 on this ground where they feel that the circumstances warrant such a finding. Thus in *Tetra Pak (No 2)*[76] the Commission held that Tetra Pak, a world leader in the manufacture of cartons for liquid and semi-liquid food, had abused its dominant position by its pricing policy on non-aseptic cartons. The company had a dominant position on the market for aseptic cartons, and the Commission found that it had used profits from this market to subsidize sales on the market for non-aseptic cartons, selling the latter at a loss below average variable cost in seven of the Member States. The Commission looked in detail at the Italian market, finding that the pricing policy was deliberately aimed at eliminating competition: it was 'difficult to conceive how behaviour so opposed to the logic of economic profitability on the part of an extremely efficient multinational company can possibly be the result of a simple management error'.[77]

7. JOINT DOMINANCE

The discussion thus far has proceeded on the assumption that one firm occupies a dominant position on the market. The majority of cases are of this nature. Yet Article 86 speaks of an abuse of a dominant position by *one or more undertakings*. What type of situation does this bring within the ambit of Article 86?

It is clear that it can cover the situation, presented by cases such as *Continental Can* and *Commercial Solvents*, where the dominant position is held by a number of firms which are part of the same corporate group or economic unit.

[76] *Elopak (No 2)*, n. 13 above. [77] *Ibid.*, para. 148.

What has been less clear is whether the phrase goes beyond this to bring within the ambit of Article 86 oligopolistic markets, in which a number of independent firms operate in a parallel manner. The ECJ appeared to have rejected this view in the *Hoffmann-La Roche* case,[78] when it held that unilateral behaviour by a single firm occupying a dominant position had to be distinguished from interactive behaviour by a number of independent firms which made up an oligopoly. It does, however, now appear to be the case, in the light of *Italian Flat Glass*, that some species of oligopolistic behaviour can be caught by Article 86:

Cases T–68, 77–78/89, Re Italian Flat Glass: Società Italiana Vetro v. Commission [1992] 5 CMLR 302[79]

A company, Cobelli, which was a wholesaler of glass, alleged that three producers of flat glass were in breach of the Treaty by maintaining agreed price lists and identical conditions of sale; and that two of these companies had engaged in practices which were designed to achieve full control, not only of the production of glass, but also of its distribution, by excluding from the market independent wholesaler-distributors. The Commission found that there had been a breach of Article 85 by the producers of the flat glass, and also a breach of Article 86. In relation to the latter, it held that the undertakings had a collective dominant position, that they were able to pursue a commercial policy which was independent of ordinary market conditions, and that they presented themselves on the market as a single entity, rather than as individual concerns. The CFI partially annulled the findings with respect to Article 85, holding that the Commission had failed to establish the requisite agreement or concerted practice between the three producers. It then proceeded to consider Article 86.

THE CFI

358. The Court considers that there is no legal or economic reason to suppose that the term 'undertaking' in Article 86 has a different meaning from the one given to it in the context of Article 85. There is nothing, in principle, to prevent two or more independent economic entities from being, on a specific market, united by such economic links that, by virtue of that fact, together they hold a dominant position *vis-à-vis* the other operators on the same market. This could be the case, for example, where two or more undertakings jointly have, through agreements or licences, a technological lead affording them the power to behave to an appreciable extent independently of their competitors, their customers and ultimately of their consumers (*Hoffmann-La Roche*).

. . .

360. However, it should be pointed out that for the purposes of establishing an infringement of Article 86 EEC, it is not sufficient, as the Commission's agent claimed at the hearing, to 'recycle' the facts constituting an infringement of Article 85, deducing from the finding that the parties to an agreement or to an unlawful

78 Case 85/76, n. 9 above, para. 39.

79 M. Schodermeier, 'Collective Dominance Revisited: An Analysis of the EC Commission's New Concepts of Oligopoly Control' [1990] 1 ECLR 28.

> practice jointly hold a substantial share of the market, that by virtue of that fact alone they hold a collective dominant position, and that their unlawful behaviour constitutes an abuse of that collective dominant position. Amongst other considerations, a finding of a dominant position, which is in any case not in itself a matter of reproach, presupposes that the market in question has been defined (Case 6/72, *Continental Can*, Case 322/81, *Michelin*). The Court must therefore examine, first the analysis of the market made in the decision and, secondly, the circumstances relied on in support of the finding of a collective dominant position.

The CFI annulled the Commission's decision on Article 86, on the ground that there were errors in its reasoning both with respect to the definition of the relevant market and because it had not adduced the necessary proof of a collective dominant position. Notwithstanding the reversal of the Commission on the facts, the decision in *Italian Flat Glass* is important in principle for its affirmation of the existence of collective dominance. A number of points should be noted about this concept and its ambit.

First, the CFI based the existence of such collective dominance on the presence of *other* links between the firms, such as technological agreements; it did not state that such dominance could arise solely from the structure of the market, which is how the Commission would like the concept to be interpreted.

Secondly, if the concept is to be of importance it will clearly have to be able to catch conduct of a kind which is not already caught by Article 85. This Article will itself capture concerted practices by oligopolists. For Article 86 to be of use collective dominance will have to embrace non-collusive behaviour, whether this takes the form of parallel pricing, refusal to supply, or discrimination.

Thirdly, some commentators question whether Article 86 should be used to catch collective dominance exercised by oligopolists. Whish is sceptical:[80]

> Theoretical models of oligopoly are insufficiently convincing to warrant a major attack on oligopolistic markets; much seems to depend on how particular markets operate, and many factors contribute to a failure of the competitive process. In the circumstances the Article 86 approach to oligopoly that is premised on the idea of *abuse*, entailing as it does the threat of fines and actions in domestic courts, seems inappropriate. The investigative system of the Fair Trading Act is useful precisely because it does not condemn, but merely confers power to try to improve conditions prospectively. There is a serious lacuna in EEC competition law, but it is not one that is likely to be successfully filled by the introduction of the notion of collective dominance.

The argument the 'other way' would be as follows. The ECJ has made it clear that Article 86 should be applied to protect the structure of the

[80] N. 36 above, 490, italics in the original. See also R. Whish and B. Sufrin, 'Oligopolistic Markets and EC Competition Law' (1992) 12 YBEL 59.

market/competitive process, and that this should be so irrespective of whether a firm has used its economic muscle to attain the end which is now being impugned. There are, as we have seen, difficulties with this approach. However, *given* that this approach has been adopted with respect to behaviour by single firms which possess a dominant position, is it not also the case that the same approach should be adopted when it is behaviour by a group of firms which are collectively dominant which is in question? One possible response would be to say that the oligopolists should not be penalized for pursuing a rational market strategy. Yet the fact that a single-firm monopolist may be acting rationally in economic terms, given its market position, has not been regarded as a reason to exonerate it under Article 86. Another, and more plausible, response would be to contend that oligopolies pose less of a threat to the competitive market structure than do dominant single firms, and that they should therefore be treated differently. This may be so, but it will be interesting to see how far the Commission tries to take the notion of collective dominance, and the reaction of the CFI and the ECJ to these attempts.[81]

The early indications are that the ECJ itself will be supportive of the idea of collective dominance. This is apparent from its decision in the *IJM* case.[82] IJM had a non-exclusive concession, granted by the government, to distribute electricity within a certain area. It supplied electricity to local distributors, mainly in urban areas, as well as supplying rural areas directly. The local distributors were bound by an exclusive-purchasing clause which prevented them from obtaining their supplies from elsewhere. IJM charged the local distributors an equalization supplement, which was designed to offset the difference between the cost of supplying electricity in urban and rural areas. The local distributors contested the legality of this charge, one of the allegations being that it was in breach of Article 86. The case came as a preliminary reference and was heard by the full Court. It held that, while one could not automatically conclude that a body, such as IJM, which held a non-exclusive concession in only one part of one Member State occupied a dominant position for the purposes of Article 86, a different assessment must apply where that undertaking belonged to a group of undertakings which collectively occupied a dominant position. It was for the national court to determine whether there existed between the regional electricity distributors in The Netherlands links which were sufficiently strong for there to be a collective dominant position in a substantial part of the common market. Much will turn on the interpretation of 'sufficiently strong links', but the case demonstrates that the ECJ is certainly willing to employ the idea of collective dominance within Article 86.

[81] See [1992] OJ L134/1, *French West African Shipowners' Committees*, and [1993] OJ L34/20, *Cewal*.

[82] Case C–393/92, n. 40 above.

8. OBJECTIVE JUSTIFICATION AND PROPORTIONALITY

We have already seen that Article 86 has no equivalent to Article 85(3): once caught by Article 86 there is no way of arguing that the behaviour or conduct should be exonerated through an equivalent to the exempting provisions of Article 85. This is explicable in part on the ground that classical monopolistic behaviour was felt to be inexcusable, and that therefore there was no need for any Article 85(3). Two developments have shaken this view.

On the one hand, there is the fact that commentators are now more circumspect than previously about whether conduct such as price discrimination should be regarded as unequivocally bad. On the other hand, the Court has extended Article 86 to cover structural abuse and detriment to the competitive market process in the manner considered above.

It is for these reasons that the Court has developed the concepts of objective justification and proportionality in order to provide some flexibility in what would otherwise be too draconian an application of Article 86. We have seen similar ideas at work in the context of Article 30 and the free movement of goods.[83] With these concepts in play Article 86 can be applied to behaviour such as refusal to supply and price discrimination while legitimate commercial behaviour can be distinguished from that which should properly be caught by the Treaty. Thus if there is an objective justification for the dominant firm's conduct, and it is proportionate, then the firm will escape condemnation under Article 86. Issues relating to objective justification and proportionality have been considered in a number of cases which have been litigated under Article 86.[84]

While the ideas of objective justification and proportionality do, therefore, imbue the application of Article 86 with added flexibility, the application of these concepts to the facts of specific cases is not self-executing. The decision, for example, whether a refusal to supply is objectively justified and proportionate in a particular case will often depend upon and reflect certain assumptions concerning the relative importance of protecting competitors and consumers, or the relative significance of single-market integration and consumer welfare. In this sense concepts such as objective justification merely serve to press the inquiry into the appropriate reach and direction of Community policy in relation to dominant firms one stage further back. They do not in themselves resolve that inquiry.

83 See above, Ch. 14.

84 See, e.g., Case 27/76, n. 14 above; Case T–69/89, n. 44 above; Case T–30/89, n. 19 above; Case 311/84, *Centre Belge d'Etudes du Marché-Télémarketing (CBEM)* v. *CLT SA* [1985] ECR 3261, [1986] 2 CMLR 558.

9. FURTHER READING

(a) Books

BELLAMY, C., and CHILD, G., *Common Market Law of Competition* (4th edn., Sweet & Maxwell, 1993)

DEMSETZ, H., *Efficiency, Competition and Policy* (Oxford University Press, 1989)

FRAZER, T., *Monopoly, Competition and the Law* (2nd edn, Harvester Wheatsheaf, 1992)

GOYDER, D., *EEC Competition Law* (2nd edn., Clarendon Press, 1992)

JOLIET, R., *Monopolisation and Abuse of a Dominant Position: A Comparative Study of American and European Approaches to the Control of Economic Power* (1970, Hague)

WHISH, R., *Competition Law* (3rd edn., Butterworths, 1993)

(b) Articles

BADEN FULLER, C., 'Article 86: EEC Economic Analysis of the Existence of a Dominant Position' (1979) 4 ELRev. 423

FOX, E., 'Monopolisation and Dominance in the United States and the European Community: Efficiency, Opportunity and Fairness' (1986) 61 Notre Dame LRev. 981

GYSELEN, L., and KYRIAZIS, N., 'Article 86 EEC: The Monopoly Power Measurement Issue Revisited' (1986) 11 ELRev. 134

KORAH, V., 'The Concept of a Dominant Position within the Meaning of Article 86' (1980) 17 CMLRev. 395

WHISH, R., and SUFRIN, B., 'Oligopolistic Markets and EC Competition Law' (1992) 12 YBEL 59

21

Competition Law: Mergers

1. INTRODUCTION

Regulation of mergers by Community law has been a long time coming. Indeed the very history of Community involvement in relation to mergers exemplifies a number of the themes which have been apparent in other areas of Community law.

Neither Article 85 nor Article 86 made specific mention of mergers. The Commission attempted to fill this gap as early as 1973 when it proposed a regulation to deal with the subject.[1] Agreement between the Member States was not, however, forthcoming. While the Member States recognized that some species of merger control was necessary, they could not agree on the more specific form which this should take. As has been noted it is often easier to agree on general principles than upon the more detailed configuration which these principles should assume. This was particularly problematic in the context of mergers since the states were divided on central issues such as the boundary line between Community merger control and that exercised at national level. There was also disagreement on the more precise form which Community control should take: what should be the minimum turnover for Community law to bite; should there be a presumption for or against mergers; how far should issues other than competition be taken into account when deciding on the legality of a proposed merger? The failure to resolve these and other issues meant that successive draft merger regulations became part of the established order of things in Community law.[2] The possibility of a 'final' regulation on mergers came to resemble *Waiting for Godot*.

The ECJ did not remain idle during this period. As with other areas in which there has been difficulty in achieving results through the legislative process, so here, too, the Court signalled that it would use its own power in interpreting the Treaty to fill the gap, in part at least. Article 86 was invoked, as we have seen, in the *Continental Can* case[3] to catch mergers by a firm in a dominant position and a competitor which strengthened the market power of the former, irrespective of whether this was achieved through pressure related to the power of the dominant firm. The Court took longer to apply Article 85

[1] Commission Proposal for a Regulation of the Council of Ministers on the Control of Concentrations between Undertakings [1973] OJ C92/1.

[2] See e.g. [1982] OJ C36/3; [1984] OJ C51/8; [1986] OJ C324/5.

[3] Case 6/72, [1973] ECR 215, [1973] CMLR 199.

to mergers. The traditional orthodoxy was that Article 85 did not apply to agreements the purpose of which was the acquisition of ownership.[4] This effectively ruled out the use of Article 85 for merger control. However, this orthodoxy was shaken in 1987 when the Court in the *BAT* case signalled its willingness to consider the application of Article 85 to some instances of share acquisition.[5]

It was in part the uncertainty generated by the *BAT* decision, and in part the need for a comprehensive merger regulation in the light of the impending completion of the Single Market in 1992, that led to the final promulgation in December 1989 of Regulation 4064/89, which became operative in September of the following year.[6] Most mergers will now be dealt with under this Regulation, but, as will be seen below, it may still be possible to use Articles 85 and 86 in certain cases. Before examining the new Regulation in detail it is important to understand the reasons why a legal system will seek to control mergers.

2. THE POLICY REASONS FOR MERGER CONTROL

Mergers can be of three kinds. *Horizontal mergers* are those between companies which make the same products and operate at the same level of the market; *vertical mergers* are those between companies which operate at different distributive levels of the same product market; *conglomerate mergers* are those between firms which have no connection with each other in any product market. Horizontal mergers are, as will be seen, potentially the most damaging to the competitive process.

(a) Arguments against Mergers

What, then, are the arguments *against* mergers? Why do legal systems seek to regulate their incidence? One of the most important reasons is that they can have a *marked impact on competition*. If there is a horizontal merger, then this may significantly reduce competition, especially if the market is already fairly concentrated and the firms which merge are large. A merger of this nature may enable the new entity to set price and output in the same manner as a single-firm monopolist, with the same consequences for consumer welfare. In some countries indices are used to measure the reduction of competition brought about by the merger.[7] The impact of vertical mergers on competition is more

4 Commission Memorandum on the Concentration of Enterprises in the Common Market.

5 Cases 142 and 156/84, *British American Tobacco Co Ltd and R. J. Reynolds Industries Inc* v. *Commission* [1987] ECR 4487, [1988] 4 CMLR 24.

6 [1989] OJ L395/1, [1990] 4 CMLR 286.

7 The best known of these is the Herfindahl-Hirschman Index which is used in the US.

controversial. In essence a vertical merger is merely one form of vertical integration: a company may relate to those downmarket by any one of a number of means, ranging from ordinary contract, through exclusive-distribution arrangements, to complete vertical merger. We have seen that such vertical relationships can be potentially anti-competitive, through, for example, foreclosing of outlets to other manufacturers. But we have also seen that commentators dispute whether such vertical relationships really do harm competition.[8] This same disagreement carries over into the field of vertical merger: such a merger may, for example, improve the distribution of a branded product and hence promote inter-brand competition. There is also disagreement on the impact of conglomerate mergers on competition. Thus, while some see them as dangerous, allowing, for example, a wealthy firm to cross-subsidize from one product to another in order to defeat new entrants, others are sceptical whether such mergers involve any detriment to competition.[9]

Another reason legal systems seek to regulate merger activity is that mergers have been used to strip the *assets of the acquired firm*, and although this may be in the short-term interests of some shareholders, it may not be in the longer-term public interest. Concerns of this nature have been indirectly fuelled by empirical research which indicates that mergers often do not produce the gains which were expected of them.[10]

Regional policy constitutes a third rationale for control of merger activity. A merger may lead to the rationalization of existing plants, with consequential effects on unemployment and regional vitality. A government may choose to use merger policy as one among a number of means whereby a balanced distribution of wealth and job opportunities around the country can be maintained.[11]

(b) Arguments in Favour of Mergers

It would, however, be mistaken to suppose that all mergers are a bad thing. There are a number of ways in which they can have a beneficial impact. The most important of these is the argument based on *economic efficiency*. There are a number of aspects to the efficiency argument which should be differentiated.

One concerns *economies of scale*. It is axiomatic that firms will produce most efficiently when they can maximize economies of scale. These are economies which can be reaped by the firm which is at the optimum size for that type of industry. A certain product may, for example, be made most efficiently with

[8] See above, 919–22. [9] R. Bork, *The Antitrust Paradox* (Basic Books, 1978), Ch. 12.

[10] G. Newbould, *Management and Merger Activity* (Cruthstead, 1970); G. Meeks, *Disappointing Marriage: A Study of the Gains from Mergers* (Cambridge University Press, 1977); A. Hughes, 'Mergers and Economic Performance in the UK: A Survey of the Empirical Evidence 1950–1990' in *European Mergers and Merger Policy*, ed. M. Bishop and J. Kay (Oxford University Press, 1993), Ch. 1.

[11] There may indeed be a conflict between regional policy and competition policy in this respect, particularly where the latter focuses exclusively on the impact of mergers on competition without taking into account other factors.

a particular piece of machinery, but this machinery may require a turnover of a specific amount before it is economically viable. Mergers are one way in which scale economies can be reaped.

Another aspect of the efficiency argument relates to *distributional efficiency*. It may, for example, be more efficient for a manufacturing firm which is seeking to extend its operations downmarket into the distributional sphere to merge with an existing distributor, rather than attempt to learn the skills of this new area from scratch.

There is also a considerable literature on the relationship between mergers and *managerial efficiency*.[12] The argument, in brief, is that the threat of a takeover is a spur for management to perform efficiently. On this view the 'market for corporate control' helps to promote economic efficiency: where the shareholders are satisfied with the performance of management they will not wish to sell to another.

The Merger Regulation, to be discussed below, recognizes the inevitability and desirability of mergers within the Community. Thus the third recital to the Regulation acknowledges that the dismantling of internal frontiers will result in major corporate reorganization; while the fourth recital states that this is to be welcomed as one means of increasing the competitiveness of European industry on world markets. The approach of the Merger Regulation itself can now be considered.

3. REGULATION 4064/89: PROCEDURAL ISSUES

The Merger Regulation is administered by a Mergers Task Force (MTF) within DG IV. Appeals from its decisions are heard by the CFI.

In order for merger control to be effective it is obviously necessary for the Commission to be informed about any such acquisition. This is covered by Article 4(1), which deals with *pre-notification*. It provides that concentrations which have a Community dimension must be notified not more than one week after the conclusion of the agreement, or the announcement of the public bid, or the acquisition of the controlling interest. Article 4(3) imposes an obligation on the MTF to publish those notifications which it considers to fall within the ambit of the Regulation. Failure to comply with the duty to pre-notify can lead to fines under Article 14(1)(a). The MTF has devised a standard form which is to be used for the notification, and this is known as Form CO.[13] This form requires the parties to submit certain information to the Commission, including copies of the documentation bringing about the concentration, copies of the accounts of the parties involved, and copies of any reports which have been prepared for the purposes of the concentration.

[12] See e.g. F. Easterbrook and D. Fischel, 'The Proper Role of a Target's Management in Responding to a Tender Offer' (1991) 94 HarvLRev. 1161.

[13] Reg. 2367/90, [1990] OJ L219/5, Art. 2.

The effectiveness of merger control also demands that a proposed concentration shall not be completed pending investigation by the Commission. This is dealt with by Article 7(1) which provides for the *suspension* of concentrations before notification and for a period of three weeks thereafter. Article 14(2) allows the Commission to impose heavy fines for breach of this obligation. The suspensive effect of notification is, however, qualified by Article 7(3) and (4). Article 7(4) allows the Commission to derogate from Article 7(1) where this is necessary to prevent serious damage to one of the parties or to a third party; the derogation may be made subject to conditions.[14]

Once the concentration has been notified the MTF can then begin its investigation. This investigation is, in effect, conducted in two stages.

At the first stage the MTF can decide pursuant to Article 6(1) that the concentration is outside the Regulation; that it is within the scope of the Regulation but is not incompatible with the common market and therefore should not be opposed; or that it is within the scope of the Regulation, that there are serious doubts about its compatibility with the common market, and that therefore proceedings should be initiated. Decisions under Article 6(1) must normally be made within one month of the date of notification.[15]

At the second stage, the Commission will proceed with investigation of those concentrations which do raise serious doubts about their compatibility with the common market. There are a number of options open to the Commission which are listed in Article 8. It can decide that the concentration is not in fact in breach of the substantive criteria, to be considered below, by which Community mergers are to be judged. Modifications may be required to the original concentration plans before the Commission decides that this is so.[16] It may determine that the merger is incompatible with the common market, because it does create or strengthen a dominant position as a result of which competition will be significantly impeded.[17] Or it may demand the reversal of a merger which has already occurred.[18] Article 10 stipulates the time limits within which such decisions must be made, the basic rule being that this must be within four months of the initiation of the proceedings.[19] If the MTF fails to comply with the time limits then the merger will be deemed to be compatible with the common market.[20] Before any decision is made under Article 8 (or Articles 14 and 15), the Commission must consult the Advisory

[14] See e.g. Case IV/M42, *Kelt/American Express* [1991] 4 CMLR 740.

[15] Reg. 4064/89, Art. 10(1); Reg. 2367/90, Arts. 6–8.

[16] Art. 8(2). Examples of clearance given to mergers subject to conditions can be found in Case IV/M18, *Alcatel/Telettra* [1991] OJ L122/48, [1991] 4 CMLR 778; Case IV/M190, *Nestlé/Perrier* [1992] OJ L356/1, [1993] 4 CMLR M17. A decision finding that the concentration is compatible with the Common Market may also cover restrictions which are directly related and necessary to the implementation of the concentration: Art. 8(2), on which see Commission *Notice on Ancillary Restraints* [1990] OJ C203/5.

[17] Art. 8(3).

[18] Art. 8(4).

[19] This period may be extended where the MTF has to obtain additional information owing to circumstances for which one of the parties is responsible, Art. 10(4). See also Reg. 2367/90, Arts. 9 and 10.

[20] Art. 10(6), subject to Art. 9.

Committee on Concentrations. This Committee consists of one or two representatives from the Member States, and the meetings are chaired by the Commission.[21]

As is common in the case of Community competition policy the Commission is given broad powers to facilitate *investigation* and *enforcement*. Thus Article 11 enables it to request information, Article 13 gives the Commission power to conduct on-site investigations, while Article 14 contains a power to impose fines which can be considerable. A fine of up to 10 per cent of the aggregate turnover of the undertakings concerned may, for example, be imposed where the parties have proceeded with a concentration which has been declared to be incompatible with the common market pursuant to a decision made under Article 8(3).[22]

4. REGULATION 4064/89: SUBSTANTIVE ISSUES

(a) Concentration: General

The Regulation will only be applicable if there is a concentration. This important issue is dealt with in Article 3(1):

> A concentration shall be deemed to arise where:
> (a) two or more previously independent undertakings merge, or
> (b) —one or more persons already controlling at least one undertaking, or
> —one or more undertakings, acquire, whether by purchase of securities or assets, by contract or by any other means, direct or indirect control of the whole or parts of one or more undertakings.

Article 3(1) must be read in conjunction with Article 3(3) which provides:

> For the purposes of this regulation, control shall be constituted by rights, contracts or any other means which, either separately or in combination and having regard to the considerations of fact or law involved, confer the possibility of exercising decisive influence on an undertaking, in particular by:
> (a) ownership of the right to use all or part of the assets of an undertaking;
> (b) rights or contracts which confer decisive influence on the composition, voting or decisions of the organs of an undertaking.

It is clear that a combination of Article 3(1) and (3) will bring a number of different situations within the ambit of the Regulation.

Article 3(1)(a) covers the case of a *complete merger*. Although the

[21] Art. 19. [22] Art. 14(2)(c).

Regulation does not define the term merger, it implies the formation of one enterprise from undertakings which were previously distinct and separate.

Article 3(1)(b) captures cases of *change of control*. This is a complex topic detailed treatment of which can be found elsewhere.[23] The essence of this Article can, however, be conveyed as follows. A change of control can result in the acquisition of *sole control* by a person or an undertaking, as in the case of *Arjomari-Prioux/Wiggins Teape*[24] where the Commission held that the acquisition of a 39 per cent shareholding in a company was sufficient to give a buyer control, given that the remaining shares were widely dispersed. It is also possible for two or more undertakings to acquire *joint control* over another. All the circumstances will be taken into account in deciding whether joint control exists in any particular case. Thus in *Northern Telecom/Matra Telecommunications*[25] both companies were held to have acquired joint control over Matra SA on the ground that the consent of both parents was necessary for all important business decisions and financial plans. Cases concerning joint control raise difficult questions of how far the Regulation captures joint ventures. It is to this issue that we should now turn.

(b) Concentration: Joint Ventures

Joint ventures are created for many purposes: the term is not one of art and covers a wide range of business arrangements, from the establishment of a new corporate entity by two competitors to a joint-purchasing scheme or joint research and development. It is this very breadth of coverage of joint ventures which causes problems for competition systems. Should they be treated by analogy with cartels, and be regarded as essentially a 'behavioural' problem to be dealt with under Article 85?[26] Should they be treated as involving a 'structural' problem and be dealt with under the Merger Regulation? As will be seen, the approach of Community law is to treat some joint ventures under Article 85, while others are considered under the Merger Regulation. However, as will also become apparent, some commentators believe that this form of differentiation is unworkable. The matter is specifically addressed in Article 3(2) of the Regulation:

> An operation, including the creation of a joint venture, which has as its object or effect the coordination of the competitive behaviour of undertakings which remain independent shall not constitute a concentration within the meaning of paragraph (1)(b).
>
> The creation of a joint venture performing on a lasting basis all the functions of an autonomous economic entity, which does not give rise to coordination of

[23] J. Cook and C. Kerse, *EEC Merger Control—Regulation 4064/89* (Sweet & Maxwell, 1991), Ch. 2; T. Anthony Downes and J. Ellison, *The Legal Control of Mergers in the European Communities* (Blackstone, 1991), Ch. 2.

[24] Case IV/M25, [1991] 4 CMLR 854.

[25] Case IV/M249.

[26] For discussion of joint ventures under Art. 85, see Whish, *Competition Law* (3rd edn., Butterworths, 1993), 430–7.

> the competitive behaviour of the parties amongst themselves or between them and the joint venture, shall constitute a concentration within the meaning of paragraph (1)(b).

Guidance on the interpretation of this provision is to be found in the Commission Notice on *Concentrative and Co-operative Joint Ventures*[27]. The notice is not binding as such, but it does provide a useful indication of the Commission's thinking on this issue. It is clear from the notice that a joint venture implies joint control, and that this will be absent if one of the parties can decide for itself on the joint venture's activities.[28] Paragraph 15 of the Notice then states that there is both a positive and a negative condition to be satisfied if a joint venture is to be treated as concentrative, and therefore within the remit of the Regulation.

The *positive condition* is that the joint venture must perform on a lasting basis all the functions of an autonomous economic entity. It must act as an independent supplier and buyer on the market, and it will only be regarded as existing on a lasting basis if it is intended to carry on its activity for an unlimited, or at least for a long, time.[29] It must, moreover, be in a position to exercise its own commercial policy independently and in accord with its own economic interests.[30]

The *negative condition* is that the joint venture will only be considered to be concentrative if it does not have as its object or effect the co-ordination of the competitive behaviour of undertakings which do remain independent of each other. There must not be such co-ordination either between the parent companies themselves or between any or all of them on the one hand and the joint venture on the other.[31] There will not normally be any such co-ordination if the parent companies withdraw entirely and permanently from the joint venture's market.[32] The Notice then proceeds to consider in more detail the likelihood of co-ordination of competitive behaviour in a number of more specific situations: where the joint venture takes over pre-existing activities of the parent companies; where it undertakes new activities on behalf of the parent companies; where the joint venture enters the parent companies' markets; and where it enters upstream, downstream, or neighbouring markets.[33]

It is none the less difficult to distinguish those joint ventures which will be treated as concentrations from those which will not. This is indeed recognized by the Commission Notice, which states that the 'dividing line between the concordance of interests in a joint venture and a coordination of competitive behaviour that is incompatible with the notion of concentration cannot be laid down for all conceivable kinds of case'.[34] The decisive factor will always be

27 [1990] OJ C203/10.
28 *Ibid.*, paras. 11–14.
29 *Ibid.*, paras. 16–17.
30 *Ibid.*, para. 18.
31 *Ibid.*, para. 20. The MTF does, however, appear to have deviated from this position: Whish, n. 26 above, 712.
32 N. 27 above, at para. 20.
33 *Ibid.*, paras. 24–36.
34 *Ibid.*, para. 23.

the economic impact of the relationship rather than the legal form through which this is expressed.

The difficulties of distinguishing between different types of joint ventures have been exacerbated by the fact that the MTF does not appear to accept all aspects of the Commission notice. As Hawk has stated, 'biblical exegesis of the guidelines is not helpful in predicting the Commission's reaction to a notified transaction'.[35] Moreover, the Commission itself appears to have subtly modified the dividing line between co-operative and concentrative joint ventures.[36]

The following case provides an example of a joint venture which was held to be co-operative rather than concentrative:[37]

Case IV/M93, Re the Joint Venture between Brau und Brunnen AG and Cadbury Schweppes plc
[1992] 4 CMLR M78[38]

Brau and Brunnen (B & B) and Cadbury Schweppes (CS) established a joint venture to make and sell mineral water in Germany and Austria and other European markets. Relevant trade marks were transferred to the joint venture. However, B & B retained its business in relation to regional mineral water and soft drinks which were sold under different trade marks; CS transferred its whole German and Austrian business to the joint venture, but retained its beverage business elsewhere.

THE COMMISSION

7. The parties' agreement to establish a joint venture for the production and marketing of non-alcoholic beverages under the Appollinaris and Schweppes trade marks will have the effect of coordinating the competitive behaviour of undertakings which remain independent.

8. It has already been pointed out that both parties will only partially transfer their non-alcoholic beverages to the joint venture. B & B will continue its activities with regard to regional mineral water and soft drinks. Likewise CS will only partially transfer the soft drinks business to the joint venture. It will remain in the same product market as the joint venture, selling those products independently in the remainder of the Community.

CS will in any event remain a competitor of B & B, although the company will transfer its present German and Austrian businesses to the joint venture. CS will in view of the nature of the products concerned have the realistic option to re-enter the German market. This is especially true for the mineral water market. Production substitutability is, for non-alcoholic beverages, in particular for

[35] B. Hawk, 'Joint Ventures under EC Law' in *Fordham Corporate Law Institute*, ed. B. Hawk (1991), Ch. 23, 571. See also W. Sibree, 'EEC Merger Control and Joint Ventures' (1992) 17 ELRev. 91.

[36] B. Hawk and H. Huser, 'A Bright Line Shareholding Test to End the Nightmare under the EEC Merger Regulation' (1993) 30 CMLRev. 1155, 1167–73.

[37] If a joint venture is held to fall outside the Merger Reg. then, under Art. 5 of Reg. 2367/90, it will be treated as an application for individual exemption under Art. 85(3).

[38] See also Case IV/M88, *Enterprise Oil plc/Société Nationale Elf Acquitaine* [1992] 5 CMLR M66.

mineral waters and soft drinks, extremely high. CS disposes of production capacities, the commercial know-how and financial means to market a mineral water. It is already selling mineral water in the U.K. market . . . Since the German mineral water market is growing, entering the German market represents for CS a commercially reasonable course in the light of all objective circumstances.

9. For the above reasons, and in particular in view of the only partial withdrawal of the parent companies which is likely to lead to a division of markets, the Commission has concluded that the notified operation does not constitute a concentration within the meaning of Article 3 of the Merger Regulation and consequently does not fall within the scope of application of that Regulation.

The decision in the preceding case can be contrasted with that which follows, in which the Commission held that a joint venture was a concentration for the purposes of the Merger Regulation:

Case IV/M72, Re the Concentration between Sanofi and Sterling Drug Inc [1992] 5 CMLR M1

Sanofi (S) and Sterling Drug (SD) are pharmaceutical companies which entered into a series of joint ventures in order to combine worldwide their prescription drug (ethical) activities, and also their European over-the-counter (OTC) activities. The Commission found that the joint ventures were concentrative for the following reasons, but cleared the merger because there was no dominance on the relevant markets.

THE COMMISSION

7. The proposed transaction is a concentration within the meaning of Article 3 of Regulation 4064/89. In arriving at this conclusion the Commission has taken into account the following elements:

—the parties merge, transfer or otherwise lease or license on a permanent basis to operating entities established by the parties their existing production, distribution and marketing assets. All material contracts, government permits and licences . . . will be licensed, transferred or assigned. Employees will be transferred to the operating entities.

—product ranges will be marketed under common trade names . . .

—with regard to research and development, which is of crucial importance for the ethical business, the parties will continue to carry out their research activities . . . independently. However, they agree to enable each other to participate in the development of future products right from the initial stages of such development . . .

To this effect a Development Committee is established, in which both parties are equally represented, which will monitor and coordinate all research efforts and which will decide whether or not development should be pursued jointly.

In the event that the committee decides against joint development the parties may not continue development individually, and instead may only assign or license such rights to third parties. With regard to the OTC business, the parties have the choice of carrying out research and development within the 'Alliance' or availing themselves of Sterling Drug's facilities outside the territory:

—new acquisitions will be carried out jointly by the parties,
—the new management structure will be fully integrated. Each venture provides for a management entity, which includes a strategic management committee responsible for all strategic management decisions . . .

. . .

8. The Commission considers that these elements taken together bring about a lasting change in the structure of the undertakings concerned. The operation implies their effective withdrawal from the markets concerned, as they place all their interests in the various joint ventures.

9. This situation leaves no room for co-ordination of conduct as between the parents amongst themselves, or between them and the joint ventures.

Some commentators have been critical of the concentrative–co-operative distinction, as the following extract indicates:

B. Hawk, Joint Ventures under EEC Law[39]

The concentrative–cooperative distinction serves a mainly jurisdictional function. It assigns a particular joint venture to different substantive and procedural systems. As a jurisdictional rule, the distinction is woefully inadequate. Jurisdictional rules must provide quick and predictable outcomes. In this respect the cooperative–concentrative distinction remains deeply flawed, despite the pragmatic efforts of the Commission to make sense of it. As this author and others predicted, the concentrative–cooperative distinction has increased legal uncertainty and transaction costs. To speak frankly, a ridiculous amount of Commission, counsel and business time is devoted to a jurisdictional issue that should be easily determinable . . .

The Commission continues its valiant but largely Sisyphean effort to make sense of the concentrative–cooperative joint venture distinction. The distinction is theoretically flawed. It exaggerates both the importance and the clarity of the economics distinction between structure and behaviour, it does not support an either/or legal distinction that results in either the application of a structural merger control test or behavioural cartel test . . .

If war is too important to be left to the generals, then the allocation of jurisdiction over joint ventures is too important to be left to the theorists. Very important practical consequences flow from the concentrative–cooperative distinction. To oversimplify somewhat, as a joint venture leaves the high-tech deadline driven world of the merger task force, one moves to the more leisurely, scarce resources of the operating divisions of DG IV. The solution is not to continue to engage in the metaphysics of refining and re-refining the cooperative–concentrative distinction. The best solution is to provide a unified analysis of joint ventures that include both behavioural and structural considerations. If this cannot be done under the existing legislation, which appears to be the case, then the second best solution is to eliminate administrative and procedural differences to the extent possible between an examination of an arrangement under the Merger Regulation and a joint venture under Article 85.

[39] N. 35 above, 575–6.

The same author has called for the replacement of the existing complex criteria by a simpler, bright-line test which would have the effect of bringing shareholdings of 25 per cent and above within the ambit of the Regulation.[40]

(c) Concentrations which have a 'Community Dimension'

In order for a concentration to be caught by the Merger Regulation it must have a Community dimension. This is defined by Article 1(2) of the Regulation:

> For the purposes of this Regulation, a concentration has a Community dimension where:
>
> (a) the combined aggregate worldwide turnover of all the undertakings concerned is more than ECU 5,000 million, and
>
> (b) the aggregate Community-wide turnover of each of at least two of the undertakings concerned is more than ECU 250 million,
>
> unless each of the undertakings concerned achieves more than two-thirds of its aggregate Community-wide turnover within one and the same Member State.

Turnover is calculated in accordance with Article 5 of the Regulation. It should be noted that the test encapsulated in Article 1(2) is purely quantitative: it does not in itself indicate that a merger will be regarded as contrary to the Regulation. The substantive criterion is contained within Article 2, which will be considered in the next section. It should also be noted that the definition in Article 1(2) can bring many non-EC undertakings within the ambit of the Regulation, provided that two of the relevant undertakings have an aggregate Community turnover of 250 million ECU.[41]

(d) Concentrations: The Substantive Criteria

The test for determining whether a merger is compatible with the Common Market is to be found in Article 2 of the Regulation:

> 1. Concentrations within the scope of this Regulation shall be appraised in accordance with the following provisions with a view to establishing whether or not they are compatible with the common market.
>
> In making this appraisal, the Commission shall take into account:
>
> (a) the need to maintain and develop effective competition within the common market in view of, among other things, the structure of all of the markets concerned and the actual or potential competition from undertakings located either within or outwith the Community;

[40] B. Hawk and H. Huser, n. 36 above.

[41] See e.g. Case IV/M24, *Mitsubishi Corporation/Union Carbide Corporation* [1992] 4 CMLR M50; Case IV/M69, *Kyowa Bank Limited/Saitama Bank Limited* [1992] 4 CMLR M105.

(b) the market position of the undertakings concerned and their economic and financial power, the alternatives available to suppliers and users, their access to supplies or markets, any legal or other barriers to entry, supply and demand trends for the relevant goods and services, the interests of the intermediate and ultimate consumers, and the development of technical and economic progress provided that it is to consumers' advantage and does not form an obstacle to competition.

2. A concentration which does not create or strengthen a dominant position as a result of which effective competition would be significantly impeded in the common market or in a substantial part of it shall be declared compatible with the common market.

3. A concentration which creates or strengthens a dominant position as a result of which effective competition would be significantly impeded in the common market or in a substantial part of it shall be declared incompatible with the common market.

It is clear from the wording of Article 2 that many of the issues which were encountered in the discussion of Article 86 will be of relevance here too. Thus, it will be necessary to define the relevant market in geographical and product terms, and also to determine whether there is a dominant position which has been created or strengthened by the concentration. It should, therefore, come as no surprise that the Commission makes reference to some of the seminal decisions under Article 86 when adjudicating on the Merger Regulation.

A sense of the Commission's approach can be conveyed by reviewing some of its decisions. We can begin by considering an instance in which it cleared the merger, holding that, although it was within the scope of the Regulation, there were no serious doubts about its compatibility with the common market. In reading this extract pay particular attention to the way in which the Commission dealt with the dynamic nature of the market and the issue of barriers to entry:

Case IV/M57, Re the Concentration between Digital Equipment International and Mannesman Kienzle GmbH [1992] 4 CMLR M99

Digital Equipment International (DEIL), a wholly-owned subsidiary of Digital Equipment Corporation (DEC), made an agreement with Mannesman Kienzle (MK) to establish a limited partnership under German law, Digital/Kienzle, which was to be owned as to 65 per cent by DEIL and 35 per cent by MK. The new company was to acquire the computer business of MK, which was then to withdraw from the computer industry (except for printers). MK also agreed not to compete with Digital/Kienzle. DEC only possessed a relatively small market share, less than 10 per cent, of the market for personal computers, and this market was, as a whole, relatively fragmented with few firms possessing more than 10 per cent. The proposed concentration did not therefore raise serious doubts about its compatibility with the common market in this sphere. DEC was one of the world's largest suppliers of networked computer systems, but MK was very much smaller. The extract which follows concerns the market for workstations. The merger was cleared under Article 6(1)(b).

THE COMMISSION

19. The workstation market is the smallest among the four markets mainly affected, but shows the highest annual growth rate (more than 30 per cent). It is also the most concentrated market with DEC, Hewlett Packard and Sun Microsystems holding an aggregate market share of about 80 per cent. DEC's market share has been in the last three years on average 22 per cent.

20. It is unlikely that the concentration will create or strengthen a dominant position because conditions of competition will not significantly change. The workstation market is a fairly new market which developed out of the PC and small computer market during the last 10 years. High market shares on a new developing market are not extraordinary, and they do not necessarily indicate market power. In fact the development of the market shares of the three leading companies over a period of time shows the dynamic nature of this market. There has been constant change including a change of market leadership.

21. DEC acquires with MK only a relatively small vendor and one which is rather insignificant for the maintenance of competition on this market. The increase in market share will not be very significant because even on the German market MK has held in the last three years on average only a 4 per cent market share . . . Finally, barriers to entry are relatively low for other computer systems manufacturers, especially for those who sell PCs and small multi-user computers. Market entry seems to be feasible even for companies on adjacent markets. Sony and Matsushita are apparently potential, if not already actual, competitors on the workstation market.

22. Thus, also with regard to the workstation market the concentration does not raise serious doubts as to its compatibility with the Common Market.

At the opposite end of the spectrum we can consider a decision in which the Commission conducted a more detailed investigation and found that the concentration was caught by Article 2(3) of the Merger Regulation:

Case IV/M53, Re the Concentration between Aérospatiale SNI and Alenia-Aeritalia e Selenia SpA and de Havilland [1992] 4 CMLR M2

Aérospatiale and Alenia controlled the world's largest producer of turbo-prop regional aircraft, ATR, and sought to take-over de Havilland, which was the world number two in this market. The Commission found that the product market was regional turbo-prop aeroplanes with between twenty and seventy seats, with sub-markets for aircraft with twenty to thirty-nine seats, forty to fifty-nine seats and sixty seats and over. The geographical market was the world, excluding China and Eastern Europe. It then considered the impact of the concentration.

THE COMMISSION

A. *Effect on ATR's Position*

27. The proposed concentration would significantly strengthen ATR's position on the commuter markets, for the following reasons in particular:

—high combined market share on the 40 to 59–seat market, and of the overall commuter market
—elimination of de Havilland as a competitor
—coverage of the whole range of commuter aircraft
—considerable extension of customer base.

(a) *Increase in Market Shares*

28. The proposed concentration would lead to an increase in market shares for ATR in the world market for commuters between 40 to 59 seats from 46 per cent. to 63 per cent. The nearest competitor (Fokker) would have 22 per cent. This market, together with the larger market of 60 seats and above where ATR has a world market share of 76 per cent, is of particular importance in the commuter industry since there is a general trend towards larger aircraft. This trend is particularly marked in Europe since airport fees favour the use of larger aircraft because of the crowded skies and limited airport capacities . . .

29. ATR would increase its share of the overall worldwide commuter market of 20 to 70 seats from around 30 per cent. to around 50 per cent. The nearest competitor (Saab) would only have around 19 per cent. On the basis of this the new entity would have half the overall world market and more than two and half times the share of its nearest competitor.

30. The combined market share may further increase after the concentration. The higher market share could give ATR more flexibility to compete on price (including financing) than its smaller competitors. ATR would be able to react with more flexibility to initiatives of competitors in the market place.

Following a concentration between ATR and de Havilland, the competitors would be faced with the combined strength of two large companies. This would mean that where an airline was considering placing a new order, the competitors would be in competition with the combined product range of ATR and de Havilland . . .

(b) *Elimination of de Havilland as a Competitor*

31. In terms of aircraft sold, de Havilland is the most successful competitor of ATR . . .

. . .

The parties argue that if the proposed concentration does not proceed, although de Havilland would not be immediately liquidated, its production might be phased out by Boeing so that de Havilland might in any case be eliminated as a competitor in the medium to long term. Without prejudice as to whether such a consideration is relevant pursuant to Article 2 of the Merger Regulation, the Commission considers that such elimination is not probable . . .

. . .

(c) *Coverage of the Whole Range of Commuter Aircraft*

32. The new entity ATR/de Havilland would be the only commuter manufacturer present in all the various commuter markets as defined above.

. . .

According to a study submitted by the parties, it is argued that the inability of a manufacturer to offer a full range of seating capacities under the same umbrella may harm the demand for other existing aircraft of that manufacturer . . . This logic flows from the fixed costs borne by the carrier for each aircraft manufacturer dealt with by that carrier. These costs include the fixed costs of pilot and mechanic training as well as the costs of maintaining in-house inventories of parts and the fixed costs of dealing with several manufacturers when ordering parts stocked only by the individual manufacturers themselves.

One of the stated main strategic objectives of the parties in acquiring de Havilland is to obtain coverage of the whole range of commuter aircraft. The competitive advantages which would arise from this would emerge over time.

. . .

In practice the advantages of having complete coverage of the market use are only present where airlines have or intend to have a fleet consisting of aircraft in different product markets. According to figures supplied by Fokker, over half of the aircraft sold in the markets of 40 seats and above for example are operated in fleets where there are also aircraft of around 30 seats. It appears therefore that at least having a more complete coverage of the market is significant.

(d) *Broadening of Customer Base*

33. ATR would significantly broaden its customer base after the concentration. On the basis of deliveries to date, the parties state that ATR has currently delivered commuters to 44 customers world-wide and de Havilland has delivered commuters to 36 other customers, giving a combination of 80 customers in all . . .

The customer base is an important element of market power for aircraft manufacturers since there is at least to some extent a lock-in effect for customers once their initial choice of aircraft is made.

. . .

B. *Assessment of the Strength of the Remaining Competition*

34. In order to be able to assess whether the new combined entity would be able to act independently of its competitors, in view of its strengthened position, it is necessary to assess the current and expected future strength of the remaining competitors. [*The Commission evaluated the strength of the other competitors and decided that it was questionable whether they could provide effective competition in the medium to long term.*]

. . .

D. *Summary of Effect of the Proposed Concentration on the Commuter Markets*

51. The combined entity ATR/de Havilland will obtain a very strong position in the world and Community commuter markets of 40 seats and over, and in the overall world and Community market, as a result of the proposed concentration. The competitors in these markets are relatively weak. The bargaining ability of the customers is limited. The combination of these factors leads to the conclusion that the new entity could act to a significant extent independently of its competitors and customers, and would thus have a dominant position on the commuter markets as defined.

. . .

E. *Potential Entry into the Market*

53. In general terms, a concentration which leads to the creation of a dominant position may however be compatible with the Common Market within the mean-

ing of Article 2(2) of the Merger Regulation if there exists strong evidence that this position is only temporary and would be quickly eroded because of high probability of strong market entry. With such market entry the dominant position is not likely to significantly impede effective competition within the meaning of Article 2(3) of the Merger Regulation. In order to assess whether the dominant position of ATR/de Havilland is likely to significantly impede effective competition therefore, it is necessary to assess the likelihood of new entry into the market.

[*The Commission evaluated the possibility of new entrants and came to the conclusion that there was no realistic potential competition in the commuter markets in the foreseeable future.*]

The Commission's decision to block the merger in the above case was not accepted unreservedly by the Advisory Committee on Concentrations. The latter was divided in its opinion. The majority agreed with the Commission. The minority disagreed with the Commission's market analysis, expressing the view that the Commission 'is not so much protecting competition but rather the competitors to this proposed concentration'.[42] The decision in *Aérospatiale–Alenia/de Havilland* has also come under fire from commentators. Fox considers that the Commission's reasoning was praiseworthy in a number of respects, but that it also had five weaknesses:

E. Fox, Merger Control in the EEC—Towards a European Merger Jurisprudence[43]

First, the Commission seemed to take an ungenerous view of economies likely to be achieved. While it counted economies of scale it seemed to disregard economies of scope; it disregarded the proconsumer aspects of savings resulting from the merged firm's full line, of opportunities for package buying, and of buyers' opportunities to save costs by concentrating on one firm's technology ('lock-in' effect). The fact that they also yield foreclosing effects simply increases the problem's complexity but does not eliminate the economies' value.

Second, the Commission viewed low pricing, also, only in its anticompetitive light and not in its procompetitive light. If the merged firm has the incentive to trigger price competition, consumers will, at least in the short run, get a better bargain . . .

Third, the Commission quickly concluded that the remaining competition would shrink from confrontation, responding with fear and retreat to the new competitive advantages of the merged firm. Might the rivals, rather, have been so challenged as to seek new efficiencies and to respond more aggressively to buyers' needs . . . ?

Fourth, the Commission readily adopted a low pricing/monopolization scenario with no mention of a dominant firm/cooperative scenario. Would ATR really engage in all out warfare with the aim of devastating its rivals, or would it more likely engage in leadership conduct inviting cooperative behaviour, with a view

[42] [1992] 4 CMLR M2, 35. [43] N. 35 above, Ch. 28, 738–9.

towards enjoying less tumultuous life and confronting fewer risks? By posing these two scenarios (both anticompetitive) as alternative possibilities, the Commission would have strengthened its case.

Fifth and finally, the commuter aircraft industry is heavily subsidized in Europe and Canada, and moreover, despite subsidies, De Havilland was in seriously weakened financial condition. The Commission did not grapple with the difficult issues raised by either situation.

The two examples considered thus far concern respectively cases in which the Commission has cleared a merger under Article 6(1)(b) and condemned a merger under Articles 2(3) and 8(3). Our third example is of a case in which the Commission cleared the merger, but only after imposing conditions. This particular case is also of more general importance because it raises the question as to how far the Merger Regulation can apply to oligopolistic markets:[44]

Case IV/M190, Re the Concentration between Nestlé SA and Source Perrier SA [1993] 4 CMLR M17

There were three major suppliers of bottled water in France: Nestlé, Perrier, and BSN. Nestlé sought to takeover Perrier and also made an agreement with BSN under which it would sell the Volvic source of Perrier to BSN if it acquired control over Perrier. The Commission held that the merger between Nestlé and Perrier, and the subsequent sale of the Perrier source to BSN, would create a duopolistic dominant position (as between Nestlé and BSN), which would significantly impede competition in the French bottled water market. Nestlé and BSN argued that the Merger Regulation did not apply to oligopolistic dominance. Did, therefore, Article 2(3) cover market situations where competition was impeded by more than one firm which firms together have the power to behave independently of the market?

THE COMMISSION

112. The Commission considers that the distinction between single firm dominance and oligopolistic dominance cannot be decisive for the application or non-application of the Merger Regulation because both situations may significantly impede effective competition under certain market structure conditions. This is in particular the case if there is already before the merger weakened competition between the oligopolists which is likely to be further weakened by a significant increase in concentration and if there is no sufficient price-constraining competition from actual or potential competition coming from outside the oligopoly.

113. Article 3(f) EEC provides for the institution of a system ensuring that competition in the common market is not distorted. One of the principal goals of the Treaty is thus the maintenance of effective competition. The restriction of effective competition which is prohibited if it is the result of a dominant position held by one firm cannot become permissible if it is the result of more than one firm. If,

[44] R. Whish and B. Sufrin, 'Oligopolistic Markets and EC Competition Law' (1992) 12 YBEL 59.

for instance, as a result of a merger, two or three undertakings acquire market power and are likely to apply excessive prices this would constitute an exercise of a collective market power which the Merger Regulation is intended to prevent by the maintenance of a competitive market structure. The dominant position is only the means by which effective competition can be impeded. Whether this impediment occurs through single firm power or collective power cannot be decisive for the application or non-application of Article 2(3) of the Merger Regulation.

114. In the absence of explicit exclusion of oligopolistic dominance by Article 2(3) it cannot be assumed that the legislator intended to permit the impediment of effective competition by two or more undertakings holding the power to behave together to an appreciable extent independently on the market. This would create a loophole in the fundamental Treaty objective of maintaining effective competition at all times in order not to jeopardise the proper functioning of the Common Market. If, in order to avoid the application of the Merger Regulation, it sufficed to divide the dominant power between two companies in order to escape the prohibition of Article 2(3), then, in contradiction to the basic principles of the common market, effective competition would be significantly impeded. In such a hypothesis the objective of Article 3(f) EEC could be overturned.

115. Seen in the light of these legal and economic considerations, Article 2(3) must be interpreted as covering both single firm and oligopolistic dominance. It is also significant to note that all other major antitrust systems with a merger control system apply or can apply their rules to both single firm or oligopolistic dominance . . .

[*Assuming that the sale of Volvic to BSN went ahead the Commission found that the resulting duopolistic dominance of Nestlé and BSN would be caught by Article 2(3) for the following reasons:*[45] *it would create a duopoly with a combined market share of 82 per cent; there was no viable Community competitor; the proposed deal would eliminate a major competitor, Perrier, from the market; this would render it easier for the remaining two parties to engage in anti-competitive parallel behaviour; prices of the goods were transparent and the duopolists monitored each other's behaviour, thereby facilitating tacit co-ordination; demand was relatively inelastic; there were high barriers to entry; and the duopolists had acted to deter the entry of a third party to the market. Even if the Volvic agreement was not implemented the Commission found that the acquisition of Perrier by Nestlé would create a dominant position for the new entity.*[46] *The Commission, none the less, cleared the merger on acceptance by Nestlé of the following conditions*:][47]

136. Nestlé has offered to modify the original concentration plan as notified by entering into the following commitments:

. . .

In order to meet the requirements of the Commission to facilitate the entry of a viable competitor with adequate resources in the bottled mineral water market or the increase in the capacity of an existing competitor so that in either case such competitor could effectively compete on the French bottled water market with Nestlé and BSN, Nestlé has undertaken that it will make

[45] [1993] 4 CMLR M17, paras. 119–31. [46] *Ibid.*, paras. 132–4.

[47] The extract below contains the main condition imposed by the Commission on Nestlé. There were a number of other related conditions, e.g. that Nestlé would keep the assets of Perrier distinct pending completion of the divestiture required by the Commission.

available for sale both brand names and sufficient capacity of water for bottling to such competitor as will permit that competitor to have not less than 3,000 million litres of water capacity per annum.

. . .

Nestlé acknowledges that the approval of the purchaser by the Commission is of the essence for the acceptance of its undertaking by the Commission. The establishment of an effective competitor *vis-à-vis* Nestlé and BSN depends on the strength of the purchaser to develop the sources and brands which will be sold to it. The purchaser must in particular have:

—sufficient financial resources to develop a nation-wide distribution organization and to adequately promote the acquired brands;

and

—sufficient expertise in the field of branded beverage or food products.

. . .

Nestlé is enjoined and restrained from re-acquiring, directly or indirectly, any of the sources or brands which it divests pursuant to this undertaking, for a period of 10 years from the date of this Decision, without the prior written approval of the Commission.

Given that the parties agreed to the conditions set by the Commission there was no reason to appeal the decision to the CFI or the ECJ. Pending any such appeal in a different case, the Commission's view on the issue of oligopoly and the Merger Regulation will continue to hold sway.[48]

(e) *Concentrations: Reflections on the Substantive Criteria*

The substantive criteria contained in Article 2 of the Merger Regulation are open to varying interpretations, and their application to the facts of particular cases will often, as seen above, be contentious. There are, however, two more general issues of interpretation which should be touched on here: one concerns the scope of the competition inquiry which is engaged in; the other is the relevance or not of non-competition issues. These will be considered in turn.

The *scope of the competition inquiry* under Article 2 raises a number of interesting issues, one of the most important of which is the meaning to be accorded to efficiency within this inquiry. The central nub of the problem can be stated as follows. The general objectives of competition policy are based on the idea that competition will secure to the consumer the desired goods at the lowest price with the sacrifice of the fewest resources. In this sense competition is a mechanism for promoting economic efficiency. Merger policy is but one part of this more general strategy. Now as we have seen, under Article 2(3) a concentration will be condemned if it creates or strengthens a dominant position as a result of which competition will be significantly impeded. But

[48] A. Winckler and M. Hansen, 'Collective Dominance under the EC Merger Control Regulation' (1993) 30 CMLRev. 787.

what if the merger does strengthen a dominant position, yet also entails economic-efficiency gains by reducing costs? Is this a factor which can or should be taken into account in the assessment under Article 2(3)? Jenny has concluded from a study of decisions that the Commission may in fact hold such efficiency gains *against* the parties:[49]

> To date the record of the Commission in the merger control area is clear. The possibility that a merger might lead to static efficiency gains . . . or to dynamic efficiency gains . . . which other non-merging firms are unlikely to achieve is interpreted as prima facie evidence that the merger will enable the merging firms to acquire a dominant position incompatible with the common market.

Whether this should be so in terms of economic theory is debatable, to say the least. It has, for example, been shown by Williamson that relatively modest cost savings can outweigh the impact of price increases when considering allocative efficiency.[50]

In any event this still leaves unanswered the question whether such an inquiry is possible within the present framework of Article 2. The response of Overbury, the Director of the MTF, to the concerns raised by Jenny is somewhat equivocal, as the following extract demonstrates:

H. Colin Overbury, EEC Merger Regulation[51]

> I think when you are considering how you apply the criteria set out in Article 2 of the Regulation, you have to bear in mind that there was a very long, hard-fought debate in getting the Regulation through, and that all the earlier proposals for a Regulation contained a specific derogation. In the final battle to get the Regulation out, any kind of derogation was totally excluded, with the result that the only test that appears on the face of it is . . . that you can examine anything you like, as long as you come to the conclusion that it does not form an obstacle to competition. If it does form an obstacle to competition, it is incompatible; if it doesn't, it is compatible and can be cleared.
>
> The idea has always been, can you dilute that in any way without having a specific derogation? To do that, therefore, you've got to go to Articles 2 and 3 and look at how they have worded it there and see if you get any comfort. You then find that a concentration which does create or strengthen a dominant position in an objective manner, as a result of which effective competition will be significantly impeded in the Common Market, shall be declared incompatible.

[49] F. Jenny, 'EEC Merger Control: Economies as an Antitrust Defense or an Antitrust Attack?' in *Fordham Corporate Law Institute*, ed. B. Hawk (1992), 603.

[50] O. Williamson, 'Economics as an Antitrust Defense: the Welfare Tradeoffs' (1968) 58 Am. Econ. Rev. 18. It might be argued by way of response that any such calculus designed to weigh the advantages and disadvantages of a proposed merger in efficiency terms would be too difficult, particularly within the tight time tables imposed by the Merger Regulation. This might be so, although the cogency of this argument would be dependent upon assessing the marginal increase of time that any such inquiry would take over and above that already taken on the issues which are presently considered by the Commission.

[51] N. 49 above, Ch. 24, 615–16.

Now, is that a one-stage test or is that a two-stage test, and does that mean that you can have a dominant position which does not significantly impede competition in the Common Market because it is, as Professor Jenny would say, very efficient? That, I suppose, to some extent is debatable.

I have some difficulty, because if you have a dominant position, you've got a dominant position. A dominant position, whether it's efficient or not, must be defined in the terms of the jurisprudence of the Court as meaning giving the holder of that dominant position the power to be able to act independently of competitors and consumers . . .

So what do you do, then, if you have a dominant position? You have to look to see whether it produces a significant effect. I think this is a question of the durability of the thing.

We have determined in the merger cases so far . . . that the question is the dynamic view . . . The question is: Is it going to last? If it isn't going to last, then it's not going to have a significant effect upon competition because the ability to act to the detriment of consumers and competitors will evaporate . . .

That, I think, is as far as one can go. I would entirely agree with Professor Jenny that the wording of Article 2 leads you up the garden path. It gives you the hope that you can achieve something which in the end you find you can't.

The other general issue of interpretation concerns *the relevance of non-competition issues.* The discussion thus far has focused principally on the competition inquiry which takes place within the framework of Article 2. But how far can other matters be taken into account? The thirteenth recital to the Regulation states that, in considering the compatibility of a concentration with the common market, the Commission should bear in mind the fundamental objectives of the EC, including the strengthening of the Community's economic and social cohesion. The Commission has, none the less, taken the view that competition is to be the prime objective of the Regulation.[52] The failure of the Commission to take account of broader concerns of industrial policy was a cause for criticism in *Aérospatiale–Alenia/de Havilland*, but it did not shake the Commission's resolve in this respect.[53] For the present, therefore, such issues will not play a role in Community merger analysis, although it is by no means impossible that this position will change, either because of Member State pressure, or because of shifts in thinking within the Commission itself.

[52] 20th Report on Competition Policy, point 20.

[53] E. Fox, 'Merger Control in the EEC—Towards a European Merger Jurisprudence' in n. 35 above, Ch. 28, 709–10.

5. RELATIONSHIP BETWEEN COMMUNITY AND MEMBER STATE MERGER CONTROL

(a) The General Principle: One-stop Merger Control

It is obviously undesirable for the same merger to be subject to investigation under differing regimes at Community and national level, given the expense that this would entail and given that they may apply different substantive criteria. A central feature of the Merger Regulation is, therefore, the idea that mergers which have a Community dimension should, in general, only be investigated by the Commission. This policy finds expression in Article 21(1), which states that only the Commission may take the decisions covered by the Merger Regulation. This is reinforced by Article 21(2) which provides that, subject to Article 9, no Member State may apply its national legislation to a merger which has a Community dimension. There are, however, a number of exceptions to this general principle.

(b) Article 21(3)

Article 21(3) allows a Member State to take appropriate measures to protect legitimate interests other than those taken into consideration by the Regulation, provided that they are compatible with Community law. Public security, plurality of the media, and prudential rules are listed as legitimate interests for these purposes. Any other public interest must be notified to the Commission which will inform the Member State of its decision within one month.

(c) Referral to the Competent Authorities of the Member State: The German Clause

When the Regulation was being drafted there was some concern that a merger might not be regarded as harmful from the Community perspective, but that it could still be detrimental at national level. These concerns found expression in Article 9 which allows a Member State to request that the Commission take action, or that the national authorities be allowed to take action, in the following circumstances. There must be a concentration with a Community dimension which threatens to create or strengthen a dominant position as a result of which effective competition would be significantly impeded on a market within that state, where the market has all the characteristics of a distinct market, irrespective of whether it is a substantial part of the Common Market or not. It is up to the Commission to decide both whether such a distinct market exists, and also whether there is in reality the relevant threat to competition.[54] The Commission has rejected a number of

[54] Art. 9(3).

such applications from Member States,[55] but accepted a request from the United Kingdom.[56]

(c) Article 22(3): The Dutch Clause

Article 22(3) provides that a Member State may request the Commission to investigate a concentration which does not have a Community dimension where that concentration creates or strengthens a dominant position as a result of which effective competition on the territory of that state would be impeded. The Commission can then take action provided that the concentration affects trade between Member States. The object of this provision was to provide a mechanism for merger control where none existed at national level. It will be rarely used, given that most states do now have their own systems of merger control.

(d) The Residual Role of Articles 85 and 86

We have already seen how the ECJ used Articles 85 and 86 to impose some control on mergers in the absence of any regulation. A question which remains to be considered is the scope of application of these Articles now. This question must be addressed both as to the powers of the Commission and as to those of the national courts.

As to the powers of the Commission, Article 22(1) of the Merger Regulation provides some guidance, albeit of a limited nature. It provides that Regulation 4064/89 alone shall apply to mergers as defined by Article 3 of the Regulation. This is reinforced by Article 22(2) which states that the main implementing regulations concerning Article 85 shall not be applicable to concentrations as defined by Article 3. It is clear, therefore, that the Commission can no longer use the general regulations designed to implement Articles 85 and 86 to oppose mergers.[57]

More problematic is the impact of Article 22 on national courts. Given that Articles 85 and 86 have direct effect it would seem to be possible, for example, for an undertaking which is opposed to a hostile takeover to raise the matter in the national courts, and seek a reference to the ECJ under Article 177, claiming that the takeover was in breach of Article 85 or 86. This strategy would, moreover, be available even though the takeover would not qualify as one which had a Community dimension under the Merger Regulation. One possible answer would be that Article 85 does not have direct effect in the absence of more detailed implementing regulations,[58] but this answer would not apply to Article 86, the direct effect of which does not seem to be

[55] See e.g. Case IV/M41, *Varta/Bosch* [1991] OJ L320/26; Case IV/M222, *Mannesman/Hoecsh* [1993] OJ L114/34.

[56] Case IV/M75, *Streetley plc/Tarmac*.

[57] Although the Commission could use the more general power contained in Art. 89, on which see Whish, n. 26 above, 725.

[58] Whish, n. 26 above, 726.

dependent on such implementing regulations.[59] Challenges in national courts of the type considered above may well therefore occur in the future.

6. JUDICIAL REVIEW

Commission decisions which are taken under the Merger Regulation are reviewable by the Community courts. Applicants who wish to challenge such decisions will, however, have to satisfy the normal criteria for annulment under Article 173.[60] They will therefore have to show that there is a decision which has legal consequences or legal effects; they will have to prove that they have been directly and individually concerned; and they must be able to attack the contested decision on substantive grounds.[61]

7. FURTHER READING

(a) Books

BISHOP, M., and KAY J. (eds.), *European Mergers & Merger Policy* (Oxford University Press, 1993)

COOK, J., and KERSE, C., *EEC Merger Control—Regulation 4064/89* (Sweet & Maxwell, 1991)

DOWNES, T. A., and ELLISON, J., *The Legal Control of Mergers in the European Communities* (Blackstone, 1991)

HAWK, B. (ed.), *International Mergers and Joint Ventures* (Fordham Corporate Law Institute, 1990)

(b) Articles

BELLAMY, C., 'Mergers Outside the Scope of the New Merger Regulation—Implications of the *Philip Morris* Judgment', in *Fordham Corporate Law Institute*, ed. B. Hawk (1989), Ch. 22

FOX, E., 'Merger Control in the EEC—Towards a European Merger Jurisprudence', in *Fordham Corporate Law Institute*, ed. B. Hawk (1991), Ch. 28

HAWK, B., 'Joint Ventures Under EC Law', in *Fordham Corporate Law Institute*, ed. B. Hawk (1991), Ch. 23

—— and HUSER, H., 'A Bright Line Shareholding Test to End the Nightmare under the EEC Merger Regulation' (1993) 30 CMLRev. 1155

[59] Case 66/86, *Ahmed Saeed Flugreisen and Silver Line Reiseburo GmbH* v. *Zentrale zur Bekämpfung Unlauteren Wettbewerbs e V* [1989] ECR 803, [1990] 4 CMLR 102.

[60] See above, Ch. 11.

[61] See e.g. Case T–83/92, *Zunis Holdings SA* v. *Commission* [1993] ECR II–1169 [1994] 5 CMLR 154; Case T–3/93, *Société Anonyme à Participation Ouvrière Compagnie Nationale Air France* v. *Commission*, 24 Mar. 1994.

Jenny, F., 'EEC Merger Control: Economies as an Antitrust Defense or an Antitrust Attack?', in *Fordham Corporate Law Institute*, ed. B. Hawk (1992), Ch. 23

Langeheine, B., 'Substantive Review Under the EEC Merger Regulation', in *Fordham Corporate Law Institute*, ed. B. Hawk (1990), Ch. 22

Sibree, W., 'EEC Merger Control and Joint Ventures' (1992) 17 ELRev. 91

Siragusa, M., and Subiotto, R., 'The EEC Merger Control Regulation: the Commission's Evolving Case Law' (1991) 28 CMLRev. 877

Venit, J., 'The "Merger" Control Regulation: Europe Comes of Age . . . Or Caliban's Dinner' (1990) 27 CMLRev. 7

Whish, R., and Sufrin, B., 'Oligopolistic Markets and EC Competition Law' (1992) 12 YBEL 59

Winckler, A., and Hansen, M., 'Collective Dominance under the EC Merger Control Regulation' (1993) 30 CMLRev. 787

22

Competition: Enforcement and Procedure

1. INTRODUCTION

In the preceding chapters we have considered the substantive rules which apply to cartels, monopoly power, and mergers. These rules must be enforced if they are to be effective, and the object of this Chapter is to describe and assess the EC regime on procedure and enforcement. The nature of the enforcement process is of interest not only in and of itself, but also because it casts further light on the more general issue of how norms of EC law are applied.

The earlier discussions of direct effect and the Article 169 action[1] revealed the interplay between private enforcement through the medium of direct effect and public enforcement through actions brought by the Commission. We have seen that one of the motivations for direct effect was to alleviate the burden that would otherwise be placed on the Commission if it were to be the sole enforcer of Community norms. If actions brought by the Commission were to be the only method of ensuring compliance with EC rules then this would be to place an impossible burden on this institution. Direct effect provides an alternative avenue through which compliance with EC law can be attained in this area. The importance of this is brought out in the following extract:

R. Whish, Competition Law[2]

In practice the Commission is hopelessly short of the resources necessary to enforce the competition rules throughout the Community while at the same time discharging its other duties, such as the development of competition policy and the drafting of new legislation. In any one year the Commission is capable of publishing only about 20 formal decisions at most, a minute number compared with the volume of agreements notified to it and complaints received by it. The decisions that the Commission does publish tend to deal with important points of principle indicating the way in which it wishes to develop competition policy or to involve serious transgressions of the competition rules where deterrent punishment is thought necessary. The Commission deals with many other cases informally, but the reality of the matter is that it cannot hope to deal with every

[1] See above Chs. 4, 5 and 9.. [2] (3rd edn., Butterworths, 1993), 285–6.

transgression of Articles 85 and 86. In *Automec* v. *Commission (No 2)*[3] the CFI delivered an important judgment dealing with various aspects of the enforcement of the competition rules in which it held, *inter alia*, that the Community was entitled to give priority to cases that involve a 'Community interest'; this is consistent with the Commission's own policy which is to encourage decentralization of the enforcement process to the national courts of Member States, leaving it to concentrate on major cases and the development of policy.

The discussion in this Chapter will, therefore, focus initially on the enforcement role of the Commission itself, to be followed by an analysis of the way in which this is complemented by actions which are brought in national courts.

In reading the material which follows you should be aware not only of the interplay between public and private enforcement, but also of the way in which the enforcement process in competition matters throws light on other issues which have been considered in earlier chapters. One such issue is the way in which the Court allows the Commission discretion on how the latter should use its own scarce resources. Another important issue which is exemplified by the process of enforcement is a topic which was considered in the discussion of preliminary rulings.[4] This is the way in which national courts are increasingly perceived as part of a Community judicial hierarchy, enforcing certain competition norms in their own right in a manner which fits in with and facilitates the task of the ECJ and the CFI.

2. PUBLIC ENFORCEMENT BY THE COMMISSION: FINDING THE VIOLATION

It is axiomatic that the Commission must know of the existence of a competition infringement in order to take appropriate action. There are, in essence, three ways in which it can become aware of a potential violation: it may find out about it from its own investigations; the parties to an agreement may notify the Commission; or there may be a complaint from a private party. These will be considered in turn.

(a) Investigation

Under Article 89 of the Treaty the Commission is charged with the duty of ensuring the application of Articles 85 and 86, and of investigating suspected infringements of these Articles. The detailed investigative powers of the Commission are contained in Regulation 17. Article 11 of this Regulation empowers the Commission to *request information* from governments, competent authorities of Member States, and undertakings. The Commission must

[3] Case T–24/90, [1992] ECR II–2223, [1992] 5 CMLR 431.

[4] See above, Ch. 10.

state the legal basis for, and the purpose of, the request, as well as making clear the penalties for supplying incorrect information.[5] If the information requested is not supplied within the requisite period then the Commission shall by decision require the information to be supplied; there are penalties for non-compliance.[6] Decisions of this nature are reviewable before the CFI.[7]

In addition to the powers contained in Article 11 the Commission may also carry out an *investigation* under Article 14 of Regulation 17.[8] It may examine company books, business records, seek oral explanations, and enter premises.[9] Investigations can be either voluntary or mandatory. Voluntary investigations are conducted under Article 14(2), and the Commission officials must produce a written authorization which specifies the subject matter and purpose of the investigation; they must also indicate the penalties which can be incurred under Article 15(1)(c). Mandatory investigations are conducted under Article 14(3). These are based on the existence of a decision which orders the investigation. Once again the decision has to state the subject-matter and purpose of the investigation, as well as the susceptibility to penalties.[10] This Article has been a potent source of Commission investigative power, acting as the legal foundation for dawn raids against suspect undertakings. Although the Commission cannot literally gain forcible entry should a firm refuse to comply with an Article 14(3) decision, the authorities of the Member State must, under Article 14(6), afford the necessary assistance to it in the event that the firm in question proves intractable. The use of the powers contained in Article 14 gave rise to the important decision in the *Hoechst* case:

Cases 46/87 and 227/88, Hoechst AG v. Commission [1989] ECR 2859, [1991] 4 CMLR 410

The Commission was of the opinion that Hoechst was taking part in an illegal cartel, and instigated a dawn raid. The company refused to admit the Commission officials and contended that it was entitled to refuse entry until a search warrant had been obtained through national procedures. The Commission did eventually obtain access in this way, but then fined Hoechst for non-compliance with the original decision under Article 14. Hoechst argued that, in so far as Article 14 purported to allow the Commission to carry out searches, it was unlawful, being incompatible with fundamental rights, in that such searches should only be carried out on the basis of a warrant issued in advance.

THE ECJ

12. It should be noted, before the nature and scope of the Commission's powers of investigation under Article 14 of Regulation 17 are examined, that that

[5] Reg. 17, Art. 11(3).
[6] Art. 11(5).
[7] Case 374/87, *Orkem SA* v. *Commission* and Case 27/88, *Solvay and Cie* v. *Commission*, both [1989] ECR 3283, [1991] 4 CMLR 502.
[8] It has been held in the *Orkem* case that the powers in Arts. 11 and 14 are independent, and hence that the existence of a decision made pursuant to Art. 14 does not prevent the Commission from using its powers under Art. 11, Case 374/87, n. 7 above, para. 14.
[9] Art. 14(1).
[10] Arts. 15(1)(c) and 16(1)(d).

article cannot be interpreted in such a way as to give rise to results which are incompatible with the general principles of Community law and in particular with fundamental rights.[11]

. . .

26. Both the purpose of Regulation 17 and the list of powers conferred on Commission officials by Article 14 thereof show that the scope of investigations may be very wide. In that regard, the right to enter any premises . . . is of particular importance inasmuch as it is intended to permit the Commission to obtain evidence of infringements of the competition rules in the places in which such evidence is normally to be found, that is to say, on the business premises of undertakings.

27. That right of access would serve no useful purpose if the Commission officials could do no more than ask for documents or files which they could identify in advance. On the contrary, such a right implies the power to search for various items of information which are not already known or fully identified. Without such a power, it would be impossible for the Commission to obtain the information necessary to carry out the investigation if the undertakings concerned refused to co-operate or adopted an obstructive attitude.

28. Although Article 14 of Regulation 17 thus confers wide powers of investigation on the Commission, the exercise of those powers is subject to conditions serving to ensure that the rights of the undertakings concerned are respected.

29. In that regard, it should be noted first that the Commission is required to specify the subject-matter and purpose of the investigation . . .

30. It should also be pointed out that the conditions for the exercise of the Commission's investigative powers vary according to the procedure which the Commission has chosen, the attitude of the undertakings concerned and the intervention of the national authorities.

[*The Court then noted the different types of investigation which can be carried out under Article 14, and more particularly the difference between those instances where there is co-operation between Commission and undertakings and those where there is not. What follows refers to the situation where the undertaking resists the Commission's investigation and the latter has to seek the assistance of the Member State under Article 14(6) of Regulation 17:*]

34. . . . if the Commission intends, with the assistance of the national authorities, to carry out an investigation other than with the co-operation of the undertakings concerned, it is required to respect the relevant procedural guarantees laid down by national law.

35. The Commission must make sure that the competent body under national law has all that it needs to exercise its own supervisory powers. It should be pointed out that that body, whether judicial or otherwise, cannot in this respect substitute its own assessment of the need for the investigations ordered for that of the Commission, the lawfulness of whose assessments of fact and law is subject only to review by the Court of Justice. On the other hand, it is within the powers of the national body, after satisfying itself that the decision ordering the investigation is authentic, to consider whether the measures of constraint envisaged are arbitrary or excessive having regard to the subject-matter of the investigation and

[11] For discussion of the issues relating to fundamental rights in this case see above, 304–5.

to ensure that the rules of national law are complied with in the application of those measures.

36. In the light of the foregoing, it must be held that the measures which the contested decision ordering the investigation permitted the Commission officials to take did not exceed their powers under Article 14 of Regulation 17.

In some cases parties have sought to resist the taking of certain documents on the ground that they are covered by legal professional privilege between lawyer and client. Regulation 17 says nothing on this issue, but in the *AM & S* case[12] the ECJ held that such a privilege was recognised by EC law to a limited extent at least:[13] the confidentiality of written communications between lawyer and client was protected, provided that the communications were made for the purposes of the client's right of defence and that they emanated from independent lawyers, i.e those not bound to the client by an employment relationship.

The ECJ has also concluded that there is a limited privilege against self-incrimination: an undertaking is not required to answer questions which would be an admission of the very offence which the Commission is investigating; but the undertaking cannot refuse to hand over documentation which could establish the offence.[14]

As might be expected, investigations of the type considered above can lead to the Commission being in possession of business secrets.[15] Article 19(3) of Regulation 17 states that publication of Commission decisions shall pay due regard to the legitimate interest of undertakings in the protection of business secrets, and this was reinforced by the *AKZO* case[16] in which the ECJ held that such secrets should not be divulged.[17]

In circumstances where the disclosure of information to, for example, interveners in an action might reveal confidential business information of the complainants, the Court has power to order that documents should be withheld. In deciding on this issue the Court will balance the applicant's legitimate interest in the non-disclosure of business secrets with the interveners' legitimate concern to have the information which will enable it to state their case before the Court.[18]

[12] Case 155/79, *Australian Mining and Smelting Europe Ltd (AM and S Europe Ltd)* v. *Commission* [1982] ECR 1575, [1982] 2 CMLR 264, paras. 21–2, 23, 27, 34.

[13] As to what should happen in the event of a dispute whether documents did come within these criteria, see *ibid.*, paras. 30–2.

[14] Case 374/87, n. 7 above, paras. 34–5; Case 27/88, n. 7 above, paras. 31–2.

[15] J. Joshua, 'Balancing the Public Interests: Confidentiality, Trade Secret and Disclosure of Evidence in EC Competition Procedures' [1994] 2 ECLR 68.

[16] Case 53/85, *AKZO Chemie BV* v. *Commission* [1986] ECR 1965, [1987] 1 CMLR 231.

[17] See also Art. 20 concerning non-disclosure of information on professional secrecy.

[18] Case T–30/89A, *Hilti AG* v. *Commission* [1990] ECR II–163, [1990] 4 CMLR 602; Case T–57/91, *National Association of Licensed Opencast Operators* v. *Commission* [1993] 5 CMLR 124.

(b) Notification

The second way in which the Commission may become aware of a potential competition violation is if the parties notify an agreement to it.

Regulation 17, Article 4(1), states that agreements, decisions, and concerted practices of the kind described in Article 85(1) which came into existence after the entry into force of the Regulation must be notified to the Commission if the parties seek the application of Article 85(3).[19] Until they have been notified no decision concerning Article 85(3) can be taken.[20]

Article 4(2) specifies certain agreements which do not have to be notified to the Commission. This provision deals principally with particular types of bipartite agreement relating to areas such as research and development and specialization, under which the parties accept only restrictions of a specified kind. Although these agreements do not have to be notified the parties may still do so.

While there is therefore no duty to notify agreements there are two reasons why parties may do so. First, the benefit of individual exemption can only be sought in respect of agreements which have been notified. Secondly, notification carries immunity from fines. Under Article 15(2) of Regulation 17 fines may be imposed for agreements which are in breach of Article 85(1) or 86. However, Article 15(5) states that such fines shall not be imposed in respect of acts taking place after notification to the Commission and before its decision concerning Article 85(3), provided that they fall within the limits of the activity described in the notification. This immunity from fines is itself then qualified by Article 15(6) which allows the Commission to remove the immunity by informing the undertakings that, after a preliminary examination, it is of the view that Article 85(3) will not apply to the agreement.[21]

(c) Complaints

The final way in which the Commission may become aware of a possible infringement of Articles 85 or 86 is through a complaint which it receives from an aggrieved party. In 1991, eighty-three such complaints were received.[22] Any natural or legal person with a legitimate interest may make a complaint.[23] The law on this issue is somewhat complex, but the main principles can be stated as follows.

It is clear that the Commission is under a duty *to consider* a complaint which has been submitted to it.[24] Failure to do so could lead to an action under Article 175 for failure to act.

[19] The notification must be formal: Case T–23/90, *Automobiles Peugeot SA* v. *Commission* [1991] ECR II–653, [1993] 5 CMLR 540.

[20] Arts. 5 and 7 deal with agreements etc which were in existence when Reg. 17 came into force.

[21] For Commission practice on this issue see Whish, n. 2 above, 301–302.

[22] *Ibid.* 312.

[23] Reg. 17, Art. 3(2)(b).

[24] Case 210/81, *Demo-Studio Schmidt* v. *Commission* [1983] ECR 3045, [1984] 1 CMLR 63.

If the Commission *does decide to conduct an investigation* then it must generally do so with the degree of care which will enable it to assess the factual and legal considerations which have been submitted by the complainant.[25]

If the Commission decides to initiate proceedings then it *shall hear* such persons who have a sufficient interest.[26]

Where the Commission decides not to pursue a complaint made to it under Article 3(2)(b) of Regulation 17 then it must *inform the applicant of its reasons* and fix a time limit for him or her to submit any further comments in writing.[27]

We have already seen that the Commission has limited resources with which to pursue competition violations. A corollary of this is that it may well have to pick and choose which possible infringements are more worthy of its attention. This may, not surprisingly, cause upset to the complainant whose claim is not then pursued. The *Automec* case provides a good example of this tension:

Case T–24/90, Automec Srl v. Commission
[1992] ECR II–2223, [1992] 5 CMLR 431

The applicant company lodged a complaint with the Commission alleging that the car manufacturer BMW had terminated its dealership in breach of Article 85(1). It sought a mandatory injunction compelling BMW to resume supply. The Commission rejected the application on the ground, *inter alia*, that the Italian courts had already taken cognizance of the matter and that there was not a sufficient Community interest to warrant the Commission continuing with the case. The complainant appealed to the CFI.

THE CFI

75. . . . it is clear from the case law of the Court of Justice (*GEMA*)[28] that the rights conferred upon complainants by Regulations 17 and 99/63 do not include a right to obtain a decision, within the meaning of Article 189 EEC, as to the existence or otherwise of the alleged infringement. It follows that the Commission cannot be required to give a ruling in that connection unless the subject-matter of the complaint is within its exclusive remit, such as the withdrawal of an exemption granted pursuant to Article 85(3) EEC.

76. As the Commission has no obligation to rule on the existence or otherwise of an infringement it cannot be compelled to conduct an investigation, because this could have no purpose other than to seek evidence of the existence or otherwise of an infringement the existence of which it is not required to establish . . .

77. In this connection it should be observed that, for an institution performing a public-service task, the power to take all the organizational measures necessary for the fulfilment of that task, including settling priorities in the framework laid down by law, where those priorities have not been settled by the legislature, is an inherent part of the work of administration. This must apply particularly where

[25] Case T–7/92, *Asia Motor France SA* v. *Commission (No 2)* [1993] ECR II–669, [1994] 4 CMLR 30.

[26] Reg. 17, Art. 19(2).

[27] Reg. 99/63, Art. 6.

[28] Case 125/78, *GEMA* v. *Commission* [1979] ECR 3173, [1980] 2 CMLR 177.

an authority has been given a supervisory and regulatory function as general and extensive as that assigned to the Commission in the field of competition. Therefore the fact that the Commission allocates different degrees of priority to the matters referred to it in the field of competition is compatible with its obligations under Community law.

. . .

79. However, although the Commission cannot be compelled to conduct an investigation, the procedural safeguards provided for by Article 3 of Regulation 17 and Article 6 of Regulation 99/63 oblige it nevertheless to examine carefully the factual and legal aspects of which it is notified by the complainant in order to decide whether they indicate behaviour likely to distort competition in the Common Market and affect trade between Member States . . .

80. Where, as in the present case, the Commission has decided to close the file relating to the case without conducting an investigation, the review to be made by the Court of the legality of that decision seeks to ascertain whether the contested decision is based on materially wrong facts, is flawed by a mistake in law or a manifest error of assessment or by a misuse of powers.

81. It is for the Court to verify, in the light of these principles, first, whether the Commission has carried out the examination of the complaint which it is required to do by evaluating with all the requisite care the factual and legal aspects adduced by the applicant in his complaint and, secondly, whether the Commission has given proper reasons for closing the file on the complaint on the basis of its power 'to accord different degrees of priority to pursuing the matters referred to it' on the one hand, and on the basis of the Community interest in the matter as a criterion of priority on the other.

82. In this connection the Court finds, first, that the Commission carried out a careful examination of the complaint . . .

83. Secondly, concerning the reasons for the contested decision to close the file, the Court points out in the first place that the Commission is entitled to accord different degrees of priority to examining the complaints it receives.

84. The second point to be considered is whether it is legitimate, as the Commission contends, to refer to the Community interest of a matter as a criterion of priority.

85. In this connection it should be observed that, unlike the civil courts, whose task is to safeguard the subjective rights of private persons in their mutual relations, an administrative authority must act in the public interest. Consequently it is legitimate for the Commission to refer to the Community interest in order to determine the degree of priority to be accorded to the different matters before it. This does not mean removing the Commission's acts from judicial review: as Article 190 EEC requires the reasons on which decisions are based to be stated, the Commission cannot merely refer to the Community interest in isolation . . . Thus by reviewing the legality of those reasons the Court can review the Commission's acts.

86. To assess the Community interest in pursuing the examination of a matter, the Commission must take account of the circumstances of the particular case . . . It is for the Commission in particular to weigh up the importance of the alleged infringement for the functioning of the Common Market, the probability of being able to establish the existence of the infringement and the extent of the investigation measures necessary in order to fulfil successfully its task of securing compliance with Articles 85 and 86.

On the facts of the case the CFI upheld the Commission's decision that it was not necessary to proceed with the matter. The CFI found that the proceedings within the national courts in Italy were an appropriate way of resolving the issues; that the Italian courts could always refer a point to the ECJ under Article 177 if they felt it necessary to do so; that although the national court could not impose fines, it could apply Article 85(2), which stipulated that agreements in breach of Article 85(1) were automatically void; and that the existence of a block exemption covering the subject matter of the dispute made it easier for the national court to apply competition law in this instance.[29]

The Commission has now issued a Notice on Co-operation between National Courts and the Commission in Applying Article 85 and 96 of the EEC Treaty.[30] The notice will be examined more fully below, but it is of relevance for present purposes in that it builds on the Court's case law, and aims to encourage national courts to apply competition law more frequently than hitherto. The Notice further states that the Commission intends to concentrate on notifications, complaints, and own-initiative proceedings which 'have a particular political, economic or legal significance for the Community'. Complainants are encouraged to go to national courts in cases where such courts can provide adequate redress.

3. PUBLIC ENFORCEMENT BY THE COMMISSION: COMPETITION DECISIONS

Having discovered, by one of the means described above, the existence of facts which might indicate a competition violation, the Commission is then empowered to make a formal decision whether there has been an infringement of Article 85 or 86. The nature of these formal decisions will be considered in the discussion which follows. However, the problem of the Commission's limited resources, which we have encountered on more than one occasion in our discussion of enforcement, has had an important impact on this area. It is precisely because of these limited resources, coupled with the time that firms may have to wait for a resolution of the issue, that the Commission has developed a technique for informal settlement. In numerical terms informal settlements now outnumber formal decisions by a significant margin, although this is not to deny the fact that the formal decisions will often be given on more important topics. None the less the comparison is a telling one: in 1990 the Commission made fifteen formal decisions on substantive matters, and

[29] [1992] ECR II–2223, paras. 87–98. While the Commission is not duty bound to investigate every complaint placed before it, the CFI will none the less review the way in which the Commission has chosen to exercise its discretion, and may annul its decision if it finds that the reasons for not taking up a complaint were not sustainable: Case T–37/92, *Bureau Européen des Unions des Consommateurs and National Consumer Council* v. *Commission*, [1994] ECR II–285.

[30] [1993] OJ C39/6, [1993] 4 CMLR 12.

eighteen in 1991; informal settlements for the same years were 158 and 146.[31] We shall, therefore, begin the discussion with a look at the informal-settlement process before moving on to consider the Commission's more formal powers.

(a) Informal Settlement

The principal technique for informal settlement is the comfort letter.[32] When firms seek either negative clearance, to be described below, or individual exemption under Article 85(3), they have to use Form A/B. This form asks the parties whether they would be satisfied with a comfort letter. In essence this is a letter in which the Commission states that it is willing to close the file on the matter, although it may only do so after a process of negotiation with the parties leading to the removal of clauses from the agreement which it regards as objectionable.

This device has proven attractive to firms, but it does suffer from the drawback that these letters are not binding on national courts.[33] It would therefore be open to a third party, or indeed one of the parties to the actual agreement itself, to challenge it before the national court which, as we shall see, is empowered to adjudicate upon many issues concerning competition violations. In order to obviate this problem the Commission has introduced a more formal variant of the comfort letter, the idea being that it would publish in the Official Journal details of those agreements which it believed were outside Article 85(1). It would then be open to third parties to submit observations before the Commission made the final decision to close the file. It was thought that this would reduce the incidence of subsequent challenges to the settlement. It appears, however, that relatively few formal comfort letters have actually been issued, and that parties have normally been willing to accept the more informal comfort letter.[34]

(b) Formal Decisions: Interim Orders

While informal settlement is very important in practice it is clear that recourse to more formal decisions will still be needed either when the parties prove to be recalcitrant, or when there is a point of principle involved.

One species of formal decision which is particularly valuable is the interim order. Competition violations can cause considerable damage to a firm. Given the work-load of the Commission it may be some time before it is able to come to a final determination. It is for this reason that interim relief is given. Regulation 17 contains no explicit provisions on interim orders, but the ECJ in the *Camera Care* case decided that such a power existed:

[31] Whish, n. 2 above, 296, 311.

[32] D. Stevens, 'The "Comfort Letter": Old Problems, New Developments' [1994] 2 ECLR 81.

[33] For a recent example of a UK court having difficulty with a comfort letter, see *Inntrepenneur Estates Ltd* v. *Mason* [1993] 2 CMLR 293.

[34] N. 2 above, 311–12.

Case 792/79R, Camera Care Ltd v. Commission [1980] ECR 119, [1980] 1 CMLR 334

The complainant was a company engaged in the repair and sale of camera equipment, and alleged that the manufacturer Hasselblad was refusing to supply it with equipment. It asked for interim relief pending final resolution of the matter, but the Commission stated that there was no legal basis for this under Community law. Camera Care then brought an action against the Commission under Article 173 seeking to annul the decision that no interim relief was available under Community law.

THE ECJ

12. The hesitation shown by the Commission stems from the fact that Regulation 17 does not expressly confer upon the Commission . . . the power to adopt interim measures pending the time when it is in a position to adjudicate upon the substance of the case.

13. It is recalled that Article 3(1) of the Regulation provides that: 'Where the Commission, upon application or upon its own initiative, finds that there is an infringement of Article 85 or Article 86 of the Treaty, it may by decision require the undertakings . . . concerned to bring such an infringement to an end.' Paragraph (3) of the same Article adds that the Commission, before taking a decision under paragraph (1), may 'address to the undertakings . . . concerned recommendations for termination of the infringement.'

14. It is obvious that in certain circumstances there may be a need to adopt interim protective measures when the practice of certain undertakings in competition matters has the effect of injuring the interests of some Member States, causing damage to other undertakings, or of unacceptably jeopardising the Community's competition policy. In such circumstances it is important to ensure that, whilst enquiries are being carried out no irreparable damage is caused such as could not be remedied by any decision which the Commission might take at the conclusion of the administrative procedure.

. . .

18. From this point of view the Commission must . . . be able, within the bounds of its supervisory task conferred upon it in competition matters by the Treaty and Regulation 17, to take protective measures to the extent to which they might appear indispensable in order to avoid the exercise of the power to make decisions given by Article 3 from becoming ineffectual or even illusory because of the action of certain undertakings. The powers which the Commission holds under Article 3(1) of Regulation 17 therefore include the power to take interim measures which are indispensable for the effective exercise of its functions and, in particular, for ensuring the effectiveness of any decisions requiring undertakings to bring an end to infringements which it has found to exist.

19. However, the Commission could not take such measures without regard to the legitimate interests of the undertaking concerned by them. For this reason it is essential that interim measures be taken only in cases proved to be urgent in order to avoid a situation likely to cause irreparable damage to the party seeking their adoption, or which is intolerable for the public interest. A further requirement is that these measures be of a temporary and conservatory nature and restricted to what is required in the given situation. When adopting them the

Commission is bound to maintain the essential safeguards guaranteed to the parties concerned by Regulation 17, in particular by Article 19. Finally, the decisions must be made in such a form that an action may be brought upon them before the Court of Justice by any party who considers he has been injured.

We have mentioned the purposive style of reasoning employed by the ECJ on a number of occasions and the decision in the *Camera Care* case provides a good example of this in one particular area: the ECJ interpreted Regulation 17 so as to embrace the power to award interim relief even though there was no specific mention of this within the legislation.

The Commission has not used this power on very many occasions; only a handful of interim orders have been made. Indeed it has on some occasions been for the ECJ or the CFI to take the Commission to task for applying too stringent a test in deciding whether to grant interim relief. Thus in *La Cinq*[35] the CFI held that the Commission could not make the adoption of interim measures conditional on proof of a clear, flagrant infringement of Articles 85 or 86. This standard was held to be too high for the adoption of interim relief.

(c) *Formal Decisions: Negative Clearance*

Article 2 of Regulation 17 allows the Commission to grant a negative clearance: the Commission certifies that, on the basis of the facts in its possession, there are no grounds for believing that the agreement or practice falls within Article 85 or 86. The parties must apply for such a negative clearance. If the Commission intends to grant negative clearance then, under Article 19(3) of the Regulation, it must publish a summary of the relevant application and invite all interested parties to submit their observations within a fixed time limit. The Commission must also consult with the Advisory Committee on Restrictive Trade Practices and Monopolies. A third party who has standing may challenge such a decision.[36] Relatively few negative clearances have been granted: out of the approximately twenty decisions which are given in a year only about five will grant a negative clearance.[37]

(d) *Formal Decisions: A Finding of Infringement*

Under Article 3(1) of Regulation 17 the Commission can require parties to bring to an end an infringement of Article 85 or 86. Article 19(1) of the Regulation stipulates that a hearing must be provided for the undertakings concerned on the matters to which the Commission has taken objection;

[35] Case T–44/90, *La Cinq SA* v. *Commission* [1992] ECR II–1, [1992] 4 CMLR 449, paras. 60–61. See also Case T–23/90, n. 19 above.

[36] Case 26/76, *Metro SB-Großmärkte GmbH and Co KG* v. *Commission* [1977] ECR 1875, [1978] 2 CMLR 1.

[37] Whish, n. 2 above, 302.

Article 19(2) extends this process right to certain other parties who have a sufficient interest in the issue. There are a number of stages to this process.

When the Commission believes that there has been a competition violation which should be ended under Article 3 then it must issue a *statement of objections*.[38] This will specify the nature of the Commission's concerns about the parties' agreement or behaviour. It will contain a factual part plus the Commission's legal assessment from those facts. A fine or penalty may be imposed only if the objections were duly notified to the parties.[39] Moreover, the Commission is only able to deal with those objections raised against undertakings in respect of which they have been afforded the opportunity to make their views known.[40] Failure to comply with the above conditions will lead to the Commission's decision being quashed.[41]

After the statement of objections and the reply by the parties there then will be *the hearing*. Under Article 8 of Regulation 99/63 the Commission shall summon the parties to attend on such a date as it shall appoint. Article 9 of this Regulation provides that hearings shall be conducted by persons appointed by the Commission for this purpose. Since 1982 the Commission has appointed a Hearing Officer whose function is to preside over the hearing and to ensure that the relevant process rights are respected. Parties may be represented by lawyers, but the hearings are not in public.[42]

The procedure for determining competition violations has been attacked by undertakings on more than one occasion. One general complaint has been that the Commission combines the function of prosecutor and judge. This matter was addressed in the following case:

Cases 100–103/80, Musique Diffusion Française v. Commission[43] [1983] ECR 1825, [1983] 3 CMLR 221

The Commission had found a concerted practice operating between four companies, the essence of which was the division of the market for Pioneer electronic equipment so that distributors in different countries had exclusive rights and cross-border sales were prevented. The companies put forward a number of objections to the Commission decision, one of which was that it infringed essential procedural requirements.

THE ECJ

6. MDF (Musique Diffusion Française) maintains that the contested decision is unlawful by the mere fact that it was adopted under a system in which the Commission combines the functions of prosecutor and judge, which is contrary to Article 6(1) of the European Convention for the Protection of Human Rights.

7. That argument is without relevance. As the Court held in its judgments in

[38] Reg. 99/63, Art. 2. [39] *Ibid.*, Art. 2(3). [40] *Ibid.*, Art. 4.

[41] Cases 89/85 etc., *A. Ahlström Oy* v. *Commission* [1993] ECR I–1307, [1993] 4 CMLR 407, paras. 152–4; Case T–11/89, *Shell International Chemical Company Ltd* v. *Commission* [1992] ECR II–757; Case T–10/89, *Hoechst AG* v. *Commission* [1992] ECR II–629.

[42] Reg. 99/63, Art. 9(3). [43] See also Case T–11/89, n. 41 above.

Cases 209 etc/78 (*Van Landewyck* v. *Commission*), the Commission cannot be described as a 'tribunal' within the meaning of Article 6 . . .

8. It should however be added . . . that during the administrative procedure before the Commission, the Commission is bound to observe the procedural safeguards provided for by Community law.

[*The Court then set out the provisions of Regulation 17, Article 19, and Regulation 99/63, Article 4.*]

10. As the Court recalled in its judgment . . . in Case 85/76 (*Hoffmann-La Roche* v. *Commission*), the above mentioned principles are an application of the fundamental principle of Community law which requires the right to a fair hearing to be observed in all proceedings, even those of an administrative nature, and lays down in particular that the undertaking concerned must have been afforded the opportunity, during the administrative procedure, to make known its views on the truth and relevance of the facts and circumstances alleged and on the documents used by the Commission to support its claim that there has been an infringement of the Treaty.

11. It follows that, although the general submission put forward by MDF must be rejected as being based on a misunderstanding of the nature of the procedure before the Commission, Community law contains all the means necessary for examining, and in an appropriate case, upholding the following submissions based on alleged breaches of the applicants' right to a fair hearing.

There have also been other more particular complaints about the hearing process. Parties have expressed concern, for example, at the fact that they do not have access to Commission files. The ECJ held in the *VBVB* case[44] that there was no legal obligation to disclose such files. The Commission chose, however, not to stick to the legal letter of this judgment and has permitted access, except where, for example, information covered by professional secrecy is involved. A more recent judgment by the CFI in *SA Hercules*[45] has now given legal force to this administrative practice: the Commission is obliged to make available all documents which it has obtained in the course of the investigation, save where they involve business secrets of other undertakings, confidential information, or internal Commission documents.

Once the hearing has been held the Commission may then come to the conclusion that there has been an *infringement which should be terminated.* A formal decision which takes note of an infringement may still be made even if the parties have, by that stage, ended their violation.[46] The precise nature of the Commission order will obviously depend upon the circumstances. It is clear that the decision can impose a positive as well as a negative obligation, such as an order to supply certain goods. However, the nature of the order will depend upon which Article of the Treaty has been broken. Thus while an

[44] Cases 43, 63/82, *VBVB and VBBB* v. *Commission* [1985] ECR 19, [1985] 1 CMLR 27, para. 25.

[45] Case T–7/89, *SA Hercules Chemicals NV* v. *Commission* [1991] ECR II–1711, [1992] 4 CMLR 84, para. 54; Case T–65/89, *BPB Industries plc and British Gypsum Ltd* v. *Commission* [1993] ECR II–389, [1993] 5 CMLR 32.

[46] Case 7/82, *GVL* v. *Commission* [1983] ECR 485, [1983] 3 CMLR 645.

obligation to supply can be ordered for a breach of Article 86,[47] the fact tha an agreement is in breach of Article 85 cannot lead to an order to, for exam ple, supply cars of a certain make to a distributor.[48] The reason for this dif ference is captured by Whish:[49]

> Articles 85 and 86 have a different logic: Article 85 prohibits agreements, and the Commission may make an order to terminate them; Article 86 prohibits abuse, and again the Commission can make an order to terminate an abuse. However, a refusal to supply under Article 85 cannot in itself be unlawful. The Commission could order an undertaking to terminate an agreement not to supply, but it does not follow that it can also make an order to supply.

Once an infringement has been found the Commission has power under Articles 15 and 16 of Regulation 17 to *impose fines and periodic penalty payments*. Under Article 15(2) it may levy a fine of up to 1,000,000 ECU or 10 per cent of turnover. In fixing the quantum of the penalty the Commission will have regard to the gravity and duration of the infringement. If the violation is blatant and one which has been clearly proscribed for a considerable period of time, such as horizontal market division, then the fine will be correspondingly greater. The ECJ emphasized in the *Musique Diffusion Française* case[50] that fines should be capable of having a deterrent impact, particularly as regards those infringements which were very harmful to the attainment of the objectives of the Community.[51] Different levels of fine may be imposed upon the participants in the same agreement if there are reasons why one party is more blameworthy, as in the case where an importer of goods from Japan, which was a wholly-owned subsidiary of the Japanese firm, was the prime instigator behind agreements which divided the European market.[52]

(e) Formal Decisions: Individual Exemption

We have already noted the extent to which the national courts have been encouraged to adjudicate more frequently on competition matters, in order to alleviate the burden which would otherwise fall upon the Commission. We shall return to this issue below. However, one matter which resides within the exclusive jurisdiction of the Commission is the decision on the grant of individual exemption under Article 85(3). This power is reserved to the Commission exclusively by Article 9(1) of Regulation 17, and it is this which has been partly the cause of the large number of cases awaiting final resolution. Sir Leon Brittan has none the less stated that the time is not yet ripe for national courts to undertake this task, and he expressed concern that any such

[47] Cases 6, 7/73, *Commercial Solvents Co* v. *Commission* [1974] ECR 223, [1974] 1 CMLR 309.
[48] Case T–24/90, *Automec* [1992] ECR II–2223, [1992] 5 CMLR 431.
[49] N. 2 above, 307.
[50] Cases 100–103/80, *Musique Diffusion Française SA* v. *Commission* [1983] ECR 1825, [1983] 3 CMLR 221.
[51] *Ibid.*, paras. 106–7.
[52] *Ibid.*, para. 132.

step would lead to divergent applications of Community law in different Member States, and also to forum shopping.[53]

Where the Commission intends to grant an exemption then it must publish a summary of the relevant notification and invite all interested parties to submit their views within a stated time.[54]

Individual exemptions are issued for a specified period and conditions may be attached.[55] The exemption may be renewed,[56] but it can also be revoked where, for example, the parties breach the conditions or where the facts have changed.[57]

(f) Judicial Review by the CFI

Decisions which have been made by the Commission may be reviewed and this species of review has, since 1989, been undertaken by the CFI rather than the ECJ. Parties who wish to contest Commission action or inaction will bring proceedings under Article 173 or 175 respectively. These will be considered in turn. The general principles concerning these actions have been considered above.[58]

A condition for bringing an action for annulment under Article 173 is that the applicant has standing. This is, as we have seen, often problematic. However, as we have also seen, this hurdle is rather less of a problem in competition matters than it is in relation to other issues.[59] It is clear that the party against whom a competition decision has been made can seek to have that decision annulled: such an applicant is directly and individually concerned by the decision. It is clear also from the *Metro* case[60] that a complainant under Article 3(2) of Regulation 17 will be accorded standing.[61]

An issue which is of some importance in this context concerns the range of measures which may actually be annulled under Article 173. There is little difficulty with the formal decisions which the Commission may make, such as negative clearances, findings of infringement, and the like: these are decisions which can be attacked and struck down. More difficulty has been encountered with less formal measures. The judicial decisions in this respect do not always sit easily together. In the *Perfumes* cases[62] the ECJ held that comfort letters were not acts which were capable of being reviewed, classifying them as purely administrative. This should be contrasted with the approach taken in the *IBM* case[63] where the ECJ held that any act which was capable of affecting the

[53] [1993] 4 CMLR 14, 15.
[54] Reg. 17, Art. 19(3).
[55] *Ibid.*, Art. 8(1).
[56] *Ibid.*, Art. 8(2).
[57] *Ibid.*, Art. 8(3).
[58] See above, Ch. 11.
[59] See above, 468–9.
[60] Case 26/76, n. 36 above.
[61] See also Cases 228, 229/82, *Ford Werke AG* v. *Commission* [1984] ECR 1129, [1984] 1 CMLR 649.
[62] An example of which is Case 99/79, *Lancôme* v. *Etos* [1980] ECR 2511, [1981] 2 CMLR 164. See V. Korah, 'Comfort Letters—Reflections on the *Perfumes* Cases' (1981) 6 ELRev. 14.
[63] Case 60/81, *IBM* v. *Commission* [1981] ECR 2639, [1981] 3 CMLR 635. Compare Cases 142, 156/84, *British American Tobacco Co Ltd and R. J. Reynolds Inc* v. *Commission* [1987] ECR 4487, [1988] 4 CMLR 24: complainants could contest letters from the Commission which constituted a final rejection of their complaint.

interests of the applicant by bringing about a change in its legal position could be reviewed, although it then went on to hold that a statement of objections could not be reviewed since it was merely a preliminary stage in the initiation of formal proceedings.[64]

Once a case has passed the admissibility hurdles review will be undertaken in accordance with the grounds listed in Article 173(1). The intensity of the review process has increased since the task has been allocated to the CFI, and a number of high-profile Commission decisions have been overturned on the facts.[65] However, the CFI has indicated that the intensity of review is limited in situations entailing complex economic assessments.[66] In such circumstances, review should be confined to verifying compliance with procedural rules and those relating to the statement of reasons, verifying the material accuracy of facts and checking to ensure that there has been no manifest error of assessment or misuse of power.

An action may also be brought against the Commission for failure to act under Article 175. One of the most common instances in which parties will attempt to use this provision will be where a complainant is dissatisfied with the Commission's response to its complaint. However, as we have seen,[67] the Commission is not obliged to make any final decision on a complaint which it has received, and it has a discretion whether to use its scarce resources to proceed at all, taking account of the Community interest in the matter.

4. PRIVATE ENFORCEMENT: THE ROLE OF THE NATIONAL COURTS

We have already noted the limited resources which the Commission possesses to enforce the EC norms on competition, and the need therefore to enlist the support of the national courts in this process. This area represents a particularly good example of the way in which public enforcement through the Commission is complemented by private enforcement through national courts. This feature is highlighted by the Notice on Co-operation between National Courts and the Commission in Applying Articles 85 and 86 of the EEC Treaty[68] produced by the Commission, to which reference will be made below. It should be remembered that the distinguishing feature of private enforcement is that the action is brought by a private party at the national level. The national court may make a reference to the ECJ if it feels that this is necessary, but it may instead follow previous ECJ or CFI decisions. What entitles

[64] For further discussion, see above, 448–51.

[65] See e.g. Cases T–79/89 etc., *BASF* v. *Commission* [1992] ECR II–315, [1992] 4 CMLR 357; Cases C–89/85 etc., n. 41 above.

[66] Case T–44/90, n. 35 above; Case T–7/92, n. 25 above, following Cases 142 and 156/84, n. 63 above.

[67] See above, 1009-11.

[68] [1993] OJ C39/6, [1993] 4 CMLR 12.

the private party to begin the action in the national forum is, of course, the doctrine of direct effect: rights are given to individuals which they may enforce through the national legal system.

It is clear that Articles 85 and 86 have direct effect and that they can be enforced in this manner.[69] The national courts can, therefore, apply Articles 85(1), 86, and the block exemptions. However, we have also seen that national courts do not have the authority to give rulings on Article 85(3).

(a) Article 85: Enforcement of Agreements

Agreements which fall within Article 85(1) are held to be automatically void under Article 85(2), subject to the fact that exemption may be granted under Article 85(3). The role of the national courts in adjudicating on agreements which fall within Article 85(1) is brought out in the following case:

Case C–234/89, Delimitis v. Henninger Bräu AG
[1991] ECR I–935, [1992] 5 CMLR 210

The case concerned a publican and a brewery. They had made an agreement which contained various clauses including an obligation on the publican to purchase a certain amount of beer from the brewery. The publican terminated the contract, the brewery claimed that money was still owed and deducted this from the publican's deposit, and the publican then sought recovery of this sum, contending that the agreement was void under Article 85(2). The case has already been considered in the context of the discussion of vertical agreements.[70] What follows concerns the relationship between national courts and Community courts when applying Article 85. The ECJ stated that the Commission had responsibility for the orientation of competition policy, and that it had exclusive competence with respect to Article 85(3). It then continued as follows.

THE ECJ

45. On the other hand, the Commission does not have exclusive competence to apply Articles 85(1) and 86. It shares that competence with the national courts. As the Court stated in Case 127/73, *BRT* v. *SABAM*, Articles 85(1) and 86 produce direct effect in relations between individuals and create rights directly in respect of the individuals concerned which the national courts must safeguard.

46. The same is true of the provisions of the exemption Regulation: Case 63/75, *Fonderies Roubaix*. The direct applicability of those provisions may not, however, lead the national courts to modify the scope of the exemption regulations by extending their sphere of application to agreements not covered by them. Any such extension, whatever its scope, would affect the manner in which the Commission exercises its legislative competence.

47. It now falls to examine the consequences of that division of competence as regards the specific application of the Community competition rules by national

[69] Case 127/73, *Belgische Radio en Televisie and Société Belge des Auteurs, Compositeurs et Editeurs (BRT) de Musique* v. *SV SABAM and NV Fonior* [1974] ECR 51, [1974] 2 CMLR 238.
[70] See above, 908.

courts. Account should here be taken of the risk of national courts taking decisions which conflict with those taken by the Commission in the implementation of Articles 85(1) and 86, and also of Article 85(3). Such conflicting decisions would be contrary to the general principle of legal certainty and must, therefore, be avoided when national courts give decisions on agreements or practices which may subsequently be the subject of a decision by the Commission.

48. As the Court has consistently held, national courts may not, where the Commission has given no decision under Regulation 17, declare automatically void under Article 85(2) agreements which were in existence prior to 13 March 1962, when that Regulation came into force, and have been duly notified: Case 48/72, *Brasserie de Haecht* v. *Wilkin Jansen*; and Case 59/77, *De Bloos* v. *Bouyer*. Those agreements in fact enjoy provisional validity until the Commission has given a decision: Case 99/79, *Lancôme* v. *Etos*.

49. The contract at issue in the main proceedings was entered into on 14 May 1985 . . . The contract would not therefore appear to enjoy provisional validity. Nevertheless, in order to reconcile the need to avoid conflicting decisions with the national court's duty to rule on the claims of a party to the proceedings that the agreement is automatically void, the national court may have regard to the following considerations in applying Article 85.

50. If the conditions for the application of Article 85(1) are clearly not satisfied and there is, consequently, scarcely any risk of the Commission taking a different decision, the national court may continue the proceedings and rule on the agreement in issue. It may do the same if the agreement's incompatibility with Article 85(1) is beyond doubt and, regard being had to the exemption regulations and the Commission's previous decisions, the agreement may on no account be the subject of an exemption decision under Article 85(3).

51. In that connection it should be borne in mind that such a decision may only be taken in respect of an agreement which has been notified or is exempt from having to be notified . . .

52. If the national court finds that the contract in issue satisfies those formal requirements and if it considers in the light of the Commission's rules and decision-making practices, that the agreement may be the subject of an exemption decision, the national court may decide to stay the proceedings or to adopt interim measures pursuant to its national rules of procedure. A stay of proceedings or the adoption of interim measures should also be envisaged where there is a risk of conflicting decisions in the application of Articles 85(1) and 86.

53. It should be noted in this context that it is always open to a national court . . . to seek information from the Commission on the state of any procedure which the Commission may have set in motion and as to the likelihood of its giving an official ruling on the agreement in issue pursuant to Regulation 17. Under the same conditions, the national court may contact the Commission where the concrete application of Article 85(1) or of Article 86 raises particular difficulties, in order to obtain the economic and legal information which that institution can supply to it. Under Article 5 EEC, the Commission is bound by a duty of sincere co-operation with the judicial authorities of the Member State, who are responsible for ensuring that Community law is applied and respected in the national legal system.

54. Finally, the national court may in any event, stay the proceedings and make a reference to the Court for a preliminary ruling under Article 177 EEC.

It is clear from the Court's judgment in the *Delimitis* case that a national court has a number of options open to it. It may be helpful to summarize these briefly. In doing so it is necessary to distinguish the situation where an agreement has not been notified from one where it has.

Let us take, first, the case where there has been *no notification*. We have already seen that notification is a prerequisite for individual exemption under Article 85(3). The options open to national courts are as follows:

—if the agreement is clearly not within Article 85(1) it can proceed and rule on the agreement (paragraph 50 above);[71]
—the same is true if the agreement clearly infringes Article 85(1), and there is no real possibility of a block exemption applying (paragraph 50 above);[72]
—the national court can apply a block exemption (paragraph 46);[73]
—the national court may seek the assistance of the Commission in the manner described above (paragraph 53);[74]
—it may request a preliminary ruling under Article 177 (paragraph 54).

The position with respect to agreements which *have been notified or which do not require notification* is somewhat different. Individual exemption is available in such cases, but cannot be given by the national court. Yet, as we have seen from the judgment in *Delimitis*, national courts do have the right and the duty to apply Article 85(1). The position is further complicated by the fact that new notified agreements, those coming into existence after the entry into force of Regulation 17, do not have the benefit of what is known as provisional validity: if such agreements are within Article 85(1) then Article 85(2) bites at that point, although any exemption will be retrospective to the date when the agreement was notified.[75] Old agreements which existed at the date of entry into force of Regulation 17 do enjoy provisional validity, pending the outcome of the Commission's decision on Article 85(3); the force of Article 85(2) does not bite in relation to these agreements until that decision has been made.[76] The options open to the national courts are as follows:

—if the agreement does not appear to fall within Article 85(1) then the national court can rule on it (*Delimitis* paragraph 50);
—the national court may also rule on the agreement where it clearly does infringe Article 85(1), and there is no possibility of individual exemption being granted (paragraph 50);
—where there is a possibility of an individual exemption then the national court may stay the action or adopt interim measures (paragraph 52);[77]
—the national court may apply a block exemption (paragraph 46);
—a reference may be made under Article 177.

[71] See also Notice on Co-operation, para. 23. [72] *Ibid.*, para. 28.
[73] *Ibid.*, para. 26. [74] *Ibid.*, paras. 33–44. [75] Reg. 17, Art. 6(1).
[76] Case 48/72, *Brasserie de Haecht SA* v. *Wilkin (No 2)* [1973] ECR 77, [1973] CMLR 287; Case 43/69, *Brauerei A. Bilger Söhne GmbH* v. *Jehle* [1970] ECR 127, [1974] 1 CMLR 382.
[77] Notice on Co-operation, paras. 32, 33–44.

(b) National Courts and Comfort Letters

We have already seen that a significant number of competition issues are settled informally and that comfort letters play a central role in this process. These letters are not binding on national courts, and therefore in theory a national court could arrive at a conclusion which is at variance with the substance of the Commission view. However, as Whish notes,[78] 'it would be unusual for a judge to disagree with the opinion of the Commission, and in cases of doubt he could stay the domestic action while the Commission re-examined its file'. Moreover, the Notice on Co-operation[79] reminds us that the ECJ has indicated that national courts may take account of comfort letters which state that Article 85 or 86 does not apply.

(c) Damages Actions

One important issue which still awaits final resolution is the availability of damages actions, in particular for those who may have suffered loss as a result of a breach of Articles 85 or 86. The discussion which follows should be read in conjunction with the more general and detailed analysis of remedies provided above.[80]

In the context of the provisions on competition the leading domestic authority is still the *Garden Cottage* case.[81] In that case the plaintiff brought an action against the Milk Marketing Board, claiming that its refusal to supply certain products was an abuse of Article 86. In the course of the application for an interlocutory injunction Lord Diplock reasoned that an injunction was not necessary since damages could provide an adequate remedy, and that the action should be framed as one for breach of statutory duty, the statute in question being the European Communities Act 1972, section 2.[82] The damages issue was not finally resolved and we still await a definitive pronouncement.

The law relating to remedies for breach of directly effective provisions of Community law has, in any event, moved on since then,[83] and the ECJ has, in cases such as *Francovich*[84], signalled that it will play a greater part than hitherto in determining the remedies which should be available in national legal systems.

It is important, when deciding on the nature of the appropriate legal rule in this area, to keep two issues distinct: one is whether there should be damages liability at all; the other concerns the proper standard of liability to impose. These questions are often elided, the assumption being that if liability is to be

[78] N. 2 above, 323. [79] Para. 20. [80] See above, Ch. 5.
[81] *Garden Cottage Foods* v. *Milk Marketing Board* [1984] AC 130.
[82] F. Jacobs, 'Damages for Breach of Art. 86 EEC' (1983) 8 ELRev. 353.
[83] See above, Ch. 5.
[84] Cases C–6 and 9/90, *Francovich and Bonifaci* v. *Italian Republic* [1991] ECR I–5357, [1993] 2 CMLR 66.

imposed it should be strict. Alternatively some would argue that a finding of fault is inherent in the proof of abuse under Article 86, and that therefore this should suffice for any subsequent damages suit. Matters are not so simple. As Whish notes:[85]

> the 'abuse' of a dominant position is an objective concept and a dominant undertaking may abuse its dominant position without intention or even recklessness. It is not obvious that an undertaking should be liable in these circumstances, since it could render dominant undertakings liable to damages on a very strict basis.

He would prefer a cause of action which would allow a court to distinguish reprehensible cases from those where any harm suffered by the plaintiff is an incidental effect of the defendant's infringement of the competition rules.[86] There is much to be said for this more discriminating approach. It would, in any event, be necessary to develop rules relating to causation and remoteness of damage which would be tailored to the way in which losses can arise in this area.

5. CONCLUSION

The pressures on the Commission mean that the recent trend of encouraging actions to be brought in the national courts will, in all probability, continue. Given that this is so, some 'devolution' of responsibility to the national courts is inevitable, thereby leaving the Commission more time to concentrate on difficult cases or those which break new ground.

From the perspective of the parties concerned there are advantages in this strategy: the action in the national court is not conditional on the approval of the Commission; damages may be claimed; restitutionary relief may be available; and the Community action can be joined with claims based on domestic law. There are also disadvantages:[87] actions at the national level are likely to be more costly than complaint to the Commission; there may be difficulties where the evidence exists in a number of different states; there may be jurisdictional difficulties in finding a suitable forum; differences in procedural rules as between states may lead to forum-shopping; and national courts which are generalist in nature may lack the expertise to be able to deal with issues of this nature. The resolution of the last of these problems may lie in the establishment of a specialist court at the national level to deal with competition issues, whether through the remodelling of the Restrictive Practices Court or the establishment of a new judicial organ.[88]

[85] N. 2 above, 326. See also R. Whish, 'The Enforcement of EC Competition Law in the Domestic Courts of Member States' [1994] 2 ECLR 60.

[86] N. 2 above.

[87] Whish, n. 85 above, 61–2.

[88] *Ibid.*, 67.

6. FURTHER READING

(a) Books

KERSE, C., *EEC Antitrust Procedure* (3rd edn., Sweet & Maxwell, 1993)

(b) Articles

DOHERTY, B., 'Playing Poker with the Commission: Rights of Access to the Commission's File in Competition Cases' [1994] 1 ECLR 8

EDWARD, D., 'Constitutional Rules of Community Law in EEC Competition Cases' (1989–90) 13 Fordham Int. L. Jnl. 111

JOSHUA, J., 'Balancing the Public Interests: Confidentiality, Trade Secret and Disclosure of Evidence in EC Competition Procedures' [1994] 2 ECLR 68

KORAH, V., 'Comfort Letters—Reflections on the *Perfumes* Cases' (1981) 6 ELRev. 14

STEVENS, D., 'The "Comfort Letter": Old Problems, New Developments' [1994] 2 ECLR 81

WHISH, R., 'The Enforcement of EC Competition Law in the Domestic Courts of Member States' [1994] 2 ECLR 60

23

Intellectual Property

1. INTRODUCTION: PROPERTY RIGHTS VERSUS THE SINGLE MARKET

Intellectual property is a generic term which covers both industrial and artistic forms of property right. The more common species of right which are normally included within this generic term are: patents, trade marks, copyright, trade names, and indications of origin.

It is important to understand at the outset why these types of rights pose particular problems for Community law. An example will serve to make this clear. Let us imagine that Digital plc, a company based in the United Kingdom, has made a new piece of electrical equipment. It patents this in the United Kingdom. Digital plc does not, however, have any corporate presence in the rest of Europe, nor does it have experience of doing business from a base in France or Italy etc. Now to be sure it could none the less seek to exploit its new invention by establishing a subsidiary in such countries. But this may involve capital costs which it cannot easily meet, and this, combined with its absence of expertise in undertaking business from a base outside the United Kingdom, may preclude this strategy. Yet Digital plc will want to maximize the return on its invention. What is it to do? One common recourse in such circumstances is for the company to license other firms to make the equipment. Why, then, does this pose any special problem for Community law? The reason is that a standard feature of such arrangements is that the licensee of the patent will possess an exclusive right to market the product in its area, *and* it will often, under national systems of intellectual-property law, have a proprietary right to prevent the import of the product into its own territory from elsewhere. In this way a series of patent licences can have the effect of dividing the Community into a number of self-contained areas within which trade and competition in the relevant goods is not possible.

The potential impact of this for Community law now begins to emerge. We have already seen that one of the essential elements of the EC is a customs union, involving the free movement of goods across national boundaries. Articles 30 to 36 have been one of the major instruments in ensuring that *Member States* do not impede intra-Community trade through tariffs, quotas, and the like. These efforts to ensure a single market shorn of trade barriers would be undermined if *private parties* could, through arrangements such as those mentioned above, effectively re-partition the Community along national lines, or indeed along any lines at all. The EC would have expended considerable legislative and judicial effort in curbing Member State behaviour which divided the market through customs barriers and the like, only to see such boundaries resurrected by private parties.

The Community's legal response to this problem was, however, constrained by the Treaty itself. Article 36 provides that Articles 30 to 34 will not preclude prohibitions on imports or exports which are justified, *inter alia*, on grounds of the protection of industrial or commercial property, subject to the caveat that such prohibitions do not constitute a means of arbitrary discrimination or a disguised restriction on trade between Member States. The message which emerged from Article 36 was reinforced by Article 222, which states that the Treaty shall in *no way* prejudice the rules in Member States governing the system of property ownership.

The judicial resolution of this problem provides a good example of the more general reasoning of the ECJ, and its teleological nature. Given the danger of market partitioning presented by the use to which intellectual-property rights could be put, the Court could not simply stand idly by, content to allow this to happen. Yet, given also the wording of Articles 36 and 222, judicial room for manœuvre was limited. The answer provided by the ECJ was to draw a distinction between the *existence* of an intellectual property right and its *exercise*. The former would be protected by the Treaty, the latter would be subject to the rigours of Articles 30 to 34, and also, as will be seen below, Articles 85 and 86. Referring to Article 36 the ECJ stated that:[1]

> However, it is clear from that same Article, in particular the second sentence, as well as from the context, that whilst the Treaty does not affect the existence of rights recognised by the legislation of a Member State in matters of industrial and commercial property, yet the exercise of those rights may nevertheless, depending on the circumstances, be restricted by the prohibitions in the Treaty. Inasmuch as it provides an exception to one of the fundamental principles of the Common Market, Article 36 in fact admits exceptions to the free movement of goods only to the extent to which such exceptions are justified for the purpose of safeguarding rights which constitute the specific subject-matter of that property.

By bringing the *exercise* of such rights within the remit of the Treaty the Court was able, as we shall see, to control the market-partitioning potential of intellectual-property licences. Licensees would not be able to assert their rights to prevent imports of the goods into their territory from elsewhere.

We shall have occasion to examine the precise meaning of the existence/exercise dichotomy in the ensuing discussion. For the present it should be noted that, in analytical terms, the distinction is questionable. It is

[1] Case 119/75, *Terrapin (Overseas) Ltd* v. *Terranova Industrie C. A. Kapferer and Co* [1976] ECR 1039, [1976] 2 CMLR 482, para. 5.

generally accepted that property as a legal concept is made up of a bundle of rights, powers, privileges, and duties. These constitute the very meaning of property. To say therefore, as the Court does, that the Treaty serves to protect only the existence of a property right and not its exercise should not delude us into thinking that the bundle of rights etc. which would normally comprise this type of property has survived unscathed. It has not. If, absent the Treaty, an intellectual-property right would normally entail the power to license the right to another, in circumstances where the licensee would be able to use the right to prevent imports from outside the territory, then if the Treaty states that this is no longer possible, the effect is to diminish the sum total of rights possessed by both the licensor and licensee of the right. The distinction between existence and exercise should not be allowed to mask this. There is another more practical way of putting the same point. An intellectual-property right, such as a patent, has, like any other species of property, a commercial value. One of the determinants of that value for the licensee, which will influence how much it is willing to pay for the right, will be the degree of protection which the right affords to it from imports of the same goods coming into its territory from elsewhere. If legal rules reduce this degree of protection then the licensee may be willing to pay less for the right. In this sense one result of the ECJ's case law may be to diminish the value of intellectual-property rights to their primary holders and licensees. The justification for this in Community terms is that it is necessary in order to ensure a market free from intra-Community barriers. This rationale may well be convincing, but it should not be forgotten that legal rules can have a distributive impact on income: the Community jurisprudence which has diminished the rights hitherto possessed by holders of intellectual property means that it is they whose property is now worth less than it would otherwise have been.

Cornish captures both the analytical difficulty of sustaining the existence/exercise dichotomy, and the ECJ's real policy object. Speaking of the distinction between existence and exercise, he states that:[2]

> The distinction has also been made to turn upon a 'definition' of the specific subject-matter of the particular right. But, as with the basic dichotomy between existence and exercise, these definitions have the appearance of being formulated only in the wake of a policy decision to give preference to EEC policies beyond a certain point. All this may seem an exercise in legal obscurantism, but the basic intent is not hard to grasp: intellectual property rights are properly exercised when used against goods that come from independent competitors in trade; but they are not to be used against the movement from one Member State to another of goods initially connected with the right-owner.

Having said this, it should also be noted that the precise degree of protection which national legal systems afford to holders of intellectual-property

[2] *Intellectual Property: Patents, Copyright, Trade Marks and Allied Rights* (2nd edn., Sweet & Maxwell, 1989), 21.

rights is itself a policy decision and one which varies from state to state. The following extract from Cornish will help to demonstrate this and place the exhaustion of rights doctrine in perspective:

W. R. Cornish, Intellectual Property: Patents, Copyright, Trade Marks and Allied Rights[3]

The manner in which intellectual property can be deployed to divide markets has been dependent upon the particular form of a right, and so it derives from the national policies behind the creation of the right in the first place . . . One general concept can usefully be introduced here. In every intellectual property law it is necessary to decide which steps in the chain of production and distribution of goods require the licence of the right-owner: manufacture, first sale by the manufacturer, subsequent sales and other dealings, export and import, use. In the past, legislators have often left the answer to the courts. In many cases, both in British and foreign laws, the rights are 'exhausted' after first sale by the right-owner or with his consent. But mostly this is confined to first sales within the territory covered by the right—it amounts to a domestic, rather than international, exhaustion. Accordingly, national rights that are subject to such limitation can still be used to prevent the importation of goods sold abroad by the national right-owner or goods which come from an associated enterprise.

Viewed from this perspective the Community law approach to intellectual property appears less novel or radical than it might otherwise have done. Given that *any* legal system will have to decide on the precise steps in the chain of production which require the consent of the right owner, then EC law is simply making this determination in the context of the Community's own legal order. Given, moreover, that *many* legal systems do operate a concept of exhaustion of rights within a particular nation state, then once again it should not be considered odd for the Community to have done so within the context of the area covered by the Member States; more especially since barriers to intra-Community trade are so anathema to the very idea of the EC.

We are now in a position to examine in more detail the ECJ's case law in this area. The main provisions of the Treaty which are relevant are Articles 30 to 36, and Articles 85 and 86. These will be considered in turn as they relate to certain specific intellectual-property rights. We will begin with patents.

[3] N. 2 above, 19.

2. ARTICLES 30–36: THE EXHAUSTION OF RIGHTS DOCTRINE

(a) Patents

Patents are a reward for inventiveness. When a company spends considerable time and money in developing a new product or a new part then it is given certain rights over the invention for a period of time. The leading decision on the application of the Treaty to patents is *Centrafarm*:

Case 15/74, Centrafarm BV v. Sterling Drug Inc
[1974] ECR 1147, [1974] 2 CMLR 480

Sterling Drug was a company based in New York which held patents in several countries, including Holland and Great Britain, covering the method of preparing a drug for the treatment of urinary-tract infections. Centrafarm imported this drug into Holland from England and Germany without the agreement of Sterling Drug. The drug was considerably cheaper in England than it was in Holland, and this was the motivation for Centrafarm's actions. The drugs had been placed on the market in England and Germany by subsidiaries of Sterling Drug. Could Sterling obtain injunctive relief against Centrafarm to prevent it from selling the drug in Holland? Dutch law said that it could. Did Community law dictate the opposite result? The ECJ reiterated the existence/exercise distinction and proceeded to apply it to the facts of the case.

THE ECJ

9. As regards patents, the specific object of industrial property is *inter alia* to ensure to the holder, so as to recompense the creative effort of the inventor, the exclusive right to utilise an invention with a view to manufacture and first putting into circulation of industrial products, either directly or by the grant of licences to third parties, as well as the right to oppose any infringement.

10. The existence, in national law on industrial and commercial property, of provisions that the right of a patentee is not exhausted by the marketing in another Member State of the patented product, so that the patentee may oppose the import into his own State of the product marketed in another State, may constitute an obstacle to the free movement of goods.

11. While such an obstacle to free movement may be justifiable for reasons of protection of industrial property when the protection is invoked against a product coming from a Member State in which it is not patentable and has been manufactured by third parties without the consent of the patentee or where the original patentees are legally and economically independent of each other, the derogation to the principle of free movement of goods is not justified when the product has been lawfully put by the patentee himself or with his consent, on the market of the Member State from which it is being imported, *e.g.*, in the case of the holder of parallel patents.

12. If a patentee could forbid the import of protected products which had been marketed in another Member State by him or with his consent he would be

enabled to partition the national markets and thus to maintain a restriction on the trade between the Member States without such a restriction being necessary for him to enjoy the substance of the exclusive rights deriving from the parallel patents.

13. The plaintiff has argued along these lines that because of the variations between the national laws and practices there are no truly identical or parallel patents.

14. On that it should be noted that in spite of the variations in the national rules on industrial property resulting from lack of unification, the essential element for the judge to decide in the notion of parallel patents is the identity of the protected invention.

15. The question should therefore be answered to the effect that the exercise by a patentee of the right given him by the laws of a Member State to prohibit the marketing in that State of a product protected by the patent and put on the market in another Member State by such patentee or with his consent would be incompatible with the rules of the EEC Treaty relating to the free movement of goods in the Common Market.

The ECJ's judgment therefore defines the *existence* or *specific subject-matter* of the patent as being the right of the patent holder itself, or through its licensees, to the initial marketing of the product, and as a necessary corollary, the right to bring actions for any infringement of this right. This, says the Court, is the reward for inventiveness which the patent is designed to secure. This is not affected by Community law.

Once the product has initially been marketed in this fashion then Community law will impinge on the *exercise* of the right. The ECJ develops the *exhaustion of rights* doctrine to give expression to the limitations which EC law imposes on the exercise of the right. The patent holder's rights are exhausted, in the sense that it cannot object to what occurred in this very case: it cannot prevent the goods from being bought by a third party in a country where the patentee or its licensee has marketed the goods, and being sold into another country. It should be noted that it is irrelevant in this respect whether the patentee and licensee belong to the same corporate group. The fact that a firm is a licensee, and hence selling with the consent of the patentee, suffices to bring the exhaustion of rights doctrine into play.[4]

The Court is willing to recognize only two situations in which the patentee or its licensee could obtain injunctive relief of the type being sought here. This is where it is sought against goods coming from a state where they are not patentable and have been manufactured by third parties without the consent of the patentee; or where the original patentees are legally and economically independent of each other (paragraph 11). Neither of these is in reality an exception to the exhaustion of rights doctrine, since in neither instance has the original patentee obtained the benefit of the initial marketing of the goods.

[4] See paras. 16–20 of the ECJ's judgment. See, however, the discussion below, 1048–50, concerning the position where intellectual-property rights are assigned rather than licensed.

It is clear, moreover, that the ECJ will strictly construe any qualifications to the exhaustion of rights doctrine. We have seen that one such qualification operates where the goods are imported from a country where they are not patentable *and* they have been made by third parties without the consent of the patentee. It is clear that both conditions must be met. Thus if the patentee chooses to market the goods in a state where there is no patent protection available, then it cannot use its patent rights in a different country to prevent the import of these products. This is evident from *Merck* v. *Stephar*.[5] Merck held a patent in Holland for a certain drug. Stephar had imported the same goods into Holland from Italy where they were not patentable, but had been placed on the market by Merck none the less. Merck argued that *Centrafarm* should be distinguished since in this case it had not been able to obtain patent protection in Italy, and hence its sales in that country did not secure it any monopoly return. The ECJ was unconvinced:[6]

> It is for the proprietor of the patent to decide, in the light of all the circumstances, under what conditions he will market his product, including the possibility of marketing it in a Member State where the law does not provide patent protection for the product in question. If he decides to do so he must accept the consequences of his choice as regards the free movement of the product within the Common Market, which is a fundamental principle forming part of the legal and economic circumstances which must be taken into account by the proprietor of the patent in determining the manner in which his exclusive right will be exercised.

The patent holder therefore has a stark choice. It can choose not to market in a country such as Italy, in which patent protection is not available, with the consequence that it could use its Dutch patent rights to prevent the import of any such goods from Italy into Holland. It can choose to make any possible gains from the Italian market by consenting to the manufacture of its goods in that country, but then it cannot legally prevent the import of the goods into Holland.

It is, then, as Advocate General Mancini stated in the *Pharmon* case,[7] the patentee or licensee's consent which 'opens the door of the common market to patented products'. It is not the actual realisation of a monopoly profit. Where this consent does not exist, as in the case where the goods are initially marketed by a third party without the consent of the patentee, then import of the goods can be prevented. So, too, can they when the initial marketing is pursuant to a compulsory licence as demonstrated by the *Pharmon* case itself:

Case 19/84, Pharmon BV v. Hoechst AG
[1985] ECR 2281

Hoechst owned patents for a certain drug in Germany, The Netherlands and Great Britain. A company in the United Kingdom, DDSA, obtained a

[5] Case 187/80, [1981] ECR 2063, [1981] 3 CMLR 463.
[6] *Ibid.*, 2081–2 (ECR).
[7] Case 19/84, *Pharmon BV* v. *Hoechst AG* [1985] ECR 2281, 2288.

compulsory licence for the product pursuant to United Kingdom law; the licence prohibited exportation of the goods and was non-assignable. In breach of this condition DDSA sold to Pharmon, a Dutch company, a large consignment of the drugs which it had made. Pharmon sought to market these in the Netherlands, and Hoechst sought an injunction to prevent Pharmon from infringing Hoecht's Dutch patent. So the key question was could Hoechst use its patent rights in the Netherlands to prevent the marketing of goods which had been obtained from a third party pursuant to a compulsory licence which that third party had been granted under a parallel patent? Pharmon argued that there was little difference between a licence freely granted and a compulsory licence: the existence of either served to exhaust the patentee's rights. The ECJ disagreed.

THE ECJ

22. It must be recalled that the Court has consistently held that Articles 30 and 36 of the EEC Treaty preclude the application of national provisions which enable a patent proprietor to prevent the importation and marketing of a product which has been lawfully marketed in another Member State by the patent proprietor himself, with his consent, or by a person economically or legally dependent on him.

23. If a patent proprietor could preclude the importation of protected products marketed in another Member State by him or with his consent, he would be able to partition the national markets and thus restrict trade between the Member States, although such a restriction is not necessary to protect the substance of the exclusive rights under the patents.

24. The Hoge Raad's question is therefore essentially intended to establish whether the same rules apply where the product imported and offered for sale has been manufactured in the exporting Member State by the holder of a compulsory licence granted in respect of a parallel patent held by the proprietor of the patent in the importing Member State.

25. It is necessary to point out that where, as in this instance, the competent authorities of a Member State grant a third party a compulsory licence which allows him to carry out manufacturing and marketing operations which the patentee would normally have the right to prevent, the patentee cannot be deemed to have consented to the operation of that third party.

26. As the Court most recently held in its judgment of 14 July 1981 (*Merck* . . .), the substance of a patent lies essentially in according the inventor an exclusive right of first placing the product on the market so as to allow him to obtain the reward for his creative efforts. It is therefore necessary to allow the patent proprietor to prevent the importation and marketing of products manufactured under a compulsory licence in order to protect the substance of his exclusive rights under his patent.

(b) Trade Marks

Trade marks, such as Coca-Cola or Martini, serve two related ends: they ensure to the holder of the mark the goodwill associated with the marked product, which may well have been built up over a period of time and with considerable expenditure by the manufacturer of the product; and they inform the customer that the product is indeed of a specific kind, as opposed to a copy. The compatibility of national rules concerning trade-mark protection with Community law has come before the ECJ on a number of occasions. The *Centrafarm* case laid the initial foundations of Community legal policy in this area:

Case 16/74, Centrafarm BV v. Winthrop BV
[1974] ECR 1183, [1974] 2 CMLR 480

This case arose out of the same facts as *Centrafarm* v. *Sterling Drug* considered above. Sterling Drug (SD) held a trade mark for its patented drug. The trade mark was 'Negram', and was held in the United Kingdom by Sterling-Winthrop Group Ltd., and in Holland by a subsidiary, Winthrop BV. Centrafarm imported the drugs into Holland from the United Kingdom and Germany where they had been placed on the market by subsidiaries of SD. Some of the goods imported bore the 'Negram' mark. Winthrop BV sought to prevent this as an infringement of the mark which it held in Holland; Dutch law afforded Winthrop BV the relief it claimed. The question for the ECJ was whether EC law forbade a trade-mark holder such as Winthrop BV from preventing the import of marked goods which originated in another country where they had been placed on the market of that other country by the trade-mark owner or with its consent. The ECJ repeated the general principles which it had enunciated in the related case on patents. It then proceeded to apply this reasoning to trade marks.

THE ECJ

8. As regards trade marks, the specific object of commercial property is *inter alia* to ensure to the holder the exclusive right to utilise the mark for the first putting into circulation of a product, and to protect him thus against competitors who would take advantage of the position and reputation of the mark by selling goods improperly bearing that mark.

9. The existence, in national laws on industrial and commercial property, of provisions that the right of the trade mark holder is not exhausted by the marketing in another Member State of the product protected by the mark, so that the holder may oppose the import into his own State of the product marketed in another State, may constitute an obstacle to the free movement of goods.

10. Such an obstacle is not justified when the product has been lawfully put, by the holder himself or with his consent, on the market of the Member State from which it is imported in such a way that there can be no question of abuse or infringement of the mark.

11. If the holder of the mark could forbid the import of the protected products, which had been marketed in another State by him or with his consent, he would be enabled to partition the national markets and thus to maintain a restriction on the trade between the Member States without such a restriction being necessary for him to enjoy the substance of the exclusive right deriving from the mark.

12. The question should therefore be answered to the effect that the exercise by the holder of a mark of the right given him by the laws of a Member State to prohibit the marketing in that State of a product bearing the mark put on the market in another Member State by such holder or with his consent would be incompatible with the rules of the EEC Treaty relating to the free movement of goods in the Common Market.

The ECJ's reasoning follows closely that which it had used in the related case on patents.

The *specific object* of a trade mark, which would be protected by Community law, was the right to place the goods initially on the market. This, said the Court, would safeguard the holder of the mark against competitors who sought to take advantage of the reputation possessed by the marked goods by selling goods which improperly bore that mark. In this sense Community law would recognize and protect the *existence* of this property right.

Beyond this the *exercise* of trade-mark rights which existed in national legal systems would be controlled by EC law. Once again *consent* becomes the key to the *exhaustion of rights*. It is the placing of the goods on the market by the trade-mark holder itself, or with its consent, which exhausts the rights of all those who derive their mark through the initial holder of the mark. It is, however, now clear that the consent principle will only apply so as to exhaust rights where the owners of the trade mark in the importing and exporting states are the same, or where, even though they are separate, they are economically linked.[8] This latter idea will cover products placed into circulation by the same undertaking, by a licensee, by a parent company, by a subsidiary of the same group, or by an exclusive distributor. It will not normally cover the situation where goods are placed on the market by an assignee of a trade mark, if there is no legal or economic link between the assignor and the assignee. The rationale for this will be considered more fully below.[9]

The application of these principles can, however, be problematic, since it may well be the case that the importer who is in the position of Centrafarm in the preceding case actually alters the packaging of the goods in some way. This occurred in the following case, in which one of the protagonists was once again Centrafarm:

Case 102/77, Hoffmann-La Roche & Co AG v. Centrafarm Vertriebsgesellschaft Pharmazeutischer Erzeugnisse mbH [1978] ECR 1139, [1978] 3 CMLR 217[10]

Hoffmann-La Roche (HLR) manufactured a drug under the mark 'Valium Roche' in Germany in batches of twenty to fifty for individual use, and 100 to 250 for hospital use. The British subsidiary of HLR marketed the same product at lower prices than in Germany in batches of 100 to 500. Centrafarm bought supplies of the drug in England, which it put into packages of 1,000 tablets. Centrafarm affixed the HLR trade mark, together with a notice that the product had been marketed by Centrafarm. Centrafarm also stated that it intended to repack tablets into smaller packages for sale to individuals. HLR sought to prevent this and under German law would be able to do so. The ECJ repeated its view from

[8] Case C–9/93, *IHT Internationale Heiztechnik GmbH* v. *Ideal-Standard GmbH* [1994] ECR I–2789.

[9] See below, 1048–50.

[10] Cf. Case 1/81, *Pfizer* v. *Eurim-Pharm* [1981] ECR 2913, [1982] 1 CMLR 406.

Centrafarm v. *Winthrop* (paragraph 8) on what constituted the specific subject-matter of a trade mark. It then continued as follows.

THE ECJ

7. . . In order to answer the question whether that exclusive right involves the right to prevent the trade mark being affixed by a third person after the product has been repackaged, regard must be had to the essential function of the trade mark, which is to guarantee the identity of the origin of the trade-marked product to the consumer or ultimate user, by enabling him without any possibility of confusion to distinguish that product from products which have another origin. This guarantee of origin means that the consumer or ultimate user can be certain that a trade-marked product which is sold to him has not been subject at a previous stage of marketing to interference by a third person, without the authorisation of the proprietor of the trade mark, such as to affect the original condition of the product. The right attributed to the proprietor of preventing any use of the trade mark which is likely to impair the guarantee of origin so understood is therefore part of the specific subject-matter of the trade mark right.

8. It is accordingly justified under the first sentence of Article 36 to recognise that the proprietor of a trade mark right is entitled to prevent an importer of a trade-marked product, following repackaging of that product, from affixing the trade mark to the new packaging without the authorisation of the proprietor.

9. It is however necessary to consider whether the exercise of such a right may constitute a 'disguised restriction on trade between Member States' within the meaning of the second sentence of Article 36. Such a restriction might arise, *inter alia*, from the proprietor of the trade mark putting on to the market in various Member States an identical product in various packages while availing himself of the rights inherent in the trade mark to prevent repackaging by a third person even if it were done in such a way that the identity of origin of the trade-marked product and its original condition could not be affected. The question, therefore, in the present case is whether the repackaging of a trade-marked product such as that undertaken by Centrafarm is capable of affecting the original condition of the product.

10. In this respect the answer must vary according to the circumstances and in particular according to the nature of the product and the method of repackaging. Depending on the nature of the product, repackaging in many cases inevitably affects its condition, while in others repackaging involves a more or less obvious risk that the product might be interfered with or its original condition otherwise affected. Nevertheless, it is possible to conceive of the repackaging being undertaken in such a way that the original condition of the product cannot be affected. This may be so where, for example, the proprietor of the trade mark has marketed the product in double packaging and the repackaging affects only the external packaging, leaving the internal packaging intact, or where the repackaging is inspected by a public authority for the purpose of ensuring that the product is not adversely affected. Where the essential function of the trade mark to guarantee the origin of the product is thus protected, the exercise of his rights by the proprietor of the trade mark in order to fetter the free movement of goods between Member States may constitute a disguised restriction within the meaning of the second sentence of Article 36 of the Treaty if it is established that the use of the trade mark right by the proprietor, having regard to the marketing system which he has

adopted, will contribute to the artificial partitioning of the markets between Member States.

A similar problem arose in *Centrafarm BV* v. *American Home Products Corporation*.[11] In this case American Home Products (AHP) owned trade marks for the same product in different Member States. Centrafarm was once again the hero or the villain of the piece depending upon one's perspective. It bought the product which had been lawfully marketed in the United Kingdom under one trade mark, and then imported it into Holland, where it sold it under the mark used for the goods in that country. The product was unaltered.

The ECJ held that importation under these circumstances *could be* prevented by AHP. The right to affix a particular trade mark to a product was, said the Court, part of the specific subject-matter of the trade mark; it went to the existence of the mark itself. AHP could therefore prevent Centrafarm from changing the mark, since this would thereby safeguard the guarantee of origin which was one of the main purposes of a trade mark. This was so even where, as here, the goods had lawfully been placed on the market of one state under one trade mark.[12]

The Court accepted that it was legitimate for a company to use varying marks in different states. It was however mindful of the possibility that a company might seek, in the light of the ECJ's reasoning, to use different marks in different states with the intention of partitioning the market. If this was so it would constitute a disguised restriction on trade within the meaning of Article 36 and would be unlawful. It was for the national courts to decide in any particular case whether this was the object of the trade-mark holder.[13]

(c) Copyright

The ECJ has, as will be seen, applied the same basic approach to copyright as it has to patents and trade marks. The application of these principles may, however, be more complex than in the cases which we have considered hitherto. This is in part because of the variety of artistic work which is covered by copyright laws. A glimpse through any work on copyright will attest to this diversity. Thus copyright law will apply, albeit in different ways, to literary, dramatic, and musical work; to artistic work; to sound recording; to film; and to broadcast or cablecast.[14] This very diversity means that the purpose behind copyright protection may not always be the same. To be sure, the basic root of copyright may well be to protect the ownership of a certain book, play, etc. from reproduction without the consent of the author. But the very form of this reproduction may differ significantly from, for example, the unauthorized reproduction of a song into a sound recording, to the illegal performance of

[11] Case 3/78, [1978] ECR 1823, [1979] 1 CMLR 326.
[12] *Ibid.*, paras. 11–18.
[13] *Ibid.*, paras. 19–23.
[14] Cornish, n. 2 above, 266–7.

a play on a number of occasions without the consent of the author. It is for these reasons that it may be difficult to state with exactitude what the 'specific subject-matter' of copyright protection actually is, with the consequence that the impact of EC law may not always be clear.

One of the early cases in which the ECJ applied the Treaty to copyright was *Deutsche Grammophon* v. *Metro*.[15] Once again, as in the cases concerning patents and trade marks, price differentials lay at the heart of the matter. Deutsche Grammophon (DG) made records and sold them in Germany under a retail-price-maintenance scheme. It exported records to France where they were marketed by Polydor, which was a subsidiary of DG. Metro obtained records sold by Polydor in France and resold them in Germany at prices which were below the established price. DG used its exclusive right of distribution under German law, which was a right similar to copyright, in order to prevent Metro's actions. The ECJ based its judgment on the notion of consent: DG had placed the records on the market through Polydor in France, and could not therefore now complain when Metro sought to import them into Germany; national laws which allowed a firm such as DG to do this would be contrary to the principles of free movement of goods.

A more complete enunciation of Community law as it applies to copyright is to be found in the next case, which also concerned records:

Cases 55 and 57/80, Musik-Vertrieb Membran GmbH v. Gesellschaft für Musikalische Aufführungs- und Mechanische Vervielfältigungsrechte (GEMA) [1981] ECR 147, [1981] 2 CMLR 44

GEMA is the German copyright-management society. Certain records were imported into Germany from other Member States. These records had been manufactured and placed on those markets with the consent of the copyright owner, but the royalties had been calculated only on the basis of distribution in the country of manufacture. GEMA claimed that its members were entitled to an extra royalty when the goods were imported into Germany, which was to be calculated on the basis of the German royalty less the amount of the lower royalty which had already been paid in the country of manufacture. This claim was recognized in German national law. Was it compatible with Articles 30 to 36?

THE ECJ

10. It is apparent from the well-established case law of the Court and most recently from the judgment . . . in Case 119/75, *Terrapin Overseas Ltd* that the proprietor of an industrial or commercial right protected by the law of a Member State cannot rely on that law to prevent the importation of a product which has been lawfully marketed in another Member State by the proprietor himself or with his consent.

. . .

16. GEMA has argued that such an interpretation of Articles 30–36 of the Treaty is not sufficient to resolve the problem facing the national court since

[15] Case 78/70, [1971] ECR 487, [1971] CMLR 631.

GEMA's application to the German courts is not for the prohibition or restriction of the marketing of the gramophone records and tape cassettes in question on German territory but for equality in the royalties paid for any distribution of those sound recordings on the German market. The owner of a copyright in a recorded musical work has a legitimate interest in receiving and retaining the benefit of his intellectual or artistic effort regardless of the degree to which his work is distributed and consequently it is maintained that he should not lose the right to claim royalties equal to those paid in the country in which the recorded work is marketed.

17. It should first be observed that the question put by the national court is concerned with the legal consequences of infringement of copyright . . . On any view its claims are in fact founded on the copyright owner's exclusive right of exploitation, which enables him to prohibit or restrict the free movement of the products incorporating the protected musical work.

18. It should be observed next that no provision of national legislation may permit an undertaking which is responsible for the management of copyrights and has a monopoly on the territory of a Member State by virtue of that management to charge a levy on products imported from another Member State where they were put into circulation by or with the consent of the copyright owner and thereby cause the Common Market to be partitioned. Such a practice would amount to allowing a private undertaking to impose a charge on the importation of sound recordings which are already in free circulation in the Common Market on account of their crossing a frontier; it would have the effect of entrenching the isolation of national markets which the Treaty seeks to abolish.

19. It follows from those considerations that this argument must be rejected as being incompatible with the operation of the Common Market and with the aims of the Treaty.

. . .

25. It should further be observed that in a common market distinguished by free movement of goods and freedom to provide services an author . . . is free to choose the place, in any of the Member States, in which to put his work into circulation. He may make that choice according to his best interests, which involve not only the level of remuneration provided in the Member State in question but other factors such as, for example, the opportunities for distributing his work and the marketing facilities which are further enhanced by virtue of the free movement of goods within the Community. In those circumstances, a copyright management society may not be permitted to claim, on the importation of sound recordings into another Member State, payment of additional fees based on the difference in the rates of remuneration in the various Member States.

The ECJ's reasoning flows neatly from its initial premise that consent is the controlling criterion: GEMA would have no right to prevent the import of goods which have been placed in free circulation with its consent in other states (paragraph 10); any claim for the extra royalty must, in effect, be based on the continuing existence in the copyright holder of a right to control the movement of such goods when they have been placed on the market with its consent (paragraph 17); but the continued existence of this right, and the consequent ability to levy the extra royalty, were inconsistent with the principle that a consensual placing of the goods on the market exhausted the rights of the copyright holder (paragraph 18). The message is clear and it is one which we have seen before in the context of patents. If the copyright holder wishes to reap the benefits of placing the goods on the market in one state then it will have to rest content with whatever return is received in that state; it will not be able to 'top up' relatively low royalties in state *A* if and when the goods are imported into state *B* (paragraph 25). The ECJ was not dissuaded from this conclusion by the fact that the effect of the United Kingdom Copyright Act 1956 was to place a relatively low ceiling on royalty levels. The resulting disparity between national laws was something which should be resolved through Community harmonization; it did not serve to justify national measures which were incompatible with EC law;[16] and it certainly did not justify the proposition that, in the absence of harmonization, national laws on intellectual property were predominant over the free movement of goods.[17]

The ECJ's decision in *GEMA* identifies its general strategy towards conflicts between EC law and national regimes on copyright. There can, however, be problems with the application of this strategy to more particular cases. Two such problems can be identified here.

The first problem revolves around the meaning to be attributed to the notion of consent, which plays such a central role in this area. This issue arose in *EMI Electrola*.[18] In this case EMI Electrola was a German company which was the assignee of rights to works by Cliff Richard. It objected to the import from Denmark of Cliff Richard records. The defendant argued that EMI's rights were exhausted, and that the records had been lawfully marketed in Denmark because the period of protection under Danish copyright law had expired. It was open to the Court to reach one of two conclusions. Either it could find for the defendant on the basis that the time for copyright protection had run out in Denmark, that the copyright holder had enjoyed his legitimate protection, and that therefore the goods could move freely from Denmark elsewhere. Or it could decide that the sale in Denmark was not with the consent of the copyright holder, but only because the copyright had run out, and that therefore this was not a consensual exhaustion of rights within the *GEMA* principle. The ECJ adopted the latter course and held that the plaintiff could prevent the import into Germany.

The second problem is more complex, and arises because of the very real differences in the types of copyright claims which can arise. The problem can be presented in the following way. Cases such as *GEMA* itself centred on copyright claims where the subject matter of the claim arose in connection with literary or artistic works, where the placing of those works at the disposal of the public involves the actual circulation of the works themselves, in the form of books or records. In this type of case the ECJ, as we have seen, has decided that the specific subject matter of copyright which will be protected

[16] [1981] ECR 147, paras. 21–4.

[17] *Ibid.*, para. 14.

[18] Case 341/87, *EMI Electrola GmbH* v. *Patricia Im- und Export* [1989] ECR 79, [1989] 2 CMLR 413.

by Community law is the right of the author to reproduce and distribute the work; where he or she has consented to that, either personally or through another, then these rights will generally be exhausted throughout the Community. The matter is more complex when the nature of the copyright differs. Films, for example, are often made available to the public through public cinema, and one characteristic of this means of distribution is repeated performances. Fees will be calculated on the basis of the actual or probable number of performances. In this type of case we may therefore need to characterize the specific subject matter of the copyright differently from the case of the one-off sale; and hence the application of EC law may also differ. Two cases exemplify this problem.

In *Coditel*[19] Ciné Vog Films (CVF) brought an action for infringement of copyright for damage caused to it by the reception in Belgium of a broadcast from Germany of a Chabrol film, *Le Boucher*, for which CVF had the exclusive-distribution rights in Belgium. The showing of the film on television had, said CVF, jeopardized the commercial future of the film at cinemas in Belgium. The action was brought against the company which gave CVF the exclusive right and against Coditel, the Belgian cable company which had transmitted the film from Germany to Belgium. The question before the Court was whether Articles 59 and 60 of the Treaty prohibited an assignment of the copyright of a film which was limited to one Member State, the argument being that a series of such assignments could lead to the partitioning of the Community market.

The ECJ held that there was no infringement of the Treaty. It accepted that, in the case of copyright works such as books or records, the specific subject-matter was the right of exclusive initial reproduction or distribution of the book or record. It was, said the Court, different where, as in the case of a film, the artistic work is intended to be infinitely repeated. In this type of case the specific subject-matter of the copyright was different: 'the right of a copyright owner and his assigns to require fees for any showing of a film is part of the essential function of copyright in this type of literary and artistic work'.[20] Given that this was so, the realization of the copyright in films, and the fees attaching thereto, could not be attained without considering the possibility of television broadcasts, since this would lessen any revenue obtainable from showings at the cinema. The ECJ therefore concluded that CVF could rely on its exclusive assignment for the film in Belgium and that this enabled it to pursue its claim for recompense for the showing of the film by Coditel, even though Coditel transmitted the film after it was shown in Germany with the consent of the original copyright holder.[21]

The next decision is more problematic and demonstrates that there may be real difficulties in actually characterizing the nature of the copyright subject matter which is at stake. In *Warner Brothers*[22] Warner owned the United

[19] Case 62/79, *SA Compagnie Générale pour la Diffusion de la Télévision, Coditel* v. *SA Ciné Vog Films* [1980] ECR 881, [1981] 2 CMLR 362.

[20] *Ibid.*, para. 14.

[21] *Ibid.*, para. 18.

[22] Case 158/86, *Warner Brothers and Metronome Video ApS* v. *Christiansen* [1988] ECR 2605, [1990] 3 CMLR 684.

Kingdom copyright in the film *Never Say Never Again.* It assigned the video production rights in Denmark to Metronome. The videocassette was on sale in London and Christiansen bought it with a view to hiring it out in Denmark. Warner and Metronome sought to prevent this. Under Danish law this was possible, since the author of a work had to give his or her consent to a hiring out. Under United Kingdom law the author could control the initial sale of a work, but had no control over any subsequent hiring out.

Advocate General Mancini had no doubt that the case *was* covered by *GEMA*. He reasoned as follows. The *GEMA* case had applied the exhaustion principle to copyright, provided that the sale of the work was by the author etc. or with its consent. Although hiring out was obviously a different factual matter than sale, both involved making the product available to the consumer. The consensual principle from *GEMA* applied accordingly: the initial sale exhausted the proprietary rights of the original owner of the work; it could henceforth move freely within the EC; this free movement would be encumbered by accepting that the author could maintain any residual or further right to control the hiring of the work.[23]

The ECJ by way of contrast was equally clear that this case *was not* covered by *GEMA*. Christiansen relied on *GEMA* to argue that the copyright owner made its own marketing choice; if it chose to sell the video in a country which then afforded the seller no control over hiring out, so be it. The seller's rights over subsequent sale or hire were exhausted irrespective of whether or not the country of import gave the author power over hiring out. The ECJ disagreed. An important factor for the Court was that royalties have traditionally only been collected on sales, not hiring out, and this has rendered it impossible for film makers to gain a satisfactory return from the rental market. It therefore held that national laws designed to provide specific protection for the film maker in the hiring market were justified in principle as a protection of an industrial property right within Article 36. The defendant's argument based on *GEMA* could not be accepted, since 'where national legislation confers on authors a specific right to hire out video-cassettes, that right would be rendered worthless if its owner were not in a position to authorize the operations for doing so'.[24]

At first glance the reasoning of the ECJ is difficult to reconcile with that in *GEMA*. The key to the ECJ's analysis in *Warner Brothers* is its acceptance of the fact that the poor return to authors from the rental market justified laws such as those in Denmark which gave the author power over hiring out, and served to qualify the exhaustion of rights principle. Yet in *GEMA* it was unconvinced by the argument that the way in which the royalty system operated in some countries meant the returns to authors etc. would always be lower from those countries, thereby justifying the extra fee which GEMA sought on import of the records into Germany. The Court was not willing to accept that this could qualify the exhaustion principle. Problems of this kind should, it said, be addressed by harmonization.

[23] *Ibid.*, 2623–2624. [24] *Ibid.*, para. 18.

The only way to reconcile the two cases is to accept, as the Court did in *Warner Brothers*, that the nature of the copyright which was at stake was different from that in *GEMA*. This was the essential reason for the difference in view between the Advocate General and the Court itself. The former simply treated any rights which the copyright owner might have over hire as but part of the rights which it might have over sale and subsequent distribution. The Court, in effect, disaggregates the two issues, and is willing to recognize that there is a valid and separate issue concerning copyright protection which relates to hire. Given this crucial step, it is then willing to accept national laws which do no more than protect the specific subject matter of *this* facet of copyright.

3. THE LIMITS OF ARTICLES 30–36: THE DEMISE OF THE COMMON ORIGIN DOCTRINE AND THE LIMITS OF CONSENT

The discussion thus far has focused upon the application of Articles 30 to 36 to intellectual-property rights. We have noted the conceptual basis of the ECJ's jurisprudence, in the form of the exhaustion of rights doctrine, and the limits which the Court itself has recognized to the reach of this idea. The Court has, however, applied Community law to intellectual-property rights beyond the exhaustion of rights doctrine. It has held that trade marks can be caught by Community law on the basis of their common origin. The relevant ECJ decisions were much criticized and, as will be seen below, the Court has now in effect departed from its own previous rulings. Some understanding of this case law is none the less important because of the light which it sheds on the more general approach of the ECJ to the relationship between intellectual-property rights and the EC Treaty. The subsequent discussion will show why it is so important to delineate accurately the specific subject matter of a particular intellectual-property right. It was confusion in this respect which caused the initial mistakes by the ECJ when it invented the common origin doctrine.

The villain of the peace was the decision by the ECJ in *Hag*.[25] The trade mark for the decaffeinated coffee 'Hag' was originally owned by Hag AG, a German company. It registered the mark in Germany, Belgium, and Luxembourg. In 1927 the mark for the latter two countries was transferred to a subsidiary of Hag AG based in Belgium. After the war in 1944 German property in Belgium was sequestered, and the shares in the subsidiary were sold to the Van Oevelen family. In 1971 this trade mark in Hag was further transferred to Van Zuylen Frères (VZF). The German Hag company then

[25] Case 192/73, *Van Zuylen Frères* v. *Hag AG* [1974] ECR 731, [1974] 2 CMLR 127.

sought to sell coffee in Luxembourg and VZF sought an injunction to prevent this, arguing that the sale infringed its trade-mark rights for that country.

One of the questions before the Court was whether the grant of such an injunction would infringe Articles 30 to 36. The ECJ held that it could, and that this was so even though there was no financial, legal, or economic connection between VZF and Hag AG, the German company. The reasoning of the ECJ was as follows. It noted that trade marks could have the effect of partitioning the common market, more particularly since they are not subject to any temporal limit.[26] It was therefore incompatible with Articles 30 to 36 to allow the owner of a mark in one state to prevent the import of goods bearing the same mark from another state, where the mark had the same origin, notwithstanding the fact that there was no connection between the relevant firms.[27] The ECJ acknowledged that a trade mark performs the function of indicating the origin of the products, but said that this could be accomplished by other means which would not have the same detrimental effect on the free movement of goods.[28] There are a number of problems with this reasoning. Two may be mentioned here.

On the one hand, the Court's reasoning reduces the specific subject matter of the trade mark to almost vanishing point. This exemplifies the point made above, concerning the need for care when identifying what is the specific function of a particular intellectual-property right. We have already noted that trade marks serve two related ends: protection of the goodwill of the manufacturer who may have expended time and money in developing that product name, while earning a reputation for quality; and an indication for the consumer that the product to be purchased is of a specific kind and quality. Yet the reasoning of the Court in *Hag* wholly ignores the first of these arguments, and purports to address the second by the weak response that this object can be met in some other ill-defined manner.

On the other hand, the case considerably exaggerates the danger of market partitioning presented by this type of fact pattern. This danger is undoubtedly a real one in the situation where a holder of a trade mark in one state then licences or assigns the right to firms in the other Member States. If each of these licensees or assignees could prevent the movement of goods into their area from outside, then the common market could easily be divided along national lines. This was the rationale for the exhaustion of rights doctrine, to prevent just such an occurrence. Yet the very facts of a case such as *Hag* mean that any *systematic* or *thoroughgoing* market division will simply not occur. This is precisely because the firms in question do not have any legal or economic links. They are merely separate holders of a mark which has the same origin. Any market-partitioning effect will therefore be limited.

The criticism which greeted the *Hag I* decision led the Court to attempt a more elaborate defence of the notion of common origin. This it proffered in *Terrapin*.[29] In that case the ECJ accepted that Articles 30 to 36 of the Treaty

[26] *Ibid.*, para. 11. [27] *Ibid.*, para. 15. [28] *Ibid.*, para. 14.
[29] Case 119/75, n. 1 above, para. 6.

did not prohibit the use of a trade-mark right in one Member State to prevent the import of goods bearing a different, but similar, trade mark, where there was no economic link between the different firms, and where the firms were independent of each other. However, the ECJ continued to accept the common origin principle from *Hag I*, and it sought to respond to the argument that the effect of its judgment in *Hag I* was to undermine one of the functions of a trade mark: that of indicating the origin of the goods. The reply offered by the Court was that in cases such as *Hag* the indication of origin was, in any event, undermined by the very subdivision of the original right. This response was clearly inadequate. Advocate General Jacobs in *Hag II* shows why this is so. The following extract is a comment on the ECJ's reasoning in *Terrapin*:

Case C–10/89, SA CNL-SUCAL NV v. Hag GF AG [1990] ECR I–3711

ADVOCATE GENERAL JACOBS[30]

That is a valiant attempt to legitimize the doctrine of common origin, but the logic on which it is based is, I think, fallacious. It is true that the essential function of a trade mark is to 'guarantee to consumers that the product has the same origin'. But the word 'origin' in this context does not refer to the historical origin of the trade mark; it refers to the commercial origin of the goods. The consumer is not, I think, interested in the genealogy of trade marks; he is interested in knowing who made the goods that he purchases. The function of a trade mark is to signify to the consumer that all goods sold under that mark have been produced by, or under the control of, the same person and will, in all probability, be of uniform quality . . . Once the owner of the mark is deprived of his exclusive right to its use, he loses the power to influence the goodwill associated with it and he loses the incentive to produce high-quality goods. Looking at matters from the consumer's point of view, the result of all this is thoroughly unsatisfactory because the trade mark no longer acts as a guarantee of origin. At best he is confused; at worst he is misled. In the circumstances, it is difficult not to conclude that the essential function of the mark, its specific subject-matter is affected and—most seriously of all—its very existence is jeopardized. But none of those consequences ensued from the fragmentation of the Hag trade mark in 1944; they ensued from the Court's judgment in *Hag I*.

It is clear from this passage that Advocate General Jacobs was strongly opposed to the common origin doctrine. His opinion in *Hag II* represents a convincing analytical indictment of it, from which the Advocate General reached the 'unpalatable but inescapable conclusion'[31] that the doctrine of common origin was not a legitimate creature of Community law. Advocate General Jacobs urged the Court to overrule *Hag I* expressly for the sake of legal certainty. The ECJ obliged in *Hag II*.

[30] At 3735. [31] Case C–10/89, [1990] ECR I–3711, 3736.

Case C–10/89, SA CNL-SUCAL NV v. Hag GF AG [1990] ECR I–3711

This case grew out of the same facts as *Hag I*. We noted earlier that the Hag mark for the Benelux countries was transferred to Van Zuylen Frères (VZF) in 1971. The company SA CNL-SUCAL NV was created as a result of changes in the constitution of VZF. CNL-SUCAL then sought to sell coffee in Germany under the Hag mark. The German company, Hag AG, tried to stop this, asserting that its coffee was superior to that sold by CNL-SUCAL. The ECJ stated explicitly that it was necessary to reconsider its earlier decision in *Hag I*, (paragraph 10). The Court began by reiterating the general principles relating to exhaustion of rights as developed in cases such as *Centrafarm*. This approach requires, as we have seen, the Court to identify the specific subject matter of the property right which is in issue. The ECJ addressed this point as it relates to trade marks in the following terms.

THE ECJ

13. Trade mark rights are, it should be noted, an essential element in the system of undistorted competition which the Treaty seeks to establish and maintain. Under such a system, an undertaking must be in a position to keep its customers by virtue of the quality of its products and services, something which is only possible if there are distinctive marks which enable customers to identify those products and services. For the trade mark to be able to fulfil this role, it must offer a guarantee that all goods bearing it have been produced under the control of a single undertaking which is accountable for their quality.

14. Consequently, as the Court has ruled on numerous occasions, the specific subject-matter of a trade mark is in particular to guarantee to the proprietor of the trade mark that he has the right to use that trade mark for the purpose of putting a product into circulation for the first time and therefore to protect him against competitors wishing to take advantage of the status and reputation of the trade mark by selling products illegally bearing that mark. In order to determine the exact scope of this right exclusively conferred on the owner of the trade mark, regard must be had to the essential function of the trade mark, which is to guarantee the identity of the origin of the marked products to the consumer or ultimate user by enabling him without any possibility of confusion to distinguish that product from products which have another origin . . .

15. For the purpose of evaluating a situation such as that described by the national court in the light of the foregoing considerations, the determinant factor is the absence of any consent on the part of the proprietor of the trade mark protected by national legislation to the putting into circulation in another Member State of similar products bearing an identical mark or one liable to lead to confusion, which are manufactured and marketed by an undertaking which is economically and legally independent of the aforesaid trade mark proprietor.

16. In such circumstances the essential function of the trade mark would be jeopardized if the proprietor of the trade mark could not exercise the right conferred on him by national legislation to oppose the importation of imported goods bearing a designation liable to be confused with his own trade mark, because, in such a situation, consumers would no longer be able to identify for certain the origin of the marked goods and the proprietor of the trade mark could be held responsible for the poor quality of goods for which he was in no way accountable.

17. This analysis cannot be altered by the fact that the mark protected by national legislation and the similar mark borne by the imported goods by virtue of the legislation of their Member State of origin originally belonged to the same proprietor, who was divested of one of them following expropriation by one of the two states prior to the establishment of the Community.

18. From the date of expropriation and notwithstanding their common origin, each of the marks independently fulfilled its function, within its own territorial field of application, of guaranteeing that the marked products originated from one single source.

19. It follows from the foregoing that in a situation such as the present case, in which the mark originally had one sole proprietor and the single ownership was broken as a result of expropriation, each of the trade mark proprietors must be able to oppose the importation and marketing, in the Member State in which the trade mark belongs to him, of goods originating from the other proprietor, in so far as they are similar products bearing an identical mark or one which is liable to lead to confusion.

20. Consequently the answer to the first question must be that Articles 30 and 36 of the EEC Treaty do not preclude national legislation from allowing an undertaking which is the proprietor of a trade mark in a Member State to oppose the importation from another Member State of similar goods lawfully bearing in the latter State an identical trade mark or one which is liable to be confused with the protected mark, even if the mark under which the goods in dispute are imported originally belonged to a subsidiary of the undertaking which opposes the importation and was acquired by a third undertaking following the expropriation of that subsidiary.

The reasoning and result in *Hag II* stand in marked contrast to those in *Hag I*. The ECJ in *Hag II* shows a willingness to re-evaluate its previous ruling, and to re-consider whether the position which it had adopted in the earlier *Hag* case was correct. Its judgment in *Hag II* possesses an analytical edge which was entirely absent from the previous case. The ECJ approached the matter from first principles, by inquiring what was the specific subject matter of a trade mark, and then reasoning from its conclusions on this issue to the specific problem in the case at hand. The Court was aided in this respect by an excellent opinion from Advocate General Jacobs. The opinion demonstrated acuity and analytical rigour, and revealed a willingness to subject the Court's previous case law to close critical scrutiny.

The change of approach exemplified by the Court's decision in *Hag II* is also evident in *IHT*.[32] This latter case has now resolved an issue which became a live one after *Hag II*. We have already seen that the exhaustion of rights doctrine will apply in circumstances where goods are placed on the market by the intellectual-property right owner itself or with its consent. The initial circulation by the owner itself, or a person who is economically linked with it, will exhaust the rights of the entire group. Thus where products are placed in circulation by, for example, the intellectual-property right owner, a subsidiary,

[32] Case C–9/93, n. 8 above.

a licensee, or an exclusive distributor, they can move freely throughout the Community. What happens, however, where the right has been assigned by the original holder to a company in one Member State and there is no economic or legal link between the assignor and the assignee? Could the assignee choose, for example, to sell into the assignor's territory? Prior to the decision in *Hag II* the answer would, of course, have been that it could. The common origin doctrine would have been applied to defeat any claim for injunctive relief by the assignor. The reason is clear. If, while *Hag I* was still good law, an *involuntary* assignment of a trade mark still had the effect of allowing sales from one territory into another in situations where the trade mark was held by separate entities, then the same must *a fortiori* be so where the assignment was *voluntary*. The common origin doctrine would have allowed the assignee to sell into the territory of the assignor, even though there was no subsisting economic or legal link between the two. The obvious question which had to be resolved following the demise of *Hag I* was whether the reasoning in *Hag II* would be applied in the same manner to voluntary assignments as well as involuntary assignments.

It was this question which the Court addressed in the *IHT* case, and it did indeed extend *Hag II* to cover voluntary assignments. The facts in *IHT* raised the issue in perfect form. Until 1984 the trade mark for 'Ideal Standard' sanitary fittings and heating equipment was held by subsidiaries of an American company in France and Germany. In 1984 the French subsidiary assigned the trade mark for its area to a company called SGF. IHT sought to import into Germany heating equipment bearing the name 'Ideal Standard' which it had acquired in France. The German subsidiary of the American parent sought to use its trade mark in Germany to prevent this. The question before the Court was therefore whether, after a voluntary assignment of a trade-mark right, one of the original trade-mark holders could prevent importation from an assignee with whom there was no economic or legal link.

The Court held that this would not entail any breach of Community law. The ECJ reiterated the exhaustion of rights doctrine. Once the goods had been placed on the market by the trade-mark owner or with its consent, they could circulate freely within the Community. The Court clarified the reach of this doctrine by stressing that it would apply either where the owners of the right in the exporting and importing states were the same, or where, even though they were separate, there was an economic link between them. The idea of an economic link would, said the Court, cover products placed into circulation by the same undertaking, by a licensee, by a parent company, by a subsidiary of the same group, or by an exclusive distributor.

The position of an assignee was, however, different. The crucial difference perceived by the ECJ was that a contract of assignment, in the absence of any economic link between assignor and assignee, gave the assignor no control over the quality of the goods which were placed on the market by the assignee. The consent implicit in the assignment itself was not the consent which was required for the purposes of invoking the exhaustion of rights doctrine. For that doctrine to apply the owner of the right must be able to determine, directly or indirectly, the products to which the mark was affixed and to apply quality control. No such power existed in the case of an assignment where there was no economic link with the assignor. IHT specifically argued before the ECJ that *Hag II* should be distinguished on the ground that the assignment in that case was involuntary, whereas here it was voluntary. The Court rejected this contention. It reiterated the basis of its judgment in *Hag II* and held that this reasoning applied irrespective of whether the splitting of the trade mark originally held by the same owner was due to an act of a public authority or a contractual assignment.[33]

Even before the decision in *Hag II* it was doubtful whether the common origin doctrine had any application outside trade marks. Good reasons could be found for arguing that it did not.[34] After the Court's rulings in *Hag II* and *IHT* it can safely be assumed that the doctrine will not apply to any species of intellectual-property right.

4. ARTICLES 85 AND 86

(a) General Principles: The Existence/Exercise Distinction

Articles 30 to 36 are not the only provisions of the Treaty which are used against intellectual-property rights. Articles 85 and 86 have also frequently been cited in litigation in order to try and limit the protection which such rights confer on their owners. Not surprisingly the ECJ has adopted the same basic starting criterion for the application of Articles 85 and 86 as it has in the context of Articles 30 to 36: it has held that the existence of intellectual-property rights cannot be said to infringe the competition rules, but that the exercise of these rights may in certain circumstances do so. The following case sets out this general principle clearly:

Case 24/67, Parke Davis & Co v. Probel and Centrafarm [1968] ECR 55, [1968] CMLR 47

Parke Davis, an American company, held patents in Holland for certain drugs. It brought an action in Holland seeking relief against the defendants which had marketed the drugs there without its consent. The defendants had acquired the drugs in Italy where patent protection was not available. The question before the Court was whether the reliance by the plaintiff on its patent could be said to infringe Articles 85 and 86 of the Treaty, considered if necessary in conjunction with

[33] The ECJ did, however, make it clear that where undertakings which were independent of each other made trade-mark assignments following a market-sharing agreement this would be caught by Article 85, and the assignments which gave effect to the agreement would be void: *ibid.*, para. 59.

[34] Wyatt and Dashwood, *European Community Law* (3rd edn., Sweet & Maxwell, 1993), 594–5.

Articles 36 and 222, on the grounds, *inter alia*, that the price of the patented product was greater than that of the non-patented version.

THE ECJ

3. . . .

A patent taken by itself and independently of any agreement to which it may be subject . . . results from a legal status granted by a State to products meeting certain criteria, and thus avoids the elements of contract or concert mentioned in Article 85(1).

But it is not impossible for provisions of that Article to become applicable if the utilisation of one or more patents, in concert between undertakings, should lead to the creation of a situation liable to fall within the bounds of agreements between undertakings, decisions of associations of undertakings or concerted practices within the meaning of Article 85(1) . . .

4. . . . For an act to be prohibited (under Article 86) it is thus necessary to find the existence of three elements: the existence of a dominant position, an improper exploitation of it, and the possibility that trade between Member States may be affected by it.

Although a patent confers on its holder a special protection within the framework of a State, it does not follow that the exercise of the rights so conferred implies the existence of the three elements mentioned. It could only do so if the utilisation of the patent could degenerate into an improper exploitation of the protection.

Besides in a comparable field, Article 36 of the Treaty, after having provided that Articles 30 to 34 do not prevent restrictions on imports or exports which are justified by reasons of protection of industrial and commercial property, provides . . . that those restrictions 'shall not amount to a means of arbitrary discrimination nor to a disguised restriction on trade between Member States.'

Consequently, since the existence of the patent right depends solely at present on internal laws, only the use made of it could fall within the ambit of Community law where that use contributes to a dominant position the improper exploitation of which would be liable to affect trade between Member States.

. . .

6. It follows from all the above that, on the one hand, the rights granted by a Member State to the holder of a patent are not affected as regards their existence by the prohibitions of Articles 85(1) and 86 of the Treaty, and, on the other hand, the exercise of those rights would fall under neither Article 85(1), in the absence of any agreement, decision or concerted practice mentioned by that provision, nor Article 86, in the absence of any abuse of a dominant position, and, finally, the higher level of the sale price of the patented product as compared with that of the non-patented product coming from another Member State does not necessarily constitute an abuse.

(b) Article 85: Assignments

In accordance with the principles set out in *Parke Davis* we must therefore examine the potential application of Article 85 to intellectual-property rights. One question which has come before the Court is the extent to which assignments of intellectual-property rights might be said to fall within the prohibition of Article 85.

This question arose in the *Sirena* case.[35] In 1937 an American company assigned its trade-mark rights in Italy for a cosmetic cream to an Italian company. At a later date the American company allowed a German corporation to use its mark in Germany. This latter company then sold the goods into Italy at a price which undercut that of the Italian trade-mark holder. The Italian holder of the mark sought to prevent this. It was for the Court to decide how far an assignment of a trade-mark right which, under national law, would have the effect of enabling the Italian company to exclude the goods coming from Germany, constituted a breach of Article 85.

The ECJ reiterated the position which it had articulated in *Parke Davis*, to the effect that trade-mark rights do not *per se* possess the characteristics of a contract or concerted practice such as to fall within Article 85(1). It then went on to say that the exercise of such rights through an agreement might fall within Article 85(1) if this was the object, the means, or the consequence of the agreement. If this 'exercise occurs by virtue of assignments to enterprises in one or more Member States it must be ascertained in each case whether it gives rise to situations prohibited by Article 85'.[36] What the Court had in mind becomes clearer from its subsequent analysis. It was concerned in particular about the possibility of a trade-mark owner making a series of assignments to different assignees in different Member States, where the terms of the assignments seek to prevent imports of the goods from other Member States. This would re-establish rigid frontiers between the states to the detriment of the common market:[37]

> Article 85 therefore applies where, by virtue of trade mark rights, imports of products originating in other Member States, bearing the same trade mark because their owners have acquired the trade mark itself or the right to use it through agreements with one another or with third parties, are prevented. The fact that national legislation makes the trade mark rights dependent on circumstances of fact and law other than the aforementioned agreements, such as the registration of the trade mark or its undisturbed use, does not prevent the application of Article 85.

One further aspect of the *Sirena* case is worthy of note. The assignments had been concluded before the entry into force of the Treaty and the referring court asked whether this would make any difference to the application of Article 85. The ECJ responded in somewhat cavalier fashion, stating that it was necessary and sufficient if the agreement continued to have an effect after the Treaty became operative.[38]

One of the difficulties of applying Article 85 to trade-mark assignments is

[35] Case 40/70, *Sirena Srl* v. *Eda Srl* [1971] ECR 69, [1971] CMLR 260.
[36] *Ibid.*, para. 9. [37] *Ibid.*, para. 11. [38] *Ibid.*, para. 12.

that the contract between the assignor and the assignee will effectively be discharged by completion of the assignment. It is for this reason that the Court in *Sirena* was forced to frame the application of Article 85 in terms of agreements which continue to have consequences thereafter.

This issue came before the Court once again in the *EMI* case.[39] The trade mark 'Columbia' originally belonged to an American company. In 1917 it transferred the mark for countries which now comprise the Community to its English subsidiary. In 1923 the United Kingdom subsidiary was sold with the trade mark. The United Kingdom trade mark was now held by EMI. CBS had the trade mark in the United States and attempted to sell under this mark in the Community through its European subsidiaries. EMI sought an injunction to prevent this.

The Court repeated orthodoxy that a trade-mark right would not *per se* come within Article 85, but could do so if the exercise of that right 'were to manifest itself as the subject, the means or the consequence of a restrictive practice'.[40] For example, a restrictive agreement between traders within the Community and competitors in a third country could have this effect if it were to bring about the isolation of the Community.[41] However, in the circumstances of the present case, where the agreements, in the sense of the assignments, were no longer in force it was sufficient that 'such agreements continue to produce their effects after they have formally ceased to be in force'.[42] The Court then gave more guidance on the meaning of this somewhat elliptical phrase:[43]

> An agreement is only regarded as continuing to produce its effects if from the behaviour of the persons concerned there may be inferred the existence of elements of concerted practice and of coordination peculiar to the agreement and producing the same result as that envisaged by the agreement. This is not so when the said effects do not exceed those flowing from the mere exercise of the national trade mark rights.

The problem with this formulation is that, if a concerted practice can be inferred, then this would itself be sufficient to bring the parties within the ambit of Article 85(1). Given that this is so the precise role to be played by the assignment is not clear. One possible explanation which has been suggested is that the existence of the prior agreement may render it easier to prove a concerted practice than might otherwise be the case.[44] There may, as we have seen from the discussion of competition policy, be difficulties in inferring the existence of a concerted practice and in particular in distinguishing such a practice from a firm's legitimate reaction to market circumstances.[45] If it could

[39] Case 51/75, *E.M.I. Records Ltd* v. *CBS United Kingdom Ltd* [1976] ECR 811, [1976] 2 CMLR 235.

[40] *Ibid.*, para. 27.

[41] *Ibid.*, paras. 28–9.

[42] *Ibid.*, para. 30.

[43] *Ibid.*, paras. 31–2.

[44] Wyatt and Dashwood, n. 34 above, 598.

[45] See above, 892–9.

be shown that the behaviour of the parties represented the continuation of a practice which was evident in the initial agreement, then this would lead to a strong presumption that there was indeed now a concerted practice and not merely independent reactions to market circumstances.

The fact that Article 85 can be applied to assignments was reaffirmed more recently in the *IHT* case.[46] We have already seen that the Court in this case held that the reasoning of *Hag II* applied to voluntary as well as involuntary assignments. The ECJ had also made some cautionary statements about the application of Article 85 to assignments. It confirmed that, where independent undertakings made reciprocal trade-mark assignments as part of a market-sharing agreement then this would be caught by Article 85(1). The market-sharing agreement and the assignment would both be void under Article 85(2). But the Court then added that this rule could not be mechanically applied to every assignment. Before a trade-mark assignment could be treated as giving effect to an agreement which would fall within Article 85, it was necessary to analyse the context, the commitments underlying the assignment, the intention of the parties, and the consideration for the assignment.

(c) *Article 85: Licensing*

The other main area to which Article 85 has been applied is the licensing of intellectual-property rights. An owner of such a right can grant a licence to another party to make and/or distribute a particular product. We saw at the beginning of this chapter the reasons it is so important for the owner of the right to be able to do this. A firm may not have the resources, know-how, or desire to make and/or market the product in all areas of the Community. A licensing system enables the holder of the right to reap rewards by authorizing others to do so instead.

It is for this reason that the ECJ recognized in *Centrafarm*[47] that the right to place the product on the market through a licensee was part of the specific subject matter of the intellectual-property right which would not be placed in jeopardy by Community law. Not surprisingly, the Court has adopted the same criterion here as in other parts of this topic: while the existence of the right will not be affected by Community law, the exercise of the right can fall foul of Article 85. Thus, while the grant of a licence will not lead to any infringement of EC law, the terms of the licence may bring it within Article 85. Whether particular terms of a licence do serve to bring it within the scope of Article 85 will be determined on a case-by-case basis. Certain general principles do, however, emerge from the Court's case law.

The most important of these principles is that the ECJ will not allow terms in a licence to result in absolute territorial protection for the licensee. This has been a consistent theme in the Court's case law from early decisions such as

[46] Case C–9/93, n. 8 above. [47] Case 15/74 [1974] ECR 1147, para. 9.

Consten and Grundig[48] through to cases such as *Nungesser*[49] and *Pronuptia*.[50] These cases have been discussed fully in the context of competition law and reference should be made to that discussion.[51] The general thrust of the Court's decisions can however be conveyed here by taking the *Nungesser* case as an example.

The case was concerned with a contract made between INRA, a French research institute specializing in the development of plant seeds, and Eisele, a German supplier of seeds. The contract gave Eisele, and through him Nungesser, absolute territorial protection: INRA would not sell the seed to any other undertaking in Germany, and would prevent third parties from doing so; Eisele could use the plant breeder's rights assigned to him by INRA to prevent third parties selling into Germany. The Commission found that the agreement was in violation of Article 85(1). The applicant argued, *inter alia*, that the exclusive licence was necessary to enable INRA to enter a new market, and compete in it with comparable products, since no trader would risk launching a new product unless he were given protection from competition by the licensor and other licensees.

The Court distinguished between an open exclusive licence, whereby the owner merely undertakes not to compete himself nor to grant licences to others in the same territory, and an exclusive licence with absolute territorial protection, under which all competition from third parties is eliminated.

It accepted that an open exclusive licence was compatible with EC law. If such a licence could not be given then no licensee might be willing to take on the project. This is, as we have already seen,[52] an application of what has become an accepted part of ECJ reasoning within the context of vertical agreements. The ECJ applied it to the facts of this case in the following terms:[53]

> In fact, in the case of a licence of breeders' rights over hybrid maize seeds newly developed in one Member State, an undertaking in another Member State which was not certain that it would not encounter competition from other licensees for the territory granted to it, or from the owner of the right himself, might be deterred from accepting the risk of cultivating and marketing that product; such a result would be damaging to the dissemination of a new technology and would prejudice competition in the Community between the new product and similar existing products.

The Court therefore concluded that 'the grant of an open exclusive licence, that is to say a licence which does not affect the position of third parties such

[48] Cases 56 and 58/64, *Consten and Grundig* v. *Commission* [1966] ECR 299, [1966] CMLR 418.

[49] Case 258/78, *L. C. Nungesser KG and Kurt Eisele* v. *Commission* [1982] ECR 2015, [1983] 1 CMLR 278.

[50] Case 161/84, *Pronuptia de Paris GmbH* v. *Pronuptia de Paris Irmgard Schillgallis* [1986] ECR 353, [1986] 1 CMLR 414.

[51] See above, 906–11. [52] See above, 919–23. [53] Case 258/78, n. 49 above, para. 57.

as parallel importers and licensees for other territories',[54] was not in itself incompatible with Article 85(1) of the Treaty.

In relation to those aspects of the agreement which conferred absolute territorial protection, the Court, however, continued to follow *Consten and Grundig*, and to hold that these were illegal. It was not possible to insulate a market wholly from any competition by way of parallel imports and attempts to do so would be prohibited under Article 85.

Clauses in licensing agreements which seek to insulate the licensees from any competition whatsoever are not the only ones which may fall foul of Article 85. The *Windsurfing* case provides an excellent example of the way in which the ECJ approaches a range of licensing terms in order to decide whether they do infringe Article 85:

Case 193/83, Windsurfing International Inc v. Commission [1986] ECR 611, [1986] CMLR 489

Windsurfing International (WI) was an American company which had a patent for the rig used on a windsurfer. It licensed certain firms within the Community to sell the rigs, but imposed conditions in the licences. The Commission held that a number of these conditions infringed Article 85. WI then sought to annul this decision before the ECJ.

THE ECJ

38. The first of the clauses at issue . . . imposed on licensees the obligation to exploit the invention only for the purpose of mounting the patented rig on certain types of board specified in the agreement, and the obligation to submit for the licensor's approval, prior to their being placed on the market, any new board types on which the licensees intended to use the rigs.

. . .

45. It is necessary to determine whether quality controls on the sailboards are covered by the specific subject-matter of the patent. As the Commission rightly points out, such controls do not come within the specific subject-matter of the patent unless they relate to a product covered by the patent since their sole justification is that they ensure 'that the technical instructions as described in the patent and used by the licensee may be carried into effect.' In this case, however, it has been established that it may reasonably be considered that the German patent does not cover the board.

46. However, even on the assumption that the German patent covers the complete sailboard, and therefore includes the board, it cannot be accepted without more that controls such as those provided for in the licensing agreements are compatible with Article 85. Such controls must be affected according to quality and safety criteria agreed upon in advance and on the basis of objectively verifiable criteria. If it were otherwise, the discretionary nature of those controls would in effect enable a licensor to impose his own selection of models upon the licensees, which would be contrary to Article 85.

. . .

[54] Case 258/78, n. 49 above, para. 58.

54. The second of the clauses at issue relates to the obligation on the licensees to sell the components covered by the German patent, and therefore in particular rigs, only in conjunction with the boards approved by the licensor, or in other words, as complete sailboards.

55. Windsurfing International takes the view that in any event a contractual provision prohibiting the sale of rigs to unlicensed manufacturers was entirely justified in view of the fact that such sales would have enabled unlicensed manufacturers to combine the rigs with their boards, which would have constituted patent infringement. It further argues that such a restriction is covered by the specific subject-matter of the patent.

. . .

57. In that regard it must be borne in mind that . . . the patent must be regarded as confined to the rig. That being the case, it cannot be accepted that the obligation arbitrarily placed on the licensee only to sell the patented product in conjunction with a product outside the scope of the patent is indispensable to the exploitation of the patent.

. . .

68. The fourth of the clauses at issue relates to the obligation on the licensees to affix to boards manufactured and marketed in Germany a notice stating 'licensed by Hoyle Schweitzer' or 'licensed by Windsurfing International.'

. . .

73. Despite Windsurfing International's contention that it was not the object of the clause to distort competition but merely to convey the information, by means of a notice affixed in a place where it was easily visible, that the product and sale were made possible by a licence from Windsurfing International, it is none the less true that by requiring such a notice Windsurfing International encouraged uncertainty as to whether or not the board too was covered by the patent and thereby diminished the consumer's confidence in the licensees so as to gain a competitive advantage for itself.

. . .

89. The seventh of the clauses which the Commission regards as incompatible with Article 85(1) relates to the obligation on the licensees not to challenge the validity of the licensed patents.

. . .

92. It must be stated that such a clause clearly does not fall within the specific subject-matter of the patent, which cannot be interpreted as also affording protection against actions brought in order to challenge the patent's validity, in view of the fact that it is in the public interest to eliminate any obstacle to economic activity which may arise where a patent was granted in error.

The approach in the *Windsurfing* case clearly exemplifies the Court's strategy in deciding whether terms in a licensing agreement fall within Article 85. The key element will be to decide if the relevant term relates to the specific subject matter of the intellectual-property right. If it does so, then it will not be condemned under Article 85. If, as in many of the examples in the *Windsurfing* case itself, the conditions in the licence do not relate to the specific subject matter of the property right then they will fall within Article 85, and will only be held to be lawful if they can come within Article 85(3) or a block exemption. The extract from the *Windsurfing* case demonstrates this. The contested conditions imposed by the patent owners in that case related to quality control,[55] tying,[56] licensed-by notices,[57] and no-challenge clauses.[58] The Court in this case also had occasion to consider the legality of the terms on which royalties were paid, and decided that these, too, were restrictive since they were calculated on the net selling price of the complete sailboard whereas the patent only covered the rig.[59]

(d) Article 85: Block Exemption[60]

We have already seen in our discussion of competition law the use which has been made of block exemptions to facilitate the decision-making process under Article 85 and to provide guidance to those who might be affected by this part of the Treaty.[61]

Block exemptions have been made both on patent licensing and on know-how licensing. The format of both block exemptions follows that which is commonly employed when drafting these measures. They have in essence three different parts: a list of the basic licensing conditions which will be entitled to exemption, a 'White list' of other permissible clauses, and a 'Black list' of impermissible clauses. The two exemptions are substantively similar[62] and therefore the Regulation dealing with Patent Licensing will be taken by way of example.[63]

Commission Regulation 2349/84[64] begins in Article 1(1) with a list of licensing conditions relating to exclusivity which will be acceptable. Some of these conditions may not, in fact, require exemption in the light of the *Nungesser* decision since they may not fall within the ambit of Article 85(1), but they are included in the block exemption none the less. The conditions which benefit from the exemption are: an obligation on the licensor not to appoint other licensees in an area given to one particular licensee; a duty on the licensor not to exploit the patent himself within the contract territory; an obligation on the licensee not to exploit the patented invention in the territory of the licensor; an undertaking by the licensee not to manufacture in the territory of another licensee or to engage actively in selling there, in the sense of advertising or setting up a branch; and an obligation imposed by the licensor on the licensee to use the former's trade mark to distinguish the product, provided that the licensee can identify himself as the maker of the product.

55 See also *Campari* [1978] OJ L70/69.

56 *Ibid.*

57 See also *Burroughs/Geha* [1972] OJ L13/53, [1972] CMLR D72.

58 See, however, Case 65/86, *Bayer* v. *Süllhöfer* [1988] ECR 5249.

59 Case 193/83, [1986] ECR 611, [1986] 3 CMLR 489, paras 60–7.

60 W. R. Cornish, n. 2 above, 190–9.

61 See above, 918-19.

62 For a summary of the block exemption on know-how licensing and some of the differences betwen this and the position in relation to patent licensing, see Wyatt and Dashwood, n. 34 above, 608–611.

63 V. Korah, *Patent Licensing and the EEC Competition Rules* (ESC Publishing, 1985).

64 The Reg. came into force on 1 January 1985 and was amended by Reg. 151/93, [1993] OJ L21/8.

Article 2(1) of the Regulation then sets out the White List of conditions which are permissible in a patent licence. These include the following: tying is permissible where this is necessary for technical reasons to ensure that the invention is exploited properly; minimum royalty payments; a duty on the licensee not to exploit the patent after the expiry of the agreement; an obligation on the licensee not to assign the licence or to grant any form of sub-licence; a duty on the licensee to comply with quality controls which are necessary in order that the invention be exploited properly; an obligation on both the licensor and the licensee to share information about the working of the patented product and to grant one another non-exclusive licences for any new applications of the patent or for improvements in the existing patent; and what is known as the 'most favoured licensee clause', which obliges the licensor to extend to the licensee any favourable terms which it may grant to other licensees.

Blacklisted clauses are found in Article 3 of the Regulation. The following list contains examples of some of the provisions which are prohibited: no-challenge clauses; no-competition clauses, other than to the degree inherent in the provisions on exclusivity contained in Article 1 of the Regulation; maximum limits on the quantity of the patented goods which may be produced by the licensee; limits on the range of customers who may be supplied by the licensee; fixing the price for the patented goods; an obligation on the licensee to assign to the licensor any patents for new applications of or improvements to the patented goods; tying, where this cannot be justified as being necessary for a satisfactory exploitation of the licensed invention; and any obligations on either the licensor or the licensee which in effect seek to impede parallel imports or parallel exports.

One of the other important provisions of the Regulation is Article 9. An Article of this kind is to be found in most block exemptions. It provides an escape clause for the Commission, which is able to withdraw the benefits of the block exemption from an agreement, even though it fulfils the conditions of the Regulation, if it has effects which are not compatible with Article 85(3). The factors which the Commission will take into account in this context are: the lack of effective competition in the licensee's territory from goods which are identical, or considered by users to be identical, to the patented goods; the refusal by the licensee to respond to unsolicited orders from the territories of other licensees where there is no objective reason for this; or action by the licensor or licensee which is designed to impede parallel exporters or parallel importers.

(e) Article 86

Our discussion thus far has concentrated on the application of Article 85 to intellectual-property rights. We must now consider what constraints Article 86 imposes on such rights. We have already seen from the *Parke Davis* case that the ECJ employs the existence/exercise dichotomy in relation to Article 86 as well as to Article 85.[65] As applied in this context this means that the monopoly power which is attendant upon the grant of an intellectual property right will not in itself constitute a breach of Article 86. Were this to be otherwise Article 86 would have the effect of outlawing all intellectual-property. It is for this reason that the Court in *Parke Davis* held that it was only the use of a patent which would bring it within Community law where that use contributed to a dominant position, the improper exploitation of which would be liable to affect trade between Member States.[66] The way in which Article 86 is applied to intellectual-property rights emerges clearly in the *CICRA* case:

Case 53/87, Consorzio Italiano della Componentistica di Ricambio per Autoveicoli (CICRA) and Maxicar v. Régie Nationale des Usines Renault[67] [1988] ECR 6039

An Italian trade association, the members of which made bodywork spare parts for cars, sought a declaration that the protective rights which Renault had for ornamental designs for spare car parts were void, as being in breach of Community law. The essence of their complaint was that these protective rights made it impossible for them to make non-original spare parts for these cars.

THE ECJ

10. It must first be stated that, as the Court held in . . . Case 144/81 (*Keurkoop* v. *Nancy Kean Gifts* [1982] ECR 2853), with respect to the protection of designs and models, in the present state of Community law and in the absence of Community standardization or harmonization of laws the determination of the conditions and procedures under which such protection is granted is a matter for national rules. It is for the national legislature to determine which products qualify for protection, even if they form part of a unit already protected as such.

11. It should then be noted that the authority of a proprietor of a protective right in respect of an ornamental model to oppose the manufacture by third parties, for the purposes of sale on the internal market or export, of products incorporating the design or to prevent the import of such products manufactured without its consent in other Member States constitutes the substance of his exclusive right. To prevent the application of the national legislation in such circumstances would therefore be tantamount to challenging the very existence of that right.

. . .

14. . . . the national court wishes to establish, essentially, whether the obtaining of protective rights in respect of ornamental models for car bodywork components and the exercise of the resultant exclusive rights constitutes an abuse of a dominant position within the meaning of Article 86 of the Treaty.

15. It should be noted at the outset that the mere fact of securing the benefit of an exclusive right granted by law, the effect of which is to enable the manufacture and sale of protected products by unauthorized third parties to be prevented, cannot be regarded as an abusive method of eliminating competition.

[65] See above, 1050–1. [66] Case 24/67, [1968] ECR 55, para. 4.

[67] See also Case 238/87, *AB Volvo* v. *Erik Veng (UK) Ltd* [1988] ECR 6211.

16. Exercise of the exclusive right may be prohibited by Article 86 if it gives rise to certain abusive conduct on the part of the undertaking occupying a dominant position such as an arbitrary refusal to deliver spare parts to independent repairers, the fixing of prices for spare parts at an unfair level or a decision no longer to produce spare parts for a particular model even though many cars of that model remain in circulation, provided that such conduct is liable to affect trade between Member States.

17. With reference more particularly to the difference in prices between components sold by the manufacturer and those sold by independent producers, it should be noted that the court has held (. . . in Case 24/67, *Parke Davis* . . .) that a higher price for the former than for the latter does not necessarily constitute an abuse, since the proprietor of protective rights in respect of an ornamental design may lawfully call for a return on the amounts which he has invested in order to perfect the protected design.

The principle which determines the area within which Article 86 will apply to intellectual-property rights emerges clearly in the above case: the ability to prevent unauthorized sales of the car bodyparts constituted the specific subject matter of the intellectual-property right and was not contrary to Article 86; it was only where the owner of the right acted abusively in the sense mentioned in paragraph 16 of the judgment that Article 86 would come into play.

Matters may not always be so clear-cut, as is apparent from the *RTE* case.[68] This decision has been discussed earlier in the general context of Article 86.[69] It will be remembered that RTE was a statutory authority providing broadcasting services, and it reserved the exclusive right to publish a weekly schedule of TV programmes for its channels in Ireland. An Irish company, Magill, sought to publish a weekly guide which would have information on all the available channels. RTE wished to prevent this, claiming that it infringed its copyright in the weekly schedule for its channels. The Commission found this to be an abuse of Article 86 and RTE challenged this before the CFI. The CFI accepted the basic principle that the specific subject matter of a copyright would enjoy protection under Community law, and in that sense the exclusive right to reproduce the protected work would not be an abuse for the purposes of Article 86. However, the copyright owner would not be protected if the manner of the exercise of the right was contrary to Article 86. The CFI then held that the case fell within the latter rather than the former category, on the ground that RTE was using its exclusive copyright to publish its weekly listings in order to prevent the emergence of a *new product*, namely a general guide for all TV channels. This was held to go beyond what was necessary to fulfil the essential function of RTE's copyright as permitted by EC law.

The potential reach of Article 86 to cases concerning intellectual property

[68] Case T–69/89, *Radio Telefis Eireann* v. *Commission* [1991] ECR II–485, [1991] 4 CMLR 586. See also Case T–70/89, *British Broadcasting Corporation and British Broadcasting Corporation Enterprises Ltd* v. *Commission* [1991] ECR II–535, [1991] 4 CMLR 649; Case 238/87, n. 67 above.

[69] See above, 961–2.

is further exemplified by the decision of the CFI in the *Tetra Pak* case.[70] In that case the CFI held that there could be a violation of Article 86 where a firm in a dominant position strengthened that position by taking over another firm and thereby acquired an exclusive licence to exploit intellectual property. In reaching this decision the CFI reasoned on the basis of the ECJ's earlier ruling in *Continental Can*[71] that a merger could be caught by Article 86. The nature of the ECJ's reasoning in this case has been explored within the general discussion of Article 86,[72] but the application of this reasoning to the facts of *Tetra Pak* is contentious, given that the licence in question came within the ambit of the block exemption. The response of the CFI was that, while there might be no objection to the licence as such, this did not mean that it was unobjectionable for a dominant firm to take over another company which possessed such rights.

5. ARTICLE 7 AND NON-DISCRIMINATION

The discussion thus far has focused on the use of Articles 30 to 36 and Articles 85 and 86 in the context of intellectual property. An individual can, however, also make use of Article 7 of the Treaty in its own right without the necessity of relying on other Treaty Articles. This follows from the *Phil Collins* case.[73] The applicant was the singer who sought to prevent the sale in Germany of a bootleg recording of one of his concerts in the United States. Under German law German nationals would have been afforded relief in such circumstances, but this was not available for non-Germans. The ECJ held that this was discrimination on grounds of nationality and constituted a breach of Article 7(1). This Article was directly effective and could be relied on by the applicant in the national courts.[74]

6. INTELLECTUAL-PROPERTY RIGHTS AND HARMONIZATION

It is readily apparent that many of the problems which have been discussed in the preceding pages flow from the fact that intellectual-property rights have traditionally been granted by nation states, and that because this is so it is unsurprising that principles of exhaustion of rights have hitherto been developed on the assumption that the basic territorial unit is the nation state. This

[70] Case T–51/89, *Tetra Pak Rausing* v. *Commission* [1990] ECR II–309, [1991] 4 CMLR 334.

[71] Case 6/72, [1973] ECR 215, [1973] CMLR 199.

[72] See above, 955–6.

[73] Case C–92/92, *Phil Collins* v. *Imtrat Handelsgesellschaft mbH* [1993] ECR I–5145, [1993] 3 CMLR 773.

[74] G. Dworkin and J. Sterling, 'Phil Collins and the Term Directive' [1994] 5 EIPR 187.

traditional approach to matters concerning intellectual-property rights could, for the reasons considered in the introduction to this Chapter, not be accepted with the advent of the EC, since it would have resulted in the partitioning of the Community along national lines. Attempts to secure a single market by removing tariffs, quotas, and the like would have been undermined by the continued existence of barriers to trade created by private parties through the use of devices such as intellectual-property rights. The ECJ's creative jurisprudence must be seen as an attempt to prevent this from happening, while at the same time not denuding such property rights of all content. The judiciary could not, however, fashion a long-term solution to the problem. This requires legislative initiatives designed both to harmonize relevant national laws, and also more radically to shift the basic territorial unit for the purpose of intellectual-property rights from the nation state to the EC itself. Such legislative initiatives have been forthcoming, but the process of securing agreement between the Member States has not proven either easy or quick.

Progress in the field of patents may be taken by way of example. A Convention on the grant of European Patents was concluded in 1973, but this did not create a Community Patent as such, but rather a method through which a number of national patents could be granted at the same time, thereby obviating the need to go through separate procedures in each of the states. The Convention for the European Patent for the Common Market,[75] which is also known as the Community Patent Convention, has more ambitious objectives. The Convention was signed in 1975, but did not come into force as there were insufficient ratifications. The Convention was amended in 1989, and Member States were given until the end of 1991 to ratify. Member State compliance with this deadline has been imperfect to say the least. The central aim of the Convention is to provide for a Community-wide patent which has a unitary character, in the sense that the patent takes effect for the whole of the Community. There will then be a single owner of the patent whose rights will be exhausted by placing the patented product on the market in any one of the Member States. There are provisions designed to prevent the granting of patent licences from dividing the common market. The Community patent does not wholly supersede national patents, but where a person decides to obtain a national patent instead of a Community patent there are provisions which enshrine the principles in the ECJ's case law on exhaustion of rights.

Legislative initiatives have also been forthcoming in other areas.[76] For example, in the case of trade marks there has been some progress towards harmonization of national laws through Directive 89/104,[77] but implementation of this Directive was delayed in order that it might coincide with moves toward a Community trade mark.

There have in addition been various legislative initiatives in the context of

[75] [1976] OJ L17/1.

[76] A. Robertson, 'Recent Developments in EEC Intellectual Property Legislation' (1992) 12 YBEL 175.

[77] [1989] OJ L40/1.

computer programs and copyright. There is no doubt that developments of this nature will continue to occur and that they will contribute to the attainment of a more truly single market. Judging from past attempts at legislation in this field one should not, however, expect agreement to be reached easily.[78] It should, moreover, be noted that the mere existence of harmonization measures in a particular area does not always mean that the Community solution is a success. There is a danger that such measures may sometimes be pressed through at the expense of a more thorough treatment of the topic.

7. FURTHER READING

(a) Books

CORNISH, W. R., *Intellectual Property: Patents, Copyright, Trade Marks and Allied Rights* (2nd edn., Sweet & Maxwell, 1989)

WHISH, R., *Competition Law*, (3rd edn., Butterworths, 1993), Ch. 19

(b) Articles

BONET, G., 'Intellectual Property' (1989) 9 YBEL 315

CORNISH, W. R., 'Intellectual Property' (1990) 10 YBEL 469

FRIDEN, G., 'Recent Developments in EEC Intellectual Property Law' (1989) 26 CMLRev. 193

MANN, F. A., 'Industrial Property and the EEC Treaty' (1975) 24 ICLQ 31

MARENCO, G., and BANKS, K., 'Intellectual Property and the Community Rules on Free Movement: Discrimination Unearthed' (1990) 15 ELRev. 224

OLIVER, P., 'Of Split Trade Marks and Common Markets' (1991) 54 MLR 587

[78] Developments in this complex field move quickly. The best source for up to date coverage of these developments is the *European Intellectual Property Review*.

24

The State and the Common Market

1. INTRODUCTION

The discussion in the previous chapters has focused upon the extent to which rules of national law, whether relating to goods, services, establishment, and the like, infringe the relevant provisions of the Treaty. We have also considered the extent to which the behaviour of private undertakings may be caught by the principles of the Treaty concerning competition policy. The discussion of the substantive law of the Community would, however, be incomplete if it did not take account of the way in which the actions of the state itself might infringe the obligations laid down in the Treaty.

The Treaty contains a number of provisions which are of relevance in this respect, including Articles 5, 30, 85, 86, 90, and 92 to 94. There are, as we shall see, valid reasons in principle for controlling state action in the ways demanded by these Articles. Thus, for example, Article 90 is designed to prevent a state from enacting or maintaining in force measures, relating to public undertakings or those to whom it has granted special or exclusive rights, which derogate from other obligations under the Treaty. Some such provision is clearly required in order to prevent a state from evading the proscriptions of the Treaty in so far as these relate to such undertakings. It is equally apparent that the Community must, for example, have some rules concerning the provision of state aids. The control of such aid forms an aspect of the Community's single-market policy: if a state were enabled to give preferential treatment to its own firms then the very idea of a level playing field would be undermined. This relationship between the Single Market and the control of state aids is brought out clearly by Ehlermann:

C.-D. Ehlermann, The Contribution of EC Competition Policy to the Single Market[1]

While the European Single Market acts as the driving force for economic growth and hence also for the raising of living standards in the Member States, it must not be forgotten that the complete dismantling of internal frontiers will create serious adjustment problems for certain firms, sectors and regions in the Community. The pressure of increasing competition will force a whole series of non-viable firms to be merged into larger economic units or to withdraw from the market. Most of

[1] (1992) 29 CMLRev. 257, 259.

the remaining firms will have to modernize their production plant, improve the marketing of their products and step up their research and development activities.

As the burden of cost increases, firms are faced with a growing temptation to resort to anti-competitive agreements and practices so as to gain a breathing space in the competitive struggle or an artificial advantage in penetrating new markets. The governments of the Member States are persuaded to provide assistance for their firms (sometimes in an effort to maintain jobs, particularly in weak areas, sometimes as part of a policy to strengthen their own industrial base) by delaying the dismantling of obstacles, introducing protectionist measures or distorting competition through the granting of subsidies.

While there are, therefore, valid reasons of principle for the existence of Community controls over such areas, the topics discussed within this Chapter raise, as will be seen, important and interesting issues concerning the very nature of the Community in which we live. Thus it will be seen that the jurisprudence under Article 90 has prompted real questions about the extent to which it is, in fact, possible for a state to entrust certain activities to a public monopoly or to a private firm which has exclusive rights. Moreover, the case law concerning Articles 92–94 raises a plethora of broader issues concerning the way in which Community policy is developed in a particular area, and the appropriate balance between market integration and the attainment of other goals such as regional policy and Community cohesion.

2. THE STATE AND PARTICIPATION IN THE MARKET: GENERAL PRINCIPLES

In mixed economic systems of a type which exist within Europe it is common for the state to play some direct or indirect role in the market place. The legal form through which this is accomplished may well vary, as may the reasons the state believes that certain activities should be within public ownership or undertaken by firms which are given a specially privileged position. It has, for example, been common in the past for utilities either to be nationalized or to have some privileged monopoly or quasi-monopoly status. More recent thinking concerning the appropriate boundaries of state participation in industry and in the market place has tended to favour a more confined role for the state, as manifested in the privatization of nationalized industries and in the deregulation of sectors of the economy. Notwithstanding these changes, there continue to be a range of undertakings which either remain within public ownership or which possess a certain privileged status in the market place. Indeed in some ways the recent changes have rendered this issue more complex than hitherto, since the legal form which this privileged status may assume has become more diverse than it was in the period from 1945 until the late 1970s.

The basic starting position of the Treaty is to be found in Article 222 which states that the Treaty shall in no way prejudice the rules in Member States governing the system of property ownership. In this sense the mere fact that certain activities are undertaken in the public or the private sphere is not in itself contrary to the Treaty.

Having said this, it should also be noted that Article 222, like any other Article of the Treaty, is subject to judicial interpretation. We have already had occasion to see the way in which the Court has construed Article 222 in the context of intellectual property in order to render Articles 30 to 36 applicable to this species of property rights, resisting demands that Article 222 should be interpreted to mean that this part of the Treaty had no application to patents, trade marks, and the like.[2] Moreover, the TEU has introduced a new Article 130 under the Title of Industry which provides that the Community and the Member States shall ensure that the conditions necessary for the competitiveness of the Community's industry exist. The Article is explicitly framed in terms of open and competitive markets and action to attain this end includes the encouragement of an environment favourable to initiative and to the development of undertakings throughout the Community, particularly small and medium-sized undertakings.

Thus, while Article 222 can be seen as providing support for Community agnosticism as to the regime of ownership which subsists within any particular state, the thrust of much else within the Treaty is against the type of dominance which often accompanies public ownership. The Treaty is also against the according of any special, beneficial position to firms which may have the consequence of distorting the competitive mechanism within the common market as a whole.

3. PUBLIC UNDERTAKINGS AND ARTICLE 90

The sentiment expressed in the preceding paragraph is readily apparent from Article 90 of the Treaty, which reads as follows:

> 1. In the case of public undertakings and undertakings to which Member States grant special or exclusive rights, Member States shall neither enact nor maintain in force any measure contrary to the rules contained in this Treaty, in particular to those rules provided for in Article 7 and Articles 85 to 94.
>
> 2. Undertakings entrusted with the operation of services of general economic interest or having the character of a revenue-producing monopoly shall be subject to the rules contained in this Treaty, in particular to the rules on competition, in so far as the application of such rules does not obstruct the performance, in law or in fact, of the particular task assigned to them. The development of trade must

[2] See above, Ch. 23.

not be affected to such an extent as would be contrary to the interests of the Community.

3. The Commission shall ensure the application of the provisions of this Article and shall, where necessary, address appropriate directives or decisions to Member States.

(a) The Scope of Article 90(1): General Principles

It is clear from the wording that Article 90 covers two types of undertaking: public undertakings and those to which Member States have granted special or exclusive rights. These will be examined in turn.

The scope of the term *public undertaking* was indirectly addressed by the ECJ in the Transparency Directive case:

Cases 188–190/80, France, Italy, and the United Kingdom v. Commission [1982] ECR 2545, [1982] 3 CMLR 144

The Commission, acting pursuant to Article 90(3), enacted Directive 80/723 on the transparency of financial relations between Member States and public undertakings. The object of the Directive was to make available information on public funds which had been given to public undertakings and the use to which such money had been put. Such information was necessary in order to ensure, *inter alia*, the proper operation of Articles 92 and 93. Three Member States sought to have the Directive annulled under Article 173 on a number of grounds. In the course of its judgment the ECJ considered the definition of public undertaking contained in the Directive. The Court acknowledged that the Commission's definition in the Directive did not set out to define 'public undertakings' for the purpose of Article 90, but it none the less approved of the definition.

THE ECJ

25. According to Article 2 of the Directive, the expression 'public undertakings' means any undertaking over which the public authorities may exercise directly or indirectly a dominant influence. According to the second paragraph, such influence is to be presumed when the public authorities directly or indirectly hold the major part of the undertaking's subscribed capital, control the majority of the votes, or can appoint more than half of the members of its administrative, managerial or supervisory body.

26. As the Court has already stated, the reason for the inclusion in the Treaty of the provisions of Article 90 is precisely the influence which the public authorities are able to exert over the commercial decisions of public undertakings. That influence may be exerted on the basis of financial participation or of rules governing the management of the undertaking. By choosing the same criteria to determine the financial relations on which it must be able to obtain information in order to perform its duty of surveillance under Article 90(3), the Commission has remained within the limits of the discretion conferred upon it by that provision.

While, as stated above, the definition in the Directive is not conclusive on the meaning of public undertakings for the purpose of Article 90(1), the fact that the ECJ approved of it, that its reasoning explicitly looks to the purpose of Article 90, and that the Commission's broad definition is in line with the Court's own emphasis upon economic reality rather than legal form, all point strongly to the conclusion that the existence of a state influence in one of the ways indicated above will be a sufficient reason for an undertaking to be characterized as public. Thus in *Sacchi*[3] the Italian Broadcasting Authority, RAI, was under the control of a state holding company, IRI; the state was represented in its organs and could intervene in its operations.

Even if an undertaking is not public in the above sense, it may none the less fall within Article 90(1) if it is an undertaking to which a Member State has granted *special or exclusive rights*. The rationale behind this second category is 'the fact that the State has deliberately intervened to relieve the undertaking concerned wholly or partially from the discipline of competition, and must bear responsibility for the consequences'.[4] An obvious example of an undertaking which would fall within this category would be, for example, a nationalized industry which had been privatized on terms that it continued to have a monopoly power in the relevant area, or, even in the absence of monopoly power *stricto sensu*, where the privatized undertaking possessed certain advantages in the market place resulting from the terms on which it had been established.

It is perfectly possible for undertakings to be caught by both of the limbs of Article 90(1). Thus in *Sacchi*[5] the RAI, as well as being controlled by the state, also possessed a statutory monopoly in relation to broadcasting, while in *Muller*[6] the state had power to nominate half of the members of the management and supervisory board of a company which controlled port facilities in Luxembourg; and the company itself had certain privileges, including that of being consulted before the development of any other port facilities within a particular area was undertaken.

Article 90(1) requires that a Member State *shall neither enact nor maintain in force* any measure which is contrary to the Treaty rules. This language serves to emphasize the peremptory force of the duty which is imposed on a Member State: it constitutes both a standstill obligation, in the sense of a duty not to enact any measure which is contrary to the Treaty, and a positive obligation to remove any such measure which currently exists. The very fact that the Article expresses the duty of the state in these two complementary ways indicates that the state may be responsible even if it has failed to correct an infringement of the Treaty. This point is well captured by Wyatt and Dashwood:[7]

> If State responsibility under this paragraph is derived, respectively, from the ability to influence public undertakings and from the assumption of risk inherent in

[3] Case 155/73, [1974] ECR 409, [1974] 2 CMLR 177.
[4] Wyatt and Dashwood, *European Community Law* (3rd edn., Sweet & Maxwell, 1993), 551.
[5] Case 155/73, n. 3 above.
[6] Case 10/71, *Ministère Public of Luxembourg* v. *Muller* [1971] ECR 723.
[7] N. 4 above, 554.

the deliberate distortion of competition by a grant of special or exclusive rights, it ought to make no difference whether the role of the State has been active, in imposing or encouraging certain behaviour, or passive, in failing to correct it. Furthermore, this view entirely reflects the steps already taken by the Court in relation to State directions or encouragement for enterprises to infringe Articles 85–86 in situations where no exclusive or special rights are involved.

It is clear from the wording of Article 90(1) that a breach of this Article presupposes that some other Article of the Treaty has also been broken. Thus the Article makes specific reference in this respect to Articles 7 and Articles 85 to 94. These are only examples of other Treaty Articles infringement of which can also lead to a breach of Article 90(1). It would, for example, clearly be both possible and feasible for a government to maintain in force a measure which constituted a breach of Article 30. The way in which Article 90(1) operates in this respect can be seen from the *Bodson* case:

Case 30/87, Bodson v. Pompes Funèbres Des Régions Libérées SA [1988] ECR 2479, [1989] 4 CMLR 984

French legislation entrusted the provision of external services for funerals (the carriage of the body after it has been placed in the coffin, the provision of hearses, etc.), to local communes. The communes then granted concessions to private undertakings and Pompes Funèbres (PF) held many such concessions. Bodson offered external funeral services at a price significantly lower than that set by PF. PF sought an injunction in the French courts, claiming that Bodson was acting in breach of its exclusive rights resulting from the concession. Bodson responded by arguing that PF had abused its dominant position in breach of Article 86 by charging excessive prices. One of the issues before the Court concerned the responsibility of the commune itself under Article 90.

THE ECJ

33. In so far as the communes imposed a given level of prices on the concession holders, in the sense that they refrained from granting concessions for the 'external services' to undertakings if the latter did not agree to charge particularly high prices, the communes are covered by the situation referred to in Article 90(1) of the Treaty. That provision governs the obligations of the Member States—which includes, in this context, the public authorities at the regional, provincial or communal level—towards undertakings 'to which [they] grant special or exclusive rights'. That situation covers precisely the grant of an exclusive concession for the 'external services' for funerals.

34. It follows from that finding that public authorities may not, in circumstances such as those in this case, either enact or maintain in force any 'measure' contrary to the rules of the Treaty, in particular the rules laid down by Articles 85 and 86. They may not therefore assist undertakings holding concessions to charge unfair prices by imposing such prices as a condition for concluding a contract for a concession.

(b) The Scope of Article 90(1): Agnosticism as to the Organization of Economic Activities?

We began this discussion by noting that the Treaty is, in formal terms, agnostic as to whether economic activity is undertaken by the state itself or those to whom it has granted special or exclusive rights, as opposed to allowing the free and unfettered interplay of market forces through private firms. A state can in this sense choose to grant exclusive rights to a particular undertaking and the normal rules of the Treaty will apply. Provided that the state itself does not, as in the *Bodson* case, infringe Article 90, and provided that the undertaking does not so exercise its exclusive rights as to constitute an abuse of a dominant position under Article 86 then all will be well. The exclusivity will not, in and of itself, infringe Article 86. On this view Article 90 simply preserves parity. It does no more than ensure that public undertakings, or those to whom exclusive rights are granted, do not thereby infringe any Treaty provision.

Yet we also noted in the earlier discussion that the thrust of the Treaty was more generally in favour of eradicating any impediment to the free movement of goods, and of ensuring that normal competitive principles apply to determine the winners and losers in the market place. Now to be sure, the result of this market place contest may well be to produce a firm which is dominant because of its very economic prowess. This is one of the reasons the Treaty does not proscribe monopoly *per se*. The Treaty is, however, against what may be regarded as artificial barriers to the normal interplay of competitive forces. This can produce tensions in relation to public undertakings or those to whom the state has granted special or exclusive rights, for the simple reason that their privileged position is not the result of economic prowess, but of state grant.

The formal way in which the ECJ resolves these tensions is to recognize that the grant of exclusive rights will not *per se* infringe, for example, Article 86, but that the exercise of such rights may do so if it can be said to be abusive. This is fine in principle. But much turns on the more precise meaning which is given to the idea of abuse. We have already had occasion to consider the elasticity of this concept in the general discussion of Article 86.[8] The interpretation accorded to the term is particularly important in this context. The point may be put quite simply: the closer the Court comes to regarding the grant of exclusive rights as abusive in and of itself the more difficult does it become for a state to choose to organize its economic activities in this manner. While the Court has not yet reached the position whereby it can be said that exclusivity is abusive, its more recent case law evidences movement in this direction. It also demonstrates the fragility of the dividing line between the legitimate and illegitimate grant of exclusive rights.

The *Hofner*[9] decision demonstrates the difficulties outlined above. The case

[8] See above, 953–4.

[9] Case C–41/90, *Hofner and Elser* v. *Macrotron GmbH* [1991] ECR I–1979, [1993] 4 CMLR 306.

concerned the legality of German rules on certain categories of persons who were seeking work. Under these rules those looking for work were placed in contact with potential employers through a state-licensed agency, and this agency was given exclusive powers in the relevant area. The effect of this monopoly was to suppress the activities of independent employment consultants. Having found that the agency was an undertaking for the purposes of Article 86, the Court went on to hold that any state rule the effect of which was to compel an undertaking to breach Article 86 would be illegal under Article 90(1). While the Court held that the grant of exclusive rights was not *per se* incompatible with Article 86,[10] it went on to find that a state would violate Article 90(1) if it placed an undertaking in such a dominant position that the very exercise of these exclusive rights could *not avoid* being abusive. On the facts of the case the ECJ held that the Member State had created such a situation because the undertaking to which it had granted the exclusive right was not in a position to satisfy market demand for activities of this kind; the effective exercise of those activities by private companies was made impossible by the retention of a legal provision which prohibited such activities, the consequence being that contracts entered into in this way would be void; and the activities in question could extend to the nationals or the territory of other Member States.[11]

The fine line which may exist between a lawful grant of exclusive rights and illegality under Articles 90 and 86 is further demonstrated by the *ERT* case.[12] The case, which will be examined in more detail below, concerned the legality of a statutory radio and television monopoly held by ERT given to it by the Greek state. Once again the ECJ stated that the existence of a statutory monopoly was not in and of itself abusive for the purposes of Article 86. But the Court then went on to hold that Articles 86 and 90 could be infringed where the grant of the exclusive right would *lead* the grantee to infringe Article 86. This would be so where an exclusive right to retransmit programmes was given to an undertaking which had the exclusive right to transmit broadcasts, since the grantee would be likely to favour transmission of its own programmes, rather than retransmission of the programmes from other companies.

The willingness of the ECJ to characterize a grant of exclusive rights as abusive within Article 86 is even more apparent in the following case which develops the reasoning in the preceding two decisions:

Case C–179/90, Merci Convenzionali Porto di Genova SpA v. Siderurgica Gabrielli SpA [1991] ECR I–5889, [1994] 4 CMLR 422

Merci enjoyed the exclusive right to organize dock work in the Port of Genoa. It would call upon a dock-work company to unload ships. Siderurgica (S) applied to

[10] Case C–41/90, *Hofner and Elser* v. *Macrotron GmbH* [1991] ECR I–1979, [1993] 4 CMLR 306, para. 29.

[11] *Ibid.*, para. 34.

[12] Case C–260/89, *Elliniki Radiophonia Tileorassi AE (ERT)* v. *Dimotiki Etairia Pliroforissis (DEP) and Sotirios Kouvelas* [1991] ECR I–2925, [1994] 4 CMLR 540.

Merci to have a consignment of steel unloaded, even though the ship's own crew could have performed the task itself. Merci called upon the relevant Genoa dock-work company to do the job. Delays arose in the unloading as a result of strikes. As a consequence S demanded reimbursement for the charges paid to Merci, claiming that they were unfair in regard to the services performed. One of the questions referred by the Italian court asked the ECJ whether Article 90, in combination with Articles 7, 30, 85, and 86, applied to the instant case. The ECJ reaffirmed that an undertaking having a statutory monopoly over a substantial part of the common market would be regarded as having a dominant position for the purposes of Article 86. It then continued as follows.

THE ECJ

16. It should next be stated that the simple fact of creating a dominant position by granting exclusive rights within the meaning of Article 90(1) EEC is not as such incompatible with Article 86.

17. However, the Court has had occasion to state, in this respect, that a Member State is in breach of the prohibition contained in these two provisions if the undertaking in question, merely by exercising the exclusive rights granted to it, cannot avoid abusing its dominant position (see Case C–41/90, *Hofner* . . .) or when such rights are liable to create a situation in which that undertaking is induced to commit such abuses (see Case C–260/89, *ERT* . . .).

18. According to Article 86(2)(a), (b) and (c) EEC, such abuse may in particular consist in imposing on the persons requiring the services in question unfair purchase prices or other unfair trading conditions, in limiting technical development, to the prejudice of consumers, or in the application of dissimilar conditions to equivalent transactions with other trading parties.

19. In that respect it appears from the circumstances described by the national court and discussed before the Court of Justice that the undertakings enjoying exclusive rights in accordance with the procedures laid down by the national rules in question are, as a result, induced either to demand payment for services which have not been requested, to charge disproportionate prices, to refuse to have recourse to modern technology, which involves an increase in the cost of the operations and a prolongation of the time required for their performance, or to grant price reductions to certain consumers and at the same time to offset such reductions by an increase in the charges to other consumers.

20. In these circumstances it must be held that a Member State creates a situation contrary to Article 86 EEC where it adopts rules of such a kind as those at issue before the national court, which are capable of affecting trade between Member States as in the case of the main proceedings, regard being had to the factors mentioned in paragraph 15 of this judgment to the importance of traffic in the Port of Genoa.

21. As regards the interpretation of Article 30 requested by the national court, it is sufficient to recall that a national measure which has the effect of facilitating the abuse of a dominant position capable of affecting trade between Member States will generally be incompatible with that Article, which prohibits quantitative restrictions on imports and all measures having equivalent effect (see Case 13/77, *GB-INNO-BM* v. *ATAB*) in so far as such a measure has the effect of making more difficult and hence of impeding imports of goods from other Member States.

22. In the main proceedings it may be seen from the national court's findings that the unloading of the goods could have been effected at a lesser cost by the ship's crew, so that compulsory recourse to the services of the two undertakings enjoying exclusive rights involved extra expense and was therefore capable, by reason of its effect on the prices of the goods, of affecting imports.

The reasoning of the ECJ and the particular language which it employs are instructive.[13] In paragraph 16 the Court reiterates the proposition that the creation of exclusive rights is not itself abusive within the meaning of Article 86. This is then qualified in paragraph 17: exclusivity can entail a breach of Articles 90 and 86 either when the exercise of the exclusive rights cannot avoid being abusive (*Hofner*), or where such rights are liable to create a situation in which the undertaking is induced to commit an abuse (*ERT*). In paragraph 19 of the judgment we then see the Court applying the latter of these two formulations to the instant case.

This comes perilously close to regarding the grant of exclusivity as abusive *per se*, albeit through the back door. The reason this is so is not hard to find. It is to be found in the very notion that an undertaking may be *induced* to commit an abuse in one of the ways identified in paragraph 19. It is, of course, true that an undertaking can be in breach of Article 86 through charging excessive prices, discriminatory pricing, and the like. Any firm which possesses the market power attendant upon a dominant position has this *potential*. Whether it actually chooses to behave in this manner is another matter. The message from the Court is, however, that the very grant of the exclusive rights can create a situation in which the undertaking is *induced* to commit such abuses.

But what does the word *induce* mean here? Are we saying that, because the holder of the exclusive right possesses a species of market power which would enable it to price in an abusive manner, therefore it is induced to do so? On this hypothesis it would always be open to say that the grantee of exclusivity is induced to price abusively, with the consequence that exclusive rights are, in effect, rendered illegal *per se*. Perhaps this is misreading the Court's reasoning. Perhaps the argument thus far ignores the fact, mentioned at the beginning of paragraph 19, that the holder of the exclusive right had in fact priced in an abusive manner. Yet if this was indeed so then Merci itself should be condemned on this basis alone. On this view nothing is to be gained from the language of inducement.

But the fact that the Court did employ the language of inducement is not in reality fortuitous. It did so because it wished to make a point about the consequence of forms of economic organization *adopted by the state*. What is distinctive about the grant of a statutory monopoly is the very fact that the

[13] See also Case C–18/93, *Corsica Ferries Italia SRL* v. *Corpo dei Piloti di Genova*, 17 May 1994. The ECJ upheld the grant of exclusive rights in Case C–323/93, *Société Civile Agricole du Centre d'Insémination de la Crespelle* v. *Coopérative d'Elevage et d'Insémination Artificielle du Départment de la Mayenne*, 5 Oct. 1994.

grantee obtains a protected sphere of activity which is immune from the normal rigours of competition. This is by way of contrast to other firms which have a dominant position. They must always be looking over their shoulder lest their market power is eroded by new market entrants. It is this which is one of the important reasons why such a firm might decide *not* to price too high, since this will act as an incentive for others to enter the market. The holder of the statutory exclusive right does not have the same fears or the same rationale for self-restraint.[14] It is for this reason that such firms might well be *induced* to charge disproportionate prices, secure in the knowledge that such excessive pricing cannot operate as a carrot to bring others into the market. It is for this reason that the ECJ is particularly concerned about monopoly power in this form. This is readily understandable when looked at from the Community's point of view. But this does not alter the fact that the reasoning employed by the Court comes close to regarding the grant of exclusive statutory rights as abusive *per se*. The argument merely provides an explanation of why the Court might be moving in this direction.

Further indication of the ECJ's mode of thinking in this respect is provided by paragraphs 21 and 22 of its judgment, in which it was willing to read across from the finding that a national measure facilitates abuse for the purpose of Article 86 to the existence of a breach of Article 30. This link provides the Court with a further weapon to tackle national measures which grant exclusive rights to particular undertakings.

The general issue of state undertakings came before the Court once again in *Corbeau*.[15] Corbeau set up his own postal service for the City of Liège; for deliveries outside this area he collected the post but sent it on via the normal postal services. He was prosecuted for contravening the Belgian laws which conferred a monoply on the official postal service. The question as phrased by the Court was whether this constituted a breach of Article 90. The ECJ reiterated orthodoxy to the effect that the mere creation of a dominant position by the state through the grant of exclusive rights was not in itself incompatible with Article 90. However, it also held that Article 90 affirms the idea that the state must not enact or maintain in force measures which might eliminate the effectiveness of provisions such as Article 86. The Court then went on to consider the application of Article 90(2) which will be analysed below.

The precise effect of the case on the legality of the grant of exclusive rights is not entirely clear. One view, put forward by Hancher, is that, notwithstanding the Court's statement that the grant of exclusivity is not *per se* incompatible with the Treaty, 'the Court appears to condemn the very existence of national rules conferring a dominant position on an undertaking *unless* the monopoly or exclusive rights at issue can be justified in accordance with Article 90(2)', on the ground that this is necessary to ensure the effectiveness of Articles 90(1) and 86.[16]

14 At any rate not to nearly the same extent.

15 Case C–320/91P, *Procureur du Roi* v. *Paul Corbeau* [1993] ECR I–2533.

16 Note (1994) 31 CMLRev. 105, 111.

The general thrust of these developments has meant that it is now more difficult than hitherto for a state to organize its economic activities by giving special or exclusive rights to particular firms. Any agnosticism which the Community may previously have had in this respect has been replaced by a more strident belief in the operation of free markets in which the actors enjoy no specially privileged position. This can be seen in the quotation from Ehlermann, the Director General of DGIV, set against the backdrop of the Court's recent judgments on Article 90:[17]

> Established case law on Article 3(f) and the second paragraph of Article 5 in conjunction with Articles 85 and 86 and the most recent judgments on Article 90 in conjunction with Articles 30 and 59 reinforce the free-market thrust of the EEC Treaty. This is all the more so if they are seen against the background of the recent judgments of the Court of Justice on the concept of aid in the relationship between the state and public undertakings. Bearing in mind the fact that all these provisions involve Community *constitutional* law, it would seem clear that the *Community* has the *most strongly free-market oriented constitution in the world.*

(c) The Scope of Article 90(2)

Article 90(2) effectively falls into three parts: it begins by emphasizing that undertakings entrusted with the operation of services of a general economic interest or which have the character of a revenue-producing monopoly are subject to the Treaty; it then excludes the application of these rules where the performance of the tasks assigned to such undertakings is liable to be obstructed; it then renders this exception subject to a proviso that the development of trade must not be affected to such an extent as would be contrary to the interests of the Community.

The first step, therefore, in the application of Article 90(2) is to determine whether an undertaking is of the kind mentioned. Not surprisingly the ECJ has stressed that the category of entrusted undertakings should be strictly defined, since the Article entails a derogation from the rules of the Treaty.[18] It is, however, not relevant whether the undertaking is public or private, provided that the service entrusted to it has been assigned by an act of a public authority.[19] While it does not seem that this act must be in any particular legal form, the state must have taken some specific steps to assign the service to the specific undertaking.[20] It has been accepted that undertakings such as utilities do serve the general economic interest, as required by Article 90(2). The ECJ has also accepted in *Ahmed Saeed* that Article 90(2) may apply to airlines which are obliged by public authorities to operate on routes which are not commercially viable, but which it is necessary to operate for the general

[17] 'The Contribution of EC Competition Policy to the Single Market' (1992) 29 CMLRev. 257, 273, italics in the original.

[18] Case 127/73, *BRT* v. *SABAM* [1974] ECR 313, [1974] 2 CMLR 238.

[19] *Ibid.*

[20] Case 7/82, *GVL* v. *Commission* [1983] ECR 483, [1983] 3 CMLR 645.

interest.[21] The Court will, however, subject claims that a service is of a general economic interest to searching scrutiny. Thus in the *Merci* case[22] the ECJ rejected the argument that dock work came within this category.

The second step in the application of Article 90(2) is to determine whether the exception applies. Undertakings will, of course, seek to bring themselves within the ambit of Article 90(2) in order to argue that the Treaty rules must be modified so as not to obstruct the performance of the tasks assigned to them. The ECJ will not readily accept such arguments. In *Ahmed Saeed*[23] the Court held that, in order for it to be possible for the competition rules to be modified by needs arising from the performance of a task of general economic interest, the national authorities responsible for the approval of airline tariffs and the courts to which disputes relating thereto were submitted must be able to determine the exact nature of the needs in question and their impact on the structure of the tariffs applied by the airlines. While in *Merci*[24] the ECJ decided that, even if dock work were to be regarded as of general economic interest, there was no evidence that this demanded the modification of the Treaty rules so as to prevent any obstruction in the performance of this task. The same approach is apparent in other cases. Thus in the *British Telecom* case[25] the Commission had made a decision holding certain practices relating to the transmission of messages to be in breach of Article 86. This decision was challenged by Italy on a number of grounds, one of which was that the measures adopted by BT should be exempted from the competition rules because of Article 90(2). The ECJ disagreed. It found that Italy had failed to establish that the application of these rules to BT would prejudice the accomplishment of the tasks assigned to it.

It is clear, then, that undertakings which seek to bring themselves within the Article 90(2) exception will face an uphill task. Even if the Court accepts that an undertaking is to be regarded as 'entrusted' for the purposes of this Article, the ECJ has made it plain that the exception will only come into play if the relevant Treaty prohibitions are *incompatible* with the performance of their assigned tasks.[26]

In the light of this criterion it is not easy to conceive of situations which would satisfy the Court that the exception should be applied.[27] The *Corbeau* case[28] does, however, provide one instance in which the Court was willing to

[21] Case 66/86, *Ahmed Saeed Flugreisen and Silver Line Reisebüro GmbH* v. *Zentrale zur Bekämpfung Unlauteren Wettbewerbs eV* [1989] ECR 803, [1990] 4 CMLR 102, para. 55.

[22] Case C–179/90, [1991] ECR I–5889, [1994] 4 CMLR 422, para. 27.

[23] Case 66/86, n. 21 above, para. 56.

[24] Case C–179/90, n. 22 above, para. 27.

[25] Case 41/83, *Re British Telecommunications: Italy* v. *Commission* [1985] ECR 873, [1985] 2 CMLR 368, para. 33.

[26] Case 155/73, *Sacchi* [1974] ECR 409, [1974] 2 CMLR 177; Case 311/84, *Centre Belge d'Etudes du Marché-Télé-marketing SA* v. *Compagnie Luxembourgeoise de Télédiffusion SA and Information Publicité Benelux SA* [1985] ECR 3261, [1986] 2 CMLR 558.

[27] One suggestion concerns the sphere of state aids, in the sense that the grant of such aid to a bus company may be essential for the provision of the service in question, Wyatt and Dashwood, n. 4 above, 561.

[28] Case C–320/91P, n. 15 above.

accept that the exception might apply. The ECJ accepted that the Belgian postal service was an entrusted undertaking, and accepted also that some restriction on competition might be necessary to enable the holder of the right to fulfil the duties which it was required to perform. If this were not so then other firms could simply cream off the profitable areas of business, since they would have no corresponding obligation to perform loss-making activities. This did not serve to exclude all competition. There could, said the Court, be services which could be dissociated from the general public service, which could be offered by other undertakings without threatening the economic stability needed by the holder of the exclusive right. It was for the national court to determine whether the services in this case came within that category.

Even if the exception does come into play, we should not forget the third requirement of Article 90(2): that the development of trade must not be affected to such an extent as would be contrary to the interests of the Community. This proviso to the exception has the effect of subjugating Member State interests to those of the Community in the relevant area.

(d) The Scope of Article 90(3)

Article 90(3) gives the Commission power to ensure the application of Article 90 through directives or decisions addressed to Member States. It is one of the relatively rare provisions of the Treaty which confers direct legislative competence on the Commission. It should not, however, be thought that this is the only way in which Article 90 can be enforced. Recourse may still be had to actions under Article 169, and the interpretation of Article 90 can still be clarified through Article 177 references.

The occasions on which the Commission has chosen to make use of Article 90(3) to pass directives have been relatively rare. They have also been the cause of conflict with the Member States which have challenged the competence of the Commission to proceed in this manner. Thus in the *Transparency Directive* case,[29] the facts of which have been set out above,[30] the Member States argued that the Directive could not be enacted under Article 90(3), which, they said, was limited to dealing with a specific situation in one or more Member States. It did not give any more general legislative power to the Commission. The Court rejected this argument: there was no warrant for construing the term 'directive' in Article 90(3) any differently from Article 189.[31] The parties also contended that the directive in question should have been adopted pursuant to Article 94 by the Council. This contention was also denied by the ECJ. The specific power to issue directives contained in Article 90(3) was in furtherance of the Commission's duty of surveillance provided for in Article 90. The fact that the rules might be laid down by the Council

[29] Cases 188–190/80, *France, Italy and United Kingdom* v. *Commission* [1982] ECR 2545, [1982] 3 CMLR 144, paras. 4–15.

[30] See above, 1068.

[31] N. 29 above, para. 7.

under its general power in Article 94 did not preclude the Commission's exercise of power under Article 90(3).[32]

The Court has had a more recent occasion on which to pass judgment on the competence of the Commission under Article 90(3) in the *Telecommunications Terminal Equipment* case:

Case C–202/88, France v. Commission
[1991] ECR I–1223, [1992] 5 CMLR 552

France sought to annul Commission Directive 88/301 on telecommunications terminal equipment which had been passed under Article 90(3). Under the Directive Member States which had granted special or exclusive rights to undertakings for the importation, marketing, etc. of such equipment were to ensure that those rights were withdrawn, and to inform the Commission of the legislation enacted to reach this end. The Directive also provided for responsibility concerning the drawing up of specifications for such equipment to be assigned to a body which was independent of those actually providing the telecommunications services. The first argument advanced by France was that Article 169 should have been used rather than the power to make a directive under Article 90(3).

THE ECJ

17. It must be held in that regard that Article 90(3) EEC empowers the Commission to specify in general terms the obligations arising under Article 90(1) by adopting directives. The Commission exercises that power where, without taking into consideration the particular situation existing in the various Member States, it defines in concrete terms the obligations imposed on them under the Treaty. In view of its very nature, such a power cannot be used to make a finding that a Member State has failed to fulfil a particular obligation under the Treaty.

18. However, it appears from the content of the Directive at issue in this case that the Commission merely determined in general terms obligations which are binding on the Member States under the Treaty . . .

[*Another argument advanced by France was that the Directive should have been passed under Article 100a, and that it was contrary to Article 87.*]

23. As regards the allegation that the Commission has encroached on the powers conferred on the Council by Articles 87 and 100a EEC, those provisions have to be compared with Article 90, taking into account their respective subject-matter and purpose.

24. Article 100a is concerned with the adoption of measures for the approximation of the provisions laid down by law, regulation or administrative action in Member States which have as their object the establishment and functioning of the common market. Article 87 is concerned with the adoption of any appropriate regulations or directives to give effect to the principles set out in Articles 85 and 86, that is to say the competition rules applicable to all undertakings. As for Article 90, it is concerned with measures adopted by the Member States in relation to undertakings with which they have specific links referred to in the provisions of that Article. It is only with regard to such measures that Article 90 imposes on the Commission a duty of supervision which may, where necessary, be

[32] *Ibid.*, para. 14.

exercised through the adoption of directives and decisions addressed to the Member States.

25. It must therefore be held that the subject-matter of the power conferred on the Commission by Article 90(3) is different from, and more specific than, that of the powers conferred on the Council by either Article 100a or Article 87.

26. It should also be noted that, as the Court held in Joined Cases 188–190/80, *France, Italy and the United Kingdom* v. *Commission*, the possibility that rules containing provisions which impinge upon the specific sphere of Article 90 might be laid down by the Council by virtue of its general power under other Articles of the Treaty does not preclude the exercise of the power which Article 90 confers on the Commission.

27. The plea in law alleging lack of powers on the part of the Commission must therefore be rejected.

It is clear from the judgment that the ECJ does not wish unduly to curtail the Commission in the use of its power under Article 90(3) in relation to the making of directives. The same message is apparent from the Court's finding in *Koninklijke PTT Nederland NV*[33] concerning the power to make decisions under Article 90(3). The reasoning in paragraph 17 of *France* v. *Commission*, although concerned with directives, had led to questions whether decisions made under Article 90(3) could be used as enforcement measures against particular Member States. In the *Koninklijke PTT* case the ECJ dispelled these doubts by holding that the power under Article 90(3) to make decisions could indeed be used to find that a particular Member State was in breach of Article 90 and the decision could specify the measures which must be taken to comply with Community law. In the context of decisions, it is apparent, then, that the Commission can proceed by way of Article 90(3) rather than Article 169. When it chooses to do so it must, however, give fair hearing rights to the affected parties.

(e) Article 90 and National Courts

We have already seen in the course of the preceding analysis that a number of the cases which the ECJ has considered have come to it by way of references from national courts under Article 177. It is time now to consider in more detail how far the provisions of Article 90 are directly effective, and what are the limits to the competence of the national courts under this Article. A distinction in this respect must be drawn between Article 90(1) and (2).

The reason there is difficulty in determining whether Article 90(1) has direct effect is because the Article points us to other provisions of the Treaty. It is in this sense a reference provision. Member States are under a duty not to enact or maintain in force, in relation to public undertakings or those to whom special or exclusive rights have been given, measures which are *contrary*

[33] Cases C–48 and 66/90, *Netherlands, Koninklijke PTT Nederland NV and PTT Post BV* v. *Commission* [1992] ECR I–565.

to the rules contained in the Treaty. A breach of Article 90 is therefore dependent upon the existence of some other Article of the Treaty which has been broken by the Member State's action or inaction. Logic would therefore indicate that whether individuals can invoke Article 90 will turn on whether the other rule of the Treaty which has allegedly been broken is itself directly effective. We can see this in operation in the *Merci* case,[34] where the ECJ held that the provisions of Articles 30, 48, and 86 have direct effect when they fall to be considered within the framework of Article 90; and that national courts must therefore protect the rights of the relevant parties.

The position with respect to direct effect and Article 90(2) is complicated by a rather different factor. We have already seen that this Article has three parts: the determination of whether a body is an entrusted undertaking, the application of the exception, and the application of the proviso to the exception.

The ECJ has long recognized the competence of national courts to answer the first of these questions. In the *SABAM* case[35] the ECJ affirmed that a national court has the duty of investigating whether an undertaking which invokes the provisions of Article 90(2) for the purpose of claiming derogation from one of the Treaty rules has in fact been entrusted by the Member State with the operation of a service of general economic interest.

There has been considerably more uncertainty about whether a national court may, if it finds that an undertaking does come within this category, apply the exception. The initial response of the ECJ was that Article 90(2) could not be invoked by individuals before national courts in this way; that it did not create rights for individuals.[36] Subsequent case law of the ECJ cast doubt on this proposition.[37] The situation has now been clarified by the decision of the Court in the *ERT* case.[38] In that case the ECJ reasoned from the justifiable premise that Article 90(2) subjects entrusted undertakings which come within this Article to the rules of the Treaty except in so far as it can be shown that those rules are incompatible with the performance of their particular tasks. From this premise it concluded that it was indeed open to a national court to determine whether the practices of such an undertaking are compatible with, for example, Article 86, and to verify whether those practices, if they are contrary to such a provision, can be justified by the needs of the particular task with which the undertaking has been entrusted. The difficulties which this may present for national courts should not, however, be underestimated.[39]

Should any applicant succeed in bringing a case within the exception, the question remains whether a national court is competent to apply the proviso in Article 90(2). The better view is that the national courts do not have such

[34] Case C–179/90, [1991] ECR I–5889, [1994] 4 CMLR 422, para. 23.

[35] Case 127/73, n. 18 above.

[36] Case 10/71, n. 6 above.

[37] Wyatt and Dashwood, n. 4 above, 563–565.

[38] Case C–260/89, n. 12 above, paras. 33–34.

[39] See, e.g., the task presented to the national courts in Case C–320/91P, n. 15 above, discussed by Hancher, (1994) 31 CMLRev. 105, 119–20.

competence, since the proviso 'may well be seen as unsuitable for determination by national courts insofar as they will neither possess the information on which to take an overview of the Community's interest nor have the political legitimacy to determine the place at which the balance should be drawn'.[40] On this view it would require a Commission decision made under Article 90(3) to decide the issue.

4. THE STATE, ARTICLES 5, 85, 86, AND 30[41]

The discussion thus far has focused on Article 90. This is not, however, the only Treaty provision which is of relevance to state action and the Community. The Court has also made important decisions on the basis of Articles 5, 85, 86, and 30. The basic principle which the Court has enunciated is that a state may not adopt or maintain in force any measure which would deprive, for example, Article 85 of its effectiveness or prejudice its full and uniform application. A state can be in breach of this obligation either when it requires or encourages undertakings to conclude cartels which are in violation of Article 85, or when it divests its national provisions of their public nature by, in effect, delegating to the firms the responsibility for taking decisions about the boundaries of competition.[42]

One way of regarding this jurisprudence is to see it as the means whereby the ECJ has extended the type of obligation imposed on a state by Article 90 to situations where the undertakings are neither public nor enjoy any specially privileged position. The following cases illustrate the Court's jurisprudence at work.

In *Vereninging van Vlaamse Reisbureaus* v. *Sociale Dienst van de Plaatselijke en Gewestelijke Overheidsdiensten*[43] a travel agent was prosecuted for violating a professional code of practice which had been incorporated into Belgian law. The Code involved horizontal price fixing which was a blatant breach of Article 85. In addition to finding this breach the Court also found that the Belgian state was in breach of Article 5 read together with Articles 3(f) and 85 by supporting the cartel through its own legal regime. A similar theme is apparent in *Van Eycke*.[44] Holders of certain Belgian savings accounts had the benefit of a tax exemption provided that the bank offered them interest rates

[40] Wyatt and Dashwood, n. 4 above, 566.

[41] P. J. Slot, 'The Application of Articles 3(f), 5 and 85 to 94 EEC' (1987) 12 ELRev. 179; L. Gyselen, 'State Action and the Effectiveness of the Treaty's Competition Provisions' (1989) 26 CMLRev. 33.

[42] For recent affirmation of this principle, see Case C–2/91, *Wolf Meng* [1993] ECR I–5751; Case C–185/91, *Bundesanstalt für den Güterverkehr* v. *Gebrüder Reiff GmbH and Co KG* [1993] ECR I–5801; Case C–245/91, *Ohra Schadeverzekeringen NV* [1993] ECR I–5851; Case C–153/93, *Germany* v. *Delta Schiffahrts- und Speditionsgesellschaft mbH*, 9 June 1994. On the facts of these cases the applicants were not in breach of the principle set out in the text.

[43] Case 311/85, [1987] ECR 3801, [1989] 4 CMLR 213.

[44] Case 267/86, *Van Eycke* v. *NV ASPA* [1988] ECR 4769.

below that set by the Minister in a Royal Decree. Those who held accounts at banks which gave higher interest rates than that stipulated by the Royal Decree lost the tax exemption, with the consequence that it was unattractive for the banks to offer these higher rates. The effect of this was to limit price competition between banks. The ECJ held that, although the duty in Articles 85 and 86 is directed towards undertakings, the state itself has an obligation derived from Article 5 not to introduce measures which render the competition Articles ineffective. This would be the case where, for example, national legislation reinforced the effects of existing agreements which were themselves in breach of Article 85; or where the state deprived its own legislation of its official character by delegating to private traders responsibility for taking decisions affecting the economic sphere.[45]

What, then, of the situation where the state intervenes not to support an existing agreement which is itself illegal under Article 85, but by way of an independent measure which undertakings must follow? In such circumstances Article 30 would be the most appropriate provision to employ in the case of goods, and Article 59 in the case of services.[46]

5. STATE AIDS: THE SUBSTANTIVE RULES AND ARTICLE 92

(a) Article 92(1)

Article 92 of the Treaty lays down the basic test for state aids within the EC. The Article has three parts: paragraph (1) establishes the general principle that state aids are incompatible with the common market; paragraph (2) provides certain exceptions for situations where the aid *will be deemed* to be compatible with the common market; and paragraph (3) lists certain types of case where the aid *may be deemed* to be compatible with the common market. Let us then begin with the basic proscription of state aids set out in Article 92(1):

> Save as otherwise provided in this Treaty, any aid granted by a Member State or through State resources in any form whatsoever which distorts or threatens to distort competition by favouring certain undertakings or the production of certain goods shall, in so far as it affects trade between Member States, be incompatible with the common market.

It is necessary to examine a number of the requirements which are mentioned in this Article. The obvious starting point is the *definition of state aid.*

[45] See also Case 229/83, *Leclerc* v. *Au Blé Vert* [1985] ECR 1, [1985] 2 CMLR 286; Cases 209–13/84, *Ministère Public* v. *Asjes* [1986] ECR 1425.

[46] Case 229/83, n. 45 above.

Article 92(1) does not itself provide any such definition. As might be expected, the ECJ and the Commission have adopted a broad view of what might constitute state aid for the purposes of Article 92(1). Substance and not form is the guide. A state will not be able to avoid the prohibition contained in the Treaty by seeking to couch its grant of aid in a form which escapes the Treaty prohibition. The Commission has furnished a full elaboration of the various forms which such aid might take. These include direct subsidies, tax exemptions, exemptions from parafiscal charges, interest rates which are preferential, loan guarantees on terms which are particularly favourable, the provision of land or buildings on special terms, indemnities against losses, preferential terms for public ordering, the deferment of the collection of fiscal or social contributions, and dividend guarantees. This list is, of course, illustrative rather than exhaustive. It is always open to the Commission and the Court to respond to a new form of providing state aid if and when it should arise.

General measures of economic policy, such as an interest-rate reduction, while benefiting industrial sales will not in themselves be classified as aid. In this sense a non-sectoral measure of general taxation policy will remain within the area of fiscal sovereignty of the state. Having said this, it is also clear that a measure will be classified as aid even if it benefits a whole range of undertakings, as in the case of a general export aid. Moreover, the dividing line between general measures of economic policy and state aids may be a fine one as the following extract makes clear:

C. Quigley, The Notion of a State Aid in the EEC[47]

Although general measures of economic policy will not constitute aid, many measures taken by the state can produce benefits to undertakings or production of goods generally. Such measures may constitute aid and, if they fulfil the other criteria in Article 92(1), will be incompatible with the common market. A distinction lies between general measures of economic policy and specific measures within that policy. Those elements of infrastructure which are normally provided by the state, such as roads, bridges and tunnels, would usually form part of the transport and environmental policy of the state and would not be regarded as aid, even though particular undertakings or regions would benefit from the improvements.[48] On the other hand, if the development is carried out, not solely as part of the general transport and environmental policy but as part of a regional or sectoral plan within that policy, there may be an element of aid. Also, where the state normally insists on such infrastructure being built by private persons, such as the roads on a private industrial estate, any provision by the state of such facilities may constitute aid.

[47] (1988) 13 ELRev. 242, 252–3.

[48] On this point see now Case C–225/91, *Matra* v. *Commission* [1993] ECR I–3203: aid for infrastructure did not fall within Art. 92 since it was not intended for the exclusive benefit of those partaking in a joint venture.

One of the areas in which there has been particular difficulty concerns the situation where the state takes shareholdings in private undertakings. When should this be regarded as state aid for the purposes of Article 92(1)? The following cases provide a guide:

Case 323/82, Intermills SA v. Commission [1984] ECR 3809, [1986] 1 CMLR 614

The Belgian government had intervened to aid a paper-making firm which was in financial difficulty. The object was to restructure the operations of the company, so that it shifted its production from the making of bulk paper to the making of special paper with a high added value. To this end the Belgian government, through the Walloon Regional Executive, made loans to the company and also injected capital into the enterprise, which gave it a controlling interest in the firm. One of the questions which arose in the case was whether the capital injection, whereby the government acquired shares in the firm, could constitute state aid for the purposes of Article 92(1).

THE ECJ

31. It is clear from the provisions cited that the Treaty applies to aid granted by a State or through State resources 'in any form whatsoever'. It follows that no distinction can be drawn between aid granted in the form of loans and aid granted in the form of a holding acquired in the capital of an undertaking. Aid taking either form falls within the prohibition in Article 92 where the conditions set out in that provision are fulfilled.

Case C–142/87, Re Tubemeuse: Belgium v. Commission[49] [1990] ECR I–959, [1991] 3 CMLR 213

In 1979 the Belgian Government acquired 72 per cent of the capital holding of Tubemeuse (T), which was in severe financial difficulty following the withdrawal of private shareholders. In 1982 the Commission approved a series of aid measures, but these were not successful and the state then acquired the remaining shares in the firm. Between 1984 and 1986 Belgium initiated a series of measures designed to increase the capital of T. These measures were notified to the Commission, but the Government did not wait for the Commission's approval of them as required by Article 93(2). The Commission then made a decision that these measures constituted unlawful aid and instructed Belgium to recover the sums. The Belgian Government contested this Commission decision. One of the grounds of this challenge was that the measures in 1984–6 did not constitute state aid at all, but were rather the normal reaction of any investor whose initial investment (made in 1979 and then in 1982) was at risk.

[49] See also Cases 296 and 318/82, *The Netherlands and Leeuwarder Papierwarenfabriek BV* v. *Commission* [1985] ECR 809, [1985] 3 CMLR 380; Case 40/85, *Re Boch: Belgium* v. *Commission* [1986] ECR 2321, [1988] 2 CMLR 301. See further, the Commission's 1987 document on *The Measurement of the Aid Element of State Acqusitions of Company Capital—Evolution of Concentration and Competition.*

THE ECJ

25. It should be pointed out that, according to settled case law, investment by the public authorities in the capital of undertakings, in whatever form, may constitute State aid where the conditions set out in Article 92 are fulfilled (see Case 323/82, *Intermills* v. *Commission* and Joined Cases 296 & 318/82, *Netherlands and Leeuwarder Papierwarenfabriek* v. *Commission*).

26. In order to determine whether such measures are in the nature of State aid, the relevant criterion is that indicated in the Commission's decision, and not contested by the Belgian government, namely whether the undertaking could have obtained the amounts in question on the capital market.

27. In the event, it can be seen from the contested measure taken together with the other documents before the Court that, in addition to the technical difficulties of its plant, which made necessary the extensive modernisation programme in 1982 carried out with the help of the public authorities and authorised by the Commission, the company has, since 1979, had to face structural financial difficulties. Excessively high production costs, continual operating losses, poor liquidity and heavy indebtedness led to the withdrawal of almost all the private shareholders from the undertaking.

28. Moreover, it is not contested that the seamless steel tubes sector whose production was intended principally for use in oil exploration, was in a state of crisis, marked by considerable surplus capacity in the producing countries and new production capacity in the developing and State trading countries. Furthermore, the restrictions which the United States imposed on the importation of steel tubes into their territory and the fall in world oil prices, which contributed to a reduction in drilling, led to a fall in demand for the tubes in question and therefore to a substantial reduction in their price and in world production. That is the reason why other Member States sought to reduce their production capacity in that sector.

29. Under those circumstances, there is nothing which suggests any error in the Commission's assessment that Tubemeuse's prospects of profitability were not such as to induce private investors operating under normal market economy conditions to enter into the financial transactions in question, that it was unlikely that Tubemeuse could have obtained the amounts essential for its survival on the capital markets and that, for that reason, the Belgian government's support for Tubemeuse constituted State aid.

The ECJ has continued to apply the same test in more recent cases. Thus it has held, in response to the argument that a private investor[50] might well invest money in a company for reasons which do not relate directly to profitability, such as the wish to maintain the company's public image, that when capital is invested by a public investor there must be some interest in

[50] In applying the private investor test the ECJ has held that it is necessary to distinguish between the obligations which a State must assume as owner of the share capital, and its obligations as a public authority. The latter cannot be included in the calculation. On the facts of the case this meant that Spain could not take into account costs arising from redundancies, payment of unemployment benefit, and money for the purpose of restructuring the industrial infrastructure: Cases C–278–280/92, *Spain* v. *Commission,* 14 Sept. 1994.

profitability in the long term, otherwise the investment will be characterized as aid for the purposes of Article 92(1).[51]

A second important aspect of Article 92(1) is the fact that the aid should be granted by a *'Member State or through State resources'*. It is clear, as we have already seen from the *Intermills* case, that this can include action by regional as well as central government. The nature of the body through which the aid is provided is irrelevant in this respect. This is demonstrated by the following case:

Cases 67, 68 and 70/85, Kwerkerij Gebroeders Van der Kooy BV v. Commission[52]
[1988] ECR 219, [1989] 2 CMLR 804

The Commission made a decision that the tariffs charged by Gasunie for gas to certain firms in the horticultural industry were preferential and constituted aid for the purposes of Article 92. Gasunie was a company incorporated under private law, but 50 per cent of its shares were held by the Dutch government and the tariffs charged by Gasunie were subject to approval by a government minister. One of the grounds on which the decision was challenged was that the fixing of the tariff did not constitute action by the Dutch state.

THE ECJ

32. In the first place, the applicants maintain that . . . the contested tariff was not imposed by the Dutch State and cannot be regarded as 'aid granted by a Member State or through State resources'.

33. They argue that Gasunie is a company incorporated under private law in which the Dutch State holds only 50% of the share capital and that the tariff is the outcome of an agreement concluded under private law between Gasunie, Vegin and the Landbouwchap, to which the Dutch State is not a party.

34. Turning to the point noted by the Commission that the Minister for Economic Affairs has a right of approval over the tariffs charged by Gasunie, the Dutch Government claims that that is no more than a retrospective supervisory power which is solely concerned with whether the tariffs accord with the aims of Dutch energy policy.

35. As the Court has held . . ., there is no necessity to draw any distinction between cases where aid is granted directly by the State and where it is granted by public and or private bodies established or appointed by the State to administer the aid. In this instance, the documents before the Court provide considerable evidence to show that the fixing of the disputed tariff was the result of action by the Dutch State.

36. First of all, the shares in Gasunie are so distributed that the Dutch State directly or indirectly holds 50% of the shares and appoints half of the members of

[51] Case C–303/88, *Italy* v. *Commission* [1991] ECR I–1433; Case C–305/89, *Italy* v. *Commission* [1991] ECR I–1635. L. Hancher, 'State Aids and Judicial Control in the European Community' [1994] 3 ECLR 134, 135–6.

[52] See also Case 78/76, *Firma Steinike and Weinlig* v. *Bundesamt für Ernährung und Forstwitschaft* [1977] ECR 595, [1977] 2 CMLR 688; Case 290/83, *Re Grants to Poor Farmers: Commission* v. *France* [1985] ECR 439, [1986] 2 CMLR 546; Case 57/86, *Commission* v. *Greece* [1988] ECR 2855.

the supervisory board—a body whose powers include that of determining the tariffs to be applied. Secondly, the Minister for Economic Affairs is empowered to approve the tariffs applied by Gasunie, with the result that, regardless of how that power may be exercised, the Dutch Government can block any tariff which does not suit it. Lastly, Gasunie and the Landbouwschap have on two occasions given effect to the Commission's representations to the Dutch Government seeking an amendment of the horticultural tariff . . .

37. Considered as a whole, these factors demonstrate that Gasunie in no way enjoys full autonomy in the fixing of gas tariffs but acts under the control and on the instructions of the public authorities. It is thus clear that Gasunie could not fix the tariff without taking account of the requirements of the public authorities.

38. It may therefore be concluded that the fixing of the contested tariff is the result of action by the Dutch State and thus falls within the meaning of the phrase 'aid granted by a Member State' under Article 92 of the Treaty.

Once it has been decided that there is a state aid which has been granted by a Member State or through its resources, the third requirement of Article 92(1) is that the aid should *distort or threaten to distort competition by favouring certain undertakings or the production of certain goods*. In many cases this will be unproblematic. The grant of, for example, a subsidy, will indubitably place the recipient in a more advantageous position than it would have been in without this financial benefit. The Court will consider the position of the relevant company prior to the receipt of the aid, and if this improved then this aspect of Article 92 will be met.[53] It is no 'defence' for the state to argue that the aid is justified because its effect is to lower the costs of a sector of industry which has, in relative terms, higher costs than other industrial sectors;[54] nor is it possible for a state to contend that its aid should be excused on the ground that other states made similar payments to firms within those countries.[55]

The final element in Article 92(1) is that there should be an *effect on interstate trade*. It is clear from the Court's case law that it takes a stringent approach to fulfilment of this requirement. If aid strengthens the financial position of one undertaking as compared to others within the Community then inter-Community trade will be affected.[56] Moreover, the ECJ has made it clear that the relatively small amount of the aid, or the relatively small size of the undertaking which receives it, does not as such exclude the possibility that Community trade might be affected.[57] As in the case of competition law,[58] the need to find an impact on Community trade will not normally hinder the Court if it is minded to press forward with an investigation of the substance of the issue.

[53] Case 173/73, *Italy* v. *Commission* [1974] ECR 709, [1974] 2 CMLR 593.

[54] *Ibid.*

[55] Case 78/76, n. 52 above.

[56] Case 730/79, *Philip Morris Holland BV* v. *Commission* [1980] ECR 2671, [1981] 2 CMLR 321.

[57] Case C–142/87, *Re Tubemeuse: Belgium* v. *Commission* [1990] ECR I–959, [1991] 3 CMLR 213, para. 43.

[58] See above, 913.

(b) Article 92(2)

Article 92(2) lists three types of aid which are deemed to be compatible with the common market.

Article 92(2)(a) states that 'aid having a social character, granted to individual consumers, provided that such aid is granted without discrimination related to the origin of the products concerned' will be compatible with the common market. It is important to note that this Article only legitimates aid if there is no discrimination which relates to the goods' origin. This limits the number of occasions on which a state will be able to take advantage of this provision, since most state aid is directed exclusively to a particular firm within the Member State providing the aid.

Article 92(2)(b) legitimates 'aid to make good damage caused by natural disasters or exceptional occurrences'. The rationale for this exception is self-evident. The limits of this Article are, however, somewhat unclear. While the notion of a natural disaster is reasonably apparent, the meaning of exceptional occurrence is open to a wider range of interpretation. It is, for example, contestable whether this would cover difficulties which are economic in nature.[59]

Article 92(2)(c) makes provision for the special position of Germany, resulting from the division of the country, in order to compensate for the economic disadvantage caused by that division.

(c) Article 92(3): Commission Discretion, Rule-Making, and Individualized Adjudication

Whereas aid which comes within the exceptions mentioned in Article 92(2) will be deemed to be compatible with the common market, the exceptions which are listed in Article 92(3) are discretionary in nature, in the sense that aid which comes within these categories *may* be deemed to be compatible with the common market. Before discussing the particular exceptions two general principles concerning the interpretation of this Article should be made clear.

On the one hand, as will become evident when considering Article 93, it is the Commission which will make the initial assessment of whether any of the exceptions is applicable.[60] While this exercise of discretion can be reviewed by the Court, the ECJ will be mindful of the fact that the assessment of the applicability of the exceptions may entail complex evaluations of social and economic data. The ECJ will not therefore substitute its view for that of the Commission. In deciding upon the applicability of Article 92(3) the Commission exercises a discretion not only as to the application of any of its particular terms, but also as to the general approach which should be brought to bear when considering the exceptions more generally. Thus the Commission

59 Wyatt and Dashwood, n. 4 above, 528.

60 A valuable guide to the various sectoral and horizontal aid frameworks used by the Commission, as well as to the way in which the Commission makes decisions pursuant thereto, is to be found in L. Hancher, T. Ottervanger, and P. J. Slot, *EC State Aids* (Chancery, 1993).

has decided to apply a principle of compensatory justification, which means that, before aid can obtain approval under Article 92(3), there must be some contribution by the beneficiary of the aid, over and above the normal play of market forces, to the attainment of Community objectives as contained in the derogations from Article 92(3).

On the other hand, the Commission's discretion manifests itself in the very choice of whether to proceed through a series of individual decisions or by a species of rule-making. This choice is open to all administrators, whether operating at national or Community level. It is unsurprising that in the field of state aids the Commission has chosen to employ rules and policy guidelines. These rules and policy frameworks have been made both in relation to particular industrial sectors and also in relation to horizontal matters, such as regional aid, environmental aid, and the like. The reasons for employing such policy documents are not hard to find. They are part practical and part conceptual. In practical terms such guidelines help an overburdened administration to cope with an increased work-load.[61] In conceptual terms they have the advantages generally associated with a rule-making system:[62] they 'reduce Member States' room for manœuvre in giving aid and the controller's margin of discretion, choice and possible arbitrariness';[63] and they facilitate 'the transparency, legal security and credibility which result from strict and consistent enforcement, to the benefit of governments and industry'.[64]

Having said this it should not be thought that the choice to proceed through this mode of rule-making is unproblematic. If the benefits which flow from giving effect to administrative policy in this way are familiar to public lawyers, so, too, are some of the problems.

One such problem is the very variety of instruments used by the Commission for the promulgation of these policy choices. Directives, policy guidelines, and statements of policy all jostle one another within the Commission's portfolio. While the legal form of the instrument may not, from the Commission's perspective, affect its binding character,[65] matters may not always be so clear-cut from the perspective of those on the receiving end of the system.[66]

Another problem concerns the extent to which such guidelines may be binding upon the Commission in so far as they could be said to have created legitimate expectations. In *Deufil*,[67] to be considered more fully below,[68] the ECJ refused to accept that the absence of mention of a certain form of aid from a particular sectoral guideline generated a legitimate expectation that such

[61] F. Rawlinson, 'The Role of Policy Frameworks, Codes and Guidelines in the Control of State Aid' in *State Aid: Community Law and Policy*, ed. I. Harden, (Bundesanzeiger, 1993), 56.

[62] P. P. Craig, *Administrative Law* (3rd edn., Sweet & Maxwell, 1994), Ch. 11.

[63] Rawlinson, n. 61 above, 55.

[64] *Ibid.* 57.

[65] *Ibid.* 59.

[66] G. della Cananea, 'Administration by Guidelines: The Policy Guidelines of the Commission in the Field of State Aids', *State Aid: Community Law and Policy*, n. 61 above, 68–69.

[67] Case 310/85, *Deufil* v. *Commission* [1987] ECR 901.

[68] See below, 1105–6.

species of aid were in fact permissible. However, in *CIRFS*[69] the ECJ was willing to accept that in the instant case the Commission was bound by the terms of its policy framework.

A third difficulty arising from the Commission's use of policy guidelines is of a broader intra-institutional nature. It concerns the relationship between this mode of developing policy and the possibility of passing Council regulations pursuant to Article 94, which would thereby involve Member State participation and consent more fully than under the guideline procedure. Rawlinson, a principal administrator within the state aids directorate, is forthright in this respect: the 'Commission does not go to the Council because it, and not the Member States, is the guardian of the Treaties in the area of state aids'.[70] While accepting that the Commission should and does consult Member States he is clear in his belief that greater use of Article 94 would not only be inappropriate for the reason just given, but because the inevitable effect of particularistic Member State interests would be that policy-making in this area would be far more protracted. Others are less happy about the effective by-passing of Article 94. Thus Cananea points to the lack of clarity which exists in relation to certain of the guidelines, to the fact that in some instances the rights of individuals are not properly safeguarded, and suggests that the time may now be ripe for the passage of a 'Council regulation to cope with the existing lacunae of Community law on state aids'.[71] Hancher has also pointed to a number of important instances where there is uncertainty, concluding that there is an 'urgent need for clearer procedural guidelines for all concerned'.[72]

(d) Article 92(3): Particular Categories

With these preliminary remarks we can now examine the particular categories of Article 92(3).

Article 92(3)(a) states that 'aid to promote the economic development of areas where the standard of living is abnormally low or where there is serious under-employment' may be considered to be compatible with the common market. There is a connection between this provision and Article 92(3)(c), in that both relate in a general sense to regional development. The wording of Article 92(3)(a) makes it clear that it can, however, only be used where the problem which besets an area is especially serious; and the Commission has taken the view, upheld by the Court, that the seriousness of the regional problem must be judged in a Community and not a national context. To this end the Commission has published criteria for deciding upon the relative development of different regions as compared to the Community average.[73] This

[69] Case C–313/90, *CIRFS* v. *Commission* [1993] ECR I–1125.

[70] N. 61 above, 60.

[71] G. della Cananea, n. 66 above, 74–5.

[72] 'State Aids and Judicial Control', n. 51 above, 150.

[73] L. Hancher, T. Ottervanger and P. J. Slot, n. 60 above, 181–182.

point, as well as the general principles mentioned above, are exemplified by the *Philip Morris Holland* case:

Case 730/79, Philip Morris Holland BV v. Commission [1980] ECR 2671, [1981] 2 CMLR 321

The Dutch Government gave aid to a tobacco manufacturer. The Commission found that the aid did not come within Article 92(3)(a),(b), or (c). What follows is an extract from the ECJ's reasoning concerning the general approach to Article 92(3), and its findings on Article 92(3)(a).

THE ECJ

16. According to the applicant it is wrong for the Commission to lay down as a general principle that aid granted by a Member State to undertakings only falls within the derogating provisions of Article 92(3) if the Commission can establish that the aid will contribute to the attainment of one of the objectives specified in the derogations, which under normal market conditions the recipient firms would not attain by their own actions. Aid is only permissible under Article 92(3) of the Treaty if the investment plan under consideration is in conformity with the objectives mentioned in subparagraphs (a), (b) and (c).

17. This argument cannot be upheld. On the one hand it disregards the fact that Article 92(3), unlike Article 92(2), gives the Commission a discretion by providing that the aid which it specifies 'may' be considered to be compatible with the Common Market. On the other hand it would result in Member States being permitted to make payments which would improve the financial situation of the recipient undertaking although they were not necessary for the attainment of the objectives specified in Article 92(3).

18. It should be noted in this connection that the disputed decision explicitly states that the Dutch Government has not been able to give nor has the Commission found any grounds establishing that the proposed aid meets the conditions laid down to enforce derogations pursuant to Article 92(3) of the EEC Treaty.

19. The applicant maintains that the Commission was wrong to hold that the standard of living in the Bergen-op-Zoom area is not 'abnormally low' and that this area does not suffer serious 'under employment' within the meaning of Article 92(3)(a). In fact in the Bergen-op-Zoom region the under-employment rate is higher and the *per capita* rate lower than the national average in The Netherlands.

. . .

24. These arguments put forward by the applicant cannot be upheld. It should be borne in mind that the Commission has a discretion the exercise of which involves economic and social assessments which must be made in a Community context.

25. That is the context in which the Commission has with good reason assessed the standard of living and serious under-employment in the Bergen-op-Zoom area, not with reference to the national average in the Netherlands but in relation to the Community level.

Article 92(3)(b) states that 'aid to promote the execution of an important project of European interest or to remedy a serious disturbance in the economy of a Member State' may be considered to be compatible with the common market. It is clear from the wording of this provision that it relates to two separate types of case. The meaning of the first limb of this Article was considered in the *Glaverbel* case. Note in the extract which follows the ECJ's more general observations concerning the discretion possessed by the Commission, and the impact which this has on the ECJ's standard of review:

Cases 62 and 72/87, Executif Régional Wallon and Glaverbel SA v. Commission
[1988] ECR 1573, [1989] 2 CMLR 771

The Belgian Government gave aid to certain glass producers. The Commission found that the aid did not come within Article 92(3). This was contested by the applicants in an Article 173 action. They argued that the aid could come within Article 92(3)(b) on the ground that the new technology made possible by the investment aid would reduce European dependence on American and Japanese producers in the relevant markets.

THE ECJ

21. It should be observed that the categories of aid set out in Article 92(3) . . . 'may' be considered by the Commission to be compatible with the Common Market. It follows that the Commission enjoys a discretion in the matter.

23. The Commission has based its policy with regard to aid on the view that a project may not be described as being of common European interest for the purposes of Article 92(3)(b) unless it forms part of a transnational European programme supported jointly by a number of governments of the Member States, or arises from concerted action by a number of Member States to combat a common threat such as environmental pollution.

In adopting that policy and in taking the view that the investments envisaged in this case did not fulfil the requisite conditions, the Commission did not commit a manifest error of judgment.

24. The two applicants further complain that the Commission failed to give any reasons in the contested decision for its negative assessment . . .

25. The Court considers that a statement of reasons which is based on a supposedly 'clear' fact must generally be regarded as insufficient. In this case, however, the applicants' arguments cannot be accepted. None of the documents laid before the Court lends any support whatever to the conclusion that the aid at issue might contribute to the implementation of an 'important' project of 'common' European interest. The mere fact that the investments enabled new technology to be used does not make the project one of common European interest; that certainly cannot be the case when, as in this instance, the products have to be sold on a saturated market.

Circumstances in which the first limb of Article 92(3)(b) has been used include the development of a common standard for high definition television, and environmental protection.[74]

[74] Wyatt and Dashwood, n. 4 above, 530; L. Hancher, T. Ottervanger and P. J. Slot, n. 60 above, Ch. 15.

The second limb of this Article concerning serious disturbance to the economy of a Member State will only rarely be used, since the Commission is of the view that the economic problem must afflict the whole of the national economy. More specific problems are dealt with under Article 92(3)(a) or (c).

Article 92(3)(c) is in many ways the most significant and interesting of the discretionary exceptions. It provides that 'aid to facilitate the development of certain economic activities or of certain economic areas, where such aid does not adversely affect trading conditions to an extent contrary to the common interest' may be compatible with the common market. There are both positive and negative conditions to be satisfied before the provision of aid can come within this Article.

In *positive terms* the conditions for the application of this Article enable aid to be legitimated by reference to the needs of a particular industrial sector, and by reference to economic areas which the Commission has recognized can have a national, and not just a Community, dimension. Thus Article 92(3)(c) is the provision under which a state can seek to justify the grant of aid to a particular region which is depressed as judged by national criteria. However the nationally based criterion is not unqualified. The Commission will consider a state's regional problems and place them in a Community context: the better the position of the Member State relative to the Community situation, the wider must be the disparity of a region in order to justify the grant of aid.[75] The following extract explains how this process works:

L. Hancher, T. Ottervanger, and P. J. Slot, EC State Aids [76]

The analysis is divided into two stages. In the first stage, the socio-economic situation of the region is considered in relation to certain thresholds which are calculated in two steps. The first step relates to a minimal regional disparity in a national context, while in the second step this minimum required disparity is adjusted to take into account the situation of those Member States which have a more favourable level of development in a Community context. There must be a minimum negative regional disparity in the national context, notwithstanding the relative situation of the Member State within the Community.

. . .

Meeting the relevant threshold in the first stage does not automatically qualify a region to receive state aid. In the second stage other indicators besides unemployment and income levels are examined, including the trend and structure of unemployment, the development of unemployment, net migration, demographic pressure, population density, activity rates, productivity, the structure of economic activity—especially the importance of declining sectors, as well as the overall geographic situation and infrastructure. Where certain regions are at the margin of the thresholds applied in the first stage of analysis, it is possible that the second stage may reveal an adequate justification for regional aid, even in regions which do not fully satisfy the thresholds established in the course of the first stage.

[75] *Eigtheenth Report on Competition Policy* (1989), pt. 147.

[76] N. 60 above, 182.

The Commission has, moreover, made it clear that aid will not normally qualify under Article 92(3)(c) unless it is linked to initial investment, to job creation,[77] and/or to a restructuring of the activities of the undertaking concerned.[78] The purpose of the aid must be to develop a particular sector or region and not merely a specific undertaking therein.[79] Environmental-aid schemes constitute one type of case which can be considered for exemption under Article 92(3)(c).[80]

In *negative terms* Article 92(3)(c) stipulates that the aid must not adversely affect trading conditions to an extent contrary to the common interest.

The application of both the positive and negative aspects of the Article is evident in the *Glaverbel* case:

Cases 62 and 72/87, Executif Régional Wallon and Glaverbel SA v. Commission [1988] ECR 1573, [1989] 2 CMLR 771

The facts of the case have been given in the earlier extract. One of the claims of the parties who sought annulment of the Commission decision was that the latter had misapplied Article 92(3)(c). The Commission had found that the aid in question, which was for periodic plant renovation, did not satisfy the requirements for the development of the relevant sector without adversely affecting trading conditions to an extent contrary to the common interest.

THE ECJ

31. It is apparent from the points made by the Commission that it based its decision on the view that the investment in question was intended to renovate a float line and that such renovation, which must be carried out periodically, cannot be regarded as designed to facilitate the development of certain economic activities, even if such renovation entails the introduction of new technology. The Commission goes on to consider that, even if such renovation could constitute a new technical development which could be regarded as economic development within the meaning of Article 92(3)(c), it could not warrant an exemption under that provision in the case of the float-glass industry because, in view of the unused capacity in that industry, the aid would affect the position of other undertakings and would thus be contrary to the common interest.

32. It must be stated first of all that that line of reasoning is comprehensible and enables those concerned to ascertain the reasons for the Commission's adverse decision and the Court to review them. The complaint of insufficient reasons must therefore be rejected.

33. As far as the application of Article 92(3)(c) is concerned, it should be observed first of all that the applicants did not challenge the facts on which the Commission relied. In particular, they acknowledged that a float line must be

[77] *Ibid.* 176.

[78] For a recent example of the Commission's insistence that a valid restructuring plan should exist before an aid package could come within Art. 92(3)(c), see Cases C–278–280/92, n. 50 above.

[79] The general approach of the Commission was approved by the ECJ in Case 248/85, *Germany* v. *Commission* [1987] ECR 4013.

[80] Hancher, Ottervanger and Slot, n. 60 above, Ch. 15.

periodically renovated and that, in this instance, the plant in question had to be renovated. The applicants did challenge the view that there was unused capacity on the flat-glass market, but their grounds for doing so have already been considered and rejected above.

34. It should also be borne in mind that the Commission enjoys a power of appraisal in applying Article 92(3)(c) as well as in applying Article 92(3)(b). It is, in particular, for the Commission to determine whether trading conditions between the Member States are affected by aid 'to an extent contrary to the common interest'. The applicants have supplied no evidence to suggest that in making that assessment the Commission misused its powers or committed a manifest error.

35. It follows from the foregoing that the complaints concerning the alleged infringement of Article 92(3)(c) and the insufficiency of the reasons given in that regard must be rejected.

It should not, however, be thought that the ECJ will always uphold the reasoning of the Commission on the application of Article 92(3)(c).[81] It will take seriously allegations that the Commission's decision is contradictory or that it has provided insufficient justification for its findings under this Article. It will also overturn Commission decisions on points of principle where it believes that the Commission has erred. This is exemplified by the *Intermills* case:

Case 323/82, Intermills SA v. Commission[82]
[1984] ECR 3809, [1986] 1 CMLR 614

The facts of the case have been given in the previous extract. The applicants sought to have the Commission's decision annulled on the ground, *inter alia*, that it misapplied Article 92(3)(c). The Commission was content with the aid granted in the form of loans, but found that the aid granted by the Belgian Government in the form of shareholdings did not qualify for exemption under Article 92(3) since this aid was not directly linked to the restructuring of the undertaking, but was rather rescue aid, intended to allow the undertaking to meet its financial commitments. Aid of this kind could, said the Commission, do serious damage to competition in the Community since the free play of market forces normally demanded that such undertakings should close, allowing more competitive firms to develop. The applicants contested the finding that the aid in the form of shareholdings was rescue aid, and argued that it was used to finance the closure of unprofitable factories, combined with the conversion to products which had a better prospect of profitability.

THE ECJ

33. . . . the criticism raised by the applicants appears to be well founded, inasmuch as the contested decision does indeed contain contradictions and does not make clear the grounds for the Commission's action on certain vital points. Such doubts and contradictions relate both to the economic justification for the aid and

[81] This is also true in relation to Art. 92(3)(a): see, Cases C–278–280/92, n. 50 above.

[82] See also Case 248/84, *Germany* v. *Commission* [1987] ECR 4013, [1989] 1 CMLR 591; Cases 296 and 318/82, n. 49 above.

the question whether the aid was likely to distort competition within the Common Market.

34. First, as regards the economic justification for the aid, the Commission concedes in the statement of reasons on which its decision is based that the restructuring aimed at by the applicants corresponds, as such, to the Commission's own objectives for the European paper industry. That factor seems to be the chief ground on which the Commission recognised the compatibility with the Treaty of the aid granted in the form of low interest loans and advances.

35. On the other hand, the Commission gave no verifiable reasons to justify its finding that the holding acquired by the public authorities in the capital of the recipient undertaking was not compatible with the Treaty. It merely stated that that holding was 'not directly linked to the restructuring operation' and in view of the losses suffered by the undertaking over several financial years, constituted purely financial 'rescue aid'; . . . In making those assessments without giving any indication of its reasons, other than the statements just referred to, the Commission did not properly explain why its assessment of the restructuring operation in question . . . called for such a clear-cut distinction between the effect of the aid granted in the form of subsidised loans and the effect of the aid granted in the form of capital holdings.

. . .

37. In relation to its claim that the contested aid damages competition in the Common Market, the Commission referred to the provisions of Article 92(1) and to the requirement in Article 92(3), according to which aid may be exempted only if it does not adversely affect trading conditions to an extent contrary to the common interest.

38. As regards the first part of that requirement, the relevant paragraphs of the preamble to the decision merely note the objections raised by the Governments of three Member States, two trade associations and an undertaking in the paper industry. Apart from that reference, the decision gives no concrete indication of the way in which the aid in question damages competition.

39. As regards the second part of the requirement, the Commission, having stated that the aid granted in the form of a capital holding is not directly linked to the restructuring of the undertaking but constitutes 'rescue aid', asserts that such aid 'threatens to do serious damage to the conditions of competition, as the free interplay of market forces would normally call for the closure of the undertaking, allowing more competitive firms to develop'. On that point it must be stated that the settlement of an undertaking's debts in order to ensure its survival does not necessarily adversely affect trading conditions to an extent contrary to the common interest, as provided in Article 92(3), where such an operation is, for example, accompanied by a restructuring plan. In this case, the Commission has not shown why the applicant's activities on the market, following the conversion of its production with the assistance of the aid granted, were likely to have such an adverse effect on trading conditions that the undertaking's disappearance would have been preferable to its rescue.

40. On those grounds, the contested decision must be declared void.

Article 92(3)(d) was added by the TEU. It provides that aid which is to promote culture and heritage conservation may be compatible with the common market where such aid does not affect trading conditions and competition in the Community to an extent that is contrary to the common interest.

Article 92(3)(e) constitutes a safety net by providing that such other categories of aid as may be specified by the decision of the Council acting by a qualified majority on a proposal from the Commission may be deemed to be compatible with the common market. As might be expected, aid which emerges in this manner will be highly likely to be approved. A number of directives on aid to shipbuilding have been adopted pursuant to this Article.

6. STATE AIDS: THE PROCEDURAL RULES AND ARTICLES 93 AND 94

(a) Review of Existing State Aids

It is readily apparent that the Community has an interest in keeping under review aids which have been granted by Member States, even if those aids have been given the green light by the Commission itself under Article 92(3) or if they come within Article 92(2). There is an analogy here with the process by which the Commission can keep under review exemptions granted pursuant to Article 85(3), in order to determine whether the circumstances warranting the exceptional treatment still exist.[83] Article 93(1) provides that:

> The Commission shall, in co-operation with Member States, keep under constant review all systems of aid existing in those states. It shall propose to the latter any appropriate measures required by the progressive development or by the functioning of the common market.

The following types of aid may be regarded as existing aid:[84] aid which existed before the entry into force of the Treaty; aid which has been given the green light under Article 93(3); aid which has been notified to the Commission pursuant to the obligation contained in Article 93(3), but in relation to which the Commission has taken no action within the requisite time period. If a Member State seeks to enlarge the field of activity of an undertaking which benefits from aid under legislation pre-dating the entry into force of the Treaty, the Court has held[85] that this will not constitute the granting or altering of aid which is subject to the notification requirements of Article 93(3), provided that the national legislation granting the aid is not altered. It is,

[83] See above, 914–19.

[84] Case C–44/93, *Namur—Les Assurances du Crédit SA* v. *Office National du Ducroire and Belgian State*, 9 Aug. 1994.

[85] *Ibid.*

however, open to the Commission in these circumstances to keep such aid under review pursuant to the powers given by Article 93(1), with the possibility of initiating proceedings under Article 93(2) to abolish the aid. Individual disbursement of aid pursuant to a general aid scheme which has been approved by the Commission counts as existing aid, provided that it comes properly within the general scheme.[86]

(b) The Procedure for New State Aids: Notification and Preliminary Review

In order for Commission monitoring of state aids to be effective, it is essential for the Commission to be notified of the existence of any aid proposal. It is for this reason that Article 93 of the Treaty establishes a two-stage procedure for state aids.

Stage one concerns prior notification of any plan to grant aid and preliminary investigation by the Commission. This is provided for in Article 93(3):

> The Commission shall be informed, in sufficient time to enable it to submit its comments, of any plans to grant or alter aid. If it considers that any such plan is not compatible with the common market having regard to Article 92, it shall without delay initiate the procedure provided for in paragraph 2. The Member State concerned shall not put its proposed measures into effect until this procedure has resulted in a final decision.

Member States are therefore under a duty to notify the Commission of any aid prior to granting it. The ECJ has interpreted this Article to impose a standstill obligation on Member States during the period in which the Commission undertakes its initial review of the proposed aid. They cannot implement the grant of aid during this time.[87] The ECJ has also held that the Commission must come to some preliminary view within two months. If it does not do so the state is entitled to carry through its aid proposal, after having notified the Commission that it intends to do so.[88]

The Commission will at this early stage engage in a preliminary review of the aid proposal. It may decide to approve the aid at this juncture, in which case it will notify the relevant Member State and the latter will then implement the aid proposal. The ECJ has emphasized that the preliminary-review procedure within Article 93(3) is 'meant to be just that':[89] it is to take a short time, typically not more than two months, and if there are difficulties in reaching a decision within this time then the Commission should proceed to the more complete review provided for in Article 93(2). This is important since,

[86] Case C–47/91, *Italy* v. *Commission*, 5 Oct. 1994.

[87] Case 120/73, *Gebrüder Lorenz GmbH* v. *Germany* [1973] ECR 1471; Case 84/82, *Germany* v. *Commission* [1984] ECR 1451, [1985] 1 CMLR 153. The Commission must also be notified of any amendment to the aid proposal: Cases 91 and 127/83, *Heineken Brouwerijen BV* v. *Inspecteur der Vennootschapsbelasting* [1984] ECR 3435, [1985] 1 CMLR 389.

[88] Case 84/82, *Germany* v. *Commission* [1984] ECR 1451, [1985] 1 CMLR 153.

[89] *Ibid.*

as we shall see below, other parties are entitled to be consulted under Article 93(2), but have no such rights under Article 93(3). Thus the Court found in *Germany* v. *Commission*[90] that if the Commission does not move briskly to the second stage, but instead engages in complex negotiations lasting sixteen months with the applicant Member State to the exclusion of other interested parties, the resultant decision can be annulled at the request of such a party. Nor can the Commission avoid this by keeping other Member States informed at multilateral meetings.

What, then, if a Member State fails to notify in accordance with Article 93(3)? It is necessary in answering this question to distinguish between the position of the Commission and that of national courts.

In relation to the Commission, the ECJ has held that failure to notify does not in itself render implementation of the aid unlawful.[91] It held that once it has been established that aid has been granted or altered without notification, the Commission has the power, after giving the Member State the opportunity for comment, to issue an interim decision which requires the state to suspend immediately the payment of the aid pending the outcome of the examination of the aid by the Commission, and its determination of whether the aid is indeed compatible with the common market. If in the light of this request for information the state still refuses to supply the requisite material, the Commission may then make an assessment of the compatibility of the aid on the basis of the information available to it. This decision may demand the recovery of the aid which has been paid.

The position of the private individual is somewhat different. The Court has established that the duty not to implement aid before notification to the Commission, and before the Commission has undertaken its preliminary investigation in accordance with Article 93(3), is directly effective.[92] More recently the ECJ has also held[93] that, although a national court which is enforcing Article 93(3) is not concerned with the compatibility of the aid pursuant to Article 92, this being a matter for the Commission, none the less the national court should indeed rule aid to be illegal when it has not been notified as required by Article 93(3). The direct effect of Article 93(3) demanded that the rights of the individual should be protected in this manner. Moreover any later Commission decision which finds that the aid was compatible with Article 92 will not be retrospective in effect.

(c) The Procedure for State Aids: Detailed Investigation and Enforcement

Stage two of the investigative process is based on the assumption that the Commission has not been able to give the green light to the state-aid proposal

[90] Case 84/82, *Germany* v. *Commission* [1984] ECR 1451, [1985] 1 CMLR 153. See also Case C–198/91, *William Cook plc* v. *Commission* [1993] ECR I–2486, [1993] 3 CMLR 206.

[91] Case C–301/87, *France* v. *Commission* [1990] ECR I–307.

[92] Case 120/73, Cases 91 and 127/83, both n. 87 above.

[93] Case C–354/90, *Fédération Nationale du Commerce Exterieur des Produits Alimentaires* v. *France* [1991] ECR I–5523.

under Article 93(3). In these circumstances the provisions of Article 93(2) come into play. This reads as follows:

> If, after giving notice to the parties concerned to submit their comments, the Commission finds that aid granted by a State or through State resources is not compatible with the common market having regard to Article 92, or that such aid is being misused, it shall decide that the State concerned shall abolish or alter such aid within a period of time to be determined by the Commission.
>
> If the State concerned does not comply with the decision within the prescribed time, the Commission or any other interested State may, in derogation from the provisions of Articles 169 and 170, refer the matter to the Court of Justice direct.

It should be noted at the outset that Article 93(2) applies both to existing aids in relation to which questions have been raised pursuant to Article 93(1), and to new aids which have not been given the green light pursuant to the preliminary investigation under Article 93(3). If an existing aid is found to be incompatible with the common market as the result of a review instigated in pursuance of Article 93(1) then it will be unlawful from the date set for compliance with that decision. In the case of a new aid, the effect of the decision made under Article 93(2) will be to render the temporary prohibition which flows from Article 93(3) permanent, unless the Member State can at some future date show that the circumstances have changed.

In either eventuality the procedure described in Article 93(2) comes into operation. A notice will be placed in the Official Journal inviting parties concerned to submit their comments. We have already seen that third parties have no right to be consulted under Article 93(3),[94] but the first sentence of paragraph of Article 93(2) provides the foundation for such procedural rights in the event of the more detailed investigation being undertaken by the Commission. The phrase 'parties concerned' covers the undertakings receiving aid and other persons or undertakings whose interests might be affected by the grant of the aid, in particular competing undertakings and trade associations.[95]

The rationale for the more expedited enforcement process contained in the second paragraph of Article 93(2) is that the Commission has already had the opportunity to make its views known, and because the parties themselves have already been heard.

While Article 93(2) does, therefore, provide a speedier method of enforcement against a recalcitrant state, the Court has set itself against any further modification of the enforcement process as suggested by the Commission. This is clear from the *British Aerospace* case.[96] The Commission had approved

[94] Cases 91 and 127/83, n. 87 above.

[95] Case 323/82, *Intermills SA* [1984] ECR 3809, [1986] 1 CMLR 614, para. 16; Case C–198/91, n. 90 above, para. 24.

[96] Case C–292/90, *British Aerospace Plc and Rover Group Holdings Plc* v. *Commission* [1992] ECR I–493, [1992] 1 CMLR 853.

certain aid to the Rover group on condition, *inter alia*, that no further aid should be granted. It was later discovered that a further capital sum had been provided in the form of 'sweeteners'. The Commission then issued a decision requiring this sum to be recovered from the beneficiaries. This decision was challenged before the Court and annulled. The ECJ held that the Commission could have used the special procedure in the second paragraph of Article 93(2); or it could have chosen to treat the extra payment as a new aid in its own right. But it could not just seek to recover the further payments.[97]

(d) Exceptional Circumstances: Article 93(2) Paragraphs 3 and 4

The third and fourth paragraphs of Article 93(2) make provision for aid to be granted in certain exceptional circumstances in derogation from the provisions of Article 92. The conditions are as follows:

> On application by a Member State, the Council may, acting unanimously, decide that aid which that State is granting or intends to grant shall be considered to be compatible with the common market, in derogation from the provisions of Article 92 or from the regulations provided for in Article 94, if such a decision is justified by exceptional circumstances. If, as regards the aid in question, the Commission has already initiated the procedure provided for in the first subparagraph of this paragraph, the fact that the State concerned made its application to the Council shall have the effect of suspending that procedure until the Council has made its attitude known.
>
> If, however, the Council has not made its attitude known within three months of the said application being made, the Commission shall give its decision on the case.

(e) Article 94: Implementing Regulations

Article 94 empowers the Council, acting by qualified majority on a proposal from the Commission, and after consulting the Parliament, to make any appropriate regulations for the application of Articles 92 and 93, and in particular to determine the conditions under which Article 93(3) shall apply and the categories of aid exempted from this procedure.

(f) Challenges to Commission Decisions

We have already seen from the previous discussion a number of instances in which parties have sought to challenge Commission decisions concerning state aids. The action will normally be brought under Article 173 of the Treaty to

[97] The Court did, however, accept that the Commission could, when considering whether the aid was compatible with the common market, take account of a previous decision on the matter and any obligations which may have been imposed on the Member State.

annul the decision.[98] The most common applicants are the state whose aid has been found to be incompatible with the common market, the undertakings who are the intended beneficiaries of this aid, and competitors. Applicants will have to satisfy the requirements of Article 173 in order to proceed.[99]

The state will, of course, have standing. The intended recipient of the aid has been readily admitted to plead the case,[100] and the Court has afforded standing to interveners who have submitted comments to the Commission and who would be likely to suffer harm if the aid were to be given to the targeted firm.[101] An important point concerning the availability of review was affirmed in *William Cook*.[102] We have already seen that interested parties do not have consultation rights under Article 93(3) during the preliminary examination phase, but do have such rights under Article 93(2). What, then, if the Commission finds that an aid is compatible with the common market under Article 93(3), but an interested party disagrees with this finding and believes that the more thorough investigation under Article 93(2) should have been initiated? In *William Cook* the Court held that the procedural guarantees contained in Article 93(2) could, in such a situation, only be properly safeguarded if such parties were able to challenge such a Commission decision before the Court.[103] The ability of a third party to challenge a final decision reached under Article 93(2) may, however, be more limited if such a party has not availed itself of the opportunity to participate in the decision-making process.[104]

The substantive grounds for the challenge will be those which are found in Article 173. It is common for applicants to argue that the Commission's decision is in breach of one of the general principles of Community law, that the reasoning is defective, or that the Commission has misinterpreted the meaning of one of the phrases in the relevant Treaty articles. However, as we have seen when considering the general issue of substantive review,[105] the Court possesses considerable discretion as to the intensity with which it will apply the various grounds mentioned in Article 173. This feature is readily apparent within this area, and is exemplified by the fact that the ECJ will often make reference to the Commission's considerable discretion concerning state aids, and by the fact that it will often only overturn such a decision if the applicant can show that there has been some manifest error.

[98] The possibility of using Art. 177 to contest a Commission decision made pursuant to Art. 93 is considered within the general discussion of Art. 177: see above, 492–6.

[99] In Case C–47/90, *Italy* v. *Commission* [1992] ECR I–4145, the ECJ held that the Commission's decision to open the Art. 93(2) procedure was itself a reviewable act which could be challenged before the Court.

[100] Case 730/79, n. 56 above; Case 323/82, n. 95 above.

[101] Case 169/84, *COFAZ* v. *Commission* [1986] ECR 391, [1986] 2 CMLR 338; Case C–198/91, n. 90 above.

[102] Case C–198/91, n. 90 above.

[103] See also Case C–225/91, n. 48 above.

[104] L. Hancher, n. 51 above, 144.

[105] See above, 501–5.

7. STATE AIDS: RECOVERY OF UNLAWFUL AIDS

The Court has, not surprisingly, held that, as a matter of principle, illegal state aids should be repaid.[106] This is, as the Court has stated, the logical consequence of a finding that the grant of the aid is unlawful.[107] The peremptory force of this obligation will not easily be deflected by claims that repayment of the aid entails difficulties for the recipient. This is demonstrated by the following case:

Case 52/84, Commission v. Belgium
[1986] ECR 89, [1987] 1 CMLR 710

The Commission had found that the acquisition by a public regional holding company of shares in a firm manufacturing ceramic ware constituted state aid, and ordered that it should be withdrawn since it considered that it was incompatible with the common market. The Belgian Government did not contest this decision, but it did stress the serious social consequences of closing down the undertaking, and it stated that Belgian law did not allow share capital to be refunded except by way of withdrawal of company profits, and no such profits were available. The Government also requested clarification from the Commission of what it meant by 'withdrawal of aid'. The ECJ held that the Belgian Government was outside the time limit for challenging the validity of the decision under Article 173. It then proceeded as follows.

THE ECJ

14. In those circumstances the only defence left to the Belgian Government in opposing the Commission's application for a declaration that it failed to fulfil its Treaty obligations would be to plead that it was absolutely impossible for it to implement the decision properly. In this connection it should be noted that the decision demands the withdrawal from the undertaking of a capital holding of 475 million Bfr . . .; that demand is sufficiently precise to be complied with. The fact that, on account of the undertaking's financial position, the Belgian authorities could not recover the sum paid does not constitute proof that implementation was impossible, because the Commission's objective was to abolish the aid and, as the Belgian Government itself admits, that objective could be attained by proceedings for winding up the company, which the Belgian authorities could institute in their capacity as shareholder or creditor.

. . .

16. It should be added that the fact that the only defence which a Member State to which a decision has been addressed can raise in legal proceedings such as these is that implementation of the decision is absolutely impossible does not prevent that State—if, in giving effect to the decision, it encounters unforeseen or unforeseeable difficulties or perceives consequences overlooked by the Commission—

[106] For a discussion of recent attempts by private parties to prevent the payment of the aid through the issue of an interim order by the Court: see Hancher, n. 51 above, 145–6.

[107] Case C–310/85, n. 67 above.

from submitting those problems for consideration by the Commission, together with proposals for suitable amendments. In such a case the Commission and the Member State concerned must respect the principle underlying Article 5 of the Treaty, which imposes a duty of genuine co-operation on the Member States and Community institutions; accordingly, they must work together in good faith with a view to overcoming difficulties whilst fully observing the Treaty provisions, and in particular the provisions on aid. However, in the present instance none of the difficulties referred to by the Belgian Government is of that nature, and that Government made no proposals whatever to the Commission for the adoption of other suitable measures.

The message from the Court is clear. The only exception to the primary obligation to obtain repayment of the illegal aid is where recovery is absolutely impossible, and this is narrowly defined. If the recipient company must be wound up, so be it. Even where the exception to the primary obligation does come into play, the state is not let off the hook entirely. There will be a secondary obligation derived from Article 5 of the Treaty, which requires the state to enter into a serious dialogue with the Commission in order to resolve the problem.

The same uncompromising approach by the Court is apparent in other cases. In *Tubemeuse*[108] the ECJ accepted that in the event that the recipient company was being wound up, then the recovery of the unlawful aid would have to take its place alongside claims to the company's assets by other creditors. This was in accord with the general principle that recovery of aid should take place in accordance with the relevant provisions of national law, subject to the proviso that those provisions were not to be applied in a way which made recovery practically impossible.[109] However, the ECJ rejected an argument that recovery of the debt would be disproportionate to the objectives laid down in Articles 92 and 93, on the ground that it would cause serious damage to other creditors. Because recovery of illegal aid was the logical consequence of the finding that the aid was unlawful, it could not be regarded as disproportionate to the objectives of the Treaty, notwithstanding the fact that other creditors might suffer.

Nor have applicants fared any better in attempting to stem the force of the duty to recover by relying on the concept of legitimate expectations. Thus in *Deufil*[110] the ECJ rejected the argument that the existence of a Commission guideline setting out the policy which it intended to adopt in approving state aids in a certain area gave rise to a legitimate expectation that, if a product was not included in the guideline, then aid in relation to that product would not have to be approved. In *Bug-Alutechnik*[111] the ECJ accepted that, as part

[108] Case C–142/87, [1990] ECR I–959, [1991] 3 CMLR 213.

[109] Case 94/87, *Commission* v. *Germany* [1989] ECR 175, [1989] 2 CMLR 425.

[110] Case 310/85, n. 67 above.

[111] Case C–5/89, *Re State Aid to Bug-Alutechnik GmbH: Commission* v. *Germany* [1990] ECR I–3437, [1992] 1 CMLR 117.

and parcel of the idea that recovery of state aid was to be determined in accordance with the relevant principles of national law, this could include the concept of legitimate expectations and legal certainty. But the ECJ went on to hold that recipients of aid could not have a legitimate expectation that the aid was lawful unless it had been granted in accordance with the procedure in Article 93; a diligent businessman should normally be able to determine whether that procedure had been followed. Moreover, the Court emphasized that a Member State which had granted aid contrary to the principles of Article 93 could not rely on any legitimate expectations of the recipients to justify refusal to recover the sums. Furthermore there were limits to the extent to which national concepts such as legitimate expectations could be relied upon: they could not be used if the effect was to make it impossible to recover the aid, as where the impact of the national doctrine was to set time limits for the revocation of administrative acts.

8. THE RELATIONSHIP OF STATE AIDS TO OTHER PROVISIONS OF THE TREATY

The provisions concerning state aids within the Treaty do not exist within a legal or political vacuum. We have already touched on this issue and will return to it more fully in the light of the discussion in this section. We must now focus upon the legal relationship between Articles 92 to 94 and other Treaty Articles, since an understanding of this relationship is essential to an informed discussion of the broader social issues raised by state aids.

The ECJ has had to consider the relationship of Articles 92 to 94 with a number of other Treaty provisions. There have, for example, been a series of cases concerned with the relationship between Article 95 and the rules on state aids. The ECJ has held that the use of receipts from a levy may constitute a state aid which is incompatible with the common market, but this is a matter to be decided by the Commission and not the national court.[112]

One of the most interesting of the points of interconnection is, however, the relationship between Articles 92 to 94 and Article 30. The approach of the ECJ has altered somewhat over the years. In *Ianelli & Volpi*[113] the ECJ held that if some aspects of aid which might contravene Treaty provisions other than Articles 92 to 94 were so closely linked to the latter, then it would not be possible to evaluate them separately; however, where certain aspects of an aid scheme were not necessary or integral to the operation of that scheme, then those aspects could be subject to scrutiny under other provisions of the Treaty. In this sense the Court articulated a severability test.

[112] Cases C–149 and 150/91, *Sanders Adour et Guyomarc'h Nutrition Animale* [1992] ECR I–3899, subject to the existing competence of the national courts in relation to Art. 93(3).

[113] Case 74/76, *Ianelli and Volpi SpA* v. *Ditta Paolo Meroni* [1977] ECR 557, [1977] 2 CMLR 688.

In its later case law the Court appears to have been more ready to apply Article 30 without too delicate an inquiry whether the measure which is caught by Article 30 is an integral part of the aid scheme or not. Thus in the *Buy Irish* case[114] the Irish Government argued that its campaign to encourage consumers to buy Irish goods should be considered under Articles 92 to 94, and not under Article 30. The Court rejected this argument, holding that the fact that Article 92 might be of relevance to the financing of the campaign did not mean that the campaign itself escaped from the prohibition laid down in Article 30. In *Commission* v. *France*[115] the Court examined the legality of a French measure which gave newspaper publishers tax exemptions on the condition that the papers were printed in France. The Commission argued that this constituted a breach of Article 30. The French Government responded to the effect that if its measures did constitute aid they should be considered under Article 92, since the tax provisions could not be separated from the general aid scheme for the newspaper industry. The ECJ was unconvinced. It noted that France had never notified such a scheme in accordance with Article 93(3). It then proffered the following strong statement of principle:[116]

> it should be pointed out that Articles 92 and 94 cannot, as is clear from a long line of cases decided by the Court, be used to frustrate the rules of the Treaty on the free movement of goods or the rules on the repeal of discriminatory tax provisions. According to those cases, the provisions relating to the free movement of goods, the repeal of discriminatory tax provisions and aid have a common objective, namely to ensure the free movement of goods between Member States under normal conditions of competition . . . The mere fact that a national measure may possibly be defined as aid within the meaning of Article 92 is therefore not an adequate reason for exempting it from the prohibition contained in Article 30. The argument relating to the Community rules on aid, which the French Republic in any case raised only by way of hypothesis in reply to the observations of the Commission, therefore cannot be accepted.

The Court has persisted with this approach in other cases.[117] Thus in *Du Pont de Nemours Italiana*[118] the ECJ considered whether Italian legislation, which required that all public bodies obtain at least 30 per cent of their supplies from undertakings established in the Mezzogiorno where the products concerned were processed, was in breach of Article 30. One of the questions raised by the referring court was whether this constituted aid, with the

[114] Case 249/81, *Commission* v. *Ireland* [1982] ECR 4005, [1983] 2 CMLR 104.

[115] Case 18/84, [1985] ECR 1339, [1986] 1 CMLR 605.

[116] *Ibid.*, para. 13.

[117] In the preceding cases the states in question had not notified the aid in accordance with Art. 93. One of the explanations of the Court's reasoning in these cases was based on this fact. However, in the *Du Pont* case Italy had notified its scheme to the Commission, but this made no difference to the reasoning employed by the Court.

[118] Case C–21/88, *Du Pont de Nemours Italiana SpA* v. *Unità Sanitaria Locale No 2 di Carrara* [1990] ECR I–889, [1991] 3 CMLR 25; Case C–351/88, *Laboratori Bruneau Srl* v. *Unità Sanitaria Locale RM/24 de Monterotondo* [1991] ECR I–3641, [1994] 1 CMLR 707.

consequence that the prohibition contained in Article 30 would not apply in the instant case. The ECJ gave a negative response. It adopted the same 'unitary' view of the purpose of Articles 30 and 92 as it had done in *Commission* v. *France*: both sets of provisions were designed to ensure the free movement of goods under normal conditions of competition. The fact that a national measure might be considered an aid within the meaning of Article 92 did not, therefore, serve to take it outside Article 30. It was incumbent on the national court to ensure the full effectiveness of Article 30.

9. STATE AIDS, MARKET INTEGRATION AND REGIONAL POLICY

Although one can appreciate the force of the Court's reasoning in the cases discussed in the preceding section it is not unproblematic. It is of course true that Articles 30 and 92 have in general terms the same objective. Yet the very structure of Articles 92 to 94 attests to the different way in which fulfilment of this general aim is played out in the context of state aids. These Articles are characterized by the existence of administrative discretion possessed by the Commission, enabling it to weigh certain social and economic variables in deciding whether aid is compatible with the common market. It is for this very reason that the provisions on state aids are directly effective only to a limited extent. If, in the event of any overlap between Article 30 and Article 92, the former is to predominate then it will rule out the type of social balancing which takes place particularly in the context of Article 92(3). Concerns of this nature are apparent in the following extract. The case to which the authors refer is the *Du Pont* decision set out above:

J .F. M. Martin and O. Stehmann, Product Market Integration versus Regional Cohesion in the Community[119]

First of all, one of the grounds on which the Court of Justice justifies its position is that both sets of rules have a common objective, that is to ensure the free movement of goods under normal conditions of competition. Although this is true, it is only partially so. One should not ignore that there is a second objective underlying Articles 92(3) and 93, namely to grant the Commission the possibility to declare compatible with the EEC Treaty those aids which are intended to close the economic, social and regional gaps existing inside the Community. Therefore, the fact that some competition distorting State aids may be permitted to operate proves that certain exceptions to the free movement of goods and to free competition principles are to be admitted . . .

Secondly, the relation of both sets of rules . . . may have certain undesirable consequences. Whereas this position might be justifiable . . . in those cases in

[119] (1991) 16 ELRev. 216, 228–30.

which no prior notification has taken place, applying Article 30 as interpreted in *Dassonville* without engaging in a deeper economic (or other) analysis risks obliterating Articles 92 and 93. After the *Dassonville* definition, almost anything would come under the 'imperium' of Article 30. State aids, by their nature, always have a negative effect on inter-State trade when they strengthen national industry or regions . . . If one follows strictly the Court's reasoning of giving priority to the application of Article 30 . . . Articles 92 and 93 would lose much of their sense.

Thirdly, from a procedural point of view the Court's reasoning may also bring difficulties. Article 30 is directly applicable while Articles 92 and 93 are not so . . .

From an economic point of view the Court's position leads to favouring rapid market integration—represented by the free movement of goods provisions—to the detriment of regional cohesion—represented by the State aids provisions. In the context of the '1992' internal market this attitude is worrying. The transition from national market economies to an European one should be achieved smoothly so as to avoid the increase of regional economic divergences. The speed with which trade barriers are dismantled in the Community increases sharply the need for quick measures to balance adverse effects on disfavoured regions . . . The whole picture is aggravated by the fact that measures undertaken at the European level to balance these effects are far from sufficient . . .

While there may therefore be concerns at the too-ready application of Article 30 to facts which would also come within Articles 92 to 94, one must be cautious about the more general relationship between national regional-aid policy and that undertaken at the Community level. We must be careful not to condemn the Community for paying insufficient attention to problems which have a regional dimension. This is in part because, as we have already seen, regional needs can and are taken into account within the fabric of Article 92; it is in part because of the existence of Community schemes for regional assistance; and it is in part because the proper boundary of regional assistance is itself a contestable issue. The legitimate bounds of regional assistance are raised, of course, because of the inhibiting effect which such aid can have on market integration. But efficiency considerations are not the only ones to be borne in mind in this respect. The TEU, in Articles 130a and 130b, places a priority on the achievement of greater cohesion within the Community. Yet the attainment of this goal necessitates the placing of real limits on the grant of aid by the richer states of the Community to regions which may be poor relative to that state, but not in relation to the Community as a whole. Only in this way will cohesion be possible. The following extract from the Director of the Commission's State Aids Directorate brings out this point forcibly:

A. Petersen, State Aid and the European Union: State Aid in the Light of Trade, Competition, Industrial and Cohesion Policies[120]

Surveys published by the Commission show that Member States spend around 36 BECU a year (1990) subsidising their manufacturing industries. Most of this

[120] I. Harden (ed.), n. 61 above, 25.

money, 80%, is spent in the four largest Member States: Germany, France, UK and Italy. The EC–12 spent over 12 BECU annually on regional aid to companies during the period 1988–90, while the Community currently spends 700 MECU for the same purpose—a ratio of over 17:1.

Despite the fact that we authorise high intensities of up to 75% for investment grants in the weakest regions, in recognition of the structural problems which they face, the practical reality is that the poorer countries cannot afford to pay such high levels and average around 25%—levels which are not much higher than those authorised in central regions in Germany, France and the Benelux. These few figures serve to underline a point which is gaining increasing acceptance: strict control of State aid in the central, more prosperous, regions is necessary in the interests of cohesion as well as of competition policy.

However, persuading the richer Member States to increase their contributions to EC spending in the weaker regions is one thing, getting them to refrain in the name of cohesion from spending so much of their own taxpayers' money locally is quite another.

10. FURTHER READING

(a) Books

HANCHER, L., OTTERVANGER T., and SLOT, P. J., *EC State Aids* (Chancery, 1993)

HARDEN, I., (ed.), *State Aid: Community Law and Policy* (Bundesanzeiger, 1993)

SCHINA, D., *State Aids Under the EEC Treaty* (ESC Publishing, 1987)

(b) Articles

EHLERMANN, C–D., 'The Contribution of EC Competition Policy to the Single Market' (1992) 29 CMLRev. 257

EVANS, A., and MARTIN, S., 'Socially Acceptable Distortion of Competition: Community Policy on State Aid' (1991) 16 ELRev. 79

GYSELEN, L., 'State Action and the Effectiveness of the EEC Treaty's Competition Provisions' (1989) 26 CMLRev. 26

HANCHER, L., 'State Aids and Judicial Control in the European Community' [1994] 3 ECLR 134

MARTIN, J. M. F., and STEHMANN, O., 'Product Market Integration versus Regional Cohesion in the Community' (1991) 16 ELRev. 216

PAPPALARDO, A., 'State Measures and Public Undertakings: Article 90 of the EEC Treaty Revisited' [1991] 1 ECLR 29

QUIGLEY, C., 'The Notion of a State Aid in the EEC' (1988) 13 ELRev. 242

JOLIET, R., 'National Anti-Competitive Legislation and Community Law' [1988] *Fordham Corp. L. Inst.*, Ch. 16

SLOT, P. J., 'The Application of Articles 3(f), 5 and 85 to 94 EEC' (1987) 12 ELRev. 179

25

Completion of the Single Market

1. INTRODUCTION: THE LIMITS OF INTEGRATION PRIOR TO 1986

In earlier chapters we have seen the contribution made by the Court's jurisprudence towards the attainment of a single market. And yet the original Rome Treaty was modified in 1986 by the passage of the Single European Act, one of the main objectives of which was to facilitate the completion of the single market. How then was the Community market incomplete prior to 1986? What were the main areas in which trade barriers of some form remained?

The answers to these questions are not hard to find. Prior to 1986 the process of single-market integration had been advanced both by legislative and judicial means.

The *legislative contribution* to the creation of a single Community market assumed many forms, one of the most important of which was harmonization of laws. We have already seen how the existence of divergences in national provisions can create real barriers to free trade within the Community. Article 100 was the original legislative technique for addressing this problem:

> The Council shall, acting unanimously on a proposal from the Commission, issue directives for the approximation of such laws, regulations or administrative provisions of the Member States as directly affect the establishment of the common market.

There were, however, two difficulties with this legislative mechanism. In *procedural terms* the passage of directives could be problematic since Article 100 requires unanimity; any one Member State might therefore sound the death knell to a proposed directive. In *substantive terms* the type of directive which the Commission normally devised in the 1970s and early 1980s demanded agreement between the states on a *detailed measure* which was often difficult to attain. Thus a typical directive passed during this period would define with great specificity what was to be regulated, for example, the packaging and labelling of dangerous substances; there would then be an obligation on the Member State not to place such a substance on the market unless it was properly labelled; the directive would indicate the type of warning which had to be placed on the product, and the national authorities would be obliged to approve appropriate packaging which complied with the directive. The process of securing agreement between twelve states on provisions such as this was slow and cumbersome. Technical developments meant, moreover, that the Commission was, in a sense, fighting a losing battle. As fast as it would succeed in securing the passage of a directive to cover one technical problem, so ten more would emerge on the horizon as the result of technical innovation combined with the emergence of new types of market, such as that generated by the revolutionary changes in telecommunications or computers.

The *judicial contribution* to market integration has been examined in the chapters dealing with goods, persons, services, competition policy, and the like. The ECJ, through Article 169 actions and direct effect, interpreted the relevant Treaty Articles in the manner best designed to give effect to the objectives of the Treaty. Judicial doctrines, such as that developed in the *Cassis de Dijon* jurisprudence, were of particular importance in breaking down barriers to intra-Community trade.[1] However, as we have already noted,[2] there were limits to the form of integration which this judicially created doctrine could achieve. The effect of *Cassis* was essentially negative and deregulatory, serving to invalidate trade barriers which could not be justified under one of the mandatory requirements, but it did not ensure that any positive regulations would be put in place of the national measures which had been struck down.

So, by the early 1980s much still remained to be done notwithstanding the efforts of the Commission and the Court. Yet it was this very sense that the Community was falling behind its agenda which itself generated a feeling of pessimism in the Community in the late 1970s and early 1980s. There seemed to be no ready way in which the Community would ever attain its goals and the reality of single-market integration appeared to be as far away as ever. This problem was not lost on the European Council, which, in the early 1980s, considered various techniques for expediting the passage of Community initiatives. It was to be in one of these meetings that the seeds of the Single European Act (SEA) were to be sown. In 1985 the European Council called on the Commission to draw up a detailed programme with a specific timetable for achieving a single market by 1992. The Commission, under the new leadership of Jacques Delors, was not slow to respond. It produced a White Paper which was to provide the foundations for the passage of the SEA.

2. THE COMMISSION'S PAPER AND THE BENEFITS OF A SINGLE MARKET

The Commission's White Paper, from which the extracts below are taken, addressed the problem in strident tones. It set out to establish the 'essential

[1] See above, Ch. 14. [2] See above, 644–51.

and logical consequences'[3] of accepting the commitment to a single market. The Commission noted that the Community had lost momentum 'partly through recession, partly through a lack of confidence and vision'.[4] But it said the mood had now changed, as testified to by the calls from the European Council for the completion of the single market. The Commission was ready to take up the challenge.[5]

The time for talk has now passed. The time for action has come. That is what this White Paper is about.

Completing the Internal Market, COM(85)310, 14 June 1985

10. For convenience the measures that need to be taken have been classified in this Paper under three headings:

—Part One: the removal of physical barriers
—Part Two: the removal of technical barriers
—Part Three: the removal of fiscal barriers

11. The most obvious example of the first category are customs posts at frontiers. Indeed most of our citizens would regard the frontier posts as the most visible example of the continued division of the Community and their removal as the clearest sign of the integration of the Community into a single market. Yet they continue to exist mainly because of the technical and fiscal divisions between Member States. Once we have removed those barriers, and found alternative ways of dealing with other relevant problems such as public security, immigration and drug controls, the reasons for the existence of the physical barriers will have been eliminated.

12. The reason for getting rid entirely of physical and other controls between Member States is not one of theology or appearance, but the hard practical fact that the maintenance of any internal frontier controls will perpetuate the costs and disadvantages of a divided market . . .

13. While the elimination of physical barriers provides benefits for traders . . . it is through the elimination of technical barriers that the Community will give the large market its economic and industrial dimension by enabling industries to make economies of scale and therefore to become more competitive. An example of this second category—technical barriers—are the different standards for individual products adopted in different Member States for health and safety reasons, or for environmental or consumer protection . . . Technical barriers are technical barriers whether they apply to goods or services and all should be treated on an equal footing. The general thrust of the Commission's approach in this area will be to move away from the concept of harmonization towards that of mutual recognition and equivalence. But there will be a continuing role for the approximation of Member States' laws and regulations as laid down in Article 100 of the Treaty. Clearly, action under this Article would be quicker and more effective if the Council were to agree not to allow the unanimity requirement to obstruct progress where it could otherwise be made.

[3] *Ibid.*, para. 3. [4] COM(85)310, para. 5. [5] *Ibid.*, para. 7.

14. The removal of fiscal barriers may well be contentious and this despite the fact that the goals laid down in the Treaty are quite explicit and that important steps have already been taken along the road of approximation. This being so, the reasons why approximation of fiscal legislation is an essential element in any programme for completing the internal market are explained in detail in Part Three.

The Commission then explained that the White Paper was not intended to cover every possible issue which was of relevance to the integration of the Member States' economies. Matters such as the co-ordination of economic polices and competition policy were relevant in this respect; while other important areas of Community action, such as transport, the environment, and consumer protection, interacted with, and would benefit from, the completion of the internal market. The next extract from the White Paper looks more closely at the Commission's reasoning in relation to the second type of barrier, that which arises from differing technical rules. In reading this section note the way in which the Commission's strategy builds upon what the ECJ had achieved in *Cassis de Dijon*:

57. The elimination of border controls, important as it is, does not of itself create a genuine common market. Goods and people moving within the Community should not find obstacles inside the different Member States as opposed to meeting them at the border.

58. This does not mean that there should be the same rules everywhere, but that goods as well as citizens and companies should be able to move freely within the Community. Subject to certain important constraints (see paragraph 65), the general principle should be approved that, if a product is lawfully manufactured and marketed in one Member State, there is no reason why it should not be sold freely throughout the Community . . .

60. Whilst the physical barriers dealt with in Part One impede trade flows and add unacceptable administrative costs (ultimately paid by the consumer), barriers created by different national product regulations and standards have a double-edged effect: they not only add extra costs, but they also distort production patterns; increase unit costs; increase stock holding costs; discourage business cooperation; and fundamentally frustrate the creation of a common market for industrial products. Until such barriers are removed, Community manufacturers are forced to focus on national rather than continental markets and are unable to benefit from the economies of scale which a truly unified market offers . . .

The Need for a New Strategy

61. The harmonization approach has been the cornerstone of Community action in the first 25 years and has produced unprecedented progress in the creation of common rules on a Community-wide basis. However, over the years, a number of shortcomings have been identified and it is clear that a genuine common market cannot be realised by 1992 if the Community relies exclusively on Article 100 of the EEC Treaty. There will certainly be a continuing need for action under Article 100; but its role will be reduced as new approaches, resulting in quicker and less troublesome progress, are agreed . . . Where Article 100 is still considered the only appropriate instrument, ways of making it operate more

flexibly will need to be found. Clearly, action under this Article would be quicker and more effective if the Council were to agree not to allow the unanimity requirement to obstruct progress where it could otherwise be made.

63. In principle, therefore . . . mutual recognition could be an effective strategy for bringing about a common market in a trading sense. This strategy is supported in particular by Articles 30 to 36 of the EEC Treaty, which prohibit national measures which would have excessively and unjustifiably restrictive effects on free movement.

64. But while a strategy based on mutual recognition would remove barriers to trade and lead to the creation of a genuine common trading market, it might well prove inadequate for the purposes of the building-up of an expanding market based on the competitiveness which a continental-scale uniform market can generate. On the other hand experience has shown that the alternative of relying on a strategy based totally on harmonization would be over-regulatory, would take a long time to implement, would be inflexible and could stifle innovation. What is needed is a strategy that combines the best of both approaches but, that above all, allows for progress to be made more quickly than in the past.

The Chosen Strategy

65. The Commission takes into account the underlying reasons for the existence of barriers to trade, and recognises the essential equivalence of Member States' legislative objectives in the protection of health and safety, and of the environment. Its harmonization approach is based on the following principles:

—a clear distinction needs to be drawn in future internal market initiatives between what it is essential to harmonize, and what may be left to mutual recognition of national regulations and standards; this implies that, on the occasion of each harmonization initiative, the Commission will determine whether national regulations are excessive in relation to the mandatory requirements pursued and, thus, constitute unjustified barriers to trade according to Articles 30 to 36 of the EEC Treaty;

—legislative harmonization (Council Directives based on Article 100) will in future be restricted to laying down essential health and safety requirements which will be obligatory in all Member States. Conformity with this will entitle a product to free movement;

—Harmonization of industrial standards by the elaboration of European standards will be promoted to the maximum extent, but the absence of European standards should not be allowed to be used as a barrier to free movement. During the waiting period while European Standards are being developed, the mutual acceptance of national standards, with agreed procedures, should be the guiding principle.

The Commission's White Paper did not rest content with the enunciation of general strategies. The Annex to the Paper listed 279 legislative measures, together with a timetable for the promulgation of each measure. The object was to complete this legislative process by 31 December 1992. The momentum behind the proposals gathered further force with the realization of the cost savings which would be generated by the completion of the internal market. The following extract examines this issue, and the economic benefits foregone by having a market which is not fully integrated:

M. Emerson, M. Aujean, M. Catinat, P. Goybet, A. Jacquemin, The Economics of 1992, The E.C. Commission's Assessment of the Economic Effects of Completing the Internal Market[6]

2. *The Nature of the Community's Internal Market Barriers*

Tariffs and quantitative restrictions on trade have been largely eliminated in the Community. The remaining barriers essentially consist of:

(i) differences in technical regulations between countries, which impose extra costs on intra-EC trade;

(ii) delays at frontiers for customs purposes, and related administrative burdens for companies and public administration, which impose further costs on trade;

(iii) restrictions on competition for public purchases through excluding bids from other Community suppliers, which often result in excessively high costs of purchase;

(iv) restrictions on freedom to engage in certain service transactions, or to become established in certain service activities in other Community countries. This concerns particularly financial and transport services, where the costs of market-entry barriers also appear to be substantial.

While quite a number of these individual barriers can be overcome at a moderate cost, when taken together with the oligopolistic structure of many markets, they add up to a considerable degree of non-competitive segmentation of the market. This is suggested by the substantial consumer price differences between countries . . .

3. *The Nature of the Economic Gains to be Measured*

The creation of a true European internal market will, on the one hand, suppress a series of constraints that today prevent enterprises from being as efficient as they could be and from employing resources to the full, and, on the other hand, establish a more competitive environment which will incite them to exploit new opportunities. The removal of the constraints and the emergence of the new competitive incentives will lead to four principal types of effect:

(i) a significant reduction in costs due to a better exploitation of several kinds of economies of scale associated with the size of production units and enterprises;

(ii) an improved efficiency in enterprises, a rationalization of industrial structures and a setting of prices closer to costs of production, all resulting from more competitive markets;

(iii) adjustments between industries on the basis of a fuller play of comparative advantages in an integrated market;

(iv) a flow of innovations, new processes and new products, stimulated by the dynamics of the internal market.

These processes liberate resources for alternative productive uses, and when they are so used the total, sustainable level of consumption and investment in the economy will be increased. This is the fundamental criterion of economic gain.

These gains in economic welfare will also be reflected in macroeconomic indicators. It is implicit, in order to attain the highest sustainable level of con-

[6] (1988), 1–10. See also P. Cecchini, *The European Challenge 1992, The Benefits of a Single Market* (Gower, 1988).

sumption and investment, that productivity and employment be also of a high order. In particular, where rationalization efforts cause labour to be made redundant, this resource has to be successfully re-employed. Also implicit is a high rate of growth in the economy. The sustainability condition, moreover, requires that the major macroeconomic equilibrium constraints are respected, notably as regards price stability, balance of payments and budget balances. It further implies a positive performance in terms of world-wide competitivity. These different objectives can, however, be achieved in different mixes; it is for macroeconomic policy to determine how to dispose of the potential gains made available by the microeconomic measures taken in order to complete the internal market.

. . .

4. *Empirical Estimates*

Any estimates of the effects of complex action like completing the internal market can only be regarded as very approximate. Apart from being subject to a number of policy conditions, such estimates are extremely difficult to make, especially as regards some of the more speculative and long-term effects. With these strong reservations to be kept in mind, some rough orders of magnitude can be suggested. For perspective, the Community's total gross domestic product in 1985 . . . was 3300 billion ECU for the 12 Member States . . .

(i) The direct costs of frontier formalities, and associated administrative costs for the private and public sector, may be of the order of 1.8% of the value of the goods traded within the Community or around 9 billion ECU.

(ii) The total costs for industry of identifiable barriers in the internal market, including not only frontier formalities as above but also technical regulations and other barriers, have been estimated . . . to average a little under 2% of . . . companies' costs. This represents about 40 billion ECU, or 3.5% of industrial value-added.

. . .

(iv) . . . industries and service sector branches subject to market entry restrictions could experience considerably bigger potential cost and price reductions. Examples include branches of industry for which government procurement is important (energy generating, transport, office and defence equipment), financial services (banking, insurance and securities) and road and air transport. In these cases cost and price reductions often of the order of 10 to 20%, and even more in some cases, could be expected. For public procurement alone the gains could amount to around 20 billion ECU. For financial services also a range around 20 billion ECU in potential savings has been proposed, although the margin of uncertainty here is particularly large.

(v) The relatively large percentage reductions for some categories of public procurement reflect the fact that these estimates include the broader effects of open competition in these sectors, including the realization of previously unexploited economies of scale . . . A study of potential economies of scale in European industry shows that, in more than half of all branches of industry, 20 firms of efficient size can co-exist in the Community market whereas the largest national markets could only have four each. It is evident, therefore, that only the European internal market could combine the advantages of technical and economic efficiency, 20 firms being more likely to assure effective competition than 4 firms. Comparing the present industrial structure with a more rationalized but still less than optimal one, it is estimated that about one third of European industry could profit from varying cost reductions of between 1 to 7%, yielding an aggregate cost-saving of the order of 60 billion ECU.

(vi) It becomes progressively more hazardous to suggest magnitudes for other types of gain resulting from enhanced competition, including the reduction of what has been termed 'X-inefficiency'. This covers a poor internal allocation of resources-human, physical and financial. Conditions of weak competition cause 'X-inefficiency', and also permit excess profit margins (monopoly profits, or economic rent) . . . The costs of 'X-inefficiency' may often be as great as those resulting from unexploited economies of scale. The total effect of moving to a competitive, integrated market, with fuller achievement of potential economies of scale and reduction of 'X-inefficiency', may be twice to three times the direct cost of identified barriers in an environment where competition is less effective.

(vii) The totality of the foregoing effects could be reflected, in the new equilibrium situation in the economy after several years, in a downward convergence of presently disparate price levels . . . Under one set of hypotheses, implying strong market integration but far from complete price convergence and with incomplete sectoral coverage, the gains amounted to about 140 billion ECU.

(viii) Overall these estimates offer a range, starting with around 70 billion ECU (2.5% of GDP) for a rather narrow conception of the benefits of removing the remaining internal market barriers, to around 125 to 190 billion ECU (4.25% to 6.5% of GDP) on the hypothesis of a much more competitive, integrated market . . . Overall, it would seem possible to enhance the Community's annual potential growth rate, for both output and consumption, by around 1 percentage point for the period up to 1992. In addition, there would be good prospects that longer-run dynamic effects could sustain a buoyant growth rate further into the 1990s.

(ix) The common assumptions underlying the foregoing estimates . . . are that (a) it might take five or possibly more years for the larger part of the effects to be reached, and (b) in any event it is assumed that micro- and macroeconomic policies would ensure that the resources released as costs are reduced, are effectively re-employed productively . . . [A] number of macroeconomic simulation exercises have been conducted, injecting some of the foregoing estimates into macro-dynamic models . . .

(x) *With a passive macroeconomic policy.* The overall impact of the measures is manifest most strongly in the initial years in the downward pressure on prices and costs, but this is followed with only a modest time-lag by increases in output. The major impacts, however, appear in the medium-run, after about five to six years, by which time a cumulative impact of +4.5% in terms of GDP and –6% in terms of the price level might be expected from a full implementation of the internal market programme . . .

(xi) *With a more active macroeconomic policy*. . . . In the middle of the range . . . lies a case in which the GDP level after a medium-term period might be 2.5% higher, in addition to the 4.5% gain suggested under the passive macroeconomic policy, thus totalling 7% . . .

(xii) *The microeconomic and macroeconomic synthesis*. The foregoing paragraphs have set out quantitative estimates on matters that are extremely difficult to evaluate at all precisely . . . The estimates have been assembled in an eclectic manner, using various techniques of microeconomic and macroeconomic analysis. These different approaches suggest consistent results. The potential gains from a full, competitive integration of the internal market are not trivial in macroeconomic terms. They could be about large enough to make the difference between a disappointing and very satisfactory economic performance for the Community economy as a whole.

. . .

5. *From the Removal of Technical Barriers to Full Market Integration*

The range of quantitative estimates just presented draws attention to the major difference between:

(a) a narrow, technical, and short-term view of the costs of 'tangibly' identifiable frontier barriers, such as customs delays and various regulations; and

(b) a broader, strategic and long-term view of the benefits from having a fully integrated, competitive and rationalized internal market.

Since the magnitudes involved under the second concept are at least twice as big as under the first one, it is important to be clear about the conditions required to achieve the larger results.

(i) The most fundamental condition is the credibility of the operation: that within a medium-term period the European market environment is to be transformed in a way that will oblige all enterprises . . . to adopt European business strategies . . .

(ii) As regards microeconomic policies, the first condition for the credibility of the programme is that the economic agents should easily be able to engage in arbitrage between national markets to profit from price differences, and so impose more nearly common and competitive price levels. This means that the frontiers must be truly open . . . Thus all the essential barriers have to be removed, otherwise the last remaining barriers may on their own be sufficient to restrain competition.

The second condition, which concerns competition policy as regards public subsidies, is that enterprises contemplating European market strategies must be assured that if they advance in their penetration of other countries' markets, they will not find themselves confronted by defensive subsidies in those countries . . .

The third condition concerns competition policy addressed to private enterprises. Here it is necessary for the business world to understand clearly that commercial practices which tend to segment markets, or lead to the abuse of dominant positions, will be vigorously countered . . .

(iii) As regards macroeconomic policies . . . It is sure that implementation of the internal market programme will put downward pressure on costs and prices, and create the potential for greater non-inflationary growth. It is not sure, however, how far this potential will materialize. From the standpoint of macroeconomic analysis there are a range of possibilities: the benefits from the more competitive market pressures may be taken mainly in the form of less price inflation, or mainly in the form of more output with unchanged inflation . . . or by a more even mix of disinflation and output gains.

. . .

7. *Final Remarks*

The study supports the following essential conclusions:

(i) In the present condition of the European economy the segmentation and weak competitiveness of many markets means that there is large potential for the rationalization of production and distribution structures, leading to improvements in productivity, and reductions in many costs and prices.

(ii) The completion of the internal market could, if strongly reinforced by the competition policies of both the Community and Member States, have a deep and extensive impact on economic structures and performance. The size of this impact, in terms of the potential for non-inflationary growth, could be sufficient to transform the Community's macroeconomic performance from a mediocre to a very satisfactory one.

(iii) In order to achieve a prize of this magnitude, all the main features of the internal market programme would need to be implemented with sufficient speed and conviction, such that the credibility of the total operation is not just safeguarded, but reinforced. Implementation of half of the actions proposed in the White Paper will deliver much less than half of the potential benefits.

(iv) In fact, more than full implementation of the White Paper is required in order to achieve the full potential benefits of an integrated European market. There must be a strong competition policy . . . Macroeconomic policy has to be set on a coherent, growth-oriented strategy. The White Paper represents a policy aimed at making the supply potential of the Community economy more flexible and competitive. The counterpart in terms of the demand side needs to be clearly agreed among policy makers and credibly communicated to business and public opinion . . .

3. THE REINVIGORATION OF EUROPE: THE POLITICS OF INTEGRATION

The force of the Commission's proposals should not, however, cause us to ignore a simple, but important, question lurking in the background. Why did this initiative succeed? Why were the Commission's proposals not left to languish, one further testimony to be added to other failed attempts at institutional and substantive reform which were posited during the late 1970s and early 1980s?[7] The success of reforms is often dependent upon the conjunction of a desire for change which is felt at the same time by the key players in any particular political system. This is all the more so within a complex multinational framework such as the EC. But who were the key players and why were they willing to accept reform at this juncture? Not surprisingly views on this question differ, and exigencies of space mean that it is not possible to do justice to the wealth of literature which has appeared on this topic. Discussion of the completion of the single market would, however, be incomplete if it did not include some consideration of this important issue. What follows are two contrasting views, both of which seek to explain the success of the single-market initiative and subsequent passage of the SEA against the backdrop of the pessimism which beset the Community in the late 1970s and the early 1980s.

Sandholtz and Zysman offer one thesis.[8] They reject explanations based on neofunctionalist integration theories, and on the domestic politics of the Member States, although they admit that certain elements of these theories have a continuing relevance even under their own preferred explanation.[9] They argue that the success of the 1992 initiative should instead be viewed in 'terms of elite bargains formulated in response to international structural change and the Commission's policy entrepreneurship'.[10] On this hypothesis there were three crucial factors which combined to promote the success of the Community's reinvigoration: the domestic political context, the Commission's initiative and the role of the business elite. The way in which these elements came together is brought out by the authors in the following way:

W. Sandholtz and J. Zysman, 1992: Recasting the European Bargain[11]

The question is why national government policies and perspectives have altered. Why, in the decade between the mid-1970s and the mid-1980s, did the European governments become open to European-level, market-oriented solutions? The answer has two parts: the failure of national strategies for economic growth and the transformation of the left in European politics. First, the traditional models of growth and economic management broke down. The old political strategies for the economy seemed to have run out. After the growth of the 1960s, the world economy entered a period of stagflation in the 1970s. As extensive industrialization reached its limits, the existing formulas for national economic development and the political bargains underpinning them had to be revised . . .

. . . the second aspect of the changed political context was the shift in government coalitions in a number of EC Member States. Certainly the weakening of the left in some countries and a shift from the communist to the market-socialist left in others helped to make possible a debate about market solutions (including unified European markets) to Europe's dilemma. In Latin Europe, the communist parties weakened as the era of Eurocommunism waned. Spain saw the triumph of

[7] For a discussion of other such efforts, see above, Ch. 1.
[8] '1992: Recasting the European Bargain' (1989) 42 *World Politics* 95.
[9] *Ibid.* 97–100. On neofunctionalism, see above, 6–8. [10] *Ibid.* 97.
[11] N. 8 above, 108–9, 111–12, 113, 116.

> Gonzalez's socialists, and their unexpected emergence as advocates of market-led development and entry into the Common Market . . . In France, Mitterand's victory displaced the communists from their primacy on the left . . . After 1983, Mitterand embraced a more market-oriented approach and became a vigorous advocate of increased European cooperation . . . In Britain and Germany, the Labour and Social Democratic parties lost power as well as influence on the national debate.
>
> . . .
>
> In an era when deregulation—the freeing of the market—became the fad, it made intuitive sense to extend the European market as a response to all ailments . . .
>
> This was the domestic political soil into which the Commission's initiatives fell. Traditional models of economic growth appeared to have played themselves out, and the left had been transformed in such a way that socialist parties began to seek market-oriented solutions to economic ills. In this setting, the European Community provided more than the mechanisms of intergovernmental negotiation. The Eurocracy was a standing constituency and a permanent advocate of European solutions and greater unity. Proposals from the European Commission transformed this new orientation into policy, and more importantly, into a policy perspective and direction. The Commission perceived the international structural changes and the failure of existing national strategies. and seized the initiative.
>
> . . .
>
> The third actor in the story, besides the governments and the Commission, is the leadership of the European multinational corporations. The White Paper and the Single European Act gave the appearance that changes in the EC market were irreversible and politically unstoppable. Businesses have been acting on that belief. Politically, they have taken up the banner of 1992, collaborating with the Commission and exerting substantial influence on their governments. The significance of the role of business, and of its collaboration with the Commission, must not be underestimated . . .
>
> Substantial support for the Commission's initiatives have come from the Roundtable of European Industrialists, an association of some of Europe's largest and most influential corporations, including Philips, Siemens, Olivetti, GEC, Daimler Benz, Volvo, Fiat, Bosch, ASEA and Ciba-Geigy.

This view has not gone unchallenged. Moravcsik tells a different tale, or at least one which has a very different emphasis. He contests the thesis that the SEA was the result of an elite alliance between the Commission, Parliament, and supranational business groups, to be seen against the backdrop of certain domestic political trends. He proffers an alternative theory, whereby the fact of reform, and its success, rested on inter-state bargains between Britain, France, and Germany. On this view the condition precedent for reform was the convergence of European economic-policy preferences in the early 1980s, combined with the bargaining leverage which France and Germany used against Britain by threatening a two-track Europe, or a Europe *a deux vitesses*, with Britain in the slow lane. Moravcsik believes that regime theory, which stresses more traditional ideas of national interest and power politics, best explains the actual occurrence of events leading up to the signing of the SEA. The essential elements of this theory are portrayed by him in the following way:

A. Moravcsik, Negotiating the Single European Act: National Interests and Conventional Statecraft in the European Community[12]

An alternative approach to explaining the success of the 1992 initiative focuses on interstate bargains between heads of government in the three larger member states of the EC. This approach, which can be called 'intergovernmental institutionalism', stresses the central importance of power and interests, with the latter not simply dictated by position in the intergovernmental system . . . Intergovernmental institutionalism is based on three principles: intergovernmentalism, lowest common denominator bargaining, and strict limits on future transfers of sovereignty.

Intergovernmentalism. From its inception, the EC has been based on interstate bargains between its leading member states. Heads of government, backed by a small group of ministers and advisers, initiate and negotiate major initiatives in the Council of Ministers or the European Council. Each government views the EC through the lens of its own policy preferences; EC politics is the continuation of domestic politics by other means. Even when societal interests are transnational, the principal form of their political expression remains national.

Lowest-common-denominator bargaining. Without a 'European hegemony' capable of providing universal incentives or threats to promote regime formation and without the widespread use of linkages and logrolling, the bargains struck in the EC reflect the relative power positions of the member states. Small states can be bought off with side-payments, but larger states exercise a de facto veto over fundamental changes in the scope or rules of the core element of the EC, which remains economic liberalization. Thus, bargaining tends to converge toward the lowest common denominator of large state interests. The bargains initially consisted of bilateral agreements between France and Germany; now they consist of trilateral agreements including Britain.

The only tool that can impel a state to accept an outcome on a major issue that it does not prefer to the status quo is the threat of exclusion. Once an international institution has been created, exclusion can be expensive both because the nonmember forfeits input into further decision making and because it forgoes whatever benefits result. If two major states can isolate the third and credibly threaten it with exclusion and if such exclusion undermines the substantive interests of the excluded state, the coercive threat may bring about an agreement at a level of integration above the lowest common denominator.

Protection of sovereignty. The decision to join a regime involves some sacrifice of national sovereignty in exchange for certain advantages. Policymakers safeguard their countries against the future erosion of sovereignty by demanding the unanimous consent of regime members to sovereignty-related reforms. They also avoid granting open-ended authority to central institutions that might infringe on their sovereignty, preferring instead to work through intergovernmental institutions such as the Council of Ministers, rather than through supranational bodies such as the Commission and Parliament.

12 (1991) 45 *International Organization* 19, 25–7 italics in the original.

There is no need to decide unequivocally between the two theories presented above. We shall in any event have occasion to revert to these analyses in the discussion which follows.

Notwithstanding these differences of opinion as to the political actors primarily responsible for reactivating the Community, most would agree that there were two connected conditions for the success of these new initiatives. There had to be *legislative reform* which would facilitate the passage of measures designed to complete the internal market. There had also to be a *new approach to harmonization* which would expedite the process of breaking down the technical barriers to intra-Community trade. These will be considered in turn.

4. COMPLETING THE INTERNAL MARKET: LEGISLATIVE REFORM AND THE SEA

The European Council, which had been the immediate catalyst for the Commission's study, endorsed the White Paper in June 1985. Intergovernmental meetings which gave shape to the Single European Act followed. The SEA was signed on 17 February 1986 and entered into force after ratification by Member States on 1 July 1987. The Act contained new procedures designed to make it easier to pass the legislation which was required to complete the internal market. These new Treaty Articles will be examined in this section. It should not, however, be thought that what finally emerged in the SEA was uncontroversial, or that there was complete agreement between the major political players on the content of the new legislative norms. There was not. The Commission pressed for more far-reaching changes than the Member States were willing to accept. The importance of the political background should not therefore be 'left behind' once one has read the materials in the previous section. Quite the contrary. It is only by understanding the politics of Treaty reform that one can make sense of what was, and what was not, included in the SEA.

The SEA contains two major legislative innovations which were of prime importance for the single market project: Article 7a[13] and Article 100a.

(a) Article 7a: The Obligation Stated

What is now Article 7 has been present since the inception of the Community and states that the common market shall be progressively established during a transitional period of twelve years. The remainder of Article 7 sets out the transitional arrangements by which this was to happen. Article 7a was added by the SEA and provides that:

[13] Prior to the passage of the TEU this was Art. 8a.

The Community shall adopt measures with the aim of progressively establishing the internal market over a period expiring on 31 December 1992, in accordance with the provisions of this Article and of Articles 7b, 7c, 28, 57(2), 59, 70(1), 84, 99, 100a and 100b and without prejudice to the other provisions of this Treaty.

The internal market shall comprise an area without internal frontiers in which the free movement of goods, persons, services and capital is ensured in accordance with the provisions of the Treaty.

Let us begin by addressing the *content of the obligation* contained in the first paragraph of Article 7a. The extent to which this is legally enforceable will be considered in due course. The Community is obliged to attain the internal market by the specified date. This obligation is imposed on the Community institutions as such, but the Member States have a duty pursuant to Article 5 of the Treaty to co-operate in the endeavour. The first paragraph of Article 7a indicates the more specific provisions of the Treaty which are to be used to achieve the internal market. All these provisions were either introduced by the SEA, as in the case of Articles 7b, 7c, 100a, and 100b, or were amended by the SEA, as in the case of the other Articles mentioned. Article 7a makes clear, however, that this list is without prejudice to other provisions of the Treaty. This is in part because there are other Treaty provisions, such as Article 43, which may form the basis for measures designed to secure the internal market. The other reason the 'without prejudice' clause of Article 7a is important is because it serves to ensure that Member States can still make use of provisions such as Article 36, or the mandatory requirements of *Cassis de Dijon* to justify rules which may hamper intra-Community trade, pending the passage of the requisite Community measures which will render such national rules otiose.[14]

The second paragraph of Article 7a contains the *definition of the internal market*. The idea of the internal market is one which could be defined in a variety of ways, some broad, some narrow. The framers of the SEA chose a two-part formulation: it is to be an area without internal frontiers, in which there can be free movement of goods, persons etc. As Wyatt and Dashwood note,[15] the first of these elements is capable of more precise specification than the second. The attainment of an area without internal frontiers can be judged by whether any border controls still exist on the free movement of goods or persons etc. Such controls are essentially formal in nature. It is considerably more difficult to determine how freely goods, persons, and capital can move within the Community, *even when* border controls have been removed. This is for the very reasons that we have come across on a number of occasions already: there may, for example, be technical rules which render it difficult to market goods from state *A* in state *B*. It may therefore not be easy to decide when the internal market really has been completed. One indirect criterion would be to ask whether the Commission has completed the legislative

[14] For discussion of this body of Community case law, see above, Ch. 14.

[15] *European Community Law* (3rd edn., Sweet & Maxwell, 1993), 356.

programme which it outlined in the White Paper. This has, as will be seen below, been largely realized. Yet it would be mistaken to assume that attaining the internal market is a once-and-for-all static objective. It is not. Given the existence of continuing technological developments there is bound to be a continuing need to ensure that barriers to intra-Community trade are not resurrected.

What, then, is the *legal effect* of Article 7a? Does it in fact have any legal effect in its own right? In the first working paper which the Commission submitted to the Inter-governmental Conference from which the SEA emerged it seems that it intended what has now become Article 7a to have direct effect. The sting of this provision was given even greater force by reason of the further Commission proposal that, if national rules on free movement were not removed by the agreed date, then they would automatically be recognized as equivalent. These suggestions 'stunned the participants at the Intergovernmental Conference'.[16] This idea was too radical for the Member States and the Commission was forced to modify its suggestions. This it did in an amended working paper submitted to the Conference.[17] The Member States were still concerned at the possibility that Article 7a could produce legal consequences and therefore they attached a Declaration to Article 7a which states:

> The Conference wishes by means of the provisions in Article 7a to express its firm political will to take before January 1, 1993 the decisions necessary to complete the internal market defined in those provisions, and more particularly the decisions necessary to implement the Commission's programme described in the White Paper on the Internal Market.
>
> Setting the date of December 31, 1992 does not create an automatic legal effect.

The possibility that Article 7a will have legal consequences cannot, however, be discounted. It is at the very least necessary to distinguish between the legal effect of the Article *vis-à-vis* the Community itself, and in relation to possible actions against the Member States via direct effect.

The possibility that Article 7a will have *legal effects against the Community itself*[18] is based in part on the mandatory wording of the Article, and in part on the fact that the Declaration, whatever its precise legal status, is seeking to preclude Member State susceptibility to direct effect through the words 'does not create automatic legal effect'. What, then, would be the consequence if the Commission failed to propose the necessary measures, or, more likely, if the Council failed to adopt them by the requisite date? Could there be an Article 175 action for failure to act? The possibility of such an action would depend on whether the criteria for actions of this kind are met in these circum-

[16] C. D. Ehlermann, 'The Internal Market Following the Single European Act' (1987) 24 CMLRev. 361, 371.

[17] *Ibid.* 371–2.

[18] *Ibid.* 372. See also H. J. Glaesner, 'The Single European Act: Attempt at an Appraisal' (1987) 10 *Fordham Intl. LJ* 446.

stances.[19] The case law of the Court has established that, for such an action to be brought, it is necessary that the measures which it is claimed should have been enacted are defined with sufficient specificity for them to be identified individually, and adopted pursuant to Article 176.[20] This will not be so where the relevant institutions possess discretionary power, with consequential policy options, the content of which cannot be identified with precision. The application of this criterion to Article 7a will, as Wyatt and Dashwood state,[21] depend upon the nature of the alleged failure to act. It would. for example, be difficult to maintain that the criterion for the Article 175 action is met if the allegation is that the Commission has failed to promote measures designed to ensure the free movement of goods, persons, services, or capital. This is 'too general an objective, and its attainment too fraught with policy choices, to be the subject of proceedings under Article 175'.[22] There may, by way of contrast, be a greater possibility for such an action where the allegation is that the Council has failed to adopt a specific Commission proposal. Even in this instance much would depend upon the nature of the proposal. Matters will become clearer when the ECJ passes judgment on a case brought by the Parliament under Article 175 alleging a breach of Article 7a by the Commission.[23]

What, then, of the possibility that Article 7a might have *legal consequences for the Member States*. We should be clear what this might entail. It could possibly mean that, even if the relevant Community measures had not been enacted, none the less it would be open to an individual to argue that Member States' rules which constituted a barrier to the completion of the internal market should not be applied if they were incompatible with Article 7a itself.

Does the Declaration set out above preclude this? Toth[24] has argued that it does not, in and of itself, prevent the Article from having direct effect; that the Declaration is merely interpretative without binding force as such, and that the ECJ would be free to determine the legal consequences of Article 7a.

Accepting this analysis, it must still be shown that Article 7a fulfils the conditions for direct effect. The ECJ's jurisprudence on direct effect has been considered in detail above.[25] The condition which would appear to be most problematic in this context is that which provides that there must be no further action required before the norm in question can have direct effect. We have seen that the ECJ has in fact been willing to ascribe direct effect to certain Treaty Articles, notwithstanding the fact that the relevant provisions of the Treaty clearly do intend further action in order to flesh out the Article.[26] However, it would still be a bold move for the Court to hold that Article 7a is directly effective, given that the Article does contemplate not only further

[19] On Art. 175 generally, see above, 483–6.
[20] Case 13/83, *European Parliament* v. *Council* [1985] ECR 1583.
[21] N. 15 above, 359–60.
[22] *Ibid.* 359.
[23] Case C–445/93, *European Parliament* v. *Commission* [1994] OJ C1/24.
[24] A. G. Toth, 'The Legal Status of the Declarations Annexed to the Single European Act' (1986) 23 CMLRev. 803.
[25] Ch. 4.
[26] See above, 156–64.

Community action, but also that, pending such action, national measures which are lawful under, for example, *Cassis*, will continue to be so, pending the passage of Community measures in the area. Moreover, even though the Declaration referred to above may not formally preclude direct effect, it does clearly signal Member State intent in this respect.

The question until now has been of the possibility of direct effect in circumstances where some relevant Community measures to implement the internal market have not been passed. Where, however, they have been promulgated matters are different. The Community measure adopted might itself have direct effect. So, too, might Article 7a. As Wyatt and Dashwood note:[27]

> Frontier controls on movement between Member States will be illegal after 1992 if, but only if, they are no longer necessary to safeguard interests recognised as legitimate by the Treaty. That will obviously be the case where harmonized rules, standards or qualifications are *fully* in place. It is further submitted that, even where the legislative framework remains incomplete, the combined effect of Article 8a[28] and the obligation of loyal co-operation in Article 5 will prevent Member States from having recourse to frontier controls, if the interests in question could be protected by some other means . . . So, while there is no automatic obligation to abolish all controls at the Community's internal frontier before January 1, 1993, as from that date the burden of proof will be on Member States to justify the retention of such controls.

(b) Articles 7b and 7c: The Obligation Qualified

Articles 7b and 7c introduce procedural and substantive qualifications to Article 7a.

Article 7b requires the Commission to report to the Council on the progress towards achieving the goals of the internal market. The second paragraph of this Article then states that the Council, acting by qualified majority on a proposal from the Commission, shall determine 'the guidelines and conditions necessary to ensure balanced progress in all the sectors concerned'.

Article 7c introduces a substantive qualification to the scope of Article 7a. It requires that the Commission, when drawing up proposals pursuant to Article 7a, shall take into account the extent of the effort that certain economies showing differences in developments will have to sustain during the period of establishment of the internal market and it may propose appropriate provisions. Article 7c goes on to make clear that, if the provisions take the form of derogations, they must be temporary and cause the least possible disturbance to the functioning of the common market. The purpose of Article 7c is captured by Ehlermann:[29]

[27] N. 15 above, 361, italics in the original.

[28] For which read Art. 7a.

[29] 'The Internal Market Following the Single European Act' (1987) 24 CMLRev. 361, 374.

It makes allowance for the fact that the Community has become more heterogeneous through the accession of new Member States. If the objective laid down in Article 8A[30] appears rather ambitious for the original Member States, it is far more so for most of the new Member States, given their relative economic weakness compared with the old-established members and the considerable risks which the complete opening up of their domestic markets would therefore entail.

(c) *Amendments to Articles 28, 49, 57, 59, 70, and 84*

The original Commission working paper presented to the Inter-governmental Conference had proposed a sweeping provision, the import of which was that qualified-majority voting would be the norm for all measures to secure the internal market, subject to limited exceptions where unanimity would be required. The Member States were not keen on this broad-brush approach, so the Commission modified its proposals, indicating with greater specificity the areas of the Treaty where changes in voting would take place. The amendments to Articles 28, 49, 57, 59, 70, and 84 all entail the replacement of a unanimity requirement with one of qualified majority, either wholly or in part.

(d) *Article 100a(1): Facilitating the Passage of Harmonization Measures*

We have already seen that one of the principal difficulties in ensuring the passage of harmonization measures was the requirement of unanimity. This problem was alleviated in part by the changes in the voting rules which applied to the specific Articles mentioned in the previous section. However if matters had rested there, the attainment of the objective laid down in Article 7a would still have been difficult for the following reason. Many of the measures aimed at harmonizing laws prior to 1986 were promulgated under Article 100. This Article gives a general power to pass directives for the approximation of laws of the Member States as directly affected the establishment or functioning of the common market. But Article 100 stipulates that unanimity is needed for the passage of such directives. The framers of the SEA correctly appreciated that the passage of harmonizing measures would be facilitated if there were to be a general legislative power akin to Article 100, without the unanimity requirement. This was provided by Article 100a which was newly introduced into the Treaty by the SEA. Article 100a(1) reads as follows:

> By way of derogation from Article 100 and save where otherwise provided in this Treaty, the following provisions shall apply for the achievement of the objectives set out in Article 7a. The Council shall, acting in accordance with the procedure referred to in Article 189b and after consulting the Economic and Social Committee, adopt the measures for the approximation of the provisions laid down by law, regulation or administrative action in Member States which have as their object the establishing and functioning of the internal market.

[30] For which read Art. 7a.

There are a number of features of this Article which should be noted.

One concerns the *range of measures* which can be taken. Article 100 authorizes only the passage of directives. Article 100a, by way of contrast, empowers the Council to pass measures, which obviously includes directives, but also legitimates the use of the Article for the passage of, for example, regulations.[31]

A second feature which is worthy of note concerns *the role of the European Parliament*. Whereas Article 100 merely requires that the European Parliament be consulted, Article 100a(1) accords the Parliament a greater say by making measures passed in this way subject to the Article 189b procedure.[32] This is, as we have seen, the procedural format which was introduced by the TEU, and gives the Parliament greater power than it would otherwise have if it only had to be consulted, or than it has under the Article 189c procedure.

The third point of importance concerning Article 100a is that it is *a residual provision*. It only operates 'save where otherwise provided in this Treaty'. This means that other, more specific Treaty provisions, such as Article 43, 54, 57, or 75, should be used for measures designed to attain the internal market where they fall within the subject matter areas of those Articles. This can generate boundary-dispute problems as to the correct legal basis for Community legislation. This may be because potentially relevant Treaty Articles stipulate different voting requirements for the enactment of legislation; it may be because the European Parliament is accorded greater rights pursuant to one Treaty Article than another; or it may be because, for example, a state wishes to avail itself of the provisions contained in Article 100a(4), discussed below, which would not be available if the measure in question were to be passed under some other Treaty Article.

How, then, does the Court indicate that boundary disputes of this nature should be resolved? The general test propounded by the ECJ is that regard should be had to the nature, aim, and content of the act in question.[33] Where these factors indicate that the measure is in fact concerned with more than one area of the Treaty, then it may well be necessary to satisfy the legal requirements under two Treaty Articles.[34] The ECJ has, however, also made it clear that this will not be insisted upon where the relevant legal bases under the two Articles prescribe procedures which are incompatible. It is, for example, not possible to combine a requirement that the Parliament should merely be consulted with one which demands that the co-operation procedure should be used.

A number of the cases which the ECJ has had to resolve concerned the boundary lines between Articles 43 and 100a.[35] Another area in which there

[31] For an expansive interpretation of 'measures' see, Case C–359/92, *Germany* v. *Council* [1994] ECR I–3681.

[32] Originally Art. 100a provided that the co-operation procedure contained within Art. 189c should be used. The substitution of the Art. 189b procedure was done by the TEU.

[33] Case C–300/89, *Commission* v. *Council* [1991] ECR I–2867.

[34] Case 165/87, *Commission* v. *Council* [1988] ECR 5545, [1990] 1 CMLR 457.

[35] Case 68/86, *United Kingdom* v. *Council* [1988] ECR 855, [1988] 2 CMLR 543; Case 11/88, *Commission* v. *Council* [1989] ECR 3799.

is a possibility of conflict is the environment, and the choice between Articles 100a and 130s. The basic rule under Article 130s, which comes within the Title of the Treaty specifically concerned with the environment, is that decision-making is by the Article 189c procedure after consulting the Economic and Social Committee.[36] Yet it is clearly contemplated that environmental norms will be made under Article 100a(1): Article 100a(3), to be considered below, states that the Commission, when making, *inter alia*, measures under Article 100a(1) which have an impact on the environment, shall take as a base a high level of protection. The precise circumstances in which the Community will have to use Article 130s as opposed to Article 100a are not clear.[37] In the *Titanium Dioxyde* case[38] the ECJ held that the Commission could legitimately use Article 100a as the basis for a directive relating to the reduction of pollution caused by the titanium dioxyde industry. The Council had sought to substitute Article 130s as the legal foundation for the measure, but the Court said that this was wrong. The directive was found to have the dual objectives of environmental protection, plus removing competitive distortions resulting from divergent national rules on pollution and hence helping to secure the internal market. This would, in the light of the principles set out above, prima facie indicate that a dual legal basis had to be satisfied. The ECJ felt, however, that the procedural rules under the two Articles were incompatible and that therefore a choice had to be made between them. It chose Article 100a.[39] However, in two more recent cases the ECJ has held that Article 130s was the proper legal basis for a measure concerned with disposal of waste, and stated that Article 100a should not be used when the impact on the functioning of the internal market was merely ancillary to the attainment of an environmental aim.[40]

(e) Article 100a(2)–(5): Qualifications to Article 100a(1)

The remainder of Article 100a contains qualifications of varying kinds on the powers given by Article 100a(1). These qualifications differ in nature, and their presence in the Treaty is the result of the political negotiations which attended the passage of the SEA.

Article 100a(2) encapsulates a straightforward exception to Article 100a(1), by providing that the latter shall not apply to fiscal provisions, to those relating to the free movement of persons, or to those relating to the rights and interests of employed persons. These areas were felt by the Member States to be particularly sensitive, hence their exclusion from the ambit of Article

36 Although Art. 130s(2) does allow the Council to specify those matters on which it is willing to act by qualified majority.

37 For discussion, see Wyatt and Dashwood, n. 15 above, 370–3.

38 Case C–300/89, n. 33 above.

39 For a critical view of this case and of the Commission's use of Art. 100a as the basis for legislation which is said by the author not to fall within the ambit of the Article, see S. Crosby, 'The Single Market and the Rule of Law' (1991) 16 ELRev. 451.

40 Case C–151/91, *Commission* v. *Council* [1993] ECR I–939; Case C–187/93, *European Parliament* v. *Council* [1994] ECR I–2857.

100a(1). Legislation for these areas will therefore have to be passed either by using Article 100 or a more specific provision of the Treaty where one exists.

Article 100a(3) instructs the Commission, when passing measures under Article 100a(1) relating to health, safety, environmental protection, and consumer protection, to take as a base a high level of protection. As Ehlermann has pointed out,[41] there is an analogy between this Article and Article 7c. The latter was demanded by relatively under-developed economies to protect them from the possible rigours of free competition under a completed internal market; Article 100a(3) was included to placate countries such as Germany and Denmark, which were concerned that the harmonization measures which emerged might not be stringent enough. The wording of Article 100a(3) does not, however, compel the Commission to enact a measure which is in accord with that pertaining in the countries with high levels of protection in these areas. It merely requires that a high level of protection constitute the starting point for further discussion.

Article 100a(4) is the qualification to Article 100a(1) which has received most critical attention. The provision is complex and therefore should be set out in full:

> If, after the adoption of a harmonization measure by the Council acting by a qualified majority, a Member State deems it necessary to apply national provisions on grounds of major needs referred to in Article 36, or relating to protection of the environment or the working environment, it shall notify the Commission of those provisions.
>
> The Commission shall confirm the provisions involved after having verified that they are not a means of arbitrary discrimination or a disguised restriction on trade between Member States.
>
> By way of derogation from the procedure laid down in Articles 169 and 170, the Commission or any Member State may bring the matter directly before the Court of Justice if it considers that another Member State is making improper use of the powers provided for in this Article.

The inclusion of Article 100a(4) gave rise to much critical comment and was one of the principal defects which was emphasized by those opposed to the SEA.[42] The genesis of this Article and its exceptional character are evident in the following extract from one who was favourably inclined to the Treaty reforms:

C. D. Ehlermann, The Internal Market Following the Single European Act[43]

Whereas paragraph 1[44] is the most significant provision of the Single European Act, paragraph 4 is the most problematic. Its purpose is the same as that of the

[41] N. 16 above, 375.
[42] P. Pescatore, 'Some Critical Remarks on the "Single European Act" ' (1987) 24 CMLRev. 9.
[43] N. 16 above, 389.
[44] Of Art. 100a.

preceding paragraph, namely to protect any Member State in a minority position from being forced to accept the majority line. However, the method devised is completely different. Whereas paragraph 3 is in keeping with the approach followed by the Community in the past, paragraph 4 represents a radical new departure.

It goes back to the fact that the United Kingdom, and later Ireland, wished to safeguard certain special measures connected with their island status against the threat of majority voting. Neither country was satisfied with the safeguard offered by paragraph 3. But they both accepted that retention of the unanimity requirement would have emasculated Article 100a.

The way out of this dilemma was paragraph 4, which was drafted by the European Council itself. The first paragraph meets the concerns expressed by the United Kingdom and Ireland and at the same time solves the Danish problem which overshadowed the entire negotiations. Subparagraphs 2 and 3 on the other hand, are intended to make this exceptional arrangement acceptable by providing a means of controlling the use made of subparagraph 1.

Any assessment of this Article must take into account legal issues of interpretation, and also more practical/political considerations which have affected the instances in which states have sought to rely on this provision.

In *legal terms* it is clear that the Article can only be used when a measure has been passed by qualified majority under Article 100a.[45] It cannot be utilized when a state has second thoughts about a directive which has been promulgated unanimously under Article 100. It is clear also that Article 100a(4) is an exceptional provision which derogates from the principles of the Treaty. It will therefore be restrictively construed by the ECJ. The Member State concerns which can legitimately trigger this Article are finite: the matters covered by Article 36, plus the environment and working environment. Other state concerns, such as consumer protection, which can justify national measures under *Cassis*[46] pending adequate harmonization measures, find no place in Article 100a(4). Moreover, it should not be forgotten that Article 100a(4), by way of contrast to Article 36 and the *Cassis* mandatory requirements, will be invoked by a state even though a harmonization measure has been passed. For this reason the ECJ should scrutinize especially carefully claims by the state that it really does need to retain its national provisions on one of the specified grounds. Now it is true that Article 100a(4) is framed in subjective terms: the state 'deems it necessary' to invoke its national laws. Yet it is also clear from the terms of subparagraphs 2 and 3 that this subjective evaluation by the state is meant to be reviewable both by the Commission and by the ECJ itself.[47]

45 There is, however, nothing in the Art. to suggest that it can only be used by a state which has actually voted against the measure.

46 See above, Ch. 14.

47 The Danish Government has argued that when a state invokes the Article, confirmation by the Commission should be a mere formality. This does not, however, fit readily with the actual wording of paras. 2 and 3 of the Art. For confirmation that the ECJ can review the use of Art. 100a (4) see, Case C–41/93, *France* v. *Commission* [1994] ECR I–1829.

In *political terms* many of the more dramatic fears about the impact of Article 100a(4) have not been borne out by state practice. Concerns that Member States would routinely seek to invoke the Article to prevent the application of harmonization measures have proven to be unfounded. In fact the machinery has been utilized on only two occasions in the five years since the enactment of the SEA, and in only one of these was the process actually carried through to the stage of a formal confirmation by the Commission of the national provisions.[48] Wyatt and Dashwood indicate why the fears expressed by commentators have not been realized:[49]

> First, the common political will to complete the internal market within the time limit set by Article 7a must have helped to overcome inhibitions. Secondly, the Member States which may have hoped to use paragraph (4) to protect the high health status of their livestock industries have been prevented from doing so by the evolution of the case law on Article 43 which has shown that Article to be the appropriate legal basis for internal market legislation in the veterinary field. Thirdly, the obligation imposed on the Commission by Article 100a(3) to propose high common standards of consumer and environmental protection may have helped to deter Member States from having recourse to paragraph (4), as it was clearly intended to do.

Article 100a(5) is the final qualification to Article 100a(1). It is much less dramatic than the preceding paragraph. The Article provides that harmonization measures may include safeguard clauses authorizing Member States to take, for one of the non-economic reasons in Article 36, provisional measures subject to Community control procedures. The rationale for this provision is as follows. It will normally be the case that recourse to Article 36 is precluded when Community harmonization measures have been enacted. The purpose of Article 100a(5) is to allow a Member State, subject to a Community control procedure, to adopt temporary measures in the event of a sudden and unforeseen danger to health, life, etc.

(f) Article 100b: Mutual Recognition in the Absence of Harmonization

The origins of Article 100b are interesting for the light which they shed on the decision-making process which led to the SEA. In the original working paper submitted to the Inter-governmental Conference, the Commission proposed what was in effect automatic mutual recognition for provisions concerning the internal market which had not been harmonized by the end of 1992. This was to prove too radical for the Member States and they rejected the proposal. What finally emerged was Article 100b which reads as follows:

[48] Wyatt and Dashwood, n. 15 above, 367.
[49] *European Community Law*, n. 15 above, 367.

1. During 1992, the Commission shall, together with each Member State, draw up an inventory of national laws, regulations and administrative provisions which fall under Article 100a and which have not been harmonized pursuant to that Article.

The Council, acting in accordance with the provisions of Article 100a, may decide that the provisions in force in a Member State must be recognised as equivalent to those applied by another Member State.

2. The provisions of Article 100a(4) apply by analogy.

3. The Commission shall draw up the inventory referred to in the first subparagraph of paragraph 1 and shall submit appropriate proposals in good time to allow the Council to act before the end of 1992.

Whereas the original Commission idea had been for automatic mutual recognition, what emerged therefore was a system under which the Council has power to decide that particular provisions should be afforded such recognition. Two related points concerning the scope of Article 100b are worthy of note.

On the one hand, the Article does not make mutual recognition the only option for measures which have not been harmonized by the deadline. Article 100b gives the Council only a discretionary power to act. It may still be felt that a harmonization measure passed after 1992 is the optimum way of dealing with an area. There is nothing in Article 100a itself which would indicate that it cannot be utilized after 1992.[50] It would indeed be odd if this were to be the case since, as we have seen above, technological changes will ensure that there is a continuing need for harmonizing measures.

On the other hand, there will be no need to have recourse to Article 100b for provisions which have not been harmonized, but which are inconsistent with the Court's jurisprudence under, for example, the *Cassis* doctrine. Article 100b will only be required for those national provisions which are consistent with norms such as Article 30 of the Treaty, but which are inconsistent with the aims of Article 7a.[51]

5. COMPLETING THE INTERNAL MARKET: THE NEW APPROACH TO HARMONIZATION

(a) The Rationale for the New Approach

We noted earlier that the successful completion of the internal market was dependent on two necessary conditions: legislative reform which would

[50] The only argument to the contrary would be that Art. 100a applies for the achievement of the objectives contained in Art. 7a. This latter Art. sets the deadline of the end of 1992. However, such a reading of Art. 100a would not be sensible for the reasons given in the text concerning the continuing need for harmonization measures. Moreover, Art. 100a is itself phrased in terms of the establishment and functioning of the internal market. The word 'functioning' connotes a continuing process which can go beyond 1992.

[51] Ehlermann, n. 16 above, 400.

facilitate the passage of measures to complete the internal market, and a new approach to harmonization which would make it easier to draft and secure the passage of these measures. Legislative reform has been considered in the previous section. This section will focus on the new approach to harmonization.

Let us begin by making clear the connection between this new approach and the legislative reforms which were considered above. It might be thought that the reforms in the legislative process would have been sufficient to secure the internal market, since harmonization measures could now be passed more easily. Did this not obviate the need for any new approach to harmonization? The answer is no. It is true that the changes introduced by the SEA served to speed the promulgation of legislation. But this by itself would not have been enough to ensure that the internal market could be attained by the end of 1992, nor that it could be maintained in the face of continuing technological innovation, prompting new national regulatory provisions.

Community harmonization initiatives in their traditional form could take a long time to implement, because of the degree of detail in such directives; they could be over-regulatory, in the sense that the result would be a Community-prescribed standard which might prove to be over rigid; and they could be inflexible in the face of new technological developments. Pelkmans[52] has summarized the disadvantages of the traditional approach to harmonization: the time-consuming nature of this technique; the fact that it generated excessive uniformity; the failure to develop links between harmonization and standardization, thereby leading to inconsistencies and wastage of time; the slowness of European harmonization relative to the increase in national regulation; a neglect of the problems of certification and testing; the incapacity to solve the third country problem; implementation problems in Member States; and lack of political interest by Ministers.

These shortcomings were recognized by the Commission in its White Paper,[53] and in other documentation. Thus in its proposals to the Council and Parliament for a New Approach to Technical Harmonization and Standards,[54] the Commission acknowledged the advances which had been made through the directives which had been passed. However it also accepted that eighteen years' experience had shown the delays and difficulties with such an approach, stemming from attempting to harmonize by means of detailed technical specification. The Commission admitted that the results of harmonization had been negligible in certain industrial fields, given the multiplicity of national technical regulations, and that the speed of technological change was too fast for there to be any realistic hope that the Community, acting through its existing harmonization techniques, could keep pace.

[52] J. Pelkmans, 'The New Approach to Technical Harmonization and Standardization' (1987) 25 JCMS 249, 252–3.

[53] COM(85) 310, para. 64.

[54] Bull. EC 1–1985.

(b) The New Approach to Harmonization

The general direction of the new approach to harmonization is apparent in the extract from the Commission White Paper on Completing the Internal Market. It was to be a mixture of mutual recognition through the *Cassis de Dijon* principle, in the sense that national rules which did not survive by coming within one of the mandatory requirements would be invalid; legislative harmonization was to be restricted to laying down health and safety standards; and there would be promotion of European standardization. This general description of the Community's new approach must be fleshed out if it is to be understood. Four elements can be identified which go to make up the Community's new strategy.

The *first building block* was the adoption of Directive 83/189 on the provision of information on technical standards and regulations. This measure, which is sometimes known as the mutual information or transparency directive, imposes an obligation on a state to inform the Commission before it adopts any legally binding regulation which sets a technical specification. The Commission will then notify the other states, and may require that the adoption of the national measure be delayed by six months, in order that possible amendments can be considered. A year's delay can result if the Commission decides to push ahead with a harmonization directive on the issue.

A *second facet* of the new approach was the willing acceptance of the *Cassis* jurisprudence. Quantitative restrictions or MEQRs would be held to be incompatible with the Treaty pursuant to the Court's case law, unless they could be saved by one of the mandatory requirements or Article 36. A product which had been lawfully manufactured in a Member State should be capable of being bought and sold in any other Member State. Mutual recognition should be the norm. No harmonization measures were required with respect to those national measures which would be condemned under the *Cassis* reasoning. Harmonization efforts should therefore be concentrated on those measures which would still be lawful under the *Cassis* exceptions or under Article 36.

This leads naturally on to the *third aspect* of the new approach. Legislative harmonization was to be limited to laying down essential health and safety requirements. The essence of this is captured by Pelkmans:

J. Pelkmans, The New Approach to Technical Harmonization and Standardization[55]

—harmonization of legislation is limited to the adoption . . . of the essential safety requirements . . . with which the products brought on the market must comply in order to qualify for free movement in the Community;

—it is the task of the competent (private) standardization organs, given

[55] N. 52 above, italics in the original.

technical progress, to formulate the technical specifications, on the basis of which industry needs to manufacture and market products complying with the fundamental requirements of the directives;

—these technical specifications are not binding and retain their character of voluntary (European) standards;

—but, at the same time, the governments are *obliged to presume* that the products manufactured in accordance with the European standards comply with the 'fundamental requirements' stipulated in the directive. It is this presumption that guarantees business free market access.

Once a standard has been approved by the Commission and published in the Official Journal all Member States must accept goods which conform to it. If a Member State disputes whether the standard conforms to the safety objectives set out in the directive, the burden of proof will be on that state to substantiate its contentions.

An analogous reversal of the burden of proof operates in the case of producers in the following sense. Given that the European standards are voluntary, it will be open to producers to manufacture according to specifications other than those laid down. The burden of proof will, however, then be on that producer to show that the goods meet the essential requirements specified in the directive.

The *final element* of the new approach is the promotion of European standardization. Standardization can be of importance both because it reduces barriers to intra-Community trade, and because it increases the competitiveness of European industry:[56]

> Standards can have a market-creating effect or, in other words, the lack of a standard between adjoining countries can make the Euromarket (i.e. trade between Member States) impossible, as is for instance the case with car telephones. Standards can also have an anticipatory effect. For instance, sufficient investment in product development, process technology and further innovations takes place in some products only when compatibility is secured first. Interesting examples of this are the recently proposed Council directives concerning standardization in the field of information technologies and telecom and concerning the mutual recognition of type approval of terminal equipment for telecommunications, the latter now having been adopted.

The principal Community bodies which are being used in the new approach are the European Committee for Standardization (CEN) and the European Committee for Technical Standardization (CENELEC). Other more specialized bodies exist for particular industrial sectors. One object is to 'ensure that standardization processes take place in parallel with harmonization at Council level and are based on "essential requirements" '.[57] Provided that standard-

[56] Pelkmans, n. 52 above, 260. [57] *Ibid.* 256.

ization does comply with these 'essential requirements' then it is very likely to be approved. It should not be thought that the efforts towards standardization relate only to product markets which are well established. They do not. Standardization initiatives will also be made in the context of newly emerging fields, or those in which rapid technological change is taking place, in order to facilitate the emergence of a more truly European market for these goods. In order to expedite decision-making the Community standardization bodies have moved to qualified-majority voting, thereby preventing the objections of one or two states from frustrating the adoption of a standard agreed upon by the remainder.

It is important to be clear about the relationship between Community harmonization of essential requirements and the standardization process. A directive which is passed pursuant to the new approach will lay down in general terms the health and safety requirements which the goods must meet. The setting of standards is designed both to help manufacturers prove conformity to these essential requirements and to allow inspection to test for conformity with them. Promoting Community-wide standards in the manner described above is designed to foster this process, by encouraging the development of consensus on what the relevant standards in a particular area should be. Flexibility is provided by allowing a manufacturer to show that its goods comply with the essential safety requirements, even if they do not comply with the Community standard.

The advantages of the new approach to harmonization are considerable and can be compared to the disadvantages of the traditional technique. Directives may be drafted more easily since they are less detailed; the excessive 'Euro-uniformity' of the traditional approach is avoided by combining stipulated safety objectives with flexibility on the particular product type which can comply with those safety requirements, and flexibility also on the standards through which this compliance can be achieved; the need for unanimity in voting is circumvented through Article 100a; harmonization and standardization are related; more Community directives can be made and hence the disjunction between the pace of Community harmonization and the increase in national technical regulations can be reduced; and incentives for proper implementation of directives by the Member States are increased through judicial doctrine such as that in *Francovich*.[58]

This is not to say that the new approach has been problem-free. The adequacy of the funding for standardization bodies, and the sufficiency of the bodies able to undertake the certification process, have both been causes for concern.[59] Improvements in these areas have, however, been made.[60] Notwithstanding these difficulties the new approach to harmonization offers an opportunity for Community progress in this important area, and one which is a good deal more realistic than would have been the case using the traditional techniques.

[58] See above, 229–38.

[59] Pelkmans, n. 52 above, 263–5.

[60] Commission Green Paper on European Standardization, 28 Jan. 1991.

(c) The New Approach to Harmonization: Legislative Format

The way in which the new approach to harmonization operates may become clearer if we consider an example. Council Directive 89/392 on the approximation of the laws of the Member States relating to machinery provides an appropriate piece of legislation to focus upon.[61]

This Directive *does not* lay down detailed requirements for how to build machinery. It concentrates on the health and safety risks arising out of the use of machinery and states explicitly that the Directive is being passed within the framework of the new approach to harmonization.

The recitals to the Directive note that the Member States have differing systems of accident prevention; that although this does not necessarily lead to varying levels of health and safety, the very disparities in the national rules can constitute barriers to trade; that approximation of these national laws is therefore necessary to ensure free movement of goods without prejudicing the protection of health and safety; that the Directive is designed to define the essential health and safety requirements; and that standards (generated in the manner described above) will enable manufacturers to prove conformity with the essential requirements and allow inspection to ensure conformity with these requirements.

The recitals also locate this Directive, and the fact that it addresses only essential health and safety requirements, within the broader framework of the Treaty as a whole. Notice the way in which the following recital from the Directive places this Community initiative, and indeed the whole of the new harmonization approach, within the context of the *Cassis* jurisprudence: national technical rules which impede trade, even if not discriminatory, are contrary to Community law, unless saved by one of the mandatory requirements or Article 36; *and* it is therefore only those national rules which survive the *Cassis* test which have to be harmonized:

> Whereas Community law, in its present form, provides—by way of derogation from one of the fundamental rules of the Community, namely the free movement of goods—that obstacles to movement within the Community resulting from disparities in national legislation relating to the marketing of products must be accepted in so far as the provisions concerned can be recognized as being necessary to satisfy imperative requirements; whereas, therefore, the harmonization of laws in this case must be limited only to those requirements necessary to satisfy the imperative and essential health and safety requirements relating to machinery; whereas these requirements must replace the relevant national provisions because they are essential.

Article 1 of the Directive then defines its scope: it is to apply to machinery,

[61] See also e.g. Dir. 88/378 on Toy Safety; Dir. 89/106 on Construction Products; Dir. 89/336 on Electromagnetic Compatibility.

which is further specified both inclusively and exclusively; the essential health and safety requirements for machinery are then set out in Annex 1 at a relatively high level of generality. Article 2(1) imposes a duty on Member States to ensure that machinery is only marketed when it does comply with the essential requirements. Article 2(2) then makes it clear that the Member States may choose to lay down provisions designed to protect workers using the machines, provided that the machinery is not modified in a manner not specified in the Directive. Article 3 states that the machinery which is covered by the Directive shall satisfy the essential requirements set out in Annex 1. Under the terms of Article 4 Member States are not to restrict the placing on the market of machinery which complies with the Directive. Article 5 refers to standards: if machinery bears the 'EC mark' and is accompanied by a declaration that it conforms to the essential health and safety requirements, the Member States shall accept that it does so conform; if there are no harmonized standards Member States shall apply existing national standards which are of relevance to the proper implementation of the essential health and safety requirements; where a national standard transposes a harmonized standard, then machinery constructed in accordance with this standard shall be presumed to comply with the essential requirements. Article 6 contains safeguards in the event that machinery which does bear the EC mark is perceived to be dangerous. The provisions of Article 8 describe the procedure whereby a manufacturer can obtain a certificate that its goods conform to the Directive; an EC mark can then be affixed to the goods.

The Safety of Machinery Directive provides a good example of the legislative format used by the Community under the new approach to harmonization. One should not, however, conclude that the Community has only one type of legislative strategy which it can use for trade barriers which are lawful under the Treaty. The following extract distinguishes three such strategies which are open to the Community:

A. McGee and S. Weatherill, The Evolution of the Single Market-Harmonisation or Liberalisation[62]

1. It may pass legislation which covers the entire field in question, albeit in a very general way. This approach is referred to here as 'Exhaustive Regulation' because it involves Community rule-making which excludes Member States' competence to regulate the area. A good example of this is provided by product safety.

2. It may pass legislation which deals with some issues in the area under consideration, but leaves others to national law. This approach is referred to here as 'Partial Regulation'. Two good examples of this are provided by the Product Liability Directive and the Regulation creating the European Economic Interest Grouping . . .

[62] (1990) 53 MLR 578, 582.

> 3. It may not act at all; there are numerous possible reasons for this. One is simply lack of resources, since there is much to be done in the pursuit of the Single Market, and some matters inevitably have higher priority than others. Another possibility is political difficulty in reaching an agreed position. This may in turn take either of two forms. There may be agreement that regulation is required, but no consensus about the form of the regulation, or there may be disagreement as to whether any form of regulation is called for . . . Such failure to act, for whatever reason, is referred to here as 'No Regulation'.

If a Community harmonization measure is exhaustive in the above sense then it will pre-empt inconsistent national rules. Whether the harmonization measure is intended to preclude any national measures which differ to any degree from the Community directive may itself be a contentious issue. In *Ratti*[63] the ECJ had to decide whether Directive 73/173 on packaging and labelling of dangerous substances precluded a state from prescribing 'obligations and limitations which are more precise than, or at all events different from, those set out in the directive'. The disputed Italian rules required more information to be attached to the packaging than specified in the Directive. The Court held that the Directive enjoined this. The rules contained in the Directive were intended to prevent the state from laying down any specific, stricter rules of its own.

It may, by way of contrast, be apparent from the directive itself that it only partially regulates the area in question. In *Grunert*[64] a French producer of food preservative containing lactic and citric acid was prosecuted for selling the food preservative for use in the making of certain pork meats. French law prohibited the use of preservatives unless they had been authorized by the national authorities, and the acids used by the accused were not on the national list. Relevant Community Directives 64/54 and 70/357 did, however, list the two acids as among those which could be used to protect food against deterioration. This was the basis of Grunert's defence. But the Directives went on to provide that they were not to affect provisions of national law specifying the foodstuffs to which the preservatives listed could be added, provided that such national provisions did not have the effect of totally excluding the use in foodstuffs of any of the listed preservatives. In the light of this, and the fact that the Directives were but the initial stage in the harmonization of national laws in this area, the ECJ decided that the Member States did have a discretion as to the foodstuffs to which listed preservatives could be added.

[63] Case 148/78, *Pubblico Ministero* v. *Ratti* [1979] ECR 1629.
[64] Case 88/79, *Ministère Public* v. *Grunert* [1980] ECR 1827.

6. COMPLETING THE INTERNAL MARKET: TENSIONS AND CONCERNS

The analysis thus far has shown the real advantages which the new approach to harmonization has over the old. It would, however, be wrong to imagine that these changes have been problem-free. Commentators have perceived a number of tensions and concerns inherent in the single market strategy. We shall address three such concerns. Whatever one's views on the correctness or otherwise of the views voiced below, they do bring into focus the interrelationship between reforms of the trading process on the one hand and broader socio-political considerations on the other.

(a) Consumer Interests and Commercial Power

One concern which has been voiced, albeit in different ways, is whether consumer interests are sufficiently protected in the process of attaining a single market. We should remember that many national rules which can, because of their disparity, impede intra-Community trade are designed to protect consumers. This has been recognized in the Treaty itself, through provisions such as Article 36; through the ECJ's jurisprudence under *Cassis*, which recognises health and safety etc. as part of the mandatory requirements justifying the retention of national rules pending Community action; and through the Commission's acceptance of the fact that harmonization under the new approach will be necessary in such areas where Member States do have legitimate health and safety interests at stake. So far so good. No conflict between the realization of the single market and consumer protection. The latter will, where necessary, be addressed through Community measures which, at one and the same time, remove or reduce disparities between national rules, thereby easing barriers to trade, and ensure the continued protection of the consumer by appropriately framed Community directives or regulations. The Directive on Machinery Safety considered above can be seen as but one of many examples of this process in action. So what, then, *is* the problem? It is that some are concerned whether the Community directives which emerge in this way really will adequately balance consumer and manufacturing interests. Consider the following discussion by McGee and Weatherill:

A. McGee and S. Weatherill, The Evolution of the Single Market-Harmonisation or Liberalisation[65]

It is submitted that there are structural reasons why the New Approach might serve the European consumer ill. The difficulty lies in the privatisation of the standards making process which supports the New Approach. For financial reasons it

[65] N. 62 above, 585, 595. See also N. Reich, 'Protection of Diffuse Interests in the EEC and the Perspective of Progressively Establishing an Internal Market' (1988) 11 Jnl. Cons. Policy 395.

is likely that business will capture the standardisation process within CEN. Consumer organisations lack resources to participate fully in CEN committee work; in any event, consumer representation is ill-organized and haphazard in several Member States . . . If standards making becomes the province of business alone, the balance between consumer protection and free trade will be distorted, prejudicing overall public confidence in the Community.

[*The authors return to the theme in their conclusion:*]

This article has highlighted some of the major difficulties which currently beset the development of the Single Market. To some extent these may be regarded as technical problems caused by diversity of national tradition which are likely to be difficult even with the full-hearted co-operation of all those involved. What is also clear is that there are vested interests at work, which in many cases want either to delay the process or at least to manipulate it for their own purposes . . .

Not surprisingly, national governments appear to be the most effective at controlling developments . . . Business and commercial interests have proved less successful in blocking developments, but have been highly effective in getting control of the standard-setting process, as in the case of Toy Safety, and in ensuring that other provisions take the form which they want. Thus, the EEIG Regulation[66] excluded worker participation, the Product Liability Directive allowed for the inclusion of the development risks defence and the Merger Regulation ignores all considerations of social policy. Again, it is not surprising to find that the highly motivated, well organised and generously resourced interests at work here have proved effective. Far less successful have been the consumer and employee interests, whose concerns seem largely to have been overridden. This too need not be a cause for surprise, but it is important to ask the fundamental question, what sort of Single Market is being created here? The answer seems to be that it is a Market in which business flourishes, relatively free from protective regulation, but the legitimate interests of other social groups are at risk of being ignored.

These concerns should be taken seriously. We should at the same time be mindful of the fact that such worries are also present when regulations about product safety and the like are made at national level. Tensions which result from the imbalance in power between consumer and commercial interests, flowing from the greater resources wielded by the latter combined with better organized pressure groups, are not *created* by or because of harmonization measures being passed at Community rather than national level. They are endemic in most Western-style market economies. Given that this is so, whether consumer interests fare better in the regulatory process at national or Community level will depend upon a complex calculus in which a number of factors will be of relevance. These will include the relative capacities of commercial and consumer interests to influence the legislative process within the Community and within the nation state; the relative organizational costs involved in operating within these differing polities; and the effect on both types of group of having to contend with a multiplicity of national governments, each of which may have its own agenda on any particular issue. This

[66] European Economic Interest Grouping.

does not mean that we should, therefore, be complacent about the existence of interest group power within the Community. Rather that we should take care when ascribing causality and be ready to address solutions which may help to redress the problem within the Community.

(b) The Single Market, Market Freedom, and Structural Balance

A second tension which flows from the single market project is that between a Community-wide free market and the impact which this might have for the weaker economies of the Community. We have already seen that the SEA addressed this problem to some extent through Article 7c.[67] Whether this will suffice to meet the difficulty remains to be seen. Consider the view of Dehousse in the extract which follows:

R. Dehousse, Completing the Internal Market: Institutional Constraints and Challenges[68]

At some point . . . a major challenge will have to be faced, for the objective of market integration itself remains unacceptable, politically speaking, for some Member States if it is not accompanied by specific effort to improve the social and economic cohesion within the Community. It is worth recalling in this respect that economically weaker countries have been reluctant to accept majority voting, precisely because they are those who might suffer most in the short term from the creation of a single market. Of the many problems linked to the completion of the internal market, this one is perhaps the most difficult: unlike the concerns for a high level of health, consumer safety or the environment, this kind of fear cannot be allayed by derogatory measures alone. A parallel in the Community's allocative and redistributive policies has been strongly advocated by recent studies, both from a theoretical and from a practical viewpoint. The Single Act pledges the Community to reinforce its action in favour of backward areas; it even explicitly states that the completion of the internal market should be pursued taking into account the existence of different levels of development within the Community [Art. 130A]. However, it fails to give the Community additional means to reach that end. The crucial point is that, at a given stage, progress towards the single European market might be conditioned by the capacity to tackle the problem of structural imbalances: if the Community does not find a way to offer some compensation to those countries which feel they have more to lose, market integration could be severely hampered. More than institutional pragmatism will be needed in order to cut this Gordian knot.

It is then apparent that the fulfilment of the single market project will generate macro-economic and social tensions between rich, poor, and middle-class economies within the Community. This should come as no surprise.

[67] See above, 1128–9.
[68] R. Bieber, R. Dehousse, J. Pinder, and J. Weiler (eds.), *1992: One European Market?* (Nomos, 1988), 336.

Reflect on experience within nation states. A free-enterprise, market-driven, national economic policy will not infrequently create regional problems within a particular country. There will be areas in which there is high unemployment, decline of traditional industries, and relative poverty. Calls for assistance to be given to these areas will emerge.[69] Small wonder that a vigorous policy of increased competitiveness and breaking down trade barriers throughout the Community as a whole will produce similar tensions, albeit on a larger scale. Some countries will be concerned about their general ability to survive and prosper within this barrier-free, competitive environment. Dehousse is therefore quite right to point to the connections between the single market project and the need to tackle structural imbalances within the Community.

(c) Politics, Economics, and the Single Market Enterprise

Conceptions of market freedom are not value-free. The meaning of this phrase, the manner in which it is to be attained, and the appropriate limits to free markets are all matters on which there is considerable disagreement. It is one of the key issues which has divided political parties. Let it be accepted that the Community has decided that removing barriers to intra-Community trade will bring economic benefits. There is sound economic evidence to sustain this decision, as we have seen above.[70] Yet even given this consensus, there is still room for considerable diversity of opinion along party lines on what the necessary or desirable scope of protective Community measures should be. These differences of opinion are, moreover, perfectly possible among those of differing political persuasion all of whom are committed to the European ideal. The politicization which in this sense accompanies the process of market integration has been noted by commentators. Thus, as Pelkmans puts it, an internal-market strategy which cuts so deeply into the regulatory environment of consumers, traders, and producers, and which severely limits the options available to Member States cannot pretend to be entirely apolitical.[71] Weiler develops the same theme:

J. Weiler, The Transformation of Europe[72]

It is an article of faith for European integration that the Commission is not meant to be a mere secretariat, but an autonomous force shaping the agenda and brokering the decisionmaking of the Community. And yet at the same time, the Commission, as broker, must be ideologically neutral, not favouring Christian Democrats, Social Democrats or others.

This neutralization of ideology has fostered the belief that an agenda could be

[69] It is, of course, the case that such calls will now be strictly constrained by the Community rules on state aids. That is not, however, of direct relevance here.

[70] See above, 1116–20.

[71] J. Pelkmans, 'A Grand Design by the Piece? An Appraisal of the Internal Market Strategy', in R. Bieber, R. Dehousse, J. Pinder, J. Weiler (eds.), n. 68 above, 371.

[72] (1991) 100 Yale LJ 2403, 2476–8.

set for the Community, and the Community could be led towards an ever closer union among its peoples, without having to face the normal political cleavages present in the Member States. In conclusion, the Community political culture which developed in the 1960s and 1970s led . . . to an habituation of all political forces to thinking of European integration as ideologically neutral in, or transcendent over, the normal debates on the left–right spectrum. It is easy to understand how this will have served the process of integration, allowing a nonpartisan coalition to emerge around its overall objectives.

1992 changes this in two ways. The first is a direct derivation from the turn to majority voting. Policies can be adopted now within the Council that run counter not simply to the perceived interests of a Member State, but more specifically to the ideology of the government in power. The debates about the European Social Charter and the shrill cries of 'Socialism through the backdoor', as well as the emerging debate about Community adherence to the European Convention on Human Rights and abortion rights are harbingers of things to come . . .

The second impact of *1992* on ideological neutrality is subtler. The entire program rests on two pivots: the single market plan encapsulated in the White Paper, and its operation through the instrumentalities of the Single European Act . . . It is not simply a technocratic program to remove the remaining obstacles to the free movement of all factors of production. It is at the same time a highly politicized choice of ethos, ideology and political culture: the culture of 'the market'. It is also a philosophy, at least one version of which—the predominant version—seeks to remove barriers to the free movement of factors of production, and to remove distortion to competition as a means to maximize utility. The above is premised on the assumption of formal equality of individuals. It is an ideology the contours of which have been the subject of intense debate within the Member States in terms of their own political choices . . . A successful single market requires widespread harmonization of standards and environmental protection, as well as the social package of employees. This need for a successful market not only accentuates the pressure for uniformity, but also manifests a social (and hence ideological) choice which prizes market efficiency and European-wide neutrality of competition above other competing values.

7. CONCLUSION

What conclusions can then be drawn about the SEA and its impact on the single market project? We will not attempt to summarize all the arguments which have been presented above. A word or two on the importance of the SEA in the more overall development of the Community may, however, be helpful.

What might in the long term prove to be one of the most significant contributions of the SEA and the single market project to the process of European integration is the very fact that it jolted the Community out of the Europessimism which had beset it from the late 1970s to the early 1980s. That there are difficulties with the SEA is undeniable; that the Member States at the Inter-governmental Conference gave short shrift to many procedural and substantive changes which would have taken the cause of Community integration even further is also undeniable. But politics is the art of the possible, not a counsel of perfection. All the more so in the international arena. Despite all this the SEA happened and without it the new approach to harmonization might never have taken hold at all. If the Community was, prior to 1986, rather like an unwieldy train struggling up an interminable hill and in danger of grinding to a halt, the SEA gave it the impetus to press forward. In this sense the SEA laid the foundations for the institutional and substantive changes which have occurred since then. Causality in international affairs is difficult to determine. But it is doubtful, to say the least, whether the TEU would ever have been negotiated had the SEA not preceded it. Talk of more complete economic and monetary union and the like would probably have not featured on a realistic agenda had the Community not shaken itself free of the Euro-sclerosis of the late 1970s and early 1980s, and had the moves towards completing an internal market not convinced many that further integration was attainable. It is this which may prove to be the most important long-term contribution of the SEA and the single market project.

8. FURTHER READING

(a) Books

Brealey, M., and Quigley, C., *Completing the Internal Market* (Graham & Trotman, 1989)

Bieber, R., Dehousse, R., Pinder, J., and Weiler, J. (eds.), *1992: One European Market?* (Nomos, 1988)

Cecchini, P., *The European Challenge—1992* (Gower, 1988)

Emerson, M., Aujean, M., Catinat, M., Goybet, P. and Jacquemin, A., *The Economics of 1992* (Oxford University Press, 1988)

(b) Articles

Bieber, R., 'Legislative Procedure for the Establishment of the Single Market' (1988) 25 CMLRev. 711

Burrows, N., 'Harmonisation of Technical Standards: Reculer Pour Mieux Sauter?' (1990) 53 MLR 597

Crosby, S., 'The Single Market and the Rule of Law' (1991) 16 ELRev. 451

Dehousse, R., '1992 and Beyond: The Institutional Dimension of the Internal Market Programme' [1989] 1 LIEI 109

Edward, D., 'The Impact of the Single Act on the Institutions' (1987) 24 CMLRev. 19

Ehlermann, C. D., 'The Internal Market Following the Single European Act' (1987) 24 CMLRev. 361

Forwood, N., and Clough, M., 'The Single European Act and Free Movement' (1986) 11 ELRev. 383

Glaesner, H. J., 'The Single European Act: Attempt at an Appraisal' (1987) 10 Fordham ILJ 446

McGee, A., and Weatherill, S., 'The Evolution of the Single Market-Harmonisation or Liberalisation' (1990) 53 MLR 578

Moravcsik, A., 'Negotiating the Single European Act: National Interests and Conventional Statecraft in the European Community' (1991) 45 *International Organization* 19

Pescatore, P., 'Some Critical Remarks on the "Single European Act" ' (1987) 24 CMLRev. 9

Pelkmans, J., 'The New Approach to Technical Harmonization and Standardization' (1987) 25 JCMS 249

Sandholtz, W., and Zysman, J., '1992: Recasting the European Bargain' (1989) 42 *World Politics* 95

Toth, A., 'The Legal Status of the Declarations Annexed to the Single European Act' (1986) 23 CMLRev. 803

Vignes, D., 'The Harmonization of National Legislation and the EEC' (1990) 15 ELRev. 358

INDEX

THE UNIVERSITY OF BIRMINGHAM
INFORMATION SERVICES